THE GREAT BOOK OF
WORLD WAR II AIRPLANES

THE GREAT BOOK OF WORLD WAR II AIRPLANES

Authors

Jeffrey L. Ethell
Robert Grinsell
Roger Freeman
David A. Anderton
Frederick A. Johnsen
Bill Sweetman
Alex Vanags-Baginskis
Robert C. Mikesh

Illustrator

Rikyu Watanabe

BONANZA BOOKS

This book was designed and produced by Wing & Anchor Press,
a division of Zokeisha Publications, Ltd.
5-1-6, Roppongi, Minato-ku, Tokyo 106/641 5th Avenue, New York, N.Y. 10022

This 1984 edition is published by Bonanza Books,
distributed by Crown Publishers, Inc., by arrangement with
Zokeisha Publications, Ltd.

Printed and bound in Japan.

Library of Congress Cataloging in Publication Data

The Great Book of World War II Airplanes.

1. Airplanes, Military. 2. World War, 1939-1945—
Aerial operations. I. Ethell, Jeffrey L.
UG1240.G68 1984   358.4'183   84-15004

ISBN: 0-517-459930

Contents

Foreword

Here is a book about twelve aircraft that changed the world, an international publishing effort, beautifully illustrated by premier aircraft artist Rikyu Watanabe. The text, written by a team of aviation experts and enthusiasts, provides indispensable information about the design and production of these aircraft, their tactical employment, the development of specialized models and variants, the decisive battles they fought in, and the daring and harrowing exploits of their pilots. But clearly the heart of this book consists of Watanabe's original illustrations—exactly rendered fullcolor profiles (some on large fold-out panels), detailed interior cutaways, control and weapons systems schematics, cockpit views, and actual squadron insignia which make this volume an invaluable possession for military and aviation historians, aircraft buffs, model builders, and the veterans who flew these airplanes.

Though each aircraft was unique and was designed to serve a different end, taking them together we can form an overview of how the war changed aviation and how aviation influenced the aims of the war. The first pattern to emerge concerns the rapid pace of technological change during wartime. Before the late 1930s aircraft design was still rather primitive, but the war accelerated the transition from wooden framed, dope and fabric biplanes to the all metal, cantilever mono-wing aircraft. The British Mosquito, with its all wood construction, was something of an exception. Yet even here, its basic design was modern, and the use of wood was dictated by the need to manufacture this remarkable fighter-bomber in different parts of the world from non-strategic materials. The overall trend was clear. The war also brought radar, modular construction, electric gun turrets, armor plate, self-sealing fuel tanks, new bomb sights, dive brakes, superchargers, complex hydraulic systems, and the IFF, the forerunner of the modern transponder so indispensable to modern air traffic control.

Of paramount importance were the enormous increases in power plant efficiency and power-to-weight ratios. By the end of the war, with 2000 horsepower engines pulling aircraft in excess of 400 mph, reaching altitudes as high as 30,000 feet, the ultimate limits of piston engine propeller technology had been reached. Never would the performance of the propeller driven aircraft be significantly improved, or its wartime parameters exceeded in any meaningful way. That would have to wait for the jets, themselves a product of a last desperate wartime effort. After several decades of groping and often unsuccessful experimentation, in the short space of six years—from 1939 to 1945—the war created modern aircraft and the propulsion system of the future.

The conduct of warfare itself was radically altered by the appearance of reliable flying machines. During the Great War of 1914 to 1918 air combat was still imbued with a sense of adventure and heroism and individual prowess. Aerial duels were just that, contests of individual skill between knights of the air. The primitive Spads and Fokkers were used in individual dogfights, for reconnaissance, and only late in the war for tactical support of infantry and tank assaults. The influence of these planes on the outcome of the war was negligible. The scope of World War II meant that the full might of air *forces* would now be employed against the enemy. Victory in the air would not come through the individual duel, but through numerical and technical superiority; it would be achieved through industrial organization, research and planning, and the commitment of a nation's resources to total war. That industrial versatility could be decisive was clearly demonstrated by the military record of the Japanese Zero. One of the most advanced fighters at the beginning of the war, it was by 1943 completely outclassed by most American aircraft and could be shot down at will by veteran pilots. The commitment of Japanese resources to production of the Zero made it impossible to manufacture an advanced replacement, whereas the Americans, initially caught off guard, gearing up their more innovative war machine after the devastating effectiveness of the Zero was known and had been carefully studied, were easily able to produce superior fighters.

The concept of total war produced a revolution in military strategy. If a nation's entire economy was to be geared for war, it followed that a nation's entire economy was now a legitimate target. The primary goal was no longer air combat itself but the massive strategic bombing of national resources with a view to dislocating basic industry. Part of the new strategy involved terror bombing—the destruction of the lives and homes of the enemy's civilian population in order to undermine the national morale. The Ju 87 Stuka dive bomber was the perfect example of this; it was equipped with sirens mounted on the undercarriage for no other purpose than to terrorize victims of the Blitzkrieg. Massive strategic bombing was not a tactic of the set piece battle but a long term war of attrition against a whole people, and nearly every aircraft represented in this book was designed either to carry out such bombing or defend against it.

Someone, somewhere, once quipped that if all the German and all the British bombers of the second World War II had stayed and dropped their bombs over their own respective countries, the same result would have been achieved with an immense saving in gasoline.

Whatever the merits of this facetious argument, and whether or not strategic bombing achieved the results claimed for it in any theater of war, the ultimate effects were to eliminate the distinction between soldier and civilian, compromise the moral position of the combatants, and prepare the way in people's minds for the even higher levels of destruction contemplated by military strategists in the nuclear age.

In spite of the horrors of World War II, we cannot help but look back upon these aircraft as wondrous machines. Though they were the products of painstaking engineering and a massive industrial effort, we see them as the pilots saw them, almost as graceful works of art, as extensions of our personal freedom, as machines with living—occasionally cantankerous—personalities. How many flight crew members will remember with affection the B-17 Flying Fortress, the plane that proved the effectiveness of high altitude precision daylight bombing, as it carried them home to safety in England, badly damaged by flack, but continuing to fly with the tenaciousness of a living creature. Or the Spitfire with its unique low-drag elliptical wing—a pilot's favorite. Or the F4U Corsair, a hot airplane, but treacherous for the inexperienced airman attempting a carrier landing.

The war is remembered as a time of fear and a time of exhilaration. The men who flew these machines had perhaps a greater measure of both these feelings than other combatants. It is to their memory that this book is dedicated.

P-38
LIGHTNING

Text by JEFFREY L. ETHELL

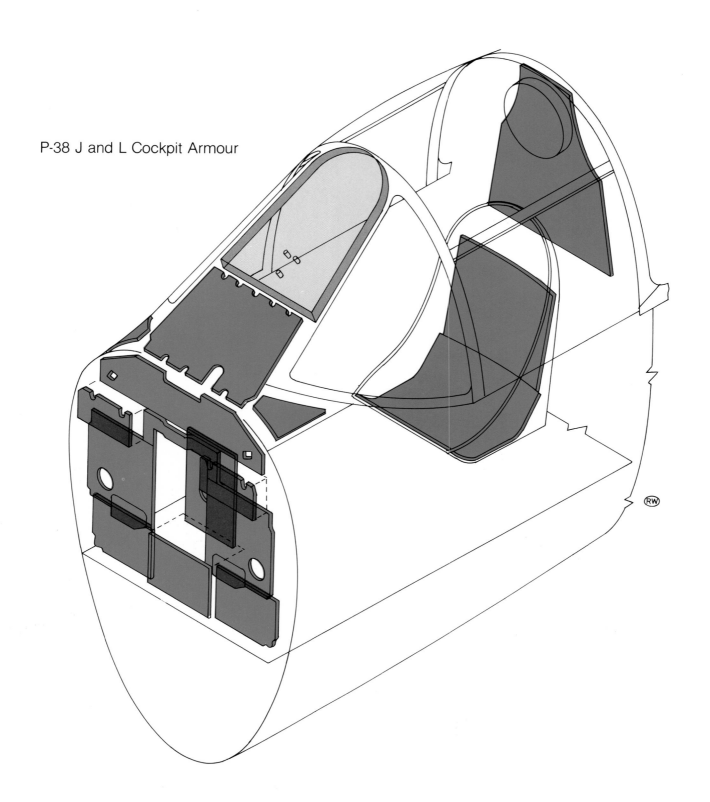

P-38 J and L Cockpit Armour

"Kelly" Johnson's six desings for 1937 Army fighter competition. (2) and (3) load two engines in each fuselage. (4) became XP-38.

Genesis

In February 1937 the US Army Air Corps asked the American aircraft industry to submit designs for an experimental pursuit having "the tactical mission of interception and attack of hostile aircraft at high altitude". Specifications called for a minimum true air speed of 360 mph (579 km/h) at altitude and a climb to 20,000 ft (6,096 m) within six minutes.

In essence the Air Corps was asking for a major breakthrough in performance since there were no engines of sufficient power to produce the expected results. 1,600 horsepower would be necessary and the only engine coming close to that kind of power was General Motors' small Allison Division V-1710-C8 which in February 1937 had yet to be tested at 1,000 hp. The isolationist climate of the 1930s had stunted military development, creating a situation where the authorities would not allocate money for even single cylinder development.

One of the solutions envisaged taking two of the Allisons and building a fighter around them; the other was to reduce the requirements and challenge the designers to refine an airframe to utilise every bit of the Allison's power. That there was some freedom to pursue almost any course of action can be laid at the feet of the officer in charge of Wright Field, Ohio's Pursuit Projects Office, Lt Benjamin S. Kelsey. As he later recalled, "We had to find a name that kept people from telling you what should go into the spec, a name that nobody was familiar with or could relate to. We came up with 'interceptor'. Of course it was a fighter in mission but we told these guys that just so we could develop what we needed in a fighter."

Lockheed's Model 22, later the XP-38, and Bell's XP-39 were entered into the competition. The Lockheed project was certainly the more radical approach to the problem, resulting in an airplane 150% the size of a normal single engine fighter. Clarence L. "Kelly" Johnson designed a twin-boomed, twin engine aircraft that was quite sophisticated. The two large propeller discs offered increased efficiency for the horsepower being generated and the resulting larger wingspan gave better high altitude performance. The guns would fire down the centre line and single engine returnability resulted.

Bell Aircraft took the other approach as Larry Bell and Bob Wood designed a fighter with an engine behind the cockpit over the aircraft's centre of gravity. The result was a machine 20% lighter through placing the main landing gear on the main spar of the wing. Since the tail did not have to carry a wheel through use of tricycle landing gear, the fuselage tail cone was lighter due to decreased stress. The engine sat on two webs directly on the wing, eliminating the need for cantilevers or other support structures.

Air Corps contract 9974, dated 23 June 1937, authorized Lockheed to build one XP-38, USAAC serial number 37-457. The Bell XP-39, AAC serial number 38-326, was ordered on 7 October 1937.

Construction of the XP-38 began in July 1938 and it was fitted with the Allison C-9 Model (V-1710-11/15), rated at 1,090 hp. Its right engine turned "backwards" (clockwise viewed from the front), thus countering the effects of propeller torque. It would weigh more than 15,000 lb (6,804 kg) loaded. The aircraft combined the latest technological innovations: tricycle landing gear, very high wing loading, Fowler flaps for good low-speed handling, butt joints and flush riveting of the skin which would share flights loads with the interior structure, a bubble canopy and metal covered control surfaces.

The XP-38 was completed in December 1938, then disassembled and loaded on three trucks, covered by canvas, and taken to March Field, California from Burbank during the early morning hours of New Year's Day 1939. Ben Kelsey began taxi tests on 9 January and made the first flight on 27 January 1939 after delays due to problems with the brakes. The aircraft was an immediate success, coming well within projected performance parameters, but a number of minor problems forced Kelsey to drag it in just above stall speed and chop the power over the end of the runway every time he landed.

After about five hours total flying time the aircraft was scheduled for delivery to Wright Field, with a possible continuaton of the flight to Mitchel Field, New York. On 11 February Kelsey took off from March, refuelled at Amarillo, Texas, and landed at Wright Field averaging 360 mph (579 km/h) true air speed at cruise power. Chief of the Air Corps, General Henry H. "Hap" Arnold, was waiting for Kelsey at Wright and the two discussed going on to Mitchel. Arnold thought a complete transcontinental dash to make some headlines and prove the US still had a top notch aircraft industry would be beneficial to Air Corps funding in Congress.

Kelsey recalled the last leg: "Descending into Mitchel, I think I probably picked up carburetor ice. This was a problem that had not been solved – there wasn't enough heat available via the superchargers at low rpms to handle carburetor ice. I had the throttle way back to lower the flaps [due to flutter problems in the new Fowler flap installation]; and then since I was faced with a landing without wheel brakes (having used them up for the Amarillo and Dayton stops – they simply weren't designed to last on such a big airplane), I had to drag it in under power at low speed.

"The flap problem and the brake problem were just waiting on one additional problem – lack of power at a critical

XP-38	Power units		Armament

Power units
Allison V-1710-11 (left) and V-1710-15 (right)
  : 1,150 hp each for take-off
    1,000 hp at 20,000 ft (6,100 m)
Fuel: 230-400 US gal (192-333 Imp gal. 871-1,514 ltr)

Performance
Max speed
  : 413 mph (665 km/h) at 20,000 ft (6,100 m)
Cruising speed
  : 350 mph (563 km/h) at 16,000 ft (4,880 m)
Landing speed
  : 80 mph (129 km/h)
Time to climb to 20,000 ft (6,100 m)
  : 6.5 min
Service ceiling: 38,000 ft (11,580 m)
Endurance: 1 hr at top speed

Armament
1 × 23 mm cannon
4 × 0.50-in (12.7 mm) machine guns

Weights
Empty: 11,507 lb (5,220 kg)
Gross: 13,500 lb (6,120 kg)
Max: 15,416 lb (6,993 kg)

Dimensions
Span: 52 ft (15.85 m)
Length: 37 ft 10 in (11.53 m)
Height: 9 ft 6 in (2.90 m)
Wing area: 327.5 sq ft (30.4 m²)

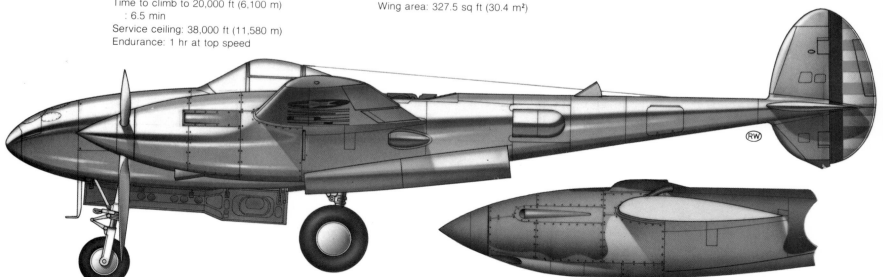

Lightning I (used by USAAF as P-322 engine-nacelle without turbo-supercharger)

YP-38

Power unit
Allison V-1710-27 (left) and V-1710-29 (right)
: 1,150 hp each for take-off
Fuel: 230-410 US gal (192-341 Imp gal, 871-1,552 ltr)

Performance
Max speed
: 405 mph (652 km/h) at 20,000 ft (6,100 m)
Landing speed
: 80 mph (129 km/h)
Time to climb to 20,000 ft (6,100 m)
: 6 min

Rate of climb: 3,333 ft (1,016 m)/min
Service ceiling: 38,000 ft (11,580 m)
Normal range: 650 mls (1,050 km)
Max range: 1,050 mls (1,850 km)

Armament
1 × 37 mm cannon
2 × 0.50-in (12.7 mm) machine guns
2 × 0.30-in (7.62 mm) machine guns

Weights
Empty: 11,171 lb (5,067 kg)
Gross: 13,500 lb (6,120 kg)
Max: 14,348 lb (6,508 kg)

Dimensions
Span: 52 ft (15.85 m)
Length: 37 ft 10 in (11.53 m)
Height: 9 ft 10 in (3.00 m)
Wing area: 327.5 sq ft (30.4 m²)

time – to produce disaster. As I attempted to ease-in power, the engines failed to respond. Both continued to idle nicely but wouldn't accelerate. I was low and slow on final, in landing configuration. Without power, there was nothing I could do to add a single inch to the approach. I struck the ground short of the runway. The aircraft was a total loss; I was uninjured."

Arnold took Kelsey to Washington the day after the crash to tell four or five top level people about the new XP-38, how fast it was, how nicely it handled. Within 60 days Lockheed had a contract for 13 service-test YP-38s. This would not have been possible had the XP survived since it would have been necessary to validate all its performance estimates with a prototype airplane full of bugs.

The P-38 remained the sweetheart of Kelsey's flying career and he saw it through most of its teething pains, including its bouts with compressibility, Atlantic ferry and combat.

The order for 13 service-test YP-38s (Lockheed Model 122) was Air Corps Contract 12523 dated 27 April 1939 but the first YP did not fly until 16 September 1940 and the last one was not delivered until eight months after that. Mass production was still far off, total production in 1941 amounting to 196 units (exclusive of the YPs) and none of these were fit for combat. Nevertheless, the performance estimates were so promising that substantial orders were in hand months before the first YP-38 had even flown: France ordered 417 Model 322-F and Britain 250 Model 322-B fighters in May 1940 (the *Armee de l'Air* order being taken over by Britain after the French capitulation late in June 1940), and the USAAC followed with initially 66 Model 222 fighters (to be known as P-38) in July 1940, augmented by another 410 the following month. By September 1940 USAAC orders totalled 673 aircraft.

The delays can be traced to a number of factors, not the least of which was the underfunded industry coming out of 20 years of neglect. The YP-38 was also a totally new aircraft, extensively redesigned from lessons learned from the XP, which was essentially a handbuilt machine. The Army had demanded the YPs be at least 1,500 lb (680 kg) lighter than

the experimental model.

Most of the testing on the YP-38s was turned over to the Army since they were service-test machines and by late May 1941, after the fifth YP had been delivered, compressibility began to rear its ugly head. Air Corps Major Signa A. Gilkie took the new YP well above 30,000 ft (9,140 m) and entered a dive. As the airspeed needle swung past 320 mph (around 500 mph/800 km/h true air speed), the plane's tail began to buffet severely. As the dive continued, the '38 became progressively nose-heavy, increasing its dive-angle to near vertical, while the control yoke oscillated stiffly and defied Gilke's utmost efforts to pull it back and effect recovery. Unwilling to bale out and lose the plane to this strange and terrifying force, he tried the only thing left and cranked in nose-up elevator trim.

This didn't seem to work at first but as the YP entered denser air below 18,000 ft (5,490 m) the nose began to come up and full control quickly returned as the aircraft entered straight and level flight at 7,000 ft (2,130 m). Two major problems had been discovered – tail buffeting and aerodynamic compressibility. It took awhile to discover that the two problems were unrelated. Kelly Johnson and Hall Hibbard (Chief of Lockheed Design Bureau) had foreseen the problem of compressibility back in 1937 when the XP-38 was laid out but there was so little information on the phenomenon that it was pushed aside, in spite of a revealing report by Johnson that predicted the effects.

Only a few Lockheed engineers believed the trouble with the P-38 was compressibility. Most maintained that the tail was improperly balanced which resulted in the installation of external mass balance weights on the elevator (which remained on all subsequent P-38s, although Kelly Johnson has always maintained they were useless). Other fixes were tried but none helped because no tail flutter was present to start with – under extreme conditions, it was simply being buffeted by a strongly turbulent airflow created at the sharp junctures where wing and fuselage were joined, as discovered by wind tunnel tests at the California Institute of Technology. By June 1941 Lockheed test pilots James Mat-

Six of the initial production P-38s over the California mountains during the latter half of 1941. The aircraft were not combat-equipped. (USAF)

tern and Ralph Virden proved this to be correct by flying with wing fillets at the wing-central pod juncture and all subsequent P-38s carried the fillets as standard.

Compressibility, however, remained to plague the aircraft as Mattern, Virden and Milo Burcham cautiously explored high altitude dives. On 4 November Virden took the first YP-38, 39-689, up for a series of dive tests. The aircraft, which had accumulated just over 23 hours flying time, had been fitted with new spring-loaded servo tabs on the elevator's trailing edge which would add to the pilot's muscle in pulling back on the control column. Virden reached true air speeds up to 535 mph (856 km/h) but the new tabs worked so well that Virden pulled the tail off of the aircraft at about 3,000 ft (910 m) in a dive recovery and was killed. The P-38 was obviously not going to be muscled out of its problem.

One of the early production P-38Ds with dummy guns in the nose. The Fowler flaps are set in fully extended position. (USAF)

Production and development

Meanwhile a total of 68 fighters had been built, not counting the XP and YP models: 29 P-38s (among them one XP-38A with a pressurized cockpit), no P-38Bs or Cs, 36 P-38Ds and three P-38Es. Delivery of the production models had begun in June and by the end of October 1941 the P-38Es were being delivered. During the next five months, only 210 P-38Es were built and the P-38F entered production in April 1942 but it was not until P-38Gs were coming off the line in October 1942 that a P-38 scale model was accepted for high-speed wind tunnel tests at NACA's Ames Laboratory. This was, perhaps, the single most significant lapse in P-38 development. Since Maj Gilke's first surprise, 17 irretrievable months had gone by.

It was discovered that the shock wave generated on the P-38s wing at Mach .67 produced airflow at certain points that reached the speed of sound, rendering the machine uncontrollable. Several aerodynamic improvements could have been made to solve the problem but America was at war and there was no time; production was all important. The stop-gap solution was to put a dive brake under each wing outboard of the engines which broke up much of the airflow.

In late February 1943 Ben Kelsey, by then a colonel, tested the flaps but Lockheed was unable to incorporate them into the production line for another 14 months. By that time 5,300 P-38s had been built, more than half of the ultimate total. The dive brake modification appeared on the last 210 P-38Js produced in June 1944.

The early P-38s, through the Ds, never left the United States, though they were shifted around the country quite a bit. All but four initially went to Selfridge, Jackson, Wright or Patterson Fields and as they were not combat-ready, served in training and familiarisation roles. Most of these P-38s participated in the September 1941 Louisiana manoeuvres as well as in the October–November manoeuvres in the Carolinas while attached to the 1st Pursuit Group.

These first production P-38s were given the name "Atlanta" by the company, until the Royal Air Force chose "Lightning" for the P-38s it had on order. Sometime in October 1941 Lockheed and the USAAF (the Army Air Corps was redesignated the Army Air Force on 20 June 1941) decided that the British were more apt at the naming of airplanes, and switched to the British appellation.

The British Lightnings, however, were useless as combat aircraft without turbo-superchargers (due to production problems) and engines that rotated in the same direction, thereby eliminating the P-38s normally gentle handling characteristics at and near stalling speed and introducing a trim problem. These Lightning Is were redlined at 300 mph

(483 km/h) indicated airspeed and soon after the first two were tested by RAF pilots in March 1942 the Air Ministry cancelled its order for 667 Lightnings.

In reality, this solved a problem for USAAF Training Command – 143 of these aircraft were given counter-rotating engines and, as AAF P-322s, became twin-engine fighter trainers. The remaining 524 Model 322s were worked into P-38F and G assembly lines.

During the early Lightning transition period in the AAF, the aircraft became known as "hot ships" that were difficult to handle, particularly when losing an engine on take-off. Ben Kelsey, Milo Burcham, Jimmy Mattern and later Tony LeVier made regular trips to P-38 units to demonstrate the aircraft and buck up morale. No one seemed to forget the amazing single engine shows these pilots would perform.

Robert L. "Curly" Johnson recalled, "The first P-38s had a stirrup mounted on a cable, like a regular horse's stirrup, and that's how you got in. It was interesting if you had a seat pack chute on and weren't practised at it. You'd put your foot in the stirrup to launch yourself, but when you got airborne you discovered that your CG [centre of gravity] was too low and you landed underneath the damn airplane flat on your back. So, you learned to throw the parachute up on the wing first and then climb up. Finally, we learned to go back and climb on the horizontal stabilizer and walk up the boom. Then, they changed it to a little trigger you could release and drop down a four-step ladder. But it was still a helluva way to get into an airplane."

The outdoor P-38 assembly line beside Lockheed Burbank factory in early 1942. (Lockheed)

Thomas H. Jones remembered, "We were sent to Muroc Dry Lake (now Edwards AFB) to P-38 checkout. Tar paper shacks with a coal burning potbellied stove at each end. Each time we fired up the stove a cloud of black smoke and soot dusted our uniforms.

"For checkout we had a few 'piggy-back' P-38s – single control where the new Second John (lieutenant) sat behind the IP (instructor pilot) and got a hair-raising 'ride.' Then he was off on his own – a self checkout. We lost a few jocks. With 3,000 rpm and 55 inches of mercury on take-off, if either engine failed it was impossible to hold torque with the one leg muscle. The drill was to *retard* the good throttle, crank in trim, then re-boost and don't forget to feather the dead engine. Otherwise the bird went up – then over – then down!"

The 210 P-38Es built were delivered between October 1941 and February 1942 with a number of detail changes – the Hispano 20 mm cannon in place of the 37 mm Oldsmobile gun, Curtiss Electric propellers in place of Hamilton Standards, improved radios, a low pressure oxygen system and other improvements over the D. An additional 99 E model airframes were built as F-4 photo reconnaissance craft and some of these were in service with the 8th Photo Group in Australia as early as April 1942. P-38Es were also rushed to the Aleutians to equip the 54th Fighter Squadron of the 343rd FG in June 1942. This version of the Lightning was the first to see combat.

Delivery of the 527 P-38s began in April 1942 and continued into September with 40 photo recce aircraft coming off the lines as F-4As and F-5As in addition to the fighter versions; from this point on, all photo Lightnings were produced in addition to the fighters though using the fighter airframe.

Even though the P-38F was the first model of the Lightning to see extensive combat service, it did not incorporate as many improvements as the USAAF would have wished – but it was still the only genuine high altitude fighter in the Army's inventory as of mid-1942. In North Africa,

New Guinea and the Solomons, the P-38F began to see action on a large scale by late 1942.

The P-38G, with Allison F-10 engines and an external bomb/fuel capacity of up to 4,000 lb/1,814 kg (equal to the B-25 and B-26), entered service in September 1942. A total of 1,082 Gs was produced, including 374 ex-322s (Lightning IIs) which had been a part of the original RAF order. An additional 160 F-5As were built with USAAF serials in the P-38G range.

The follow-on P-38H was fitted with 1,425 hp Allison F-15s, the first fully automatic supercharger controls and automatic control of its enlarged oil coolers. By August 1943 601 P-38Hs had been delivered.

Although 2,970 P-38J models were produced, it was not until the last 210 of these machines came off the line in June 1944 that the Lightning's true potential was tapped. By the time that dive brakes, aileron boost, improved cockpit heating, electrical system circuit breakers, an adequate inter cooler system were added to such previous improvements as manoeuvring flaps, flat bullet-proof windshield, better engines and dependable automatically controlled supercharging, the Lightning belatedly became a long-legged combat aircraft.

The P-38L was equipped with F-30 engines which delivered 1,600 hp at 28,700 ft (8,750 m), but this advantage was largely diluted by the L's 500 lb (227 kg) of additional weight. The last of the 3,810 P-38Ls built was rolled out in August 1945.

During 1943 Lockheed built and tested a single P-38K (actually a modified P-38E, 41-1983), which was fitted with paddle-blade propellers and Allison F-17 engines which, with better supercharger control, promised a definite increase in performance at 30,000 ft (9,145 m) and above. The K model was not produced because Allison could not guarantee delivery of the F-17 engines in sufficient quantity so the P-38L followed with F-30s as the next best combination for high altitude bomber escort.

One of the Lockheed company's modified P-38Fs in flight. Fitted with a simple second seat but no dual controls, a small number of these aircraft named "Piggy-Back" were used for P-38 pilot familiarisation training. (Lockheed)

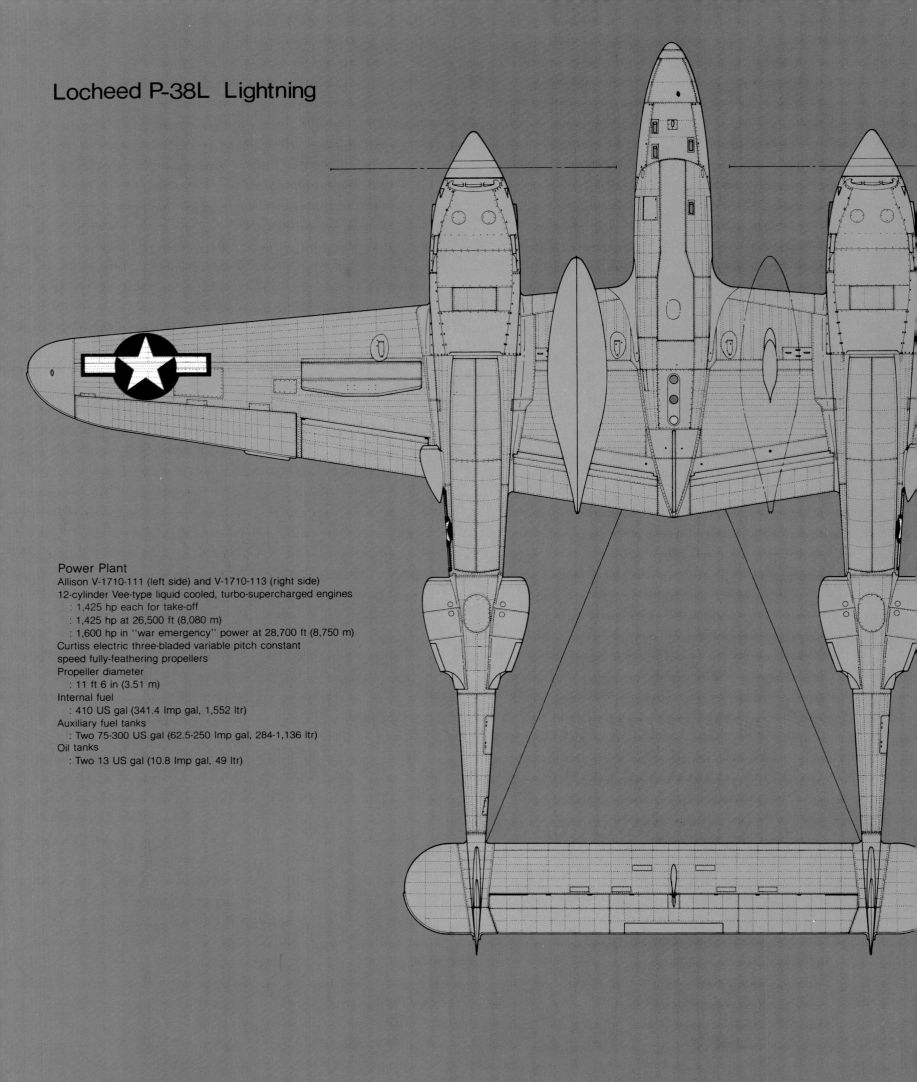

Locheed P-38L Lightning

Power Plant
Allison V-1710-111 (left side) and V-1710-113 (right side)
12-cylinder Vee-type liquid cooled, turbo-supercharged engines
  : 1,425 hp each for take-off
  : 1,425 hp at 26,500 ft (8,080 m)
  : 1,600 hp in ''war emergency'' power at 28,700 ft (8,750 m)
Curtiss electric three-bladed variable pitch constant
speed fully-feathering propellers
Propeller diameter
  : 11 ft 6 in (3.51 m)
Internal fuel
  : 410 US gal (341.4 Imp gal, 1,552 ltr)
Auxiliary fuel tanks
  : Two 75-300 US gal (62.5-250 Imp gal, 284-1,136 ltr)
Oil tanks
  : Two 13 US gal (10.8 Imp gal, 49 ltr)

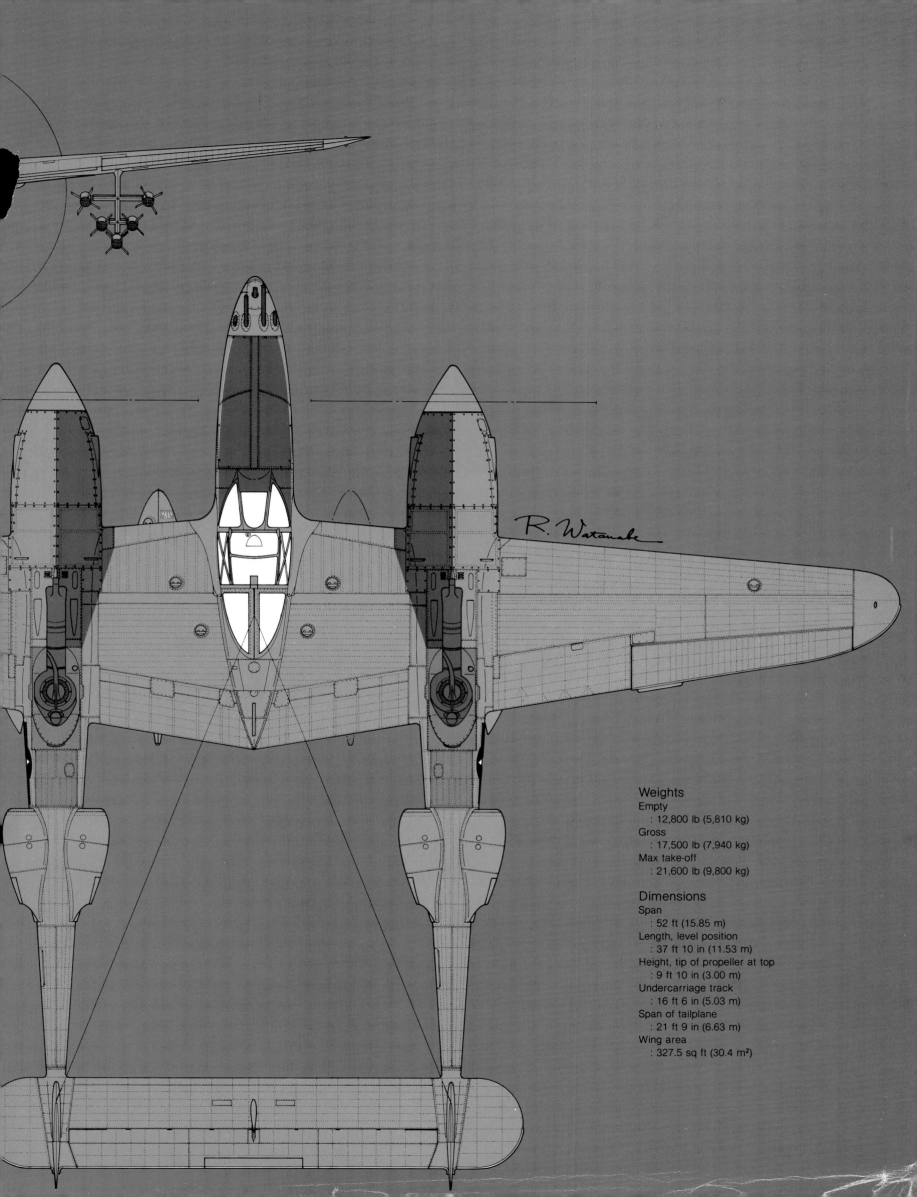

R. Watanabe

Weights
Empty
  : 12,800 lb (5,810 kg)
Gross
  : 17,500 lb (7,940 kg)
Max take-off
  : 21,600 lb (9,800 kg)

Dimensions
Span
  : 52 ft (15.85 m)
Length, level position
  : 37 ft 10 in (11.53 m)
Height, tip of propeller at top
  : 9 ft 10 in (3.00 m)
Undercarriage track
  : 16 ft 6 in (5.03 m)
Span of tailplane
  : 21 ft 9 in (6.63 m)
Wing area
  : 327.5 sq ft (30.4 m²)

Lockheed P-38L Lightning flown by Colonel Charles
H.MacDonald, Commander of the 475th Fighter Group,
5th Air Force

Charles H.MacDonald, the fifth highest ranking ace in the USAAF
(the seventh highest score of all American aces), was born in
Dubois, Pennsylvania, and was appointed the second commander
of the 475th FG "Satan's Angels" in November, 1943. He scored
his first and second victories on 15 October, 1943, and shot down
his 27th and final Japanese aircraft on 13 February, 1945. This illustration shows Col Charles H.MacDonald's P-38L at Tacloban
airfield, Leyte Island in the Philippines, on 25 December, 1944, just
after scoring a triple victory that day bringing his total to 24.

THRUST LINE

CENTRE LINE

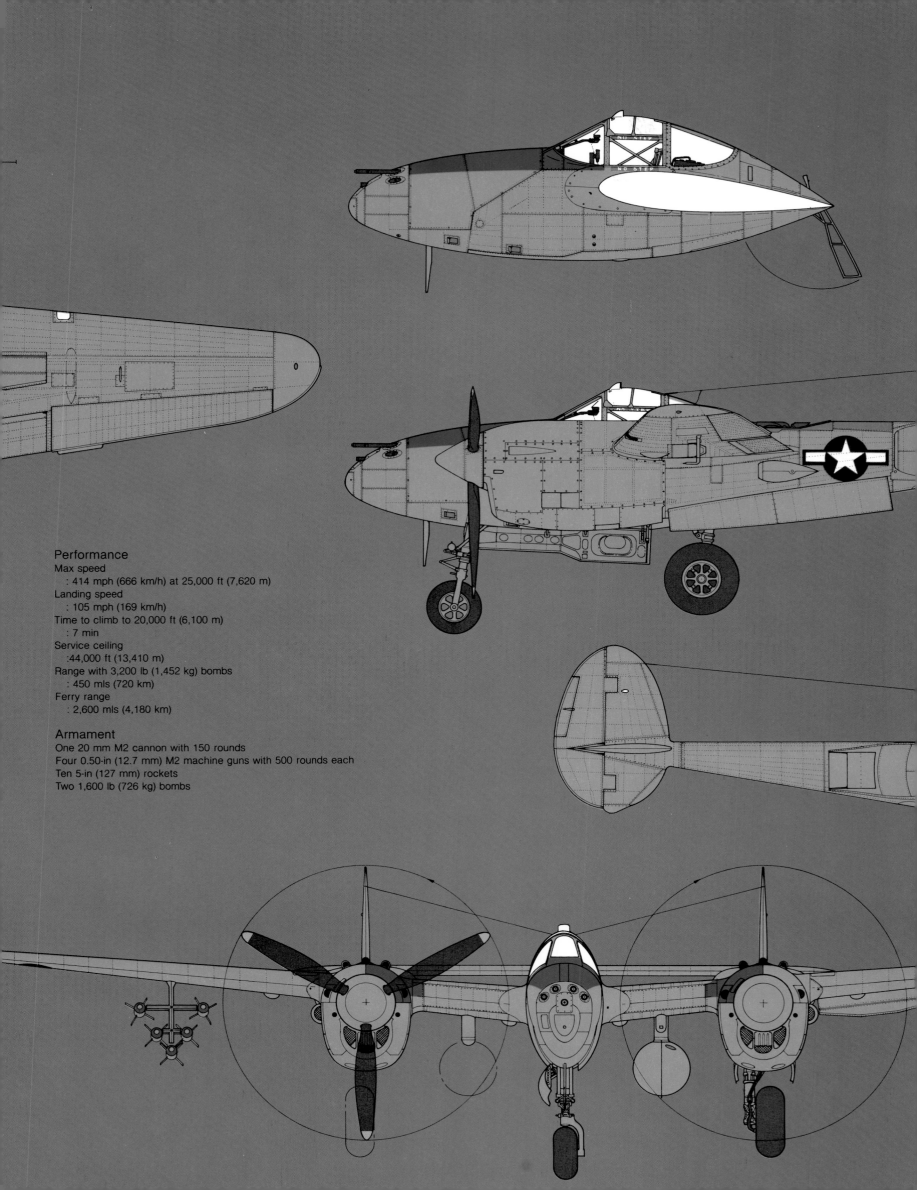

Performance
Max speed
 : 414 mph (666 km/h) at 25,000 ft (7,620 m)
Landing speed
 : 105 mph (169 km/h)
Time to climb to 20,000 ft (6,100 m)
 : 7 min
Service ceiling
 :44,000 ft (13,410 m)
Range with 3,200 lb (1,452 kg) bombs
 : 450 mls (720 km)
Ferry range
 : 2,600 mls (4,180 km)

Armament
One 20 mm M2 cannon with 150 rounds
Four 0.50-in (12.7 mm) M2 machine guns with 500 rounds each
Ten 5-in (127 mm) rockets
Two 1,600 lb (726 kg) bombs

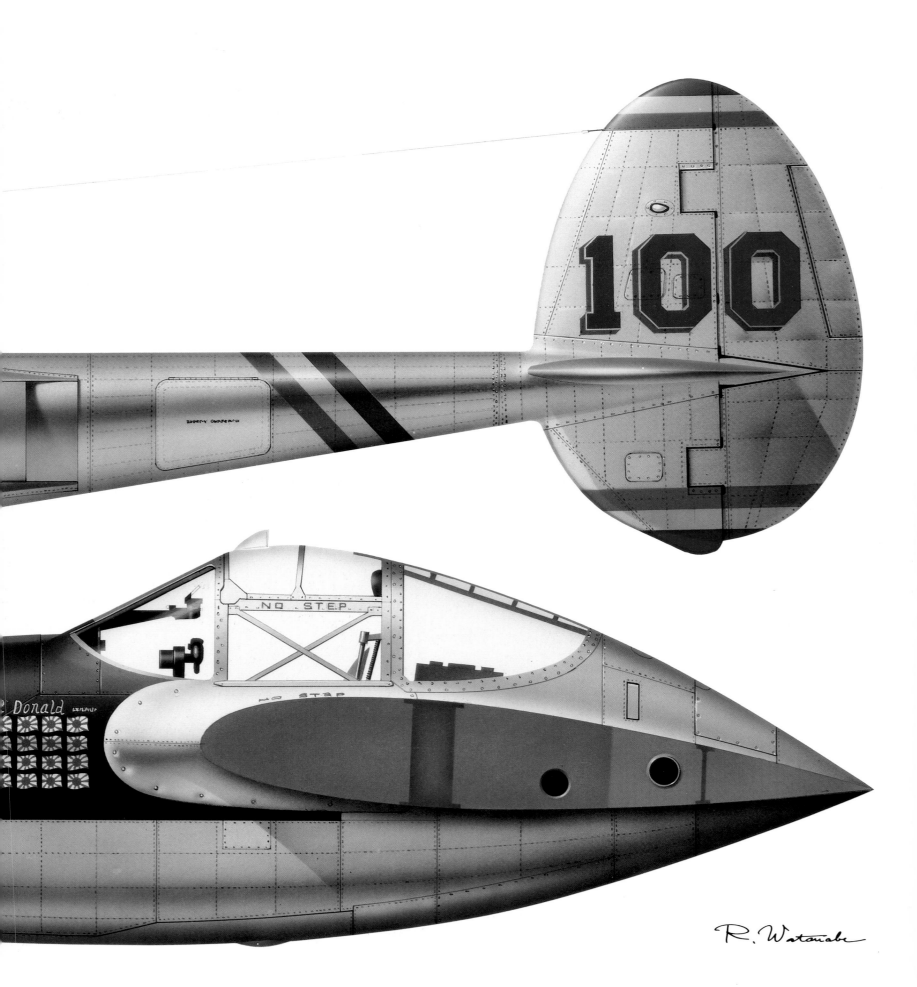

P-38M

Converted from P-38L-5-LO at the Dallas Modification Centre, and made the first flight on 5 February, 1945. Seventy five similar conversions were ordered as P-38M, but only several aircraft were completed.

Power unit
Allison V-1710-111 (left) and V-1710 (right)
: 1,475 hp each for take-off
1,600 hp in "war emergency" power at 28,700 ft (8,750 m)

Performance
Max speed: 391 mph (629 km/h) at 27,700 ft (8,440 m)
Service ceiling: 44,000 ft (13,410 m)

Armament
1 × 20 mm cannon
4 × 0.50-in (12.7 mm) machine guns
Radar equipment : AN / APS-4

Weights
Gross: 17,646 lb (8,000 kg)

Dimensions
Span: 52 ft (15.85 m)
Length: 37 ft 10 in (11.53 m)
Height: 10 ft 4 in (3.15 m)
Wing area: 327.5 sq ft (30.4 m²)

Crew
2 (pilot and radar operator)

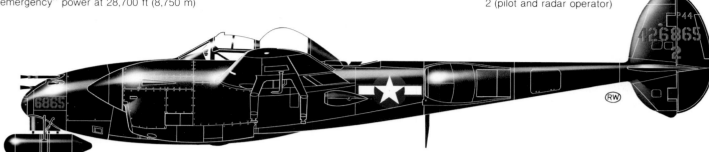

XP-49

Lockheed Model 522, designed as P-38 improvement with 24-cyl Pratt & Whitney HX-2600 engines and ordered in October, 1939. Only one prototype completed and first flown with lower-powered Continental XIV-1430 engines on 11 November, 1942. Neither armament nor the proposed pressurised cockpit were fitted.

Power unit
Continental XIV-1430-13 (left) and XIV-1430-15 (right)
: 1,350 hp each for take-off
Fuel: 300-600 US gal (250-500 Imp gal, 1,135-2,270 ltr)

Performance: 18,500 lb (8,390 kg)
Max speed: 406 mph (653 km/h) at 15,000 ft (4,570 m)
361 mph (581 km/h) at 5,000 ft (1,520 m)
Time to climb to 20,000 ft (6,100 m)
: 8.7 min
Rate of climb: 3,075 ft (937 m)/min
Range: 679 mls (1,093 km)

Armament
2 × 20 mm cannon
4 × 0.50-in (12.7 mm) machine guns

Weights
Empty: 15,410 lb (6,990 kg)
Gross: 18,750 lb (8,505 kg)

Dimensions
Span: 52 ft (15.85 m)
Length: 40 ft 1 in (12.22 m)
Height: 9 ft 10 in (3.00 m)
Wing area: 327.5 sq ft (30.4 m²)

XP-58

An advanced development of the P-38, designed as a heavy long-range bomber escort fighter and confirmed in July, 1940. Due to non-availability of the specified engines and official changes of proposed role the XP-58 prototype not flown until 6 June, 1944. Two months before, the second prototype was cancelled without settlement when 65 per cent complete.

Power plants
Allison V-3420-11 (left) and V-3420-13 (right)
: 2,600 hp each for take-off
3,000 hp at 25,000 ft (7,620 m)
Fuel: 656-760 US gal (546-633 Imp gal, 2,483-2,877 ltd)
max 1,690 US gal (1,407 Imp gal, 6,397 ltr)

Performance
Max speed: 436 mph (702 km/h) at 25,000 ft (7,620 m)
Cruising speed: 274 mph (441 km/h)
Time to climb to 25,000 ft (7,620 m): 12 min
Rate of climb: 2,660 ft (666 Imp gal, 3,028 ltr)
Service ceiling: 38,400 ft (11,700 m)
Absolute ceiling: 39,975 ft (12,184 m)
Range with 800 US gal (666 Imp gal, 3,028 ltr)
: 1,250 mls (2,010 km)

Armament
2 × 20 mm cannon
8 × 0.50-in (12.7 mm) machine guns
4 × 1,000 lb (454 kg) bombs

Weights
Empty: 31,624 lb (14,345 kg)
Gross: 39,192 lb (17,777 kg)
Max: 43,020 lb (19,514 kg)

Dimensions
Span: 70 ft (21.34 m)
Length: 49 ft 5 in (14.95 m)
Height: 13 ft 7 in (4.14 m)
Wing area: 600 sq ft (55.7 m²)

Crew
2 (pilot and turret gunner)

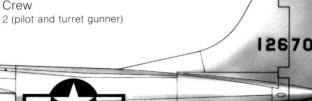

Scale 1/63

P-38E of the 343rd FG, 54th FS, 11th AF on the ramp at Adak, Aleutian Islands in 1942. The weather was more hostile than the Japanese forces. (Frank Shearin)

The Aleutians

Even though the Japanese diversion of landing 3,000 soldiers on the Aleutian Islands of Attu and Kiska in June 1942 failed to lure the US Navy from the Battle of Midway, the enemy threat to Alaska and the North American continent, though an unknown quantity, had to be challenged. As things turned out, the weather was a far more formidable enemy to both sides.

Though the aircraft were not considered fully combat capable, P-38Es were thrown into the gap to fly with the 28th Composite Group, making up the 54th Fighter Squadron. The Lightning was the only fighter capable of operations up and down the 1,200 mile Aleutian Archipelago but pilots often flew in fog so dense that a flight leader lost sight of his Nos 3 and 4 which were flying wing. Of the initial batch of pilots to go into action with the 54th, only 10 survived – the majority were lost to bad weather. Most of the missions from the autumn of 1942 were flown against Attu and Kiskaj from Umnak, usually to bomb and strafe since there were few enemy fighters to tangle with. As Adak and Amchitka became available for P-38 operations, the 54th FS moved up the island chain and by May the Army successfully conquered Attu, and two months later Kiska was recaptured.

By October 1943 the 54th moved to the island of Shemya to stand guard for an enemy that never returned yet continued to battle the enemy of weather until the war ended.

North Atlantic Ferry

After the attack on Pearl Harbor, the United States became aware of just how unprepared it was to fight a global war. Not only would aircraft have to be shipped to the war theatres, but they would have to be flown over to save time.

Operation "Bolero", the build-up of US forces in England, began in the spring of 1942 with the ferrying of aircraft across the North Atlantic. Bombers and transports were no problem but fighters were another matter. Since there was no official interest in external fuel tanks before the war, increasing the range of fighters could have been impossibly complicated – except for some behind the scenes manoeuvring before the war.

General Oliver Echols, Chief Engineer at Wright Field before going to Washington as a Deputy Chief of Staff in charge of Procurement, is looked upon as the man most responsible for what readiness existed in America before the war. Ben Kelsey remembers being "ordered into his office one morning and finding out that General Arnold wanted to know about ferrying fighters across the ocean. So Arnold said, 'Spaatz here says we got to find out whether we can fly our fighters across to Europe. What can we do about it?' I thought he was going to say, in his typical fashion, 'Tell me why you can't do it?' I had already worked on the problem and it just so happened that the 13th version of the drop tank we had been flying on the P-38 had just flown 2,200 miles.

P-38F just airborne from the dusty La Senia airfield in Algeria, North Africa. (US Army)

"I told this to Arnold and he reacted, 'Who authorized that?!' I answered, 'Nobody, General. Remember that it is prohibited to carry external fuel on our fighters.' Arnold came back, 'How long is it going to take you?' 'A month I guess. If we recycle the 1st Fighter Group that's already got them back through the factory, we should have them out in 90 days.' Arnold: 'What the heck's going to take you so long?' Answer: 'General, you know we can't have them – we haven't got them.' Arnold's classic reply, 'Oh go on, get the hell out of here, get going!' "

As a result of this classic exchange, the Air Corps was able to develop reliable external fuel tanks, as proven by the 1st and 14th Fighter Groups taking their P-38s across the Atlantic Ocean beginning on 27 June 1942. The Lightnings went across in fours led by a B-17E for navigation. In all, 178 P-38s made it across the Atlantic to England on the ferry route while 656 reached Britain by sea.

The 1st Fighter Group P-38Fs arrived in England between 9 July and 25 July while the 27th Fighter Squadron of the Group stayed in Iceland until 28 August for air defence. On 15 August 1942 Lt Elza E. Shahan of the 27th FS shared with P-40 pilot J. K. Shaffer (33rd FS) credit for the first German aircraft destroyed in the European Theatre of Operations (ETO) by the USAAF in the Second World War when they shot down an FW 200 Condor off the Icelandic coast.

The 48th and 49th Fighter Squadrons of the 14th Fighter Group reached England during the last two weeks in August, permanently leaving behind in Iceland the 50th FS which relieved the 27th to go on to England.

Both the 1st and 14th Fighter Groups were attached to the US 8th Army Air Force in England but Operation "Torch," the invasion of North Africa, had been finalised in late July so the Lightnings were committed to that action even as they were being broken in over England. Beginning 1 September the P-38s flew several missions over the European continent, although no contact with the Luftwaffe resulted.

On 24 October the Groups were alerted for movement and by 8 November the aircraft landed at Gibraltar as Torch was launched across the Mediterranean.

North Africa

By 11 November the 14th Fighter Group flew the first Lightning mission from African soil when 48th FS pilots got airborne at 1330 hours from Tafaraoui. The ground echelon had not arrived yet so the pilots had to be their own mechanics and armourers, scrounging from the British; fuel was poured into the aircraft by hand with five gallon cans, using a rag to filter the sand out.

In combat the pilots soon found that the separate firing buttons for the 20 mm cannon and the .50 calibre machine guns were unnecessary. Arthur O. Beimdiek, a 48th pilot, recalls making things a bit easier by modifying this battery of fire power: "Several of us did something else with our guns. There was a lot of heavy equipment down in front of your left knee for charging a gun that jammed. In combat, you haven't time to try to figure if one of your .50 calibers wasn't firing, so we had this heavy junk taken out. It lightened the load a lot. Also, on the control wheel, there was a thumb button for the cannon and a finger button on the back side for the four machine guns. When I pressed the button, I wanted everything possible going out the front end, so I had all guns wired to the finger button."

Before long the 1st and 14th Fighter Groups were flying their Lightnings as units but it was rare to get more than 10 aircraft up on a single mission. Aircraft and spare parts were scarce, and would continue to remain so well into 1943. General Dwight Eisenhower, in overall command of Torch, had yet to learn the proper use of tactical airpower; he soon had General Jimmy Doolittle's US 12th Air Force spread thinly over 600 miles of Northwest Africa to serve, piecemeal, the presumed needs of his ground commanders. The two P-38 Groups, particularly the 14th, would pay heavily as a result.

During early operations with the 48th FS, Lt Ervin C. Ethell recalled a sweep near Tunis. After turning around for the return trip to Maison Blanche, the P-38 pilots realized they had overextended their range. It was late and as nightfall settled they received a vector from the British to land at Boné, a field manned by the French with no runway lights. Open five gallon cans were half filled with dirt and soaked with petrol, then lit to outline the runway. As each Lightning landed the pilot was signalled to brake, get out and leave his aircraft unmoved until daylight. Ethell, upon getting out of his P-38F *Tangerine*, walked to the rear of his aircraft instead of, as usual, towards the nose. The next morning he found his nosewheel less than three feet from the precipice of a 200 foot cliff overlooking the sea.

By the end of November both Groups had tangled with the enemy enough to know there was quite a disparity in experience. The Lightning pilots would have to learn things the hard way, living in rugged conditions. The primary problem, particularly with the Lightnings based at Youks`les Bains, was mud which mired the aircraft after every rain, forcing the pilots to take-off and land on the adjacent 1,700 ft (520 m) smooth slope of rock.

Tents were the highest style of living until empty five gallon petrol cans were formed into an officer's club and Group HQ. Food was usually K-Ration except for what could be traded with the Berber tribesmen (always called Arabs) to get coveted eggs or mutton.

As pilots became more experienced, they found that the concentrated fire power of the P-38 offered exceptional strafing capability and more often than not, the Lightnings were sent out to hit ground targets rather than escort bombers, though they did both, as well as some tactical reconnaissance due to superior range.

In December 1942 two new Lightning groups arrived in Africa, the first being the 3rd Photo Recon Group, flying F-4s and F-5As and commanded by the President's son, Col Elliot Roosevelt. Just before Christmas Day, the 82nd FG entered the theatre along with the first batch of replacement pilots for the other two Lightning fighter units.

Norman W. Jackson, one of the 26 replacement pilots, remembers what it was like, "I had only 30 hours in a P-38 and no aerial gunnery. By the time I had 30 hours of combat, I had bailed out, crash-landed in the desert, come home on one engine and brought one more home so shot up that it was junked."

With the New Year came more ground attack missions, and the Lightning was doing most of Eisenhower's ground support of a stalled offensive due to its versatility and range. William Hoelle, a pilot with the 49th FS who had earlier survived, along with his P-38, a collision with a telephone pole, recalled a particularly rough low level fighter recon sweep over Kairboun on 8 January. The eight P-38s were strafing tanks when they were bounced by about 20 Bf 109s and Fw 190s. The first inkling he had of a fight was the Lightning on his left going down under fire. Hoelle pulled up immediately into an Immelmann which brought him out of the fight. No sooner had he rolled out than he found himself in another fight with a Messerschmitt in front of him, which he quickly shot down.

With more Germans on his tail, he dropped the flaps to the manoeuvring stop but a cannon shell hit jammed them down, eliminating the possibility of running away from the fight. After some desperate manoeuvring, Hoelle's left engine was hit and burst into flames when he was a bare 50 ft off the ground. Nothing to do but get out – the terrain was too rough to crash land. He pulled the Lightning up into a stall and jumped out between the booms at 500 ft (150 m) as the aircraft fell into a spin. He landed behind Allied lines, suffering shrapnel wounds, but was returned to base by friendly Arabs and Frenchmen.

Robert J. Moffatt recalled that "the P-38 was definitely a low altitude fighter. It compared very well with the Bf 109G and Fw 190 even to manoeuvrability in low altitudes, but the manoeuvrability dropped off as altitude increased. We were faster in straight and level flight. The 109G could out-dive us on the initial dive, but we could hold our

An armourer checks the machine guns on P-38J-15-LO of the 14th FG, 49th FS, 12th AF, at Mateur, Tunisia in 1943. (Ken Sunny)

speed longer. Both 190 and 109G could initially outclimb us, but again we could soon overtake them."

When flaps were placed in the manoeuvre detent, pilots found they could out-turn any of the opposition; this was aided quite often by reducing power on the inside engine and increasing power on the outside engine. Pilots fighting the very manoeuvrable Japanese fighters in the Pacific found they could do the same thing after gaining some experience, although the standard directive given to new pilots was never to turn with an opposing single-engined fighter.

It was not until March 1943 that the P-38 pilots began to gain superiority over the enemy: enough aircraft were finally being supplied to the theatre, though at the expense of the units that were flying the Lightning in England which had to give up P-38s for P-47s.

In April, during Operation "Flax", the Lightnings joined other Allied fighter units to intercept the masses of Axis transport aircraft that were attempting to resupply the remains of the *Afrika Korps*. Skip bombing of ships was also being perfected.

On 13 May 1943 the last German and Italian troops surrendered in North Africa which would now be a base for the coming landings in Sicily and Italy. The campaign for Tunisia had established the worth of the P-38 and the commanders in the Mediterranean, in the words of General Carl "Tooey" Spaatz, considered the aircraft to be "in a class by itself."

The Mediterranean

The first stepping stone to Europe's "soft underbelly" (which turned out to be anything but) was the island of Pantelleria. In May and June 1943 the entire North African Strategic Air Force, with P-38s in the forefront, attacked the island. Most of the Lightnings were used to strafe and dive bomb but Ernest C. Young, Deputy Group Commander of the 82nd Fighter Group, decided to skip bomb the well protected underground hangar in the side of a mountain. He skipped a 1,000 lb (454 kg) bomb directly into the hangar doors, but unfortunately the bomb only dented them. Pantelleria was the first objective totally neutralised by airpower alone.

As all Lightning units were moved to Tunisia in June 1943, the Northwest African Photo Reconnaissance Wing was growing to meet the increasing need for accurate assessment of Axis movements and strength. The primary recce aircraft was the Lightning and among the new units to fly the aircraft was the French *Groupe de Reconnaissance* II/33 (later GR I/33) which had to start operations with war-weary F-4s. Among the unit's pilots was the legendary *Capitaine* Antoine de Saint Exupéry who, at 43, was too old for combat operations but his talent with words worked in his behalf. He was delighted to be flying for France but a year later, on 31 July 1944, he went missing in action in an F-5A, No 223. Sicily was invaded on 9–10 July 1943 and six days before Lt Thomas H. Jones flew his first mission with the 95th FS of the 82nd Fighter Group from Constantine, North Africa to Milis, Sardinia: "After take-off and climb over the

sea, some jock above and ahead of me cleared his four .50s with a burst of fire (as we always did) and the empty casings rattled off my windscreen, scaring the hell out of me. Thought the Jerries had me zeroed in – and I was gonna be shot down!"

In August and early September, the Lightnings of the 1st and 82nd Fighter Groups began to encounter fierce enemy fighter resistance as Sicily was captured and plans were made to invade Italy. Distinguished Unit Citations were given to both groups (the second for each) for facing close to 75 enemy fighters at a time while escorting bombers – the 1st FG battled things out on 30 August 1943 over the coast of Italy and the 82nd FG ran into severe opposition over Italy on 2 September.

Tom Jones was flying with the 82nd that day: "The Germans and Italians first put up about 70 fighters (Macchi 202s, Reggiane 2000s and Bf 109s). As we approached at about 14,000 feet from the sea we could see the dust trails made by their take-offs from several fields. What an air battle – never before (or since) have I seen so many aircraft in one area in combat – 220 aircraft, of which 145 were fighters. We were using our escort formation of flights of four P-38s in trail scissoring (crossing over) with other four-ship P-38 flights above and around the B-25s when they hit us. Everywhere one looked, a P-38 or an enemy fighters was in a steep dive or spiral, some smoking, to plunge into the Bay of Naples or the adjacent sea. Looked like one of those old war movies *Hell's Angels* or *Wings* or *Lilac Time*! Of course we had to drop our two 165-gallon pylon tanks immediately – and it was 350 miles over water back to home base. They followed us out to almost 100 miles from Naples. Some of us just couldn't make it – headed for the 31st American Spitfire strip on the north shore of Sicily to refuel. Our flying suits were salt-encrusted from good old scared sweat! I got an Bf 109 that day – right on the deck – not 100 yards away crossing in front of me – the battle had worked down to just above the sea." Every one of the escorted B-25s made it back to base.

Johannes Steinhoff, *Kommodore* of JG 77 in North Africa, Sicily and Italy, flying Bf 109s, had this to say about the P-38, "I had encountered the long-range P-38 Lightning fighter during the last few days of the North African campaign. Our opinion of this twin-boomed, twin-engined aircraft was divided. Our old Messerschmitts were still, perhaps, a little faster. But pilots who had fought them said that the Lightnings were capable of appreciably tighter turns and that they would be on your tail before you knew what was happening. The machine guns mounted in the nose supposedly produced a concentration of fire from which there was no escape. Certainly the effect was reminiscent of a watering can when one of these dangerous apparitions started firing tracer, and it was essential to prevent them manoeuvring into a position from which they could bring their guns to bear."

Oberleutnant Franz Stiegler, a 28 victory ace in the Bf 109 with JG 27 in North Africa, said the P-38s "could turn inside us with ease and they could go from level flight to climb almost instantaneously. We lost quite a few pilots who tried to make an attack and then pull up. The P-38s were on them at once. They closed so quickly that there was little one could do except roll quickly and dive down, for while the P-38 could

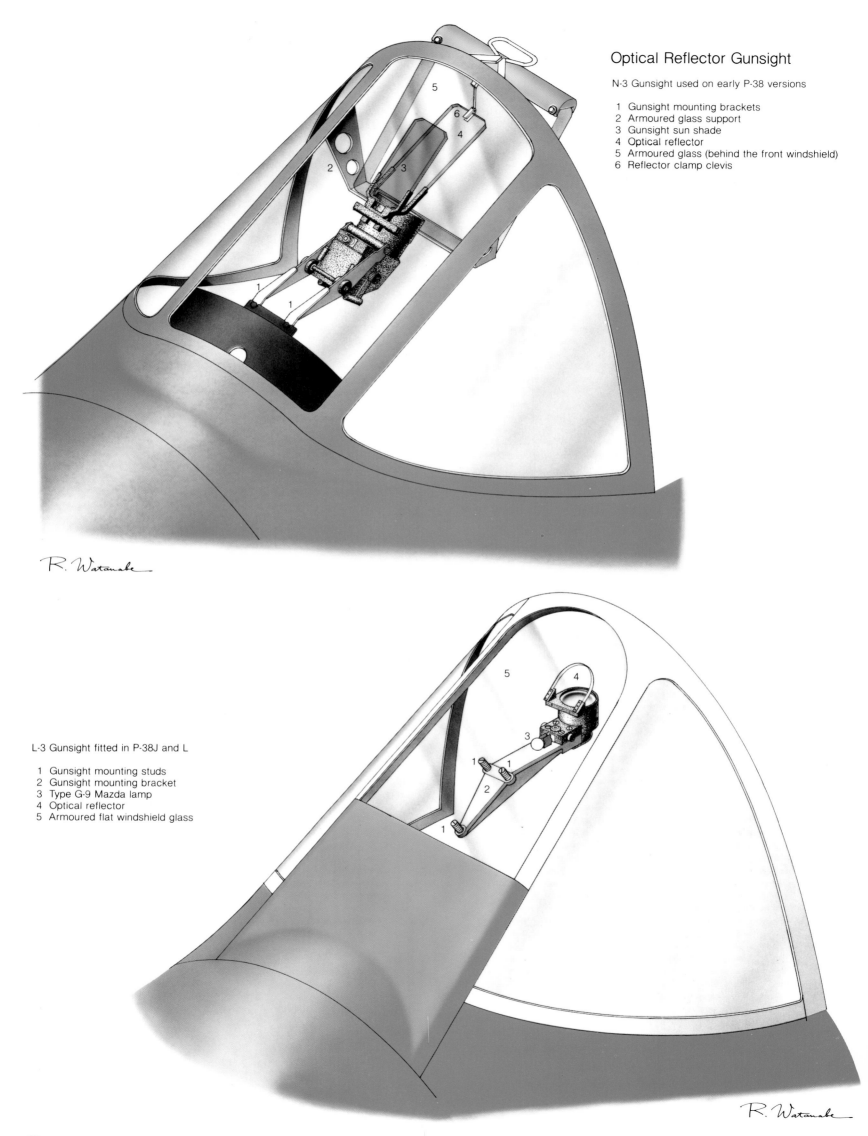

Optical Reflector Gunsight

N-3 Gunsight used on early P-38 versions

1 Gunsight mounting brackets
2 Armoured glass support
3 Gunsight sun shade
4 Optical reflector
5 Armoured glass (behind the front windshield)
6 Reflector clamp clevis

L-3 Gunsight fitted in P-38J and L

1 Gunsight mounting studs
2 Gunsight mounting bracket
3 Type G-9 Mazda lamp
4 Optical reflector
5 Armoured flat windshield glass

R. Watanabe

turn inside us, it rolled very slowly through the first 5 or 10 degrees of bank, and by then we would already be gone. One cardinal rule we never forgot was: avoid fighting a P-38 head on. That was suicide. Their armament was so heavy and their firepower so murderous, that no one ever tried that type of attack more than once."

After the surrender of Italy in September, a new US Air Force, the 15th, was formed in November to become the second strategic arm of the Combined Bomber Offensive against Germany – the 1st, 14th and 82nd Fighter Groups were transferred along with the recce units from the 12th to the 15th Air Force and based at the fields around Foggia, Italy. A problem that began to show up was sabotage of American aircraft by Italians who were still sympathetic to the Germans; a number of Italian fighter pilots had chosen to stay on the German side.

On 25 December 1943 the 82nd FG was assigned a fighter sweep and Jules J. Hymel of the 95th FS remembers being at 23,000 ft (7,010 m) over the Alps when enemy fighter came up through the overcast. An immediate break was called, Hymel pulled back on the control yoke and the wheel hit him square in the chest, also knocking off his oxygen hose connection. He was convinced it was sabotage. Beginning to pass out, he jettisoned the canopy and released his belts, then caught his right foot within the cockpit. The next thing he remembers is floating in mid-air, waking enough to see his Lightning hit the ground without its tail. He pulled the ripcord, swung twice and hit a mountain which knocked him out cold. He woke up with civilian clothes on and a fractured right ankle; due to his injuries, the Italian underground had him turned over to the Germans.

Col Oliver B. Taylor, Commander of the 14th Fighter Group in 1944, analysed the P-38's effectiveness is the theatre with the following recollections:

Bad Points

1. Ease of Handling: It required at least twice as much flying time, perhaps more, to achieve the level of skill which was necessary to realise the full capability of the ship, as compared with what it took with a single engine fighter. Only after about 150 or 200 hours could a man hope to be an expert, but when he reached that point he could be unbeatable in the 38.

2. Vertical Dives: The 38 could not be controlled in a vertical dive if allowed to build up speed, and that happened awfully damned fast, with speed rapidly building up thereafter until something came apart. The Jerry knew this well.

3. Distinctive silhouette: The Jerry, on seeing a lone plane off in the distance, would generally leave it be unless he had absolutely nothing else in prospect at the moment. On seeing the unique P-38 silhouette, however, there would be no doubt at all, and after it he would go, knowing that it would not be a waste of time.

Good Points

1. Stability: The plane could be pulled into a tight turn, essentially right at the stall point, without snapping out or dropping. The counter-rotating props eliminated any torque problems when passing through a range of speeds. This was particularly useful during dive bombing and strafing runs because the longitudinal axis of the plane remained on the flight path along which we were aiming.

2. Manoeuvrability: Generally we found the 38 could out-manoeuvre anything else, friend or foe, between about 18,000 and 31,000 ft (5,490 and 9,450 m). Below 18,000, it was sort of a toss up, except that very near the ground we could run Jerry right into the dirt, since he apparently couldn't get quite such a fast pull-out response as we could.

3. Range: A 500 mile (800 km) distant target was easily reached allowing for 30 to 45 minutes for possible diversions. Being something less than modest about it, I feel I initiated the first really big step toward extending our escort range, when I prevailed upon out Wing (Gen Atkinson) to let us join the bombers out somewhere near the target area, rather than burn up fuel accompanying them from their bases. This created quite a stir among the bomb group COs, but a foul up helped me convince them.

4. Single Engine Flight: The 38 was just as controllable turning into, as away from, the dead engine. Quite a number of our ships returned on one engine without mishap.

5. Engine configuration: Aside from having another engine to bring you home in case one is lost, the two-engine arrangement provided exceptionally good visibility forward for the pilot, and provided protection from flanking enemy fire, especially during low-level strafing runs.

6. Rugged Construction: The 38 could take a phenomenal amount of beating up and still make it home. One [flown by Lt Thomas W. Smith, 37th Squadron] was hit by an Me 109, one wing of the 109 having slashed along the inside face of the right boom, carrying away the inside cooler and slicing the horizontal stabilizer/elevator assembly in two. The 109 lost its wing and crashed. The 38 flew 300 miles (480 km) on one engine to belly land on my orders at our base. The pilot wanted to try the wheels, but figured he had gone far enough in disobeying two previous orders from me to bale out.

7. Ease of maintenance: I can only go by reports from maintenance types. The general feeling seemed to be that both the P-38 and the Allison engines were very easy to maintain. In our Group, we had an exceptionally high level of experienced ground crew types, and they did an extraordinary job. During the winter of 1943, when no replacement 38s were coming through, they kept the few we had operating under the most adverse conditions, so that we were always able to meet our commitments when called upon. I would say that the vast majority of our early returns due to malfunction were the fault of the pilot.

The photo reconnaissance Lightnings were heavily engaged in first part of 1944 and another recce group, the 5th, had been added to the 15th Air Force. On 19 May Lt R. L. Luce, assigned to the 5th, was sent to the east coast of Italy near Venice. Heading north at 1030 he found an Bf 109 and an Fw 190 on his tail, one half mile behind and closing fast at his altitude of 140 ft (40 m). Luce dropped tanks and went full bore but he could not outdistance the enemy aircraft which had closed to 800 yards.

Heading north, Luce then turned inland above Venice, deciding to make his photo runs with the Germans still on his tail. Flying parallel to the coast at 300 ft (90 m), Luce started taking pictures, receiving sporadic machine gun fire from the ground. The Germans were still clinging to him. The American pointed his Lightning east, passing *under* some high tension wires running across Lake Veneta.

Dense smoke appeared to be coming from a burning oil refinery or oil storage plant at Porto Marghera – a damage assessment could well be made so Luce turned north along the east side of the refinery, taking pictures. The 109 and 190 were still there. A quick 180° turn into the smoke and

P-38J-15-LO "Billy Boy" flown by Ben A. Mason, Jr., Deputy Commander of the 82nd FG, 12th AF, in 1944 when the Group was based at Foggia, Italy. (Ben Mason)

another 180° turn while in the smoke at 200 ft (60 m); the Germans had been chasing the recon Lightning for 30 minutes and if something wasn't done, Luce knew he would never make it back.

The blue Lightning popped out of the smoke over the north coast of Lake Veneta and the Germans were gone. Taking more photos as he came over the coast, he dashed for home. Dangerously low on fuel, Luce feathered one engine. Calling MAYDAY as he neared friendly territory, he received a direct vector to Vasto where he landed at 1245, on single engine, with only seven gallons of fuel left. Luce re-fuelled and flew home, an example of the unheralded recce pilots who flew the Lightning alone and unarmed.

On 10 June 1944 the 82nd Fighter Group dive-bombed the Romana Americana Oil Refinery at Ploesti, Rumania while the 1st Fighter Group provided escort – an all-Lightning show. The 1st went ahead of the 82nd to engage enemy fighters and the reaction was overwhelming as German and Rumanian pilots scrambled. Lt Herbert B. Hatch of the 71st FS shot down five German fighters on the way home; it was his first mission. The 82nd's P-38s, each carrying a 1,000 lb (454 kg) bomb, went in at tree top level, then pulled up over the refinery to make their runs. Dogfights were numerous over the target area and on the way back with heavy claims on both sides. Sending fighters on strategic missions was a rough way to operate and it was not tried again.

Enemy air activity was consistently heavy in the summer of 1944 – on 14 June the 14th Fighter Group supported the 55th Bomb Wing to the Petfurdo oil refineries in Hungary and had a day pilots still remember, particularly in the 49th FS.

As smoke rose over the target up to 20,000 ft (6,100 m), the 37th and 48th FS went east of the column while the 49th went west alone. As 49th pilot Don Luttrell remembers, "Suddenly the whole sky erupted with German fighters against our 15 P-38s." 40 to 50 109s attacked in two

groups simultaneously at 1105. Lt Louis Benne was leading the squadron but got separated on the first pass. Lt Clyde Jones called a break to the right and brought the flights into a large Lufbery turning circle, destroying enemy aircraft as the manoeuvre was initiated. As the flights got into position, belly tanks were dropped, falling directly through some of the formation and miraculously hitting none of the P-38s.

Benne attempted to get into the Lufbery, shooting down two 109s in the process but just as he destroyed the second Messerschmitt he was hit by another 109 that had come in on his tail. The right engine was knocked out, the instrument panel shattered, the left engine caught fire and he was hit in the left shoulder by 20 mm shrapnel. Kicking the Lightning into a spin to get away, he recovered at 14,000 ft (4,270 m), pulled the nose up to kill speed, crawled out on the wing and dived down through the booms, then opened his parachute. He was immediately captured after being buzzed by the victorious 109.

The battle had developed into a mass of aircraft. Jones was one of the first to fire on a 109 passing through but as he rolled out slightly to fire his instrument panel disintegrated as a Messerschmitt pounded him. Jones kicked bottom rudder and went straight down. The small incendiary charge carried in the aircraft to set it on fire after a crash landing in enemy territory was ignited, burning the oxygen lines and fuel lines and a roaring fire developed.

Still going straight down, Jones began to claw his way out but his leather gloves had become slick from the heat and he could grasp nothing. The canopy finally popped open and the suction pulled Jones, still strapped to the seat, into the slipstream; the seat sprung to full extension and spread him over the back of the canopy. Reaching down, he managed to release the belt and was sucked out of the cockpit, catching his feet on the wheel and fracturing his legs. As he was thrown over the canopy, his back was broken and then his head hit one of the mass balances on the elevator, knocking him out.

When Jones came to, he was trying to pull the chute

open with his hands, tearing his finger nails off, then came to his senses and pulled the D-ring. The chute opened – the first good thing that had happened all day. Coming down within 50 feet of his crashed P-38, Jones was roughed up and arrested by civilians before being sent to a hospital in Budapest and then Stalag Luft III.

As the fight progressed, two turning circles formed at 18,000 ft (5,490 m), one to the right and one to the left. Lt Thomas S. Purdy recalled, "There wasn't one split moment went by that I couldn't see Bf's in front, above, beside and below; they came from above and every direction."

One turning circle got down to 14,000 ft (4,270 m) and Purdy called, "Climb Hangmen, climb," using the call name for the 49th. Jack Lenox was in awe as "no one could tell who was leading who as we continued the circle.... Every muscle in my body ached and I wondered how much longer this could last." It lasted for 25 minutes, an eternity in combat. When the Lightnings broke to run, the 109s did not follow. The 49th claimed 13 destroyed and five damaged for the loss of five P-38s. No one single pilot who returned shot at less than eight Bf 109s. Not one bomber was lost.

During the first week in August the second and final shuttle mission to the Soviet Union for the Lightnings was flown. On the way to Russia on 4 August 1944 1st Lt Richard E. Willsie ran into heavy ground fire and got his left engine shot out; shortly thereafter the right engine began streaming glycol. He radioed to his flight that he was going in and back came the reply, "Pick a good spot. I'm coming down after you." It was Flt Off Richard T. Andrews.

Willsie didn't answer as he set his damaged aircraft down in a Rumanian pasture. Since the ground was furrowed, Andrews made two passes to get a look, then carefully landed the heavy Lightning on the mushy ground close to Willsie as the rest of the Group provided top cover. Andrews threw out his parachute as Willsie ran over to the idling P-38. Squeezing into the cockpit on Andrews' lap, Willsie took the controls and made the long take-off run. They completed the two and a half hour flight to Poltava, Ukraine, with a long stretch of blind flying through rain.

In September 1944 the P-38L entered combat for the first time but by then enemy air opposition had all but disappeared; the 82nd, for example, would score only four more aerial victories before the war's end. Bombing and strafing became the order of the day.

On 7 November, however, the 82nd Fighter Group under Col C. T. "Curly" Edwinson got in serious trouble. Giving ground support to the Soviet troops the day before in Yugoslavia, which had been praised by the Soviet commanders, the Group went back not knowing the battle lines had changed and strafed the Russian columns, killing Soviet Lt Gen Kotov. Not able to communicate with the Americans, the ground commander called in Yak fighters to bounce the Lightnings. Two P-38s went down quickly and the 82nd fought its way out, getting four or five Yaks.

The Soviets immediately demanded Edwinson be shot in exchange for Kotov. The response was Americans did not do things that way, particularly since it was a mistake, so the Russians shot the Yak leader who had jumped the P-38s

and demanded, again, that Edwinson be done away with. "Curly" was quickly spirited out of the theatre and the incident hushed up.

For the remainder of the war in the Mediterranean, the P-38 made its major contribution as a ground attack aircraft: concentrated fire power that did not have to converge made strafing a bit easier in the Lightning. In April 1945 the 14th Fighter Group alone destroyed 111 locomotives, 84 on just one mission as the P-38s roamed southern Germany.

The P-38 was considered the major fighter in the theatre, setting the record for the most sorties flown with only 16% early returns or aborts from missions. Lightnings claimed 608 enemy aircraft destroyed in the air, 123 probables and 343 damaged for 131 P-38s lost. The aircraft was operational 75% of the time versus 72% for the Mustang.

Europe

While the Lightning was regarded as an effective weapon in other theatres, it failed miserably in the European Theatre of Operations until it was given the primary mission of ground support with the US 9th Air Force. When the 20th and 55th Fighter Groups brought their P-38Hs to England in the autumn of 1943, they were immediately faced with long hours above 30,000 ft (9,140 m) to escort the bombers. Cockpit heating in the P-38 was a disaster and there was not enough heat even to keep the windshield defrosted. Pilots found that they quickly became numb in the −60°F (−51°C) temperatures and it was an effort simply to fly, let alone fight.

In addition the supercharger, inter-coolers caused regular engine failures being prone to overboosting. Engine problems also led to many missing airmen and by winter 1943/44, after the P-38s had seen a fair amount of combat, pilot morale suffered badly.

The 55th Fighter Group was the first to fly a mission, on 15 October 1943, and the major asset of the aircraft soon became evident: it had much longer range than the P-47 Thunderbolt which equipped the other fighter groups in the US 8th Air Force. By November a few Lightnings of the 20th Fighter Group were flying with the 55th to gain experience. The 55th lost 12 P-38s, claiming 18 enemy aircraft, while the 20th lost five without claiming any kills.

The first major air battle for the Lightnings took place on 13 November 1943 over Bremen when the Americans traded seven for seven. Mark Shipman, a veteran of North Africa with the 48th FS recalled leaving in foul weather and poking "into the clouds at around 8,000 feet over the channel. The guys stayed in like they were glued together, climbed to 32,000 without topping, ended up then half frozen because the heaters were worthless above 20,000 (outside −57°F), so I let down to 24,000 continuing an occasional evasive turn even though we did not actually see flak. About 15 minutes before target ETA we broke out into absolutely clear air. 50 miles away and about that far apart were two very large boxes of bombers – B-24s – and we could already begin to assess the fighter coverage from the contrails. I put Joe Myers on the lead box with eight and headed for the rear

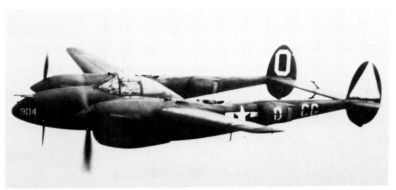

P-38J of the 55th FG, 8th AF, over England in 1944. (T.R. Bennett)

bunch with my eight, trying to top their 25,000 with another two.

"About the time of our arrival two squadrons of roughly 30 109s each had gained position in front of the bombers ready for their head-on attacks. I would hate to guess how many twin-engine rocket launchers were in position to the rear of the boxes. Our tactic was to break up the 109s, make them split-S if their leadership would go for the pitfall, and let us return to escort position.

"Our worst position came when our eight had about that many 190s above us. However, that threat which could have – and on many previous missions would have – tied our hands was soon dealt with and we went back to the primary business of busting up the big threatening gaggles.

"The net result was six scored for my squadron, no losses, and I did not see a single bomber in trouble after we made rendezvous." Shipman told Lt Gen William Kepner, CO of VIII Fighter Command, that this was a breakthrough

in seeing effective escort become a reality.

By the spring of 1944 several more P-38 groups had been added to the 8th and 9th Air Forces – the 370th, 474th and 367th in the 9th and the 364th and 479th Fighter Groups and the 7th Photo Group in the 8th. "Droop Snoot" P-38Js began to appear, first being modified at Langford Lodge, but the Lightning was losing favour as the new P-51 Mustang began to go even farther into enemy territory to escort the bombers.

Lloyd Wenzel of the 474th Fighter Group recalled, "we had solved the problem of predetonation at altitude because of too much cooling in the inter-cooler and did a field-fix, anchoring the nacelle fillet to reduce buffet. We moved the inter-cooler switch up to the control yoke and ganged that switch with the gun sight and guns' hot switch so we wouldn't forget to open it.

"The 474th was the only '38 outfit in the ETO at the end of the war – we had petitioned General Pete Quesada [9th Commander] to let us keep the bird when other groups were changing to P-51s and P-47s."

P-38L Pylon Mechanism

1 AN-N-6 gun sight aiming point camera
2 Camera fairing
3 Front sway brace
4 Wing nut
5 Auxiliary fuel tank shackle clevis
6 Bomb rack
7 Bomb hoist supports
8 Rear sway brace
9 Auxiliary fuel tank fairing aft door
10 Lower failing

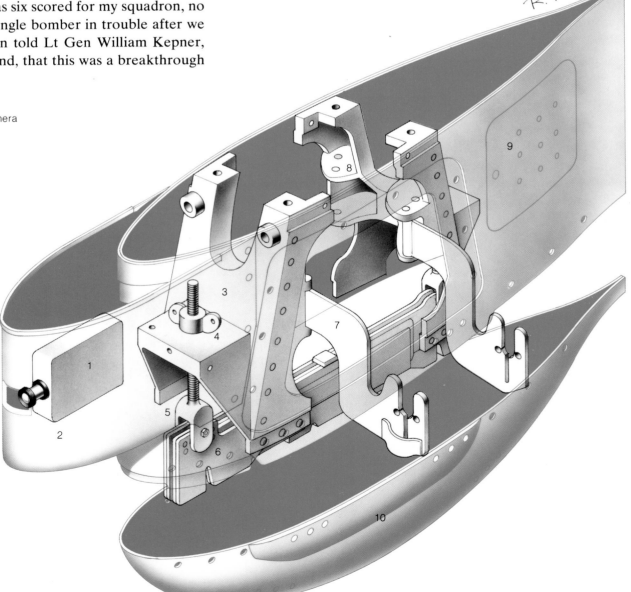

The Lightnings flew through D-Day with bombing and strafing missions in addition to supporting the bombers but soon the P-38s began to disappear, for the most part due to 8th Commander MajGen Jimmy Doolittle's desire to replace his P-38s and P-47s with P-51s. Since the other theatres, particularly the Mediterranean and the Pacific, were continually begging for more P-38s, the solution fit almost everyone. The Lightning had been called an "ice wagon", with some justification, in Europe and it seemed to be doing a much better job on the whole in other parts of the world.

The Pacific

The first six months of the Second World War in the Pacific was disaster for an unprepared United States. Into this arena arrived the Lightning in April 1942, not to fire guns but to take pictures.

Four F-4s (converted P-38Es) were assigned to the 8th Photographic Squadron under the command of Maj Karl Polifka at Melbourne, Australia. Polifka's "A" Flight of four Lightnings, organized on 7 April, took the distinction of pioneering use of the large twin boomed Lockheed in combat. By 16 July 1942 "B" and "C" Flights were operating from Laloki at Port Moresby, New Guinea and Polifka himself mapped a large portion of eastern New Guinea and eastern New Britain. The 8th's Lightnings were the only source of hard data on what the enemy was doing with the normal recon route leading from Port Moresby up to Rabaul and back to Lae and Salamaua.

Polifka and his "Eight Balls," as the squadron came to be known, managed to elude the enemy with great success; far deadlier was the tropical weather. On the way up to Rabaul the F-4s had to cross the equatorial front with its attendant towering cumulus and low ceilings.

General George Kenney, US 5th Air Force commander, grew increasingly impatient in 1942 for P-38 fighters in the Southwest Pacific. Every time he pleaded with "Hap" Arnold for Lightnings, he was told that Europe and Africa would have to be taken care of first. The 13th Air Force was also begging for P-38s to patrol the long overwater Pacific distances. The outclassed P-39s and P-40s were only holding their own.

In August 1942 the first 30 P-38s arrived at Brisbane and Kenney ordered BrigGen Carl Connell to take personal charge getting them ready. Kenney assured Arnold of the usefulness of both the P-39 and the P-40 but they did not have the altitude performance to be effective against the Japanese formations. Kenney recalled that he was looking for the day when he had enough P-38s to engage "the Zero coverage up top-side while the P-39s and P-40s take on the bombers." Issuing a contract to the Australian sheet metal industry, Kenney also ordered about 10,000 150 US gallon (125 Imp gal/568 ltr) drop tanks for added range.

Capt George Prentice was placed in command of the new P-38 unit, the 39th FS, 35th Fighter Group, having been pulled from the veteran 49th Fighter Group. By September 65 Lightnings had arrived at Amberly but Kenney

had to begin grounding them on the 9th. First the fuel tanks began to leak, requiring rubber experts to solve the problem, and the first 25 to arrive had no feeds for the guns.

By 19 September 16 P-38s were being flown out of Laloki but more problems surfaced. Leaks in the intercoolers appeared, forcing an almost total rebuild of the forward wing sections on 10 fighters in New Guinea and 38 in Australia. Problems with inverters and armament showed up as well. If nothing else went wrong, combat for the Lightnings would not be possible until mid-November.

Eight 39th FS P-38s were loaned to MajGen Millard Harmon, 13th Air Force commander, for operations out of Guadalcanal in anti-shipping strikes. On 14 November, when the P-38s landed at Henderson Field, the newly arrived P-38s of the 339th FS were already performing the mission, and by the 22nd Kenney had his Lightnings back.

John Mitchell was the first 339th pilot to fly the P-38 after P-39s and P-400s (P-39 Airacobra variant originally intended for Britain) and he recalled that when the Squadron started to get used to their "hot" ships they bounced every P-39 and P-40 they could find. Maj Dale D. Brannon brought the first 12 of the 339th's Lightnings in to Henderson Field on 12 November, but that night one was lost to enemy shelling. Three more arrived on the 15th and the Squadron began to operate with a mixed bag of P-38s and P-39s.

On 18 November the 339th FS became the first Lightning unit in the Pacific to fire its guns in anger while escorting Col "Blondie" Saunders' 11th Bomb Group B-17s; three Zeros were claimed as destroyed.

Mitchell took command of the Squadron and developed tactics that took into account the bigger, heavier Lightning. Four fighter sections would fly in a loose one mile radius ball, protecting each other's tails. Since the Lightning would not easily out-turn the Zero, pilots would dive under the enemy and zoom up for the kill to keep airspeed high. With the manoeuvring stop on the flaps, the P-38 in the hands

F-4A over heavy clouds. (Lockheed)

of a good pilot could stay with the lighter Japanese fighters in a turn long enough to brings the guns to bear.

In December 1942 Col Henry Viccellio brought up the 70th FS P-39s to begin joint operations with the 339th; both were attached to the 347th Fighter Group. The pilots began to rotate through the Lightnings, which would fly patrol as the Airacobras went low to strafe and dive-bomb. Escort was also provided for Marine Corps SBD Dauntlesses.

As the Lightning pilots honed their skill in fighting the Japanese, they began to give more than take. According to Jiro Horikoshi (in his book *Zero*), "the peculiar sound of the P-38's twin engines became both familiar and bitterly hated by the Japanese all across the South Pacific." By the New Year the P-38s at Guadalcanal had claimed 21 destroyed and seven probables for the loss of four pilots in combat and six in accidents. The fighter pilots were more than pleased with their new Lightnings, though some of them were averaging five or six hours of combat flying a day.

Millard Harmon, now Commanding General, South Pacific, joined Kenney in requesting more P-38s; he had only 41 and wanted an immediate 100.

Kenney's 5th Air Force fighter pilots were still trying to get their Lightnings into combat. On 24 November 1942 the 39th FS hung one 500 lb (227 kg) bomb on each of eight Lightnings, a drop tank being carried on the other shackle. A mission was launched to Lae but very little damage was done. However, Lt Robert Faurot made the first P-38 kill of the 5th Air Force. Overshooting the runway, his bomb landed in the water off the end of the base. Just as the bomb exploded an intercepting Zero of the 582nd Kokutai flew into the wall of water thrown into the air and went in.

When Faurot returned and asked Kenney if he was going to get a medal for his feat, Kenney replied, "Hell, no. I want you to shoot them down, not splash water on them!" Faurot got the Air Medal.

It was not until 27 December 1942 that the 39th FS came face to face with the Japanese in a fight. With good weather, 12 Vals (Aichi D3A) and 12 Zekes (A6M Zero) of the Imperial Japanese Navy Air Force's 582nd Kokutai and 31 Oscars (Ki.43 Hayabusa) of the Japanese Army Air Force's 11th Sentai took off from Rabaul at 0930 hours. The 12 Zekes and eight of the Oscars escorted the Vals while the other 23 Oscars made up the top cover for an attack on Dobodura.

On alert at Laloki, the 39th scrambled 12 P-38s around noon, led by Capt Thomas J. Lynch in flights of four each. Crossing the Owen Stanley Mountains, the Lightnings were called by P-40s of the 49th Fighter Group escorting C-47s, "Hey, P-38s, bandits coming into Dobo 18,000 feet up." Lynch replied, "OK, P-40s, thanks. We'll drive a few down to your level." About 20 minutes after take-off Lynch spotted the Japanese formation as the Vals were making bomb runs from about 6,500 ft (1,980 m).

A milling dogfight developed as Capt Miyabayashi, 1st Chutai leader, opened fire. Before long 9th FS P-40s arrived to help and the Oscars escorting the Vals left the bombers to jump into the fight.

The Lightning pilots made a number of mistakes in their eagerness to engage the long awaited enemy, from firing at too great a distance to manoeuvring with the Oscars and Zekes. They inadvertantly jumped the P-40s a number of times but Lynch claimed two Oscars, Ken Sparks a Zero and a

P-38F of the 35th FG, 39th FS, 5th AF, at Port Moresby, New Guinea in late 1942. (Bruce Hoy)

F-5A shortly before a sortie. (USAF)

P-38Fs in formation flight. (Lockheed)

Val. Andrews, Eason, Planck, Gallup and Bills also made claims. A quiet Wisconsin farm boy named Richard Bong claimed his first two victories, a Val and a Zeke. In all the 39th claimed nine enemy aircraft destroyed while the Japanese claimed four P-38s shot down and three probables.

Japanese records indicate Warrant Officer Tadashi Yoshitake went down in his 1st Chutai Ki.43 Hayabusa, one Navy Zero went down with its pilot while another Zero and another Hayabusa crash-landed: four aircraft and at least two pilots lost. Ken Sparks nose wheel would not come down so he was forced to land at Dobodura but the P-38 was flown back to Laloki a few days later, the only loss.

Four days later, on 31 December, the 39th FS escorted bombers to Lae. Twelve Japanese fighters tangled with the P-38s and seven victory ace 1st Lt Hironojo Shishimoto of the 11th Sentai was lost in his Hayabusa. 39th FS pilots claimed nine destroyed, one probable and two damaged. Ken Sparks was in trouble again – he ran head on into one of his opponents, losing two feet of his right wing. He flew back home but the Japanese fighter lost its right wing and went in. Dick Bong, who himself was well aware of his poor shooting, claimed one of the probables after connecting with the eighth enemy aircraft he shot at.

By early January the 9th FS had transitioned to P-38s, entering combat over Lae. Bong claimed an Oscar on the 8th, bringing him to ace status, while Lynch had six and Sparks four so a "race of aces" was in the making.

For the next two months only single major air action took place in New Guinea, the Japanese raiding Dobodura on 6 February 1943. Kenney's major battle was with Washington for more P-38s. After receiving eight P-38s

under a replacement schedule of 15 per month initiated in January, Kenney got word in February that the crucial situation of North Africa would mean no more P-38s until summer. The only consolation given to Kenney, by General George Marshall himself, was that the 348th Fighter Group, originally scheduled for Europe, would be coming to the theatre with P-47s by 12 June. Of the 330 worn out fighters under General Paul "Squeeze" Wurtsmith's V Fighter Command, only 80 were P-38s.

The lull ended on 2 March 1943 when Kenney launched 28 Flying Fortresses escorted by 16 Lightnings to stop eight destroyers and eight transports dispatched by the Japanese from Rabaul to land 6,000 troops at Lae. Hayabusas (Ki.43 Oscar) from the 1st and 11th Sentais covered the convoy and intercepted the Lightnings as the B-17s sank one transport; the Battle of the Bismarck Sea was underway.

On 3 March Kenney put up 109 aircraft: the 39th FS provided 18 P-38s for top cover while 10 P-38s of the 9th FS provided close escort for the B-25s, Beaufighters and A-20s. In a raging battle, with the Lightnings coming home to refuel and rearm, then go back out to the action, numerous claims were made. Kenney's brilliant bomber-strafers and the Australian Beaufighters left only four destroyers out of the 16 ship convoy on the water's surface. The Japanese had lost their gamble to hold ground in New Guinea and two aircraft had emerged as the key weapons of airpower in the Pacific – the strafing, skip-bombing B-25 and the long ranging P-38 with its heavy fire power.

In late March Kenney was in Washington begging for more airplanes but he could only squeeze one P-38 group out of Arnold and even at that he would have to man it himself with pilots and mechanics in the theatre. Kenney replied, "Give me the planes and I'll find the men if I have to dissolve my own headquarters staff to get the people to fly them!" The 475th Fighter Group was born but it would not be operational until August.

The third squadron in the 5th Air Force to get Lightnings, the 80th, flew its first mission under Capt Edward Cragg on 24 March but its first real tangle came on 11 April when Capt Danny Roberts led a four-fighter scramble over Oro Bay at 1215 and three enemy aircraft were claimed destroyed. On 12 and 14 April Admiral Isoruku Yamamoto continued to hit Milne Bay, Port Moresby, Oro Bay and Guadalcanal with Operation "I-go" using the total strength of the Japanese carrier fleet which had been land based at Rabaul for the action, which lasted through the 18th.

The only new Lightning unit to arrive in the Solomons to fly with the 13th Air Force was the 17th Photo Squadron with F-5s. In January the unit set up camp at Cactus, as Fighter Two base on Guadalcanal had become known. Capt Eugene R. Brown flew one of the more memorable early missions when he was jumped by two Zeros while taking pictures over Kahili under an overcast. His left engine was shot out and a 20 mm shell nicked the right propeller, throwing it out of balance. Regaining control at 300 ft (90 m) above the ocean, he could not find the enemy and limped home for over 400 miles (644 km) on one engine as the F-5 rattled and kicked itself to death. He received the DFC.

The 347th Fighter Group (339th and 70th Fighter Squadrons) was still the only 13th Air Force Lightning fighter unit in early 1943 and it took the brunt of the fighting. With the arrival of Marine Corps' VMF-124 and its F4U Corsairs on 12 February, the joint Navy-Army-Marine effort in the air had some real teeth to stop incoming bombers. When a raid was inbound, all the fighters on the field scrambled: the Lightnings went to 30,000 ft (9,100 m), the Corsairs to 25,000 ft (7,600 m) while the Wildcats, Airacobras and P-40s stayed below around 12,000 ft (3,660 m). Stacked in position, they simply waited for the Japanese to show up, and the number of claims rose sharply.

The Lightnings and Corsairs found themselves dealing with ships when other targets failed to present themselves. On 29 March the P-38s heavily damaged a Japanese destroyer on the way back from strafing a seaplane base. Lt Rex T. Barber of the 339th FS flew smack into the warship's foremast, leaving three feet of wing behind, then flew back to Guadalcanal. On 2 April the Lightning pilots took on a small freighter off Vella Lavella. Thomas G. Lanphier, Jr., Douglas Canning and Delton C. Goerke took three P-38s against the ship but after a few runs there was no visible result. As Canning recalled, "We decided to drop our belly tanks on it and then set it on fire with our incendiary bullets. Tom and I

This view of F-5A clearly shows the rearview mirror on the canopy and the turbo-superchargers. (Lockheed)

F-5B-1-LO Camera Configuration

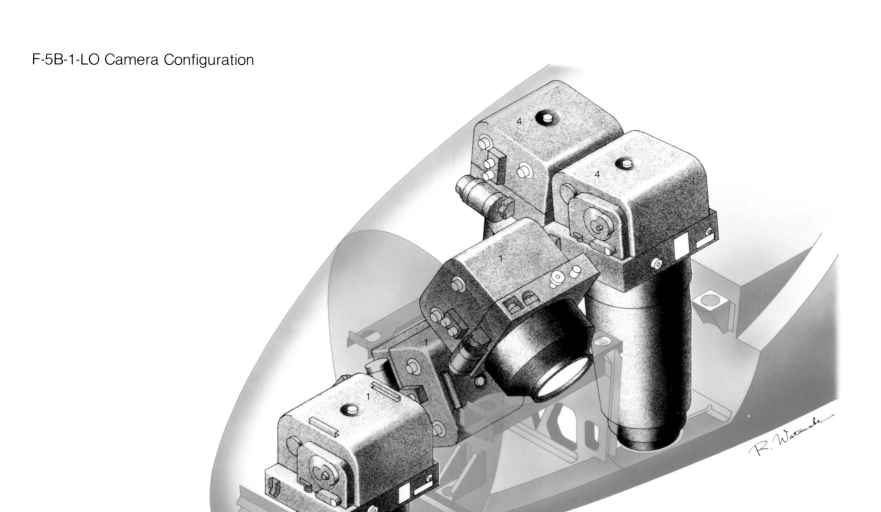

1 K-17 camera of 6-in (152 mm) focal length
2 K-17 camera of 12-in (305 mm) focal length
3 K-18 camera of 24-in (610 mm) focal length
4 K-17 camera of 24-in (610 mm) focal length

Exposure size
K-17: 9 × 9 in (229 × 229 mm)
K-18: 9 × 18 in (229 × 457 mm)

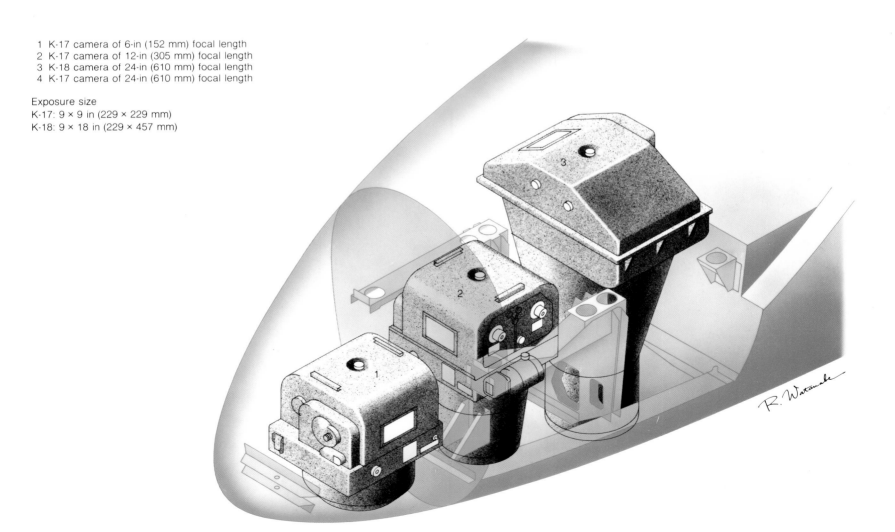

P-38L Cockpit

1 Outer wing tank low level check button
2 Auxiliary fuel pump switches
3 Starboard tank selector valve
4 Port tank selector valve
5 Window crank hatchet handles
6 Port window crank
7 Spotlight alternate position socket
8 Cockpit ventilator control
9 Bomb or tank release selector switches
10 Landing gear control handle
11 Landing gear control release
12 Propeller lever vernier knob
13 Friction control
14 Elevator tab control
15 Landing gear warning light
16 Throttle levers
17 Propeller controls
18 Propeller selector switches
19 Mixture controls
20 Coolant shutter controls
21 Supplemental light switch box
22 5-in (127 mm) rockets fuse box
23 Nose gun compartment heat control
24 Instrument panel light
25 Propeller circuit breaker buttons
26 Main fuel tank quantity gauge
27 Reserve fuel tank quantity gauge
28 Standby magnetic compass
29 Compass indicator
30 Altimeter
31 Hydraulic pressure gauge
32 Suction gauge
33 Clock
34 Directional gyro
35 Airspeed indicator
36 Landing gear warning light
37 Empty cut out
38 turn and Bank indicator
39 Gyro horizon
40 Rate of climb indicator
41 Compass correction cards
42 L-3 optical reflector gun sight
43 Dual manifold pressure gauge
44 Dual tachometer
45 Port engine gauge (oil temperature, oil pressure and fuel pressure)
46 Starboard engine gauge (same as above)
47 Ammeters
48 Generator switches
49 Coolant temperature gauge
50 Carburetor air temperature gauge
51 Empty cut out
52 Oxygen pressure gauge
53 Ignition switches
54 Oil dilution switches
55 (left to right) Starter switch. Engage switch. Flourescent light switch. Position light switches. Landing light switches
56 Fluorescent light rheostat
57 Voltmeter
58 Propeller feathering switch warning lights
59 Propeller feathering switches
60 Parking brake handle
61 Oxygen flow indicator
62 Oxygen pressure warning light
63 Emergency knob
64 Auto-mix lever
65 Engine primer
66 Rudder trim tab control
67 Auxiliary fuel tank and bomb manual release handle
68 Rudder pedals
69 Automatic coil cooler flap switches
70 Battery disconnect switch
71 (left to right) Generator switch. Battery switch. Pilot tube heat switch. Coolant flap override switches.
72 Cockpit light rheostat
73 Circuit breakers
74 Contactor heater switch
75 Flap control lever
76 Radio OFF push button and frequency selector push buttons
77 Selector switch
78 Cockpit light
79 Recognition light switches
80 Detrola receiver tuning knob
81 Detrola receiver volume control
82 Starboard window crank
83 Surface controls lock (stowed)

84 Cockpit heat control
85 Hatch locking arm (released position)
86 Hatch release buttons
87 Hatch release handle
88 Hatch locking arm (locked position)
89 Rubber pad

P-38L
Control column

1 Gun handles
2 Radio button
3 Dive recovery flap control switch
4 Microphone switch
5 Cannon button
6 Chart
7 Gun sight light rheostat

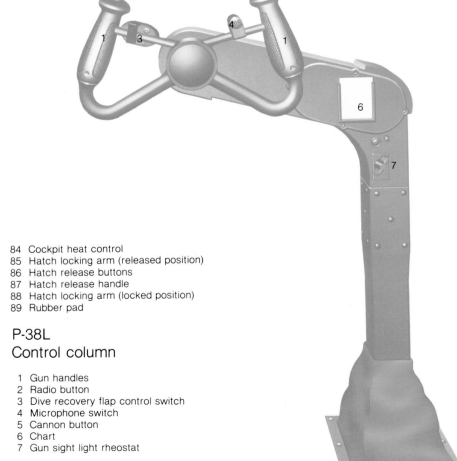

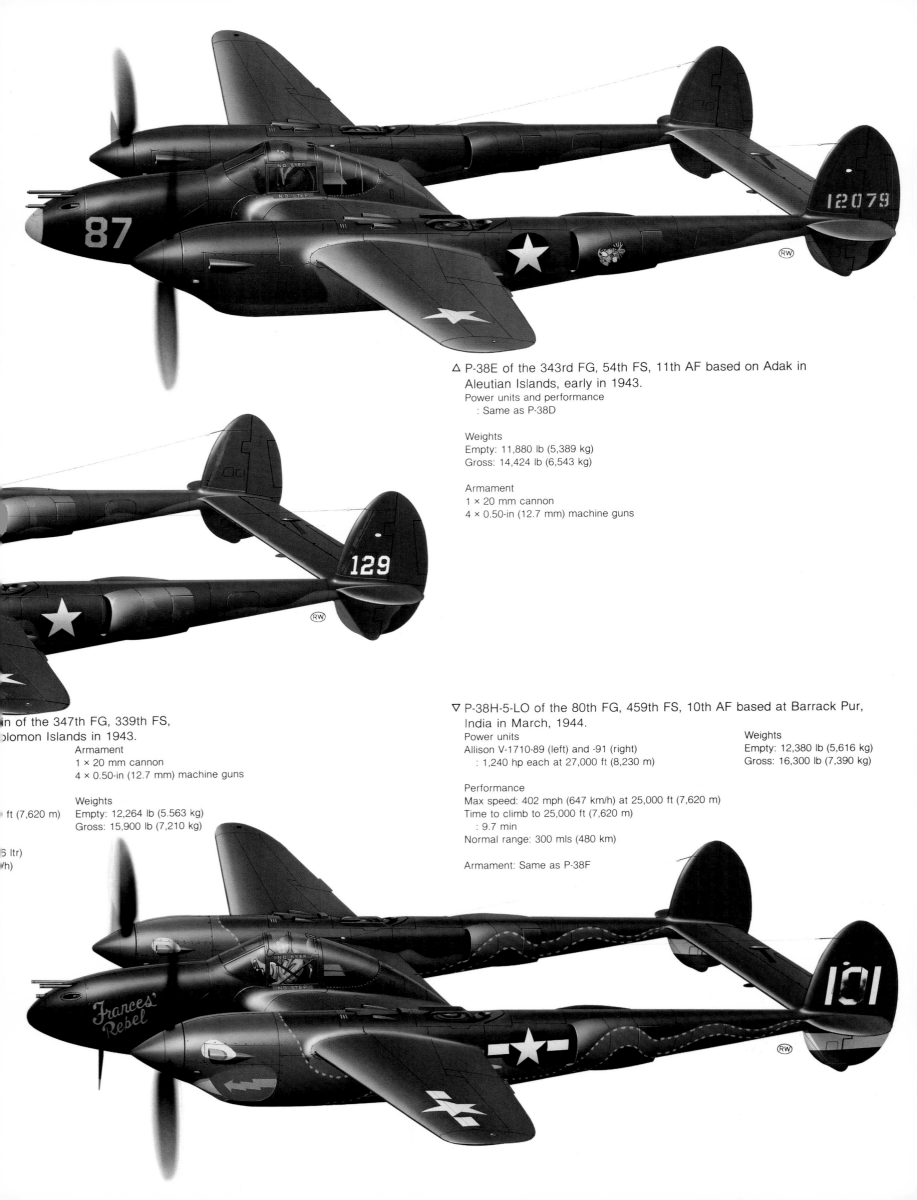

△ P-38E of the 343rd FG, 54th FS, 11th AF based on Adak in
Aleutian Islands, early in 1943.
Power units and performance
 : Same as P-38D

Weights
Empty: 11,880 lb (5,389 kg)
Gross: 14,424 lb (6,543 kg)

Armament
1 × 20 mm cannon
4 × 0.50-in (12.7 mm) machine guns

n of the 347th FG, 339th FS,
olomon Islands in 1943.
Armament
1 × 20 mm cannon
4 × 0.50-in (12.7 mm) machine guns

Weights
ft (7,620 m)   Empty: 12,264 lb (5.563 kg)
          Gross: 15,900 lb (7,210 kg)
6 ltr)
/h)

▽ P-38H-5-LO of the 80th FG, 459th FS, 10th AF based at Barrack Pur,
India in March, 1944.
Power units   Weights
Allison V-1710-89 (left) and -91 (right)   Empty: 12,380 lb (5,616 kg)
 : 1,240 hp each at 27,000 ft (8,230 m)   Gross: 16,300 lb (7,390 kg)

Performance
Max speed: 402 mph (647 km/h) at 25,000 ft (7,620 m)
Time to climb to 25,000 ft (7,620 m)
 : 9.7 min
Normal range: 300 mls (480 km)

Armament: Same as P-38F

△ P-38D of the 1st Pursuit Group based in USA, November, 1941.

Power units
Allison V-1710-27 (left) and -29 (right)
 : 1,150 hp each in Max power

Performance
Max speed: 390 mph (628 km/h) at 25,000 ft (7,620 m)
Time to climb to 20,000 ft (6,100 m)
 : 8 min
Normal range: 400 mls (640 km)

Armament
1 × 37 mm cannon
2 × 0.50-in (12.7 mm) machine guns
2 × 0.30-in (7.62 mm) machine guns

Weights
Empty: 11,780 lb (5,343 kg)
Gross: 14,456 lb (6,557 kg)

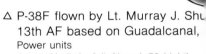

△ P-38F flown by Lt. Murray J. Shu...
13th AF based on Guadalcanal,

Power units
Allison V-1710-49 (left) and -53 (right)
 : 1,150 hp each at 25,000 ft (7,620 m

Performance
Max speed: 395 mph (636 km/h) at 25,0
Time to climb to 20,000 ft (6,100 m)
 : 8.8 min
Range with 300 US gal (250 Imp gal, 1,
 : 425 mls (684 km) at 305 mph (491 k

▽ P-38G-15-LO of the 14th FG, 49th FS, 12th AF based in North
Africa, spring 1943.

Power units
Allison V-1710-51 (left) and -55 (right)
 : 1,150 hp each at 25,000 ft (7,620 m)

Performance
Max speed: 400 mph (644 km/h) at 25,000 ft (7,620 m)
Time to climb to 20,000 ft (6,100 m)
 : 8.5 min
Range: 350 mls (560 km) at 310 mph (500 km/h)

Armament: Same as P-38F

Weights
Empty: 12,200 lb (5,530 kg)
Gross: 15,800 lb (7,170 kg)

P-38L Cockpit

P-38L Control column

Comparison of twin-engined single seat fighters
Scale 1/75

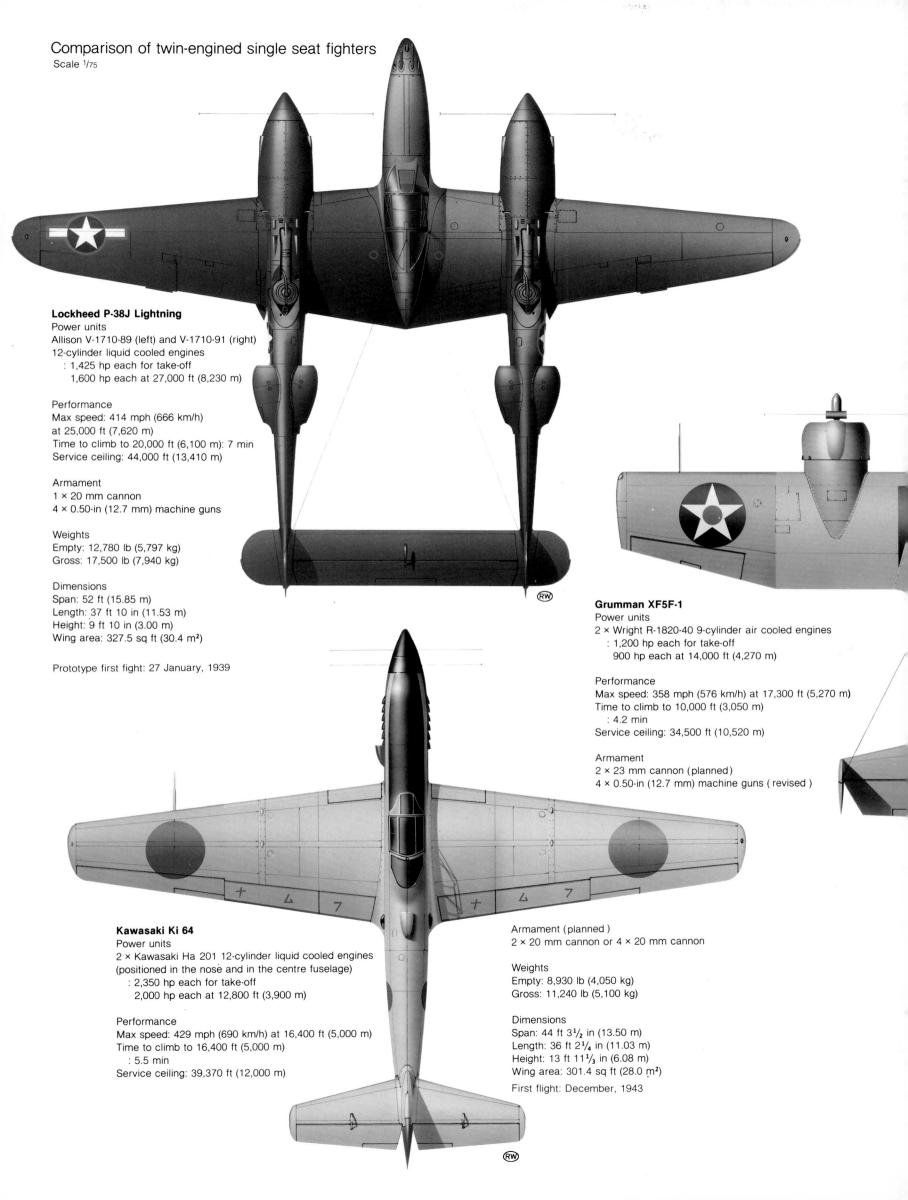

Lockheed P-38J Lightning
Power units
Allison V-1710-89 (left) and V-1710-91 (right)
12-cylinder liquid cooled engines
: 1,425 hp each for take-off
1,600 hp each at 27,000 ft (8,230 m)

Performance
Max speed: 414 mph (666 km/h)
at 25,000 ft (7,620 m)
Time to climb to 20,000 (6,100 m): 7 min
Service ceiling: 44,000 ft (13,410 m)

Armament
1 × 20 mm cannon
4 × 0.50-in (12.7 mm) machine guns

Weights
Empty: 12,780 lb (5,797 kg)
Gross: 17,500 lb (7,940 kg)

Dimensions
Span: 52 ft (15.85 m)
Length: 37 ft 10 in (11.53 m)
Height: 9 ft 10 in (3.00 m)
Wing area: 327.5 sq ft (30.4 m²)

Prototype first fight: 27 January, 1939

Grumman XF5F-1
Power units
2 × Wright R-1820-40 9-cylinder air cooled engines
: 1,200 hp each for take-off
900 hp each at 14,000 ft (4,270 m)

Performance
Max speed: 358 mph (576 km/h) at 17,300 ft (5,270 m)
Time to climb to 10,000 ft (3,050 m)
: 4.2 min
Service ceiling: 34,500 ft (10,520 m)

Armament
2 × 23 mm cannon (planned)
4 × 0.50-in (12.7 mm) machine guns (revised)

Kawasaki Ki 64
Power units
2 × Kawasaki Ha 201 12-cylinder liquid cooled engines
(positioned in the nose and in the centre fuselage)
: 2,350 hp each for take-off
2,000 hp each at 12,800 ft (3,900 m)

Performance
Max speed: 429 mph (690 km/h) at 16,400 ft (5,000 m)
Time to climb to 16,400 ft (5,000 m)
: 5.5 min
Service ceiling: 39,370 ft (12,000 m)

Armament (planned)
2 × 20 mm cannon or 4 × 20 mm cannon

Weights
Empty: 8,930 lb (4,050 kg)
Gross: 11,240 lb (5,100 kg)

Dimensions
Span: 44 ft 3½ in (13.50 m)
Length: 36 ft 2¼ in (11.03 m)
Height: 13 ft 11⅓ in (6.08 m)
Wing area: 301.4 sq ft (28.0 m²)

First flight: December, 1943

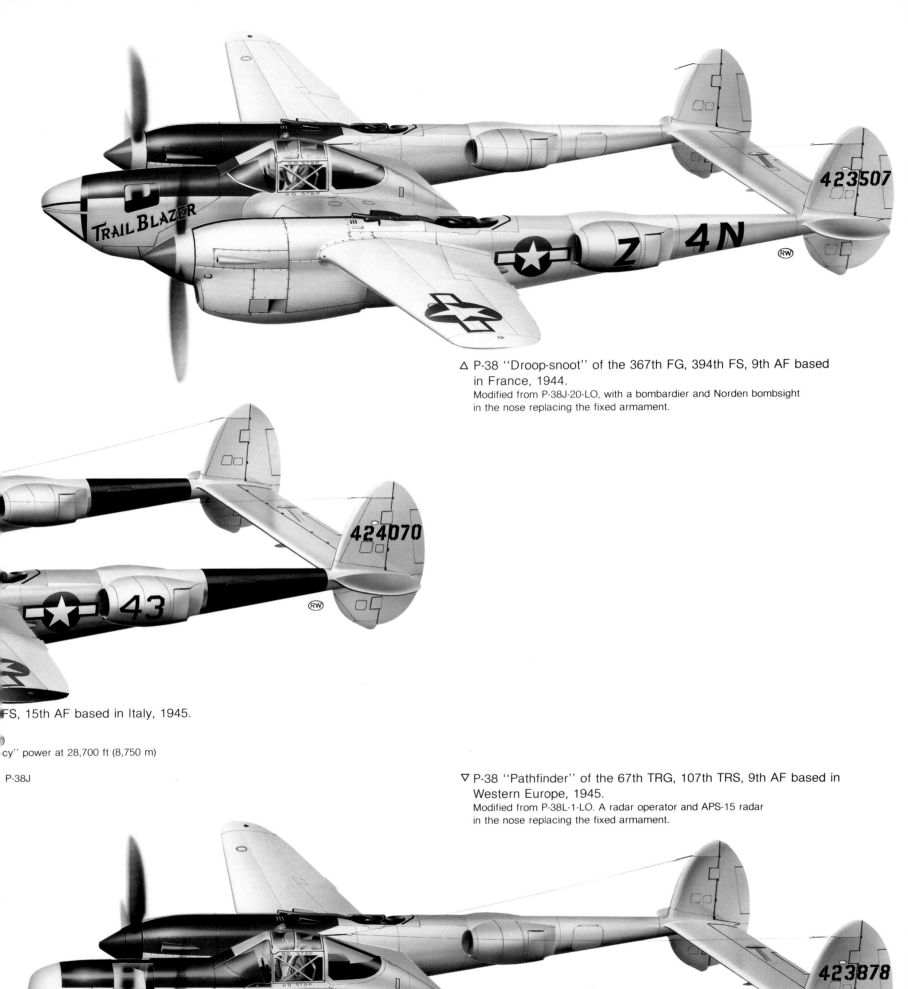

△ P-38 ''Droop-snoot'' of the 367th FG, 394th FS, 9th AF based
in France, 1944.
Modified from P-38J-20-LO, with a bombardier and Norden bombsight
in the nose replacing the fixed armament.

FS, 15th AF based in Italy, 1945.

cy'' power at 28,700 ft (8,750 m)

P-38J

▽ P-38 ''Pathfinder'' of the 67th TRG, 107th TRS, 9th AF based in
Western Europe, 1945.
Modified from P-38L-1-LO. A radar operator and APS-15 radar
in the nose replacing the fixed armament.

△ P-38J-15-LO flown by Lt. Edwin Wasi of the 20th FG, 55th FS,
8th AF based at Kingscliff, England in 1944.

Power units
Allison V-1710-89 (left) and -91 (right)
: 1,600 hp each with "War emergency" power

Performance
Max speed: 414 mph (666 km/h) at 25,000 ft (7,620 m)
Time to climb to 20,000 ft (6,100 m)
: 7 min
Range with 3,200 lb (1,451 kg) bombs
: 450 mls (720 km)

Armament: Same as P-38F

Weights
Empty: 12,780 lb (5,797 kg)
Gross: 17,500 lb (7,940 kg)

△ P-38L-1-LO of the 1st FG, 71
Power units
Allison V-1710-111 (left) and -113 (r
: 1,600 hp each with "War Emer

Performance and armament: Same

Weights
Empty: 12,800 lb (5,810 kg)
Gross: 17,500 lb (7,940 kg)

▽ F-5E-4-LO of the 21st PRS, 14th AF based at Kunming, China in 1945.
Modified from P-38L-1-LO. Fitted with K-17, K-18 and K-22 cameras.

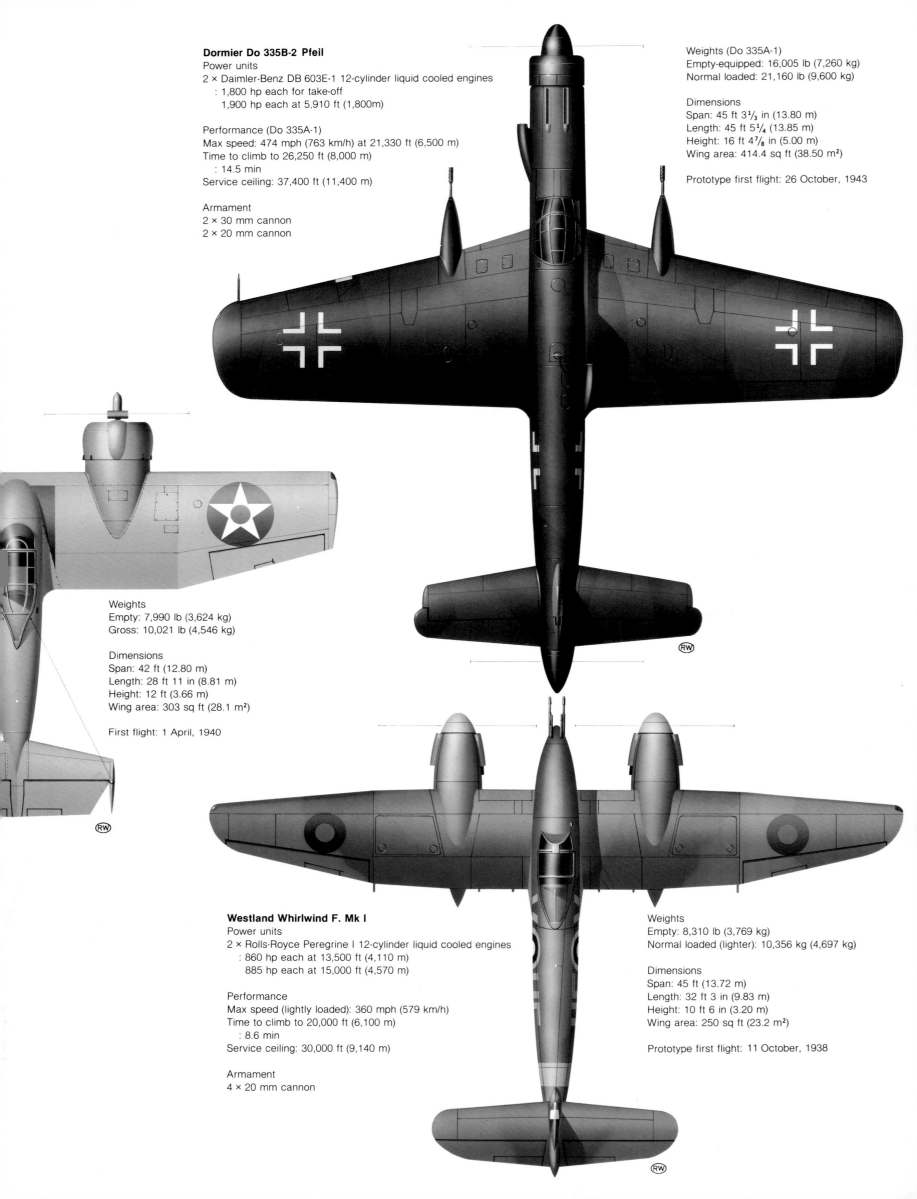

Dormier Do 335B-2 Pfeil
Power units
2 × Daimler-Benz DB 603E-1 12-cylinder liquid cooled engines
: 1,800 hp each for take-off
1,900 hp each at 5,910 ft (1,800m)

Performance (Do 335A-1)
Max speed: 474 mph (763 km/h) at 21,330 ft (6,500 m)
Time to climb to 26,250 ft (8,000 m)
: 14.5 min
Service ceiling: 37,400 ft (11,400 m)

Armament
2 × 30 mm cannon
2 × 20 mm cannon

Weights (Do 335A-1)
Empty-equipped: 16,005 lb (7,260 kg)
Normal loaded: 21,160 lb (9,600 kg)

Dimensions
Span: 45 ft 3⅓ in (13.80 m)
Length: 45 ft 5¼ (13.85 m)
Height: 16 ft 4⅞ in (5.00 m)
Wing area: 414.4 sq ft (38.50 m²)

Prototype first flight: 26 October, 1943

Weights
Empty: 7,990 lb (3,624 kg)
Gross: 10,021 lb (4,546 kg)

Dimensions
Span: 42 ft (12.80 m)
Length: 28 ft 11 in (8.81 m)
Height: 12 ft (3.66 m)
Wing area: 303 sq ft (28.1 m²)

First flight: 1 April, 1940

Westland Whirlwind F. Mk I
Power units
2 × Rolls-Royce Peregrine I 12-cylinder liquid cooled engines
: 860 hp each at 13,500 ft (4,110 m)
885 hp each at 15,000 ft (4,570 m)

Performance
Max speed (lightly loaded): 360 mph (579 km/h)
Time to climb to 20,000 ft (6,100 m)
: 8.6 min
Service ceiling: 30,000 ft (9,140 m)

Armament
4 × 20 mm cannon

Weights
Empty: 8,310 lb (3,769 kg)
Normal loaded (lighter): 10,356 kg (4,697 kg)

Dimensions
Span: 45 ft (13.72 m)
Length: 32 ft 3 in (9.83 m)
Height: 10 ft 6 in (3.20 m)
Wing area: 250 sq ft (23.2 m²)

Prototype first flight: 11 October, 1938

went in, Tom first, and then me and both of us hit the wheel house and just below it, spreading fuel all over the place. Goerke, following me, fired into it and it started burning all over the place but didn't sink. Because of fuel we went home, called in the results and the Navy sent a PBY up to watch it. Late that night it blew up and sank."

With Yamamoto's Operation "I-go" commencing on 2 April, the enemy formations began to come down the "slot" in larger numbers. The fighters on Guadalcanal had their hands full. As more intelligence came into Allied headquarters, decoded messages revealed that Yamamoto was going to make an inspection tour of his front-line forces on 18 April 1943 and after some initial discussion, an interception was planned with the only aircraft that possessed the range, the P-38.

John Mitchell was told on the 17th to lead the interception with 16 Lightnings just before the fanatically punctual Yamamoto was to reach Ballale, Bougainville. Four Lightnings were given the job of shooting down the Betty bomber as the rest took on the Zero escort. "Killer flight" was to be Tom Lanphier, Rex Barber, Jim McLanahan and Joe Moore.

As the Lightnings got off the next day, McLanahan blew a tyre and veered off the runway; he was out of it. Moore's drop tanks would not feed and he was forced back. Besby Holmes and Ray Hine were then ordered to take up the slots in "Killer flight". Flying from 10 to 50 ft (3 to 15 m) off the water, the P-38s would have to take four different headings in loose formation to avoid detection.

Yamamoto left Rabaul precisely on time in a 705th Kokutai G4M1 Betty flown by veterans, accompanied by Admiral Ugaki in another G4M1 and six Zeros of the 309th Kokutai.

At 0934 hours, dead on course and only one minute from estimated interception, Doug Canning called, "Bogeys 11 o'clock high." Climbing for altitude, the Lightnings took their places, although Holmes tanks would not jettison, forcing him to break with Hine. That left Lanphier and Barber to go in for the kill.

Lanphier was a mile east of the Japanese formation when he saw the Zero drop tanks flutter away. The enemy fighters nosed down and turned into the P-38s as the lead bomber winged over violently. A quick shot at the lead Zero and Lanphier had another kill. Barber pressed in to one of the Betty's after overshooting, raking it with his guns as they came down to treetop level. Three Zeros chased him only to be driven off by two P-38s. Fifteen seconds had gone by since Lanphier began his climb into the Zeros.

Lanphier had pulled up and rolled over onto his back to look out the top of his canopy for the bombers. He saw Barber with the Zeros and the bomber "skimming along the surface of the jungle headed for Kahili." Closing in with two Zeros desperately chasing him, Lanphier got off a long burst before he was in range. The right engine and then the right wing began to burn as the Zeros shot over his head. The Betty's right wing came off and the bomber plunged into the jungle to explode. Lanphier escaped by entering a shallow high speed climb for 20,000 ft (6,100 m), a manoeuvre no

enemy fighter could follow.

Holmes finally got rid of his tanks to dive back in and protect Barber who was chasing the second Betty. Two Zeros were shot off Barber's tail by Holmes, who then got a few shots into the bomber before it crashed into the sea. Barber remembered seeing two P-38s chase the Betty before he went in to finish it off, being hit by the debris from the disintegrating bomber. Barber, Holmes and Hine formed up to go home – as they turned eastward, Holmes saw a Zero dive on Barber. With a high speed loop, Holmes rolled around and destroyed the Zero. Hine's P-38 was smoking and that was the last anyone saw of him, the only casualty of the mission. Holmes made it to the Russell Islands due to low fuel while the rest landed at Cactus. With Yamamoto's death came the end of Operation "I-go".

16 June 1943 was to be the highlight of 1943 for the 339th FS. Shortly after noon two formations of Japanese aircraft, one with 38 and the other with 80, converged on the Russell Islands, headed for Guadalcanal. Out of the total of 49 Zeros and 32 Vals claimed by the Cactus fighters, the 339th claimed 12 while one P-40 and three F4Fs were lost. Lt Murray Schubin got two Zeros on his first pass, then found himself alone with five Zeros near Cape Esperance. For 40 minutes he fought the nimble Navy fighters, shooting down four out of the five.

By mid-1943 the P-38 was firmly established as the leading fighter in the Pacific with Lightning pilots emerging as the top fighter leaders. Tommy Lynch was acknowledged as possibly the most talented of the early group. He led the 39th FS until late 1943 with great skill and had the reputation of being able to lead while shooting at twice the number of enemy aircraft than any of the others in the formation.

By May 1943 George Prentice was assigned as commander of the 475th Fighter Group. Kenney "liberated" 20 Chinese from the Aussies who had impounded them in jails and they became the mess personnel. As Prentice picked a staff of New Guinea veterans, the first all P-38 group in the Pacific was at long last a reality. By 11 August the 431st and 432nd FS of the Group were operating from Twelve Mile Strip and Ward's Drome at Port Moresby. The 433rd FS moved up to Jackson Drome on the 16th.

As the 348th Fighter Group entered action with its P-47s, commander Maj Neel E. Kearby went after the enemy with a ferocity that ran his score to 14 by October 1943, placing him firmly in the "race of the aces" with Bong, Lynch and Sparks.

Dick Bong was certainly the centre of attention in the 9th FS. On 26 July 1943, flying wing to the commander, Jimmie "Duck Butt" Watkins, Bong got four as did Watkins. That brought Bong's score to 15, just one behind Lynch who was on leave in the States. Bong described the action in his usual terse manner, "I dropped my tanks, shot at one and missed. I dove out and shot at a Zeke head-on and he burst into flames. I shot at another and he burst into flames." He left it to other men in the flight to describe his other two kills. Gerald R. Johnson got his fifth kill on this mission – he would go on to command both the 9th FS and the 49th Fighter Group, shooting down 22 enemy aircraft in the process.

P-38G carrying two auxiliary fuel tanks under the inner wings. (Lockheed)

Two days later nine 9th FS Lightnings were escorting bombers just north of Cape Gloucester, New Britain when 15 Japanese fighters bounced the Americans. During the melée Bong saw an enemy fighter diving after a '38 that had lost an engine so he slid in between the two fighters and feathered an engine, allowing the other American to escape. Restarting his engine, Bong pulled away from the dogfight only to have his P-38 vibrate badly. Looking back, he saw about half his tail shot away but made it to a friendly field by nursing his mount carefully. The ailerons were also shot up but he got the aircraft down with no brakes and a punctured tyre. The P-38 wound up in a ditch beyond the end of the runway, a total loss. Bong's comment to an incredulous General Kenney was, "Boy, I'll bet that guy wondered what kept that P-38 flying and he sure must have been mad when he saw that I had foxed him into thinking I had only one engine."

On 18 August 1943 a 1st Lt who had been pulled from the 9th FS to fly with the 431st FS got his first aerial victories: two Zekes and a Ki.61 Tony were chalked up for Thomas B. McGuire, Jr.

With Lae and Nabzab captured in September, the entire lower Markham Valley became a major air base and by early October the 5th Air Force was concentrated at Dobodura for the all-out assault on Rabaul in concert with the 13th Air Force. By this time Kenney had standardized four aircraft as ideal for operations in the Southwest Pacific – B-24 bombers, B-25 strafers, C-47 transports and P-38 fighters.

The fighter pilots mirrored Kenney's feelings. Harry W. Brown, who shot down two Japanese aircraft over Pearl Harbor on 7 December 1941 in a P-36, and later flew with the 475th Fighter Group considered those days in the P-38 the highlight of his military career: "A thousand kaleidoscopic views come rushing in when I sit down to think about that wonderful bird. The thrill of the first check-out; the loss of canopies by those who forgot to latch it (try flying a traffic pattern to land with one hand while trying to hold the canopy on with the other after you first discover it's about to blow away after you're fully committed on your take-off roll); the ability to manoeuvre at 20,000 feet when in P-40s you lost 300 feet with a one-needle width turn at that altitude; the extra range provided by the belly tanks; the ability to cut out throttle to reverse directions; having one of the engines stop 200 rounds when you are stalled out after a pass at another enemy, and then flying 300 miles across the ocean on one already strained engine; the awesome fire power of four .50s and a 20 mm; the tumble that resulted from an attempt to cut a throttle and execute an Immelmann; the buffeting during a dive and the inability to get out of the airplane except at either relatively low or relatively high airspeeds – all these things were attributes that were inscribed on my memory forever. I think the superiority of the airplane may be reflected in the fact that I flew better than 200 combat missions in P-40s without a kill, where I flew about 70 in P-38s both with the 9th Fighter and the 431st Fighter Squadrons with five kills."

And the P-38's ammo cans could hold exactly four cases of Australian gin or whisky. Thomas D. "Robbie" Robertson remembered making gin runs from Australia when new planes had to be ferried to the combat zone. Even though General MacArthur had prohibited such goings on, the normal technique was to have three planes in each flight loaded with alcohol while the fourth would fly escort to protect the precious cargo: a bottle of gin could buy a side of beef from the quartermaster warehouse. Harry Brown remembers loading the ammo cans with beer for the early morning flights where they were chilled at 20,000 feet, and the maximum performance dive for the ground was watched with eager anticipation by all.

During the give and take air battles to and from Rabaul in October 1943, Lt Tom McGuire flew what he remembered as his most exciting mission. On the 17th the 431st FS of the 475th Fighter Group met an incoming Japanese formation head on at 23,000 ft (7,010 m). On the first pass Mac got a Zeke and was promptly jumped from behind by three more. Getting separated from his flight, he was left with one course of action – dive away. Going down to 12,000 ft (3,660 m), Mac later noted to the Group Information Officer, Dennis Glenn Cooper, that he felt as if he were on a huge circular stage: Zekes all around but not a single '38. Nothing to do but fight it out.

Both Mac and the enemy exchanged numerous passes. Spotting a smoking Lightning, he attempted to help but was bounced by a flock of fighters. He turned into the formation and engaged. One Zeke blew up, then another. With three for the day, it was time to leave, but before he could bank away the instrument panel disappeared under enemy fire, the left engine broke into flames and a 7.7 mm round hit him squarely in the wrist. Instinctively he pushed forward on the control yoke to get away, going straight down, then the right engine began pouring black smoke and a 20 mm exploded in the cockpit, hitting the yoke.

The rear of the canopy flew off and five pieces of shrapnel entered his arm and leg. The Lightning was out of control, giving no response to Mac's movements. Only one fear crept into his mind, "Boy, will Nick be sore at me!" (McGuire was flying Maj Franklin A. Nichols' aircraft). Trying to get out, Mac became wedged halfway – the oxygen mask was firmly attached over his eyes as the wind tore at him. Kicking like crazy, he finally came sailing out after falling 5,000 ft (1,520 m). Find the rip cord – it was gone, torn off! Another 5,000 ft was gone before he found the D-ring wire trailing behind.

At 800 ft (240 m) Mac yanked the wire, the chute opened and he hit the water. Getting away from the chute and harness, he inflated his rubber dinghy, but it was full of bullet holes and sank away. As he was going under, a PT boat picked him up and got him to the hospital.

Up through 7 November Kenney hit Rabaul as often as he could. During the campaign a pilot emerged who was fast catching up with the leading aces and who had assumed command of the 433rd FS of the 475th Fighter Group on 4 October. Quiet and unassuming, he was already a legend among his peers and an uncommonly talented leader of men. Daniel T. Roberts had left teaching music to fly fighter planes. He didn't drink or curse and was genuinely interested in people. He had flown P-39s in the 80th and 40th FS before finally leaving to join the 475th Fighter Group.

Little is known about Danny Roberts in the official records. According to those who flew with him, he was very possibly the finest Lightning pilot of the war when judged from all around ability. Teddy Hanks, Roberts' crew chief, recalled that "from the moment Captain Roberts entered the Squadron area, morale of the 433rd FS did an about face." The unit had suffered badly in leadership.

For a mission "usually 16 P-38s, plus two to four spares, would be lined up wing tip to wing tip. The commander's plane normally was placed at the extreme end of this line since he would take off first. Our first commander would go directly from the operations shack to his plane, say nothing or very little to the crew chief, get in and take off. Danny, at least during those first days he led the squadron, would leave the ops shack early enough to permit him to walk the entire line. He made it a point to speak or at least nod to every man he met. And always – always – that warm, sincere, friendly smile. He never failed to greet me in some form that demonstrated his appreciation for my efforts on his behalf."

Roberts used to say to the 433rd, "We'll stay together like a pack of wolves, like a pack of wolves!" The pilots operated as a team and Roberts made it clear to all of them that the enlisted men were the backbone of the outfit. During missions Roberts' primary concern was the squadron, not his own personal score, although he managed to get 15 claims without a bullet hole in his P-38. The pilots openly stated they would willingly follow Capt Roberts even if he were headed directly for a solid wall.

Since Roberts had led all seven of the escort missions to Rabaul during the campaign, the 475th Fighter Group flight surgeon, Capt Frank Bosse, ordered him to go to Sydney on leave but he refused, saying, "There are still a couple of tough ones coming up, but as soon as they are over I'll go."

On 9 November 1943 Danny led a low cover escort for the strafing B-25s to Alexishafen. 15 to 20 enemy aircraft jumped the formation over Sek Harbor and Roberts quickly shot down a Hamp (Zeke 32). Danny latched on to another enemy fighter with his wingman, Lt Dale O. Myers. The Japanese pilot made a sudden turn to the right and Myers, flying to the left of Roberts, tried to follow. The wingman's right propeller cut through Danny's left boom just aft of the wing and the two stricken Lightnings tumbled the 200 feet down into the marshy area between the coast line and the Japanese airfield. Danny Roberts, along with Dale Myers, was dead.

Teddy Hanks and the rest of the 433rd FS could not believe it when the other P-38s got back. At the empty revetment, waiting for Danny, Hanks openly wept as did many others. Laying on his canvas cot that night at Dobodura, Teddy Hanks, with tears flowing from his eyes, vowed that should he survive the war he would name his first son Daniel Robert Hanks. This kind of devotion seemed universal to Roberts, later known as the "Gentle Ace."

The "aces race" took another blow on 15 December when 80th FS commander Ed Cragg was killed after claiming 15 victories. George Welch, another pilot who gained fame over Pearl Harbor by claiming four destroyed in a P-40, had gone home with 16 victories. Bong was home on leave with 21 victories with orders not to come back until

P-38L Cutaway

1 Four 0.5-in (12.7 mm) machine gun barrels
2 20 mm cannon barrel
3 Camera-gun aperture
4 Four 0.5-in (12.7 mm) Colt-Browning M2 machine guns
5 Ammunition boxes (2,000 rounds in all) and feed chutes
6 Case ejection chute
7 Ejection chute exits
8 Nose armament cowling hinges
9 Chatellerault-feed cannon magazine (150 rounds)
10 Hydraulic brake reservoirs
11 Nosewheel lower drag struts
12 Shimmy damper oil tank
13 Torque links
14 Actuating cylinder
15 Fork
16 Nosewheel
17 Tyre (diameter 27 in, 686 mm)
18 Radio antenna
19 Instrument panel
20 Rudder pedal supports
21 Armour plate
22 Gunsight mounting bracket
23 Flat bullet-proof windshield
24 L-3 optical reflector gunsight
25 "Spectacle grip" cantilevered control wheel
26 Radio controls
27 Starboard window crank
28 External rear-view mirror
29 Rearward-hinged canopy
30 Armoured headrest
31 Pilot's armoured seat back
32 Downward winding side windows
33 SCR 522A radio range receiver
34 Radio rack
35 Entry ladder release
36 Entry ladder
37 Fuel filler caps
38 Hydraulic reservoir access hole cover
39 Port reserve fuel tank (60 US gal, 50 Imp gal, 227 ltr)
40 Port main fuel tank (90-93 US gal, 74.9-77.4 Imp gal, 341-352 ltr)
41 Wing inner surface corrugations
42 Main spar
43 Rear spar
44 Flat structure
45 Propeller hub
46 Curtiss-Electric three-blade (right) handed propeller
47 Spinner bulkhead cover plates
48 Coolant header tank
49 Cowling formers
50 Spark-plug and magneto cooling intake
51 Allison V-1710-111 (right: -113) twelve-cylinder
   liquid cooled engine (1,475 hp for take-off)
52 Intake fairing
53 Port outer oil cooling radiator
54 Oil cooling radiator shutters
55 Carburetor air intercooler
56 Intercooler inlet duct
57 Intercooler flap
58 Turbo-supercharger cooling intakes
59 Oil tank (13 US gal, 10.8 Imp gal, 49 ltr)
60 Insulated exhaust shroud duct
61 Turbine cooling duct
62 Exhaust turbine
63 GE B33 turbo supercharger
64 Supercharger air intake
65 Supercharger air filter duct
66 Supercharger oil tank
67 Mainwheel (retracted position)
68 Main landing gear actuating cylinder
69 Drag link
70 Drag strut
71 Mainwheel oleo leg
72 Side strut
73 Torque links
74 Cantilever axle
75 Removable wheel disc cover
76 Tyre (diameter 36 in, 914 mm)
77 Fulcrum
78 Flap outer section
79 Landing light
80 Zero-length launcher front support
81 Five 5-in (127 mm) rockets
82 Fixed tab
83 Aileron structure
84 Junction box
85 Port navigation lights (red)
86 Port wing fuel tank (55 US gal, 45.8 Imp gal, 208 ltr)

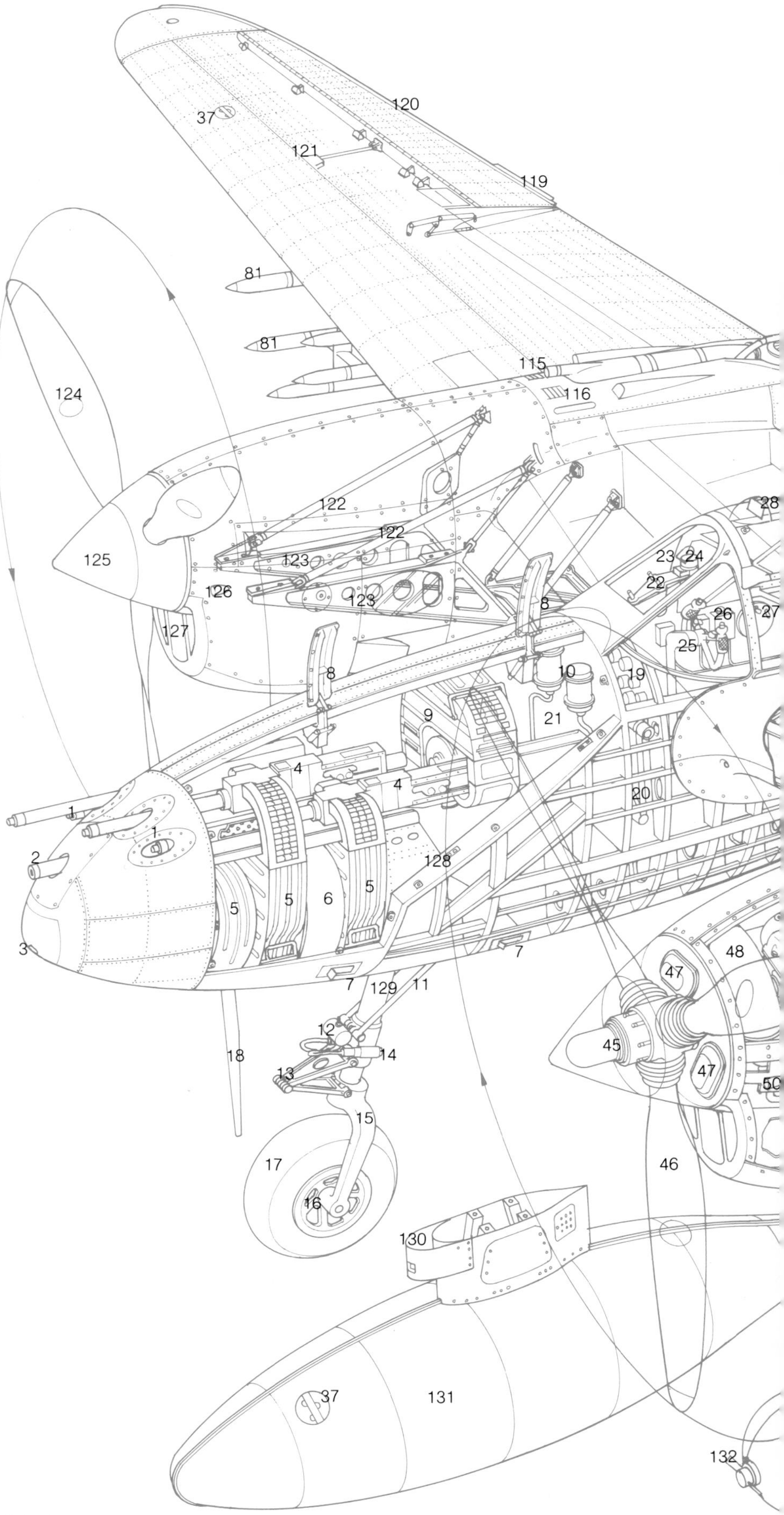

87 Mainwheel doors
88 Mainwheel door actuator
89 Oxygen Type F-1 low pressure bottles
90 Coolant/radiator return pipe
91 Radiator/coolant supply pipe
92 Engine coolant radiator assembly
93 Radiator exit flaps
94 Battery compartment
95 Elevator pulley access
96 Fixed tip structure
97 Elevator pulley access
98 Rudder tab drum access
99 Tail running light

100 Aerodynamic mass balance
101 Rudder structure
102 Rudder trim tab structure
103 Aerials
104 Elevator structure
105 Elevator trim tab
106 Upper and lower mass balances
107 Elevator trim tab control cables
108 Rudder trim tab
109 Starboard rudder
110 Rudder trim control cable
111 Tail surface control cables
112 Tool and baggage compartment

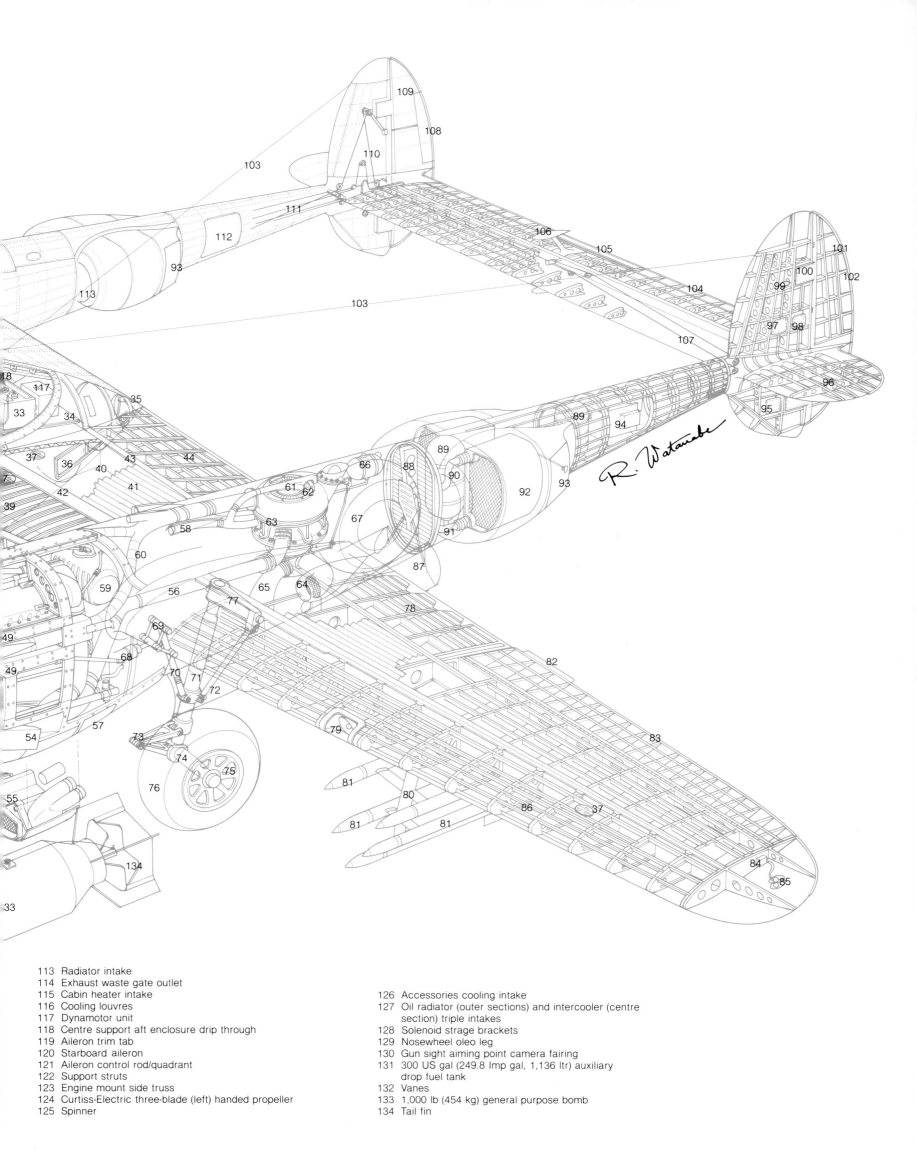

113 Radiator intake
114 Exhaust waste gate outlet
115 Cabin heater intake
116 Cooling louvres
117 Dynamotor unit
118 Centre support aft enclosure drip through
119 Aileron trim tab
120 Starboard aileron
121 Aileron control rod/quadrant
122 Support struts
123 Engine mount side truss
124 Curtiss-Electric three-blade (left) handed propeller
125 Spinner

126 Accessories cooling intake
127 Oil radiator (outer sections) and intercooler (centre
     section) triple intakes
128 Solenoid strage brackets
129 Nosewheel oleo leg
130 Gun sight aiming point camera fairing
131 300 US gal (249.8 lmp gal, 1,136 ltr) auxiliary
     drop fuel tank
132 Vanes
133 1,000 lb (454 kg) general purpose bomb
134 Tail fin

February. Lynch was also on leave and Kearby was the only one left to stay in the race but he was too busy getting his P-47s honed in the New Britain fighting to score significantly. Tom McGuire had shot down three Vals over Cape Gloucester on 26 December to bring his score to 16 but he would not score again until May.

The Lightning was thrown into a role ill suited to its ability in late 1943. Having trained on P-70s and waiting for P-61s, the 418th, 419th and 421st Night Fighter Squadron were given P-38s. The 419th was intended for night work over Guadalcanal without radar, using "searchlight co-op." 2nd Lt Donald M. Dessert was the first member of the 419th to check himself out in the Lightning, flying the first co-op mission on 10 December between 1945 and 2145 hours, but he couldn't find the enemy aircraft.

The experiment turned out to be a flop. In 368 night sorties, the 419th shot down three Japanese aircraft. The 418th got two P-38s in February 1944. Without any stateside thinking on converting Lightnings into radar-carrying night fighters, Lt Richardson and a radar mechanic installed a P-70 radar in a war-weary Lightning, receiving the Legion of Merit for the first true "Night Lightning." This was the name given to the P-38M which carried a radar observer in a second seat. It never saw combat, even though a few had reached the 421st Squadron by the end of the war.

With Bong and Lynch back from leave by mid-February 1944, the race was ready to pick up if the Japanese would co-operate. Lynch was assigned as General Wurtsmith's staff operations officer with Bong as his assistant. No longer attached to a specific group, they could roam free as a team with any 5th Air Force fighter unit. By 4 March Bong had number 24 while Lynch had 19, just one behind Kearby. On this day Kearby and four of his Thunderbolts tangled with 15 enemy fighters near Wewak. He got two before being shot down and killed.

Five days later, on the 9th, Bong and Lynch went on a sweep. Finding no aircraft to shoot at, they came upon a Japanese corvette escorting some transports to Hollandia. The return fire caught one of Lynch's engines. Turning for shore with a smoke trail, the Lightning looked OK to Bong who felt sure Lynch could put it down on the beach. As the '38 got to the shoreline three things happened in succession – a prop flew off, Tommy tried to bail out and the Lightning exploded. Bong circled for several minutes hoping for a miracle but Lynch was dead just three weeks after this unique "flying circus" had begun. Bong remembered this time with Tommy Lynch as the most enjoyable during his career as a fighter pilot.

By 12 April 1944, after the effective Allied raids on Wewak and Hollandia, Bong had No 27 (later No 28 was confimed) to make him the first American pilot to equal Eddie Rickenbacker's aerial score from the First World War. (Don Gentile, flying with the 4th Fighter Group in the ETO, claimed 27 the previous 5 April but some of those were ground kills). With that Kenney sent Bong back to the States for a gunnery course. Bong readily admitted his poor gunnery – he simply got close enough to his quarry so that he could not miss. This left Tom McGuire eager to catch up at 16 victories.

By 16 June McGuire was up to No 20, just eight behind Bong, but Hollandia proved to be in the doldrums of air combat and mid-1944 turned out to be a very slow period for the P-38 pilots. It was ideal for another newly arrived fighter pilot, however – Charles A Lindbergh flew his first combat mission in P-38s with the 35th FS on 20 June, then moved over to fly with the 475th Fighter Group. Although officially a civilian, Lindbergh had manoeuvered himself into combat saying that he needed to gather actual performance statistics for the aircraft manufacturers he represented.

After a few missions Lindbergh noted the pilots were using more fuel than was required: on 1 July he had flown a 6 hr 50 min flight, returning with 210 gallons of fuel. Lindbergh suggested 1,600 rpm with sufficient manifold pressure to maintain a slow cruise speed to get nine hours flying time. Amid cries that this would foul the spark plugs and burn up the engines, the Allison technical representatives said this was within the limits of the engine. The next mission proved the method to work, and it was then Lindbergh found that most of the pilots were flying at high rpm in auto rich.

On 28 July 1944 Lindbergh shot down a Ki.51 (Sonia) light bomber while flying with the 475th Fighter Group.

The day before McGuire bagged No 21 after staying eight behind Bong. McGuire the person remains largely hidden behind his lofty position as America's second ranking ace. That he was a top notch fighter pilot no one will question. John A. Tilley, a squadron mate of McGuire's and an ace himself, remembers that Mac was notorious for going "round and round" with Japanese fighters. McGuire told those under his command never to turn with an enemy fighter in the heavy '38 but he did it anyway with great success, particularly at low altitudes and low airspeeds of 90 mph (145 km/h).

This excellence in combat made him appear to his squadron as a driven man, obsessed. His P-38s took tremendous abuse from his violent flying. Tilley can remember flying behind Mac, noticing his plane always seemed to be flying slightly cock-eyed, like some dogs trot with their hind legs out of line with their front legs. Every member of the 431st FS absorbed some of this fighting spirit when flying with him but on the ground Mac was still number one in his own eyes. As a result, virtually none of the pilots liked him personally, though they came to look upon him as near invincible. When he was promoted to captain in late 1943 he was notorious for pulling rank. Always referred to previously as "Mac" or "Tom" (never Tommy), it was subsequently "Captain McGuire" to all junior officers. After he took command of the 431st FS the "Mac" was rarely heard when he insisted it be dropped.

On the ground people avoided him as much as possible because he took pleasure in making junior officers run errands for him. This even extended to Lindbergh (they shared the same tent) as some vividly remember seeing McGuire, much to their horror, lying on his cot ordering the famous flyer around like a servant, "Hey Charlie, get me this" or "Hey Charlie, do that."

Although dogfighting in the Lightning was often played down officially, it was more common than not. Tilley remembered "most of out fights with the Japanese started out above 20,000 feet but damned soon everyone was milling around on the deck. And that lovely Lightning just didn't have any competition at low altitude. I've flown the P-51 (liked it very much) and the P-47 (disliked it very much), and I've engaged in mock dogfights against just about all out WW II fighter planes. The only one the ole Lockheed Rocking Chair and I had trouble staying behind was a pretty savvy Navy type in an F4F Wildcat.

"During stateside training I had been told many times never to attempt to turn with a Jap fighter. Everyone agreed it was a good way to get creamed. I believed! Before going into combat with the 475th Fighter Group I was told by all the 'old hands' who bothered to talk to me 'never turn with a Jap, it's suicide.' I believed, I believed! The first time I got behind one of those made in Japan secret weapons called a Zero (Zeke) I was looking at his tail one minute and the next thing I knew I was looking at the same guy coming at me head on. I still don't know how he got that thing cranked around so fast, but brother, did I ever BELIEVE!

"Alright, so how come I got my second kill by turning a full 360° circle to the left, at low speeds and on the deck with an Oscar? Primarily I think it happened because the Jap and I both believed he could out turn me. I never would have tried to stay with him if there hadn't been 12 of us and only two of them. I figured I could always holler for help if I got in a jam. And I'm sure the Jap figured the usual tight turn was his best bet when he didn't have enough air under him for a split-S. Miracle of miracles, the big old P-38 actually turned inside the nimble little Oscar. I was on the deck, in a vertical

bank, the airspeed under 90 mph, and the yoke was bucking and shuddering in my hands. That turn was nothing more nor less than a controlled stall. But without torque (good old counter-rotating engines) I didn't worry about 'snapping' out of control and into a spin, as with a single engine aircraft, so I was able to pull enough lead for my guns to really hit him hard. By the time we had completed 360° of this turn he was a ball of flames and my aircraft was drenched with oil from his engine. I couldn't see a thing through the windshield so I had to ask a squadron mate to lead me home. Then I had to crank down the side window and reach around to wipe a clear spot on the windwhield so I could see enough to land the aircraft."

By September 1944 the Far East Air Forces began strikes against the Philippines and the Lightnings were providing most of the escort and fighter sweep duties. With the capture of Morotai, Kenney had a base from which to hit the major oil target in the theatre, Balikpapan, Borneo, 830 miles (1,335 km) away.

On 10 October 58 B-24s escorted by Lightnings encountered a large force of Japanese fighters over the target. Dick Bong was along with his old outfit, the 9th FS, and Warren Curton recalled, "Just about the time we arrived over Borneo, Dick broke radio silence to say, 'Red One, this is Red Three. We have a bandit following us in.' Col [George] Walker replied, 'Red Three from Red One, Roger, you lead.' We turned around and flew for what seemed to be to be ten minuted before I spotted the bandit. It wasn't that long but it was a long time before I saw the Japanese plane, which we were now approaching head on. This was one of Dick's secrets of success – his uncanny eyesight. Dick manoeuvred

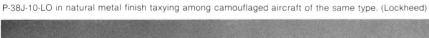
P-38J-10-LO in natural metal finish taxying among camouflaged aircraft of the same type. (Lockheed)

directly astern of the Nick and at about 150 feet opened fire. The Jap plane immediately burst into flames and went out of control. I honestly believe that the tail gunner bailed out before Dick opened fire!"

Bong got another enemy aircraft that day, all while he was ostensibly to see how his gunnery pupils were doing. Kenney had said no combat, just teach gunnery at Nadzab now that he had come back from that course in the States. Bong claimed a flimsy self defence to a twinkle-eyed Kenney and the "race of the aces" was back on.

McGuire was fit to be tied: MacDonald had told him he was commander of the 431st FS and that was his job, not chasing the free-lancing Bong around to even up the score. Typically, McGuire disobeyed orders and went on the next Balikpapan mission of 14 October without MacDonald's permission. Attaching himself secretively to the 9th FS, Mac was in on the fight with 50 enemy fighters to shoot down three for a total of 24. MacDonald was furious, restricting the feisty little fighter pilot to the 431st FS from that point on.

Capt Joe Forster of the 432nd FS would remember the 14th of October for a different reason. Tangling with a Zeke after shooting down another previously, Forster got hit and went straight down, having to use dive flaps to pull out. Left engine oil pressure was gone so he had to feather the propeller, then watch the rest of the squadron pull away. He would have to fly home for 900 miles on one engine.

"I certainly prayed to the Lord to keep that right engine running, for my gas to hold out and to do some good navigation," he recalled. After three hours he got in radio contact with another squadron mate, then the tower which gave him the correct steer for home. He landed with a few gallons after four hours and 15 minutes. It was a single-engine record in the P-38 but Forster didn't care, "After a total time of eight hours and twenty minutes in the air, all I wished was rest. I was discouraged too, for my brand new airplane was all shot up."

With the landings on Tacloban and Dulag at Leyte Gulf, the Philippines campaign opened officially on 20 October. On the 27th the 49th Fighter Group brought its Lightnings into the 2,800 ft (854 m) strip at Tacloban, the first American aircraft on Philippine soil since 1942. The last to pull up, as Kenney and MacArthur greeted the pilots, was Dick Bong who busily explained to a surprised Kenney that General Whitehead had said it was OK to come but no combat and was it OK sir if he just flew a little bit of combat. Kenney relented.

By mid-December the P-38 could be counted in greater numbers than any other aircraft in the Southwest

Allison V-1710-113 (F-30) Starboard Engine for P-38L

Twelve-cylinder Vee-type liquid cooled turbo-supercharged engine
: 1,475 hp for take-off
: 1,600 hp in "War emergency" power at 28,700 ft (8,750 m)

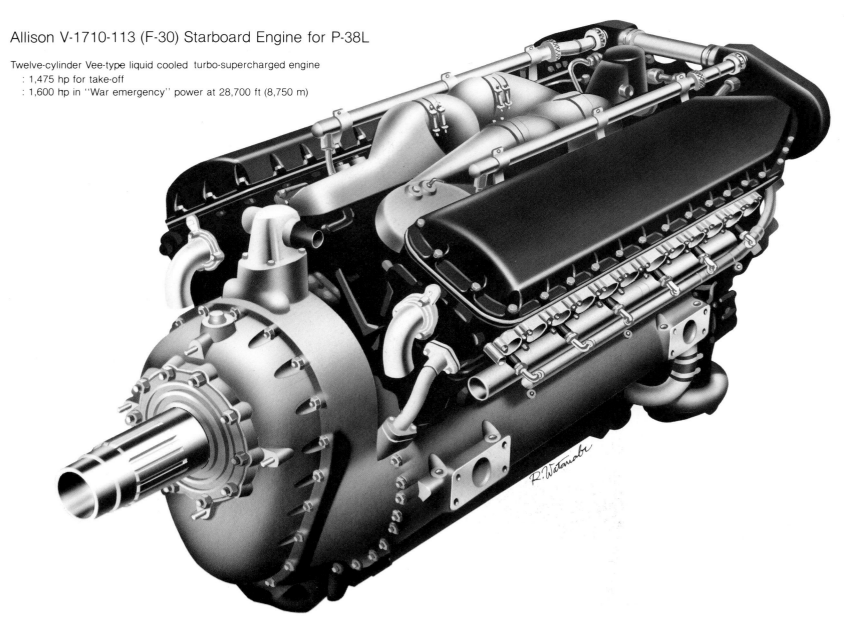

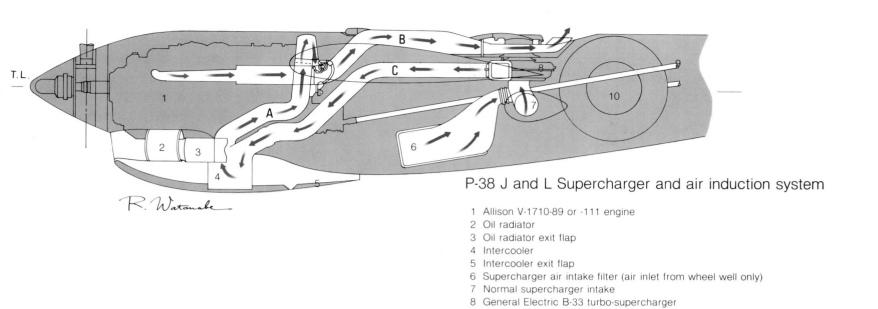

P-38 J and L Supercharger and air induction system

1 Allison V-1710-89 or -111 engine
2 Oil radiator
3 Oil radiator exit flap
4 Intercooler
5 Intercooler exit flap
6 Supercharger air intake filter (air inlet from wheel well only)
7 Normal supercharger intake
8 General Electric B-33 turbo-supercharger
9 To engine coolant radiator
10 Port main wheel
A Carburetor air from intercooler
B Exhaust
C Supercharger to intercooler

P-38 J and L Supercharger Installation

1 Bearing blast tube
2 Tail pipe side cover
3 Transition
4 Nozzle box air duct
5 Cooling cap tube
6 Turbo cooling shaft cap
7 General Electric B-33 turbo-supercharger
8 Waste gate
9 Turbo warning flexible shaft
10 Turbo warning unit
11 Supercharger oil tank
12 Waste gate control rod
13 Supercharger regulator push rod
14 Discharge duct gasket
15 Supercharger inlet and discharge ducts hose
16 Air intake scoop
17 Intercooler inlet duct
18 Supercharger air filter duct
19 Air filter
20 Air filter duct support

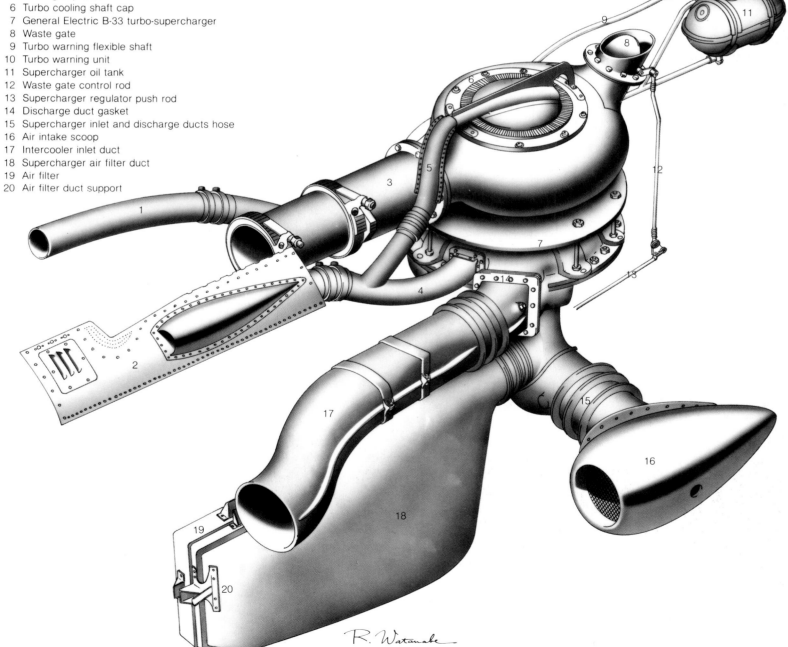

Pacific Area, topping 500. It was a far cry from the days when Kenney knew that 10 Lightnings could easily make the difference in a battle. On 10 November, as the fourth Japanese reinforcement convoy steamed into Ormoc, Bong and McGuire were up. Lt Chris Herman, a 431st FS pilot who was later killed, wrote in a letter home of the events on the 10th, "Our CO knocked off two more for a total of 26; Bong now has either 34 or 36 [the former]. The CO got nicked too – part of a Nip plane he shot up tore off the top of his canopy and creased his noggin; later he got an engine shot out in strafing a troop convey. So maybe he's tamed down a bit for awhile! He's still hot after Bong's record, though; rather got behind now. Mac will break it or his neck trying, I guess!" Herman's thoughts were prophetic.

On 22 November another leading ace, Robert Westbrook, led his 18th Fighter Group Lightnings over the Philippines and was killed in action. With 20 victories he stands as the leading ace of the 13th Air Force.

By December Bong had attached himself to the 475th Fighter Group and on 7 December, covering the landings at Ormoc, his score rose to 38. On the 12th he received the Medal of Honor from MacArthur. By the 15th it was Bong 39, McGuire 31: Mac couldn't seem to break his "eight behind Bong" jinx.

On 17 December 1944 Bong got number 40, an Oscar, over San Jose. Bong pleaded for the chance to make 50 but Kenney knew it was time to pull the quiet, unassuming pilot out after 146 missions and 400 hours in combat.

On Christmas Day McGuire downed three fighters and four more the next day but Kenney grounded him on the 27th – he looked very tired – and Kenney did not want Bong to be No 2 before reaching the States.

Turning P-38J-10-LO with two 165 US gal (137 Imp gal, 625 ltr) auxiliary fuel tanks.

(Lockheed)

McGuire's furious flying caused Chris Herman to write home, "I flew with both 'Macs' [McGuire and MacDonald] in a couple of fights and now need a new plane. Both wings were sprung and wrinkled from racking around at excessive speeds and dive recoveries – it's one hell of a job to fly with McGuire, and his plane is in the same shape. . . . I'm usually No 3 man in his flight when he takes the Squadron out – expects me to stay for at least three or four passes, or till we get things split up and going our way. Then he doesn't give a damn what happens, but hates to find himself suddenly all alone down on the deck!"

On 7 January 1945 McGuire led three other Lightnings from Dulag as Daddy Flight on a sweep in poor weather. A low overcast had forced the Americans to patrol at 1,400 ft (430 m). About ten miles from Fabrica Capt Edwin Weaver, Mac's wingman, called out a lone enemy fighter: Warrant Officer Akira Sugimoto was taking his 54th Sentai Ki.43 Hayabusa (Oscar) back to Fabrica after a fruitless try at bombing with his aircraft.

Sugomoto passed underneath the Lightnings when McGuire pulled his P-38 around and Sugimoto met the challenge. Sgt Mizunori Fukuda, who had briefly flown formation with Sugimoto on the way back a few minutes earlier, had his 71st Sentai Ki.84 Hayate (Frank) on final at Manapla with gear and flaps down. Glancing around, he saw Sugimoto engage the Lightnings.

Sugimoto pulled in tighter, heading for the formation, and fired at Daddy Three, Lt Douglas Thropp, who started to drop his external tanks when McGuire called, "Daddy Flight. Save your tanks." This was an unusual order since the '38s were heavy and slow. One can only guess at McGuire's reasoning – perhaps an easy kill before continuing on with precious fuel to hunt.

Maj Jack Rittmayer, on loan from the 13th Air Force, fired at Sugimoto from his No 4 position. The Hayabusa was boring in on Weaver. McGuire pulled his Lightning around on the edge of a stall, as he had many times before, to bring his guns to bear. The P-38 shuddered as it neared position for a good shot – only a bit more. The drop tanks were now a great liability but Mac's wingman was in trouble. The big fighter was almost there when it entered a full stall, snap-rolling inverted at 200 ft (60 m). Going in upside down at a 30° angle, the P-38 exploded in a huge ball of flame. Only three victories away from first place in his ace race with Dick Bong, "Feisty" Tom McGuire was dead at 0708 hours. The "race of aces" was over, never to be duplicated again.

Sugimoto pulled up into the overcast and crash-landed his badly damaged Oscar only to be killed by the Filipinos. Fukuda entered the fight, seeing the blazing crash of McGuire's Lightning and Sugimoto's zoom into the overcast. The 21 year old Japanese fighter pilot placed fire directly into the centre section of Rittmayer's Lightning, and the American went in. Fukuda got a shot at Thropp as the two Lightnings pulled up into the overcast. Weaver had placed a few rounds into the Hayate and Fukuda had to crashland at Manapla.

Herman noted in a letter home that "it was quite a shock to us – sort of took the spark plug out of the

P-38J-15-LO of the 23rd FG, 449th FS, 14th AF, parked at Tingkwak Sekan, Burma in August, 1944. After refuelling the P-38 would return to China by way of Myitkyina. (Kenneth M. Sunney)

Squadron. . . . Our red nosed planes are known all over and wherever we go we're asked, 'What happened?' " As John Tilley remembered his boss, "To sum it all up, McGuire was an unpleasant individual with a talent much bigger than he was, and an unnatural lack of fear. I did not like him and I'm sure he knew it. But to his everlasting credit, I will say he was about the fairest boss I've ever worked for . . . ; he would go to bat for the squadron and the men without hesitation." Bong, who had gone home to fly jets, was killed in a P-80 on 6 August 1945.

Though the Lightnings were able to wrack up good scores against enemy aircraft through December in the Leyte and Luzon campaigns, hunting became scarce with the New Year and FEAF fighters were flying more bombing and strafing missions far beyond the Philippines into Formosa, China, Indo-China and against shipping.

Ross T. Humer recalled these kinds of missions while flying with the 12th FS, 18th Fighter Group, "One of the missions which stands out is a fighter sweep of Surabaya while based at Palawan – a round trip of more than 2,000 miles lasting 10½ hours. I believe this must be one of the longest fighter missions attempted during the war.

"Of course, most wars are long periods of waiting; dull, boring missions with only an occasional bright or exciting action. We were no different, for one of our duties was convoy cover, sometimes lasting five hours. With the P-38, however, we made it as easy on ourselves as possible, for when on station we would fly a four mile radius circle, all planes in trail, and when trimmed properly, we could sit back,

eat, smoke, write letters, and even read a little while the plane did all the work. About the only thing we couldn't do was catnap."

Although the commanders in the China-Burma-India Theatre wanted more Lightnings, only two squadrons of P-38s saw action, the 449th and 459th. The 449th FS was formed in July 1943, with pilots in North Africa who volunteered to fly their fighters to China while the 459th FS was born two months later as the 4th FS of the 80th Fighter Group flying out of Upper Assam, India.

Enemy air activity was not the major threat in the CBI so the Lightning pilots found themselves doing a great deal of ground support work. From Kunming the 449th FS, attached to the 14th Air Force, produced a number of aces in spite of the lack of targets. One of its better known pilots was Lt Tom Harmon, a football player and present-day TV sportscaster. In an air battle over Klukiang he was shot down and despite painful burns, walked back to home base in 32 days.

The 459th FS became known in the theatre as the "Twin Dragons" of the 10th Air Force. Their primary mission was to protect the terminals in India and the Air Transport Command cargo aircraft that flew over the Himalayas to China. The 459th FS did its share of ground support as well, particularly in Northern Burma, but several aces emerged from this squadron as well.

Attached to RAF 224 Group out of Chittagong on the Bay of Bengal, the 459th FS got most of its aerial victories in March and May 1944 and then became adept at bridge-

P-38Ls of the 318th FG, 7th AF, waiting their turn to take off on a mission at Isley (Isely) field, Saipan Island in November, 1944. (USAF)

busting by early 1945 while flying out of Rumkhapalong. China, at the end of one of the longest supply lines in the world, remained somewhat overlooked as the Allies decided against landings on the China coast, preferring instead to take Iwo Jima and Okinawa.

Across the Pacific the P-38 entered combat with the 7th Air Force's 318th Fighter Group. Also flying the P-47, the Saipan based Group was assigned to the 20th Air Force for long range B-29 escort. The 28th Photo Recon Squadron mapped Iwo Jima with five F-5s escorted by 12 P-38s and four B-29s, bringing back 1,720 photos for the mid-February 1945 invasion. Once the P-38 units got into the crowded airstrip on Iwo in March, they found themselves in hand to hand combat with Japanese soldiers. The 7th Air Force Lightnings finally moved on to Ie Shima in preparation for the invasion of the Japanese home islands. By June the 5th Air Force was flying off Okinawa and Ie Shima for the coming assault, to be launched 1 November.

The atomic bombings in August 1945 brought the war to a rapid end. On 6 August the 25th Photo Squadron had been out photographing the Japanese home islands in preparation for the invasion when on the way back Charles Lerable saw a strange mushroom-shaped "thunderstorm" and photographed it for one of the more unusual shots of the Hiroshima explosion.

In late August the 49th Fighter Group, under the command of LtCol Clay Tice, Jr, was making fighter sweeps of southern Japan with orders not to shoot unless shot at. On 25 August Tice and a wingman, F/O Douglas C. Hall, were escorting some recon Lightnings over Honshu when Hall reported 240 gallons of fuel left – 550 miles (885 km) from the base on Okinawa. Thirty minutes later Hall radioed 120 gallons left. "I told Hall," recalled Tice, "we could pick out an airstrip to land. Meanwhile we contacted a B-17 rescue plane and told them to go back to Ie Shima and return with

gasoline."

Tice selected Nittagahara on the eastern shore of South Central Kyushu. Around noon Tice settled his Lightning down, the first American to touch Japanese soil not to be captured. Hall quickly followed. The two sat in their aircraft but the Japanese had vanished, and Tice finally got out to examine two Betty bombers sitting on the field. A Japanese officer and seven soldiers approached, smiling. The officer saluted and shook hands, "then everybody started talking but nobody knew what the hell anybody was saying."

When the B-17 arrived the Japanese swarmed over it, admired its .50 caliber guns and then helped pump the fuel aboard the P-38s. In exchange for some C-Rations the Japanese offered candy. The war was truly over and, significantly, the P-38 Lightning had been there, representing the aircraft that had shot down more Japanese aircraft than any other and the type most numerous in the Pacific: 808 were in the Far East Air Forces at the time.

MacArthur selected the 49th Fighter Group to be the first fighter unit assigned to the Japanese mainland. They flew to Atsugi on Honshu on 8 September to serve as the occupational fighter force. By December the beloved Lightnings were beginning to be replaced by P-51s: when a P-38 was grounded for maintenance, it was simply pushed aside on the field. James Watkins flew the last operational P-38 in the FEAF, the 49th's "piggy-back", with Capt Guy Watson aboard. They jumped a Navy floatplane for a quick dogfight, then it was back to Atsugi.

For three and a half years Lockheed's pride and joy had dominated the Pacific, along with the Grumman F6F Hellcat, to earn a record of success and popularity far in excess of what had been dreamed. Unloved in Europe on the whole, the P-38 had been the primary fighter in both the Mediterranean and the Pacific and a major instrument in the Allied victory.

TEXT BY
ROBERT GRINSELL

P-51

MUSTANG

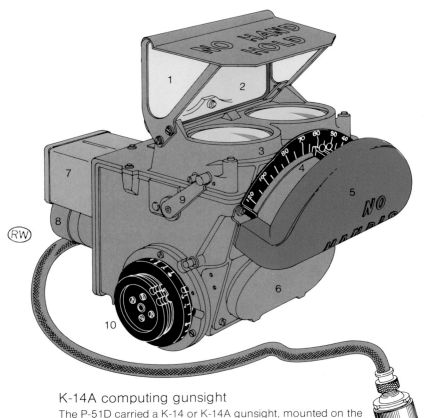

K-14A computing gunsight

The P-51D carried a K-14 or K-14A gunsight, mounted on the instrument glare shield centre line. It contained both fixed and gyro-actuated optical systems and computed the correct lead angle for all targets. The K-14A sight differed from the K-14 only in having range lines on the fixed reticle used for aiming rocket projectiles.

1 Sun filter glass
2 Reflector plate
3 Span dial
4 Span knob
5 Crash pad
6 Lamp cover
7 Silica gel cell
8 Gyro motor
9 Fixed reticle mask lever
10 Range dial

Introduction

Much as we liked the P-38, we knew what the P-51 "Spam Can" could do and we wanted a piece of the action. For the pilots who had never flown a single engine fighter, the conversion was something of a minor trauma. This little beauty had torque aplenty, and we quickly found it necessary to convert our strong right arms to strong right legs. We also learned that the most important control, aside from stick and rudders, was the rudder trim knob. It also took a bit of self-hypnosis to ignore the peculiar sounds the Merlin engine always made the moment you flew over any stretch of water.

In addition, it was weeks before any of us became even the slightest bit accustomed to the soul-shattering thump that occurred each time we climbed or descended through the altitude where the supercharger blower cut in or out. This is not to mention the sheer panic the first time

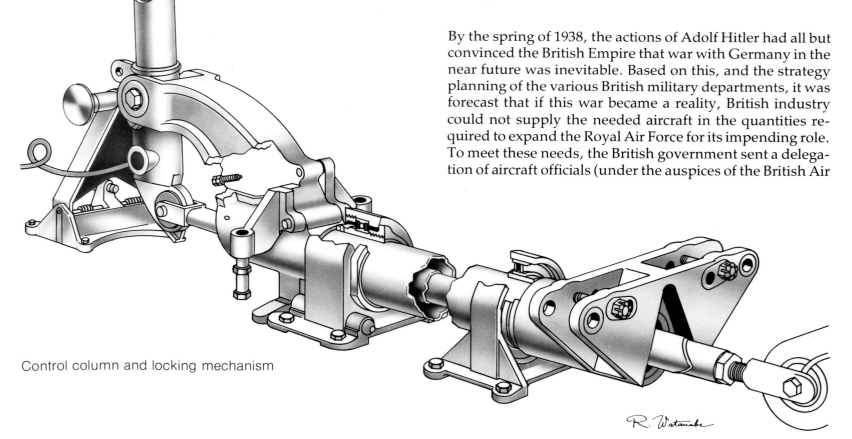

Control column and locking mechanism

you ran a drop-tank dry deep over Germany and the engine instantly cut out. But the joy of flying that absolutely fabulous little machine far out-matched any of its annoying little habits. At last we sat in comfort, plenty of room for legs, arms, shoulders, and head, ample heat at any altitude, fantastic pilot visibility all around (except over the nose of course—and who cared what was in front) and a range capability we hadn't dreamed of.

There were a few minor annoyances of course. Centre-of-gravity (C.G.) was crucial with the fuselage tank filled. But we learned to cope. Trim was critical if you wanted to hit anything with those six wing-mounted fifties—but that was what the rudder trim was for and you learned to use it. Landing was sporty, but you soon took pride in placing the bird gently on the runway in a three-point attitude. Even taxiing in a constant "S" turn to afford forward visibility either side of that long engine cowling became a matter of routine habit.

The ultimate proof and moment of truth came in your first air combat. Here was a fighter! High or low, straight down, or in a shuddering Lufberry, you knew no one could match you. The gyro sight was deadly accurate. The firepower devastating. Gun camera results were like Hollywood, a far cry from the blurred, jumping imagery produced by the gun camera in the P-38 (some knothead had mounted that one right under the 20-mm gun).

As for actual combat performance, the P-51 was good at everything, matching the German machines in all they could do. In all, the P-51 was a fighter pilot's dream. If you don't think I'm right, just ask any pilot who ever strapped a Mustang to his bottom and set out across the North Sea to do battle with the wily Hun.

General Robin Olds
USAF, *Retired*

Background

By the spring of 1938, the actions of Adolf Hitler had all but convinced the British Empire that war with Germany in the near future was inevitable. Based on this, and the strategy planning of the various British military departments, it was forecast that if this war became a reality, British industry could not supply the needed aircraft in the quantities required to expand the Royal Air Force for its impending role. To meet these needs, the British government sent a delegation of aircraft officials (under the auspices of the British Air

Ministry) to the United States, which at that time had not entered the war or made any commitments to the war effort. The delegation was to survey the American aircraft fabrication potential in the hopes of augmenting the aircraft industry of the Commonwealth.

One of the companies visited by the British was North American Aviation in Inglewood, California. North American had been established by Clement Keys as an aircraft holding and investment company, having been incorporated in the state of Delaware in 1928. The company had held interests in almost every major American aircraft producer as well as a number of emerging airline services. General Motors, recognizing the potential of this new concern, purchased a major interest in North American in the mid-thirties and established a manufacturing division under the North American name, headed by James (Dutch) Kindelberger, a former top-design executive with Douglas Aircraft.

The British tour of the American firms resulted in the placing of a pair of orders, one to Lockheed Aircraft in Burbank, California, for 200 Hudson reconnaissance bombers and a second to North American Aviation for 200 advanced flight trainers.

The trainer was simply a modified version of the AT-6 (the AT designation representing Advanced Training) that was being produced for the United States Army Air Corps (USAAC). The plane incorporated a North-American-built variant of the Pratt and Whitney R-1340 powerplant, (rated at 600 hp), and had provisions for installation of both forward and aft armaments. The cockpit was laid out in military fashion and included combat aircraft type instruments and navigational gauges.

The AT-6 Texan (as it was called by North American) was more than likely one of the most widely used and longest life aircraft ever produced. It had been designed and developed by Kindelberger in 1934, and it was an order of 42 of these aircraft from the USAAC that had kept the North American company on the positive side of the ledger and made possible its 1935 move from Maryland to California—where the weather was more conducive to flying, and thus also to the development of new aircraft.

The aircraft ordered by the British was actually an improved BC-1 design (the BC designation standing for Basic Combat) which had evolved into the AT-6 after the addition of retractable landing gear. The British aircraft were designated AT-6C (Harvard IIA) and AT-6D (Harvard III) and were somewhat heavier than the American version in that they were produced with non-essential materials (such as steel) to save critical aluminum which made up a major portion of the airframe structure and skin of the American version.

Within four months of the issue of the contract, North American delivered the first trainer to England. This was the beginning of a course of events and action which would culminate two and a half years later in the first flight of the North American NA-73X (the initial P-51 Mustang prototype).

On 3 September, 1939, with the invasion of Poland, both France and England declared war on Germany. This meant that the industrial output of both countries would now definitely be stressed and they would again look to the United States for added production capabilities and needed war materials. Again a complete review and tour of the American aircraft producers was carried out by

officials of the British Government. The group decided in April, 1940, that the best available fighter they could purchase was the Curtiss P-40 which was just entering service with the USAAC.

Because of commitments to American needs, Curtiss could not guarantee deliveries of the new plane to England until the end of 1940, thus the British Commission decided to try and establish another, less committed, manufacturer as a second source for the Tomahawk. Based on their success and satisfaction with North American on the Harvard trainer contract, the British approached Kindelberger with their proposition. They were, however, rejected and instead, offered a North American proposal for a new fighter design utilizing the Allison V-1710-39 powerplant of the Curtiss P-40, but which would provide the Royal Air Force with improved performance, armament and range. Leaving the British delegation with a tentative agreement on his proposal in early May, 1940, Kindelberger wired the North American plant in Inglewood. Working through the night, the design team provided Kindelberger with its sleek, low-profile fighter concept the next morning when he arrived. Kindelberger liked what he saw and mailed the design drawings to the British delegation in New York for review and approval.

North American was given the authorization to proceed on detail designs and specifications as well as long-lead material orders while negotiations continued on the cost of the proposed fighter. The contract was finally settled on 29 May, 1940, when the British signed an order for 320 of the new aircraft, designated NA-73 (NA representing North American, as the fighter was not for the USAAC and therefore had no official American government code letter), at a cost of over $15 million.

The conditions of the contract were restrictive. The prototype aircraft would be required to meet all specification goals and was to be ready for flight testing within eight months. However, an internal North American time limit target was agreed to, based on the projected time it would have taken them to tool for production of the Curtiss P-40, if it had accepted the initial offer of the British. This meant they would try to roll-out the NA-73 within 120 days.

One additional stipulation of the British contract was that, due to their lack of experience in the actual design and construction of an advanced fighter aircraft, North American was to obtain all current data on the P-40 development from the Curtiss company.

The design team, headed by Raymond Rice, began their efforts in earnest on 30 May. The chief designer on the team was Edgar Schmued, a German (Bavarian) engineer who had migrated to the United States in 1930. The main goals were reduced weight and a streamlining of the design to reduce drag to a minimum, resulting in maximized performance from the selected Allison powerplant. The cowling of the aircraft was fitted tightly around the engine with only a single carburetor intake on the topside to spoil its smooth lines. The fuselage cross section was minimized and the cockpit canopy was actually semi-buried into the sidewall to reduce its protrusion into the airstream. The radiator inlet required for all liquid-cooled powerplants was located under the center fuselage between the wings, and utilized a unique and new design for the entry scoop. The shape and location of the ducting scoop resulted in the delay of the drag factor imposed

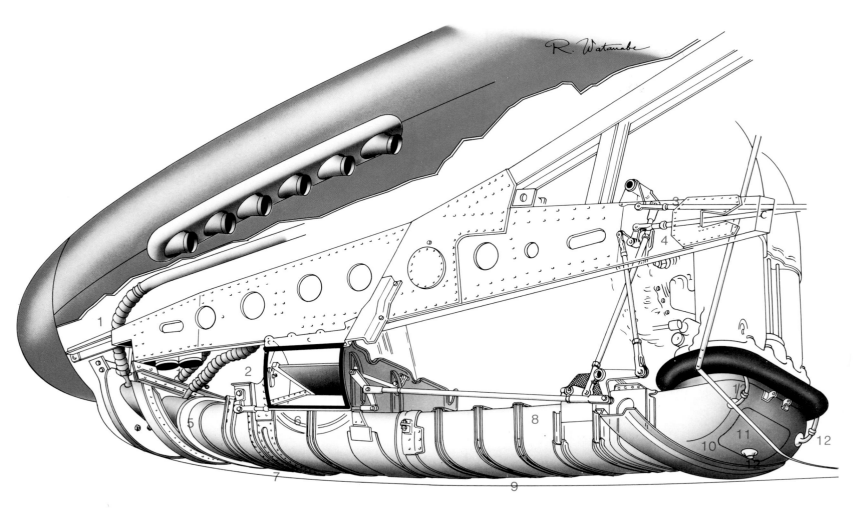

Radiator air scoop

1	Spark plug blast tubes	5	Duct front (scoop) section	9	Duct rear section
2	Generator blast tube	6	Ram air gate	10	Duct elbow
3	Hot air control	7	Duct intermediate section	11	Access door
4	Cold air control	8	Icing screen	12	Drains

negative effects on the aircraft's airspeed because of the aft location. In addition, the air would flow into the duct, be slowed in the ducting, heated through contact with the hot engine-cooling lines of the radiator, and then expand as it flowed out from the plane, to further reduce drag losses.

Armament for the NA-73X design included a pair of 0.50-caliber Browning 53-2 machine-guns housed in the lower engine cowling, and a pair of 0.30-caliber Browning MG40 machine-guns in each wing.

Perhaps the most innovative feature of the NA-73 design was its incorporation of a laminar flow wing. This concept, developed by the National Advisory Committee for Aeronautics (NACA), involved moving the thickened section of the wing aft, or toward the middle, which provided a long sloping incline to the middle of the wing for an even flow prior to the air's breaking into turbulence at the thickened point. This increase in the area of even airflow layers reduced the drag created by turbulent air currents (common on previous wing designs) and greatly improved the aircraft's overall performance and range capabilities through increased fuel efficiency.

The laminar flow concept was adopted by the North American engineering team and modified for compatibility with the specific flight regime envisioned for the NA-73. The completed wing contour was then tested at the California Institute of Technology for flight characteristics with the experimental results correlating almost exactly to the North American calculations.

One additional unique feature that was embodied in the NA-73 design was the extensive use of secondary curves in place of straight angles (used for ease of fabrication) or single curvatures. In simple terms, this concept utilized compound, or non-uniform curvatures and fillet radii, to streamline the entire aircraft from planeview to frontal view in an effort to reduce drag and create smooth airflow over the aircraft's outer surfaces. This innovation was also tested at California Technology Institute for design calculation verification.

Work proceeded at an accelerated pace as the month of August neared, and the only major problem that occurred was the lack of availability of the 1,150 hp V-1710 Allison engine, which at the time was in short supply due to its use in the Lockheed P-38 Lightning, Curtiss P-40, and Bell P-39 Airacobra (all in, or entering, production in American factories). The USAAC had committed to supply the powerplant, but on an "as available" basis.

By August the airframe was ready for marrying to the engine, but North American had still not received clearance, or the powerplant, from the USAAC. The Allison was finally delivered on 7 October and was preliminarily fitted to the NA-73X airframe in only one day; however, it took four days to finalize mounting and connections. This short time was the result of working around the clock and a unique feature of the aircraft's cowling and powerplant attach structure design which allowed quick and simple assembly, dismantling and inspection of the entire powerplant unit.

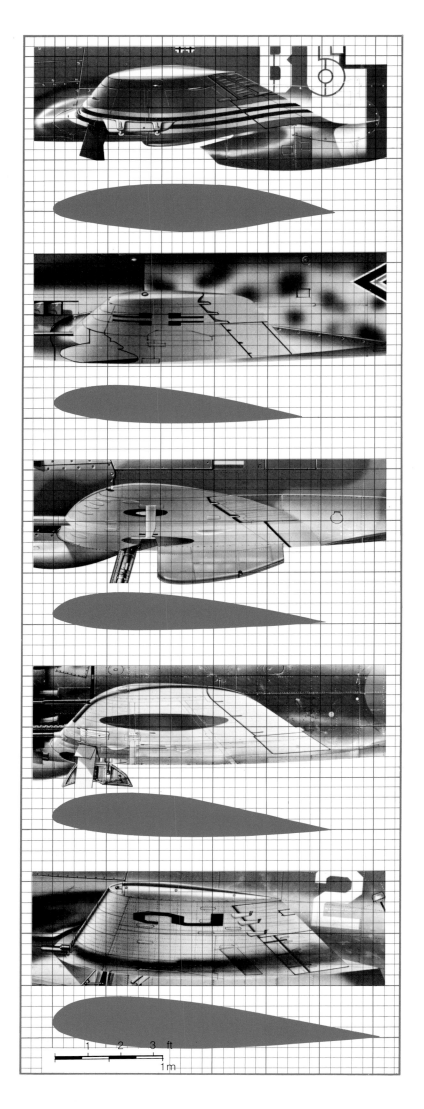

The NA-73X rolled out onto the runway at Mines Field, California, on 26 October, 1940, almost five months to the day from the time the rough design sketches had been submitted to the British Commission for approval. At the controls was Vance Breese, project test pilot, who had conducted all the taxying trials.

Although the initial flights exposed a few shortcomings and minor design problems, the evaluation produced the expected results, which verified that the NA-73X represented a major breakthrough in the design and performance of fighter aircraft. The main problems exposed by the trials related to the overheating of the V-1710 Allison (not uncommon with any new aircraft, radial or in-line) and design drawings were immediately drafted to increase the cooling ducting. However, before these modifications could be incorporated, the aircraft met with disaster. On its fifth flight, an airspeed calibration test on 20 November, 1940, the powerplant failed and Paul Balfour, the North American test pilot, attempted a dead-stick landing at a nearby farm. The aircraft hit the field and flipped over on its back resulting in major structural damage to the airframe. The crash was the result of fuel starvation of the engine resulting from the pilot's having forgotten to switch to another fuel tank, and was not caused by any mechanical failure of the design.

The crash, of course, resulted in a major stumbling block to North American's development plans. However, the initial trials with the NA-73X had already shown that the sleek little fighter was exceptionally easy to handle, and, between altitudes of 10,000 to 15,000 feet (3,000 to 4,600 m), it had exhibited a 25 mph (40 km/h) increase in airspeed over the Curtiss P-40 Tomahawk it had been designed to replace. Based on this limited data and the enthusiasm of the North American design team, headed by Raymond Rice, the British placed an order for 300 additional aircraft bringing their total order to 620 fighters. This order was sent during the height of activities of the Battle of Britain and the aircraft included several modifications based on combat experience over Britain. The North American designation for these aircraft was NA-83.

At the same time as the British Government was increasing their production order, the United States Government, as part of the agreement to allow North American to build fighter aircraft for a foreign power, requested a pair of the production aircraft allocated to the USAAC for evaluation. These two aircraft, given the designation XP-51, were delivered to Wright-Patterson Field in Ohio, where they were logged in and then stored on a little-used portion of the base.

The initial pair of USAAC XP-51s were given the name "Apache," however, these were the only two aircraft in the P-51 series that were to carry this name. The name

Comparison of the P-51 laminar-flow wing with other aerofoils (cross-section at the wing root)

Type	Wing area	Maximum speed
NA P-51D Mustang:	235 sq.ft (21.83m²)	437 mph at 25,000 ft (703km/h at 7625m)
Fw 190D-9:	196.98 sq.ft (18.2m²)	426 mph at 21,650 ft (with MW 50 boost) (686km/h at 6600m)
Spitfire Mk XIV:	242 sq.ft (22.48m²)	448 mph at 26,000 ft (with RR Griffon 65) (721km/h at 7925m)
Reisen 52-Otsu (A6M5):	229.27 sq.ft (21.3m²)	351 mph at 19,685 ft (565km/h at 6000m)
Grumman F6F-3 Hellcat:	334.09 sq.ft (31.04m²)	373 mph at 23,700 ft (600km/h at 7220m)

The prototype North American NA-73X provided the aviation industry with an advanced and highly innovative design.

"Mustang" was recommended by the British Purchasing Commission in an official communique with North American in December, 1940. The new name was based on a song that had made the rounds of both the American and European Continents during the late 1930's. The name contained both an American flavor (representing a small wild horse of the Western U.S.) and was indicative of the speed and independence that were critical ingredients for a successful fighter. By the end of World War II in 1945, over 15,500 P-51s had been produced while nearly 6,000 more were on order by the USAAF (changed designation of the United States Army Air Corps on 20 June, 1941).

The first production Mustang (AG 345) was completed and test flown on 25 April, 1941, and accepted by the British Purchasing Commission on 1 May. The first finished Mustang I to reach the Royal Air Force arrived at Liverpool on 24 October, 1941, in a large wooden crate. It was the second aircraft to roll off the assembly line at North American (the first remaining in the United States for further testing by RAF evaluation teams), and carried the serial number AG 346. The crate was transported to nearby Speke airfield and assembled for flight testing by the Royal Air Force. The tests confirmed the results that had been generated in California. The Mustang possessed excellent handling characteristics and gave a superior performance, not only in comparison to the Curtiss Kittyhawk I but, in comparison to the Spitfire Vb as well. It was, in fact, 35 mph (56 km/h) faster than the Spitfire.

The trials also confirmed the seemingly singular drawback of the new Mustang, this being its performance losses above 11,300 feet (3,440 m). By the time the Mustang reached altitudes over 20,000 feet (6,100 m), the performance degradation was so significant that the aircraft became difficult to handle. It was this latter fact, coupled with the British concern that the selection of an American aircraft as primary inventory equipment would present difficulties in obtaining spare parts and maintenance training, that resulted in the decision by the RAF to concentrate their future fighter development programs on the Supermarine Spitfire airframe for the interceptor role. The Mustang, therefore, was restricted to the lower altitude role of Army Co-operation combat missions, including reconnaissance and ground attack/support.

The initial RAF unit to receive the Mustang I was 26 Squadron based at Gatwick, which took delivery of one of the new aircraft from Speke in January, 1942. By March, the Mustang began to appear in the inventories of several other Army Co-operation units whose main task was to support the British army in training exercises up and down the length of Britain in preparation for future combat operations on the European mainland. Due to the fact that the Mustang was essentially in training, and no current need existed for it as a fighter interceptor, delivery of it to the various units was slow and several experimental modifications were evaluated. The one which was to have not only a major impact on the air supremacy of the Allied Forces in later years, but one which may have also played a major role in determining the overall outcome of World War II, was the installation of the Rolls-Royce Merlin powerplant into four Mustang Is. The success of these aircraft convinced the U.S. Government to place an order for two Packard-built Merlin powered prototypes, designated XP-78 (North American designation NA-101). These aircraft were to provide the basis for the later model P-51B model of the Mustang which offered long-range high-altitude bomber escort and interceptor capabilities.

The first combat operations in which the Mustang was used as an offensive weapon occurred on 10 May, 1942, when a single aircraft of 26 Squadron took off from Gatwick on a reconnaissance sortie to the French coast. The pilot photographed parked Luftwaffe aircraft at Berck airfield and then swung his Mustang around for a strafing pass at the various vehicles and supplies lined up along the outskirts of the field. On his way home, the pilot sighted a supply train and again banked his aircraft to attack. In less than two hours the Mustang was back at Gatwick, but it had set the stage for almost continuous Mustang "reconnaissance and destroy" (called "Popular" by the RAF) sorties into German-held French territory. The first known casualty of a Mustang occurred two months later when, in July, 1941, 26 Squadron reported the loss of aircraft AG 415 during a strafing mission near Le Touquet, France.

With the combat worthiness of the Mustang I being proven daily, the RAF decided to expand its role and during the late summer and early fall of 1941 assigned the aircraft to Coastal Command duties which included the escort of slower more cumbersome anti-shipping bomber aircraft, and in low-altitude fighter interception sorties against wave-top flying Fw 190s which were carrying out deep interdiction raids against British coastal harbors and ports. In addition, the Mustang units were assigned to "Seek-and-Destroy" sorties over the coast of France to strafe specific targets such as trains, transport convoys and military installations.

P-51-NA

The first aircraft to carry the official P-51 designation were the Mustang IA's ordered by the British under the American Government's Lend-Lease Act of March, 1940. The reason for the designation lay in the conditions of the Lend-Lease Act itself. To maintain its veil of neutrality, the American Government halted the selling of aircraft to foreign powers, and instead drew up an agreement through which military equipment could be leased to a foreign power, but only after it had been originally ordered by an American Agency of Military Service and carried American serial numbers and designations.

The only difference in the P-51-NA (NA designating production at the North American Inglewood plant) and the original British ordered Mustang lay in the installation of a pair of 20-mm cannon in each wing in place of machine guns, and the deletion of 0.50-caliber machine-guns in lower engine cowling.

Although impressed with the test performance of the early Mustangs, and with the combat results being forwarded from Europe, the USAAF still could not identify a need for the North American fighter, as it already had committed itself to the Lockheed P-38, Republic P-47, Curtiss P-40 and Bell P-39 in late 1941. In addition, America was not currently at war and could not foresee any near-term requirement for the P-51. However, the events of 7 December 1941, had a significant impact on these influencing factors.

With the attack on Pearl Harbor by the Japanese, America was no longer an observer, but was now a participant in the worldwide conflict. The USAAF immediately initiated an in-depth test and evaluation program of the initial two prototypes (XP-51s) they had received from the first production run of the British order. Based on the results of these tests, conducted at Wright-Patterson Field, the USAAF diverted 55 of the P-51-NAs from the British order and after installation of oblique cockpit cameras, assigned them to photographic reconnaissance units in the United States and gave them the designation F-6A.

A-36A

Based on the performance and handling of the P-51 in a dive mode of operation, North American decided to propose a dive-bombing version of the aircraft to the USAAF. North American was aware of the USAAF's interest in a ground support/attack dive bomber based on the success of the Luftwaffe's Junkers Ju 87 Stuka in Europe. With the superior ratings submitted by Army pilots who had flown the two XP-51s, the USAAF approved the North American proposal and ordered 500 P-51s under the designation of A-36 (A for Attack). USAAF assigned serial numbers for the 500 A-36A's were 42-83663 to 42-84162. The actual official designation change from P-51 to A-36A was prior to initial deliveries of the aircraft in September, 1942.

The A-36A utilized the basic P-51 airframe and Allison V-1710-87 powerplant, but structural reinforcing in several high stress interfaces was incorporated to insure that the added loadings of steep dives and quick, low-altitude, pull-outs could be accommodated. Bomb racks were added under each wing just outboard of the armament bays. In addition, a set of hydraulically operated dive brakes were installed in each main wing plane. The four 0.30-caliber wing machine-guns were also replaced by 0.50-caliber guns in keeping with the USAAF tendency towards larger caliber armament.

The initial A-36A, nicknamed "Invader," was rolled out of the North American plant at Inglewood in September, 1942, with the first aircraft reaching USAAF units by October. The first units to deploy overseas with the A-36A were the 27th and 86th Fighter Bomber Groups which arrived in North Africa during the spring of 1943. The 86th contained a full four squadron complement of the new plane (approximately 150 aircraft) while the 27th initially was composed of both the A-36A and the Douglas A-20 Havoc. Despite the transitioning problems of the 27th, the unit was the first to enter combat with the A-36A. In June the unit carried out continuous dive-bombing sorties against the German airfield at Pantelleria, and the following month supported the Allied invasion of Sicily where it was joined by the 86th Fighter Bomber Group.

The method of attack with the A-36A consisted of a level approach from an altitude of approximately 8,000 feet (2,440 m) until the aircraft was nearly over the target. At this point the pilot would activate the dive brakes and nose down into a nearly vertical dive, releasing his bombs at between 2,000 and 4,000 feet (600 and 1,200 m), and then pulling sharply up. The main problem with this attacking

The second Mustang I carried the RAF Serial AG 346 and was evaluated in Britain in late summer 1941.

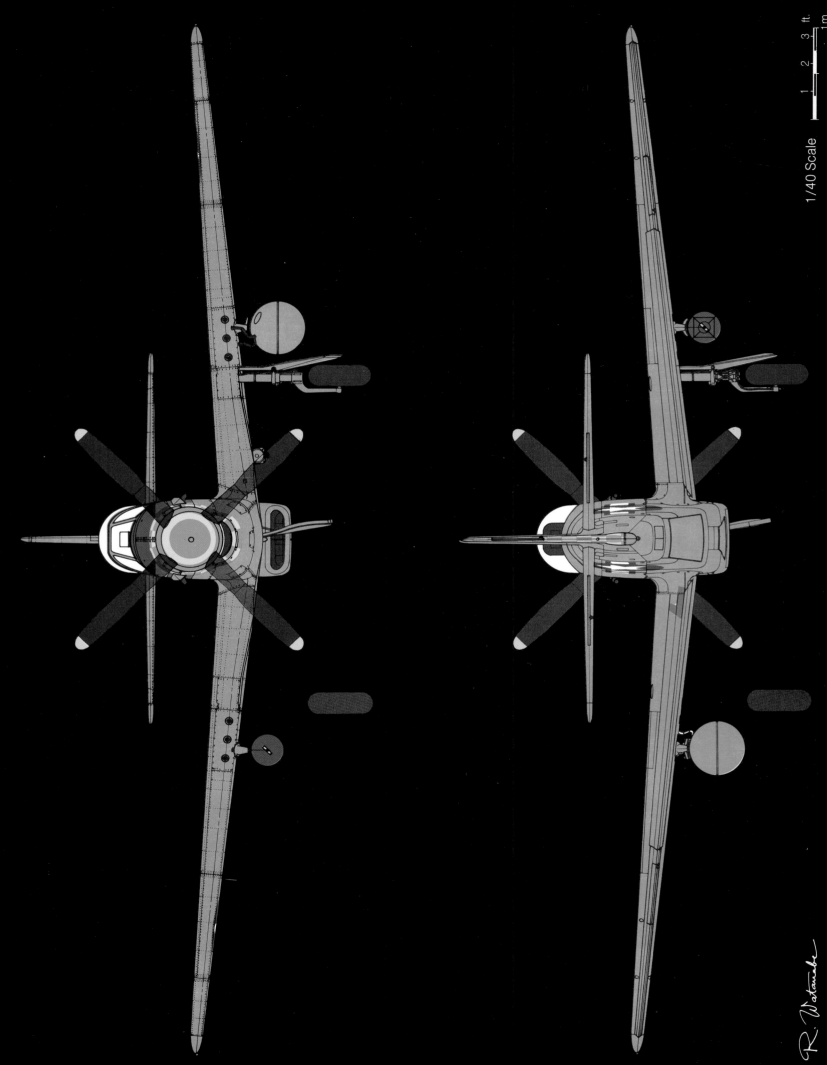

1/40 Scale

1 2 3 ft.

1m

R. Watanabe

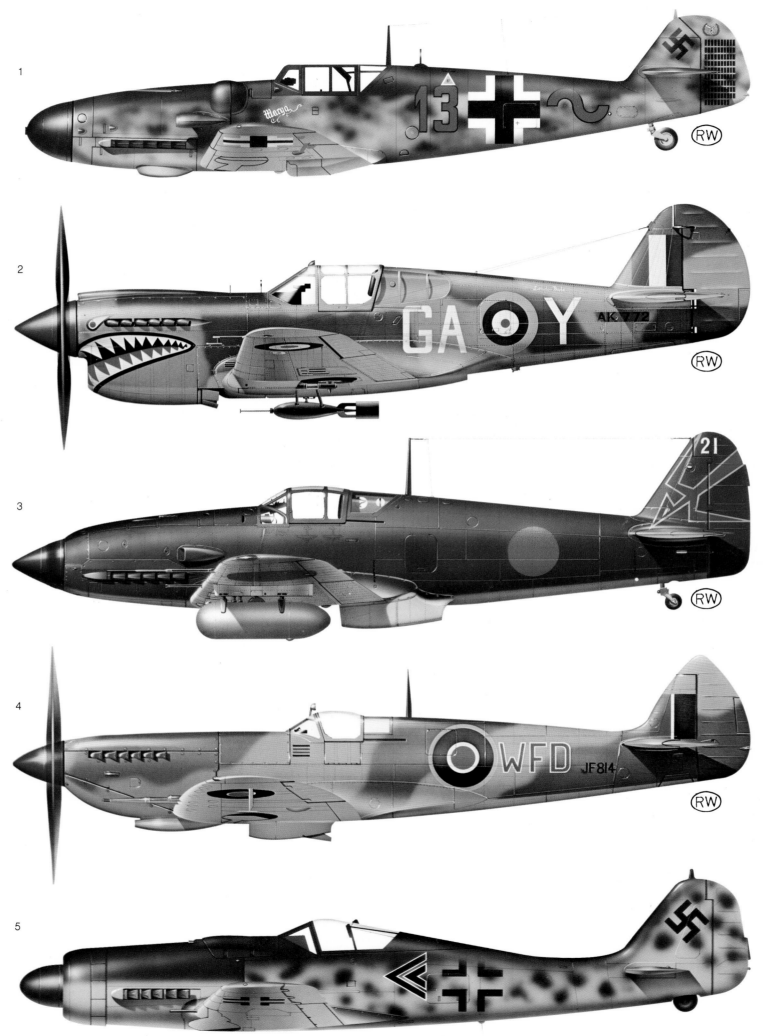

R. Watanabe

| 1 | 2 | 3 | ft |

1m

5 **Focke-Wulf Fw 190D-9**

Weight loaded (normal):	9480 lb (4300 kg)
(max):	10,670 lb (4840 kg)
Max speed (clean):	426 mph at 21,650 ft (686 km/h at 6600 m) with MW 50
Climb rate (initial):	approx 3300 ft/min (16.8 m/sec)
Time to 19,685 ft (6000 m):	7 min 6 sec
Service ceiling:	32,810 ft (10,000 m)
Range (clean):	520 mls (837 km) at 18,500 ft (5640 m)

Flown by *Oberleutnant* Oskar Romm, *Kommandeur,* IV/JG3.

North American P-51B-15-NA Mustang

Weight loaded (normal):	9800 lb (4450 kg) with extra 85 US gal (322 ltr) fuselage tank fitted on this series
(max):	11,200 lb (5080 kg) with 2000 lb (907 kg) bomb load
Max speed (clean):	435 mph at 30,000 ft (700 km/h at 9144 m)
Climb rate (initial):	3900 ft/min (19.8 m/sec)
Time to 20,000 ft (6100 m):	6 min 54 sec
Range (clean):	815 mls (1311 km)

Flown by Captain Clarence E. Anderson, 357th FG, 363rd FS, 8th AF at Leiston in England in June, 1944.

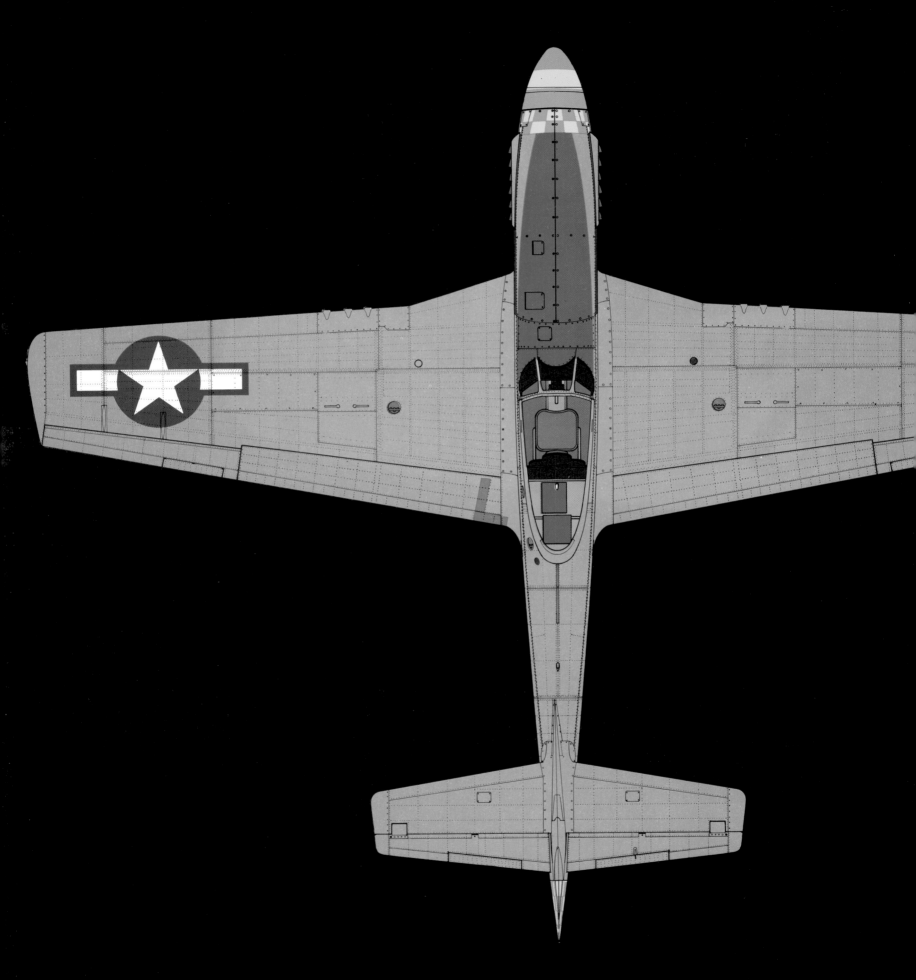

R. Watanabe

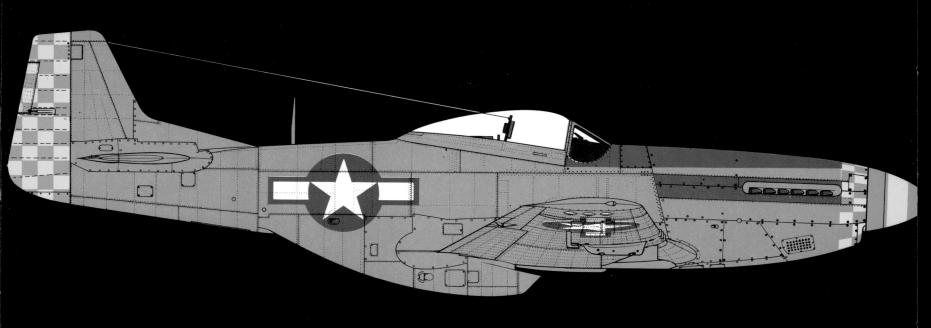

North American P-51D
Performance details:
Max speed (clean): 395 mph at 5000 ft (636km/h at 1525m)
413 mph at 15,000 ft (665km/h at 4575m)
437 mph at 25,000 ft (703km/h at 7625m)
433 mph at 30,000 ft (665km/h at 9150m)
Rate of climb: 3475 ft/min at 5000 ft (17.7m/sec at 1525m)
Time to 20,000 ft (6100m): 7 min 18 sec
Time to 30,000 ft (9150m): 12 min 36 sec
Range (clean): 950 mls (1529km) at 25,000 ft (7625m) at
max cruise power
Range (with max fuel): 1650 mls (2655km) at same alt, same power

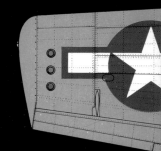

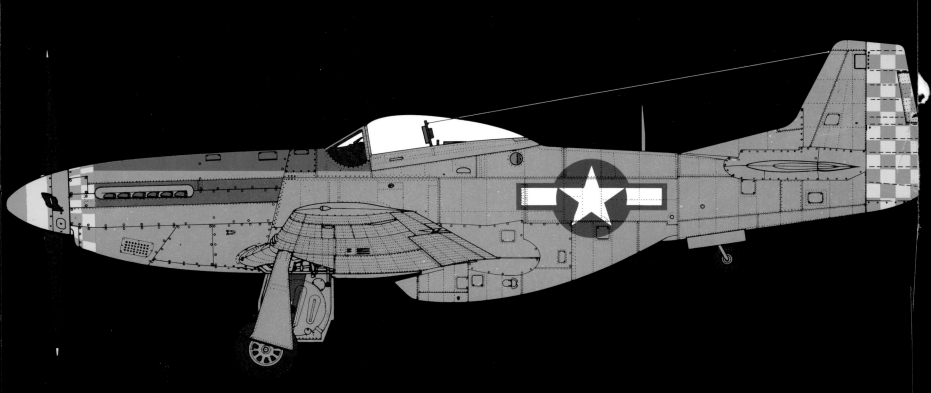

1/40 Scale

3 Kawasaki Ki-61-I Otsu Hien
Weight loaded: 7650 lb (3470 kg)
Max speed: 348 mph at 16,400 ft
(560 km/h at 5000 m)
Time to 16,405 ft (5000 m): 7 min
Service ceiling: 32,810 ft (10,000 m)
Range (clean): 684 mls (1100 km)
Flown by Master Sergeant Iwao Tabata, 39th Flight Training Unit.

4 Supermarine Spitfire F. Mk VIII (data: LF Mk VIII)
Weight loaded (normal): 7767 lb (3523 kg)
(max): 8000 lb (3629 kg)
Max speed: 408 mph at 25,000 ft
(656.6 km/h at 7600 m)
Climb rate (initial): 3000 ft/min (15.24 m/sec)
Time to 20,000 ft (6100 m): 7 min
Service ceiling: 41,500 ft (12,650 m)
Range: 660 mls (1062 km)
Flown by Air Vice Marshal W.F. Dickson, RAF.

Liquid cooled engine fighters in WWII
(Not to scale)

Messerschmitt Bf 109G-6/R6
Weight loaded (normal):   6944 lb (3150 kg)
Max speed: 386 mph at 22,640 ft (620 km/h at 6900 m)
                              with MW 50 (methanol-water injection)
Climb rate (initial):   3346 ft/min (17.0 m/sec)
Time to 18,700 ft (5700 m):   6 min
Service ceiling: 37,890 ft (11,550 m)
Range: 350 mls (563 km) at 330 mph
                              (530 km/h) at 19,030 ft (5800 m)
Flown by *Oberfeldwebel* Heinrich Bartels, 15/JG 27.

2 Curtiss P-40E Warhawk (RAF: Kittyhawk I)
Weight loaded (normal):   8400 lb (3814 kg)
              (max):   9100 lb (4131 kg)
Max speed (clean):   362 mph at 15,000 ft
                              (582 km/h at 4575 m)
Climb rate (initial):   2580 ft/min (13.1 m/sec) clean
Time to 15,000 ft (4575 m):   7 min 36 sec clean
          25,000 ft (7625 m): 18 min 12 sec clean
Service ceiling: 30,600 ft (9327 m)
Range (clean):   525 mls (845 km)
Flown in 112 Sqn., RAF.

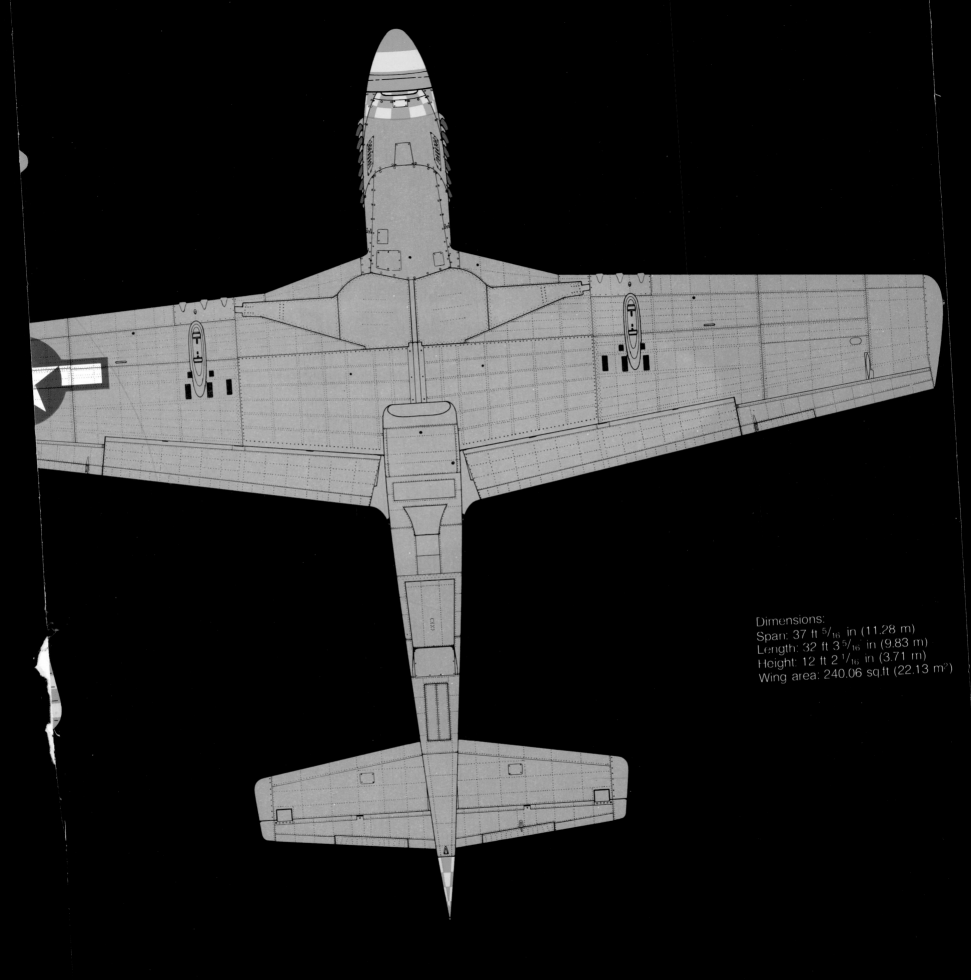

Dimensions:
Span: 37 ft $^{5}/_{16}$ in (11.28 m)
Length: 32 ft 3 $^{5}/_{16}$ in (9.83 m)
Height: 12 ft 2 $^{1}/_{16}$ in (3.71 m)
Wing area: 240.06 sq.ft (22.13 m²)

3 ft.
1m

concept was, that due to manufacturing tolerances and symmetry, an occasional imbalance in the extension of the dive brakes was encountered which resulted in unequal loadings on the port and starboard sides of the plane. These unequal pressure forces created an unstable dive and could result in spins, loss of control, and even structural failures.

Modifications were, therefore, incorporated into the dive brake system to eliminate this unequal extension during bombing runs. However, before these changes could be made in the field, and/or newer aircraft delivered, the units flying the A-36A were ordered to restrict their attack angle to 70 degrees, instead of near 90 degrees, and to refrain from use of the dive brakes. Several of the units ignored this order in an effort to maintain bombing accuracy, but others wired their dive brakes shut until the modifications were made.

In addition, due to the predictable method of attack, German flak was normally encountered in strength and with regularity. This resulted in the last aircraft in the formation of four often being shot down. This led to an increase in target approach to 10,000 feet (3,000 m) and a bomb release height of 4,000 to 5,000 feet (1,200 to 1,500 m).

Although only a few units utilized the A-36A dive bomber during the war, those that did had few complaints with regard to its performance. With its inherent handling capabilities, long range, speed and accurate bombing systems, the A-36A became a well respected, even though relatively unknown, aircraft and served as the cornerstone for the ordering and production of future P-51 Mustang fighters.

P-51A-NA

The P-51A was also ordered by the USAAF under the Lend-Lease Act for the RAF. However of the 310 aircraft ordered only 50 were delivered to the RAF (as Mustang IIs) while an additional 35 were modified with the addition of K-24 cameras for use as reconnaissance F-6B aircraft by the USAAF. Remaining P-51A-NAs were accepted by the USAAF and assigned to Air Commando Groups and dive-bombing units in the China-Burma-India (CBI) Theater where they performed both the function of fighter-interceptor and fighter-bomber. USAAF serial numbers allocated for the 310 P-51As were 43-6003 to 43-6312.

The P-51A-NA incorporated a pair of 0.50-caliber machine-guns in each wing in place of the 0.30-caliber weapons of the P-51-NA, and utilized the improved performance of the 1,200 hp Allison V-1710-81 in-line engine. The aircraft also included low drag wing racks for the carrying of bombs, rocket launchers or auxiliary fuel tanks.

The first P-51As (which followed the A-36As off the production line at Inglewood) were delivered to the 311th Group in India. The unit, although originally designated for dive-bombing sorties, had assumed reconnaissance, patrol, interception and ground attack roles on its arrival at Dinjan. For these varied missions the P-51A was much more suited than the A-36A.

It was the 311th which conducted the initial long-range escort duty mission for the Mustang, when they flew cover from Kurmitola in Bengal in November, 1943, for a formation of American B-24 and B-25 bombers. The formation was assigned to attack Japanese positions in the Rangoon area. The Mustangs also made use of 75 (US) gallon (284 liter) auxiliary fuel tanks to extend their range. This was the first time Mustangs had used the wing drop tanks.

Another unit to receive the P-51A was the 1st Air Commando Group which was a self-contained unit created specifically for the air support of Wingate's Raiders which were operating behind the Japanese lines in the China-Burma-India theater. The P-51As would operate from small, almost inaccessible landing fields, striking deep into Japanese-held territory with dive-bombing runs, strafing sorties and rocket attacks. In addition to the Air Commando units, P-51As also served with the 23rd Fighter Group (formerly part of the "Flying Tigers") and with the 51st Fighter Group before the arrival of the P-51Bs.

P-51B-NA

Although over 650 Mustang I, IA, and II models were delivered to the RAF and a further 350 P-51 and P-51A models were accepted by the USAAF, the aircraft did not possess, nor exhibit, the performance which could classify it as a superior fighter. Its overall performance deficiencies due to the limited capabilities of the Allison powerplant had restricted its mission roles and had raised only minor interest in decision-making military circles. The experiments conducted in Britain with the Rolls-Royce Merlin 65 and

The P-51 Mustang I, fitted on British request with four 20mm wing cannon in the USA in 1941, was known as the Mustang IA in RAF service. This variant was also the first used by USAAF, in photo-reconnaissance role.

(Robert Grinsell collection)

shortly after, similar tests by North American with a Packard-built Merlin 65 (V-1650-3), were to provide the impetus for the modification of the early P-51 into a truly great all-around fighter.

The actual concept of installing a Rolls-Royce Merlin in the Mustang to improve its high altitude interceptor capabilities was instituted in several arenas, all within a matter of weeks. Ideas came from both British aerodynamic engineers who theorized and calculated the high altitude performance improvements that could be expected with the changeover to the improved Merlin power-plant, as well as from pilots whose personal test and combat experience with the P-51 convinced them that, although the Mustang was superior in a number of respects to other fighters of the day, to be truly great it would have to be given an altitude performance boost of some kind. The major driver in this project was Ronnie Barker, a Rolls-Royce test pilot, who had familiarized himself with an "early" Mustang Mk I late in April, 1942.

The Rolls-Royce engineers estimated that the incorporation of the Merlin engine would increase the P-51s maximum airspeed to over 441 mph (709.7 km/h) at an altitude of over 25,000 feet (7,600 m) (an increase of over 90 mph (144.9 km/h) compared to the Allison-powered Mustang and at nearly twice the altitude). The proposal for the installation and testing of the Merlin in the Mustang was made to the British Air Ministry in mid-1942 and four Mustang Is (Serial numbers AM 203, AM 208, AL 963 and AL 975) were delivered to Rolls-Royce at Hucknall to be fitted with the Merlin 65 and were designated as Mustang Xs.

The Assistant Air Attache for the USAAF in London at the time was Major Thomas Hitchcock who had flown in the first World War and had the reputation of being somewhat of an adventurer. Because of his position as a representative of the US Embassy, Major Hitchcock was informed of the program to fit the Mustang with the Rolls-Royce powerplant. As the same engine was being manufactured in the United States by Packard, under license to Rolls-Royce, for delivery to Canadian and British aircraft manufacturers, Hitchcock drew up a proposal to conduct the same type of test program in the United States. He took his proposal to General "Hap" Arnold in Washington and on 25 July, 1942, the USAAF contracted with North American for the installation of Packard-built Merlin engines in a pair of P-51s. These two aircraft were aircraft requisitioned from the Lend-Lease production series.

The actual design of the Merlin engine, which when married to the P-51 airframe provided the USAAF with what would become the best overall fighter aircraft of World War II, was actually initiated in 1915 when Sir Henry Royce demonstrated his 12-cylinder in-line Vee power-plant delivering 225 hp. During the next ten years, improvements in the basic design, combustion efficiency and

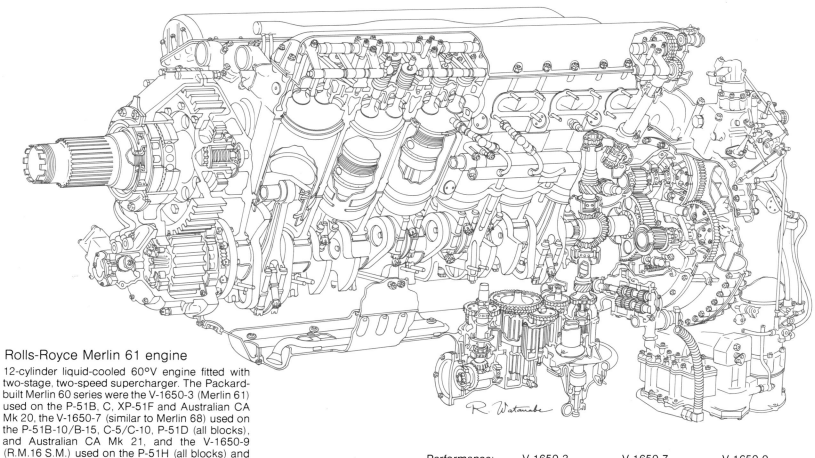

Rolls-Royce Merlin 61 engine

12-cylinder liquid-cooled 60°V engine fitted with two-stage, two-speed supercharger. The Packard-built Merlin 60 series were the V-1650-3 (Merlin 61) used on the P-51B, C, XP-51F and Australian CA Mk 20, the V-1650-7 (similar to Merlin 68) used on the P-51B-10/B-15, C-5/C-10, P-51D (all blocks), and Australian CA Mk 21, and the V-1650-9 (R.M.16 S.M.) used on the P-51H (all blocks) and XP-51M. (The V-1650-9 was developed from the Merlin 100 series and could be fitted with or without water injection).

	V-1650-3	V-1650-9
Total swept capacity:	1647 in³ (27 ltr)	1647 in³ (27 ltr)
Compression ratio:	6:1	
Dry weight:	1690 lb. (766.6kg)	1745 lb. (791.5kg)
Length:	87.108 in (2212mm)	87.141 in (2213mm)
Width:	29.97 in (761mm)	30.76 in (781mm)
Height:	41.63 in (1057mm)	44.97 in (1142mm)

Performance:	V-1650-3	V-1650-7	V-1650-9
Take-off power:	1380 hp (max 5 mins)	1490 hp (max 5 mins)	1830 hp (wet)
Low blower:	1600 hp at 11,800 ft (3600m)	1720 hp at 6200 ft (1890m)	—
Low blower:	1490 hp at 13,750 ft (4190m)	1590 hp at 8500 ft (2590m)	1930 hp at 10,100 ft (3080m) (wet)
High blower:	1330 hp at 23,000 ft (7010m)	1370 hp at 21,400 ft (6520m)	—
High blower:	1210 hp at 25,800 ft (7860m)	1065 hp at 23,400 ft (7130m)	1630 hp at 23,500 ft (7160m)

Mustang III was the first Merlin-powered P-51 version in RAF service. (Robert Grinsell collection)

material changes increased its output to 2,550 hp. This latter engine was incorporated into the Schneider Trophy winning Supermarine S6B seaplane in 1931 and set what then was a world speed record of over 407 mph in September, 1931.

The high performance engine was, of course, not suited for military use, as its capabilities for long duration operation were minimal. Rolls-Royce, therefore, in 1932, decided to modify its record-setting engine and produce it as a high performance military powerplant for the RAF. The basic powerplant specification included a delivery of 1,000 hp and capability of maintenance free operational durations of up to 100 hours flying time. The project was designated PV 12 (PV = Private Venture).

Named the ''Merlin'' in 1933, the new engine's development was filled with mishaps and problems. In striving for 100-hour operational capability, the engine suffered numerous material failures as well as severe mechanical problems, including cracked cylinders, bearing failure and rod fractures. However, in July, 1934, the first successful 100-hour run was made at a rating of 750 hp and the powerplant was selected for installation into the Hawker Hart and Hawker Fury as flight test evaluations were initiated.

By the time of the Battle of Britain, every first-line RAF fighter used the Merlin powerplant. The Merlin III, as it was designated, delivered 1,030 hp at 6,250 feet (1,900 m), and provided more than adequate performance up to, and over, 20,000 feet, offering the RAF Hurricanes and Spitfires needed airspeed and climb rates to counter low flying Luftwaffe fighter inderdiction sorties. Before the war was over, nearly 70,000 Allied aircraft would be fitted with one or another model of the Rolls-Royce Merlin, and all-in-all, over 150,000 Merlin engines would be produced over the powerplant's lifetime.

Later Merlin variants were fitted with a two-stage supercharger and an injection type carburation system (for high altitude performance). The supercharger was automatically controlled by altitude and cut-in at 19,000 feet (5,800 m); however, it could be manually over-ridden by pushing the throttle past its normal stop, breaking the safety wire.

The instant the supercharger cut-in, the pilot knew it. There was a loud thudding noise and the P-51 vibrated violently. This was especially true for an inexperienced pilot. The vibration could, however, be controlled through throttle manipulation if the pilot anticipated the cut-in and reduced power. When the supercharger cut-out, usually at about 15,000 feet (4,670 m), a less severe shuddering was encountered and in some cases the only indication was a drop in manifold pressure.

The only drawback to the Merlin was its susceptibility to damage by enemy fire. However, this was inherent in all liquid-cooled in-line powerplants, including its Allison predessor, and was not considered critical when compared to all the other advantages offered by the Packard-build engine.

The first flight of a Merlin-powered Mustang X took place on 13 October, 1942, when RAF aircraft serial number A1 975 taxied down the runway at Hucknall and lifted into the sky. The results were immediate, with speeds up to 435 mph (700 km/h) attained at altitudes above 25,000 feet (7,600 m). The Mustang had now proven its high-performance high-altitude interceptor potential.

Efforts on the North American version of the Merlin-powered Mustang (designated XP-78) were initiated in September and completed by late October. The first flight of the XP-51B, as it was redesignated, occurred on 30 November 1942, but was terminated short of the scheduled duration due to overheating of the Merlin caused by clogged radiator cooling vents. Nevertheless, the results of the initial flight and the performance data from the British Mustang Xs were enough to convince the USAAF to place a production order for the Merlin-powered P-51B on 28 December.

Other changes that were incorporated into the North American Merlin (Packard built) powered prototypes included deletion of the carburator intake on top of the forward engine cowling and incorporation of a small intake scoop just aft and under the powerplant.

Whereas the original Allison powered Mustang used a three-bladed 10 feet 6 inch diameter propeller, the Merlin version utilized a four-bladed Hamilton-Standard 11 feet 2 inch diameter which was necessary to effectively use the increased power of the big Merlin powerplant.

In addition, the aircraft required several minor structural and powerplant interface changes to accommodate the new engine, and permanent wing pylons for carrying up to 2,000 lbs (900 kgs) were added to the wings.

The promising results of these test aircraft were recognized immediately by the USAAF and orders were placed for the P-51B from North American. Nearly 2,000 models of the P-51B were produced by North American at Inglewood with 71 of these being converted to F-6Cs (with incorporation of a pair of K-24 cameras or a combination of a K-17 and K-22 camera) and 275 being delivered to the RAF as Mustang III's.

In addition, several field modifications were made to the P-51B including the fitting of a bulged Malcom canopy. This canopy was initially utilized on early models of the Spitfire to increase overall visibility and provide increased head room for the pilot.

Several blocks of orders for the P-51B were received by North American, each armed with four Browning MG 53-2 0.50-caliber wing machine-guns and wing racks for carrying a 1,000 lb (450 kg) bomb. A total of 1,260 rounds of ammunition was carried, with the inboard guns having 350 rounds per gun and the outboard having 280 rounds. The seven blocks of P-51B Mustangs, serial numbers, and total produced are presented below.

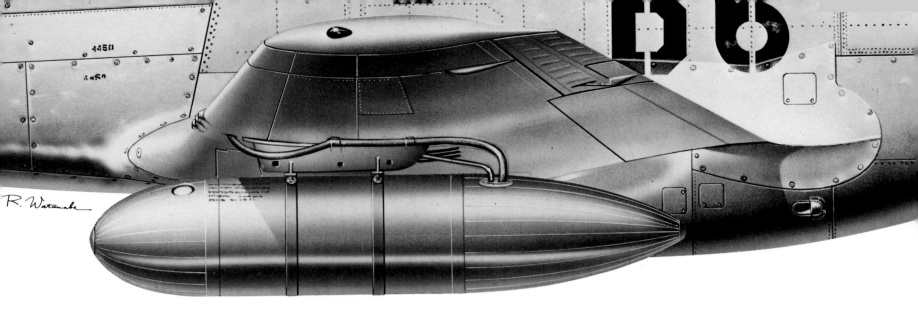

DESIGNATION	SERIAL NUMBERS	TOTAL PRODUCED
P-51B-1NA	43-12093 to 43-12492	400
P-51B-5NA	43-6313 to 43 43-7112	800
P-51B-10NA	42-106429 to 42-105638	110
P-51B-10NA	42-106541 to 42-106738	198
P-51B-10NA	43-7113 to 43-7202	90
P-51B-15NA	42-106739 to 42-106978	240
P-51B-15NA	43-24752 to 43-24901	150
		1,988

The -1, -5, and -10 aircraft used the Packard (Merlin) V-1650-3 powerplant rated at 1,400 hp for take-off while the -15 aircraft were fitted with the more powerful Packard (Merlin) V-1650-7 which was rated at 1,450 hp at take-off. While the V-1650-3 had maximum continuous power ratings of 1,450 hp at 19,800 feet (6,030 m) and 1,190 hp at 31,000

Fuel selector valve

feet (9,450 m), the V-1650-7 offered 1,695 hp (war emergency) at 19,300 feet (5,880 m) and 1,550 hp (combat rating) at 13,000 feet (3,960 m). Changes that accompanied the various block, or contract, identification quantities in addition to the powerplant changeover, included the standardized incorporation of the 85 (US) gallon (322 liter) fuel tank located behind the cockpit, minor component changes (especially in the radio transmission area), and the increase from four to six 0.50-caliber machine-guns. The latter modification was made in the last block of aircraft.

Although not directly related to the development of the Mustang airframe proper, the development of the 108 (US) gallon (409 liter) expendable auxilliary wing drop tanks played a significant role in the long-range escort capabilities of the P-51. The design and evaluation of these tanks was initiated in October, 1942, the same month as the first flight of the initial Merlin-powered RAF Mustang I. After receipt of the test results of the Merlin-powered Mustang and notification of the USAAF's order for the P-51B, the Eighth Air Force identified the need for added fuel capacity for long-range bomber escort missions into Germany. To accomplish this, auxilliary fuel tanks that could be jettisoned after fuel usage, or before if necessary, had to be developed. Maximum tank availability at the time was 75 (US) gallon (284 liter), and with departure from bases in England, did not provide sufficient fuel for escorting the bombers out and back.

Thus, the Eighth Air Force instituted a program to demonstrate an inexpensive 108 (US) gallon (409 liter) droppable wing tank that would be of no use to the enemy if recovered (the aluminum construction 75 (US) gallon (284 liter) tanks available could be used by the enemy for aircraft structural parts and were considered to be a critical material). The new design was based on work that both American and British scientists had worked on in the late thirties, that of paper layers bonded with glue. The only drawback to this concept was the incompatibility of the fuel and the glue. Storage of fuel in the tanks was limited to less than eight hours due to the corrosive interaction and eventual degration of the bond. This constraint, however, posed no problem, as the tanks could be fueled prior to a mission, attached to the aircraft, and jettisoned approximately four hours later.

In addition, the jettisoned tanks provided no military use to the enemy and also offered a unique weapon for heavily entrenched enemy forces. By dropping full tanks and following them down with machine-gun fire, the

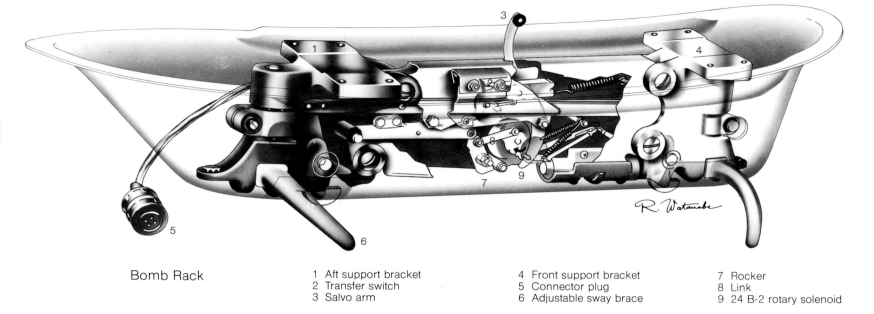

Bomb Rack

1 Aft support bracket	4 Front support bracket	7 Rocker
2 Transfer switch	5 Connector plug	8 Link
3 Salvo arm	6 Adjustable sway brace	9 24 B-2 rotary solenoid

tanks acted like napalm (jellied gasoline), spreading flames over wide target area.

When production of these tanks started in 1943, over 24,000 a month were being fabricated. However, after only a couple months of production, the Eighth Air Force ordered the production halted and reverted to all-metal tanks for the duration of the war.

P-51C-NT

The P-51C-NT was identical to the P-51B-NA except for the fact that it was built by the North American plant in Dallas, Texas. Production began in mid-1943 with over 1,750 P-51Cs being delivered during late 1943 and early 1944. The P-51C-NT was ordered and delivered in 11 separate blocks, with 636 aircraft being delivered to the RAF as Mustang IIIs and another 20 planes being modified to incorporate the K-24 camera installation and redesignated as F-6Cs by the USAAF.

The blocks, serial numbers and total production of the P-51C is presented below:

DESIGNATION	SERIAL NUMBERS	TOTAL PRODUCED
P-51C-1NT	42-102979 to 42-103328	350
P-51C-5NT	42-103329 to 42-103778	450
P-51C-10NT	42-103779 to 42-103978	200
P-51C-10NT	42-23902 to 42-25251	350
P-51C-10NT	44-10753 to 44-10782	30
P-51C-10NT	44-10818 to 44-10852	35
P-51C-10NT	44-10859 to 44-11035	177
P-51C-10NT	44-11123 to 44-11152	30
P-51C-11NT	44-10783 to 44-10817	35
P-51C-11NT	44-10853 to 44-10858	6
P-51C-11NT	44-11036 to 44-11122	87
		1,750

Like the P-51B, the different block designations (-1, -5, -10, etc.) were made to identify minor component or structural improvements that were incorporated into the C-variant as production proceeded.

The Packard (Merlin) V-1650-3 was installed in only the three-hundred and fifty -1 block deliveries, while all other blocks were fitted with the Packard (Merlin) V-1650-7 powerplant.

P-51D-NA

While the P-51Bs and Cs were making their presence felt in both Europe and the Pacific, North American Aviation and the USAAF were busily gathering data from pilot's reports in an effort to improve future blocks of the Mustang and correct any minor difficulties or irregularities that were inherent in the design. Basically the reports were unanimous in their praise of the new fighter, however, one negative point continually appeared. The lack of rearward vision for the pilot, especially unit commanders who were responsible for keeping formations together, was marginal with the cockpit/aft fuselage arrangement. The addition of the British-developed bulged Malcolm hood improved the situation, but the problem was not solved.

In late 1943, the USAAF requested North American to modify the Mustang to increase pilot visibility. Two production P-51B-10NAs were taken from the assembly line and given the North American designation NA-106. These aircraft were to become the prototypes for the P-51D. At this time, the late series Hawker Typhoon Ibs were entering service with the RAF, and these aircraft incorporated a new full-view "blown" canopy. North American decided to fit this type of canopy to the P-51D.

To fit the "tear-drop" shaped canopy to the Mustang required the cutting-down of the section of the aft fuselage behind the cockpit. In addition the P-51D incorporated a strengthened main wing spar to accommodate increased and varied underwing armament, extended chord wing roots, the 85 (US) gallon (322 liter) fuel tank behind the cockpit that was installed on later P-51Bs and Cs, the Packard built Merlin V-1650-7 powerplant and a wing armament of six (instead of four) MG 53-2 Browning 0.50-caliber machine-guns. Ammunition capacity for the machine-guns was also increased from 1,250 rounds to 1,880 rounds.

The P-51D went into full production at Inglewood in February, 1944, with the Dallas plant initiating production of this variant in July. A total of 6,502 P-51D-5NA to -25NAs were produced by North American at the Inglewood plant while a further 1,454 P-51D-5NT to -20NTs were produced and delivered by the Dallas facility.

Serial number blocks for the P-51D-NA variants were 42-106539 to 42-106540, 44-13253 to 44-15752, 44-63160 to 44-64159, and 44-72027 to 44-75026. Serial number blocks for the

P-51D-NT were 44-11153 to 44-11352, 44-12853 to 44-13252, 44-84390 to 44-84989, and 45-11342 to 45-11742. The P-51D, like the earlier variants, was improved with several minor modifications to structural interfaces as well as being fitted with updated models of instrumentation and radio equipment as the various blocks of the D-model were produced. These changes of the basic configuration were identified by the -5, through -25 designations assigned to the aircraft contract. Later models also featured a small dorsal fin to compensate for the reduced side area that resulted from the addition of the "tear drop" canopy.

The P-51D production also included 136 aircraft modified for photo-recon tasks as F-6Ds. Lend-lease deliveries to the RAF totaled 271, which like the P-51Ks were designated Mk IV in British service.

One unique modification was made on the P-51D-NT. This was to modify it into a trainer version with dual controls. The P-51D canopy was removed and a second set of controls and instrumentation panels were installed aft of the normal cockpit. The seat in the aft cockpit was slightly raised to insure visibility over the forward pilot's head, and an elongated canopy was installed. Because of the additional space necessitated by the aft cockpit, re-arrangement of some of the radio equipment was required. A total of ten of these modifications were made at the Dallas plant and were given the designation TP-51D-NT.

A pair of other developments greatly added to the capabilities of the P-51 and its pilot. These were the development of the K-14 gyroscopic gunsight and the G-suit. The K-14 sight was a modification of an English developed system which allowed a pilot to make accurate deflection shots during high speed dogfights.

The G-suit came in two versions, the Berger (American) and the Frank (British). Both worked on the same principle of applying pressure to the legs and lower abdomen of the pilot during tight turns and steep dives, during which, forces experienced by the body caused blood

to rush from the head resulting in dimming of vision, and oft times, total blackout. The principle of the G-suits was to put pressure on the lower body thus restricting blood flow.

While the British design used water to pressurize it, the Berger concept utilized air which was transmitted from the P-51s vacuum system. Although the British suit was first available, it was found to be excessively heavy and uncomfortable and was discarded by most pilots in the Eighth and Ninth Air Force. By June, 1944, the production of the Berger had reached capacity and suits were being delivered to both P-51 and P-47 Fighter Groups. It proved to be tremendously successful and resulted in still another advantage for the P-51 pilot and his plane.

P-51F-NA

The P-51 variants, although improved in armament and performance, had grown in weight since the early prototype was delivered to the British in October, 1941. The P-51D was almost 300 lb (140 kg) heavier than the B and C variants, and nearly 1,500 lb (680 kg) heavier than the A model. This increase was due to the change from the Allison V-1710 to the Packard V-1650 powerplant, the increase in armament, increased fuel capacity and structural improvements. The Mustang was still a superior performer, even with the increased weight, but the USAAF approved a North American proposal in July, 1943, to design a variant that would represent a lightweight version of the basic Mustang design. The new design was designated the XP-51F.

The new design utilized the British system of establishing limit load factors (less conservative than the American method), simplified structures, smaller components were feasible, and the use of new materials, such as

The P-51D was delivered in greater quantities than any other variant.

(Robert Grinsell collection)

The P-51H was the final Mustang production version and incorporated many optimum refinements of previous lightweight experiments.

(Robert Grinsell collection)

plastic. The main wing was thinned and the wheel struts, brakes and wheel size were reduced. The armament was also reduced from six to four Browning 0.50-caliber machine-guns, and the fuel tank behind the pilot was eliminated since light weight was more necessary than extended range. In addition, the four-bladed Hamilton-Standard propeller was replaced by a three-bladed Aeroproducts design. The only added weight was due to the fitting of a longer "blown," or tear-drop, canopy to reduce drag and provide increased pilot visibility.

When the first XP-51F (NA-105) made its initial flight on 14 February, 1944, the overall weight had been reduced by over 1,500 lb (680 kg) and the top speed had been increased by over 25 mph (40 km/h) in level flight. Although designed to be powered by the Packard (Merlin) V-1650-3, the prototypes were refitted with the more powerful V-1650-7 before they were completed. The second and third XP-51Fs flew on 20 and 22 May, after which the number three plane was shipped to the RAF for their evaluation.

The remaining two prototype of the original five aircraft contracted for were projected to be powered by the Rolls-Royce R.M. 14SM engine (Merlin 100 development) and subsequently became the XP-51G prototypes.

The XP-51F proved to have exceptional speed and climb capability. However, handling control due to high loading and an inconsistent flight stability problem forced abandonment of this variant in favor of the XP-51H.

P-51G-NA

Identical to the XP-51F except for the incorporation of a Merlin 14SM powerplant and a five-bladed Rotol propeller, work on the XP-51G (NA-105) prototype began in January, 1944, with the first flights taking place on 9 August. Again, impressive performance figures verifying North American calculations resulted, however, the improved Merlin powerplant was not at that time in full production and therefore, like the XP-51F, the XP-51G was by-passed in favor of the P-51H.

P-51H-NA

The P-51H (NA-126) was the final production Mustang and embodied many of the innovations and lightweight mate-

rials of the earlier XP-51F and G prototypes. Similar in appearance to the XP-51F, the H model was fitted with the standard type P-51D canopy rather than the lengthened XP-51F design, a 50 (US) gallon (189 liter) fuel tank in the fuselage, carried a standard armament of six 0.50 caliber machine-guns, and incorporated a dorsal fin extension for increased stability. The P-51H also included a shallower carburator air intake under the forward cowling (which reduced drag) and was fitted with a straight forward-cowling slope, rather than the smooth ojive of the earlier variants. The aircraft was powered by a Packard-built Merlin V-1650-9 with a war emergency horsepower of 2,250 at 10,200 feet (690 at 3,100 m) and a maximum continuous rating of 1,470 hp at 21,300 feet (6,490 m). The engine drove a four-bladed Aeroproducts propeller.

The first production P-51H was test flown on 3 February, 1945, and was followed shortly by the delivery of nineteen additional aircraft to the USAAF for operational assignment. The P-51H arrived in Europe too late to see actual combat, but fighter groups in the Pacific Theater used the P-51H in the final months of the war. One of this type was also delivered to the RAF for test and evaluation.

A total of 555 P-51Hs were produced with an additional 1,845 cancelled with the end of hostilities. The USAAF serial numbers for the 555 completed P-51Hs ran from 44-64160 to 44-64714. All aircraft were built at the Inglewood facility and were produced in the blocks noted below:

P-51H-1NA	20
P-51H-5NA	280
P-51H-10NA	255
	555

The -5 and -10 versions incorporated an enlarged tail and rudder area and several minor equipment modifications.

P-51J-NA

At the same time initial efforts on the XP-51F and G lightweight prototypes was being conducted by North American, design was also initiated on another lightweight model, designated XP-51J. Serial numbers for the XP-51Js were 44-76027 and 44-76028. The J variant was similar to the F and G, in so far as it utilized new construction, improved structural design, new materials, and modified components; however, it was fitted with an Allison V-1710-119 powerplant, incorporating a water injection system, which offered over 1,700 hp at 20,000 feet (6,100 m). The XP51-J also reflected design attempts at streamlining (reducing drag) the nose contours. These included moving the carburetor intake to the ventral radiator location which smoothed out the nose surface. The aircraft was also some 9 inches (23 cm) longer than the XP-51F, measuring 32 feet 11 inches (10.03m), compared to 32 feet 2 inches (9.80m).

The initial XP-51J (NA-105) rolled off the assembly line in April, 1945, and was test flown on the 23rd. Problems with the still not fully developed engine, however, restricted the amount of testing that could be done, and full power settings were never accomplished. Although a maximum speed of nearly 500 mph (805 km/h) was predicted for the P-51J at altitudes of 27,000 to 30,000 feet (8,200 to 9,100 m), this figure was never verified.

Because of the problems with the powerplant of the initial prototype, the second aircraft was delivered to Allison for use in their-engine test program. The aircraft was never flown, and instead, was scavenged for spare parts in an attempt to correct the difficulties being encountered with the first prototype.

P-51K-NT

The P-51K was identical to the late model P-51D production blocks, incorporating the latest radio equipment and the dorsal fin modification, except that it included an 11 foot Aeroproducts four-bladed propeller in place of the 11 foot 2 inches Hamilton-Standard. All P-51Ks were produced at the North American Dallas facility and carried the NT designation.

The P-51K, and its different airscrew, was necessitated by USAAF's fear that with the Mustang production lines in full gear, insufficient supplies of the basic Hamilton-Standard propellers could result in delivery delays of this critical fighter aircraft. Therefore, a second-source contract was awarded to Aeroproducts to supply their hollow-steel blade design to the Dallas facility. As Aeroproducts had been one of the firms to work on the four-blade propeller design when the initial Merlin powered Mustang was in development their selection was natural.

In addition, the new propeller was over 50 lb (23 kg) lighter than the Hamilton-Standard, and, if successful, would offer this added weight advantage. Several problems, however, occurred with the Aeroproducts propeller. Excessive vibration resulting from imbalance resulted in several minor incidents and as a result, production delays were incurred. After completing the basic order for 1,500 P-51Ks, the Dallas facility reverted to the use of the Hamilton-Standard propeller and the P-51D designation.

Of the total of 1,500 P-51Ks produced, 594 were delivered to the RAF as Mustang IVs. Of these, 163 were completed as F-6Ks with the addition of the K-17, K-22 or K-24 camera systems for reconnaissance. Early model P-51Ks, the -1NT and -5NT, did not include the wing racks for zero launched rockets; however, all further blocks did. Serial numbers for the P-51K ran from 44-11353 to 44-12852.

P-51L-NT

The P-51L was identical to the P-51H airframe except that it was to be manufactured and assembled at the North American Dallas plant, and was scheduled to utilize the Packard (Merlin) V-1650-11 engine with direct fuel injection. None of these aircraft were built due to the end of the war, which occurred prior to the initiation of production; a total of 1,700 aircraft had been ordered on this contract.

P-51M-NT

The P-51M was identical to the Inglewood built P-51H. However, of the 1,628 ordered by the USAAF, only one was completed before the order was cancelled due to the surrender of the Axis forces. The serial number assigned to the sole P-51M was 45-11743.

The P-51K was essentially a P-51D with a light-weight Aeroproducts hollow steel blade propeller, but due to prolonged vibration problems only the basic order was completed.

(Robert Grinsell collection)

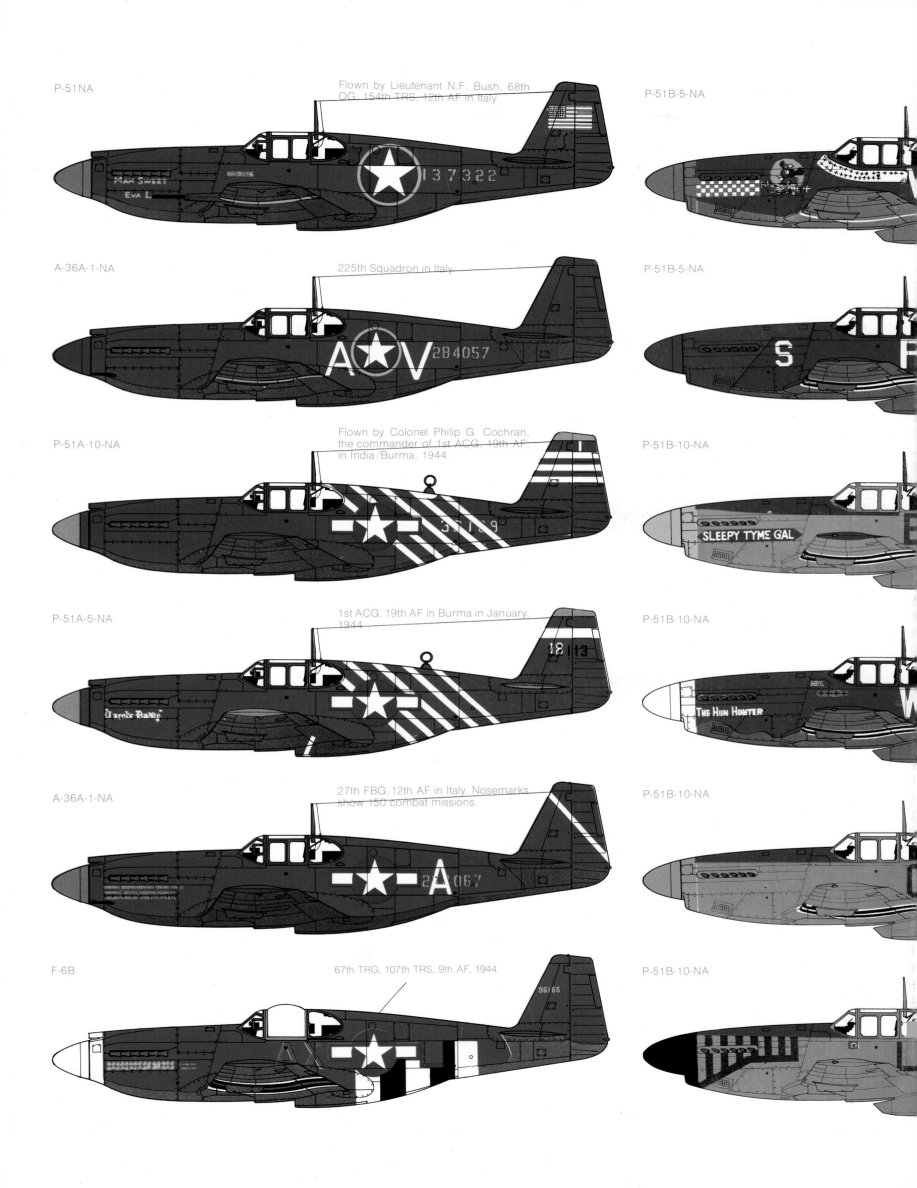

P-51NA

Flown by Lieutenant N.F. Bush, 68th OG, 154th TRS, 12th AF in Italy.

P-51B-5-NA

A-36A-1-NA

225th Squadron in Italy.

P-51B-5-NA

P-51A-10-NA

Flown by Colonel Philip G. Cochran, the commander of 1st ACG, 19th AF, in India/Burma, 1944.

P-51B-10-NA

P-51A-5-NA

1st ACG, 19th AF in Burma in January, 1944.

P-51B-10-NA

A-36A-1-NA

27th FBG, 12th AF in Italy. Nosemarks show 150 combat missions.

P-51B-10-NA

F-6B

67th TRG, 107th TRS, 9th AF, 1944.

P-51B-10-NA

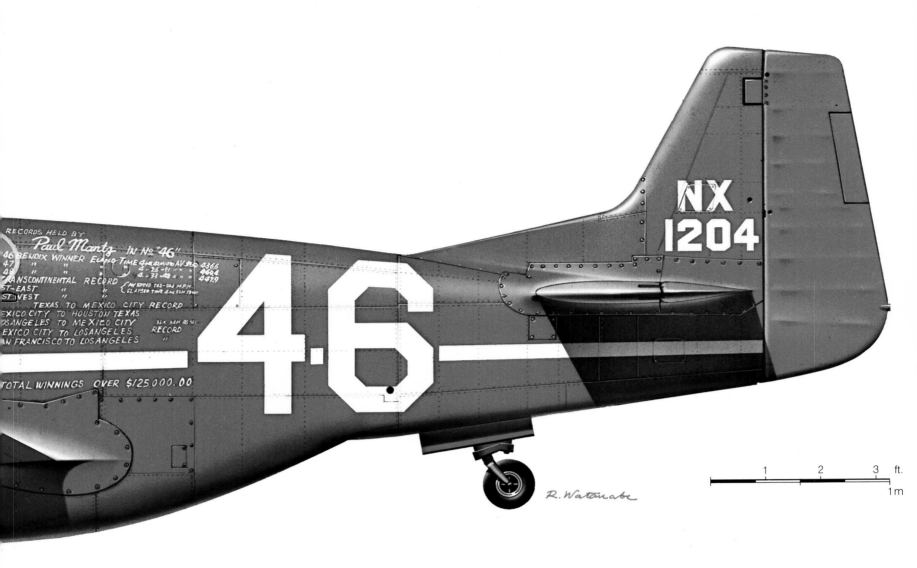

RECORDS HELD BY
Paul Mantz IN No "46"
'46 BENDIX WINNER ELAPSED TIME 4 HR 42 MIN AV SPD 435.5
'47 "   "   4 - 26 - 41   464.4
'48 "   "   4 - 33 - 49   447.9
TRANSCONTINENTAL RECORD
ST-EAST   "   (AV SPEED 582-584 M.P.H.
ST-WEST   "   ELAPSED TIME 4 HR 52M 58 SEC
     TEXAS TO MEXICO CITY RECORD
EXICO CITY TO HOUSTON TEXAS
OS ANGELES TO MEXICO CITY   31 K 34M 05 SEC
EXICO CITY TO LOS ANGELES   RECORD
AN FRANCISCO TO LOS ANGELES   "

TOTAL WINNINGS OVER $125,000.00

46

NX
1204

R. Watanabe

1   2   3 ft.
1m

provided quite enough fuel: an additional 406 US gallons (337 Imp.gal) were added to the Mustang's normal 269 US gallon (224 Imp.gal) internal capacity. Finally, both planes were finished in bright red.

Mantz's NX1202 won the Bendix races in both 1946 and 1947. The earlier victory established a new Bendix speed record, an average of 435.5 mph (700.85km/h), covering the entire distance in 4 hours, 42 minutes, and 14 seconds.

In 1947 he cut 16 minutes off the record he had set the previous year. In 1948 his NX1204 was again first across the finish line, averaging 447.9 mph (720.8km/h), and making Mantz the first and only winner of three consecutive Bendix races. These two modified Mustangs then went on to make and break records all over the hemisphere.

The P-51 Mustang NX1204

After the end of Word War II, a number of P-51 Mustangs were sold on the civil market. Though listed at $64,569 when new, they were disposed of for a fraction of their value, some going for as low as $5,000 apiece. Two of these were purchased by A. Paul Mantz,

famous as a film flyer and a racing pilot. When the Bendix Transcontinental Races (Van Nuys, California to Cleveland, .Ohio) were begun again in 1946 after a seven year lapse, he decided to enter his new planes.

Both were carefully serviced, irregularities in the laminar-flow wing contours were filled and smoothed, and their wings were modified to hold fuel. These 'wet wings' eliminated all need for external fuel tanks, and

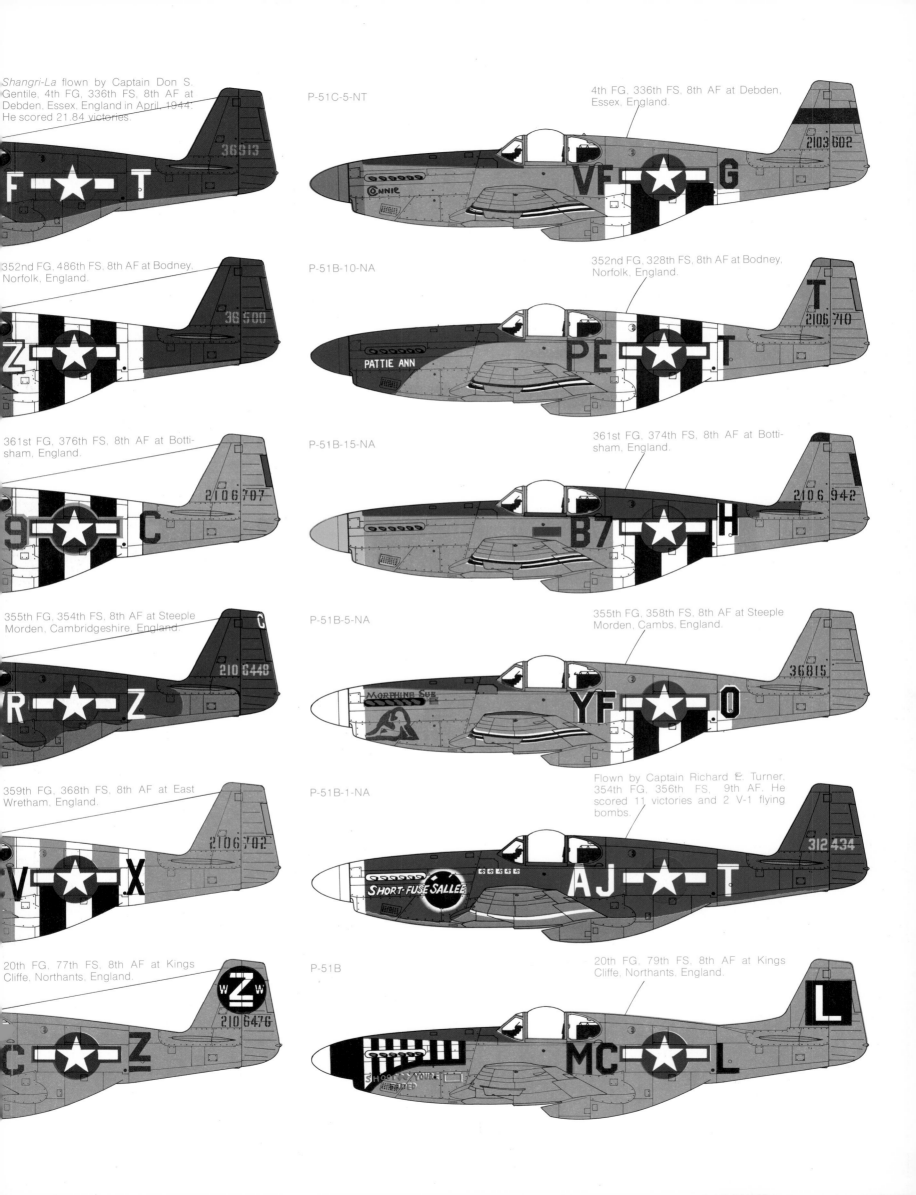

Shangri-La flown by Captain Don S. Gentile, 4th FG, 336th FS, 8th AF at Debden, Essex, England in April, 1944. He scored 21.84 victories.

P-51C-5-NT

4th FG, 336th FS, 8th AF at Debden, Essex, England.

352nd FG, 486th FS, 8th AF at Bodney, Norfolk, England.

P-51B-10-NA

352nd FG, 328th FS, 8th AF at Bodney, Norfolk, England.

361st FG, 376th FS, 8th AF at Bottisham, England.

P-51B-15-NA

361st FG, 374th FS, 8th AF at Bottisham, England.

355th FG, 354th FS, 8th AF at Steeple Morden, Cambridgeshire, England.

P-51B-5-NA

355th FG, 358th FS, 8th AF at Steeple Morden, Cambs, England.

359th FG, 368th FS, 8th AF at East Wretham, England.

P-51B-1-NA

Flown by Captain Richard E. Turner, 354th FG, 356th FS, 9th AF. He scored 11 victories and 2 V-1 flying bombs.

20th FG, 77th FS, 8th AF at Kings Cliffe, Northants, England.

P-51B

20th FG, 79th FS, 8th AF at Kings Cliffe, Northants, England.

P-51D-5-NA

20th FG, 55th FS, 8th AF at Kings Cliffe, Northants, England.

P-51D-15-NA

JERSEY JERK

P-51D-20-NA

Big Beautiful Doll flown by Lieutenant Colonel John D. Landers, the commander of 78th FG, 8th AF at Duxford, Cambs, England. He scored 14.5 victories.

P-51D-10-NA

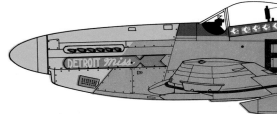

DETROIT Miss

P-51D-20-NA

Ridge Runner flown by Major Pierce W. McKennon, the commander of 335th FS, 4th FG, 8th AF at Debden, Essex, England. He scored 12 victories.

P-51D

BOOMERANG, JR.

P-51D-5-NA

357th FG, 362nd FS, 8th AF at Leiston, Suffolk, England.

P-51D

P-51D-25-NA

Flown by Lieutenant Colonel Donald A. Baccus, the commander of 359th FG, 8th AF at East Wretham, Norfolk, England. He scored 5 victories.

P-51D

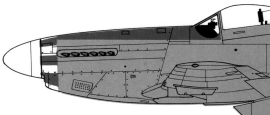

P-51D-10-NA

Petie 2nd flown by Lieutenant Colonel John C. Meyer, the group executive of 352nd FG, 8th AF at Asche, Belgium on January 1, 1945. He scored 24 victories in WW II.

P-51D-15-NA

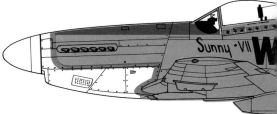

Sunny ·VII

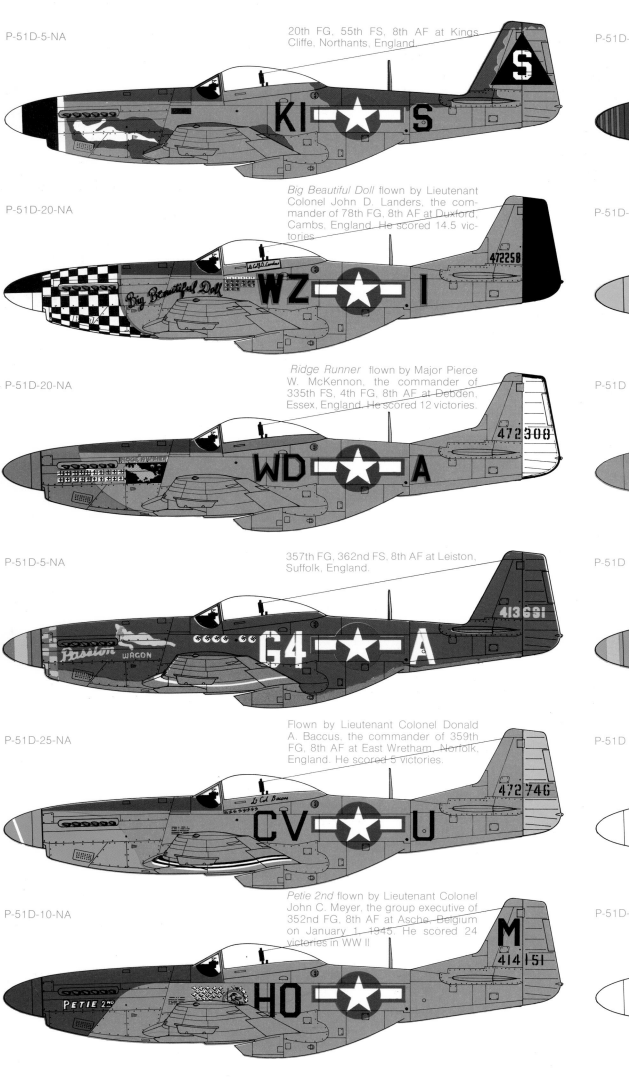

The P-51 Roto-Finish Mustang

Destined to become the most famous of all civilian Mustangs this aircraft was produced in 1944 as a P-51D-25, serial number 44-84961. Although built as a military weapon this airplane never entered combat.

Its trek to fame began in 1966 when Charles R. (Chuck) Hall, a Seattle-based airline pilot purchased the 44-84961 to participate in the Reno National Championship Air Races. The aircraft was officially assigned racing

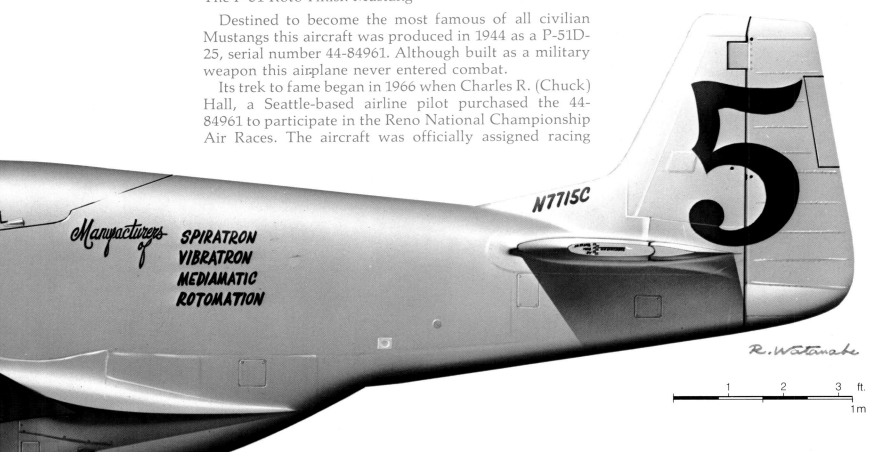

number 5. It entered its first competition in nearly stock configuration.

During the following years it underwent a systematic sequence of airframe and engine modifications which ultimately lead to the most extensively modified Unlimited Class racing plane ever built. From 1967 through 1970 'Race 5' was assigned to Jim Larsen, an aeronautical engineer with the Boeing Company, to design and build airframe changes that would make it one of the fastest racers in competition. Changes included a resurfaced wing of reduced span, a low profile canopy and a specially modified Rolls-Royce Merlin engine.

In 1971 the racer was sold to Gunther Balz, a Michigan-based industrialist, who retained Jim Larsen to further modify the aircraft for racing. Extensive engine and airframe modifications were completed in 1972 and under the racing banner of 'Roto-Finish' it won the 1972 Reno National Air Race at a record pace of 416.16 mph (669.73km/h).

The aircraft was then sold to Ed Browning of Idaho Falls, Idaho, in 1974 and was thereafter campaigned as the 'Red Baron'. During its carrer as the 'Red Baron' the racer underwent further modifications including the installation of a Rolls-Royce Griffon engine with contra-rotating propellers. In this configuration it won numerous Championship races and in 1979 established a new World speed record for piston-engine aircraft—499.018 mph (803.07km/h). The 'Red Baron' was destroyed in a spectacular crash during the 1979 Reno National Championship Air Races, thus ending the career of the most famous of all civilian Mustangs.

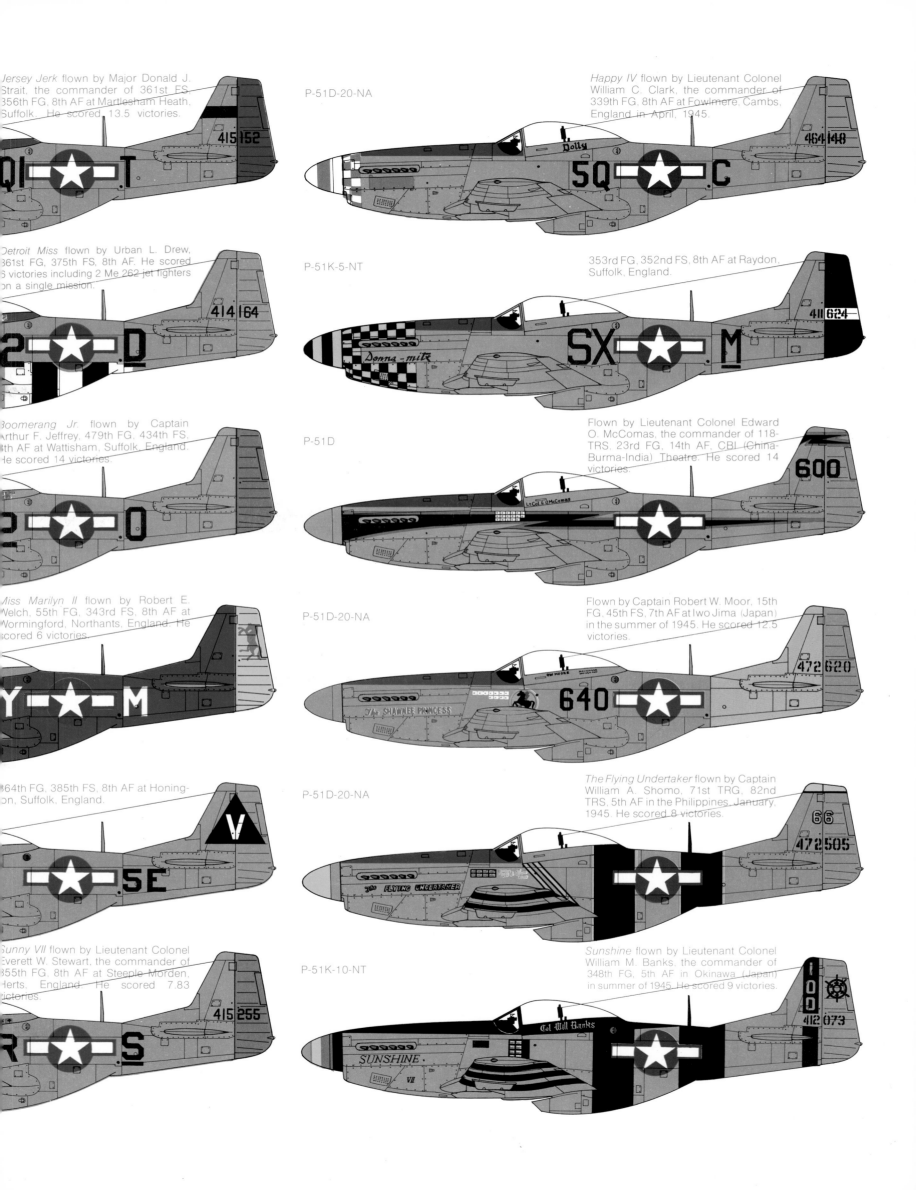

Jersey Jerk flown by Major Donald J. Strait, the commander of 361st FS, 356th FG, 8th AF at Martlesham Heath, Suffolk. He scored 13.5 victories.

P-51D-20-NA

Happy IV flown by Lieutenant Colonel William C. Clark, the commander of 339th FG, 8th AF at Fowlmere, Cambs, England in April, 1945.

415152

Dolly

QI · T

5Q · C

464148

Detroit Miss flown by Urban L. Drew, 361st FG, 375th FS, 8th AF. He scored 6 victories including 2 Me 262 jet fighters on a single mission.

P-51K-5-NT

353rd FG, 352nd FS, 8th AF at Raydon, Suffolk, England.

414164

Donna-mite

2 · D

SX · M

411624

Boomerang Jr. flown by Captain Arthur F. Jeffrey, 479th FG, 434th FS, 8th AF at Wattisham, Suffolk, England. He scored 14 victories.

P-51D

Flown by Lieutenant Colonel Edward O. McComas, the commander of 118-TRS, 23rd FG, 14th AF, CBI (China-Burma-India) Theatre. He scored 14 victories.

Lt Col E O McComas

2 · O

600

Miss Marilyn II flown by Robert E. Welch, 55th FG, 343rd FS, 8th AF at Wormingford, Northants, England. He scored 6 victories.

P-51D-20-NA

Flown by Captain Robert W. Moor, 15th FG, 45th FS, 7th AF at Iwo Jima (Japan) in the summer of 1945. He scored 12.5 victories.

RW Moore

The SHAWNEE PRINCESS

Y · M

640

472620

564th FG, 385th FS, 8th AF at Honing-ton, Suffolk, England.

P-51D-20-NA

The Flying Undertaker flown by Captain William A. Shomo, 71st TRG, 82nd TRS, 5th AF in the Philippines, January, 1945. He scored 8 victories.

The FLYING UNDERTAKER

V

SE

66

472505

Sunny VII flown by Lieutenant Colonel Everett W. Stewart, the commander of 355th FG, 8th AF at Steeple Morden, Herts, England. He scored 7.83 victories.

P-51K-10-NT

Sunshine flown by Lieutenant Colonel William M. Banks, the commander of 348th FG, 5th AF in Okinawa (Japan) in summer of 1945. He scored 9 victories.

415255

Col Will Banks

R · S

SUNSHINE

VII

412073

P-82 TWIN MUSTANG

Without question the most unusual, and last, Mustang variant to be produced was the P-82 Twin Mustang. The design was a natural outgrowth of earlier P-51 models.

Although reports on the initial Mustangs to enter combat in the Pacific had been laudatory, the problems of pilot fatique and boredom on long flights over the ocean became a primary concern of American military planners as well as North American engineers. The P-82 offered a unique two-pilot concept to solve this problem.

The P-82, though based on the original Mustang, was, in truth, an entirely new aircraft. Instead of utilizing a pair of P-51 fuselages and outer main wing sections, as originally conceived, the P-82 was actually some six feet (1.8m) longer than the P-51 and incorporated numerous new technological innovations. It represented a radical departure from conventional aircraft design in that it had a pair of lifting bodies that were joined by a center wing and horizontal stabilizer with provisions for a pilot in each of the fuselages (the two-pilot concept was, as noted earlier, to resolve the problem of pilot fatigue on the long range Pacific escort missions). In addition, a simplified cockpit arrangement was devised to improve pilot comfort. This included an adjustable seat to reduce discomfort extended flights.

The original P-82 was powered by a pair of Packard-built Rolls-Royce Merlin V-1650-23 engines with counter-rotating propellers to eliminate any torque problems on take-off and landings. Throttles and propeller controls were located in both cockpits, the left side containing the primary overall control while the right cockpit (co-pilot's side) contained sufficient instruments for emergency and/or relief operation. The first of two prototypes (designated NA-120) by North American and XP-82 by the USAAF flew on 15 April, 1945, a year and a half after the basic effort was initiated. A third prototype (designated NA-123) by North American, and XP-82A by the USAAF, was also initiated with a pair of improved Allison V-1710 powerplants with common rotating propellers, however, this aircraft was never completed.

On 8 March, 1944, the USAAF ordered 500 P-82s, however, only twenty of the order (designated P-82Bs) were completed before the war ended and the contract was cancelled. Two of the twenty produced were converted to night-fighting versions, being designated P-82C (SCR-720 radar) and P-82D (APS-4 radar) after the war. Each of the aircraft incorporated a specially fabricated pod beneath the center wing section and the righthand cockpit was refitted as a radar operator's station.

On 12 December, 1945, the USAAF placed an order for 100 P-82E (North American NA-144) escort fighters and additional orders for 100-82Fs with SCR-720 radar (NA-149) and 50 P-82Gs with APS-4 AI radar (NA-150) night-fighters, all powered with a pair of the improved Allison engines following in September and October of 1946. The night-fighters were earmarked to replace the then aging Northrop P-61 Black Widows.

Between 1946 and 1949 the total order of 250 aircraft was produced; however, nine of the P-82s and five of the P-82Gs were diverted from the assembly line and converted to P-82H models, which incorporated cold weather equipment for operation at the Air Defense Command bases in Alaska.

Like its predecessor the P-51, versatility was a major strongpoint of all P-82s. It was capable of carrying a wide variety of underwing stores, including rockets, auxiliary fuel tanks and bombs, and, in addition, its middle wing section could be modified to incorporate an additional eight Browning 0.50-caliber machine-guns.

The F-82 (changed from the "P" designation in 1948) was the aircraft in which the initial USAF air victory of the Korean conflict was achieved when five P-82Gs from the 68th Fighter Squadron were vectored to Kimbo airfield outside of Seoul on 27 June 1950, to intercept a flight of prop-driven Soviet-built North Korean Yak-9 fighters strafing Allied aircraft. Lt. William Hudson was officially credited with the first victory of the engagement and his fellow pilots destroyed two other of the enemy fighters without a loss. Soon after this engagement the F-82s were relegated to air defense of Japan and Okinawa until they were replaced by jets in 1951.

The P-82 Twin Mustang. Below is the specially modified P-82B 'Betty Joe' on a test flight over Hawaii in Feb., 1946, shortly before its record 14 hr. 33 min. flight from Hickam Field/Hawaii to Mitchell Field/N.Y. on 28 Feb., 1946.

(KOKU-FAN)

Entering service too late to play an influencial role in World War II, the F-82 was, in reality, almost obsolete when it did enter combat during the initial stages of the Korean conflict. Nevertheless, it served in the critical role of maintaining the USAF long-range-fighter capabilities during the post-World-War-II era. The F-82 was the last piston-powered fighter to be produced in any quantity by the USAF and provided a stepping stone into the jet era of aviation.

Postwar Mustangs

No further basic Mustang production was undertaken after the end of the war, however, the Mustang's career as a potent fighting machine was not over. Service with several smaller countries and a number of unique modifications prolonged its life for another ten years.

In the years immediately following the war, the USAAF offered the excess P-51 fighter inventory for use by a number of the Allied powers and emerging nations. Russia received a small quantity from Britain while the Italian Air Force, Swedish Air Force, Swiss Air Force, Royal Canadian Air Force, National Chinese Air Force, Royal Australian Air Force, Royal New Zealand Air Force, French Air Force, the Philippines, and Indonesia all took delivery of the Mustang during 1945 through 1947, to provide the backbone of their post-war peace-keeping forces.

Also in 1947, a number of South American countries, under the assistance terms of the Rio Pact, received P-51Ds. These included Bolivia, Cuba, Haiti, Honduras, Guatemala, Uruguay, San Salvador, Dominican Republic and Nicaragua, where the Mustang remained in service until the late sixties and early seventies.

Interest in the performance characteristics of the P-51 also led to its use by civilian pilots (who purchased these aircraft for less than $5,000) on the National Air race circuit. The success of the P-51 in this role was again immediate.

The interest exhibited by civilian pilots led a small aircraft firm in Florida, called Trans-Florida Aviation Incorporated, to purchase several surplus P-51s and convert them to a two-seat executive plane, called the Cavalier 2000 for large business firms. These aircraft were offered in two basic forms: as the Cavalier Special, and the Cavalier 2000 (with wingtip fuel tanks). The popularity of this aircraft led to the changing of the company's name in 1962 to the Cavalier Aircraft Corporation.

In February, 1967, Cavalier developed a company-sponsored modified counter-insurgency version of the Mustang based on the needs being experienced in the various Southeast Asia conflicts. The concept behind the design was to offer the USAF an inexpensive and yet effective ground attack/support plane in place of being forced into the long and costly development of an entirely new aircraft.

Known as the Cavalier Mustang II, the aircraft utilized the basic P-51D airframe with strengthened wings to carry a large variety of underwing armament and bombs. It incorporated new instrumentation and the latest avionics as well as being fitted with the 1,760 hp Rolls-Royce Merlin

620. To allow for increased range and for the added underwing stores (totaling over 4,000 lbs (1,800 kg)), a pair of auxiliary fuel tanks were fixed to the wingtips increasing fuel capacity by over 200 (US) gallons (760 liter). The initial prototype was first flown in December, 1967, but, although results proved impressive, the Air Force did not order any of this aircraft.

Not dissuaded in their enthusiasm, Cavalier next developed a turbo-powered Mustang III which used the basic Mustang II airframe, but was fitted with a Rolls-Royce Dart 510 turpoprop. After flight testing in October, 1968, Cavalier produced two more prototypes of the Mustang III (a single- and dual-seat version) that were powered by the American-built Lycoming T55-L-9. Cavalier was then purchased by Piper Aircraft and the name of the Mustang III was change to Enforcer.

The Enforcer was one of three aircraft evaluated by the USAF in 1971 for its Pave Coin counter-insurgency Forward Air Control operations. However, the Enforcer was never produced in quantity.

Foreign Production

The only foreign production of the P-51 Mustang variants was completed in Australia by the Commonwealth Aircraft Corporation under license to North American. The reasons behind this foreign production lay in the need of the Royal Australian Air Force for a late model fighter aircraft, an item it was unable to get from Britain due to the concentration of the British production in supplying European combat units.

In 1943, North American sent 100 sub-assembly sets of components for the P-51D to the Australian manufacturer, as well as a crated production aircraft to be used for tooling patterns. Commonwealth assembled 80 of the supplied aircraft under the designation CA-17 Mustang XXs, the first of which flew in April, 1945.

Having sufficiently tooled up to meet their own needs, Commonwealth then produced 120 aircraft before hostilities ceased and remaining orders were cancelled. These 120 included 40 Mustang XXIs with Packard (Merlin) V-1650-7 engines, 14 Mustang XXIIs, with similar engines but incorporating the K-24 oblique camera, and 66 Mustang XXIIIs with Merlin 66 and 70 engines supplied by Rolls-Royce from Britain.

Construction Details

The basic concept, and driving force, behind Kindelberger's P-51, was that it would be not only the finest and most reliable fighter in combat, but that it would be also an inexpensive and highly reproducible plane. The Mustang proved to be all that, and more. The basic construction was comprised of five separate sub-assemblies. The fuselage consisting of three sections and the main wing consisting of two.

One of the driving reasons behind the five subassembly approach to fabrication can be laid on "Dutch"

Kindelberger. It was his belief in the mass-production concept developed by the American auto industry in Detroit that actually led him to turn down the original request of the British Government to produce the Curtiss P-40. The P-40, like most aircraft of its time, was produced by manufacturing and assembling the entire aircraft structure and skin and then proceeding to install all the internal components, wiring and control lines. Kindelberger, who had made a tour of European aircraft facilities in the middle 1930's, was adamant in his support of the complete sub-assembly method of mass production. This resulted not only from his European tour, especially influenced by German aircraft companies, but as much by his knowledge of the General Motors assembly line techniques.

Each sub-assembly of the P-51 was produced as a total unit within itself with selected interfaces and connecting points for critical wiring and control lines. For instance, the wing assembly before mating to the fuselage sub-assemblies was complete with all necessary electrical and hydraulic control harness and lines, which mated to a connecting interface on the fuselage section. This production method allowed North American at its peak, to produce 22 finished aircraft in one 24-hour period.

When historians and authors speak of the great American industrial war machine of World War II and its capability to produce the weapons and arms required by not only our forces, but in support of our Allies, some mention ought surely be given to the innovations and success of Schmued, Kindelberger, North American and the P-51 Mustang.

The three fuselage sections were of all metal semi-monocoque construction and was made up of the forward, (or engine) compartment, the cockpit, and the aft fuselage which included the tailplane and fin. The powerplant was mounted to the frame on a pair of cantilever-designed load bearing structures, each interfacing to the firewall at two points. Longerons ran from the firewall bulkhead to the tail and were reinforced along the outer surface by stringers and vertical supporting frames. The overall aircraft was covered with a skin of stressed metal.

The wing, as noted previously, was constructed in two sections, right and left. The two halves, including armament bays and landing gear systems, were bolted together at the fuselage centerline. The center section of both halves was flat and formed the cockpit floor upon mating. The wings were a two-spar, all-metal structure with spaced longitudinal stringers and frame support braces. Each half included the installation of a self-sealing 92 (US) gallon (348 liter) fuel tank between the two main spars. The wing's outer surfaces were covered with an aluminum skin flush-riveted to the spars and framing. Lightning holes (holes in structural components to reduce weight) were utilized throughout the internal wing structure for running vital hydraulic, fuel feed, electrical and control lines.

The tail assembly was fabricated similarly to the main fuselage, but on a smaller scale. The tail plane and fin utilized two main spars and support stringers covered with an aluminum skin, while the rudder and elevators were built of aluminum alloy frames with spars and support webs covered with fabric for light weight and ease of repair.

The P-51 cockpit was neatly arranged with all critical control gauges within easy view. The right side cockpit

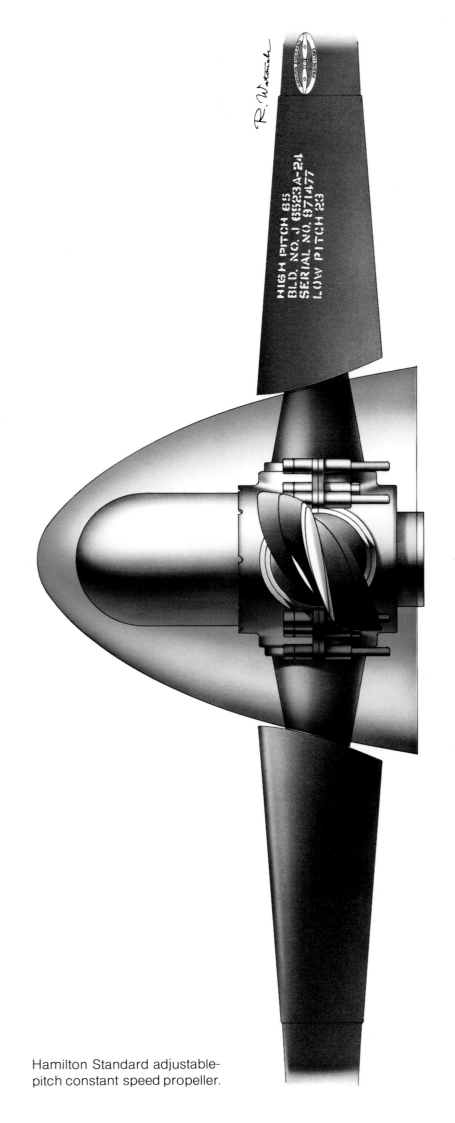

Hamilton Standard adjustable-pitch constant speed propeller.

P-51D Cutaway

1 Spinner
2 Propeller hub
3 Four-blade Hamilton Standard Hydromatic propeller
4 Armour plate
5 Propeller governor
6 Coolant header tank
7 Carburettor air intake
8 Engine leads
9 Packard (Rolls-Royce) Merlin 61 series V-1650-7 engine (1,450-hp)
10 Exhaust pipes
11 Generator
12 Aftercooler pump
13 Air duct
14 Air filters
15 Engine bearer assembly
16 Cowling panel frames
17 Magneto
18 Engine aftercooler
19 Carburettor
20 Oil inlet line
21 Oil tank
22 Filler cap
23 Hydraulic reservoir
24 Instrument panel
25 Rudder pedal
26 Aileron trim tab control knob
27 Rudder trim tab control knob
28 Elevator trim tab control knob
29 Carburettor hot air control lever
30 Carburettor air intake control lever
31 Signal pistol discharge tube
32 Throttle lever
33 Propeller control lever
34 Control column
35 K-14A gun sight
36 Laminated glass windscreen
37 Bubble-type canopy
38 Head rest
39 Head/back armour plate
40 Pilot's seat
41 BC-457 transmitter
42 BC-451-A transmitter control box
43 BC-453 receiver
44 BC-454 receiver
45 Battery
46 BC-442 antenna relay
47 SCR-274-N antenna
48 BC-458 transmitter
49 SCR-515-A radio set
50 BC-455 receiver
51 Fuselage auxiliary fuel tank, capacity 85US gallons (322 ltr.)
52 Fuel filler cap
53 Coolant radiator assembly
54 Ventilation flap
55 Oxygen filler valve
56 Low pressure oxygen bottle
57 Radio bay aft plywood bulkhead
58 Fuselage aft bulkhead/breakpoint
59 Lifting tube
60 Rudder control cable
61 Rudder trim tab control cable
62 Elevator trim tab control cable

63 Control cable pulley brackets
64 Antenna mast
65 Tailwheel retraction mechanism
66 Forward-retracting tailwheel
67 Tailwheel steering mechanism
68 Rudder actuating bellcrank
69 Elevator operating horns
70 Rudder trim tab actuating drum
71 Dorsal fin
72 Vertical stabilizer
73 Rudder

74 Rudder trim tab
75 Rudder trim tab control link
76 Rear navigation light
77 Elevator balance weight
78 Horizontal stabilizer
79 Elevator
80 Elevator trim tab
81 Elevator trim tab control link
82 Main spar
83 N-6 gun camera
84 Flap control linkage

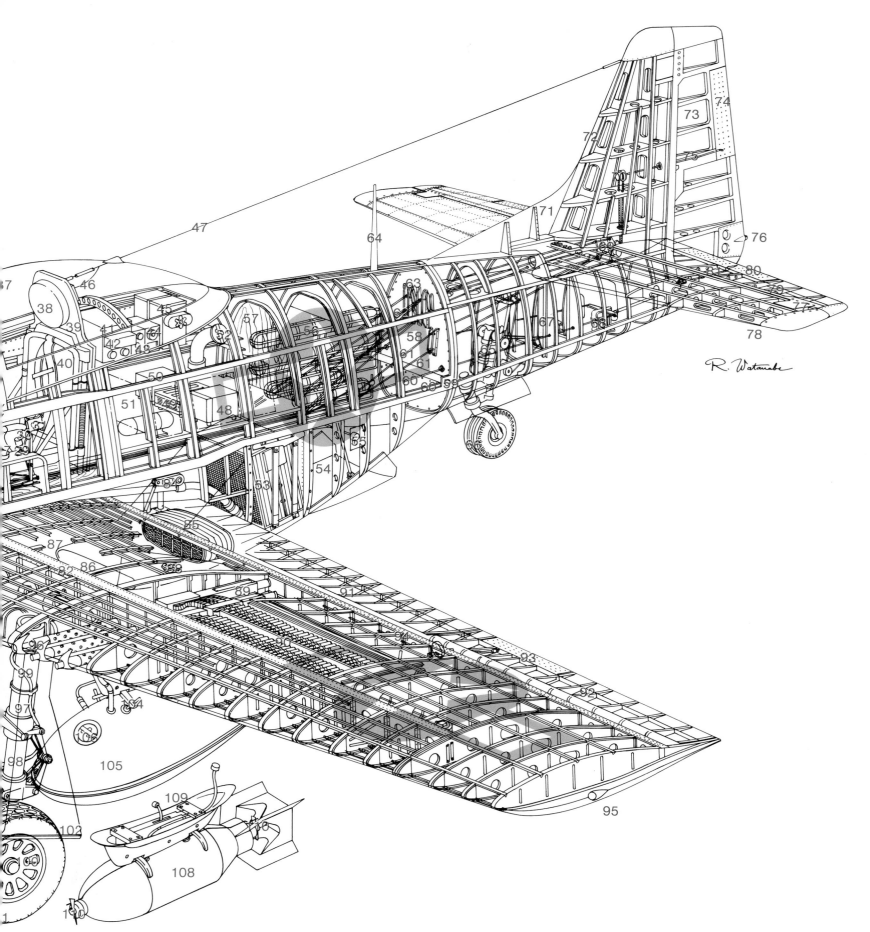

85 Oil radiator
86 Ventral air intake
87 Wing fuel tank, capacity 92 US
   gallons (348 ltr.): total 184 US
   gallons (696 ltr.)
88 Fuel filler cap
89 Browning 0.50-in (12.7mm)
   machine-gun
90 Ammunition boxes
91 Flap
92 Aileron

93 Aileron trim tab
94 Wing rear spar
95 Navigation light
96 Blast tube (inboard guns only)
97 Main landing gear
98 Shock strut
99 Brake tube
100 Main wheel, 27in (68.6cm)
101 Tire, smooth contour,
    27in (68.6cm)
102 Main landing gear cover

103 Main wheel cover
104 Pylon
105 Auxiliary fuel tank, metal,
    75 US gallons (284 ltr.)
106 Fuel filler cap
107 Auxiliary fuel tank, plastic-pressed
    paper, 108 US gallons (409 ltr.)
108 Bomb 500 lb. (227 kg)
109 Bomb rack
110 Fuse
111 Disc-type brake

wall was uncluttered, with the radio control box (normally a SCR-522), the overall electrical control panel, and the oxygen hose and regulator. The emergency canopy release was also located on the right side, just forward of the oxygen regulator. The left panel was covered with a built-in column that housed the flap controls, elevator trim, carburetor air flow regulation, landing gear position, aileron control, propeller pitch and fuel mixture ratio control, rudder trim, and bomb release. In addition, emergency equipment, such as a first-aid kit and signal pistol, were attached to brackets on the forward portion of right side wall.

The radio receiver and battery pack were located just behind the pilot in the aft fuselage. The radio array included the receiver, transmitter and antenna transfer lines.

The Mustang was fitted with a Bell and Howell optical gunsight which was located in the center of the forward cockpit dash just behind the 1½ inch (38 mm) thick bulletproof windscreen of the canopy. The sight utilized a series of lenses and mirrors to project a target ring onto a slanted glass surface directly in the pilot's forward line of sight. The quality of the materials and workmanship of the gunsight provided the pilot with distortion-free target-zeroing during even the tightest turns and dives.

In case of a failure in the reflector sight, a set of standard rings, and ring-and-post, visual sights were located on either side of the optical unit. These could be used by sighting thru the iron rings and visually lining up the enemy aircraft on either the bulls-eye dot or on the post.

The wing mounted Browning MG 53-2 machine-guns were manually cocked prior to take-off and automatic from that point on. In combat, the firing button released a solenoid (which locked the bolt in the cocked position until activated) and the first round was fired. The recoil of the expended cartridge was absorbed by a oil filled damping piston at the rear of each gun mechanism. The guns always locked in the open or cocked position once the firing button was released. To activate the guns, pressing the trigger again released the solenoid which initiated the firing sequence all over again until all the ammunition was-consumed.

The armament system of the P-51 was, in general, one of the most sensitive components on the aircraft. After each sortie the guns had to be checked to see if they had been fired, and if they had, they were frequently removed from the bay for cleaning and inspection for any worn or damaged parts. However, if properly maintained, according to the applicable technical manuals (and the inherent insight of a number of armourers), the guns were highly reliable and accurate.

The major problem occurring with the machine-guns, which became apparent when the P-51B arrived in England, was that random jamming occurred during tight turning. An investigation of this critical problem (critical because of the already limited armament of the P-51B with its four machine-guns compared to six and eight for most other fighters), uncovered that when exposed to greater than 2G loads the ammunition was restricted by centrifugal forces, causing the bolt to lock up. The addition of a belt-feed booster motor solved the problem.

Also, like most military aircraft, the P-51 had its negative points. Apart from its liquid-cooled engine, the most feared of these was the difficult bail-out in level flight where the slipstream could jam the pilot against the armor plate, thus keeping him from climbing out of the cockpit.

Combat Operations

The P-51, as noted earlier, entered combat with the RAF as the Mustang I, and shortly after saw action with USAAF Fighter Bomb Groups and Air Commando Units (using both the P-51 and A-36A in the CBI. While RAF Mustang IAs and Mustang IIs were delivered to England and assigned to operational units, it wasn't until late 1943 that USAAF P-51s reached operational squadrons in Europe.

The first production Mustangs, Merlin-powered P-51Bs, arrived in Europe in October and were assigned to the 354th Fighter Group of the Ninth Air Force. Although the Eighth Air Force was the strategic force in England, and was the unit that requested the new long-range fighter, the Ninth, or tactical force being formed to support the Allied invasion of the continent, was the first to receive the Mustang. The reasoning behind this decision was based on the influence of a few Pentagon officers who still believed that the P-51 was only a high-performance tactical type fighter in the mold of the A-36A.

The 354th Group, however, was still under the control of the Eighth Air Force, as the Ninth was just forming and lacked the control chain and facilities to fully absorb the 354th. The Eighth, therefore, actually had control of the first USAAF Mustang unit. They took the opportunity and made the most of it. Based at Boxted, England, the 354th arrived in November and its pilots immediately engaged in simulated combat training as none of the pilots had ever flown the new fighter, having been trained on the Bell P-39 Airacobra. With a combination of experienced officers from the Eighth giving advice, and constant flying by the new pilots of the 354th, the unit was declared operational on 1 December, 1943. The new fighters took part in numerous short escort missions during the next two weeks, engaging the Luftwaffe for the first time on 13 December while on an escort mission for Boeing B-17s who were bombing Kiel. A

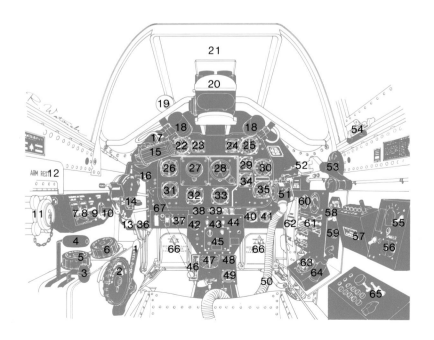

P-51D Cockpit

 1 Landing gear control lever
 2 Elevator trim tab control wheel
 3 Carburettor hot air control lever
 4 Carburettor cold air control lever
 5 Rudder trim tab control
 6 Aileron trim tab control
 7 Radiator air control (coolant)
 8 Radiator air control (oil)
 9 Landing light switch
10 Fluorescent light switch, left
11 Flare pistol mount cover cap
12 Arm rest
13 Mixture control lever
14 Throttle quadrant locks
15 Throttle lever
16 Propeller control lever
17 Selector dimmer assembly
18 Instrument light
19 Rear warning radar lamp
20 K-14A gun sight
21 Laminated glass
22 Remote compass indicator

23 Clock
24 Suction gauge
25 Manifold pressure gauge
26 Airspeed indicator
27 Directional gyro turn indicator
28 Artificial horizon
29 Coolant temperature
30 Tachometer (rpm counter)
31 Altimeter
32 Turn and bank indicator
33 Rate of climb indicator
34 Carburettor air temperature
35 Engine T gauge
36 Bomb salvo release lever(s)
37 Engine control panel
38 Landing gear warning light(s)
39 Parking brake handle
40 Oxygen flow blinker
41 Oxygen pressure gauge
42 Ignition switch
43 Bomb and rocket switch
44 Cockpit light control
45 Rocket control panel

46 Fuel shut-off valve
47 Fuel selector valve
48 Emergency hydraulic release
   handle
49 Hydraulic pressure gauge
50 Oxygen hose
51 Oxygen regulator
52 Emergency canopy release handle
53 Canopy crank and lock handle
54 Emergency release indicator
55 IFF control panel
56 IFF detonator button(s)
57 VHF radio control box
58 Rear warning radar control panel
59 VHF volume control knob
60 Fluorescent light switch, right
61 Electrical control panel
62 Circuit-breakers
63 BC-438 control box
64 Cockpit light
65 Circuit-breakers
66 Rudder pedals
67 Control column

brief scuffle with Bf 110s occurred, but no victories were scored by either side. On this mission the USAAF made use of 75 (US) gallon (284 liter) auxiliary wing tanks to increase range.

The initial victory of the European campaign to be scored by an American-flown Mustang was accomplished on 16 December, 1943, when Lt. Charles Gumm of the 355th Fighter Squadron destroyed a Bf 110 over Bremen while flying a P-51B-1-NA (S/N 4312410). The 354th Group was back over Bremen four days later and on this mission was credited with three Bf 110s. The die had been cast. The Eighth and Ninth Air Force, cooperating in the use of the 354th had proven that a single-engined fighter could escort the American heavies all the way to the target and home again. This meant minimizing losses to the bombers, and more accurate overall bombing results. These round trip missions of 900 to 1,000 miles (1,450 to 1,600 km) could be accomplished with the P-51B and P-51C, but not by any other fighter. The P-51 had finally proven its capability as a long-range high-altitude escort fighter/interceptor.

The reputation of the Mustang continued to grow as the 354th, which was now permanently attached to the Ninth Air Force, was credited with the destruction of 18 Bf 110s on 5 January, 1944, while again escorting B-17s over Kiel.

On 11 January, while escorting B-17s to Oschersleben and Halberstadt (locations of German aircraft factories), the 354th claimed 11 enemy fighters destroyed and 24 others as probably destroyed or damaged. During this mission, Major James Howard was awarded the Congressional Medal of Honor. In his P-51B, Howard found himself separated from the main formation and the sole fighter escort for a box of B-17s. When attacked by over 30 Luftwaffe fighters, Howard did not hesitate. Even though two of his four guns jammed (common in early P-51Bs), he fought for over 30 minutes before both forces broke off contact. Howard scored four victories in this engagement.

On 19 January, Lt. Gumm (who was killed in action 1 March, 1944, when his P-51B-15-NA, S/N 42-106749, crashed and burned after developing engine trouble) and the 354th again returned to Bremen. Following is a brief description of the action from Gumm's flight report of that day. "Talbot sited four (4) Bf 110s attacking our bombers (Lt. Gilbert F. Talbot, wingman, Rouge River, Oregon-5 victories). When we came within 400 yards (360 m), two saw us and broke away. We closed on the other two and I dropped back to cover Lt. Talbot's tail, but the German saw him and dived away.

"I was then almost in position to fire on the lone Messerschmitt, who was still headed straight for the bombers. Talbot then pulled up to cover my tail as I closed to within 100 yards (90 m) of the enemy plane. I fired a two second burst at him, noticing no effects. I closed to about 50 yards (45 m) and fired again. This time I noticed a thin trail of smoke coming from the right side of his engine. I gave him another burst at close range, so close that I was showered with smoke, oil and pieces from his plane. I pulled up through it and glanced back to see him going down in a large roll of smoke coming from his engine."

During this period, the resemblence of the Mustang to the Bf 109 became apparent, as many P-51s were fired upon by both American and RAF fighters and bombers. To eliminate this potentially critical situation, all P-51s were painted with a white ring around the cowl just aft of the spinner and single white stripes were painted on the surfaces of both main wing and tail for identification and recognition by Allied aircrews.

A second P-51 unit, the 357th Fighter Group, arrived in England to join the Ninth Air Force in November and began the transition to the P-51B in December. On 23 December, the 363rd Fighter Group, like the 354th trained on the Bell P-39, arrived at Keevil. The 363rd, based at Rivenhall, Essex, became the second operational Mustang unit in Europe when it was declared combat ready late in February, 1944.

The first operational Mustang unit assigned to the Eighth was the 357th Fighter Group at Leiston in Suffolk which had transferred from the Ninth Air Force in January in exchange for the P-47 Thunderbolt equipped 358th Fighter Group. The unit entered combat with its P-51Bs on 11 February 1944, on a fighter sweep over the coast of France. Two weeks later, the 4th Fighter Group, under Colonel Donald Blakeslee (former RAF Eagle Squadron pilot) became operational at Debden (the now famous 24-hour conversion to P-51s).

The success of the 354th Fighter Group was followed by that of other P-51B units and after only two months of operational combat duty the Mustang had become the first escort fighter to fly escort missions of over 1,000 miles (1,600 km) and had been credited with a victory rate of over 13 enemy fighters for every 100 sorties. This was over three times that of the P-47 and the P-38. The 4th Fighter Group alone, during their first month of operations, set a new USAAF victory total by destroying 156 enemy aircraft. The loss to the 4th was 29 pilots and aircraft for a positive victory ratio of more than 5 to 1. The following month they increased this record to 207. Serving the USAAF as a ground attack aircraft, the P-51 was equally as successful as it was as an interceptor. A brief description of piloting the P-51 in the ground attack role is related by Major William Hovde (10.5 victories) who served with the 358th Fighter Squadron at Steeple Morden, England, during the summer of 1944. In Hovde's words; "As the month of July came to a close, I recorded a pair of ground victories while on a strafing mission to Luftwaffe airfields. Every German plane we got on the ground was just one less that we had to fight in the air.

"Light caliber flak and small arms fire was coming at us as we started across the German airdrome. That stuff was plenty rough, and a few of the boys got some holes in their planes. We were going like hell, right down on the tree-tops. I picked out a Dornier 217, a twin-engined plane, parked in the middle of the field. After I polished that one off I kept right on going and nailed a Junkers 88, another twin-engined plane, which was right in line with the Dornier. Our group knocked off thirteen Luftwaffe planes on that mission, as well as a lot of assorted targets, including shooting up hangars, gun emplacements, a control tower, flak cars, railroad cars, locomotives, oil tanks, and even a couple of tugboats. It was a good day for hunting, but a plenty rough ride."

The first operational use of the Merlin powered P-51B and C in the Pacific theater occurred during the Spring of 1944 with the arrival of the new fighters for the 311 Fighter Group, which had been utilizing the older A-36A and P-51A. A few of the new aircraft were also assigned to

Browning M2HB
('Heavy Barrel')

Evolved from the .50 calibre Browning M1921A1 water-cooled machine gun via the M2 water-cooled and later M2 air-cooled heavy ground and aircraft machine gun. Cooling problems due to the powerful .50 cartridge led to the development of the M2HB ('Heavy Barrel') during the 1930s which was capable of absorbing more heat and dissipating it faster, permitting longer firing periods, without the danger of overheating. This version was evolved for fixed, flexible and anti-aircraft use for single or coupled mounts.

System of operation: Short recoil
Length of weapon: 65 in (1651mm)
Length of barrel: 45 in (1143mm)
Weight (on P-51):   65 lb (29.5kg)
Weight (standard):   84 lb (38.1kg)
Weight of one round: .637 lb (290g)
Weight of one bullet: .10614 lb (50g)

Barrel: 8 grooves, right-hand twist
Feed: Disintegrating metallic link belt
Cyclic rate of fire: 550 rpm
Muzzle velocity: 2900 ft/sec (884m/sec)
Effective range: 3280 ft (1000m)

the 1st Air Commando Group. By the end of 1944, the 23rd and 51st Fighter Groups (which transitioned into the P-51s in September and October) were also declared combat-ready for the Mustang.

Unlike their counterparts in Europe, which utilized the long-range capabilities of the Mustang for bomber escort duties, the CBI based units used the long-range P-51s for interdiction attacks against advancing Japanese forces and strafing and bombing sorties against the enemy airfields and storage depots.

The varied missions assumed by the Mustang in the Pacific is illustrated by the assignments of the 23rd, 51st and 311th Fighter Groups during late 1944 and early 1945. While the 23rd provided ground support and top cover for the advancing Chinese Armies, the 51st was assigned escort functions for the 1st Bomb Group of the Chinese-American Composite Wing operating over southwest China, Burma and Indochina. The 51st was also responsible for fighter support and protection for the transport runs over the famous "hump". The 311th, as part of the 312th Fighter Wing, provided fighter defense for the Chengtu area of China and operated in an offensive mode by attacking railway and communication links of the Japanese forces in Northern China.

An example of the effectiveness of the Mustang in the CBI occurred on 5 January 1945, when P-51s of the 311th, after completing bombing and strafing of the railyards, engaged a dozen Japanese fighters over Sinsiang. Five of the enemy planes were destroyed without a loss to the 311th.

A number of F-6Cs (P-51B/C photo reconnaissance aircraft) also were delivered to the CBI. The advantages of these aircraft in the photographic role was obvious. The F-6C was identical to the P-51B except that, in addition to normal armament, it carried cameras. These aircraft were used by the 118th Tac Recon Squadron, not only for reconnaissance, but in a ground support/attack role.

On 23 December, 1944, 16 of the F-6Cs of the 118th (part of the 23rd Fighter Group) left Suichwan to bomb and strafe the port at Wuchang-Hankow. After successfully carrying out their attack and photographing the results, the unit moved to the Japanese airfield at Wuchang to strafe the enemy aircraft parked there. They were jumped by a formation of Nakajima Ki.43s. The Commander, Major Edward McComas, who ended the war with 14 victories, destroyed five of the enemy fighters to become the only pilot in the Fourteenth Air Force to destroy five enemy planes in a single day.

In mid-1944, the improved P-51D variant started to appear in USAAF units in Europe and the Pacific. The 4th Fighter Group, which had been the initial Eighth Air Force Group to take delivery of the Mustang P-51B, started to receive their new mounts in June, as did the 352nd Fighter Group.

On 21 June 1944, the 4th and 352nd Fighter Groups again displayed the exceptional range of the P-51 when they took part in the first "shuttle" mission (coded FRANTIC) escorting one-hundred and forty Boeing B-17s targeted to an oil plant near Berlin. Seventy P-51s left Debden, England, picked up the bomber formation, and flew to Poland and on to Piryatin, Russia. Four days later, on the 25th, 55 airworthy P-51s picked up B-17s over Leszno, Poland, and escorted them to their target at Drohobycz,

and then on to Lucera, near Foggia, Italy.

The P-51Ds, Hs and Ks initially were used to replace earlier models which had been lost in combat or by other means and were supplied in bulk to newly forming units. Once these two situations had been satisfied, the later P-51s were supplied to most units for transitioning from the P-51B and C models.

Although not directly related to the combat characteristics of the P-51D, nor yet a hair-raising tale of aerial combat, an interesting and almost comical story involving a pair P-51D Mustangs is described by Henry Brown of Dallas, Texas, who at the time of the following incident was the leading American ace in Europe (including both air and ground victories). The story does, however, give an insight into the complete dominance the Allies had achieved by late 1944, describes both the correct and incorrect methods of strafing an enemy airfield with the Mustang, and explains the loss of an Allied aircraft. As Captain Brown, flying with the 354th Fighter Squadron, recalls:

"At this stage of the war, the American Forces had completed the invasion beachhead of France and had pushed the German Army back to the Rhine. Eighth Fighter Command was daily engaged in escorting bombers to all points in Germany, with very little opposition from the Luftwaffe. They, suffering from heavy aircraft losses, would often refuse to send up intercepting fighters to challenge this invading force. They would occasionally mass all their power and attack one of the bomber missions, but these attacks were well selected and undertaken only when the Luftwaffe could inflict heavy losses on the bombers. They could always outnumber our fighter escort by massing all their fighter strength and striking at a certain point on the bomber route, sometimes when the bombers were going into the target, other times when they were on their way home. As a result, many of our missions were accomplished without the slightest German fighter interference.

"I was the leading American ace in Europe at the time, with 30 destroyed German aircraft to my credit. I had completed one tour of duty in Europe, flying the P-47 Thunderbolt, and had come back to begin flying another tour, this time in the P-51 Mustang. At that time a 'tour of duty' consisted of flying 50 combat missions. I was flying my 70th mission when the events of October 3, 1944, took place.

"Major Charles W. Lenfest had recently been assigned duty as my Squadron Commander, and Captain Alvin S. White was flying his last mission with our unit prior to being rotated back to the United States. He jokingly made the announcement at the mission briefing that since this was his last mission and the German Air Force wasn't too active, he would appreciate it if anyone who saw a German plane would hold on to it until he got there so that he could shoot it down. We laughingly said, 'Yeah, Al, we'll hold him for you.'

"But the mission was a rather dull one. There were no German airplanes observed or reported in the air. We escorted the bombers into Neurnburg, Germany, and our part of the mission was completed. Since there were no enemy aircraft reported in the area, the fighter group split into squadrons, each taking a separate route home, to look for targets of opportunity. Possible targets were aircraft parked on the ground, trains, troop concentrations, anti-aircraft guns; in fact, anything of a military nature.

"While on the route out, I spotted a Messerschmitt 110, a twin engine bomber parked on an airdrome near the town of Nuernburg. I called Captain White and asked if he wanted to take a shot at it. He yelled, 'Roger!' Captain White told the remainder of his flight of three Mustangs to stay high and give him cover while he went down and strafed the airplane. His flight was off to my right and slightly low. I saw him dive away from the remainder of his flight and saw that he was using the correct technique in establishing his attack. The technique we were using when strafing an airdrome was to initiate the dive away from the direction we wanted to attack. We held the airplane in a dive until we reached the treetops and then made a 180 degree turn and flew back into the target area. Captain White made two passes at the aircraft, but could not fire his guns because he could not center his gun sight on the German airplane due to the high trees at the edge of the airfield.

"I called Captain White after his second pass and brazenly told him to watch me and I'd show him how it should be done.

"I peeled off in a steep dive right over the airdrome and pulled out just above the ground. I screamed in toward the parked aircraft as fast as the Mustang would go with the propeller three to four feet off the ground. At maximum firing range, I squeezed the trigger. My shots were hitting the aircraft and the area around the aircraft, filling the air with smoke, dust, and chunks of the German airplane. Diving on any enemy airfield in plain sight was the poorest type of maneuver. The enemy gunners had already been alerted by Captain White's attacks and undoubtedly were watching the other aircraft circling above the airfield, just waiting for someone to make a mistake such as this. In my excitement, evidently I had forgotten all the caution and finesse learned in 72 previous missions.

"At the same time I was shooting at the German

Engine control quadrant
Later models equipped with single-position carburettor.

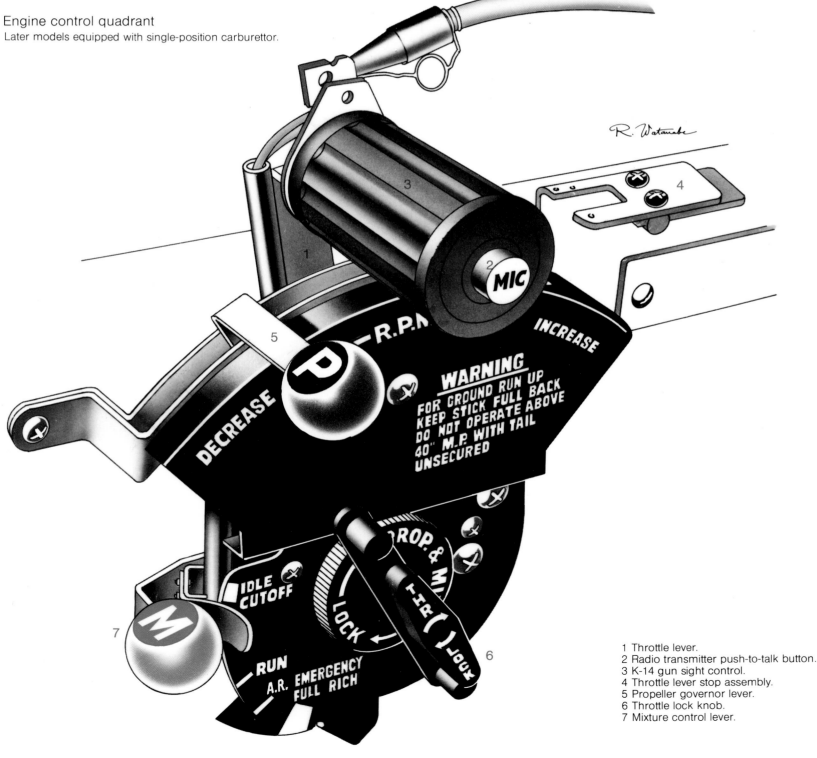

1 Throttle lever.
2 Radio transmitter push-to-talk button.
3 K-14 gun sight control.
4 Throttle lever stop assembly.
5 Propeller governor lever.
6 Throttle lock knob.
7 Mixture control lever.

airplane, the German anti-aircraft gunners around the base were blasting at me. The aircraft that I was shooting at exploded and parts flew into the air. I don't know whether the anti-aircraft knocked me down or if it was parts from the exploding aircraft that hit my Mustang. Regardless which it was, my Mustang's engine suddenly began to run very rough, and I yelled over the radio that my engine had been hit and I was going to bail out.''

Although the P-51 was basically utilized by both the USAAF and the RAF as a long range interceptor and escort fighter once it had been re-engined with the Merlin powerplant, it continued to be employed as a ground attack/support aircraft and in many other unique and difficult missions. Among these were anti-"Diver" interceptions and flight qualification from the deck of an aircraft carrier.

In Europe, the advent of Germany's V-1 flying bomb created a new mission for the USAAF and RAF, the defensive interception and destruction of the pulse-jet powered missiles prior to their impact on English soil. For the most part, the missions would consist of patrolling a segment of the coastal area, flying back and forth in a predetermined pattern. These so-called ''Diver'' patrols would be vectored to the flying bomb by coastal radar and then attempt to shoot it down.

Typhoons, Tempests, Supermarine Spitfires and P-51 Mustangs were pressed into this role due to their high airspeeds at all altitudes. Bringing down one of the flying bombs was anything but an easy task, even though they could not fire back and normally were programmed for a straight flight path. The problem was in their high speed and their small size.

To attack, the interceptor, or the chase plane, would come in behind the bomb and open fire from approximately 400 yards (360 m). To get too much closer was a dangerous risk as the explosion of the bomb under the 300 to 400 yard (270 to 360 m) range could bring down the chase plane. The 400 mph (640 km/h) speed of the bomb, in most instances, also gave the pilot only one pass to make his hits.

Another RAF method of bringing down the

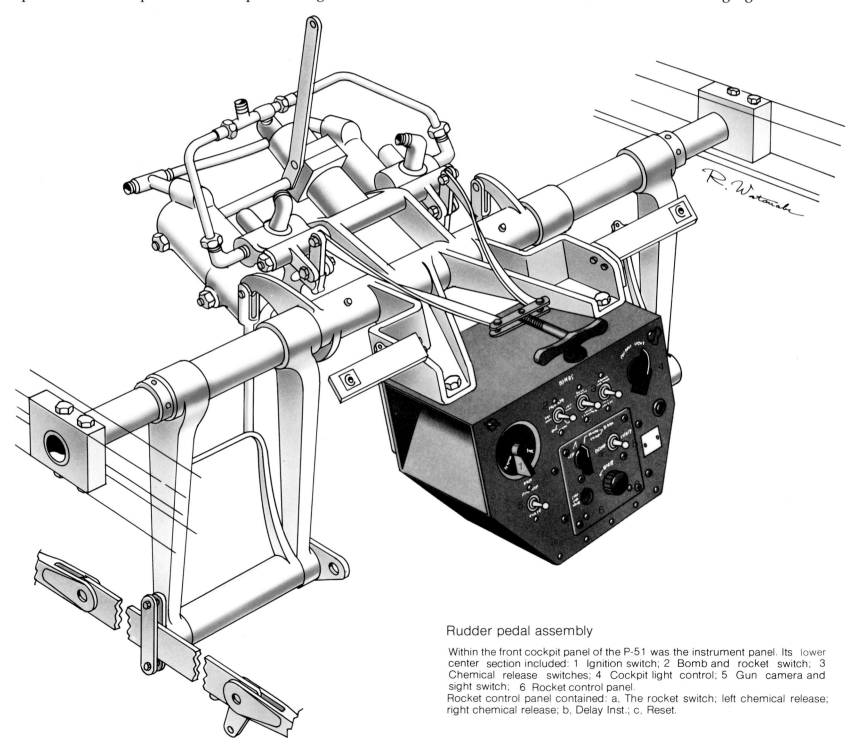

Rudder pedal assembly

Within the front cockpit panel of the P-51 was the instrument panel. Its lower center section included: 1 Ignition switch; 2 Bomb and rocket switch; 3 Chemical release switches; 4 Cockpit light control; 5 Gun camera and sight switch; 6 Rocket control panel.
Rocket control panel contained: a, The rocket switch; left chemical release; right chemical release; b, Delay Inst.; c, Reset.

"Divers" consisted of flying the chase plane up next to the bomb and locking the bomb's wingtip on top of the interceptor's wing. A quick tip of the chase plane, and the V-1 would roll over under the momentum of the tipover and head for the surface below in a steep dive. This proved to be very successful, but also very dangerous.

One extremely unique, and unpublicized, use of the versatile P-51 Mustang was in its qualification by the United States Navy for carrier operations. In mid-1944, the Navy took delivery of a P-51D-5NA (S/N 414017) at Mustin Field, a small airstrip within the confines of the Philadelphia Navy Yard. The aircraft was modified for carrier use at the Navy Yard through the addition of a strengthened fuselage bulkhead in the area of the simplified arrester hook (which was also added), and the main fuselage was extended in the aft tail area to allow for the arrester hook mechanism. Catapult hooks were bolted to the main landing gear struts and the air pressure in the main oleos was increased to insure a dampening of any shock transmittal due to launching.

During September and October, initial testing was completed on a marked out carrier deck at Mustin, with approximately 150 arrested landings and a like number of catapult assisted launches recorded. The P-51 and its pilot, Robert Elder, were then put aboard the USS *Shangri-La*, and on 15 November, the carrier headed sout to a location off the Virginia coastline for actual carrier qualification. As Elder describes this singular experience:

"Early on in the testing it became evident that the airspeed band between minimum approach speed as defined by available rudder control, and maximum engaging speed as defined by wind over the deck and aircraft structural tolerances, was indeed narrow. To be exact, hard-over right rudder occurred when stablized at 82 mph (132 km/h) in the approach configuration and structural limitations under specified hook loads peaked out at slightly less than 90 mph (145 km/h). I, therefore, used 85 mph (137 km/h) as target approach speed. Fortunately, the little lady exhibited marvelous speed control characteristics and even though

operating at near minimum margins of directional and lateral controllability (limited by torque), waveoffs could be executed by judicious application of power.

"Landing attitude was the one critical factor most worthy of comment because of either premature main wheel contact with the deck prior to hook engagement or an inflight engagement prior to tail contact, would certainly have configured the test airplane and possibly the pilot.

"Visibility forward during the approach was quite good and caused no problem at all in alignment or landing the airplane. In fact, some of the radial engine fighters of that era, notably the F4U and F6F with cowl flaps open, had considerably more restricted forward visibility. In any case, I simply made a turning approach almost to touchdown as was the practice at that time.

"Although I have had the privilege of several firsts' in qualifying Navy aircraft aboard ship, none was more interesting or satisfying than my experience with the Mustang."

The reasons for the Naval interest shown in the P-51 is obvious. With it's extended range, the susceptibility of the launching carriers to enemy detection was much less, and with the great distances existing between the targets of the Pacific Campaign, the Mustang appeared to be a logical answer. However, with the capture of Iwo Jima and Okinawa in early 1945, coupled with the growing Allied air supremacy, the urgency of this long-range need subsided and the project was cancelled.

The P-51 made aces out of a number of pilots among them Lieutenant Sidney Woods (7 victories) from San Marcos, Texas who had flown the Curtiss P-40 and Lockheed P-38 Lightning in the Pacific during the first four years of the war before being transferred to the 4th Fighter Group at Debden, England, in early 1945. Woods describes the mission in which he reached ace status:

"I was leading the 'A' Group on an escort mission to Ruhland. After taking the bombers through the target, I turned and took 'A' Group on a sweep to the east of Berlin. While at 5,000 feet (1,500 m), flying from east to west, the

American mechanics at work on an F-6D of 10th Photo Reconnaissance Group, US 9th AAF, at St. Dizier airfield, France, in September, 1944. Note the radio 'call number' on the fin, an abbreviated form of the serial number used as individual identity marking. The burned-out wreck is a Ju 88G night fighter.

(U.S. ARMY PHOTOGRAPH)

bomber made a 180-degree turn to the right and headed back to the Russian lines. The aircraft bore 3rd Division markings (a red tail with diagonal red markings on the wings). I tried to call the B-17 on 'C' channel, but was unable to contact him. I was following the Fortress east of Berlin when I saw four aircraft making a circle over the town of Furstenwalde. I chased them across the town and identified them as Fw 190s. They were carrying bombs, and appeared to be forming up for a sortie over the Russian lines.

"I closed behind the No. 4 man in the flight and gave him a two-second burst from about 50 yards (45 m). I got strikes along the fuselage, in the cockpit, and along the left wing. My flight observed the enemy pilot slumped over in the cockpit, and saw him nose over and hit the deck.

"I pulled up to clear my tail and observed an enemy aircraft firing at me from above, 90-degrees to my left. I shoved the stick down and he missed and went over the top of me. I pulled straight up and rolled off the top and came down behind his tail. I followed him down in an aileron roll, hit him during the roll and observed him crash on Fuerstenwalde airdrome.

"At this point I saw all members of my group were getting intense, light, accurate flak from the airdrome, town and fields in the vicinity. Then I saw another flight of four Fw 190s turning between Eggersdorf and Fuersten-walde airdromes. Again, I closed in on the No. 4 man, gave him two two-second bursts. He jettisoned his bombs, then his canopy and started smoking. The pilot bailed out, but as I had observed strikes in the cockpit I believe he was dead when he came out.

"After destroying this aircraft, I pulled up and looked down my left wing to see some gunners in a pit below me shooting light flak that was just coming by my tail. I broke to the right and then observed two Fw 190s on the tail of a P-51. I closed behind one right on the deck, gave him several short bursts and he crashed and burned.

"I then climbed back to 3,000 feet (900 m) and sighted still another flight of four aircraft circling between Furstenwalde and Eggersdorf. I closed in behind the No. 4 man and all four aircraft broke violently to the left. I pulled in so tight, in order to stay behind him that my gyro spilled and I was giving him lead with the fixed sight. He pulled up in a steep, climbing turn to the left and as he did I saw my tracers going just into his tail. I pulled back slightly on the stick and the tracers went into the Fw 190 cockpit. The aircraft caught fire, crashed and burned.

"I climbed up to 5,000 feet (1,500 m), circled once and picked up three members of my group and went home. Through all these engagements, my wingman, 2d Lt. Richard E. Moore, 336th Fighter Squadron, stayed with me, protecting my tail."

One of the most publicized missions to come out of the Pacific Theater was carried out by a pair of F-6 camera equipped Mustangs attached to the 71st Reconnaissance Group, Fifth Air Force. Captain William Shomo, Commander of the 82nd Squadron, and Second Lt. Paul Lipscomb were conducting a low level photographic sortie over Japanese airfields in Northern Luzon on 11 January, 1945, after having taken off from their base on Mindoro Island. Prior to this mission, Captain Shomo had sighted only one enemy aircraft, that being an Aichi dive-bomber only two days before as he was attempting a landing at his base. The dive-bomber had become his only sighting and

his only victory, as he quickly turned his reconnaissance fighter into the enemy plane and sent it to the jungle below.

On the 11th, Shomo, who had received his pilot's wings in March, 1942, sighted a formation of twelve enemy fighters escorting a lone bomber flying at approximately 2,000 feet (600 m) over him. He motioned to Lipscomb and together they made a wide sweeping climb to position themselves slightly above and behind the enemy formation. Diving to attack, Shomo destroyed a pair of the escorting Kawasaki Ki. 61s on the first pass. Meanwhile, his wingman, Lipscomb had had similar success. Shomo turned toward the bomber and in the process had another of the fighters cross his sights. He promptly sent it to the jungle in flames and continued to press his attack at the underbelly of the bomber. As the bomber burst into flames, Shomo peeled away and flamed still another fighter in a head-on attitude. Before the encounter was over, Shomo had been credited with seven enemy aircraft destroyed and for his actions, was awarded the Congressional Medal of Honor, the only Mustang pilot to receive this in the Pacific.

Also, in the Pacific, the P-51D was the first fighter to escort Allied bombers over the Japanese mainland when on 7 April, 1945, Mustangs of the 15th and 21st Fighter Groups from their base at Iwo Jima escorted a formation both to and from the target, the fighters also destroyed a total of 21 Japanese interceptors over the target area.

In Europe, the P-51 met and bested everything that the Luftwaffe sent against it during the war. Its great success can be at least partially credited to the superior numbers and better training of the Allied forces, especially during the later years of the war. When pilots of equal ability in the P-51 and later model Luftwaffe aircraft were matched, ex-pilots of the P-51 readily admit, it wasn't an easy victory and one of the P-51s most interesting adversaries was the Me 262 twin-jet fighter that began appearing over the skies of Europe during the summer of 1944. Faster than the P-51, the Me 262 was also the most heavily armed fighter interceptor of the war with its four 30-mm nose mounted cannons.

A testimony to the P-51s ability to engage on equal terms with the Luftwaffe's Me 262 is related by First Lt. Urban Drew, who, in a matter of two weeks with the 375th Fighter Squadron, encountered the new jet fighters on two separate occasions being credited with the destruction of two of them. As Drew recalls:

"I was leading Cadet Blue Flight in Cadet Squadron. We had just sighted the bombers and the marker flares in the vicinity of the target at Hamm, Germany. We were flying at about 2,000 ft (600 m), when this unidentified aircraft crossed under me at about 10,000 ft (3,000 m). It was flying on a course 90 degrees to ours, and I could see it was a twin engine ship of some sort. I called the Squadron Leader and got permission to go down on a bounce. I started down in about a 60 degree dive with my wing tanks still on, but, as I got lower, I could see I wasn't gaining any on the aircraft so I dropped my tanks. I was hitting about 500 mph (800 km/h) and didn't seem to be closing on the aircraft at all. He actually was pulling further away from me.

"Just about that time, I saw the spurts of smoke that actually come out of the jet-propelled aircraft. He was still diving at about 30 degrees. I called out to the group that I was chasing a jet-propelled aircraft and wasn't having too much luck. By this time we were right on the deck, and I could see I wasn't gaining on the jet. I was about to give up the chase when it started a shallow turn to the left, so I immediately started a sharper turn to cut him off. As I was cutting him off, he also started tightening his turn. When we finally passed each other all I could get was about a 90-degree deflection shot, which didn't do me any good at all. I racked my ship around and started after him again, thinking that his speed would have been cut down some in his turn. As we straightened out I could see he wasn't pulling away from me, but I couldn't gain on him either. I had everything wide open and was indicating about 410 mph (660 km/h) straight and level on the deck. I chased him on this leg of the hunt for about 30 seconds when I observed this airfield directly ahead of me. I could see the jet pilot intended to drag me across the field behind him.

"I called my flight and told them to hug the deck as closely as they could and I started a sharp right turn to skirt the edge of the airfield. The flak was terrific and one of my wingmen was hit and had to bail out. The jet was still ahead of me and flying on a fairly straight course. I had been firing on the ship in his turns and every time I thought I was anywhere near being in range, so I had used up quite a bit of my ammunition. Just then, another jet-propelled aircraft dropped out of the lower cloud layer, which was about 4,000 feet (1,200 m), and headed for my flight. My wingman started a sharp turn into him but the Me 262 pilot kept right on going and made no attempt to stay around and mix it up. The first jet started another shallow turn and I started firing from about 1,000 yards (900 m). I was too far out of range and couldn't get any hits on him at all. The Me 262 ship then headed back for the airfield, and I sighted still another aircraft taking off. I had fired all my ammunition except a couple hundred rounds and my wingman had been separated when he turned into the other jet, so I decided it was just about time I left. I climbed up, after pinpointing myself for the rest of the group, and headed for home." Drew's next encounter with the Me 262 came on 7 October 1944, and it was during this action that he was credited with two of the swift fighters:

"I was leading a decoy squadron when I went down to join a fight that was going on under the box of bombers behind our group. When I got there the fight had been dispersed and I could not locate any enemy aircraft. I had left my Red Section with the bombers, and I had just one flight with me due to a number of previous abortions. I couldn't locate our bombers so I joined up with some red-tailed B-17s that were short on escorting fighters. I stayed with them until I spotted two aircraft on the airfield at Achmer. I watched them for awhile and saw one of them start to taxi. The lead ship was in take-off position on the east-west runway and the taxiing ship got into position for a formation take-off. I waited until they both were airborne and then I rolled over from 15,000 ft (4,600 m) and headed for the attack with my flight behind me. I caught up with the second Me 262 when he was about 1,000 ft (300 m) off the ground; I was indicating 450 mph (720 km/h) and the jet could not have been going over 200 mph (320 km/h). I started firing from about 400 yards (360 m), 30-degree deflection, as I closed on him. I observed hits all over the wings and fuselage. Just as I passed him I saw a sheet of flame come out near the right wing root. As I glanced back I saw a gigantic explosion and a sheet of red-orange flame shot out over an area of about 1,000 ft (300 m).

"The other Me 262 was about 500 yds (400 m) ahead of me and had started a fast climbing turn to the left. I was still indicating about 400 mph (640 km/h) and I had to haul back on the stick to stay with him. I started shooting from about 60-degree deflection, 300 yards (270 m), and my bullets were just hitting the tail section of the enemy plane. I kept horsing back on the stick and my bullets crept up the fuselage to the cockpit. Just then I saw the canopy go flying off in two sections and the plane rolled over and went into a flat spin. He hit the ground on his back at about a 60-degree angle. The aircraft exploded violently and as I looked back at the two wrecks there were two mounting columns of black smoke."

In RAF service, the P-51 Mustang saw combat duty with a number of fighter and reconnaissance units until the end of the war. The first RAF fighter formation to equip with the Mustang Mk III was 122 Wing (19, 65 and 122 Squadrons), late in 1943. This unit was also the first to use the Malcolm hood, later adopted on many USAAF Mustangs. Before

Tail gear assembly

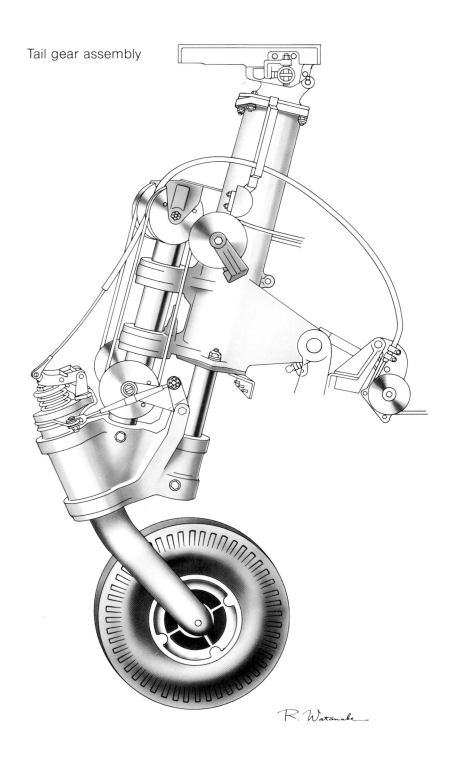

R. Watanabe

being diverted to a more tactical role in preparation for the D-Day invasion on 6 June, 1944, 122 Wing flew escort missions for USAAF bombers between February and April, 1944. Subsequently, RAF Mustangs were operational over France, Belgium, Holland and Germany until hostilities ceased in May, 1945. A total of 18 RAF squadrons were equipped with the Mustang Mk III, eight of which later changed to Mk IV (plus another two squadrons formerly flying other aircraft). In addition, low level photographic and visual reconnaissance missions were flown in the P-51 by RAF units such as 2, 168, 268, 414 and 400 Squadrons in 1943 and 1944, but due to high losses, only 268 Squadron had Mustangs left by January, 1945.

Major maintenance difficulties in Europe were never a problem with the P-51 and its Merlin engine. The only real problem was the reorientation of American ground crews on the principles and repair of the Merlin powerplant. (In Europe, this was normally conducted at RAF bases). The P-51s engine had an overhaul and replacement time of 200 hours, but this was rarely met due to the heavy combat flying done by the P-51 groups. The major disadvantages of the P-51 was its continuous use of spark plugs. These would normally be changed at least every 12 to 15 hours of flying time, and often after every 7 to 8 hour long-range escort mission had been completed.

The Pacific offered the Mustang a much different kind of environment than did the European Continent, where mechanical failures, losses and weather and climate-related down-times of the Mustang were much higher. The crushed volcanic rock airfields of islands like Iwo Jima created havoc with pilots and aircraft due to the dust that was kicked up during take-off and landings. Pilots would have to stagger take-offs in order to let the volcanic dust whipped into the air by the propwash settle and be provided sufficient visibility. The dust and volcanic particles also was a constant hazard to the filtering systems of the powerplant as they would oft times clog, resulting in engine cut out. Although this normally occurred during the takeoff run, it sometimes happened after the aircraft had cleared the runway and forced a crash-landing attempt into the nearby water or onto the rocky outer peripheries of the airfield.

The humid weather of the Pacific also resulted in numerous problems for maintenance crews and pilots through corrosion of critical seals and the leaving of unwanted residue on exposed electrical components. The unpredictability of the weather also resulted in numerous aircraft being lost due to sudden and extensive cloud and storm activity.

A comparison of the nominal performance characteristics of the P-51D and four other famous fighters of World War II is presented below. Each aircraft, including the P-51 Mustang, was produced in number of variants, each of these exhibiting a variety of performance characteristic differences, however, the selections shown, are believed to give a representative evaluation based on time period, technology, number delivered and mission objectives.

The last American use of the Mustang in combat was during the Korean War, where the P-51D was operated as a ground attack/support aircraft for Allied Forces. The Mustang was selected for this role because it was still available (some 100+ P-51s were parked on a Japanese airfield awaiting scrapping) and because it possessed the slow speed maneuverability that was absent in the new high speed jet aircraft. This ability to maneuver under the direction of a Forward Air Controller on the ground made it much more effective than the higher speed Lockheed P-80 Shooting Stars which were filling the fighter/intercept role.

The major drawback in this type of operation was, of course, the susceptibility of the Mustangs' liquid-cooled in-line Merlin engine to anti-aircraft and small arms fire while attacking. This fact led to the Mustang having the highest loss ratio of any aircraft in Korea. A total of 194 Mustangs were lost during the less than three years it fought in Korea (with US, South African and South Korean Air Forces) with only ten being lost to enemy aircraft.

Spanning over a decade of warfare with the American air arm, and longer with several emerging nations, the P-51 Mustang more than lived up to its expectations. Without question, it was the finest all-around USAAF fighter of World War II, and most likely the best overall fighter aircraft of the war. The P-51s capabilities, after its marriage with the Rolls-Royce Merlin powerplant, as a high-altitude escort fighter shortened the war in Europe and unquestionably saved an inestimable amount of life on both sides. This later fact in itself could well serve as a fitting epitaph to this superb fighting machine.

Acknowledgements

Without the interest, trust and cooperation of the following individuals and organizations, this book on the P-51 Mustang could not have possibly been completed. I want to extend my thanks to each of them for their assistance in this project.

Henry Brown

Urban Drew

Robert Elder

William Hovde

General Robin Olds, USAF, Ret.

Sidney Woods

C. E. "Rocky" Ruckdashel

United States Air Force
Office of Information

North American Division
Rockwell International

B-17 FLYING FORTRESS

Text by ROGER FREEMAN

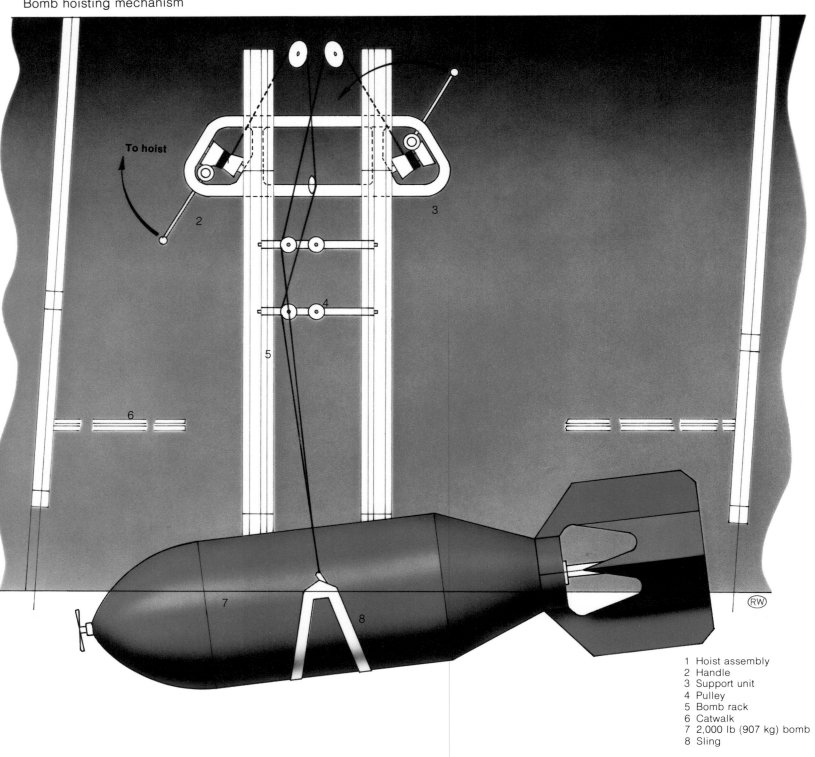

To hoist

1 Hoist assembly
2 Handle
3 Support unit
4 Pulley
5 Bomb rack
6 Catwalk
7 2,000 lb (907 kg) bomb
8 Sling

Newly rolled-out Boeing B-17F-40-BO Flying Fortress in flight. (BOEING)

Legend

Such is the fame of the B-17 Flying Fortress that stories of its exploits have already become legendary. Blurred by time and hearsay, it is not always easy to separate fact from fiction and assess just what contribution the aircraft made to the Second World War. Few would dispute that bombing played a major part in inducing the surrender of the Axis powers; and in this respect it can be stated that two-fifths of the total tonnage of bombs dropped by the US Army Air Forces were delivered to their target areas by Fortresses. To achieve this, crews had to fight their way through the enemy's airspace, enduring the hazards and discomforts of high altitude flying to minimize the effect of anti-aircraft fire, yet be alert to man the guns to ward off enemy fighters. The aircraft had to be large to permit heavy bombs to be lifted and carry the fuel necessary to fly

long distances. In view of the enemy defences on the ground and in the air, they were of necessity heavily armed and armoured – in fact, they were literally flying fortresses. The name itself has a magic ring and supports the legend – but here is their story in fact.

The bomber had its origins in the US Army Air Corps' doctrine of high altitude precision daylight bombing to attack strategic targets and deny an enemy the means to sustain their opposition. By establishing air power as a major force in warfare the air leaders were hopeful that they would gain autonomy for their own service, as Britain had done in 1918 with the establishment of the Royal Air Force. This was an expectation not to be fully realized until 1947 – when the Fortress was already outdated. When the potential of a new Boeing bomber was first recognized in the mid-1930s, it was seen as the means to foster this doctrine, and so the Fortress spearheaded the American offensive in Europe and remained operational throughout the Second World War.

Lineage

The genesis of the aircraft can be traced to a design project originated by Boeing in the summer of 1934. At that time the future of the company seemed uncertain as the US government had forced the break-up of United Aircraft, an aeronautical consortium which included engine, airframe and component manufacturers plus an airline. The government viewed this as a cartel and, indeed, Boeing had an order for 60 of its Model 247 passenger transports from the consortium airline, United. This was seen as unfair competition and legislation ensured that Boeing would no longer have the benefit of a guaranteed market for its products. The company was experienced and enterprising, as were most of its competitors, but the national economy was severely depressed and few commercial or military orders were being placed. Despite this the period witnessed a rapid advance in aeronautical technology with Boeing among the leaders.

William Boeing had started building seaplanes at Seattle, Washington state, in 1916 and his business prospered with orders from the US Army and Navy and for civil transports. In 1930 the company flew an all-metal low-wing monoplane, the Model 200 *Monomail*, featuring a simple retracting undercarriage – an innovation for the period. The substantial low-wing configuration, employing tubular-truss spar construction, featured in following designs; these were the progressive but unsuccessful Model 215 twin-engined bomber (later designated YB-9) and the successful ten-seat Model 247 twin-engine airliner. All these aircraft, powered by Pratt & Whitney air-cooled radial engines producing top speeds ranging from 150–200 mph (241–322 km/hr), outpaced the biplanes that predominated at that time. The expertise gained in producing these aluminium structures encouraged Boeing to pursue designs for even larger monoplanes when a requirement arose.

The US Army's Materiel Division pursued a policy of circulating requirement specifications for new aircraft to the industry, inviting manufacturers to submit entries for competitive evaluation. Normally the cost of producing a prototype was met by the manufacturer. In the biplane era of wood, wire and fabric this system did not usually impose a great strain on company resources. However, with the advanced technology involving the widespread use of metal in airframes not all companies could sustain the investment necessary for such a gamble. For the US Army Air Corps there were tight military budgets and only a small number of active flying squadrons permitted, yet despite this they continued to make efforts to promote new technology. While many senior officers nurtured an interest in a bomber capable of long-range strategic operations, this was no part of official Army policy and certainly not in line with the then isolationist stance of Congress. Development of a long-range bomber could only be pursued if seen as a necessary means of defending the United States' overseas possessions or protectorates, such as the Hawaiian and Philippine islands.

In early 1934 the Army offered a contract for the design, wind tunnel testing and technical data of an experimental long-range bomber, appropriately designated XBLR-1 (Experimental Bomber Long-Range Number 1). The Boeing company, seizing the chance to further their monoplane designs, tendered. Their submission was accepted in June 1934 which led to an order for a prototype a year later. This was truly a giant aircraft, spanning nearly 150 ft (45.72 m) and weighing 20 tons. Difficulties encountered during its construction delayed the first flight of the aircraft until October 1937, by which time it had been redesignated XB-15.

While design of the XB-15 and tail-off work on fighter and transport production kept Boeing in business, their future did not look bright unless a substantial airline or military order could be obtained. The company therefore decided to work up preliminary designs for two multi-engined aircraft types – one military and one commercial. It was expected that later in the year the Army Air Corps would issue requirements and invite bids for a bomber to replace the Martin B-10 currently serving in bomber squadrons. This would be of the then conventional size, which later became the "medium" classification. The manufacturer of the successful prototype could expect an order in excess of 100 aircraft, a prize well worth the gamble. Paralleling this design would be a commercial transport utilizing as many components of the bomber design as practical. The Boeing design team under Claire Egtvedt started work in the summer of 1934 and included several features proven in previous aircraft in their preliminary drawings. Understandably, work on Model 294, the large experimental bomber that was to become the XB-15, was a major influence and the new bomber project, Model 299, included several similar features and looked rather like its scaled-down version.

The anticipated "Circular Proposal" for a new bomber for the Air Corps was received early in August that year. Stated requirements included a top speed of 250 mph at 10,000 ft (400 km/hr at 3,050 m) carrying a "useful load", and a 220 mph (354 km/hr) cruising speed at the same height at which endurance was to be 10hr. The aircraft was to reach this operating altitude in 5min and it was also required to maintain level flight carrying its useful load at a minimum of 7,000 ft (2,130 m) with any one engine out. In view of this final requirement and the overall high performance, Boeing engineers considered using four instead of two engines to power their entry. The specification had stipulated only "a multi-engined 4 to 6 place land type airplane". While a twin-engine design was the general expectation of the Air Corps officers drafting the specification, Boeing's enquiry on this point brought assurance that there would be no objection to the use of four powerplants.

Prototype

Boeing was authorized to design and build the prototype on 26 September, 1934 with an initial funding of $275,000. Subsequently additional funds had to be found and well over double the original sum was expended before the prototype flew. Egtvedt's design team was steered by the Project Engineer, E. Gifford Emery, and his assistant, Edward C. Wells, who had a major influence on the design of the aircraft. In basic configuration Model 299 had a wingspan of 103 ft 9 in (31.6 m) and would be powered by four Pratt & Whitney Hornet radials developing 750 hp each. The wing utilized the extremely robust tubular form strutting developed by Boeing and additional strength was built in by the use of a corrugated underskin. Within the wing, between the two engine nacelles, aluminium fuel tanks were sited. A 68 ft 9 in (20.95 m) long streamlined fuselage was divided into five compartments, the centre-section housing up to 4,800 lb (2,177 kg) of bombs in two vertical racks. Both mainwheels and tailwheel were retractable although part of the tyres remained exposed. An innovation was the use of the new Hamilton Standard constant-speed propellers which offered automatic pitch control to suit various power and altitude requirements. In contrast to the open defensive gun positions found on many military aircraft of the day, four closed gun cupolas were provided, their teardrop shape contributing to the smooth lines of the aircraft. The nose gun installation was also fully enclosed and the whole Plexiglas nosepiece could be turned to extend the field of fire of this weapon. A bombardier's sighting panel was installed in a rather ungainly fold in the underside of the nose. Side-by-side pilot and co-pilot dual controls in the cockpit were common to all Air Corps twin-engine bombers, so to facilitate four-engine operation a novel arrangement of throttle levers allowed either pilot easy manipulation of one, two or all engines with one hand. Features were added and changed during design and construction, despite the urgency of the aircraft being ready on time to compete in the evaluation trials at the Air Corps' experimental establishment at Wright Field, Dayton, Ohio.

Origin of the Famous Name

Model 299 was first "rolled out" for public display on 17 July, 1935. Boeing promoted it as the world's first all-metal four-engined monoplane bomber, but press representatives viewing it that day seemed more impressed by its sheer size and streamline. One reporter, Richard Williams of the *Seattle Daily Times*, fascinated by the prominent gun positions, was moved to write of a "flying fortress" in his report. An accompanying photograph captioned "15 ton flying fortress" was brought to the attention of Boeing public relations men and at a later date the term Flying Fortress was adopted as a company registered name. The appeal of the name lay in the United States' defensive posture as a fortress, alert to meet any attacker.

Eleven days after its first public appearance, Model 299 made a first test flight with Leslie Tower in the pilot's seat. The aircraft behaved well in this and subsequent flights, the only major problem being tailwheel oscillation during taxiing. On 20 August the bomber was flown from Seattle to Dayton for evaluation by the Air Corps. The flight, made in 9hr 3min averaging 233 mph (375 km/hr), no doubt impressed the examining officers at Wright Field. Even so, top speed was not as high as Boeing expected although it was considerably better than that of two other prototypes – from Martin and Douglas – also being evaluated. The Boeing was superior in

almost every aspect except price, which was more than double that of its competitors. For a small production run the Martin 146 entry was priced at $85,910; the Douglas DB-1 was offered at $99,150; but the Boeing 299 was $196,730.

On 30 October, towards the end of the evaluation programme, disaster struck. The Boeing, after taking off from Wright Field, immediately went into a steep climb, stalled and just failed to level out before crashing into the ground. The pilot, Major Ployer Hill, chief of the Wright Field Flight Test Section, was killed and the Boeing test-pilot, Leslie Tower, died from injuries received. Although the forward section of the aircraft was almost completely destroyed by fire, the tail suffered little damage and revealed the cause of the accident. One of the innovations of Model 299 was a system of control surface locks which could be operated from the cockpit. These locks prevented damage to ailerons and elevators from wind gusting when the aircraft was parked. Evidently Major Hill had failed to release the lock control and neither he nor Tower noticed this. The tragedy was a major setback for Boeing and there was little consolation to be had from the fact that the crash was due to human error and not to some fundamental weakness in the design.

The Boeing Company had committed the major proportion of its resources to the building of this aircraft and, as the outstanding tests could not now be completed, the contract would be lost to one of the other competitors. The superiority of Model 299 was unchallenged, but the fact that the Army could have two Douglas DB-1s for every Boeing purchased was an important consideration. The crash of the Boeing entry resulted in the decision late in the year to give Douglas a contract for 133 aircraft, to be known as the B-18, based on the successful DC-3 transport. All was not lost for Boeing as they were the recipients of an order for 13 Model 299s, to be designated YB-17 for service evaluation. The contract, issued on 17 January, 1936 for $3,823,807, covered the 13 aircraft, an additional airframe for static tests, spares and back-up. This was sufficient to keep Boeing solvent and their factory occupied for two years. Additionally, contracts were

Model 299 parked in front of the final assembly hangar at Boeing field in Seattle on 16 July, 1935. (BOEING)

Y1B-17 of 96th Bomb Squadron. (USAF)

received from airlines for individual examples of the transport design utilizing the wing form and empennage of the Model 299, plus a large flying boat transport embodying several components similar to those of the earlier XB-15. While at this date Boeing had no substantial production orders, the future began to brighten.

Prior to the first flight of a service test Flying Fortress on 2 December, 1936 the official Army Air Corps designation was changed from YB-17 to Y1B-17 to indicate that the aircraft was specially funded. In practice the revised designation was rarely used and the aircraft were generally referred to as YB-17s, even on official documentation. The Y1B-17s, although externally very similar to the Flying Fortress prototype, incorporated a number of changes. The most important was the substitution of Wright R-1820 Cyclone engines for the Pratt & Whitney Hornets. Although a similar nine-cylinder single-row radial engine, also originating in 1927, the development potential of the Cyclone was greater; the R-1820-39 version, selected for the Y1B-17, was rated at 930 hp for take-off as against the Hornet's 750 hp.

Another notable difference between the Y1B-17 and the prototype was to be found in the main undercarriage. Model 299 had hoop-type legs which made tyre changing extremely difficult as the whole axle had to be dropped to remove the wheel. To simplify matters the landing gear was redesigned to feature a single oleo-type leg. The mainwheels, however, still retracted forward and up into the nacelles, remaining partly exposed. Rubber de-icer boots were fitted to the leading edges of wings and tailplanes. These were pneumatically operated with their inflation dislodging ice accumulation. The aluminium-covered landing flaps were fabric-covered on the Y1B-17 and there were several minor internal changes to vacuum pump equipment, fuel and oil tanks and instrumentation.

Early Service

The first Y1B-17 was delivered to the Air Corps in January 1937 and the 13th early in the following August. That same month 12 of the bombers were sent to an elite bombing unit of the Air Corps, the 2nd Bombardment Group based at Langley Field, Virginia. This Group was under the control of General Headquarters Air Force, created in 1935 as a special air strike force, having equal status to the Air Corps, while being also a corporate part of it. This anomaly nevertheless provided General Headquarters Air Force with the opportunity to develop a bomber organization with strategic capability, in spite of the presence of many senior officers in the Army hierarchy who opposed any tendencies towards developing separate missions for the Air Corps. They

firmly believed that all Army aircraft should be committed to supporting ground forces and be subservient to them. General Frank Andrews, commanding General Headquarters Air Force, together with many of those within his command, believed in the promotion of an independent role for air power. They were also wise enough to appreciate the opposition which lay not only in the Army, but also with the US Navy and certain factions of government.

The doctrine of strategic bombardment had been quietly nurtured for some time, although the idea of long-range bombers destroying an enemy's war industry was not new – Britain's Royal Air Force, having been instituted in the latter stages of World War I, was such an example. With the arrival of the Y1B-17s many officers within General Headquarters Air Force saw that at last there was an opportunity to investigate and develop strategic bombing. In view of the critics who deplored the expenditure on these large advanced aircraft, every effort was made to prevent accidents that might draw adverse publicity. On the other hand every opportunity was taken to show off their acquisition to good effect. In what was a carefully orchestrated publicity campaign, flight records achieved by the Y1B-17s were brought to public notice and in 1938 goodwill missions were flown to Argentina and Brazil. The publicity surrounding an incident where three B-17s intercepted the Italian liner *Rex* over 700 miles (1,130 km) out to sea as a navigational exercise, brought unexpected results when the US Navy demanded that the Air Corps restrict its activities to within 100 miles (161 km) of the shoreline.

In developing their bomber ideas, Air Corps officers promoted operation from high altitudes where, it was reasoned, a bomber aircraft would be at less risk from intercepting fighters and anti-aircraft artillery. To operate at altitudes where air density was lower, engine supercharging was necessary. The additional Y1B-17 airframe built for static tests had eventually been upgraded for development flying. It was this machine, known as the Y1B-17A, that was fitted with exhaust driven turbo-superchargers. Such boosting had been featured on earlier experimental and service aircraft, but the system had not been found reliable. There were many prob-

lems involved in the installation of superchargers and ancillary equipment on this Y1B-17A, delaying its first flight until April 1938, three months later than scheduled. Both supercharger and exhausts were fitted above the nacelles and early test flights showed that their operation caused excessive turbulence over the wing, setting up vibration. Efforts to correct this problem came to nothing and eventually Boeing decided that the system would have to be repositioned on the underside of the engine nacelles.

The cost of reworking these installations, nearly $100,000, the Army refused to meet. Perfecting the installation took a considerable number of man-hours and it was not until the early spring of 1939 that all the major problems had been solved. The advantage it bestowed upon the Y1B-17A in performance was considerable. The service ceiling was raised 10,000 ft (3,050 m) more than that of the Y1B-17, and top speed increased by over 40 mph (64 km/hr). The Air Corps, greatly impressed, specified turbo-superchargers in subsequent heavy bomber orders. Meanwhile, later in 1937, Boeing had obtained production orders for ten B-17B models featuring turbo-superchargers and a redesigned nose section; other improvements included a larger rudder, hydraulic brakes, the addition of external bomb racks under the wings, fuel system changes and a reversion to all-metal wing flaps.

Smoothly contoured, the new nose section on the B-17B greatly enhanced the looks of the aircraft in addition to improving its aerodynamic qualities. The restructuring, however, was basically functional. In the Y1B-17 the navigator/bombardier sat behind the pilots and had a restricted outlook. In the B-17B his position was moved to the nose compartment where forward visibility was good and side observation windows gave additional views. By dispensing with the novel, but impractical, revolving nose gun structure of the Y1B-17 and substituting a framed fixture that included a large flat panel, the bombardier's sight could be moved forward. A ball and socket fixture in the Plexiglas framing allowed a 0.30-in (7.62 mm) machine gun to be used for defence. Although the contract for ten B-17Bs was signed in November 1937, followed by orders for an additional 29, technical problems – notably with the turbo-supercharger – delayed production

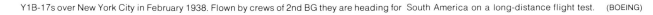

Y1B-17s over New York City in February 1938. Flown by crews of 2nd BG they are heading for South America on a long-distance flight test.　(BOEING)

B-17B with enlarged rudder and larger flaps. (BOEING)

and the first did not fly until late June 1939. Deliveries began in October and were completed in the following March. This order gave the Air Corps sufficient aircraft to fully equip two bombardment groups, one on the Atlantic and one on the Pacific coast of the United States; these were the 2nd Group at Langley Field, Virginia, and the 7th Group at Hamilton Field, California.

With the outbreak of war in Europe, US defence chiefs changed their attitudes towards the development and operation of long-range bombing aircraft and advocates of strategic bombardment propounded their doctrine more openly. Even before delivery of the first B-17B, Boeing had won a contract for 38 improved models, designated B-17C. Moreover, that availability of the B-17B with its supercharged engines allowed investigation and experimentation in high-altitude bombing.

High Altitude Precision Bombing

The Flying Fortress had become the prime instrument in the development of a technique and the promotion of a doctrine. Not only had the Air Corps been furthering the development of turbo-supercharging engines for some years, but also oxygen equipment for crews in the rarefied atmosphere. Another significant development was a high-altitude bomb-sight, (known as the Norden after its inventor) originally procured by the US Navy. Employing gyroscopes and an advanced computing system, it provided a degree of precision far in advance of any other existing bomb-sight. From altitudes of 10,000 ft (3,050 m) bombardiers, using their Norden sights in B-17Bs, could repeatedly place their bombs on or in close proximity to a range target. At higher altitudes the degree of accuracy declined, but it could still be acceptably near to the aiming point even from 20,000 ft (6,100 m) and above.

Thus encouraged, Air Corps planners envisaged these bombers attacking from high altitudes where their speed would make them difficult for contemporary fighters to

reach or pursue, while at the same time they would be above maximum range for most anti-aircraft artillery. Nevertheless, the advance of fighter capability as exhibited in the latest British and German designs and new directing systems, indicated that the B-17B could and would be intercepted. As a defensive measure it would be necessary to fly the bombers in large formations where the massed firepower of their defensive armament would form a formidable deterrent to intercepting fighters.

Although the B-17 had been labelled the Flying Fortress because of its many gun positions, in reality it was poorly armed by European standards. The British – and the French – were busy ordering aircraft from many US manufacturers by the end of the 1930s and were particularly critical of the Boeing's armament. RAF bombers were being fitted with powered turrets and this service considered a tail gun position imperative on large bomber aircraft. The streamlined cupolas on the B-17B – similar to those on the Y1B-17 – proved to have limited field of fire as well as being awkward to operate. The B-17C model was, basically, an attempt by the manufacturers to improve the aircraft's defences. The teardrop-shaped gun cupolas were dispensed with. The two fuselage side waist positions were transformed into open hatches through which

B-17B of 11th Bomb Group. Fitted with C type waist hatches. (USAF)

B-17F-10-BO

B-17F ''Memphis Belle'' of 91st GB, 324th BS, based at Bassing-bourn, north of London. Flown by Captain Robert K. Morgan's crew, the Fortress commenced combat operations on 7 November, 1942, the target being Brest in France. ''Memphis Belle'' completed 25 missions on 17 May, 1943 with an operation against Lorient. The bomber and crew were the first from the 8th AF to be returned to the USA on completion of an operational tour but probably the second to fly 25 missions.

Boeing Model 247D
Modified from Model 247 in 1934. The plane was operated by United Airlines
Power units: 2 × 550 hp Pratt & Whitney Wasp S1H1-G engines
Max speed: 202 mph (325 km/h) at 8,000 ft (2,440 m)
Cruising speed: 189 mph (304 km/h) at 12,000 ft (3,660 m)
Range: 890 mls (1,430 km) at 8,000 ft (2,440 m)
Service ceiling: 25,400 ft (7,740 m)
Span: 74 ft 0 in (22.56 m)
Length, tail up: 51 ft 7 in (15.72 m)
Height, tail down: 12 ft 1.75 in (3.70 m)
Wing area: 836 sq. ft (77.7 m²)
Gross weight: 13,650 lb (6,192 kg)
Crew: 2 pilots and a stewardess
Passengers: 10

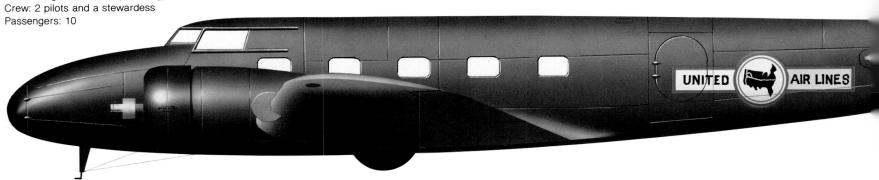

Boeing XB-15
Made its first flight in October, 1937
Power units: 4 × 850 hp Pratt & Whitney R-1830-11 engines
Max speed: 197 mph (317 km/h) at 6,000 ft (1,830 m)
Cruising speed: 171 mph (275 km/h)
Range: 3,400 mls (5,470 km) with 2,511 lb (1,139 kg) bombs
Service ceiling: 18,850 ft (5,750 m)
Span: 149 ft 0 in (45.42 m)
Length, tail up: 87 ft 7 in (26.70 m)
Height, tail down: 18 ft 1 in (5.51 m)
Wing area: 2,780 sq. ft (258.3 m²)
Gross weight: 65,068 lb (29,515 kg)
Armament: 3 × 0.30-in (7.62 mm) and 3 × 0.50-in (12.7 mm) machine guns,
          8,000 lb (3,630 kg) bombs
Crew: 10

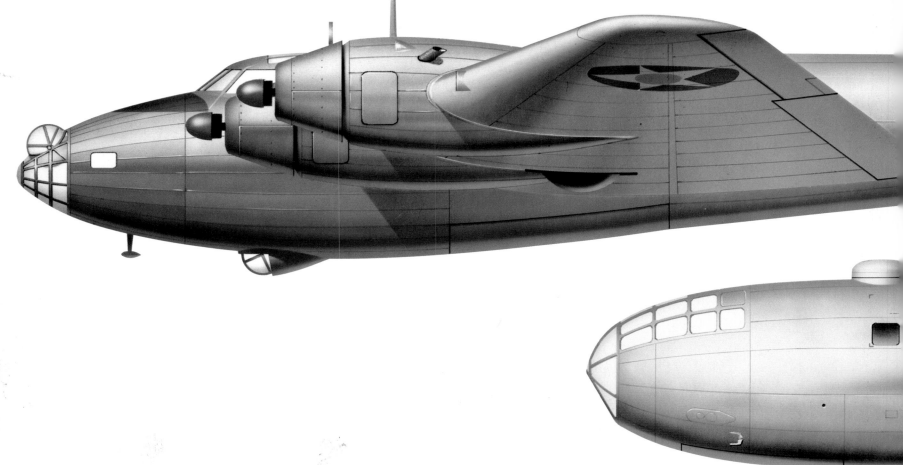

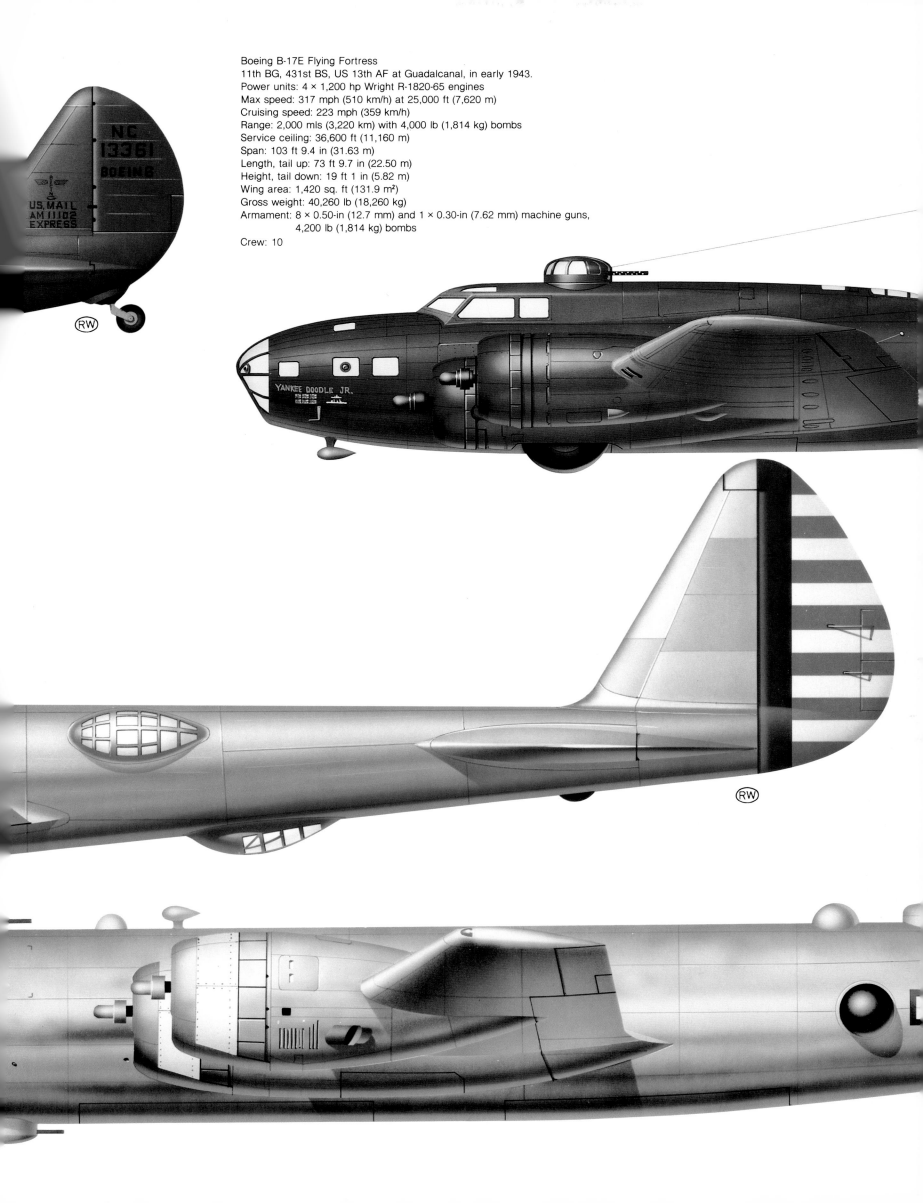

Boeing B-17E Flying Fortress
11th BG, 431st BS, US 13th AF at Guadalcanal, in early 1943.
Power units: 4 × 1,200 hp Wright R-1820-65 engines
Max speed: 317 mph (510 km/h) at 25,000 ft (7,620 m)
Cruising speed: 223 mph (359 km/h)
Range: 2,000 mls (3,220 km) with 4,000 lb (1,814 kg) bombs
Service ceiling: 36,600 ft (11,160 m)
Span: 103 ft 9.4 in (31.63 m)
Length, tail up: 73 ft 9.7 in (22.50 m)
Height, tail down: 19 ft 1 in (5.82 m)
Wing area: 1,420 sq. ft (131.9 m²)
Gross weight: 40,260 lb (18,260 kg)
Armament: 8 × 0.50-in (12.7 mm) and 1 × 0.30-in (7.62 mm) machine guns,
          4,200 lb (1,814 kg) bombs

Crew: 10

Boeing B-29 Superfortress
9th BG, 313th BW, US 20th AF at Tinian, Marianas, in 1945.
Power units: 4 × 2,200 hp Wright R-3350-23 engines
Max speed: 358 mph (576 km/h) at 25,000 ft (7,620 m)
Cruising speed: 230 mph (370 km/h)
Range: 3,150 mls (5,070 km) with 20,000 lb (9,070 kg) bombs
Service ceiling: 31,850 ft (9,710 m)
Span: 141 ft 3 in (43.05 m)
Length, tail up: 99 ft 0 in (30.17 m)
Height, tail down: 27 ft 9 in (8.46 m)
Wing area: 1,736 sq. ft (161.3 m²)
Gross weight: 134,000 lb (60,780 kg)
Armament: 12 × 0.50-in (12.7 mm) machine guns and
1 × 20 mm cannon,
20,000 lb (9,070 kg) bombs
Crew: 11

a gunner could manoeuvre a single machine gun fixed on a pedestal mount inside the fuselage. In place of the teardrop blister in the roof of the radio room a removable low-profile transparent canopy covered a machine gun hatch. To improve the rearward defence a lowered compartment on the underside of the aircraft, frequently likened to a bathtub, held another machine gun and provided a gunner with a fair field of fire.

The four weapons used to defend the rear and beam of the aircraft were all 0.50-in (12.7 mm) Brownings, whereas frontal defence rested on a lone 0.30-in (7.62 mm) rifle calibre machine gun. The only improvement in this weak area was two additional ball and socket fixtures in the nosepiece as alternative locations for the machine gun. Influenced by developments in Europe, the B-17C also featured some armour plate to protect crew members, and self-sealing fuel tanks. Uprated engines were installed, the R-1820-65 model of the Cyclone rated at 1,200 hp, pushing the top speed to 323 mph at 25,000 ft (520 km/hr at 7,620 m). As with the B model, the C was subject to numerous changes between the singing of the contract and the acceptance of the first aircraft in August 1940. Also, as with the B, the quantity ordered was increased. However, so many changes ensued that the additional 42 aircraft were given a new model number as B-17Ds. Again steps were taken to improve the

Flying Fortress's firepower, this time by installing two 0.50-in (12.7 mm) Browning machine guns in the upper and lower gun positions.

Carrying heavy loads to high altitude brought high engine temperatures and, in an effort to improve cooling, trailing edge flaps were fitted to the engine cowlings of the D model. In fact, this was the only major external difference between the C and D and although most Cs and many Bs went for modification and received many D features, these apparently did not include the cowling flaps. The D also had revised electrical, fuel and oxygen systems, extra armour plate, bomb rack changes and improved self-sealing fuel tanks – the original type having been prone to leaks!

From a half-dozen US companies working on power turret designs Boeing planned to install those being produced by Sperry on late production B-17Ds. But as development problems delayed the production of these turrets, only one experimental installation was carried out, the turret being positioned just aft of the cockpit where the gunnery controller's Plexiglas dome was sited on the B-17C and D. The majority of B-17Ds were delivered to the Air Corps during the early spring of 1941, most being sent to reinforce the 5th Bomb Group in Hawaii and to re-equip the 19th Bomb Group which moved from the US to the Philippine Islands later in the year.

B-17C under flight test. (BOEING)

B-17D with cowl flaps that were introduced with this model. (BOEING)

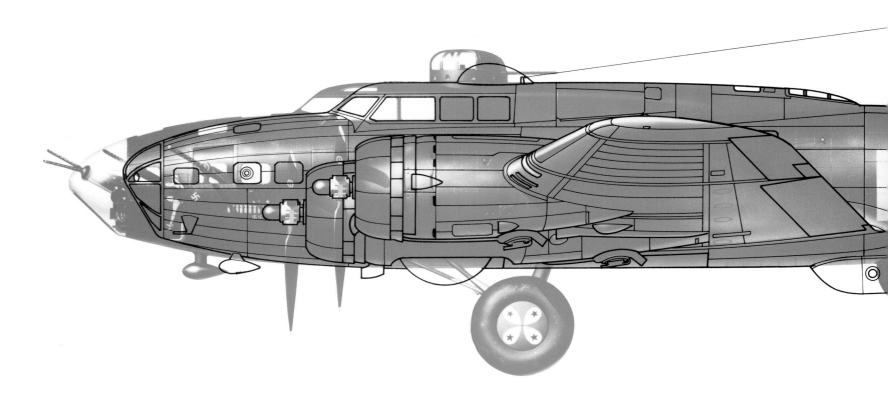

First Combat

The first Flying Fortresses used in war operations were flown by Royal Air Force crews. This acquisition of the B-17s by the British is in itself interesting and although the episode can hardly be said to have been successful, it provided some important information on the operation of the aircraft and high-altitude bombing over Europe.

When, in the summer of 1940, Great Britain stood alone against the Axis powers, she was anxious to acquire as much war material as possible from the United States. High on the shopping list were aircraft, and large quantities were supplied at first by direct purchase and then under Lend-Lease. The B-17 was not a priority as, prior to hostilities, RAF bomber leaders had inspected the aircraft and considered both its bomb-carrying capacity and defensive armament inadequate. Nevertheless, they knew the aircraft to be well made and to have good handling qualities. It appeared to them to be ideal for maritime-reconnaissance in view of the growing U-boat menace.

The US government, eager that the public should see some return for their money being lavished on armaments, particularly aircraft, thought it would be useful if the pride of the Air Corps could exhibit some of its prowess and gain some publicity on the quality of their goods. The British government, on the other hand, was interested in any move

that would appear to align the United States with their war aims. The propaganda value of being able to launch the vaunted American Flying Fortress against Germany was considerable. The US and British governments came to a decision whereby 20 B-17Cs revamped to D standard would be sent to the United Kingdom and an RAF squadron be specially trained to operate them according to the method of high-altitude precision bombing developed by the Air Corps. Although reluctant to part with their precious B-17s, particularly to a service known to be sceptical of their use in bombing, the US Army Air Corps (USAAC) – which became the US Army Air Force (USAAF) in April 1941 – was anxious to see that the aircraft had a good press. Although the United States was officially still neutral, arrangements were made for a small number of experienced pilots and technicians to go to England to train and advise RAF personnel on the use of the bomber.

In RAF service the B-17 was known as the Fortress, as it was British policy to use names rather than designations to identify their aircraft types. The RAF, like the Luftwaffe, had tried daylight bombing operations with large aircraft and found them extremely vulnerable to interception. In consequence RAF heavy bomber operations were conducted under cover of darkness and only fast low-level attacks by light bombers were carried out in daylight. From their experience, RAF Bomber Command considered that the only way the Fortresses could be employed in high-altitude day bombing

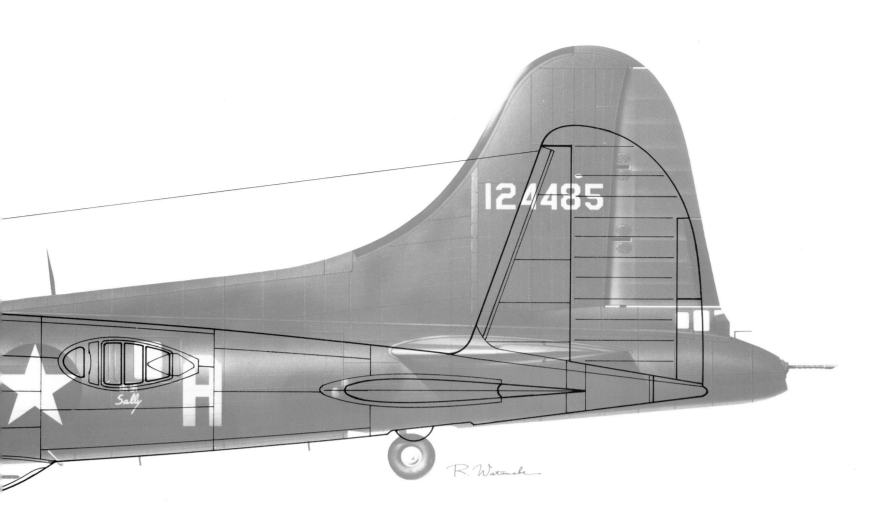

R. Watanabe

Fortress I of No. 90 Squadron, RAF. This aircraft was involved in the air fight on 2 August, 1941.

raids was to make maximum use of their then very high ceiling. The plan was to operate the Fortresses at an optimum 32,000 ft (9,750 m), a height which the known types of enemy fighter would have difficulty in attaining. This was, however, some 10,000 ft (3,050 m) higher than the Air Corps had planned in developing their technique of high-altitude bombing; in the event, this extra altitude proved critical. The still secret Norden bomb-sight had not been released to the British and a Sperry sight was substituted.

RAF crews specially selected and trained were allotted to 90 Sqn re-formed for this task on 7 May, 1941 at RAF Watton in Norfolk. Their first operation was not flown until 8 July due to various problems with the aircraft, airfield moves and awaiting suitable weather – a clear day was essential for target location and bombing. Three Fortresses were despatched from Polebrook in Northamptonshire on the first operation with the Wilhelmshaven naval base as the objective. Only one bomber was able to complete the mission as planned; the other two were plagued by technical problems caused by the high humidity of the atmosphere and the extremely low temperatures. Windshields and Plexiglas frosted thus obstructing vision, bomb release and gun mechanisms were also frozen and a supercharger failed. The engines of one Fortress began to throw oil from the crankcase breathers after the bomber had reached 23,000 ft (7,010 m) and, continuing to do so, forced the pilot to abandon his mission. Oil throwing remained a major problem but, strangely, only certain engines were affected. From problems encountered on this and subsequent operations it became evident that the Fortress could only rarely be operated at the desired altitude of 32,000 ft (9,750 m). Consequently Fortresses were used mainly singly and often had to attack their targets from lower altitudes with the attendant risk of interception.

The first brush with the enemy occurred on 2 August, 1941 when Pilot Officer F. W. Sturmey's crew flying Fortress AN519 were attacked off the Dutch coast at 22,000 ft (6,710 m) by two Bf 109s. The result of the exchange of fire was in the Fortress crew's favour as, unknown to them, one Messerschmitt receiving hits in the engine was abandoned by the pilot. The other Bf 109 was also hit and the pilot had to make an emergency landing in Holland. This incident proved the exception for, in following actions between RAF Fortresses and enemy fighters, it was the bombers which suffered. Two weeks after this successful engagement Pilot Officer Sturmey was flying another Fortress near Brest, when it was repeatedly attacked and severely damaged. Two of the gunners were killed but Sturmey managed to bring the aircraft back for a crash-landing in England.

On a mission to Oslo on 8 September, 1941, a Fortress was shot down, the first of its kind to fall to enemy action. Another Fortress also failed to return from this operation although it was believed to be lost through an accident. At the end of the month the squadron was taken off operations. Bombing accuracy had been poor due to the physical and mental strain imposed using oxygen and heating equipment. Although the armament was found inadequate, no enemy fighters had been able to intercept when the aircraft

Wright R-1820 nine-cylinder air-cooled radial engine.
(CURTISS-WRIGHT CORPORATION via BRIAN D. O'NEILL)

were flying above 32,000 ft (9,750 m). Had the aircraft been able to maintain altitudes above this level it might have been able to operate with impunity. The RAF was also critical of the average bomb-load which they considered uneconomical in relation to the manning and maintenance effort.

Despite the lack of success some favourable propaganda was produced for this effort by both British and US news media. A great deal of useful information had been gathered which was put to good use by both the USAAF and Boeing. Perhaps not enough attention was paid to the problems of operating in the moisture-laden air of Europe, for difficulties encountered by the RAF in 1941 were still to be solved when the USAAF brought the Fortress to Europe again late the following year.

Revamping Design

While RAF experience had again underlined the poor defensive firepower of the B-17, Boeing had already taken some positive steps to really transform the B-17 into a flying fortress. Advances in military aviation technology were so rapid during the late 1930s that, by the time hostilities had commenced in Europe, Boeing were aware that the advanced bomber design they had created in 1934 was fast approaching obsolescence. Another US manufacturer, Consolidated, was producing a new four-engined bomber, the B-24, which would have an all-round performance superior to the B-17. It had also been designed to take a power-operated gun turret in the tail, the most vital defence point on any large bomber. With the possibility that the United States herself might soon be involved in the war, it seemed likely that funds for a substantial order for an improved B-17 type would be forthcoming.

The immediate problem was whether the B-17 could be developed further to meet the defensive requirements that were bound to be imposed by the Air Corps or if it would involve a completely new design. Time was a critical factor and Boeing decided to revamp the B-17 by designing a completely new rear fuselage in which the tail gun position could be incorporated. At the same time a larger tailplane was developed to overcome complaints of lateral instability at high altitudes. These and other changes proposed to the Air Corps in the summer of 1940 were duly accepted, resulting in the new B-17E being put into production early the following year. As everything aft of the radio compartment was new, it is surprising that the Air Corps did not bestow a completely new model designation. Certainly the change gave the Fortress a completely different appearance for the shape of the empennage bore no resemblance to the earlier models. The outstanding visual feature was the large fin which was derived from that on the Boeing Model 307 Stratoliner, the commercial airliner developed in conjunction with, and using the same basic wing and powerplants as, the B-17.

Although a major reason for the redesign was the need for a tail gun position, Boeing did not install one of the new power-operated turrets. Being bulky, their inclusion would have involved a larger diameter rear fuselage or a bulge behind the tail. To avoid increasing drag Boeing preferred to maintain the tapering fuselage, terminating in a small gunner's compartment where twin 0.50-in (12.7 mm) guns would be hand-operated by a gunner in a sit-kneel position. The two beam or waist gun hatches were retained but were now in rectangular form. The entrance door, previously placed near the starboard wing root, was repositioned on that side between the tailplane and the waist gun hatch. For ventral defence a compact two-gun remotely controlled under-turret was located in the forward part of the new

fuselage section. It was sighted by a gunner in prone position using a periscope device projecting through the bottom of the fuselage to the rear of the turret – a method that proved far from satisfactory.

This Bendix turret was really a stopgap until the new manned Sperry under-turret became available. A Sperry electrically powered upper-turret was installed aft of the cockpit in the position worked out for the B-17D. Nose armament remained unchanged as frontal interception of such a fast bomber was considered unlikely to be attempted.

The B-17E, however, was less speedy than its predecessor, as the larger tailplane and the drag induced by the turrets reduced top speed by some 6 mph to 317 mph at 25,000 ft (510 km/hr at 7,620 m). The revised fuselage increased the length of the aircraft from 67 ft 11 in to 73 ft 10 in (20.7 m to 22.5 m), and the height at rest from 15 ft 5 in to 19 ft 1 in (4.7 m to 5.82 m). Another feature incorporated was a fully retractable tailwheel. Certainly in the B-17E Boeing had achieved an improvement in both firepower and field of fire (there were now eight 0.50-in [12.7 mm] guns) with minimal effect on the aerodynamic qualities of the airframe. Indeed, they had produced a classic configuration with undeniable aesthetic appeal.

The first B-17E did not fly until 5 September, 1941, more than four months behind schedule. The problem then was shortage of materials. Faced with the prospect of involvement in hostilities the US government had placed huge orders for a vast range of military equipment, temporarily swamping America's industrial capacity. Orders for 512 B-17Es had been obtained in the late summer of 1940, and to boost production still further agreements were established with Douglas and Lockheed-Vega for additional production of the B-17E in their plants. Boeing themselves were now trying to expand as rapidly as possible, building new factories and expanding old. A completely new bomber design was in the pipeline, the B-29, but if the US became involved in a war at an early date the B-17 and Consolidated's B-24 would be the only heavy bombers ready for operation.

A new B-17E at Boeing's Seattle plant on 19 February, 1942. (BOEING)

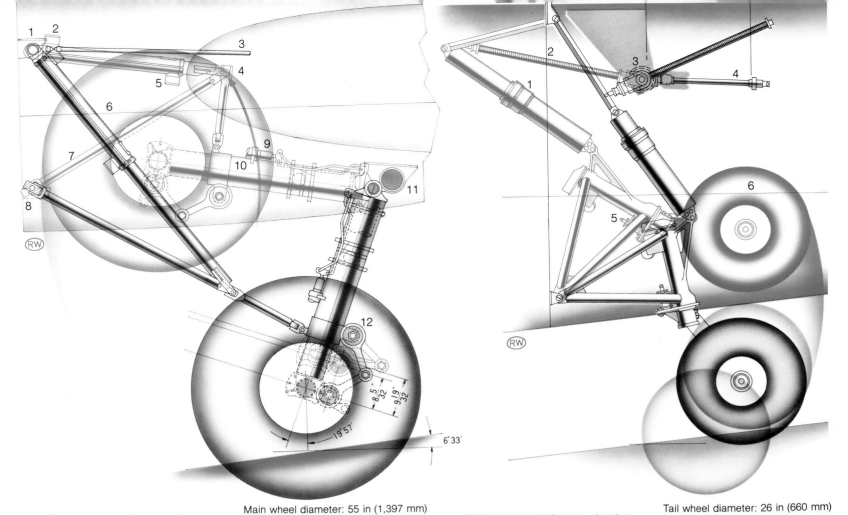

Main wheel diameter: 55 in (1,397 mm)

Tail wheel diameter: 26 in (660 mm)

Landing gear retracting mechanism
1 Retracting screw support
2 Upper limit switch
3 Control installed hand retraction
4 Drag strut universal assembly
5 Lower limit switch
6 Retracted tyre
7 Drag strut
8 Drag strut support
9 Return booster valve
10 Strut assembly
11 Landing gear support
12 Torsion link assembly

Tail gear retracting mechanism
1 Oleo
2 Retracting gear
3 Tail wheel motor
4 Hand retracting mechanism
5 Tail wheel lock assembly
6 Retracted tyre

In Action Against the Japanese

B-17s in fact became involved at the very opening of hostilities between Japan and the United States when a small number, sent from the US to Hawaii as reinforcements, were caught up in the Japanese attack on Pearl Harbor. In the following days 53 B-17Es were despatched to the Philippines, Java, Australia and Hawaii to help combat the Japanese invasion through the Central and South-east Pacific. During the initial attacks on bases in the Philippines most of the 35 B-17C and D models assigned to the 7th and 19th Bombardment Groups were destroyed by strafing Japanese fighters. Surviving aircraft moved to Java and Australia, to be joined by the reinforcements from the United States for flying maritime-reconnaissance and occasional bombing attacks on enemy shipping. With a range of 2,000 miles (3,220 km), the B-17 was one of the few aircraft available that could be used to reconnoitre the vast stretches of ocean and report on Japanese movements. But the small number of aircraft available, lack of parts and poor maintenance facilities limited the average strike force to only three or four and there was little effective bombing.

Nevertheless, the Flying Fortress was able to give quite a good account of itself and live up to its name on occasions. With one exception, current Japanese fighters were only armed with two rifle calibre machine guns with unsuitable ammunition including rounds with a 6.35 mm (0.25-in) armour-piercing core. It proved extremely difficult

for Japanese fighter pilots, in even the most advantageous circumstances, to bring down a B-17C or D. Their armour-piercing ammunition was not effective against the Boeing's armour and though riddled with bullet holes, B-17s usually survived combat with Japanese fighters. The famed Zero, the Japanese Navy Type 0, was at that time the only antagonist equipped with 20 mm cannon capable of inflicting serious damage. However, B-17s could survive Zero attacks due to the fact that the lack of 20 mm shell fuzing resulted in impact explosion causing only superficial damage. At this stage of the war Japanese fighters lacked adequate armour protection and self-sealing fuel tanks and so were particularly vulnerable to accurate defensive fire. The B-17E's tail guns proved particularly useful in warding off attacks.

Japanese pilots developed a healthy respect for the B-17 and as a result of these early encounters improvements were made in the firepower of their fighters. Subsequently it became regular practice to make frontal attacks on B-17s where it was known their defensive armament was poor. Combats in the South-west Pacific War theatre also revealed that the early B-17E's remotely controlled under-turret was ineffectual, leading to its removal. Hand-held guns were often mounted to fire through the open space where the turret had been located. With the 113th B-17E in production, the manned Sperry under-turret was introduced. Because of its unique spherical structure, it was termed a "ball turret". Unlike most powered turrets where the guns were elevated or depressed manually, those in the Sperry ball were fixed and it

B-17Es shortly after delivery to USAAF.

was the whole turret that moved. The gunner sat in a foetus-like position between the guns, using a reflector sight aimed between his feet. His back was to the entry door through which access could be gained on the ground.

In practice a gunner would not be in position during landing or take-off in case of undercarriage failure. For entry, usually made once the bomber was airborne, it was necessary to revolve the turret so that the guns pointed downward to expose the door. The whole electrically operated assembly was supported on a yoke and gimbal which, while looking rather unsubstantial, was actually very robust and in a crash would tear the fuselage rather than break the attachments. Even so, the ball turret was not a place for the claustrophobic; it was extremely compact and men of small size were usually picked for this position. Owing to space restriction a parachute could not normally be worn and in an emergency the gunner had to go back into the fuselage to get his.

The ball turret proved highly successful and was of great value in fighting off attacks from below. It did, however, bring one problem that was never satisfactorily resolved: cases from the two 0.50-in (12.7 mm) guns were ejected outside the turret and on occasions caused damage to other Fortresses in the formation.

A total of 812 B-17Es were ordered from Boeing, but only 512 were completed as such as the rest came under a new designation, B-17F. The F can be described as the first really battle-worthy Fortress – this name had also been officially accepted by the USAAF. Apart from the nosepiece devoid of framing, the F was externally similar to the E model. Internally, it was subject to some 400 changes, albeit most of them minor. One of the most important was the Wright R-1820-97 model of the Cyclone turning Hamilton Standard "paddle blade" propellers which had a diameter of 11 ft 7 in (3.53 m), an inch more than the type previously fitted. The changes necessitated the leading edge contours of engine cowlings being remodelled to avoid the wider blades striking them when fully feathered. Other improvements were to the landing gear, brakes, and the oxygen system. There were also changes in the bomb racks, ball turret, and the addition of an automatic pilot/bomb sight link. While the new model engines developed the same power as those in the B-17E, and were subject to only detail changes such as carburettor dust filters, the new wide blade propellers gave improved performance at high altitude, raising the service ceiling to 38,000 ft (11,580 m) and increasing top speed to well over 320 mph (515 km/hr). During the production run another 10,000 lb (4,536 kg) weight was added through various equipment improvements which in turn adversely affected performance, reducing the top speed to 299 mph (481 km/hr).

The Wright R-1820 Cyclone was near the limit of its

XB-38

Modified from B-17E

Power plants
 4 × Allison V-1710-89 liquid cooled engines:
 1,425 hp at 25,000 ft (7,620 m)

Performance
 Max speed: 327 mph (526 km/h)/25,000 ft (7,620 m)
 Cruising speed: 226 mph (364 km/h)
 Service ceiling: 29,700 ft (9,050 m)
 Max range: 3,600 mls (5,790 km)
 Range with 6,000 lb (2,720 kg) bombs: 1,900 mls (3,060 km)

Weights
 Empty: 34,748 lb (15,762 kg)
 Gross: 56,000 lb (25,400 kg)
 Max take-off: 64,000 lb (29,030 kg)

Dimensions
 Same as B-17E

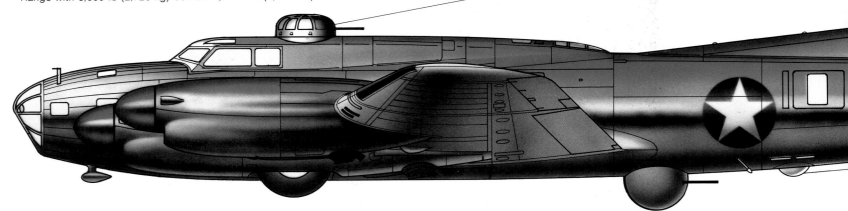

development and further improvements in the Fortress's performance were only likely to be achieved by installing a completely new engine type. The liquid-cooled supercharged Allison V-1710-89 engine rated at 1,425 hp offered a potential improvement in performance, although the Army Air Forces had long favoured air-cooled radials for their reliability and simpler maintenance. Lockheed-Vega were asked to carry out an experimental installation of Allisons in a Fortress airframe to be designated XB-38, in line with the USAAF policy of bestowing a new aircraft model number when major changes in powerplants were made. A B-17E previously obtained by Lockheed for familiarization purposes when setting up their Fortress production line at Burbank, California, was used for the conversion.

Work began in the summer of 1942 and progressed slowly and it was not until 19 May, 1943 that the XB-38 took to the air. It performed well in early tests, but had to be grounded for some days when exhaust manifold leaks were discovered. During a subsequent test, four weeks after its first flight, the XB-38 had to be abandoned by its crew because of an uncontrollable engine fire, the co-pilot being killed when his parachute failed to open; the aircraft crashed in open country. The data obtained from test flights attributed a performance comparable to that of the B-17F at similar weight. Apparently there had been no opportunity to find the service ceiling that the turbo-supercharged Allisons would give the XB-38, a calculated figure being substantially less than that of a Cyclone-powered Fortress. Plans to build two more B-38s, and the actual conversion of the Lockheed-Vega Fortress production line to the type, were dropped when it was decided that its extra weight would limit endurance and offer few, if any, advantages over the radial-engined types.

Deliveries of B-17Fs began in late May 1942 from the Boeing plant, followed by the first from the Douglas line at Long Beach in California, and later in the summer from

Lockheed-Vega. The two new factories took time to build up to a mass production schedule and by the end of the year Douglas had only delivered 85 aircraft and the Vega plant 68, whereas Seattle turned out 850. By the time the F was superseded by the G model in the late summer of 1943 the combined production from all three plants was averaging 400 aircraft a month.

Large-scale service use of the Fortress highlighted the need for many improvements or modifications to the aircraft and its equipment. Changes could not usually be introduced quickly on the production line without some disruption and as the priority was to build increasing numbers of aircraft, production flow took first place. To effect the desired changes speedily, modification centres were set up to receive aircraft after they left the factory. This policy was continued with much success until the end of hostilities, while other modification centres overseas incorporated changes desirable in particular theatres of war.

A theatre modification carried out to many B-17Es and most Fs was the installation of additional defensive firepower in the nose of the aircraft. Japanese frontal attack tactics had resulted in many hastily improvised nose gun installation in B-17Es operating in the South-west and Central Pacific battle zones. These varied from a twin-gun mount firing through an opening in the top of the Plexiglas nose, to single 0.50-in (12.7 mm) weapons in openings made by removal of the side window Plexiglas. In the light of this requirement, modification centres in the US installed a 0.50-in gun and mount to fire through an aperture made in Plexiglas observation windows on both sides of the nose. These were staggered to allow more freedom of operation in the compartment and could be used by either the bombardier or the navigator, although in practice it was usually the navigator who manned these guns. Larger gun windows later became standard, allowing a wider field of fire forward.

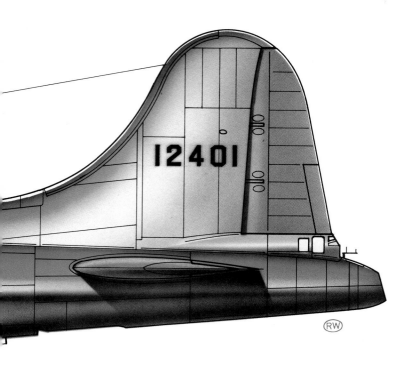

The Main Air Front

In July 1942 the USAAF began moving B-17 units to the United Kingdom with the intention of building a strategic bombing force for operations against Germany. The first unit to arrive, the 97th Bombardment Group equipped with B-17Es, commenced operations over France on 17 August. During that month other groups arrived with early B-17Fs and a few weeks later the E models were relegated to operational training duties. The two most experienced Fortress groups were sent down to French North Africa following the Allied invasion of November 1942. This left four B-17 groups and a small number of B-24s in England to conduct strategic bombing missions during the winter and following spring. Initially the high-flying bombers, usually in group formations of 18 to 21 aircraft, gave a good account of themselves against enemy fighter attacks. Bombing results, varied at first, improved when experienced crews led and sighted on target, with the rest of the formation briefed to follow their signal for bomb release. Luftwaffe fighter tactics then changed and included frontal attacks on the B-17s.

As in the Pacific, defensive armament improvements were carried out locally with one or two 0.50-in (12.7 mm) machine guns on special mounts firing through an aperture in the Plexiglas nosepiece. The 0.30-in (7.62 mm) machine gun was abandoned completely, although it continued to be specified for production B-17Fs for some time. With the field additions B-17Fs operating from England were carrying 12 or 13 0.50-in machine guns, making the aircraft the most heavily armed bomber in service with any of the belligerents. The authorized crew of a B-17F was ten men, the official change having been recorded with the introduction of the "big tail" Fortresses. Early models had six-man crews, increased to seven or eight when hostilities commenced. Of the ten-man crew, four in the forward part of the aircraft were officers – the pilot (who sat in the left-hand seat), the co-pilot and the navigator and bombardier in the nose section. The remaining men were all non-commissioned officers. The flight engineer monitored engine operation and fuel supply amongst other duties and also manned the top turret guns. The radio operator also doubled as a gunner using the machine gun in the roof of his compartment. The remaining four men were gunners manning the tail and ball turrets and the two waist positions. Fortresses used for leading formations often carried one or two additional men for special purposes. In some theatres of war only one waist gunner was carried, reducing the average crew number to nine.

In early 1943 the USAAF operating agency in the United Kingdom, the 8th Air Force, extended its bombing missions into Germany. On some operations losses were high but the Fortress performed so well, both in fighting off enemy interceptors and returning safely to base after sustaining heavy battle damage, that the USAAF were encouraged to commit larger forces to these unescorted high-altitude daylight bombing missions. In May 1943 the B-17 force in the UK was doubled and by August a total of 16 B-17F groups were in action. Two other B-17F groups scheduled for the 8th Air Force had been diverted to North Africa earlier in the year to give a total of 20 groups fully equipped with this model in action against Germany and Italy.

Douglas Long Beach plant built B-17F-30-DL of 381st BG, 535th BS, US 8th AF flying over English countryside in 1943. (USAF)

XB-40 armed with 14 Browning 0.50-in (12.7 mm) machine guns, which reduced the maximum speed to 292 mph (470 km/h) at 25,000 ft (7,620 m). (LOCKHEED)

Among new arrivals in England in the spring of 1943 was a squadron equipped with special Fortresses designated YB-40. These aircraft had extra heavy armament and armour for acting in an escort role. The intention was that they would draw the attention of intercepting fighters and afford the B-17 bomber formation they were covering some protection. A prototype, the XB-40, was converted by Lookheed-Vega from the second Boeing-built B-17F. Firepower was increased by installing twin machine guns in each waist window position, a second two-gun upper turret in the radio compartment and a remotely controlled two-gun turret in the chin position under the nose for forward defence. The chin turret, developed by Bendix and based on the earlier ventrally situated remote-control turret on some B-17Es, was operated and sighted by a gunner sitting in the bombardier's position above.

Altogether, the XB-40 had 14 0.50-in (12.7 mm) machine guns, only one more than many B-17Fs already operating from England. However, the additional power turrets plus power boost to the manipulation of both tail and waist guns, gave the XB-40 the potential of being far more effective against enemy fighters than the B-17. To feed the battery of guns more than 11,000 rounds were carried, approximately three times that specified for a B-17F. In fact, the XB-40's ammunition load could be boosted to over 17,000 rounds by utilizing the space available in the bomb-bay, as it was not intended that the XB-40 should be used for bombing.

Approved by the USAAF during the winter of 1942–43, the prototype XB-40 was followed by an order for 12 YB-40s to be used for an operational test from England. The conversions were carried out on Lockheed-Vega production B-17Fs, the modifications and equipment being similar to those on the XB-40. However, the YB-40's armament was further increased to 16 guns by the addition of two nose side guns, as the standard modification fixture on all B-17Fs. YB-40s were assigned to the 327th Bombardment Squadron at

YB-40

Modified from B-17F-10-VE
Armed with 16 × 0.50-in (12.7 mm) machine guns. Assigned to 92nd BG, 327th BS of US 8th AF based at Alconbury in England, June 1943.

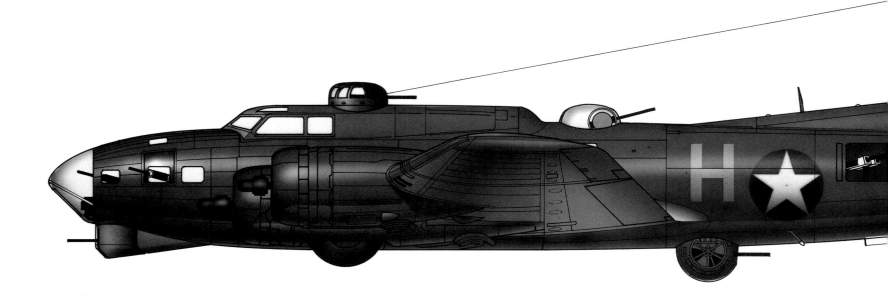

Alconbury, England, and they were despatched on a number of missions between late May and late July.

The aircraft was not a success primarily because of weight distribution; its flying characteristics were poor because of a shift in the centre of gravity towards the rear of the aircraft which made control at high altitudes and formation flying difficult. Moreover, once the B-17s had dropped their loads, the YB-40s were unable to keep up with them, as they were still laden with ammunition and were already a ton heavier than a B-17F empty. With such flight problems the YB-40s could afford little help to a Fortress formation under attack – indeed, it appeared to be more of a liability than an asset as Fortress formations sometimes had to reduce power to stay with them. Meanwhile a further 11 YB-40s had been ordered, but as far as is known only seven were completed before the USAAF decided to abandon the type.

While modification centres made many changes to Fortresses before they reached combat units, changes were constantly effected on the production line. To ease identification of variations in a model, a system of production block numbers had been introduced in 1942 whereby most changes made on a production line were identified. As the three B-17 factories did not always produce identical models with the same equipment at the same time, block numbers were further identified by code letters distinguishing the manufacturer. The B-17F received 26 different block changes at Seattle, 17 at Long Beach and 11 at Burbank. The majority of changes involved internal equipment, usually the substitution of improved types.

The most important and major improvement to the B-17F model came with the B-17F-80-BO, B-17F-25-DL and B-17F-30-VE when two additional fuel tanks of 270 US gal (1,022 ltr) capacity each were placed in each outer wing. This raised the total built-in tankage of the B-17 from 1,730 US gal capacity to 2,810 (6,550 to 10,636 ltr), increasing the stated range from 1,300 miles to 2,200 (2,092 to 3,540 km) at

comparative loadings and settings. In the high altitude operations conducted over Europe the additional fuel gave an extra 3 hr endurance. However, the increased fuel load, by adding another 6,360 lb (2,885 kg) to the B-17F's gross weight, reduced the rate of climb, so that it took 38 min to reach 20,000 ft (6,100 m) compared with 25 min in the earlier B-17Fs. The additional tanks became popularly known as "Tokyo Tanks" because it was said that they would enable a B-17 to make a one-way trip to Tokyo. Although bestowing increased range the Tokyo Tanks came to be seen as something of a mixed blessing. Fuel fumes collecting in the outer wing sections were vulnerable to incendiary ammunition by explosion and fire hazarding the bomber. It was some time before a system of natural air venting was installed in Fortress wingtips to reduce this risk.

As previously stated, the B-17F could absorb a considerable amount of battle damage and survive. The flying qualities of the aircraft were so good that it could lose one side of a tailplane or considerable areas of fin and rudder and still return to make a safe landing. Aircraft often returned with one or two engines out of action and sometimes with a main fuel tank burned out. Damage to hydraulic systems forced a number of wheels-up or "belly" landings and provided the ball turret was jettisoned and the tailwheel lowered, the damage to the airframe in landing could be slight and soon repaired. If the ball turret remained in place and the tailwheel was not extended, the turret suspension frame was usually forced through the base of the fuselage causing it to distort. In such instances economic repair was not possible and the aircraft was written off.

Service Troubles

The Fortress was a fairly viceless aircraft, but operation in the rarefied air of the sub-stratosphere put considerable strain on both crew and aircraft. Engine temperatures ran to near critical limits and had to be constantly monitored. The sub-zero temperatures caused equipment to seize up with frost, particularly in the early days of the offensive before the art of keeping moisture from gun and bomb rack mechanisms was more practised. A major problem was freezing of the hydraulically actuated turbo-supercharger regulators. To prevent this they had to be worked at frequent intervals. Sluggish operation of the turbos was a frequent complaint from pilots. Another problem encountered, whether caused by enemy action or mechanical failure, was the inability to feather a propeller. It was found that when an engine was damaged or failed, loss of fluid would not allow hydraulic adjustment of the propeller blades to a position where the propeller would remain stationary and not windmill. In consequence idling propellers could pick up a low turning rate causing such severe vibration that the safety of the aircraft was in jeopardy. A number of aircraft were lost both directly and indirectly to this cause; it was some months before the extent of this trouble was realized and modifications were introduced.

Crew discomfort was considerable: the heavy clothing needed to keep out the cold impeded movement about

US general purpose bomb

Total weight: 500 lb (227 kg)
Explosive weight: 255 lb (116 kg)
Length overall: 4 ft 11⅕ in (150.3 cm)
Fin width: 1 ft 7 in (48.1 cm)

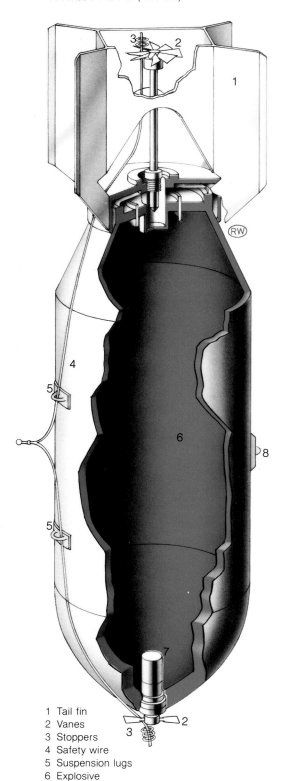

1 Tail fin
2 Vanes
3 Stoppers
4 Safety wire
5 Suspension lugs
6 Explosive
7 Exploder container
8 Lug

US semi-armour piercing bomb

Total weight: 1,000 lb (454 kg)
Explosive weight: 310 lb (141 kg)
Length overall: 5 ft 10⅖ in (178.8 cm)
Fin width: 1 ft 8⁷⁄₁₀ in (52.6 cm)

1 Tail fin
2 Vane
3 Stopper
4 Safety lug
5 Suspension lugs
6 Explosive
7 Exploder containers
8 Lug

US armour piercing bomb

Total weight: 1,000 lb (454 kg)
Explosive weight: 145 lb (66 kg)
Length overall: 6 ft 1 in (185.4 cm)
Fin width: 1 ft 4⅔ in (42.2 cm)

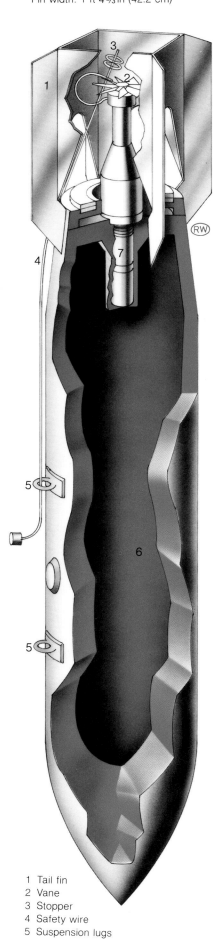

1 Tail fin
2 Vane
3 Stopper
4 Safety wire
5 Suspension lugs
6 Explosive
7 Exploder container

the aircraft; frostbite was always a risk if a bare hand was exposed; and wearing an oxygen mask, sometimes for six hours at a stretch, was not pleasant. Long flights under these conditions were very fatiguing. A failure in the oxygen supply to any crewman could quickly cause unconsciousness and sometimes death.

A major criticism of the Fortress was its small bomb-load in comparison with some other four-engined bombers. With the use of underwing racks the B-17 could, and did on occasions, lift operational loads of 12,000 lb (5,440 kg) whereas its normal internal load averaged between 4,000 and 5,000 lb (1,814 and 2,270 kg). The maximum load that a B-17F could carry was 9,600 lb (4,355 kg), made up of six 1,600 lb (726 kg) armour-piercing bombs, a load that was rarely carried and could only be used on short-range targets. This compared favourably with the maximum for a B-24 Liberator of 12,800 lb (5,806 kg) under similar conditions. A marked contrast was in the actual average operational tonnages carried by RAF Lancasters and 8th Air Force Fortresses to the same target area – 10 and 4 tons respectively. The B-17's limiting factors were the size and construction of the bomb-bay. The aircraft had been designed as a medium bomber. Not only did bomb-bay size limit the overall tonnage carried, but it also restricted individual bombs to a 2,000 lb (907 kg) type maximum. On the face of it, the USAAF's method of taking 4,000 lb (1,814 kg) of bombs to a target appeared highly extravagant in manpower, materials and fuel.

The USAAF argued that the really important factor was the actual destruction wrought at the target, and that their form of precision bombing had a much greater chance of success than the RAF's area bombing at night. Indeed, during the summer and autumn of 1943 8th Air Force Fortresses were able to cause considerable destruction at a number of German war plants. The success of their operations was evident by the efforts the enemy made to thwart the raids, diverting fighters from the Eastern Front and causing losses which threatened to make these daylight raids prohibitive. Priorities then shifted to the introduction of long-range fighters for escort but these did not become available in substantial numbers until the early months of 1944. Meanwhile a notable improvement in the Fortress's forward firepower was made. Efforts to develop a power turret had been concentrated on the Bendix remotely controlled unit which appeared in pre-production form on the YB-40s. Production units became available in late July 1943 and were initially fitted to the last 86 Douglas-built B-17Fs. These later became B-17Gs, the designation used for all chin-turreted Fortresses from Boeing and Lockheed-Vega production. They became the major Fortress production model with the three plants jointly turning out a total of 8,680 during nearly two years of production.

B-17Gs were really an ongoing production development of the B-17Fs, the new designation simply acknowledging the fitting of the chin turret; no other major changes followed worthy of recognition. Significant changes in functioning and performance would follow during the course of production but from a pilot's point of view the early

A bombardier checks 100 lb (45 kg) bombs in a B-17 bomb bay. (USAF via G. S. WILLIAMS)

G models were simply late B-17Fs with chin turrets. The new turret was operated by the bombardier through controls on a column which folded back against the starboard side of the nose, so as not to impede his bomb-sighting activities. The computing sight was suspended from the top of the fuselage and projected just inside the Plexiglas nosepiece. There was some criticism of the rate of traverse of these guns and also of their limitations in the field of fire. Fortress manufacturing plants omitted the nose side or cheek guns when the chin turret was introduced. In combat theatres this installation was reinstated for navigators' use and subsequently cheek guns were reintroduced on the production lines.

The first B-17Gs arrived in combat theatres during September 1943 and were soon in action. The B-17F soldiered on for another year, although attrition was such that by the early spring of 1944 groups that had been equipped with the model had only about a half-dozen remaining. The 8th Air Force strength was built up during the winter of 1943–44 to 40 bombing groups, 21 equipped with the B-17 and the remainder with the B-24. Subsequently five B-24 groups were

Angles of defensive fire in B-17G

1 Chin turret: 2 × 0.50-in (12.7 mm) guns
2 Starboard cheek gun: 1 × 0.50-in (12.7 mm)
3 Port cheek gun: 1 × 0.50-in (12.7 mm)
4 Upper turret: 2 × 0.50-in (12.7 mm) guns
5 Lower ball turret: 2 × 0.50-in (12.7 mm) guns
6 Starboard waist gun: 1 × 0.50-in (12.7 mm)
7 Radio compartment gun: 1 × 0.50-in (12.7 mm)
8 Port cheek gun: 1 × 0.50-in (12.7 mm)
9 Tail turret: 2 × 0.50-in (12.7 mm) guns

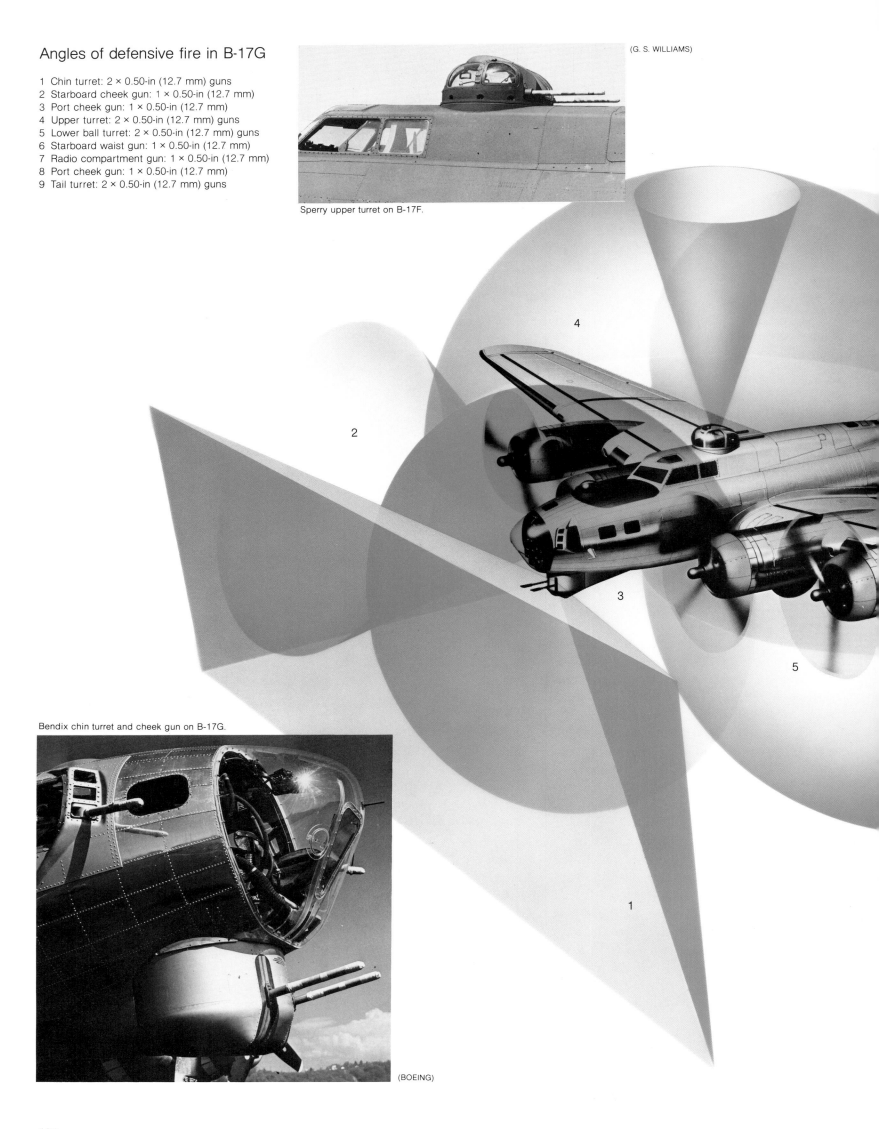

(G. S. WILLIAMS)

Sperry upper turret on B-17F.

Bendix chin turret and cheek gun on B-17G.

(BOEING)

7

9

8

46868

338660

Ball type "Cheyenne" tail gun turret developed by the United Airlines bomber modification centre. It was fitted on late production B-17Gs.

(BOEING)

Sperry ball turret.

(G. S. WILLIAMS)

B-17G Specification

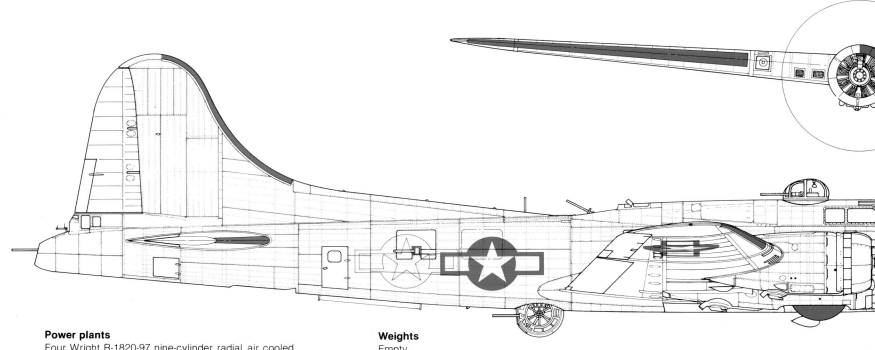

Power plants

Four Wright R-1820-97 nine-cylinder radial air cooled
turbo-supercharged engines
  : 1,200 hp each at 25,000 ft (7,620 m)
  : 1,380 hp in "war emergency" power at 25,000 ft (7,620 m).
Hamilton Standard three-bladed hydromatic variable pitch
constant speed fully-feathering propellers
Diameter
  : 11 ft 7 in (3.53 m)
Total fuel in the wings
  : 2,810 US gal (2,340 Imp. gal. 10,637 ltr)
Provision for two overload tanks in bomb-bay
  : 820 US gal (682 Imp. gal. 3,104 ltr)

Performance

Max speed
  : 287 mph (462 km/h) at 25,000 ft (7,620 m)
Max speed in "war emergency" power
  : 302 mph (486 km/h) at 25,000 ft (7,620 m)
Cruising speed
  : 182 mph (293 km/h) at 10,000 ft (3,050 m)
Most economical climbing speed
  : 140 mph (225 km/h)
Max permissible diving speed
  : 305 mph (491 km/h)
Take-off speed
  : 110-115 mph (177-185 km/h)
Landing speed
  : 90 mph (145 km/h)
Time to climb to 20,000 ft (6,100 m)
  : 37.0 min
Service ceiling
  : 35,600 ft (10,850 m)
Take-off distance
  : 3,400 ft (1,040 m)
Landing distance
  : 2,900 ft (880 m)
Range with 6,000 lb (2,722 kg) bomb-load at 10,000 ft (3,050 m)
  : 2,000 mls (3,220 km) at 182 mph (293 km/h)
Max range (ferry) at 10,000 ft (3,050 m)
  : 3,400 mls (5,470 km) at 180 mph (290 km/h)

Weights

Empty
  : 36,135 lb (16,391 kg)
Normal gross
  : 55,000 lb (24,950 kg)
Max take-off
  : 65,500 lb (29,710 kg)

Armament

Bendix chin turret
  : Two 0.50-in (12.7 mm) Browning M2 machine guns with
    365 rounds each
Sperry upper turret
  : Two similar guns with 375 rounds each
Sperry ball turret
  : Two similar guns with 500 rounds each
Tail turret
  : Two similar guns with 500 rounds each
Cheek gun positions
  : Two similar guns with 610 rounds in all
Radio compartment (removed from later aircraft)
  : One similar gun
Waist gun positions
  : Two similar guns with 600 rounds each

Bombs

Normal max six 1,600 lb (726 kg) and two 4,000 lb (1,814 kg)
  : 9,600 lb (4,355 kg) in all
  : 8,000 lb (3,629 kg) in all

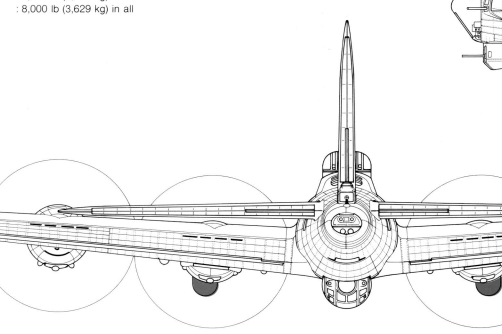

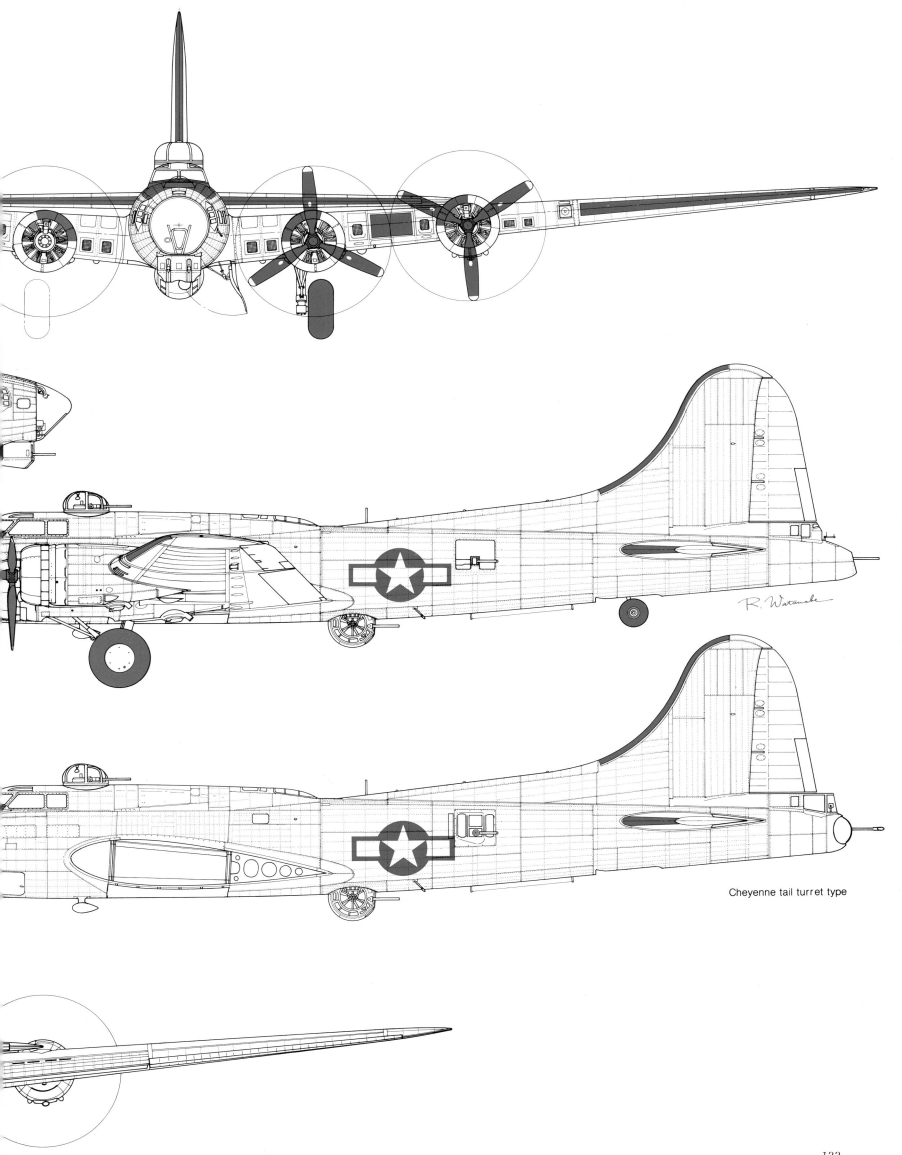

Cheyenne tail turret type

R. Watanabe

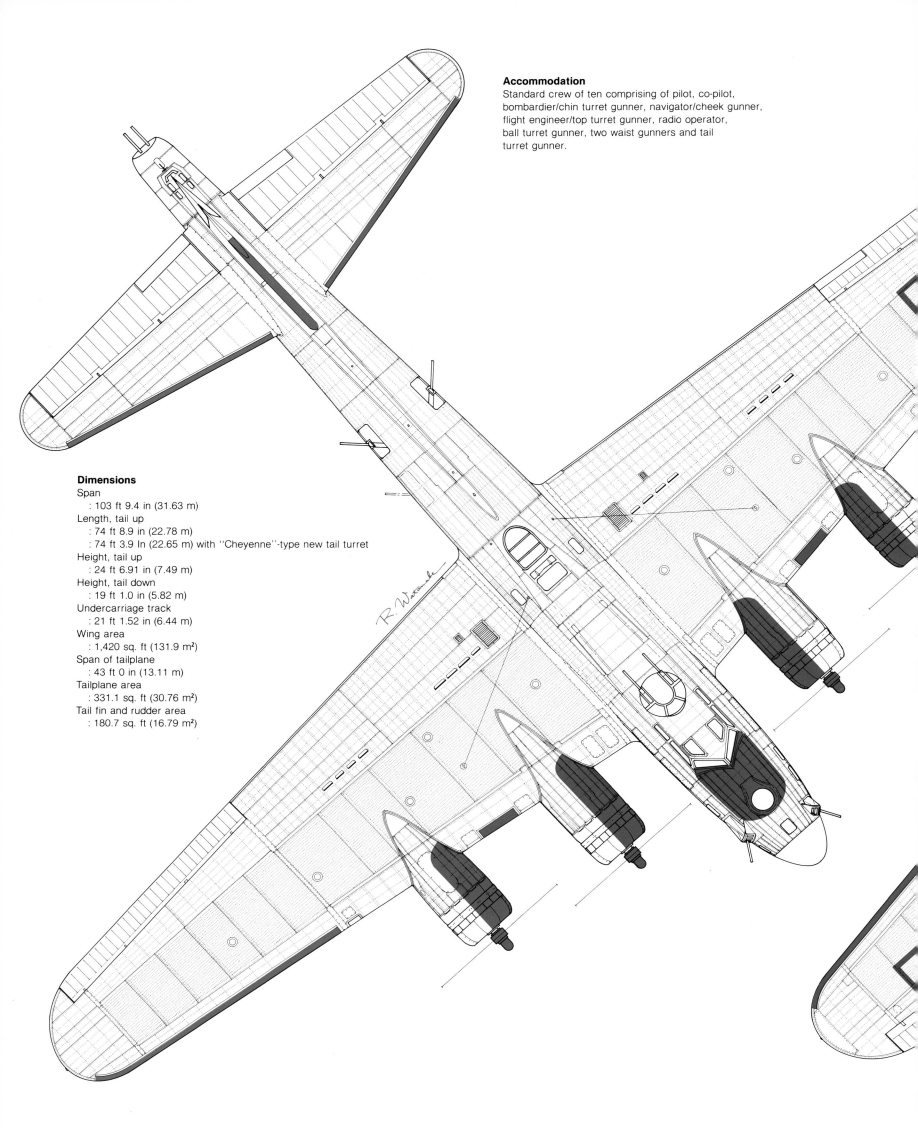

Accommodation
Standard crew of ten comprising of pilot, co-pilot, bombardier/chin turret gunner, navigator/cheek gunner, flight engineer/top turret gunner, radio operator, ball turret gunner, two waist gunners and tail turret gunner.

Dimensions
Span
  : 103 ft 9.4 in (31.63 m)
Length, tail up
  : 74 ft 8.9 in (22.78 m)
  : 74 ft 3.9 In (22.65 m) with ''Cheyenne''-type new tail turret
Height, tail up
  : 24 ft 6.91 in (7.49 m)
Height, tail down
  : 19 ft 1.0 in (5.82 m)
Undercarriage track
  : 21 ft 1.52 in (6.44 m)
Wing area
  : 1,420 sq. ft (131.9 m²)
Span of tailplane
  : 43 ft 0 in (13.11 m)
Tailplane area
  : 331.1 sq. ft (30.76 m²)
Tail fin and rudder area
  : 180.7 sq. ft (16.79 m²)

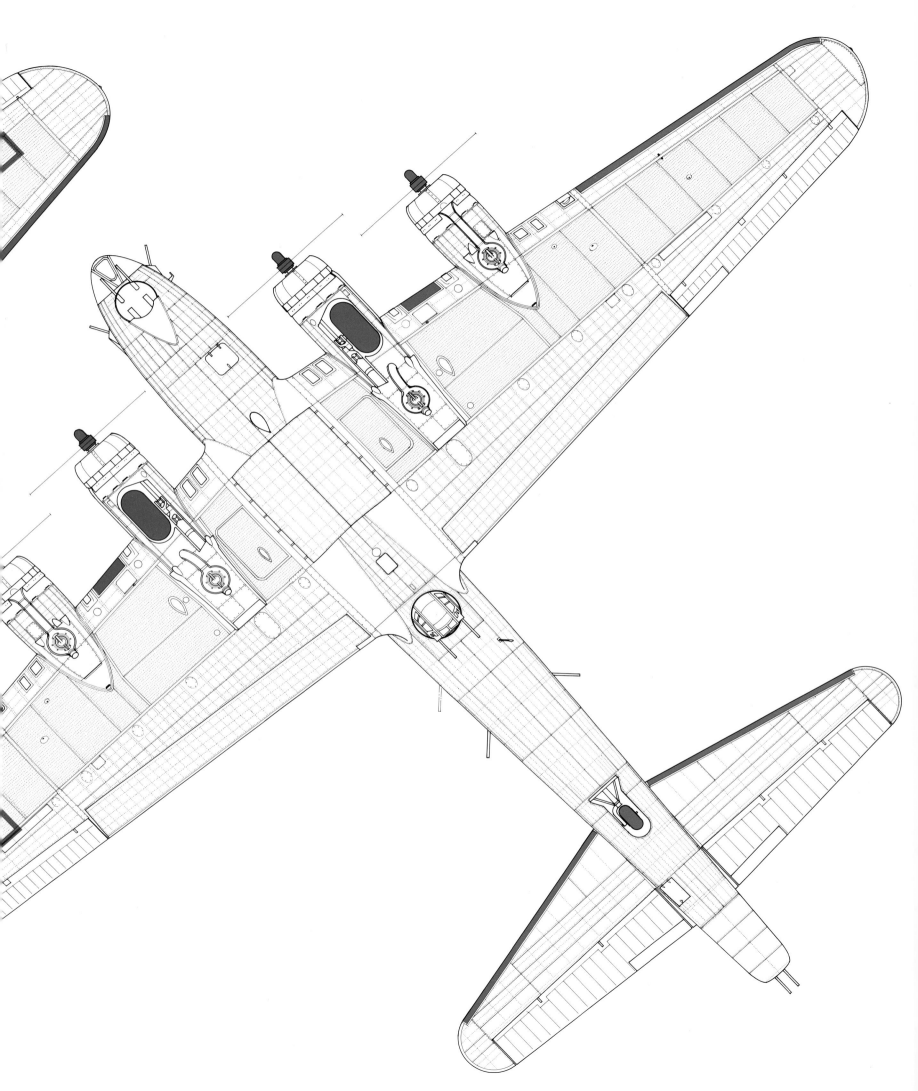

converted to the B-17 to make a total of 26 Fortress groups, which remained in England until the end of the war. Additional units, equivalent to the strength of another combat group, engaged in special activities with the B-17.

In the Mediterranean area a new air force, the 15th, was formed in late 1943 to conduct strategic bombing operations from bases in southern Italy. To the nucleus formed by the four B-17 and two B-24 groups already in that war zone, 15 heavy bomber groups originally earmarked for the 8th Air Force were added to bring the 15th's total to 21, of which six were equipped with B-17s. The Fortress had been completely withdrawn from operations in Pacific war zones in the autumn of 1943 and numbers had been small for many months previous.

There were a number of armament feature improvements during B-17G production and the first during the winter of 1943–44 was the replacement of the Sperry top-turret by a Bendix model. The new turret had a higher profile that looked rather ungainly in comparison with the neat Sperry, but it allowed the gunner better visibility and response to control. Trouble was experienced with fires in these turrets, eventually traced to fraying electrical wiring and oxygen lines. During operational missions the waist posi-

tions were open so that the gunners in the rear of the aircraft were exposed to the icy blast of the slipstream. Also, being directly opposite, the two gunners frequently bumped each other, sometimes dislodging an oxygen connection with serious consequences. Moving the starboard position forward removed this risk and gave each man more room to manoeuvre. Plexiglas coverings were introduced into production and in early 1944 modification centres began installing a framed type cover at waist positions, also fitted to many older B-17s in combat areas.

The radio room gun hatch was also open during combat missions and modification centres devised a change so that this could remain screened with the machine gun installed. A similar installation was made on production with the G-45-DL from Douglas, the G-55-VE from Lockheed-Vega and in the G-80-BO at Boeing. Another important armament change was planned at the same time as the enclosed radio room gun position. This was the "Cheyenne" tail turret, so called because it had originally been developed by the Cheyenne, Wyoming, B-17 modification centre.

The original B-17 tail position featured a tunnel opening at the extremity of the fuselage through which the guns projected, their traverse being restricted to about 30° in

B-17Gs on the assembly line at Boeing plant.   (BOEING)

136

B-17G-20-DL (the first of this block) of 95th BG, US 8th AF heads for a target at Bremen, Germany. (USAF)

both the horizontal and vertical planes. The sighting of these weapons was by a ring and bead placed just outside the gunner's armoured glass panel and linked to the gun movement by a series of cables and pulleys. Both in layout and operation there had been need for improvement. The Cheyenne conversion gave the gunner a reflector sight and better visibility by enlarging the window area in his position, and a greater field of fire for the guns which were brought closer to him in a pivoting cupola. These turrets were also fitted to a number of older Fortresses at repair depots in combat zones.

By the summer of 1944 the provision of long-range fighter escort had made attacks by Luftwaffe interceptors on 8th and 15th Air Force bombers more the exception than the rule. Many B-17 gunners completed their tour of 30 or more combat missions without ever firing their guns in action. By this time factory, modification centre and battle zone additions to the B-17 plus the maximum fuel, bomb and ammunition loads and other paraphernalia ranging from extra radio equipment to body armour, meant that many of these bombers grossed as much as 30 tons at take-off. The penalty of this overload was reduced range, marred control and engine strain. Concern at the situation led to a reduction in defensive armament in view of the lessened risk of enemy fighter interference.

The value of the radio room gun had always been in question. Here the gunner's outlook was poor and he was rarely able to see the approach of an enemy aircraft; his contribution to defence was usually a hasty burst of fire as an enemy fighter flashed by. The use of this gun position was discontinued by combat groups in Europe and it was eventually omitted on the B-17 production lines. Reducing the quantity of ammunition carried was another measure to cut down the gross weight – during the great air battles of the previous

autumn and winter as many as 10,000 rounds were being carried on some Fortresses. The lessened fighter activity also reduced the number of waist gunners per aircraft from two to one. In the last few months of the war, when enemy fighter attacks were predominantly from the rear quarter (sometimes by fast closing jet aircraft) limited evasive action by the bombers was often considered to be more effective than defensive armament.

In the 8th Air Force an experimental programme of further armament reductions was introduced to lessen weight and drag in order to enhance performance and manoeuvrability. In some units no waist guns or gunners were carried, in others the ball or chin turrets were removed. One group removed chin and ball turrets and cheek and waist guns, increasing top speed by over 20 mph (32.2 km/hr) and giving benefits in rate of climb and endurance. The top speed of a standard B-17G was officially given as 278 mph (447 km/hr). Top speeds, however, had little bearing on the combat performance of the B-17s as the mode of operation entailed flying formations where a specified cruising speed had to be maintained and this varied from 165 to 180 mph (266 to 290 km/hr) IAS (Indicated Air Speed).

With the demise of the German fighter defences came an increase in anti-aircraft artillery fire against the USAAF bomber formations. Flak weapons with controlling radars had been developed to a point where 88 mm and 105 mm shells could be exploded at a selected proximity with great accuracy even 6 miles (9.7 km) up. Some targets were defended by as many as 300 flak guns and the barrages they put up were formidable. Countermeasures were difficult although some success was obtained in jamming the gun-laying radars and by frequent bomber formation deviations in course and altitude. A large amount of armour plate had been added for crew and component protection during the produc-

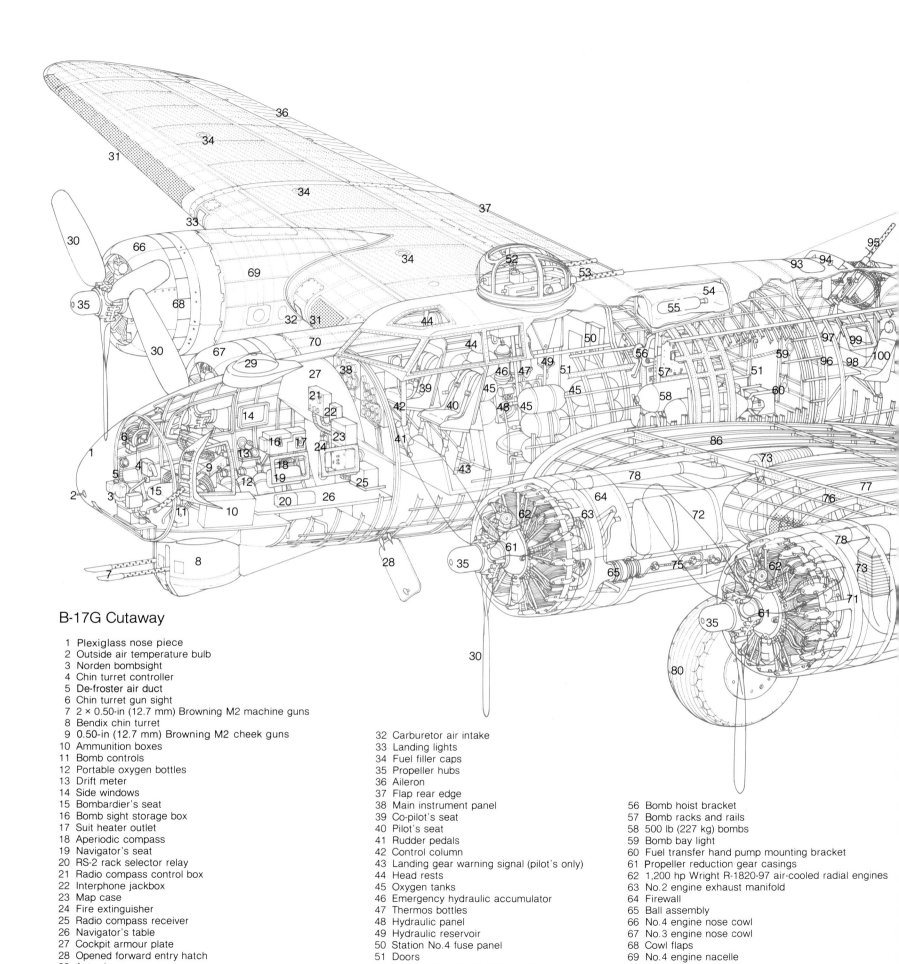

B-17G Cutaway

1 Plexiglass nose piece
2 Outside air temperature bulb
3 Norden bombsight
4 Chin turret controller
5 De-froster air duct
6 Chin turret gun sight
7 2 × 0.50-in (12.7 mm) Browning M2 machine guns
8 Bendix chin turret
9 0.50-in (12.7 mm) Browning M2 cheek guns
10 Ammunition boxes
11 Bomb controls
12 Portable oxygen bottles
13 Drift meter
14 Side windows
15 Bombardier's seat
16 Bomb sight storage box
17 Suit heater outlet
18 Aperiodic compass
19 Navigator's seat
20 RS-2 rack selector relay
21 Radio compass control box
22 Interphone jackbox
23 Map case
24 Fire extinguisher
25 Radio compass receiver
26 Navigator's table
27 Cockpit armour plate
28 Opened forward entry hatch
29 Astrodome
30 Hamilton standard hydromatic constant-speed propellers
   (paddle bladed type)
31 Wing leading-edge de-icer boots

32 Carburetor air intake
33 Landing lights
34 Fuel filler caps
35 Propeller hubs
36 Aileron
37 Flap rear edge
38 Main instrument panel
39 Co-pilot's seat
40 Pilot's seat
41 Rudder pedals
42 Control column
43 Landing gear warning signal (pilot's only)
44 Head rests
45 Oxygen tanks
46 Emergency hydraulic accumulator
47 Thermos bottles
48 Hydraulic panel
49 Hydraulic reservoir
50 Station No.4 fuse panel
51 Doors
52 Sperry upper turret (later type)
53 2 × 0.50-in (12.7 mm) Browning machine guns
54 Left-hand life raft
55 Life raft CO₂ inflation bottle

56 Bomb hoist bracket
57 Bomb racks and rails
58 500 lb (227 kg) bombs
59 Bomb bay light
60 Fuel transfer hand pump mounting bracket
61 Propeller reduction gear casings
62 1,200 hp Wright R-1820-97 air-cooled radial engines
63 No.2 engine exhaust manifold
64 Firewall
65 Ball assembly
66 No.4 engine nose cowl
67 No.3 engine nose cowl
68 Cowl flaps
69 No.4 engine nacelle
70 No.3 engine nacelle
71 No.1 engine exhaust manifold
72 Oil tank (36.9 US gal/30.7 Imp. gal/140 ltr)
73 Intercooler

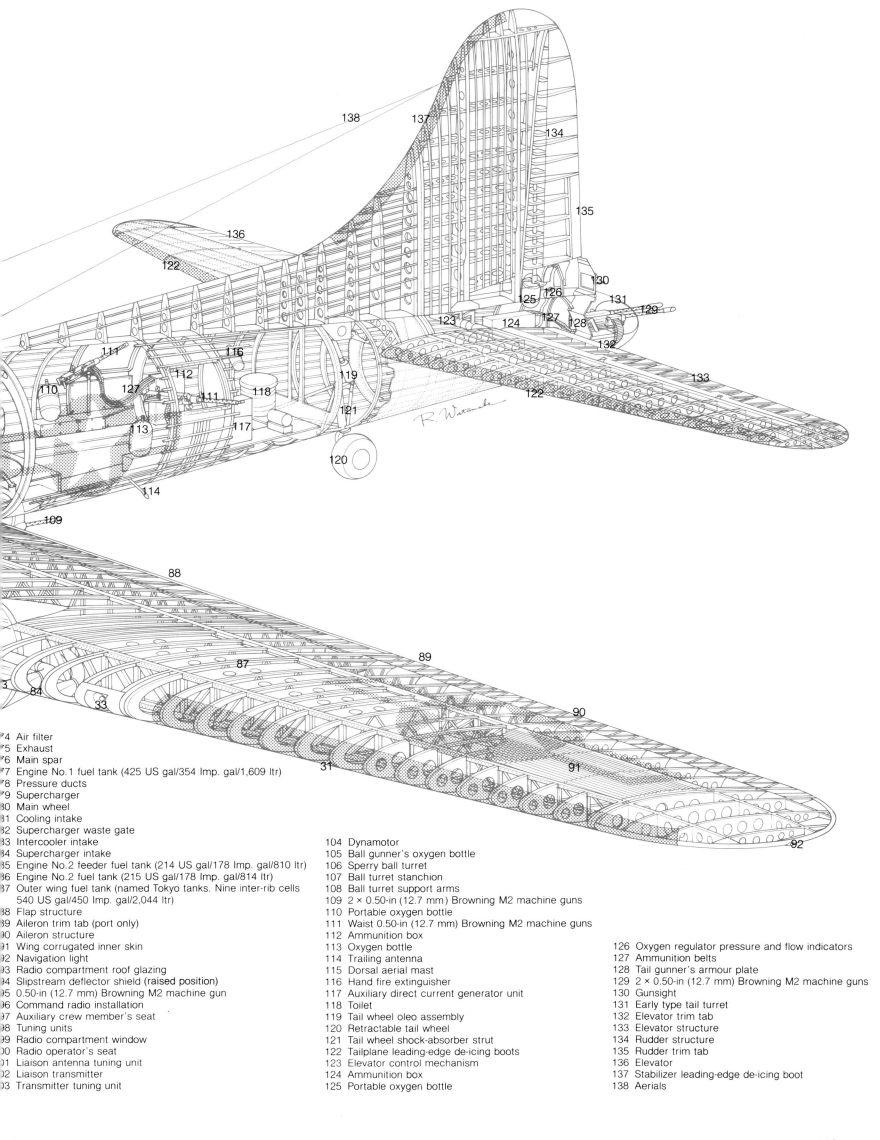

74 Air filter
75 Exhaust
76 Main spar
77 Engine No.1 fuel tank (425 US gal/354 Imp. gal/1,609 ltr)
78 Pressure ducts
79 Supercharger
80 Main wheel
81 Cooling intake
82 Supercharger waste gate
83 Intercooler intake
84 Supercharger intake
85 Engine No.2 feeder fuel tank (214 US gal/178 Imp. gal/810 ltr)
86 Engine No.2 fuel tank (215 US gal/178 Imp. gal/814 ltr)
87 Outer wing fuel tank (named Tokyo tanks. Nine inter-rib cells
540 US gal/450 Imp. gal/2,044 ltr)
88 Flap structure
89 Aileron trim tab (port only)
90 Aileron structure
91 Wing corrugated inner skin
92 Navigation light
93 Radio compartment roof glazing
94 Slipstream deflector shield (raised position)
95 0.50-in (12.7 mm) Browning M2 machine gun
96 Command radio installation
97 Auxiliary crew member's seat
98 Tuning units
99 Radio compartment window
100 Radio operator's seat
101 Liaison antenna tuning unit
102 Liaison transmitter
103 Transmitter tuning unit

104 Dynamotor
105 Ball gunner's oxygen bottle
106 Sperry ball turret
107 Ball turret stanchion
108 Ball turret support arms
109 2 × 0.50-in (12.7 mm) Browning M2 machine guns
110 Portable oxygen bottle
111 Waist 0.50-in (12.7 mm) Browning M2 machine guns
112 Ammunition box
113 Oxygen bottle
114 Trailing antenna
115 Dorsal aerial mast
116 Hand fire extinguisher
117 Auxiliary direct current generator unit
118 Toilet
119 Tail wheel oleo assembly
120 Retractable tail wheel
121 Tail wheel shock-absorber strut
122 Tailplane leading-edge de-icing boots
123 Elevator control mechanism
124 Ammunition box
125 Portable oxygen bottle

126 Oxygen regulator pressure and flow indicators
127 Ammunition belts
128 Tail gunner's armour plate
129 2 × 0.50-in (12.7 mm) Browning M2 machine guns
130 Gunsight
131 Early type tail turret
132 Elevator trim tab
133 Elevator structure
134 Rudder structure
135 Rudder trim tab
136 Elevator
137 Stabilizer leading-edge de-icing boot
138 Aerials

B-17Gs of 99th and 301st BG, US 15th AF release their bombs on the Luftwaffe Me 262 jet fighter base at Lechfeld in southern Germany on 12 September, 1944. (USAF)

tion development of the B-17 but with the change in the form of opposition encountered much of the armour plate was removed at crew positions and so-called flak curtains substituted. These consisted of a series of laminated plates in canvas designed to check low velocity shell splinters.

From a pilot's viewpoint one of the most important improvements to the B-17 was the change from hydraulic to electrically operated turbo-supercharger regulators. The sluggish operation and unreliability of the hydraulic regulator system caused power setting difficulties and added to the problems of flying close formations. The failure of a hydraulic regulator could also precipitate the malfunction of a super-charger. The electrical system gave immediate turbo response, cut down failures and greatly eased control problems in the cockpit. The electric regulators were first installed on production blocks G-10-BO from Boeing, G-15-DL from Douglas, and G-5-VE from Lockheed-Vega. This change was followed a few weeks later by the introduction of a new model turbo-supercharger, the B-22, which through increased turbine speed gave better high altitude performance and improved the B-17's critical altitude. The new turbo came with the G-35-BO, G-35-DL and G-25-VE blocks.

Radar-carrying Models

The main obstacle to high altitude precision bombing was the European weather. Cloud frequently obscured primary targets, forcing bombers to attack targets of opportunity in place of planned targets and sometimes to return with their bombs. To alleviate such frustration, the USAAF turned to the British-developed ground-scanning radar used by RAF night bombers. In the latter half of 1943 twelve installations of this device, known as H2S, were made in B-17Fs of the 8th Air Force. The scanning antenna was installed under the nose of the aircraft and covered with a plastic blister reminiscent in shape of the original Model 299 gun blisters. From late September 1943 these radar Fortresses were used as pathfinders for bomber formations, the technique being to fly one in the leading position, the other bombers dropping their bombs on its release signal.

Fortresses equipped with a US-developed version of H2S, designated H2X, commenced operations in November 1943. The first 11 were conversions on Douglas-built B-17G types; the radar scanner, which was partly retractable and

B-17E "Little Skunkface" of 97th BG, US 8th AF in 1942.

Power units
4 × Wright R-1820-65 engines
: 1,200 hp each at 25,000 ft (7,620 m)

Performance
Max speed
: 317 mph (510 km/h) at 15,000 ft (7,620 m)
Cruising speed
: 195—223 mph (314—359 km/h)
Service ceiling
: 36,600 ft (11,160 m)
Range with 4,000 lb (1,814 kg) bombs
at 15,000 ft (4,570 m)
: 2,000 mls (3,220 km) at 224 mph (360 km/h)

Armament
8 × 0.50-in (12.7 mm) and
1 × 0.30-in (7.62 mm) machine guns
14 × 300 lb (136 kg) bombs (max)

Weights
Empty
: 32,250 lb (14,630 kg)
Max take-off
: 53,000 lb (24,040 kg)

Dimensions
Span
: 103 ft 9.4 in (31.63 m)
Length, tail up
: 73 ft 9.7 in (22.50 m)
Height, tail down
: 19 ft 1 in (5.82 m)
Wing area
: 1,420 sq. ft (131.9 m²)

Crew
10

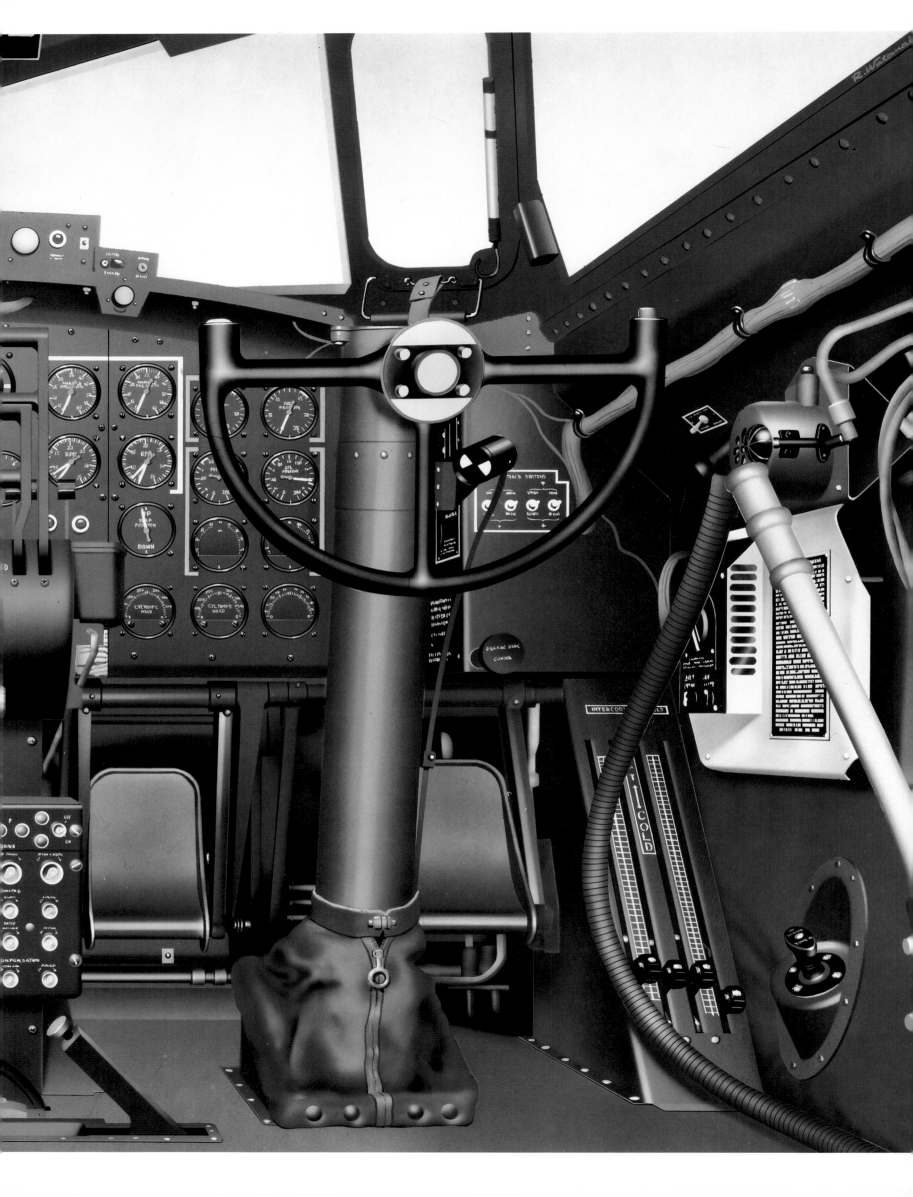

B-17D of the 11th BG, US Army Air Corps, captured by Japanese forces in the Philippines, January, 1942.

Power units
4 × Wright R-1820-65 engines
  : 1,200 hp each at 25,000 ft (7,620 m)

Performance
Max speed
  : 323 mph (520 km/h) at 25,000 ft (7,620 m)
Cruising speed
  : 227 mph (365 km/h) at 25,000 ft (7,620 m)
Service ceiling
  : 37,000 ft (11,280 m)
Range with 4,000 lb (1,814 kg) bombs at 2,500 ft (7,620 m)
  : 2,000 mls (3,220 km) at 250 mph (402 km/h)

Armament
6 × 50-in (12.7 mm) and 1 × 0.30-in (7.62 mm) machine guns
8 × 600 lb (272 kg) bombs (max)

Weights
Empty
  : 30,600 lb (13,880 kg)
Max take-off
  : 49,650 lb (22,520 kg)

Dimensions
Span
  : 103 ft 9.38 in (31.63 m)
Length, tail up
  : 67 ft 10.56 in (20.69 m)
Height, tail down
  : 15 ft 4.5 in (4.69 m)
Wing area
  : 1,420 sq. ft (131.9 m²)

Crew
8

B-17F-25-DL ''Winsome Winn'' of 381st BG, 534th BS, US 8th AF in July, 1943.

Power units
4 × Wright R-1820-97 engines
  : 1,200 hp each at 25,000 ft (7,620 m)
  1,380 hp in ''war emergency'' power at 25,000 ft (7,620 m)

Performance
Max speed
  : 314 mph (505 km/h) in ''war emergency'' power
Cruising speed
  : 200 mph (322 km/h) at 10,000 ft (3,050 m)
Service ceiling
  : 37,500 ft (11,430 m)
Range with 6,000 lb (2,722 kg) bombs at 10,000 ft (3,050 m)
  : 1,300 mls (2,090 km) at 200 mph (322 km/h) (Tokyo Tanks)
  : 3,200 mls (3,540 km) at 200 mph (322 km/h) (Tokyo Tanks)

Armament
11 × 0.50-in (12.7 mm) machine guns
8 × 1,000 lb (454 kg) bombs (max)

Weights
Empty
  : 34,000 lb (15,420 kg)
Max take-off
  : 65,500 lb (29,710 kg)

Dimensions
Span
  : 103 ft 9.4 in (31.63 m)
Length, tail up
  : 74 ft 8.9 in (22.78 m)
Height, tail down
  : 19 ft 1 in (5.82 m)
Wing area
  : 1,420 sq. ft (131.9 m²)

Crew
10

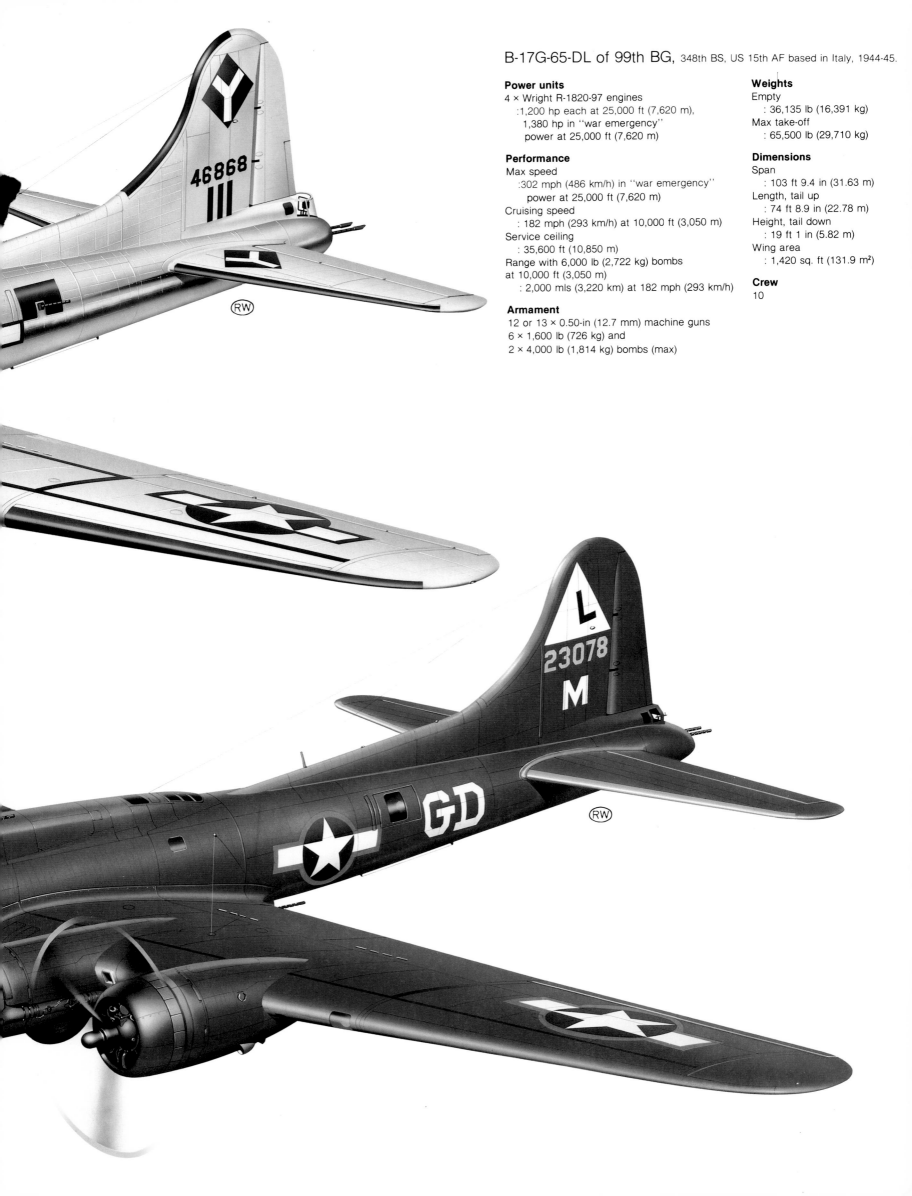

B-17G-65-DL of 99th BG, 348th BS, US 15th AF based in Italy, 1944-45.

Power units
4 × Wright R-1820-97 engines
  :1,200 hp each at 25,000 ft (7,620 m),
  1,380 hp in ''war emergency''
  power at 25,000 ft (7,620 m)

Performance
Max speed
  :302 mph (486 km/h) in ''war emergency''
  power at 25,000 ft (7,620 m)
Cruising speed
  : 182 mph (293 km/h) at 10,000 ft (3,050 m)
Service ceiling
  : 35,600 ft (10,850 m)
Range with 6,000 lb (2,722 kg) bombs
at 10,000 ft (3,050 m)
  : 2,000 mls (3,220 km) at 182 mph (293 km/h)

Armament
12 or 13 × 0.50-in (12.7 mm) machine guns
6 × 1,600 lb (726 kg) and
2 × 4,000 lb (1,814 kg) bombs (max)

Weights
Empty
  : 36,135 lb (16,391 kg)
Max take-off
  : 65,500 lb (29,710 kg)

Dimensions
Span
  : 103 ft 9.4 in (31.63 m)
Length, tail up
  : 74 ft 8.9 in (22.78 m)
Height, tail down
  : 19 ft 1 in (5.82 m)
Wing area
  : 1,420 sq. ft (131.9 m²)

Crew
10

covered by a plastic dome, was positioned directly behind the chin turret. This arrangement caused very cramped conditions in the nose compartment, particularly for the bombardier. Meanwhile, experiments in the US showed that the H2X antenna could be moved further back under the aircraft without spoiling signal transmission or reception. All other H2X-equipped B-17Gs, the first of which arrived in England in late January 1944, had the scanner antenna in a retractable radome placed in the well normally occupied by the ball turret. The radar operator and the display screen (or scope) were situated in the radio room of these aircraft. Initially assigned to the special Pathfinder Group, as more H2X B-17s became available, special units were set up in combat bomber groups. Eventually every B-17 station had a small number of these radar-equipped aircraft for leading missions. The 15th Air Force in Italy also established H2X B-17 units during 1944.

Another form of radar bombing, known as Oboe, was tried out in B-17s in late 1943 but abandoned after only a few trial missions. The system depended upon a signal sent from ground stations in England but this could not be satisfactorily received at high altitude over a long distance. Externally Oboe B-17Fs could only be distinguished from other F models by additional fuselage aerial masts. A very accurate form of short-range radar bombing known as G-H, which reversed the principle of the Oboe system in that the bomber transmitted signals to ground stations in order to obtain its position, was introduced in 8th Air Force B-17s during the spring of 1944. A further development, Micro-H using micro wavelengths, was even more precise and was used with considerable effect during the last six months of the war. Both G-H and Micro-H equipped B-17 lead aircraft and were outwardly only distinguished by additional aerial masts.

A new form of ground-search airborne radar developed in the US was produced in late 1944 and employed during 1945 in special test bombing operations by both 8th and 15th Air Forces. Known by the name *Eagle* it featured an antenna housed in a 1 ft 4 in by 18 ft (40.6 cm by 5.5 m) aerofoil shaped section suspended under the nose of the B-17 giving the appearance of a forward stabilizer. The antenna swept from side to side through approximately 60°, the beam being formed in the forward path of the aircraft in contrast to the revolving 360° sweep of H2X. Using a much higher frequency than the latter, *Eagle*, officially designated AN/APQ-7, gave a clearer presentation of ground images on the operator's scope. In addition to pathfinder radars, the Fortress was also used for specialized work carrying jamming devices for use against enemy radars. This work was later taken on by B-24s which had more internal space to accommodate the bulky transmitters and equipment.

Other Duties

In their offensive role Fortresses carried a variety of explosive and incendiary bombs. External wing racks were used occasionally but mostly for special weapons. The 8th Air Force experimented with a 2,000 lb (907 kg) glide bomb suspended from each wing rack of a B-17, with the object of attacking heavily flak defended targets without the bomber

aircraft having to fly through the defences. Used operationally on only one occasion during the spring of 1944, the weapon was found inaccurate and did not justify the effort involved in delivery. More success was achieved with concrete-piercing rocket bombs during the final stages of the war. This British-made missile was used to penetrate U-boat and E-boat shelters on the Dutch and German coasts. Each rocket bomb grossed over 4,500 lb (2,040 kg) and represented the heaviest combat bombing loads carried by B-17s.

Greater quantities of high explosive were aimed at enemy targets using Fortresses in a unique experiment. Under the codename *Aphrodite*, this highly secret operational project used old B-17Fs and Gs as radio-controlled flying bombs. The Fortresses had all armour, armament and most crew equipment removed, and a load of 20,000 lb (9,070 kg) of high explosive was packed into various parts of the fuselage together with a radio control receiver. A volunteer crew of two would fly the aircraft off its English base and put it on course before bailing out prior to crossing the coast. A following B-17 mother aircraft with special radio transmitters would then take over control of the explosive-laden aircraft and guide it towards its target. The radio control system was in an early stage of development and frequently failed with the result that there was little success in hitting a target. One of these drone B-17s exploded in Sweden and another crash-landed in Germany without exploding, so presenting most of its secrets to the enemy. The experiments were terminated in early 1945 and the designation QB-17 was introduced retrospectively for these Fortresses.

During hostilities USAAF Fortresses were used for purposes other than offensive. A number were converted for photo-reconnaissance under the designation F-9. The cameras varied in number and type but most of the original batch of 16 B-17Fs converted to F-9s carried a total of six situated in the nose, radio room and tail. One squadron equipped with these aircraft was sent to England in late 1942 and moved to North Africa. However, these aircraft could rarely be operated in a combat area without fighter escort and were eventually withdrawn from service. Some 35 other B-17Fs were converted to F-9A and F-9B standard differing only in camera equipment, most being used in non-combat areas for high altitude photography. The F-9C was the designation given to an unspecified number of B-17Gs similarly converted. Although the F-9 photographic designation was retained for some years, some B-17Gs converted for camera work in the latter part of 1944 were not given the F-9C designation. A squadron equipped with photographic B-17Gs carried out mapping surveys in the Middle East, West Africa and Europe during 1945.

The Fortress's excellent high altitude performance led to its employment for weather reconnaissance in the Mediterranean and western European areas. A special weather reconnaissance squadron operated B-17Gs on regular sorties over the Atlantic to collect meteorological information with their special monitoring equipment. Another B-17 squadron was assigned to drop propaganda leaflets over occupied territories and Germany during darkness. The same unit had, during the autumn of 1943, conducted night bomb-

B-17G Cockpit

B-17G Bombardier's compartment

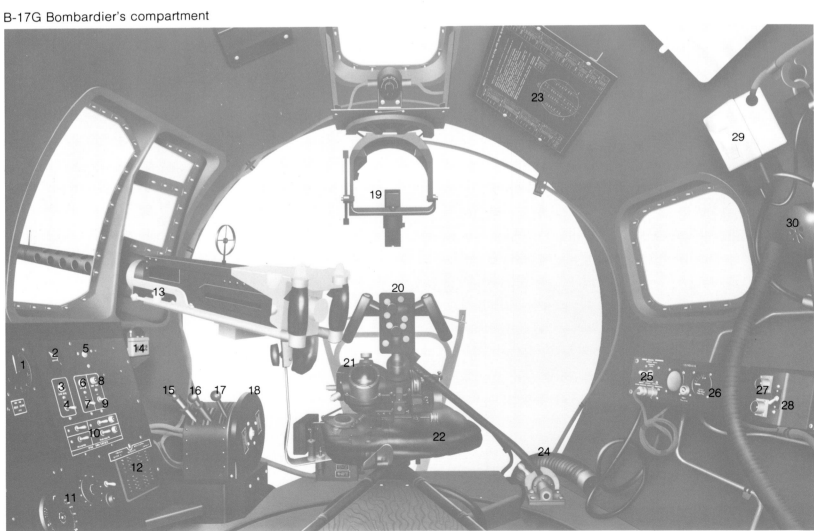

B-17G Cockpit

1 Demand oxygen regulator
2 Cabin air control
3 Vacuum selector valve
4 Suit heater outlet
5 Aileron trim tab control
6 Pilot's control panel
7 Pilot's control panel lights
8 Ammeters
9 Voltmeter
10 Panel lights
11 Fluorescent lights switches
12 Voltmeter
13 Pilot's control column
14 Pilot's rudder pedals
15 Remote compass indicator
16 Pilot's directional indicator
17 Bomb door position light
18 Hydraulic oil pressure gauge
19 Suction gauge
20 Pilot's oxygen flow indicator and pressure gauges
21 Co-pilot's oxygen flow indicator and pressure gauges
22 Co-pilot's oxygen supply warning light
23 Air speed alternate source switch
24 Radio compass position
25 Marker beacon light
26 Altimeter
27 Propeller feathering switches
28 Air speed indicator
29 Turn indicator (Directional gyro)
30 Flight indicator (Gyro horizon)
31 Throttle levers

32 Bank and turn indicator
33 Rate of climb indicator
34 Throttle control lock
35 Propeller pitch controls
36 Propeller pitch control lock
37 Elevator trim tab control wheel
38 Auto flight control panel
39 Elevator and rudder locking lever
40 Rudder tab control wheel
41 Tail wheel locking lever
42 Co-pilot's rudder pedals
43 Co-pilot's control column
44 Tail wheel lock light
45 Landing gear warning light
46 Mixture controls
47 Manifold pressure gauges
48 Tachometers
49 Flap position indicator
50 Cylinder-head temperature gauges
51 Fuel pressure gauges
52 Oil pressure gauges
53 Oil temperature gauges
54 Carburetor air temperature gauges
55 Oil dilution switches
56 Starter switches
57 Parking brake control
58 Intercooler controls
59 Suit heater outlet
60 Demand oxygen regulator
61 Engine primer
62 Hydraulic handpump
63 Interphone jackbox

B-17G Bombardier's compartment

1 Altimeter
2 Ultra-violet light control
3 Bomb formation light
4 Bomb formation switch
5 Bomb indicator light switch
6 Bomb arming light
7 Bomb arming switch
8 Pilot call light
9 Pilot call switch
10 Bomb rack selector switches
11 Intervalometer control panel
12 Bomb indicator
13 Browning M2 0.50-in (12.7 mm) machine gun
14 Bomb release switch
15 External bomb control lever
16 Internal bomb control lever
17 Bomb door control handle
18 Emergency rewind wheel
19 Gunsight setting position
20 Chin turret controller
21 Norden bombsight (phantom view)
22 Bombardier's seat
23 Bomb loading chart
24 De-froster air duct
25 Glide bombing attachment static pressure selector valve
26 Oxygen panel
27 Camera receptacles
28 Camera switch
29 Interphone jackbox
30 Oxygen regulator

A B-17H Dumbo rescue plane (modified from B-17G-105-BO) of 4th Emergency Rescue Squadron, US 20th AF based at Iwo Jima. When photographed, this B-17H was returning from an attempt to save a ditched P-51 pilot with the air-dropped lifeboat. (USAF)

ing experiments with B-17Fs in conjunction with RAF raids on German targets. Fortresses also took part in other night sorties over enemy territory on a very limited scale until the end of hostilities. These were usually to test experimental radar equipment or to obtain photographs of the radar images produced by potential target areas.

The British had successfully developed lifeboats which could be carried under aircraft and dropped by parachute to airmen down in the sea. Late in 1944 a US-developed airborne lifeboat was introduced for carrying under the trusty B-17. The boat was 27 ft (8.2 m) long and

could be carried by any Fortress providing the lower area of the bomb-bay was reworked to accommodate attachment. Early in 1945 a few B-17Gs in England were modified to take airborne lifeboats and used by the Emergency Rescue Squadron operating over the North Sea. During that year some 50 B-17Gs were specially modified in the United States for lifeboat use and several despatched to Pacific war zones. B-17s with airborne lifeboats operated regular patrols from the island of Iwo Jima during the B-29 Superfortress raids on Japan and made a number of drops to the crews of bombers forced down in the sea. Fortresses converted to this air-sea

PB-1G

Modified from B-17G-VE (similar to USAAF B-17H). Fitted with an airborne lifeboat. (US Coast Guard)

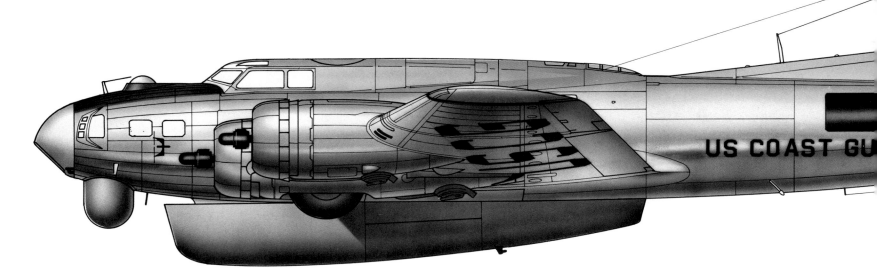

rescue configuration were later given the identity B-17H but, as far as is known, the majority of wartime conversions operated under their original service designations.

The good handling qualities of the B-17 led to many war weary bombers retired from combat being converted into staff transports, air ambulances, target towers or general "hacks". The few B-17s remaining in the Pacific theatres of war after the type had been withdrawn from bomber units during 1943 were all converted for staff transport use. The most celebrated example was a B-17E specially for use by General Douglas MacArthur, commander of the US forces in the South-west Pacific. This aircraft had all camouflage and remaining armour removed. The radio equipment and operator were repositioned to the rear of the cockpit, the bomb doors were sealed and the bay was used as a storage compartment; the waist windows were also sealed, and the forward waist area was fitted out with five airline-type seats. The original door was discarded in favour of a swing-down type with steps. Additional small windows were fashioned in the fuselage, a galley with cooking and refrigeration facilities was fitted out in the former radio room, and a streamlined fairing was placed over the former tail gun position. This officially sanctioned conversion, carried out in 1943, was designated XC-108 and a similarly reworked B-17F, serving the US Command in Europe and the Middle East, received the designation YC-108. Neither aircraft had any experimental or test programme before being despatched to their combat areas. Stripped of war equipment and having smooth contours, these aircraft were potentially the fastest Fortresses flying. In practice they were operated at altitudes where oxygen was not required for crew and passengers and the top speed attained was only about 300 mph (483 km/hr).

Further investigation of B-17 transport possibilities resulted in two more conversions under the C for Cargo designation, XC-108A and XC-108B. The former was a B-17E in which the interior of the fuselage from the bomb-bay aft was

stripped to allow the maximum in storage space. A large upward folding cargo door was constructed in the left-hand side of the fuselage just aft of the wing trailing edge, and the radio and navigation positions were relocated behind the pilots. The XC-108B was a B-17F turned into a flying fuel tanker. Fuel cells were fitted into the bomb-bay area to give a thousand gallon load. The restrictions imposed by the B-17's comparatively narrow fuselage made both the cargo and tanker adaptations uneconomical. The B-24 Liberator, with its deeper fuselage and more rectangular section, was better suited to such conversions, in the absence of a sufficient number of cargo transports. While this investigation of the B-17's transport potential was taken no further in the US, a considerable number of B-17s had been and were employed in transport work. As early as the autumn of 1942 stripped

Fortress IIA

Modified B-17E armed with a 40 mm Vickers "S" gun. This aircraft was at one time operated by No. 220 Squadron, RAF Coastal Command, over the Central Atlantic.

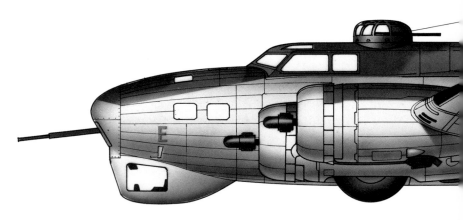

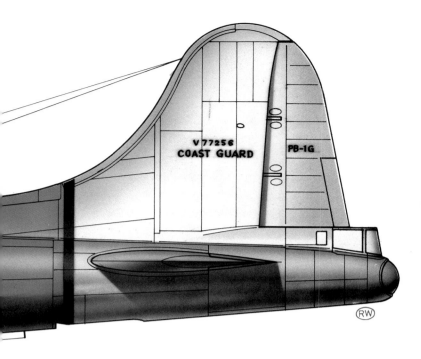

down B-17Es had been used to move supplies from Australia to New Guinea in the absence of sufficient true air transports. Both in Italy and England air depots carried out conversions, removing armament and bombing equipment and installing seating. Although fuselage space and access were restricted, Air Forces Services Command employed lightened Fortresses on a regular basis to carry spares and equipment to combat bases.

In Allied Service

When hostilities terminated in Europe in May 1945, the USAAF had 133 squadrons equipped with Fortresses in that theatre. The Royal Air Force and Royal Canadian Air Force were the only other services with the

Fortress in regular use at this time, the RAF having six squadrons and the RCAF one partially equipped. Despite the unsuccessful use of the Fortress I by RAF Bomber Command in 1941, Britain was scheduled to receive a substantial number of improved B-17F Fortresses for bombing use during 1942 as the Fortress II. America's entry into the war, and the USAAF's desperate need for aircraft to meet its own expansion, brought a revision of plans, and a large number of B-17Es and B-17Fs complete with RAF markings and serial numbers reverted to the USAAF. Later it was decided to supply 45 B-17Es from earlier production to the British and, as these differed from the original planned allocation, they were designated Fortress IIA. These aircraft arrived in Britain during the early summer of 1942 and, as the USAAF was in the process of establishing its own bombing organization equipped with Fortresses in the United Kingdom, the RAF decided to use them for maritime reconnaissance and anti-submarine work.

The RAF eventually received 19 B-17Fs from the earlier contract, and these Fortress IIs reached them in the early autumn of 1942. Both versions were used by RAF Coastal Command. Equipped with submarine-detecting radar, these aircraft carried out oceanic patrol from airfields in the north-west of the UK and in the autumn of 1943, when agreement was reached with the Portuguese Government, two squadrons moved to the Azores. The Command's Fortresses made a number of successful attacks on U-boats during their service before the longer-ranged Liberators replaced them the following year. Remaining Mk II and IIA Fortresses were then used by squadrons in the meteorological role.

The RAF selected the Fortress as the vehicle for a number of test installations, perhaps the most notable being a 40 mm Vickers "S" gun. This was the largest calibre weapon installed in a wartime Fortress – there were a few experimental installations of 20 mm cannon by the USAAF. A gondola had to be constructed below the Fortress's nose to

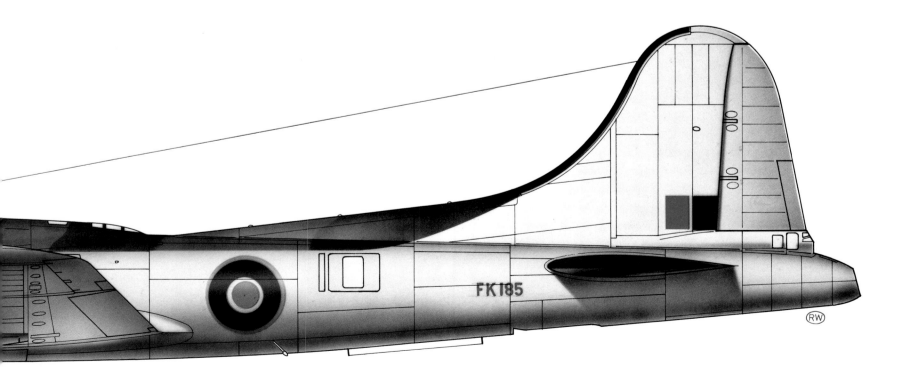

accommodate the gunner who sighted for and fired the 40 mm cannon. Tests revealed unacceptable vibration when the gun was fired and the project was discontinued. Britain did not acquire further production Fortresses until the summer of 1944 when 85 B-17Gs, to be known as Fortress IIIs, were earmarked for delivery. Only 69 actually reached the RAF in Britain, the other 16 apparently being diverted to the USAAF. It is probable that deletions were made because the RAF had received a similar number of Fortresses (B-17Fs) direct from the USAAF in the United Kingdom, most during January 1944. These aircraft were acquired for use in a special radar-jamming squadron and were selected because of the Fortress's superior high altitude performance and the depth of the bomb-bay which could more easily accommodate the bulky jamming transmitters.

In service these lately acquired Fortress IIIs also fitted H2S ground-scanning radar with the antenna housed in a plastic fairing under the nose very similar to that of the early 8th Air Force H2S-equipped pathfinders. Fortress IIIs, similarly modified and with chin turrets removed, were used as replacements in the two radar countermeasures squadrons forming part of RAF No. 100 Group supporting RAF Bomber Command night operations. Various radio and radar countermeasures equipment was carried and these Fortresses usually displayed a number of aerial masts along their fuselages. A few examples of the RAF's B-17G acquisition ended up in Coastal Command meteorological squadrons but for the most part the type was used by RAF Bomber Command.

Canadian squadron use of the Fortress was confined to six aircraft converted for transport duties. In November 1943 three B-17Es and three B-17Fs which had seen service at US training bases were purchased for use in a transatlantic airmail service. Assigned to the RCAF's 168 Heavy Transport Squadron, the aircraft were employed on regular transatlantic flights over the next two years, during which time one disappeared at sea, two were written off in crashes in Europe and another at home base in Canada.

Enemy Fortresses

An unexpected operator of Fortresses during the Second World War was the Luftwaffe. Most combatant nations managed to capture examples of their enemy's warplanes and there were usually flown for evaluation purposes. The Japanese acquired a number of disabled B-17C, D and E models when they overran the Philippines and Java. Subsequently they rebuilt three examples and tested them in Japan. The Germans obtained their first Fortress in December 1942 when a battle-damaged B-17F of the 8th Air Force made a wheels-down forced landing in northern France during a bombing mission. This aircraft was duly evaluated and used to develop effective fighter tactics against the US bomber formations. Two other B-17Fs and a B-17G were acquired in later months. The Luftwaffe, impressed with the high altitude performance and useful range of the B-17, employed the aircraft in clandestine operations behind the Allied lines. KG 200, the organization involved in this work, used Fortresses for agent and equipment deliveries to the Middle East and North

Africa. These activities came to the Allies' notice when a Luftwaffe-operated Fortress with mechanical difficulties made a crash-landing in Spain on return from one of these secret operations.

During 1944 the Luftwaffe secured other Fortresses, two when the crews thought they were landing in neutral or Allied-controlled territory. KG 200 extended its operations to liberated France and the UK after the Allied cross-Channel invasion, and it was during a night sortie over Brest to drop supplies to the beleaguered German garrison that the only enemy-operated B-17 to be lost in action was shot down by a British night fighter. At least six different B-17s are known to have been operated by KG 200 which referred to them by the cover name of Do 200. Three are believed to have been destroyed on the ground by Allied air attacks and one was recaptured by US forces at the end of the war.

Postwar Employment

The last of the 12,731 B-17s built was delivered by the Lockheed-Vega plant on 29 July, 1945. Prior to that production at Boeing had been terminated in mid-April of that year and by Douglas in June. Of this total some 5,000 Fortresses had been lost in operational sorties and another 2,000 had been written off as a result of crashes or damage beyond economical repair. Around 2,500 Fortresses returned from Europe at the end of the war were sent to storage depots. Most would never fly again, ultimately to be broken up for salvage. A similar fate awaited the great majority of warplanes but the Fortress's military service was far from over. While the B-29 Superfortress would form the basis of the USAAF's (and later the USAF's) bomber force during the immediate post-war years, the B-17 was relegated to a wide variety of tasks, indicated by the various designations bestowed upon them.

CB-17s were passenger transport conversions which rated as VB-17s if they were to a de luxe standard for high ranking and other VIPs. TB-17 identified a Fortress used for training. FB-17 was a designation for those aircraft fitted out for camera work which, to some extent, clashed with the RB-17 designation for Fortresses with similar equipment in reconnaissance units. In any event, the FB-17 tag apparently faded out while the RB-17 endured. Weather-reconnaissance Fortresses collected the appropriate W prefix and WB-17Gs survived in USAF service well into the 1950s. The model designation B-17H, given to lifeboat carrying B-17Gs in 1945, became identified later as SB-17s (the S standing for search).

Following on the operational trials carried out with radio-controlled Fortresses from England during the war, considerable experimentation in this art at United States' establishments was based on the same reliable airframe. Radio-controlled Fortresses, whatever their mission, were distinguished as QB-17s from 1948 and the controlling aircraft as DB-17s, the D standing for director. MB-17 was a little-used designation applied to Fortresses used to launch guided missiles in the early post-war years. The Fortress in its QB-17 form was to become the first choice for a real target on which to test

A crewless QB-17 Drone starts 2,600 mile flight from Hilo Naval Air Station, Hawaii, to Muroc Army Air Base on 6 August, 1946. This QB-17 was a modified B-17G-110-VE and was used in the Bikini nuclear bomb tests.
(USAF)

the growing assortment of air-to-air and ground-to-air missiles. Radio-controlled B-17s were also used in the Bikini Atoll atom bomb tests of 1946–47, to provide information on blast turbulence and radiation.

Perhaps the most unusual of the conversions were the three five-engined Fortresses. The first of these were the two JB-17Gs, flying test beds for engines, with an additional engine under test mounted in the nose; the flight deck was in consequence repositioned further back. One JB-17G was transferred to Curtiss-Wright to flight test the Wright XT-35 experimental turboprop engine. Later this aircraft was used to test the Wright XJ-65 experimental turbojet mounted under the nose. The other JB-17G, operated by Pratt & Whitney, tested their trial XT-34 turboprop engine. In the early 1950s a third B-17G became a flying test bed. This involved the Allison T-56 turboprop but the installation was made without repositioning the cockpit. In this way the Fortress played its part in bridging the gap to the jet age.

The last Fortress in regular squadron service with the USAF was an SB-17G of the 57th Air Rescue Squadron

Israeli Air Force's B-17Gs flying over the Mediterranean.

based in the Azores until withdrawn in 1956. DB-17 and QB-17 Fortresses continued to be used in missile firing tests until mid-1960.

In 1945 the US Navy had acquired 48 Douglas and Lockheed-Vega-built B-17Gs, 31 of which were fitted out for radar early warning duties under the designation PB-1W. They featured an APS-20 scanner in a large radome under the fuselage centre-section and extra tankage was installed. The remainder of those acquired went to the US Coast Guard, administered by the Navy, under the designation PB-1G. Among their tasks was that of long-range iceberg reconnaissance. The last Coast Guard-operated aircraft, one specially modified for aerial survey work, was not withdrawn until October 1959.

While Britain discarded its Fortresses soon after the war ended and returned the survivors to the US under Lend-Lease agreements, some foreign air forces purchased the type for service. The newly formed state of Israel acquired three B-17Gs, to the apprehension of the Arab world, basing them at Ramat David where they formed the nucleus of a bomber unit for the Israeli Defence Force. The Rio Pact of Mutual Defence of 1947 opened up South American republics as markets for US war surplus armaments, including Fortresses. Dominica used a few B-17Gs ostensibly in the bombing role and as late as 1958 eight B-17Gs were taken out of store in the US to equip a bombing squadron in Bolivia. Chile also acquired B-17Gs but used them in the search-and-rescue role and Brazil bought SB-17Gs for this purpose. In mid-Atlantic the Portuguese for many years stationed three SB-17Gs for long-distance sea search and rescue.

During the Second World War nine B-17Fs and 60

B-17Gs had landed or crashed in Sweden or in Swedish territorial waters. Over 30 of these that were undamaged or only slightly damaged were returned to the USAAF during May and June 1945, but eight others in good condition were bought for commerical use by the Swedish ABA airline to run a transatlantic service. In this venture they were partnered by the Danish line DDL, also operating an ex-USAAF Fortress from the same source. As Denmark had been under German occupation, Fortresses crashed or force-landing in Denmark (nearly 50 in all) were salvaged by the Luftwaffe. DDL sold their Fortress to the Royal Danish Air Force who used it for communications duties with Greenland.

The French l'Institut Géographique National based at Creil, near Paris, operated a small number for over 30 years in high altitude photographic mapping; altogether a dozen B-17Gs were registered in France for civil use. The Fortress was preferred for photographic work because it did not have fuselage pressurization, allowing cameras to be used from open hatches and avoiding the risk of distortion posed by window glazing. Fortresses used by a forest fire-fighting company for the aerial application of borate in fire suppression were operated until the early 1980s. By this date remaining airworthy Fortresses were mostly in the hands of air show enthusiasts who flew the veteran aircraft for the delight of spectators.

Boeing have produced many other fine bomber aircraft and become the world's premier manufacturers of commercial transport aircraft bringing the company international respect. Many of their products are renowned for reliability and durability, but it is highly unlikely that any will ever eclipse the fame of the venerable B-17 Flying Fortress.

B-17G-DL of 401st BG, US 8th AF, on final approach to Deenethorpe aerodrome, England.

TEXT BY
DAVID A. ANDERTON

HELLCAT

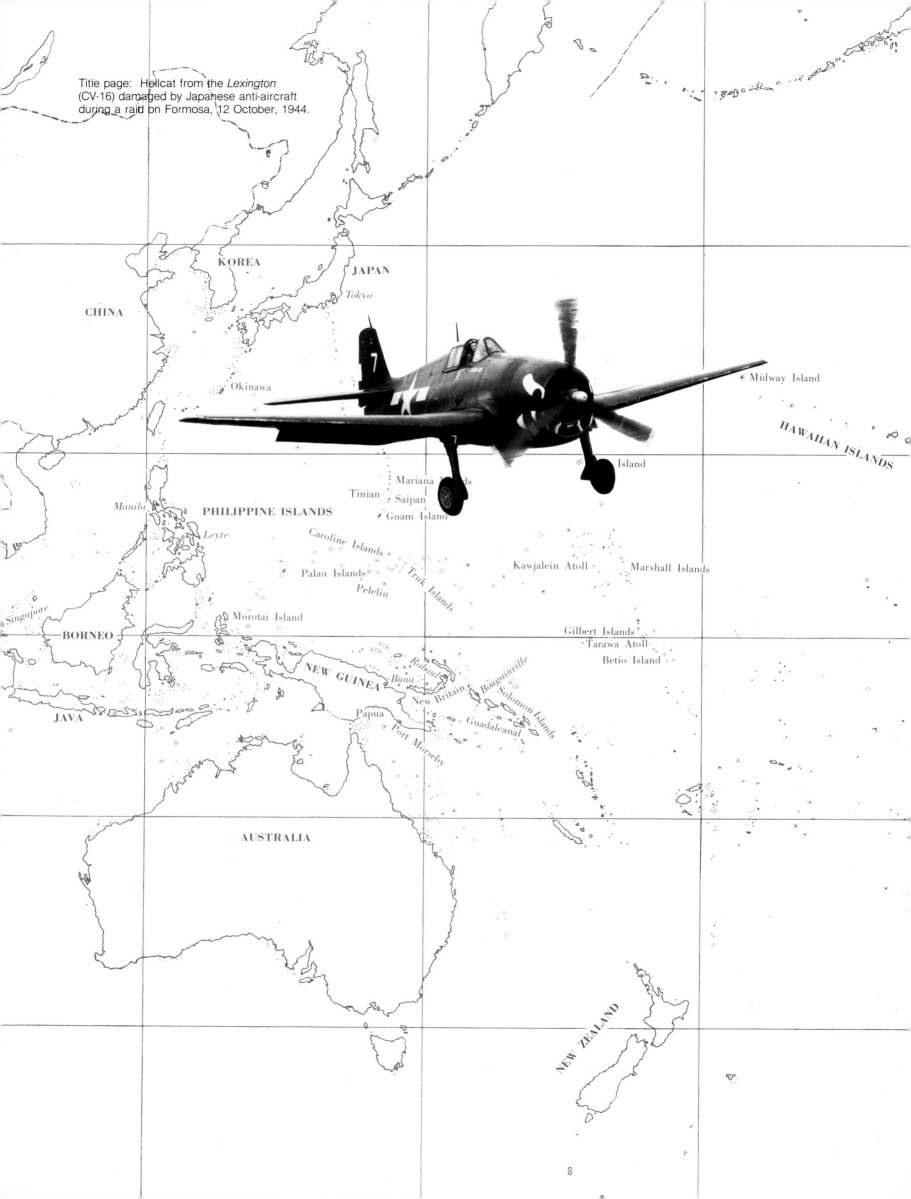

Title page: Hellcat from the *Lexington* (CV-16) damaged by Japanese anti-aircraft during a raid on Formosa, 12 October, 1944.

KOREA

JAPAN

CHINA

Tokyo

Okinawa

• Midway Island

HAWAIIAN ISLANDS

Manila

PHILIPPINE ISLANDS

Mariana Islands

Tinian : Saipan

• Guam Island

Island

Leyte

Caroline Islands

Kawjalein Atoll · · Marshall Islands

Singapore

Palau Islands

Peleliu

Truk Islands

BORNEO

Morotai Island

Gilbert Islands

Tarawa Atoll

Betio Island

Rabaul

NEW GUINEA

Buna

New Britain

Bougainville

Solomon Islands

JAVA

Papua

Guadalcanal

Port Morseby

AUSTRALIA

NEW ZEALAND

"A Bigger and Better Wildcat..."

An F6F-3N, factory-fresh, on the aft deck of the *Charger*. October, 1943. (National Archives)

A dozen humpbacked Hellcats cruised the high skies above the Pacific atoll of Tarawa on 23 November, 1943. With engines cut back to their most efficient cruise power settings, the twelve Grummans orbited in a steady racetrack flight pattern. The midday sun flooded into the cockpits through the canopies, lighting the side consoles. Crazy-house mirror images of portions of flight suits, arms and hands danced on the inner surfaces of the canopy and windshield, and rebounded from the small faces of the instruments.

"Fighting Sixteen", skippered by Lt. Cdr. Paul D. Buie, was flying combat air patrol, a defensive screen for its carrier, the USS *Lexington*, and other ships in the task force lying in the waters off the atoll.

The taking of Tarawa had been assigned to an amphibious assault force of U.S. Marines. They stormed the beach, established a beachhead, and doggedly moved inland, taking fierce fire from the Japanese defenders. Cornered on the atoll, the trapped Japanese made a last desperate charge during the night of 22 November. Now it was about noon on the following day, and the Marines were still moving methodically through the ruined defences, flushing out individual Japanese soldiers. It would take another day to complete their task, but by then the ground defences on the atoll had crumbled.

There was still Japanese air strength to reckon with, long-range bombers and torpedo aircraft, escorted by the agile Zero, dog-fighter supreme in the Pacific skies, and a most effective fighter-bomber besides. That threat, if it appeared, was the reason for the flight of Hellcats assigned to combat air patrol (CAP).

Picket destroyers cruised well offshore, far below the fighters; their radars searched the alloted sectors of sky out to the limits of their sightlines, watching for the telltale echoes that would signal the impending arrival of a Japanese air strike.

"Bogies!", said one of the radar operators, spotting the first signs of a return on the circular screen that played back the patterns seen by the rotating antennae. Other obser-

vers confirmed the sighting, and concentrated their attention on the motion and direction of the luminous blob on the screen.

It advanced, and began to break into a clearly discernible formation of aircraft. There were no incoming signals from IFF (Identification, Friend or Foe) systems that now were standard in the U.S. fleet. They were Japanese, 21 of them, probably fighter-bombers escorted by fighters. And that meant a sky full of Zeros.

The Fighter Director Officer on board the destroyer vectored Buie's squadron toward the incoming strike. They were at altitude, and up-sun from the Japanese, in a classical offensive position of advantage for the attacker. The Hellcats, flying at about 23,000 feet (7000 m) were at least 4,000 feet (1220 m) above the incoming force.

The distance between the two air units closed; Buie called the tallyho, rolled and ruddered his Hellcat toward the "Zekes" and "Hamps," followed by eleven eager Navy pilots looking for a good fight.

They got it. They tore into the Japanese formation in a high-sided, overhead attack that flamed a few of the Zeros on the first pass. And then the sky was filled with individual combats, flashes of white stars and red suns, dark blue fuselages and wings chasing blue-green shapes with polished black cowlings, spurts of flame from wing leading edges and atop cowlings, longer tongues of flame blossoming into great gouts of fire and smoke. Here and there a parachute, pilot dangling below, headed for the water.

The fight raged for ten minutes, between 23,000 feet (7000 m) and about a mile above the Pacific's rolling swells. When it was over, only the Hellcats remained in the air, in complete control of the skies over Tarawa. No Navy pilots had been lost in the swirling combat; they had learned how to fight with their Hellcats, and particularly how not to fight with the nimble Zeros. Don't ever dogfight with those guys, they had been told, or you will be dead. Use your power, your speed, and your altitude advantage to get them on the first pass; if they get on your tail, roll and dive fast, You'll make it OK.

Lt. (jg) Ralph Hanks had learned well. It was his first real combat, and he was now an ace. He got five Zeros in about five minutes, the first of many Navy pilots who were to make ace in a single engagement.

24 November saw action again in the same arena with the same combatants. But on that day, the Japanese entered the scene with an altitude advantage. They did not exploit it properly and, within minutes, they were caught in a replay of the previous day's slaughter. The Hellcats shot down 13 of the attacking force, and claimed credit for six more. One Hellcat pilot was killed in the combat.

The two engagements added up to a remarkable record for the Hellcat. From the beginning it had been designed to kill Zeros, and it was doing just that. In these two fights, U.S. Navy pilots had downed 30 Zeros certainly, ten more probably, and had lost one of their own. The kill ratio was an impressive 30 to one. It was the pattern, if not the dimension, of the Hellcat's combat record during its action in the Pacific.

Genesis of the Hellcat

The design process that produced the Grumman F6F series of Hellcat fighters was evolutionary, rather than revolutionary. It had its roots in the early wartime combat experience of its immediate predecessor in U.S. Navy service, the Grumman F4F-3 Wildcat. Those tubby fighters were front-line equipment on Navy carriers and with Marine land-based units when war broke out on 7 December, 1941. They had the expected modest performance of a fighter that had been

recognized by an anonymous cartoonist at Grumman who, soon after the Hellcat was a matter of public knowledge, drew an arrogant-looking Hellcat being told by a self-righteous Wildcat, "Hellcat, Hell! Copycat!"

The resemblance was not accidental, either at Grumman or at the home of any other aircraft line that is developed. But it was part of the basic Grumman design philosophy, which required the designers to "Make it strong, make it work, and make it simple." Known components give more confidence in their operation than do unknown ones, so Grumman – and other companies – built successive generations of fighters on the lines of the predecessors.

F4F-4 (1942)

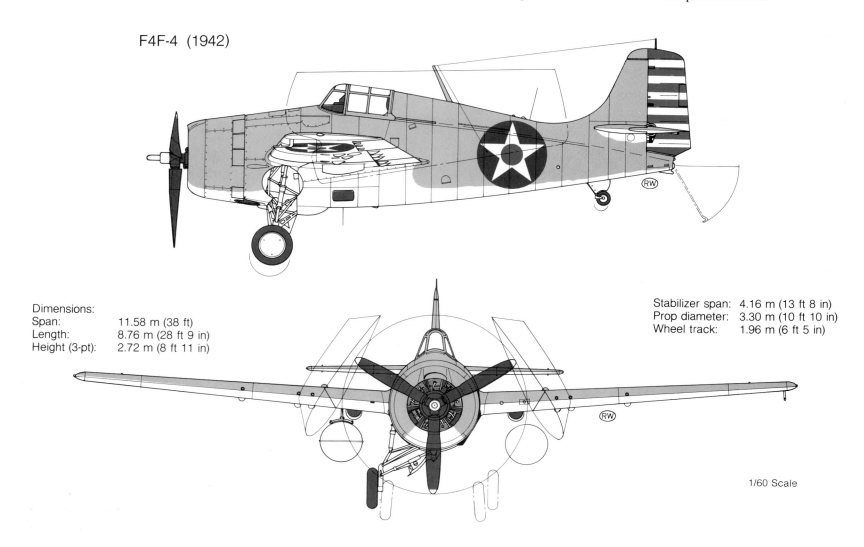

Dimensions:
Span: 11.58 m (38 ft)
Length: 8.76 m (28 ft 9 in)
Height (3-pt): 2.72 m (8 ft 11 in)

Stabilizer span: 4.16 m (13 ft 8 in)
Prop diameter: 3.30 m (10 ft 10 in)
Wheel track: 1.96 m (6 ft 5 in)

1/60 Scale

designed in the mid-1930s, and the first and most obvious way to improve that performance was to fit an engine of increased horsepower.

Faded Grumman blueprints and ozalid copies of original design drawings show the gradual evolution of the Hellcat. The requirement for more horsepower led to the use of a larger propeller to absorb the greater horsepower. Increased propeller diameter meant that the landing gear had to be taller, to give sufficient ground clearance. A heavier powerplant demanded more wing area, and a physically larger wing was reflected in the increased areas of vertical and horizontal tail surfaces.

Thus Grumman's proposal to the Navy was an entirely new fighter, no longer a modified Wildcat, but still bearing a definite family resemblance. That similarity was

There were a couple of other guiding principles that every new designer at Grumman soon learned. The first was Roy Grumman's idea: The last part of a Grumman aircraft to fail was to be the cockpit. Grumman, himself a qualified pilot with years of experience, wanted to give Navy pilots the best possible chance to survive the accidentally destructive landing or minor crash. The second was called the "Schwendler factor", after Grumman's chief engineer, William T. Schwendler. It was based on the quite simple principle that if something was strong enough according to the specifications, it surely wouldn't hurt to make it twice as strong. In that case, the designer applied a "Schwendler factor" of 2, and the resulting piece easily met Navy specifications.

Schwendler also told the story of the Hellcat's evolution in an article in the Grumman plant newspaper,

Plane News, for 16 September, 1943. In the first official announcement of the Hellcat, he wrote:

"The Grumman Hellcat – which Grumman men and women have been turning out in such large numbers – bears the distinction of being the first U.S. fighter plane designed and produced in quantity since Pearl Harbor.

"The early Pacific battles – Coral Sea, Marshall and Gilbert Islands, defense of Midway and the attack and conquest of Guadalcanal – all served to write, through experience, the requirements for the type of fighter most needed by the Navy. The Hellcat's specifications were roughly drafted in those distant parts of the Pacific by such men as Thach,

describe what was, simply, the best carrier-based fighter ever developed and built.

It had been designed and built specifically for one kind of war – fighter versus fighter. And fighter meant even more specifically, the Japanese Mitsubishi Zero. It was developed with the thought that it would be flown by a large number of relatively inexperienced, young pilots who needed a forgiving aircraft in the demanding environment of Naval air warfare. And, thought the Grumman officials, if it is going to be built, we're going to need an awful lot of them, so let's make it easy to produce.

The Hellcat was a forgiving aircraft, easy to fight with. It was an excellent gunnery platform, stable and con-

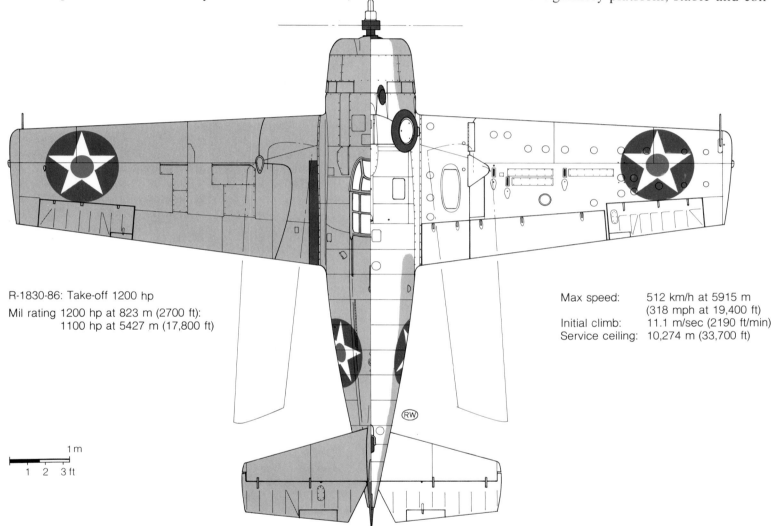

R-1830-86: Take-off 1200 hp

Mil rating 1200 hp at 823 m (2700 ft):
1100 hp at 5427 m (17,800 ft)

1 m
1 2 3 ft

Max speed: 512 km/h at 5915 m
               (318 mph at 19,400 ft)
Initial climb: 11.1 m/sec (2190 ft/min)
Service ceiling: 10,274 m (33,700 ft)

Flatley, O'Hare and Gaylor of the Navy and Smith and Carl of the Marines.

"With the insistent demands of these men as the basic design objective, the Hellcat airplane was engineered to provide greater rate of climb and increased speed over that of the Wildcat, heavier fire power and more and better disposed armor protection for both the pilot and vital parts of the airplane." There was a little licence in that statement. The Grumman reports and specification for the XF6F-1 were dated 24 February, 1941; those for the F6F-3 1 August, 1941. Both dates were well before Pearl Harbor, so that very little input of the Pacific combat could have been an initial design influence. But the details of long-forgotten contracts and specifications are unimportant. What remains is the record of the Hellcat, and the words and phrases that only begin to

trollable. It was rugged; its great strength and its ability to take punishment were legends in the fleet. It was easy to maintain, consistently setting the highest availability marks in the fleet. A very high percentage of Hellcats – between 90 and 95 per cent – was always ready for operations. No other Naval aircraft of its time could make that claim, and probably none since.

It ended the war with a kill ratio of 19:1, another mark that has not since been touched. Nor was it within reach of any other fighter at the time.

It was, in every respect, an absolutely remarkable aircraft, and one that can safely be called unmatched.

This is the story of the Grumman F6F Hellcat series, and how they won the Naval air war in the Pacific in World War II.

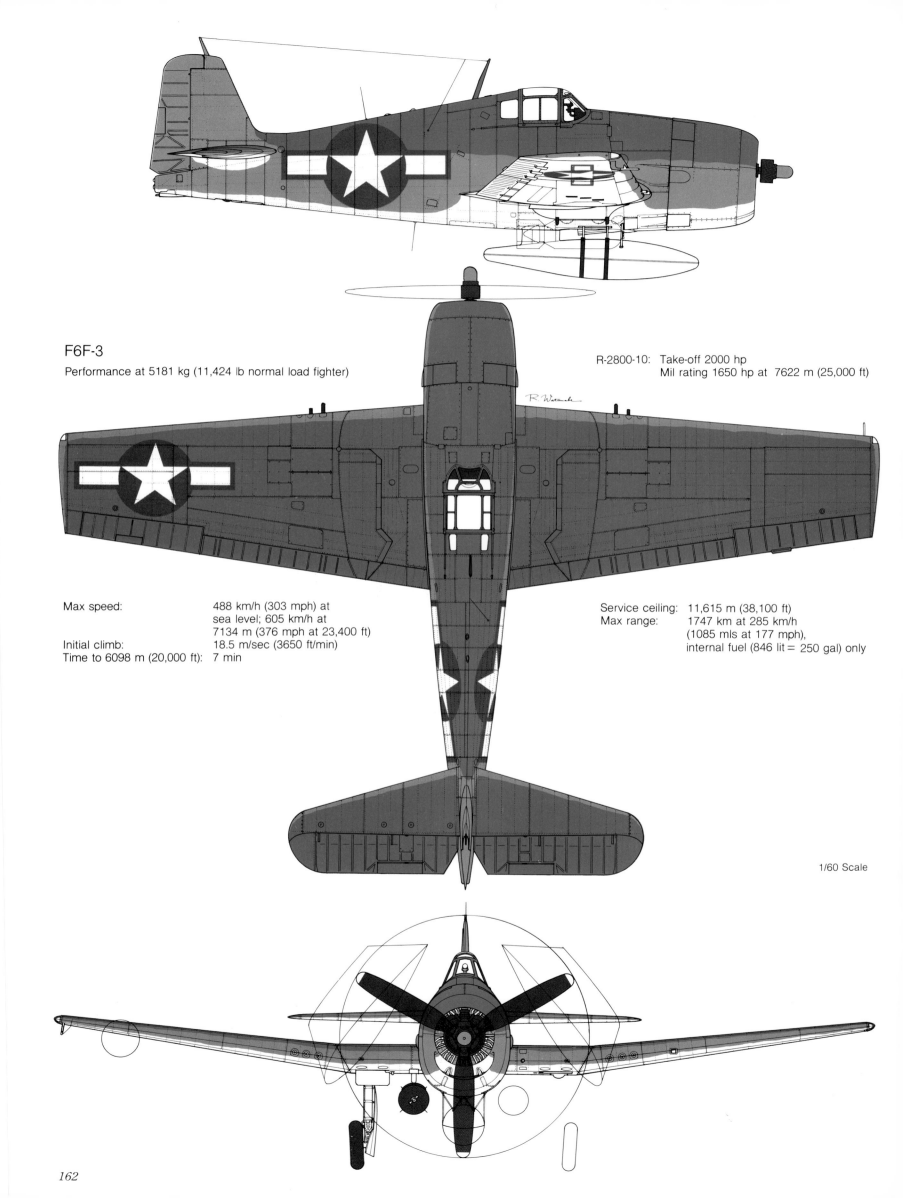

F6F-3

Performance at 5181 kg (11,424 lb normal load fighter)

R-2800-10: Take-off 2000 hp
Mil rating 1650 hp at 7622 m (25,000 ft)

Max speed: 488 km/h (303 mph) at
sea level; 605 km/h at
7134 m (376 mph at 23,400 ft)
Initial climb: 18.5 m/sec (3650 ft/min)
Time to 6098 m (20,000 ft): 7 min

Service ceiling: 11,615 m (38,100 ft)
Max range: 1747 km at 285 km/h
(1085 mls at 177 mph),
internal fuel (846 lit = 250 gal) only

1/60 Scale

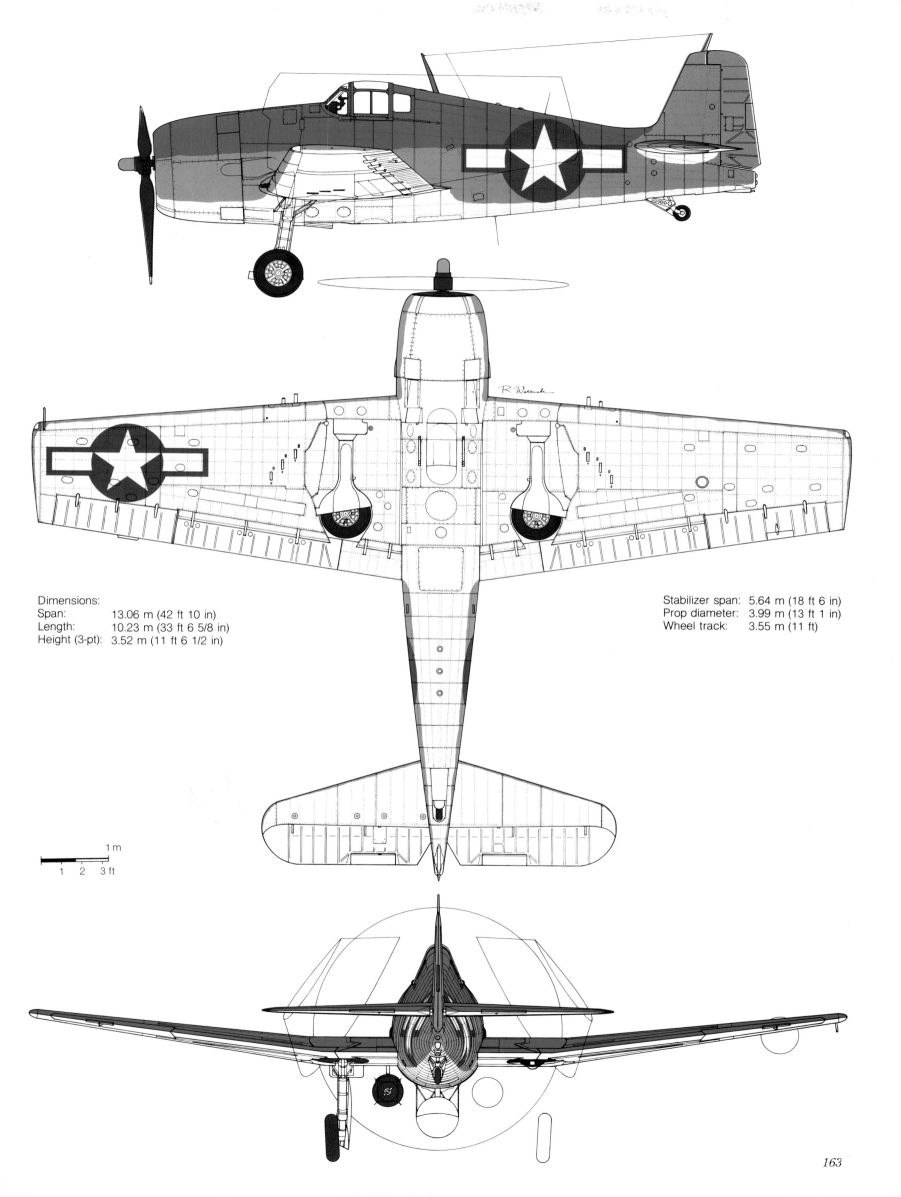

Dimensions:
Span: 13.06 m (42 ft 10 in)
Length: 10.23 m (33 ft 6 5/8 in)
Height (3-pt): 3.52 m (11 ft 6 1/2 in)

Stabilizer span: 5.64 m (18 ft 6 in)
Prop diameter: 3.99 m (13 ft 1 in)
Wheel track: 3.55 m (11 ft)

1 m
1   2   3 ft

The Hellcat Family

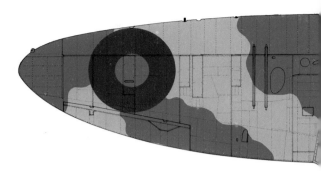

Spitfire MkIa

Span:	11.323 m (35 ft 10 in)
Length:	9.116 m (29 ft 11 in)
Height:	3.480 m (11 ft 5 in)
Wing area:	22.3 sqm (242 sq ft)

Although six different models of Hellcat were developed by the Grumman Aircraft Engineering Corporation, only two of them reached production status: The F6F-3 and the F6F-5. All of them retained the characteristic Grumman shape: Chunky fuselage lines, moderate aspect ratios on the tail surfaces, a simple tapered wing with squared-off tips. The Hellcat had its own unique shapes, also. The deep cowl with its bottom inlet for the carburetor and cooler air was one trademark of the series. The wing, seen from the front, was another; it had a thick section, and the dihedral began outboard of the root. The wide-treaded landing gear was a third.

But most characteristic were the humpbacked fuselage lines, drawn to give the pilot the best possible visibility forward. He sat high in the fuselage; the dorsal spine sloped down and aft, and the cowling sloped down and forward. When he sat up straight in the cockpit, his eyes were more than ten feet above the ground.

The Hellcat was not elegant, in the sense of a Spitfire, a Zero, or a Mustang. But it had its own kind of rugged beauty, a functional and tough geometry that spoke volumes. There were good reasons for the angular lines. Parts with straight lines are a lot easier and less expensive to build than parts with curves. A flat surface is easier and less costly than one with multiple contours. Elliptical wings are the theoretical aerodynamic ideal; but a set of properly tapered wings with straight leading and trailing edges come fairly close to the ideal and presented fewer production problems.

As early as February, 1938, Grumman designers were carefully studying the installation of a larger engine in the Wildcat series. Design 33 seems to have been the first of the more formal approaches to the problem; it showed the Grumman XF4F-2, the experimental forerunner of the production Wildcat series, modified to install a big – for that day – Wright Aeronautical Corp. R-2600 engine, model unspecified. That same month, Design 33-A appeared, this time modifying the XF4F-3 with an R-2600 engine. In March, another revision: Design 35 called for a single-engined fighter built around an R-2600 engine, still basically the Wildcat, but beginning to close in on the eventual shapes and sizes of the Hellcat.

There was one more intermediate stage on paper: Design 50, an F4F-4 modified by the installation of an R-2600-10 two-stage engine. It was a powerplant that would deliver 1,290 horsepower at 22,000 feet (6700 m) altitude, and it changed the basic contours of the Wildcat out of almost all recognition.

For reference, the Wildcat had a wingspan of 38 feet (11 m 59 cm) and an overall length of 28 ft. 9 ins (8 m 76 cm). Its wing area was 260 square feet (24 m²). Production Wildcats were powered by the reliable Pratt & Whitney R-1830-86 engines, developing 1,200 horsepower for takeoff and 1,100 horsepower at an altitude of 17,800 feet (5420 m).

Design 50 showed a wingspan of 41 ft. 6 in. (12 m 64 cm) that reflected its greater wing area of 290 square feet (27 m²). Its overall length was 31 ft. 4 in. (9 m 55 cm). The

Zero 21 (*Reisen* A6M2)

Span:	12 m (39 ft 4 7/16 in)
Length:	9.06 m (29 ft 8 11/16 in)
Height:	3.05 m (10 ft 0 1/16 in)
Wing area:	22.44 sq m (241.54 sq ft)

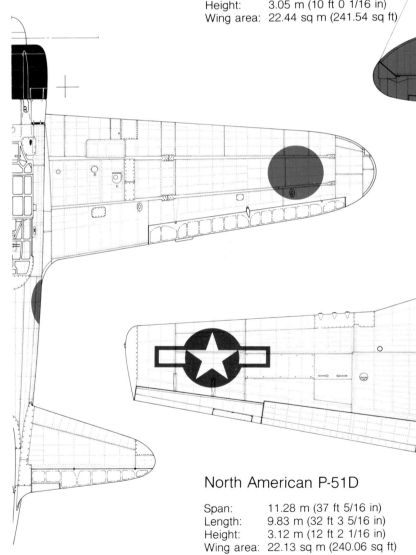

North American P-51D

Span:	11.28 m (37 ft 5/16 in)
Length:	9.83 m (32 ft 3 5/16 in)
Height:	3.12 m (12 ft 2 1/16 in)
Wing area:	22.13 sq m (240.06 sq ft)

R. Watanabe

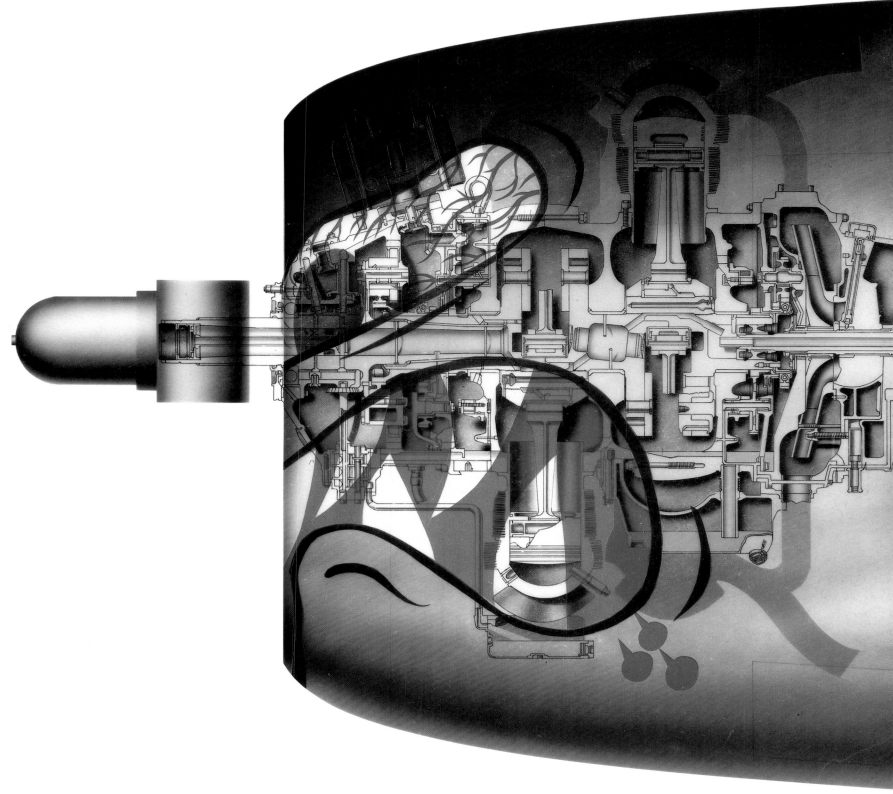

Pratt & Whitney R-2800-10W

These big twin-row, 18-cylinder air-cooled radials were the engines installed on F6F-5 production aircraft. All were equipped with two-stage, two-speed superchargers, and with anti-detonant injection (ADI, or "water injection") systems. The latter generally were removed in the field to reduce weight and eliminate one maintenance headache. The −10W was rated at 2,000 hp. for takeoff, and swung a three-bladed Hamilton Standard Hydromatic propeller of 13 ft. nominal diameter. The powerplant was 52 inches in diameter, and weighed 2,496 pounds in the −10W version. Its displacement, part of its designation, was 2,800 cubic inches. The engine had a reputation for being reliable and rugged; it delivered power when it was needed.

Grumman F6F-3 Hellcat of VF-27
(see page 207)

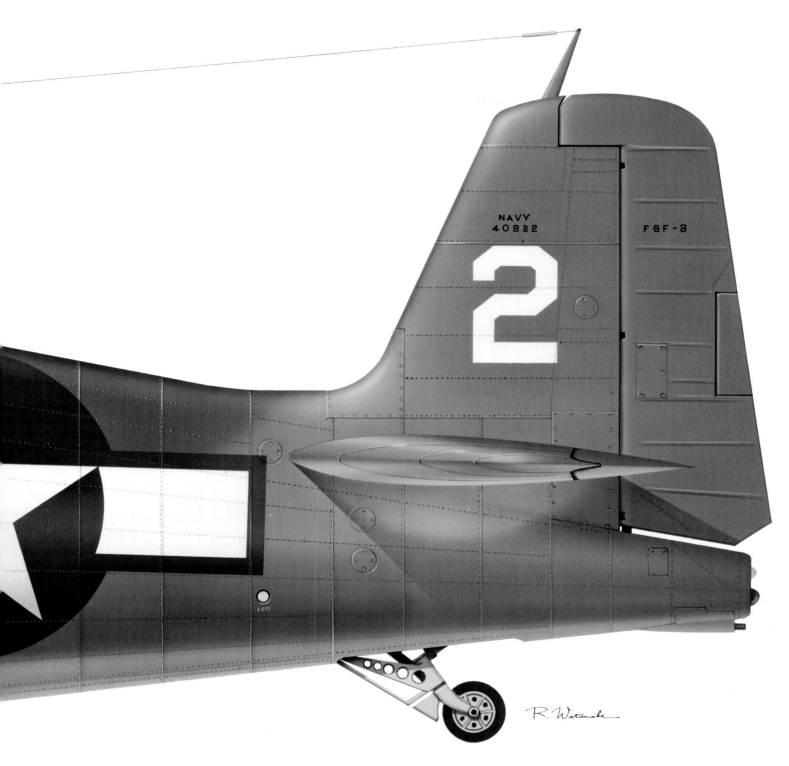

NAVY
40882

2

F6F-8

R. Watanabe

1 m

1   2   3   ft

USS YORKTOWN (CV10)

She was fast and clean. Her bulbous bow was designed to help speed her passage through the dark Pacific waters. She boarded an air group of new fighters, bombers and torpedo bombers. She became a keystone of the fast carrier task forces, the major Navy component in World War II.

She was called "The Fighting Lady", following the age-old Naval tradition that all ships are feminine. She was the USS *Yorktown*, designated CV-10, the second of the *Essex*-class heavy carriers.

She logged a formidable combat record, spending about 22 months in combat during the war, with time out only for an overhaul. She ended her fighting career in the South China Sea on station with Task Force 77 during the war in Southeast Asia. Decommissioned in 1970, she now is on permanent display at Patriot's Point Naval and Maritime Museum, Charleston Heights, South Carolina.

She was the fourth U.S. Navy ship and the second carrier to bear the name *Yorktown*. Her immediate predecessor, the USS *Yorktown* (CV-5), had been laid down in 1934 and was only in combat for about six months of her life; but in that time, she lived and fought well, playing an important part in two of the significant naval battles in history: Coral Sea and Midway. In that latter battle, she took three bomb hits, recovered, and then was hit twice by torpedoes that jammed her rudder, and flooded her port compartments. Abandoned, and then reboarded by her captain and a volunteer crew, she was showing signs of recovery when a Japanese submarine evaded the anti-submarine guard, fired a spread of four torpedoes, and hit the *Yorktown* with a pair. It was the end, and she sank in the early morning light of 7 June, 1942.

Her name was soon given to another carrier on the ways, orginally named the USS *Bonhom me Richard*, that had been ordered from the Newport News Shipbuilding and Drydock Co. on 3 July, 1940. Laid

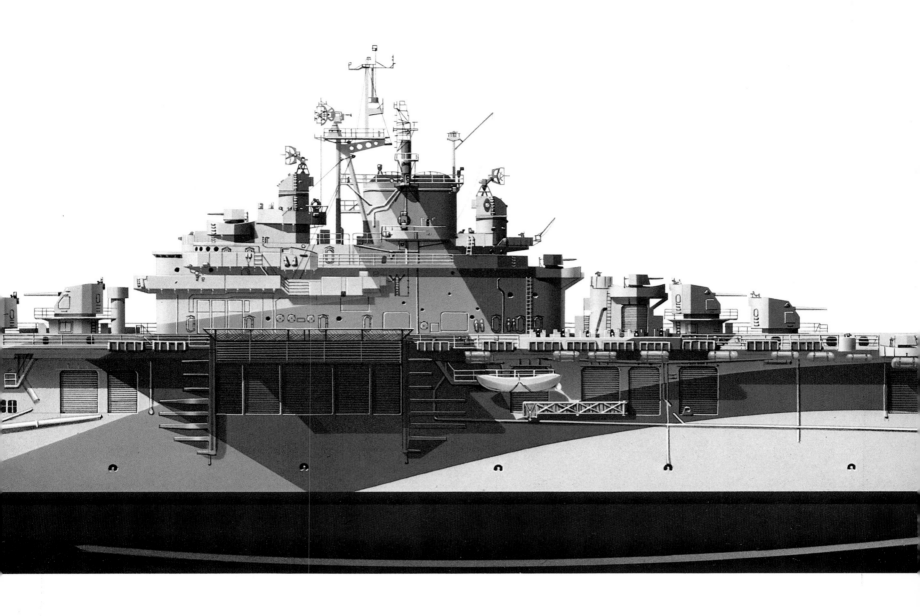

down six days before the attack at Pearl Harbor, the declaration of war lent speed to her construction. *Bonhom me Richard* was renamed *Yorktown* on 26 September, 1942, and was launched 21 January, 1943. She was commissioned 15 April, joining the Navy just 17-1/2 months after keellaying and almost a year ahead of schedule.

After a shakedown cruise—during which much of the famous film, *Fighting Lady*, was photographed—she became the flagship of Rear Admiral Charles A. Pownall, commanding Task Force 15. She sailed from Pearl Harbor on 22 August, 1943, headed for the Marcus Islands and the first strike by her aircraft.

In succession, she took part in raids against Japanese installations on Marcus and Wake Islands, supported the invasion of the Gilbert and the Marshall Islands, hammered Truk, Saipan, Tinian, Palau, and the New Guinea coast. During the invasion of the Mariana Islands, her Hellcats took part in the "Great Marianas Turkey Shoot," that aerial massacre that was the high-altitude portion of the

battle of the Philippine Sea. Then it was a series of raids on Iwo Jima, Chichi Jima, Yap and Ulithi before returning to the United States for overhaul at the Bremerton, Washington, Navy Yard.

Yorktown was out of action for three months, most of the time laid up at Bremerton. But on 3 November, she rejoined the task force off Ulithi, then supported the invasion of the Central Philippines. She fought in the South China Sea near Cam Ranh Bay, a place she would return to decades later, then sailed to launch strikes against Formosa, southern Japan, Okinawa, and finally Tokyo itself.

Yorktown was planned according to Navy specifications dated June, 1939, and drew heavily on the design and experiences of her namesake. Fully loaded, she displaced 36,200 tons. She was 820 feet long and had a 93-foot beam at the waterline. Overall, she stretched 855 ft 10 in, and had a beam of 147 ft 6 in. She drew a maximum of 28 ft 4 in of water, fully loaded.

Her reason for being was her carrier air group: four squadrons,

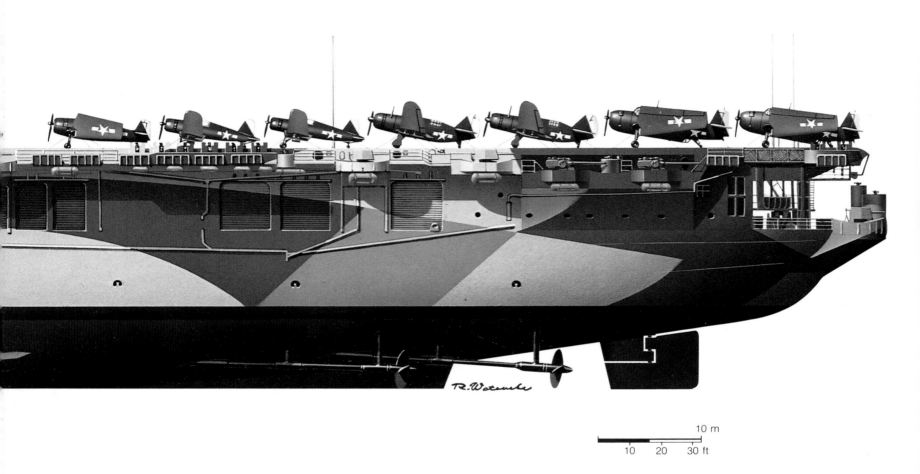

10 m

10   20   30 ft

five if necessary. That meant not only airplanes, but fuel, ordnance, and spare parts, as well as a large crew of technical specialists to keep the aircraft flying. Stored away in the endless compartments and on deck space below was the equivalent of 25% of her aircraft strength in knocked-down spare parts. In her belly lay 231,650 gallons of aviation-grade gasoline and tons of bombs, machine gun bullets and anti-aircraft shells.

Her flight deck was scarred by the long cuts of two forward catapults and the rectangular outlines of two centerline elevators and a single deck edge elevator. For a while, she carried a transverse catapult on her hangar deck, to launch scouting aircraft when her deck was otherwise occupied.

Her crew complement was 246 officers and 2,436 men, the population of a small town.

Her defense was in armor, curiously enough not designed for protection against the 8-in guns of the heavy Japanese cruisers she had

been planned to fight, but against American 6-in armor-piercing shells. She was triple-bottomed, and had four layers of torpedo defense. Her armored main deck could resist a 1,000-lb. general purpose bomb. Her gun batteries consisted of eight paired 5''/38 cal. and four single guns of the same bore and caliber, plus an ever-increasing number of 40-mm quad-mounted anti-aircraft cannon. She was built with eight of those, and by mid-1944 had 17. Her 20-mm cannon mounts also proliferated, from 46 at the time of her launching to 61 by the end of 1944.

Under the thrust of her four screw propellers, driven by 150,000 shaft horsepower, she made nearly 33 knots in test runs. Less urgently, she could cruise at 15 knots for about 19,000 miles. In these days of billion-dollar carriers, it's interesting to note that she cost less than $44 million, not counting her armor and armament.

She won eleven battle stars in World War II. She was, truly, "The Fighting Lady".

Grumman drawing for the design study – SP56, "B" change – was initialed by Richard Hutton, the brilliant young designer of so many of Grumman's aircraft, on 6 January, 1941. Just nine days later, a draughtsman put the finishing touches on drawing SP-799, "C" change, defining once and for all the final lines of the XF6F-1.

The growth process that had started with more power had produced the Hellcat. The lines that it started with were, by and large, the lines that it finished with. The basic changes to successive models of the Hellcat were minor and none involved any modification that changed the outlines of the F6F in any major way.

The XF6F-1 spanned 42 ft. 10 in. (13 m 6 cm); its overall length was 33 ft. 6¼ in (10 m 21 cm) from the tip of its propeller spinner to the rearmost portion of the tail-fuselage fairing. It stood 11 ft. 6½ in. (3 m 52 cm) high from the three-point static ground level to the highest part of its rearward folding wings.

The folding wing concept was an idea of great simplicity and it has been credited, in Grumman legend, to Roy Grumman's inspired work with a straightened paperclip and a pink gum eraser. Since Grumman legends are, in happy contrast to most, invariably true, that's how the inclined single hinge system was born. It was a brilliant and simple idea, typical of the company's approach to design. It was developed originally for a special version of the Wildcat, and was adapted later to both the Hellcat and the TBF-1 Avenger.

The XF6F-1 received its final definition in Grumman Specification SD-286, and Report No. 2421, dated 24 February, 1941. The Navy awarded the company Contract No. 88263 and the Hellcat was on its way.

Experimental Grumman aircraft were built in a small shop presided over by a resident genius with an occasional temper. He was Julie Holpit, and the craftsmen that worked in his experimental shop were as exceptional as the products of their hands. They were Rodins who worked in sheet aluminium alloys. They knew what to do and how to do it before the first engineering drawing ever hit the shop, and they saved many a young engineer from embarrassment by their skills and their understanding. You got only one chance, though; the second mistake brought a scathing and profane commentary down on your head.

The contract for the XF6F-1 was signed on 30 June, 1941, and on the same day, the Vought XF4U-1 was ordered into production. The coincidence of the dates is important; Vought's Corsair had a head start, but it was a year later getting to the fleet. The Navy had approved the initial design of the Hellcat after running a series of wind-tunnel tests on a one-sixteenth scale model at the Aerodynamical Laboratory. Navy Yard, Washington, DC. The Navy bought two prototypes with that first contract, and specified concurrent testing of the planes.

On 26 June, 1942, the XF6F-1 stood on the ramp at Bethpage, serviced and ready to fly. Its Wright R-2600-16 engine had been run in on the ground, and all of the basic aircraft and engine systems had been checked and rechecked. Bob Hall, who had been responsible for flying the most recent Grumman experimental aircraft, hauled his lanky frame up on the wing and stepped over the sill into the cockpit. He conferred briefly with the plane captain, primed the big Wright powerplant, and started the engine. It coughed into life, jerking and shaking on its mount, spewing exhaust out over the upper surface of the wing.

Hall taxied out, took off uneventfully, and landed after discovering what thousands of Navy pilots were to find out later: the Hellcat was a very fine aircraft, and it flew very well indeed.

But although it flew well, it didn't fly fast enough nor did it climb rapidly enough to meet the requirements the Navy had laid down some months before. Hall's flight tests and their analyses by Grumman aerodynamicists clearly showed the need for more horsepower. Fortunately, there was an engine about to be available, an engine of approximately the same dimensions as the Wright R-2600, but of substantially more horsepower. It had been scheduled for production versions of the Navy's Vought F4U-1 Corsair and the Army's P-47 Thunderbolt; both those planes were delayed, and a production flow of Pratt & Whitney R-2800-10 engines became available. The Navy assigned one to Grumman, and Holpit's men installed it to replace the Wright engine in the XF6F-1, while engineers took notes and sketched. Development programmes moved fast in those days, under the pressures of war and the lesser demands of a simpler era and uncomplicated aircraft. Remember that the first Hellcat-1 prototype had flown 26 June, 1942. On 30 July, Bob Hall clambered into the new XF6F-3, fired up the engine, and made the first test flight of the Pratt and Whitney-powered Hellcat. It lasted less than fifteen minutes, but Hall had found out all he needed to know in that time. Power made the difference and the new Hellcat had it.

On 17 August, though, it didn't have it. The R-2800 quit, and suddenly Hall was flying a very quiet and very heavy glider. He landed it in one of the many farm fields that then covered much of Long Island, Grumman's long-time venue. It wasn't to be the last dead-stick landing in a nearby farmyard for the Hellcat, and this first one, although it did considerable damage to the aircraft and somewhat less to Bob Hall, was taken in stride by both the Navy and Grumman.

The flight tests showed that some minor changes could be made, or needed to be made. The spinner that had covered the propeller hub and delighted the aerodynamicists was an early casualty; nobody else was sorry to see it go. The Curtiss electric propeller, matched to the Wright R-2600 engine, was replaced by one made by Hamilton Standard, a Hydromatic model, matched to the Pratt & Whitney engine.

The production F6F-3s were in the construction phase while the experimental aircrafts were being tested. Grumman's confidence and foresight paid off; the first production Hellcat was ready for its initial flight 3 October, 1942, and from that date there was a constant flow of -3 models rolled out of the Plant 3 doors and parked along the concrete ramps that lined the factory area at Bethpage.

To look ahead of this phase of the story for a moment, the first F6F-3 models were assigned to VF-9 at Naval Air Station (NAS) Oceana. They took them on board the fast carrier USS *Essex* in February, 1943, for carrier qualification

F6F-3 with 1,000 lb (454 kg) bomb.

trials. On 13 March, Hellcats were assigned to the *Essex* Air Group for duty with the fleet, and by the following August they were ready to go into combat. The time between the first flight of the first prototype and the first combat use of the Hellcat totalled 14 months.

The F6F-3 was succeeded in production by the -5 model, an improved version with minor modifications that made it a better fighter and also a better fighter-bomber. The avowed purpose of the Hellcat design had been to fight the Japanese Zeros. It was optimized, as much as it could be, for that task. It had power, speed and the heavy firepower of a sextet of .50-cal machine-guns, and an airframe that could take an unbelievable amount of damage and still fly.

During the combat life of the Hellcat, the proportion of fighters to other types on board carriers steadily increased. In the latter years of the war, fighters predominated; they had been found to be versatile, able to bomb point targets just as well as the Navy's standard dive bombers could. They packed the equivalent of a destroyer broadside in the half-dozen five-inch high-velocity rockets they carried on underwing racks. It was the F6F-5 model that gave the fleet that advantage.

The -5 had a redesigned engine cowling, to help cut down the drag of cooling the mighty R-2800. More power meant more heat, both to the cylinder fins and to the cooling oil, and both demanded increased airflow. To get that without increasing the drag was a neat trick, and the Grumman engineers did it. To drop the drag a few more points, the Navy decided to supplant the paint scheme that had been one of the features of the fleet's aircraft during the middle years of the war. A glossy dark sea blue replaced the three hues of non-specular paint that had contributed its share of skin friction drag to the detriment of Hellcat speed.

The Hellcat's ailerons were redesigned, and a spring tab system was added to reduce the control forces. Grumman spent many hours and dollars during the Hellcat programme trying to come up with a set of ailerons that met the Navy's requirements for the control surfaces, but never succeeded. The spring tab system got them closer than they had been before.

The windshield was cleaned up, and a couple of metal braces were removed for better visibility. The cockpit armour plate was increased somewhat in size, for better protection of the pilot, and the side window behind the cockpit, which had survived in early production units of the -5 model, was removed later in production blocks.

The stabilizer and the fuselage tail structure were strengthened, which meant the heavier-handed Navy pilots could dive the Hellcat faster, and pull out more abruptly, than they had been able to with the -3 model. (It is true that catastrophic failures were almost unknown on the Grumman products of that time. Grumman was often facetiously called "The Iron Works" because of its reputation for building very, very rugged aircraft.)

The Navy made the F6F-5 a fighter-bomber by adding bomb racks to the wing centre section, one on the centreline for ordnance or a droppable fuel tank, and one on each side of the centreline, each capable of holding a 1,000-lb. (450 kg) bomb. The first of the F6F-5 models flew in April, 1944, and they quickly replaced the older -3 aircraft in the fleet.

All together, there were five experimental types of Hellcat and two production models, plus five different sub-types and at least six design studies of other variations on the same theme. The XF6F-1 was the progenitor of the breed. Numerically it was followed by the XF6F-2, although chronologically that specific modification came after the F6F-5 was well into production. The XF6F-2 began as a study for the installation of a special type of turbo-supercharger designed and developed by an expatriate Swiss engineer, Rudolf Birmann. Tests had shown that the supercharger could maintain engine sea-level power to an altitude of at least 40,000 feet (12,200 m), and the promise of such performance was the reason for the design of the XF6F-2. The final engine selection was the Pratt & Whitney R-2800-16; Birmann's Model P14B turbosupercharger was installed for the flight test programme, which began with the first flight of the experimental machine on 7 January, 1944. By July the combination of airframe, engine and turbocharger had shown little significant improvement in standard Hellcat performance, so the programme was stopped, and the XF6F-2 was delivered to the Navy for use in training.

The XF6F-4 was the third stage in the life of the original XF6F-1 prototype. That first experimental Hellcat had then been converted to serve as the -3 prototype; Grumman took it one step further by using it for the -4, a test installation of the Pratt & Whitney R-2800-27, an engine with a single-stage, two-speed built-in supercharger. While it was being converted, the standard armament of six .50-cal machine guns was changed to four 20-mm aircraft cannon, each with 200 rounds of ammunition. The aircraft first flew on 3 October, 1942, and was extensively tested by Grumman and Navy pilots, but was not placed into production. Instead, after the completion of the test programme, it was once again reworked to correspond to a production F6F-3 and was delivered in that state.

Last of the experimental Hellcats was the XF6F-6, powered by the Pratt & Whitney R-2800-18W engine, one of the new "C" type powerplants. Its internal two-stage, two-speed supercharger and water injection for War Emergency Power gave a further boost to the available takeoff and high-altitude military power. That Hellcat first flew 6 July, 1944, as a modified standard production F6F-5 with the XF6F-6 designation. A second XF6F-6 also flew in the test programme, and the results of the increased power were impressive. The Hellcat's top speed was increased substantially, to 417 mph (671 km/h). The Navy had planned to build that high-powered version, but cancelled the programme abruptly on V-J Day, in August, 1945.

Five suffixes were used with Hellcat designations during the life of the aircraft. The first few to carry drop tanks were designated as F6F-3D, but that suffix was soon abandoned as the use of drop tanks became part of the standard configuration. It was later reinstated after the war to indicate aircraft used as drone controllers.

Both the F6F-3 and -5 carried an "E" suffix to indicate that they were equipped with the AN/APS-4 search radar, or an "N" suffix if they were carrying the later AN/APS-6

intercept radar. A number of each production version were built to incorporate camera installations in the fuselage, for post-strike bomb damage assessment; those sub-types carried a "P" suffix.

Postwar, many Hellcats were converted to drone configurations, and were so designated by using a "K" suffix.

The first F6F study to receive a Grumman number after Pearl Harbor was Design 54, the installation of a totally new wing on a standard Hellcat. The wing, of greater area and different geometry, was to have had a low-drag, "laminar flow" airfoil section that had been developed at the National Advisory Committee for Aeronautics' (NACA, the forerunner of today's National Aeronautics and Space Administration) Langley Memorial Aeronautical Laboratory. Work never progressed beyond some drawings, dated February, 1942, and a performance analysis.

Designs 59 and 60 studied the installation of the 28-cylinder R-4360 "Wasp Major" engines in the Hellcat. The two-speed supercharger engine was Design 59: the two-stage engine was Design 60. Both carried a drawing date of August, 1943, and neither went beyond the drawing boards. The reason may have been found in the first analysis of Design 61, cryptically called "F6F with GE unit". The GE unit referred to was the first jet engine in America, and the design was a study of a Hellcat with a mixed powerplant, standard reciprocating radial engine in the nose, and the new General Electric turbo-jet engine in the fuselage with a tailpipe exhausting the jet aft of the Hellcat's rudder. It was a formula that Grumman was to try again and again, and that the Navy experimented with for some years, but it was not a technical success, in any form, and was very soon overtaken by the performance of all-jet aircraft. Last of the identifiable Hellcat studies was Design 69, the installation of the Pratt & Whitney R-2800-22 "C" engine with a two-speed supercharger in what would have been a bomber version of the Hellcat. The two-speed engine developed its power at a lower altitude than a two-stage unit, and so was more suitable for low-level attack and bombing work.

Since the Hellcat could carry bombs, the next logical step was to turn the F6F into a torpedo carrier. This plan was actually carried out but never progressed beyond the test installation.

Grumman F6F-5 Hellcat Cutaway

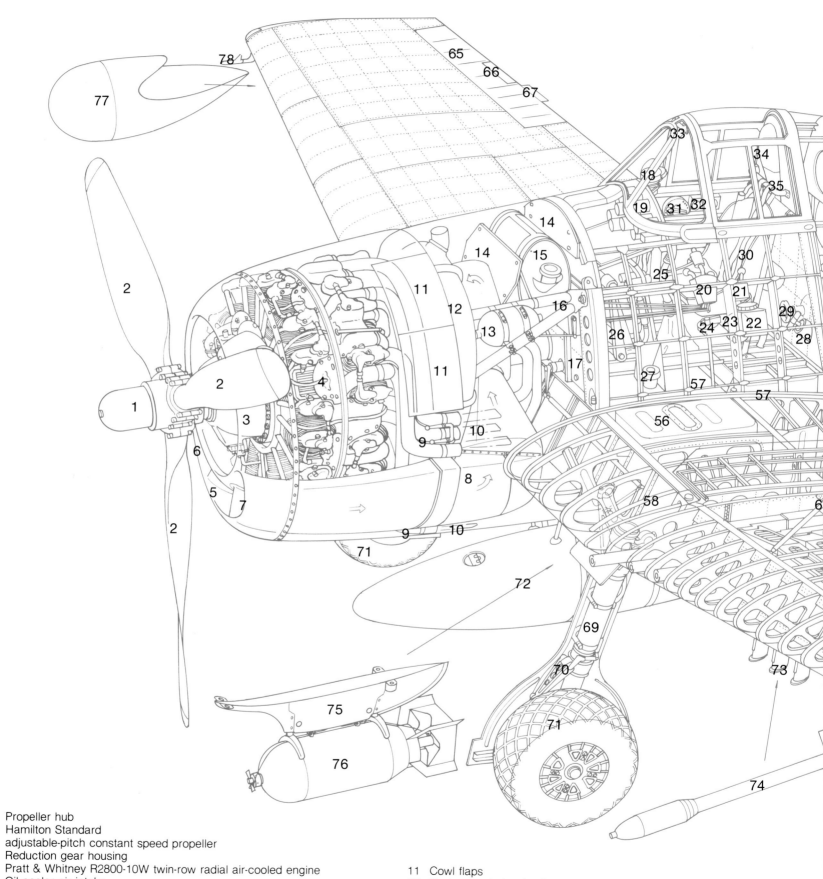

1 Propeller hub
2 Hamilton Standard
   adjustable-pitch constant speed propeller
3 Reduction gear housing
4 Pratt & Whitney R2800-10W twin-row radial air-cooled engine
5 Oil cooler air intake
6 Supercharger air intake
7 Supercharger air intake
8 Supercharger air intake duct
9 Exhaust pipes
10 Exhaust flame damper (F6F-5N only)

11 Cowl flaps
12 Engine carried-on-load mounts with rubber bushing
13 Hydraulic fluid tank
14 Armour plate
15 Engine oil tank
16 Engine mounting frame
17 Main bulkhead

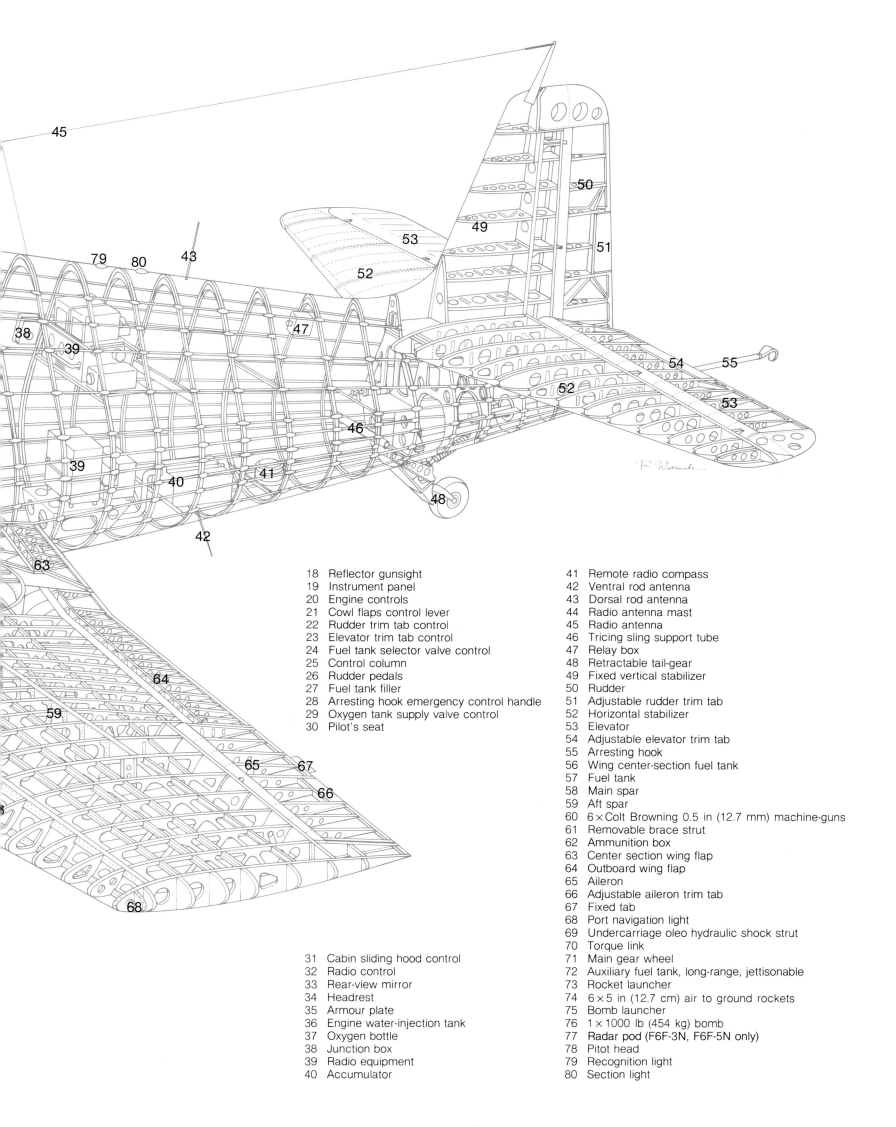

18 Reflector gunsight
19 Instrument panel
20 Engine controls
21 Cowl flaps control lever
22 Rudder trim tab control
23 Elevator trim tab control
24 Fuel tank selector valve control
25 Control column
26 Rudder pedals
27 Fuel tank filler
28 Arresting hook emergency control handle
29 Oxygen tank supply valve control
30 Pilot's seat

31 Cabin sliding hood control
32 Radio control
33 Rear-view mirror
34 Headrest
35 Armour plate
36 Engine water-injection tank
37 Oxygen bottle
38 Junction box
39 Radio equipment
40 Accumulator

41 Remote radio compass
42 Ventral rod antenna
43 Dorsal rod antenna
44 Radio antenna mast
45 Radio antenna
46 Tricing sling support tube
47 Relay box
48 Retractable tail-gear
49 Fixed vertical stabilizer
50 Rudder
51 Adjustable rudder trim tab
52 Horizontal stabilizer
53 Elevator
54 Adjustable elevator trim tab
55 Arresting hook
56 Wing center-section fuel tank
57 Fuel tank
58 Main spar
59 Aft spar
60 6 × Colt Browning 0.5 in (12.7 mm) machine-guns
61 Removable brace strut
62 Ammunition box
63 Center section wing flap
64 Outboard wing flap
65 Aileron
66 Adjustable aileron trim tab
67 Fixed tab
68 Port navigation light
69 Undercarriage oleo hydraulic shock strut
70 Torque link
71 Main gear wheel
72 Auxiliary fuel tank, long-range, jettisonable
73 Rocket launcher
74 6 × 5 in (12.7 cm) air to ground rockets
75 Bomb launcher
76 1 × 1000 lb (454 kg) bomb
77 Radar pod (F6F-3N, F6F-5N only)
78 Pitot head
79 Recognition light
80 Section light

In December, 1942, the Navy requested Grumman to study a Hellcat with floats for off-water operations, and the company followed through with tests of a 1/16th scale model at the Navy's Washington wind tunnel. The floats were designed by the Edo Aircraft Co. They were almost 29 feet (8 m 84 cm) long, and each float had a cross-section that was about 40 per cent of the fuselage cross-section area. It would have created a major drag increase and the performance of the Hellcat would have been degraded far too much. The water-borne Hellcat was never developed any further than the wind-tunnel tests and some analyses.

Out of all these prototypes, modifications and design studies, only two standard Hellcats entered production, and they became the backbone of the Navy's fighter strength in the Pacific.

Building the Hellcat

The U.S. Navy accepted its first production Hellcat on 30 September, 1942, and its last on 16 November, 1945. Between those two dates, distanced in time by only 25½ months, Hellcat acceptances totalled 12,275. That's a sustained, average production rate of 481 units each month, a formidable mark for a wartime production effort.

All of those Hellcats were built by Grumman, unlike other Grumman aircraft that were produced and further developed by General Motors. And almost all of them were built in a new plant, erected specifically for the Hellcat. It was built from, among other materials, steel salvaged from New York's Second Avenue Elevated Railway, when that imposing system of mass transit was torn down just before the war.

The angular lines of the Hellcat were chosen to simplify production. Its simple, tapered wing and tail surfaces, its slab-sided fuselage, its internal systems and unseen components were designed, developed and produced by people who, some months before, knew literally nothing about the construction of aircraft and who may never even have seen one up close.

Grumman began its history in a small town on Long Island, New York, at one of the many airports that dotted the chequerboard of flat farmland and villages characteristic of pre-war times. Through successive moves, the company had stayed on the Island, and had drawn its labour force from the area surrounding its plants and airport. That keystone of Grumman policy was one of its great strengths; when the time came to expand production, Grumman was able to call in people from every profession and occupation, to train them to build aircraft and – more importantly – to retain them in that vital task until it had been completed.

The basic Hellcat production programme had its inception in a Navy letter of intent to Grumman, dated 6 August, 1941. The formal contract was signed 23 May, 1942, and by mid-June the first tooling was being built. The first direct labour on the Hellcat had begun, without benefit of production tooling, the previous January.

Leroy R. Grumman, President of what was then called the Grumman Aircraft Engineering Corporation (GAEC), was a quiet, introspective thinker who tended to concentrate on technical problems and to leave the running of the company on a day-to-day basis in the very capable hands of Leon A. Swirbul. Swirbul, who was universally known as "Jake", was an extroverted manager, thoroughly at home with people of all stations in life. His visibility was so high that it frequently seemed as if he, and not Grumman, was the real mover and shaker in the company. No matter; each man was essential, and each was complementary to the other.

But because Jake was always to be seen, moving around the shop floor, greeting visiting Navy pilots, travelling to the Pacific to find out firsthand how Grumman aircraft were holding up, Jake is the one who gets credit for many of the innovative and pioneering aspects of Grumman's approach to production.

The first necessity for Hellcat production was a place to make the aircraft. Grumman's existing facilities were already crowded with lines that were turning out components, assemblies and complete aircraft for the Navy, and for foreign customers. There was no room to sandwich any F6F production among the long aisles that were crowded with Wildcat fuselages, Avenger wings, and even the last of the of J2F-5 "Duck" line.

Accordingly, Plant 3 was designed and built, using – as mentioned – steel from the Second Avenue El. Before the mortar was dry on the brickwork, and before the roof or the fourth wall had been finished, Grumman had moved tools and workers into the plant. It opened officially 1 June, 1942, according to Grumman records; that probably means that the plant was dedicated that day. It is a matter of record that the first production wing panels for the Hellcat were being assembled by stiff-fingered workers during the cold winter months of 1942. The heating plant for the building had yet to be completed; wartime priorities had delayed its delivery, and there was no chance of salvaging something like a heating system from an abandoned factory somewhere. All of the country's industrial base was moving into high gear, and plant space was at an absolute premium.

By the end of 1942, Grumman had delivered ten complete Hellcats; the press releases of the time referred to the quantity as a "full squadron" which was not quite accurate, but forgivable. And from then on, there was no looking back. During 1943, 2,547 Hellcats – a mix of the single XF6F-3/-4 experimental prototype, 2,441 standard F6F-3 Hellcats, and 104 F6F-3N night fighters – were accepted by the Navy. Consider the magnitude of that increase in production: From 10 in one year to 2,547 the very next. To understand that accomplishment a little better, one has to understand the general attitude that prevailed at Grumman among both labour and management.

The population of Long Island was made up of duck farmers, potato farmers, clam-diggers, fishermen and housewives. They became skilled metalsmiths, machinists, crew chiefs, electrical experts, assemblers, inspectors, tool designers, draughtsmen. Grummen recruited, and then trained thousands of personnel during the war years, putting them through programmes that assumed no prior knowledge and that began by telling them what an aircraft was.

More than 30 per cent of the Grumman work force were women, and they proved a point in the war years that still is largely unappreciated: Women can do anything that men can do, and often do it better. They learned as rapidly, and worked as hard. They became any of the hundreds of technicians needed for the efficient production and testing of the Hellcat. Women were aircraft captains, the industrial equivalent of the military crew chief. And some of them became test pilots, lifting the roaring Hellcats off the runway and into the air on acceptance flight tests that demanded much skill and no little bravery.

Grumman pioneered in the introduction of blacks and the credit has been given to Jake for the way it was done. Jake, who knew his shop people, also knew that they felt some hostility to blacks. It was a common social phenomenon in those days. But he knew that they recognized superior performance when they saw it. So Jake recruited a top-level black basketball player, put him through training school, and made him an inspector. He was soon joined by other blacks, picked for their local renown as athletes, and introduced into the work force with no fuss. Within a short time, Grumman workers had accepted the presence of blacks on the assembly lines, in the component shops, and at the lunch tables in the cafeteria. It was a model programme; it resulted in more than 800 blacks employed in the company. And it was accomplished with a minimum of problems.

Among other Grumman innovations was the "Little Green Truck". Wartime priorities made it difficult to keep personal automobiles in good repair, and they frequently broke down on the way to work. A telephone call to the plant brought out "The Little Green Truck", with assistance for the stranded motorist. It was also available to go back to a worker's home and turn the heat off under a forgotten pot roast or to perform some other important errand.

Many of the women workers were the young wives of servicemen, doing their part for the war effort. Many of them had small children at home; so Grumman introduced nursery schools, an industry first. Three were opened in key locations, staffed with full-time nurses, and a consulting pediatrician on call. The schools were open 12 hours a day, and served five meals at different hours to match the mothers' work schedules. The fees that were charged varied, according to the mothers' salaries.

The result of all this was to weld the work force and management closely, and to enable both of them to direct their maximum efforts to the production of aircrafts. Grumman's salary scale was not the highest in the aircraft industry at the time, but the extra benefits were unusual. The company developed an incentive bonus system, to reward workers for goals reached or exceeded. Additionally, there was a bonus for seniority, in effect. The longer one stayed at Grumman, the more that portion of the bonus was. Every Christmas, Grumman, Swirbul and a plant executive lined up in one of the large assembly areas, and handed out bonus cheques and a Christmas turkey to each employee.

It has been called "paternalism"; but most Grumman employees looked on the company's attitude as a good one, and gave their best in return. The semantics were not important.

Five plants contributed to Hellcat production. Plant 1 held the experimental shop, and produced the first prototypes of any Grumman design, including the Hellcats. Plant 3 was where Hellcat production was concentrated, and where components were built and assembled. Plant 11 in Syosset was responsible for building the control surfaces; Plant 13 in Lindenhurst made engine mounts for all the Grumman aircraft; and Plant 14 in Babylon produced the electrical system harness and other wiring for the company.

During 1943, Hellcat production reached its full stride, and by early autumn, Grumman was turning out about 100 F6F-3s every week. The figure continued to climb as the months went by, and by late 1944, Swirbul told the Navy that Grumman was headed for a figure of 700 Hellcats a month. It was more than the Navy could handle; the need did not exist for such a quantity, and they asked Grumman to cut back production to no more than 600 fighters every month.

The peak was reached in March, 1945; Grumman produced 664 aircraft of all types during those 31 days, and of the total, 605 were Hellcats.

The Navy had high praise for the Grumman production effort. James Forrestal, then the Secretary of the Navy, wrote:

"I think everyone has heard of your Hellcats and of the reputation you achieved in 1943 when you set an all-time record in the aviation industry for accelerating production. I have no doubt that you would still be beating your own record month after month if the Navy had not had to slow you down a little."

The Navy also was on record with a statement that Grumman produced more pounds of airframe per taxpayer dollar than any other company in the fighter business. To give dimension to that general statement, the Hellcat's original contract price was $50,000, exclusive of what was then known as GFE: Government Furnished Equipment. By the end of the production run, the price had been cut to $35,000, a 30 per cent reduction in cost to the government. Grumman also liked to point out that the Hellcat was delivered to the Navy for 2/3 of the price of the Vought F4U "Corsair" series.

So the "embattled farmers" – their own description – established production records that set marks for the industry. During the last years of the war, rivalry was intense between Grumman and North American Aviation, then in full production of the elegant P-51 Mustang series. Monthly production rates of the two fighters were posted on bulletin boards, broadcast over the public address system and discussed at lunch. And when, in March, 1945, Grumman set the mark that soundly beat NAA's deliveries for that month, it was announced over the loudspeakers in every factory by Jake Swirbul himself, and it produced a small pandemonium among the workers.

Production was not the only mark that was beaten by the Grumman work force. Absenteeism and turnover were two of the most bothersome factors in the aircraft industry, which has long been noted for having a population of "gipsies" who move with the contracts. Grumman again was the exception; its unavoidable absenteeism figures were consistently under one per cent during the war, and its annual turnover rate was about three per cent, including those men who were drafted to serve in the armed forces. Those two numbers beat all aircraft industry figures by a substantial margin.

Tested before the Battle

XF6F-2

(David A. Anderton)

Flight-testing has been, and always will be, a vital part of any aircraft development programme. It first seeks to establish the basic safety of the aircraft under test; the early steps explore level flight, simple manœuvres, approaches to the stall, low-speed handling, and other aspects of getting the craft off the ground, into the air, and back down again safely. Subsequent test flights extend those manoeuvres, increase the speed and altitude range, perform more abrupt turns. Gradually the entire flight envelope – the aerodynamic and structural limits that completely define the extremes of performance – is explored and the aircraft is judged as safe for other pilots to fly.

Flight-testing is a requirement in any aircraft development programme, because it alone can prove that the operating parameters are what the designers say they are.

The Hellcat flight test programme started when Bob Hall made the first flight on the experimental XF6F-1 and was generally satisfied with what he found. Hall's long experience as a pilot, coupled with his technical and design background, fitted him for the job of initial evaluation of the Hellcat. Later test flying was done by Seldon Converse and, still later, other Grumman test pilots were brought into the programme.

The Navy, as the interested purchaser, also evaluated the Hellcat. Navy pilots flew the aircraft at Bethpage and at the Naval Air Station at Anacostia, Maryland, home of much of the Navy's wartime flight-test activity. And later, when the British bought Hellcats, Royal Navy pilots took F6Fs into the air on a series of detailed test and evaluation missions to see that the planes met the standards the Fleet Air Arm had established.

Finally late in the war and too late to have much influence on Hellcat design, the fighter was tested by NACA pilots at the Langley Memorial Aeronautical Laboratory. Their approach was much more academic and research-oriented; their major concern was with understanding the qualities of flight, and trying to define them for future generations of test pilots.

In the early war days, the popular concept of a test pilot was drawn from the movies: Handsome devil-may-care types who casually risked their lives in screaming power dives and pullouts. Occasionally something went wrong, and then there was an opportunity for some really dramatic moments while the test pilot tried to free himself and parachute to safety. The image was based on some fact, of course. Part of every flight-test programme was a series of pullouts, entered at high speed. Those manoeuvres are severe tests of the structure of an aircraft, and also of its pilot, because they call for imposing "G" loads several times the normal force of gravity. Grumman's contract with the Navy specified that the company was to demonstrate one aircraft. That meant that it was up to Grumman to show the Navy, through a series of flight tests, that the Hellcat had been designed so that it met the Navy's requirements for flight performance, structural strength and operational flexibility. The preliminary flying was done at the Bethpage plant; for the serious work, the programme moved to the Naval Air Station at Anacostia, down the Potomac River from Washington.

The aircraft chosen for demonstration flying was Bureau No. 04775, the first production F6F-3. The flying at Anacostia began in March, 1943, and proceeded without a hitch until the scheduled dives and pullouts. On the fourth and fifth dives, the horizontal stabilizer was overstressed. It distorted, and cracked, and neither was acceptable in an aircraft designed for the rigours of combat. That ended the demonstration, while the Grumman engineering team went back to report the details of the problem and to ask for a fast solution. Parallel to the piloted flights of the Hellcat, a radio-controlled, pilotless Hellcat was being tested in a series of high-speed dives called Project Fox. The work was done at the Naval Air Station at Cherry Point, South Carolina, and the purpose was to determine whether or not the Hellcat would hold together at speeds greater than the restricted limits that had been imposed on the plane. There were then " . . . grave doubts about the control characteristics . . ." in a high-speed dive. Pilots had reported earlier that, in their dives to a Mach number of 0.67 maximum, they had the feeling that a loss of control was imminent.

The radio-controlled dives were begun from 27,000 feet (8230 m); the Hellcat was put into a 70-degree dive, measured from the horizontal, and was allowed to accelerate under full power to an altitude of 10,000 feet (3050 m), where the pullout signal was given by one of the two Grumman Wildcat fighters that controlled the tests. There are reports that one of the dives exceeded 500-mph (805 km/h).

The stabilizer failure took a long time to analyse and fix. Grumman's standard procedure was to strengthen something first and test it again, repeating that cycle until a fix had been achieved. Later, if there were time and reason to do so, the engineers would attempt to analyse what went wrong and why. Remember that this was during a war, and quick fixes, with analyses afterwards, were the rule.

The failure first occurred in an 8G pullout from a dive at 276 mph (444 km/h) indicated airspeed. Subsequent failures happened at higher speeds, in the range of 270 to 390 mph (435 to 628 km/h) indicated, and at load factors above 6.8G. The flow field around the aircraft produced a forced vibration at 3,600 cycles per minute at the tail; that high-speed shake plus the stress of the pullout produced permanent buckling and failure of the skin on the leading edge of the horizontal stabilizer.

In June, 1943, the Navy began a series of static tests on a horizontal tail at the Naval Aircraft Factory, Philadelphia, in an attempt to analyse what was causing the problem. Meantime, the Hellcat was restricted from high-G, high-speed pullouts until the problem was cleared up to the satisfaction of the Navy and company.

Grumman test pilot Corwin H. Meyer, who flew the structural demonstration tests of the Hellcat, remembers what was happening. "The Hellcat was the first Grumman airplane, to my knowledge, that hit the buffet boundary. It was a fairly new phenomenon then, and the first thought was that it was some sort of tail flutter that was causing the trouble with the stabilizer. But somebody in the aerodynamics department came up with the idea that maybe it was the wing wake that was creating the problems with the tail. So we stuck a bunch of long yarns on the wing, long enough to almost reach the tail, and I went up to pull some G. Sure enough, at high speed and just above 6G, those yarns were pointing straight at the horizontal tail. It was the wing wake that was producing the buffeting and the problem.

"After we got past that, we had a very, very fine aircraft, an old man's aircraft. It flew itself off and onto the runway. The cockpit was well-organized, and you could see – really see well – out of the canopy and windshield. I could see the runway ahead of me on the flareout; you couldn't say that about any other fighter, Army or Navy, at that time.

"It was stable laterally, and gusts and crosswinds were no problem. The stall was great. My only complaint – and it was shared by every test pilot who flew the aircraft, whether he was Navy, British or NACA – was that the ailerons were heavy. It seemed to me that we spent most of our flight-test time trying to improve the ailerons to get them to do what the Navy wanted. But nothing seemed to help. The F6F had high lateral damping, and we were working against that."

"Corky" Meyer started his flight-test experience with the Hellcat series with a few flights in the XF6F-1 and the XF6F-3, and did all the structural and powerplant test flights and most of the aerodynamic tests on the production F6F-3 and -5 models. He also flew the sixth production F6F-3 (BuNo. 04780) from its first to last test flight. That machine, like any other aircraft in Grumman's test programme, was called a "dog ship"; the origins of the name are lost in time.

"I flew the 'dog ship' on an altitude test," Meyer remembers, "And when I got to 32,600 feet (9930 m) the engine quit just as suddenly as if it had been turned off. So I glided down, and got the engine restarted at about 7,000 feet (2130 m). I phoned Carl Bellinger (a Republic Aviation test pilot with long experience on the P-47 and its similar powerplant) and talked it over with him, and he told me about the pressurized ignition harness they had on the P-47s. Pratt & Whitney had orders to deliver all their production to Republic, so we got the Navy to lean on them through the

proper channels, and six weeks later we got a harness for our own work. On the first flight with the pressurized ignition system, I got up to 37,000 feet (11300 m) with no problem."

Meyer emphasized the strength of the Hellcat: "You could still pull 3G at 420 knots, and about all you could stand at the low-speed end of the envelope. The Dash 3 had a 6.5G limit, and the Dash 5 let you go to 7.5G. And about there the average pilot is beginning to feel the strain a bit.

"The landing gear was one of the more rugged features of a very rugged aircraft. The Navy requirements called for a six-foot free drop with the aircraft at landing weight. But the 'Schwendler factor' came in here again; Grumman kept on going after making the six-foot (1.8 m) drop successfully, and took it up to ten feet (3 m). They couldn't go any higher, because the canopy was practically up against the ceiling in the test building."

NACA pilots made a series of 30 flights in the second production F6F-3 (Bu. No. 04776), beginning in February, 1944, and ending 15 May. They reported, in NACA Memorandum Report L5B13, that " . . . pilots were favourably impressed with the longitudinal stability and control of the F6F-3 aircraft. They considered it an easy airplane to fly. The control forces in abrupt and steady manoeuvers were satisfactory. Also, the airplane was very easy to land."

But the NACA research pilots noted some problems, including the fact that the aileron control characteristics did not completely fill either Navy or NACA minimum requirements. There was objectionable rudder shake in all flight conditions, and it occurred right through the speed range. The least stable condition tested was one that was going to cause some problems in carrier operations: The wave-off. And they noted that the Hellcat was difficult to control in highspeed flight.

The thorough NACA analysis of the Hellcat's stall characteristics reported that "Stall warnings existed in steady flight for glide, climb and landing conditions in the form of increased vibration, a duct howl in power-off conditions, and gentle buffeting." That buffeting only happened if the approach to the stall was made very slowly and deliberately; otherwise it was not among the warnings. And there was no warning of stall in either the approach or wave-off conditions, further aggravating that latter manoeuver. The NACA tests confirmed Meyer's opinion of the stall: " . . . roll-off was mild, checked easily by ailerons and rudder."

The Navy's Board of Inspection and Survey made its final performance flight tests of the F6F-3 over the better part of a year, between August, 1944, and June, 1945. There were four basic items that had been guaranteed by Grumman in the contract; Grumman met two of them, and nearly made the other two. Maximum speed had been guaranteed to be greater than 377 mph (607 km/h), using military power at 23,400 feet (7130 m); the Hellcat under test did 376 mph (605 km/h). Its stalling speed, power off, at sea level, had been guaranteed to be less than 80.6 mph (129.7 km/h); the actual number in the Navy tests was 81.5 mph (131.2 km/h).

The company had said that the service ceiling – that altitude where the rate of climb is 100 feet (30 m) per minute – would exceed 38,000 feet (11580 m), and the Navy

A formation of F6Fs over Guam.

achieved 38,100 feet (11610 m). Finally, the takeoff distance in a 25-knot wind, a critical factor in carrier-based operations, had been promised to be less than 285 feet (87 m) by Grumman. The Navy got its test Hellcat off the deck in 265 feet (80 m).

By then, of course, Navy pilots by the hundreds had flown the Hellcats off carrier decks, had fought with them from sea level to the thin blue edge of the stratosphere, had jammed the throttles forward for all the power they could get, and had manoeuvered abruptly, violently, recklessly, in their fights with the Japanese aircraft. The flight-test reports, if they knew about them, were of no interest whatever except as they imposed limitations that were clearly stated in large capital letters in their pilots' handbooks.

Those limitations were few. When diving the F6F-3 or -3N, do not exceed 415 knots IAS below 10,000 feet (3000 m); for most of the -5 and -5N models, do not exceed 440 knots. Maximum permissible speed for unlimited use of the ailerons is 260 knots IAS (Indicated Air Speed). Don't exceed +5G and −2G limits of acceleration. Don't lower the landing gear above 135 knots, or it will trail and not lock down. (Pilots later took advantage of that to dive-bomb with the landing gear trailing to act as an air brake.)

But there was one limitation on the Hellcat that did not appear in the handbooks. It was taught in training for combat, and it was repeated and repeated at every level by instructors, flight leaders, squadron commanders, air group commanders, and probably task force admirals. It was simple: Don't dogfight with a Zero.

And even so, it was a lesson that had to be learned again and again in combat. Some of those who learned were lucky and escaped, to fight again. But those who ignored that advice and tried to stay with the Zero in its agile aerobatics too often died.

Combat, in the final analysis, was the ultimate set of limitations imposed on the Hellcat.

Hellcat's First Fight

"BULLETIN: Washington, DC, Oct. 12 (Delayed) – Grumman Hellcats shot down 21 Japanese planes with a loss of only two in an air battle over an unidentified South Pacific island, the Navy disclosed today. The raid was the Hellcats' first appearance in combat.

"A special Navy bulletin also announced that Hellcats at Wake Island on October 5 and 6 accounted for 61 Jap planes without the loss of a single Grumman fighter.

"It is presumed that the delayed Navy announcement regarding the 21–2 victory in the South Pacific refers to a battle which took place before the September 3 raid on Marcus Island. The score for the two battles – that one and the Wake Island action – now stands at 82 – 2 in favor of the Grumman fighters."

That news dispatch, reprinted in *Plane News*, the Grumman plant newspaper, for 14 October, 1943, was greeted with wild enthusiasm in Plant 3, where the Hellcats were being produced. Like many other wartime reports on both sides, that one contained its exaggerations, and later, more detailed analysis of the battles reduced the claims somewhat. But the basic truth was there: The Hellcats had been in their first combat, and had acquitted themselves outstandingly.

It was quite different from the news of the initial combat of the Grumman TBF-1 Avenger. Six of the then-new torpedo bombers, based on Midway Island as part of Torpedo Squadron 8, attacked the Japanese fleet early on the morning of 4 June, 1942. Five had been shot down and the sixth just managed to get back, badly damaged and with a dead rear gunner.

Zero 22 of the Tainan *Kokutai* on its way from the Rabaul airbase to attack Guadalcanal, 11 October, 1942.

The Battle of Midway was a turning point in the war. From then on, the power of America's sea and air forces was to grow rapidly, to overwhelm the Japanese. The U.S. Navy had a single fleet carrier left at the end of 1942; but in little more than one year, it had added eight *Essex*-class fast carriers, each with a 90-aircraft air group, nine *Independence*-class carriers, each with a 35-aircraft group, and 25 escort carriers.

Further, there was a new generation of Naval aircraft entering service. The Avenger was rapidly replacing the aged Douglas Devastator; Curtiss SB2C Helldiver bombers promised much better performance than the Douglas Dauntless they were supplanting – a promise, incidentally, that was a long time in the keeping – and the Hellcat was taking over from the Wildcat as the first-line fighter.

The first combat-ready batch of Hellcats was assigned to Fighting Squadron Nine (VF-9, in Navy shorthand) and they learned how to handle the new planes at NAS Oceana. The squadron boarded the *Essex*, in February, 1943, for carrier qualification trials to prove out both the aircraft and the pilots. The squadron was officially assigned to the *Essex* on 13 March, 1943, and declared ready for combat. The time and place had yet to be chosen.

The Pacific was about to become the stage for a massive, island-hopping series of assaults that were to roll the Japanese garrisons back, one by one, either by defeat or by bypassing them. Amphibious task forces, supported by massive Naval – and frequently Army Air Forces – air strength, were assembling and provisioning for the battles that lay ahead. The tactical plan was similar for each: A saturation bombardment of the Japanese defences by Navy divebombers and fighter-bombers, supported in strength by covering fighters and by shelling by off-shore battleships, cruisers and destroyers. After this softening of the defenders, the Marines would storm the beaches, establish a beachhead, and

fight their way inland until the Japanese surrendered or were slaughtered.

The envisioned role of the Hellcat in these battles was a dual one. It was responsible for maintaining combat air patrol above its carriers and the fleet, knocking down any Japanese aircraft that attempted to attack the ships. It was also responsible for ground attack, bombing and strafing the Japanese positions ahead of the invading Marines, and working with Marine fighters that were giving close support to the Leathernecks on the ground.

A dress rehearsal was to be a strike against Marcus Island, a lone mountain top lying about halfway between Wake Island and the Japanese Bonin Islands. Marcus had been hit earlier by Navy bombers in March, 1942, but the damage they did then was light and ineffective militarily. The second Marcus strike was scheduled for 31 August, 1943, and the Navy sent Task Force 15 against it. TF15, commanded by Rear Admiral Charles A. Pownall, was built around two fast carriers, the *Essex* and the *Yorktown*, plus the light carrier *Independence*.

TF15 sailed from its Hawaiian rendezvous on 23 August, headed on a course to bypass Marcus to the north-west. The plan was to turn south and hit the northern side of the base, expected to be the weaker sector of the defences. Primary target was the Japanese airfield and its aircraft, rumoured to be a fairly large air unit.

The two carriers launched their aircraft in darkness, because the tactical plan called for strikes against the airfield no later than one hour after dawn. Both "Fighting Nine", from the *Essex*, and "Fighting Five" from the *Yorktown*, dispatched their Hellcats as part of the first strike. Commander James H. Flatley, CAG (Commander, Air Group) aboard the *Yorktown*, made the last takeoff from that carrier. His job that day was to be air boss to direct the strike from his Hellcat. Because he was expected to stay on the scene for the duration

A photographic F6F-5P on the deck of the *Bunker Hill* being readied for missions over Iwo Jima, 19 February, 1945. (National Archives)

Fighting Nine, from the *Essex* (CV-9), takes off for an attack on Truk on 16 February, 1944. (National Archives)

of the fight, his plane was carrying a pair of auxiliary fuel tanks. Flatley later wrote this description of the engagement; it appeared in *Plane News* on 16 September, 1943.

"A Grumman 'Avenger' was the first plane over Marcus at 6:08 a.m. The pilot found a bright light burning in the air base's control tower, so he turned on his own running lights so that any watching Japs might think his plane was one of their own. Then he dropped his bombs from low altitude and was away before the anti-aircraft woke up.

"The island was immediately lighted by fires as the heavy bombs exploded. At the same time the supporting fighters began their strafing.

"The anti-aircraft opened up after about three minutes. Meanwhile the fighters in the light of the fires saw seven Mitsubishi bombers beautifully parked in a line on the runway. Four Hellcats immediately commenced low-altitude strafing runs through heavy ack-ack. They made repeated passes dodging over the targets in a series of wingovers and destroyed the seven bombers one by one. They finished the job in ten minutes. It was a beautiful job and the highlight of the day . . . Incidentally, this is the first time I know of that carrier fighters have done night strafing."

The Japanese were taken by surprise, and were unable to get any defending aircraft into the air. Only the anti-aircraft gunners were able to fight back, and their firing downed two Hellcats and a TBF. The Hellcats assigned to combat air patrol over the island orbited with nothing to do, and watched the fight develop below them. The F6Fs from Fighting Five and Nine continued to strafe the field, working over the anti-aircraft battery positions to draw their attention away from the slower dive bombers that were hitting the buildings and potholing the runways.

The task force launched nine strikes against Marcus Island that day, and by late in the afternoon all Japanese defensive activity had ground to a halt. The last sporadic firing of the anti-aircraft guns stopped, and left the Navy in complete possession of the skies above Marcus. It was an early, and classical, example of the gaining of air superiority, and the importance of that superiority in determining the way the rest of the battle would go. It was a demonstration that the U.S. Navy would repeat, time after time, as it advanced inexorably across the broad reach of the Pacific.

The combat debut of the Hellcats in the Marcus strike triggered a long-lasting argument about which squadron first flew the planes into battle. Recently, Barrett Tillman, a careful researcher and fine writer, set the record straight for that day at Marcus Island. He pointed out that Fighting Five launched first, and could rightfully be credited with first going into battle with the Hellcats. But Fighting Nine, a few minutes later to launch, diverted two of its Hellcats on the way to the primary targets at Marcus to strafe a pair of Japanese picket boats. So VF-9 gets credit for the first shots fired in anger by Hellcats. Among the things that plague historians are the difficulties of proving, once and for all, any particular "first". The case of the Hellcat's first combat is one of those specific examples.

On 5 October, 1943, Lt. (JG) H. A. Cantrell, of Fighting Squadron 33 ("Hellcats"), wrote a letter to his brother:

"Our squadron was the first one in action with this new plane and not that squadron that made a raid on the Marcus Island.

"While we were in action we made a good record. I can't tell you how many planes our squadron shot down, but it was quite a few. I only got credit for half a Zero. My division leader and I shot down one together. One other day our division of four were jumped by eight Zeros. We went into our weave [The so-called 'Thach weave', a mutually supporting attack maneuvre developed by Cdr. James Thach while flying 'Wildcats'] and that was the only thing that saved us. I am sure that I got one of them that day but it wasn't confirmed. I could see part of his plane fly over my wing and my division leader saw two splashes but didn't actually see the plane hit the water."

Now, almost 40 years later, the details fade from memories. Records were often poorly kept in the pressure of daily combat, and we may never know exactly which squadron, let alone which pilot, first took the Hellcat off on a combat mission, first fired the guns in anger, first scored a victory over a Japanese aircraft. One fact remains. The Hellcat entered combat early in the autumn of 1943 and, from then on, the dimensions of air war in the Pacific changed. The Navy had a fighter that could gain control of the skies over the battleground.

Hellcat Actions and Aces

Neither the Japanese nor the Americans were able to gain a decisive advantage during early air combat in the Pacific. Neither country had an overwhelming quantity of skilled pilots available and neither held the technological edge in aircraft design that might have turned the tide of battle.

The development and deployment of the fast carrier force by the U.S. Navy introduced a new – and eventually decisive – factor into naval air power. The task force was mobile airpower, positioned in the Pacific on fast carriers that were supported by the traditional fighting ships. The fast carrier forces – later designated as numbered Task Forces – became the leading edge of the campaigns that were to destroy one Japanese outpost after another and finally reach the Japanese home islands themselves.

The fighter was the key element in the development of the tactics used by the task force. Fighter primary missions were seen first as combat air patrol, to defend their carriers, and second as escort, to defend the dive-bombers and torpedo planes set out on strikes. But the fighter soon proved itself to be a versatile and rugged weapons platform that could launch rockets or drop bombs with precision.

It was a stroke of good fortune, because as the war progressed, the other major elements of the air strike force did not measure up to their expected potential. The Douglas Dauntless dive-bombers were supposed to be replaced in fleet service by the greatly improved Curtiss Helldiver, but that latter aircraft was long delayed in reaching the fleet. When it did arrive, it was not greatly admired; it was quickly nicknamed "The Beast". The role of the torpedo bomber diminished steadily during the war. It was a high-risk way to attack shipping, and torpedo designers had not produced a

The F6F-5 is about to leave on a fighter sweep over Northern Luzon province in the Philippines, part of the Task Force 38 assault before the scheduled invasion by MacArthur's forces.

The humidity of this October, 1944, day condenses behind the propeller tips and is visible as vapor trails corkscrewing aft in the slipstream.

(National Archives)

dependable weapon that could be counted upon to run true and detonate after the drop from an aircraft.

Although it was not recognized at the time, the Navy was very dependent on the performance and the versatility of the Hellcat. And the F6F itself was unproven in long and continuing combat.

The strike against Rabaul on 5 November, 1943, was the first major air battle for Hellcats of the fast carrier force. It was, in a way, a test of the concept itself. Rabaul's harbour was the anchorage for a large number of Japanese merchant ships and warships; the latter were a potential threat to the thinly spread fighting ships of the U.S. Navy, just beginning their long advance across the Pacific. A clutch of cruisers lay at anchor and the mission of the Navy's Task Force 38 was simple: Get in, get the cruisers, get out.

Rabaul was heavily defended by anti-aircraft and fighters; at least 50 Zeros were routinely available as top cover for the base. Supplementing the ground-based anti-aircraft batteries would be the guns of the cruisers and any other warships in the harbour.

Toward this bastion sailed TF38, built around the 16-year old *Saratoga*, and the eight-month old *Princeton*. They launched their aircraft more than 200 miles (320 km) to the southeast of Rabaul, under rain clouds and an overcast sky. All available aircraft went; the striking force was a mix of about two dozen each of SBDs and TBFs, escorted by 52 Hellcats. Sixteen of them, from Fighting Twelve aboard the *Saratoga*, flew about 1,000 (305 m) feet above the bombers; in the lead fighter was VF-12's skipper, Cdr. Joseph C. Clifton. VF-12's executive officer, Lt. Cdr. R. G. Dose, led another 16 F6Fs stepped 3,000 feet (914 m) above Clifton's group. Well above both formations were the Hellcats from VF-23, off the *Princeton*, led by Cdr. Henry L. Miller. The air boss for the battle was the Air Group Commander, Cdr. Howard H. Caldwell, flying a TBF escorted by one Hellcat from the *Sara* and one from the *Princeton*.

Japanese radar had picked up the strike force and the Zeros were already in the air when the lead pilots sighted Rabaul. Their orders were to go straight to the target and to stick together for that run. The fighters were to fly escort, and not to be enticed away to tackle the three-plane flights of Zeros. Protection of the bombers was the primary mission.

The bombers ploughed into the heavy flak and drove straight through to their targets. The Zeros, unwilling to enter their own flak zones, hung around the edges until the bombing was over and the planes were leaving the area. And then the fight erupted. And, as "Jumping Joe" Clifton said later: "The F6F proved to be far and away the best fighter in the air . . . definitely faster at sea level than the Zeke . . . did not have the maneuverability or the climb advantage, but again the Thach weave plus the rugged construction and pilot protection offset these . . . The F6F's superior diving speed proved a Godsend in places where weaving was impossible."

The cruisers were hit and three were heavily damaged. Five Hellcats and five bombers were lost; the U.S. pilots claimed 11 Japanese planes shot down and 14 more probably shot down. Those claims were exaggerated, like most of the air combat claims made during the war. But the important point had been made. The Hellcat had shown its abilities within the framework of a difficult mission and the melee that followed. The Rabaul strike was the real baptism of fire for the F6F. Within a few days, Rabaul was hit again; and then the campaign against the Gilbert Islands, led by Task Force 50 re-emphasized the Hellcat's capability. In that latter campaign, the F6F came into its own, and established, once and for all, its superiority over anything the Japanese could put into the air. After the Gilberts, came assaults on the Marshalls. On 29 January, 1944, Rear Admiral Marc Mitscher opened the fight to take Kwajalein with a strike by about 700 carrier-based aircraft. Mitscher, commanding Task Force 58 with its 15 heavy battleships, 18 cruisers, about 100 destroyers and a mix of 17 carriers of heavy, light and escort types, directed "Operation Flintlock", the beginning of the end for Japan.

Kwajalein was followed by the occupation of the Marshall Islands, strikes on the Western Caroline Islands, landings at Hollandia in New Guinea and the assault against the Marianas Islands, slated to become the bases for the gigantic Boeing B-29 Superfortress long-range bombers that were to destroy Japanese industries, armaments and cities.

There was however an unusual Hellcat action far removed from the Pacific during mid-1944. Said a Navy dispatch in August, 1944:

"New Hellcats piled up an impressive record of destruction during landings in Southern France. Based on baby flattops, the F6F-5s gave close support to the U.S. Army troops and blasted the Nazis along the shore during their northward retreat."

Two U.S. Navy carriers – the *Kasaan Bay* and the *Tulagi* – supported that landing with Hellcats. In their fighter-bomber role, they first struck the beaches before the landing of the amphibious assault force, then spotted shell bursts for the off-shore naval artillery firing. After that, they chased retreating German columns. VFO-1, flying off the *Tulagi*, claimed to have shot up 487 motorized transports and other vehicles.

On 19 August, a pair of Hellcats shot down three Luftwaffe Heinkel 111s, caught near Lyon, France; another F6F duo searching for a fight found and shot down three Junkers Ju 52 transports.

The reputation of the "Grumman Iron Works" was upheld time and again in combat. One Hellcat of VF-5 aboard the *Yorktown* came back from a raid against Palau and grazed a gun turret after a shaky landing. The plane continued up the deck, shedding its wing, then its empennage, then finally its after fuselage up to the armour plate bulkhead behind the pilot. Ensign Black threw back the canopy and climbed out of the ruins, his only injury a forehead scratch.

Normal landings incorporated post-flight checks while the plane was still in motion. Once the Hellcats picked up the arresting gear wires, they were quickly brought to a halt while the "airedales", the plane crews on the carrier deck, disengaged the wire and gave the taxi signal. When the pilot passed the bridge, he held up his open hand with fingers tallying his victories. As he passed the radioman on deck, that

'Hangar Queen,' a Hellcat grounded several times in one week for minor repairs, is about to be launched on a mission to Sakishima.   (Marine Corps)

specialist would tap his ear, asking the pilot if the radio worked properly. Finally the Hellcat was spotted forward on the deck and the wheels were chocked. The engineering officer then moved toward the plane, holding up his thumb. If the pilot answered with the same gesture, he knew the plane was mechanically OK. If not, he waited for the pilot to climb down and start the list of complaints.

The compression of action into the space of a carrier deck made for a few furious minutes during each launch and recovery of aircraft. Not all the landings were good, nor were all of them as fortunate as Ensign Black's escape. One Hellcat came in for a landing on a strange carrier, a common practice when fuel was low after the return from combat. Just as the pilot was about to cut the power, the sea lifted the ship's stern and the F6F slammed onto the deck in a very hard landing. The guns fired a short burst; apparently they had not been safetied. The belly tank broke loose during the arresting and its momentum carried it into the propeller, which sliced it into chunks and sprayed the remaining gasoline over the aircraft. The fire was extinguished, and the pilot only received minor burns. But 11 men on the carrier island were wounded by bullets, and five planes spotted on the forward deck were holed. Another Hellcat, being respotted with its wings folded, somehow triggered off a burst from the six .50-cal machine-guns. The bullets went right through the flight deck, wounded six men on the hangar deck, and a man in sick bay on the third deck below.

Hellcats flew a classic escort action over Manila in October, 1944, that was a textbook example of that type of mission.

They were from Task Force 38.4, commanded by Rear Admiral Ralph Davison. The fast carrier *Enterprise* was in the group, which was tasked to send its planes against Nelson Field, a Japanese air base on Luzon. The *Enterprise* launched at 0900 on 15 October; its strike force consisted of nine Helldivers and eight Avengers with an escort of 16 Hellcats from "Fighting Twenty" under Cdr. Fred Bakutis. The Helldivers and Avengers were carrying bombs; the Hellcats were armed with rockets in addition to their standard ration of .50-cal ammunition.

The bombers cruised in at 15,000 feet (4570 m), with Hellcats above and to the sides. Bakutis led the top two elements – four Hellcats – at 22,000 feet (6706 m). They were still 40 miles out of Manila Bay when Bakutis saw the Japanese fighters. There were about 40 Oscars, and they knew the first part of their business. They boxed in the bombers and their escorts, cruising along a parallel course, while the Navy pilots watched and waited.

And then, singly, the Oscars began runs against the formation, as feints to attempt to draw off the Hellcats. That didn't work; the F6Fs stayed in formation and refused to break off for battle. The Japanese continued to run in, still singly, and pressed their attacks until they had to be fought. A Hellcat element would swing wide to meet the thrust, and then shoot down the intruder. It was, in retrospect, a very one-sided fight. The Japanese were unable to get through the protective screen, and were shot out of the sky, one at a time, until nearly all of the intercepting force had been destroyed. There were no American losses, either to the heavy flak, or to the fighters. And, said Cdr. A. E. Riera, who was flying the leading Helldiver, "Not one enemy fighter approached within gun range.'

By the end of 1944, the fleet was calling its airpower "The Big Blue Blanket". The Hellcats had seized air superiority and, except for an occasional nuisance raider, no Japanese aircraft penetrated the defences to attack the fleet.

Cdr. James S. Thach organized fighter sweeps by day and interdiction strikes by night to seek out and destroy what was left of Japanese air power. On 14 October, the day before the classic escort mission described earlier, Thach's

A Hellcat lands heavily and its six HVAR rockets bounce along the deck of the *Essex*. (National Archives)

Six Aces In The F6F

The complete list of U.S. Navy and Marine Corps aces who achieved their string of five or more victories while flying the Hellcat is far too long for the scope of this book. Dozens of pilots earned the title "ace," some in a single combat sortie. Others made their scores one at a time, over a period of some months in battle.

The six aces named here head the list, and their exploits are a representative cross-section of the ways in which Navy and Marine pilots became aces.

Cdr. David McCampbell, Medal of Honour winner, rolled up a total score of 34 aerial victories and 20 aircraft destroyed on the ground. He commanded Air Group 15 on board the fast carrier *Essex* in strikes against Marcus Island in May, 1944, and later in the attacks against Saipan, the battles of the Philippine Sea and of the Leyte Gulf. On 19 June, 1944, the day of the Great Marianas Turkey Shoot, McCampbell got seven Japanese fighters. On 12 September, over the Philippines, he got four more and the next day shot down three. His best day's shooting was 24 October, when he and his wingman Lt. (jg) Roy W. Rushing of VF-15 attacked a formation of 40 Zeros. In a one-sided slaughter, McCampbell shot down nine while Rushing got six. The fight lasted about ten minutes, and not once did the Japanese attempt to defend themselves or to attack the two Navy pilots.

Second-ranking Hellcat ace was Lt. Eugene A. Valencia, of Fighting Nine aboard the *Essex* during his first combat tour in 1943. He shot down seven Japanese planes during three sorties over Rabaul, Tarawa and Truk. Valencia developed a variation on the Thach weave which used a four-plane section instead of the usual two-plane flight. When he returned to combat in the Pacific in 1945, he tried the new tactic – which was to become known as "Valencia's mowing machine" – in action over Tokyo on 16 February. Valencia himself got six planes on that first time out. By the end of his tour he

sweeps nailed 46 out of 69 Japanese aircraft while they were trying to take off from their home bases to defend them against the marauding Hellcats. Eight F6F-5s from "Fighting Eighty" ran into a formation of 27 Zeros and Oscars moving into the Philippines from Formosa as reinforcements, and proceeded to shoot down 20 of them in a short brawl.

Toward the end of the war, it was almost embarrassingly easy to down Japanese fighters. By then, the Empire had long since lost the training battle; its pilot schools were turning out eager and enthusiastic pilots whose knowledge of the rudiments of air fighting and tactics was very sketchy. There were many instances of Japanese fighter formations that simply held course while they were picked off, one by one, by Hellcats that harrassed them. The best-known of all such one-sided engagements was the "Marianas Turkey Shoot," an air action which is described in the next chapter.

This Hellcat, taking off from the *Hornet* for a strike against Formosa nearly went over, but the pilot made it. (National Archives)

had shot down 16 more, and had made aces out of each of his three wingmen in the section. His final victory tally was 23.

Lagging Valencia by only one victory was Lt. Cecil E. Harris. He'd bagged two Japanese while assigned to a Wildcat Squadron, and got 22 more after joining VF-18 aboard the *Intrepid*. But Harris' unique claim to fame is that, on three separate occasions, he shot down four Japanese aircraft in a day's combat.

Reading anything about Lt. Alexander Vraciu gives one the impression that he liked to fight. His final score, before he was knocked down over the Philippines in December, 1944, totalled 19 aerial victories and 21 destroyed on the ground. Vraciu did two tours; the first was with Fighting Six on the *Independence* and, later, on the *Intrepid*. That tour accounted for nine of the planes that he shot down. The remaining ten victories were achieved while with VF-16 aboard the *Lexington*. The most outstanding of his air combats was over the Marianas; he shot down six Japanese bombers in eight minutes of a fierce fight. He escaped from his aircraft after being knocked out of combat that December, and continued to fight the Japanese as a member of a Philippine guerrilla band until the end of the war.

Lt. Patrick D. Fleming also did two combat tours. His first, with VF-80 on the *Ticonderoga*, netted him ten Japanese planes; his second, as a pilot in VBF-80 on the *Hancock*, accounted for eight more Japanese victories. On the latter tour, he shot down five enemy aircraft in a single combat 16 February, 1945. But since he was already an ace twice over, the feat attracted little attention. Besides, by the end of the war it was not uncommon.

Lt. Cornelius N. Nooy also did that little trick, but he did it the hard way: With a 500-lb. (230 kg) bomb still in the rack on his Hellcat. Nooy, who flew two tours with VF-31 on the *Belleau Wood* got into a fight on 21 September, 1944, with his Hellcat still armed for dive-bombing. He turned to the attack and shot down five Japanese aircraft in the single combat. His final tally was 19 victories.

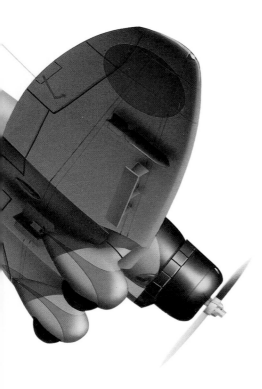

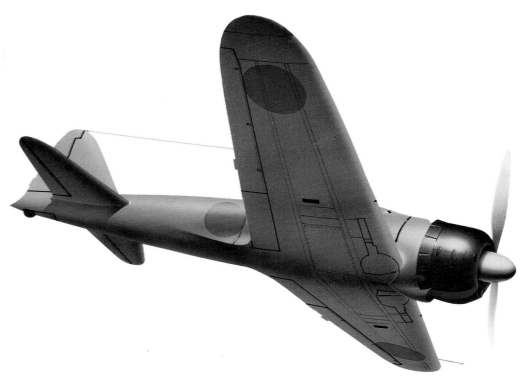

Mitsubishi A6M2 *Reisen* ("Zeke")

Dogfighter supreme, the Zero fighters achieved instant fame and a reputation as very tough adversaries in aerial combat. Until the campaign for Midway Island, they maintained the offensive, and supplied air cover for attack aviation.

Koku-Gijutsusho D4Y2 *Susei* ("Judy")

This advanced design, prematurely introduced into the fleet as a reconnaissance aircraft, later in the war took up its primary role as a dive bomber. Hellcats shot them out of the sky in the Turkey Shoot, and their major effort was in *kamikaze* attacks off Okinawa

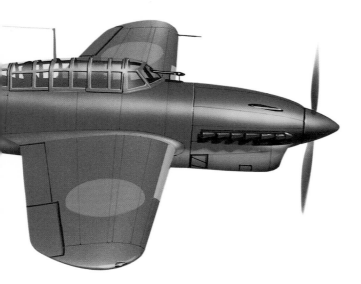

Mitsubishi A6M5 *Reisen* ("Zeke")

This upgraded Zero was developed to stop the Hellcats; it failed because by then U.S. Navy pilots had developed a superior set of combat tactics. Working in teams, they defeated the nimble Zero decisively.

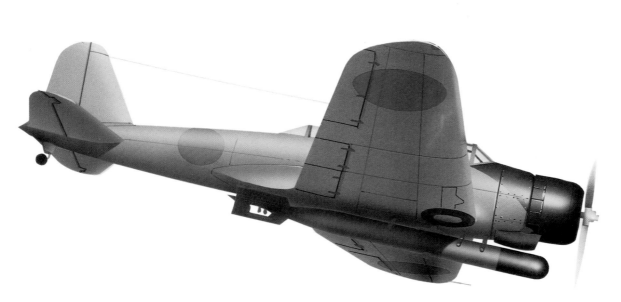

Nakajima B5N2 (ATIU Code name: ''Kate'')

Responsible for sinking three major U.S. carriers—the *Lexington, Yorktown,* and *Hornet*—the Japanese Navy Type 97 Carrier Bomber Model 12 was the world's most modern carrier-based torpedo bomber at the beginning of the Pacific War.

Aichi D3A1 (''Val'')

These were antiquated designs, but wreaked havoc at Pearl Harbor as the first Japanese planes to bomb an American objective. They fought in all the Naval actions until Midway, where heavy losses forced a redeployment to landbased units. They were never a threat again.

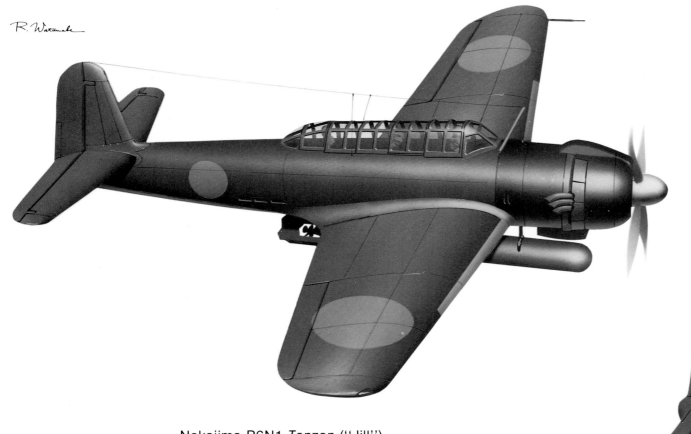

R. Watanabe

Nakajima B6N1 *Tenzan* (''Jill'')

Designed to replace the B5N series, the Tenzan arrived too late in the war to be effective. By then, pilot quality and training were poor, and the Hellcats were on the scene. In the Marianas campaign, Tenzan's first combat, the Hellcats decimated the Japanese planes.

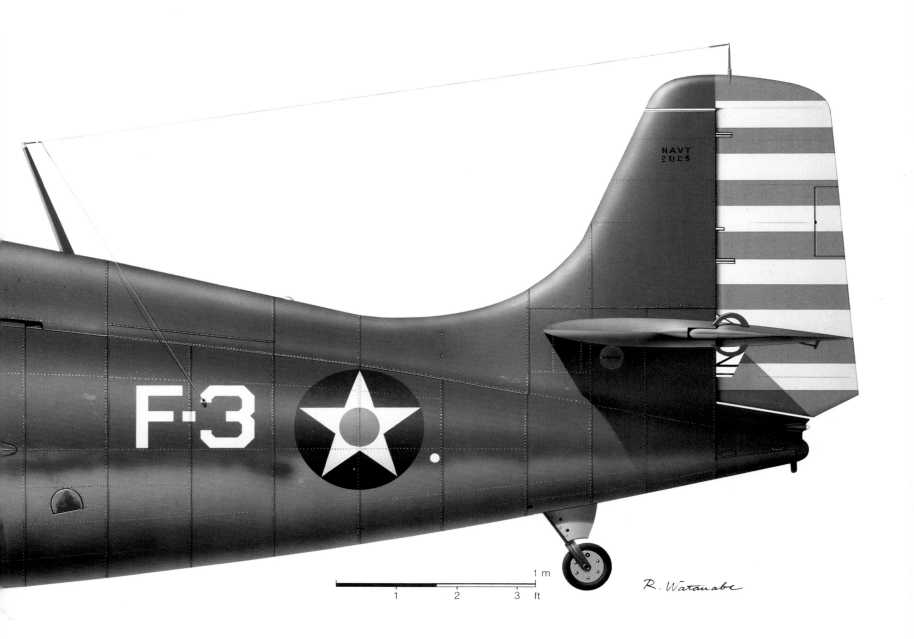

Grumman F4F-3 Wildcat

'Felix the Cat' insignia identifies this Wildcat as part of Fighting Squadron Three (VF-3); The row of Japanese flags and the stenciled line below the sliding canopy further mark the airplane as one flown by Lt. Edward H. O'Hare. He was flying combat air patrol 20 February, 1942, when nine twin-engined Mitsubishi G4M1 bombers, out of Rabaul, hurtled down on the task force. *Lexington* had 12 of her VF-3 Wildcats in the air; in the ensuing fight, more were launched and some

were recovered. The Japanese lost five, fast; the remaining four headed for the horizon, with all but two of the Americans in pursuit. From another heading came nine more G4M bombers, now with only Wildcats between them and the *Lexington*. The guns of one F4F jammed; only O'Hare was left to blunt the attack. He sliced into the formation, shot down five in four minutes and scored hits on three others. For that daring feat of arms, O'Hare received the Medal of Honor. Differences persist today about the specific markings of the airplane he flew in that epic combat; he was photographed at another time in F-13.

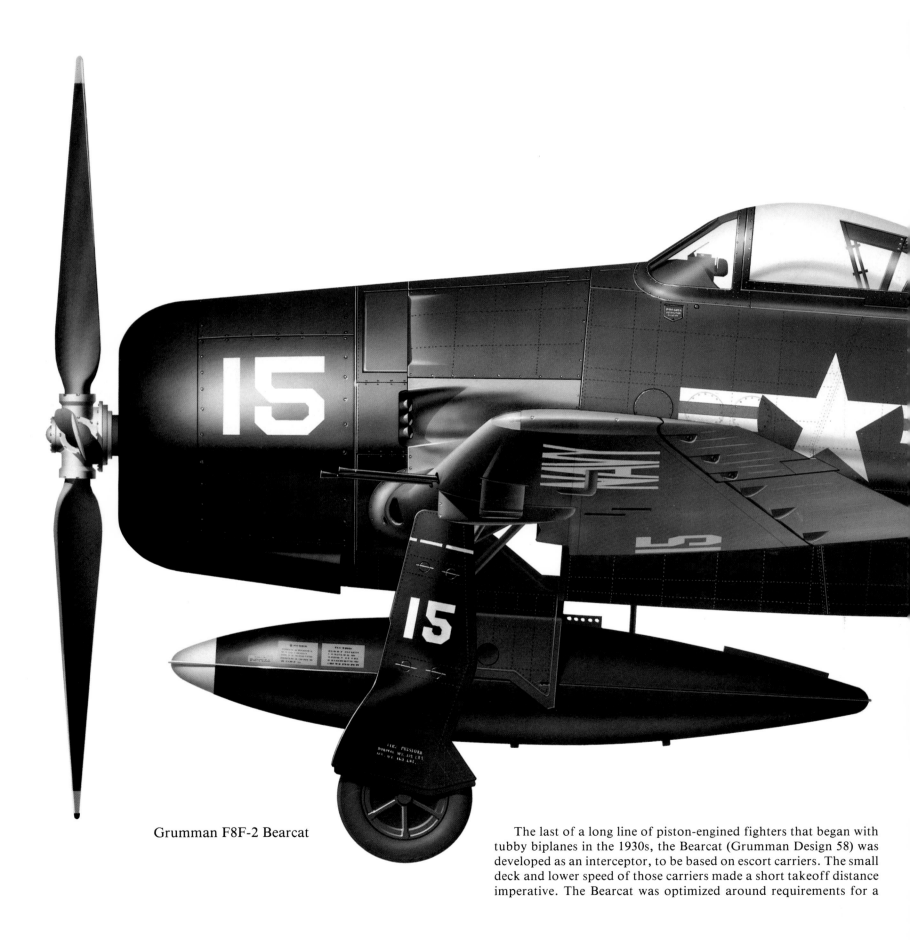

Grumman F8F-2 Bearcat

The last of a long line of piston-engined fighters that began with
tubby biplanes in the 1930s, the Bearcat (Grumman Design 58) was
developed as an interceptor, to be based on escort carriers. The small
deck and lower speed of those carriers made a short takeoff distance
imperative. The Bearcat was optimized around requirements for a

Douglas TBD-1 Devastator

If ever a plane was misnamed, it was the TBD. They were the Navy's first production monoplane on carriers, and fought from Pearl Harbor to Midway. In that latter battle, their losses were devastating, and they were withdrawn from service.

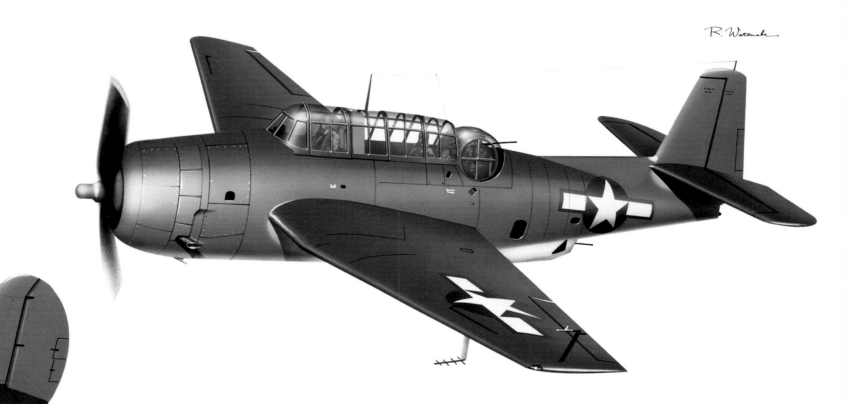

Curtiss SB2C-1 Helldiver

Heir to a great name, the SB2C was late in living up to its promise. Deliveries were delayed because of operational difficulties; their first combat occurred late in 1943. From then on, they assumed the offensive against Japanese shipping and other targets.

Grumman TBF-1 Avenger

The versatile TBF entered combat at the Battle of Midway, when six were sent against the Japanese fleet. Five were destroyed, and the sixth badly damaged. But from that unfortunate begining they sprang back to become a primary offensive component of the Fleet.

Grumman F4F-3 Wildcat

This chunky fighter, standard with U.S. Navy and Marine Corps air units at the beginning of the war, saw service in most later Naval actions. No performance match for the Zero, it became superior because it was flown by pilots with a better grasp and use of fighter tactics.

Douglas SBD-3 Dauntless

Each delivering more than one ton of bombs, Dauntless dive-bombers accounted for a major share of Japanese naval losses in the Pacific war. They served with both the Navy and Marine Corps, and were reliable, rugged and ready.

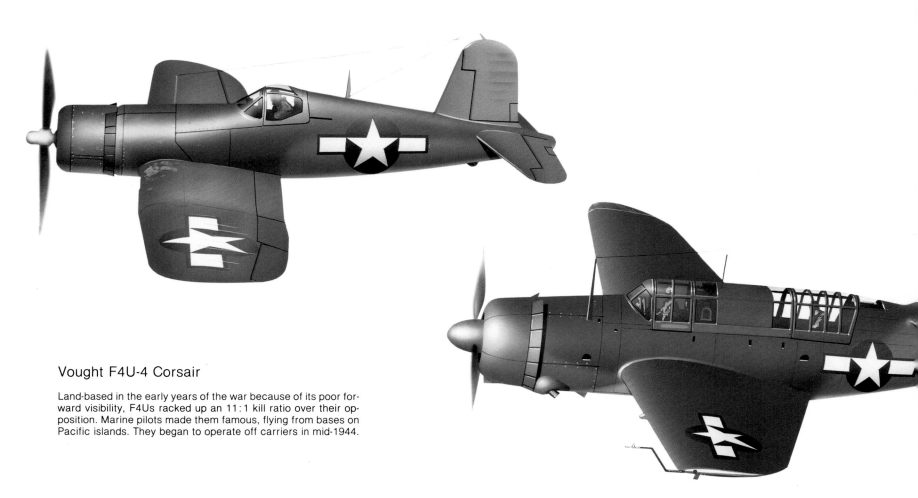

Vought F4U-4 Corsair

Land-based in the early years of the war because of its poor forward visibility, F4Us racked up an 11:1 kill ratio over their opposition. Marine pilots made them famous, flying from bases on Pacific islands. They began to operate off carriers in mid-1944.

1 m

1 2 3 ft

R. Watanabe

minimum takeoff, maximum climb, and heavy armament; range was a secondary consideration. It just missed the war in the Pacific; it was scheduled for operational deployment with the Fleet during the summer of 1945. The F8F-2 model was built in 1948 and 1949, and differed from the F8F-1 models in the taller vertical tail assembly, a re-

vised cowling, and the installation of four 20-mm. cannon instead of .50-cal. machineguns. A modified F8F-2 set a new world speed record of 483. 041 mph. for piston-engined planes in August, 1969. This Bearcat is pictured as it looked around 1950 when flown by pilots of a Naval Reserve unit at Denver, Colorado.

The Great Marianas Turkey Shoot

The largest naval air battle of all time took place off the Mariana Islands in the Philippine Sea on 19 June, 1944. When it was over, Japan's naval air strength was devastated. Only 35 aircraft were left operational in Admiral Ozawa's First Mobile Fleet.

The fight was in the hands of the Hellcat pilots from the very beginning. Their average kill ratio during combat was better than ten to one. But there was a final twist to the battle; a late night recovery, after the longest mission flown by Naval aircraft during the war, cost the U.S. Navy 80 aircraft and 38 aircrew.

battle. The air arm was embarked on nine carriers, and totalled 430 aircraft, of which about one-third were Zero fighters. The supporting force consisted of 13 cruisers, with an air component of 43 floatplanes for scouting and observation, and 28 destroyer escorts. Additional air power was to be drawn from the First Air Fleet, 540 land-based naval aircraft strung out in detachments along a great arc from Chichijima in the Bonin Islands to the East Indies and the Philippines. To reinforce that air fleet, Japanese planners hoped to be able to fly in aircraft from the home islands and from Southeast Asia.

Ozawa's fleet was based at Tawi-tawi in the southern Philippines, where they were near the oil resources of Borneo. From there, they could strike anywhere in the Philippine Sea. The Japanese battle strategy was to wait for

Fighting Fifteen Cdr. Dave McCampbell in the lead, prepares for launch from the *Essex* (CV-9). The white bar is the unofficial recognition marking; later, *Essex* aircraft would sport a geometric 'butterfly' made of white triangles.　(National Archives)

This is the story of that great battle which officially is known as the Battle of the Philippine Sea, but best known as the "Great Marianas Turkey Shoot".

The Japanese were ready to make a major naval offensive in the Pacific by mid-1944. After some earlier indecisive battles and some reverses, they had built their warship and aircraft strength to substantial numbers. The First Mobile Fleet, under Vice Admiral Jisaburo Ozawa, centred on the Imperial Navy's first-line strength. Five battleships, including the massive *Yamato* and the *Musashi*, headed the order of

the next American amphibious assault to form. Then Ozawa's force would sail to intercept it and force the battle. His aircraft, plus the half-thousand from the First Air Fleet, would ravage the U.S. naval air strength while his bombers and torpedo planes attacked and destroyed the surface vessels.

The Japanese aircraft had a range advantage; everyone, from fighters to bombers, could out-cruise anything the U.S. Navy had in the air. That range offered a tactical advantage to Ozawa; he would attempt to use it, and

Bataan-based F6F-5s, their rudders carrying the letter T for identification, fly above Japanese waters, 21 June, 1945. (National Archives)

to supplement it by landing his carrier-based aircraft at shore bases so that they could be rearmed and refuelled to return to the fight. That shuttle technique and the basic striking range of about 800 miles (1300 km) that the First Mobile Fleet used in planning its air battles, were expected to give Ozawa the edge over his adversaries.

He needed some kind of an advantage, because on a one-for-one basis, he was inferior. He was up against Task Force 58, already a Navy legend, and then a tough, disciplined, skilled and driven fighting combine. TF 58 had seven large fast carriers and eight light fast carriers, with a total complement of 891 aircraft. They were the foundation of the fleet's strength; but just in case a gunnery battle developed, Vice Admiral Marc Mitscher had seven heavy battleships in the task force. There were additional warships: 21 cruisers with 65 floatplanes and 69 destroyers. The amphibious force they were supporting and defending included its own carriers, seven escort types with a total of 169 embarked aircraft. Mitscher also had available some long-range aircraft, Consolidated PB4Ys out of Admiralty Island, and PBYs operating from Saipan.

The two air fleets were about equal in numbers: 1,013 Japanese planes of all types against 1,125 American aircraft. In all classes of ships, Ozawa was outnumbered and outgunned. An unseen and unknown number of submarines could become part of the action on either side.

Mitscher's airmen had been in the Marianas since about 11 June, seizing and holding air superiority there as the amphibious forces landed and secured the ground. Japan's naval strategists decided that it was now, or perhaps never, and ordered Ozawa to sea. The First Mobile Fleet sailed from its anchorage at Tawi-tawi on June 13. They were tailed by U.S. submarines as they entered the Philippine Sea through the San Bernardino straits.

The U.S. fleet, now aware that Ozawa was on the move, sailed out to meet him and concentrated west of Tinian Island, about 180 miles at sea. Both sides had scouting planes aloft, flying search patterns they hoped would reveal the enemy's fleet. The Japanese scored the first success; they spotted Task Force 58 and were not seen by the Americans.

Ozawa launched the first element of his air strike at 0830 on 19 June, and, in a little more than a half-hour, was in trouble. The U.S.S. *Albacore*, one of the subs that had been at Ozawa's heels, fired a torpedo spread that hit the Japanese flagship carrier *Taiho*. Between the first launch and 1130, Ozawa's carriers sent off three more waves of attackers. It took them three hours to get their 326 planes airborne.

Soon after the last wave had left, the *Shokaku* was torpedoed by the U.S.S. *Cavalla*. Hit by three tin fish at 1220, *Shokaku* fell behind the main force, burning.

Mitscher had split his Task Force 58 into five Task Groups that included four separate carrier components. They took up a loose, widespread formation and steamed into the easterly trade winds. Their Hellcats began the continuous cycle of combat air patrol launches, orbits and recoveries.

At three minutes after ten, the battleship *Alabama* picked up the first radar returns from the oncoming Japanese. Lt. Joe Eggert, Fighter Director Officer, saw what was about to happen and scrambled Hellcats from five carriers: *Cowpens*, *Essex*, *Hornet*, *Monterey*, and *Princeton*. Within minutes they were climbing to 25,000 feet (7600 m) under full military power. The Hellcats coming back from a strike on Guam were held in orbit west of the fleet to intercept any torpedo bombers in the attacking force.

Then the Japanese did an incredible thing. They orbited for about 15 minutes, miles away from the target area, while their leaders gave very detailed briefings on the attack to the flight elements. On board the *Lexington*, Lt. Charles A. Sims intercepted the transmissions, which were broadcast in the clear, and translated them for Eggert's benefit.

All of Mitscher's carriers had turned southeast for the scramble takeoff of every available Hellcat. There were 82 already airborne, either on CAP or returning from Guam, and the carriers fired another 140 into the blue in about 15 minutes. All the bomber and torpedo aircraft were launched also, to clear the carrier decks for continuous Hellcat CAP operations.

First visual contact was made by Cdr. Charles W. Brewer, leading two sections of Hellcats from VF-15. He spotted the Japanese, who were about 50 miles (80 km) from the fleet and at 18,000 feet (5500 m) At 1035 Brewer keyed his mike: "Tallyho! Twenty-four rats (bombers), 16 hawks (fighters) and no fish (torpedo planes)!" He missed seeing another 16 fighters that were high above and well behind the first attacking wave.

Brewer half-rolled, pulled through and dived into the Japanese fighter escort, his seven wingmates close behind. He destroyed four Zeros in the first few minutes of a fierce combat that broke and dispersed the raiders with heavy losses. The second wave was sighted at 1107, seen by radar in the same incredible briefing orbit. Once again, the *Essex* Hellcats were first on the scene, led by Air Group Commander McCampbell. They hammered the Japanese hard; McCampbell himself got five torpedo bombers. The second wave of attackers suffered heavy losses and, like the first, was driven from the target area after an ineffective assault.

There was a two-hour midday lull, another tactical error by the Japanese, and then their third force arrived at 1320. Some had become lost on the way, and so only about 20 aircraft tried to attack. They were beaten off, losing seven in the uneven combat.

The fourth strike was vectored in error by the Japanese controllers to a stretch of open sea without a target in sight. They split into three separate groups with the hope of finding their targets. One group, carrier-based, turned for home, but others continued on. One formation sighted and attacked a Navy task group, but did little damage. The other formation headed to Orote field on Guam.

The dive-bombers that had been launched to wait out the battle tired of doing nothing, and got permission to

Someone just got that Zeke! (National Archives)

strike Orote airfield. They hit it hard, cratering the runways extensively with their bombs. The Japanese 652nd Air Group, hoping to recover at Orote, made their approach and were jumped in the landing pattern by some fifty Hellcats. The Americans claimed 30 Japanese aircraft.

The Japanese heading back to their carriers were sighted by two TBFs and their single Hellcat escort. The Navy trio swung their aircraft into the attack, and were joined almost immediately by another pair of Avengers and a Hellcat. Among them, they shot down seven Zeros. One TBF was hit in the tail, doing no serious damage.

The day's last fight took place over Orote. Brewer was leading a fighter sweep when his section was bounced by Zeros. He and his wingman were killed on the first pass. Perhaps a dozen Japanese fighters mixed it up with the remaining pair of F6Fs. The fight broke; the two Hellcats escaped. And all the Japanese aircraft were either destroyed or severely damaged in their attempts to land on the potholed airfield.

The Japanese stragglers returned to their remaining carriers, now two fewer. At about 1500, an explosion had ripped the *Shokaku* apart, and she sank. Within minutes, a frightening roar erupted from within the *Taiho* and, mortally wounded, she also sank.

After the engineering officers had made their inspections, Ozawa got the bad news: He had about 100

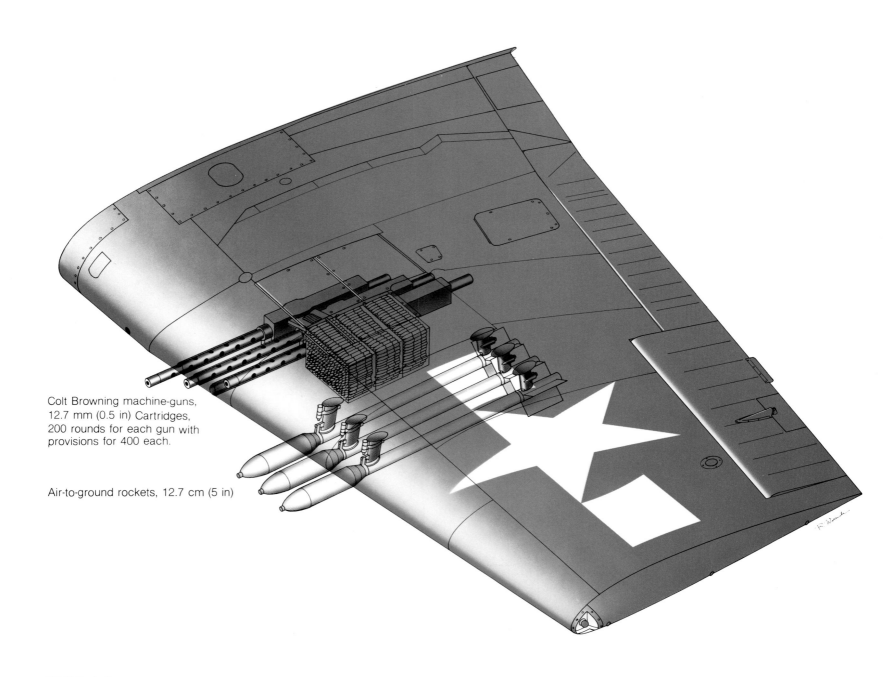

Colt Browning machine-guns,
12.7 mm (0.5 in) Cartridges,
200 rounds for each gun with
provisions for 400 each.

Air-to-ground rockets, 12.7 cm (5 in)

F6F-5 Cockpit

1 Map case
2 Elevator trim tab control
3 Rudder trim tab control
4 Aileron trim tab control
5 Tail wheel lock control
6 Cowl flaps control
7 Oil cooler shutter control
8 Fuel tank pressure control
9 Oil dilution switch
10 Fuel tank selector valve
11 Fuselage droppable tank manual release control
12 Anti-blackout regulator
13 Propeller pitch control
14 Propeller pitch vernier control
15 Engine control quadrant friction knob
16 Mixture control
17 Supercharger control
18 Throttle control
19 Mask microphone switch
20 Wing flaps electric control switch
21 Droppable fuel tank release switch
22 Cockpit light
23 Water injection control switch
24 Auxiliary electric fuel pump switch
25 Intercooler shutter control
26 Fuel tank pipe
27 Landing gear control
28 Landing gear and wing flap position indicator
29 Carburetor protected air control
30 Ignition switch
31 Altimeter
32 Instrument panel light
33 Clock
34 Spare lamps
35 Directional gyro
36 Airspeed indicator
37 Rate of climb indicator
38 Compass
39 Electric gunsight
40 Rear-view mirror

41 Gyro horizon
42 Turn and bank indicator
43 Manifold pressure gauge
44 Gyro horizon caging knob
45 Tachometer
46 Raflector panel
47 Water quantity gauge—A.D.I. system
48 Cylinder head temperature gauge
49 Oil-in temperature gauge
50 Fuel pressure gauge
51 Fuel quantity gauge
52 Oil pressure gauge
53 Cabin sliding hood control
54 Radio controls
55 Cockpit light
56 Landing gear emergency dump pressure gauge
57 Hydraulic system pressure gauge
58 IFF destructor switch
59 Hydraulic pump selector valve
60 Recognition light switch
61 Hand microphone
62 Main electrical distribution panel
63 Generator warning light
64 Radio master control switch
65 Starter switch
66 Manual reset circuit breaker panel
67 Armament panel
68 Radio channel selector
69 IFF controls
70 Hydraulic hand pump
71 Pilot's seat
72 Control column
73 Fresh air duct control
74 Fresh air duct
75 MK-I rocket selector
76 Check-off card
77 Gun charging control
78 Landing gear emergency lowering control
79 Wing folding safety lock control
80 Rudder pedals

Five-inch HVAR rockets being racked on the underwing of one of the *Enterprise*'s Hellcats. (National Archives)

Ammunition (.50-cal. rounds) being loaded in the ammunition bay of folded Hellcat wing. (National Archives)

airworthy aircraft left. The Japanese had lost 315, including those knocked out of the skies over Guam, and 22 that went down with the two carriers.

U.S. losses were light; 16 Hellcats were downed, and some ships had been hit, despite the protective screen that the fighters put up over the fleet. But no ships were damaged seriously, and none had been sunk.

Another day was coming, and both sides planned to strike again. They manoeuvered without encountering each other, and the searches flown by both sides turned up no results. Finally, late in the day, Navy planes sighted Ozawa's fleet. It was out near the end of the effective cruising radius of American fighters and bombers, and to launch an attack then meant that the Navy aircraft would be operating at extreme range. The two fleets were about 275 miles (440 km) apart, and Mitscher decided to risk the launch, even though he knew that his aircraft would be returning after dark.

The first Hellcat was fired off the *Lexington* at 1624; 12 minutes later, the last of 236 aircraft, an SBD from the *Lexington*, lifted off her deck.

They found the Japanese, in a formation of three carrier groups and one oiler group, and charged into battle. The Japanese, over home territory, had the advantage; they launched about 75 Zeros. Those fighters and the anti-aircraft shot down 12 U.S. planes. But it was a very uneven trade; the Japanese lost the carrier *Hiyo* to a torpedo attack. Other ships were hit and damaged, and about 30 Japanese aircraft planes were shot down.

By 1935, all the U.S. Navy aircraft were headed homeward, leaving behind three Japanese ships sunk and seven damaged. Their toughest times lay ahead; they were coming home long after dark.

Mitscher, who had been sweating out the return of his pilots, passed a curt order to turn on the lights of the ships. It was unheard of in wartime; the fleet always travelled in a complete blackout at night. But this time, Marc Mitscher had

his pilots out there in the dark, and he wanted to give them the best possible chance to get home safely.

It may be a little harsh to call what followed a panic. But the recovery of so many aircraft, all of them low on fuel and manned by pilots relatively inexperienced in night operations, was just that. The order was to land on any carrier, and they did. Aircraft shot the approach in formation, with pilots jockeying for position. Planes landed on top of planes. Others landed alongside the carriers or the covering destroyers in the water, out of fuel. Machines landed in tandem on carrier decks, one picking up the aft wires and one picking up the forward, or worse, missing them and crashing into the barrier or other aircraft.

The losses were heavy. The two days of fighting with the Japanese in the greatest naval air battle of all time had cost the U.S. Navy 49 planes. But that night landing cost 80 aircraft and 38 aircrew.

But the results still favoured the American force. The Japanese fleet was withdrawing at speed to the temporary shelter of Okinawa. It had lost three heavy carriers, and two more were heavily damaged, out of action for the rest of the war. Only 35 operational aircraft were left to Ozawa. And in contrast, the U.S. Navy had lost no ships at all, all were operational, and they had more than 700 aircraft still embarked.

The U.S. Navy was in undisputed possession of the Philippine Sea, and of the sky above it. The Navy had won one of the decisive battles of World War II, had protected the landings on Saipan, had driven the Japanese out of the arena and had inflicted such losses on them that there was no possible recovery.

Ozawa had lost three-quarters of his airmen, and it was not only the first team that he had lost. It was the only team he had. There were no reserves, and there was no full pipeline of pilots from training schools. It was the end of Japan's carrier air effort.

Cat's Eyes at Midnight

The F6F-5N's cockpit radar display.   (David A. Anderton)

Night raids by both Pacific antagonists were, if not routine, at least not uncommon. Given a moonlit night, and some recognizable landmarks defined by reflections from water, it was within the capabilities of the more-experienced pilots to handle a night mission.

But intercepting and attacking a night mission was a problem of another order of magnitude. Visually, it had to be largely a matter of luck. Perceptions are deceptive in the environment of night flying, and unless a keen-eyed pilot could spot the pale blue exhaust flames from an enemy plane's engines, he stood little chance of completing the intercept.   Radar held the promise of solving that problem. Before the United States had been drawn into the conflict of World War II, the Navy developed a requirement for an airborne intercept (AI) radar with a three-centimeter wavelength. Its primary envisioned use was for night intercepts; its secondary was for attacking surface vessels. The Radiation Laboratory at the Massachusetts Institute of Technology was assigned the job in January, 1941, and straightaway scientists began component development on a prototype set, the AI-3 (AN/SCR-537). Design of the specific system for the Navy began in August. In December, because the Radiation Laboratory was a prototype shop only, the Navy awarded a production contract to the Sperry Gyroscope Co. for a set designated the AIA. By late 1942, Sperry had the unit in full production for Hellcat deliveries.

The company delivered 604 sets of the equipment for installation in F6F-3E and – 3N aircraft. By late 1943, the AIA designation had been changed to AN/APS-4 (APS = Airborne Pulse Search). It was mounted in a pod on the Hellcat's right wing, in an unsightly protuberance that caused all manner of comment and not a little apprehension on the part of pilots who wondered what that thing would do to the drag, and particularly to the stall, characteristics of the Hellcat. (It slowed the aircraft by about 20 mph (32 km/h), and it triggered a right-wing drop in a stall.)

A proficient operator of the APS-4 could pick up a target at a maximum distance of about four miles (six kilometers). As a first attempt, the equipment was not too bad, but there was room for improvement, and Westinghouse Electric Corp. got a Navy contract for a follow-on set designated the APS-6. It turned out, as all developments of a basic unit seem to, considerably heavier. It was still installed in the same pod on the right wing. But the reliable range was about five miles in the search mode, and it would work down to a minimum range of about 120 yards (110 m). Ideal firing range during night interceptions was about 250 yards (230 m). The APS-6 weighed 242 pounds (110 kilograms), and it cost $10,936 for each unit. Westinghouse produced 2,161 of them by the end of the war, and they were installed on both the Hellcat and the Corsair night fighter versions.

Four sub-models of the Hellcat carried the new electronic gear into the air: The F6F-3E, -3N, -5E and -5N. The first of these, the F6F-3E, was equipped with an early form of the airborne search radar designated ASH or ASD-1. Only 18 aircraft were so equipped and may never have reached the fleet as operational planes.

The real developmental night fighter was the F6F-3N, carrying the new AIA radar into battle. It was a basic -3 Hellcat with some special equipment and modifications to fit it for the night-fighter mission. In addition to the radar, the -3N had a redesigned instrument panel with red lighting to interfere the least with the pilot's night vision. The panel mounted a radar altimeter (AN/APN-1) and the relatively new IFF (Identification Friend or Foe) equipment (AN/APX-2). The standard Hellcat windshield was curved plexiglass in front, backed by a protective slab of bullet-proof glass. The combination caused internal reflections in the cockpit, and so it was replaced by a single flat panel on production F6F-3N Hellcats and all subsequent models.

First deliveries of the AIA equipment began with the receipt of six sets in September, 1943, by which time Grumman had delivered 19 of the aircraft supposed to carry those radars.

The final version of the night-fighting Hellcat, the F6F-5N, differed only in the type of radar installed. Deliveries of the APS-6 unit began in February, 1944, and continued at a rate that considerably exceeded the Navy's acceptances of the fighters. It was probably just as well; early radar sets were noted for their unreliability and, in the pressure of wartime, a malfunctioning set was likely to be yanked out entirely and replaced by a completely new unit. Lots of spares were necessary, and perhaps that explains why the production rate of APS-6 sets was about three times the rate of F6F-5N production.

According to a Navy Aviation Planning Directive 85-A-44 of 26 September, 1944, night-fighter Hellcats were to be assigned to carrier air day-fighter groups as well as to the dedicated night-fighter groups formed and attached to both heavy and light carriers. In a standard carrier air group aboard one of the fast carriers, there were to be four -5N and two -5E Hellcats. Each dedicated night-fighter group attached to a heavy carrier was to be equipped with the -5E and -5N in equal numbers. On the light carriers, only the -5N fighters were to be assigned.

The same directive showed that the Navy envisaged a final total of 54 Hellcat squadrons assigned to the heavy carriers. Of these, 46 would be fighter squadrons for daytime operations. Four would be -5N squadrons, and two would be -5E squadrons; all six would be dedicated night-fighter units. There would be 16 squadrons each of the -5E and -5N models, equipping the planned 32 night-fighter squadrons to be assigned to carrier air groups that would be dedicated only to night fighting. And 16 squadrons of -5N models were to be assigned for dedicated night fighting air groups on board the light carriers.

As finally put into service, the night-fighter Hellcats served with considerably fewer squadrons than the grand plan had foretold. Eight Navy Squadrons and five Marine squadrons were the only night-fighter units to see combat during the war. The Navy's night fighters worked as a team, using the powerful shipboard search radars and fighter directors as the primary source of attack information. The position of the bogie, detected on the radars, was relayed to the airborne "Bat" team, generally a single radar-equipped TBF accompanied by a pair of night-fighter Hellcats. Steering vectors guided the team to the general vicinity of the enemy, and at that point, the radar of the TBF was used to direct the fighters on the closing intercept. Their own radars would be brought into use then, and would supply the primary information to make the intercept and attack the enemy. But the final judgment was made by the old-fashioned human eyeball. After the radar indicated that the fighter had closed to firing range, the pilot almost invariably turned his vision from the scope presentation to look forward through the windshield, and would complete the attack visually.

Hardly two months after the first APS-4 sets had been delivered, the first attempts at night interception were made by U.S. Navy pilots in the campaign in the Gilbert Islands. They resulted in both triumph and tragedy. And, as is so often the case, the price paid was far too high for the results achieved.

Task Group 50.2 was lying off Makin Island in the Gilberts. The fast carrier *Enterprise*, keystone of the force, had been on the receiving end of night attacks by a few Japanese "Betty" (Mitsubishi G4M) bombers. For two nights, the bombers attacked, unmolested. Then, on 24 November, a "Bat" team from Fighting Two, led by Lt. Cdr. Edward H. O'Hare, tried an intercept which failed. "Butch" O'Hare had become intensely interested in night fighting; as commander of Air Group Six, he was responsible for the defence of the *Enterprise*. Any means that would improve his chances of staving off a Japanese attack interested him.

Two nights later, the bombers came back in a force of about 30. A "Bat" team was aloft, and the TBF picked up the telltale returns of the bomber formation on the radar scope. The Hellcats were vectored into the area, but found nothing. O'Hare, flying an F6F-3N, and his teammate, flying a standard day model, stayed in the area and waited. Soon after, the radar on board *Enterprise* picked up the Japanese, and gave the Hellcats a course to bring them nearer to the formation. The three planes, flying a fairly tight formation for night-time operations, closed on the bombers. The pilot of

the TBF found the target on his scope was within effective gunnery range. He fired the forward machine-gun, a single synchronized .50-cal on the starboard cowling, and then pulled up and to the left to give his turret gunner a chance to use the twin fifties back in that position. The inflammable "Betty" staggered, caught fire, and plunged to the dark water below. In the manoeuvring, the formation had opened up and O'Hare was, he believed, too far away from the Avenger. The Fighter Director below, still working the radar screen, called a second set of bogies, and immediately after, the TBF pilot sighted a pair of bombers. O'Hare asked him to turn on his recognition lights so that the fighters could form on him, but the Avenger pilot understandably refused, not wanting to give the Japanese a chance to spot him in the night sky. He did, however, flash his lights once or twice, and then proceeded to shoot down a second "Betty" with his forward gun while his turret gunner fired at a third.

Once again under control of the Fighter Director, the TBF began an orbit and turned on its recognition lights. The Hellcats switched on theirs and began to move in close to the torpedo bomber. As O'Hare closed in from astern, the TBF turret gunner fired at what he believed was an unidentified plane crossing the formation from behind. It was, probably, O'Hare's Hellcat that he hit, and it was the last combat for the Medal of Honour winner. Two Japanese bombers had been downed in this first successful night interception and attack by the radar-equipped "Bat" team. But the loss of O'Hare was not an even trade.

During the Marshall Islands campaign, detachments of night-fighter squadrons were assigned to five carriers, and occasionally they were sent out against the Japanese. But the trouble of night launches and recoveries after a day full of hard work for the deck crew didn't seem worth it, and the night 'cats were seldom sent out as a result.

That was in early 1944. By late in the year, the situation had been changed by the formation of dedicated night-fighter squadrons attached to a specified carrier for after-dark operations only. The *Independence* was the first carrier so designated. She carried a complement of 14 F6F-5Ns manned by the pilots of VF(N)-41, plus eight TBM-1Ds equipped with search radar. Five standard day-fighter F6F-5s were also assigned, to fly combat air patrols during the daylight hours.

Typical of their action was the job they did on the night of 12 October. The Japanese routinely sent out long-range bombers to act as fleet shadowers; they spotted the positions of the ships, reported activities, and occasionally pressed home a bombing attack. That night, the "Bat" teams of VF(N)-41 were airborne when they were directed to a group of Mitsubishi G4Ms that were up to the usual trick. One after another, the Hellcats approached, fired, and shot down five "Betty" bombers.

Marine NF squadrons were active with the radar-equipped Hellcats, and racked up an impressive total score before the war was over. But the most remembered association of the Marine units with night-fighting requirements was summed up tersely in the war diary of Marine Night Fighting Squadron 541 (VMF(N)-541) for December, 1944:

A formation of F6F-5Ns. (National Archives)

"The Commanding General, Far East Air Forces, requested that the F6F night fighters replace the (Army Air Forces) P-61 night fighters at Tacloban Drome (on Leyte, in the Philippines) for several weeks. The P-61 had not sufficient range or speed to perform the necessary duties required by the 308th Bomb Wing."

In December, 1944, and January, 1945, the Marine VMF(N)-541 Hellcats shot down 22 aircraft at night. Their efforts were not unrewarded; the squadron received an Army Distinguished Unit Citation, the only Marine Corps aviation unit to be so recognized.

Marine unit night victories totalled 106, most of them scored in Hellcats. "Black Mac's Killers," the informal name for VMF(N)-533, was the highest scorer, with 35 Japanese to its credit. VMF(N)-542, based at Yontan field, Okinawa, began its night-fighting career late in the war. From 16 April, 1945, to V-J Day, they accounted for 17 Japanese aircraft and lost only two of their own.

In the closing months of the war, studies and tests were still being conducted to improve the quality and effectiveness of night fighting. One such series was a tactical evalu-

ation of searchlights flown at NAS Patuxent River, Maryland. Two Hellcats – one a -3N model and the other a -5N – were fitted with two different types of searchlights and sent up to intercept a variety of aircraft of different size and performance, varying from other F6Fs to a USAAF Consolidated B-24 bomber.

The planned tactic was to use the radar for finding the target, and for closing for the attack. The searchlight would then be turned on for the attack itself. No matter that the British had tried the same idea earlier in the war and had abandoned it in favour of concentrating on radar. The programme ran from 3 March, 1945, until June 11, and required 36 hours of flight tests. The conclusion: The disadvantages outweighed the advantages and, besides, airborne intercept radar was coming along nicely by then.

There were Navy and Marine night-fighter aces, although for apparent reasons their scores were less than the top tallies achieved by such pilots as McCampbell and Vraciu. But their contribution was a major one to the development of radar for interception and attack.

The Lingering Death of an Empire

Japan's carrier force had been decisively beaten in the battle of the Philippine Sea, and Saipan had been lost. The irreplaceable pilots that perished in the "Great Marianas Turkey Shoot," and the further decimation that had resulted from continuing combat losses, left few aviators of any competence and fewer with any knowledge and experience to lead. Attacks on Japanese merchant shipping, particularly tankers, had reduced drastically the flow of supplies to the home islands. The Japanese Navy was so low on fuel that it could not have the freedom it once enjoyed. Instead of putting to sea, it stayed in port, scraping together enough reserves for an occasional foray.

It must have been painfully apparent to any Japanese who thought about the situation that the country was doomed to lose the war. But those were different times, and there were different customs. It has never been easy for people with totally different cultural heritages to understand each other. And so, from here and now, it may seem strange that the Japanese continued to resist, and to do so desperately and bravely, even suicidally. There and then, however, that was the situation.

It must be said that the Japanese did not seem very adept at learning from bitter experience. They never mastered the strategies, tactics or techniques of sustained carrier air war. A few brilliant strikes were overshadowed by a long succession of unimaginative campaigns and battles fought poorly. In aircraft design, they did not realize, until too late, that air war was not entirely a matter of individual combat, pilot against pilot, in a mad melee of manoeuvring. Air war was a matter of striking fast first, and getting out to strike again. The important design requirements were firepower, armour, and self-sealing tanks. Low wing loading, and the ability to perform astounding aerobatics, had gone out in the '30s with the death of the biplane.

It's an old story now, but the Hellcat was inferior to the Japanese fighters in many respects. If the contest had been to see who could turn tighter, loop faster, roll more quickly, zoom vertically, or split-S in a split second, the Zeros would have won, hands down. But it wasn't that kind of a contest, and the Hellcat was designed for a different kind of air combat. And in that role, doing that job, it was infinitely superior to anything the Japanese aircraft industry ever thought of producing.

And the Americans continued to learn from combat experience, and to apply the lessons to the design of their aircraft and other weapons – in most cases. True, they stayed with an atrocious torpedo, an absolutely appalling performer that accounted for many Americans lost in attacks. The U.S. Navy also never fully appreciated the importance of really long-range scouting and search planes; the Japanese had it all over them in that regard. But when it came to finding out what a Hellcat could do, and using it in the best way possible, the Americans had no peers.

Hellcat 24, from the *Bunker Hill*, over Subic Bay, Manila.　(National Archives)

And so the F6F became a fighter-bomber. It would haul bombs further, and drop them more accurately, than the "Beast", the Helldiver that had been designed specifically to do that very job. (In fairness, it must be said that late models of the Curtiss aircraft resolved many of the difficulties of the earlier models, but they were too late to have any real effect on the Pacific war.)

Carrier air groups cannot afford to be tied to a single concept of employment for their aircraft. Portable air power demands a versatile, flexible and dynamic force structure, using aircraft that themselves are versatile and flexible. During the war, the basic structure of the carrier air groups, and the uses of their aircraft, changed to reflect the changing demands of the campaigns.

For most of the war described to this point, the standard makeup of a carrier air group was 36 fighters, 36 bombers, and 18 torpedo planes. In August, 1944, that was changed to a mix of 54 fighters, 24 bombers and 18 torpedo planes. Further, those 54 fighters were to include four night fighters and two photographic conversions of the standard fighters.

The U.S. Navy continued to roll westward, striking in the Western Carolines in late July, 1944, supporting the occupation of Palau and Morotai in September, and then heading for the Philippines and the invasion and occupation of Leyte.

And there, the Japanese introduced a new weapon of air war with frightening potential. It inflicted more punishment on the U.S. Navy than that service had ever felt before. And, for a while, it appeared to be unstoppable.

That weapon was, of course, the suicide attack by individual Japanese pilots who deliberately guided their aircraft to crash on Navy ships. On 25 October, off Leyte, the first of these planned attacks hit and sank the escort carrier

St. Lo CVE-63. In later action, a dozen more carriers of all three classes were hit and damaged, some severely, by kamikazes from Japanese bases in the Philippines.

As one countermeasure, the Navy increased the complement of fighters on board their iron carriers. From late November, a carrier air group on board one of the large fast carriers was to have 73 fighters, and only 15 each of bombers and torpedo planes. The fighters were formed into two squadrons of 36 each, with one more Hellcat for the Air Group Commander himself, and they included four F6F-5N, two F6F-5P, and two F6F-5E aircraft.

The damage done by the Japanese kamikazes in the battle of Leyte Gulf was only part of the toll. The light carrier *Princeton*, with its "cat-mouth" Hellcats of VF-27 embarked, was bombed. She burned, and later exploded, killing many of a rescue force from the cruiser *Birmingham* that had pulled alongside to assist.

In December, the fleet supported the landings on Mindoro Island in the Philippines. Task Force 38 under Vice Admiral John S. McCain, sent its seven heavy and eight light carriers to launch fighter sweeps over the island on 14 December, holding down the Japanese air elements and assuring air supremacy over the battleground. McCain's pilots flew a continuous cycle of combat air patrol over the fleet and over the landing areas, relieving the Hellcats on station in the air. Fighters were always airborne and ready for any Japanese aircraft that came by. If any did, it was quickly

hammered out of the sky by the "Big Blue Blanket". The Japanese lost 341 aircraft in that campaign, and the major share of that loss was credited to the carrier-based Hellcats of TF38. In early January, it was the turn of Luzon Island. Again, the kamikazes hurtled past the protective fighter screens, through the thick anti-aircraft fire, and slammed into the decks or hulls of carrier after carrier. The escort carrier *Ommaney Bay* was sunk, and her sister-ships *Manila Bay* and the *Savo Island*, were damaged in early attacks. Later, it was the turn of two more *Bay* class escorts, the *Kadashan Bay* and the *Kitkun Bay*, as well as the *Salamaua*.

Those attacks on the carriers really harrassed the Navy. The escorts, lightly built and nicknamed "Kaiser coffins" after the shipyards that developed their construction techniques, were singled out by the Japanese as targets. It is surprising, in the light of the vulnerability of those small carriers, that more were not fatally stricken when the kamikazes hit. But superb damage-control work and fire-fighting by their crews saved most of the carriers from severe destruction and probable sinking.

McCain's TF38 was subdivided into four battle groups. Seven heavy carriers and four light carriers were apportioned among three of the groups. The fourth – a dedicated night operations battle group – deployed a single heavy carrier and a single light carrier. Their pilots concentrated on hitting enemy aircraft, in the air when they were there, but mostly on the ground, where they were kept by the incessant

Fighting Twenty-Seven's "Cat-Mouth" Hellcats

(National Archives)

Nose art was conspicuous by its absence from the side cowling panels of the average Hellcat. There were a few land-based Marine F6Fs that are known to have carried some decorations, but all fleet Hellcats were marked only with numbers, the standard insignia, and carrier identifiers.

All, that is, except for the Hellcats of VF-27, aboard the *Princeton*. Three VF-27 pilots – Carl Brown, Richard Stambook, and Robert Burnell – conceived the idea of marking their Hellcats with a distinctive "cat-mouth" design, borrowing the concept from the many "shark-mouth" noses that have been used through the years on fighters. Burnell personally hand-painted most of the designs on the planes.

The *Princeton* was attached to Task Group 38.3, under Rear Admiral Forrest C. Sherman. On 24 October, 1944, the force was off the coast of eastern Luzon in the Philippines, about 150 miles (240 km) out of Manila. They were seen by a Japanese observation plane, which radioed a warning to its main force. The Japanese launched an attack, using land-based bombers from Luzon, and carrier-based aircraft from Admiral Ozawa's fleet. They arrived over the Task Group in the early morning, and *Princeton* Hellcats were flying combat air patrol when they spotted the Japanese.

It was an uneven battle. VF-27 had only eight of its F6F-5s aloft, a standard number for the job, and they roared into the fight at odds of ten to one. "We held off 80 planes for about 15 minutes," Lt. Carl Brown said later. "We had to get them before they got our ships . . . It had been drilled into us that the primary task of a Navy fighter pilot is to protect his ship."

But heroics on that scale couldn't save the *Princeton*; she was hit by a single bomb at 0938. Normally a single bomb does limited damage and causes casualties; but this single missile hit the aft elevator. Six Avengers, fully gassed and loaded with weapons for a strike, blew up almost simultaneously. The *Princeton* crew fought the fires, but it was a hopeless task. In mid-afternoon, a thunderous blast rocked the ship. Her stern was blown off, and the explosion, the fireball, the concussion, and flying debris caused hideous and high casualties.

With the carrier in flames and her deck unable to receive aircraft, the Hellcats of VF-27 had to land on other carriers. And there they ran afoul of the Navy's official views on nose art. No matter that they had just lost their ship, in spite of extreme efforts to save her. No matter that the fighter pilots of VF-27 had developed an esprit-de-corps built around those "cat-mouth" designs The decorations had to go; they were not Navy.

And so they were removed; with a few days all the VF-27 Hellcats looked like any other Hellcats in the fleet.

But some photographs remain, and from them, the artist has re-created a typical Hellcat of VF-27 as it looked on the day the *Princeton* was lost. It's a tribute to VF-27, and to all naval fighter pilots whose first thoughts were of the defence of their ships.

pressure of the Hellcats' combat air patrol. When Luzon was declared secure by the commanders of the ground force, McCain took TF38 into the South China Sea and spent a few days there sinking Japanese shipping with well-timed air strikes. At the end of the fight for Luzon and the excursion into the South China Sea, McCain's men reckoned they had destroyed about 700 Japanese aircraft and had sunk about 365,000 tons of shipping.

Once again the force structure changed. In early January, the Navy began the commissioning of 18 new VBF (Heavier-than-Air Bomber Fighter) squadrons within the existing carrier air groups. The reason was that the Japanese were no longer believed capable of mounting a serious air threat. More bombers would be needed for the coming planned invasion of Japan and the prerequisite air interdiction that would be orchestrated with strategic bombing by the B-29 force. One of the necessary tasks to be accomplished before the B-29s could operate effectively from the Marianas bases was the capture of Iwo Jima. Garrisoned by the Japanese, and base for an air element that included bombers and fighters, Iwo was about halfway between the Marianas and Japan. It was to become a valuable emergency landing area for troubled B-29s, and would justify the bloody losses that were suffered in taking it.

Task Force 58, under Mitscher, was deployed on a covering operation to hit Tokyo on 16 and 17 February, with the Iwo Jima invasion scheduled for 19 February. They struck that city again on 25 February, bombing and shelling air and naval installations and ships. Following those strikes, Mitscher's pilots claimed the destruction of 648 aircraft and 30,000 tons of shipping.

And off Iwo, the kamikazes struck again, sinking the escort carrier *Bismarck Sea*. Their attacks hit and severely damaged the *Saratoga*, and did minor hurt to the *Lunga Point*.

Iwo Jima was declared secure 16 March, although B-29 crews making emergency landings there a few days later were still reporting Japanese small-arms fire as they approached the field. Two days later, Mitscher's Task Force 58 joined the campaign against Okinawa, a fortress island. His first task was to strike Japanese installations on Kyushu Island, the departure point for reinforcements on the way to

A Zero (A6M5a) diving on the *USS Essex*.

(National Archives)

Okinawa. His ten heavy carriers and six light carriers launched their aircraft against the Japanese home island in a series of devastating strikes. They destroyed 482 planes by air attack, most of them on the ground, and an additional 46 were pulverized by naval gunfire. By March 23, TF58 was back off Okinawa and had begun to send combat sorties over that island.

The kamikaze was the only offensive weapon left to Japan. Her carrier force was destroyed, her airmen lost, her navy reduced to a few ships cowering in port, her distant garrisons overwhelmed. The kamikaze effort was potentially a deadly weapon; yet it required more skill than the young and inexperienced pilots had absorbed in their brief training. Like so many of the Japanese tactics, this one also leaves the question "What if . . .?" hanging in the air.

To the best of their abilities, these highly motivated, deeply patriotic, devoted subjects of the Emperor coolly and deliberately dashed themselves and their planes against the unyielding steel hull, the planked deck, or the armoured superstructure of Naval vessels.

In their last action, coded "Kikusui" (Floating Chrysanthemum), Army and Navy pilots together pledged to die in their attacks against the American fleet off Okinawa.

They came in formations, their war-weary aircraft scattered in loose geometries across the skies. Often they were intercepted on the way, and they died in the air instead of the way they had planned.

USS Essex takes a *kamikaze* hit aft of the forward elevator. She was able to survive thanks largely to damage-control improvements.

(US Navy Collection in the US National Archives)

The *Yamato* off Kushu on 7 April, 1945.

One such intercept tells the whole story. Lt. Eugene Valencia, on his second combat tour, was up with his "Flying Circus," also known as the "VF-9 Mowing Machine". His three hand-picked wingmen – Lts. James French, Harris Mitchel, and Clinton Smith – orbited with him at 5,000 feet above a picket destroyer. The ship's radar was being interpreted by a Fighter Director Officer on board, and he was reading the bearing and height of an approaching gaggle of Japanese aircraft. He vectored the Hellcats toward them. Valencia's section slashed into the formation and began the one-sided blood letting. Out of 38 planes in the attacking group, the "Mowing Machine" destroyed 14. They claimed nine more as probably destroyed, and six damaged. And there was not a single bullet hole in any of the four Hellcats.

The Navy, after it had time to collect battle reports and apply some objective thought to the raw data, estimated that the Japanese expended as many as 1,500 aircraft in a series of seven kamikaze attacks between 6 April and 28 May. Certainly the Navy had never been so punished.

No carriers were sunk; but 12 were hit and damaged and some of those had to be returned to a naval shipyard for major repairs. The list reads like a roll-call of the carriers on the scene: *Enterprise*, *Intrepid*, *Yorktown*, *Franklin*, *Wasp*, *San Jacinto*, *Hancock*, *Essex*, and *Bunker Hill*, all from TF58; *Wake Island*, *Sangamon* and *Natoma Bay*, all from TF52.

Not only aircraft featured in these suicidal attacks. The Japanese Navy finally sortied on its last attempt to strike the Americans, and it was a mission of deliberate self-destruction. They were to attack the U.S. ships lying off Okinawa and fight to the end. If they exhausted their ammunition while they were still above water, they were instructed to run aground so the crews could join in the defence of Okinawa. Flagship on this last attack was the huge *Yamato*. She was escorted by a light cruiser and a screen of eight destroyers. Bottled in the Inland Sea by effective mining that had been done by the B-29s, the *Yamato* force had only one way out. It sailed through the Bungo strait and was seen by American subs, which were operating almost openly in the Japanese waters.

The Japanese ships were found the next morning by a scout from the *Enterprise*; the pilot radioed his position back and the battle began to take shape. Task Force 58 with three of its fast carrier groups already under way toward the threat, launched 75 bombers and 131 torpedo planes with an escort of 180 fighters.

The Japanese had no air cover; the glossy blue planes drove to their targets and pounded the big battleship hard with bombs and torpedoes. She took five direct bomb hits and ten torpedo strikes, rolled over and sank with 2,500 men. The cruiser and four of the destroyers joined her on the bottom. Only the remaining four destroyers escaped, running to Sasebo at their top speed.

The Americans lost a dozen planes. Once again, capital ships had been sunk by air power, and once again the aircraft proved itself to be the basic unit weapon of naval strength.

Finally the ghastly Okinawa campaign ground to a halt. The island had become a charnel-house. Japanese soldiers and civilians had been cut down by every means known to the technology of war, and by a much older and stranger means: Suicide.

If statistics are meaningful in that context, here are some of the Navy's numbers for that campaign:

Naval aircraft flew more than 40,000 combat sorties. They dropped more than 8,500 tons (18,700,000 pounds) of bombs, fired about 50,000 rockets, and shot off countless rounds of ammunition. The pilots claimed a total of 2,516 enemy aircraft destroyed. Marine squadrons, operating from shore bases, claimed 506 Japanese planes downed or otherwise destroyed, and reported that they had dropped 1,800 tons (3,600,000 pounds) of bombs and fired 15,865 rockets during their close air support missions.

The *Essex*, prototypical ship for an entire class of heavy, fast carriers, once again distinguished herself. She had been in combat for 79 consecutive days, a record untouched by any other U.S. carrier during the war.

Now all that remained was the final assault on Japan itself, an invasion that was expected to be the most costly operation of World War II. The forces began to gather their strength for that final battle.

VF-40/USS SUWANEE (CVL 27) July 1945

VF-81/USS WASP (CV 18) February 1945

VF-45/USS SAN JACÍNTO (CVL 30) March 1945

VF-83/USS ESSEX (CV 9) April 1945

VF-46/USS COWPENS (CVL 25) March 1945

VF-84/USS BUNKERHILL (CV 17) February 1945

VF-47/USS BATTAN (CVL 29) April 1945

VBF-87/USS TICONDEROGA (CV 14) June 1945

VF(N)-53/USS SARATOGA (CV 3) February 1945

VF-94/USS LEXINGTON (CV 16) July 1945

The Last Battle

Early in March, 1945, a cigar-chomping Army Air Forces general made a fateful decision. He ordered his B-29 crews to strip their aircraft of the defensive armament except for tail guns, and to get rid of all unnecessary equipment on board. Then, said Maj. Gen. Curtis E. LeMay, load 'em with incendiaries and bomb the cities from five or six thousand feet (1500 or 1800 metres). The first fire raid, which hit Tokyo, was successful beyond belief, and it was followed by another fire-bombing mission, and another, and another. One by one, the great industrial cities of Japan, the cities built around naval bases, army garrisons and airfields became funeral pyres for thousands.

Much of Japan's dispersed industrial support was destroyed in the raids, burned in the relentless and consuming flames of thermite bombs. Vast numbers of the population had been displaced, were homeless, had lost families, relatives, friends, homes and places to work. And still the Japanese summoned enough reserves of strength and courage to talk of defending their country to the death.

Old men and women trained with bamboo spears. Factory workers slaved to turn out one more aircraft, one more gun, one more shell, knowing that every one would count. Aircraft in every state of repair were prepared for one more flight, and hidden under camouflage or in the ruins of villages and towns, waiting for their last missions. Fuel was collected, barrel by precious barrel, and stored near the concealed aircraft. And all over Japan, the people prepared to face a frightening future.

The U.S. Navy's Third Fleet, commanded by Admiral William F. Halsey, detached Task Force 38 to operate against the Japanese homeland. Vice Admiral McCain, TF38 commander, had 14 available carriers in the strike force, and his operations were supported by a replenishment group and a group dedicated to anti-submarine warfare. Both these support units included escort carriers whose aircraft normally flew CAP, but were also available for supplementing the air strength of the main body of the task force.

The British detached their Carrier Task Force 37 under the Royal Navy's Vice Admiral H. B. Rawlings, and ordered its four carriers and screening ships to join in the assault against Japan.

It was the seaborne half of the total air campaign against the islands, the other half coming from hundreds of Superfortress bombers from the Marianas, aided by other hundreds of medium and light bombers based on the islands and land masses of the Pacific. They were to join a single great bombing and interdiction offensive that would break the Japanese and leave the country as defenceless as possible against the invasion.

The targets were airfields, any and all that were known or could be spotted. Warships and merchant shipping were to be attacked. Military installations and naval bases completed the roster. The area covered was to extend throughout the island empire, from Kyushu in the south, Hokkaido in the north.

The offensive opened for the Navy on 10 July, with a strike on the airfields in the plains around Tokyo. By now, the Americans had such a degree of air superiority that the fighters, although they still flew as escorts on strikes, carried bombs and were part of the strike force.

After the first Tokyo raid, the Navy shifted its attention to the northern regions of Honshu and Hokkaido, hitting airfields and shipping. They went back to Tokyo on 17 July, then pounded Japanese shipping at Yokosuka, the big naval base. They struck ships on the Inland Sea near Kure on the 24th, and attacked airfields on the northern end of Kyushu Island the same day. Then they moved up the Inland Sea to bomb Osaka and Nagoya the next day, and repeated the move northward on 25, 28 and 30 July.

The typical Hellcat bombing mission started with a climb to a cruise altitude around 20,000 feet/6100 m. (Individual aircraft varied, but maximum performance of the F6F series was obtained at altitudes between 18,000 ft/5500 m and 21,000 ft/6400 m, at that height, the Hellcat would cruise at a true airspeed of 205 to 210 knots with the engine in automatic lean mixture and turning about 2,000 rpm. (In these days of fuel shortages, it is interesting to remember that the Hellcat could cruise that way for an hour on just 75 gals/280 l of aviation grade gasoline.)

The mission had been launched before dawn, so that the planes would approach the coast while it was still dark, in order to catch the defenders by surprise. Running with the navigation lights on, the Hellcat formation would mark the 50-mile (80 km) distance from the coast and check the guns. Their flight plan would put them just over the coast at daybreak and, upon crossing the coast, the pilots flipped off their running lights and began the search for the familiar landmarks that would lead them to the target.

In the Tokyo area it was always Mount Fuji, with its characteristic shape and prominence, that gave them their bearings. At about ten miles from the target, the Hellcats would slide into a loose echelon formation, generally led from the left aircraft, and would cut back the power to start a long, quiet and speedy glide to the target. Somewhere around 10,000 feet (3000 m) the formation pushed over for the dive-bombing run. The pilots, if they remembered to do so, unlocked the landing gear and let it extend partially in a trail position, to serve as a stabilizing dive brake. The flight opened its formation to leave about 1,000 feet (300 m) between successive F6Fs in the dive. The pilots eyed their targets and the altimeter alternately, and when the gauge read about 3,000 feet (900 m), they pressed the bomb release on the control stick handgrip. A split second later they hauled back on the stick in a gut-wrenching pullout, jinking up and away if there were any anti-aircraft fire.

They did this, time after time, across the breadth and along the length of Japan. After the July 30 strike at the northern end of the Inland Sea, they stood down and moved south to avoid the typhoon that was roaring up into the area.

By the time they had returned, the top level commanders had been told about the highly secret operation that was scheduled soon. Hiroshima, they knew, was one city that was on the target list for a special operation, and the area

around it was to be kept clear for the Army Air Forces bombers. So McCain steamed well north of the doomed city. A few days after the news of that first nuclear weapon attack had electrified the world, TF38 again struck the Honshu and Hokkaido areas. Apparently, thought the Navy, the Japanese needed more convincing that they ought to surrender.

And they did, on 15 August, after a second city – Nagasaki – had vanished in a fireball brighter than the sun. At 0635 on the morning of the 15th, Halsey passed the word to his fleet. But he was too late to catch the first strike of the day which had been launched, according to custom, well before dawn and was at that moment dropping its bombs on the assigned targets. The second attack wave was on its way to the coast when it heard the commands radioed in the clear to all planes of the strike force: Return to base. Return to base. Do not attack; repeat, do not attack. The war is over; the war is over.

The Hellcats of VBF-87, from the *Ticonderoga*, were diving on Chosi airfield when the orders came through. All 12 planes continued, committed to the dive and the drop, ignoring the order. It would be easy to explain later, and besides, nobody really cared whether or not a few more bombs were dropped on the Japanese.

All through the target areas, the blue planes swung their noses around and headed back to their carriers. Several formations were jumped by Japanese fighters, who either had not heard the word, or who chose to ignore it in favour of one last opportunity to strike a blow for their country.

A mixed gaggle of VF-88 Hellcats from the *Yorktown* and Corsairs from the *Wasp* and *Shangri-La* were out on a fighter sweep with assigned targets in the Choshi Point area. The dozen Hellcats, led by Lt. Howard Harrison, had left their carrier in three flights of four. It was the first combat tour for many of the pilots; VF-88 had entered combat on V-E Day and had not yet accumulated that much experience in the real world of aerial combat. They had lost their skipper on their first day of combat, and had other losses since. It was felt to be a hard-luck outfit.

The twelve, with the lead flight high and the two trailing flights stepped down, penetrated a thunderstorm area. In its turbulence and low visibility, the formation was sundered. When they came out the other side, "Howdy" Harrison was leading a smaller formation, and they headed for a rendezvous point.

On the way, their radios picked up the return to base order and they began the easy turn back. Choshi Point had a lighthouse, and they decided to go down and shoot out the light as a last gesture, and then cruise past Fuji, to see that mountain without having to watch for Japanese interceptors.

They peeled off, blasted the lighthouse, reformed and headed for Fuji. In the distance they spotted a group of Hellcats headed toward them on a course that would take them back to the carriers. The Hellcats turned out to be a batch of Japanese fighters and they got one free pass at Harrison's formation. And then the sky was full of turning, diving, zooming planes, blue and metal, starred and red-balled.

That last dogfight, an unnecessary one, cost the Navy four pilots, including Harrison and the squadron "low-man," a pilot who was trying to log a fifth combat mission so that he would be eligible for a decoration.

The Hellcat was in combat with the U.S. Navy for a little less than two years. When the claims were added at the end of the war, the Navy said that the F6F had accounted for a total of 5,155 Japanese aircraft. The greatest number of those fell to the guns of the Navy's carrier-based Hellcats. Land-based Hellcats did considerably less damage to Japanese aircraft; they had other work to do.

Against those 5,155 victories was balanced the loss of only 270 Hellcats in combat during the war. The kill ratio is a little better than 19 to one, a phenomenal figure.

Its record as an escort for the strike forces was exceptional; the Navy lost only 42 dive-bombers and torpedo bombers to enemy air action during the Hellcat's day with the fleet.

The Hellcat seized and held air superiority over the Pacific. It defended the fleet and the strike forces with outstanding success. It achieved an enormous kill ratio over its opponents.

And, said Grumman's Dick Hutton, that's what we wanted it to do.

F4U
CORSAIR

Text by FREDERICK A. JOHNSEN

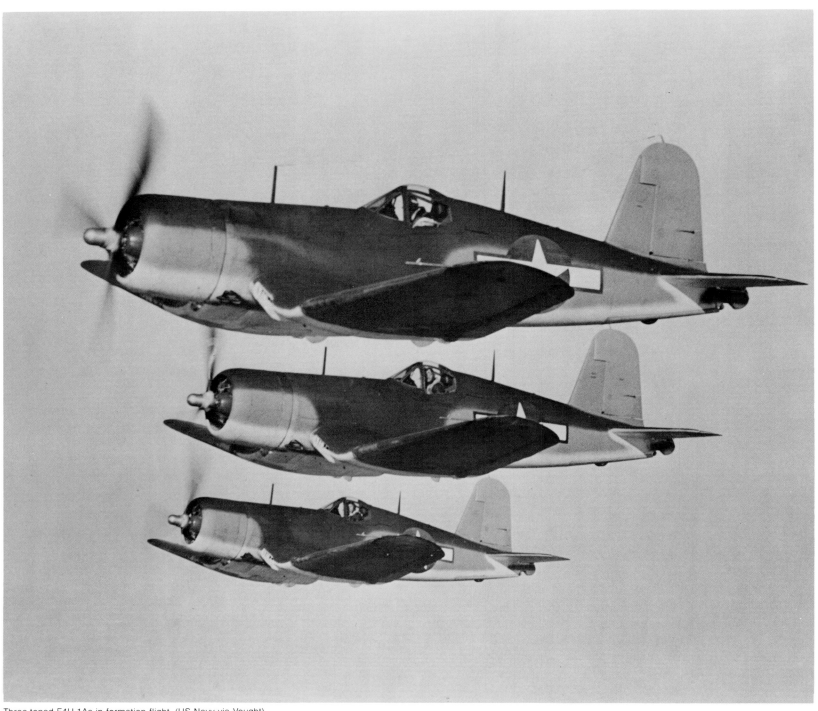

Three-toned F4U-1As in formation flight. (US Navy via Vought)

USMC F4U-1As with 500 lb (227 kg) bombs moving out to take off from their parking positions on Majuro Atoll, Marshall Islands in August, 1944. (USMC via Vought)

Introduction

Long after its combat career has ended the Vought Corsair still enjoys a public image as a powerfully successful fighter, its distinctive inverted gull wing prompting instant recognition even by those who do not profess to be aircraft enthusiasts. Aviation history has entered an enlightened era now, in which the press-inflated heroics and propaganda which first accompanied most aircraft into combat in World War II can be lifted away, revealing a truer picture of the machine, the pilots and the actions they faced together.

In the case of the Vought Corsair, the record shows an impressive, innovative design which delivered outstanding performance, but at a price. The cost was a series of teething troubles which delayed shipboard deployment of the F4U, and which destroyed an alarming number of aircraft, killing many pilots who had not mastered its intricacies.

The Corsair story is one of determined American engineers and fliers, as well as worthy opponents in Japan. Now, more than three decades after the end of World War II, the former antagonists of the war in the Pacific can frequently be seen together at museums and air shows, where Japanese and American veterans mutually agree the Vought Corsair was an inspired design and one to be reckoned with.

Many people and organizations helped with the preparation of this Corsair story. They include: Mike Hatfield and Bob Nelson of the Vought Corporation; Jeff Dorroh, Jeff Endicott, W. Buckner Hanner, Richard E. Harmer, Mal Holcomb, Don Keller, Keith Laird, Jim Landry, Jim Larsen, Dave Menard, Jim Morrow, the US Navy, Pat Palmer, Barrett Tillman, and my father, aeronautical engineer Carl M. Johnsen. How well I remember, as a boy of eight, racing over back roads leading to the Salt Lake City, Utah, airport with my father at the wheel, hurrying to beat the arrival of a rare and wonderful sight for 1959 – a surplus Corsair fighter from the stable of Frank Tallman. More recently, my father spent hours poring over old magazines and cuttings, gleaning bits of wartime information about the Corsair for my use in this book. To all who helped, thank you.

Frederick A. Johnsen

Design and Development

Most people would assume that aircraft specifications are fixed and readily determinable. Yet a host of variables in measuring techniques invariably gives several sets of specifications for the same aircraft. Figures referred to in this text may be considered reliable guidelines, gleaned in many instances directly from the official Erection and Maintenance Manual for the Corsair. However, variations still exist from source to source.

In the case of performance figures, different readings can be obtained from various factors such as winds, and from far more subtle changes including roughness of the aircraft's finish, ordnance or ordnance attachments in place, and, ultimately, the skill of a particular pilot. For example, where the handbook suggested a deadstick glide ratio of about 13 to 1 for a Corsair, discussion by Naval Aviation safety experts suggested a clean Corsair on a windless day might achieve a glide of 15 to 1!

XF4U-1

Power unit
Pratt & Whitney XR-2800-4 Double Wasp
: 1,850 hp for take-off
: 1,460 hp at 21,500 ft (6,550 m)
Internal fuel: 273 gal (227.3 Imp gal, 1,033 ltr)

Performance
Max speed: 405 mph (652 km/h)
Cruising speed: 185 mph (298 km/h)
Service ceiling: 35,200 ft (10,730 m)
Rate of climb: 2,660 fpm (811 m/min)
Range: 1,070 mls (1,720 km)

Armament
2 × 0.50-in (12.7 mm) machine guns with 600 rounds in all and
2 × 0.30-in (7.62 mm) machine guns with 1,500 rounds in all
20 × 5.2 lb (2.36 kg) anti-bomber-formation bombs

Dimensions
Span: 41 ft (12.50 m)
Length: 31 ft 11 in (9.73 m)
Wing area: 314 sq. ft (29.2 m²)

Weights
Empty: 7,505 lb (3,404 kg)
Gross: 9,357 lb (4,244 kg)
Max take-off: 10,074 lb (4,570 kg)

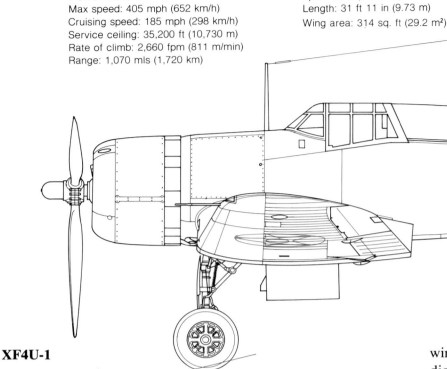

XF4U-1

The first Corsair was Vought's response to a set of operational requirements set forth by the US Navy early in 1938, calling for a shipboard fighter which could match performance with the best of the current land-based pursuit aircraft, while catering for the demands of operations and stowage aboard an aircraft carrier. Rex Beisel led the Vought design group which concocted an innovative reverse-gullwing fighter, pulled through the sky by the new and mighty Pratt and Whitney XR-2800 Double Wasp radial engine. The big power-plant was rated at 1,850 horsepower for takeoff – a phenomenal amount of power in an age where existing Navy pursuits mustered from about 940 to 1,200 horsepower. Later, Corsairs would fly with improved versions of the R-2800 engine delivering 2,000 horsepower and more.

To harness properly all the energy available from the Pratt and Whitney engine and convert it to propulsion, Beisel's design team had to cope with a huge propeller with an arc of 13 feet, 4 inches (4.06m). Clearance for the big three-blade propeller had to be maintained in a takeoff or landing attitude, rolling on the mainwheels with the nose lower to the ground than when the aircraft was resting on its tailwheel. Typical straight-wing designs would impose extremely long landing gear struts to assure propeller clearance, and a spidery main gear was not desirable, especially for abrupt aircraft carrier landing.

A solution was reached by dropping the stub wings at an angle as they left the fuselage, and then canting the outer wing panels upwards again with a dihedral of eight degrees, 30 minutes in the outer sections. At the lowest point in the Vee formed thus on each wing, a short landing gear leg would still be long enough to keep the big propeller out of trouble. Another happy result of this arrangement was low drag at the wing root/fuselage joint, a product of the virtually perpendicular mating of the wing roots to the round fuselage.

The stub wings featured open vents in their leading edges to draw cooling air for engine oil, and air for supercharger intercooler equipment. On the XF4U-1, the pilot sat over the wing in a ribbed canopy. Offensive armament originally specified for the XF4U-1 consisted of a .30 and a .50 calibre machine gun in the top of the cowling and a .50 calibre weapon in each wing. Unique to the prototype Corsair were small bomb bays in the wings capable of holding 5.2-pound (2.36kg) bombs. The small bombs were to be dropped on enemy formations in flight. This feature was discarded on production Corsairs.

The outer wings of the prototype Corsair also featured fuel tanks. These were located near the leading edge of the wing. The wings of the Corsair were designed to hinge at the gullwing bend, with the outer wing panels folding overhead. Fabricated of metal frames, the outer wing panels featured large portions skinned in cloth fabric, somewhat of a novelty for American fighters, although in England the Hawker Hurricane was employing fabric covering on its fuselage.

While designer Rex Beisel was busy refining Vought Model V-166B into the design the Navy would order as the XF4U-1, the US Army Air Corps was attempting to persuade Pratt and Whitney, makers of the R-2800 engine, to concentrate instead on liquid-cooled inline aircraft engines. However, Beisel pressed ahead, producing the smallest airframe which could handle the power of the massive R-2800 radial powerplant. Ultimately, the prototype Corsair would clock an exciting speed of 404 mph (650 km/h) in 1940, a feat which some observers credit with helping get the Air Corps to back off in its insistence that Pratt and Whitney build liquid-cooled engines instead of motors such as the R-2800.

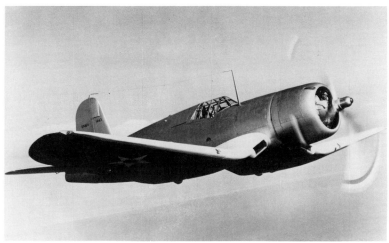
XF4U-1, the first of more than 12,000 Corsairs. (US Navy via Vought)

The first Corsair was shorter than the rest, measuring 31 feet, 11 inches (9.73 m). Smooth fuselage skin was achieved by a spot-welding process.

In June 1938, the US Navy approved Beisel's bentwing proposal, and placed an order for a prototype, the XF4U-1. By the following February, after wind tunnel tests, a mock-up was on hand for Navy inspection. But it was not until 29 May, 1940, that the number one Corsair transferred its weight from wheels to wings, and sailed into the sky from the Vought runway at Stratford, Connecticut. Test pilot Lyman A. Bullard, Jr., took the Corsair up for its maiden flight, following taxi tests intended to give him a preview of the fighter's handling characteristics. Bullard's first landing in the big new Vought appeared to follow a routine shakedown hop, as observers recalled, but the chief test pilot for Vought was visibly irritated when he dismounted from the aircraft.

During his manoeuvres, flutter had briefly attacked the elevators, and the spring trim tabs had shimmied off in flight. Nevertheless, Bullard had been able to control the vibrating aircraft, returning safely to Stratford.

But in July 1940 the first F4U was wrecked in an off-airport landing. Another Vought pilot, Boone Guyton, found himself beset with problems as his fuel ran low, storms blocked his way back to Stratford, and radio communications could not be established with any other field in the area. Deciding he would have to attempt a landing before fuel exhaustion forced him down, Guyton set up an approach to a long fairway on a Connecticut golf course. To keep the use of terrain at a minimum, Guyton set up an aircraft-carrier style landing, with flaps fully deployed, and the engine still carrying power as the fighter descended in a nose-high attitude.

The touchdown on the grass of the golf course was good, and Guyton's troubles appeared over. But the rain-slippery grass robbed the Corsair of effective braking ability. Not even an intentional groundloop could be induced as a desperate means of halting the coasting fighter. The tyres sliced straight ahead, sending the XF4U-1 into woodland where it swapped tail for nose, and continued to slide along on its back, rudder first. A stout tree trunk halted the fighter, and the shaken Boone Guyton wriggled out of the overturned XF4U-1. The right wing was gone, and fuselage damage looked terrible. But the very fact that Guyton survived was due in part to the aircraft's rugged construction which kept some of its structural integrity even in the crash. Vought mechanics pounced on the crippled machine, rebuilding it for flight in a few months. It was this rebuilding which allowed the fighter to achieve its 400-plus clocking on 1 October, 1940. Soon, US Navy pilots got their turn at the amazing Corsair. Though impressed by its speed and ceiling, the service pilots offered suggestions based on experience – suggestions that would manifest themselves as changes to the design of the F4U-1 variant to follow.

F4U-1

The major production version of the Corsair series was the F4U-1, characterized by a slender, circular cowling and three-blade propeller. Within the basic designation F4U-1 were several modifications and offshoots which earned suffix letters for identification, as in F4U-1A.

On 30 June, 1941, the US Navy ordered the F4U-1

F4U-1

Power unit
Pratt & Whitney R-2800-8 Double Wasp
: 2,000 hp for take-off
: 1,650 hp at 21,000 ft (6,400 m)
Internal fuel: 363 US gal (302.3 Imp gal, 1,374 ltr)
Auxiliary fuel tank: 1 × 160 US gal (133.2 Imp gal, 606 ltr)

Performance
Max speed: 417 mph (671 km/h)
Cruising speed: 182 mph (293 km/h)
Service ceiling: 36,900 ft (11,250 m)
Rate of climb: 2,890 fpm (881 m/min)
Normal range: 1,015 mls (1,630 km)

Armament
6 × 0.50-in (12.7 mm) machine guns with 2,350 rounds in all
2 × 100 lb (45.4 kg) bombs

Dimensions
Span: 41 ft (12.50 m)
Length: 33 ft 4 in (10.16 m)
Height: 15 ft (4.57 m)
Wing area: 314 sq. ft (29.2 m²)

Weights
Empty: 8,982 lb (4,074 kg)
Gross: 12,039 lb (5,461 kg)
Max take-off: 14,000 lb (6,350 kg)

F4U-1A

Modified from F4U-1. Fitted with bulged clear-view
canopy instead of "Greenhouse" type. Specification
is almost same as F4U-1.

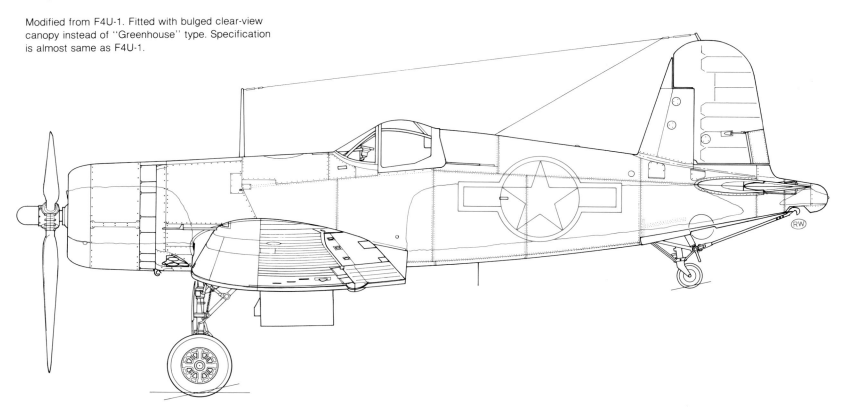

FG-1A

Fitted with bubble canopy for performance
tests. Not put into production.

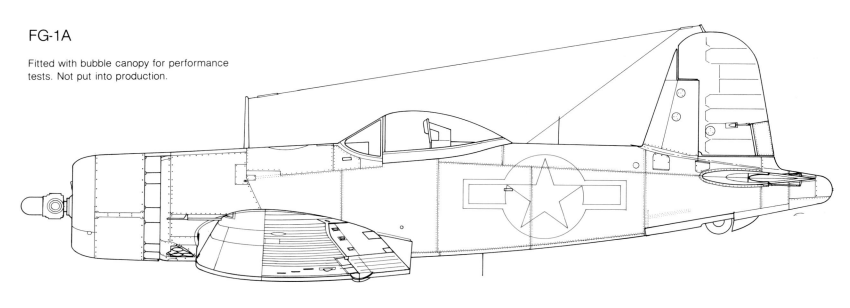

F4U-1C

Armed with four 20 mm Hispano M-2 cannon with
880 rounds in all.

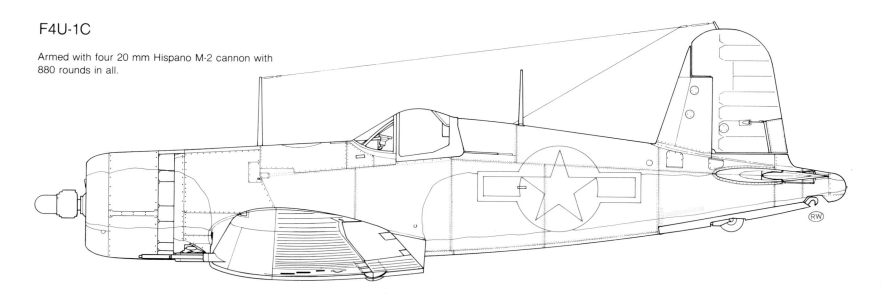

into production for an initial run of 584 of the Voughts. Length was increased to more than 33 ft, 4⅔ in. (10.18 m), to split hairs with the official Erection and Maintenance manual for the F4U-1. Initially, another .50 calibre machine gun was added to each wing of the production F4U-1, making the total in the wings four, while the fuselage guns were deleted entirely. Soon, production F4U-1s would have the wing armament upped again for a total of six .50 calibre M-2 machine guns. To accommodate the extra wing guns, the leading edge fuel tanks of the prototype were removed. This petrol capacity was replaced with a 237-US gallon (896 l) self-sealing fuel tank in the fuselage. By mounting this tank near the Corsair's centre of gravity, the aircraft would not require attitude changes as the fuel was burned off. So the cockpit was positioned aft about three feet (91 cm) farther than on the XF4U-1, with the fuel tank ahead.

With his relocation aft, the Corsair pilot had an immense stretch of nose obstructing his view in a nose-high attitude for landings – a shortcoming that would later receive attention as part of a continuous effort to make the F4U as suitable for aircraft carrier operations as possible.

The engine for the F4U-1 in production was the Pratt and Whitney R-2800-8 Double Wasp with a two-stage supercharger for performance at altitude. Takeoff horsepower of this engine was rated at a full 2,000. Top speed was 417 mph (671 km/h) achieved at an altitude of 19,900 feet (6066 m). Pilots sitting behind this monster engine quickly discovered a defect in the hydraulically-operated cowl flaps which spewed fluid on the windscreen, mixed with engine oil. The ultimate solution would be to seal the upper section of cowl flaps.

When the cockpit was moved aft, the number of metal ribs in the canopy was reduced as an aid to vision, and fuselage cutouts similar to those employed on P-40s behind the canopy were introduced behind teardrop-shaped windows, to provide a measure of rear vision. Armour plating was added around the cockpit and oil tank on production Dash-1 Corsairs, and after the wing gun installation had necessitated the removal of the original wing fuel tanks, new wing fuel cells were devised to add 62 more US gallons (234.7 l) to each wing.

By slightly diminishing the span of the landing flaps, the ailerons were increased in size on the F4U-1, prompting a quicker roll rate than possible in the prototype. This would serve the Corsair well in its combat career. The wings still retained the use of fabric-covered panels. According to the Erection and Maintenance manual for this model of the Corsair, the moveable control surfaces were made "of either wooden or fabric-covered metal construction".

So equipped, the production F4U-1 could weigh in at nearly 6.5 US tons. First of the production models flew late in June 1942, with the first deliveries to squadrons, US Marine VMF-124 and Navy VF-12, commencing early September and 3 October. The next month, the Navy added the Brewster Aeronautical Corporation into the Corsair programme, followed in December by the entry of the Goodyear Aircraft Corporation into the pool of manufacturers turning out Corsairs. Brewster versions were called F3A-1s;

Goodyear's equivalents were known as FG-1s. Brewster's production record was not impressive, and its F3A-1s did not see delivery until July 1943, while Goodyear began delivering FG-1s in April 1943. At last, combat Corsairs were on the way.

The British Royal Navy received 95 F4U-1 Corsairs under the designation Corsair I. These were fitted with the ribbed birdcage canopy as were early US F4U-1s. The 689th F4U-1 featured a raised pilot's seat under a bulging canopy. To denote the changes, the nomenclature was changed to F4U-1A, or Corsair II in British service. Goodyear equivalents were the FG-1As, made without the wing folding mechanism. They served with Marine shore-based squadrons.

Some accounts reserve the designation F4U-1B for the British versions which had clipped wingtips to permit stowage aboard low-ceilinged British aircraft carriers.

The F4U-1C was armed with four 20-mm cannon in the wings instead of the six .50 calibre guns of other Dash-1s.

The ultimate sub-type of the Dash-1 Corsair was the F4U-1D, echoed by Brewster as the F3A-1D and Goodyear as the FG-1D. Many Goodyear FG-1Ds became Royal Navy Corsair IVs. The F4U-1D did away with the outboard internal wing fuel tanks, relying instead on a belly-mounted 160-US gallon (604.6 l) droppable tank for extended range. Or, two 1,000-pound (454 kg) bombs could be lugged aloft by the D-model. Using the Pratt and Whitney R-2800-8W engine with water injection, emergency power of the D-model could be pegged at 2,230 horsepower. The F4U-1D was said to achieve a top speed of 425 mph (684 km/h) at 20,000 feet (6096 m) altitude. Eight hard points for five-inch (127 mm) rockets were mounted under the wings of the F4U-1D. In addition to superlative service as a fighter in the Pacific, these Corsairs would work admirably well as dive bombers against surface targets. In fact, some Corsair manuals refer to the forward-opening landing gear strut doors as dive brakes, since extension of the landing gear brought these flat doors into play as air brakes to slow the rate of descent during an ordnance-delivery dive.

When fitted with cameras for reconnaissance, F4U-1s were called F4U-1Ps.

F4U-1A carrying 160–170 US gal (606–644 ltr) 'Duramold' type auxiliary fuel tank beneath the fuselage. (US Navy via Vought)

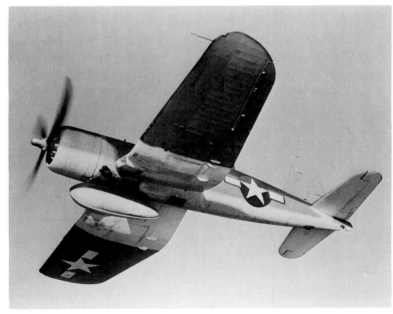

F4U-1D Cockpit

1 Armoured glass
2 Mk 8 reflector gunsight
3 Gun switch box
4 Bomb switch box
5 Water injection quantity warning light
6 Stall warning light
7 Carburetor air temperature warning light
8 Engine speed indicator
9 Auxiliary droptank fuel control switch
10 Altimeter
11 Manifold pressure gauge
12 Directional gyro
13 Airspeed indicator
14 Compass
15 Turn and bank indicator
16 Artificial horizon
17 Rate of climb/descent indicator
18 Elapsed time clock
19 Cylinder temperature indicator
20 Oil temperature indicator
21 Oil pressure gauge

22 Fuel pressure gauge
23 Instrument panel lights
24 Flap control/indicator
25 Ignition switch
26 Alternate air control
27 Throttle lever
28 Supercharger control lever
29 Landing gear and dive brake control lever
30 Gun charging control
31 Surge chamber
32 Mixture control lever
33 Propeller control lever
34 Aileron trimming tab control wheel/indicator
35 Fuel tank selector
36 Hydraulic hand pump
37 Elevator trimming tab control wheel
38 Elevator trimming tab indicator
39 Rudder trimming tab control wheel/indicator
40 Tail wheel locking handle
41 Wing-folding control lever
42 Manual wing hinge pin lock
43 CO$_2$ bottle for emergency landing gear
44 CO$_2$ bottle for vapour dilution

45 Rudder pedal adjustment screw
46 Rudder pedals
47 Control grip with gun-firing button
48 Control column
49 Cockpit ventilator
50 Signal pistol cartridge container
51 Rocket station distributor box
52 Main tank fuel contents gauge
53 Hydraulic pressure gauge
54 Voltmeter
55 Fuel tank pressure gauge
56 Accelerometer
57 Radio control box
58 Cooling flap control levers
59 Pilot's distribution box
60 Light
61 Map case
62 Arrester hook control lever
63 Landing gear and wing folding claxon
64 Signal pistol
65 24 Volt battery
66 Cockpit heating duct
67 Oxygen bottle

F4U-1D Cockpit

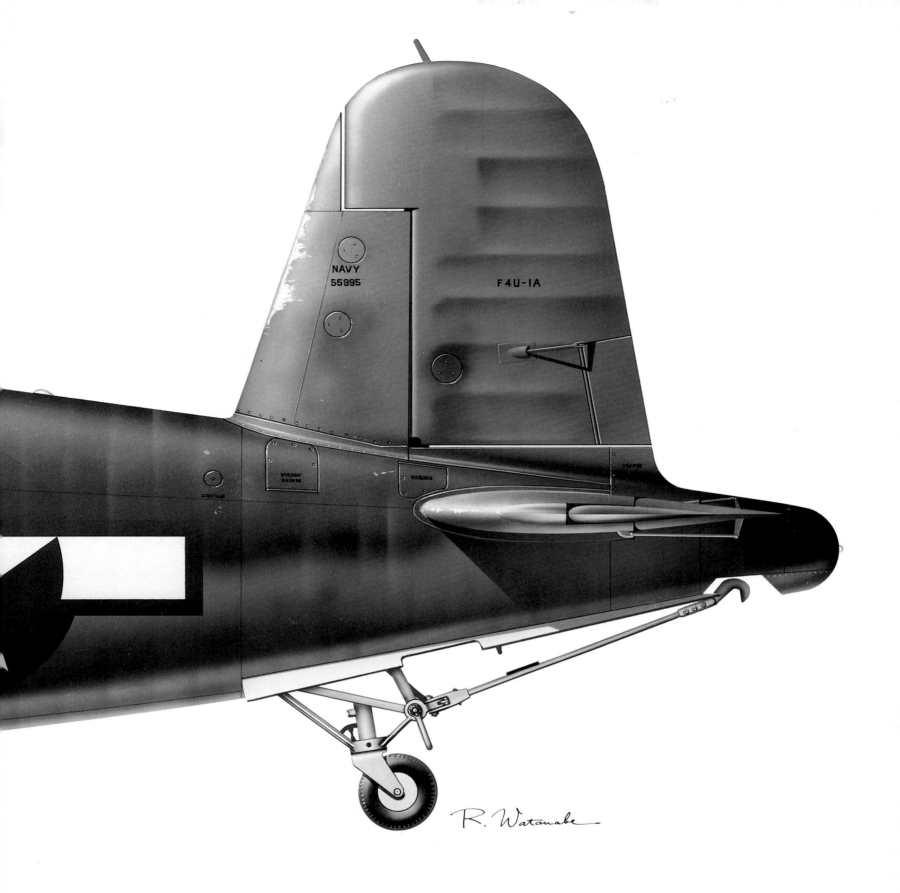

NAVY
55995

F4U-1A

R. Watanabe

F4U-1A Corsair flown by Lt (jg) Ira Cassius Kepford of VF-17, US Navy.

Naval Fighter Squadron VF-17 "Blackburn's Irregulars" became the first to enter into action with Corsair in the US Navy. During 8,577 combat hours, VF-17 destroyed 156 Japanese aircraft over the Solomon Islands as against 12 pilots lost by the unit.

Ira C. Kepford, the top scoring ace of VF-17 and the fifth highest ranking in the US Navy, achieved 17 victories including one unconfirmed from November 1943 to February 1944. He shot down four zero fighters in only ten minutes over Rabaul area on 29 January, 1944, and downed one Zero (his last victory) without firing a shot three weeks later. Awarded the DFC, "Ike" Kepford was promoted to the rank of Lieutenant on 1 May, 1945.

This illustration shows his second "No 29" aircraft based on Bougainville Island in March, 1944, just before homecoming. The "Jolly Roger" (skull and crossbones) insignia and victory markings were displayed both sides of the fuselage.

R. Watanabe

F4U-1D Starboard wing

hinge details

 1 Outer wing flap
 2 Outer wing flap inboard hinge
 3 Folded outer wing
 4 Flap control rods
 5 Aileron control links
 6 Aileron control lever
 7 Main hinge bolt
 8 Fuel swivel position (for F4U-1)
 9 Wing folding swivel
10 Gun charging swivel
11 Gun heater swivel
12 Auxiliary hinge pin position (for F4U-1)
13 Load and fire valve
14 Gap door mechanism
15 Wing folding rod
16 Hinge pin pulling strut
17 Flap control lever
18 Flap strut
19 Flap control by-pass valve
20 Inner wing
21 Centre flap outboard hinge
22 Centre flap
23 Landing gear well door
24 Drag links
25 Locking springs
26 Locking linkage
27 Lifting cable
28 Oleo strut
29 Fairing
30 Brake tube
31 Tyre
32 Removable wheel disc cover

R. Watanabe

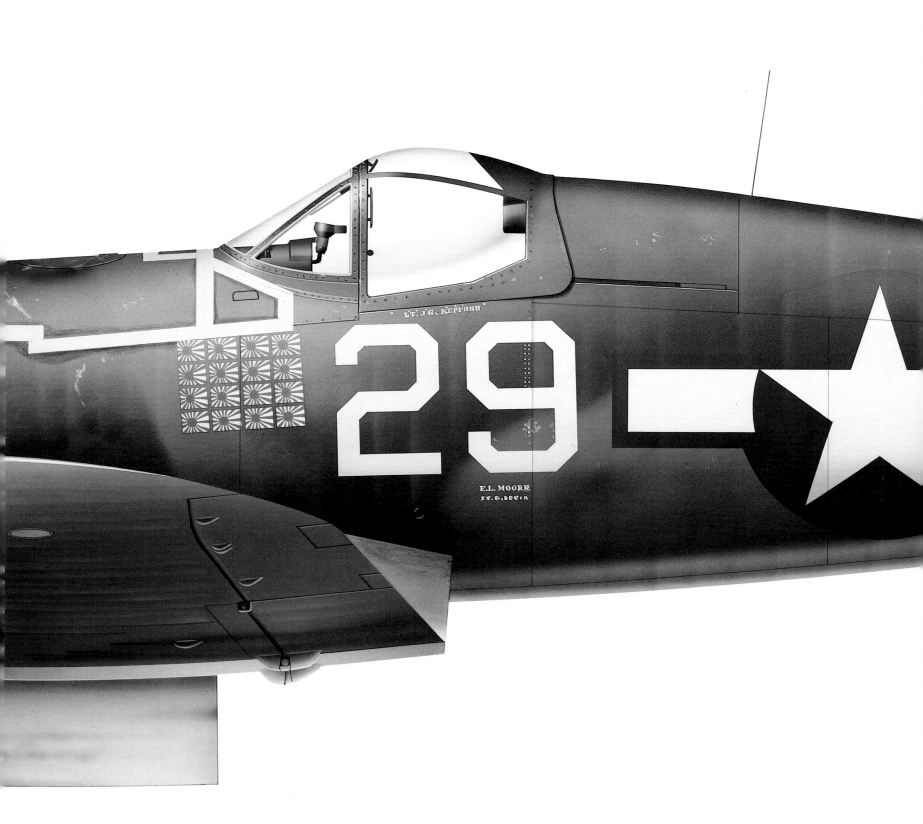

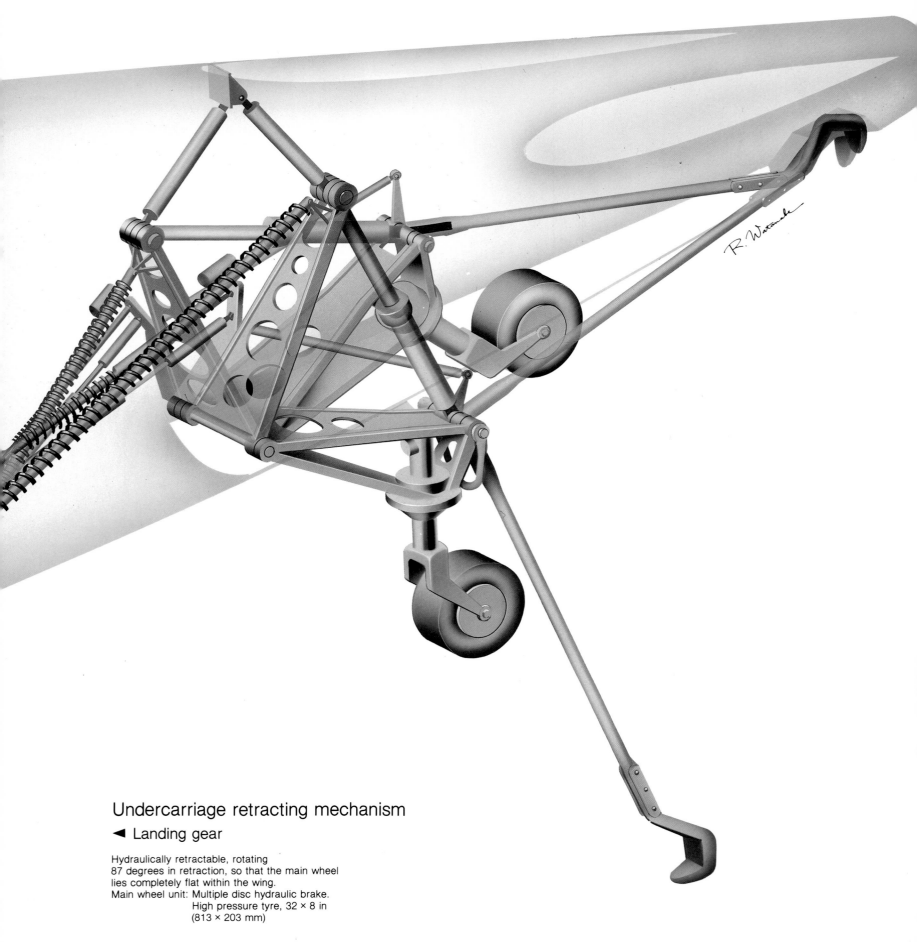

Undercarriage retracting mechanism

◄ Landing gear

Hydraulically retractable, rotating
87 degrees in retraction, so that the main wheel
lies completely flat within the wing.
Main wheel unit: Multiple disc hydraulic brake.
High pressure tyre, 32 × 8 in
(813 × 203 mm)

▲ Tail wheel and arrester hook

Both gears are also hydraulically retractable.
The arrester hook (1) is attached to an arm assembly (2)
moving in the joint at the after part of the tail
wheel housing.
Tail wheel unit: Fully-swiveling with locking device.
High pressure tyre, 12$\frac{1}{2}$ × 4$\frac{1}{2}$ in
(318 × 114 mm)

R. Watanabe

(Vought)

Comparison of propeller diameters

F4U-4
: Hamilton-Standard four-bladed hydromatic
constant-speed propeller
Diameter
: 13 ft 2 in (4.01 m)

A6M5 (Zero Mk 52)
: Sumitomo (under a licence from
Hamilton-Standard) three-bladed hydromatic
constant-speed propeller
Diameter
: 10 ft 1/8 in (3.05 m)

F4U-2	Power unit	Armament	Weights

F4U-2

Power unit
Pratt & Whitney R-2800-8 Double Wasp
: 2,000 hp for take-off
: 1,650 hp at 21,000 ft (6,400 m)
Internal fuel: 178-363 US gal (148.2-302.2 Imp gal, 674 ltr-1,374 ltr)

Armament
5 × 0.50-in (12.7 mm) machine guns with 1,975 rounds in all

Radar equipment
AN/APS-4

Weights
Empty: 9,170 lb (4,160 kg)
Gross: 11,446 lb (5,192 kg)
Max take off: 13,112 lb (5,948 kg)

Performance
Max speed: 381 mph (613 km/h) at 23,500 ft (7,160 m)
Cruising speed: 187 mph (301 km/h)
Service ceiling: 33,900 ft (10,330 m)
Rate of climb: 2,970 fpm (905 m/min)
Normal range: 955 mls (1,540 km)

Dimensions
Span: 41 ft (12.50 m)
Length: 33 ft 4 in (10.16 m)
Height: 15 ft (4.57 m)
Wing area: 314 sq.ft (29.2 m²)

F4U-2

Radar-equipped night fighters for fleet and shore-base protection were sought by the Navy. The Naval Aircraft Factory's plant at Philadelphia, Pennsylvania, took 32 F4U-1s and mounted radomes from the right wings for use as night fighters, calling the finished product the F4U-2. As the Corsair was still basically a land-based fighter at the time of the modification, early F4U-2 successes were scored by pilots of VF(N)-75 flying from Munda, New Georgia, against nocturnal Japanese prowlers. Later, Dash-2s would serve aboard carriers for fleet defence. Additional night fighter Corsairs would be made from F4U-4s and -5s.

XF4U-3

By mating a new two-stage turbo-supercharger to the R-2800 engine, the -16C version of this powerplant promised to keep delivering 2,000 horsepower on up to altitudes as high as 40,000 feet, where the ratings on other R-2800s would be lower. This high-altitude package, with a recessed air inlet in

a "chin" position near the cowl flaps, was mounted to a converted F4U-1 to create the XF4U-3 high-altitude version of the Corsair. Progress was slow, and "bugs" in the project plagued engineers. The XF4U-3 and its Goodyear FG-3 counterparts did not become production models.

F4U-4

Even as the F4U-1D and its twin the FG-1D were turning in impressive missions against Japanese aircraft and ground targets, Vought was reaching for a still better Corsair. The R-2800-18W engine promised 2,100 horsepower for takeoff. Five F4U-1 airframes were mated to the new engine, and the resulting aircraft were all tagged as XF4U-4s. First of these flew on 19 April, 1944, pulled along by a new four-blade propeller instead of the familiar three-blade airscrew of the earlier production Corsairs.

The F4U-4 hit a top speed of 446 mph (718 km/h) at an altitude of 26,200 feet (7986 m) — higher than the F4U-1 by about 30 mph (48 km/h). Carburettor inlets for the Dash-4 Corsairs were removed from the wing root inlet loca-

XF4U-3B

Power unit
Pratt & Whitney XR-2800-16 (C) Double Wasp
: 2,000 hp at 30,000 ft (9,140 m)

Performance
Max speed: 412 mph (663 km/h) at 30,000 ft (9,140 m)
Cruising speed: 180 mph (290 km/h)
Service ceiling: 38,400 ft (11,700 m)
Rate of climb: 2,990 fpm (911 m/min)
Normal range: 780 mls (1,255 km)

Armament
6 × 0.50-in (12.7 mm) machine guns

Dimensions
Span: 41 ft (12.50 m)
Length: 33 ft 4 in (10.16 m)
Height: 15 ft (4.57 m)
Wing area: 314 sq.ft (29.2 m²)

Weights
Empty: 9,039 lb (4,100 kg)
Gross: 11,623 lb (5,272 kg)
Max take off: 13,143 lb (5,962 kg)

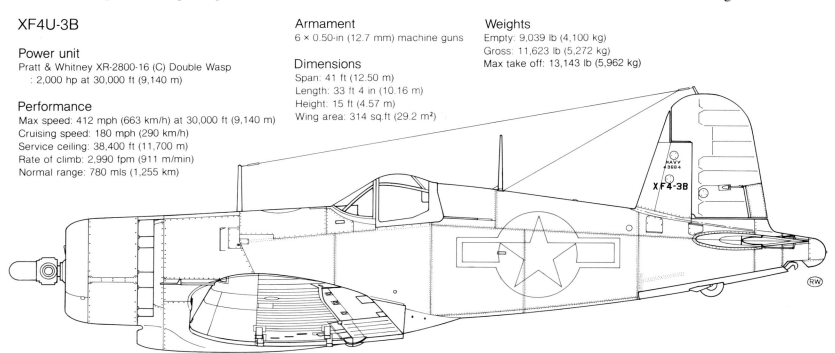

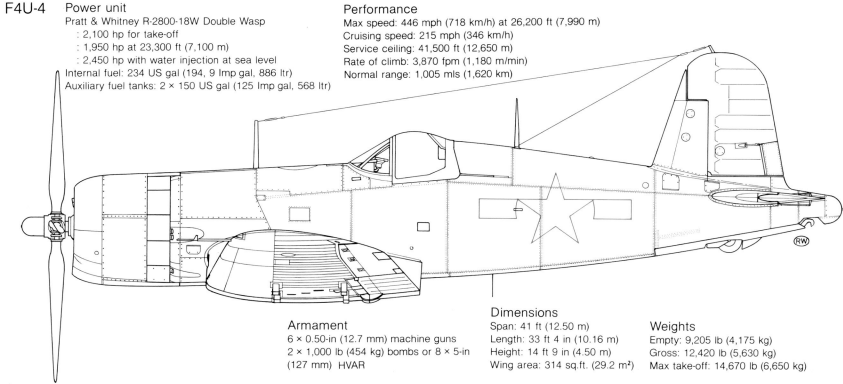

F4U-4

Power unit
Pratt & Whitney R-2800-18W Double Wasp
: 2,100 hp for take-off
: 1,950 hp at 23,300 ft (7,100 m)
: 2,450 hp with water injection at sea level
Internal fuel: 234 US gal (194, 9 Imp gal, 886 ltr)
Auxiliary fuel tanks: 2 × 150 US gal (125 Imp gal, 568 ltr)

Performance
Max speed: 446 mph (718 km/h) at 26,200 ft (7,990 m)
Cruising speed: 215 mph (346 km/h)
Service ceiling: 41,500 ft (12,650 m)
Rate of climb: 3,870 fpm (1,180 m/min)
Normal range: 1,005 mls (1,620 km)

Armament
6 × 0.50-in (12.7 mm) machine guns
2 × 1,000 lb (454 kg) bombs or 8 × 5-in
(127 mm) HVAR

Dimensions
Span: 41 ft (12.50 m)
Length: 33 ft 4 in (10.16 m)
Height: 14 ft 9 in (4.50 m)
Wing area: 314 sq.ft. (29.2 m²)

Weights
Empty: 9,205 lb (4,175 kg)
Gross: 12,420 lb (5,630 kg)
Max take-off: 14,670 lb (6,650 kg)

tion, and were mounted in the lower lip of the cowling. This revision, plus the use of a four-blade propeller, considerably altered the countenance of the Corsair from the long, lean "hose-nose" look of the F4U-1.

As designed, the F4U-4 carried six .50 calibre machine guns in the wings, and had provisions for slinging a pair of 1,000-pound (454 kg) bombs or eight five-inch (127 mm) rockets, with the rocket launchers being retrofitted to some of the earlier F4U-4s.

Some of this variant, variously identified as F4U-4Bs or F4U-4Cs, were armed with four 20-mm cannon instead of six .50-calibre machine guns. A handful were fitted with cameras as F4U-4Ps, and at least one was a night-fighting F4U-4N.

In mid-1944 the Brewster plant closed. Most of its F3A-1 Corsairs had gone to Britain; Brewster was not involved in producing a corresponding version of the F4U-4. But Goodyear had built prodigious quantities of FG-1s, and that company was selected to build F4U-4s under the designation FG-4. In 1945, with knowledge of the atom bomb's experimental development a closely-kept secret, some military planners envisaged several more years of war with Japan. Accordingly, Goodyear was awarded a contract to build 2,500 FG-4 Corsairs at its Akron, Ohio, factory. About a

dozen FG-4s were built by Goodyear when the abrupt end of the war in August 1945 caused cancellation of the order. A former Goodyear employee recalled that as late as the early 1950s, one of the FG-4s hung from the girders in the Akron plant, a souvenir of the company's Corsair production.

Vought F4U-4s reached the Pacific theatre before the end of the war, matching their increased speed to that of new and improved Japanese fighters as the war neared the Japanese islands. With the end of the war in 1945, the US Navy teetered on the brink of the jet age. Not yet able to commit its aircraft resources entirely to new jets, the Navy kept Vought's F4U-4 production line open after the war. About 400 post-war F4U-4s were built up to 1947. Many Dash-4s would see combat again over Korea from 1950 to 1953.

F4U-5

The result of wartime planning, the F4U-5 Corsair was not ready for flight until after the war. This model roared with still greater takeoff horsepower than the F4U-4. Now, 2,300 horsepower from an R-2800-32W engine could be realized, with a top speed reported variously as 462 or 470 mph (743 or 756 km/h). Cheek inlet gills on the cowling were a visible

F4U-4N   Radar equipment: AN/APS-6

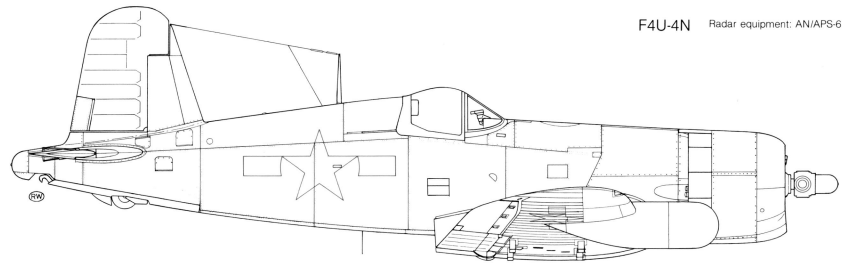

indicator of the F4U-5. For mechanics, access to the radio bay and cockpit heater was improved via a large door behind the cockpit. The pilot was favoured with a power-actuated canopy surrounding a cockpit redesigned for comfort. A new adjustable seat featured folding armrests; the foot brake pedals could be lowered to make leg rests on long flights.

And for the first time in the Corsair's long production history, the outer wing panels were completely metal-skinned.

The powerful R-2800-32W engine of the F4U-5 was attached with a two-degree downward angle of thrust as a fix for longitudinal stability problems. This allowed for improved forward vision over the long nose.

A valued feature at high speed especially were spring tabs put on the elevators and rudder assisted pilot input for control movements.

Armed with four 20-mm cannon, F4U-5s often sported flared muzzle flash-hiders on the guns. The provision for carrying two 1,000-pound (454 kg) bombs was retained in the Dash-5, and some were rocket-equipped. More than half the F4U-5s were built as night fighter versions, with the large radar pod on the right wing. Electric heat for the guns and pitot system allowed high altitude operation for the F4U-5, and some of the F4U-5N night fighters received extra heating equipment and de-icing gear for use in the cold Korean winter during that war, under the nomenclature F4U-5NL. The F4U-5 series also used a redefined contour for the sliding canopy.

F4U-5PS were camera-equipped Corsairs which proved their worth in Korea.

XF4U-6/AU-1

During F4U-5 production, Vought's plant was moved from Connecticut to a site near Dallas, Texas. At Texas, the Corsair design evolved a pure ground attack version, acknowledging the prop-driven F4U's inferiority as a dogfighter in a jet world, but capitalizing on the sturdy Vought's proven abilities as a bomb-carrier. Logically, this new ground attack Corsair was initially called the XF4U-6. Later, to reflect the fighter's specific role, it was renamed AU-1 – A for Attack, U the code letter for all Vought aircraft at that time, and -1 indicating the first of this series.

The AU-1 was not equipped for high-altitude performance, since its hunting was to be done close to the ground. Power was supplied by a Pratt and Whitney R-2800-83W engine with only a single-stage supercharger. Though takeoff power for the AU-1 was rated at 2,300, speed was considerably slower than the F4U-5. But gross weight of the AU-1 was more than 5,000 pounds (2268 kg) heavier than the Dash-5 – more than two and a half US tons of extra ordnance could be lugged into the sky by the AU-1.

Armed with four 20-mm cannon in the wings, 10 underwing rocket launchers, and the ability to carry as many as four 1,000-pound (454 kg) bombs, the AU-1 roared into combat over Korea in 1952. It was an updated version of a design which had been a decade in production. Besides its low-altitude high performance, a top speed of 438 mph (705 km/h) at 9,500 ft (2896 m), this armoured Corsair packed a deadly wallop.

Because it would be exposed to all kinds of groundfire, the AU-1 was fitted with sheets of armour plating to protect the undersides, and the precious cargo of pilot and equipment. Oil coolers were not placed directly in the stub wing inlets on the AU-1, but were moved inside the fuselage at the wing root, where air from the traditional wing ducts was channelled. The inlet for the single-stage supercharger was moved aft, near the wing centre section, where it too could be sheltered under the armour umbrella. Thus no cheek or chin gills were used on the ring cowl of the AU-1.

About 111 AU-1s were built, these going mainly to the US Marine Corps in 1952.

F4U-5NL winterised night fighter. (US Navy via Vought)

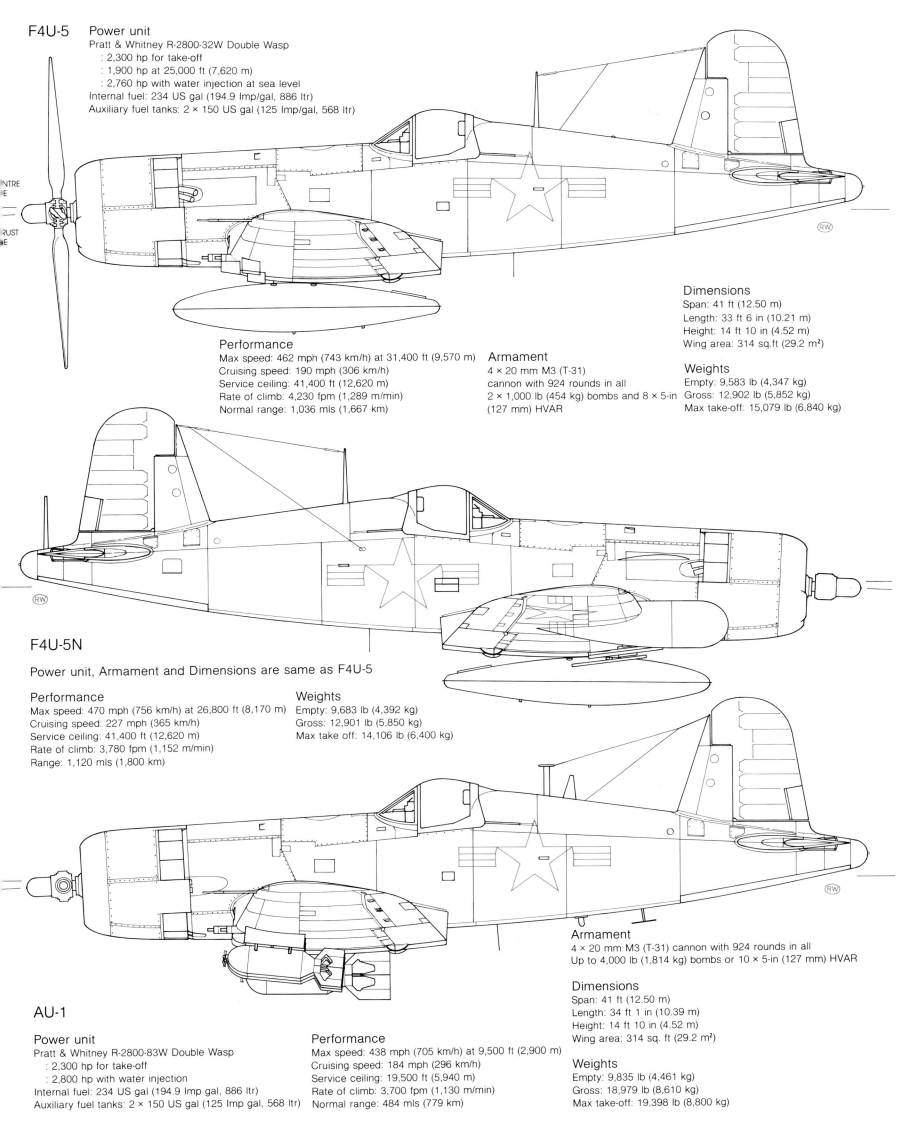

F4U-5
Power unit
Pratt & Whitney R-2800-32W Double Wasp
: 2,300 hp for take-off
: 1,900 hp at 25,000 ft (7,620 m)
: 2,760 hp with water injection at sea level
Internal fuel: 234 US gal (194.9 Imp/gal, 886 ltr)
Auxiliary fuel tanks: 2 × 150 US gal (125 Imp/gal, 568 ltr)

Performance
Max speed: 462 mph (743 km/h) at 31,400 ft (9,570 m)
Cruising speed: 190 mph (306 km/h)
Service ceiling: 41,400 ft (12,620 m)
Rate of climb: 4,230 fpm (1,289 m/min)
Normal range: 1,036 mls (1,667 km)

Armament
4 × 20 mm M3 (T-31)
cannon with 924 rounds in all
2 × 1,000 lb (454 kg) bombs and 8 × 5-in
(127 mm) HVAR

Dimensions
Span: 41 ft (12.50 m)
Length: 33 ft 6 in (10.21 m)
Height: 14 ft 10 in (4.52 m)
Wing area: 314 sq.ft (29.2 m²)

Weights
Empty: 9,583 lb (4,347 kg)
Gross: 12,902 lb (5,852 kg)
Max take-off: 15,079 lb (6,840 kg)

F4U-5N

Power unit, Armament and Dimensions are same as F4U-5

Performance
Max speed: 470 mph (756 km/h) at 26,800 ft (8,170 m)
Cruising speed: 227 mph (365 km/h)
Service ceiling: 41,400 ft (12,620 m)
Rate of climb: 3,780 fpm (1,152 m/min)
Range: 1,120 mls (1,800 km)

Weights
Empty: 9,683 lb (4,392 kg)
Gross: 12,901 lb (5,850 kg)
Max take off: 14,106 lb (6,400 kg)

AU-1

Power unit
Pratt & Whitney R-2800-83W Double Wasp
: 2,300 hp for take-off
: 2,800 hp with water injection
Internal fuel: 234 US gal (194.9 Imp gal, 886 ltr)
Auxiliary fuel tanks: 2 × 150 US gal (125 Imp gal, 568 ltr)

Performance
Max speed: 438 mph (705 km/h) at 9,500 ft (2,900 m)
Cruising speed: 184 mph (296 km/h)
Service ceiling: 19,500 ft (5,940 m)
Rate of climb: 3,700 fpm (1,130 m/min)
Normal range: 484 mls (779 km)

Armament
4 × 20 mm M3 (T-31) cannon with 924 rounds in all
Up to 4,000 lb (1,814 kg) bombs or 10 × 5-in (127 mm) HVAR

Dimensions
Span: 41 ft (12.50 m)
Length: 34 ft 1 in (10.39 m)
Height: 14 ft 10 in (4.52 m)
Wing area: 314 sq. ft (29.2 m²)

Weights
Empty: 9,835 lb (4,461 kg)
Gross: 18,979 lb (8,610 kg)
Max take-off: 19,398 lb (8,800 kg)

F4U-7 Power unit
Pratt & Whitney R-2800-18W Double Wasp
: 2,100 hp for take-off
: 1,950 hp at 23,300 ft (7,100 m)
: 2,450 hp with water injection at sea level
Performance
Max speed: 450 mph (724 km/h) at 26,000 ft (7,920 m)
Max take-off weight: 13,426 lb (6,090 kg)
Other data are almost same as AU-1

F4U-7

The French Navy faced the same difficult decisions regarding the switch from propeller-driven aircraft to jets in the late 1940s and early 1950s. Like their American counterparts, the French opted for a revised postwar version of the Corsair to meet some of their needs. The F4U-7, last Corsair in production, was specifically built for France, although they were obtained by the US Navy, and then transferred to the French *Aéronavale* as part of the United States' Military Assistance Program (MAP). The F4U-7 shared many of the airframe and armour features of its immediate predecessor, the AU-1. In fact, the French would also fly AU-1s along with their new F4U-7s in a dreary little brushfire war somewhere in French Indochina in the 1950s. It was here, in Vietnam, that Corsairs would take part in two wars, the first against Japanese occupiers and the second against insurgents.

The re-used ex-Marine AU-1s of the French numbered about 25 in 1954. Their companion Corsairs were the French Dash-7s, delivered by Vought in 1952. With the roll-out of the last F4U-7 in December 1952, the Corsair ceased production.

The Dash-7 flew behind a Pratt and Whitney R-2800-18W engine, much as had the wartime F4U-4. The two-stage supercharger of the engine gave the Dash-7 a better performance at altitude than the AU-1. The Dash-7 also incorporated a chin scoop in the front of the cowl – a readily visible clue when differentiating French F4U-7s from their stablemate AU-1s. Like the AU-1s, the F4U-7s carried five long streamlined hardpoints beneath each wing instead of the older two-point rocket holders used on previous Corsairs. The F4U-7, AU-1 and even the F4U-5 also used a flat armoured glass windscreen – a feature which may have even been introduced on some F4U-4s in place of the curved front windscreen. Canopy design on the F4U-7, AU-1 and back to the F4U-5 also was humped in a slightly different contour from previous models.

The 94 French F4U-7s served well into the jet age, and as a result several survived to become the property of private owners back in the United States after retirement by the *Aéronavale*.

F2G-1D Power unit
Pratt & Whitney R-4360-4 Wasp Major
: 3,000 hp for take-off
: 2,400 hp at 13,500 ft (4,110 m)
Internal fuel: 309 US gal (257.3 Imp gal, 1,170 ltr)
Auxiliary fuel tank: 2 × 150 US gal (125 Imp gal, 568 ltr)

Performance
Max speed: 435 mph (700 km/h)
Cruising speed (F2G-2): 190 mph (306 km/h)
Service ceiling (F2G-2): 38,800 ft (11,830 m)
Rate of climb (F2G-2): 4,400 fpm (1,340 m/min)
Normal range (F2G-2):
1,190 mls (1,915 km)

Armament
4 × 0.50-in (12.7 mm) machine guns with 1,600 rounds in all
2 × 1,600 lb (726 kg) bombs

Dimensions
Span: 41 ft (12.50 m)
Length: 33 ft 10 in (10.31 m)

Weights
Empty (F2G-2): 10,249 lb (4,649 kg)
Gross: 13,290 lb (6,030 kg)

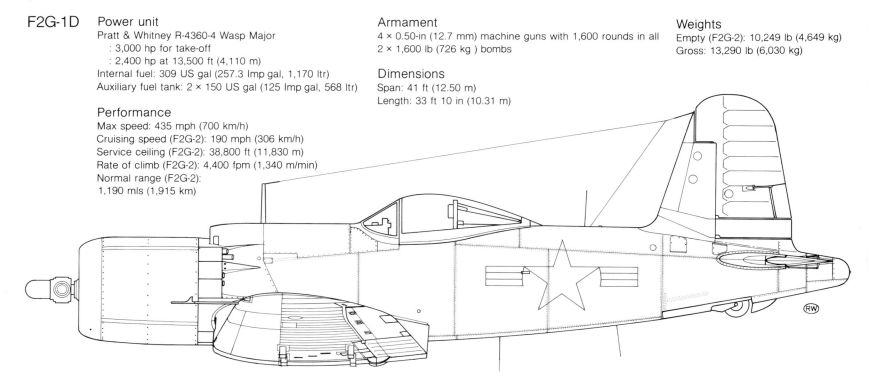

F2G

A spectacular non-production variant of the Corsair was created by Goodyear during World War II. Called the F2G, this Corsair was to have gone into mass production specifically as an answer to the threat posed by Japanese kamikaze aircraft which were ramming US ships in the Pacific in increasing numbers as the Americans sailed nearer to Japan. Heart of the F2G design was the massive 3,000-horsepower Pratt and Whitney R-4360-4 radial engine. This was an earlier version of the powerplant which would be used in the behemoth Convair B-36 Peacemaker strategic bomber of the late 1940s and 1950s, and in the Boeing B-50 and C-97 bomber and transport. The R-4360's 28 cylinders were arranged in four rows, aptly earning the nickname "corncob" for this layout.

Emphasis was put on low-altitude interception capability, to stop the kamikazes before they could hit surface ships. Thus, where the FG-1D Corsair at sea level was expected to reach a top speed of 328 mph (528 km/h), and the F4U-4 could hit 381 (613 km/h) at minimal altitude, the F2G could cut through the dense low-level air at 399 mph (642 km/h), while hitting a maximum speed of 431 mph (694 km/h) at 16,400 feet (4999 m). These figures showed the F2G to excel where it was meant to – down low – while the Dash-4 Corsair still could top it at altitude.

Instead of cowl-lip inlets, the F2G used a unique top-mounted duct behind the actual ring of the cowling. Most significant as a recognition feature, the F2G used a large teardrop-shaped bubble canopy with a cut-down aft fuselage for an improved field of vision for pilots stalking kamikazes.

Armament equipment including machine guns, rocket launchers and bomb racks – just in case – were incorporated into the F2G design. A contract was let in March 1944 calling for 428 F2Gs to be built. Most would be F2G-1s with non-folding wings, while 10 would be F2Gs with folding wings and carrier-compatible equipment. But development of a production-worthy F2G took time, due in part to problems with the engine. Between May 1945 and early 1946, only five of each type of F2G were built, the major production batch being cancelled.

In fact, statistics show the postwar F4U-5 Corsair could top 400 mph (644 km/h) at sea level, without resorting to the huge R-4360 engine. But the racy lines of the bubble-topped F2G caught the fancy of some civilians, including race pilot Cook Cleland, who won the crash-riddled 1947 Thompson trophy race in an F2G achieving 396 mph (637 km/h) average on the closed-circuit race course.

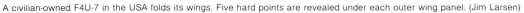

A civilian-owned F4U-7 in the USA folds its wings. Five hard points are revealed under each outer wing panel. (Jim Larsen)

Miscellaneous

Otherwise stock Corsairs participated in a number of test programmes which produced one-of-a-kind modifications. Among these was a two-seat F4U-1 trainer prepared by Vought in 1946 as one possible way to keep the U-machine in production; an experimental Dash-4 with tip tanks; and a Dash-4 with a counter-rotating six-blade propeller. During

any extra gills or vents which characterized later models. The close-cowled nose, because of its smaller diameter, deceptively looks even longer than the snouts of the later versions.

A three-blade Hamilton Standard propeller caps the nose of the FG-1D, dividing the prop arc into thirds. The propeller looks leaner than the four-blade fans of later models, and the overall countenance of the FG-1D/F4U-1 series is that of the leanest, sleekest Corsair produced.

FG-1D of a US Naval Reserve squadron after the war. (Balogh/Menard)

World War II, it is reported, an FG-1 put the vaulted space beneath its inverted gull wing to use by slinging a Westinghouse turbojet engine to give in-flight test data on the new jet powerplant.

First flown in 1940, last built in 1952, several airworthy Corsairs still fly in the hands of civilian and museum owners – monuments to a successful design that has held up to time.

Corsair in Close-up

When designed in 1938, Rex Beisel's Vought Corsair was a herald of the future of aeronautics. Today, the surviving Corsairs still show aesthetic lines that recall a significant milestone in design and construction techniques. A walk-around inspection of a Goodyear FG-1D and the last of the series, a French F4U-7, reveals salient differences and family traits common to the Corsair line.

The FG-1D, ultimate version of the first major Corsair production variant known as the F4U-1 series, is probably the most aesthetically pleasing of the entire bentwing line. Its R-2800 radial engine is cowled in a neat circular ring, free from

Throughout, the skin of the Corsair is smooth and remarkably stiff: it does not "oilcan" under light pressure, but stays firm. A key to this smooth rigidity is in the use of spot welding to attach longerons and stringers to the inside of the skin. On the surface, the spot-welding machine leaves a barely-visible flat circular dimple on each place it welds the skin and underlying structure together. At any distance, this blends under a coat of paint to produce a slick finish.

Where sections of aluminium join together, they are butt-jointed to avoid a drag-producing overlap. At these section joints, the fuselage pieces are flush-riveted together, again minimizing drag. The entire fuselage is covered in aluminium, except for small sheets of stainless steel in the engine area in high-heat locations.

The fuselage's integrity depends heavily upon the important centre wing-fuselage section. A heavy spar, shaped like the inverted gull portion of the wings and carrying through the fuselage, bears heavy structural loads. To the centre wing-fuselage section are hung the engine section, aft fuselage, wings and landing gear. With screws loosened and forward fuselage panels removed for inspection or maintenance, the long nose of the graceful Corsair reveals that its strength lies in a heavy steel-tube truss, welded as a frame to support the Pratt and Whitney engine. Behind the engine, inside the cage formed by the steel load-bearing motor mounts, a yellow oil tank shares cramped quarters with ducts and accessories for the supercharger and fuel-feed equipment.

Behind the oil tank, the arms of the motor mount tie into the canted portion on top of the spar which forms a major load-carrying frame of the centre section of the fuselage. The stiff-skinned, spot-welded semi-monocoque construction of the fuselage replaces the steel-tube load-bearing members on the aft side of the fuselage spar member. It is here, behind the spar and ahead of the cockpit, that a fuselage fuel tank is situated beneath a large circular access panel into which a petrol filler cap is set. Placed so close to the Corsair's centre of gravity, this fuselage tank's depletion in flight causes little change in trim.

Compared with smaller fighters of World War II, the Corsair's cockpit is cavernous. The FG-1D still uses twin footrails instead of a full floor, and the distance to the actual bottom of the fuselage – or bilge as some Corsair men call it – adds to the feeling of spaciousness. Because this is a bubble-topped FG-1D instead of an earlier "birdcage" canopied F4U-1 with a ribbed, low cockpit enclosure, this place has its pilot's seat raised to give the flier some advantage when trying to peer over and around the long "hose nose" ahead of him. The raising of the seat made it necessary to bulge the canopy upward.

Inside the cockpit, a straightforward instrument panel confronts the pilot with vital information relayed by flight instruments. Grouped in the centre of the panel are gauges used for instrument flying. Three of these, on the bottom row of the panel, from left to right, are the airspeed indicator, turn-and-bank indicator, and climb indicator. Above the climb indicator is an artificial horizon, with which the pilot can tell at a glance whether or not his wings are level and if the nose is above or below the horizon. Other instruments available on the frontal panel include: tachometer, altimeter, directional gyro, magnetic compass, elapsed time clock (crucial in navigational and fuel-consumption maths plotting), oil temperature regulator, oil temperature gauge, manifold pressure gauge, cylinder temperature gauge and fuel pressure gauge. Above these instruments, the FG-1D pilot would encounter an optical gunsight (probably a US Navy Mark VIII) featuring an angled clear glass panel on which crosshairs are illuminated, and through which the pilot sights his target.

Within reach of his left hand by the side console, the pilot has a throttle quadrant with engine and propeller control levers. Another lever, mounted for use by the pilot's left hand, serves a unique dual role as landing gear handle and dive brake lever. The Corsair is a steady diving aircraft, with a recorded percentage of hits on 250-foot (76 m) target circles only about seven per cent less than that of the vaunted Douglas SBD Dauntless, an aircraft designed from the ground up as a dive bomber.

The two-purpose handle rests at the bottom of a squared "U" channel. Much like an automobile gear shift

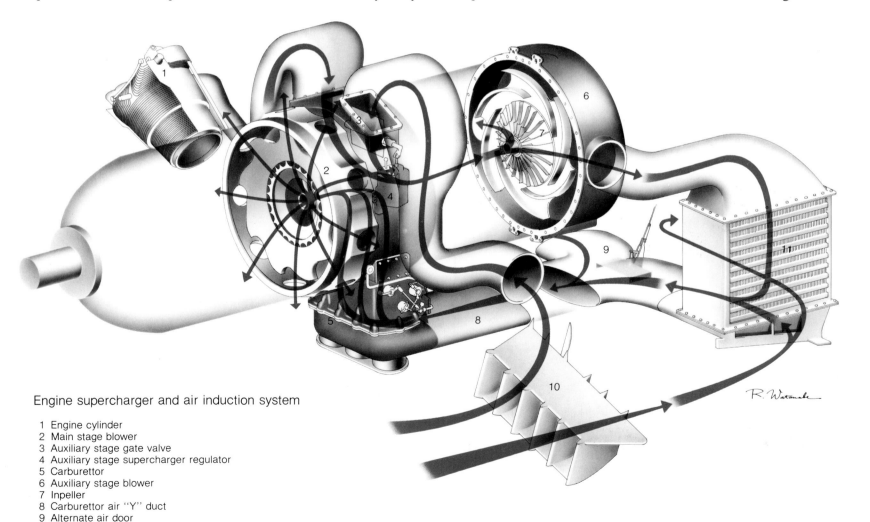

Engine supercharger and air induction system

1 Engine cylinder
2 Main stage blower
3 Auxiliary stage gate valve
4 Auxiliary stage supercharger regulator
5 Carburettor
6 Auxiliary stage blower
7 Inpeller
8 Carburettor air "Y" duct
9 Alternate air door
10 Wing root air intake
11 Intercooler

lever, the handle is pushed to the left and then up to lower the Corsair's landing gear. It is pushed to the right and up when the pilot elects to lower the dive brakes instead. The dive brakes allow the Corsair to pursue a steep dive angle without building up excessive speed. They consist of the flat aluminium doors attached to the main landing gear struts.

When the dive brake option is selected, the main landing gear drops from the wheel wells, causing extra drag to slow the plane down. If the pilot uses the brakes above a set safe speed – about 225 knots – the hydraulics will refuse to push against the excessive slipstream, and the gear will dangle until the plane slows sufficiently to permit the hydraulics to push the gear down and lock it. The tailwheel doors stay closed with the tailwheel within when the dive brake option is chosen, because the tailwheel doors might rip free of their piano hinges at high speeds. The aft main gear doors similarly could rip off if the pilot ignores the maximum dive brake speed warning. When extended, the flat doors on the fronts of the main gear struts make very effective brakes.

The flap lever sticks out at a right angle from the left cockpit wall near the instrument panel of the FG-1D, further emphasizing that the fighter is meant to be flown with the curved control stick in the right hand, allowing the left hand to perform the chores of raising and lowering the landing gear, dive brakes, and landing flaps, and controlling the engine performance.

Also on the left console, a wheel allows for trimming the aircraft's pitch attitude, gently nosing the FG-1D up or down as needed to obtain a specific angle of flight. Rudder and aileron trim-tab controls are mounted on the left console also, under scalloped clear Plexiglas knobs designed for easy gripping.

The cockpit control which opens and closes the cowl flaps for engine cooling purposes actuates a hydraulic pump which holds a braided steel cable attached to spring-loaded flap actuators. With the cable slack, the flaps spring open, allowing more air to circulate through the cowling. As the cable is drawn tight by the hydraulic mechanism, the flaps are drawn shut.

If the view forward from the cockpit resembles looking out over the boiler of a steam locomotive, as the cowling extends into the distance, the view aft reveals a vertical tail surprisingly close behind, and noticeably offset as a built-in correction for torque from the powerful R-2800 engine and Hamilton-Standard propeller. The closeness of the tail and the vast length of the nose are the direct result of the redesign of the prototype Corsair which saw a fuel tank installed in the forward fuselage over the centre of gravity, necessitating the removal of the cockpit to a site further aft.

Stepping out of the FG-1's cockpit, the pilot can place a foot on a rough-surfaced foot plate on the top of the sloping gull wing section next to the fuselage. The foothold is a spring-loaded section which depresses under the weight of the pilot to make a more level stepping surface. The flap section on the righthand wing has a permanent cutout foothold to aid getting in and out of the Corsair.

Scanning the wings of the FG-1D, the out-of-place use of fabric to cover the outer panels seems ironic for a fighter as fast and rugged as the Corsair. Yet thousands of the bentwing fighters were built with cloth covering the major parts of the outer wings.

But the use of cloth wing covering over the centre section of the outer panels is only one seemingly contradictory construction method employed on the same fighter

F4U-1D immediately before take-off from USS *Franklin* in March, 1945. (National Archives)

which pioneered spot-welded fuselage assembly – the Corsair's ailerons are made of wood, skinned over with fabric. Wooden ribs and a light, tough plywood skin form the shape of the ailerons on the wing of the Corsair. Engineers found the wooden structure stronger than fabric stretched over metal ribs when high-speed rolling manoeuvres or dangerous wing-flutter conditions arose in the Corsair.

The trailing edge wing flaps are metal-skinned; the moveable tail surfaces are built up of metal ribs covered with cloth. The horizontal stabilizers are interchangeable from left to right, simplifying combat repair chores as well as original construction headaches. Therefore it is not unusual for a combat Corsair to have a horizontal stabilizer pitted and dented on the upper part of the leading edge from gravel damage on the runway, instead of the traditional lower part, indicating that the upper part of the stabilizer has been removed from the opposite side of another aircraft for use on the present owner, and flipped upside down for mounting.

However, the location of pushrods for trim tabs on the elevators precludes swapping the elevators right for left.

The six .50 calibre machine guns of the FG-1D are buried in the wings, staggered to allow for ammunition feed of successive guns from the side. Smooth rounded ports in the stiff aluminium leading edge of the wing announce the presence of the weapons, but no muzzles protrude, resulting in a streamlined appearance. To capitalize on the streamlined gun installations, many Corsair pilots used tape to cover the gun ports. This has the effect of blocking airflow from pressurizing the gun bays, and results in less drag. In the event of combat, the first rounds fired quickly burst open the temporary tape.

As it rests on the main landing gear, the FG-1D seems to be collapsing the oleo shock absorbing struts. The scissors of the main gear are virtually closed, indicating that little possible compression remains in the struts. Early Corsairs suffered a serious bouncing tendency when landing, especially with the high vertical descent rate of an aircraft-carrier deck landing. The leaping phenomenon was tamed by modifying the oil and air pressures in the strut to give the gear a longer, softer stroke which dissipated the high energy of landing impact. Vought Corsair specialist Bob Nelson explained that the stiffer stroke of early Corsair transferred some of the energy down to the tyres. Nelson, who headed a Vought project to rebuild a flying Corsair for the Confederate Air Force museum, said the old stiff legs "would just compress the tyres and you would get a lot of bounce out of it like a rubber ball".

The FG-1D Corsair is a fighting machine, without frills or non-essential touches. But its functional design is a happy marriage of engineering and aesthetics, resulting in a classic aircraft design which functioned superbly in the hands of a skilled pilot.

When the last Corsairs were rolled into the warm Texas sunshine in 1952 under the designation F4U-7, changes in technology, equipment and tactics all had left a mark on the fighter. The trademark bent wing was still there; the elevators still perched well aft of the rudder: the first impression was much the same. But closer inspection reveals a very different machine from the earlier FG-1D or its Vought counterpart, the F4U-1D.

The Dash-7 Corsair swings a massive four-blade propeller, as have all F4Us since the wartime F4U-4. The cheeks of the F4U-7 cowl bulge where the F4U-5 had introduced air gills, but the bulges are smoothly faired over on the Dash-7, making the cowl look like a made-over adaptation of the Dash-5. A slightly jutting chin scoop gives the F4U-7 a larger cowl diameter than the old hose-nose FG-1D. Coupled with the four-blade propeller, this countenance makes the Dash-7 look larger than the FG-1 even when the two sit together in a common hangar.

Where the F4U-1D/FG-1D have only a cutout in the right wing flap to use as a step for climbing aboard, the F4U-7 has an extendable step mounted in the right side of the fuselage. Supported by two tubes about an inch in diameter, the step can be lowered about a foot. During filming of the television show "Baa Baa Black Sheep" in the 1970s, recalls Corsair pilot John Schafhausen of Hayden Lake, Idaho, his F4U-7 was often selected for scenes in which actors were required to scramble in and out of Corsairs, since the fuselage step made this task easier.

The F4U-7 shares a trait finally introduced after World War II beginning with the F4U-5: the outer wing panels are metal-skinned. But the ailerons remain wooden sheet over wooden ribs, skinned in cloth.

As equipped by the factory, the F4U-7 has five hard points in streamlined fairings under each wing, extending forward near the leading edge. This style of streamlined pylon serves notice that this is a post-World War II aircraft with equipment more modern than its predecessors.

The cockpit layout also has been considerably changed, from the use of a new style landing gear handle to the installation of a real cockpit floor instead of the twin footrails of the FG-1D.

The F4U-7 reflects 1950s technology in its adapted construction and use of weaponry. Where the FG-1D evokes memories of Pappy Boyington roaring into combat over Rabaul, with the wingtips of his Corsair streaming vapour condensation, the F4U-7 belongs to a different set of wars – French action in Indochina and the Suez Canal conflict in the 1950s. Heavily armoured and sprouting four long 20-mm gun barrels in fat housings from its wings, the F4U-7 represents the basic Corsair design adapted about as far as it could go, and still remain a Corsair.

F4U-1A owned by Chance Vought Aircraft in 1954. (G. S. Williams)

Into Action

The first two F4U-1 Corsairs were officially transferred from Vought to the Navy in July 1942. The fighters were like spirited racehorses, capable of incredible speeds, but needing experienced care to match their temperaments. Two months after the first deliveries, the Navy waved the seventh F4U-1 aboard the carrier USS *Sangamon* in Chesapeake Bay for the Corsair's first carrier trials.

Pilot Sam Porter, a Lieutenant Commander, quickly perceived visibility problems with the long nose, compounded by the spattering of oil and fluid on the windscreen from a leaky cowl flap actuating mechanism. A few months later, the production line responded by sealing over the top portion of the cowl flaps, eliminating the source of the leaks.

More serious was a tendency of the big Vought to bounce, a trait that was tamed, as has been explained, with revisions to the oleo shock-absorbing strut in the landing gear – but not before some Navy planners had made up their minds the F4U was not desirable for aircraft carrier operations.

Other notes were made from the 1942 carrier trials: the huge flaps and low-set tailwheel conspired to make directional stability a problem for the F4U-1. This would be corrected on the production line with the use of an inflatable tailwheel, and with the introduction of a stilted tailwheel leg.

In mid-1943, the first F4U-1A was characterized with a more extensively glazed, bulged canopy to accommodate a seat raised seven inches (18 cm), providing better pilot visibility over the long nose. Vought and the Navy were working to make the F4U a valuable carrier aircraft.

Meanwhile, the British Fleet Air Arm (FAA) was forming its Corsair squadrons in June 1943, determined to use the fighters on aircraft carriers even as American doubts persisted among some Navy planners.

The smallest, most insignificant-looking alterations in aerodynamic design can often have the most profound effects on performance. When early Corsair carrier trials revealed a nasty tendency for the F4U-1 to stall left wing first due to propeller wash effects, a small triangular strip of metal about six inches (15 cm) in span was bolted to the right leading edge of the Corsair at a location that would cause the right wing to stall simultaneously at the proper nose-high attitude and low speed, thereby equalizing the stall and removing the potentially vicious roll to the left just at touchdown.

Owing to all the modifications being concocted to tame the Corsair's deck habits, the first combat Corsairs were land-based US Marine squadrons sent to the South Pacific in 1943. Runway landings did not require the high vertical descent rate of carrier landings, and some of the handling problems were less apparent when landing on a long runway instead of slamming into a small carrier deck.

Squadron VMF-124 (the "M" indicating Marines) was brought into being at Camp Kearney, near San Diego, California, in the first week of September, 1942, a few weeks before its first Corsairs were scheduled to arrive from the east. Major William E. Gise headed the squadron. Schedules called for Gise to take his squadron into the Pacific war in January 1943, allowing about three months to iron out problems in the new F4U-1s. This is a short time, when the aircraft are not combat-proven, and the crews do not really know what to expect. Modifications and directives were forthcoming, based on Corsair tests, and Gise's machines were tinkered with until they were pronounced fit for war.

Because the maintenance and changeover programmes had kept the new Corsairs on the ground, many of VMF-124's pilots could hardly be considered old hands when the unit left San Diego in January 1943 – some of the fliers

The first production F4U-1s of US Navy before deployment overseas. (Vought)

had only 20 hours' flying time in the new bentwing fighters before leaving for combat. The F4U-1s of VMF-124 still had the old "birdcage" canopy and short tailwheel strut, making even ground operations difficult at first.

A Navy squadron, VF-12, was also outfitting itself with Corsairs about this time. Carrier landings were made by VF-12 pilots, and one was killed trying to come aboard the USS *Enterprise* near Hawaii; earlier, another of VF-12's F4U-1s was written off in a carrier mishap aboard the USS *Core*, and the inflatable tailwheels which had been recommended as an aid to stability showed themselves prone to explode on hard landings.

Ultimately, in 1943, VF-12 was assigned to sail with the USS *Saratoga*, and Grumman F6F Hellcats replaced the squadron's Corsairs for combat sea duty. Uncertainty over the F4U-1's deck qualities, coupled with a possible shortage of parts aboard the carriers prompted the switch.

Next came Navy squadron VF-17, nicknamed "Blackburn's Irregulars", and commanded by Lieutenant Commander John T. Blackburn. The squadron was intended originally to fly into combat from the USS *Bunker Hill*, and Blackburn's Irregulars made sea duty a goal of their training and qualification programme, even in the face of six fatal Corsair accidents while flying the bentwing aircraft on the east coast of the United States.

Brought into being on New Year's Day, 1943, VF-17 first flew from Norfolk, Virginia. In July of that year, the squadron's F4U-1s, still with the too-stiff, bounce-inducing oleo struts, participated in the shakedown cruise of the new aircraft carrier *Bunker Hill*. Squadron and Vought personnel decided to soften the shock of landing by altering the fluid/air mixture in the oleo compression cylinders. Fluid is virtually incompressible; gas has a high degree of compressibility. Increasing the amount of air in the strut caused a softer cushioning effect.

VF-17 was the recipient of brand-new F4U-1As, featuring the first of the raised canopies, the stall-taming wing spoiler, and the modified oleo landing gear struts. Blackburn and his men were looking forward to finally taking the Corsair into battle aboard a US Navy aircraft carrier. But it was not to be so. The supply system servicing the carriers was equipped to keep spare parts flowing for F6F Hellcats, not F4U Corsairs, and Navy brass made a last-minute replacement of VF-17 with a Hellcat squadron for sea duty aboard the USS *Bunker Hill*. Blackburn's efforts to reverse the order replacing his squadron were fruitless, and he took his U-machines to the Solomons in November 1943 where they distinguished themselves as a ground-based squadron.

By 12 February, 1943, Squadron VMF-124 was in Guadalcanal, running up for takeoff on the first Corsair combat mission ever. Scarcely an hour after arriving at the strip named Cactus, some of VMF-124's Corsairs were already given the task of escorting a Catalina on a rescue flight to Vella Lavella.

Next day, VMF-124 again took its Voughts out on escort duty, scanning the skies for Zero-Sen interceptors expected to bounce a formation of PB4Y-1 Liberators attacking Buin Harbour shipping, some 300 miles (483 km) distant.

This was the longest escort mission of the Solomons campaign at that time, and took advantage of the big Corsair's range. Combat was not found on either of these first two missions, although a lone Mitsubishi Zeke paced the new Voughts for a while, and then left.

On 14 February, 1943, a force estimated at 50 Japanese fighters tangled with a mixed bag of American P-38s, VMF-124 Corsairs and PB4Y-1s as the bombers targeted Buin-Shortland area. Four P-38s were shot down, as were two each of the P-40s, Liberators and Corsairs.

Only three or four Japanese fighters were downed in the fight, one of these being involved in a collision with one of the wrecked F4Us. The stark realities of war came home to the VMF-124 airmen as they watched one of their comrades ditch his Corsair after the fight, where he was strafed in the water by Japanese fighters. (Attacks on downed fliers by fighter pilots occurred on both sides of the war, with some Corsair pilots going after enemy aircrews if it appeared the downed fliers had a chance of reaching friendly land, where they could rejoin the fight.)

As Gise's VMF-124 crews piled up more Corsair time, they became more adept at putting the big Vought's strength to advantage in combat. A major dogfight involved the squadron on 1 April, 1943. Japanese aircraft were flying south en masse to thwart American attempts to construct a landing strip at Banika, and VMF-124's Corsairs teamed up with older Wildcats and some Army P-38 Lightnings in a fight with 58 Zekes. First Lieutenant Ken Walsh of VMF-124 nosed his blue-grey Corsair into position behind one of the Zekes and shot it from the sky, following his success by destroying another Zeke fighter and a Val bomber.

The Corsair was showing itself to be a viable combat tool, and other Marine squadrons were rushed to a rear area base at Espiritu Santo to retire their weary Wildcats and pick up a few quick hours in the new Voughts which were arriving from the United States. Some of the Marines roared into combat in Corsairs after flying the type for only about 15 hours.

On 25 April, one of the USMC Corsair squadrons, VMF-213, pitted four Corsairs against about 16 Japanese dive bombers and 20 Zekes. Two of the long-nosed Voughts went down, but five Japanese aircraft were knocked out also, routing the bombers from their intended raid. One of the two downed Corsair fliers was rescued.

Thirteenth May, 1943, saw one of the last major Japanese attempts to attack Guadalcanal from the air. Two squadrons put 15 Corsairs up to meet 25 Japanese machines escorting reconnaissance aircraft. Included in the F4U brigade were VMF-124's skipper, Major Gise, and the aggressively talented Ken Walsh. Gise was one of the three Corsair losses in the fight; Walsh scored three more kills, making him the first Corsair ace.

A VMF-112 flier who earlier had scored one victory in an F4F Wildcat now bagged four Zekes in the same combat, making him the first ace for that squadron.

Corsair combat in the Solomons continued through 1943 as the Marines became increasingly confident in their big fighters. The Japanese were clearly aware of the bentwing menace. At last, a fighter with speed and diving abilities to match or top the nimble Zero series was in American service. No longer would American fighter responses be limited to tactics slow P-40s and Wildcats could employ; now the big Voughts could readily engage the Zeros with competence.

The Solomons campaign marked only the beginning of the combat career of the Corsair, and yet perhaps no image of the Corsair more conjures up its successful role as a fighter than that of a blue and white F4U-1, vapour streaming from its wingtips, as it gracefully dispatches a Zeke into the waters of "The Slot" south of Kahili. Like the cavalry of the old West, the blue Corsairs appeared on the horizon just in time to suit the needs of beleaguered Allied forces who were putting up fighters which were admittedly inferior in many respects to the quick Zero-Sens of Japan.

By September 1943, battle-wise VMF-124 was ready to rotate home. Its pilots claimed 68 enemy aircraft downed in combat, and acknowledged the deaths of seven fellow Corsair fliers from the squadron. The Corsair was a viable weapon, but it was no kiddy-car to handle – of the seven VMF-124 fliers dead, four were claimed in non-combat mishaps. In fact, the unit had lost or retired as unsuitable 32 F4U-1s and F4U-1As, with only 11 of them the result of enemy action.

About two months after the pioneering VMF-124 left combat, Tommy Blackburn's VF-17 squadron was ready for action from its station at Ondonga, New Georgia, squarely in the middle of the Solomons chain. On 1 November, 1943, Blackburn's Irregulars warmed up the big Pratts in their hump-canopied F4U-1As in preparation for their first combat mission. They intercepted a formation of Val dive bombers under the protective escort of Zekes over Empress Augusta

Bay at nine in the morning. "More by luck than good management", Blackburn later said, "we made the initial interception and, to our pleasure, shot down six Zekes and helped break up the attack." The pattern was becoming familiar – wherever the U-aircraft went, they stood a better chance of bringing home victories than did the other fighters in the area. The P-40s and F4Fs were too old and slow, and the P-38s were too few in number. It was becoming a Corsair show.

Ten days later, the squadron's Corsairs, readily identifiable with the small black and white pirate Jolly Roger flag they carried on their cowlings, flew as cover for a carrier-launched raid against Rabaul. Ironically, VF-17 returned with the carrier strike force and landed aboard the same flattop – the *Bunker Hill* – they had fought so hard to sail with earlier that year. All of the Corsairs made the carrier safely.

During their operation with the carriers, Blackburn's Irregulars claimed 18 and a half kills as they protected the fleet. Lieutenant (jg) Ira C. Kepford pressed home an attack on a lone Kate torpedo bomber, destroying it moments before it would have launched a torpedo at close range against the *Bunker Hill*, according to Navy accounts.

A section of F4U-1As of VF-17, one of the most famous fighter squadrons in US Navy, early in 1944. The nearest Corsair numbered "29" is flown by Lieutenant (jg) Ira C. Kepford. (US Navy via Vought)

Major Gregory Boyington (centre) and his VMF-214 "Blacksheep" squadron pilots.

The men of "Fighting Seventeen" took pride in an ironic interception made by four F4U-1As under the leadership of Lieutenant M. W. Davenport the morning of 21 November, 1943. Davenport's gaggle of Corsairs caught a flight of six Zekes, and shot all of the Japanese fighters down. One of the downed Japanese turned out to be a Japanese Army major dispatched to find out why so many Japanese aircraft were being shot down!

In January 1944, VF-17 flew escort for a variety of bombers on missions to Rabaul, heavily defended by the Japanese. In five frantic days in January, the skull-and-crossbones Corsairs claimed 60 and a half kills. Twelve aces returned to the States in April 1944 when VF-17 came home.

It has been argued that Hollywood made a better bomber of the B-17 Flying Fortress than did Boeing; press propaganda and television have done much the same for the Corsairs of VMF-214, the legendary Black Sheep squadron under Major Greg Boyington. Casting aside heroic tales about drunken, hell-for-leather misfits, the truth about the Black Sheep is exciting enough – Greg Boyington became the first Corsair ace in one day when he dispatched five fighters over enemy-held Ballale on 16 September, 1943. That same mission, other Black Sheep were credited with downing six more Zekes, while another eight were listed as probable kills. A month into combat, the Black Sheep tallied 47 confirmed victories.

Boyington exhibited a willingness to fight, and ran his score of victories to 25 by early January 1944. This was one fewer than the year-old high mark set by Joe Foss. On 3 January, 1944, Boyington ended a spell with no victories and quickly destroyed one of about 60 Japanese aircraft over Rabaul. Other squadron fliers lost track of Boyington and his wingman in the mêlée, and when "Pappy" Boyington failed to return from the fight, his fate was left open to conjecture for the remainder of the war.

That day over Rabaul, Boyington and his wingman Captain George Ashmun were chasing after one formation of Zekes when more Japanese fighters came in after the two Voughts. Protecting each other, Boyington and Ashmun each shot down one more Zeke before Ashmun's fighter was seriously hit, splashing down at sea. Boyington tried to keep the attackers away from the faltering Corsair of his wingman, and killed yet another Zeke before his own Corsair began to burn, forcing him to bail out at low altitude.

Picked up by a Japanese submarine, Greg Boyington's fate was not reported until he was liberated from a Japanese prison camp at the end of World War II. By that time, his disappearance had further exalted his reputation as an American hero. During his imprisonment, when he was assumed dead by many Americans, Boyington was awarded the Medal of Honor for his wartime exploits. When he returned after the war, those last two frantic shoot-downs were officially added to his tally, even though unconfirmed by other observers. This ranked Boyington as the top wartime Marine ace, including in his tally of 28 kills several he achieved while flying Curtiss P-40s as a volunteer detached from the Marines and incorporated into the Flying Tigers before America's official entry into World War II.

To the Marines goes credit for introducing the swift Corsair to combat. When the Navy first put the Voughts in action, it was the radar-equipped F4U-2s of night fighting squadron VF(N)-75. By 2 October, 1943, the night fighter Corsairs were installed at Munda, flying nocturnal patrols or simply sitting around waiting for an alert to launch into the darkness. Early intercepts were often foiled by faulty radar or effective jamming by the Japanese who prowled overhead often in single aircraft. The first VF(N)-75 kill was made visually after a ground radar station vectored Lieutenant H. D. O'Neill towards a Betty bomber which could be seen by the light of its exhaust flames; later, the pod-mounted radar aboard the F4U-2s helped the fliers home in on a variety of targets in the dark.

As the Allies worked up the Marshall Islands in 1944, Corsairs participated in operations which required less dogfighting and more ground-attacking. To be sure, Zekes and bombers occasionally were targeted by the gullwing warriors, but after VMF-111 rigged 1,000-pound (454 kg) bomb racks to its F4Us for a March 1944 raid on Mille, the role of the Corsair as a bomber was cast.

Initially, the Marine fliers experimented with lowering their wheels to slow the rate of descent in a dive. Later, bomb racks and a special slot for the landing gear handle which dropped only the main gear as brakes would be built into Corsairs to better suit them for the dive-bombing role.

Radar-equipped F4U-2 of VF (N)-101 cleared for take-off on USS *Enterprise* in 1944.

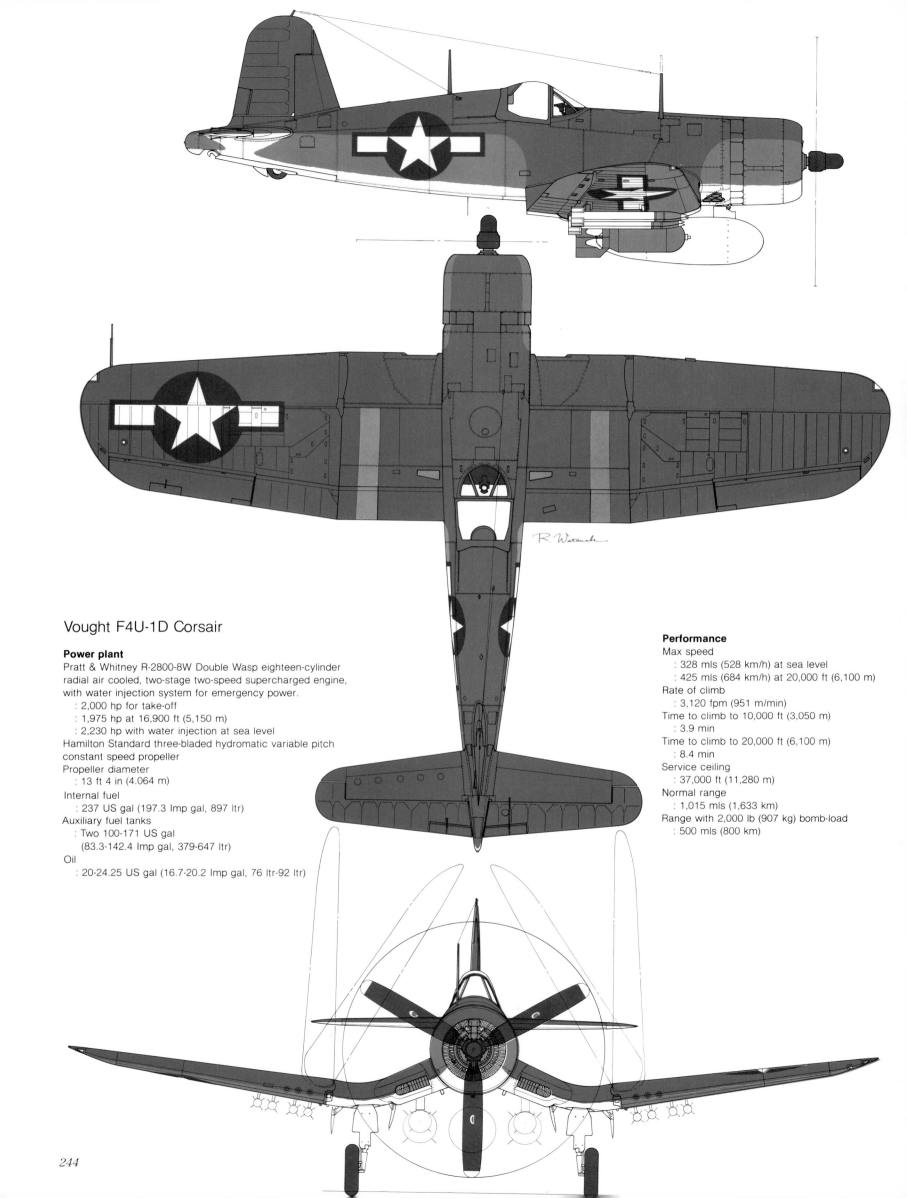

Vought F4U-1D Corsair

Power plant

Pratt & Whitney R-2800-8W Double Wasp eighteen-cylinder
radial air cooled, two-stage two-speed supercharged engine,
with water injection system for emergency power.
: 2,000 hp for take-off
: 1,975 hp at 16,900 ft (5,150 m)
: 2,230 hp with water injection at sea level
Hamilton Standard three-bladed hydromatic variable pitch
constant speed propeller
Propeller diameter
: 13 ft 4 in (4.064 m)
Internal fuel
: 237 US gal (197.3 Imp gal, 897 ltr)
Auxiliary fuel tanks
: Two 100-171 US gal
(83.3-142.4 Imp gal, 379-647 ltr)
Oil
: 20-24.25 US gal (16.7-20.2 Imp gal, 76 ltr-92 ltr)

Performance

Max speed
: 328 mls (528 km/h) at sea level
: 425 mls (684 km/h) at 20,000 ft (6,100 m)
Rate of climb
: 3,120 fpm (951 m/min)
Time to climb to 10,000 ft (3,050 m)
: 3.9 min
Time to climb to 20,000 ft (6,100 m)
: 8.4 min
Service ceiling
: 37,000 ft (11,280 m)
Normal range
: 1,015 mls (1,633 km)
Range with 2,000 lb (907 kg) bomb-load
: 500 mls (800 km)

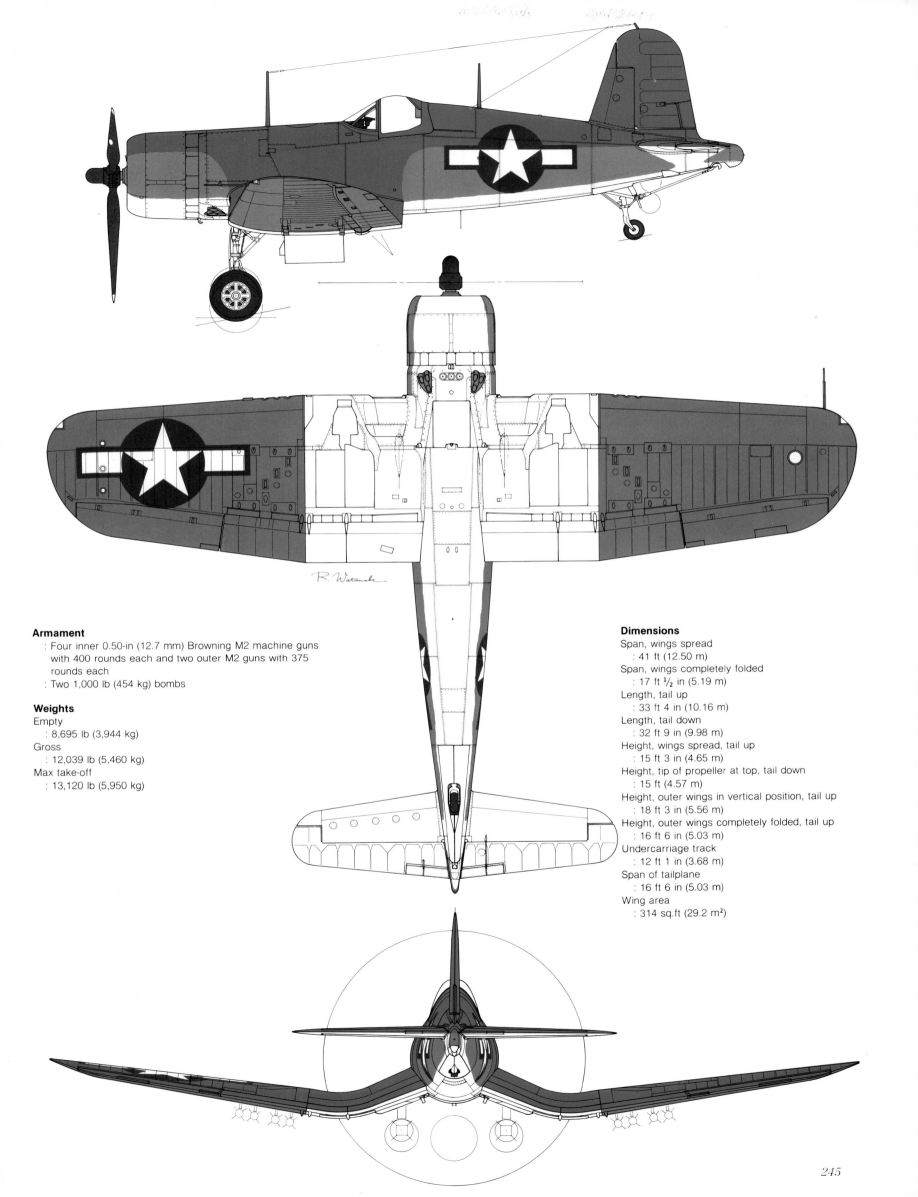

Armament

: Four inner 0.50-in (12.7 mm) Browning M2 machine guns with 400 rounds each and two outer M2 guns with 375 rounds each

: Two 1,000 lb (454 kg) bombs

Weights

Empty
: 8,695 lb (3,944 kg)

Gross
: 12,039 lb (5,460 kg)

Max take-off
: 13,120 lb (5,950 kg)

Dimensions

Span, wings spread
: 41 ft (12.50 m)

Span, wings completely folded
: 17 ft ½ in (5.19 m)

Length, tail up
: 33 ft 4 in (10.16 m)

Length, tail down
: 32 ft 9 in (9.98 m)

Height, wings spread, tail up
: 15 ft 3 in (4.65 m)

Height, tip of propeller at top, tail down
: 15 ft (4.57 m)

Height, outer wings in vertical position, tail up
: 18 ft 3 in (5.56 m)

Height, outer wings completely folded, tail up
: 16 ft 6 in (5.03 m)

Undercarriage track
: 12 ft 1 in (3.68 m)

Span of tailplane
: 16 ft 6 in (5.03 m)

Wing area
: 314 sq.ft (29.2 m²)

F4U-1A loaded with a 1,000 lb (454 kg) bomb. (US Navy via Vought)

The six heavy machine guns in the wings of the Corsairs soon proved effective in suppressing Japanese anti-aircraft fire while the big F4Us dived on their targets from angles as steep as 85 degrees or in shallow glides, depending on the preference of the pilot.

Charles Lindbergh served in an experimental advisory capacity in the Pacific during World War II, flying combat missions and working to solve combat problems. In the early autumn of 1944, Lindbergh worked with Marine Air Group 31, carrying increasing bomb loads under Corsairs, reaching a maximum of 4,000 pounds (1814 kg) – a 2,000-pound bomb under the centre section and a pair of 1,000-pounders under the wings, which he released on Japanese gun batteries in the Marshalls campaign.

It was the adaptability of the F4U to dive-bombing which would keep the Vought in production and service long after companion fighters had been stricken from the rosters with the advent of jet interceptors.

Throughout 1943, the US Navy's plans seemed to be entrenching the Vought Corsair as a land-based aircraft, while the Grumman F6F Hellcat went to sea as the principal carrier-borne fighter. But early in January 1944, four F4U-2 night fighters of VF(N)-101 were loaded aboard the USS *Enterprise* as the carrier prepared to sail for Pacific battles, while another small detachment from the squadron joined the USS *Intrepid*.

Interceptions directed by shipborne radar, and concluded by the radar in the wing pods of the Corsair night fighters, were made against bomber formations which attempted to get close enough to the task force to do damage. In the eerie darkness, tracer bullets would stitch back and forth between Corsair and prey, with the Corsairs coming out on top. The *Intrepid*'s detachment left the combat zone early when that carrier was damaged by a torpedo; the *Enterprise* contingent shot down at least five Japanese bombers without loss of its own. Arguments against taking Corsairs to sea were withering in the face of experience with the handful of F4U-2s.

The latter half of 1944 saw a serious new Japanese tactic threaten the security of Allied fleets: suicide aircraft were penetrating defences in alarming numbers, and were getting hits on ships by intentionally crashing into their decks. At this time, a temporary surfeit of Marine fliers and not enough Hellcat pilots to meet the expanded fighter quotas needed to protect the aircraft carriers suggested an obvious solution: put Marine Corsair squadrons aboard the fast carriers to offer additional protection against the kamikaze suicide attackers. Meanwhile, Goodyear was working on a special Corsair, powered by the huge new R-4360 engine, intended specifically to chase down kamikazes. But as the war unfolded, the special kamikaze-hunting F2G Corsair would not see service, while regular F4U-1Ds and F4U-4s would launch from ships repeatedly in 1945 to do combat.

Another factor in favour of the Corsair going to sea was a Navy report filed in 1944 which described the F4U as better than the F6F as a fighter and bomber, and just as good at deck operations. Corsairs were welcomed aboard fleet carriers late in December 1944, with three spectacular crashes on the USS *Essex* as the Marine pilots tried for a little pre-combat landing practice.

Task Force 38 dispatched Corsairs to French Indochina on 12 January, 1945, the same combat arena that would host newer French Navy F4U-7s some nine years later.

Japanese shipping and airfields took a terrific beating that day. Strikes against Chinese targets occupied by Japanese forces followed, often carried out in muggy, rainy, sloppy weather with extremely subdued visibility – prime time for mistakes and losses other than to the enemy.

Leaving the South China Sea in January, the task force had to pass close enough to shore to permit attacks by land-based bombers, which the big blue Voughts dispatched. The Corsair was proving a viable tool at sea, and in part the operational losses suffered by the Marines on the carriers were due to inexperience with any kind of aircraft at sea, and not specifically the Vought F4U.

By February 1945, Iwo Jima was being attacked as the fleets moved closer to Japan. Now F4U-1Ds on the USS *Bunker Hill* joined the Marines in Corsairs at sea. That same month, the bentwing fighter-bombers attacked targets near Tokyo. The work for the Corsairs was varied, and reflected the adaptability of the Vought design as the big fighters switched quickly from bombing and rocket attacks against ground targets to serious dogfighting overhead.

By now, Corsairs entering service were being painted dark glossy blue overall, a style applied to carrier planes since 1944. During the Korean War several years later, Navy discussions of the value of the dark blue paint as camouflage would include a concession that the use of dark navy-blue paint was in part a morale-booster. Just as olive drab identified virtually everything in the Army, navy blue was seen as a symbol of the Navy.

Japanese air opposition occasionally held surprises in 1945. Just when it seemed the home defence was manned by youthful and inexperienced pilots, teams of aggressive and obviously knowledgeable Japanese fighters would tear into American formations, as they did to VMF-123 on 19 March, 1945. Six Corsairs went down as a result. The war was definitely not over yet. That month, Japanese aircraft pressed home an attack which knocked three American carriers – the *Franklin*, *Wasp* and *Enterprise* – out of commission, reducing the Corsair contingent at sea while the flattops retired for repairs.

With the seizure of Okinawa, land-based Corsair units moved close to the fighting. At sea, the carriers continued to take occasional kamikaze hits which had the effect of removing them from the fight, at least temporarily, while repairs were effected.

F4U-1P of VF-84 aboard USS *Bunker Hill* head out for a photo-reconnaissance mission against Iwo-Jima in February, 1945. (National Archives)

Vought F4U-1D Corsair Cutaway

1 Hamilton-Standard hydromatic constant-speed propeller
2 Spinner
3 Distributors
4 Dual magneto
5 Front section oil scavenge pump
6 Pratt & Whitney R-2800-8W Double Wasp 18-cylinder
  two-H row radial air cooled engine
7 Exhaust pipes
8 Hydraulic reservoir
9 Supercharger housing
10 Fire suppressor cylinder
11 Oil tank forward armour plate
12 Oil tank (overload: 20 US gal, 16.7 Imp gal, 75.7 ltr)
13 Exhaust stacks
14 Intake air duct
15 Intercooler
16 Engine support frames
17 Navigation light (green)
18 Formation light
19 Ammunition box retaining doors
20 Ammunition box cover
21 Aileron
22 Aileron trimming tab

23 Outer wing flap
24 Aerial mast
25 Fuel filler cap
26 Fuselage self-sealing fuel tank
27 Engine control runs
28 Electric fuel quantity gauge
29 Armoured glass (behind the front windshield)
30 Bomb switch box
31 Mk 8 gunsight
32 Gun switch box
33 Control column
34 Landing gear and dive brake control lever
35 Engine control quadrant
36 Radio control box
37 Rearward-sliding cockpit canopy
38 Headrest
39 Pilot's seat
40 Wing-folding control lever
41 Centre/aft fuselage bulkhead
42 Aileron and rudder trimming tab control wheel/indicator
43 CO_2 bottles
44 Bulkheads
45 Radio transceiver

46 Dynamotors
47 Aerial mast
48 Elevator/rudder control runs
49 Elevator/rudder controls strut
50 Arrester hook shock-absorber
51 Remote compass installation
52 Lifting tube
53 Oleo strut
54 Tail wheel
55 Arrester hook
56 Tail wheel/hook doors
57 Elevator
58 Rudder structure
59 Rudder trimming tab structure
60 Tail cone
61 Elevator trimming tab
62 Elevator structure
63 Aileron trimming tab
64 Aileron structure
65 Aileron balance tab (port only)
66 Outer wing flap
67 Centre flap
68 Inboard flap

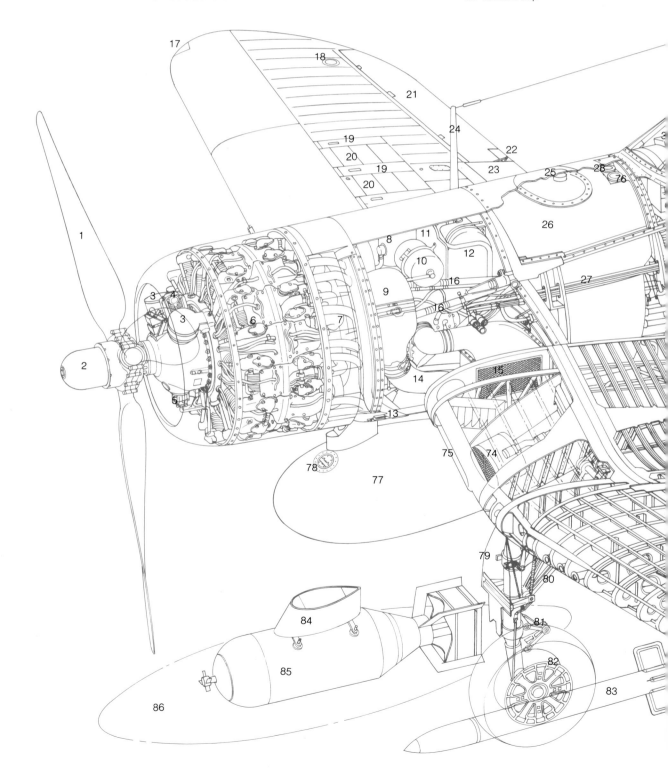

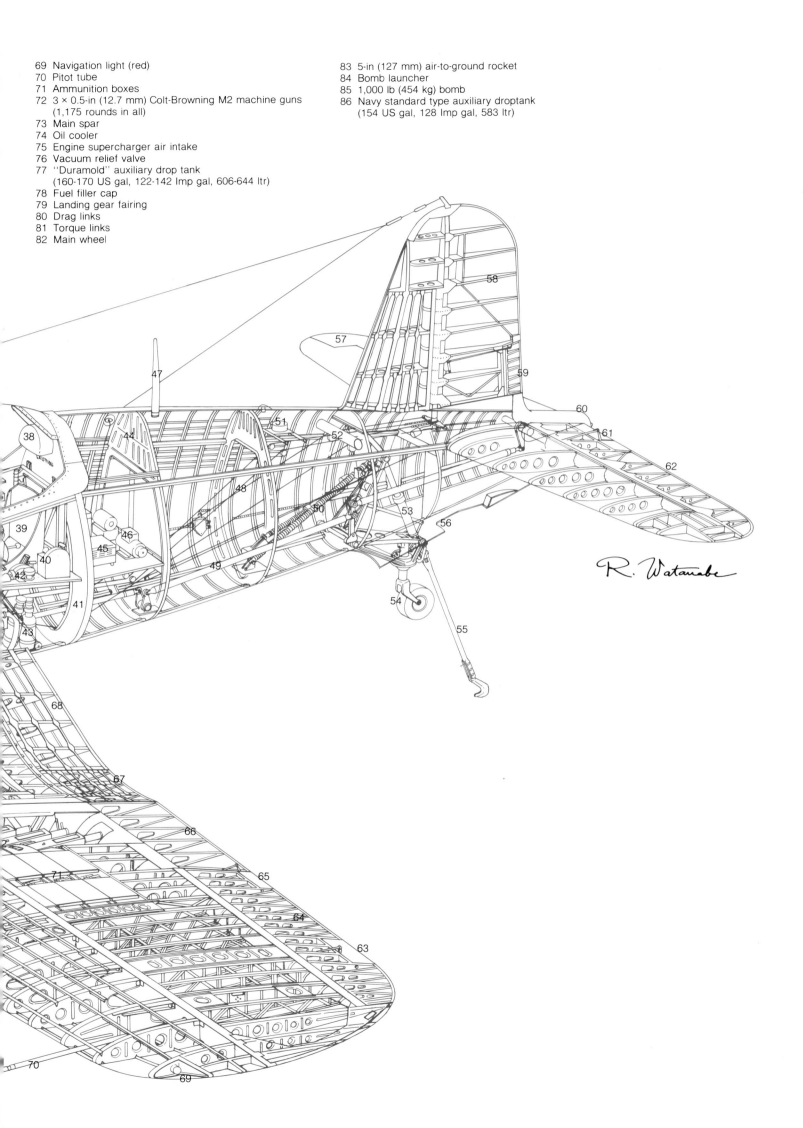

69 Navigation light (red)
70 Pitot tube
71 Ammunition boxes
72 3 × 0.5-in (12.7 mm) Colt-Browning M2 machine guns
  (1,175 rounds in all)
73 Main spar
74 Oil cooler
75 Engine supercharger air intake
76 Vacuum relief valve
77 "Duramold" auxiliary drop tank
  (160-170 US gal, 122-142 Imp gal, 606-644 ltr)
78 Fuel filler cap
79 Landing gear fairing
80 Drag links
81 Torque links
82 Main wheel

83 5-in (127 mm) air-to-ground rocket
84 Bomb launcher
85 1,000 lb (454 kg) bomb
86 Navy standard type auxiliary droptank
  (154 US gal, 128 Imp gal, 583 ltr)

R. Watanabe

Ammunition handlers fasten 5-in (127 mm) HVARs on F4U-1D for strike on Kyushu, Japan, 21 March, 1945. (National Archives)

In June 1945, Marine Air Group 14 flew into Kadena, Okinawa, with a new Corsair – the four-blade propeller and chin scoop on the cowl identified it as the F4U-4, viewed as a hot rod for chasing down kamikazes. The Corsairs, in concert with a variety of American military units, were claiming more Japanese aircraft destroyed than the number of lost F4Us. But still the carriers were being hit. When destroyers were sent out ahead of the fleet to act as warning pickets every time a kamikaze attack was launched, the picket boats took unacceptably high losses. As 1945 wore on, nobody knew when the war would end, and most were reluctantly admitting the probability of a land invasion of Japan which would meet determined resistance all the way. A popular saying among Americans, with reference to returning to the United States via San Francisco in peacetime, was "The Golden Gate in '48". Some Navy Privateer crews mused over the possibility of a full ten more years of war after 1945.

When President Franklin Delano Roosevelt died in April 1945, the succeeding chief executive of the United States, Harry Truman, had to be advised of the existence of an atomic bomb programme in the country, so secret had its development been. Weighing the gravity of the atom bomb's destructive power against the inevitable loss of life to be expected in an invasion of Japan, Truman chose to unleash nuclear war in an effort to end the fighting with Japan. The Corsair's first war ended abruptly in August following the explosions of two atomic bombs, when the Japanese government, relaying messages through neutral Switzerland, sued for peace.

It was a time for reflection. When all the tallies were in, the Vought Corsair claimed well over 2,100 Japanese aircraft shot down in flight for a loss in combat of only about 190 F4Us. Far larger were non-enemy-action losses of this fighter which demanded alert, competent pilots.

But when handled by such fliers, it is hard to argue that a better fighter served the Navy and Marines in World War II. The Corsair had the numbers in its favour.

The British experience with Corsairs included 2,012 supplied under Lend-Lease to the Royal Navy, while 424 were sent to the Royal New Zealand Air Force. In April 1944, before American acceptance of the Corsair, British Corsair IIs were launched from HMS *Victorious* during battles with the German battleship *Tirpitz* which was lodged

Corsair I (F4U-1A) of Royal New Zealand Air Force lands on an airstrip in the South Pacific, probably late in 1943. (Sommerich via G. S. Williams)

in a cold Norwegian fjord. Roaming high above the dive bombers and other fighters which succeeded, that brisk April day, in knocking the German battleship out of the war for a three-month period, the British Corsair pilots scanned the skies in vain for a German fighter response which did not materialize. In later months, repeat attacks on the *Tirpitz* and its retinue would include strafing by British Corsairs, costing one of the Voughts shot down by anti-aircraft gunnery.

In the Indian Ocean, British Corsairs flew a variety of missions, notably around Japanese-held Sumatra in 1944 and 1945. Along with the American carriers, British flattops steamed ever closer to Japan, and took their share of kamikaze hits. British Corsair fliers ended the war with about 50 air-to-air kills.

The New Zealanders converted all P-40 squadrons to Corsairs in 1944 – too late for the hottest Solomons fighting. Theirs was not to be an exciting war, though newly-arrived FG-1Ds built by Goodyear did pitch in to help the occupation forces in Japan after the surrender. Most of these were destroyed when no longer needed, but now an ex-New Zealand FG-1D is being groomed for flight by its American civilian owner at Everett, Washington. As planned in 1981, this Corsair will be something of a hybrid, bearing US markings but specially-clipped wings reminiscent of the British Corsairs. Not only did the shorter wings allow stowage on low-ceilinged British hangar decks, but some pilots claim the stubbier span makes for an even quicker than normal rate of roll.

Additionally, both the British and the New Zealanders have seen fit to preserve a Corsair apiece in museums in their countries.

Corsairs in Korea

The Korean War of 1950–53 was a bizarre mixture of high-technology weapons and old World War II machines fighting side by side. The bentwing F4U was there in force.

With the end of World War II in the late summer of 1945, the US Navy was faced with an immediate surplus of almost all types of aircraft. Production of Corsairs by contractors like Goodyear was halted, but the line at Vought would still build the crank-winged aircraft for eight years to follow. Jet propulsion promised to power Navy aircraft of the future, but the technology was not yet sufficiently perfected to permit the scrapping of all propeller-driven carrier machines. While planners could envisage carrier jets with speeds about 100 mph faster than Corsairs or their piston-engined contemporaries, the early jets could not haul as great a load over as long a distance as could a traditional propeller-driven aircraft. And, especially crucial to aircraft carrier operations, the early jets suffered a sickening time delay from when the throttle was advanced to the time the engine "spooled up" sufficiently to accelerate the aircraft. This slow response time could prove fatal if a jet had to be waved off a landing at the last minute, its power and speed too low to recover effectively.

The big bite of a variable-pitch propeller ahead of a reliable radial engine allowed quick acceleration to get a carrier pilot out of a tight situation. So while jets were being perfected for carrier operations, in the years immediately after World War II the US Navy continued to purchase new Corsairs from Vought, and to maintain many of the F4Us still in the inventory. As late as 1947, battle-proven F4U-4s were delivered from Vought's production line to the US Navy. In 1946, Vought created the fastest production Corsair yet – the XF4U-5, which boasted a top speed of about 470 mph (756 km/h). Over the next two years, more than 500 of the F4U-5 were sold to the Navy.

By May 1949, Grumman F9F Panther jet fighters were being delivered to operational squadrons. Jets would dictate air-to-air combat policies, but the Corsair had proved its worth as a dive bomber in World War II, and the piston-engine Voughts were placed in ground-attack roles in the postwar Navy.

In June 1950, troops from North Korea crossed the border into South Korea. The South Korean response was backed by United Nations military assistance in the form of combat units from several anti-communist countries. It was a large-scale commitment by the United States which saw modern jets and helicopters do battle alongside many of the classic aircraft of World War II – B-29 Superfortresses, A-26 Invaders, P-51 Mustangs, and the big blue Vought Corsairs.

A joint task force of one British and one American aircraft carrier set up for a strike against Pyongyang, capital of North Korea, on 3 July, 1950. Loaded with a brace of heavy air-to-ground rockets, 16 Corsairs joined Douglas AD Skyraiders and faster-flying F9F Panther jets in ruining the city's airfield. The Corsair was now involved in its second major war.

Perhaps the world was still trying to forget about its last war; maybe the deadly advances in the state of the art of warfare by 1950 neutralized the last vestiges of popular romance associated with warriors. Whatever the reasons, Korea was not a glamorous fight. Although courageous fliers abounded in Korea, the Corsairs and their pilots there did not receive the same hero worship which had been accorded the F4U aces like Greg Boyington in World War II over the Solomons.

US Navy documents indicate Corsairs flew more than four-fifths of all Navy and Marine close-support strikes during the first 10 months of Korean fighting. Launched from carriers and land bases in South Korea, the sturdy Voughts continued to attack ground targets until the end of Korean fighting in 1953.

Contemporary stories in *Naval Aviation News* claimed the first air-to-air combat over Korea involving Corsairs happened on 21 April, 1951 when two Marine F4Us of Squadron VMF-312 were attacked by piston-engined Yak-9 fighters. Cruising near Chinnampo, the Corsairs were on a ground-attack mission when one of the pilots, First Lieutenant Harold Daigh, spotted four fighters closing the distance between them and the other Corsair, flown by Captain Phillip DeLong.

At that moment Captain DeLong radioed to Daigh:

"Start shooting; they are putting holes in my plane." Daigh later said he saw enemy bullets pass nearby. "I saw big red balls large as baseballs going over my wing. I figured it was time to shoot," Daigh reported.

As DeLong took evasive action, Daigh scored hits on a Yak and shot it down. DeLong then took the offensive and destroyed two more Yak-9s while Daigh got hits on the fourth and last enemy fighter, which smoked its way out of the combat, and probably crashed later.

In June 1951, *Naval Aviation News* claimed the DeLong/Daigh dogfight with Yak-9s was the Corsairs' first air-to-air combat of the Korean War. Later research by naval aviation historian Barrett Tillman, in his book *Corsair – The F4U in World War Two and Korea*, detailed a Corsair kill against a Soviet aircraft operated by a Soviet crew which took place on 4 September, 1950.

Four Corsairs from Squadron VF-53 were flying cover for their aircraft carrier, the USS *Valley Forge*, and Task Force 77 that day when shipboard radar spotted two unidentified aircraft heading from the vicinity of Manchuria at about 60 miles (97 km) out. Directed to the heading of the two radar blips, the Corsairs intercepted one aircraft; the other had turned north and left the area. Visual inspection of the aeroplane showed it to be a twin-engine craft, emblazoned with Soviet red star insignia.

The Russian pilot pushed his aircraft into a power dive and raced for North Korea. The quicker Corsairs caught up with their potential adversary. This Cold War confrontation turned hot when the Corsairs were shot at by the Soviet machine. Leader of the F4U flight, Lieutenant (jg) Richard E. Downs, radioed the situation back to the USS *Valley Forge*, and was informed he could return fire. Downs and his wingman made firing runs, and the wingman's cannons sent the Soviet aircraft spinning into the sea, trailing flames. According to Tillman's account, a US destroyer later recovered the body of a Soviet airman at the scene of the crash.

Whether kept quiet for political reasons or merely overlooked when *Naval Aviation News* prepared its Corsair dogfight story, the downing of a Soviet aircraft by Corsairs in 1950 was a grim indication of the state of affairs between the two giant nations in the years following their sometimes precarious alliance during World War II.

By September 1950, it was apparent the American and United Nations intervention in the Korean War was not likely to produce an end to the fighting before the onslaught of the cold Korean winter. Radar-equipped F4U-5N Corsairs used as night-fighters would stand a high chance of flying in dangerous icing conditions. The Navy's Bureau of Aeronautics (BuAer) asked Vought in September if the F4U-5Ns could quickly be prepared for the impending cold weather over Korea.

An uncommon aspect of the proposal was the idea of attaching rubber de-icer boots to the leading edges of the wings and tail surfaces of the Corsair. Such boots were a routine de-icing device on slow-speed transports and bombers, but their application to the speedy Corsair would break new ground for the Navy and Vought. On the wings, the boots were confined to the outer wing panels outboard of

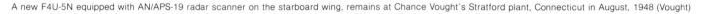

A new F4U-5N equipped with AN/APS-19 radar scanner on the starboard wing, remains at Chance Vought's Stratford plant, Connecticut in August, 1948 (Vought)

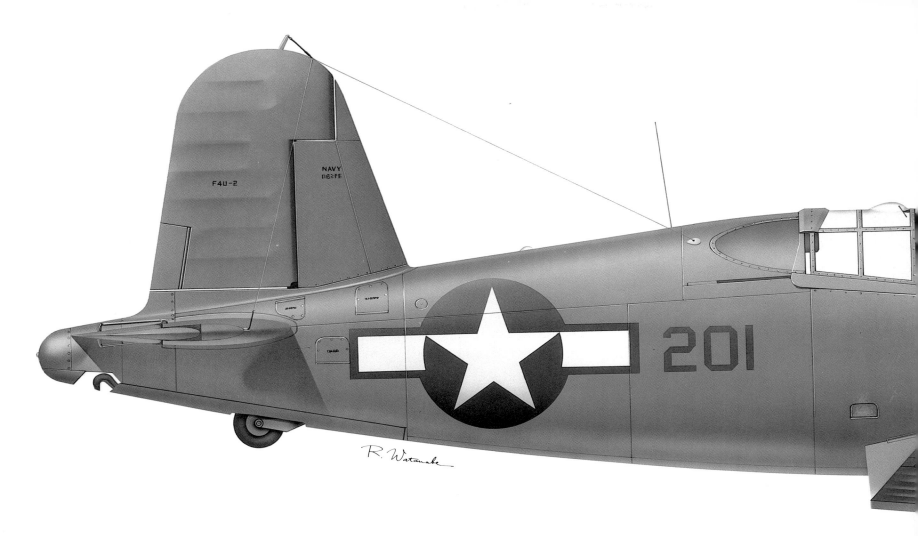

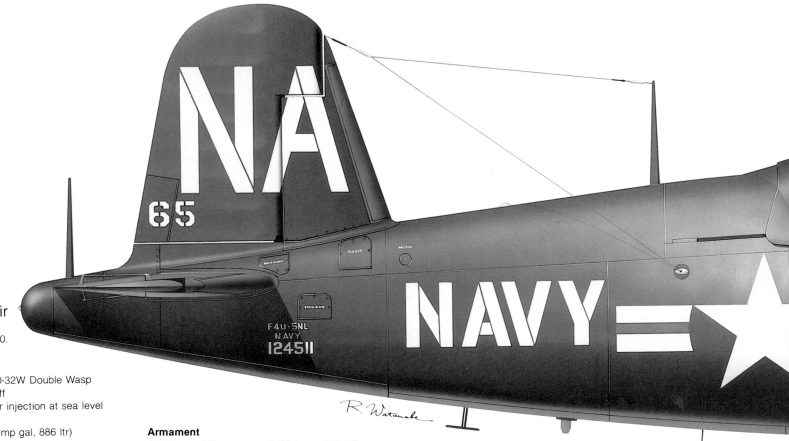

F4U-5NL Corsair
of VC-4 on USS
Antietam (CV-36) in 1950.

Power unit
Pratt & Whitney R-2800-32W Double Wasp
: 2,300 hp for take-off
: 2,760 hp with water injection at sea level
Internal fuel
: 234 US gal (194.9 Imp gal, 886 ltr)
Auxiliary fuel tanks
: 2 × 150 US gal (124.9 Imp gal, 568 ltr)

Performance (F4U-5N)
Max speed
: 470 mph (756 km/h) at 26,800 ft (8,170 m)
: 379 mph (610 km/h) at sea level
Cruising speed
: 227 mph (365 km/h)
Service ceiling
: 41,400 ft (12,620 m)
Rate of climb
: 3,780 fpm (1,152 m/min)
Range
: 1,120 mls (1,800 km)

Armament
4 × 20 mm M3 cannon with 924 rounds in all
2 × 1,000 lb (454 kg) bombs and 8 × 5-in (127 mm) HVAR

Radar equipment
AN/APS-19

Dimensions
Span
: 41 ft (12.50 m)
Length
: 34 ft 6 in (10.52 m)
Height
: 14 ft 10 in (4.52 m)
Wing area
: 314 sq. ft (29.2 m²)

Weights (F4U-5N)
Empty
: 9,683 lb (4,392 kg)
Gross
: 12,901 lb (5,852 kg)
Max take-off
: 14,106 lb (6,398 kg)

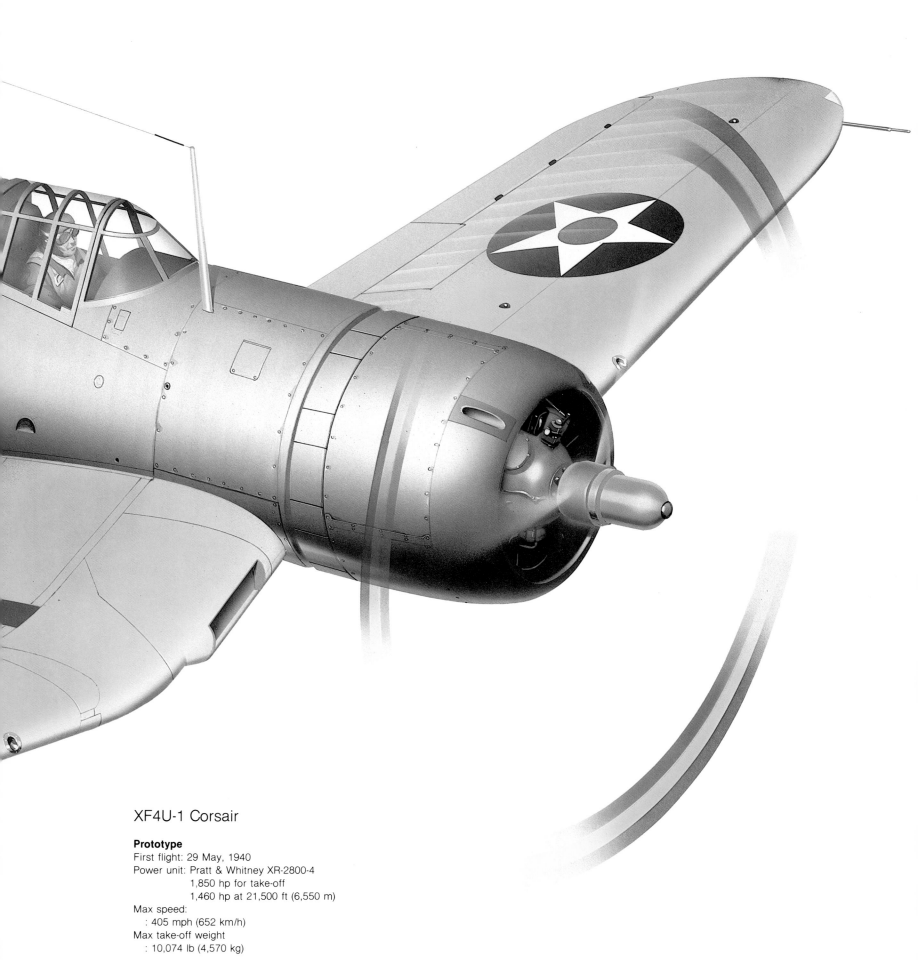

XF4U-1 Corsair

Prototype
First flight: 29 May, 1940
Power unit: Pratt & Whitney XR-2800-4
    1,850 hp for take-off
    1,460 hp at 21,500 ft (6,550 m)
Max speed:
 : 405 mph (652 km/h)
Max take-off weight
 : 10,074 lb (4,570 kg)

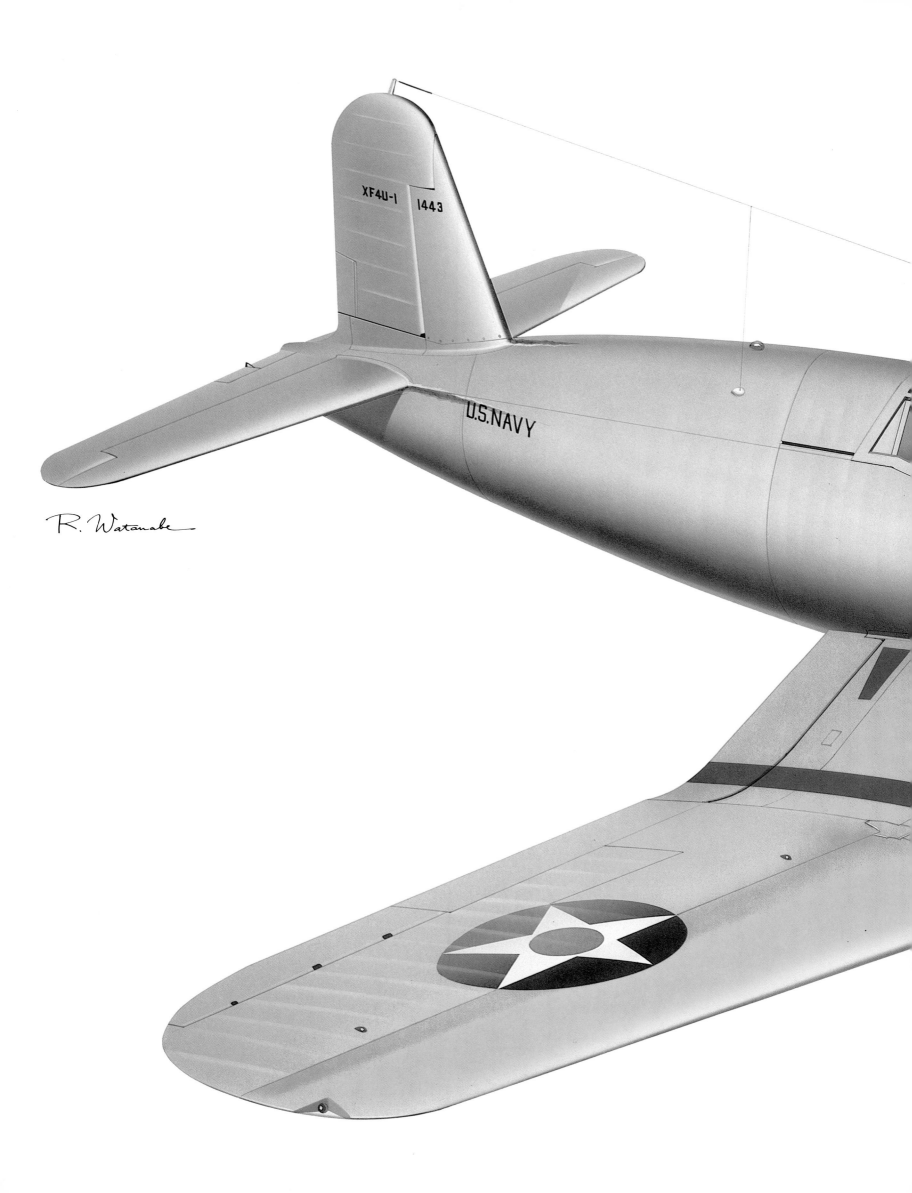

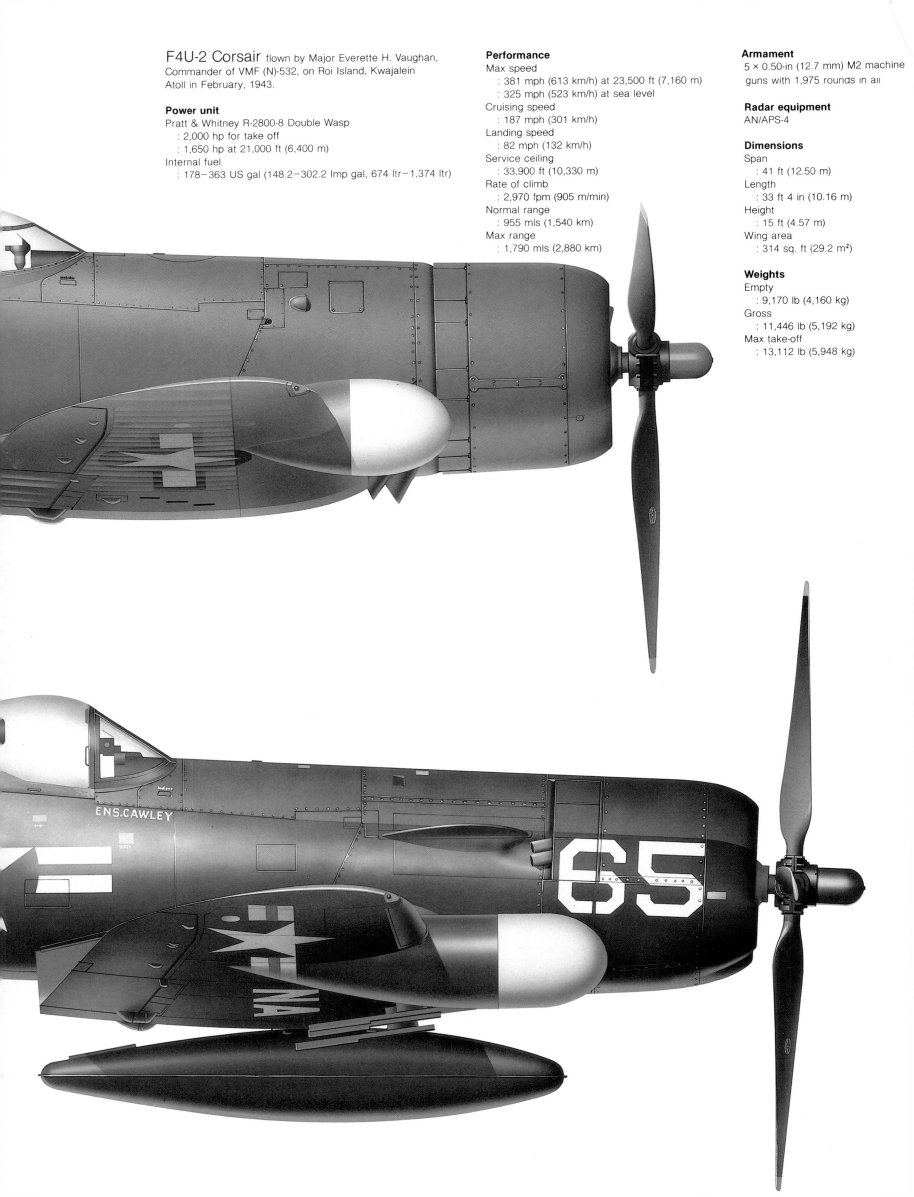

F4U-2 Corsair flown by Major Everette H. Vaughan, Commander of VMF (N)-532, on Roi Island, Kwajalein Atoll in February, 1943.

Power unit
Pratt & Whitney R-2800-8 Double Wasp
  : 2,000 hp for take off
  : 1,650 hp at 21,000 ft (6,400 m)
Internal fuel
  : 178–363 US gal (148.2–302.2 Imp gal, 674 ltr–1,374 ltr)

Performance
Max speed
  : 381 mph (613 km/h) at 23,500 ft (7,160 m)
  : 325 mph (523 km/h) at sea level
Cruising speed
  : 187 mph (301 km/h)
Landing speed
  : 82 mph (132 km/h)
Service ceiling
  : 33,900 ft (10,330 m)
Rate of climb
  : 2,970 fpm (905 m/min)
Normal range
  : 955 mls (1,540 km)
Max range
  : 1,790 mls (2,880 km)

Armament
5 × 0.50-in (12.7 mm) M2 machine guns with 1,975 rounds in all

Radar equipment
AN/APS-4

Dimensions
Span
  : 41 ft (12.50 m)
Length
  : 33 ft 4 in (10.16 m)
Height
  : 15 ft (4.57 m)
Wing area
  : 314 sq. ft (29.2 m²)

Weights
Empty
  : 9,170 lb (4,160 kg)
Gross
  : 11,446 lb (5,192 kg)
Max take-off
  : 13,112 lb (5,948 kg)

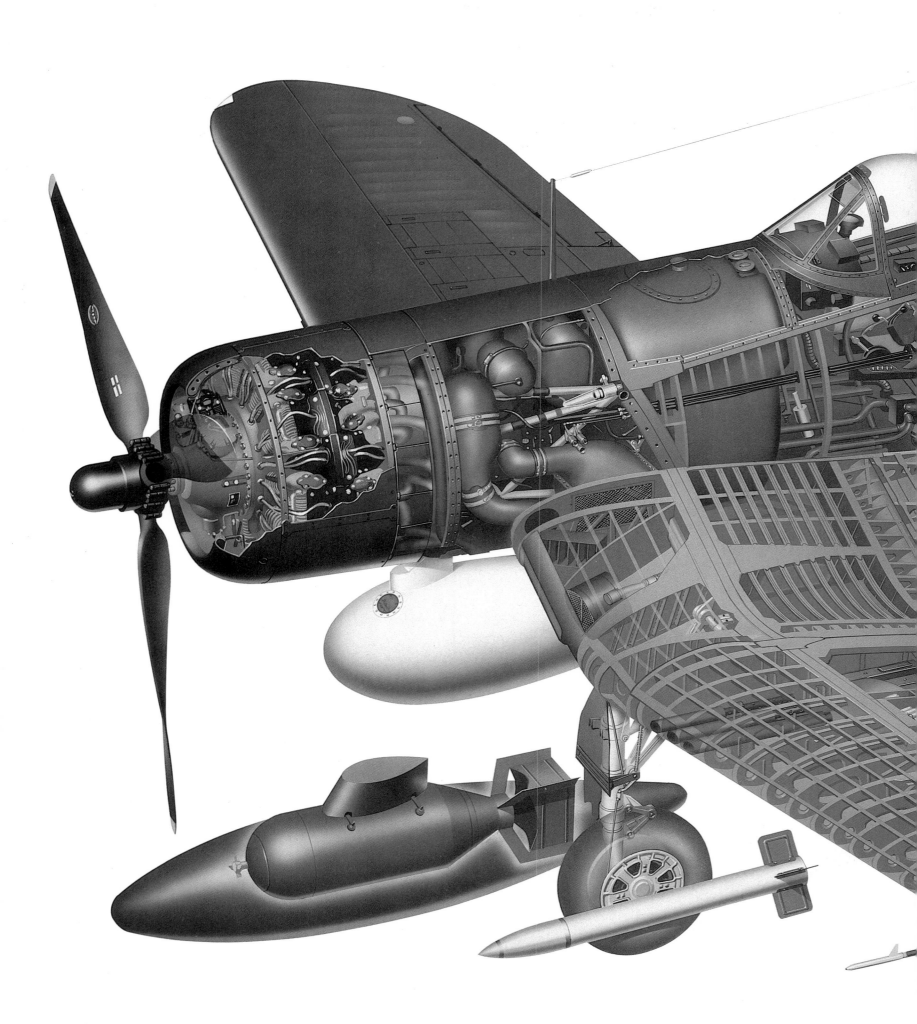

F4U-7 Corsair

Final model (French Aeronavale)
First flight: 2 July, 1952
Power unit: Pratt & Whitney R-2800-18W
       2,100 hp for take-off
       1,950 hp at 23,300 ft (7,100 m)
       2,450 hp with water injection at sea level
Max speed
  : 450 mph (724 km/h) at 26,000 ft (7,920 m)
Max take-off weight
  : 13,426 lb (6,090 kg)

R. Watanabe

F4U-5NLs of VC-4 pose for a daytime flying portrait in 1953. These aircraft have rubber de-icer boots on leading edges of outer wings and tail. (Sommerich via G. S. Williams)

the 20-mm guns. An improved cockpit heater was used, and a system for spreading alcohol on the whirling propeller blades to prevent the accumulation of ice was devised. Nozzles to spray anti-icing alcohol on the windshield were incorporated in the Corsair winterizing project.

The alcohol sprayed on the windscreen worked, but had a tendency to damage the plastic canopy until a protective coating was applied around the canopy edge where the alcohol usually gathered. Perhaps more seriously, alcohol fumes were entering the cockpit, according to pilots of the winter version. This posed a pilot-alertness problem as well as a fire hazard aboard these Corsairs.

The inventive quality Americans fondly call "Yankee Ingenuity" came into play as engineers tried to track down the source of the potentially deadly alcohol fume leaks. For safety reasons, a mixture using the spice peppermint was substituted for alcohol on an F4U-5N. The unmistakeable odour of peppermint filtered into the cockpit, until the source of the fumes was pin-pointed as being the heater airscoop. Mounting the heater scoop internally and adding cockpit sealing kept first the peppermint, and later the alcohol, from seeping into the pilot's enclosure.

Boots applied to the leading edges of the Corsairs' four-blade propeller contained troughs which conducted alcohol to the end of each blade, where ice would tend to form without its presence. A cup at the end of each blade fed the alcohol under pressure.

A new cockpit heater of 50,000 BTU output was provided in the winter Corsairs, and gave more than enough

warmth. According to Navy reports, "this revised system just about drove the pilot out" because of excessive cabin heat.

Frost covers – sleeves to keep ice formations from encrusting the wings, tail, and other parts of the Corsair on the ground – were manufactured as part of the F4U-5N – preparations for winter, because experienced aviators know how a seemingly insignificant rash of frost can destroy lift and ruin the performance characteristics of an aircraft if not removed before flight.

Requested in September 1950, the adapted Corsairs entered testing in Newfoundland in January 1951. By the first week of March 1951, winter-booted Corsairs were in Japan, ready for Korean missions. In time for the remainder of the Korean winter that year, the F4U-5Ns would face two more Korean winters before the shooting stopped.

According to a story in the December 1951 issue of *Naval Aviation News*, "External de-icing equipment is removed for summer operation but internal plumbing is permanent."

The Corsairs over Korea carried both iron bombs and a variety of rockets. Five-inch (127 mm) High Velocity Aircraft Rockets (HVARs) and monstrous 11.75-inch (298 mm) "Tiny Tim" rockets had been tried under the wings of Corsairs during World War II. A 6.5-inch (165 mm) warhead attached to a standard five-inch HVAR was a special anti-tank missile perfected by the Navy based on Korean War combat reports which indicated that regular HVARs merely bounced off enemy tanks and armour steel.

Called ATAR (Anti-Tank Aircraft Rocket) the

6.5-inch projectile was a shaped charge – an entirely different type of warhead from that on conventional HVARs. Based on a 19th-century ordnance principle discovered by a Naval torpedo engineer, the explosive charge in the ATAR is funnel-shaped. When it explodes, the force of the blast focuses superheated gases which are propelled forward with velocity sufficient to penetrate armour steel. According to Navy accounts, "The process of penetration of a tank by a shaped-charge jet is much like that of a high speed jet of water from a fire hose nozzle penetrating a bank of soft mud. Target material is splashed out at high velocities radially from the point of impact. The strength of the armour plate is of little consequence because the pressures produced at the point of impact are far above the yield point of most materials."

The ATARs went to war with the Navy, Marines and Air Force in Korea. With deadly certainty, a tank hit by an ATAR would be destroyed as the superheated gases and molten steel bored through the tank's armour. Once inside the tank, red hot bits of metal would rattle around, probably killing the vehicle's occupants. Crew members who survived the ricocheting metal might die of suffocation shortly thereafter as the superheated gases fired all the oxygen in the tank. The Corsair in Korea was a messenger of a new and terrible death.

The technology which developed terrible new weapons for the Korean War also evolved the helicopter into a rescue vehicle without peer. Where World War II fliers were often lost for weeks, or fell into enemy hands because quick rescues could not be effected in remote areas, their Korean War counterparts could be plucked literally from the enemy by helicopter, and whisked home safely.

With a blunt nose reminiscent of a grasshopper, Sikorsky's HO3S helicopter was used by the Navy to pluck downed airmen far inland, as well as to pick up fliers who crashed on takeoff or landing aboard the carriers at sea.

In 1950, two Marine Corsair pilots, Wilbur Wilcox and Charles McClain, flew to the aid of a downed US Air Force pilot north of Pyongyang. Flying cover for the grounded flier was a common mission shared by all services in Korea. But the two Marines stayed on station too long, using up their fuel in an effort to protect the Air Force pilot from capture by North Korean ground forces. Out of fuel, McClain was able to put his F4U down inside friendly lines. His partner Wilcox was not so fortunate. Wilcox went down within reach of the enemy, and soon was no better off than the Air Force pilot he had sought to protect.

Wilcox climbed out of his Corsair as soon as it stopped and scrambled 200 yards (180 m) to some tall, concealing grass. As he hid in the grass, Wilcox saw about 10 communist soldiers approach his Corsair with tree branches, which they placed over it in an effort to conceal it from American search aircraft. The soldiers then spread out and searched for Wilcox until after dark, but failed to catch him. Next morning, Wilcox saw villagers carrying South Korean flags. He took a chance on their truthfulness in waving the flags, and signalled to the Koreans. Still not sure of their loyalty, Wilcox held the Koreans at a distance with his pistol while using smoke grenades to signal two friendly aircraft

overhead – one of which was piloted by Wilcox's flying buddy McClain.

Wilcox was surprised to hear one of the Koreans say, "American soldier, I want to talk to you." The Korean went on to describe living in Los Angeles, California and brought food to Wilcox. Meanwhile, McClain vectored a Marine helicopter to the site, and Wilcox was plucked from the ground and returned to safety.

In June 1952, Colonel Robert Galer's Corsair was shot down while making a minimum altitude sprint along a valley. The engine was mortally shot, and Galer injured himself jumping from the crippled Corsair, according to Barrett Tillman's book, *Corsair – The F4U in World War Two and Korea*. Galer spent the next several hours dodging communist troops while first his Corsair squadron mates from Marine Air Group 12 and later Air Force and even South African fliers buzzed overhead, shooting up ammunition to provide cover for their downed fellow pilot. Around dusk, a Navy helicopter appeared, and lowered a sling for Galter. He scrambled aboard, and the whirlybird chugged down the valley amid enemy fire, taking hits.

Galer was safely rescued by the helicopter. Time and again, Korean battle reports are filled with stories of fliers loitering over downed comrades to protect them from enemy troops, even if it meant the ultimate loss of more aircraft. But lives were saved and captures were put off until the remarkable new helicopters could reach the scene and rescue the grounded pilots.

While the Panther jets stayed at altitude to provide fighter cover, the ground-attacking Corsairs used the war as a licence to break all the low-flying rules in spirited attacks that must surely have been fun to watch, had they not been so deadly to be near. One Corsair pilot who had already expended his ammunition spied telephone lines which he took for North Korean communications. Improvising an attack quickly, the pilot lowered the tailhook of the big F4U and roared down on the lines, snagging them with the hook and cutting communications.

Captain A. K. Phillips of Marine Squadron VMF-214 – the illustrious Black Sheep squadron – took a flight of F4U-4s laden with 1000-pound (454 kg) bombs on a bridge-busting mission to Pyongyang. Pull-out for the flight was so low that as the Corsairs left the target area, they actually had to nose up to clear several taller buildings in the enemy's capital city. Viewing the structures as fair game, the cannon-wielding Corsairs cut loose with bursts as they climbed over the structures. "It was the first time we ever shot upwards to strafe buildings", Phillips was later quoted as saying.

Low flying – "flat-hatting" in the pilots' jargon – was a way of life for the speedy Corsairs in Korea. Getting useful damage assessment photos was difficult at first, and sometimes involved the use of a separate photo aircraft following the F4U in its diving run. A better answer was the field modification of Corsair baggage hatches in the bellies of the F4Us to mount a K-25 aerial camera with a 90-degree prism, allowing the camera to get rear views of freshly-attacked targets as the flat-hatting Corsair sped away. In this way, the Corsairs doing the attacking became their own photo aircraft, bringing a film record of their exploits back with them as they returned from missions.

The Corsairs' exploits over Korea spawned many tales which were tributes to the rugged design of the F4U. A "Nightmare" squadron nightfighting F4U flown by Major George Herlihy ripped into a 5/8-inch stranded guy wire as Herlihy manoeuvred to avoid a pall of smoke in his path. With a chunk torn free from its right wing, Herlihy's Corsair nonetheless returned home safely, trailing a piece of the wire as mute evidence of the collision.

Ensign Dan Bryla, when launched in his Corsair from the USS *Valley Forge* for a hydro-electric powerplant strike, little realized the unusual adventure he and his Corsair would go through together. In dive bomber fashion, Bryla pushed the nose of his dark blue fighter earthward from 17,000 feet (5180 m), according to Navy accounts published in 1953. As the dive progressed, the big F4U set up a shuddering, buffeting vibration.

Bryla first attributed the bumpy ride to nearby flak bursts, but the sensations increased, and the pilot recognized the dreaded effects of compressibility shock waves which indicated near-supersonic speed. Control of the Corsair was nearly impossible in the throes of compressibility so Bryla jettisoned his heavy bombs and brought the throttle back to reduce power, while pulling the stick to try to nose the fighter up out of its dive.

The screaming Corsair rolled over on its back as Bryla wrestled to control the dive. At the tremendous speed he was travelling, the ailerons refused to deflect enough to allow Bryla to roll the aircraft upright again. Still in a dive and inverted, Bryla tried to pull his machine through a half loop. But this brought the angle of dive even steeper, rendering the elevators almost as useless as the ailerons. With both hands drawing back on the stick, and one foot on the left rudder pedal to keep the course true, Bryla managed to bring his fighter through a partial loop and into level flight. Now dead ahead of the still-speeding F4U was a 4,000-foot (1200 m) ridge. Bryla skimmed over the top of the mountains, avoided flak, and found the rest of his flight winging back to the *Valley Forge*.

On the journey back to the aircraft carrier, the pilot began to register intense pains in his left hip, stomach and shoulders. He switched his oxygen regulator to 100 per cent to combat faintness, and droned on for the carrier.

Near the *Valley Forge* Bryla rocked his F4U's gull wings to signal the need for an immediate landing. Down with a jolt, Bryla was safe on deck. Subsequent medical examination aboard the ship revealed Bryla had suffered a broken left hip and strained back and shoulder muscles in his life-or-death pullout against gravity. But his Corsair returned to duty the next day on another combat strike, the survivor of a dive and high-g pullout which had broken its pilot's bones!

In the first few months of the Korean conflict, communist jets were scarce. A writer in the September 1950 issue of *Naval Aviation News* said, "Military authorities have conceded that the Corsair is an excellent fighter to use against any piston-engine enemy planes. When the enemy starts using jets, our own jets will have to take over VF (fighter squadron) missions."

The appearance of MiG-15 jets came sooner than some expected. On 9 November, 1950, F9F Panther jet pilot Lieutenant Commander W. T. Amen tucked in behind a MiG and sent bullets into the communist fighter, knocking it from the sky. Ominously for the pilots of propeller-driven aircraft the vanquished MiG had been one of a flight of about six enemy jets dispatched to attack a mixed bag of Corsairs and Skyraiders which were working over the highway and rail bridges at Sinuiju on the Yalu River bordering North Korea and communist China. Amen's Panther from VF-111, the "Sundowners", ably defended the slower Corsairs and Skyraiders in a dogfight that rambled from minimum altitude to more than three miles (5 km) up. But someday the MiGs were bound to get through to the Corsairs; the jet age would catch up to Corsairs in combat.

On 9 September, 1952, MiGs engaged Corsairs from VMA-312, but the Corsair pilots, in a premeditated plan, turned on their attackers to confuse them, and then dived for the ground, where they streaked away safely. On the following day the bentwing F4Us of VMA-312 were launched from the USS *Sicily*. Flying two of the blue fighter-bombers were Captain Jesse G. Folmar and Lieutenant W. L. Daniels. Four MiG-15s spotted the two Marines, and went after them in pairs. Following a pass by the first two MiGs, the last pair of enemy jets overtook the Corsairs and pulled ahead in a climbing turn to the left, Folmar was quoted as saying. Seizing an opportunity, Folmar cranked his slower Corsair into a tighter turn, and loosed a five-second barrage from his fighter's 20-mm cannon.

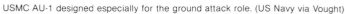

USMC AU-1 designed especially for the ground attack role. (US Navy via Vought)

An F4U-5NL moments before take-off aboard a US Navy carrier. The propeller tip vortices are caused by high air humidity. (US Navy via Vought)

The jet began to smoke and Folmar watched its pilot eject from the smoke-filled cockpit. It appeared the communist pilot's clothing and possibly his parachute were on fire as he left the burning jet.

Folmar's victory could not be savoured long. Another of the MiGs got off a shot, as the Marines were diving away to avoid the jet threat, and cannon shells chewed up the left wing of Folmar's Vought. Unable to control the severely mauled Corsair, Folmar bailed out over the ocean.

Another ironically quick rescue was effected by an Air Force Grumman Albatross amphibian 15 minutes after Folmar hit the water. Friendly anti-aircraft guns nearby had opened up on the MiGs, driving them away as Folmar bailed out.

The Corsair had downed a jet MiG, but the inevitable performance superiority enjoyed by the jets ultimately bested the propeller-driven F4U.

As the Korean War neared a truce in 1953, on detached service from the carrier *Princeton* was Navy pilot Guy Bordelon whose job was to shoot down low-flying, night-raiding communist hecklers who were too slow to be intercepted by some of the Air Force F-94 or Marine F3D jet night fighters. Bordelon skilfully used his F4U-5N Corsair to become an ace, dropping five Yak-9 and possibly also a La-9 intruders. For this work, Bordelon was stationed south of Seoul at Pyongtaek. Even in a war rapidly being dominated by fast jets, the durable Corsair became an ace-maker one last time.

Twenty-seven July, 1953, was the date set for peace in Korea – a peace that was never very far from erupting again into open war. The Corsair's last American war was over, but several foreign countries would put the U-aircraft into combat in the 1950s and even into the 1960s.

Perhaps one last anecdote from the Korean War sums up the role of the big Vought in that conflict, and characterizes the strength of the Corsair design: Ensign Ed Hofstra of Squadron VF-64, nicknamed the Freelancers, was flying a ground-attack sweep along a road near Wonsan early in the war. Hofstra's Corsair was loaded to kill – eight 100-pound (45 kg) bombs, one napalm bomb and a 150 US gallon (568 l) belly fuel tank were all suspended beneath the blue fighter.

On a sea coast road, Hofstra identified two uniformed communist soldiers, according to Navy accounts. Roaring in for an attack, the Corsair was put into a steep dive. Unable to pull out in time, the VF-64 Corsair struck the ground in a level attitude, neatly wiping all the ordnance and the fuel tank off the bottom.

The big Pratt and Whitney engine slammed to a halt as the propeller blades bent back from the impact. But the rugged Corsair did not disintegrate on impact; Hofstra found himself airborne again in a deadstick aircraft which sailed about 500 yards (460 m) out to sea before Hofstra set it down in a textbook example of a ditching.

Once in his emergency raft, the Corsair flier had to use his paddle to fight sea currents which threatened to push the raft back to the enemy shore off which he had just bounced. Other squadron aircraft flew cover for him until darkness, when they were relieved by night fighters. A British Short Sunderland flying boat, another veteran from World War II, lumbered in close to shore in the darkness and rescued Hofstra about three hours after his literal scrape with death.

Odd Jobs

Corsairs entered the civilian market in the United States following World War II, where they became air show curiosities or air racers. In the 1946 Bendix trophy race, Thomas F. Call entered a newly-surplused FG-1; the following year saw F. P. Whitton put a Corsair into contention for the Bendix. Cook Cleland won an early postwar Thompson trophy race in the radical bubble-canopied F2G. FG-1s, F4U-4s and the F4U-7 piloted by Los Angeles attorney Bob Gulford all made a run for the money when air racing was revived in the United States in the 1960s and 1970s.

In the 1950s, Hollywood pilot Frank Tallman learned of plans to film a movie about Major Greg Boyington's World War II Corsair squadron, to be based on Boyington's book, *Baa Baa Black Sheep*. Wanting to be ready with Corsairs when the movie moguls arrived, Tallman needed Corsairs in his stable of motion-picture aircraft. He found them in the Arizona boneyard used by the Navy near Phoenix. "I bought four Corsairs at Litchfield Park for $420 each and flew them out", Tallman told the author in 1976.

For years, the four Corsairs were kept licensed and hangared, running up maintenance and storage costs amounting to more than their original purchase prices. The "Black Sheep" movie was delayed and postponed repeatedly, until Tallmantz Aviation, operated by Tallman and another legendary Hollywood pilot, Paul Mantz, gave up on the idea and sold or traded the graceful Corsairs away. Some were sold at auction in the late 1960s when Tallman paid off some company debts; another was traded for a biplane amphibian Grumman J2F Duck which Tallman used in films and at air shows.

Long after the Corsairs were sold by Tallman, the "Black Sheep" movie materialized as a television series, and

Six F4U-4s of a US Navy Reserve squadron at Oakland, California, in stepped-up echelon formation framing Mt. Rainier in 1954. (US Navy via P. Palmer)

Tallmantz Aviation found itself working with the new owners of some of the same Corsairs, at last chronicling the Boyington saga, albeit with the whimsical licence of Hollywood scriptwriters who managed to set back the real story of the Pacific in World War II with their concoctions.

The Corsairs which the late Frank Tallman picked up for $420 apiece in the 1950s could now easily be valued at more than $200,000 on the American wartime aircraft collector market – a tribute to the longevity of the F4U.

When Tallman was picking up bargain Corsairs in Arizona, the Voughts were finding military employment with other countries, fighting other wars. France made use of the more than 90 F4U-7s expressly built for them, augmenting this propeller-driven strike force with AU-1 ground-attack Corsairs lent by the US Navy in April 1954.

French Navy squadrons including 12F, 14F and 15F lugged bombs and rockets under the wings of their dark-blue Corsairs in an effort to stop the Viet Minh in French Indochina in 1954, long before large-scale American combat involvement in southeast Asia. Squadron 14F sent 25 AU-1s into the Viet conflict before a cease-fire divided the country that year. Six of the borrowed Corsairs would not be coming home, and two French aviators went down with their Voughts. The cease-fire created a divided North and South Vietnam which later would spark into a bloody war involving the United States as an ally of South Vietnam.

The French would see combat in their Corsairs yet another time, halfway around the world. After sending the borrowed AU-1s home, Aéronavale bought some of them outright. Fighting insurgents in Algeria, squadrons 12F, 15F and 17F took Corsairs into combat from land bases and an aircraft carrier in 1955 and 1956. The French were in danger of losing control of Algeria, but the Corsairs could not change the final outcome of this struggle in a time when many traditional powers were being shorn of their colonies.

France took an active part in another piece of combat diplomacy in October 1956 when fighting between Israel and Egypt threatened to close the Suez Canal. With Britain as a partner, the French decided to intervene in the Israeli–Egyptian fighting by mounting air attacks against Egyptian targets. The Israelis, by virtue of previous victories, held enough strategic territory to come out in favour of a cease-fire. But the Egyptians perceived no benefit to be derived from this, and vowed to keep battling Israeli forces. It was at this point that the French and British launched their attacks, from 1 November to 7 November, 1956. The United Nations called for a cease-fire, prompting an end to the Anglo-French intervention, after the loss of two French Corsairs, including one shot down over Cairo by anti-aircraft gunners.

It was for the Suez intervention that the French painted their own version of invasion stripes on their Corsairs. Instead of black and white bars as had been used on Allied aircraft flying low over the Normandy beaches in World War II, the Suez Corsairs carried yellow and black bumblebee stripes on their wings and aft fuselage to aid quick recognition by Anglo-French ground troops which had been landed during the brief encounter.

French Corsairs remained in Aéronavale service into the early 1960s, with most of the F4U-7s being scrapped by 1964. A few of the distinctively-French Dash-7s came back to the United States where they became museum pieces and air show attractions.

From the late 1950s well into the 1960s, Argentina launched F4U-5s emblazoned with the large anchor insignia of

F4U-5 flown by Captain Fernand Soto, Honduras Air Force. Three kill marks are seen alongside the cockpit. (J. R. Bassett via B. Tillman)

the Argentine Navy, from a former British aircraft carrier. But the Latin American Corsair users who took the spotlight with their U-aircraft were Honduras and El Salvador, who pitted Corsair against Corsair in a political flare-up in July 1969. Salvadoran FG-1Ds and North American P-51 Mustangs squared off against Honduran F4U-4s and F4U-5s.

Claims have been disputed in this war, but Honduran Captain Fernando Soto's Dash-5 was painted with three "kill" symbols – signifying two Corsairs and a Mustang – during the 1969 fighting.

Later that year, El Salvador sent an FG-1D to the United States to be restored as a monument in Connecticut to the Vought employees who conceived and executed the Corsair design. The Honduran Corsairs were maintained for several more years in that country, and were flown only occasionally by the Hondurans. Some of the Honduran Corsairs have since entered the civilian wartime aircraft market in the United States.

The durable Corsair almost figured in yet another military action in 1958 during a time when Cuban revolutionary Fidel Castro had not yet declared his communist intentions, and was in fact being supplied in his guerrilla war against the Batista regime by the US Central Intelligence Agency.

The US Navy had Corsairs in desert storage in Arizona at that time. One observer who worked at Herlong Field, a small civilian airport at Jacksonville, Florida, recalled that the Navy designated its Naval Station at Jacksonville a surplus disposal site. Not long after, several Corsairs were shipped by train from Arizona all the way across the United States to Florida, supposedly to be declared surplus in Florida rather than in the southwestern United States.

The surplus Corsairs were purchased by a company with a civilian name, and trucked to Herlong Field for refurbishing. A Jacksonville airport worker recalled that the Navy permitted some mechanics to take leave from the Jacksonville Naval Air Station to assist the civilian owners in making the big Voughts airworthy. The peculiarity of shipping obsolete Corsairs right across the United States from Arizona just to have them declared surplus in Florida, and then letting

mechanics from the Navy help overhaul the fighters, did not escape the attention of the airport employee. He watched the Corsair restorations progress, and occasionally asked the man in charge of the machines what was to become of them.

They were to become high-speed personal transportation for civilians wealthy enough to keep them, the man answered.

But the presence of such military equipment as gunsights, armament panels and wiring for bomb racks on the dark blue fighters seemed to indicate a far different intention on the part of the rebuilder, and so the airport employee persisted in his cross-examination. When asked what branch of the military he had served, the man in charge of the F4U project denied ever having had any military connections – but the airport worker could clearly make out the design of the mystery man's West Point military academy ring.

As the Corsairs neared completion, Fidel Castro announced to the world his communist beliefs. Suddenly the bearded Latin guerrilla was considered as foe instead of tacit friend, and covert aid from US government agencies came to a halt. The Florida Corsairs languished after Castro's announcement. The mechanics and the mysterious supervisor with the West Point ring packed up and left.

A Corsair gunsight became a dashboard ornament in the car of a friend of the airport employee. Eventually the big blue fighters deteriorated, and may have ultimately been sold for scrap. They never served Fidel Castro, and their strange trip from Arizona to Florida went down as a quirk of Cold War diplomacy, unnoticed by almost everyone – everyone except one Jacksonville airport worker who kept his eyes open, read the newspapers, and put two and two together.

A hangar tale repeated by American fliers has just enough credibility to be true. Stories persist that a wealthy Texan sought to be rid of his wife, who fancied herself a pilot. Doing things with the grand, larger-than-life flourish which Americans have come to expect of Texans, the unhappy husband bought his spouse a plaything – a Vought Corsair. However, as Barrett Tillman has chronicled, the Corsair could be its own worst enemy, with 56 per cent of the World War II Corsair crashes attributable to non-combat causes. So the story goes, the eager wife gladly jumped into her gift surplus Corsair, and was killed when the difficult Vought brought her down. The husband, it is claimed, committed the perfect crime and got away with it!

Its days of wars and intrigues over with, the Vought Corsair can still be seen plying the skies over many major air shows in the United States and Canada, where a mixed bag of FG-1Ds, F4U-4s, -5s and -7s sport an equally mixed array of paint schemes in an effort to recapture the essence of the Corsair in combat. Still other examples of the long-nosed Vought design are permanently grounded in museums such as the National Air and Space Museum, which has painstakingly rebuilt a Corsair, tearing the big fighter down for complete and thorough corrosion control and repair as if to fly, although this Corsair's only mission will be to show museum visitors for many years to come the aesthetic harmony of this sleek milestone in aircraft development.

Pages From the Pilots' Logs

The Corsair's combats are long past; its warrior pilots are now civilian accountants, lawyers, businessmen. Indistinguishable from the rest of society, until perhaps the sound of an R-2800 engine boring overhead rekindles a spark of fire from the old days. When they talk about the U-aircraft, it is nearly always with pride and respect. The Vought Corsair will never suffer for lack of endorsements.

Jeff Dorroh, who as executive officer for VMF-323 on Okinawa in 1945 splashed six Japanese Val dive bombers in one engagement, can still breathe some life into his Corsair recollections from the past. Dorroh participated in only one aerial combat, on the fateful day he became an ace. His Marine Corps training – and a little extra-curricular activity in the States – prepared him well for that day. "Stateside when you were training," Dorroh relates, "you'd raise all kinds of hell." This meant going out as brash young aviators and dogfighting with any friendly fighter, Army or Navy, which would take up the challenge. "We jumped anybody and everybody we could; that's what young fighter pilots do." Base commanders frowned on such eager contests, but Dorroh and his squadron mates learned from these bouts to respect the capabilities of their swift, big Corsairs. Compared to the F4U, Dorroh says the Grumman F6F Hellcat "felt like you were flying a rocking chair". This he learned first hand by trying out a Hellcat one day.

When Dorroh and six other VMF-323 "Death Rattler" squadron mates saw 39 Vals apparently winging towards American picket destroyers on 22 April, 1945, Jeff figured on a long aerial engagement. To prolong his supply of ammunition, he switched on only four of his Vought's six .50 calibre machine guns. "I'd use four at a time, and switch around to make it last longer."

The rest of his combat tour, flying out of Kadena, was spent in ground attacks against heavy gun emplacements and vehicles. High Velocity Aircraft Rockets (HVARs), bombs, napalm tanks and .50 calibre ammunition all were expended by Dorroh in pursuit of these targets. The optical gunsight was used as an aiming device for the rockets, and in fact, the rocket launchers had been installed after Dorroh and the squadron left the United States, and were routed to Espiritu Santo for the attachment of the launchers and some training in their use.

"I always used them in pairs," Jeff Dorroh says, recalling the rushing noise the rockets made as they sped away from the diving Corsair. "You can hear the 'swish' as the leave," he explains. He found the unguided rockets to have good accuracy when sighted through the optical gunsight. The unmistakeable rush of the rockets could be employed to a Corsair pilot's advantage when attacking gun emplacements. "On Okinawa, if we had to go after a big gun in a cave, we'd practically fly right into the mouth of the cave" in a shallow glide angle, Dorroh remembers. In an effort to quieten the guns during an attack, Dorroh says he would fire a pair of rockets, hoping the distinctive noise of the missiles would send the gunners scrambling for cover, instead of trying to return the fire at the Corsair. "I don't know if it did any good, but it made me feel better," he recalls.

The roar of the Pratt and Whitney engine up front drowned out many other noises, but there was still no mistaking when all six .50s were armed and firing – Dorroh says his entire Corsair would shake from the recoil of the rattling guns.

A typical day for VMF-323 – if indeed there can be a typical day in a rapidly-changing war scenario – included a pre-dawn warm-up at Kadena of four or more Corsairs on early morning picket duty. These aircraft were expected to destroy kamikazes and conventional bombers or dissuade them from attacking radar destroyers used as early-warning posts, screening the main American fleets from Japan. As the sun rose, another flight of four to eight of the dark blue Corsairs would depart to relieve an earlier picket flight, either from VMF-323 or from another squadron. Assignments were made at the Marine Air Group 31 level, and involved several units covering for each other.

Later in the day, whether in hot tropical sunshine or in a torrential downpour, more VMF-323 fliers would huddle around as Dorroh or another officer would use rudimentary maps to locate a target for ground attack prior to a launch.

Lieutenant Commander Richard E. Harmer took F4U-2 night fighters aboard the USS *Enterprise* in 1944, the first US Navy combat Corsairs to fly from carriers. Though he says the addition of the radar pod on the right wing did not seem to adversely affect flight characteristics of the Corsair, the night fighters did not punish the radar sets with violent aerobatics. "We gave up any idea of stunting when we had that radar in there. Being 'hotshots' was just out of the question," Harmer explains.

Rather than flying rough-and-tumble dogfights at night, Harmer and his VF(N)-101 detachment practised precision intercept runs against aircraft obscured by the darkness. Initial direction was made by a shipboard or ground-based station, with final acquisition of the target made with the aircraft's own set. The field of coverage for the radar was a cone emanating from the pod, covering an ever larger area as it expanded away from the pod. "If your target is trying to evade you, you just hang in there back about 800 to 1,000 feet [245–305 m]," Harmer explains. At that distance, the field of view covered on the radar scope usually allowed the Corsair pilot enough time to correct for any evasive action taken by his targeted aircraft before it had a chance to fly out of the scope. Harmer says visual identification of enemy targets was mandatory, so the fliers would close the range to about 400 feet (122 m) where even in darkness the machine could be made out, and then the Corsair stalker would drop back to fire his guns.

The F4U-2s were hard to see from the front – the view most adversaries would get – because special flame dampers on the exhaust stacks hid the fire. "They narrowed the exhaust stacks down to a narrow slit and extended them about six inches," Harmer explains.

The early night fighter Corsairs occasionally spewed oil on the windscreen. This film could be overlooked in the bright daylight if it did not get too thick, but in dim night light, it was sufficient to blind the pilot to the outside world, Harmer says. So the Naval Aircraft Factory in Philadelphia modified the aircraft with the installation of a perforated copper tube in front of the centre windscreen panel which squirted a flammable cleaning fluid under pressure from a special cockpit-mounted hand pump. "After one or two squirts, it was just like someone lifted a curtain," Lieutenant Commander Harmer recalls.

An experienced Naval aviator with time in both Hellcats and Corsairs, Harmer has definite opinions about the two friendly rivals. "As a night fighter, the Corsair was a steadier platform; I felt better in it. But the F6F was such an easy-flying airplane, it was an old friend." Adding that the F6F Hellcat was a more forgiving fighter to fly, Harmer says he might choose to use Hellcats instead of Corsairs for a night fighter squadron if the experience levels of some of the pilots were low. From bitter experience, Harmer knows the Corsair and new pilots don't mix for carrier operations, whereas the stable Hellcat works well, keeping more of a squadron's aircraft intact if pilots are green.

Harmer got back together with the Corsair during the Korean War, flying F4U-5N night fighters on nocturnal convoy raids. He says the radar in the aircraft was not used to spot ground targets, but was an aid in homing in on the friendly fleet on the flight home. Corsair carrier crashes were not then a major issue. "I think the people were better trained" by the time of the Korean War, he explained.

In the years between World War II and the Korean fighting, squadrons like VMF-123, a Marine Corsair reserve outfit at Los Alamitos, California, were filled with ex-wartime fliers with experience. Such a pilot was W. Buckner Hanner whose previous Marine experience included flying most types of fighters in tests, as well as North American PBJ versions of the B-25 Mitchell twin-engine bomber.

"The Corsair, compared to any other fighter I've flown, is like comparing a Cadillac to a Model T." For Hanner, one word sums up his hours in the F4U: "Exhilarating!" But he is quick to recall that landing the Corsair took an extra measure of skill and practice. All landings, whether actually on an aircraft carrier or at a shore base, were executed in carrier-approach style for practice and consistency. A nose-high descent in a lefthand turn brought the Corsair to its final approach. On the base leg of the pattern, just before turning on final approach, Hanner remembers looking out to the left to make sure no other traffic was still on the runway.

Then, when the big-nosed F4U-4 turned onto final, the runway was obscured from view, leaving Hanner to pray "God, I hope there's nobody on that runway!" During the pattern approach, Hanner would be cranking in a total of 20 degrees right rudder trim, balancing this with a rudder pedal offset to the left. But the 20-degree input was vital, he says, in the event of a go-around, whether at sea or on land. Without that right rudder trim, the massive addition of power needed for a go-around could very well put the Corsair on its back in a vicious – and usually fatal – roll to the left from torque.

Carrying power down on final approach, the fuel mixture would be set full rich and the propeller pitch selector lever all the way forward for flat pitch. Then, if a go-around was signalled, the addition of power would be most efficiently transmitted to the huge propeller for quick acceleration. If the landing looked good, the throttle was chopped, and "you're all through", as the Corsair would drop quickly with the power off. Once on the ground, the long high nose still obstructed forward vision, so the Corsair pilot would look to the right or left, trying to keep his big Vought rolling parallel with the side of the runway as an indicator he was on path, Hanner says. With speed finally bled off to a taxi, it was mandatory to S-turn the big Corsair to get a glimpse of the ramp ahead by turning the big nose first to one side and then the other.

Jeff Dorroh, Richard Harmer and Buck Hanner each flew both Hellcats and Corsairs, and all concluded, in their own ways, that the Hellcat was an easier aircraft to fly, and therefore might have wider appeal among squadrons of relatively inexperienced fliers, where the F6F's ease of operation and maintenance could allow squadrons to put up greater numbers. But, for the performance edge, there was nothing to match the powerful Corsair in the hands of a precision aviator.

Mechanics and their F4U-1A at Torokina Point, Bougainville Island. (USMC via Vought)

SPITFIRE

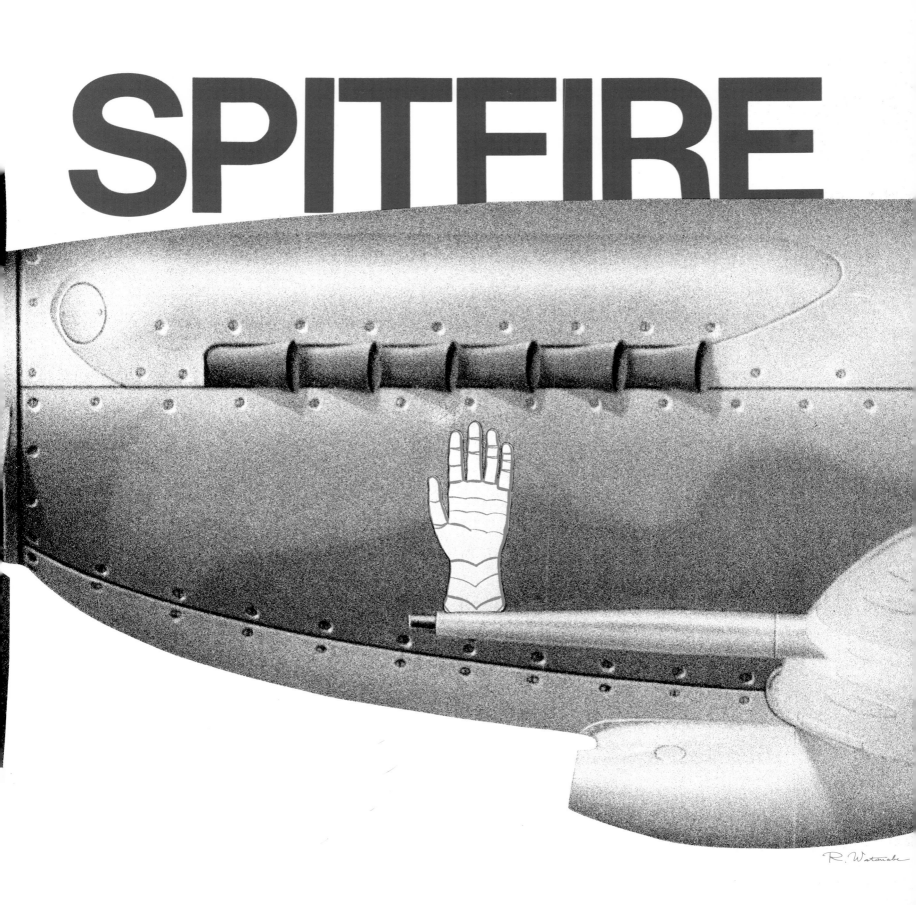

Text by Bill Sweetman

Spitfire control column head with
oamera switch and (Va model only)
gunfiring button.

Spitfire MX IID Gyro gun sight

Control Column and Rudder Pedal Assembly

1 Gun firing button
2 Brake operating lever
3 Control column chain
4 Brake operating cable
5 Rudder pedal
6 Rudder pedal adjustment star wheel
7 Aileron torque shaft
8 Cable drum
9 Elevator lever

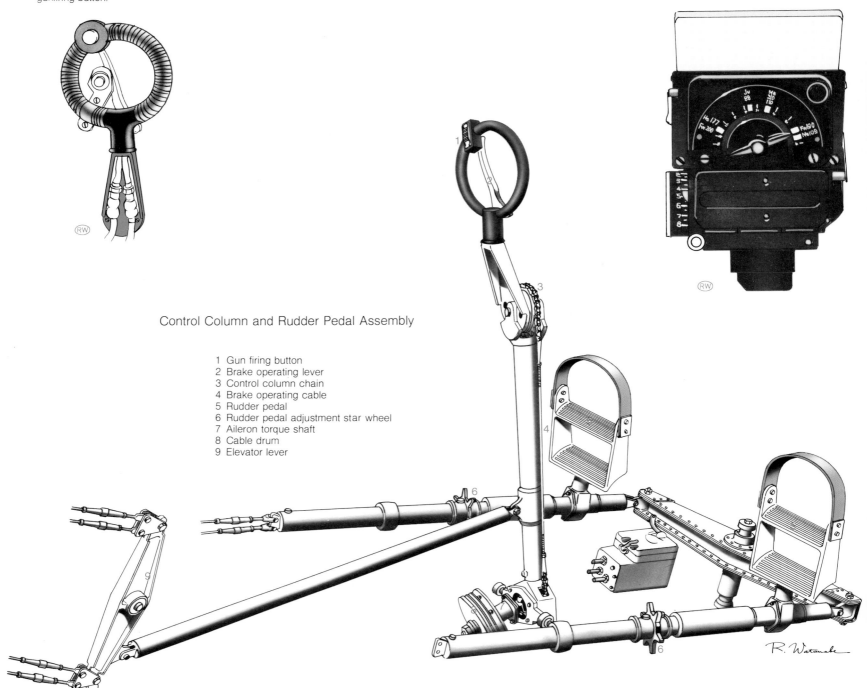

R. Watanabe

Something about a Spitfire

There are few of mankind's artifacts which have stood for so much in the consciousness of an entire nation as the Spitfire. Those to whom the Spitfire is part of history—and this number includes the author—can experience only at second-hand the identification of the graceful shape of the Supermarine fighter with that 'finest hour' of tension and conflict—yet it was of that identification that the legend was made.

The fact that the Hurricane—the dashing Spitfire's trusty but unimaginative esquire—bore by far the greatest weight of the Battle of Britain, and that without the sturdy and easily built Hawker fighter the control of the air over Southern England would have been lost, seem to count for nothing. The Hurricane was just never photogenic; it looked like a monoplane which had not quite shrugged off the chrysalis of the biplane. But neither are the inevitable deficiencies of the Spitfire taken into account in the formation of the legend: it was a production engineer's nightmare, a torment for the armourer and a tricky and weak-kneed carrier fighter. This is not to denigrate the design, but to view it as simply one more military aircraft.

But there is one respect in which the Spitfire and Seafire are equalled by no other aircraft in history: development. The Spitfire was one of the first all-metal, low-wing, retractable-undercarriage, enclosed-canopy monoplane fighters, but it was also one of the last to remain in production, only the Sea Fury and Corsair (both of much later design) outlasting it. In the eleven years between the delivery of the first Spitfire I and the completion of the last Seafire FR.47, a constant and dynamic development process, ever flexible and always ready to incorporate the latest technology, had kept the fighter fully competitive with its contemporaries.

The Spitfire was conceived when the importance of speed and rate of climb was beginning to be recognised. Turning performance had been sacrificed to some extent with the demise of the biplane, while forward and downward vision was traded off against lower drag with the move from the Supermarine 224, built for the F.7/30 contest, to the Type 300 Spitfire. However, what had not been foreseen was the extent to which success in combat was to depend on the advantages of momentum and surprise, calling as never before on speed and rate of climb to give the fighter leader the option of giving or refusing combat. Of equal importance was the firepower to deal out a lethal burst before concentration on the target proved fatal.

It was in the crucial aspects of speed, rate of climb and firepower that the Spitfire was developed as no other aircraft has been. Compare the mighty FR.47 with the dainty Spitfire I: Top speed, 25 per cent greater; time to 20,000 ft (6,100 m), 49 per cent less; weight of fire per second, trebled. The increased performance meant more power, a hefty 128 per cent more in point of fact, delivered through a massive six-blade contraprop instead of a two-blade fixed-pitch airscrew. Part of the 111 per cent weight increase was accounted for by 81 per cent more fuel to slake the thirst of the Griffon engine; part by the heavier armament; another slice by the 80 per cent heavier powerplant, and the rest by the extra stainless steel and aluminum required to make the thing hang together. All in all, the resulting Seafire FR.47 had barely a component in common with the Spitfire I, but retained the general arrangement and the balance of flying qualities which had characterised the original.

Development of the Spitfire was the result of two factors: the massive increase in power made available from a package of broadly similar dimensions—and, particularly, similar cross-sectional area—and the ability of the airframe to absorb such power. The former was the product of the intense development efforts which Rolls-Royce placed on the design of mechanical supercharging systems from the late 1920s, allowing the increase of power without increase in cross-section area. An equally important engine development was the design of the Griffon engine to offer 36 per cent more capacity in a package the same size as a Merlin.

The ability of the airframe to take such power, however, is barely comprehensible. It stemmed from the fact that the wing was both large enough in area to support the consequent weight growth and thin enough in section to avoid the problems of 'compressibility' which would have cropped up with a thicker wing as fighting speeds increased. The risk inherent in designing such a wing is that it will be either excessively heavy or insufficiently rigid, but the wing of the Spitfire was designed in such a way that it avoided both risks. Admittedly, a lack of torsional rigidity in the wing affected the Spitfire's ability to roll in a high-speed dive, at least until the Mark 21 appeared, but in the test of combat this defect was never proved crucial until the late stages of the war.

It was the great span of the Spitfire's wing which endowed it with lower induced drag—air resistance related to lift—than its contemporaries, while the thin section freed it from the profile drag which limited the Hurricane. Its aerodynamic efficiency was therefore outstanding, particularly at the high altitudes and relatively low air speeds where induced drag becomes of greatest importance. Hence the Spitfire's outstanding turning performance at low airspeeds, and the ease with which it was adapted as a high-altitude strategic reconnaissance aircraft.

One can only wonder how much R.J. Mitchell foresaw of the future development of the little fighter which he watched on its maiden flight in March, 1936. Mitchell himself had little more than a year to live; and the design of the Spitfire was redolent of second sight, the last inspired work of a dying artist.

Creation of a Legend

There must be as many legends surrounding the story of the Supermarine Type 300 Spitfire and its many descendants as there were examples of the aircraft itself. This is a pity, because the facts are themselves remarkable enough. What distinguishes the Spitfire from almost all other aircraft which can be accurately described as 'classic' is that neither its forbears nor its descendants can make any claim whatsoever to that status. The quality of the Spitfire, both in its basic design and its prodigious capacity for development, was apparently an unrepeatable combination of elements, a classic case of the whole being greater than the sum of its parts. Had you told a seasoned aviation observer in 1930 that the next generation of fighting aircraft for the Royal Air Force would be predominantly of Supermarine design, he would have nodded and smiled politely; if you had told the same man in 1945 that within two generations of aircraft the Supermarine name would have vanished completely, he would probably have considered you insane. However, that is exactly what did happen: the name of Supermarine came and went, leaving the world's most famous aircraft as its memorial.

The name itself was coined in September, 1913, when it was adopted as the telegraphic address of a small aircraft factory on a Southampton wharf. Its founder, Noel Pemberton-Billing, was an enthusiastic aviator and designer of indifferent marine aircraft, some of which were distinguished by removable wings without which the hull was intended to function as a cabin cruiser. In 1917, after a career with the Royal Naval Air Service, Pemberton-Billing entered Parliament and on one occasion was expelled from the chamber when his expostulations against the unprepared state of the British air defences grew too extreme.

The factory he founded, which in a later conflict was to be synonymous with those defences, was by this time in other hands. Headed by Hugh Scott-Paine, the Supermarine Aviation Works had in 1916 employed a 21-year-old engineer from the Midlands, named Reginald J. Mitchell. Within three years he was the company's chief designer: a high-sounding position, but less secure than it might have been given the state of British aviation at the time. Post-war cuts in military expenditure had hit the emerging Royal Air Force heavily—the Cinderella service's two older and uglier sisters had more political muscle and no interest in a third independent service—and the consequent sales of redundant military aircraft reduced the market for new commercial aircraft to virtually zero. However, the company continued to produce small marine aircraft sharing a similar basic layout: biplane wings with the engine between them, above the hull. Not only was this basic layout visible in service for the next 20 years, in the comfortingly sturdy shape of the Walrus rescue and reconnaissance amphibian, but despite its apparent lack of aerodynamic qualities it succeeded in winning races, bringing the Schneider Trophy back to Britain in 1922.

By that time, however, the Schneider Trophy seaplane race was on its way to becoming a contest of international machismo on a grand scale. The races of the 1923 and subsequent years would see a strong field of much more modern competitors, with speeds rising from the 145 mph (233 km/h) of the 1922 winner to well above 200 mph (320 km/h). Mitchell and his team—which now included another young Midlander, Joe Smith—set to work on a radical new machine which would beat even the US navy's purpose-built Curtiss racers.

After a brief flirtation with a flying-boat design in which the propeller was to be driven via shafts and gearing from an engine buried in the hull, R.J. Mitchell drew up the

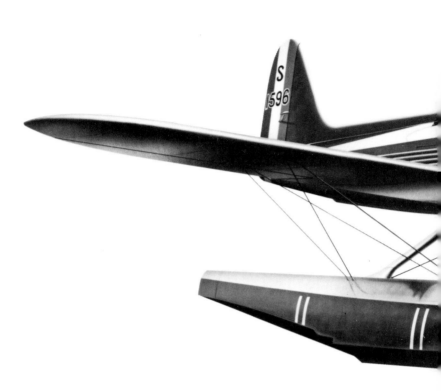

Supermarine S.6B (S1695), winner of the final 1931 Schneider Trophy race at an average speed of 340.08 mph (547.29 km/h). This and the subsequent new speed record of 408.8 mph (657.88 km/h) were achieved thanks to very careful streamlining combined with (for those days) high wing loading and the light water-cooled Rolls-Royce R engine developing 2300 hp at only 1630 lb (739.4 kg) weight.

design of a seaplane called the S.4. The new floatplane was flown for the first time in August, 1925, a mere five months after receipt of an Air Ministry contract to develop a high-speed seaplane 'for research purposes.' The most revolutionary feature of the S.4 was its unbraced (cantilever) monoplane wing, and this may also have been its weakest point. After setting a new world air speed record, the S.4 crashed in practice over the 1925 Schneider course at Baltimore. Not enough of the thin plywood wing was fished from the harbour to permit the cause of the accident to be determined, but Mitchell's later seaplanes reverted to streamlined bracing wires on their wings. They also had all-metal fuselages instead of the wooden structure of the S.4.

In the 1927 race at Venice, Mitchell's less lovely but sturdier S.5 took the first of three successive victories for the British Government team. The S.5, like the S.4, was powered by a Napier Lion engine with a 'broad arrow' configuration, having three banks of four cylinders converging from above on a single crankshaft. The US victors of the 1923 race at Cowes, however, had sparked off a chain of events that was to provide a powerplant not only for the last and fastest of the Supermarine racers, but also for their more warlike descendants.

British aircraft manufacturer C.R. Fairey had been among the spectators in 1923 as Lt. David Rittenhouse raced the Curtiss CR-3 to victory. He was more impressed, however, by the racer's powerplant, a narrow-angle V-12 engine of 'monobloc' construction—the cylinders were cast into a solid block rather than comprising separate liners and cooling jackets. Arthur Nutt's Curtiss D-12 offered a tremendous

R. Watanabe

advantage in streamlining over the bulky wartime engines then in service. A month after the race, Fairey had agreed with Curtiss to import a batch of D-12s, with an option on licence production, and had started the design of a light bomber based on the American engine.

The speed performance of the resulting Fairey Fox was sensational, but its impact was hardly what Fairey had anticipated. The Air Ministry remained profoundly uninterested in buying large quantities of Foxes powered by Curtiss-Fairey engines, and instead dispatched a D-12 (called the Felix in Britain) to Rolls-Royce. The august British company dropped its first postwar development, the powerful but complex Eagle 16, and produced a narrow-angle V-12. At first referred to as the Falcon X, the engine later became known as the Rolls-Royce F before being finally christened the Kestrel, and it was Kestrel-powered, Hawker-built Harts rather than Foxes which became the RAF's fastest light bombers.

It was a call to patriotism that persuaded Rolls-Royce to convert its scaled-up Kestrel, the 36.7-litre Buzzard, into a racing engine for Mitchell's 1929 Schneider contender, the S.6. (Racing was, of course, anathema to the utterly conservative Derby company.) The ingredient which Rolls-Royce added to the basic V-12 engine to produce the R racing powerplant was a massive mechanically driven supercharger, with a centrifugal rotor tailored to the S.6 fuselage. The advantages of supercharging were many; above all, the compression of the air before induction into the engine increased the power output without the increase in weight and frontal area which would have been incurred had the engine simply been scaled up. The supercharger was moreover fed by a ram inlet, gaining extra compression and power virtually as a free by-product of the aircraft's forward speed.

By 1931, when the ultimate S.6B set a world's air speed record at 407 mph (655 km/hr), the R engine was generating 2,530 hp. This was a long way from a service rating; after every full-power run, the engine had to be stripped and overhauled, and its consumption of a specially developed cocktail of benzol, methanol, acetone and lead was phenomenal. As well as pioneering the use of high supercharger boost ratios, the R was the first Rolls-Royce engine to feature high-strength aluminum forgings and sodium-cooled valves.

At that time Rolls-Royce's military hopes largely rested on the Goshawk, an engine closely related to the Kestrel but featuring a novel system of cooling in which the water was allowed to boil and was then condensed into steam in pressurised surface radiators. This powerplant was embodied in several of the designs being prepared to meet Air Ministry specification F.7/30, which called for a new 250 mph fighter for the RAF.

One of the designs was from Supermarine, which had been taken over by armaments giant Vickers-Armstrong in 1928. (Vickers had its own aviation division, which remained in business separately and produced the Jockey fighter to F.7/30.) However, neither Supermarine nor Vickers nor Rolls-Royce emerged victorious from the F.7/30 competition, since the conservative evolutionary design of the Bristol-powered Gloster Gauntlet biplane turned out to meet what had been regarded as revolutionary specifications. For Supermarine and Rolls-Royce, it was time to adopt a policy of *reculer pour mieux sauter*.

Flown in February, 1934, the Supermarine F.7/30 or Type 224 was a mix of old and new. The wing was of cantilever design, but the type featured a fixed undercarriage and a fixed-pitch propeller and lacked landing flaps. Retractable gear, variable-pitch propellers and split flaps had been demonstrated on the American Douglas DC-1 airliner in the previous year, and the airframe of the 224 was similar in its technology level to that of the Boeing P-26 of 1932. Flight-testing of the Goshawk in the 224 and other F.7/30 contenders was also to prove that steam-cooling (or surface evaporation cooling) was not a practical proposition for combat aircraft. A beneficial result of this failure was that the British industry avoided the long flirtation with zero-drag evaporative cooling which was to plague many German aircraft programmes.

In any event, developments in aviation between the issue of F.7/30 and the appearance of the prototypes designed to meet it had rendered the specification obsolete. The appearance of the Heinkel He70 Blitz light transport in late 1932 had confirmed that Germany was not far behind the United States in airframe technology. F.7/30 had been founded on the premise that higher speeds would be needed if aircraft comparable to the Hart were to be intercepted successfully; only something altogether more potent would suffice if an enemy was to introduce a bomber based on the 1933 technology of the Blitz or the DC-1. It was also becoming accepted that the tight-turning dogfight of the 1914-18 war was no longer the

K5054, one of the most famous of aircraft prototypes. Accepted by the Air Ministry for construction in January, 1935, it first flew on 5 March, 1936.

(Imperial War Museum)

best way to prevent an escorted bomber force from reaching its target; speed to overhaul an enemy aircraft, and firepower to destroy it in a single burst, became the targets of the aircraft industry.

The Royal Air Force, responsible for drawing up specifications for such aircraft, had survived the savage blows of the immediate post-war era, and in 1923 won the significant victory of parity in authority with the Army and Navy. Under Stanley Baldwin's administration some sort of air-defence force and organisation had been created. In the absence of any device for giving advance warning of the approach of enemy bombers, however, defence against air attack was regarded as of low priority. Fighter development advanced hardly at all between 1920 and 1930, and production of the Fury was curtailed in favour of the cheaper but slower Bulldog. Defence spending in general was governed by the 'ten-year-rule,' which laid down that hostilities in Europe would be heralded by ten years of increasing tension. This policy ceased to carry weight from 1930 onwards, and, although the Air Estimates remained constant through 1932-34, spending virtually trebled over the next two years and rose by another 50 per cent in 1936-38. The years of 1934-36 were not unnaturally a period of great fertility in new technical ideas.

As often happens in the development of aircraft, it was the engine manufacturer which made the first move. By 1932, possibly in anticipation of trouble with the Goshawk, Rolls-Royce was working on an engine 20 per cent bigger than the Kestrel but using some of the racing engines' technology to yield an output similar to that of the much larger Buzzard. Initially, Rolls-Royce proposed that the engine should be inverted to allow the pilot a better view over the nose, but manufacturers reactions to this unfamiliar arrangement were negative. Accordingly, it was an upright V-12 engine which made its first run in November, 1933. Known as the PV-12, it was later to join the other birds of prey in the company aviary as the Merlin.

The Merlin was designed to yield about 1,000 hp for combat, in its initial service version. The ratio of supercharger speed to crankshaft speed was fixed. In consequence the speed of the supercharger could not be adjusted to cope with variations in atmospheric pressure at various altitudes.

The engine thus had to be throttled back to prevent excess pressure, detonation and damage below the altitude at which the supercharger and engine were best matched: the 'rated altitude' at which the engine would give its best power. This 'tuning' of the engine to the role performed by any particular variant of the aircraft was a highly important factor in the versatility of the aircraft powered by the Merlin.

Another element of the Spitfire's design originated in 1933, when the Armament Research Department of the Air Ministry organised a design competition to find a replacement for the Vickers machine-gun. The 1914-18-vintage Vickers was so prone to jam that it had to be located within the pilot's reach. It hence fired through the airscrew disc, incurring penalties in rate of fire and the complexity of a mechanical synchronising system. The American 0.300-in Colt was selected from a field of six weapons as the best basis for a replacement and was put into production as the Browning, firing standard British 0.303-in ammunition.

By early 1934, the Air Ministry was looking for a new fighter to carry these weapons, and was suggesting that it should be ten per cent faster than the Gladiator (a refined version of the F.7/30-winning Gauntlet). Hawker responded with a monoplane incorporating several features of the Fury, while Supermarine's proposal was a refined extrapolation of the disappointing 224 featuring a retractable undercarriage, enclosed cockpit and split flaps on a smaller wing. Both were offered with the Goshawk until late 1934, when steam-cooling was abandoned in favour of the new PV-12, and were armed with four wing-mounted machine guns. At the beginning of 1935 the manufacturers received specification F.37/34, written around their new aircraft, and in the course of the year the Air Ministry decided to investigate the possibility of installing no fewer than eight of the new machine guns to give greater lethality against the new twin-engined bombers then under development in Germany. This requirement, set out in specification F.10/35, suggested that the eight guns might be made movable in some way; armament policy was not irrevocably committed to the use of eight machine guns, and in late 1934 the rival concept of the two-seat turret fighter was being pursued in parallel with the Supermarine and Hawker fixed-gun studies.

Throughout 1935 R.J. Mitchell led his team in the

creation of the Supermarine Type 300, probably aware that he might never live to see it fly; he had fallen victim in 1933 to the cancer which was to kill him four years later. Joe Smith later recalled the chief designer's technique: 'He would modify the lines of an aircraft with the softest pencil he could find, and then remodel over the top with progressively thicker lines, until one would finally be faced with a new outline of lines about 3/16ths of an inch thick. But the results were usually worthwhile and the centre of the line was usually accepted when the thing was redrawn.' In this way the shape of the Spitfire emerged from the chrysalis of the 224. To begin with, the 224 fuselage could be modified in light of the relaxation of requirements on forward view in favour of greater speed. The fuselage of the new aircraft was faired neatly from the PV-12 engine and supercharger, flowing past the tightly hooded cockpit in unbroken straight lines to the tail in the original manner of the S.4 and its successors.

The wing was the unique feature which was to distinguish the Spitfire from all its contemporaries and endow it with most of its outstanding qualities. That the elliptical wing shape represented something close to an ideal had been acknowledged for some years. It combined the long span needed for aerodynamic efficiency at high altitudes with some of the structural attributes of a short-span wing, because so much of its area was carried well inboard. The comparatively long chord of the wing roots meant that the landing gear and (in early 1935) four-gun armament of the Type 300 could be buried completely within a wing of low thickness-to-chord ratio and correspondingly low drag. (After the unhappy experience with the thick wing of the 224, this consideration must have weighed heavily on Mitchell's mind.) Eventually, the Type 300 emerged with a wing section thinner than any other fighter of its day, and this was probably the most important factor in the extraordinary potential for development which it was to display over the next ten years.

The structure of the wing was unique, and in part a legacy from the 224. The steam-cooling system of the Goshawk engine demanded that the entire leading edge of the wing be devoted to condensers, and to this end the leading edge forward of the single mainspar was sealed and formed into a structural torsion box. This technique was refined on the 300 to provide sufficient stiffness and strength in the thin, large-area wing. The mainspar itself was formed of square-section tubes 'telescoped' together so that the narrowest and longest extended to the tip of the wing; the number of concentric tubes forming the spar decreased from root to tip. The spar was close to the structural ideal, being tapered in fore-and-aft and up-and-down axes, and nowhere thicker than it had to be. The spar could also be fairly readily 'beefed up' in development by extending the inner tube sections. The wing ribs forward of the spar and the heavy-gauge skin of the leading edge formed the rest of the torsion box that gave the wing its strength and light weight. Later in the development of the Spitfire it was found how exactly R.J. Mitchell and Joe Smith had tailored the strength of the wing to the job which it had to do.

The Spitfire was to take advantage of two other innovations before it reached the RAF squadrons. Possibly the most important was the ducted radiator developed at the Royal Aircraft Establishment, Farnborough, which considerably reduced the extra drag incurred with the replacement of the surface-evaporation-cooled Goshawk by the PV-12. Instead of being simply thrust out into the airflow, the radiator was housed in an aerodynamic duct which was designed so that some of the heat shed by the radiator was recovered in the form of thrust as the heated air escaped from the duct. Another new feature, similarly offering a benefit from otherwise wasted energy, was the ejector exhaust nozzle, which simply directed the energy of the escaping exhaust rearwards. The extra power was worth about 70 hp at 300 mph.

The move to an eight-gun armament in the course of 1935 reduced the new fighter's fuel capacity, which in any event was based on home-defence requirements. From the initially specified 94 Imp gal (427 lit), adequate for two hours at cruise power and half an hour's combat, capacity was reduced to 85 Imp gal (378 lit) enough for 1.65 hours cruising and 15 minutes combat. Range and endurance were never improved to the point where the Spitfire could be compared with later fighter aircraft, although some of the breed were, paradoxically, among the longest-ranged single-engined aircraft of the war years.

At the time of the new type's first flight from

Spitfire F.Mk Ia of No 19 Sqn.

(Imperial War Museum)

275

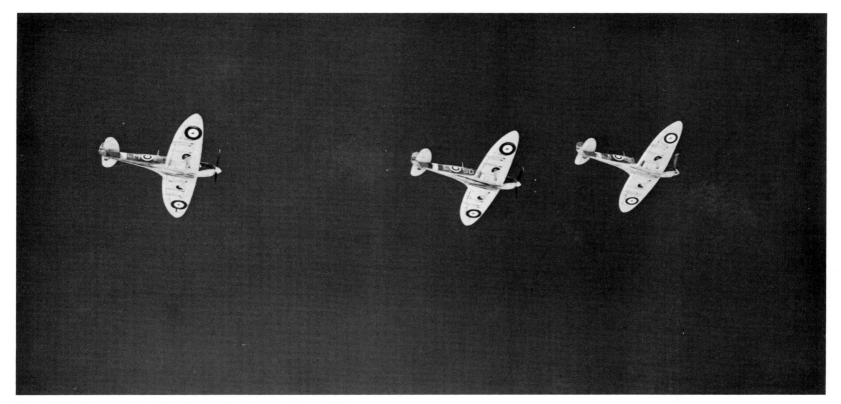

Three Spitfire F.Mk Ia fighters of No 501 (Auxiliary) Sqn in autumn, 1940.

Southampton's Eastleigh airport on 6 March, 1936, it was still referred to in public as the F.37/34; by July of that year the name 'Spitfire' had been officially adopted, but is not clear at what point the aircraft had been christened. The new aircraft changed little during its flight tests, beyond the addition of the newly developed ejector exhausts, camouflage and armament. It was rapidly realized that it was both faster and more manoeuvrable than its Hawker contemporary, by then named Hurricane, and in June, 1936, the Air Ministry ordered 310 Spitfire Is.

The first Spitfire production order formed part of Scheme F, the latest of a series of expansion plans for the RAF; the very first had appeared in mid-1934 as developments in Europe became perceptibly more threatening. Scheme F was the first to include modern fighters, but although earlier schemes were to be criticised as encouraging the production of obsolescent aircraft, they had been invaluable in building up a trained workforce before the new designs were ready to be put into production. In addition, facilities used for cars and commercial vehicles in peacetime were designated as 'shadow factories' for the construction of military aircraft. The Spitfire was due to be built at the Nuffield factory at Castle Bromwich.

Scheme F called for 310 Spitfires to be delivered by March, 1939, but the program soon slipped behind schedule. There were two basic reasons for this. The first, which also affected the Hurricane, was the delayed development of the Merlin engine. In March, 1937, the prototype Spitfire belly-landed after a connecting rod failed. The original Merlin C had failed its 100-hour type test in the month the Spitfire flew, while the initial production Merlin (Merlin F or Merlin I) only passed its type test with a limitation on valve life in November, 1936. It was decided to apply this engine to the Fairey Battle bomber and fit the new fighters with the improved Merlin II, and this understandably caused some delay.

The other problem was confined to the Spitfire. Whereas the Hurricane was structurally still closely related to its ancestor the Fury, the Spitfire introduced stressed-skin construction throughout (apart from fabric-covered control surfaces). New techniques had to be devised to mass-produce the new fighter's sophisticated airframe, the Pressed Steel Company's work on the production of the complicated mainspar being particularly noteworthy. However, by September, 1939 only 306 Spitfires had been delivered, six months after the scheduled handover date for the last of the initial 310-aircraft order. By that time, however, production of the Hurricane and Spitfire—together, it is easily forgotten, with that of the misconceived Defiant—was in full swing.

A number of changes were either introduced in the production of the Spitfire I or incorporated during the early production stages. After early service experience the flat-topped cockpit canopy, which tall pilots had found a little restrictive, was replaced with the characteristic bulged hood from the Malcolm Company. A fixed tailwheel replaced the prototype's skid. A more significant change came about from the 78th aircraft, which was the first to boast a three-blade metal two-pitch propeller made by de Havilland. From the 175th aircraft the Merlin III was standardised, this engine being modified to yield about 10 per cent more power than the Merlin II at a slightly lower altitude.

The manually controlled two-pitch airscrew was a considerable advance, reducing the take-off run by 30 per cent and increasing the speed of fastest climb from 175 mph (281 km/hr) to 192 mph (310 km/hr). However, it created another problem for the pilot: it was all to easy to forget, and the propeller was a poor substitute for a genuine constant-speed unit which would automatically adjust the pitch of the blades to the speed of the aircraft.

This, then, was the standard Spitfire at the outbreak of war, after the ironing out of remarkably few prob-

Spitfire Mk Vb

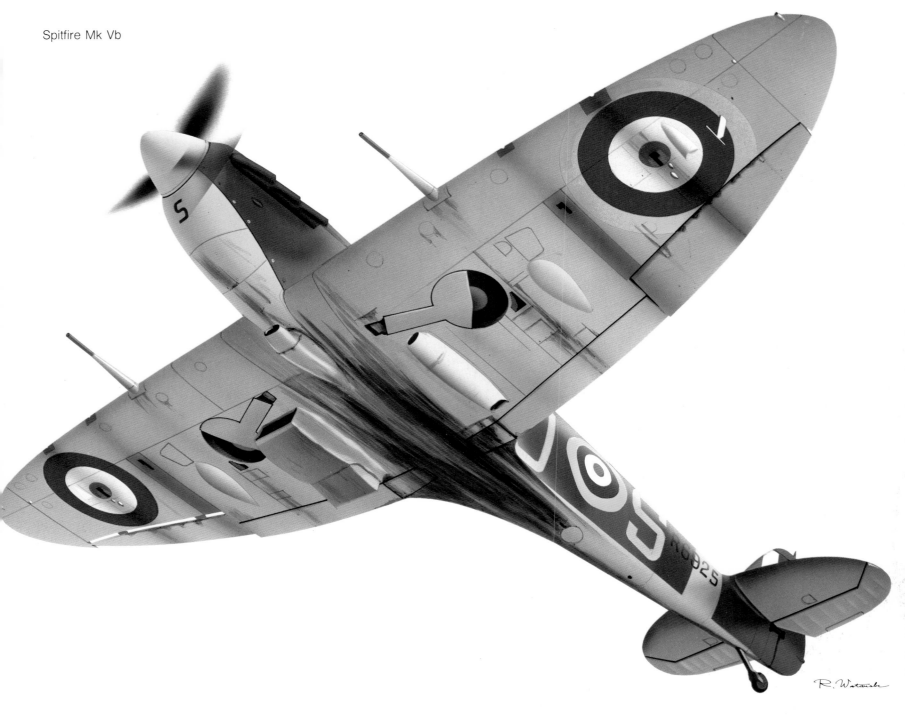

Armour protection

1 Front of header tank
2 Ammunition boxes
3 Front of fuel tank
4 Top of fuel tank
   (cowling panel)

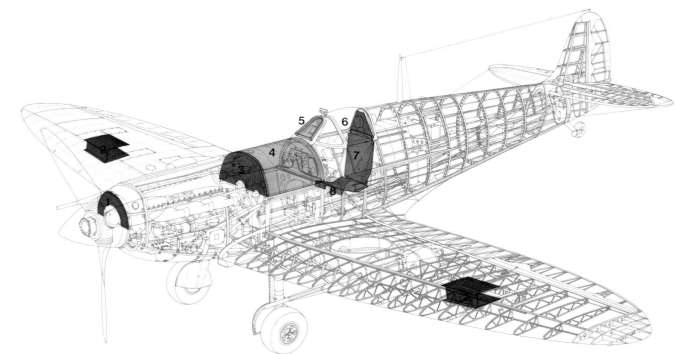

5 Windscreen
6 Pilot's head
7 Back of pilot's seat
8 Bottom of pilot's seat

Spitfire Mk IA, N3029 'K' of 610 'County of Chester' Sqn, based at Biggin Hill.
The N3029 'K' was one of the second production batch of two hundred Mk Is
ordered from Supermarine in 1937. It took part in the Battle of Britain but was
lost on 8 January, 1943, while being shipped overseas—after having surived four
years of air combat.

1m

1   2   3   ft

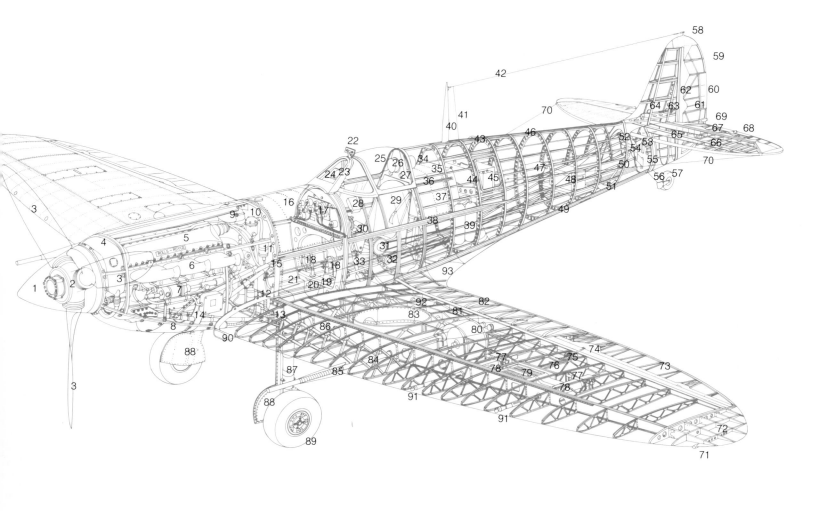

ermarine Spitfire Vb Cutaway

inner
opeller hub
tol, R.X. 5/10 35° pitch range three-blade
nstant-speed propeller
ycol header tank
lls-Royce Merlin 45 engine
shtail' exhaust manifold
enerator
posed oil tank
draulic tank
ewall
filter
el filter
pipe
in engine support member
gine bearer attachment
in fuselage fuel tank (48 Imp. gal/218 ltr)
trument panel
dder pedals
dder bar
g post
selage lower fuel tank (37 Imp. gal/168 ltr)
ar-view mirror
lector gunsight
oured windscreen
xiglass canopy
adrest
uctural bulkhead
dio controller
t's seat

30 Engine control lever
31 Elevator trim controller
32 Rudder tab controller
33 Control column
34 Voltage regulator
35 Cockpit aft glazing
36 Canopy track
37 Auxiliary long-range fuel tank (29 Imp. gal/132 ltr)
38 Datum longeron
39 Air bottles (alternative rear fuselage stowage)
40 Aerial mast
41 Aerial lead-in
42 HF aerial
43 Dorsal formation light
44 Radio compartment
45 Access door
46 Backbone longeron
47 Rear oxygen bottle
48 Battery compartment
49 Lower longeron
50 Tailwheel oleo shock-absorber
51 Fuselage angled frame
52 Elevator control lever
53 Rudder control lever
54 Cross shaft
55 Fuselage double frame
56 Tailwheel strut
57 Castoring non-retractable tailwheel
58 Aerial stub attachment
59 Fabric-covered rudder
60 Rudder tab
61 Rudder tab hinge
62 Sternpost

63 Fin rear spar (fuselage frame extension)
64 Fin front spar (fuselage frame extension)
65 Tailplane front spar
66 Port tailplane
67 Port elevator
68 Elevator tab
69 Rear navigation light
70 IFF aerial
71 Port navigation light
72 Wingtip structure
73 Port aileron construction
74 Aileron hinge
75 Bellcrank
76 Aileron push tube
77 Machine-gun support brackets
78 0.303-in machine-gun, with 350 rounds of ammunition
79 Ammunition boxes (350 rpg)
80 Cannon magazine drum (120 rounds)
81 Aileron control cables
82 Flap structure
83 Mainwheel well
84 Hispano 20mm cannon, with 120 rounds of ammunition
85 Cannon barrel support fairing
86 Main spar
87 Mainwheel leg shock-absorber
88 Mainwheel fairing
89 Mainwheel
90 Carburettor air intake
91 Machine-gun ports
92 Gun heating pipe
93 Wingroot fillet

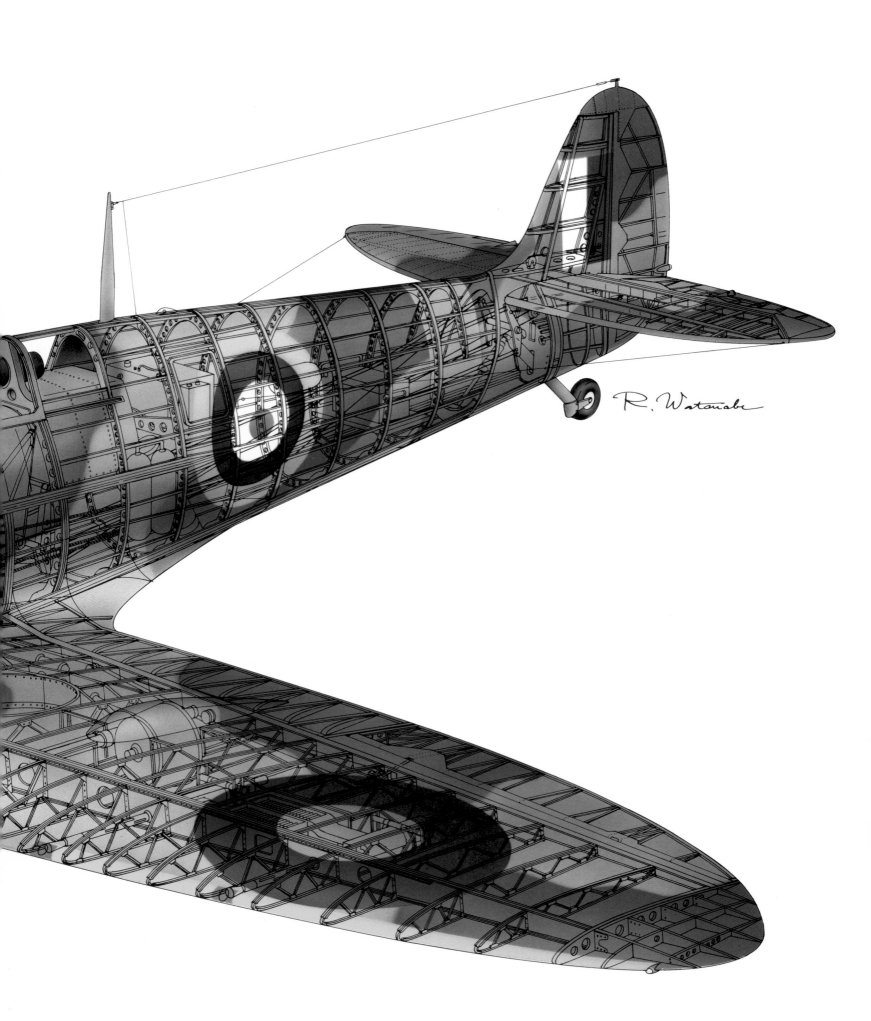

R. Watanabe

lems and the inevitable lag in the introduction of some of the features of the definitive service aircraft. By September, 1939, however, the Spitfire had revealed little of its true class. Technically and operationally, the most remarkable part of the story was still to unfold.

Room for Improvement —1

Most of the Spitfires built before mid-1942 were broadly similar, at least three major groups of modified aircraft appearing on the scene thereafter. The first group, however, can be identified by one common feature: their Merlin engines were supercharged by a single centrifugal impeller stage, and were similar enough in general layout to be interchangeable. Built in larger numbers than subsequent 'generations,' they pioneered many of the armament and systems variations later to be available on the Spitfire, and thus existed in a vast range of subtypes and variants.

The first Spitfire I variant to appear was a one-off type, and the second an improvisation, and both were capable of extremely high performance. The first was the High Speed Spitfire N17, and the second was the start of a long series of Spitfires modified for strategic reconnaissance. The different degrees of success enjoyed by the two aircraft indicate some of the Spitfire's stronger and weaker points.

The High Speed Spitfire was based on a standard aircraft, just as Germany's 463 mph He100 record-breaker was adapted from an experimental fighter, and was in sharp contrast to the purpose-built Messerschmitt Me209V1. It was the He100's run which put paid to Supermarine's hopes of the record even before any attempt was made. However, the exercise was not a complete waste of time. The airframe modification, admittedly, had little direct relevance to a production aircraft. A low-drag, curved windscreen was fitted, and the radiators were removed. A large detachable radiator bath was fitted for normal flight testing, and for the record run an enlarged coolant tank was to be used and the coolant simply allowed to boil away. The two-bladed propeller of the standard aircraft was replaced by a fine-pitch four-bladed wooden propeller optimised for high speed. The airframe was polished to achieve the smoothest possible finish, and the wingtips were clipped.

The High Speed Spitfire's engine was a harbinger of what the Merlin would later achieve under service conditions. It was a stock engine apart from strengthened connecting rods, pistons and gudgeon pins, and was not only rated at 2,160 hp for a record run but managed a 15-hour endurance test at 1,800 hp. Even with the aid of a racing cocktail similar to the brew used for the Schneider Trophy engines, this was a remarkable performance. The High Speed Spitfire was expected to attain 410 mph at sea level, slower than the maximum speed at altitude of many subsequent service Spitfires.

In November, 1939, the Photographic Development Unit (PDU, later the Photographic Reconnaissance Unit or PRU) at Heston put into service the second Spitfire I derivative, starting a series of photographic reconnaissance Spitfires. Specially converted from standard production aircraft, these were originally designated Spitfire A and B and so on. The Spitfire A was an unarmed, cleaned-up Spitfire I, but in the course of time the series was to embrace much more extensive modifications of the standard aircraft, with extra fuel and oil capacity. The PDU was led by Sidney Cotton, who had laid the foundations for aerial reconnaissance of Germany before the war in a Lockheed transport fitted with concealed cameras. The PR Spitfires benefited from this experience, and were fitted with progressively more powerful photographic equipment.

A less successful experiment was the service introduction of the Spitfire IB. Armed with four Brownings and two Mk 1 Hispano cannon of 20-mm calibre, the IB was ordered into production after trials of the new guns under the wings of a Hurricane in early 1939. (When the so-called 'B' wing carrying four guns and two cannon was introduced, the original eight-gun aircraft was retrospectively designated Spitfire IA.) Placed into service in July 1940, the Spitfire IBs soon acquired an unenviable reputation for high rates of cannon stoppages. The heavy recoil force of the opposite cannon made the aircraft virtually uncontrollable and useless as a gun platform, and the squadron chosen for the trials insisted on being re-equipped with IAs.

Production at Castle Bromwich began to build up rapidly in the second half of 1940, this facility concentrating on the Spitfire II. Powered by a Merlin XII of higher take-off power and higher rated altitude than the powerplants of Spitfire Is, the new type also featured additional armour protection for the pilot and the coolant tank. The engine was started by a cartridge-activated Coffman starter instead of an electric motor, and a constant-speed propeller was fitted as standard. Spitfire IIAs and IIBs were produced with similar armament to the IA and IB, while a few aircraft were fitted with the universal C wing which could accommodate either the A or B armament or, alternatively, four Hispano cannon. Despite the development of the Hispano to an acceptable level of reliability, however, the armament carried by most Spitfires and favoured by the squadrons was the B wing with its mix of cannon and machine guns.

If the Spitfire II was the definitive version of the first Spitfire subtype, the Spitfire V was the first version to offer a substantial increase in performance. It was also, taking the VA, VB and VC versions together, the most widely produced single Mark of the aircraft. Previous Merlin engines had been designed to accept the 85 octane fuel which was the best the RAF could guarantee during the early war years; by the end of 1940 the supply of 100 octane fuel was building up and the boost pressure from the supercharger could be increased without fear of detonation. The early Merlin had also been found to suffer from a very restricted airflow to the supercharger, and at first it was thought that modified impeller ducting necessary to solve this problem would also lengthen the engine. However, by reversing the carburettor the increase in length was cancelled out; the new Merlin 45 series was both more powerful and more efficient than its predecessors and could be installed in a similar airframe.

Most of the aircraft produced in this series were fitted with the B (four Brownings, two cannon) wing, but about 20 per cent of the output comprised eight-gun VAs and

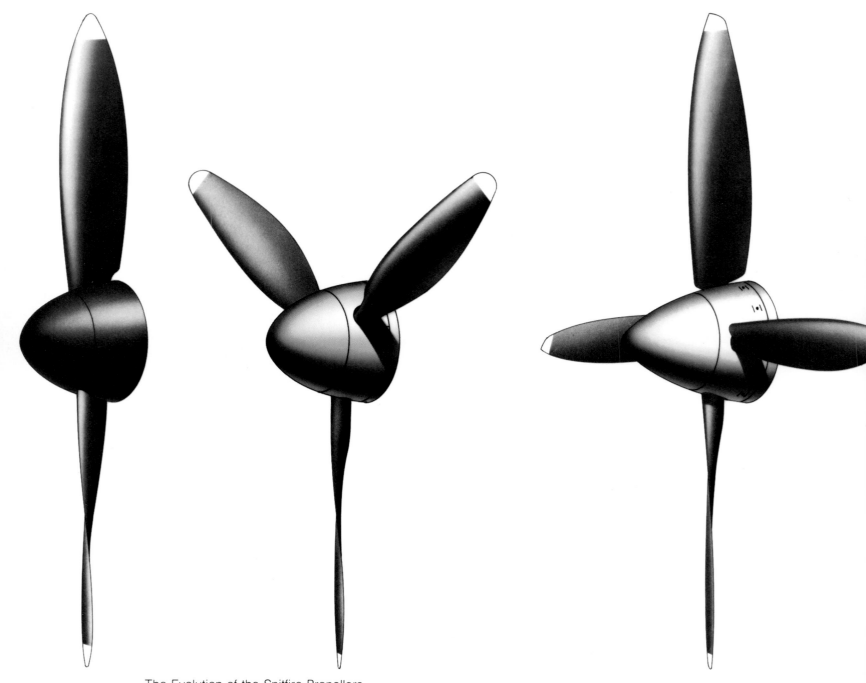

The Evolution of the Spitfire Propellers

The two-blade de Havilland wooden fixed pitch propeller was initially used in the Mk I and those models which preceded it. The Mk Ia used the same construction propeller sometimes triple-bladed with metal blades. The following model, Ib used a three-blade de Havilland two-position propeller as well. The three-blade Rotol Jablo variable pitch propeller was used in the IIa. Both IIb and IIc used a three-blade de Havilland hydromatic constant speed propeller. Other aircraft using three-bladed propellers were the PR III and IV, as well as the V series.

another tenth were delivered as four-cannon VCs with additional armour and bomb pylons. A number of Spitfire Is and IIs were modified at maintenance and repair units to V standard, with some strengthening of the fuselage and installation of the Merlin 45.

The Spitfire V entered service in March, 1941, and although it was the dominant production version for most of 1941-42 at Castle Bromwich and Supermarine—by that time dispersed throughout Southern England—within two years it was outclassed as a medium-altitude fighter. Many surviving aircraft were then converted to low-level fighters, under the designation LF.V. The wingtips were removed outboard of the ailerons and a smaller supercharger impeller was fitted. The effect of the latter modification, indicated by the suffix M on the engine designation, was to allow the engine to develop more power at low level without detonation, at the same time reducing the power demands of the blower; however, the smaller impeller was incapable of maintaining full power at

altitudes above 2,750 ft (838 m). Dubbed 'clipped, cropped and clapped' by their pilots, the LF.V.s were mainly used as improvised ground-attack fighters. Other Mark Vs were converted into PR.VII and PR.XIII tactical reconnaissance fighters with oblique cameras, the PR.XIII being a factory conversion.

The Spitfire V was the basis for numerous Spitfire derivatives, both successful and abortive. One of the most remarkable was the Spitfire D or PR.IV long-range reconnaissance aircraft, developed in mid-1941. Although the Spitfire had not been developed with long-range operations in mind, the legacy of the Goshawk included the torsion-box leading-edge which, with armament removed, made an impressive integral fuel tank. The addition of 133 Imp gal (605 lit) of fuel more than doubled the fuel capacity of the PR.IV and endowed it with a range of 2,000 miles (3,220 km). An enlarged oil tank was housed in a modified lower engine cowling. The long-span, low-drag wing of the Spitfire was the other contributor to this long-range performance, which

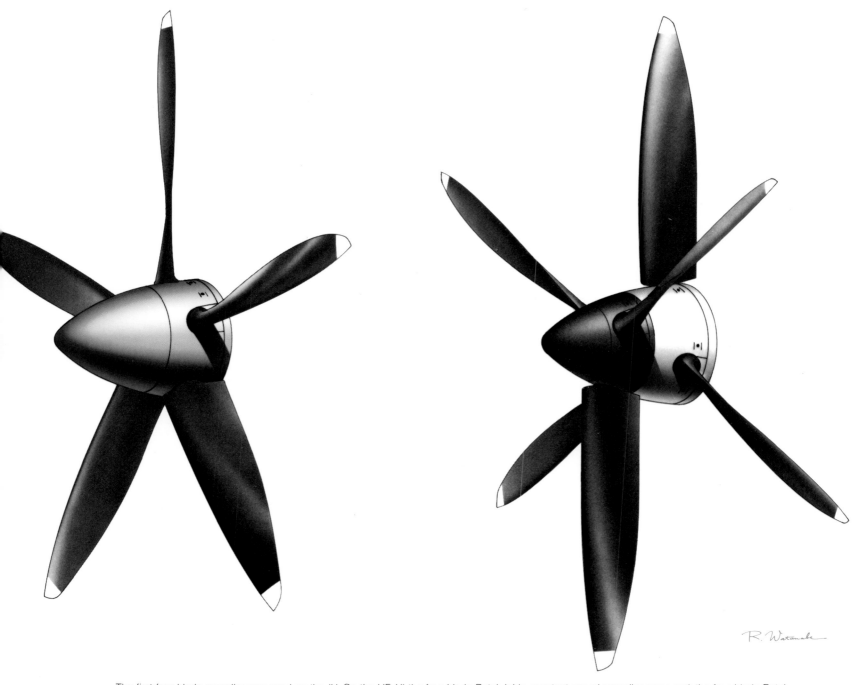

The first four-blade propeller was used on the IV. On the HF. VI the four-blade Rotol Jablo constant speed propeller was used; the four-blade Rotol hydulignum being used on PR. VIIs, F. VIIIs, F. IXs, PR. XIs and other aircraft. The first five-blade propeller was used on the XIVe. It was a Rotol constant speed model and used reinforced wooden blades. Other aircraft used five-blade propellers were the F. XVIII, the FR. XVIII, the PR. XIX and the F.21 and 22, these latter two models using a five-blade Rotol constant speed. Six-blade propellers (Rotol counter-rotating) were used on the FR.XIV, and those F.21s and F.22s equipped with the Griffon 85 engine.

combined with the high speed of the Spitfire allowed it to roam over Germany in daylight without incurring prohibitive losses.

The Spitfire V was also the basis for the Seafire, conceived in 1941 when it was realised that the carrier-based Hurricanes and Martlets of the Fleet Air Arm were no match for the latest generation of Luftwaffe fighters. The Seafire IBs were converted from existing Spitfire VBs; the IIC was a more thorough modification, built from the outset as a naval fighter but lacking folding wings. The first IICs were delivered in mid-1942. The Seafire LIIC, a low-level-optimised successor to the basic IIC with a cropped-impeller engine and a four-blade propeller (among single-stage Merlin aircraft, only Seafires had these), entered service in the following year.

The Fleet Air Arm, defending targets which at that time were invulnerable to high-altitude level bombing, attached less importance to high-altitude operations than their dry-shod brethren, and never used any Merlin derivative other than the single-stage 45 and the low-altitude 32 series. Although the Seafire had been conceived as a stopgap pending delivery in late 1943 of purpose-built American naval fighters (Grumman F6F Hellcats and Chance Vought F4U Corsairs), there was some doubt that these could be delivered on time and the development of the Seafire continued. The Seafire III was the first of the family with folding wings, a system having been devised which retained 90 per cent of the thin wing's rigidity without excessive weight increase. Most of these aircraft—built by a separate Seafire production organisation, headed by Westland—were completed as LIII low-altitude fighters with cropped-impeller engines, which served alongside the US-built fighters. The Seafire LIII was the most widely produced version of the type, and the last to enter service during the war. The Seafire LIII was also the only single-stage-engine version to feature the new exhaust stacks introduced on the later variants of the type. The replacement of collector pipes with individual ejector ports for

Merlin 60 series engine section

The Spitfire is always associated with the Merlin engine. Though it was a Rolls-Royce engine, the Griffon, which gave the plane its later boosted performance, the Merlin was its first and in some ways its most important engine. The two-stage two-speed Merlin 60 series driving four-bladed reinforced wood propellers was the initial powerplant which carried the Spitfire into the skies of Europe. Its largest drawback was its 27 litre capacity. This limited performance and led to the development of the 36.7 litre two-stage Griffon. This development had certain parallels in Germany where in an attempt to gain more power the 33.9 litre capacity of the DB 601 series was increased to 35.7 litres in the DB 605A series, and to not less than 44.5 litres in the DB 603A series.

Merlin 61	V-1650-3	V-1650-7	V-1650-9 (Merlin 100)
Take-off Power:	1380hp max 5 min	1490hp max 5 min	1830hp wet
Griffon	III, IV	65	85
Take-off Power:	1720hp	1540hp	1915hp

Rolls-Royce Merlin 61 Engine

1 Valve gear cover
2 Propeller shaft
3 Volute chamber
4 Supercharger components
5 Exit guide vane ring
6 Valve
7 Rocker arm
8 Coolant outlet connection
9 Valve spring
10 Overhead camshaft
11 Cylinder sleeve
12 Camshaft bevel-drive gear
13 Connecting rod
14 Piston and rings
15 Spark plug
16 Exhaust port
17 Tachometer drive
18 Magneto cross-shaft driving gear
19 Air intake
20 Twin choke carburettor
21 Throttle oil heating pipe
22 Crankcase lateral bolts
23 Balanced crankshaft
24 Supercharger two speed driving gear
25 Scavenge oil suction pipe
26 Oil pump
27 Reduction gear
28 Propeller constant speed unit
29 Automatic boost control unit

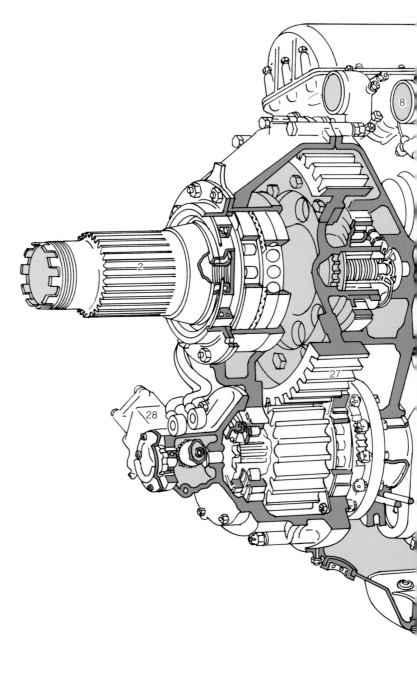

each cylinder was credited with a 4 mph (6.5 km/hr) increase in maximum speed.

Another derivative of the Mark V was the first pressurised Spitfire, developed to counter expected high-altitude bombing. The Spitfire VI was fitted with a Marshall cabin blower and a sealed, non-jettisonable canopy, together with extended, more pointed wingtips. Rated altitude of its Merlin 47 engine, however, was only 14,000 ft (4,270 m), limiting the performance of the Spitfire VI to the point where it was regarded as a stopgap pending development of the more extensively modified Mk VII, and only 100 Spitfire VIs were built.

The long family of Spitfire V descendants included some smaller subgroups; among these were the PR.VI or Spitfire F and the PV.VII Spitfire G, field modifications of the basic type. There was also the small batch of Spitfire V

floatplanes, converted in 1942. The Spitfire had been earmarked for float conversion in early 1940, in a panic programme to provide a fighter which could fly from fjords in defence of Norway. One conversion, known as the 'Narvik Nightmare,' was completed but never flown: a Spitfire I fitted with floats developed for the lumbering Blackburn Roc turret fighter, its performance would have been poor. The Spitfire V conversion, by contrast, was designed by the Supermarine team and produced what was probably the best float fighter of the war, even compared with the purpose-built Japanese Kawanishi N1K1 'Kyofu.' Specially designed floats were attached to the wings by slender cantilever pylons with no cross-bracing, and the water and air handling of the conversion was reported to be excellent. The 11 ft 3 in (3.43 m) four-blade propeller was the largest fitted to any Spitfire.

The three Mk V conversions completed were ferried

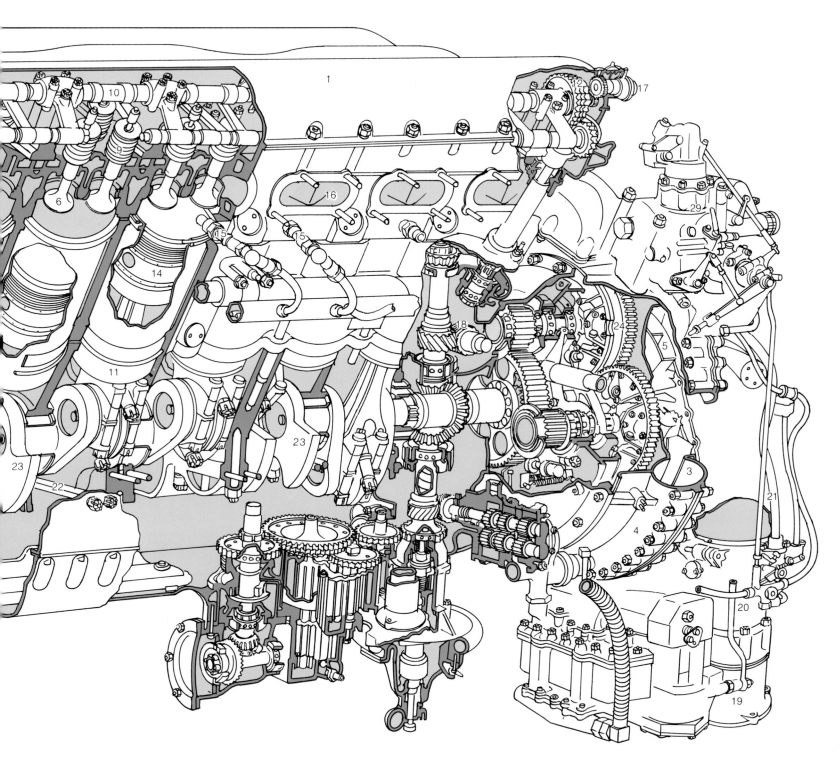

in great secrecy to Alexandria in the autumn of 1943. In an exercise worthy of the grandest fictional feats of arms, it was intended to operate the Spitfires from an uninhabited Greek island to harry Luftwaffe transport aircraft, supplying and controlling them by submarine. However, the German counter-attack in the Aegean overran the intended launching point for the operation while the floatplanes were still working up on the Great Bitter Lake, and the plan was abandoned.

One of the last derivatives of the Spitfire V to appear was one of the most unusual and was certainly not intended as a production version. It is not quite clear when or how Spitfire V EN380 fell intact into German hands, but in November, 1943, it was modified by the experimental and flight-test department of Daimler-Benz to accept a DB605A-1 engine and VDM propeller in a modified Bf 109G cowling, together with German instruments and a 24v electrical sys-

tem. The aircraft as modified was reported to be far more pleasant to fly than the Bf 109, particularly in take-off and landing. It was slower than the Bf 109 at low and medium altitudes but could climb much faster, despite the fact that the engine was some 200 lb (90 kg) heavier than the original Merlin. The DB605 Spitfire was destroyed during a USAAF bombing raid in August, 1944.

The development of the Spitfire V had left the Spitfire more heavily armed and better protected than the aircraft envisaged in 1935. Its performance, however, had not greatly improved; the higher speeds at low level attained by modified LF.Vs were in the future when that type entered service. By that time, moreover, development along a number of parallel lines was under way, with a view to further exploiting the immense potential, by now being appreciated, of the basic design.

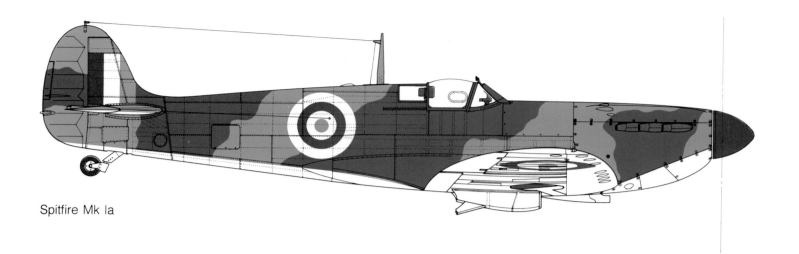

Spitfire Mk Ia

Room for improvement — 2: Which stage next?

Aircraft development in wartime seldom follows a logical sequence, and the Spitfire typifies this tendency more than any other type does. Repeatedly, developments were started only to be overhauled by improvisations stimulated by urgent operational needs, the improvisation being sufficiently successful to postpone the production of the original development still further. To comprehend the life cycle of the aircraft, it is necessary to look at the options available for short-term and medium-term developments in 1939 and 1940, which could be considered for application to future production aircraft once the crisis of the Battle was over.

One early proposal was to produce a generally cleaned-up version of the original design. Relatively simple modifications such as switching from a fixed to a retractable tailwheel, and the addition of small doors to cover the retracted mainwheels (semi-exposed on the Spitfire I) would yield a useful increase in maximum speed for a small increase in cost and complexity. Also becoming available at that time was the Merlin XX series engine, using the same supercharger as the 45 series with a two-speed mechanical drive. This engine could work to its full potential over a wider range of altitudes than the single-speed engine of the original Spitfire, and could be installed with only minor modifications.

The Merlin XX and other refinements mentioned above were fitted to the Spitfire III, which appeared in the form of a single prototype late in 1939. However, that was not the most auspicious moment to present the Ministries with a new version of the Spitfire; logical as the development of the Spitfire III might be, deliveries of the standard aircraft were still behind schedule and the introduction of more modifications could only delay production. Plans to build the III at Castle Bromwich were cancelled, and it was the Mark II version of the better established Hurricane that received the first Merlin XX powerplants. When an improved Spitfire was ordered, it was the Spitfire V, with an almost unmodified airframe and an engine which achieved similar results to the XX with less modification and weight. By the time that production constraints permitted consideration of more radi-

cal derivatives of the Spitfire, other developments had improved vastly on the single-stage, two-speed Merlin XX.

The first radical change to be embarked upon was the second to be used. In 1939, Rolls-Royce and Supermarine had collaborated closely in the design of an engine which, although much larger in capacity than the Merlin, would fit with few airframe modifications in aircraft designed for the smaller engine. This placed very tight restrictions on length (because an engine as long for its capacity as the Merlin would have made a re-engined fighter nose-heavy) and frontal area, and after considerable work on the mock-up the design of the Griffon was frozen. The Griffon had been conceived as a high-power, low-altitude engine, and a heavily armed low-level intercepter version of the Spitfire was designed around it. This prototype was tested with a wing carrying a mock-up of a six-Hispano armament. It was originally designated Spitfire IV, but the designation PR.IV had been allotted before the first Griffon-powered aircraft flew. Incorporating the design refinements of the Spitfire III, this aircraft became the sole Spitfire XX.

The Mark XX never went into production. Instead it became the first of the ultimate Mark 20 series Spitfires, another line of development which was to be largely overhauled by improvisation. Designed to overcome the Spitfire's only major weakness, these aircraft underwent a protracted gestation and finally entered service as the war drew to a close. In concept, however, they antedated most of the wartime production aircraft.

Early trials at Martlesham Heath with the Spitfire I had revealed that the ailerons became increasingly heavy at high diving speeds, and a modified design of fabric aileron was introduced during Spitfire I production to alleviate the problem. However, the unexpected development of the 'diving race' style of air combat in wartime took the Spitfire into the high-speed regime where its lateral control became increasingly heavy. The Spitfire V introduced metal ailerons of the Frise type, in which the leading edge was shaped to aid the upward deflection of the aileron, but this was still no more than a palliative. The 'clipped' wings of LF Spitfires were intended to reduce rolling inertia, but also worsened performance at altitude.

Investigation of the problem revealed by late 1940

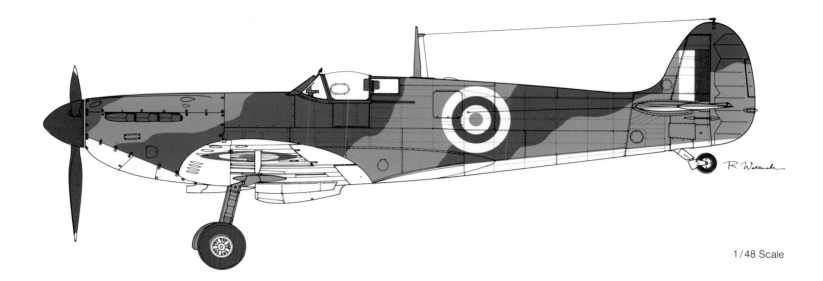

that the existing Spitfire wing, with its simple torsion-box leading-edge, could not be fitted with more powerful ailerons without encountering 'reversal,' a phenomenon in which the aileron twists the wing as a tab deflects an aileron, reversing the control input. The design of a new wing with plain ailerons and a structure of multiple torsion boxes was started, and this was to be combined with the Griffon engine of the Spitfire XX to produce the Spitfire XXI (generally written as 21). A parallel if slightly later development was an alternative new wing based on the 'laminar-flow' symmetrical aerofoil already in use on the North American P-51 Mustang, deeper in section than the Spitfire wing but offering similar performance. Neither wing retained the original elliptical platform of the earlier Spitfires, but Mitchell's classically beautiful shape had more life in it than many people imagined.

The development that was to have most influence on the wartime Spitfire, unexpectedly extending the production life of the basic airframe, originated during 1940, when the Air Staff became increasingly interested in the threats and opportunities presented by the possibility of aircraft operations above 40,000 feet (12,190 m). It has to be recognized that the Air Ministry went a little overboard in its enthusiasm for high-altitude aircraft. High-altitude, pressurized versions of the Wellington bomber were built, as well as two specialised high-altitude interceptors; one of the latter, the Westland Welkin, was put into production but never fired a shot in anger. However, the high-altitude requirement produced one very useful result in the shape of the special Merlin engine developed for the Wellington and Welkin.

This, the Merlin 60, differed from its predecessors in possessing a two-stage supercharger to achieve much higher boost levels and maintain power at high altitudes. With a two-speed drive, it could also produce high power at lower levels. In addition, the Merlin 60 featured an 'aftercooler': an air cooler between the supercharger and the inlet manifold which lowered the temperature of the air and increased the boost pressure which could be achieved without detonation. The Merlin 60 had vastly better high-altitude performance than the earlier Merlins, and was significantly better at all but the lowest altitudes. However, in the long run its most significant attribute was the ease with which it could be applied to the standard aircraft.

Room for improvement—3: A Successful Panic

Understandably, in view of the apparently increasing danger that the Luftwaffe would make a large-scale switch to high-altitude bombing from outside the reach of conventional fighters, the first version of the Spitfire to be ordered into production with the two-stage-supercharged Merlin was a high-altitude type. Predictably, in view of the tortuous path taken by the development of the type, the first actually to enter service was the third to be allotted a Mark number; it was an improvisation, and it was to be built in greater numbers than any other version of the type except the Spitfire V series.

In 1941, Spitfire pilots returned from fighter sweeps over Northern France reporting encounters with a new and formidable German radial-engined fighter. This, the Focke-Wulf Fw 190, was superior by a substantial margin to the Spitfire V, only then entering service, and with the increasing employment of the new German fighter the development of a version of the Spitfire offering superior straight-line and climbing performance at all altitudes became a matter of urgency.

Development of two parallel Spitfire versions combining the airframe refinements pioneered on the prototype Spitfire III with the Merlin 60 engine was under way, but it was considered more important to speed up as far as possible the shift of Spitfire production from the Mk V to a more potent aircraft. In theory, the greater power and speed of a Spitfire with the new engine would demand a certain amount of strengthening to the airframe, while the four-blade airscrew needed to absorb the greater output of the new engine would call for a slightly larger tailfin to counteract its destabilising effect. None of these modifications was applied to the Spitfire IX, which in its standard production form was virtually identical to the Spitfire V aft of the firewall, apart from the aftercooler in the enlarged port radiator duct. Ahead of it, all was changed, with a 1,710 hp Merlin 60, a four-blade Rotol airscrew and the more efficient multiple ejector exhausts. The reduction in structural load safety factors inhe-

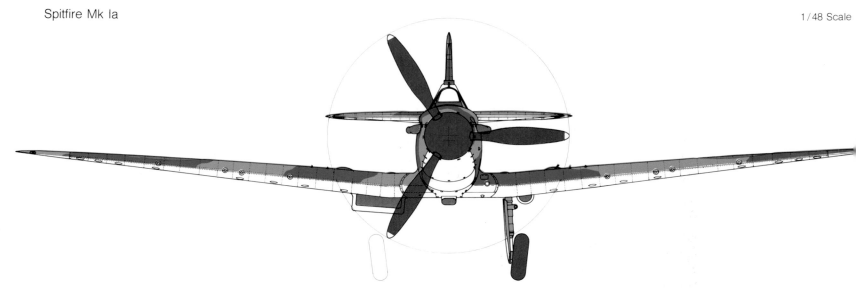

rent in such a simple modification was accepted as the price of a speed gain which included an improvement in level speed of 70 mph (112 km/hr), or upwards of 20 per cent, at all altitudes. Climb, acceleration and sustained turning ability were increased in proportion: in modern terms, the Spitfire IX enjoyed higher 'specific excess power' than the Mark V.

Most of the 5,600 Spitfire IXs were built as LF.IXs, their supercharger gearing optimised for best performance below 6,000 feet (1,830 m); less than a quarter had the medium-altitude-rated Merlin, and a tenth of the IXs built were HF models with engines rated at 22,500 ft (6,850 m) in top gear. (None had 'cropped' superchargers, so all were multi-level fighters unlike the LF.V.) Although none of the Spitfire IXs was actually delivered with clipped wingtips, the variant followed the Spitfire V in being so modified in the field or at maintenance units once more advanced versions had taken over the task of medium-altitude interception. Some later aircraft were also fitted with a larger tailfin. The wing of the Spitfire IX was basically that of the VC, production of the A and B wings having ceased. The C wings of the Mark IX invariably carried the two-cannon, four-Browning armament; in 1944, however, the E wing was introduced and replaced the four 0.303 fin (7.7 mm) guns with a pair of 0.5 in (12.7 mm) weapons, and this equipped later Spitfire IXs. An advantage of the E wing was that the guns were housed in two bays instead of six, simplifying maintenance.

The Spitfire IX was the progenitor of the usual quota of experiments, two of the most remarkable being concerned with marine operations. In the United Kingdom, one of the conversion kits developed for the Spitfire V float-plane was applied to a single Spitfire IX. The Spitfire IX floatplane appeared some time after the plans to operate the marine Mark V from hidden bases in the Mediterranean had been abandoned, and it is not clear for what theatre the aircraft was intended; however, it was unquestionably the fastest float fighter ever built, with a maximum speed of 377 mph (607 km/hr), and helped to inspire development of the Saunders-Roe SR.A1 flying-boat fighter ordered in 1944.

Another maritime experiment involved one of the 1,288 Spitfire IXs delivered to the Soviet Union, which in 1947 was converted for tests of a rail-type catapult similar to that used for British Hurricane-equipped CAM (Catapult-Armed Merchantman) ships in the Battle of the Atlantic. This Soviet venture into maritime air power was apparently a failure, and was not proceeded with.

Rarely can any aircraft have absorbed a 70 per cent power increase with as little external and internal modification as the Spitfire did between the Mark I and the Mark IX, and certainly no aircraft has exploited it so well. The advantage in power which the Mark IX enjoyed over the V is well illustrated by the floatplane version; with two massive pontoons slung below the wings, the Mark IX was still slightly faster than the landplane Mark V. The implications in terms

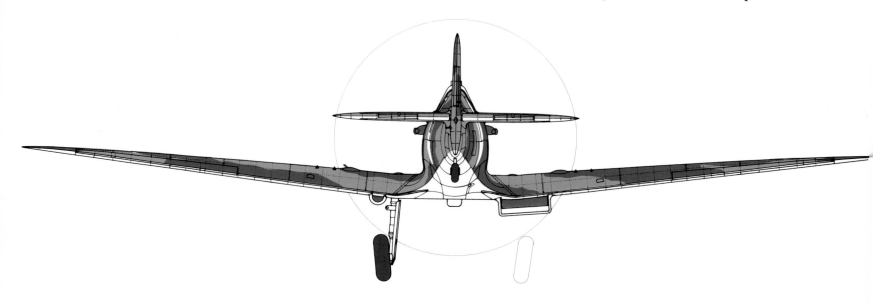

▼ Spitfire L.F. Mk VB

Flown by Wing Commander I.R. 'Widge' Gleed, No. 601
Sqn, AR502. A Battle of Britain veteran, Gleed had at least
15 victories to his credit when he failed to return from a 16
April, 1943, fighter sweep.

Rolls-Royce Merlin 45M/50M/55M engines: 1,585 hp

Performance:

Max speed:	369 mph at 19,500 ft (594 km/h at 5950 m)
Time to 5000 ft (1520 m): 1 min 36 sec	
Service ceiling:	36,500 ft (11,100 m)
Range:	470 mls (760 km) with 85 Imp.gal (386 ltr)
Weight:	6,650 lb (3016 kg)

Dimensions:

Span:	32 ft 7 in (9.928 m)
Length:	29 ft 11 in (9.116 m)
Height:	11 ft 5½ in (3.491 m)
	Airscrew vertical, 11 ft 4¾ in (3.472 m)
Wing area:	231 sq.ft (21.3 m²)
Armament:	2 x 20 mm Hispano-Suiza cannon
	4 x .303-in Browning machine-guns

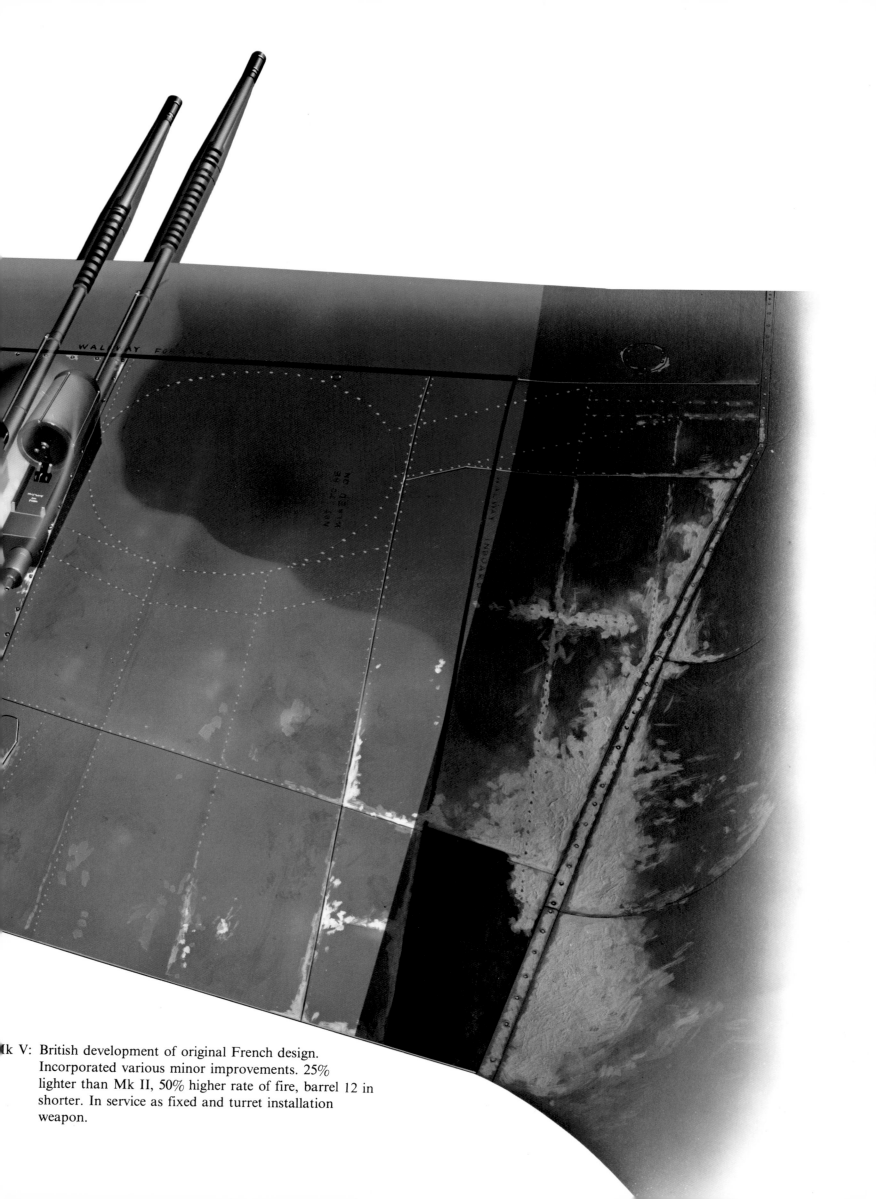

Mk V: British development of original French design.
Incorporated various minor improvements. 25%
lighter than Mk II, 50% higher rate of fire, barrel 12 in
shorter. In service as fixed and turret installation
weapon.

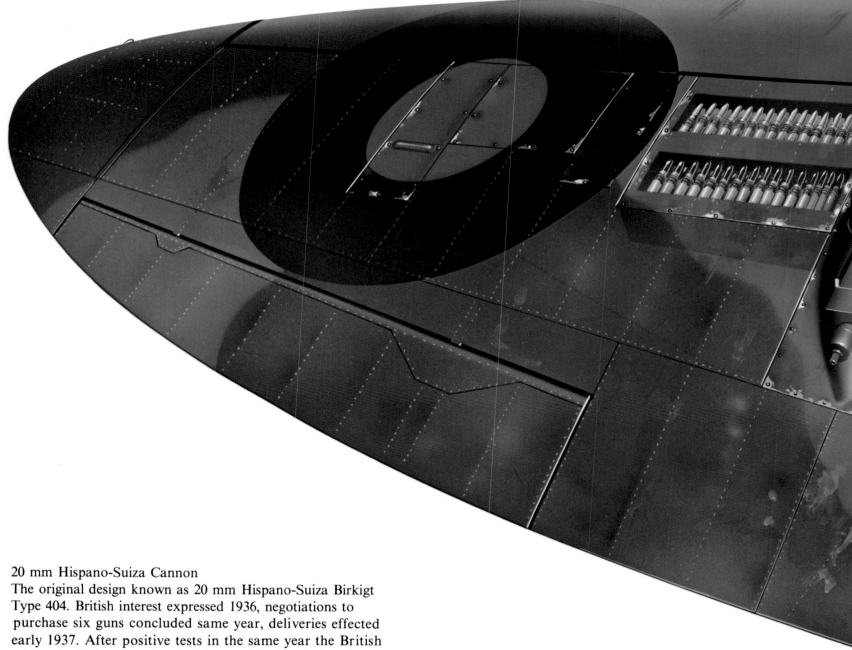

20 mm Hispano-Suiza Cannon

The original design known as 20 mm Hispano-Suiza Birkigt Type 404. British interest expressed 1936, negotiations to purchase six guns concluded same year, deliveries effected early 1937. After positive tests in the same year the British accepted a HS proposal to build a special plant in Britain to manufacture a minumum of 400 guns. Guns manufactured in Britain were initially known simply as 20-mm Hispano-Suiza Type 404; later, 20-mm Automatic Gun Mk I (etc.).

Mk I: Initial British production from French drawings. Small series only due to difficulties with (metric) drawings.

Mk II: British manufacture from new (British) drawings which included various minor changes and improvements to suit British manufacturing methods and large-scale production.

Mk III: Designed to have fabricated gun body for cheaper production and reduced weight. Test examples only: no production.

Mk IV: Identical to Mk II but barrel 12 in shorter; also, a shoulder 9 in further to rear. Intended mainly as turret gun, but only small number produced.

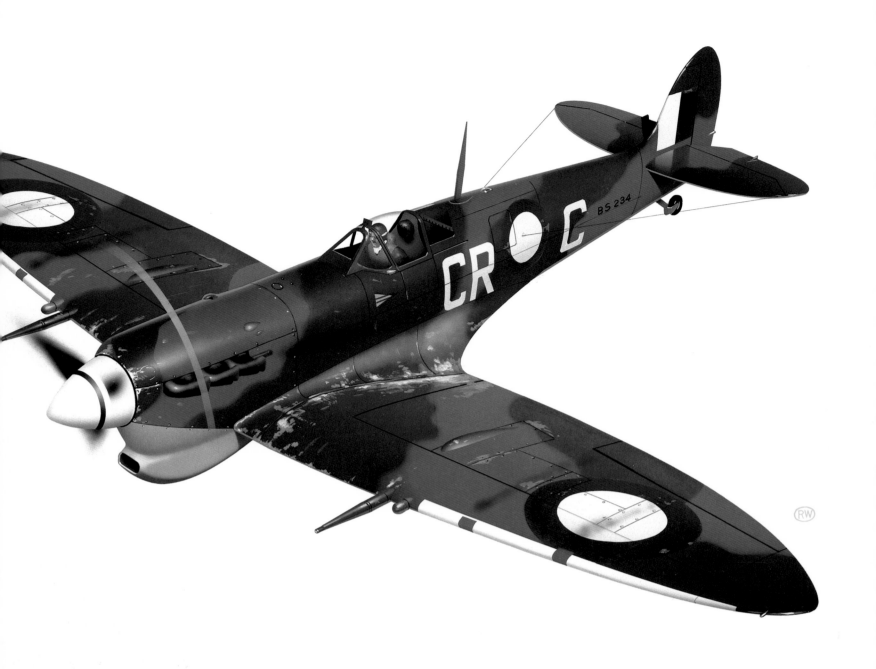

▲ Spitfire Mk VC

Flown by Wing Commander Clive R. Caldwell, probably the
most celebrated of all Australian fighter pilots, Wing Leader No. 1
Fighter Wing, Royal Australian Air Force; Darwin, Australia,
1942–43. Serial BS234.

Rolls-Royce Merlin 45/46/50/50A engines: 1,470 hp

Performance:

Max speed:	374 mph at 13,000 ft (602 km/h at 3960 m)
Time to 20,000 ft (6100 m): 7 min 30 sec	
Service ceiling:	37,000 ft (11,300 m)
Range:	470 mls (760 km)
	1,135 mls (1830 km) with 175 Imp. gal (796 ltr)
Weight:	6,785 lb (3078 kg)

Dimensions:

Span:	36 ft 10 in (11.323 m)
Length:	29 ft 11 in (9.116 m)
Height:	11 ft 5½ in (3.491 m)
	Airscrew vertical, 11 ft 4¾ in (3.472 m)
Wing area:	242 sq.ft (22.3 m²)
Armament:	2(4) x 20 mm Hispano-Suiza cannon
	4 x .303-in Browning machine-guns

▼ Spitfire H.F. Mk VI

No. 616 'South Yorkshire' Squadron, June, 1942. BS111.

Rolls-Royce Merlin 47/49 engines: 1,415 hp

Performance:

Max speed:	364 mph at 22,000 ft (586 km/h at 6700 m)
Time to 20,000 ft (6100 m): 8 min	
Service ceiling:	40,000 ft (12,200 m)
Range:	510 mls (820 km)
Weight:	6,797 lb (3083 kg)

Dimensions:

Span:	40 ft 2 in (12.239 m)
Length:	29 ft 11 in (9.116 m)
Height:	11 ft 5½ in (3.491 m)
	Airscrew vertical, 11 ft 4¾ in (3.472 m)
Wing area:	248.5 sq.ft (22.9 m²)
Armament:	2 x 20 mm Hispano-Suiza cannon
	4 x .303-in Browning machine-guns

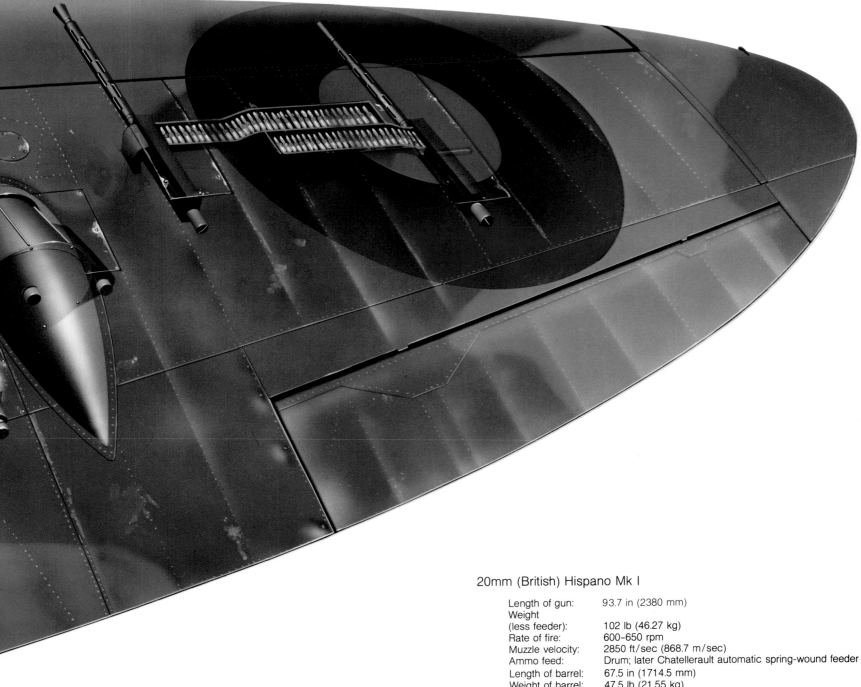

20mm (British) Hispano Mk I

Length of gun:	93.7 in (2380 mm)
Weight (less feeder):	102 lb (46.27 kg)
Rate of fire:	600–650 rpm
Muzzle velocity:	2850 ft/sec (868.7 m/sec)
Ammo feed:	Drum; later Chatellerault automatic spring-wound feeder
Length of barrel:	67.5 in (1714.5 mm)
Weight of barrel:	47.5 lb (21.55 kg)
Bore:	8 grooves, RH twist
Rifling length:	63.08 in (1602 mm)
Cartridge:	20 mm Hispano-Suiza (M75 series)

20 mm (British) Hispano Mk V

Length of gun:	77 in (1955.8 mm)
Weight of gun:	99.5 lb (45.1 kg)
Rate of fire:	700–750 rpm
Muzzle velocity:	2850 ft/sec (868.7 m/sec)
Ammo feed:	Automatic spring-wound feeder using metallic links
Length of barrel:	52.5 in (1333.5 mm)
Weight of barrel:	26$^{1}/_{4}$ lb (12.1 kg)
Bore:	9 grooves, RH twist
Cartridge:	20 mm Hispano-Suiza (M75 series)

Browing .303 Machine Gun Mk II

Calibre:	.303 in (7.7 mm)
Belt feed:	Recoil operated
Weight of gun:	21.9 lb (9.93 kg)
Rate of fire:	1200 rpm (cyclic)
Weight of bullet:	.022 lb (10.0 g)
Muzzle velocity:	2600 ft/sec (811 m/sec)

R. Watanabe

▲ Spitfire Mk 24

Similar to the Mark 22 (from which several had been converted)
the Spitfire 24 had internal differences, among them the ability
to carry eight 60 lb rockets. No. 80 Squadron was the sole Royal
Air Force unit to use this version. It flew Mark 24s until
January, 1952, and was the last fighter unit to operate Spitfires.

Rolls-Royce Griffon 61/85 engines: 2,050 hp

Performance:

Max speed:	454 mph at 26,000 ft (731 km/h at 7900 m)
Time to 20,000 ft (6100 m): 8 min	
Service ceiling:	43,500 ft (13,250 m)
Range:	490 mls with 120 Imp. gal (790 km with 546 ltr)
	640 mls with 150 Imp. gal (1030 km with 682 ltr)
	880 mls with 210 Imp. gal (1420 km with 955 ltr)
Weight:	9,900 lb (4490 kg)

Dimensions:

Span:	36 ft 11 in (11.249 m)
Length:	32 ft 11 in (9.801 m)
Height:	Airscrew vertical, 13 ft 6 in (4.114 m)
Wing area:	244 sq.ft (22.5 m²)
Armament:	4 x 20 mm Hispano-Suiza cannon

of the ability of the Mark IX to climb and accelerate in combat are clear: and this was an improvisation?

Once the Spitfire IX was established at the massive but inflexible plant at Castle Bromwich, the smaller but more versatile Supermarine production group could turn its attention back to the original two-stage-engine derivatives which had been overhauled with such good effect by the Mark IX. The first to appear was the high-altitude Spitfire VII (a different aircraft altogether from the confusingly designated PR.VII, which was a field-modified Spitfire VA), combining the long-span wing and pressure cabin of the interim Mark VI high-altitude fighter with the two-stage engine and other design refinements such as a sliding hood (the pilot of the earlier Mark VI could not escape in an emergency), a retractable tailwheel and a stronger airframe.

After 140 Mark VIIs had been built, it was decided that the high-altitude threat had receded and the pressurized aircraft was replaced in production by the unpressurized Mark VIII, which essentially amounted to a refined and strengthened Spitfire IX with a slightly higher speed due to its retractable tailwheel. It also differed from the Mark IX in being delivered with extended-span and clipped wings as well as the standard planform. Most of the Mark VIIIs had clipped wings and low-level Merlins and at least some of the type had four 20-mm Hispano cannon. Later aircraft shared the taller, more pointed tailfin of later Spitfire IXs. Supermarine delivered 1,650 examples of the Mark VIII before it was superseded by Griffon-powered versions.

Logical offshoots of the two-stage-engined Spitfires were the high-altitude, long-range PR.X and PR.XI reconnaissance aircraft, combining the extra fuel tankage de-

veloped for the Spitfire D/PR.IV with the two-stage Merlin and the refined airframe of the Mark VIII. As readers of this history will now have come to expect, the Mark XI preceded the Mark X into service. In fact only 16 of the pressurized Mark X Spitfires were delivered, most PR sorties being flown in unpressurized Mark XIs (of which 471 were delivered) despite the extremely high altitudes of which the lightened, highly polished aircraft were capable. Production of the Mark XI started in 1942 and the Mark Xs followed in 1944.

By 1944 the Griffon-powered Spitfires were in production, within the Supermarine organisation, but Castle Bromwich was being held ready to produce the new-generation Spitfire 21 and development of this aircraft was taking longer than expected. This doubtless was part of the inspiration for the Spitfire XVI, a low-level fighter-bomber powered by a Packard-built Merlin 266—in fact, the only difference between a late-production Spitfire LF.IX and an early Mark XVI was the production source of its engine. Both were designated Type 361 by Supermarine. Most of the XVIs featured clipped E-type wings, and a substantial proportion of them featured the all-round-vision canopy and cut-down rear deck tested on a Mark VIII. This allowed the deletion of the rear-view mirror and slightly reduced the drag of the aircraft. The later XVIs also featured the taller fin of later Merlin-powered Spitfires and a low-drag whip aerial replacing the mast type of earlier aircraft. Castle Bromwich built 1,054 Spitfire XVIs, making the Type 361 Spitfire IX/XVI the most widely built *type* of Spitfire, although the Mark V was the most abundant Mark. By the time the XVI gave way to the Mark 21 the war was almost over.

The termination of Spitfire XVI production brought

Following the successful trials with three Spitfire Mk V floatplane conversions, Folland built the Type 385 Spitfire IX floatplane conversion in 1943. Only one example was completed and test-flown.

(Imperial War Museum)

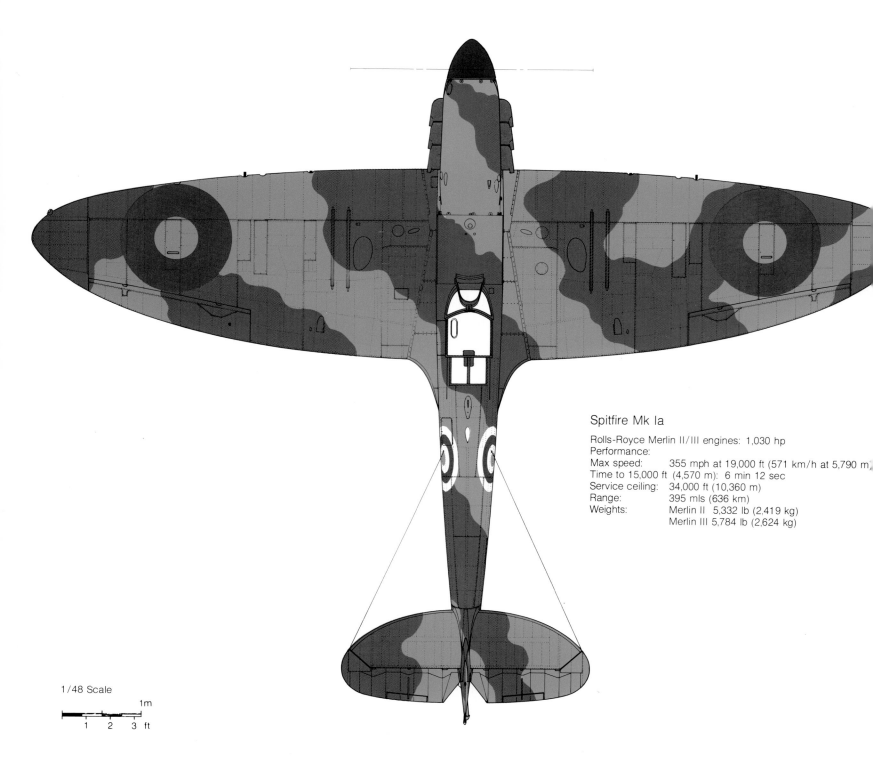

Spitfire Mk Ia

Rolls-Royce Merlin II/III engines: 1,030 hp
Performance:
Max speed: 355 mph at 19,000 ft (571 km/h at 5,790 m)
Time to 15,000 ft (4,570 m): 6 min 12 sec
Service ceiling: 34,000 ft (10,360 m)
Range: 395 mls (636 km)
Weights: Merlin II 5,332 lb (2,419 kg)
                 Merlin III 5,784 lb (2,624 kg)

1/48 Scale

1m

1   2   3 ft

to an end the line of two-stage-Merlin Spitfires, of which the vast majority had been IXs and XVIs stemming directly from the original conception of a minimally modified Spitfire V. These versions, identified by their fixed tailwheels, outnumbered the 'definitive' Mark VII and its variants by three to one, ample evidence were it needed of the enormous capacity of Castle Bromwich. On the debit side, the XVI appears to have been a stopgap, put into production when the Merlin-powered Spitfire was falling increasingly far behind fighters of later conception and used mainly for ground attack. However, the development of the Spitfire IX was astonishing proof of the potential for development designed into the first prototype Spitfire I, aerodynamically almost identical. And even if the Merlin had reached the peak of what it could achieve on 100/130 octane petrol, the Spitfire—by now primarily identified as a short-range air-to-air fighter, or 'air-superiority fighter' in modern terms—still had some way to go.

Room for improvement—4: Griffon Spit

The big Griffon engine, 36 per cent larger in capacity than the Merlin and inherently more powerful by half than its smaller ancestor, had nonetheless been conceived as a powerplant suitable for the Spitfire from its earliest days. The installation of the engine in a Spitfire airframe was basically simple, but the modification of the airframe to take full advantage of the extra power was another matter. The development was also to some extent outpaced by the continuing increases in the power of the Merlin obtained through design refinements and improved supercharging. Such technology could, of course, be applied directly to the very similar Griffon, but the potential output of the larger engine at such ratings demanded innovation in both airframe and propeller design. There was thus a tendency for the development of Griffon-Spitfires to be viewed as a long-term activity while Merlin improvements

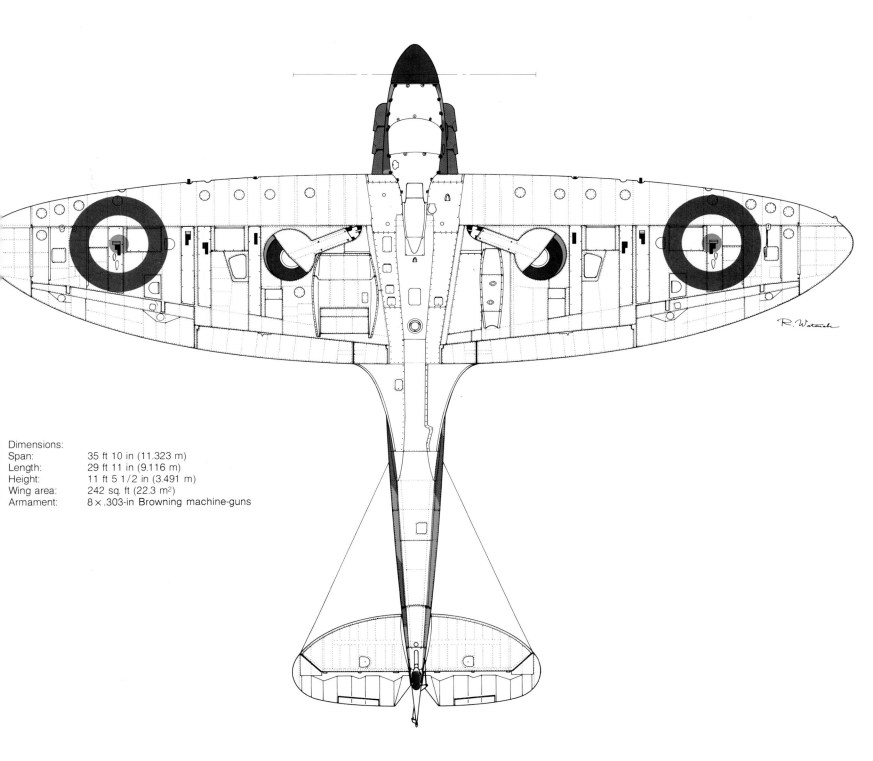

Dimensions:
Span: 35 ft 10 in (11.323 m)
Length: 29 ft 11 in (9.116 m)
Height: 11 ft 5 1/2 in (3.491 m)
Wing area: 242 sq. ft (22.3 m²)
Armament: 8 × .303-in Browning machine-guns

filled the gap until the ultimate Griffon variant should become available.

    Given these attitudes, it was logical that the Spitfire IV or XX should be regarded as a technology demonstrator for the improved Supermarine Type 356 or Spitfire 21. However, in the summer of 1942 the Luftwaffe adopted a new tactic: high-speed, low-level nuisance raids on targets in Southern England by aircraft such as the Fw 190A and Me210. The new Spitfire IX lacked the speed to intercept these raiders successfully at low level, its highly supercharged engine being most effective at higher altitudes. However, it pointed the way to the first Griffon-powered production Spitfire, which entered service in early 1943 with two home-defence squadrons in Southern England. This, the Spitfire XII, was strictly an improvisation, and represented one of the more marked bars sinister in the fighter's lineage: Of the 100 Mark XIIs built by Supermarine, half used Spitfire VC airframes and the rest were based on Spitfire VIIIs, all of which were

converted before assembly. Clipped wingtips were standard. Externally distinguished by asymmetric underwing radiators similar to those of the Spitfire V, the XII was the only land-based Spitfire variant to feature the single-stage-supercharged Griffon; the absence of an aftercooler between the supercharger and the engine accounted for the small port radiator. Another peculiarity of the Griffon was that the propeller turned in the opposite direction to that of the Merlin, creating some traps for the newly converted Merlin pilot.

    Although a two-stage Griffon was expected to be the powerplant for the definitive Griffon-Spitfire, the single-stage, two-speed engine developed for the Mark XII was suited to the Fleet Air Arm's requirement for a low/medium-altitude interceptor. The Seafire XV was more akin to a navalised Spitfire XII than any other variant, with folding wings similar to those of the Seafire III. In the course of Seafire XV production the change was made from the A-frame arrester hook, which was attached beneath the aft fuselage and tended to tip the aircraft forward on arrest, to a 'sting' hook at the extreme tail. The sting necessitated a new rudder with a higher base and broader chord. Additionally, the last batch of Seafire XVs built by Westland featured the cut-down rear fuselage and all-round-vision bubble hood introduced on all Spitfire production lines in 1944-45. The Griffon-Seafire missed the war, reaching operational squadrons in September, 1945.

Meanwhile, the introduction into service of the two-stage Griffon had taken an unexpected turn. Six Spitfire VIIIs had been allocated to test and develop this engine for the Spitfire 21, one of these aircraft being the first Spitfire to feature a contra-rotating propeller, and trials of these aircraft proved so successful that it was decided to produce yet another interim variant in the Supermarine organization, to yield a faster medium-altitude Spitfire for the RAF until Castle Bromwich commenced Spitfire 21 deliveries. Perhaps predictably, this type was to be produced in greater numbers than any other Griffon-Spitfire.

The Mark VIII adaptation was known as the Spitfire XIV, entering service in the first days of 1944. The two-stage Griffon 65 drove a five-blade airscrew, and the airframe was similar to that of the Mark VIII with the exception of some strengthening and the enlargement of the fin and rudder to counteract the higher solidity of the propeller. The Supermarine-built Mark XIV was roughly contemporary with the Castle Bromwich-built, Merlin-powered Mark XVI and underwent similar changes during its production life, the most important being the introduction of the E-type wing, bubble hood and whip aerial. Nearly half the Mark XIVs were completed as FR.XIV reconnaissance-fighters with clipped wingtips and oblique F.24 camera installations in the rear fuselage in addition to full fighter armament, this dual-purpose configuration becoming increasingly popular with the British services.

There was still a need for unarmed, specialised long-range photo-reconnaissance aircraft, and the Spitfire's capability in this role attained its ultimate expression in the PR.XIX, the only Griffon-powered strategic reconnaissance version of the type. Like most of the PR variants, the Mark

XIX was a hybrid, combining the fuselage of the Spitfire XIV with the high-fuel-capacity wing evolved from that of the Spitfire V and used on the PR.X and PR.XI. A few unpressurised pre-production aircraft were followed by 225 pressurised production aircraft, which appeared in time to operate in both main war theatres. Due to pressurised cabins and the fact that stern attack from above was considered unlikely (the Spitfire XIX penetrated defences at altitudes of 49,000 ft (15,000 m) during post-war exercises) the PR.XIX retained the raised rear decking and Malcolm hood throughout its production life, and possessed the distinction of being the last Spitfire to see front-line operational service.

A less successful development was the Spitfire XVIII, a high-weight version in which the original 'telescopic' mainspar was replaced by a single extrusion and the undercarriage was strengthened and increased in track. The fuel capacity of the type, which had been steadily increased by the addition of small extra tanks in successive versions as the power and fuel consumption of the powerplant was stepped up, was further augmented by extra rear-fuselage and wing tanks. Production delays due to the new wing spar caused the XVIII to miss the war, the first examples of the type being delivered in mid-1945—deliveries running behind those of the more advanced Spitfire 21. Like the XIV, the XVIII (often, after 1945, written Mark 18) was delivered in fighter and fighter-reconnaissance versions, 200 of the 300 aircraft delivered being FR.XVIIIs. Most of the type were delivered into storage, some entering service in the late 1940s.

The Mark XVIII/18 had a maritime counterpart in the Seafire XVII/17, similarly representing a beefed-up, higher-fuel-capacity development of its predecessor and, like the Mark XVIII/18, entering service after the war. One of the advantages of the stiffer landing gear of the Seafire 17 (which retained the single-stage engine and four-blade propeller of the XV) was increased deck clearance, particularly at high weights; the increased weight and larger propeller of the Griffon had conspired to produce a great many chipped decks and bent blades, and the stiffer undercarriage conferred a great improvement in deck handling. The Seafire 17 super-

PR.Mk XIX 2305hp Griffon-powered unarmed photo-reconnaissance variant. After operating over Europe during the last weeks of the war, the PR.XIX appeared in the Far East.

(Imperial War Museum)

seded the XV as the sole front-line fighter in FAA service in 1947, US-built carrier fighters having retired by that time.

Once again, with the development of the Spitfire XIV, the Supermarine fighter had shown that the basic wing shape and structure could be taken further than the theoretical stiffness limits might suggest, there being little to choose in terms of performance between the Mark XIV and the more advanced, much more radically modified Mark 21. In fact, the Mark XIV was close to the ultimate in pure flying performance, although increasing speed and weight was beginning to take its toll of the type's handling qualities. Considering that the Spitfire was now absorbing the power of two Merlin Is, however, this degradation in handling quality might be regarded as understandable; and at least the Spitfire XIV was available as a defence against Fi103 flying bombs and new jet fighters while the teething troubles of the Mark 21 were still being eradicated.

Room for improvement—5: The New Look

According to the design numbers applied by Supermarine, the Spitfire Mark 21 was the first major version of the type on the drawing boards after the Mark V, preceding the Mark IX and following closely on the limited-production high-altitude Mark VII. Given this background, it is perhaps hardly surprising that in its early days there was some question as to whether such a radically redesigned aircraft should be a Spitfire at all, and other names—including Victor—were considered. By the time the Spitfire 21 appeared, the basic aircraft had advanced so far that grounds for renaming the type no longer existed.

The design of a completely new wing for the Spitfire, similar in general characteristics to that of the existing aircraft but with a completely new structure to withstand the torsional loads imposed by more sensitive ailerons, was under way in earnest by early 1942. Whereas the ailerons of previous Spitfires had been balanced by area ahead of the hinge line, those of the new Type 356 were plain and devoid of aerodynamic balance. Instead the pilot's controls were connected to tabs on the trailing edge of each aileron, so that the surface itself was actuated aerodynamically. The wing structure was changed to incorporate multiple torsion boxes, but in the process the classic elliptical wing was modified to a more angular planform which could accommodate the more complex structure without too many production difficulties. The more effective ailerons were expected to eliminate the need for clipped wingtips and to improve high-altitude performance it was intended that the Type 356 should be fitted as standard with the extended wingtips of the Marks VI, VII and HF. VIII.

Evolving in parallel with the new elliptical wing, but with a slightly later schedule, was a more radically revised wing using a 'laminar-flow' section in which the point of maximum thickness was moved closer to the 40 per cent chord line and the curvatures of the top and bottom surfaces were made more similar. The new wing could be made deeper than that of the Spitfire without risking encounters with compressibility or increasing drag, and was designed with compound straight taper so that chord and thickness near mid-span would be adequate for the installation of a wide-track, inward-retracting undercarriage. The new laminar-flow wing also departed from Spitfire philosophy in featuring dual mainspars.

The fuselage of the Spitfire 21 was to be based on that of the Mark VIII, suitably modified and strengthened to accept the two-stage Griffon 60-series engine. As outlined above, the Mark VIII airframes used to test the fuselage modifications and engine installations proved so successful that the modified aircraft went into production as the Mark XIV. The new wing, however, still promised improvements in warload, weaponry (both the elliptical and laminar-flow designs were intended to accept four 20-mm cannon) and handling. The greater strength of the modified airframe and landing gear—the latter incorporating Seafire lessons—would increase the weight available for weapons and fuel, improving the Spitfire's endurance which by then was regarded as minimal in comparison to more modern aircraft. The taller landing gear would also permit installation of a larger propeller, increasing the speed of the aircraft. Spitfire

PR.Mk X, one of the sixteen built with a pressurized cockpit and a 1655hp Merlin 77 engine for high altitude photo-reconnaissance.

(Imperial War Museum)

21 was ordered in large quantities in mid-1943, preparations being made before the prototype had flown for the construction of 1,500 of the type at Castle Bromwich. The Castle Bromwich aircraft were to have the elliptical wing, but an order placed slightly later in the year with Supermarine was quickly amended to specify the more angular laminar-flow wing.

Fortunately, the 'interim' Marks XIV and XVI were well established in production by the time it was found that the Spitfire 21 with the elliptical wing was a very bug-infested aircraft. Almost a year after the first prototype had flown, and following an extensive series of modifications, the Mark 21 was rejected for service use on account of instability and control difficulties which rendered it generally inferior to the Mark XIV. Substantial modifications followed, and eventually made an acceptable aircraft out of the 21 in time for it to carry out a few patrols over Europe in the closing days of the war. The 120 production aircraft from Castle Bromwich were nearly all delivered post-war.

Meanwhile, the development of the laminar-flow wing had taken a somewhat different course. The new wing was married to a modified, Griffon-powered Spitfire VIII fuselage in mid-1944, but by this time it had been decided to apply the new wing to a completely new fuselage under the name Spiteful. The fuselage was deeper than the Spitfire's, offering a better view for the pilot and more volume for fuel. In order to make use of this space, however, it was necessary to improve the Spiteful's stability when loaded fully aft. The third Spiteful was therefore fitted with a new tail assembly in which the tailplane and elevators were enlarged by means of a 'plug' at the root and the fin was replaced by an altogether new and larger design. Like the tail of the first Spiteful prototypes, this was interchangeable with the Spitfire unit. Another modification introduced by the third Spiteful, the true prototype of the planned Spiteful XIV production aircraft (the choice of the designation has never been fully explained, but may have been a hangover from the original plans to use a fuselage similar to that of the Spitfire XIV), was an engine air intake extended to the nose of the aircraft, resulting in a deeper cowling.

With the end of the war, it was decided that the effort involved in putting the Spiteful into production was unjustified; continuing requirements for piston-engined fighters for close support (and to tide the Royal Air Force and Fleet Air Arm over until jets could take over completely) could be mainly met by cheaper continued production of Spitfires. Additionally, the FAA put its longer-term faith in the radial-engined Sea Fury, less vulnerable to damage of the cooling system than aircraft with liquid-cooled engines. The latter policy stopped development of the Seafang, a navalised Spiteful, although a handful of fixed-wing Seafang 31s and fully navalised 32s were delivered.

Some experimental work with the Spiteful continued, however, and this was to have an impact on the development of the last Spitfires and Seafires. The Seafang was intended from the outset to feature the Griffon 80-series engine, with a modified reduction gear driving contra-rotating propellers. The six-blade Rotol unit finally solved the handling problems caused by propeller torque, and its advantages were clear, especially in the difficult environment of carrier flying. Contra-rotating propellers were also tested on two Spitfire 21s and the single Spiteful XV. The ultimate Spiteful, however, was the XVI; powered by a three-stage-supercharged Griffon 101, the sole Spiteful XVI attained 494 mph (795 km/hr) in level flight during tests in 1947. Only one piston-engined fighter (the Republic XP-47J) can claim a higher speed in a controlled test.

Some of the Spiteful features were fed back into the Spitfire line. In March, 1945, Castle Bromwich started production of the Spitfire 22, differing from the 21 mainly in featuring the all-round-vision hood and cut-down rear fuselage; later aircraft, however, were fitted with the tail unit of the Spiteful, restoring to a great extent the handling qualities which had begun to deteriorate with the Spitfire XIV. The 260 Mark 22s were followed by the slightly heavier, longer-range Mark 24, and 27 of these aircraft were the last to be delivered

from Castle Bromwich before the massive shadow factory reverted entirely to its peacetime role. A further 54 Mark 24s were completed at the Supermarine works at South Marston, and delivery of the last of them in February, 1948 brought production of the Spitfire to a close.

This was not the end of the line for the Supermarine fighter. The Fleet Air Arm had been interested in the Type 356 from its earliest days, and Cunliffe-Owen was tasked early in 1944 with the development of a navalised version of the Spitfire 21. Up to the end of 1945 about 50 of these Seafire 45s were built at Castle Bromwich, but they lacked folding wings and it was discovered that the handling characteristics of the type were not acceptable for carrier operations. Application of contraprops to two Seafire 45s vastly improved the aircraft, and in addition it was found that the stiffer Mark 21-type wing improved gun aiming. The next Seafire variant was the interim FR.46, with contraprops, all-round-vision hood and the Spiteful's fin; a small batch of these aircraft preceded the definitive FR.47 with folding wings, the Spiteful tailplane and—the only member of the whole line to feature the system—fuel injection directly into the cylinders of the Griffon 88 engine. The nose shape of the FR.47 was altered by adoption of the Spiteful's extended air inlet, with the exception of a few early FR.47s which were completed with carburated engines. The last of 90 of the mighty FR.47s left the South Marston line in March, 1949, sharing hardly a single component with the dainty Supermarine 300 of 1936 but still, recognisably, a member of the same family.

The Spitfire and its descendants left their mark on Supermarine, and it could be said that the company rested on its laurels too much, aided by the suddenly slowed pace of development and learning in the British aircraft industry. Supermarine's next aircraft was the Attacker, a competent jet fighter designed in 1944 and using the wing and landing gear of the Spiteful, but by the time the Attacker entered service with the FAA it was outclassed by contemporaries of later design. The Swift, which had started its design life as a swept-wing Attacker, was even less fortunate, being afflicted with stability problems which could not be alleviated in time to avert cancellation of most Swift production. Another long gestation produced the frankly mediocre Scimitar naval fighter, development of which dated back to 1946 but which was almost a contemporary of the Blackburn Buccaneer and McDonnell Phantom when it finally became operational. With the delivery of the last Scimitar in 1960, the name of Supermarine finally vanished from the scene.

The Battle Line

So much has the Spitfire become identified in the lay mind with the Royal Air Force's fighter operations in the 1939-45 war that it is sometimes almost forgotten that the RAF operated other aircraft during that period, or that the Spitfire remained in service, firing its guns in anger, long after 1945 and in many other markings other than RAF roundels. However, it was in the campaign over Southern England in the summer of 1940 that the Spitfire achieved its greatest fame, perhaps because it was the only time that the Spitfire was used in the role for which it was originally designed.

The Spitfire was conceived as an interceptor, with high speed, heavy armament, high rate of climb and the agility to make repeated attacks on its targets as well as to fight off escorting aircraft. It was high level speed and rapid climb which between them shaped the wing of the aircraft, while the modest requirement for range was to affect it throughout its development life and limit its participation in air combat later in the war.

As an element in an air defence system the Spitfire knew few equals even with the appearance of early jet aircraft. In 1940 the Spitfire and Hurricane were incorporated into the world's most effective air defence system, and to explain the success of the aircraft it is necessary to examine this system as a whole, and in particular the technical innovation which had been applied by the RAF to revolutionise the entire concept of air defence. Baldwin's 1930 warning to the citizen that 'there is no power on earth that can protect him from the bomber . . . the bomber will always get through' was based on a simple fact of life. At that time there was no way in which an approaching aircraft or force of aircraft could be detected before it was almost over the territory of the target country. It would then be necessary to scramble aircraft, climb to engage the intruders and identify them before attacking. The air defence structure which had been built up following the raids on London by German aircraft in the 1914-18 war recognised this, leaving a 50-mile 'zone of identification' between the British coast, where the intruders would first be detected, and the 'interception line.' By 1930, increasing speeds of aircraft were inevitably deepening this area to the point where many strategic targets would be vulnerable to air attack before any co-ordinated interception could be made. The bombers would arrive over the target unchallenged in broad daylight: hence Baldwin's pessimism. The most the defences could expect to do would be to harry the attackers as, relieved of their bomb loads, they headed for home. The lumbering RAF bombers of the early 1930s regularly sauntered unscathed past Furies and Bulldogs in the course of exercises.

Radar, developed almost accidentally in the United Kingdom following a search for an electrical 'death ray,' would alter the picture beyond recognition if intelligently used. Fighter Command, formed in 1936 and dedicated primarily to the defence of the United Kingdom, had by 1939 come to rely mainly on radar for the detection and classification of threats, and had integrated it completely into its command structure. The entire air battle was to be conducted from underground command centres fed by radar, with secondary inputs from human observers and commands being issued to the operational groups by telephone.

It was within this system that the Spitfire was to make its vital contribution. At the time of the Munich crisis of September, 1938, the monoplane strength of Fighter Command comprised two squadrons of Hurricanes, but the Spitfire began to join the front line from the following month. It was only in mid-1940, however, that production difficulties with the Spitfire were overcome to the point where the production rate was half that of the simpler Hurricane; the massive Castle Bromwich plant did not begin to open up to its full production rate with the Spitfire II until the second half of the year. It is a comment on the state of German reconnaissance and intelligence that the Woolston factory, the sole source of the only British fighter which could effectively challenge the best of the German fighters, was not attacked until late September, 1940.

Appropriately enough, the Spitfire's first combat encounter was with another new and highly successful type, when a group of Spitfire Is from 603 Squadron attacked a formation of the new Junkers Ju88A-1s, then on final service tests with KG30. Two of the unescorted German bombers were shot down. The Spitfire's combat career in 1939-40 was affected by the insistence of Sir Hugh Dowding, Commander-in-Chief of Fighter Command, that none of the Supermarine fighters should be sent to join the Allied Air Expeditionary Force in France. The only Spitfires to be based in France were a few Spitfire C photo-reconnaissance aircraft of 212 Squadron, which were briefly based near Paris in the spring of 1940. At least one of these aircraft appears to have

Patrol of three Spitfire F.Mk Is, Sqn 19. Spring, 1940.

(Imperial War Museum)

fallen into German hands during the collapse of France. Otherwise, the only Spitfires to land in France were the 92 Squadron aircraft which escorted Winston Churchill's Flamingo transport to Paris in May, 1940, the occasion of the last British refusal to spare the Supermarine fighters for the defence of France.

With the start of the Battle of Britain, the Spitfire came up for the first time against Professor Willy Messerschmitt's Bf 109. Seldom have two aircraft been so equally matched, the advantage switching from one to another according to the manner of combat and the place of action. The Bf 109 and Spitfire represented extreme contrasts in design and philosophy; the wing of the German fighter was nearly 30 per cent smaller than that of the Spitfire, while the capacity of its similarly rated engine was 25 per cent greater. Faster to accelerate in a dive than the Spitfire, and slightly faster in level flight, it became progressively less manoeuvrable than the British fighter as the combat speed was reduced, and at low speeds the bigger-winged Spitfire could roll faster than the Bf 109E, the standard service version of the German fighter during the battle. The Bf 109E was definitely superior to the Spitfire I above 20,000 ft (6,100 m); a considerable part of the credit for this must be laid at the door of Daimler-Benz, who had fitted the German fighter's DB601 engine with an infinitely variable hydraulic transmission to drive the supercharger. The DB601 was unaffected by the drop in output which afflicted the early single-speed Merlin above 'rated altitude'—a concept about which the German pilot did not have to worry.

Two other important features distinguished the adversaries. The Bf 109 was armed with cannon, either two in the wings on the E-4 or one between the cylinder banks of the engine on the E-3, while the 1940 Spitfire was confined to rifle-calibre machine-guns—as mentioned earlier, the service trials of the cannon-armed IB in 1940 were successful only inasmuch as they demonstrated conclusively that the installation was not ready for service use. Experience in the Battle of Britain, however, showed also that the eight-gun armament was not enough to ensure lethality against a target such as the Heinkel He111 bomber, with its self-sealing fuel tanks and 600 lb (272 kg) of armour.

The other major technical difference between the two types lay, like the supercharger drive, in the engine. In developing the DB601 from the basic DB600, Daimler-Benz had installed a system of direct fuel injection into the cylinders. The pilot of the Bf 109, attacked from the rear, could simply push forward on the stick and dive away at full power. A Merlin-powered aircraft treated similarly would suffer an immediate engine cut as the transient negative G force prevented fuel droplets from reaching the engine through the vertically-mounted carburettor. Rolls-Royce had deliberately refrained from using fuel injection in its engines, on the grounds that the fuel from the carburettor, evaporating downstream of the supercharger, cooled the charge entering the cylinder and produced an effect similar to a higher octane rating or higher supercharger boost rating. Neither had the negative-G cut-out been anticipated. Eventually carburetor modifications alleviated the problem, and the last of the whole line—the Seafire FR.47—had fuel injection, but not

before the negative-G cut had provided the Bf 109 with a useful means of escape.

In the opening stages of the Battle of Britain, the Bf 109-equipped *Jagdgeschwader* adopted tactics which best exploited the attributes of their aircraft, providing top cover for the bomber formations above the British fighters' best altitude and engaging British fighter formations when conditions were most favourable. This 'free-chasing' tactic also involved the sort of combat at which the Bf 109 excelled: high-speed diving attacks, a single firing pass with the highly destructive armament and a dive away. The Luftwaffe was moreover adopting a far better combat formation than the British squadrons' three-aircraft 'vics'; the German fighters flew in a loose *Schwarm* of four aircraft, fighting in a *Rotte* of two. Each pilot could scan the sky beyond his companion so that formation flying did not impede the scan for the enemy, and the responsibility was cleanly split between the offensive leader and the defensive wingman. In the early stages of the Battle this formation was adopted by some Fighter Command units. However, it was still difficult for the British fighters to meet the free-chasing Bf 109s on anything like equal terms. In late July, Bf 109s were first reported to be using the pushover-and-dive tactic to escape from pursuit; around the same time, Fighter Command acknowledged that the Hurricane was outclassed by the German fighter and instituted the policy of using the Hurricanes against the bombers while the Spitfires took on the fighter escort. This was only a partial solution to Fighter Command's loss rate. Fortunately, despite the fact that the Luftwaffe tactics were highly damaging to Fighter Command they were not seen as such by the Luftwaffe *Kampfgeschwader* whose pilots and gunners saw only the apparently unopposed attacks of those British fighters which managed to engage them. A succession of increasingly authoritative orders were transmitted to the *Jagdgeschwader,* requiring them to escort the bombers ever more closely. The fighter leaders understandably protested that this forced them into the slow-speed, medium-level defensive combats, with a great deal of tight turning, where the Spitfire's virtues came to the fore. This was the context of Adolf Galland's much-quoted comment to Hermann Goering, when asked if there was anything he needed for the air battle: 'I should like an outfit of Spitfires for my squadron.' Galland certainly did not believe that the Spitfire was intrinsically a superior aircraft to the Bf 109—he would have been a very unusual fighter pilot if he had believed it—but that he appreciated that the performance and characteristics of the British fighter would have been ideal for the job his squadron was now being asked to do.

The reduced effectiveness of the German fighter force, coupled with the deeper penetration and correspondingly shorter combat endurance consequent on the switching of the brunt of the attack to London, gave the British intercepters the chance they needed to attack the main bomber formations with a steadily decreasing degree of interference. The Bf 109s were even assigned to escort the Bf 110 'destroyer' fighters which were themselves intended to provide support for the bomber squadrons but had proved incapable of defending themselves against the RAF fighters. By mid-September the bomber losses had mounted to the point where the daylight campaign was untenable. A minor incident that month marked the end of the Spitfire IB's brief career; eight of the aircraft, on service trials with 19 Squadron, attacked a formation of Bf 110s, no fewer than six of the Spitfires suffering gun stoppages almost immediately. The Spitfire squadron subsequently exchanged its IBs for a scratch team of IAs drawn from maintenance units.

Late September and early October, however, brought a new problem. Now that the Luftwaffe bomber squadrons were raiding by night without fighter escort, the Bf 109 units were left free to conduct nuisance bombing raids, generally releasing their single bombs from high altitude before the population of the attacked area could be alerted. The Spitfires sent up to intercept these high-flying intruders, which were now unencumbered by bombers, found themselves at a serious disadvantage, but the raids were eventually stopped by a combination of worsening weather, increasing Fighter Command strength and the introduction of the Spitfire II and Hurricane II, with much improved high-altitude performance.

By the end of 1940 the Photographic Development Unit (PDU) was well established, and was relying almost entirely on Spitfire conversions. The PDU was unusual in that it owed its beginnings to an ostensibly civilian operation, headed by Sidney Cotton, which before the war had operated an apparently innocent Lockheed transport around Europe. In fact the Lockheed was equipped with long-focal-length cameras in a concealed installation, and the lessons learned about heated lenses and other necessary items of equipment were applied in the conversion of Spitfire Is to photo-reconnaissance aircraft. Between July and December of 1940 the PDU carried out 841 sorties over German-occupied areas, losing ten aircraft.

The work of the PDU—later renamed the Photographic Reconnaissance unit or PRU—became increasingly important as the RAF bombing campaign against Germany intensified, but some of its most valuable and hazardous early work involved the investigation of new systems being put into service by the German forces. In the first two months of 1941 PRU Spitfires revealed the shape of the Freya early warning radar, allowing its performance and characteristics

to be assessed. In this area, one of the greatest strengths of the PRU was the ability of successively improved reconnaissance Spitfires to maintain *routine* surveillance of important sites so that British Intelligence would be immediately alerted to any development by changes in the picture. An advantage of the Spitfire in this role was that it was a dual-purpose aircraft: as well as carrying long-focus cameras at high level the PR Spitfires could be fitted with an oblique camera facing to port for low-level 'Dicer' sorties, which were highly dangerous but justified when the reward was a detailed photograph of a new electronic installation.

A more aggressive role was taken by the Spitfire squadrons—by now including an increasing proportion of the much improved Spitfire V—in the 'fighter sweeps' which the RAF conducted against German fighter forces in Northern Europe in 1941. A small force of bombers was used as bait to draw the Luftwaffe into combat with a massive fighter escort divided into a close escort, escort cover groups and free-chasing target-support wings. However, the introduction of the Spitfire V yielded less of a combat advantage than had been expected, because its service entry coincided with that of the aerodynamically refined Bf 109F and only just preceded that of the Focke-Wulf Fw190, an aircraft of later design that outclassed and outperformed the Spitfire V in every operational characteristic except turning circle. Development and introduction into service of the Spitfire IX was not in time to prevent the Luftwaffe from achieving local air superiority over the Channel during the escape of the warships *Scharnhorst, Gneisenau* and *Prinz Eugen* from Brest to Wilhelmshaven and Kiel in February, 1942; nor was the improved type available in sufficient numbers to prevent heavy RAF losses (amounting to 106 aircraft) in the air operations supporting the abortive Dieppe raid in August of that year. This was also the period of the first high-speed hit-and-run raids by German fighter-bombers on British targets, and only with the introduction of the Spitfire XII could the British fighter effectively counter these low-level intruders.

The year of 1942 was the first in which the Spitfire was deployed in any numbers outside the United Kingdom. Following the entry of the Soviet Union into the war, 143 Spitfire Vs (some converted from earlier Marks) were deliv-

Spitfire F. Mk I

(Imperial War Museum)

Spitfire F. Mk Vc

(Imperial War Museum)

ered to the Soviet Union. It was the intensifying North Africa campaign, however, which made the greatest demands on the Spitfire force. At that time the Spitfire was still the only Allied fighter available in any quantities which could meet contemporary German combat aircraft on equal terms, and the deployment of a force of Spitfires into the Mediterranean theatre became a high priority. The problem was that the strengthened Luftwaffe forces in Sicily were a well-nigh impenetrable obstacle to the shipment of Spitfires to Malta—the unsinkable aircraft carrier around which the air strategy in the Mediterranean revolved—while the Spitfire apparently lacked the range to be ferried by air from the nearest secure base at Gibraltar. Starting in March, 1942, therefore, standard Spitfire Vs modified by the addition of a non-jettisonable ventral fuel tank were carried to a point off the Algerian coast by aircraft carriers and launched to fly the remaining 660 miles (1,060 km) to Malta. Between March and October, 367 Spitfires were safely delivered to Malta in this way, and as the campaign developed the fighters were transferred from Malta to North African bases. Special procedures were developed to get the overloaded Spitfires, manned by land-based pilots making their first carrier take-offs, safely into the air. Later in the year, Spitfires fitted with 170 gal (770 lit) drop tanks were ferried non-stop to Malta from Gibraltar; the aircraft were also fitted with 29 gal (132 lit) auxiliary oil tanks similar to that installed in the modified nose of long-range reconnaissance Spitfires, which replaced the usual tropical filter. (The ungainly tropical air filter installed on Mediterranean Spitfires and early Seafires was later replaced with a more discreet and streamlined design.) Non-stop ferrying from Gibraltar would have become the standard method of delivering Spitfires to the Mediterranean theatre in 1943, but the collapse of the German forces in North Africa after El Alamein eliminated the need for such expedients.

October, 1942, also saw the operational debut of the Seafire in support of the Allied invasion of French North Africa, the type being blooded in action in the following month against Dewoitine D.520 fighters of the Vichy French forces. The Seafire's first kill, in fact, was an American-built Martin 167 light bomber of the Vichy forces. Seafires were not the only Supermarine fighters used in support of the Operation Torch landings; Spitfire VBs of the US Army Air Force 31st and 52nd Fighter Groups also took part in the action. The USAAF Spitfire groups stemmed from the Eagle squadrons which, manned by American volunteers, had supported the RAF in the Battle of Britain, and the Supermarine fighter was used on a larger scale by the US units based in the United Kingdom. (The only US fighters available in quantity before the end of 1942 were the mediocre Curtiss P-40 and Bell P-39.) Before the North African invasion the USAAF Spitfires had participated in some RAF fighter sweeps and had also provided escorts for early short-range daylight bombing missions. After the USAAF fighter force had converted to newer American fighters the 8th Air Force continued to use a few of the photo-reconnaissance versions in Europe.

Both in North Africa and in Europe the Spitfire encountered a new threat in 1942, taking the ungainly shape of the Junkers Ju86. This pre-war German bomber/transport had been retired from the front-line bomber squadrons before the Battle of Britain, but had been made the subject of development work aimed at producing a high-altitude bomber and reconnaissance aircraft. In May, 1942, the first version of this aircraft, the Ju86P, commenced operations from Crete over Cairo and Alexandria, photographing defence preparations and military installations with impunity. It was a stripped-down Spitfire V which carried out the first successful interception of the high-flying but unprotected Junkers, bringing the reconnaissance aircraft down with the mighty armament of two 0.5 in (12.7 mm) machine guns.

By the time the Junkers Ju86 was used for resumed flights over Britain, however, the aircraft had undergone some changes. The most obvious of these was a further massive extension of the wingspan, but the two Ju86Rs deployed to Northern France in August, 1942, were modified to carry a single 550 lb (250 kg) bomb. The extra span and engine modifications of the Ju86R put it outside the reach of the Spitfire V, and even the high-altitude, pressurised Mark VI was, due to its single-stage Merlin, incapable of intercepting the new aircraft. The Mark VII with two-stage Merlin and pressure cabin was not yet ready, and the German bombers were able to raid British targets unopposed. Air raid warnings

Spitfire F. Mk IX (left)

(Imperial War Museum)

Spitfire F. Mk IXc

(Imperial War Museum)

Spitfire Mk Vb Cockpit

1 Seat
2 Control column
3 Heel board
4 Rudder pedal adjusting wheel
5 Rudder pedal
6 Radiation flap control lever
7 Map case
8 Oil dilution pushbotton
9 Rudder trimming tab handwheel
10 Pressure head heater switch
11 Elevator trimming tab handwheel
12 Bomb switch
13 Crowbar
14 Door catch
15 Camera indication supply plug
16 Mixture lever
17 Throttle lever
18 Propeller control lever
19 Boost control cut-out
20 Radio controller
21 Ignition switch
22 Brake triple pressure gauge
23 Clock
24 Elevator tabs position indicator
25 Oxygen regulator
26 Navigation lights switch
27 Flap control
28 Airspeed indicator
29 Altimeter
30 Gun and cannon three-position
   pushbutton (Spitfire Vb)
31 Cockpit light switches
32 Direction indicator and setting nob
33 Artificial horizon
34 Reflector gun sight, type GM-2
35 Rear view mirror
36 Ventilator control
37 Rate of climb indicator
38 Turning indicator
39 Booster coil pushbutton
40 Engine starting pushbutton
41 Oil pressure gauge
42 Oil temperature gauge
43 Fuel contents gauge and pushbutton
44 Radiator temperature gauge
45 Boost pressure gauge
46 Fuel pressure warning lamp
47 Engine speed indicator
48 Ventilator control
49 Stowage for reflector sight lamp

50 Cockpit light
51 Signalling switchbox
52 Remote contactor and switch
53 Fuel tank pressurising cock control
54 Slow running cut-out control
55 Priming pump
56 Fuel cock
57 Compass
58 Undercarriage control lever
59 Harness release
60 Oxygen hose
61 I.F.F. controls
62 CO₂ cylinder for undercarriage emergency
   system
63 Oxygen supply cock
64 Windscreen de-icing pump
65 Windscreen de-icing needle valve
66 Undercarriage emergency lowering control
67 Windscreen de-icing cock

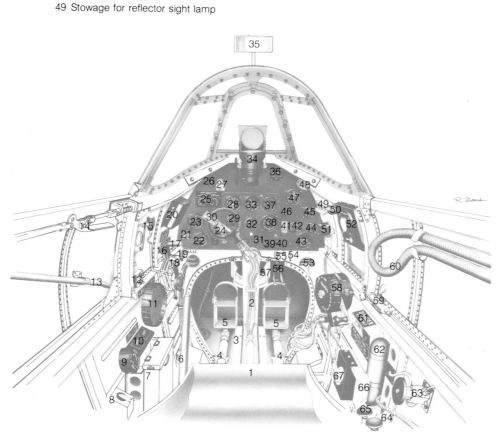

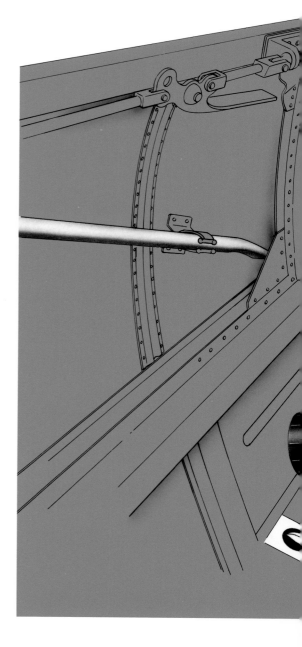

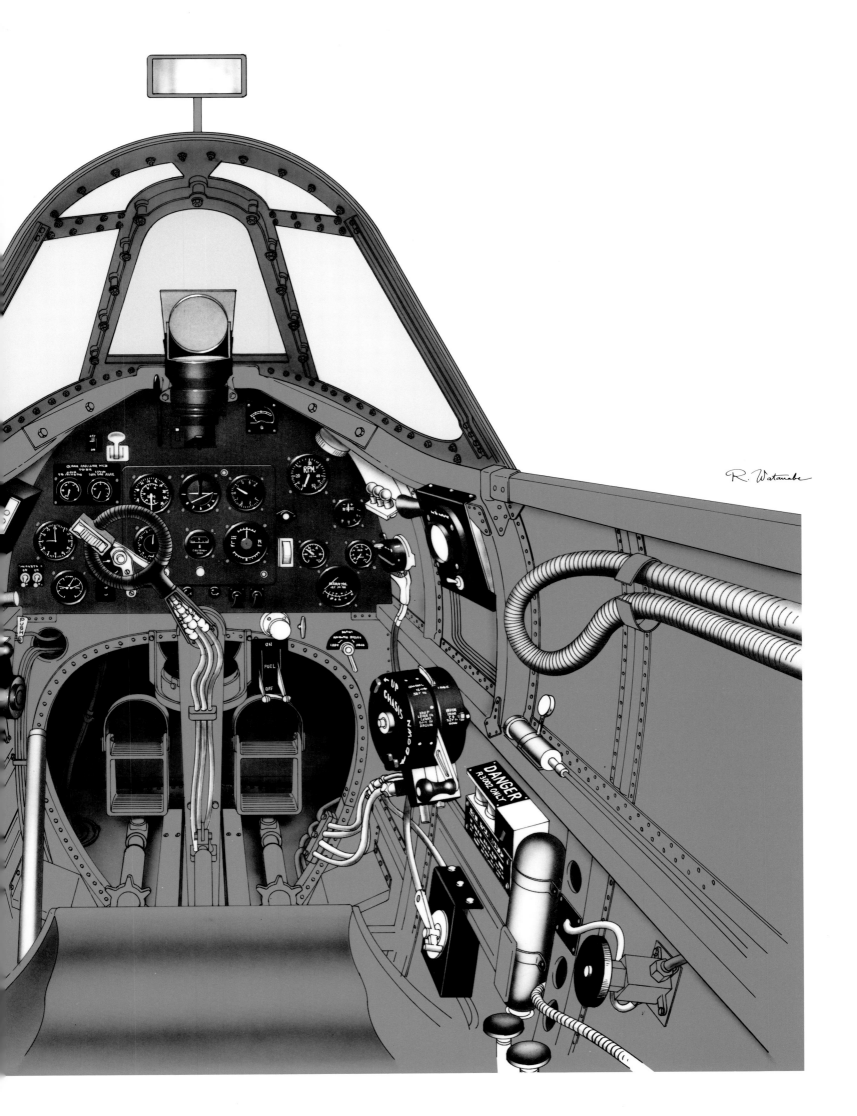

R. Watanabe

were not sounded for single intruders, with the result that on August 28 a single bomb from a Ju86R killed 48 people at Bristol. After this incident, a special unit was formed at Northolt, flying Spitfire IXs modified by removal of the machine guns, armour and other equipment and fitted with a lightweight wooden propeller. Medically selected pilots were trained to fly at high altitudes without pressurisation. On September 12 one of the modified aircraft put a cannon shell through one of the intruders at 44,000 ft (13,400 m), and although the Ju86R regained its base operations over Britain were halted.

With the increasing tempo of Spitfire production and the availability of newer fighters in the European theatre, the Spitfire began to spread its wings more widely in 1943. Early in the year 54 Squadron took its Spitfire Vs to Darwin to protect the Australian mainland from the Japanese air forces. In August the Portuguese air force, which had ordered a batch of Spitfire Is before war broke out, finally took delivery of 15 of the type; these rather elderly aircraft were supplemented soon after by Spitfire Vs. One unit which had an eventful year was 155 Squadron, which took its new Mark VIIIs (including some unusual four-cannon aircraft) to the Soviet Union before joining a rapidly expanding Spitfire force in Burma late in 1943. Operations in the Far East brought the Spitfire up against the Japanese Navy and Army fighters, of which the foremost was the redoubtable Mitsubishi A6M Zero-Sen. The A6M was an unusual opponent for the Spitfire, in that the British fighter enjoyed superiority in the areas where it was inferior to its other contemporaries, and vice versa. For example, it was faster in level and diving flight than the A6M, but the Japanese fighter could turn inside it at low speeds, and the tactics adopted against the A6M by the Spitfire tended to be the reverse of those used against its other adversaries.

September, 1943, saw the first extensive combat use of the Seafire. The decision to invade Italy at the 'knee' rather than fighting all the way up from Sicily created problems in providing air cover over the invasion beaches, because the selected invasion site at Salerno was too far from the Allied air bases in Sicily for effective air cover to be maintained. Accordingly it was decided to provide air support for the operation from a force of Royal Navy carriers equipped mainly with Seafire IICs and LIICs. The Seafires brought down few of the German and Italian aircraft, partly because the tactics used were predominantly defensive and many of the raiders were bomb-carrying *Jabo* Bf 109s and Fw190s. But in 713 sorties, no fewer than 42 of the 120 Seafires involved had been lost or written off, including 32 wrecked in landing accidents, while 39 more of the fighters had been damaged in deck accidents. Although the operation served its purpose of providing air cover until the land forces could provide secure airstrips, the Seafire force had virtually ceased to exist by Salerno D-day plus 3. The bad experience of Salerno not unnaturally coloured the Navy's subsequent view of the Seafire; although development of a Seafire version with a stronger undercarriage was initiated shortly after the Salerno operations, it was to be another three years before this aircraft, the Seafire 17, entered service. Meanwhile, deliveries of purpose-built American carrier fighters to the Fleet Air Arm were picking up speed, and the Seafire suf-

fered by comparison.

The Spitfire, however, continued to be one of the mainstays of Fighter Command as the invasion of Europe approached. In 1943 the Mark XII had joined the home-defence force to help counter the threat of 'tip-and-run' attacks by German fighter-bombers, and at the beginning of the following year the Spitfire XIV appeared, keeping the Spitfire well in the front line despite the delayed appearance of the Mark 21. The US daylight bombing offensive was by this time drawing away an increasing proportion of the German fighter force in Western Europe, and the Royal Air Force found itself concentrating on low-level fighter sweeps and ground-attack operations. The steady re-equipment of the squadrons with Mark IXs from Castle Bromwich or the new Mark XIVs, both with the ability to carry unguided rockets or bombs, helped this trend; the remaining Mark Vs were also converted in 1943 to a low-altitude configuration.

Tactics of close support developed in the Western Desert and Italy were naturally developed and improved in the campaign in Northern France. The lesson learned in the early stages of the Desert campaign was that close co-operation was essential at all levels if the Army and Air Force were to work together. Air Marshal Harry Broadhurst, supporting British forces in Europe in command of 83 Group, moved his headquarters alongside that of the commander of the army group he was supporting. At the air force bases, Army liaison officers kept the squadrons informed about what was going on in the ground battle, while at the front operations were controlled by RAF personnel in radio-equipped vehicles. Another part of this system was the fighter-reconnaissance aircraft, a low-level fighter with a specially trained pilot and an oblique camera; the FR Spitfires not only reported on enemy movements but provided the British commanders with exact and up-to-date information on the positions of their own forces. The fighter pilots' tallies of 'kills' were expanded to include enemy vehicles; the Spitfire, however, was less suitable for attacks against armoured vehicles or locomotives than the more heavily armed Typhoon and Tempest.

The Spitfire played an important part in the fight against the German 'revenge weapons' on which Hitler had ordered a tremendous development effort in the belief that there was no effective defence against them. In the case of the Fieseler Fi103 or V-1 flying bomb this was certainly not true, because the missile's straight flightpath made it a relatively easy target and its speed was not quite sufficient to ensure its escape from the latest fighter aircraft. Spitfire XIVs and Tempest Vs were the only fighters with enough speed to catch the V-1s—either overhauling them and toppling the relatively cheap and crude guidance system with their wingtip vortices or blasting the bomb at perilously close range with cannon—until the first RAF Meteor jet fighters entered service. The Fi103 could thus be countered by conventional means; not so the A-4 or V-2, a ballistic missile which presented an impossible target once it was off the ground. After heavy bombers had wrecked the massive concrete bunkers from which the rockets were originally to have been launched, the German Army switched to small, mobile launch teams carrying their missiles on the Meilerwagen transporter/erector. The search for these sites, well hidden and inevitably protected by heavy flak, was a difficult task; bomb-carrying Spitfires attacked the sites to some effect, but the missile firings on London only ceased when the front line was pushed out of range. Firings at Antwerp and Rotterdam, however, continued until the end of the war. Some of the armed reconnaissance patrols over suspected A-4 sites towards the end of the war involved Spitfire 21s, one squadron of which became operational before the end of the war in Europe.

Meanwhile, the first Seafires had been heading for the Far East. By now the Fleet Air Arm had largely re-equipped with Seafire IIIs and LIIIs, the folding wings of the new type facilitating carrier operations and allowing more aircraft to be carried. By this time it was accepted that the high climb speed and rapid acceleration of the Seafire, which was superior to the American fighters in these respects, suited it mainly to the defence of the fleet against air attack; and by early 1945, when the first Seafire units were engaged in support of carrier-aircraft strikes against oil refineries in the East Indies, suicide tactics were increasingly being used by the Japanese Army Air Force. In normal air-to-air combat, however, the fighters employed in South-East Asia by the Japanese were outclassed by the Seafire. In March, 1945, Seafires became operational with the carriers of the British Pacific Fleet in time for the invasion of Okinawa, in which the Supermarine fighter again filled its role of protecting the carriers against Kamikaze suicide attacks. Only in the last days of the war were the Seafires used on ground attacks against Japanese air bases.

The post-war run-down of the British Spitfire force was rapid. The Merlin-engined variants went first, being replaced by Griffon-powered aircraft built towards the end of the war or shortly afterwards and held in storage. Spitfire IXs based in Palestine, for example, were replaced with Mark 18s (Arabic numerals replacing Roman shortly after the war) and the Spitfire 22 re-equipped many of the Auxiliary Air Force squadrons until these received jets in 1950-51. The RAF fighter force had not fought its last combat with the end of the 1939-45 war, however. In 1948, the RAF Spitfires of 32 Squadron, based at Ramat David in Palestine, were attacked by Egyptian Mark IXs, apparently mistaking them for Spitfires acquired by the Israeli Air Force. The second wave of four attacking aircraft failed to escape before they were pursued and easily overhauled by the faster Mark 18s of 208 Squadron, which destroyed them without further loss.

Mark 18s also saw action in Malaya, being used for cannon and rocket strikes against suspected guerilla hideouts. The effectiveness of such tactics was doubtful due to the lack of precise information as to where the hideouts were, and later the RAF switched to using more heavily armed aircraft such as Bristol Brigands (which also had a much longer loiter endurance than the Spitfire) and even carpet-bombed suspected areas with Lincolns. The last RAF fighter unit to use the Spitfire was No 80 Squadron, which operated its Mark 24s from Kai Tak airfield at Hong Kong until January 1952.

With the Royal Navy, the Seafire enjoyed increased importance when the Lend-Lease Corsairs and

Hellcats were returned to the United States after the end of the war. The new Griffon-powered Seafire XV replaced the Merlin-engined versions by mid-1946, at least as far as front-line units were concerned; between that time and mid-1947, however, operations with these aircraft were severely restricted after a succession of accidents caused by a faulty design feature in the supercharger clutch. This was remedied in time for the improved Seafire 17—with its stronger landing gear—to be issued to front-line units and the newly formed Royal Naval Volunteer Reserve squadrons. It was an RNVR squadron which took delivery of the first Seafire FR.46s, more advanced than the contemporary front-line Seafire but lacking folding wings, in July, 1948. The definitive FR.47 embarked later in that year aboard HMS *Triumph,* and arrived in Singapore in September, 1949; in the following month the ultimate descendant of the Supermarine 300 fired ordonance in anger for the first time, carrying out rocket strikes against guerilla bases in Malaya. With the outbreak of war in Korea, *Triumph* took the Seafires to the Yellow Sea, where the fighters carried out strafing, ground attack and air defence missions until normal attrition forced the retirement of the carrier and its few remaining aircraft. The disembarkation of *Triumph's* last Seafires in November 1950 marked the end of the type's career with the Royal Navy's first-line units, the last RNVR and training units retiring their Mark 17s and FR.47s in 1954.

The year 1954 saw the replacement of the last strategic reconnaissance Spitfire PR.19s in Royal Air Force service, the last of this variant soldiering on for meteorological reconnaissance until 1957, when the last aircraft of the type was retired from British service. By this time the Spitfire had also come to the end of its career under foreign flags, a career which might be said to have started with the pre-war Portuguese order for 12 Spitfire Is. Eventually, Portugal took delivery of Spitfire Is in August, 1943, these aircraft being retired in 1948; the more modern Spitfire VBs delivered in the same year as the older aircraft were retired in 1952. The Portuguese Spitfires were noteworthy in that they were the only aircraft of the type to operate outside Allied command during the 1939-45 war.

Post-war reconstruction of European air forces was helped in some instances by the pilots who had flown with the wartime RAF while in exile from their occupied homelands. Norway, Denmark and Greece all took delivery of surplus Mark IXs in 1947; the first two also received a trio of PR.XIs each, while Greece became the only export customer for the Mark XVI. Some Spitfires reached Eastern Europe, serving briefly in Yugoslavia; another group of Mark IXs was supplied to Italy. The Royal Dutch Air Force was one of two European air forces to use the Supermarine fighter in combat, employing its clipped-wing Mark IXs against insurgents in Indonesia before that country's independence.

The other European air arm to use the type in anger was the French Aeronavale, which took delivery of 48 refurbished Seafire LIIIs in March 1946. The Seafires departed for France's South-East Asian possessions abroad *Arromanches* in October 1948, and a few air strikes were carried out against Viet Minh insurgents late in that year. Landing accidents were common, as they had been with the Royal Navy's

Seafires and by early 1949 *Arromanches* has so few serviceable aircraft that there was no longer any point keeping the ship in the Vietnam area. The Seafires were replaced by equally elderly but more reliable Grumman F6F Hellcats in 1950.

Seafires were also exported to Canada, two squadrons of Royal Canadian Navy Seafire XVs being formed in 1945. They were replaced by Hawker Sea Furies in mid-1948. The last Seafires to see combat, however, were probably a batch of 20 Seafire XVs delivered to Burma for counter-insurgency operations in 1951. These aircraft had been extensively modified by the installation of non-folding Spitfire 18 wings and the removal of carrier equipment, and were thus very similar to the Spitfire 18s also operated by the Union of Burma Air Force, the main difference between the two types being the Seafires' single-stage Griffon engines and the Spitfires' all-round-vision hoods. The Seafire also took off its seaboots for the Irish Air Corps, which took delivery of 12 denavalised Seafire IIIs in 1947; the same air force was one of two purchasers for the two-seat Spitfire T.IX, converted from the standard aircraft by the installation of a second, separate cockpit behind and above the first.

A major Spitfire operator in Europe was the Royal Swedish Air Force, which acquired 50 unused surplus Spitfire PR.19s from the United Kingdom in 1948. Designated S31 in Swedish service, the aircraft were operated by the F11 wing based at Nykoping until they were superseded by more modern jet aircraft in August 1955. The biggest Spitfire operator other than the RAF, however, was the Royal Indian Air Force (as it was named between 1945 and 1948) which took delivery of 250 Spitfire VIIIs towards the end of the 1939-45 war. From 1945 these aircraft were supplemented by Griffon-powered Mark XIVs, and in 1947 the Indian Air Force gained a conversion-training capability with the delivery of half-a-dozen two-seater T.IXs. Four years later, India acquired from British stocks a squadron of Mark 18s and a squadron of PR.19s, these being the last Spitfires delivered from the UK. India's last Spitfires were retired in 1955.

Egypt and Syria also took delivery of Spitfires, the former receiving Mark 22s to replace its Mark IXs in 1950, and as far as the British were concerned these were the last Spitfires to be delivered to the Middle East. The State of Israel had other ideas, and despite an arms embargo the emerging Israeli air force managed to conclude a contract with dollar-hungry Czechoslovakia for the supply of 50 Spitfire LF.IX fighters, as these were being replaced at that time by Soviet aircraft. The Spitfires were preceded into service by Avia C-210s—developments of the Bf 109—with the result that Spitfires and Messerschmitts were to find themselves fighting side by side against Egyptian Spitfires.

The first C-210s had been ferried to Israel abroad Douglas C-54s acquired in the USA, but in 1948 the French closed the airport of Ajaccio to the transports and the air route to Zatec in Czechoslovakia was blocked. An attempt to fly the Spitfires non-stop from Zatec to Ramat David in Israel succeeded only in part, two out of the five Spitfires in the formation being forced to land at Rhodes. Eventually, however, 50 Spitfires reached Israel from Czechoslovakia, proving very much more popular than the unwieldy Junkers-powered Avia. In early 1949, Israeli Spitfire IXs shot down a number of RAF Spitfire 18s based in the Canal Zone when the British fighters were carrying out reconnaissance missions over Israeli-held territory to check compliance with the ceasefire which had ended the 1948 war: thus, the last RAF Spitfires to be destroyed in fighter-versus-fighter combat were shot down by Spitfires, just as their last victims had been Spitfires.

The Israeli Air Force acquired 35 more Spitfires HF.IXEs from Italy in 1950-51, and these aircraft replaced the Avia fighters. In 1954, however, Israel acquired Gloster Meteor jet fighters and the Spitfires were retired. Thirty of the newer aircraft were sold to Burma, but once again there was a problem of delivery because Arab states would refuse landing and refuelling rights to any aircraft originating in Israel. An attempt to deliver the aircraft via Sicily, complete with false flight plans alleging that they originated in Britain, was unsuccessful, and the aircraft had to be refitted with long-range fuel tanks and delivered by a northerly route. These reconditioned Spitfire IXs joined the motley Burmese force of Mark 18s and denavalised Seafire XVs, operating against insurgents in Burma into the late 1950s. By 1956, only these aircraft and a few RAF meteorological reconnaissance PR.19s remained in service out of the 22,000 Spitfires and Seafires built, and by the end of 1957 the aircraft passed into history.

A number of Spitfires, however, have remained in flying condition, preserved by the RAF, by groups of enthusiasts or by wealthy individuals. In the making of the film *The Battle of Britain* in 1968, a force of 12 airworthy Spitfires was assembled, including one Spitfire II which had actually participated in the 1940 conflict. Some of these still fly, and have actually been joined in the air recently by newly restored aircraft; such is the appeal and fascination of the Spitfire that the last of the type seem set to continue flying indefinitely.

(Imperial War Museum)

MOSQUITO

Text by BILL SWEETMAN

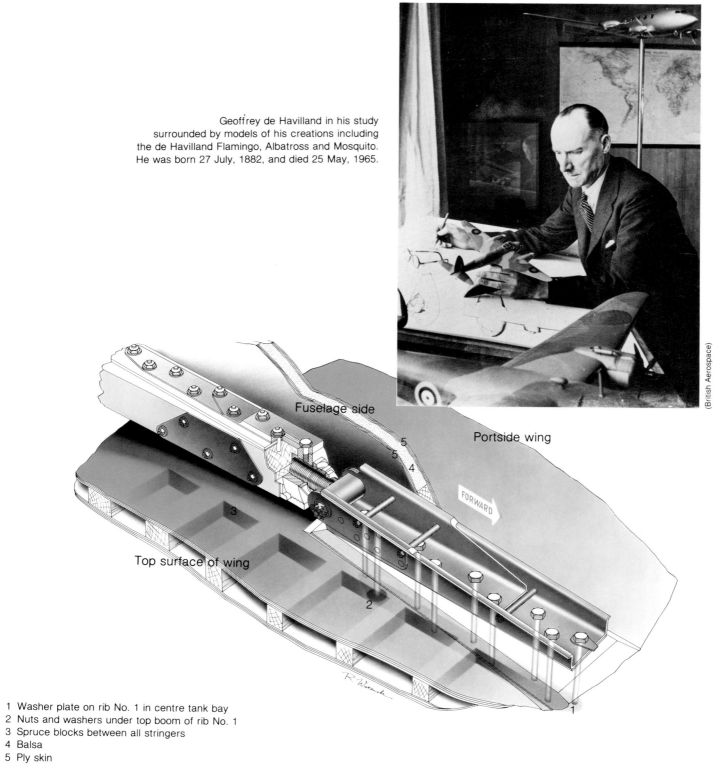

Geoffrey de Havilland in his study surrounded by models of his creations including the de Havilland Flamingo, Albatross and Mosquito. He was born 27 July, 1882, and died 25 May, 1965.

(British Aerospace)

Fuselage side

Portside wing

Top surface of wing

FORWARD

1 Washer plate on rib No. 1 in centre tank bay
2 Nuts and washers under top boom of rib No. 1
3 Spruce blocks between all stringers
4 Balsa
5 Ply skin

Introduction

In our own time, as the cost of military aircraft has steadily risen, so there has been increasing concern on the part of planners, air staffs and governments to ensure that any new military aircraft can function efficiently in as wide a variety of roles as possible. This concern is not always rewarded, and efforts to produce such an ideal machine often result in an aircraft which costs more than it need have done and can often perform only one or two of the roles originally proposed for it.

The de Havilland Mosquito of the Second World War by contrast was a truly successful multi-role combat aircraft. Following the scepticism which initially greeted the concept, the Mosquito was adopted as high-speed bomber, reconnaissance aircraft and night fighter, going on to pioneer one of today's most important warplane categories, that of the heavy, long-range interdiction/strike aircraft.

The chief problem with the Mosquito was that it was relatively late in the war before it was put into large-scale production, and its very versatility conspired with the tardiness of the production decision to ensure that there were never enough Mosquitos for each of its many applications as many commanders would have wished. Neither was the potential of the Mosquito as the mainstay of a strategic bombing offensive fully put to the test, for the simple reason that the Luftwaffe was much reduced in strength by the time even a medium-sized force of Mosquito bombers could be assembled. It was a year after Stalingrad and Midway before the Mosquito was available in any large quantities, and it never had a chance to show its full potential before a new breed of whistling propellerless aircraft had rendered it obsolescent. It is an indication of the pace of change of aircraft technology that the jet-propelled Arado Ar234 bomber was flying by the time Mosquito operations got into their stride.

The Mosquito never underwent the sort of massive development which took place over the lifespan of the Spitfire; the main changes introduced during production were the switch to the two-stage supercharged Merlin engine and the introduction of a lightly pressurized cabin to ease some of

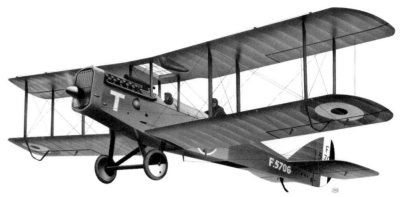

The de Havilland D.H.4, designed by Geoffrey de Havilland for the Aircraft Manufacturing Company in 1916 and one of the most successful light bombers of the First World War.

the physiological stress on crews at altitude. Neither affected the external shape of the Mosquito to any great extent, and all changes to the Mosquito (with the exception of the folding wings of the naval TR.33 and TR.37) were carried out without major changes to the structure.

It was the external shape and internal structure of the Mosquito which were the keys to its load-carrying ability and speed, the two parameters to which its success can be attributed. Aerodynamically, the Mosquito was the outcome of a chain of development which started with the D.H.88 Comet racer, aimed at extracting the maximum cruising speed from minimum power in the interests of maximum range. Minimum size, neat packaging and above all clean design enabled the de Havilland designers to achieve this aim, while wrapping the Mosquito around a bomb-bay which, with a little extension, could accommodate a larger weapon than that of a Boeing B-17.

More is said below of the Mosquito's radical internal structure. Suffice it to remark here that wood, being composed of fibres bonded together with resin, is a naturally occurring "composite" material. In contemporary military aircraft, fine filaments of carbon have replaced wood fibres, and the resins are artificial polymers, while glass-fibre sailplane and lightplane wings are built up around cores of polyurethane foam rather than balsa. Perhaps composites simply are better adapted to the structural requirements of flight than metals.

Few aircraft have been designed in such fidelity to the original concept as the Mosquito. The pioneering in its

(Planet News)

design was not achieved without some cost. The wooden structure was subject to unsuspected ills away from the mild climate of England and the loving care of the flight-test shed. The small wing, mighty engines and delicately harmonized flight controls unquestionably laid the foundations for the Mosquito's astonishing performance, but at the same time laid pitfalls for the unwary, unsympathetic or badly trained pilot. The Mosquito was a slightly nervous thoroughbred which would perform impressive feats in the hands of the courageous and competent – such as lifting a 4,000 lb bomb and carrying it to Berlin – but would occasionally deal out a kick or a bite. Some of its wartime achievements were off limits to peacetime pilots, and some of its variants were less pleasant to handle than others.

But a Mosquito without these quirks would have been an aircraft far less optimized for maximum performance above all things, and would have been just another heavy combat aircraft among others rather than the outstanding machine which it was.

Genesis

In 1930, it would have been hard to tell either from the Hatfield drawing offices of the de Havilland Company or from the front line of the Royal Air Force that the initials "D.H." had once been synonymous with the light bomber, or even with military aircraft of any type. Neither was there any sign that the situation was to change as dramatically as it did, within a little more than ten years.

Captain Geoffrey de Havilland's D.H.4 light bomber of 1917 had already inscribed its designer's name in the history of the bomber. With the D.H.4, bomber pilots could at last feel that they were something more than second-class citizens of the air, fit only to augment the "kill" tallies of the fighter pilots' chivalry. (Much has been written about the sportsmanship of the fighter pilots in sparing an enemy whose interrupter gear had collapsed in a shower of cogwheels and left him defenceless in the middle of his adversary's ring-and-bead sight; rather less has been said about the fact that this sportsmanship rarely extended to bomber pilots.) For a short time after its introduction in March, 1917, the D.H.4 even possessed a slight ascendancy in speed over opposing fighters, and together with its American-engined derivative the D.H.9A achieved the distinction of being built under licence in the United States.

Rarely has a business collapsed so quickly as did the supply of military aircraft following the Armistice. De Havilland's company, Airco, was faced with massive cuts in its orders. The Royal Air Force, itself only a few months old as an independent organization, narrowly escaped complete submergence in the Army, and the paths of the company and its erstwhile main customer diverged.

Airco plunged heavily into the embryo airline business, supporting a new airline called Air Transport & Travel in a bid to start air services with rudimentary, semi-weatherproof adaptations of the D.H.4 and D.H.9. Larger, heavier airliners along similar lines followed, but AT & T had

Two D.H. Gipsy Six engines: 224 hp each
Max. speed: 235 mph (376 km/h)
Ceiling: 19,000 ft (5,795 m)
Span: 44 ft (13.42 m)
Length: 29 ft (8.87 m)
Height: 9 ft (2.74 m)
Wing area: 212.5 sq.ft (19.74 m²)

already collapsed in the face of competition from subsidized foreign airlines, and was not re-established when the British Government retaliated with its own system of subsidies. Airco instead sold its airliners to other companies; Daimler Air Services' D.H.34s were said to be the first aeroplanes to carry a uniformed steward. The D.H.34 had a brief career; Britain's smaller airlines were amalgamated into Imperial Airways in 1924, and the new company decreed that future airliners should have at least two engines. Handley Page took the lion's share of Imperial Airways' business, although de Havilland designed the D.H.66 Hercules which the airline used on some particularly demanding route sectors.

It was a completely different aircraft which brought fame and commercial success to the de Havilland Company, as Airco was now known. As recovery started after the 1914–18 war, the idea took root that the aeroplane would follow the same path as the motor-car, leading to almost universal ownership. Private sponsors, the *Daily Mail* newspaper and the Air Ministry offered prizes for the design of light aircraft using small engines or a restricted quantity of fuel; the Air Ministry's interest extended well beyond the design of such an aircraft, because the Government planned to aid the formation of flying clubs as a means of developing a national force of trained pilots.

D.H. 88 Comet Racer

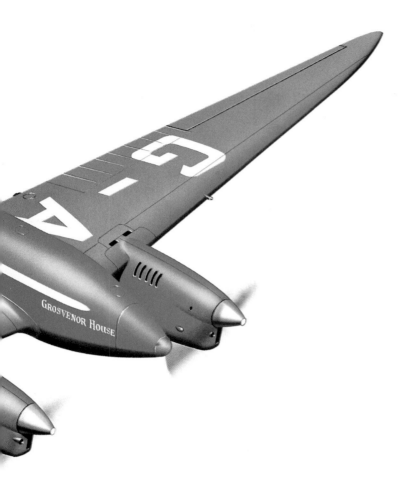

The de Havilland Company made its mark in the design of long-range, high speed aircraft with the D.H.88 Comet long-range racer. After fulfilling its design objective by winning the 1934 London-Melbourne air race for Britain, the Comet went on to set a number of speed-and-distance records.

As so often happens in aviation, the officially sponsored design efforts were more significant in showing designers what to avoid than in generating good designs directly. The ground-rules set for the competitions were shown to be too restrictive by the performance limitations of the aircraft they produced. Geoffrey de Havilland, whose D.H.53 Hummingbird was a runner-up in the Air Ministry's 1923 contest, learned these lessons and proceeded with the design of a rather more conventional, slightly larger aircraft. This, the D.H.60 Moth, totally eclipsed the older competition-winners on its appearance in 1925, and was adopted for the Air Ministry's training scheme; the Gipsy Moth, with a specially developed de Havilland engine, won fame in the hands of pilots such as Amy Johnson and Sir Francis Chichester; its descendants, derivatives and relatives established de Havilland as the major force in the world market for light aircraft, and included the Tiger Moth, the British Commonwealth's standard trainer. Demand for light aircraft led to the establishment of a de Havilland subsidiary in Australia in 1927, and a facility in Canada in 1928.

Meanwhile, the Royal Air Force was buying replacements for the D.H.4 and D.H.9A from other manufacturers. Fairey, Hawker and Westland light bombers and army co-operation aircraft closely followed the layout of the original de Havilland designs: single-engined aircraft using the same engines as contemporary fighters, and slightly slower due to their two seats and small bomb-load. The bomber strength of the RAF comprised these aircraft, and the very different "night bombers": large, very slow and unwieldy machines of twice the power and three times the weight. Compromise aircraft such as the Boulton Paul Sidestrand and Overstrand, faster than the night bombers but carrying a more effective armament than the day bombers, were treated with very little enthusiasm. When a technical revolution overtook the aircraft industry in the first half of the 1930s, the deficiencies of such a polarized bomber force became a source of potential disaster.

Part of the reason why the inadequacies of bomber designs were not appreciated lay in military conservatism. It was the United States' airline industry which generated the impetus behind the 1930s upheaval in aircraft design, as the U.S. West Coast produced new aircraft which took advantage of a whole range of completely new techniques. All-metal, smooth-skinned construction, retractable undercarriages, wing flaps and variable-pitch propellers combined to produce a massive improvement in airliner performance.

The potential of these new airliners as military aircraft could not be overlooked, and could be used as a deliberate instrument of propaganda and persuasion. Lord Rothermere, proprietor of the London *Daily Mail*, ordered a personal transport from the Bristol company; the fact that it could outrun any RAF fighter with ease was widely publicized, and the Type 142 formed the basis of the Blenheim bomber. In Germany, the Dornier Do 17 was the subject of similar claims that its speed rendered it relatively invulnerable to fighter interceptions.

But the bomber designers and those responsible for drafting bomber specifications had overlooked a vital point. The new technology could be applied just as easily to the fighter as to the bomber, but the new all-metal bombers were designed to survive against the 1920s' fabric-skinned biplane fighters. A new generation of fast, powerfully armed all-metal fighters would more than reverse the new bombers' speed advantage and render completely inadequate their single defensive machine guns. In the case of the RAF, however, it was to be 1938 by the time the new fighters entered service and could conduct mock attacks on the new and much vaunted Blenheims and Fairey Battles. By the time their vulnerability was exposed it was too late to eliminate them from the RAF's expansion plans without creating chaos out of the ordered working-up of the aircraft industry. Battles and Blenheims went into action, unescorted, against Bf 109s which were not only faster than the British bombers but were armed with cannon. Blenheim operations suffered heavy losses; some Battle missions verged on the suicidal.

The official answer to the problem was to specify larger aircraft with new, more powerful engines, which could carry a worthwhile bomb-load as well as a credible defensive armament. But two design teams, entirely separately and in the face of a great deal of scepticism, maintained their conviction that a properly designed bomber could rely on speed alone for its protection. Fortunately for the Western Allies, perhaps, official disbelief triumphed over the first to demonstrate results: the brothers Siegfried and Walter Gunter attained 363 mph (585 km/hr) with their coupled-engine Heinkel He119 in September 1937, but despite successful flight trials the German Air Ministry remained unimpressed. The other team to persist with the unarmed bomber, the de Havilland design office under Geoffrey de Havilland's supervision, were to have better luck.

Wooden Wonder

The de Havilland company's move from light training aircraft and light transports to a multi-purpose combat type arose from the company's interest in air racing. In the year that the Douglas company flew the first prototype of the aircraft that was to become the DC-3 – 1933 – Australian airline pioneer Sir Macpherson Robertson offered a £15,000 prize for the winner of an air race between London and Melbourne, to be held in the following October. Either a DC-2 or a Boeing 247 seemed certain to win; this was enough to spur de Havilland into the design of a specialized long-range racer. Geoffrey de Havilland announced that his company would build such aircraft to order for the race, and three customers came forward. They were given barely any information about the racer they had bought, except that it was guaranteed to cruise at 200 mph (320 km/hr) or more.

Eventually, it was one of the three D.H.88 Comets entered for the race which took the absolute prize, although a DC-2 in full airline trim took second place behind the specialized racer. The Comet was an unusual aircraft in many ways. Its slender wings were too thin for fuel tanks, so the fuel was carried in the slim fuselage which de Havilland had tailored around a pilot and navigator in tandem seats. More surprising, in an aircraft designed to race with a new generation of metal aeroplanes, was the fact that the airframe was built of wood.

The Comet and its de Havilland descendants have been described as "throwbacks", but in fact the method of construction used represented as important a change from the wooden-and-steel-framed fabric-covered aircraft of the 1920s as did stressed-skin metal construction. Two basic technical advances in the bonding of wood were the foundation of the de Havilland method and the reason why it had not been used earlier.

Carpenters had traditionally used glue made from animal products to assemble their products, but it breaks down in water and is thus unsuitable for outside use. In the early 1930s, however, the boat-building and aircraft industries discovered casein glue, which had been used in Ancient Egypt, lost until 1800 and then rediscovered by some carpenters in Germany and Switzerland. Casein is the protein in milk and is the basis of cheese, taking its name from the same root. It reacts slowly with lime to form a solid, highly effective as a glue and relatively impervious to moisture. Glued joints, more effective than mechanical fasteners, thus became practical for aircraft use.

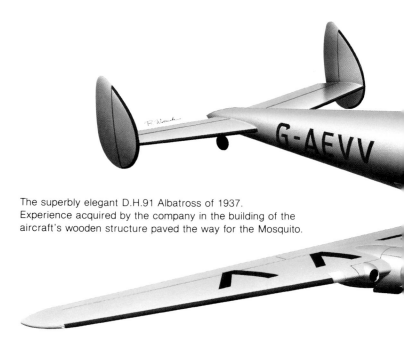

The superbly elegant D.H.91 Albatross of 1937. Experience acquired by the company in the building of the aircraft's wooden structure paved the way for the Mosquito.

The other technical advance used in the de Havilland wooden structure was the early plastic, Bakelite. Used in the form of phenol-formaldehyde glues, it could provide a strong and weather-proof bond in wood. Unlike casein, which was relatively easy to use, phenol-formaldehyde glues have to be cured under heat and pressure, making it almost impossible to use them for structural joints. However, they were used very successfully in making strong, waterproof plywood from very thin veneers.

Three weeks after the Comet *Grosvenor House* arrived victorious in Melbourne, de Havilland proposed the development of a high-speed intercontinental mailplane of wooden construction, designed to carry a 1,000 lb (450 kg) payload over 2,500 miles (4,025 km). An official rejection was reversed in time for the D.H.91 Albatross to fly in May 1937. The type went into production as a 22-seat airliner for Imperial Airways, which badly needed a modern airliner, having for the previous few years been operating lumbering biplanes in competition with DC-2s and Lockheeds.

The Albatross – the immediate ancestor of the Mosquito – was an aircraft of surpassing aerodynamic refinement, possessing a flowing gracefulness of line which would have been hard if not impossible to achieve in an aluminium structure. The cambered fuselage was built in one piece around a jig that could be dismantled and removed from inside the fuselage. The shell was formed of two layers of plywood, braced apart by a layer of balsa. The wing spars were spruce, and the skin was spruce planking covered with synthetic resin film. The wing was assembled in one piece, and fitted into the fuselage from underneath. A final touch of artistry was the engine installation, the four Gipsy Twelve engines being housed in pencil-slim cowlings and cooled by air which entered tiny ram-air inlets in the wing leading edge, passed forwards through the cowl and was exhausted via a flap behind the de Havilland variable-pitch propeller.

By the time the Albatross entered service in November 1938 there could be little doubt that the time for elegant airliners was running out. The de Havilland com-

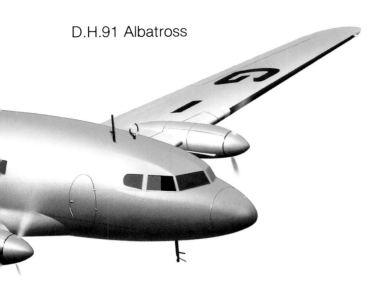

D.H.91 Albatross

pany's own studies of military aircraft had been under way for some time, investigations having started in earnest once the Albatross had flown. The company had taken as a starting point the specification for an advanced, high-powered medium bomber issued by the Air Ministry in 1936. This specification, P.13/36, called for prototypes of a twin-engined bomber which would not be far short of the B.12/36 four-engined heavy bomber (of which Shorts and Supermarine were building prototypes) in bomb-load, range and armament. In April 1938 de Havilland started design work on a version of the Albatross powered by two Rolls-Royce Merlins, an engine which at that time promised a great deal and was to achieve considerably more. As called for by P.13/36, the Albatross bomber featured powered multi-gun turrets in the nose and tail. With two Merlins, however, the performance was well short of the specification, and a radically different approach was called for. (P.13/36 led, ultimately, to the Lancaster and Halifax.) The de Havilland company was already under pressure to become more fully involved in military work, and in the absence of any military project of the company's own design it was being threatened with subcontract work building the products of other companies.

It was during 1938 that the idea emerged of a completely unarmed bomber which, like the Comet and Albatross, would achieve speed and range through aerodynamic refinement rather than brute force. Even a light defensive armament, together with the structure to carry it and the space to house the crew, represented one-sixth of a bomber's total weight. Eliminate that, and the bomber might be able to evade fighters primarily through speed. As the Günter brothers of Rostock had found with the He 119, this argument met a wall of resistance in official circles. Like their German counterparts in the *Reichsluftfahrtministerium*, the civil servants and RAF officers in the Air Ministry had seen proposals for high-speed, almost-unarmed aircraft before. The argument that the Luftwaffe would simply deploy a new generation of 500 mph (800 km/hr) fighters and leave an unarmed bomber a sitting duck was hard to oppose. Another objection to the concept was that the workload on a two-man crew – the pilot getting no relief at the controls, and the second crewman having to navigate, operate the radio, aim the bombs and keep a lookout – would be excessive.

Throughout 1939 Geoffrey de Havilland continued to lobby the Air Ministry on behalf of the unarmed wooden bomber, while the design office studied bigger or smaller aircraft with Merlins, Rolls-Royce's bigger Griffons or Napier Sabres. A gun turret might make the aircraft more acceptable to the Ministry, but would knock 20 mph (32 km/hr) off the maximum speed. Conventionally armed with defensive guns, the aircraft became just another slow medium bomber. Without guns, the de Havilland team discovered, a highly efficient twin-Merlin aircraft, with a wing area twice that of the Spitfire, could outrun the fighter by a significant margin.

There was, however, one factor going de Havilland's way. Until the aircraft industry switched to metal construction, aluminium had never been used on a very large scale. The facilities for the mining of bauxite and the extraction of aluminium were only just gearing up to the demands of aviation. The vast scale of the heavy-bomber production programme contemplated by the Air Ministry depended entirely on the availability of aluminium, and even in 1938 there was interest in anything that offered an insurance against restricted supplies. More than a year before serious interest was expressed in de Havilland's proposal, specification B.17/38 had been issued for a medium bomber making use of "non-strategic" materials such as wood, synthetic or compressed wood, or laminates. (The Bristol 155 design was reworked by Armstrong Whitworth to meet the requirement, resulting in the mediocre Albemarle.)

Finally, the de Havilland project found an ally in Air Marshal Sir Wilfrid Freeman, Air Member for Research and Development on the Air Council, the Government/ military body set up to give expert advice on air policy. When de Havilland submitted the unarmed bomber for reconsideration, three days after the outbreak of war, Freeman took up its cause and won approval for prototype construction despite the high priority being given to existing types. By this time, the potential of a fast, long-range basic airframe in the fighter and reconnaissance roles was appreciated, and some of the official objections to the project had been mollified by laying stress on the photo-reconnaissance role; the military were beginning to be acutely aware that the RAF lacked a vehicle for long-range reconnaissance, and the value of air photography was beginning to be appreciated.

The decision to support development of the de Havilland D.H.98 was taken officially in late 1939, and the prototype became the subject of specification B.1/40. Already, in October, Geoffrey de Havilland had moved his D.H.98 design team away from the prominent bomber target of the Hatfield works to the moated manor house of Salisbury Hall a few miles away. A hangar was erected close to the house, disguised as a barn, where the couple of dozen people who were admitted to the secret of Salisbury Hall could build the first prototypes. (The workforce grew to 60 by June and some 230 by the time the first aircraft flew.)

March 1940 saw an order for 50 production B.1/40 bomber/reconnaissance aircraft, but soon the baleful and unsympathetic eye of Lord Beaverbrook, the new Minister of Aircraft Production, fell on the activities at Salisbury Hall. Beaverbrook was not interested in supporting development of any aircraft which would reach the squadrons later than 1941. The production order was cancelled on 15 May, and it has been said that Beaverbrook told Freeman on three occasions to stop work on the B.1/40 prototypes, but failed to give a written instruction; Freeman allowed work to continue. The contract was reinstated on 12 July, Freeman having told Beaverbrook that 50 aircraft could be delivered by July 1941. This target was not to be achieved, but by that time the immediate production crisis had passed and the B.1/40 had shown what it could do.

The external design of the aircraft which neared completion in the autumn of 1940 was conventional, apart from its remarkable cleanliness of line and the relative lack of straight lines in its fuselage shape. The crew sat well forward, giving a good view on landing but making rearward visibility something of a problem in later years. As with the Albatross, the designers had merged the engine cooling system with the wing, so that it added nothing to the frontal area; the radiators were installed ahead of the front wing spar, between the nacelles and the fuselage, endowing the aircraft with a distinctive "stepped" leading edge in plan view. Like the contemporary Messerschmitt Bf 109 and Bf 110 fighters, the B.1/40 featured automatic Handley Page slots on its outer leading edges; in common with the German fighters, it possessed a relatively high wing-loading for its day.

Under the skin, the B.1/40 was completely different from any other combat aircraft. The company's third high-performance wooden airframe, it incorporated the lessons learned in development of the Comet and the Albatross. Plywood and lamination were used extensively; the largest spruce components, for instance, were made up of laminations only 0.4 in (10 mm) thick, so that construction would not make unrealistic demands on the supply of solid high-quality timber.

The fuselage assembly was different from anything before or since. The two layers of plywood which formed the inner and outer skins of the fuselage were only 0.06 in to 0.08 in (1.5 mm to 2 mm) thick, and could be formed without heat or pressure around the male moulds on which the fuselage was made. Each mould comprised the entire left or right half of the fuselage: the Mosquito fuselage, unlike that of the Albatross, was built in two halves and joined down the centreline, greatly facilitating production. First, the inner skin was fastened to the mould; then the balsa core was glued in place. The balsa gave way to spruce where strength was required, such as at the edges of doors and cutouts, at the wing attachment points or on the joint line between the fuselage halves. All doors were made as integral parts of the fuselage. After the top skin had been glued in place, the half-shells were removed from the mould; the doors were removed by sawing through the plywood skin, and as much internal equipment as possible (including control runs and hydraulic lines) was installed before the two half-shells were joined together, saving a great deal of time-consuming fitting in the confined space of the fuselage.

The construction of the wing was similar to that of the Albatross, except that the skins were of plywood, rather than spruce planking. Upper and lower wing skins consisted of two layers of birch plywood, sandwiched around spanwise spruce stringers. The front and rear spars, like those of the Albatross, were of box section and were the only major assemblies to be bonded under heat and pressure. The wooden structure was to prove extremely sturdy and resistant to gunfire, probably because wood contains its own natural crack-stoppers and because the wooden airframe had the minimum of fastener holes to generate stress concentrations. But at the time of the first flight of the B.1/40 prototype, made at Hatfield on 1 October, 1940, the new aircraft was very much an unknown quantity, and the merits of its radical structure were far from proven.

The wooden fuselage of the Mosquito was first assembled in two halves which were partially equipped with internal fittings before being joined down the centre lines.

(Hawker Siddeley)

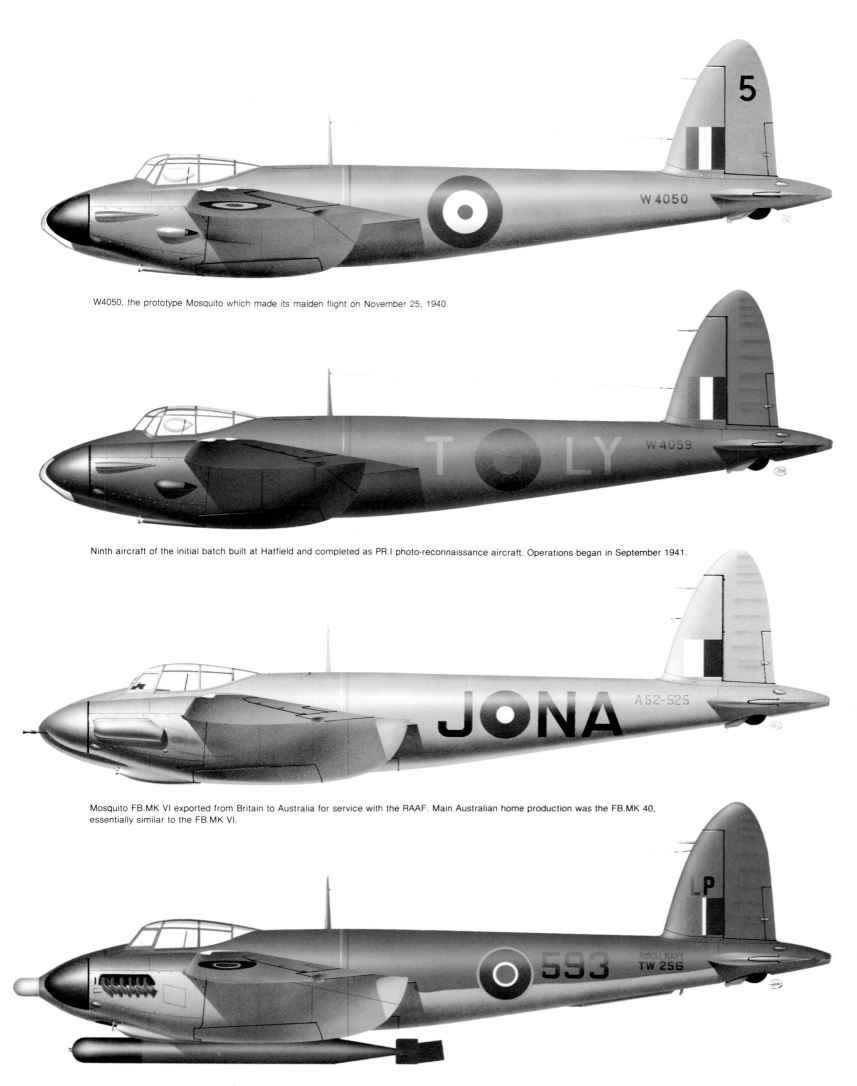

W4050, the prototype Mosquito which made its maiden flight on November 25, 1940.

Ninth aircraft of the initial batch built at Hatfield and completed as PR.I photo-reconnaissance aircraft. Operations began in September 1941.

Mosquito FB.MK VI exported from Britain to Australia for service with the RAAF. Main Australian home production was the FB.MK 40, essentially similar to the FB.MK VI.

TR.MK 33. This torpedo-reconnaissance fighter-bomber was developed for Royal Navy carrier operations from the FB.MK VI. It had folding wings, a thimble nose, radome and arrester hook.

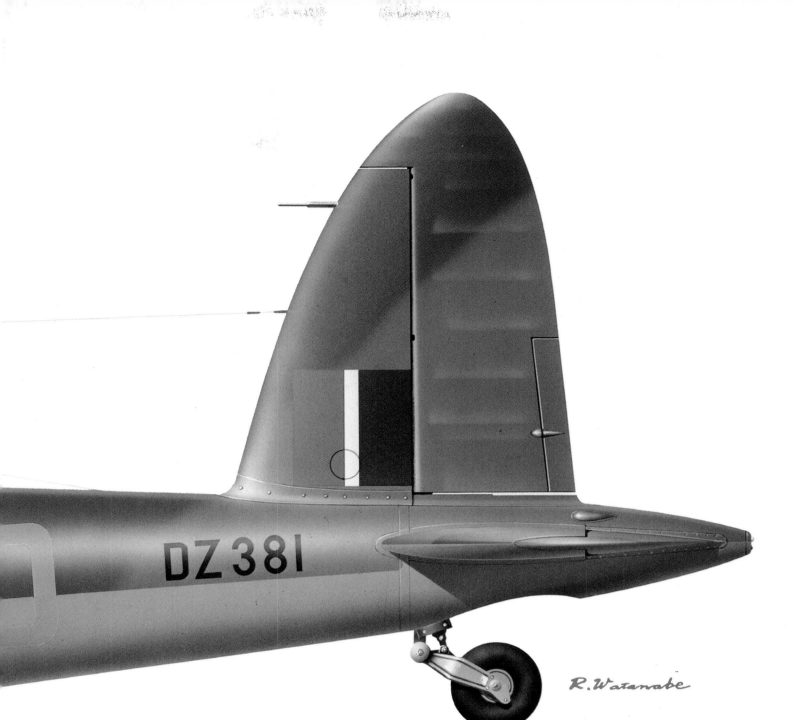

R. Watanabe

Mosquito F.MK II ▶

De Havilland Mosquito F.MK II W4087 of No. 157 Squadron, the first to operate all-black night fighting Mosquitoes. The arrow head on the nose is the transmitting aerial for the AI.MK IV radar set. The first nocturnal interceptions by Mosquitoes were made in May 1941.

Two Rolls-Royce Merlin 21 engines, 1,460 hp each.

Performance

Max speed: 370 mph (595 km/h)
Service ceiling: 36,000 ft (10,973 m)
Range: 1,705 ml (2,744 km)
Weight loaded: 19,670 lb (8,922 kg)

Dimensions

Span: 54 ft 2 in (16.5 m)
Length: 41 ft 2 in (12.54 m)
Height: 12 ft 6 in (3.75 m)
Wing area: 454 sq ft (42.1 m²)

Armament

4 x 20mm Hispano cannon,
4 x .303-in Browning machine guns

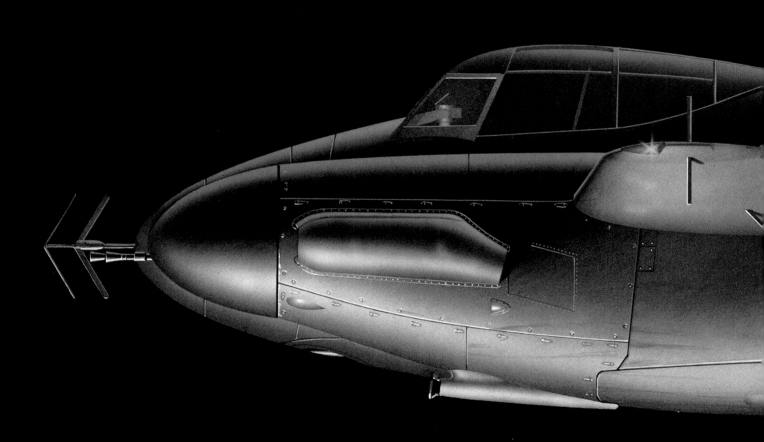

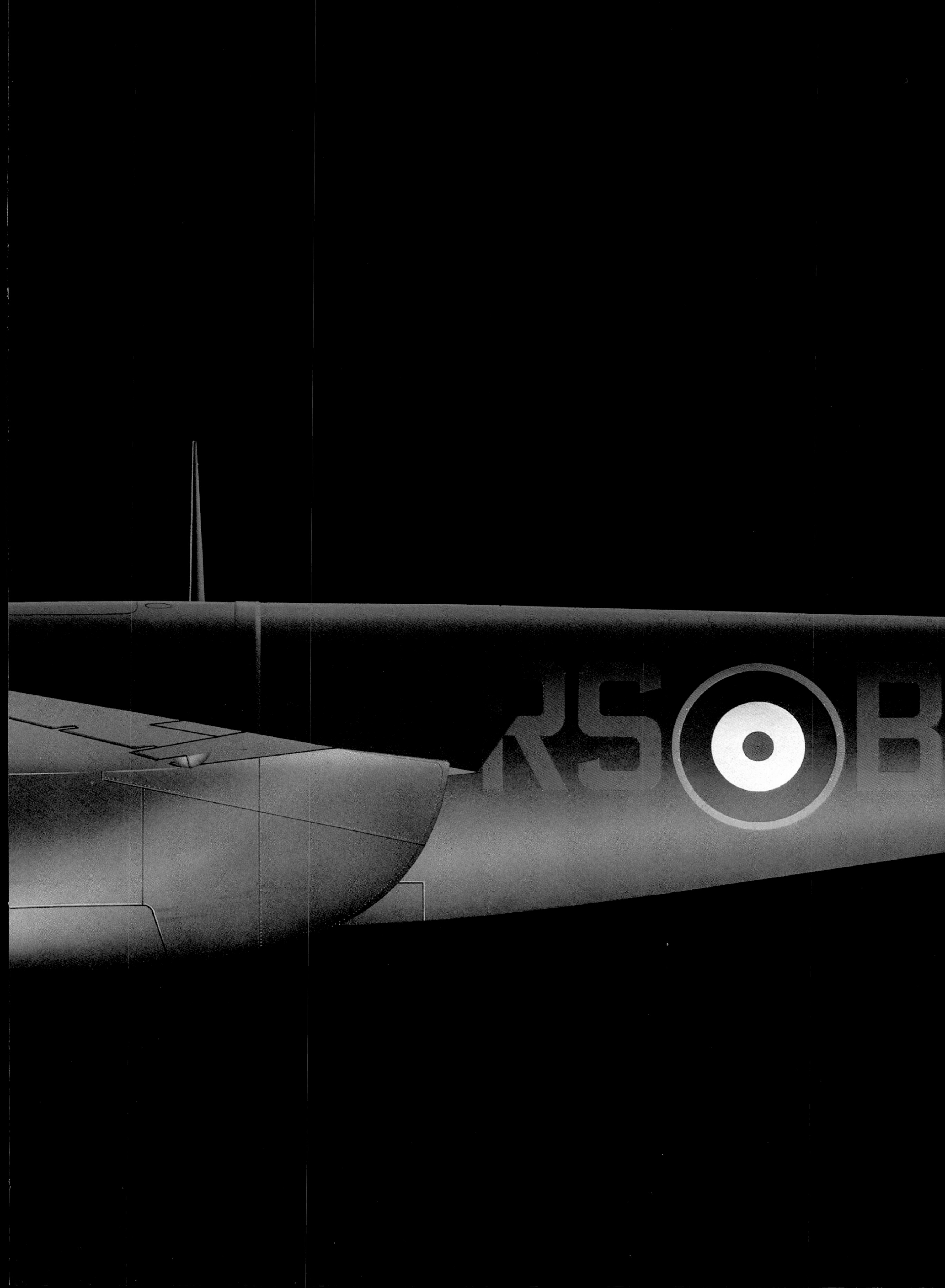
RS

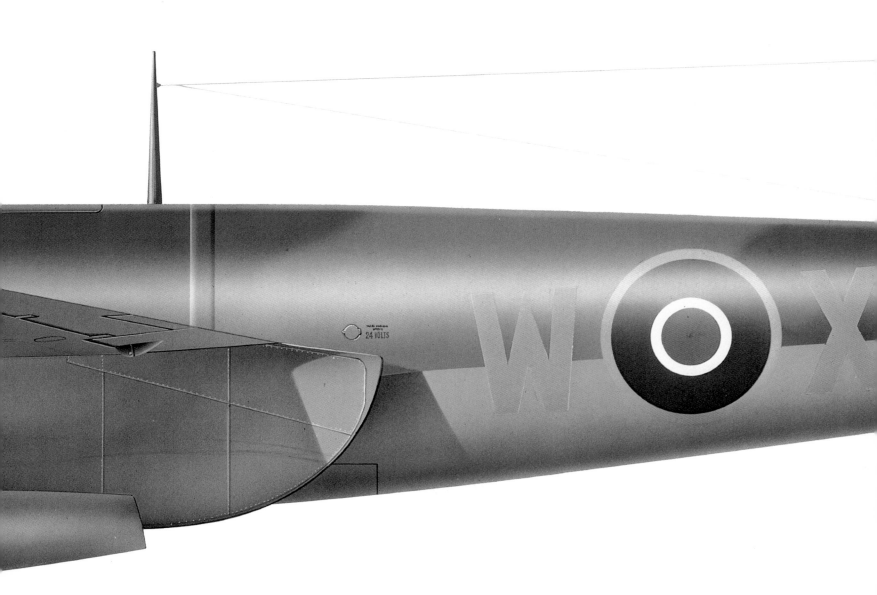

Mosquito B.MK IV

Hatfield built B.MK IV, DZ381. This aircraft first flown in March 1942, exemplified operationally the concept of the fast unarmed bomber.

Two Rolls-Royce Merlin 21 engines, 1,460 hp each.

Performance

Max speed: 380 mph (611 km/h)
Service ceiling: 34,000 ft (10,363 m)
Range: 2,040 ml (3,283 km)
Weight loaded: 21,462 lb (9,737 kg)

Dimensions

Span: 54 ft 2 in (16.51 m)
Length: 41 ft 2 in (12.55 m)
Height: 16 ft 4 in (4.98 m)
Wing area: 454 sq ft (42.18 m²)

Armament

No guns. 1 x 1,000 lb (454 kg) and 2 x 500 lb (227 kg) or 4 x 500 lb (227 kg) or 4 x 250 lb (114 kg) bombs or with Mod 537 installed, 1 x 4,000 lb (1,816 kg) bomb.

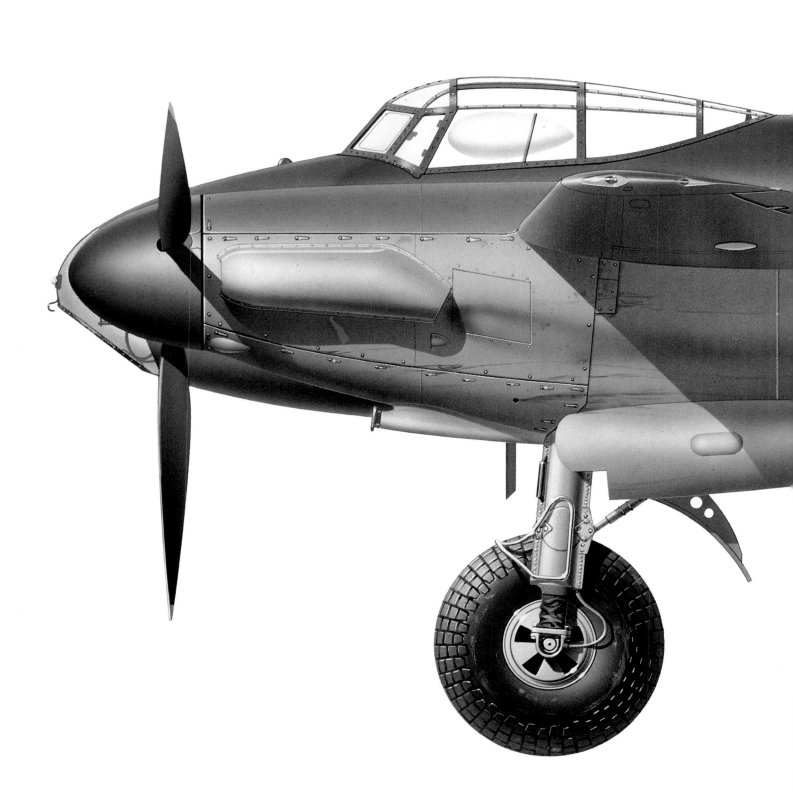

Into Action

Nearly two months elapsed between the first flight of the B.1/40 on 1 October, 1940, and the second and third flights at the end of November. Thereafter, the bomber romped through its trials with a minimum of modification and few serious problems. On 29 December the aircraft showed its paces before Lord Beaverbrook, Minister of Aircraft Production, Sir Henry Tizard, Britain's senior scientific civil servant, the Canadian Minister of Supply and Sir Wilfrid Freeman. It must have been a satisfying day for Freeman, now Vice-Chief of the Air Staff, who had done more than anyone else outside de Havilland to get the project going. The day after the demonstration took place, the Air Ministry ordered another 150 examples.

Around this time, the name Mosquito was bestowed on the prototype: prophetically, perhaps, in view of the immense irritation the type was to arouse in the Luftwaffe. It was apparent at an early stage that the performance of the new aircraft was outstanding, even before the first prototype was delivered to the Aircraft & Armament Experimental Establishment at Boscombe Down. Indeed, the Air Ministry's main problem – one which was to affect the Mosquito programme throughout its life – was deciding how many aircraft to allot to each role. The first change to the mix of production types took place in January 1941. The Photographic Reconnaissance Unit (PRU) was to receive more than half the first batch of aircraft, enabling it to extend its coverage of Occupied Europe and the Reich well beyond the range of its Spitfires. Meanwhile, there was increasing concern about the safety of shipping in the North Atlantic, and in particular about the menace of the small force of Focke-Wulf Fw 200 Condors which the Luftwaffe had installed in Western France. Derived from a pre-war transatlantic mailplane, the Fw 200s presented a direct threat to shipping with their bombs, and an indirect menace with their ability to guide U-boats to their targets. The second production type of Mosquito was therefore to be the F Mk II, second only to the PR.I. Although the type had been designed as a bomber, the first batch of 50 aircraft was initially planned to include only one prototype in bomber configuration.

Development of the Mosquito advanced smoothly. The prototype's stalling behaviour proved sufficiently innocuous to allow the removal of the automatic leading-edge

The prototype Mosquito rolled out for the first time at Hatfield on 19 November, 1940.

(British Aerospace)

(Planet News)

Armourers tending the machine guns and pulling through the .303-in (7.7 mm) ammunition belts of a No. 23 Squadron Mosquito.

slots. A slight "dithering" under certain conditions detracted from otherwise excellent stability and control, and after a series of modifications had been tested it was cured by extending the engine nacelles rearwards (dividing the flaps into inboard and outboard sections) and fitting a slightly larger tailplane; the problem had been caused by interaction of the tailplane and the slipstream of the nacelles. Slightly smaller airscrews were found to eliminate a vibration problem. The only serious incident to befall the first aircraft was a failure of the rear fuselage caused by a malfunction of the castoring tailwheel. The fuselage of the first photographic reconnaissance aircraft was used to keep the first prototype flying.

By any standards, however, the problems encountered in the development of the Mosquito were none too serious, and the initial production aircraft were closely similar to the prototype. The external shape of the Mosquito underwent few changes during the life of the aeroplane, and the individual variants were also largely similar. The bomber and reconnaissance versions were, externally, virtually identical, with a glazed nose incorporating a flat aiming panel through which the second crewman could take a ground sighting or aim bombs in a level attack. Apart from the interim PR.VIII, the high altitude PR.32 and the long-range PR.34, all the reconnaissance versions were parallel to bomber variants. The fighter version, as it entered service, was more closely similar to the other two major variants than was at first envisaged; a strong faction within the Air Ministry was in favour of turret-mounted armament for heavy fighters, and not until flight trials with a dummy turret demonstrated that this would cut 20 mph (32 km/hr) off the maximum speed was the idea dropped. Instead of the turret, the fighter Mosquito was to be equipped as "secondary armament" with a battery of four of the RAF's standard 0.303-in (7.7 mm) Colt-Browning machine guns in a solid nose replacing the forward crew position. The main armament, however, was a quartet of the new and formidable Hispano 20 mm cannon. The deceptively graceful fuselage of the Mosquito was in fact capacious enough to house these weapons under the cockpit floor and in the forward half of the bomb-bay without any change to the external lines of the aircraft. The cockpit area of the fighter featured two concessions to Fighter Command philosophy: a control stick instead of a wheel, despite the fact that many pilots found that the Mosquito was more agile with the former, which gave greater leverage, and a flat windscreen. V-shaped windscreens such as those of the reconnaissance and bomber Mosquitos were anathema to Fighter Command, which preferred the drag of the flat screen to the aiming difficulties associated with the swept screen. One improvement studied for the fighter, but not adopted in production, was an airbrake in the form of a frill, or retractable ruff, around the entire circumference of the fuselage aft of the wing. The airbrake was intended to overcome a difficulty common to all heavy, fast and aerodynamically clean fighters: how to lose speed fast enough to deliver an effective attack on a slow bomber. In the absence of an effective airbrake this was to remain a problem for Mosquito fighter pilots.

Nearly all the fighter variants, however, were to be delivered either as specialized night-fighters or as fighter-bombers, the latter variant being the most versatile and widely produced Mosquito in the series. The fighter-bomber was essentially the long-range fighter with the rear part of the bomb-bay re-activated to accommodate two 250 lb (113 kg) bombs, and with the wings strengthened to carry external loads.

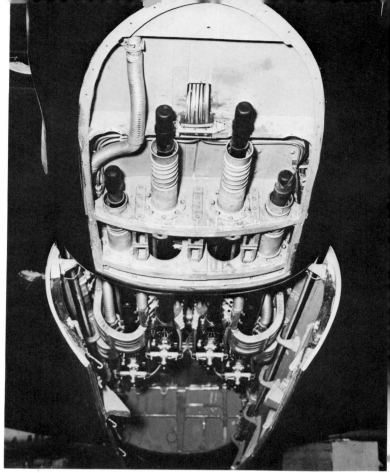

Four 20 mm cannon installation in the belly of F. MkII/NF.II.

Mosquito orders mounted rapidly, and the tremendous effort of putting an aircraft of completely unfamiliar structural concept into large-scale production took up a great deal of time in 1941. In that year only 20 Mosquitos were delivered (Freeman had promised Beaverbrook 50 by July, but the Mosquito was performing so well that it was safe from any reprisals). The de Havilland headquarters factory at Hatfield was the first line to gather speed, using track assembly techniques which had been introduced under the guidance of Standard Motors, and was to remain by far the largest single source of Mosquitos. Components for the Hatfield assembly line came from a wide variety of sources, including furniture factories, bus depots and luxury coachbuilders. Second in importance to Hatfield was nearby Leavesden, which had been set up under de Havilland direction as a "shadow factory" and was successively designated as a source of Albemarles and then Wellingtons before being taken over for Mosquito production. Hatfield was to produce 3,054 Mosquitos and Leavesden 1,390. Later, Standard Motors, Percival Aircraft and Airspeed were to contribute to British production, of which only the first was to produce the Mosquito in large quantities: a total of 916 fighter-bombers stemmed from Standard's works at Ansty, Coventry.

In retrospect, it appears that one of the most important single procurement decisions of the entire 1939–45 war was the September 1940 agreement between Rolls-Royce and Packard, providing for the American company to manufacture the Merlin under licence. Packard Merlins in the P-51B Mustang saved the US Army Air Force from defeat over Germany, and at the same time augmented production of a number of British types. In the case of the Mosquito, the flow of Merlins from Detroit opened up the possibility of licence manufacture of the Mosquito. Curtiss-Wright looked at the idea, but it was de Havilland's own subsidiary in Canada which was eventually selected as a second source for the

Elevator and aileron controls

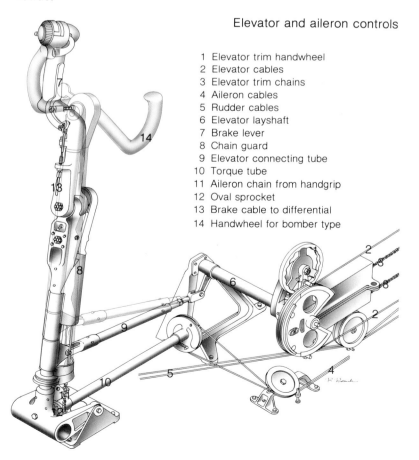

1 Elevator trim handwheel
2 Elevator cables
3 Elevator trim chains
4 Aileron cables
5 Rudder cables
6 Elevator layshaft
7 Brake lever
8 Chain guard
9 Elevator connecting tube
10 Torque tube
11 Aileron chain from handgrip
12 Oval sprocket
13 Brake cable to differential
14 Handwheel for bomber type

European theatre of operations. Despite the difficulty of setting up production of a new and unfamiliar type, a torpedo-streaked ocean away from the design office, the de Havilland factory at Downsview and the Atlantic ferry service managed to deliver nearly 500 bomber and fighter-bomber Mosquitos to Europe by the end of May 1945.

Production in Australia was even more badly affected by distance than de Havilland Canada's efforts, and despite the fact that the decision to go ahead with production was taken in March 1942 it was May 1945 before the Royal Australian Air Force was fully operational with Mosquitos. Deliveries had taken place a year earlier, but operational use had been delayed by two mysterious accidents, and the difficulty of getting investigations under way from the other side of the world.

Production in Australia and Canada was adversely affected by the only major technical problem to hit the Mosquito. As soon as the position in Europe had become more favourable to the Allies, consideration was given to the durability of the Mosquito structure in the tropics. It soon became clear that casein glue was a potential disaster; as mentioned above, it is closely related to cheese, and like cheese it is susceptible to micro-organic attack under warm, moist conditions. Time-expired Camembert, which rotten casein glue sometimes resembles, is not a good structural material. The search for a synthetic replacement for casein was long and difficult as the strong synthetic glues available at that time required either heat and pressure treatment or destructive acid catalysts (the latter problem contributed to the failure of Dr Kurt Tank's Ta154 "Moskito" wooden fighter). Finally, urea-formaldehyde glues were found to be an acceptable substitute, using a system whereby the hardener was painted on one face of the joint and the glue on another. Nevertheless, some casein-glued Mosquitos were used in the tropics, resulting in at least one fatal accident in October 1944 and a spate of groundings. According to Professor J.E. Gordon, who worked on the glue problems at the Royal Aircraft Establishment, rumour had it that some casein-glued aircraft in the tropics were held together by the small nails used to hold the parts together while the glue set. "In most cases this was slander," the scientist wrote later, "but I have seen instances where it was not far from the truth."

A more serious problem with Mosquitos in the tropics was caused by the fact that the plywood webs of the spars would shrink or swell with water soakage at a different rate than the heavier spruce booms. In the European theatre of operations, this presented few problems, because the level of humidity was rarely extreme or consistent enough to affect the wood seriously. With the more stable seasons and extreme conditions of the tropics, however, differential shrinkage could lead to destructive internal tensions and severe and dangerous damage to the spar. However, like problems with water soakage the effects of this phenomenon could be contained within safe limits provided that the airframe was properly inspected and maintained.

Usually, only the most proficient and experienced crews were selected to fly Mosquitos. The Luftwaffe remarked on the fact that the crews of the first two Mosquitos shot down over Germany were of fairly high rank, and speculated that the British must consider the aircraft particularly safe. (They were also led to believe by some of the first Mosquito crews to be captured that the early Mosquito was capable of 450 mph at 38,000 ft – had they captured a de Havilland sales team?) This was not the case: in fact, although the Mosquito was regarded as a delightful aircraft to fly under most circumstances, it was also a demanding machine. Like most contemporary high-powered twin-engined aircraft, the Mosquito could be a handful with asymmetric power, and the loss of an engine just after a high-weight take-off was unquestionably dangerous. In peacetime, Mosquitos were not normally operated at gross weights as high as those used during active hostilities. The Mosquito also had a high wing loading and landing speed, coupled with a very steep approach path once the undercarriage was down. The elevators were particularly light, and it was possible to overstress the airframe in pulling out of a dive without too much difficulty; this problem was dealt with by warning pilots against ham-handed use of the controls rather than by technical means. The Mosquito was generally sensitive in pitch; heavily laden bombers with shorter, lighter single-stage engines were seriously tail-heavy, while night-fighters with bigger engines, radar and cannon forward tended to go the other way.

Once the main service variants of the Mosquito were established in production, studies of future developments started. One immediately obvious area of potential improvement was the powerplant. The Mosquito had been designed with the most advanced version of the Merlin available in 1939–40, the XX series with a two-speed supercharger drive permitting operation over a wider range of altitudes than was possible with the early engines' single-speed supercharger. By 1941, however, Rolls-Royce was working on a new version of the Merlin with a two-stage supercharger, promising a considerable increase in output for a slight increase in length and weight and no change in frontal area. In October 1941 the first Mosquito prototype was selected to test the Merlin 61, and flew with them in mid-1942, attaining an altitude of 40,000 ft (12,195 m) on one test flight. Mosquitos with two-stage Merlins could be distinguished externally by the additional air intake below the propeller, which fed the intercooler between the two supercharger stages. To begin with, the use of two-stage-supercharged engines on the Mosquito was delayed because the Spitfire IX, urgently needed to counter the threat posed by the Fw 190, had higher priority for limited supplies of the new engines. PRU managed to get some of the new engines by late 1942, but most Mosquitos used single-stage engines until the second half of 1943. Fighter-bombers continued to use the older engines until the end of Mosquito production, because their need for altitude performance was not so great as in the case of bombers, PR aircraft and night-fighters.

Following closely behind the development of the two-stage engine, and ideally complementing it, was the development of a pressurized cabin to allow the crew to operate as efficiently as the engines at high altitude. To be accurate, the system first tested in a Mosquito in July 1942 was a partial-pressure cabin, the differential having been kept

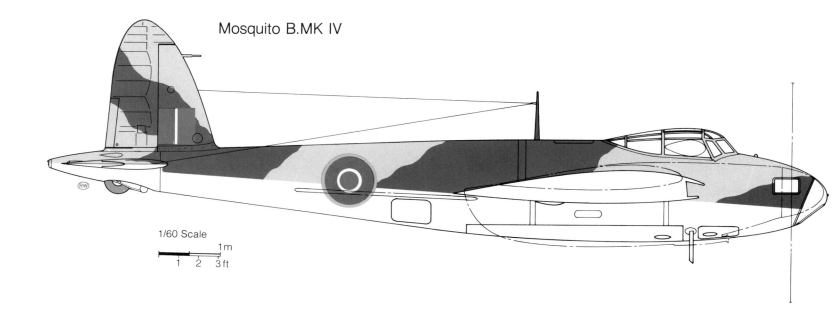

Mosquito B.MK IV

1/60 Scale

1m
1 2 3 ft

to 2 lb/sq in (0.145 kg/cm²) to minimize the risk of the design and to reduce the danger of explosive decompression. It was, however, enough to make 42,000 ft (12,800 m) cruising altitudes physiologically acceptable for long missions.

The highest altitude reached by a Mosquito was 44,600 ft (13,594 m), attained by one of five NF.XV high-altitude night-fighters produced in 1942–43 to counter nuisance raids by Ju86P bombers. These aircraft were pressurized, carried radar and had their wings extended to 59 ft 2 in (18.03 m) span. To save weight, armament was reduced to four 0.303 in (7.7 mm) machine guns in a ventral blister. This was felt to be adequate to deter the slow, unarmoured Junkers Ju86P, but in the event the NF.XVs never made a successful interception. In late 1944 a similar version, the PR.32, was introduced to counter the increasing threat from German jet and rocket fighters.

The fastest Mosquito recorded, remarkably, was the first prototype. In November 1942, fitted experimentally with the long-span wings of the NF.XV and testing Merlin 77 engines, the hard-worked airframe was measured at 437 mph (704 km/hr) at 29,000 ft (8,838 m).

It is unlikely that the Mosquito was ever the fastest aircraft in service. The maximum speed of the production aircraft stabilized around 410 mph (660 km/hr) after the introduction of the two-stage Merlin engine at the end of 1942; this was slightly slower than the contemporary Spitfire IX and Fw 190, and significantly slower than the Corsair or P-47B Thunderbolt, both of which entered service about the same time. The prototype's top speed in late 1942 was among the highest attainable by any combat-type aircraft at that time, but was probably being matched during flight-tests of the P-47D Thunderbolt, Merlin-powered Mustang and Tempest V. What saved the Mosquito from being overtaken by the new generation of fighters which the pessimists had predicted was the unforeseen performance plateau which all propeller-driven aircraft encountered during the 1939–45 war. This was due partly to the declining efficiency of the propeller above 375 mph (605 km/hr), and partly to aerodynamic compressibility around the airframe, neither

phenomenon having been fully appreciated at the time the Mosquito was designed. The tactical implications of this speed plateau were vital. The "fast unarmed bombers" of the early 1930s had been rendered obsolete when the Spitfire and Bf 109 increased fighter speeds from 250 mph to 370 mph (400 km/hr to 595 km/hr) in three years up to 1938; the next 80 mph (130 km/hr) increase took the fighter designers six years. The Bf 109 had enjoyed a 50 per cent speed margin over the doomed Fairey Battles of April 1940; five years later, a handful of Luftwaffe jet fighters could wield a 25 per cent margin over the de Havilland bomber, but they were too few and too late to cause significant Mosquito casualties.

More significant than high-speed trials were the continuing tests of Mosquitos at higher weights: by April 1943 one example had been tested at 23,000 lb (10,350 kg), representing full fuel for a bomber version and a 2,000 lb (900 kg) weapons load. The heaviest of all Mosquitos, however, were B.XVI aircraft fully loaded with bombs and fuel, which under wartime conditions were cleared to take off at 25,917 lb (11,715 kg). This was a 35 per cent increase over the original design weight of the Mosquito, and most of it represented fuel and bombs.

The success of the basic design militated to some extent against the development of more ambitious projects by de Havilland. The first of these to take shape on the drawing board was the subject of a de Havilland proposal to the Air Ministry in November 1941. The D.H.101 (originally designated D.H.99) was known informally as the Sabre-Mosquito, but in the course of design grew into a new and larger aircraft intended to replace heavy bombers such as the Stirling. Using two of the very powerful and compact Napier Sabre NS19M engines driving counter-rotating propellers, the DH.101 could have carried a 16,000 lb (7,260 kg) bomb-load to Berlin, with a maximum speed of 430 mph (692 km/hr). However, Sabre development could not be guaranteed to match the D.H.101 timetable; de Havilland wanted to fly their new bomber by 1943, but were told that they would have to adapt the design to Rolls-Royce Griffons if it was to be ready on time. The Griffons did not make such an attractive aircraft,

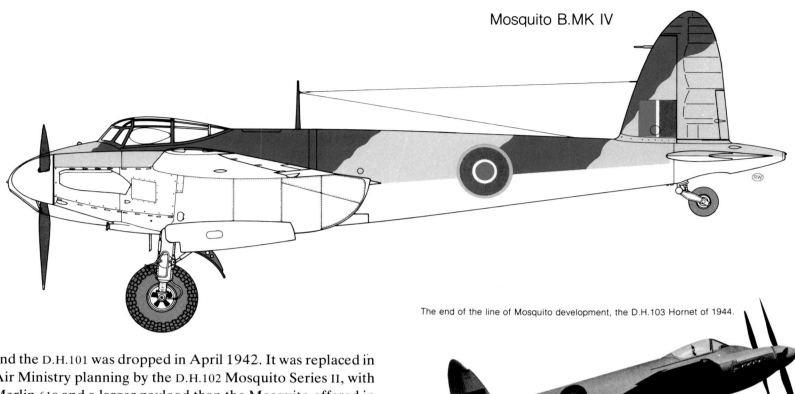

Mosquito B.MK IV

The end of the line of Mosquito development, the D.H.103 Hornet of 1944.

British Aerospace (via Philip Birtles)

and the D.H.101 was dropped in April 1942. It was replaced in Air Ministry planning by the D.H.102 Mosquito Series II, with Merlin 61s and a larger payload than the Mosquito offered in 1942. There was little enthusiasm for the D.H.102, which was rather slower than the basic Mosquito, and at the end of 1942 it was itself abandoned in favour of continued development of the existing aircraft. The Mosquito's only descendant, in the true sense of the word, was the D.H.103 Hornet single-seat fighter using metal/wood bonding; appearing too late for the 1939–45 war, the Hornet was used by the Royal Air Force and the Fleet Air Arm. The de Havilland company also made some use of the Mosquito's constructional techniques in the D.H.100 Vampire jet fighter, but as an all-wooden production combat aircraft, the Mosquito was destined to remain unique.

Photo-Reconnaissance

Whatever the arguments about the merits of an unarmed bomber, the Royal Air Force had very quickly learned to accept the idea of the unarmed, high-flying reconnaissance aircraft. Throughout the 1939–35 war, the Photographic Reconnaissance Unit, formed at the outbreak of war as the Photographic Development Unit and headquartered at RAF Benson, maintained its ability to penetrate enemy airspace in broad daylight, in the clearest weather, to reconnoitre high-priority military targets and, more often than not, return safely with the evidence. It was rewarded for its success with high priority in deliveries of the latest, fastest and highest-flying aircraft, and this was part of the reason why PRU was the first unit to use the Mosquito operationally. Bomber Command's scepticism concerning the survivability of an unarmed bomber also helped PRU as it scavenged and fought for extra Mosquitos in the first few months of production.

The prototype Mosquito PR.I was flown in June 1941, and although the type was initially plagued with engine troubles at high altitude PRU had five PR.Is on strength by September 1941. Hereward de Havilland, reporting from the

PRU after the first deliveries, recorded the first of many compliments the Mosquito was to receive from its pilots, albeit rather negatively phrased: "In my experience," he wrote, "this is the only aircraft which has not initially been branded by the pilots as a death-trap in some way or another." Operations nonetheless started inauspiciously; an otherwise successful mission to Brest and the Franco-Spanish border was somewhat marred by the fact that the cameras failed to work. Three days later, on September 20, the Mosquito flew its first successful mission.

The first PR.Is were simply camera-carrying versions of the basic bomber prototype – some featuring the shorter engine nacelles of the first aircraft – but the later aircraft featured extra fuel tanks bringing the total capacity of 700 gal (3,180 lit) compared with the standard 550 gal (2,450 lit). The long-range PR.Is extended the PRU's area of operations into Scandinavia and Central Europe, as far as Bergen and Danzig.

PRU suffered its first Mosquito loss in December 1941, when an aircraft failed to return from a mission to Bergen, but in general the Mosquito's high speed and altitude enabled it to evade all but the best planned and most determined interception attempt, successive modifications denying attackers a useful margin of performance over the de Havilland aircraft. During 1942 the original PR.Is – supplemented by a few F.IIs which PRU had managed to divert from the night-fighter conversion line and equip as rudimentary reconnaissance aircraft – were joined by PR.IVs, equivalent to the B.IV production bomber.

In mid-1942 PRU's capability was significantly improved when the Mosquitos were fitted with the new F.52 camera developed by the Royal Aircraft Establishment, and this remained the primary equipment of PR Mosquitos. Later

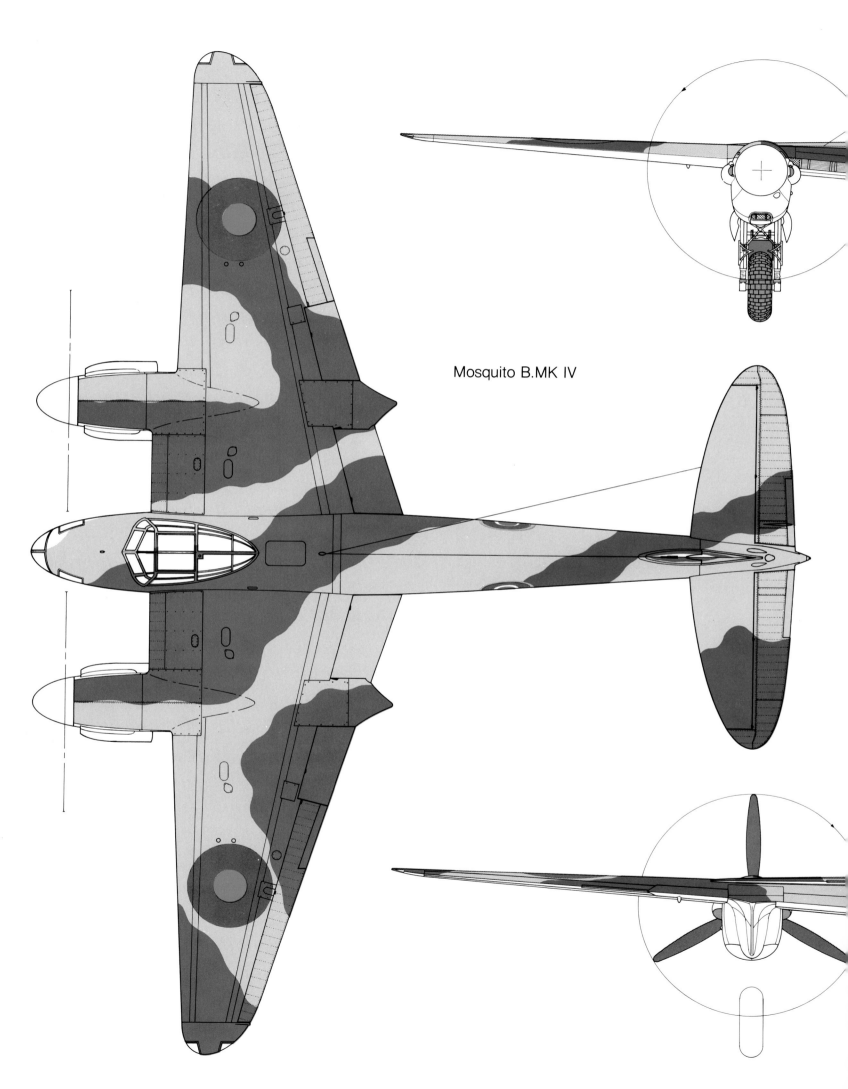

Mosquito B.MK IV

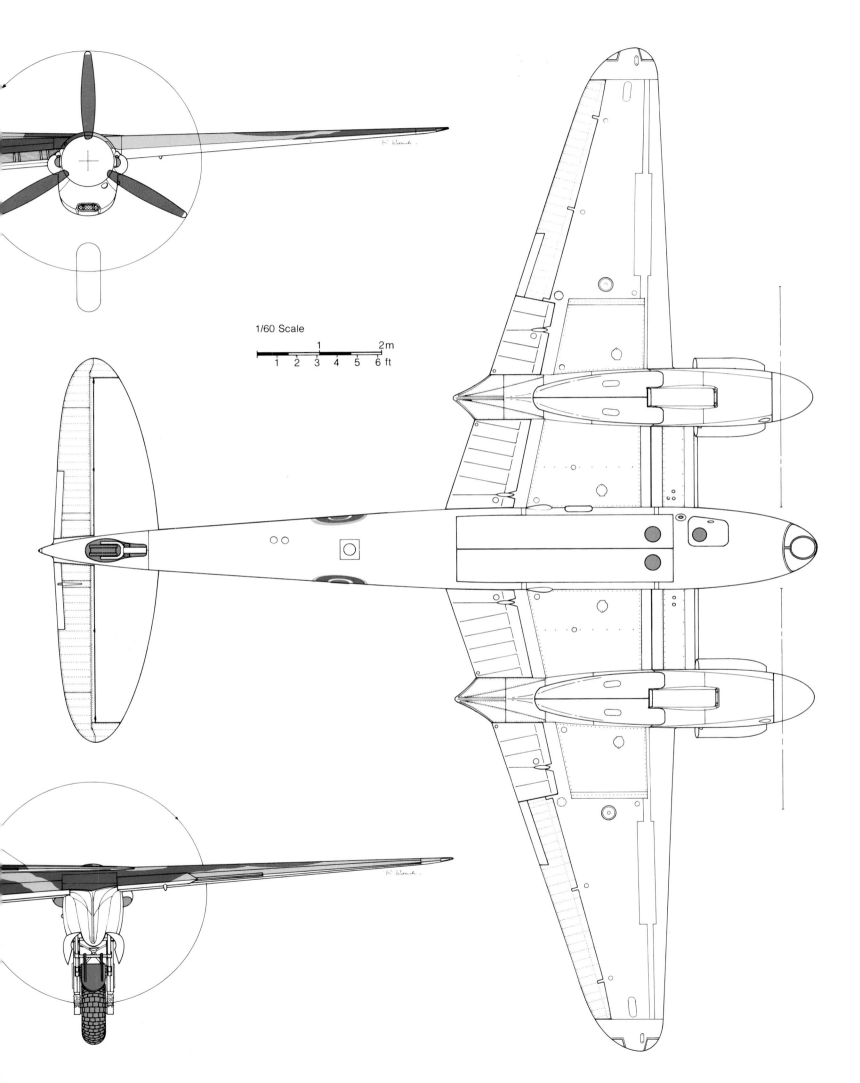

1/60 Scale

Mosquito FB. Mk VI Cutaway

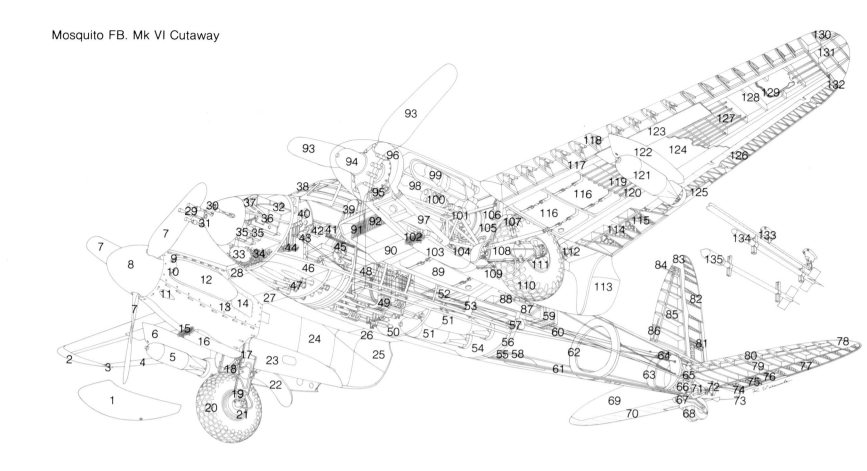

1 Dump fuel tank
2 Starboard wing tip
3 Resin lamp
4 Starboard aileron
5 500lb bomb
6 Universal bomb carrier
7 De Havilland hydromatic
  propeller
8 Starboard spinner
9 Cooling spout for exhaust
  manifold flanges
10 Sparking plug cooling duct
11 Bulge for coolant pipe
12 Exhaust flame damper shroud
13 Fuel pump cooling duct
14 Inconel heat resisting insert
15 Ice guard
16 Carburettor air intake
17 Undercarriage compression legs
18 Wheel door guides
19 Gaiter
20 Starboard mainwheel
21 Disc brake
22 Mudguards
23 Main undercarriage doors
24 Wheel bay
25 Nacelle aft fairing
26 Starboard flap
27 Radiator flap
28 Radiator air intake
29 Four .303-in (7.7-mm)
   Browning Mk 11 machine guns
30 Camera gun spout and port
31 Nose cone
32 Inspection door for instrument
   panel
33 Cover to used cartridge-case
   chamber
34 Empty cartridge cases
35 Empty case chute
36 Ammunition boxes
37 Ammunition feed chutes
38 Flat bullet-proof windscreen
39 Pilot seat & harness
40 Instrument panel
41 Throttle quadrant
42 Junction box
43 Control column

44 Rudder pedal assembly
45 Elevator trim handwheel
46 Floor
47 20-mm cannon
48 Ammunition boxes
49 Cannon ammunition feed chutes
50 Cannon bag
51 500lb bombs
52 Long range fuel tank
53 Bulkhead No.3
54 Bomb bay
55 Downward identification lamp
56 Bulkhead No.4
57 Elevator & rudder pulleys
58 Aft fuselage entry/access
59 T.R. 1143 wireless
60 Control cables
61 Fuselage bottom joint
62 Bulkhead No.5
63 Bulkhead No.6
64 Rudder control linkage
65 Bulkhead No.7
66 Retraction mechanism unit
67 Axle fork
68 Retractable anti-shimmy tailwheel
69 Tailplane
70 Elevator
71 Elevator (internal) static balance
72 Elevator linkage
73 Tail formation light
74 Tail navigation light
75 Tab control link
76 Tab control link
77 Elevator
78 Elevator mass balance
79 Tailplane structure
80 Aerial
81 Rudder trim tab
82 Rudder frame
83 Rudder mass balance
84 Pitot head
85 Fin structure
86 Aerial
87 Inboard flap
88 Flap hinge
89 Inboard fuel tank
90 Radiator flap
91 Cabin heater unit

92 Coolant radiator
93 Paddle blade Hamilton Standard
   hydromatic propeller
94 Propeller boss
95 Constant speed unit
96 Coolant header tank
97 Coolant pipe
98 Rolls-Royce Merlin 25 1640 hp
   12-cyl. Vee engine
99 Exhaust stubs
100 Generator
101 Engine bearer supports
102 Ice guard
103 Carburettor air intake
104 Carburettor air duct
105 Fireproof bulkhead
106 Boost gauge fuel trap
107 Radius rod
108 Compression legs
109 Wheel hub
110 Port main wheel
111 Wheel hub
112 Flap jack and crank
113 Nacelle aft fairing
114 Flap hinge
115 Outboard flap
116 Outboard fuel tank
117 Front spar
118 Leading-edge ribs
119 Landing lamp
120 Rear spar
121 500lb bomb
122 Universal bomb carrier
123 Stiffener
124 Single plywood skin (lower)
125 Aileron trim tab
126 Aileron
127 Wing stringers
128 Wing outer ribs No.13
129 Spaced double skin (upper)
130 Port navigation light
131 Port wing tip
132 Resin lamp
133 Rocket launcher
134 25lb armour-piercing rockets.
    4 × each wing
135 60lb semi armour-piercing rockets.
    4 × each wing

Mosquito FM.MK XIX

This night fighter variant was fitted with a new 'universal' nose to accept either British or American radar. First flight was in April 1944.

Two Rolls-Royce Merlin 25 engines, 1,635 hp each.

Performance

Max speed: 378 mph (608 km/h)
Service ceiling: 34,500 ft (10,516 m)
Range: 1,830 ml (2,945 km)
Weight loaded: 21,750 lb (9,865 kg)

Dimensions

Span: 54 ft 2 in (16.51 m)
Length: 40 ft 6 in (12.3 m)
Height: 15 ft 3½ in (4.65 m)
Wing area: 454 sq ft (43 m²)

Armament

4 x 20mm Hispano cannon

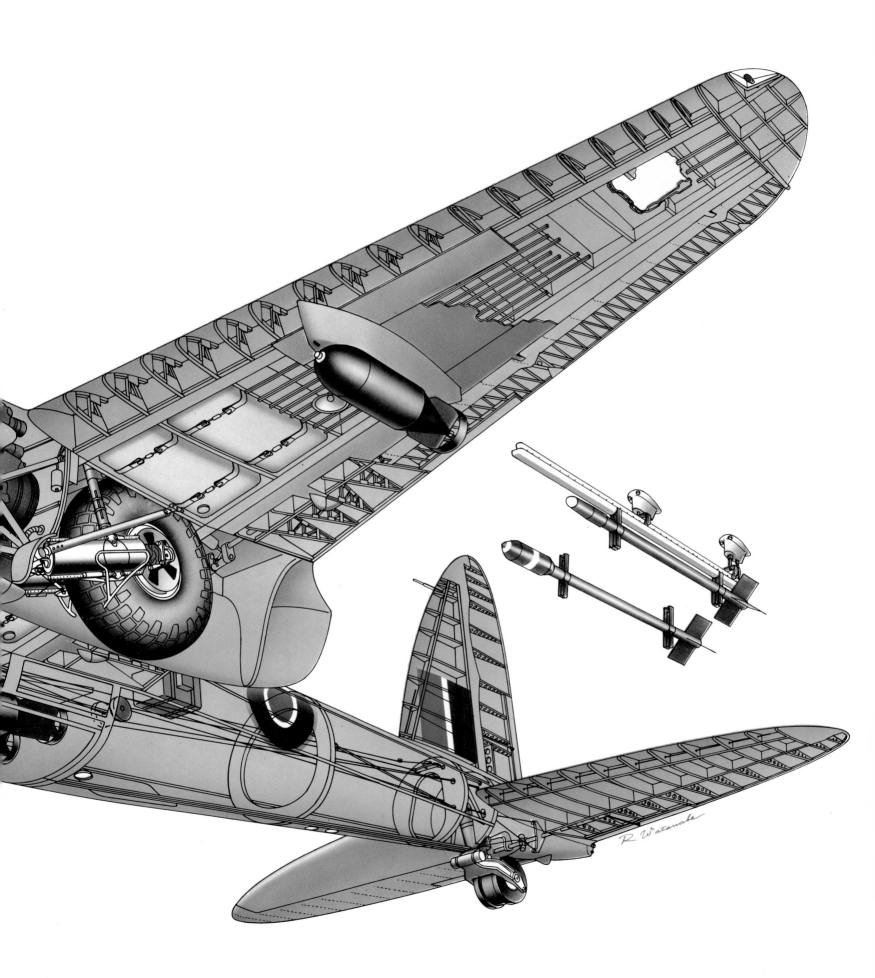

R. Watanabe

Mosquito B.MK XVI

This Mark represented the highest stage of development as a bomber. With a pressure cabin the type could operate at altitudes up to 40,000 ft (12,192 m) and the bulged bomb bay could accomodate a 4,000 lb (1,814 kg) bomb.

Two Rolls-Royce Merlin 72/73 or 76/77 engines, 1,680 hp or 1,710 hp each.

Performance
Max speed: 408 mph (656 km/h)
Service ceiling: 37,000 ft (11,277 m)
Range: 1,485 ml (2,390 km)
Weight loaded: 25.917 lb (11,756 kg)

Dimensions
Span: 54 ft 2 in (16.5 m)
Length: 40 ft 10 in (12.3 m)
Height: 15 ft 3$\frac{1}{2}$ in (4.65 m)
Wing area: 454 sq ft (43 m²)

Mosquito PR.MK XVI

This pressurised high altitude unarmed
photo-reconnaissance version first become
operational in July 1943.

Two Rolls-Royce Merlin E 72/73 engines,
1,680 hp each.

Performance

Max speed: 408 mph (656 km/h)
Service ceiling: 37,000 ft (11,277 m)
Range: 1,485 ml (2,390 km)
Weight loaded: 25,917 lb (11,756 kg)

Dimensions

Span: 54 ft 2 in (16.5 m)
Length: 40 ft 10 in (12.3 m)
Height: 15 ft 3$\frac{1}{2}$ in (4.65 m)
Wing area: 454 sq ft (43 m²)

Armament: None

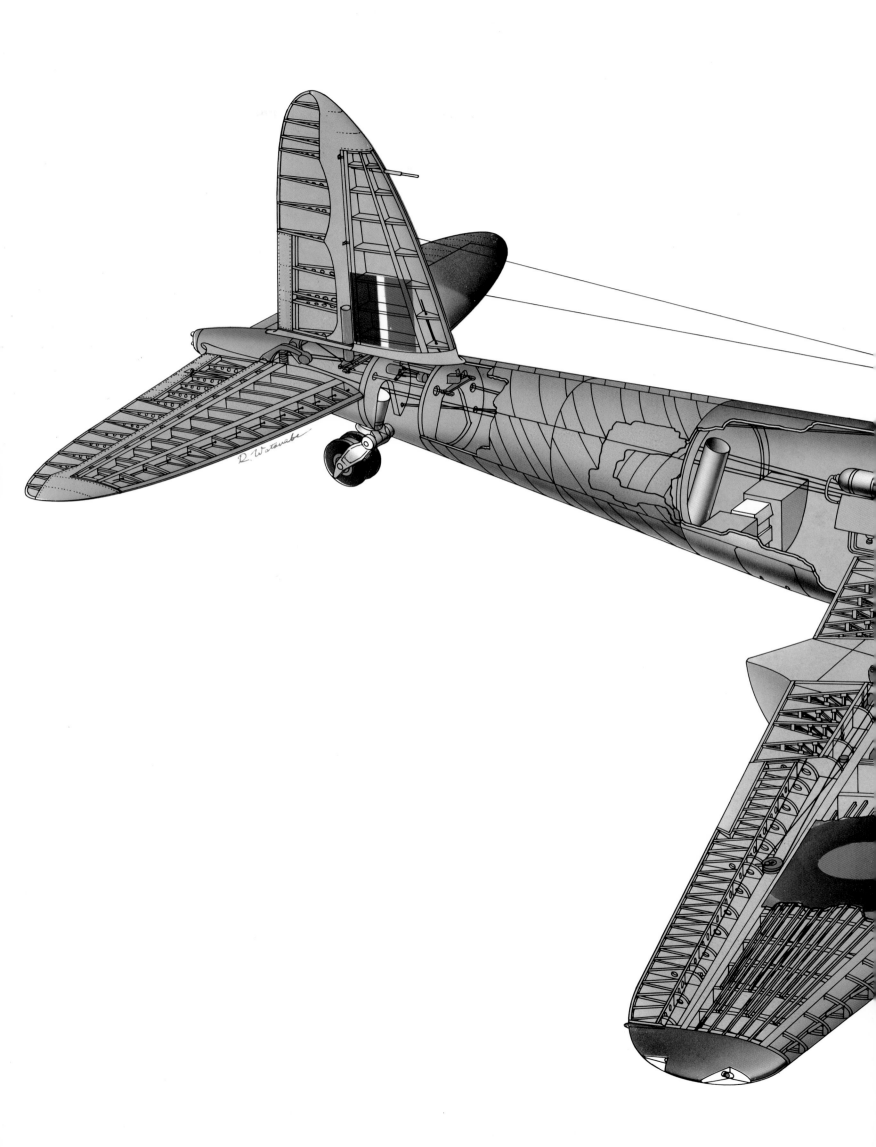

Mosquito FB.VI

FB.VI of No. 143 Squadron Coastal Command based at Banff in Scotland. Armed with rockets and cannon they commenced operations in November 1944 and specialized in anti-shipping strikes against German vessels operating in Norwegian waters. On April 9, 1945, squadron leader David Pritchard of 143 squadron flying Mosquito NE-D led his wing into an attack which claimed three German U-Boats in the Kattegat.

Two Rolls-Royce Merlin 21 engines, 1,460 hp each.

Performance	Dimensions	Armament
Max speed: 358 mph (576 km/h)	Span: 54 ft 2 in (16.5 m)	4 x 20mm Hispano cannon,
Service ceiling: 33,000 ft (10,058 m)	Length: 40 ft 6 in (12.35 m)	4 x .303-in Browning machine guns
Range: 1,855 ml (2,985 km)	Height: 12 ft 6 in (3.75 m)	
Weight loaded: 20,804 lb (9,463 kg)	Wing area: 454 sq ft (42.1 m²)	

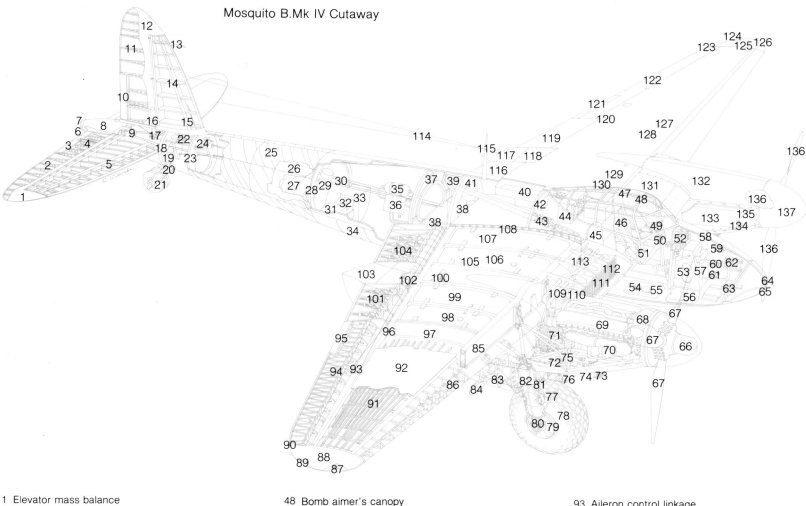

Mosquito B.Mk IV Cutaway

1 Elevator mass balance	48 Bomb aimer's canopy	93 Aileron control linkage
2 Elevator	49 Engine & propeller control box	94 Aileron
3 Elevator trim tab	50 Control column	95 Aileron trim tab
4 Elevator trim tab control linkage	51 Pilot's seat	96 Rear spar
5 Aerial	52 Instrumental panel	97 Wing rib No.6
6 Formation keeping lamp	53 Rudder pedal box	98 Outboard fuel tanks
7 Tail nagivation lamp	54 Drift sight	99 Outboard fuel tanks
8 Tail cone	55 Entrance door	100 Undercarriage strut/rear spar
9 Elevator internal mass balance	56 Bomb-aimer's kneeling cushion	attachment
10 Rudder trim tab	57 Nose compartment side windows	101 Outboard flap
11 Rudder structure	58 Windscreen de-icing jet	102 Flap jack and crank
12 Rudder mass balance	59 Signal cartridges	103 Nacelle aft fairing
13 Pitot head	60 Signal cartridges	104 Inboard flap
14 Fin structure	61 Signal cartridges	105 500lb bombs × 4
15 Aerial	62 Thermos bottles	106 Inboard fuel tanks
16 Rudder torque shaft	63 Bombsight	107 Inboard fuel tanks
17 Rudder control linkage	64 Navigation headlamp	108 Double wing upper skin
18 Bulkhead No.7	65 Bomb-aimer's windscreen	109 Engine controls/coolant pipes
19 Tailwheel retraction mechanism	de-icing jet	110 Oil cooler
20 Tailwheel leg	66 Propeller boss	111 Coolant radiator
21 Tailwheel	67 Three-blade de Havilland	112 Cabin heater unit
22 Rudder Internal mass balance	hydromatic propeller	113 Electro-pneumatic ram
23 Bulkhead No.6	68 Coolant header tank	114 Aerial
24 Rudder control linkage	69 Rolls-Royce Merlin XXI liquid-cooled	115 Aerial mast
25 Plywood outer skin	12-cylinder Vee engine	116 Inboard flap
26 Balsa	70 Exhaust (fishtail) stubs	117 Nacelle aft fairing
27 Plywood inner skin	71 Magneto	118 Flap jack inspection/access panel
28 Bulkhead No.5	72 Electric starter	119 Outboard flap
29 Flare chute	73 Ice guard	120 Aileron servo inspection panel
30 Control cables	74 Carburettor air intake	121 Aileron trim tab
31 Camera mounting box	75 Engine bearer assembly	122 Aileron
32 F.24 camera	76 Wheel guards	123 Resin lamp
33 Camera mounting box	77 Wheel guards	124 Formation light
34 Aft entry/access door	78 Mainwheel tyre	125 Wingtip
35 Air bottle	79 Wheel hub	126 Navigation light
36 Pneumatic panel	80 Gaiter	127 Filler cap
37 Bulkhead No.4	81 Roller	128 Ventpipe access holes panel
38 Oxygen bottles	82 Compression leg	129 Filler cap
39 Hydraulic reservoirs	83 Undercarriage wheel doors	130 Vent pipe access holes panel
40 Dinghy stowage	84 Mudguard	131 Radiator inspection panel
41 Bulkhead No.3	85 Front spar	132 Nacelle
42 HT power unit	86 Leading-edge ribs	133 Flame-trap exhaust
43 Attachment joint wing to	87 Navigation lamp	134 Spark plug cooling intake
fuselage	88 Starboard wing tip	135 Cooling spouts
44 T.1154 transmitter	89 Formation light	136 Three-blade de Havilland hydromatic propeller
45 Observer's seat	90 Resin lamp	137 Spinner
46 Harness	91 Wing outboard stiffeners	
47 Emergency exit canopy section	92 Spaced double skin (upper)	

in the year, the PRU – now divided into four squadrons – took delivery of PR.IVs modified with more efficient ejector exhausts which added 10 mph (16 km/hr) to the maximum speed. Other means to increase speed, such as maintaining the aircraft in a high state of polish, were found to be less effective.

Despite the performance of the Mosquito, interceptions were still possible. The usual evasive tactic was a very shallow dive to 395 mph (636 km/hr) as soon as an interceptor was spotted, but with the increasing use of Fw 190s and Bf 109Gs by the Luftwaffe this speed margin began to be eroded. The PR squadrons asked for more performance, and received it in the form of the PR.VIII with Merlin 61 two-stage-supercharged engines. The first of five of these interim high-speed, high-altitude aircraft was delivered to 540 Sqn in January 1943. The first sortie in the following month suffered the same fate as the initial Mosquito PR.I sortie: the cameras failed. On 3 March, however, a lone Mosquito PR.VIII penetrated the defences of Berlin in broad daylight. The PR units always found that the twin-engined Mosquito always aroused a fiercer response from the defences than the Spitfire, and this was no exception. Despite the efforts of Fw 190s and Bf 109s, the new Mosquito's 410 mph (658 km/hr) speed brought it back safely to its base. That sortie may have done a great deal more than simply provide proof of the PR.VIII's ability to flout the daylight defences of *Festung Europa*: it has been suggested that the overflight of 3 March convinced Adolf Hitler that Germany needed a high-speed bomber and inspired his decision to have the Messerschmitt Me 262 adapted from its intended role of bomber destroyer.

The PR.VIIIs were rapidly followed in service by the definitive PR.IX, basically similar but fitted with more powerful Merlin 72s. The remaining PR.IVs and PR.VIIIs were withdrawn by October. Like the PR.VIII, the PR.IX could exploit the greater power available by using 50 gal (228 lit) drop tanks, but a new and welcome feature (and an external distinguishing mark) was an observation blister in the roof to improve rearward view. Successful evasive action, obviously, depended on being able to see the attacker, and in this respect the early Mosquitos were not too well equipped.

The greater speed, altitude and fuel capacity of the PR.VIII and PR.IX made some remarkable sorties possible. During 1943 one of the new PR.IX Mosquitos made a grand tour of South-Eastern Europe from RAF Benson to Catania in newly occupied Sicily, crossing Regensburg, Vienna, Budapest, Bucharest and Foggia in 6½ flying hours. The average speed was 292 mph (470 km/hr) and the total distance covered was 1,900 miles (3,060 km). Before the Mosquito could taxi to its parking place at Catania, both its Merlin 72s cut from fuel exhaustion.

The winter of 1943–44, however, was a difficult one for the strategic PR units. The RAF's bomber offensive against Germany was at its peak, and the need for photographs of the damage caused by raids, and for surveys of new targets, was greater than ever. The series of raids on Berlin launched in November presented a particularly difficult problem, because Berlin was at the outer limit of range for the Spitfire PR.XI and the defences were particularly well supplied with fighters. In the cold of the winter, the Mosquitos could no longer adopt the traditional reconnaissance pilots' trick of flying just below contrailing height, which ensured that any fighter manoeuvring for a "bounce" would betray its presence by a trail; contrailing heights were too low for safety in the cold air. Instead, the reconnaissance crews went up to 33,000 feet (10,000 m) where the contrails of interceptors climbing to meet them could be seen well in advance. Eight of the PR.IXs were fitted with the more powerful Merlin 76/77s, and larger-area "paddle-bladed" propellers – the latter were American-designed, and had their maximum chord further outboard than the British-style propeller, and improved performance at high altitude at the expense of low-level performance – as an interim improvement to the performance of the Mosquitos at high altitudes.

Greater heights, however, brought their own problems. Persistent canopy icing and engine failures resulted from the extreme cold, and Luftwaffe fighters were still being sighted at altitudes of 40,000 feet (12,200 m) and upwards. The pressurized PR.XVI had made its first flight in July 1943, but due to shortages of heat exchangers the first aircraft were delivered without cabin heating. Neither did they have observation blisters in the canopy, and the PR squadrons deemed them unsuitable for operational use until these problems were solved. It was not until May 1944 that the PR.XVI was sufficiently developed to be considered operational.

The relative invulnerability of the two-stage-engined Mosquito was to suffer a dramatic setback in the summer of 1944. On 25 July a PR.XVI was attacked from astern at 29,000 ft (8,800 m) by an aircraft which enjoyed a marked superiority in straight-line performance – a Messerschmitt Me 262. The Mosquito managed to evade the jet fighter by turning into the attack repeatedly, depriving the attacker of its speed advantage, and finally dived into cloud to escape. An earlier Mosquito had not enjoyed such luck, one of the British aircraft having already been claimed destroyed by the Me 262 operational trials unit to which the attack of 25 July belonged.

Intelligence – largely informed by the Mosquitos' own reconnaissance – had predicted and followed the development of the Me 262 from an early stage, and studies of a specialized high-altitude reconnaissance Mosquito had been set in motion early in 1944. The basis of the new version was the long-span wing originally tested in 1942, and used on the NF.XV high-altitude night-fighter. Special Merlin 113/114 engines, featuring superchargers adjusted to high altitudes, were fitted to a long-span conversion of a PR.XVI, and all equipment that could be dispensed with was removed. Five production PR.32s were built, and although their 42,000-foot (12,800 m) cruising altitude did not render them immune to Me 262 attacks – one of the PR.32s was intercepted at maximum altitude in December 1944 – it rendered interceptions more difficult in the closing stages of the war.

The ultimate reconnaissance Mosquito, however, was conceived mainly for the Far East, and was intended to reconnoitre the mainland of Japan in support of an expected campaign of conventional bombing in 1945–46. Merlin 113/114s were married to a basic PR.XVI airframe, but with a massive increase in fuel capacity. The extra fuel was carried in a large auxiliary tank in the bomb-bay, the doors of which were bulged to a slightly greater extent than those of the later bomber versions of the Mosquito. In addition, a pair of 200 gal (900 lit) drop tanks were carried under the outer wings; not surprisingly, the wings drooped measurably when the big tanks were filled. Carrying so much weight on or behind the centre of gravity, and nearly all of it behind the wheels, the new Mosquito PR.34 was not a particularly easy aircraft to fly at its maximum all-up weight, despite the greater power of its engines, but its performance was outstanding. A small unit of PR.34s became operational from an improvised base in the Cocos Islands in July 1944, and made a few flights over Japanese-held territory before the war came to its unexpectedly early end. After the Japanese surrender, the PR.34s continued their activities over the Far East, covering up to 2,900 miles (4,670 km) in one nine-hour sortie.

After the war, the long-range PR.34 became the standard RAF reconnaissance aircraft, and 58 Sqn used the type on long and clandestine sorties over Eastern Europe and the Soviet Union in the immediate post-war years. Other examples were used in the Far East, locating terrorist installations in Malaya, and the type was used to set a number of point-to-point speed records: one was the London to Cape Town record, which a PR.34 captured at more than twice the speed achieved ten years before by its ancestor, the D.H.88 Comet. The Royal Air Force flew its last operational PR.34 sortie over Malaya in December 1955, and the type gave way to the English Electric Canberra in front-line service.

Night Fighter

Public fear of the conventional bomber in the pre-war years has been compared to the fear of nuclear warfare in the modern age. The bomber was regarded as a weapon against which there was no defence, capable of levelling whole cities in a single raid: and this was in the 1930s, when the average heavy bomber could carry barely a ton of bombs. The exaggerated fears of the public mirrored the exaggerated hopes of the air power strategists, who had disregarded the problems of navigation and bomb-aiming in their belief that the bomber "would always get through". The Mosquito was to play an important part in the development of the bomber force as a reasonably accurate offensive weapon; but it was also to prove very significant in countering the bomber, as the Western Allies' primary night-fighter in Europe.

The first Mosquito fighters, differing from the bombers in armament, cockpit detail and stronger wing skins, were intended as long-range day interceptors to counter Fw 200s over coastal waters. By mid-1941, however, one of the many changes of policy which were to affect the start of Mosquito production so adversely had placed fresh emphasis on the night-fighter force. The risk of a renewed night-bombing offensive by the Luftwaffe remained present despite the opening of the Eastern Front, and nuisance raids were a continuing problem. Some of the Mosquito F.IIs nearing completion were to be transferred to the PRU at Benson,

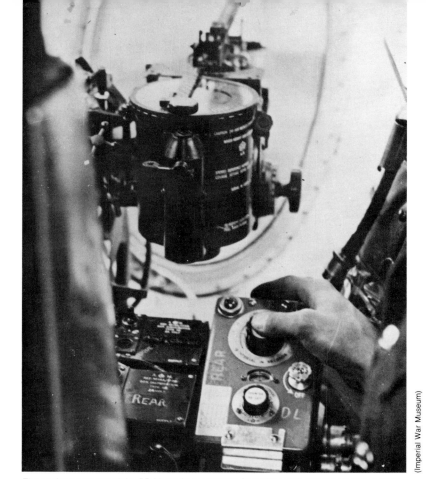

(Imperial War Museum)

The navigator operated the PR Mosquito's cameras from the bomb aimer's glazed position in the nose. (Below) Examining the results.

(Imperial War Museum)

PR Mosquito photograph of a Fw 190 factory destroyed by USAAF B-17's.

(Imperial War Museum)

351

Mosquito NF.II on a test flight.   (Charles E. Brown)

while others were to be fitted with Air Interception (AI) equipment – from 1944, to be known by the US-originated term "radar".

Prototype AI had been flight-tested as long ago as August 1937, and in July 1940 a Blenheim used the early AI.III to stalk a Luftwaffe night bomber to the point of visual contact, and shot it down. A more efficient set, the AI.IV, was used on the much faster Beaufighter, which became the standard Fighter Command night fighter through 1941.

The Beaufighter had one particular drawback: although it was sturdy, tractable and could carry a heavy armament, it was not particularly fast. Luftwaffe aircraft operating from bases in Northern France included the Dornier Do 217 and the Junkers Ju 88 as well as the slower Heinkel He 111s which had borne the greater share of earlier bombing efforts; and with a relatively short distance to reach home, they could afford to use their height and escape in a dive. Speed became more important to the Royal Air Force night fighters than it was to be for the Luftwaffe in its struggle against Bomber Command.

The first Mosquito NF.IIs were delivered in December 1941. Sixteen aircraft had been handed over by the following April, but only seven crews had been trained, and initial teething troubles had not yet been overcome. One of the most serious problems was the flash from the nose-mounted machine-guns. For some reason these had never been fired at night during trials at Boscombe Down, and it was left to the squadrons to discover that they completely wrecked the crews' laboriously acquired night vision (developed through acclimatization in a darkened room rather than by eating carrots as the Government told the British public). The exhaust shrouds, needed to prevent the flames from the engine exhaust betraying the fighter's position at night, not only slowed the fighter down by 10 mph (16 km/hr) but also wore out frequently. Even worse was the RDM.2 night camouflage finish, which accounted for another 16 mph (26 km/hr) in maximum speed through the increased skin friction of its velvet-black surface; if ever there was an object demonstration of the degree to which the Mosquito relied on aerodynamic cleanliness for its performance, this was it. RDM.2 was abandoned, initially in favour of a plain matt black.

The NF.II's radar equipment was comparatively free from troubles. Designated A1.V, it was basically similar to the preceding AI.IV, which had been the first practical AI radar in service; the main difference was that it included an indicator screen for the pilot in addition to the radar operator's controls. Initially regarded with some misgivings by the more experienced radar operators, who felt that it reduced them to the status of machine-minders, the pilot-indicating philosophy and the Mosquito eventually won acceptance. The crew's quarters were more cramped than in the Beaufighter, the Mosquito NF.II lacking the bomber's nose compartment and having to accommodate bulky display avionics as well; on the credit side, the belt-fed Hispano cannon installation of the Mosquito eliminated the painful and annoying job of changing ammunition drums in a manoeuvring aircraft.

One feature of the design which was less than ideal for a night fighter was the wing radiators; nocturnal interceptors specialized in destroying explosive-laden targets at short range and were more exposed than most aircraft to damage from debris. One NF.II was tested with less vulnerable chin radiators, but like several other experiments it cost more speed than it was worth. Throughout the Mosquito's active career it was not uncommon for a successful night-fighter sortie to be followed by a single-engined landing. Another experimental installation was that of a Turbinlite airborne searchlight in an unarmed Mosquito NF.II which was expected to illuminate a target for accompanying single-engined fighters. The idea proved too unwieldy for effective operational use and was abandoned.

The NF.II achieved its first kill in May 1942, and during the rest of the year the fighter squadrons enjoyed priority in Mosquito deliveries; 159 NF.IIs were in service by the end of January 1943, 60 per cent of the entire Mosquito force. The effectiveness of the Mosquito night-fighter was, however, to be immeasurably improved by one of the most important of all wartime operational advances.

Early AI radars such as the AI.V fitted to the NF.II Mosquito operated in the very-high-frequency spectrum of electromagnetic waves, with frequencies in the region of 0.2–0.5 GHz and relatively long wavelengths. Maximum and minimum range alike were very limited. The radar produced a circular pulse of energy, and if the target was further away from the radar than the ground, the reflection from the ground would swamp the screen. The receiver also had to be switched off while each pulse was transmitted, and because of the long wavelengths used the radar had a minimum range of around 1,000 ft (300 m); any target closer than that could not be detected because the echo returned while the receiver was still switched off.

Shorter "centimetric" wavelengths would solve many of these problems, because they could be accurately focussed and directed by a reflector small enough to be carried in an aircraft. Until May 1940, however, there was no way of generating such short waves – known as microwaves – at sufficient power to generate a useful echo from a distant target. The breakthrough that made British and American airborne radars far superior to German equipment for the rest of the war was made by J.T. Randall and A.H. Boot of Birmingham University, who succeeded in producing a magnetron, or microwave generator, of vastly increased power. The Telecommunications Research Establishment (TRE) at Malvern immediately realized the significance of this development and set out to turn it into practical AI radar. Very soon afterwards, in September 1940, the magnetron was revealed to the U.S. Government, which immediately accorded similar priority to development of the so-called "centimetric" radar in the USA.

The British and Americans tested their first pre-production centimetric AI radars in 1941. The first production centimetric radar to be installed on the Mosquito was the British AI.VIII. Mosquito NF.IIs were fitted with the new radar by Marshall Aviation at Cambridge, being redesignated NF.XII. The loss of the machine-guns, displaced by the new radar in its thimble-nose radome, was a minor inconvenience compared with the immense improvement in the ability of the Mosquito to find its targets.

Just after NF.XIII conversions started to reach the squadrons, the Luftwaffe adopted a new tactic: nocturnal nuisance raids by high-speed aircraft such as the attack versions of the Fw 190 and the new Messerschmitt Me 410. The older A1 equipment was virtually useless against these "hit-and-run" raiders, which took advantage of the very limited range of the NF.II radar at low altitude. On the night of 16–17 May, 1943, the Mosquito NF.XIIs of 85 Sqn accounted for five Fw 190s, and even the Me 410 had trouble escaping from the new Mosquitos. It was still a close race, and in late 1943 some of the NF.XIIs and NF.XIIIs were fitted with nitrous-oxide boost to catch the Me 410s.

The Mosquito NF.XIII, built from the start with centimetric AI.VIII and fitted with the strengthened wing and drop-tank attachments of the fighter-bomber series, followed the converted NF.XIII into service. By this time, however, even more capable radar equipment was well advanced in development. The TRE at Malvern was working in conjunction with Metropolitan-Vickers on the very advanced AI.IX; while earlier radars simply scanned the sky in the same preset pattern, the AI.IX could be steered like a spotlight to obtain a much stronger echo from the target, and could hold the target even against jamming. It could also be set to track the target automatically, constantly aiming its beam at the point where its signal was strongest. Disaster struck the AI.IX programme, however, at the end of 1942, when a Canadian Spitfire pilot on his first operation shot down the Beaufighter carrying the prototype AI.IX, killing the radar's designer.

Development of the AI.IX continued, but at a lower key.

Part of the reason for the slowing-down of AI.IX after the loss of the prototype was the promise of an American radar of lighter weight and comparable effectiveness, particularly in the face of heavy jamming. This was the Western Electric SCR-720, which had been developed from the original US centimetric radar using some AI.VIII features and other modifications to reduce its sensitivity to jamming. The USA could afford to spare SCR-72s because the aircraft for which it had been designed, the Northrop P-61 Black Widow, was taking rather longer than expected to develop, so the system was readily available for the Mosquito. Following flight tests in early 1943, some of the remaining NF.IIs were converted by Marshalls to NF.XVIIs with the American radar, redesignated AI.X by the RAF. It was to be the RAF's main night-fighter radar until 1958.

The NF.XIII was succeeded in production by the NF.XIX, which was more powerful than the earlier night-fighters and could be fitted with either the British AI.VIII or the American AI.X. The more advanced radar was in action at the beginning of 1944, in time to be used against the Operation *Steinbock* raids on London in the early part of the year. Despite the use of "chaff" (aluminium strips which created a dense fog on the radar screen) and the use of fast bombers operating from France, the Luftwaffe suffered heavy losses to the upgraded night-fighters.

By this time the NF.IIs had all been retired from the home-defence squadrons for conversion to NF.XIII and NF.XVII standard. The Air Ministry, however, had always been highly sensitive to the possibility that night-fighter Mosquitos lost over enemy territory might betray vital secrets. Intruder and bomber-support squadrons were not even issued with the AI.V-equipped NF.II until mid-1943, by which time the equipment was well on the way to obsolescence. NF.XIXs with centimetric radar were not allowed over enemy territory until May 1944, by which time the German night-fighters had driven Bomber Command out of Germany. The long delay is curious in the light of the fact that the most vital secrets of centimetric radar had already been given to the German industry through the installation of H2S bombing radar on RAF heavy bombers. The first H2S-equipped bomber had crashed in enemy territory before even the NF.II was released for intruder operations, and H2S technology was already being used for the German FuG 240 Berlin N-1a long before the AI.VIII and AI.X were allowed into the night-fighter battle over Germany. The impact of the night-fighter Mosquito on the war was therefore somewhat less than it might have been.

Intruder and Bomber Support night-fighters were equipped with a battery of electronic devices in addition to their primary radars. Some were fitted with Monica tail-warning radar. This was less of a disadvantage to the Mosquito than it was to the heavy bombers. Any aircraft closing on a Mosquito from the rear, for example, was almost certainly hostile, while on a heavy bomber the Monica set gave frequent false warnings caused by other bombers in the stream. The Mosquitos also carried the Serrate series of homers, each successive model being designed to locate and

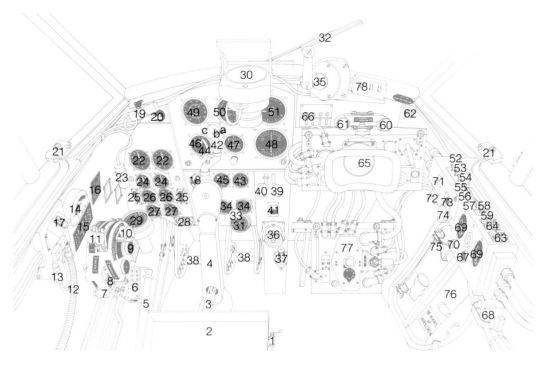

1	Harness release lever
2	Pilot's seat
3	Elevator connecting tube
4	Control column
5	Seat control lever
6	Radio control unit
7	Mixture control lever
8	Supercharger gear change switch
9	Friction adjusting knobs
10	Propeller speed control levers
11	Throttle levers
12	Pilot's oxygen pipe
13	Intercom jack
14	Elevator trimming tab indicator
15	Undercarriage emergency label
16	Engine limitations date plate
17	Beam approach switch
18	Ventilator
19	Instrument light
20	Boost control cut-out
21	Bottom ball slide
22	R.P.M. indicators
23	Compass light
24	Boost pressure gauges
25	Oil pressure gauges
26	Oil temperature gauges
27	Coolant temperature gauges
28	Landing lights switches
29	Compass
30	Gun sight
31	Triple pressure gauge
32	Windscreen wiper
33	Mark VIIIc oxygen regulator
34	Oxygen-contents gauge and oxygen-flow indicator
35	Rudder trim tab control handle
36	Aileron trimming tab control and indicator
37	Windscreen de-icing pump
38	Rudder pedal
39	Flaps selector lever
40	Undercarriage selector lever
41	Gun master switch
42	Control column hand grip (a) Ciné camera gun button (b) Machine gun firing plate (c) 20 mm gun firing lever
43	Flaps position indicator
44	Brake control lever
45	Undercarriage position indicator
46	Altimeter
47	Direction indicator
48	Turn indicator
49	Air speed indicator
50	Artificial horizon
51	Rate of climb indicator
52	Camera gun switch
53	Navigation lights switch
54	Ultra-violet lighting switch
55	Pitot head heater switch
56	Immersed fuel pump switch
57	Generator switch
58	Navigation headlamp switch
59	I.F.F. switch
60	Propeller feathering buttons. Right
61	Propeller feathering buttons. Left
62	Immersed fuel pump warning light
63	Fire extinguisher switches
64	I.F.F. detonator buttons
65	Radar screen
66	Radiator flap switches
67	Air temperature gauge
68	Mark VIIIc oxygen regulator
69	Fuel contents gauges
70	Windscreen wiper rheostat
71	Identification lights selector switch
72	Air recognition lights switch
73	Voltmeter
74	Identification switch box and key
75	Emergency door-jettison handle
76	Cockpit entrance door
77	A.R.I. 5093 receiver
78	Rudder trimming tab control and indicator

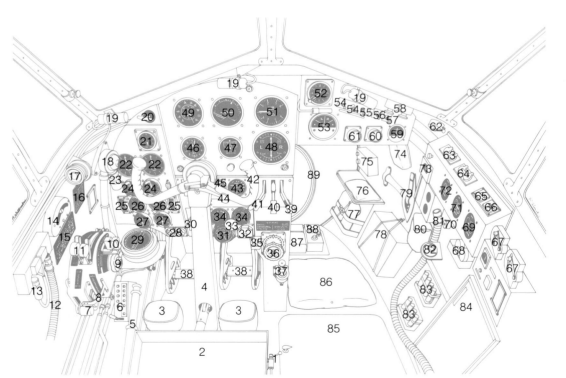

1	Harness release lever
2	Pilot's seat
3	Foot rest
4	Control column
5	Seat control lever
6	Radio control unit
7	Mixture control lever
8	Supercharger gear change switch
9	Friction adjusting knobs
10	Propeller speed control levers
11	Throttle levers
12	Pilot's oxygen pipe
13	Intercom jack
14	Tail trim indicator
15	Undercarriage emergency label
16	Engine limitations data plate
17	External fuel tanks jettison switch
18	Ventilator
19	Instrument light
20	Boost control cut-out
21	Steering indicator
22	R.P.M. indicators
23	Compass light
24	Boost pressure gauges
25	Oil pressure gauges
26	Oil temperature gauges
27	Coolant temperature gauges
28	Landing lights switches
29	Compass
30	Master and ignition switches
31	Triple pressure gauge
32	Bomb container jettison switch
33	Mark VIIIc oxygen regulator
34	Oxygen-contents gauge and oxygen-flow indicator
35	Bomb jettison handle
36	Aileron trimming tab control and indicator
37	Windscreen de-icing pump
38	Rudder pedal
39	Flap control lever
40	Undercarriage and tail-wheel control
41	Compass
42	Handwheel
43	Flaps position indicator
44	Brake lever
45	Undercarriage position indicator
46	Altimeter
47	Direction indicator
48	Turn indicator
49	Air speed indicator
50	Artificial horizon
51	Rate of climb indicator
52	Time of flight clock
53	Beam approach visual indicator
54	Radiator flap switches
55	Navigation lamp switch
56	Fuel pump switch
57	Pitot head switch
58	Dimmer switches for instrument and chart table floodlamps
59	Outside air temperature indicator
60	Propeller feathering buttons. Right
61	Propeller feathering buttons. Left
62	Identification lamp signalling switch box
63	Fire extinguisher switches
64	I.F.F. detonator buttons
65	Navigation headlamp switch
66	Downward identification lamp switch
67	Radiator flap control and indicators
68	Mark VIIIc oxygen regulator
69	Fuel contents gauges. Inner tank
70	Ventilation control
71	Fuel contents gauges. Center tank
72	Fuel contents gauges. Outer tank
73	Voltmeter
74	Extension lead stowage
75	Fuse box
76	Elbow cushion
77	Emergency oxygen bottles stowage
78	Syko apparatus stowage
79	Fireman's axe
80	Camera stowage
81	Observer's oxygen pipe
82	Observer's cold air punkah louvre
83	Stowage for signal pistol cartridges
84	Navigator's hinged table
85	Front entrance door
86	Knee cushion
87	Bomb panel fuse box
88	Bomb fuzing switches
89	Front bombsight dome

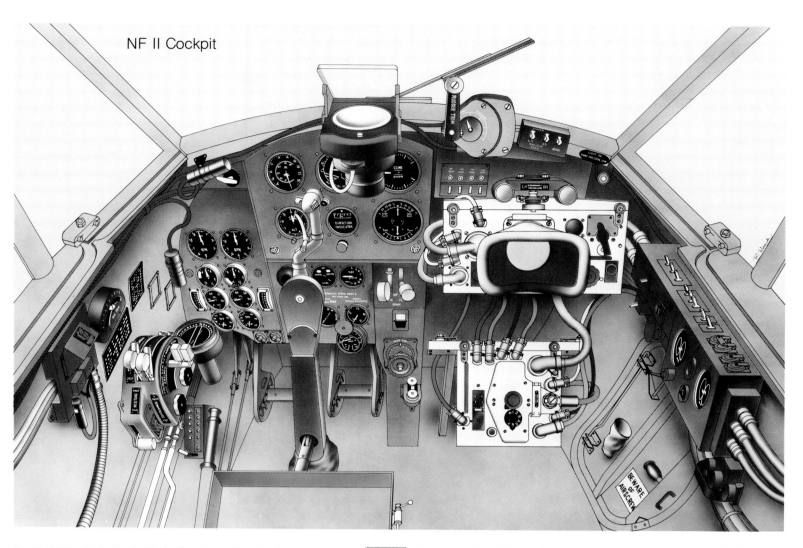

NF II Cockpit

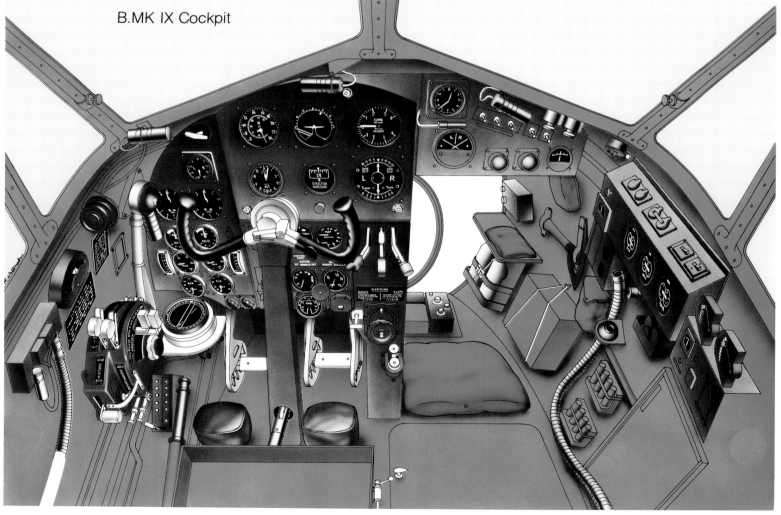

B.MK IX Cockpit

track the latest Luftwaffe radar. From 1944 – thanks to a Ju 88G crew who flew a reciprocal compass heading and landed their aircraft at Woodbridge in Essex by mistake – the intruders also carried Perfectos, which located German aircraft by triggering their identification friend-or-foe (IFF) equipment. The intruding night-fighters caused alarm among German night-fighter crews out of proportion to their numbers; some Luftwaffe crews were known to return to their bases at high speed and low level to escape the patrolling Mosquitos.

The improved two-stage Merlin came late to the night-fighters, with the exception of the few long-span, pressurized, stripped-down and lightly armed NF.XV high-altitude fighters produced in 1942–43. The NF.30 was the first version to be so equipped, but was dogged by problems, mainly with its exhaust shrouds, and was not in full-scale service until early 1945. It was fitted with the Western Electric AI.X radar, as was its immediate successor, the NF.36, which differed in having the improved Merlin 113/114 engine with better high-altitude performance than earlier engines. The NF.36s remained in front-line RAF service until 1952.

The invasion of Northern France in June 1944 found the two-stage-engined Mosquitos still wrestling with introductory problems, and it was the NF.XII, NF.XIII, NF.XVII and NF.XIX which saw most action. Some of the RAF night-fighter units were added to the 2nd Tactical Air Force for the defence of the invading forces, but seven squadrons were retained for defence against the Fi 103/V-1 missiles launched against England from Northern France. It was found that the Mosquito could usually cause a V-1 to crash by cutting rapidly across the missile's bows, and upsetting it with its slipstream. This was preferable to a cannon attack, which rendered the

Mosquito vulnerable to damage from the bomb's explosion. Other Mosquitos were used in the hunt for the He 111s which were used for air-launching V-1s after the bases in Northern France had been overrun. Destroying the slow bombers at low altitude over the North Sea, usually at night, was a hazardous occupation.

In the last stages of the war, the number of high-speed targets began to diminish; 85 Sqn was assigned to preventing the escape of any senior Nazis from the dwindling pocket around Berlin, and possibly the last German target to feature on the radar screen of a Mosquito was a Fieseler Fi 156 Storch caught by an 85 Sqn aircraft. Flying at 65 mph (105 km/hr), the Storch was flying too slowly for the Mosquito to attack it.

The final Mosquito variant, the NF.38, was also the least successful. Its radar was the British AI.IX, which had been so tragically set back at the end of 1942. Despite the large-scale purchase of American AI.X, work on the British radar had been continued as an insurance policy. The NF.38 was flown in November 1947, five years after the AI.IX prototype had been destroyed. The AI.IX and its associated equipment were bulkier than the AI.X installation, and the cabin had to be slightly extended to accommodate the new equipment. The combination of the longer and heavier nose with the longer and heavier two-stage Merlin 114 engines had unforeseen and unpleasant effects on the handling of the Mosquito, and the NF.38 was rejected for squadron service. Even so, 101 NF.38s were completed, some being sold to Jugoslavia two years after production ended. The last NF.38 was delivered in November 1950, ten years after the original B.1/40 prototype flew.

Radiator installation

1 Cabin heater coolant inlet
2 Cabin heater coolant outlet
3 Electro-pneumatic ram
4 Cabin air heater shutter control
5 Front spar
6 Warm air inlet to cabin
7 Cabin air heater shutter
8 Cabin cold air extractor
9 Back plate
10 Flap (drawn closed)

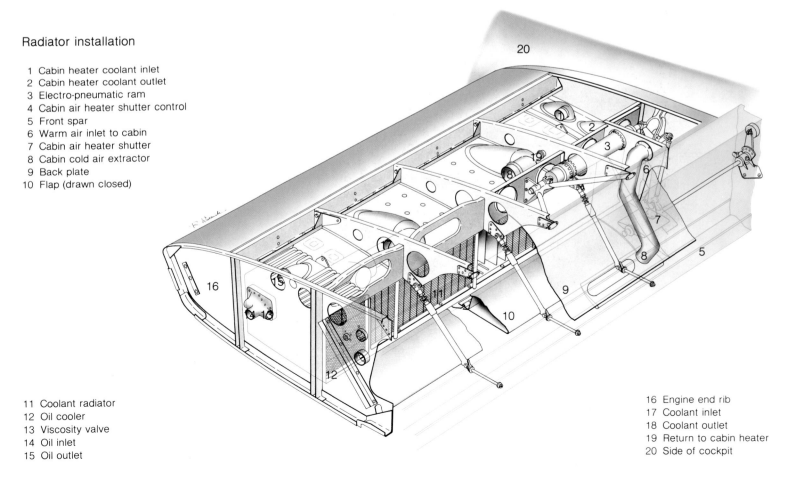

11 Coolant radiator
12 Oil cooler
13 Viscosity valve
14 Oil inlet
15 Oil outlet

16 Engine end rib
17 Coolant inlet
18 Coolant outlet
19 Return to cabin heater
20 Side of cockpit

Strategic Weapon

RAF Bomber Command had been unconvinced by the de Havilland Company's promises of a high-speed unarmed bomber at the start, and there is little doubt that the Command thereby deprived itself of the chance to make maximum use of the Mosquito. It was only at a late stage in the war that the type started to see action as part of a large high-speed bomber force, but never again did Bomber Command specify a single defensive gun on one of its aircraft. It was 30 years before the US Strategic Air Command finally abandoned the security blanket of a tail gun turret, and Soviet bombers still have guns, but the Mosquito had converted Bomber Command by 1945.

The lack of enthusiasm for the Mosquito in Bomber Command accounted for the fact that the reconnaissance and night-fighter versions were deployed rather earlier than the bombers and took the larger share of production in 1942 and 1943. By the time Bomber Command began to appreciate the Mosquito's potential as a strategic weapon, this imbalance of production was difficult to reverse, and the Command only started to receive Mosquitos in larger numbers when the Canadian production lines started to move at the end of 1943.

However, Bomber Command did equip two units – 105 and 139 Squadrons – with Mosquitos in the spring of 1942. A few of these were converted from aircraft destined for the reconnaissance squadrons, with the smaller tailplane and shorter nacelles of the prototypes; these were known as Mosquito B.IV Series i aircraft. Most were B.IV Series ii machines, with definitive-standard airframes, provision for 50 gal (228 lit) underwing drop tanks and single-stage-supercharged Merlin engines. All Mosquito bombers to see action up to late 1943 were of this version, and in addition all the Canadian-built bombers (B.VIII, B.XX and B.25) were completed to a roughly similar standard.

The Mosquitos of Bomber Command took over the task of carrying out daylight precision bombing attacks from the obsolete Blenheims, which had begun to suffer crippling losses in 1941. Typical targets were administrative or industrial targets of military importance, located in a populated area in one of the occupied countries, where Bomber Command was still concerned to avoid civilian casualties. (The introduction of the Mosquito took place at the time Bomber Command was beginning to adopt a policy of area bombing for German targets.)

Originally designed to carry four 250 lb (114 kg) bombs internally, the Mosquito had demonstrated considerably better load-carrying capability in its flight tests, and to exploit this capacity a modified 500 lb (228 kg) bomb with shortened fins was developed. Four of these weapons could be carried internally by the B.IV, and this 2,000 lb (912 kg) load was standard for early Mosquito operations. Bomber Command's aircraft also received the same Mk XIV vector bomb-sight as the force's heavier aircraft.

Operations started on 31 May, 1942, when four Mosquitos followed up the first "1,000-bomber raid" on Cologne with a daylight attack. One of the raiders was shot down by flak but although details of the Mosquito were now clearly apparent to the Luftwaffe, the aircraft was still a closely guarded secret in Britain, and in June one British newspaper was reprimanded for referring to the existence of the Mosquito. Meanwhile, the Luftwaffe was taking the measure of the new British bomber. Just as the Hawker Typhoon was to counter the Me 410 on daylight raids, so the new Fw 190 began to exact an increasing toll of Mosquitos, which lacked any speed margin over the German aircraft. Losses on early raids averaged 16 per cent of all sorties flown, leading to some improvised measures aimed at increasing the speed of the Mosquito. Exhaust shrouds were removed, trading stealth for speed; other detail changes were tried, but only the removal of the exhaust shrouds was found to produce a worthwhile improvement. An additional modification was the installation of a rear-view blister in the canopy roof.

These modifications started to take effect after the 26 September, 1942 raid on the Gestapo headquarters in Oslo, in which one of four Mosquitos was lost to defending Fw 190s. Evaluation was greatly assisted by the RAF's acquisition of an Fw 190 in July. Its pilot had followed a reciprocal compass bearing and had inadvertently delivered the Luftwaffe's latest fighter to an RAF base in Wales. It was found that height was the Mosquito's ally, increasing its speed advantage. Increasingly, the Mosquitos were used at higher altitudes over well defended targets in daylight. The recommended tactic under attack was to enter a shallow dive and perform a high-speed corkscrew manoeuvre. Unlike most fighters, the Mosquito did not suffer excessively from hardening of the controls at high speed (this was not an unmitigated benefit, because it made it rather too easy for a pilot to overstress the airframe) and a diving, turning evasive tactic stood a good chance of success.

High-level raids, however, ruled out the sort of accuracy needed for attacks on "pinpoint" targets in occupied cities, and the hazardous low-level attacks continued. Better training and planning, occupying two weeks at least before the date of the raid, helped to reduce losses to some extent, but the loss rate remained high. By the end of November, 24 Mosquitoes had been lost out of 282 sorties flown; a loss rate of 8 per cent compared with a current rate of 5 per cent among the slow, turret-studded night bombers. The crews felt more than a little vulnerable, knowing that they had no defensive armament and knowing that the Luftwaffe knew it. Various types of rear defence had been studied, if only to discourage the "take your time, he can't shoot back" mentality the Mosquito crews were beginning to notice in their attackers. A trial installation of machine guns in the engine nacelles was made and tested, but found to offer no benefit.

The losses fell gradually, however, and the Mosquitos' ability to bite the Luftwaffe eagle's tail and survive was excellent propaganda. A Nazi rally in Berlin addressed by Göring and Goebbels was effectively disrupted by a Mosquito raid on 30 January, 1943; only one of the raiders was caught by the defences. Göring referred to the Mosquito squadrons' "contempt" for the Luftwaffe after the defences failed to account for any of the bombers which hit the Zeiss optical

Mosquito B.MK XVI used for trials with experimental H2S bombing radar installations. (De Havilland)

factory in Jena, deep inside Germany, in May. By the end of March, the Mosquitos had dropped a total of 2,000 tons of bombs, with a 7.5 per cent missing rate, and by the end of May, after exactly a year of operations, the Bomber Command units had lost 48 Mosquitos in 726 sorties, a 6.7 per cent loss rate; over the second half of the year, losses had averaged 5.4 per cent.

The latter rate was on the high side of tolerable, however, and the Mosquito units represented a higher concentration of valuable crew experience than the average bomber squadron. However, Bomber Command was about to embark on a radical change in the way it used the Mosquito, and like many of the changes which affected the design it stemmed from the Telecommunications Research Unit "boffins" at Malvern. It was to elevate the Mosquito in Bomber Command from the status of an experiment to that of a necessity.

Bomber Command had entered the war in 1939 committed to night bombing of military targets, despite the fact that no means of hitting individual targets with any accuracy existed. The Luftwaffe had pioneered the use of radio beams for navigation, using two systems operationally against Britain in late 1940. One of these systems, the X-Gerät, had introduced the concept of a specialized target-finding squadron, using selected aircrew and advanced electronic equipment aboard the aircraft, which would find and mark the target for the main force. After the beam-assisted raids of late 1940, the TRE started work on an even more accurate navigation aid, capable of marking and bombing a given target such as a factory in completely blind conditions.

This system was Oboe. It relied on two ground stations – "Cat" at Dover and "Mouse" at Cromer – linked to each other by land lines and communicating with a device in the aircraft which received and repeated the synchronized pulsed signals from the two ground stations. The time between transmission and return of the signal gave the ground station an accurate measurement of the distance of the aircraft from the station. The aircraft fitted with Oboe flew an arc of constant radius around the Cat station, guided by an audible signal in the pilot's headphones. The distance of the

aircraft from the Mouse station naturally changed as it flew on its arc around Cat, and when the distance between the aircraft and the Mouse station corresponded to the location of the target along the flightpath – with compensation for the ballistics of the bombs or markets, and the height and airspeed of the aircraft – the Mouse station signalled for bomb or marker release.

Once corrected for the inaccuracies in standard maps used in Britain and Germany, Oboe could aim bombs to within an average of 150 yards of the target, irrespective of weather. It had two limitations: its range was limited by the curvature of the earth, because its beams propagated only in straight lines, and two stations could guide only one aircraft at a time. The high altitude and speed of the Mosquito were essential to extend the range of Oboe as far as possible, because the range of the system increased with the operating height of the Oboe aircraft. The speed of the Mosquito meant more aircraft could be handled by the ground stations in a given period of time, and reduced the risk that Oboe hardware would fall into German hands and facilitate jamming or deception.

Operational trials of Oboe-equipped Mosquito B.IVs started in late 1942. The existence of Oboe was one of the motives for the formation of a new force within Bomber Command which was to become almost the sole user of Mosquitos within the command. 8 Group, or the Pathfinder Force, had been formed amid some controversy in July 1942, and was responsible for Oboe marking of targets. The Pathfinders also included Lancaster squadrons, which dropped their own markers on the Target Indicator flares aimed by the Oboe Mosquitos.

Bomber Command suddenly found that it could not get enough Mosquitos. The 28,000 ft (8,530 m) cruising altitude of the de Havilland bomber was just enough to allow Oboe marking of the industrial cities of the Ruhr, the Command's main target during most of 1943. The first Oboe-marked heavy raid on Essen took place in March 1943, bringing a dramatic increase in accuracy. Not until July was a Mosquito with Oboe brought down and examined, and by the time the information extracted from the wreckage had been

The B.MK XVI's bulging bomb bay could accomodate a 4,000lb bomb.

used to create an effective jamming system the British were ready to switch to another frequency.

After a year of Mosquito day bomber operations, 105 and 139 Sqn were transferred to 9 Group – the Pathfinder Force – in mid-1943. They formed the nucleus of 8 Group's Light Night Striking Force (LNSF), formed to carry out high-speed night raids using precision bomb-aiming and navigation devices. The activities of the LNSF formed a counterpoint to the Main Force raids of hundreds of heavy bombers. When the Main Force was operating, the LNSF would stage a diversionary raid, marking a completely different target and dropping bombs to simulate the opening stages of an attack. The Mosquitos would carry large quantities of "window", the British term for "chaff" – strips of aluminium foil intended to confuse radar – in an effort to make German radar controllers believe that they were a large force of heavy bombers. By the autumn of 1943 the LNSF was losing less than two aircraft for every 100 sorties flown, the Mosquito being usefully faster than most of the Luftwaffe's night-fighters. When the heavy bombers were not flying, the LNSF continued its raids to ensure that the German night-fighters would get no rest.

Deliveries of the improved B.IX – basically similar to the PR.IX, which went into service a little earlier – with two-stage Merlin engines started in April 1943, although it was much later in the year before the improved aircraft formed a large proportion of the LNSF strength. More significantly, work had started in April 1943 on the task of converting the Mosquito to carry a 4,000 lb (1,814 kg) thin-case blast bomb. As well as increasing the offensive capacity of the aircraft, the conversion would allow the LNSF to provide a much more convincing imitation of the opening stages of a Main Force raid. The addition of so much weight behind the centre of gravity and the landing gear did nothing to improve the Mosquito's handling, and the bulged bomb-bay doors covering the dustbin-shaped weapon did nothing for its looks, but after some modifications to alleviate the worst handling problems the Mosquito was cleared for service with the 4,000 lb bomb. A few B.IVs were converted to carry the big bomb, but the more powerful B.IX was better suited to the heavier weights required, especially since the longer and heavier engines offset the weight of the bomb. The 4,000 lb installation became standard on the B.XVI, the pressurized-cabin bomber equivalent to the PR.XVI. The B.XVI was the ultimate wartime bomber Mosquito, and could carry 100 gal (455 lit) drop tanks under its wings in addition to the internal bomb. Superseding the B.IX in production after only six months, it entered service in early 1944, about the same time that the Mosquitos started dropping 4,000 lb bombs in anger. The British-built aircraft were by now being supplemented by deliveries of the Canadian-built B.XX, and 8 Group's Mosquito force was expanding.

At the end of March 1944 Bomber Command's "heavies" suffered disastrously heavy losses during a raid on Nuremberg, and the RAF's main strategic bomber force was re-assigned to operations directly linked to the invasion of France. 8 Group's commander, Air Vice-Marshal Donald Bennett, asked for 200 more Mosquito B.XVIs to conduct an independent night campaign. Targets were to be marked with Oboe if they were within range; otherwise, Mosquitos fitted with the new K-band H2S Mk VI air-to-ground bombing radar were to find and mark the targets. A variety of H2S installations were used; most aircraft carried it in a solid nose, an experimental aircraft carried it in the fuselage, and others beneath the rear fuselage. (The scanner aerial for the Mk VI equipment was smaller than that of the earlier, longer-wavelength versions, and fitted more neatly beneath the Mosquito.)

In the closing stages of the war, the Light Night Striking Force came closer than any other unit to achieving Geoffrey de Havilland's ideal of fast, unarmed bombers, using speed for protection. On the night of 21–22 March, 1945, the Mosquitos raided Berlin, losing one aircraft out of 138 and marking by H2S; the last RAF raid of the war involved 125 aircraft against Kiel, marking with Oboe, and every aircraft returned safely. In the long winter nights of 1944–45, it was not unknown for a single LNSF Mosquito to bomb Berlin twice in a single night with different crews. All in all, 8 Group flew 27,239 Mosquito sorties from which 108 aircraft failed to return: less than a tenth of the loss rate among the "heavy" squadrons, and representing a loss of aircrew (killed and missing) about one-third as great as the total loss on the single raid to Nuremberg in March 1944. It is fair, however, to point out that the conventional "heavies" had crippled the Luftwaffe's fuel supply by the time extensive LNSF raids started.

It has been argued that Bomber Command could have done far more damage to Germany, with far less loss of life among its own crews and far less wastage of wartime production capacity, had it embraced the concept of the fast unarmed bomber earlier. Certainly, the Command's post-war policy reflected this experience, with its jet bombers being designed around advanced H2S and electronic countermeasures and relying on speed and altitude for defence.

It takes fairly simple arithmetic to calculate that the Mosquito in its ultimate form could deliver more weapons over the same distance than the typical heavy bomber, when the two aircraft were compared on the basis of crew man-hours, total engine hours and fuel consumption; also, that the average Mosquito could be expected to deliver far more bombs during its far longer life expectancy, and its crew could expect to survive a far longer tour of operations. The only serious weakness of this argument is that the relative invulnerability of the Mosquito was itself indirectly brought about by Bomber Command's own policies. Because the RAF concentrated on producing the four-engined heavy bombers, the Luftwaffe's main task was to destroy these; Germany's aircraft-production chief Erhard Milch accordingly opposed production of the Heinkel He 219 night-fighter, which was faster than the Mosquito, in favour of the slower Ju 88G, which was adequate to deal with the heavy bombers and could be built more cheaply than the He 219. The practical difficulties of a shift to the unarmed bomber philosophy would have been enormous at any stage (including the need to train crews to the high standards demanded for the Mosquito) and would have given the Luftwaffe time to re-equip with the He 219, undoubtedly increasing Mosquito losses.

The final Mosquito bomber version was the B.35, basically similar to the B.XVI but powered by the high-altitude-rated Merlin 114. It remained in front-line service with the RAF until 1953, when the English Electric Canberra replaced it. Even the B.35, however, was restricted to operational weights and loadings in peacetime which were well below those of wartime B.XVIs; the "war emergency" weights at which the B.XVI operated were 4,000 lb (1,815 kg) higher than the peacetime weights, which limited the Mosquito's bomb-load to 1,500 lb (680 kg). These restrictions could, of course, be lifted in wartime, and were an excellent indication of the abuse which the Mosquito would put up with in the hands of a skilled and dedicated crew.

Fighter Bomber

Considering the versatility of the Mosquito, and the initial difficulty in deciding what role it should be used for first, it was hardly surprising that the version produced in greater numbers than any other was a compromise. Oddly, considering the Mosquitos reputation for speed, it was also the slowest

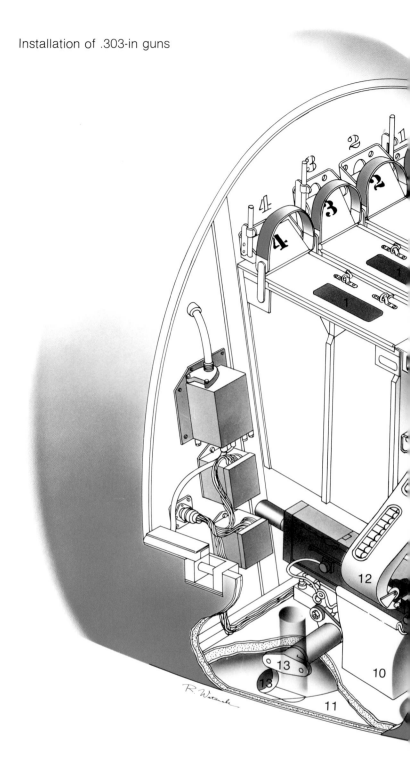

Installation of .303-in guns

version to see action. The fighter-bomber version of the Mosquito was also ideally suited to the air campaign waged by the Royal Air Force in the latter stages of the 1939–45 war, and unlike the other main variants of the type it needed no major development to match improvements in enemy air power. Every FB built in Britain, Canada and Australia was an unpressurized aircraft with single-stage Merlin engines, with the exception of a single Australian prototype.

The fighter-bomber version of the Mosquito was conceived as a specialized aircraft for "intruder" missions. These had developed from the "fighter sweeps" which Fighter Command had started in 1941 following the end of the Luftwaffe's daylight bombing offensive against the British mainland. In the absence of enemy aircraft over Britain,

1 Ammunition boxes
2 Ammunition chutes (drawn empty)
3 Tube in fuselage for exit of gun heating air
4 Blast tube & spring
5 Ciné camera mounting for G42 or G45 camera
6 Spout
7 Browning MK.II .303-in machine guns
8 Removal of empty cartridges
9 Link chute
10 Empty case chute
11 Space for collecting empties
12 Ammunition chute (drawn loaded)
13 Warm air passages for gun heating

Fighter Command would send formations of aircraft to harass the Luftwaffe over Europe. When the Luftwaffe ceased rising to the bait of patrolling Spitfires, the RAF started to send light bombers to accompany the fighters and provoke the enemy into battle.

The suitability of the Mosquito for these operations was demonstrated by 23 Sqn in the second half of 1942, using some of the very few Mosquito F.IIs which were not converted to NF.II standard with AI radar. These replaced Havocs on night intruder operations, and in the absence of radar – not yet security-cleared for operations over enemy territory – the RAF had to rely on enemy pilots leaving their navigation lights on. Long-range fuel tanks were added in the rear fuselage, to give an extra 1½ hr endurance.

Intruder operations using Mosquitos were gradually expanded in the autumn of 1942, using NF.IIs withdrawn from the night-fighter role. These aircraft were converted by removal of the radar and the addition of long-range fuel tanks and extra ammunition for the 20 mm cannon.

The F.IIs and converted NF.IIs were, however, to be joined by a version rather better adapted to the Intruder mission. In late 1941 it was envisaged that the existing Mosquito II day and night fighters would be replaced by a heavier version with provision for bombs or fuel tanks under the outer wing. The F.VIA was to be a night fighter and the F.VIB a specialized fighter-bomber, with room for internal bombs aft of the cannon bay. With the advent of more advanced night-fighters, the F.VIA was dropped and the intruder renamed FB.VI. Originally, two 250 lb (113 kg) bombs were to be carried, but the internal weapon load was doubled when the short-finned 500 lb (227 kg) bomb specially developed for the Mosquito was approved. Most of the FB.VI versions were equipped to take two of the heavier bombs internally plus another pair on the wing pylons – a 2,000 lb total load, in addition to the four cannon and quartet of machine guns.

The FB.VI was flown in prototype form in July 1942, but an accident to the prototype and the endemic confusion about production priorities for different Mosquito subtypes conspired to delay production deliveries until May 1943, when the type replaced some of the intruder units' old F.IIs. The pace of operations quickened, and several different types of mission were defined. Intruder missions were directed at pre-planned targets. Day or Night Rangers were freelance patrols mainly aimed at keeping the air defences awake, and became steadily riskier as more Fw 190s were deployed. "Instep" patrols were flown to protect Coastal Command operations from long-range Luftwaffe day fighters over the Bay of Biscay. These operations occupied the intruder squadrons from mid-1943 until the run-up to the invasion of Northern France.

The activities most closely associated with the Mosquito FB.VI, however, were those of the 2nd Tactical Air Force (2TAF). This force was formed in June 1943, just after the Bomber Command Mosquito day-bomber units had been transferred to 8 Group to join night and Pathfinder operations. Two "big wings" of Mosquito FB.VIs were formed at Sculthorpe and Lasham, launching operations in October 1943 against the same sort of precision targets which had been the objective of the day bombers' efforts in 1942–43. Power stations, in particular, were the objectives of early raids.

Towards the end of 1943, however, the Germans started building large number of curious concrete emplacements in Northern France. Intelligence partly provided by reconnaissance Mosquitos confirmed that these were launch sites for V-1 flying bombs. 2TAF was to take a major share in the attacks on these sites, which were well concealed, hard to find and heavily protected by concrete and anti-aircraft guns.

The most celebrated exploit of 2TAF was the raid on Amiens Prison in February 1944, intended to breach the wall and free Resistance prisoners facing execution by the Gestapo. More than 250 prisoners were "sprung" in a carefully

The Mosquito FB.XVIII that was specially developed for anti-shipping strike operations with a nose armament of 4 x .303-in machine guns and one 57mm anti-tank gun.

planned operation carried out despite unfavourable weather. 2TAF Mosquitos continued to attack Gestapo headquarters in various towns, SS barracks and similar targets, all of which tended to be located in friendly populated areas. The last raids of this type took place on Gestapo HQs in Denmark towards the close of the war, in an attempt to reduce the scale of reprisals in the collapsing Reich.

Mosquitos of the Intruder squadrons and the 2TAF were in great demand after the D-Day landings of 6 June, 1944. Some of the units were assigned to "Flowers" Operations – strikes against German communications – while others continued the battle against the V-1 sites until the Allied forces finally pushed the launching sites out of V-1 range from London.

The only production fighter-bomber to differ significantly from the FB.VI was the FB.XVIII, conceived in March 1943. Enemy U-boats had to cross the Bay of Biscay on the surface to return from their Atlantic patrols, and they were vulnerable, in theory, to air attack. This was appreciated by the Luftwaffe, which deployed Ju 88 and Bf 110 long-range day fighters to protect the submarines from Coastal Command patrol aircraft. Mosquitos had the range and air-to-air fighting ability to counter this opposition, but until the advent of the FB.XVIII lacked a weapon of sufficient power and accuracy to sink a U-boat. The new variant carried a 57 mm Molins gun – familiar to the Army as the 6-pounder anti-tank gun – in place of the four Hispano cannon, and a small batch was produced. The anti-shipping Mosquito, known as the Tse-Tse, was intended to be used in composite strike squadrons with FB.VI escorts. The Tse-Tse enjoyed some success,

Installation of 20 mm guns

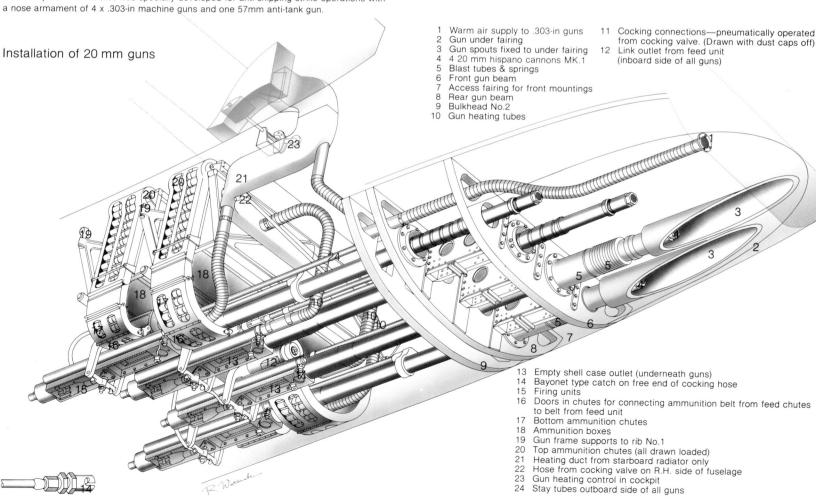

1 Warm air supply to .303-in guns
2 Gun under fairing
3 Gun spouts fixed to under fairing
4 4 20 mm hispano cannons MK.1
5 Blast tubes & springs
6 Front gun beam
7 Access fairing for front mountings
8 Rear gun beam
9 Bulkhead No.2
10 Gun heating tubes
11 Cocking connections—pneumatically operated from cocking valve. (Drawn with dust caps off)
12 Link outlet from feed unit (inboard side of all guns)

13 Empty shell case outlet (underneath guns)
14 Bayonet type catch on free end of cocking hose
15 Firing units
16 Doors in chutes for connecting ammunition belt from feed chutes to belt from feed unit
17 Bottom ammunition chutes
18 Ammunition boxes
19 Gun frame supports to rib No.1
20 Top ammunition chutes (all drawn loaded)
21 Heating duct from starboard radiator only
22 Hose from cocking valve on R.H. side of fuselage
23 Gun heating control in cockpit
24 Stay tubes outboard side of all guns

but better results were attained in the closing months of the war when the FB.VI was cleared to carry the 60 lb unguided rocket, which had been used to great effect already by ground attack aircraft. Nevertheless, one Mosquito was fitted experimentally with the 3.7 in (94 mm) anti-tank gun after the war, and successful air firings were made.

A number of specialized Mosquito versions stemmed from the FB.VI. After the restrictions on the use of centimetric AI radar over enemy territory were abandoned in mid-1944, some of the FB.VIs used by 100 Group to harass German night-fighters were fitted with American-built Sperry AN/APS-4 radar, designated AI.XIV by the RAF. Originally designed for use in single-seat naval fighters, the AI.XIV was not as bulky or as heavy as the more usual night-fighter radar, but was less powerful.

The FB.VI also had the distinction of being the first twin-engined aircraft to land on the deck of an aircraft carrier. (The first to take-off from a carrier had been the US Army Air Force B-25s which made a one-way raid on Tokyo in April 1942.) There was considerable doubt as to whether the Mosquito, larger than any other carrier aircraft and with something of reputation as a "hot ship" due to its rapid sink rate and high landing speed, could touch down safely on the deck of a carrier. However, the Royal Navy had outstanding requirement for long-range reconnaissance/strike aircraft and night fighters, so it was decided to modify an FB.VI for deck landing trials. Four-blade propellers were fitted and the rear fuselage was strengthened to withstand the loads imposed by the arrester hook. The first successful deck landing was made on 25 March, 1944, and trials were generally successful although the arrester hook broke on the fourth attempt and the aircraft performed a "bolter" off the end of the deck.

The Royal Navy was sufficiently impressed by the results of the trials to order the Sea Mosquito TR.33, with manually-folding wings which used the same metal/wood skin construction as those of the Hornet. Other modifications included four-blade propellers, of larger diameter than those of the standard aircraft, and a completely different undercarriage, that of the land-based aircraft being much too "bouncy" for carrier operations. The TR.33 carried American ASH radar, a relative of the APS-4/AI.XIV; the weapons fit was augmented by ventral attachments for a torpedo or similar heavy store, and to persuade the aircraft to leave the deck rocket-assisted-take-off gear (RATOG) could be fitted on the rear fuselage. After all this development work and the production of 50 TR.33s, followed by 14 TR.37s with British radar, the RN never used the Mosquito from carriers, all the Sea Mosquitos being issued to training units.

The installation of the two-stage Merlin engine in the fighter-bomber had been considered quite early in development, but because the FB.VI operated mainly at low altitudes the higher power available at high levels was not as significant. The designation FB.XI was applied to a two-stage equipped fighter-bomber Mosquito, but it never reached the prototype stage. Meanwhile, improved single-stage Packard-Merlins were fitted to later Canadian-built fighter-bombers: the FB.21 was the initial version and the FB.26 had

The sinking of three U-boats in the Kattegat.   British Aerospace (via Philip Birtles)

FB.VI attacking shipping off Norwegian coast.   British Aerospace (via Philip Birtles)

Rocket strike in a Norwegian fjord.   British Aerospace (via Philip Birtles)

the improved engines. Australian production was based on the FB.40, directly equivalent to the FB.VI, trainer and reconnaissance aircraft alike being FB.40 derivatives. These included the PR.41 with two-stage Packard engines and the similarly powered FB.42.

The contribution of the fighter-bomber Mosquito was a reflection of its versatility. Essentially a high-speed bomber with guns, the FB.VI combined with bomb- and rocket-carrying fighters to create a new concept of tactical air power, infinitely more flexible than the "light bomber" operations of the pre-war RAF and capable of precision strikes well behind the battle line in the face of determined air defences.

This Mosquito NF.XII was badly burned in combat with a Ju 188 but managed to return to base. (British Aerospace via Philip Birtles)

Soldiering On

There were few wartime aircraft which did not see service in a variety of roles other than that for which they were originally designed, and the Mosquito was typical in this respect. Its post-war career was equally varied, if not so long as that of some of its contemporaries such as the Mustang.

One of the most interesting and little-known weapons with which the Mosquito was armed was "Highball", installed on 60 modified Mosquito B.IVs (making the Highball Mosquito a more abundant version of the type than the FB.XVIII). Highball was a junior version of the spinning depth mine or bouncing bomb invented by Barnes Wallis and used by the Lancasters of 617 Sqn on the famous "dambusting" raid in May 1943. Its primary target was the battleship *Tirpitz*, sister-ship to the *Bismarck* and probably the most powerful warship then afloat, which was in early 1943, sheltering in a heavily defended anchorage in Norway and presenting a constant threat to the Russian convoys.

The Wallis mine was launched from a spinning cradle

and intended to bounce across the surface of the water in a predictable fashion, leaping over torpedo nets, striking the side of the target and using its residual spinning energy to crawl underwater until it was detonated by its depth fuse. It could be placed more accurately against a marine target than a conventional bomb, and by taking advantage of the tamping effect of deep water it could lethally damage a heavy target with a relatively small charge.

Highball carried less than a tenth of the explosive charge used in the "Upkeep" weapon carried by the Lancasters on the dams raid, roughly 600 lb (272 kg). It retained the spherical shape originally planned for the larger weapon (which was used without the planned spherical fairing after development problems) and two could be carried in a modified Mosquito in which an open belly fairing replaced the bomb doors. A ram-air turbine (an early application of this means of generating power) provided the necessary impetus to give the weapons a 1,000 rev/min backspin before release.

Trials with the Highball Mosquitos started in March 1943, the decision to use the Wallis mine against *Tirpitz* having been taken well before the raid on the Ruhr dams. 1 April saw the formation of 618 Sqn to use the weapon. However, development presented even more problems than had that of the larger weapon, and it was not until July that a successful drop was achieved. Even then, the weapon was not judged ready for operational use, and 618 Sqn was temporarily assigned to conventional shipping strikes while the Highball Mosquitos continued trials. In May 1944 these began to show some success, including the first successful double drop from a single aircraft.

By this time, the German fleet no longer offered any worthwhile targets for the Mosquitos, and it was decided to convert the squadron for carrier-based operations in the Pacific against the Japanese fleet. A Highball Mosquito made the type's second successful series of deck-landings in September 1944, and at the end of the following month the aircraft embarked for Australia. Based at Fisherman's Bend near Melbourne and later at Narromine, the squadron remained inactive while the Allied commanders in the Pacific argued about a suitable use for the British carrier force, and it was never used operationally. After the war, the Navy continued to take an interest in Highball, and a Mk 2 version was developed by Vickers for installation as a self-contained package on standard Mosquito TR.33s and Sea Hornets, but work on this had been abandoned by 1947. The basic details of the Highball and Upkeep bombs remained wrapped in secrecy until mid-1963, despite the fact that atomic weapons and air-to-surface missiles had, between them, rendered them obsolete long before.

The Mosquito also saw wartime service in an unusual role: as an airliner with British Overseas Airways Corporation. The type was introduced into BOAC service in late 1942, because the important air link between Britain and neutral Sweden was in danger of being broken by increasingly strong night defences over Germany and the Skagerrak, which was patrolled by German flak-ships carrying radar-directed guns. Originally the Mosquitos were used to supplement Douglas DC-3s and Lockheed Lodestars, which had

Highball under test. This anti-shipping bouncing bomb was based on the Barnes Wallis dam-bustung weapon.
(British Aerospace via E. Morgan)

been forced to take a slower, more northerly route, and were used to carry high-priority cargo such as ball-bearings and mail. In the latter half of 1943, however, an urgent requirement arose to carry British officials to Sweden, and the Mosquitos were converted to carry passengers. Couches, oxygen and heating equipment, an intercom and a reading light were installed above the bomb-bay doors. Among the distinguished passengers who made the three-hour trip in these somewhat Spartan conditions were the conductor Sir Malcolm Sargent, the Danish physicist Niels Bohr and the historian Sir Kenneth Clark.

The first Mosquito assigned to BOAC was a PR.IV, but later aircraft totalled 12 FB.VIs, with all armament removed. These aircraft were not as fast as the original PR.IV, lacking ejector exhausts and having the fighter's less efficient flat windscreen. Four of the Mosquitos were lost in the course of 520 round trips before the service ended on 17 May, 1945.

Another use to which the Mosquito was adapted rather than born was the mundane task of target-towing, in which the aircraft ended its days in RAF and Royal Navy operational service. It fell to the Royal Navy to perform the most severe act of vandalism on the Mosquito, engaging General Aircraft Limited to convert a number of surplus B.XVIs into TT.39 target tugs. A massive glazed nose of singularly air-defying aspect was added to house a camera operator, who could also dispense chaff, while a dorsal cupola housed the drogue operator. The TT.39s were replaced by Short Sturgeons in 1950. A somewhat longer career awaited the TT.35, which was adapted by the Royal Air Force from surplus B.35s. A few of these remained in service with the civilian organizations which provided the RAF with target-towing services until 1963, when the Mosquitos flew their last sorties for the RAF.

By this time the last export customers for the Mosquito had retired their aircraft. The first and briefest overseas operator of the type had been the U.S. Army Air Force, which took some 40 B.VII and B.20 aircraft from the Canadian production line as F-8 reconnaissance aircraft. (The F prefix was used for reconnaissance aircraft until 1948.) A few of these were delivered to the 8th Air Force in Great Britain, but most of the Mosquitos operated by the 8th were British-built PR.XVIs which carried no US service designation. A number of these aircraft were equipped with H2X, the US equivalent of H2S. Also used by the USAAF were a few Mosquito NF.30s, handed over to USAAF units on North-West Africa. All the USAAF Mosquitos were, however, returned to the British at the end of the 1939–45 war, when lend-lease arrangements expired. The only other wartime users were South African Air Force units in the Mediterranean, and the Soviet Union, which received a few used B.IVs in 1944.

At the end of the war the British found themselves with a large number of unused combat aircraft. In addition to aircraft which had been completed but had never reached the squadrons, more were being produced by a wartime industry which could not immediately be slowed down. Most contracts were cancelled, but the stock of surplus aircraft was nevertheless large. Many of them were delivered to the re-established air forces of Europe: Belgium took delivery of FB.VIs and

A BOAC Mosquito MK.VI prepares for take off for Sweden on the 'ball-bearing run' from a Scottish airfield in 1943.   (BOAC)

NF.30s; France received more than 100 Mosquitos, including NF.30s, PR.XVIs and FB.VIs, and used some of the last-named type in Indo-China in the first half of 1947. Turkey took delivery of a large number of FB.VIs and a few T.III trainers. Czechoslovakia and Norway received a few FB.VIs as the wartime émigré squadrons which had fought as part of the RAF returned home. Dominica also took delivery of a few ex-RAF FB.VIs.

The export of surplus Mosquitos continued for some time. Sixty ex-Royal Air Force NF.XIX night-fighters were delivered to Sweden in 1948–49, serving as J30s until the delivery of J32A Lansen jets in the mid-1950s. The J30s differed from the standard NF.XIX in featuring four-blade airscrews. Among the last deliveries of any *unused* Mosquitos were the NF.38s, which had been pronounced unsuitable for RAF service and were sold to the Jugoslav Air Force. Deliveries of these aircraft began in 1952, nearly two years after the last of them had been completed. Even then, the last Mosquitos had not left the UK for export, a number of second-hand Mosquitos being handed over to the Burmese Air Force on its formation in 1955. It is possible that the Mosquito, like the Spitfire, fired its last shots in anger against Burmese insurgents in the late 1950s.

Mosquitos from the Canadian and Australian production lines also served post-war. Australia's FB.40s served with both kangaroo and kiwi centres to their roundels, some of the Australian-built aircraft supplementing the Royal New Zealand Air Force's British-built Mosquitos. The history of the Canadian aircraft is more interesting. The whole of Canadian production waš directed into the European theatre of operations, for the Mosquito never flew with the Royal Canadian Air Force in Canada, and at the end of 1947 an agreement was reached to sell more than 200 of the surplus aircraft to the government of Nationalist China, then fighting for its life against the forces of Mao Tse-Tung. A mixed batch of FB.26 and T.27 versions was prepared for disassembly and shipping to China, and throughout 1948 the de Havilland technical team in China supervised the setting-up of an

assembly line. By August 1948 the Chinese were assembling aircraft at the rate of one a day, and a total of 144 were successfully test-flown. The surviving aircraft were withdrawn to Formosa in the face of the revolutionaries' advance, and formed the nucleus of the Nationalist Chinese air force.

Meanwhile, the French *Armée de l'Air* had retired its force of Mosquitos, and the surviving aircraft were awaiting demolition when they were acquired by the Israeli Air Force and reconditioned for service. Serving alongside Mustangs purchased from the Swedish Air Force, the Mosquitos were used as interceptors as well as bombers and reconnaissance aircraft, and played a limited part in the 1956 Suez conflict. Israel, skilled at scavenging for combat aircraft, was to acquire some 300 Mosquitos of various marks, most of which were cannibalized for spares. Among the last to be delivered were 14 "denavalized" TR.33s. The Mosquitos served until the late 1950s, when they were replaced by Vautour jet bombers supplied by France.

A few Mosquitos found their way on to civil registers after the war, following the trail blazed by the BOAC aircraft. British European Airways was provided with a couple of PR.34s in 1947 to equip a research unit intended to investigate the nature of clear-air turbulence, but financial stringencies led to the closure of the unit in January 1950. A number of other ultra-long-range PR.34s were acquired by a Los Angeles-based company, Jack Amman Photogrammetric Engineers, in 1955–56, and were converted at Hatfield to undertake survey flights over Libya. A number of B.35s were acquired by Spartan Air Services of Canada after their retirement from the RAF, and were converted to carry extra fuel and aerial cameras. Some of these remained in service until mid-1963.

The speed and range of the Mosquito attracted a number of would-be racers and record-breakers in the immediate post-war years, but efforts were hampered by the fact that most of the aircraft immediately available were Canadian or Australian aircraft with single-stage engines and, in many cases, flat windscreens. The speeds demonstrated by these aircraft were thus slower than the Mosquito might have achieved, while the racing scene was dominated by the Merlin-powered Mustang. A Canadian-built B.25, named "Miss Flying Tiger", was used for attempts to break the round-the-world speed record in 1950 and 1954, but both attempts were frustrated by weather and technical problems. A highly modified Australian PR.41 was entered for the London–Christchurch air race in 1953, but was forced down en route following navigational difficulties.

The surviving British-owned Mosquitos, which ceased towing targets for the RAF in 1963, were to have one final fling: five remained airworthy for use in making the film *633 Squadron*, a fictitious celebration of the exploits of the 2TAF fighter-bombers. Three of those aircraft, together with the target-towing unit's T.III, took part in *Mosquito Squadron*, produced in 1966 as a follow-up to the previous epic. The T.III is now the only Mosquito which is flown regularly; it belongs to British Aerospace, which uses it for occasional demonstrations. Generally, however, it has been found that the wooden airframe of the Mosquito lacks the virtual indestructibility of wartime metal structures; restoring a Mosquito to flying condition and keeping it there is considerably more difficult than maintaining something like a Mustang. Like the Spitfire force assembled for the movie *The Battle of Britain*, the Mosquitos of *633 Squadron* represented the closing chapter in the career of this most versatile of combat aircraft.

Mosquito Marks and Variants

Mosquitos were produced in a great variety of versions, but an even greater number of subtypes were conceived but never placed in production or, in some cases, even test-flown. Some of these were allocated Mark numbers, accounting in part for the high Mark numbers reached. 7,781 Mosquitos were built.

PR.I   Early-series aircraft issued to PRU. Some with long-range tanks

F.II   Originally planned as long-range fighters with machine-guns, cannon and flat windscreen. Completed as NF.II night-fighters with AI.V radar or F.II (Special Intruder) with extra fuel and ammunition. Some early aircraft adapted to reconnaissance role at PRU. Later aircraft ordered as F.IIs delivered as NF.XII or NF.XVII versions

T.III   Unarmed trainer with dual controls. Used as trainer for all versions. Fighter-type solid nose and windscreen

B.IV   *Series i:* a few early bombers converted from PR.1s on production line, with short engine nacelles and small tailplane. *Series ii:* Initial standard bomber with provision for underwing fuel tanks. Canadian B.VII, B.XX and B.25 essentially similar

(Aircraft Production)

The rubber block main undercarriage assembly was simple to make and effective in action.

1   11 rubber blocks
2   11 separator plates
3   Radius rod
4   Bakelite piston
5   ½ rubber block
6   Rebound rubber
7   Telescoping tube
8   Gaiter
9   Wheel door guides
10   Compression legs

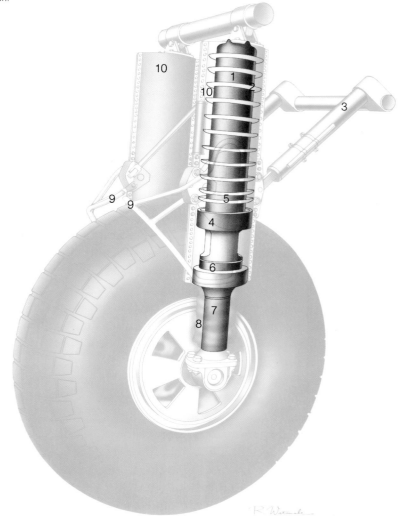

(Pilot Press)

Mosquito B.MK XVI

PR.IV Reconnaissance conversion of B.IV

B.V Improved bomber with wing bombs, prototype only

FB.VI Intruder and fighter-bomber with provision for wing and internal bombs and (from late 1944) rocket projectiles. Basis of FB.21, FB.26 and all Australian-built versions. Most widely produced of all Mosquitos

B.VII First Canadian-built bomber. Some to USAAF as F-8 reconnaissance aircraft

PR.VIII First version with two-stage-supercharged Merlin engines. Interim conversion of B.IV pending availability of PR.IX

PR.IX Definitive two-stage-engined reconnaissance aircraft. Further increase in fuel capacity

B.IX Bomber equivalent of PR.IX. Some modified with provision for 4,000 lb bomb

NF.X Night-fighter with two-stage Merlins. Not built

FB.XI Fighter-bomber with two-stage Merlins. Not built

NF.XII Conversion of NF.II by Marshall Aviation, with British centimetric AI.VIII radar

NF.XIII New-production night-fighter: airframe based on FB.VI with AI.VIII radar

NF.XIV NF.XIII derivative with two-stage engines. Not built

NF.XV Prototype Mosquito XV developed as high-altitude bomber with extended span, pressure cabin and two-stage engines. Adapted to emergency high-altitude fighter with AI.VIII and machine-gun armament. A few production conversions

PR.XVI Developed from PR.IX with partial-pressure cabin. Some used by USAAF in Britain with H2X radar

B.XVI Bomber equivalent of PR.XVI and ultimate wartime bomber. Most with provision for 4,000 lb bomb. Wide variety of electronics carried

NF.XVII Conversion of NF.II by Marshall Aviation, with American-built AI.X (SCR-720) radar. Preceded Mosquito XVI in service

FB.XVIII FB.VI derivative with 57 mm cannon

NF.XIX New-production night-fighter: airframe based on FB.VI with "universal nose" housing British or American radar

Canadian production

B.XX Equivalent to B.IV

FB.21 Equivalent to FB.VI

T.22 Equivalent to T.III

B.23 Equivalent to B.IX. Not built

FB.24 Two-stage-engined fighter-bomber. Not built

B.25 B.XX with improved single-stage Packard-Merlins

FB.26 FB.21 with improved single-stage Packard-Merlins

T.27 T.22 with improved single-stage Packard-Merlins

28 Designation not used

T.29 Some trainers converted from FB.26 after completion

Later British Developments

NF.30 Night-fighter with two-stage Merlin engines. Entered service late 1944 after development difficulties

NF.31 NF.30 derivative with Packard-Merlins. Not built

PR.32 Reconnaissance aircraft developed in response to deployment of jet interceptors by Luftwaffe. Similar to Mosquito XV

TR.33 Carrier-based torpedo-reconnaissance fighter based on FB.VI with many detail changes. Produced in quantity but not used in first-line units

PR.34 Very-long-range reconnaissance aircraft with extra fuel in bulged belly. Standard reconnaissance aircraft in RAF service post-war

B.35 Development of B.XVI with higher-altitude-rated engines. Post-war service only

NF.36 Similar to NF.30 with later, higher-altitude-rated Merlins

TR.37 Similar to TR.33 but with British radar. Built but not issued to first-line units

NF.38 Similar to NF.36 but with British radar. Rejected for RAF service due to handling problems. Some sold to Jugoslavia

TT.39 Surplus B.XVIs converted as target-tugs for Royal Navy

Australian production

FB.40 Equivalent to FB.VI

PR.40 Reconnaissance conversion of FB.40

PR.41 Development of PR.40 with two-stage engines

FB.41 Prototype fighter-bomber with two-stage engines

T.43 Trainer, equivalent to T.III

AVRO
LANCASTER

Text by BILL SWEETMAN

Fraser-Nash FN.50 mid upper turret

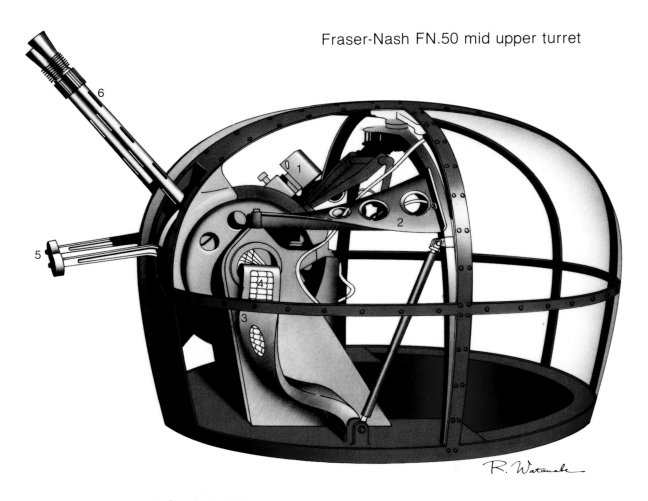

R. Watanabe

1 Gun aiming sight
2 Left side support arm
3 Left side ammunition duct
4 Ammunition belt
5 Gun barrel stoppers
6 Two Browning 0.303-in (7.7 mm) machine-guns

Lancaster I, SR-Z, of No.101 Squadron about to take off. The aircraft is equipped with the H2S radar bombing system.   (Imperial War Museum)

Introduction

The Avro Lancaster bomber is one of the most significant combat aircraft to have taken part in World War II. The legend of British technological invincibility that has grown up around the raid by 617 Squadron on the Ruhr dams in 1943, and the resulting popular fame of the Lancaster, have tended to obscure its true importance.

That the Lancaster was an outstanding design among its contemporaries was realised during 1941, when the design emerged from the heavy, ugly chrysalis of the Manchester. That a direct descendant of the design would still be in first-line service with the RAF in 1982, nearly half a century after the original specification was issued, was then unimaginable.

The Lancaster was never intended as a multi-role aircraft. Together with its descendant, the Lancaster IV/V or Lincoln, it formed the basis of a number of transport aircraft which ranged from the mediocre to the dangerously useless. Notwithstanding the sterling qualities of the Shackleton it was hardly considered in the same class as the contemporary Neptune.

There was, however, one quality in which the Lancaster was genuinely outstanding – its supreme suitability for its intended role. The leaders of Bomber Command wanted to deliver large quantities of explosives and incendiaries to German cities, at night and without an escort. By virtue of its slow speed such an aircraft was vulnerable to damage or destruction by the defences. The Lancaster was tough and able to survive attacks, simple in construction for easy repair if it came home damaged, and easy to build in quantity, to replace the aircraft which never returned. It was the ideal bomb truck, with a far greater weapons load than any of its contemporaries. For an aircraft designed in 1936, its ability to carry its payload and more in the form of a single weapon was extraordinary. The bomber's handling, although not faultless, was to prove reasonably unaffected by the high operating weights.

It could be argued that the history of Bomber Command would have been very different had it not been for the Lancaster. Had the Manchester not been developed into the Lancaster with such unexpected success, Bomber Command would have had nothing better than the Halifax, and the crisis of early 1944 would have come a great deal earlier, possibly proving too great a defeat for the advocates of area bombing for the policy to survive.

The evolution of the Lancaster presents an interesting contrast to the development in Germany of the contemporary Heinkel He177 heavy bomber. The He177 was developed to a specification issued in 1936, like the Manchester, and flown in the same year as the British bomber. It was a twin-engined heavy bomber similarly plagued by troubles with heavy, complicated engines, which had an unfortunate tendency to catch fire. Design teams at Rostock and Manchester were roughing out the lines of modified aircraft with four smaller, more reliable powerplants in early 1940, but whereas the Manchester III prototype made its first flight in January 1941 and was selected for production within a matter of months, the parallel He177 did not appear until the end of 1943. By that time it was too late.

The Lancaster's greatest significance, however, was that it was both the last of the old generation and the first of the new. Designed for an Air Staff which believed that the bomber was invincible and still envisaged the bomber as a slow and heavily armed aerial battleship, the Lancaster first demonstrated that the bomber was vulnerable, and that the hopes of the bomber enthusiasts had been wildly exaggerated. Later, it was to show the way to what the bomber was eventually to become – a stealthy intruder rather than a brazen raider, concealing itself behind subtle electronic smokescreens and finding its way along webs of electromagnetic waves.

By 1945, the British Air Staff had turned from the blinkered and self-deluded supporters of the pre-war heavy bombers to embrace some of the most advanced thinking in the world on the best way to penetrate an enemy's airspace. Never again did a new British bomber carry a single defensive gun – speed, altitude, stealth and, above all, electronic countermeasures were to assure the bomber's ability to penetrate defences. Many of the devices used to the present day on Chadwick's last design, the extraordinary Vulcan, are descendants of the mysterious black boxes developed for Bomber Command Lancasters. The Avro bomber contributed greatly to the history of aviation in testing out the tremendous changes in bomber philosophy, by its continued and dogged service over Germany.

The ultimate weapon

On the 14th anniversary of the armistice which ended the Great War of 1914–18, a leading article in *The Times* of London dealt with the subject of aerial warfare. "The supreme menace and the supreme horror of war comes from the air," intoned the Thunderer, "and unless Mars can be dethroned in the sky, there will be small gain in pinpricking him on the earth and sea." *The Times*, in short, was calling for international agreement to abolish or severely restrict the use of the bomber aircraft, in terms which are more familiar in the modern world from the opponents of nuclear weapons.

The fear of the bomber which was prevalent in the 1930s was something very different from the apprehension aroused by more conventional, familiar problems of defence such as land war in Europe or the defence of sea lanes. One reason for the extent of this fear was that in the past there was very little evidence of the effects of air attacks on any large scale, the forays of Imperial Germany's airships and bombers having been little more than experimental operations. Since that time bomber fleets had expanded, and there were clear signs that the aeroplane was on the point of evolution into a far more reliable, faster machine, carrying a much greater load. Above all, however, the bomber's range and mobility gave an enemy the chance to carry the war to the homes of the civilian population in a way which only slow land war or invasion could have done before.

It was this last aspect of bomber warfare which particularly alarmed the British. Despite their pride in a 900-year clean record in defeating would-be invaders, and their professed faith in the invincibility of the Royal Navy, the British had become used to terrifying their children with the threat of the foreign invader ("Bonaparte may come this way", concluded a 19th-century nursery rhyme) and could also panic themselves, as in 1870 and the early 1900s. The idea of a bomber force sailing impudently over the iron walls of the Home Fleet was enough to tie the stomach of the body politic in a sickening knot.

Bomber phobia was not confined to the general public or even to the politicians. One internal memorandum within the Admiralty went so far as to describe the bombing of civilian populations as "revolting and un-English". The effectiveness of air attack was a controversial subject among military experts, and there were many who supported and encouraged popular fears. Generally, however, the British Admiralty and the War Office (which controlled the Army) were reluctant to concede that bombing would be effective at all. This attitude was based less on detailed studies of bombing techniques than on resentment of the funds being appropriated by the Air Ministry for the development of the Royal Air Force's Heyford and Hendon bombers.

Urged by the public and the Foreign Office, the government of Stanley Baldwin took the view that the effect of bombing could be devastating, even to the point where a heavy air attack could cause civilian morale to collapse and force surrender before land or sea battle could be joined. The question was what to do about it. The politicians' view was that bombing should be curtailed by international agreement, and preliminary discussions under the auspices of the League of Nations were held in Geneva in February 1932. Baldwin himself took the extreme view that all bombing should be abolished, and civil aviation discouraged by the removal of subsidies in order to slow the advance of aeronautical technology. More moderate proposals included the international control of commercial aviation, and a ban on bomber research and development. This was seen as entirely practicable; warships, after all, were already limited by international agreement.

In the worsening international tensions of the early 1930s, and in particular with the realisation that Germany's National Socialist government – elected in 1933 – would not be a party to any agreement on restricting bombers, the opposing view of the Air Ministry began to gather weight. The Air Ministry had opposed any ban on bombing from the start, because it argued that the bomber was the cheapest and most efficient way of policing the North-West Frontier. Moreover, it preached that devastating air attack was inevitable in the event of war. The only defence, the Air Ministry said, was counter-attack, and this was reflected in the RAF expansion which started in 1934.

The first steps in RAF expansion were rightly identified by Lord Swinton, Secretary of State for Air in the early years of the expansion programme, as the enlargement of the industrial base and the RAF's human and fixed resources rather than the development of new aircraft types. The first of the expansion schemes were based on the obsolete Hendon and Heyford. Scheme C of 1935 included the Whitley and Harrow, both developed from existing "bomber-transport" prototypes, while the newer Wellington and Hampden would follow in later schemes.

These two later aircraft were already well into their development by late 1935, when the eyes of the British Air Staff turned enviously westwards. July 1935 had seen the first flight of the Boeing 299 bomber. The first four-engined aircraft to use modern aerodynamic and constructional technology, the 299 – later to become the B-17 – displayed a combination of defensive and offensive armament, speed, altitude and range which astonished the aviation world. The Air Staff, under Sir Edward Ellington, asked the Air Ministry to approve development of a new class of heavy bombers superior to the Boeing 299, and the Air Ministry gave its approval in February 1936.

Boeing Y1B-17, the first production version of the Model 299/B-17, in flight.　(USAF)

Because Germany was now regarded as the most likely enemy, a range of at least 2,000 miles (3,200 km) was basic to the new requirements. The new bombers were also expected to be able to defend themselves in daylight, as were the Wellington and Hampden. However, they were able to take advantage of a weapon in which Britain had established an early and valuable lead, and in which Bomber Command placed great faith – the powered gun turret.

The powered turret had been developed by two ex-Royal Flying Corps pilots, "Tommy" Thompson and "Archie" Frazer-Nash. The latter was an engineer of no mean ability, and the designer of the unconventional but much admired chain transmission of the sports cars which bore his name. Foreseeing that the only way in which defensive guns could be used on high-speed aircraft was to power the guns in elevation and traverse against the force of the slipstream, Frazer-Nash and Thompson obtained a contract to fit an experimental turret to a Hawker Demon fighter in 1933. This early start was important, because the development of the powered turret was not easy – the movement of the guns had to be smooth and manageable at low speeds for aiming and tracking, but had to move fast for acquiring a new threat from another quarter. The size and weight restriction compounded the engineering and production problems, but from the formation of the Nash & Thompson company to build turrets in early 1935, production built up steadily and was in full swing by 1939.

The new RAF bombers combined the speed of the day bombers with a greater weapon load than the slower night bombers – such as the Whitley and Harrow – and a heavy defensive armament. In July 1936 the Air Staff issued two specifications for the new "heavies" and invited manufacturers to compete for contracts. One of the specifications, B.12/36, was relatively conservative, calling for some increase in performance over the Boeing 299, using four engines derived from types then well advanced in development. In the summer of 1937 prototypes to B.12/36 were ordered from Shorts and from Vickers-Supermarine. The former was to become the Stirling, but the Supermarine 318 lost development priority to the Spitfire and was abandoned in 1940 after a bombing raid destroyed the partly completed prototype.

The other specification was P.13/36, and as the prefix implied it called for prototypes rather than a production bomber, being rather more advanced and more risky than B.12/36. More a "heavy-medium" bomber than a heavy, P.13/36 was designed to be very fast, with a cruising speed of 275 mph (443 km/hr), and a range of 3,000 miles (4,830 km) with a 4,000 lb (1,800 kg) load. Powered turrets were to be installed in the nose and tail. High speed was to be attained by high wing loading, and by the use of new engines in the 2,000 hp class – twice the power of the Merlin, which was then starting flight tests in the Hurricane and Spitfire. The heavily loaded bomber was to be launched with the aid of a catapult, like a carrier-based aircraft, increasing permissible take-off weight and making a smaller wing possible. Handley Page, suppliers of heavy bombers to the British services since 1915, proposed the HP.56, a derivative of an earlier day-bomber design which had been proposed to the same specification as

the Vickers Warwick, and prototypes of this aircraft were ordered to P.13/36 in early 1937. Rather more surprisingly, the second firm chosen to build an aircraft to P.13/36 was that of A. V. Roe and Company, trading as Avro.

Avro was second only to Shorts in seniority among the British aircraft industry. Alliott Verdon-Roe – later knighted for his achievements – became the first Briton to fly an all-British aeroplane in July 1909 and was promptly threatened with prosecution as a danger to public safety. Roe's subsequent efforts were more successful. His Type E biplane of 1912 was the basis for the Avro 504. After a brief combat career, the 504 became the Royal Air Force's standard trainer, until it was replaced in the late 1920s by another Avro machine, the Tutor.

Avro had gained some experience with larger aircraft in the late 1920s, when the company took out a licence to build the Fokker F.VIIB/3m tri-motor transport as the Avro Ten. One of the first monoplane airliners to be built in Britain, the Ten was followed by the smaller Avro Five (designed along Fokker lines by Avro's chief designer Roy Chadwick), and the Avro 642. The company's first substantial success with larger aircraft, however, was the Avro 652. Structurally similar to the early Fokker-based designs, with a one-piece wooden wing, the 652 differed from them in being a low-wing aircraft with a retractable undercarriage. By the time Chadwick was preparing the company's P.13/36 design, the 652 had been adopted by Coastal Command as the Anson maritime-reconnaissance aircraft, entering service in 1936 as the RAF's first type with retractable landing gear. Nevertheless, the Avro P.13/36, known to the company as the Type 679, was more than four times the size of any aircraft the company had designed before, and was moreover the first Avro aircraft to be built in metal. The attention to the industrial base which had been part of the early RAF expansion plans had paid off – as the Avro P.13/36 prototype was assembled, Avro's workforce under the leadership of Roy Dobson (later to head the company), was gaining experience and growing in size through a production contract for Blenheims, and factory buildings near the Newton Heath plant were being taken over by the rapidly growing aircraft company. Employees numbered 5,000 by August 1938, when Secretary of State for Air Sir Kingsley Wood announced that £1 million was to be invested in a new factory for Avro, and that the workforce would be doubled by mid-1939.

Avro's star was rising so dramatically mainly because of some important changes in British aviation policy. RAF expansion Scheme J had been approved in October 1937 by Lord Swinton, then the Secretary of State for Air, and reflected concern about the growing numbers of Luftwaffe bombers. Scheme J proposed the creation of a numerically equal RAF bomber force by mid-1941, before the P.13/36 designs would be ready for production, but it was rejected by the British Cabinet in favour of greater fighter output. Swinton was replaced as Air Minister by Sir Kingsley Wood in May 1938.

Although fighters had temporarily been granted priority over bombers, the long-term importance of offensive air power was not seriously questioned. More bombers would be bought, but because they would be acquired rather later than Swinton had envisaged they could include a greater proportion of new types such as the P.13/36 and B.12/36. While this policy was evolving, a team of Air Staff officers prepared a paper on "The Ideal Bomber" which had a considerable influence on Air Staff planning, particularly in its advocacy of a few, powerful bombers rather than a numerically larger force of smaller aircraft. In the summer of 1938, the Air Ministry prepared Scheme M, covering the expansion of the RAF up to early 1942. It was expected by that time that the bomber squadrons would very nearly reach the strength proposed for mid-1941 in Swinton's rejected scheme. The equipment planned for these squadrons represented an even bolder gamble, because the Air Ministry wanted to order 500 heavy bombers off the drawing board, among them 200 Avro P.13/36 types.

The cost and boldness of this plan led to queries from some Cabinet members. However, the Air Ministry's mind was made up. Swinton's 1937 scheme had aimed at numerical parity with the Luftwaffe's bombers, but now the Air Ministry wanted an equivalent total bombload, and this could be achieved by a smaller force of heavy bombers. Economies would be possible in flying time, maintenance, accessories and, most important, the number of pilots required. Casualties would also be reduced, because the heavies could carry a satisfactory defensive armament. "Developments in recent years," the Air Ministry hinted to Cabinet, had somewhat reduced the threat of air attack to Britain, and the absolute priority to fighters could be relaxed – even the Cabinet was not openly told of the existence of radar. The heavy-bomber contracts were approved, and hence the expansion of Avro went ahead.

British aircraft production was to be led by the experienced aircraft companies, but in addition to their new and existing factories they organised production in facilities owned by the motor and general engineering industries. Production of the Avro P.13/36 was to be carried out by Avro itself, in charge of a group including Metropolitan-Vickers and Rootes. In November 1938, delicate negotiations started to enable British bomber designs to be produced in Canada. Although there were domestic political objections to the overseas funding of military programmes, it was finally agreed that a consortium of Canadian companies would cut their teeth on the Hampden before putting one of the British heavies into production.

The new heavy bombers were developed under a mantle of secrecy unprecedented in peacetime experience, because of the Air Ministry's fear that their existence might spur Germany into developing a rival strategic bomber force. As it happened, German work on heavy bombers remained half-hearted, the Do19 and Ju89 *Ural-Bomber* programmes being terminated in 1937 and the He177, which replaced them in Luftwaffe planning, being fatally compromised in favour of the tactical-support role. The very existence of the heavy bombers was ostensibly a secret, although in a country the size of the United Kingdom a large aircraft in flight test is hard to conceal. C. G. Grey of *The Aeroplane* could not resist remarking, in an account of the Shorts factory published just

before the secret Stirling made its first flight, "Unfortunately, these machines are a deadly State secret to everybody except the few hundreds of thousands of people . . . within, say, a 50-mile radius of the Shorts works." Accordingly, there was no champagne Press reception at Woodford when Avro test pilot Capt. H. A. Brown took the first Avro P.13/36 on its maiden flight. British cities provided the theme for the names of the new heavy bombers – the Shorts Stirling, Handley Page Halifax, and now the Avro Manchester.

The problem child

Development of the Manchester coincided with the crisis of 1940, but nevertheless was accorded high priority. The architects of the pre-war expansion schemes had accepted the risks involved in ordering large quantities of aircraft types which had not been flight tested, and Manchester production was built up as flight trials continued. Any modifications found necessary were either incorporated at a later stage in production or could be fitted retrospectively to aircraft already built. Despite the interruptions of the Battle of Britain in the summer of 1940, the first production Manchesters were delivered in October 1940, just over a year after the first flight of the prototype.

The Manchester never attained the ambitious performance envisaged by P.13/36, which had been superseded by B.19/37 for production aircraft. One reason was that the proposals for catapult launching of the Manchester had been discarded as impracticable. Bomber Command operated from new bases far more hurriedly and crudely equipped than the pre-war stations, and the provision and maintenance of massive mechanical launching gear was rejected at an early stage. The abandonment of the catapult played a part in the decision to enlarge substantially the Manchester's wing after early flight trials. New outer wings were fitted to the existing centre-section, increasing the span from 80 ft 2 in (24.43 m) to 90 ft 1 in (27.46 m), and take-off and climb performance were improved at the expense of maximum cruising speed.

Directional stability was inadequate, and the second prototype and subsequent Manchester I sported a stumpy third tailfin above the rear fuselage. Defensive armament had been increased by the addition of a ventral gun turret, again at the expense of speed and range, while combat experience in 1939 dictated the need for more passive protection measures, such as armour and self-sealing fuel tanks. The Manchester began to put on weight, as did nearly every aircraft developed for military purposes around that time. The complexity of the new aircraft also caused problems, the hydraulics giving trouble (so extensive a system was completely new to the British industry) and the undercarriage proving weak-kneed.

All these troubles were overshadowed utterly and comprehensively by the failure of the Manchester's heart, the Rolls-Royce Vulture engine. This had been designed in 1937 as the Derby firm's main contender for the military engine market beyond the Merlin. It was considered then that new and more powerful engines would oust powerplants in the class of the Merlin by the early 1940s, and nobody expected the basic V-12, 27-litre Merlin to stay in production throughout the war and to yield an eventual 2,000 hp in service. All three of Britain's manufacturers of large aero-engines – Rolls-Royce, Bristol and the tiny Napier company – had engines in the 2,000 hp class under development in 1937–38, but in the prevailing climate of rationalisation it seemed unlikely that all three of them would be put into production. The Vulture was, in that respect, of the greatest importance to Rolls-Royce.

The Vulture was an X-type 24-cylinder engine, basically consisting of two of the company's Kestrel V-12s vertically opposed and connected to a single crankshaft. (Nearly all 24-cylinder wartime engines used two crankshafts, either in H or double-V layouts.) In detail, though, it was considerably more advanced than the Kestrel. Rolls-Royce's managing director, Ernest (later Lord) Hives, noted in late 1937 that "to get the Vulture going is going to be a terrific job, the biggest we have ever had to tackle".

One of the problems with the Vulture, from Rolls-Royce's point of view, was that it was too complex an engine for a new "shadow factory" to take on. If the Vulture was to be built on the scale envisaged in early 1937, Rolls-Royce would have to transfer the whole of the Merlin production line to shadow factories, running the risk that the supply of engines for the Hurricane and Spitfire might be interrupted. It may have been the desire to reduce the planned 1940 production of the Vulture which led to the decision to redesign the Handley Page aircraft as the HP.57 with four Merlins, only months after the original P.13/36 prototype contracts went out. This redesigned aircraft was to be the Halifax.

The Vulture posed a dilemma for Rolls-Royce. The company needed it in one sense, because of the threat that the RAF would switch to Napier Sabre and Bristol Centaurus power if Derby backed out of the 2,000 hp business. On the other hand, in 1938 Rolls-Royce recognised some of the development potential of the Merlin, and was working on a more powerful V-12, the Griffon. Not much smaller than the Vulture in terms of capacity and output, the Griffon had one overwhelming advantage over the big 24-cylinder engine – it could be fitted to any aircraft which used Merlins, thanks to some very clever detail design. Concentration on the Merlin, with the Griffon to follow, made a great deal of sense to Rolls-Royce.

The Manchester and the Vulture were irrevocably linked in 1938–39, because neither the Centaurus nor the Sabre had been ordered early enough, or in sufficient quantities, to match Manchester production. By the time it became apparent that the Vulture was a problem-filled engine, the inertia of the production programme was irresistible. The Vulture was just not powerful enough for the now heavier Manchester, yielding only 1,760 hp in its initial service form. The Manchester lost height rapidly on one engine and had a lower service ceiling than even the Hampden, never regarded as the best of pre-war bombers. The engine itself suffered early problems with coolant circulation, but oil circulation presented a far more serious difficulty, leading to seizure of the big ends and broken connecting rods – at best the engine would stop dead, but frequently it would catch fire. One of Rolls-Royce's test pilots was among the victims of the Vulture whilst the company wrestled with the technical problems of the engine.

The engine problems were unsolved when 207 Squadron was reformed at Waddington to operate the top-secret new bomber, the first of the new heavies to enter service. (The Stirling, which had been planned to enter service earlier, was delayed by the loss of the first prototype and a bombing raid on the production line.) The first two aircraft

 Ground crew check Manchester I of No.207 Squadron.

 (Imperial War Museum)

were used for 500 hours of intensive endurance trials in November, and the squadron's next six aircraft were used for Vulture development. It was not until February 24, 1941, a fortnight after the Stirling's operational debut, that the Manchesters of 207 Squadron flew their first operational mission. Six aircraft joined a force of Hampdens to attack enemy shipping at Brest, and one was lost in a landing accident.

The equipment of 207 Squadron comprised basic Manchester Is, but production switched in mid-1941 to the improved Manchester IA. Modified Vultures yielded 1,845 hp at take-off, still with no real reliability, but this barely compensated for the fact that the weight at take-off had risen from 45,000 lb (20,412 kg) for the prototype to 56,000 lb (25,400 kg) on the Manchester IA. Tail armament was increased from two to four machine-guns. The most significant modification, however, was the removal of the central fin and a 50 per cent increase in tailplane span, from 22 ft (6.7 m) to 33 ft (10 m), alleviating the Manchester's stability problems and setting a pattern for future members of the family.

The second Manchester squadron, No 97, became operational in April 1941, three days before a spate of bearing failures in the Vulture caused the grounding of the entire force. Another grounding for modifications to the cooling system followed in June, but the problems continued. Sometimes the airscrews would not feather, turning an engine failure into a slow crash. By that time, although the crews did not know it, the recalcitrant, unreliable, dangerous bomber was dead on its feet. Production and operations nevertheless continued. To the Air Ministry, if not to the crews of 97 and 207 Squadrons, this was preferable to interrupting the re-equipment programme.

Before the P.13/36 flew, Rolls-Royce had concluded internally that a Merlin/Griffon programme would be best for the company. As early as August 1939, Ernest Hives advised the Air Ministry that the Vulture should be scrapped, along with its half-size development, the V-12 Peregrine, and the pressure-air-cooled 24-cylinder Boreas or Exe which the company was developing for the Fairey Firefly naval fighter. The Exe was abandoned, but the other two engines continued in production.

The pressure on the Vulture programme mounted in mid-1940. Lord Beaverbrook, as Minister of Aircraft Production, wanted to rationalise the production of large aero-engines, reducing the number of types in production to five – the two air-cooled Bristol radials (Hercules and Centaurus) and three liquid-cooled units. One of the latter was the Merlin; the Peregrine was certain to be terminated; the Griffon, the Vulture or the Napier Sabre had to go.

While Rolls-Royce wrestled with the Vulture's problems, the full potential of the Napier Sabre was being recognised. Smaller in capacity than the Vulture, and roughly equal in size to the Griffon, the Sabre was promising much higher outputs than either from a tiny, streamlined package of far smaller frontal area than the Rolls-Royce X-24 engine. The Centaurus was also shaping up as a far better engine than the Vulture. Avro had already designed a Manchester II with Bristol or Napier engines, and there seemed little doubt that

the Rolls-Royce Vulture would be ousted from both the Manchester and the new Hawker fighter. The latter, indeed, was eventually produced in quantity with Bristol and Napier engines.

In mid-1940 Hives proposed to the Air Ministry that both his own company's Vulture and the Napier Sabre should be scrapped. Rolls-Royce could continue with the Merlin and the Griffon, while Napier would be deprived of its only product and could slide quietly into history. Whether Rolls-Royce saw the matter in those precise terms is not clear, but the company was clearly worried by the performance of the Sabre, and paid it the ultimate (and for Rolls-Royce, unique) compliment of copying its basic layout for the Griffon's planned successor, the 3,500 hp Eagle. Hives' suggestion was not accepted, and the Vulture and Sabre programmes continued. A few months later, Hives himself rejected a proposal from Rolls-Royce's chairman that an all-out effort to stop the Sabre should be mounted, saying that "the answer to the Sabre is for us to show that the Vulture is a better engine". Whether or not Hives considered that this could be done, in view of the frequent engine failures and airborne conflagrations being experienced by 207 Squadron at that time, is not clear, but at the end of 1940 Rolls-Royce was still committed to production of the Vulture.

The ultimate solution to the problem was beginning to emerge as the Manchester entered service. In September 1940, Rolls-Royce had agreed with Packard to set up a production line for the Merlin in the United States, and the programme went ahead with astonishing speed. Deliveries started within little more than a year of the agreement. Merlin engines would henceforth be in abundant supply.

In the Air Ministry's eyes this removed the main obstacle to production of the Avro Type 683 Manchester III, which had been designed in parallel with the Sabre/Centaurus Manchester II. A Manchester I had been removed from the production line in 1940 for conversion to the Manchester III prototype, and this aircraft was flown on January 9, 1941. The outer wings were extended once more, Merlin X engines in standard Wellington/Whitley/Halifax installations replaced the Vultures, and two extra Merlins were mounted outboard, on simple cantilever frameworks attached to the lower booms of the front and rear spars. Apart from the new outer wings, the Manchester III was structurally identical to the Manchester I.

The success of flight tests with the Manchester III, the apparent inability of Rolls-Royce to solve the Vulture's problems, the availability of abundant Packard Merlins before Sabre or Centaurus engines could be available for a Manchester II, and the urgent need to phase out the Manchester I and IA as soon as possible all pointed in the early months of 1941 to one course of action. By the time the existence of the Manchester was revealed to the British public, in the same month that Metropolitan-Vickers delivered its first production aircraft, and before the second squadron had been declared operational, the decision had been made to end Manchester I development after 200 production aircraft. The remaining 300 aircraft on current contracts would be completed as Manchester IIIs.

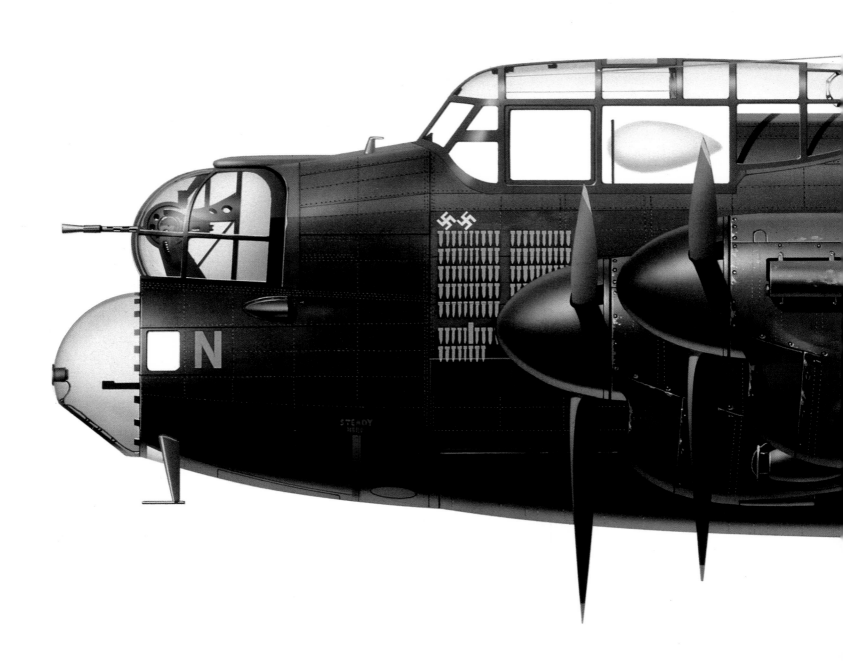

Avro Lancaster B.Mk.III of No. 91 Squadron

Avro Lancaster B.Mk.III flown by Flight Lieutenant Basil Turner from Skellingthorpe, England in the summer of 1944. The 120 bombing operation marks and the two victories over German aircraft are painted under the cockpit. This plane retired from bombing duties after completing 130 missions in October 1944.

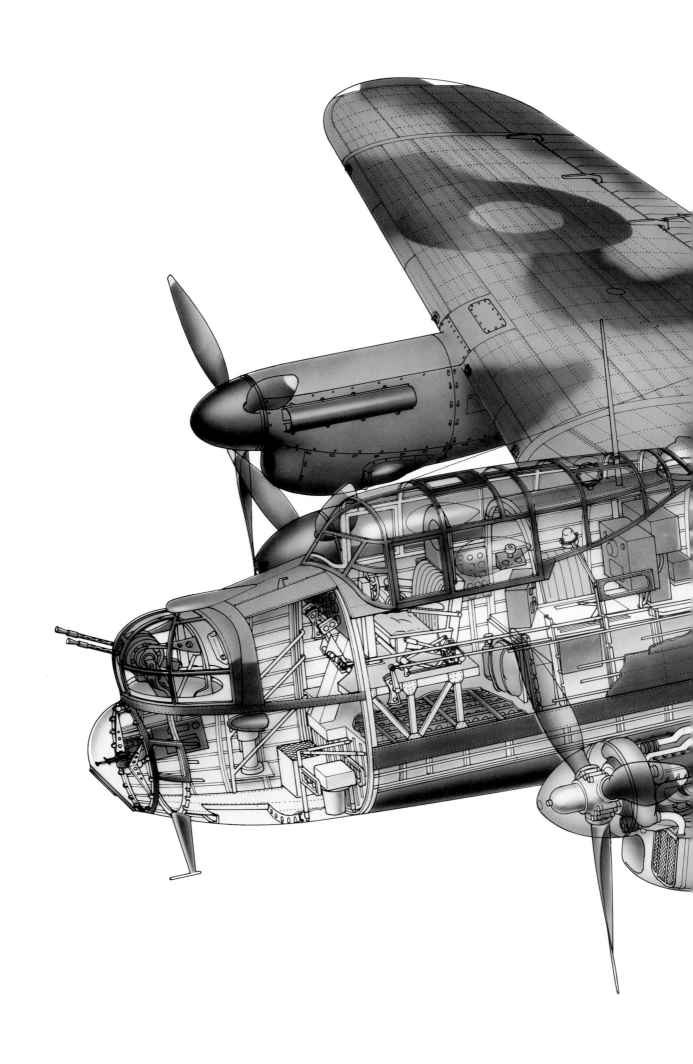

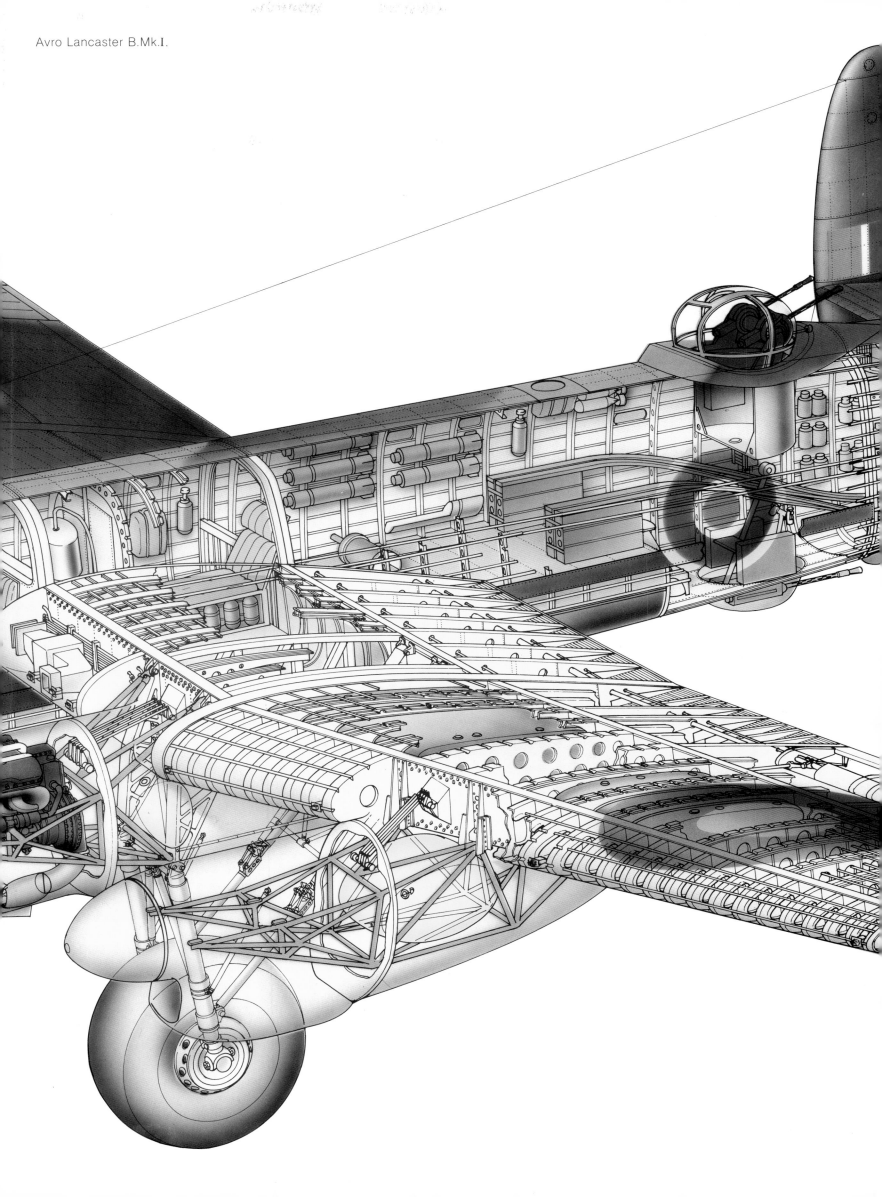

Avro Lancaster B.Mk.I.

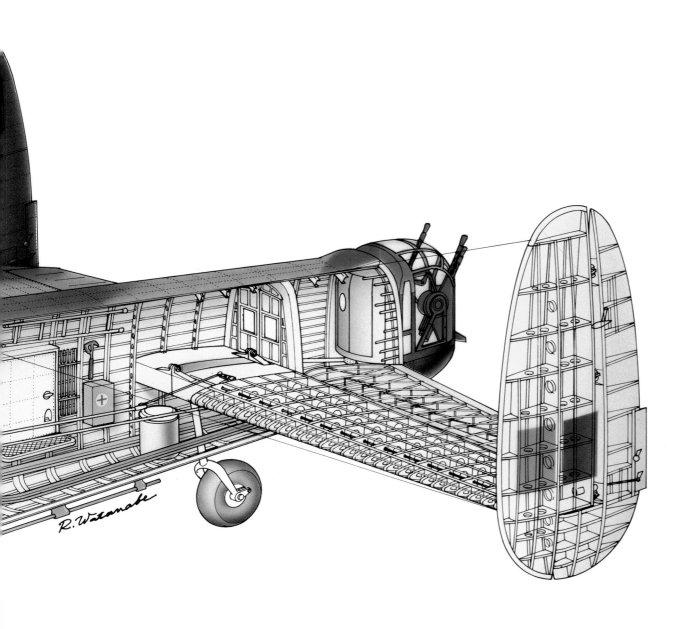

R. Watanabe

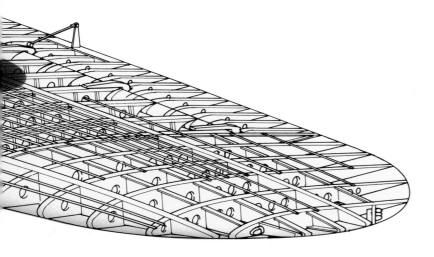

The first Lancaster prototype as originally flown, retaining the Manchester's small span tailplane and triple fins.

(Imperial War Museum)

The Manchester I had not quite ended its career, however. In July 1941 a number of aircraft with fully modified cooling systems were flown for 15 hours a day by the squadrons. By August, seven units were equipped with Manchesters, and by November the type outnumbered the Halifaxes in Bomber Command. But the first production example of the four-engined variant had flown in October 1941 (unlike the first aircraft, it had the later twin-fin tail of the Manchester IA), and in January 1942 a relieved 97 Squadron converted from the Manchester to its descendant. By the time production ended, Avro had delivered 159 Manchester Is and IAs, including the two prototypes, and Metropolitan-Vickers had delivered 43. In June 1942 the type was withdrawn from operations and sent to operational training units, where the last was retired in the following year.

Before production of the Manchester III began, it was decided that in view of the miserable reputation which the Manchester I and IA had earned in service, it would be advisable to reflect the major modification to the aircraft in a new name. The Type 683 became the Lancaster I.

The durable Lancaster

The Lancaster underwent very little fundamental alteration during its production life compared with other wartime aircraft. Detail modifications were legion, but any major modifications proposed were rigorously examined by the Air Staff in the light of the cold calculations behind the British bomber offensive. If they would allow more bombs to be dropped on Germany for a given expenditure of effort they were approved, whether they achieved this aim by increasing production output, increasing the bombload or reducing losses to enemy action. If the cost of any new modification in terms of money or interrupted production could be better spent on simply building more aircraft, the modification was rejected.

The bottom line was the tonnage of explosives and pyrotechnics unloaded on German cities by Bomber Command, and very few major modifications achieved a credit balance sufficient to be implemented during the height of the campaign.

Paradoxically, the number of smaller modifications introduced during the production life of the Lancaster was very large. Any alteration which could be adopted in the field or which would not seriously interrupt production had a good chance of being accepted, and the design of the Lancaster was such that modifications could often be incorporated easily. The result was that the Lancaster fleet, although comprising basically similar aircraft, embraced an enormous range of detail variations.

From the start of flight trials with the production Lancaster I, it became increasingly clear that the tortuous path of development had yielded an aircraft which totally outclassed the similarly powered Halifax. From the beginning it equalled the range and warload of the much heavier Stirling and could attain rather greater altitudes. The Lancaster accordingly replaced the Halifax in plans for production in Canada, and during 1942–43 the Avro bombers started to roll out of Vickers-Armstrongs and Armstrong Whitworth factories as well. Although plans for production by Shorts at Belfast – replacing the Stirling – and in Australia by Government Aircraft Factories never materialised, more than 7,300 Lancasters were built.

The development of the Lancaster was as smooth as might have been expected, considering that both the engine and the airframe were already known quantities. The prototypes were fitted with the Merlin X engine, which was the first subtype to be fitted with a two-speed supercharger drive. It delivered 1,280 hp for take-off, and at altitude the supercharger could be shifted into high gear, increasing the boost pressure, and the engine's output was 1,010 hp at 17,500 ft (5,330 m). The first production aircraft had the Merlin XX rated at 1,390 hp on take-off, and 1,435 hp at 11,000 ft

(3,350 m). All production Lancasters used the same basic Merlin 20 series, with a single-stage, two-speed supercharger. Only the Mark II and a few later Mark VI conversions differed in this respect.

The first few Lancaster Is differed from later aircraft in their fuel system, with standard tankage for 1,710 Imp gal (7,774 lit) in four wing cells; all subsequent aircraft carried 2,154 Imp gal (9,792 lit) in six tanks, and could take-off at 63,000 lb (28,577 kg) all-up weight instead of 61,500 lb (27,896 kg). This was the standard Lancaster I, in all essentials similar to the aircraft being produced at the end of the war.

The only serious technical problems encountered by the Lancaster concerned the structure and the fuel system. Problems with the system of immersed pumps originally installed halved the operational strength of the Lancaster force in autumn 1942, before a series of temporary fixes and permanent modifications cured the difficulties. Another early problem involved failures of the outer wingtip under high load, leading to a brief grounding in March 1942 until the joint could be strengthened. The Lancaster's Achilles heel, however, was its tail unit. Early aircraft were subject to fin failures under high loads (such as evasive manoeuvring) until the fin-tailplane junction was reinforced. Then, in the second half of 1943, nearly a dozen Lancasters were lost on training

flights under similar and mysterious circumstances, usually involving uncontrollable high-speed dives. No single cause was ever found for these accidents, and sabotage was suspected at one time, but the most likely theory was that the fabric covering of the elevator may have separated from the ribs because of wear and tear. Pilots were warned not to use the elevator trim tab to assist the entry to a dive, but to keep it in reserve to help the pull-out, and that the engineer should stand by to help the pilot pull the stick back in any long dive. Other than these problems, the Lancaster's record was good, certainly far better than that of the mulish Halifax. The type's loss rate from all causes was consistently the lowest of any of the Bomber Command heavies.

The Lancaster I was the most widely produced version of the type, the vast majority of aircraft being either Lancaster Is or Lancaster IIIs, the latter differing solely in having Packard-built engines and associated changes to engine accessories and controls. The only production version to differ externally from the Merlin-powered types was the Lancaster II. This version, powered by Bristol Hercules VI or XVI radial engines, was developed as an insurance against the failure of the supply of Merlins from the USA. The Avro-built prototype was flown in November 1941. After the USA entered the war the following month it was decided to produce the Lancaster II in quantity, in case the Packard Merlin

Lancaster I of No.83 Squadron, built by Metropolitan Vickers. The aircraft had transferred from No.207 Squadron with the original code EM-R.   (Imperial War Museum)

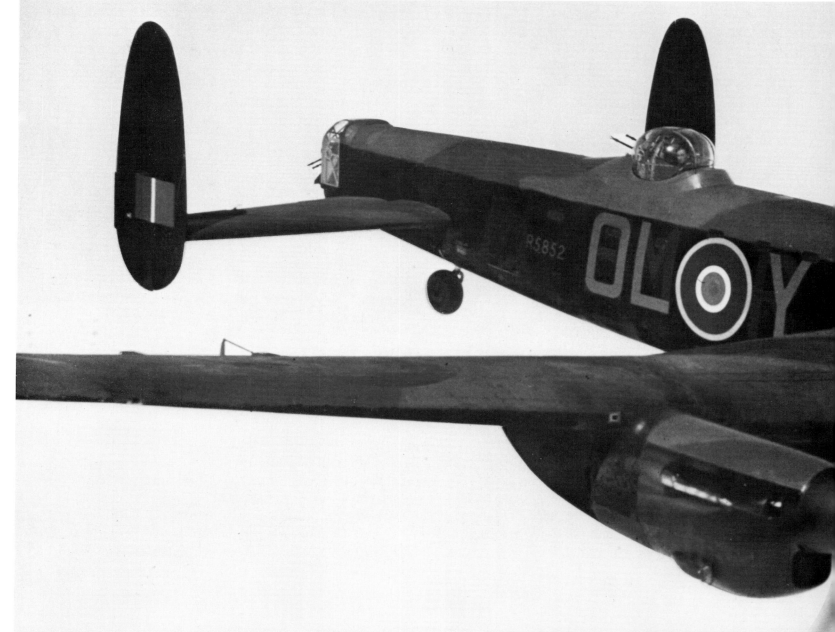

production was diverted to the US forces. Three hundred Lancaster IIs were built by Armstrong Whitworth at Baginton, but the altitude performance of the Hercules was not as good as that of the Merlin and the Lancaster II was replaced in production by the basic aircraft. Most of the Lancaster IIs were delivered as standard with ventral gun turrets and enlarged bomb-bay doors.

The Lancaster I and III were operated with a variety of Merlins. The Merlin 22 from Derby and the Packard-built Merlin 28 and 38 had basically the same ratings as the original Merlin XX, but could deliver slightly more power at sea level and were preferred for operations at high weights. Some fortunate squadrons – usually the crack units or those selected for special operations – had the more highly boosted Merlin 24 or 224 (the latter being the American-built engine) rated at 1,610 hp for take-off, 16 per cent more than the normal engines. Some Packard-engined Lancasters had the US-developed large-area "paddle-bladed" propellers, which improved high-altitude performance and climb significantly, but which gave inferior performance below 16,000 ft (4,877 m).

Chadwick's heavy bomber was successful because it was perfectly suited to its intended role. It represented exactly the right balance between effectiveness and cost, and the fact that it did so was in large measure due to the basic design produced by the Avro team.

Lancaster II, powered by four 1,725 hp Bristol Hercules VI radial engines.   (Imperial War Museum)

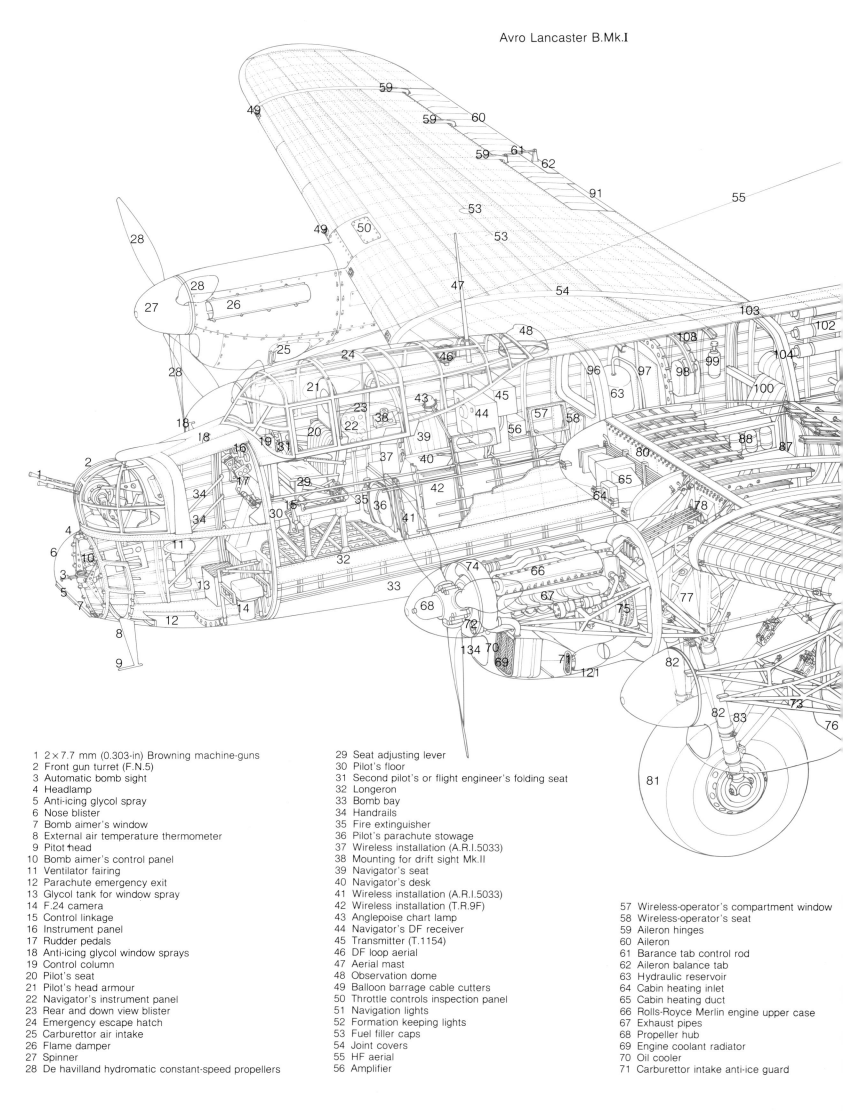

Avro Lancaster B.Mk.I

1 2 × 7.7 mm (0.303-in) Browning machine-guns
2 Front gun turret (F.N.5)
3 Automatic bomb sight
4 Headlamp
5 Anti-icing glycol spray
6 Nose blister
7 Bomb aimer's window
8 External air temperature thermometer
9 Pitot head
10 Bomb aimer's control panel
11 Ventilator fairing
12 Parachute emergency exit
13 Glycol tank for window spray
14 F.24 camera
15 Control linkage
16 Instrument panel
17 Rudder pedals
18 Anti-icing glycol window sprays
19 Control column
20 Pilot's seat
21 Pilot's head armour
22 Navigator's instrument panel
23 Rear and down view blister
24 Emergency escape hatch
25 Carburettor air intake
26 Flame damper
27 Spinner
28 De havilland hydromatic constant-speed propellers

29 Seat adjusting lever
30 Pilot's floor
31 Second pilot's or flight engineer's folding seat
32 Longeron
33 Bomb bay
34 Handrails
35 Fire extinguisher
36 Pilot's parachute stowage
37 Wireless installation (A.R.I.5033)
38 Mounting for drift sight Mk.II
39 Navigator's seat
40 Navigator's desk
41 Wireless installation (A.R.I.5033)
42 Wireless installation (T.R.9F)
43 Anglepoise chart lamp
44 Navigator's DF receiver
45 Transmitter (T.1154)
46 DF loop aerial
47 Aerial mast
48 Observation dome
49 Balloon barrage cable cutters
50 Throttle controls inspection panel
51 Navigation lights
52 Formation keeping lights
53 Fuel filler caps
54 Joint covers
55 HF aerial
56 Amplifier

57 Wireless-operator's compartment window
58 Wireless-operator's seat
59 Aileron hinges
60 Aileron
61 Barance tab control rod
62 Aileron balance tab
63 Hydraulic reservoir
64 Cabin heating inlet
65 Cabin heating duct
66 Rolls-Royce Merlin engine upper case
67 Exhaust pipes
68 Propeller hub
69 Engine coolant radiator
70 Oil cooler
71 Carburettor intake anti-ice guard

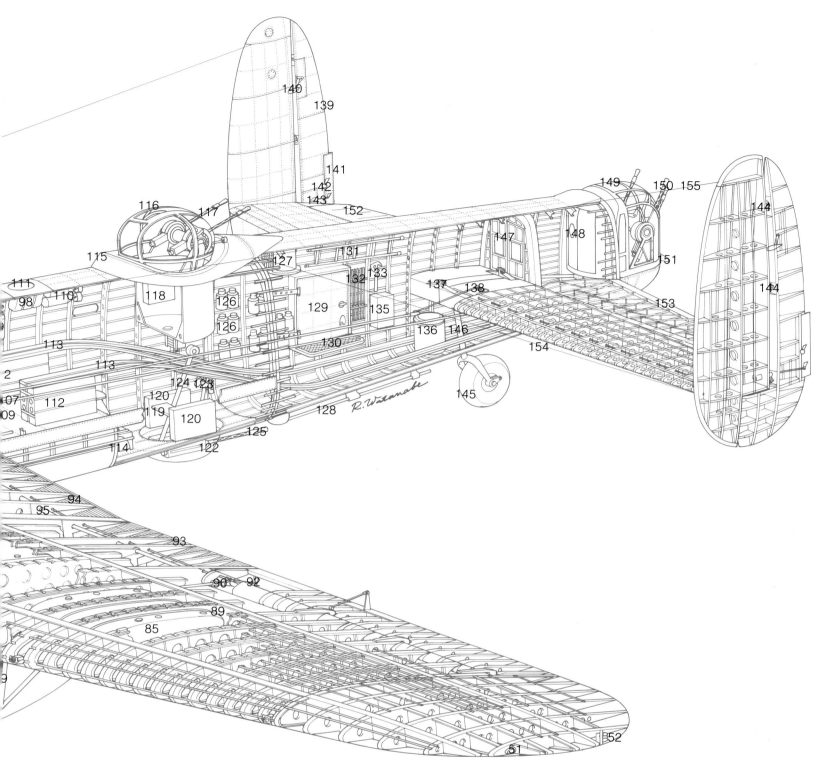

72 De Havilland constant-speed unit on motor casing
73 Engine support frames
74 Glycol header tank
75 Super charger components
76 Firewall/engine bulkhead
77 Oil tanks
78 Throttle controls
79 Engine sub-frame
80 Main spar
81 Main wheel
82 Main wheel shock-absorber struts
83 Undercarriage door operating link rod
84 Undercarriage retraction jack
85 No.3 fuel tank (518 ltr/114 Imp. gal)
86 No.2 fuel tank (1,741 ltr/383 Imp. gal)
87 No.1 fuel tank (2,637 ltr/580 Imp. gal) position
88 Oxygen bottles stowage (15 bottles)
89 Rear spar
90 Aileron control
91 Aileron trim tab
92 Trim tab control rod
93 Outboard split flap
94 Inboard split flap
95 Flap operating tube
96 Spar flange reinforcement
97 Armoured doors
98 Parachute stowages
99 Portable oxygen stwages

100 Rest bed
101 Flap jack
102 Reconnaisance flares
103 Fuselage joint
104 Rear spar fuselage frame
105 Flare chute extension (stowed and in position)
106 Rudder control cable
107 Elevator control cable
108 Windows
109 Main floor
110 Sea markers and flame floats
111 Emergency exit
112 Tail turret ammunition boxes
113 Ammunition ducts
114 Flare chute
115 Dorsal turret fairing
116 Upper mid turret (F.N.50)
117 2 × 7.7 mm (0.303-in) Browning machine-guns
118 Upper turret ammunition box
119 Lower mid gunner's seat
120 Lower turret ammunition boxes
121 Control shutter
122 Lower mid turret (F.N.64)
123 Lower turret control fitted with firing button
124 Gun control (up and down) arm
125 2 × 7.7 mm (0.303-in) Browning machine-guns
126 Vacuum flasks
127 DR compass housing

128 Dipole aerial (Lorenz beam blind approach)
129 Crew entry door
130 Step over ammunition ducts
131 Ladder
132 Dipsticks stowage
133 Crash axe
134 Air intake
135 First aid kit
136 Elsan closet
137 Tailplane joints
138 Rudder control lever
139 Rudder
140 Rudder balance weight
141 Rudder trim tab
142 Rudder tab balance weight
143 Rudder tab actuation rod
144 Datum hinges
145 Fixed tail wheel
146 Tail wheel shock-absorber strut
147 Draught proof doors
148 Tail turret entry door
149 Tail turret (F.N.20)
150 4 × 7.7 mm (0.303-in) Browning machine-guns
151 Cartridge case ejection shute
152 Elevator
153 Elevator trim tab
154 Aerial for A.R.I.5033
155 Aerial for navigator's DF receiver and T.F.9

The Lancaster differed from the Stirling and Halifax in carrying all its bombs in the fuselage, shunning the use of small bomb cells in the inner wing. The massive, uninterrupted, constant-section bomb-bay was the heart of the design, and the reason why the Lancaster could carry a bigger bomb than any other wartime aircraft. Around this bomb-bay, the aircraft was put together in a manner reminiscent of a DC-3 or other Northrop-inspired design, with the centre-section of the wing built integral with the centre fuselage and carrying the outer panels. The outer wings were secured by bolts, pins and shackles to the centre-section, therefore it had not been too hard for Chadwick's team first to increase the span of the Manchester prototype and then to attach the new outer wings of the Lancaster. Simple curved wingtips completed the planform. Thanks to its basis in the much shorter wing of the original Manchester, together with the absence of wing bomb cells, the Lancaster's wing was unusually slender and thin for a British aircraft of the period, and this may have been the secret of its high performance.

Like the wing, the fuselage was designed in large independent sections held together by bolted joints, immensely facilitating repair. Damaged components could be removed rapidly and replaced by relatively unskilled crews. The comparative ease with which the major sub-assemblies could be handled was a major convenience in production, and Avro took full advantage of this by ensuring that as much equipment as possible was installed before the components arrived on the final assembly line.

One of the Lancaster's descendants was defined as "20,000 rivets flying in close formation", and this somewhat unkind phrase reflects the Lancaster's structure quite neatly. Instead of using sophisticated machining techniques, most of the Lancaster was built up from basic components joined by riveting. The main exceptions to this philosophy were a number of high-strength aluminium extrusions, including the booms of the front and rear spars and the highly stressed longerons at the top of the bomb-bay. The spars were built up from these extrusions, riveted to a web of Alclad sheet. The structural heart of the fuselage, firmly bolted to the wing spars, was a heavily ribbed double-skinned floor which carried the fuselage loads and the weight of the bombload.

Simplicity of structure was allied to labour-intensive production. The workforce in the Avro manufacturing group, not including Metropolitan-Vickers (although the latter's aircraft were assembled at Avro's workshop) rose from 10,000 in mid-1939 to 23,500 in 1941, and peaked at over 40,000 in 1943–45. The average working week was more than 66 hours, and 44 per cent of the workers were

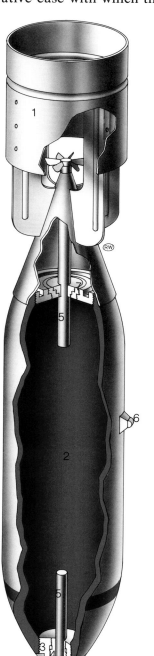

British general purpose bomb

500 lb (227 kg) MC
Used by RAF in the early years of WWII

1 Tail unit
2 Explosive (Amatol)
3 Nose bushing
4 Locking screw
5 Exploder containers
6 Suspension lug
7 Tail bushing

German general purpose bomb

250 kg (551 lb) SC 250
Used by Luftwaffe through WWII

1 Brace
2 Tail fin
3 After fuze pocket
4 Suspension lug
5 Forward fuze pocket
6 Explosive (Amatol and TNT)
7 Suspension

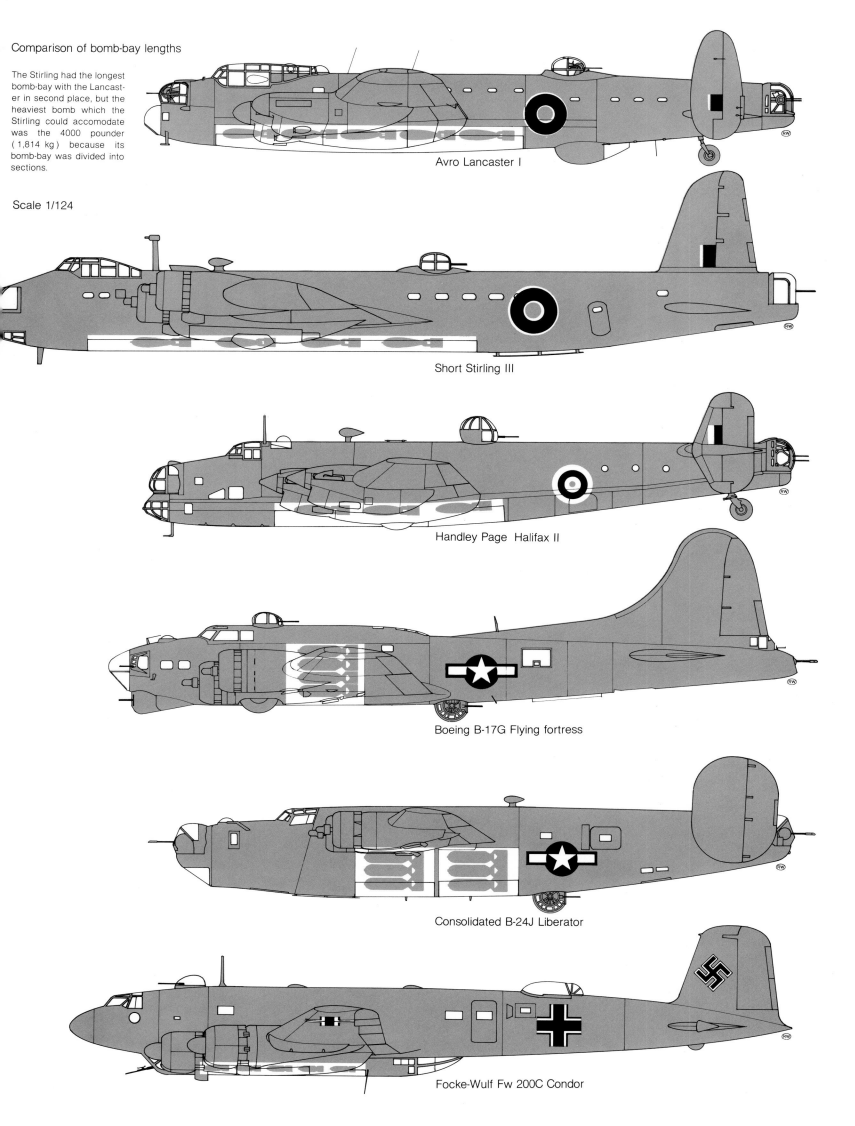

Comparison of bomb-bay lengths

The Stirling had the longest bomb-bay with the Lancaster in second place, but the heaviest bomb which the Stirling could accomodate was the 4000 pounder (1,814 kg) because its bomb-bay was divided into sections.

Scale 1/124

Avro Lancaster I

Short Stirling III

Handley Page Halifax II

Boeing B-17G Flying fortress

Consolidated B-24J Liberator

Focke-Wulf Fw 200C Condor

Avro Lancaster B.Mk.I

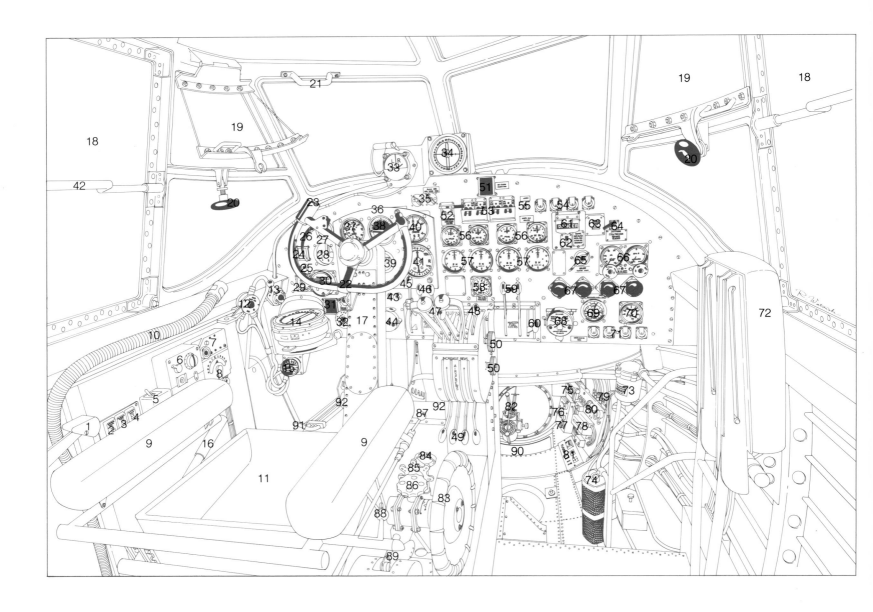

Avro Lancaster B.Mk.I

1 Bomb-bay door control lever
2 Navigation-light switch
3 T.R.9 switch
4 Autopilot master switch
5 Mixer box
6 Beam-approach control unit
7 Intercom call light
8 Autopilot altitude control
9 Folding armrests
10 Oxygen connection
11 Pilot's seat
12 Autopilot lock
13 Autopilot
14 P.4 magnetic compass
15 Autopilot pressure gauge
16 Seat-raising lever
17 Control column
18 Sliding windows
19 Direct-vision windows
20 Window catches
21 Hand grip
22 Control wheel
23 Bomb-release button
24 A.S.I. correction card holder
25 Flap indicator switch
26 Brake lever
27 Watch holder

28 Beam-approach visual indicator
29 Flap indicator
30 Undercarriage indicator
31 P.4 compass-deviation card holder
32 Autopilot speed and heading levers
33 D.F. indicator
34 D.R. repeater compass
35 Landing-light switches
36 Instrument-flying panel
37 A.S.I.
38 Artificial horizon
39 Direction indicator
40 Rate of climb/descent indicator
41 Turn-and-flip indicator
42 Sliding-window hand grips
43 Identification-light colour selector switches
44 Recognition-light signalling switchbox
45 Boost-control cut-out
46 Port master engine fuel-control cocks
47 Throttle levers
48 Mixture lever
49 Propeller pitch controls
50 Friction adjusters
51 D.R. compass-deviation card holder
52 Undercarriage indicator switch
53 Ignition switches
54 Engine-starting pushbuttons
55 Booster coil switch
56 Boost gauges
57 Engine speed (r.p.m.) indicators
58 Steering indicator
59 Starboard master engine fuel-control cocks

60 Two-speed supercharger control
61 I.F.F. detonator buttons
62 I.F.F. switch
63 Bomb-container jettison button
64 Bomb jettison control
65 Vacuum change-over cock
66 Oxygen regulator gauges
67 Propeller Feathering switches
68 Identification-light signalling switchbox
69 Brake pressure gauge
70 Air temperature gauge
71 Fire-extinguisher pushbuttons
72 Folded flight engineer's seat
73 Oil transfer pump
74 Oil filter
75 Bomb selector switches
76 Stick-bombing trim device
77 Bomb-interval trimming dial
78 Bomb-dropping selector box
79 Master switch
80 Camera controls
81 Automatic bombsight
83 Elevator trim-tab control
84 Flap control
85 Aileron trim-tab control
86 Rudder trim-tab control
87 Pilot's harness-release lever
88 Undercarriage-control safety bolt
89 Undercarriage control
90 Emergency exit
91 Pilot's microphone socket
92 Rudder pedals

women. Only a small proportion of the staff had more than a couple of years' experience of aircraft production. Maximum output, attained in August 1944, was 155 Lancasters a month. This was equivalent to something like 2.5 man-hours per pound of airframe empty weight, whereas modern airliners take rather less than one man-hour per pound weight. But the predominantly riveted structure could be produced easily and reliably by people with little training, with minimal need for costly tooling and machinery.

Contributing to the ease of maintenance and repair which characterised the Lancaster was the "power egg" concept, applied for the first time to the heavy bombers. The engine, cooling system and all other accessories were installed as a single unit, with control lines going in and electrical, hydraulic and pneumatic power for the aircraft systems coming out. The engines were mounted in cradles cantilevered from the wing, slightly below the chord line. Chadwick's design of the inner engine mount was particularly ingenious – a pair of forged members attached to the front spar not only took the loads from the engine but carried the main undercarriage pivots on their lower ends. The front and rear spars were fitted with attachment points for a specially designed gantry for engine removal and replacement.

By 1941 standards, a heavy bomber was a complex aircraft, but in comparison with modern aircraft the Lancaster was relatively simple. The simple split flaps, for example, were operated by a single hydraulic jack, the sections being connected with torque tubes. The main hydraulic system – operating the landing gear, flaps and bomb doors – was fed from pumps on the inboard engines, as were the pneumatic brakes and the electrical system. A Lancaster could therefore lose either inboard engine and continue functioning, and there was an emergency compressed-air system for the landing gear and flaps.

The "standard" Lancaster as defined by the official manual had a defensive armament of ten 0.303 in (7.7 mm) Colt-Browning machine-guns, mounted in twin-gun Frazer-Nash turrets in the nose, dorsal and belly positions, and a four-gun turret in the tail. The tail gun was provided with nearly twice as much ammunition as the rest of the turrets put together. The majority of Lancasters, however, lacked a ventral turret, and this created a dangerous blind spot which the Luftwaffe would later exploit. A Lancaster with its full design complement of ten guns would have a crew of eight, but the more common three-turret aircraft carried seven men.

Captain of the aircraft, irrespective of rank, was the pilot. Originally designed to be flown by a pilot and co-pilot, the Lancaster was used operationally with a single pilot and a flight engineer. This crewing system had been introduced by the RAF as the Lancaster entered service to reduce the demand for pilots, but placed a heavy strain on the captain – he was not only in charge of the aircraft but had no qualified relief at the controls. The Lancaster was equipped with a Mk IV automatic pilot, consisting of three air-driven gyroscopes linked to pneumatic servo motors. The servos drove the controls via chain drives. The system was powered by an air compressor on the port inboard engine and could, in theory,

Above: Nose mounted F.N.5 turret on a Lancaster B.Mk.III. The aerials on either side are for the Rebecca blind approach landing system.　　　(Imperial War Museum)
Below: F.N.20 tail turret. Many gunners removed the perspex panel as here for greater visibility.　　　(Imperial War Museum)

hold the aircraft straight and level with one outboard engine stopped and feathered. The autopilot could not be used over enemy territory, because disengagement of the autopilot could cause a fatal delay in taking evasive action under attack. There were no Lancaster trainers, but dual-control kits could be fitted.

Behind the pilot was the Lancaster's administrative office, containing the navigator and wireless operator. Originally a somewhat bare and cavernous space in the early Lancasters, by the end of the war this area was to contain equipment totally undreamt of when Chadwick mapped out the Lancaster's crew compartment in 1936. The bomb-aimer lay prone in the nose for the run into the target, his head projecting into a perspex dome. He could also man the front turret. The crew complement comprised the mid-upper gunner, his feet dangling into the rear fuselage (where the ventral gunner's head would be in a four-turret Lancaster) and, last, coldest, but often the most important, "Tail-End Charlie", the rear gunner. All the turrets except the rear guns included their own ammunition supply, but the 10,000-round tanks for the rear turret were located near the end of the bomb-bay and fed the guns via long steel chutes which snaked towards the tail. The Lancaster's armour protection consisted of a bulkhead across the centre fuselage, ahead of the mid-gun positions, with some armour around the pilot. The standard escape routine, even for the tail gunner, was for all the crew to leave by the escape hatch provided under the nose – use of the normal entrance door was cautioned against because of the risk of striking the tail. Only just over a tenth of Lancaster crewmen survived if their aircraft were destroyed by enemy action.

The Lancaster was an aircraft of few vices, and could be thrown around very violently in the "corkscrew" evasive manoeuvre practised by Bomber Command. A determined corkscrew was a test of the aeroplane itself and the pilot – a sequence of wingover, maximum-rate descent and climbing turn in which vertical and horizontal airspeed and attitude fluctuated wildly to the maximum permissible values. The aircraft was restricted to straight and level flight at the higher operational weights introduced later in its life, but would usually have burned off sufficient fuel to be free of restrictions over enemy territory. However, only the Merlin 24 and 224 were really powerful enough to restore the Lancaster's initial climb performance at the gross weights of up to 68,000 lb (30,850 kg) that were used on some long-range missions towards the end of the war, and the more powerful engines were relatively scarce.

The standard Lancaster had been designed to accept bombs as big as the 4,000 lb (1,815 kg) "cookie" thin-cased bomb but many aircraft were built or field-converted with larger bomb doors to accommodate the 8,000 lb (3,630 kg) "blockbuster" or the larger 12,000 lb (5,445 kg) demolition bomb, the former being introduced in 1943 and the latter in 1944. Defensively, the possibility of using heavier guns than the relatively ineffective 0.303-in (7.7 mm) Colt-Browning had been considered in the Air Staff's 1938 "ideal bomber" paper. However the supply of the obvious substitute, the American 0.5-in (12.7 mm) machine-gun, was never sufficient to allow change on any large scale before 1944, when some Lancaster Is and IIIs were fitted with Frazer-Nash FN.82 or Rose Brothers tail turrets, mounting two of the American weapons. When Austin Motors became the last company to commence Lancaster production it was intended to produce a new version, the B.VII, with 0.5-in guns in the dorsal and tail turrets, the former being moved further forward than on earlier versions. The shortage of heavier guns led to some aircraft being completed as B.I (Interim) types with the existing turrets in the new position, but a few B.VIIs were completed before the end of the war.

The advanced Merlin with two-stage supercharger was never used in significant numbers on the Lancaster. The Lancaster IV and V, extensively redesigned to take full advantage of the new Merlin's high-altitude performance, became the post-war Lincoln – Bomber Command's constant demands for more Lancasters prevented the Lincoln from being produced any earlier. Rolls-Royce fitted the two-stage Merlin 85 to a few Lancasters. These, designated Lancaster VI, were used by 635 Squadron for electronic-countermeasures work. Externally the standard production Lancaster remained very much the same throughout its career, although internal changes were many and vital. Despite the enthusiasm with which 44 Squadron at Waddington received their new aircraft in December 1941, the Lancaster B.I was then virtually useless as a weapon system. The story of its increasing effectiveness reflects the campaign of Bomber Command from 1942–45.

Bombing blind

It was not Roy Chadwick's fault that the Lancaster was ineffective, and neither could the blame be laid at Rolls-Royce's door – it was simply that the Lancaster was unable to defend itself in daylight and unable to find its targets at night. This was because the pre-war proponents of bombing had believed, like those who called for the bomber to be outlawed, that the effects of bombing would be far more devastating than they actually were.

The pre-war staff of Bomber Command considered that they alone presented a workable alternative to the terrible trench warfare of the 1914–18 war. Their aim was to build up a bomber force which would realise for its victims the most nightmarish fantasies of the early 1930s. The attitude of the bomber enthusiasts towards the practitioners of more traditional forms of warfare could, on occasion, slip over into

Canadian-built Lancaster B.Mk.X with enlarged bomb-bay to carry the 8,000 lb (3,629 kg) bomb. This plane was used for trials of Martin dorsal turret (two 0.50-in/12.7 mm guns) which is shown just after the bomb-bay doors. (Imperial War Museum)

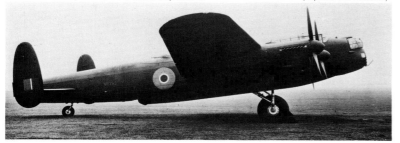

open contempt. A staff Group Captain noted to the Chief of the Air Staff in September 1936 that he anticipated that the War Office would, in time of war, experience "natural difficulties" in finding "sufficient morons willing to be sacrificed in a mud war in Flanders". The author of this memorandum was Group Captain Arthur Harris, of whom we will hear rather more later.

Like the advocates of disarmament, Bomber Command believed that an efficient air campaign would cause a rapid and total collapse of civilian morale, and force an enemy to sue for peace. Although there was, at this time, no overt decision to bomb civilian populations, there was little ground for supposing, given the state of the art of the bomber force, that the non-combatant could be effectively spared from damage. The belief of some officers that the attack on the civilian centres should be the primary purposes of bombing was only to be expressed publicly at a later stage of the war.

There were two dangerous and connected fallacies underlying Bomber Command's confidence in its ability to win the war through such a campaign of bombing. The first was the belief that unescorted bombers could survive in daylight against fighter defences by using their multiple guns, mutual fire-support between aircraft and their speed. Even in July 1939 this policy was being questioned by the Commander-in-Chief of the bomber force, Sir Edgar Ludlow-Hewitt. Gunners, he noted, "have no real confidence in their ability to use this equipment [powered turrets] effectively, and captains and crews have little confidence in the ability of the gunners to protect them". These misgivings were well founded, daylight attacks on the German fleet at anchor being badly mauled by German fighters in the last quarter of 1939. Even though some officers blamed the losses on poor formation-keeping and flak rather than fighters – Harris, by January 1940 in command of 5 Group, still believed after these losses that three bombers in company "considered themselves capable of taking on anything" – the fact that daylight operations were near-suicidal was slowly driven home.

But if the bombers could not attack by day, they would have to go by night, and it was in the art of night bombing that Bomber Command's most gaping deficiencies were exposed. Between 1937 and 1939 no fewer than 478 of the Command's aircraft force-landed after getting lost on training flights over a friendly country spangled with the lights of peacetime. Sir John Slessor, recalling his time as a Group Captain with the Air Staff in the pre-war years, noted that the RAF had no Bomber Development Unit charged solely with improving tactics and methods until 1939, and that the results of bombing trials carried out sporadically in the pre-war years "should have depressed us more than they did". Unless the crew could identify a pin-point on the ground – and over a blacked-out country this would be impossible – the only means of navigation was dead-reckoning based on predicted winds, which could be no more than intelligently guessed at over enemy territory.

Civilian navigators could use radio direction-finding, but these basic beacon aids were easy to jam and there was a high risk of flying a reciprocal heading. Skilled navigators could take a star-shoot, all bombers being fitted with an astrodome for this purpose, but this required long periods of straight, level flying which would be risky in a hostile area. The commander of 3 Group summed the problems up in May 1939, when he stated that without any outside aid, the average crew could only be expected to get within 50 miles (80 km) of the target.

Even if the crews succeeded in finding the target against all odds, the chances of a Bomber Command strike causing any serious or irreparable damage were small. The Mk VII bomb-sight, standard at the outbreak of war, was more

Lancaster I of No.1661 Conversion Unit, flying over heavy clouds.

(Imperial War Museum)

suited to the Command's old biplane bombers than to the Lancaster, early examples of which carried the Mk VII. The sight could not take account of banked turns on the run into the target, so the aircraft had to approach straight and level if the bombs were not to go wide. Finally, RAF bombs were of 1914–18 design, and compared with Luftwaffe bombs of the same gross weight contained a smaller quantity of less powerful explosive. Not surprisingly, Bomber Command entered the war initially committed to conserving its forces until the heavy bombers could be brought into service and more advanced tactics developed. Meanwhile, in Slessor's words, the early bomber campaign advanced "under the cloak of a complacent publicity which kept everyone happy" while efforts were made "to build up a force which could do what the optimists imagined was already being done".

This cloak was rudely rent asunder by a report submitted to Prime Minister Churchill by his cabinet staff in August 1941. It was already known that one-third of bomber crews returned without claiming to have found the target, and it was found that of the remainder, only one in three had bombed within five miles of the aiming point. This report coincided with an appeal by the RAF for a massive increase in bomber production, to the point where Bomber Command could deploy 4,000 heavy bombers. This would have meant virtually the entire output of British war production being devoted to the manufacture of heavy bombers. The Bomber Command enthusiasts wanted to defeat Germany by bombing to the point where an invasion could land unopposed, but in the aftermath of the report to Churchill they were unlikely to win approval for this plan. Bombing continued to enjoy high priority, but henceforth there would be constant tension between the leadership of Bomber Command, who believed that any effort not put into bombers was wasted, and the supreme leadership of the Royal Air Force and the Allied war effort in general.

The Lancaster entered service just as Bomber Command began to overcome some of its more serious deficiencies. By March 1942, when 44 Squadron started experimental minelaying sorties with the new bomber, one-third of Bomber Command's aircraft were equipped with receivers for the new Gee navigation aid. More sophisticated and flexible than the German beam devices used in 1940–41, Gee transmitted two circular patterns of radio pulses and, with the aid of the receiver and a set of special charts, the navigator could find his position with reasonable accuracy. Relatively difficult to jam, Gee was also protected by a series of elaborate deception operations. Although it was not accurate enough for blind bombing, it was good enough for target-finding.

The Lancaster force grew at an increasing pace after a slow start. The 29 Lancasters which took part in the 1,000-bomber raid on Cologne at the end of May 1942 – the first major operation organised by Bomber Command's new commander-in-chief, Sir Arthur Harris – were the largest force of the type to be used up to then. Bomber Command was suffering from a general shortage of aircraft at that time, due to the failure of the Manchester and the slow deliveries of the new heavy bombers, and the Cologne raid was organised by the expedient of milking training and conversion units of every available aircraft.

Bomber Command's policy was to make the crack 5 Group an all-Lancaster unit, and in the second half of 1942 this Group explored the Lancaster's potential. Daylight raids were attempted – the MAN factory in Augsburg, a main source of submarine engines, was attacked by 12 Lancasters from 44 and 97 Squadrons on 17 August. The flight involved a 750 mile (1,200 km) unescorted penetration of enemy territory, and all but one of the Lancasters were destroyed by the defences. On 17 October a shorter-range, low-level raid met with far greater success. Virtually every available Lancaster in 5 Group joined a 94-aircraft raid on the Schneider armaments factory at Le Creusot in Northern France, losing only one of their number.

By the end of 1942 it was confirmed that the Lancaster was far superior to the Halifax or Stirling. It was well on the way to becoming numerically the most important type in the Command, as production increased at Armstrong Whitworth and Metropolitan-Vickers. The Lancaster was to be used in future for all Bomber Command's most demanding missions. In January 1943, as 1 Group started to convert from Wellingtons to the Avro bomber, Lancasters formed the largest single element in a Bomber Command night raid for the first time. In the same month the Lancaster II was first used operationally, by 61 Squadron. On the type's first operation, it was found that the radial-engined bomber could only attain a maximum altitude of 18,400 ft (5,610 m). The career of the Mk II was relatively short.

The effectiveness of the RAF's bombing was improving rapidly. In the summer of 1942 Harris had been forced to create a new force, comprising hand-picked crews, which would be tasked with leading the main force of bombers to the target and "marking" it with pyrotechnic flares. These were the Pathfinders, or 8 Group, and they wielded a range of new electronic devices. Among them were Oboe, a highly accurate marking aid carried on Mosquitos, and Gee equipment operated by skilled navigators. In addition, the Pathfinders were the first unit to use a revolutionary new aid which offered unlimited range (unlike Oboes) and far greater accuracy than Gee. This was H2S, the world's first ground-mapping radar.

H2S had been made possible by a British invention – the high-powered magnetron, which for the first time made feasible the design of powerful radar on very short "centimetric" wavelengths. Development of a "town-finding" air-to-surface radar using the new magnetron proceeded in

A navigator watches GEE indicator unit.　　　　(Imperial War Museum)

parallel with advanced night-fighter radar. Despite appeals from the Admiralty for priority in H2S deliveries to be allotted to Coastal Command, the bombers were equipped first with the new aid. Scientific Intelligence had also opposed the early deployment of H2S with Bomber Command, on the grounds that the secret of the magnetron would be lost to the Germans as soon as an H2S-equipped aircraft was shot down, but while almost equally good results could be attained with Gee and Oboe, the urgent requests of the bomber leaders carried the day.

A range of devices designed to weaken the enemy's night defences was also coming into action in the winter of 1942–43. Tinsel was the code-name for a crude jammer consisting of a microphone in the Lancaster's engine nacelle, connected to the radio. The wireless operator swept the available frequencies, listening for an exchange between a German controller and a night-fighter, and blotted it out with a roar of engine noise. More sophisticated was Monica, a simple radar related to early long-wavelength night-fighter equipment, designed to give an audible warning of any aircraft at close range within a 45° arc to the rear. There were always many of those, however, because the German night-fighters were controlled by a system of sector controls running from Denmark to the Swiss border, and Bomber Command had countered by attempting to saturate a single sector with a "stream" of bombers, flying individually but following roughly the same course. Most of the warnings from Monica were generated by other bombers in the stream.

Another innovation preceded Bomber Command's campaign in the first half of 1943 – the introduction of the Mk XIV bomb-sight. It was gyroscopically stabilised to compensate for aircraft manoeuvres and was linked to a primitive analogue computer which took account of the ballistic behaviour of the bombs being used, the direction and speed of the wind over the target (worked out by specially trained crews called Windfinders) and the aircraft's airspeed and altitude. A vast improvement on the old Mk VII, the Mk XIV began to be introduced from late 1942.

Bomber Command's target was Germany's heavy-industry workforce. Saturation bombing of heavy-industry centres was intended to damage factories, but more importantly it was aimed at the homes, morale and lives of the civilian population. The typical raids up to July 1943 involved around 400 aircraft. Although this force was numerically no larger than the experimental raids of 1941, the increasing use of heavy bombers vastly augmented its destructive power. The first Bomber Command raid on Berlin since 1941 took place on March 1, 1943, and was also distinguished by being the first large raid to be composed entirely of Lancasters. The Ruhr was the focus of the Command's efforts, however, leading the March–July period to be labelled the Battle of the Ruhr. Pathfinders and Oboe, the latter used on a heavy raid for the first time in March, were by that time making their full contribution to improved bombing accuracy.

The early attacks on the Ruhr, carried out against the sector-based German night-interception system known as the Kammhuber Line, delivered a total of 58,000 tons of bombs and incendiaries to German targets. Bomber Command flew 18,506 sorties, losing 872 aircraft (4.7 per cent of those dispatched) to the defences.

The odds against any crew surviving a tour of operations in 1943–44 were unfavourable. It has been calculated that 51 out of 100 crew in an Operational Training Unit at that time would be killed on operations, and another nine killed in crashes. Twelve would survive the destruction of their aircraft to be taken prisoner (sometimes seriously injured) implying that roughly one man in five escaped after an aircraft was hit. Three out of 100 would be injured badly enough to be taken off operations. Statistically, one man among the 100 would survive a crash in enemy territory and find his way back to England without being captured or killed. Less than a quarter – 24 out of 100 – would complete their tour of operations unscathed and at liberty. On the German side, the citizens of the Ruhr reacted as the citizens of London had done under heavy bombing, and the effectiveness of the RAF's campaign was not highly rated by the German leaders. The 4.7 per cent loss rate, however, was only just acceptable to Bomber Command, which feared that morale among its crews might collapse if the loss rate rose above five per cent of its sorties.

Still the campaign continued, because there seemed to be no alternative to the mass night raids. The US Army Air Force was building up to its doomed campaign to carry out precision daylight attacks with unescorted, heavily armed, lightly loaded bombers, but was to be driven from the skies by the Luftwaffe. In May 1943 also, Bomber Command experimented with a different form of attack, in a single raid which earned the Lancaster immense popular fame.

This was the raid on the Moehne, Eder and Sorpe dams by a specially formed 5 Group unit, 617 Squadron. The squadron's Lancasters were modified by the removal of bomb doors and mid-upper turrets and fitted with launching gear for the special mine developed by Barnes Wallis of Vickers – the famous bouncing bomb. The weapon was cylindrical, carried with its axis at right angles to the line of flight, contained 6,600 lb (2,994 kg) of RDX explosive (which had replaced the pre-war Amatol) and weighed 9,250 lb (4,196 kg). The bomb was carried by calipers at its ends, and the Lancaster carried a hydraulic motor in the fuselage to spin the bomb backwards at 500 rpm before launching. Dropped at a carefully set altitude, speed and distance from a dam, the weapon would bounce predictably across the water surface, clearing the torpedo nets with which the dams were protected, and with its residual spin energy would crawl down the face of the dam and explode at a pre-set depth. Avro converted 23 Lancaster IIIs to take the mine, and 19 of these aircraft took part in the attack on May 16–17, 1943. Two of the aircraft aborted, and eight were destroyed, but the Moehne and Eder dams were breached, depriving a large area of hydro-electric power and industrial water supplies, and causing considerable flood damage.

The spectacular dams raid drove home a hard operational lesson – a highly trained force of experienced and proficient pilots had successfully attacked a precision target at night and at low level, but had lost 42 per cent of their number. This was no alternative to nocturnal area bombing.

War in the dark

The weapon system which ushered in the crucial phase of Bomber Command's strategic offensive against Germany had been understood in principle since shortly after the invention of radar, and had been ready for operational use in the first half of 1942. It was then, and remains now, one of the most effective, and certainly the simplest means of confusing a radar system. Now known as chaff, it consists of a cloud of aluminium strips which create a dense fog on the radar screen. It was known to its inventors in Britain as Window.

The use of Window was delayed because of the realisation that it would be equally useful to an enemy, and that operation of the device would inevitably betray it. Unknown to the RAF, the Luftwaffe had independently discovered the use of chaff, and had followed the same course of action, suppressing it in the interests of security. But as bomber losses increased in the summer of 1943, a number of factors were favouring the introduction of Window by the British. It was increasingly unlikely, for example, that the Luftwaffe would ever be in a position to mount an air offensive against Britain on the scale now being carried out by Bomber Command against Germany. Fighter Command was also taking delivery of night-fighters equipped with the new AI.X radar, which had much improved resistance to Window jamming. Finally, it was pressure from Bomber Command to introduce a system that promised to reduce losses which overcame the resistance to the use of Window. It was decided to introduce the new weapon on Operation Gomorrah, the raid on Hamburg on July 24, 1943.

Bomber Command could now field nearly 800 aircraft for a single raid – nine in ten of them were heavy bombers and nearly half the heavies were Lancasters. Hamburg presented an ideal target for H2S, because the coastline gave a clear image on the radar screen. The defenders' radars were a mass of flickering light and random echoes, and the tightly organised German night-fighter system disintegrated. Repeat raids on succeeding nights laid waste to the centre of Hamburg, with the loss of 50,000 lives.

The RAF never repeated the initial surprise of Window, although Bomber Command followed the attack on Hamburg with increasingly devastating attacks on targets successively deeper within Germany. By now, the Halifaxes with their inferior payload and range were being used mainly to carry incendiaries, while the withdrawal from service of the Stirlings with their much lower cruising altitude was only a matter of time.

August 1943 saw two notable and significant raids. The secret base at Peenemunde, where the cream of Germany's aeronautical engineers were working on the Fi 103 and A-4 missiles, was the subject of an attack during which 40 out of the 597 raiders were destroyed by flak and fighters. However, a spoof attack, in which aircraft carrying Window simulated a larger bomber force aimed at Berlin, deceived the night-fighter controllers to such an extent that most of the aircraft bombed successfully before the night-fighters could attack, and the high-priority research centre was heavily damaged. In the same month, Bomber Command returned to Berlin, suffering 7.2 per cent losses, but this figure broke down into 12.9 per cent for the Stirling, 8.8 per cent for the Halifax and 5.4 per cent for the Lancaster. After these early raids, only Lancasters were used for attacks on Berlin.

The early successes using Window led to a reorganisation of German night-fighter tactics. Initially, the destruction of Hamburg provided the opportunity for Major Hajo Hermann to gain acceptance of his proposal for freelance interception by single-engined fighters. These *Wilde Sau* (wild boar) interceptors achieved some success intercepting and destroying night bombers in the brightly lit area above the target, where searchlights, RAF marker flares and the flames of the city below conspired to turn night into day. They experienced high accident rates, however, and their most important contribution was to point the way to two other Luftwaffe tactics. *Zähme Sau* (tame boar) was the use of radar-equipped night-fighters on the same sort of freelance operations that Hermann had advocated. The fighters were simply vectored towards the bomber stream by ground controllers and left to find their own individual targets. The other main innovation was *Helle Nachtjagd* (bright night-fighting), based on the assumption that good visibility favoured the cannon-armed fighter rather than the bomber. Wherever possible, the sky was illuminated by searchlights on the ground and parachute flares dropped from high-altitude aircraft.

The equipment of the fighter squadrons was also improving, while development of improved versions of the Lancaster remained subordinate to the increasing of production rates. The Messerschmitt Bf 110, with its limited range, was replaced by the Junkers Ju88G, which could follow the bomber stream over a far greater distance and was thus better suited to *Zähme Sau* fighting. More importantly, the new fighters were equipped with *Lichtenstein* SN-2 radar which was far less susceptible to Window jamming. However, perhaps the biggest contribution to the Luftwaffe's recovery from Window jamming was made by Bomber Command itself.

In January 1943, a Pathfinder Stirling carrying H2S was shot down near Rotterdam, and the city's name was used as the German code-name for the revolutionary radar device. In the following month, a Bomber Command aircraft carrying the Monica tail-warning radar was shot down and the equipment was discovered. In addition, Bomber Command crews had persuaded themselves that they could discourage searchlight-control radars from locking onto their aircraft by switching on their identification friend-or-foe (IFF) transponders. There was no foundation whatsoever for this rumour, but Bomber Command nevertheless fitted its aircraft with a "J-switch" to activate the IFF transmitter, in an effort to boost morale. Crews also got into the habit of switching on their H2S radars soon after taking off from Britain.

Bomber Command totally failed to appreciate that in electronic terms every bomber dispatched over Germany in late 1943 was carrying two or three long-range identification lamps. The Luftwaffe was quick to fit its aircraft with systems to detect them. The Ju88s carried the Monica-homer – code-named Flensburg – and the FuG 350 Naxos-Z to

Lancaster B.I RA530 of No 57 Squadron, based at East Kirkby, Lincs, in February 1945. Fitted with H₂S radar. Destroyed in a crash on the night of 20/21 March, 1945.

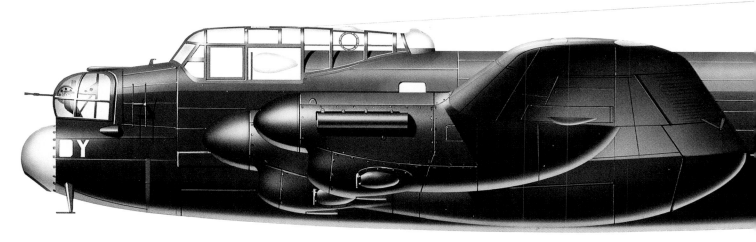

Lancaster B.II DS626 of No 115 Squadron, based at East Wretham, Norfolk, in March 1943. Flown by Sgt G.P. Finnerty (RCAF). Subsequently served with No 426 (RCAF), No 408 Squadron (RCAF) and No 1668 Heavy Conversion Unit. Retired on 20 March, 1945.

Lancaster B.I HK541 modified as experimental long-range bomber for use against Japan. Fitted with 5,460 ltr (1,200 Imp gal) saddle tank. Tested by Aircraft & Armament Experimental Establishment at Boscombe Down in 1945.

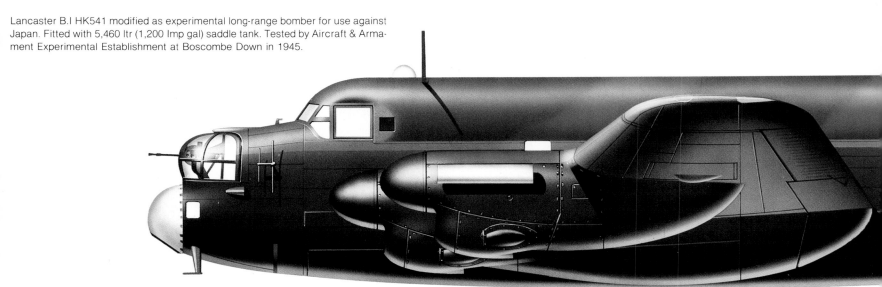

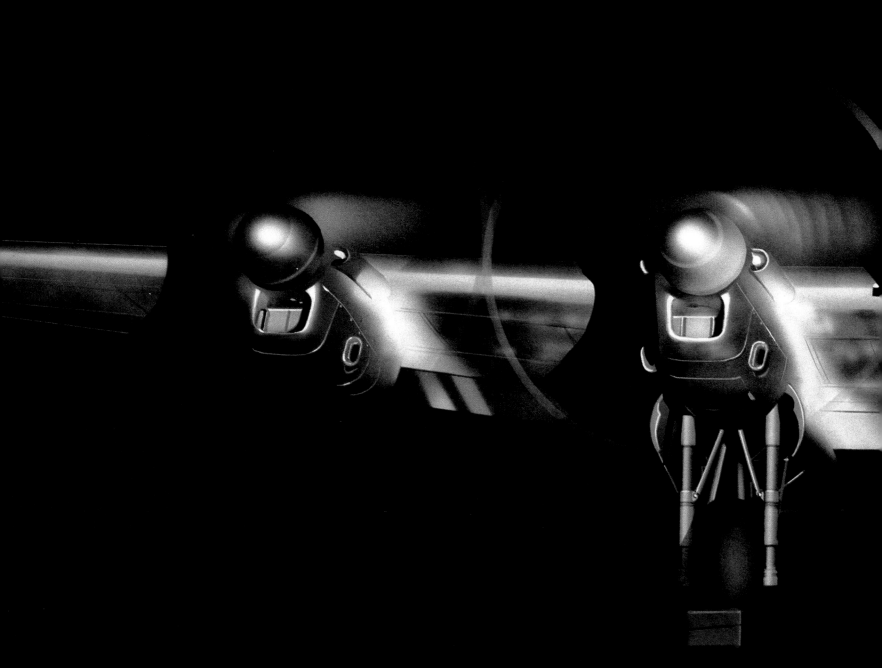

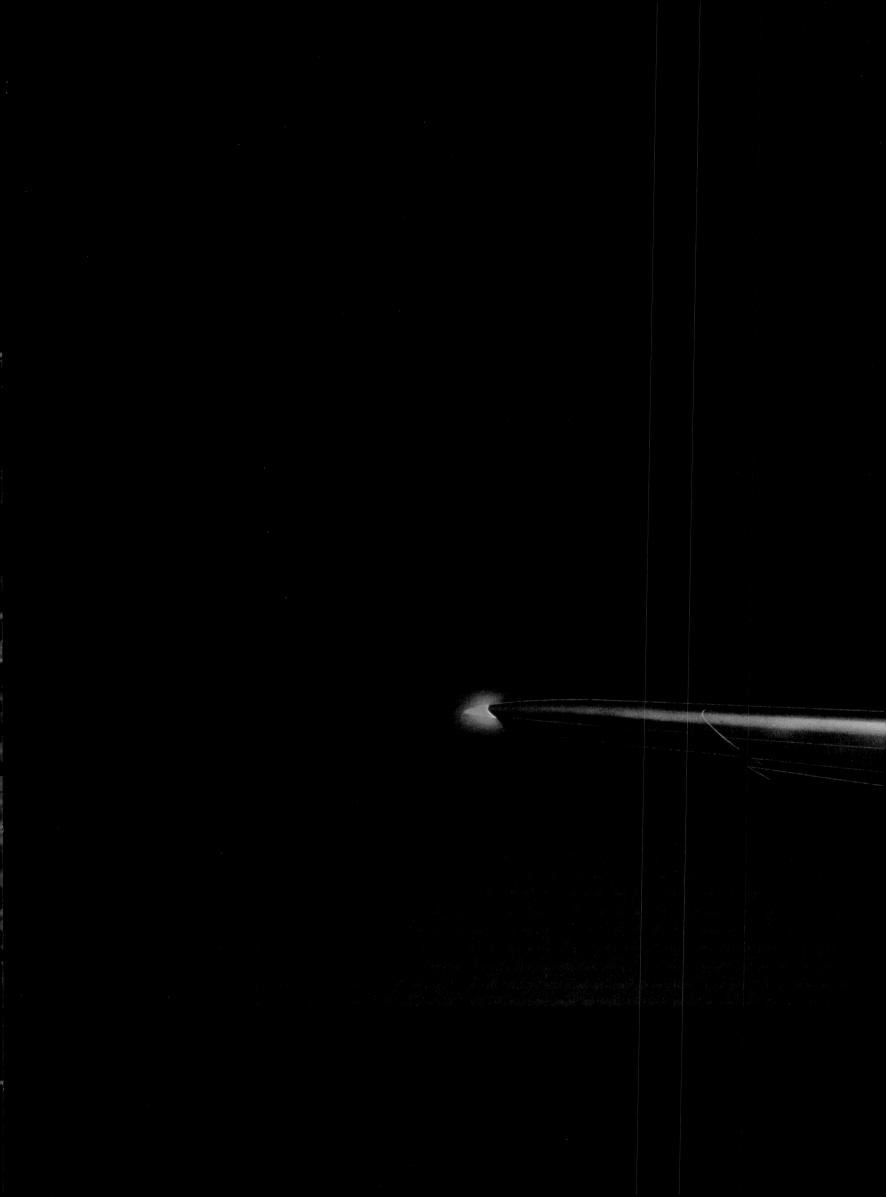

Lancaster B.I (Special) PD131 of No 15 Squadron. Carried 10,000 kg (22,000 lb) Grand Slam bomb for trials against U-boat pens after the end of the war. Scrapped in May 1947.

Lancaster ASR.III SW324 with a lifeboat about 1950. Used for rescue duties by No 210 Squadron. Scrapped in May 1957.

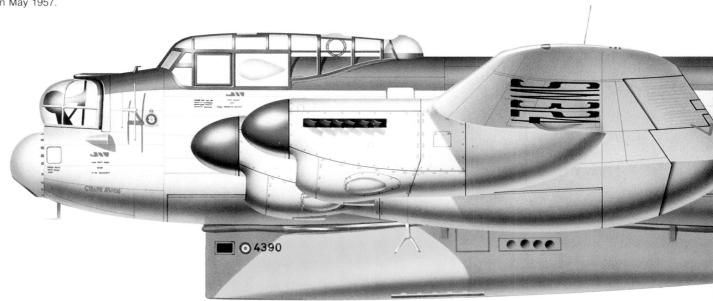

Lancaster 10AR KB882 of No 408 (Goose) Squadron, RCAF, at Rockcliffe, Ottawa, in 1963. Used for photographic and Arctic reconnaissance.

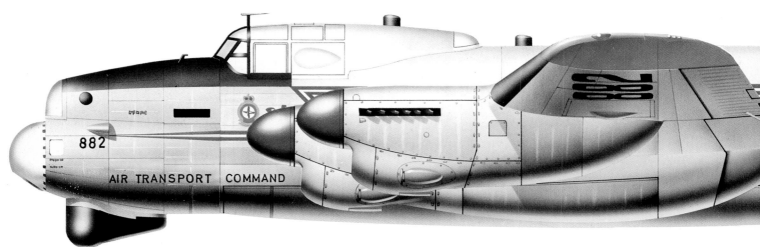

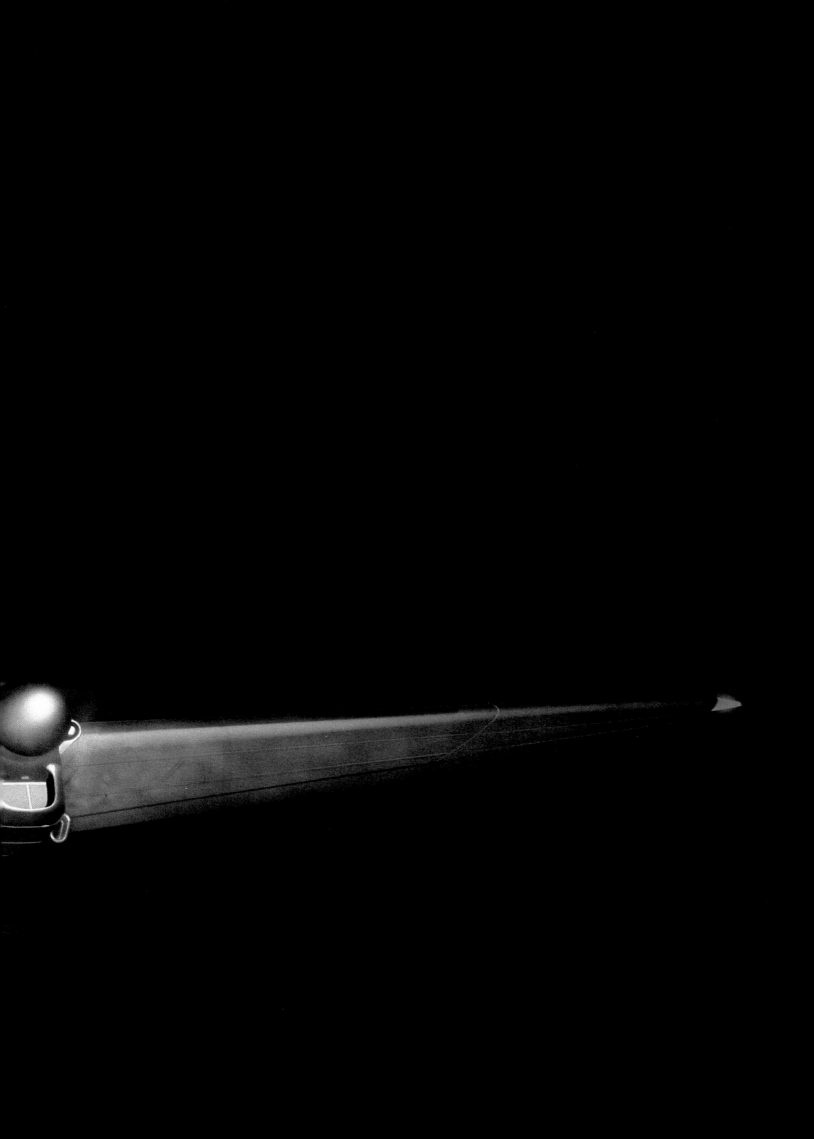

home on H2S emissions. Ground stations were equipped with a combination of both devices, called Naxburg, together with a system which detected the bombers' "flames" or IFF transmissions. Meanwhile, Bomber Command steadily increased the proportion of its fleet equipped with H2S, in either its British version or the American-built H2X, known to the RAF as H2S Mk III and operating on shorter wavelengths.

The German night-fighters were also being equipped with another new device, as simple as it was deadly. This was *Schräge Musik* (jazz music or, literally, "oblique music"), a pair of 20 mm (0.79 in) or 30 mm (1.18 in) cannon installed in the fuselage to fire upwards and forwards. The advantages of this weapon for use against the RAF night bombers were many: the fighter could approach the target from below, reducing its own visibility while silhouetting the victim against the sky; the bomber presented a large target with no deflection required; the fighter could approach without wandering into the cone of detection from the rear turret or Monica radar; and above all the RAF's bombers were almost all completely blind to an attack from below. So lethal was *Schräge Musik* that its existence went unsuspected for many months as victims of an attack did not return to report it and very seldom even escaped into captivity.

It could be argued that the introduction of H2S, which with its ventral scanning aerial was installed on the mounting ring for the original mid-lower turret, was a twofold menace to the bomber as it supplanted its ventral defensive position and provided the predator with a homing beacon. Throughout the bomber offensive, therefore, some Lancaster units discarded H2S in favour of the ventral guns, particularly the Canadian 6 Group.

There is no conclusive proof of the effectiveness of ventral armament. Many of the Lancasters delivered with the Frazer-Nash FN.64 ventral turret were the lower-flying, more vulnerable Lancaster IIs, so direct comparisons with the I and III would probably be inaccurate. The ventral turret was sighted through a periscope, so the gunner could not fulfil his most effective role, which was that of a lookout rather than an active combatant. The FN.64 was also restricted in traverse to 100° either side of the centre-line. It was probably better than nothing though, and its removal did not make very much difference to the Lancaster's bombload. Also used in small numbers, especially by 6 Group, were simpler ventral defence positions fitted with single manually operated 0.5 in (12.7 mm) or 0.303 in (7.7 mm) machine-guns.

The whole question of the effectiveness of defensive armament was raised in a paper produced in the Operational Research Section of Bomber Command in 1944. Essentially it argued that the defensive armament and gunners were simply heavier and created more drag than they

Lancaster B.Mk.III sets out on a night bombing mission.

(Imperial War Museum)

were worth, and that the speed of the Lancaster could be increased by 50 mph (80 km/hr) by dispensing with guns. Its payload would also be increased, so fewer aircraft would be needed to carry the same tonnage of bombs, the faster aircraft would be less liable to interception, and casualties per aircraft would be lower when they were destroyed. On this question, as on so many other technical matters, it was simply impossible to gather enough data in wartime to present a convincing case for change to the hardline bomber enthusiasts in Command HQ at High Wycombe. There were numerous crews in Britain whose gunners had saved them by driving off an assailant, or more commonly by spotting the attacker in time for evasive action to be effective. Many more crews had found the protection and observation of the gunners inadequate, but often these men were not in Britain – they were in Germany, either in captivity or dead.

While the Luftwaffe improved its night-fighters and bomber development stagnated, Sir Arthur Harris was preparing to launch Bomber Command's biggest offensive. "We can wreck Berlin from end to end," he told Churchill. "It will cost us 400–500 aircraft. It will cost Germany the war." Between November 1943 and March 1944, Bomber Command embarked on a series of raids against major German cities, more than half being against Berlin itself. The Stirlings were withdrawn from raids on Berlin after the second operation, when it became clear that the German defences were too much for them, and the Halifaxes were withdrawn from Berlin a few weeks later.

Harris's appetite for Lancasters was never quite slaked. Victory Aircraft – a consortium of Canadian constructors – completed its first aircraft in August 1943. The Canadian Lancaster X was basically similar to the Lancaster III, with the exception of some Americanised equipment. The aircraft were completed externally, except for their gun tur-

rets, and ferried across the Atlantic for finishing and fitting out. Vickers-Armstrongs completed their first Lancaster in October 1943, the company's Castle Bromwich plant producing 25 aircraft a month by the end of 1944, and the Chester works building 36 a month by the end of the war. This volume of production was necessary because by early 1944, the Lancaster had become a semi-expendable aircraft. The ultimate bomber raids, meeting the fiercest opposition ever from the Luftwaffe, cost more than 1,000 aircraft, twice Harris's estimate.

Losses continued to rise despite the use of specialised jammers such as the Airborne Cigar (ABC) system, a Lancaster modified to jam the night-fighter control, and the similarly intended Corona jamming and deception operations launched from ground transmitters in Britain. Undoubtedly the chief reason for the rising losses was the use of passive homing and the improved SN-2 radar by the Luftwaffe, especially as the new equipment was issued to the best pilots first. By February 1944, the Luftwaffe had 200 SN-2 sets in service, and 28 aircraft equipped with Naxos-Z homers. The RAF's losses rose. At the end of January, 43 out of 683 were lost over Berlin; and in mid-February, 78 out of 823 failed to return from Leipzig. The effect of spoof attacks was variable. It was noted at that time that the German night-fighter system was unstable. If the controllers reported enemy aircraft in a certain spot, the ground observers would hear the approaching Junkers and confirm the report of an attack. This led to some "milk runs" where the losses were in single figures, even in the early part of 1944, but the general trend was upwards and the milk runs were more than offset by the nights where the bombers' luck was out. The last and most infamous of these was Nuremberg, when 94 bombers out of a force of 795 were lost. The bombers' over-use of H2S had been crucial in betraying the nature of a spoof raid towards Kassel – the would-be deceivers were not fitted with H2S.

After the defeat of Nuremberg, the bombers were never again sent to face an unbroken German night-fighter force. In any event, they were needed to prepare the ground for the invasion of Europe, an operation which the Bomber Command enthusiasts had hoped to reduce to a formal occupation of a bomb-wrecked enemy. To that extent the bombers had failed, and there will no doubt be controversy for many years as to the exact degree to which they succeeded. But for the time being, apart from being harried by the Light Night Striking Force Mosquitos, Germany's towns and cities had a period of relief.

The more successful raids had, however, pointed the way to new concepts in bomber tactics, based on subtle electronic systems rather than defensive guns and dead reckoning. More effective developments of H2S would eliminate the problems experienced over Berlin. The city was out of range of Oboe marking, often covered in cloud, and was too widespread to present a clear target to the H2S radar screens. Newer systems would offer better definition. With better training, new bomb-sights and new navigational systems and techniques, Bomber Command was on the point of being able to operate as a precision strike force when the main offensive against Germany was suspended.

Destruction with precision

From April 1944 Bomber Command concentrated on targets directly associated with the forthcoming invasion of Northern France. A series of trial attacks on railway marshalling yards in France in March 1944 had provided startling proof of the RAF's ability to attack precision targets at night without inflicting more than a minimum of damage on the surrounding urban areas. Attacks on the transport system were to receive high priority, although they were ordered with little enthusiasm by the Bomber Command staff. Harris still wanted to organise a full-scale bomber offensive against Germany's industry, and the support of the invasion was incredibly regarded as a distraction.

The most remarkable demonstrations of precision bombing by the Lancaster force were carried out by 617

Squadron, the "dambusters" of May 1943. After the dams raid, 617 was withdrawn from the line to recover from its losses, while 5 Group considered a use for them. No love was lost between 5 Group (which had always considered itself an élite) and 8 Group, the newly formed Pathfinders, and this relationship may have played a part in the decision to use 617 Squadron as the élite precision-bombing unit of 5 Group.

Also influential in this decision was the emergence of a new category of German weapon, the surface-to-surface missile, two of which were under development at the research establishment of Peenemunde. Despite the damage caused by Bomber Command in August 1943, production of the Fi103 cruise missile and the ballistic A-4 continued. In late 1943 it also became apparent that these weapons were to be stored and launched from massive concrete-covered bunkers. Bomber Command was by then using 12,000 lb (5,443 kg) bombs, but these were intended to demolish city houses and were little more than light metal cases filled with explosive. On solid concrete, they would simply shatter. Barnes (later Sir Barnes) Wallis of Vickers-Armstrongs had studied the problem of attack on such installations as part of the process which led to the invention of the spinning mine used on the dams raid in May 1943. Until the advent of the new German missiles his designs had remained in a pigeon-hole at the Air Ministry, but late in 1943 they were taken out again.

Bouncing-bomb spinning mechanism

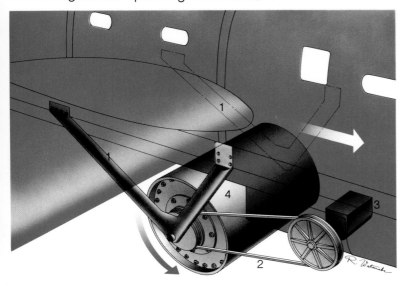

◄ 1 Side arms
2 Driving belt
3 Motor
4 9.250 lb (4,196 kg) bouncing bomb

▼ 1 Lancaster B.III (Special) ED932 "G for George"
of No.617 Squadron, flown by Wg. Cdr. Guy P. Gibson
flies at a height of 60 ft (18 m)
2 Bouncing-bomb launch
3 Converging searchlight beams indicate precise
height for launch
4 Water surface
5 Torpedo nets
6 Net's buoys
7 Dam walls

The attack against Moehne Dam on the night of May 16-17, 1943

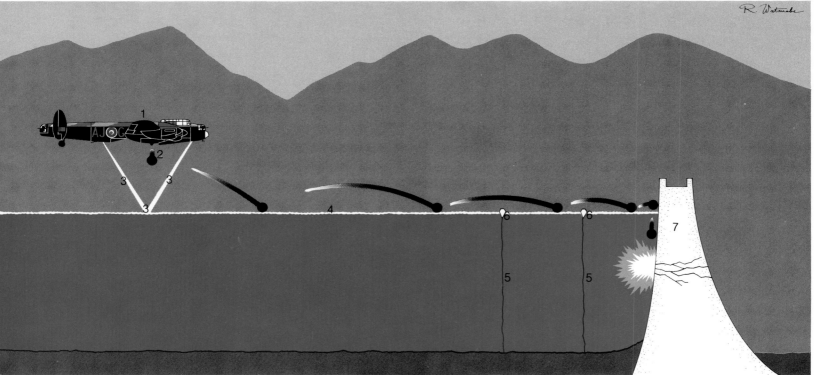

Lancaster B.Mk.I in service with No.617 Squadron carrying a 22,000 lb (9,979 kg) "Grand Slam" bomb. (Imperial War Museum)

Wallis's idea was for a heavy, strongly-cased and very streamlined bomb dropped from as high as possible. With a terminal velocity well above the speed of sound, such a bomb would bury itself very deep underground before exploding, creating underground shock waves which would destroy the heaviest structure. The initial version was Tallboy, a 12,030 lb (5,457 kg) weapon, but the ultimate development of the series was Grand Slam, weighing no less than 22,000 lb (9,979 kg).

Vickers-Armstrongs had started to build Tallboys as a private venture in mid-1943, and it was later in the year before the Air Ministry realised that there would be enough targets to justify the procurement of the "earthquake" bombs. Not only were there shelters for missiles, but there were U-Boat and E-Boat pens on the coast and other, more mysterious installations such as that for the V-3 or HDP (from the German initials of its code-name, High-Pressure Pump), a multi-barrel long-range gun. Go-ahead was given for both weapons, Tallboy development running ahead of that of Grand Slam.

Meanwhile, 617 Squadron had been developing the bomb-aiming skills needed to use such expensive weapons effectively. They were helped by the new Stabilised Automatic Bomb Sight (SABS), invented at Farnborough in 1941. Similar in principle to the American Norden sight, SABS incorporated a telescopic sight in which the aimer acquired the target, having fed in the usual information on ballistics, performance and weather. The sight was mounted on a gyro-stabilised platform, and the SABS automatically generated aiming corrections as the aimer held the sight on the target. The drawback was that the aircraft had to make a 20-second straight-and-level aiming run, which was considered unacceptable unless special tactics could be devised and executed by a highly trained unit such as 617 Squadron. Eventually, 617 Squadron could bomb at night with such accuracy that three-quarters of the weapons launched landed within a 75 yd (68.5 m) radius of the aiming point.

Tallboy was first used in action just after the invasion of June 6, 1944, when the weapons were used to block the railway tunnel through which a Panzer Division was due to pass. They were also used to attack the V-weapon launching sites, until the Luftwaffe's loss of air superiority and the increasing weight of the Allies' Operation Crossbow attacks forced the Germans to switch to mobile launching. One of the most important Tallboy operations, however, was the attack on the battleship *Tirpitz* at its anchorage in Tromso fjord, in the north of Norway.

This was a long-range mission for the Lancaster, even with a reduced bombload. To carry the Tallboys to Tromso, the 617 Squadron Lancasters were equipped with extra fuel tanks in the fuselage, and the mid-upper turrets were removed. All the aircraft were fitted with Merlin 24 engines specially overhauled and modified by Rolls-Royce. *Tirpitz* was a relatively small target, well defended by flak and a nearby fighter station, and she had to be attacked in daylight with sufficient surprise to permit bombing before the extensive smokescreens could be activated. An attack plan was formulated with the aid of electronic intelligence "ferret" aircraft, which found a gap in Norwegian radar defences. The Lancasters crossed the coast at low level, breached the airspace of neutral Sweden and flew north, keeping the mountains of Norway between themselves and the radar chain. Crossing into Norway and climbing at the last moment, the bombers took the defences by surprise and wrecked the *Tirpitz* with three Tallboy hits. One Lancaster was lost. The contrast between the *Tirpitz* attack and the early Bomber Command raids over the Schillig Roads and Wilhelmshaven was indescribable – they were a generation of weapons and a revolution in military electronics apart, but were separated by only five years.

When the first Grand Slams were delivered in February 1945, there were few targets worth attention. Production had been delayed by the difficulties of casting the main casing of the massive 25 ft 6 in (7.77 m) weapon. The casing was cast in one piece around a concrete core in a sand mould, and needed special handling equipment even when empty. The Grand Slam bomb was placed in production in Britain and the United States, but 617 was the only squadron to use it operationally, dropping 41 of the weapons on targets such as U-Boat pens. Those at Farge near Bremen were covered with 23 ft (7 m) of solid reinforced concrete, but two direct Grand Slam hits penetrated and wrecked the roof.

Even the Lancaster had to work hard to carry the "special store", the name first used for the Grand Slam and later for other even more destructive weapons. About 30 Lancasters were modified to B.I (Special) configuration, with the nose and mid-upper turrets removed, reinforcement fitted to the bomb-bay, fuselage and undercarriage, and the bomb doors replaced by a fairing into which the Grand Slam was partly recessed. Without the Lancaster, the weapon would have been unusable, but the B.I (Special) could carry the bomb to 20,000 ft (6,100 m) for maximum penetration effect.

For Bomber Command in general, however, the time after the invasion was an opportunity to resume the campaign of bombing against German cities. In July 1944 Harris proposed Operation Thunderclap, aimed directly at the lives and morale of the German population – although it was disapproved in form, Bomber Command largely adhered to it in substance. Only a quarter of the Command's effort was directed against energy supplies, despite the devastating effect this was having on the German war machine and the fact that new navigational devices finally had made such precision attacks possible at night. Bomber Command now threw the bulk of its strength – more than 1,000 Lancasters, over 300 Halifaxes and 200 Mosquitos were available – against Germany's cities, in the Ruhr and elsewhere. Bomber Command's accuracy had improved and its losses plummeted, and the German population was to suffer for it.

Losses were falling largely because of the invasion. The Luftwaffe's early-warning line was being pushed backwards, and the forward bases which the night-fighters could use as they harried the bombers across Western Europe were in Allied hands. By day, even bases well behind the lines were attacked by the Tactical Air Forces, and the aircraft factories were under pressure to build day fighters to protect the troops. The USAAF was back in the daylight skies, with hordes of Mustang and Thunderbolt escorts, destroying the Luftwaffe in the skies and the factories, and wrecking its fuel supplies.

The survival chances of Bomber Command crews were given another boost on July 13, 1944, when a Luftwaffe night-fighter crew committed the classic navigational mistake of taking a reciprocal direction-finding reading and landing their Ju 88G-1 at Woodbridge in Suffolk. Bomber Command realised for the first time the extent to which Monica, the "security-blanket" of the useless J-switch and the excessive use of H2S had been telegraphing the positions of individual bombers over hundreds of miles. Monica was removed and the use of IFF and H2S restricted. Against the weakened German night-fighter force, bombers became safer places. In January 1944 Bomber Command had lost 314 aircraft in 6,278 sorties; by September, when the campaign against German cities was resumed, this fell to 96 losses for 6,428 sorties; and in the following month Bomber Command flew 10,193 missions and lost only 75 aircraft, less than one per cent of the raiders. As losses fell, the numbers and experience of the raiders began to mount.

The Lancaster was also being equipped with a new series of navigation and bomb-aiming devices. Oboe's range had been extended by the invasion, as transmitters were moved further forward, and a new and more accurate version operating on shorter wavelengths was coming into use. More important was a new device known as Gee-H, combining the universal applicability of Gee with near-Oboe levels of accuracy, using a transmitter-receiver in the aircraft to measure distance from ground beacons. Gee-H was introduced by Lancasters of 3 Group in October 1944. Almost simultaneously the K-band H2S Mk VI was introduced, alleviating some of the system's limitations over poorly defined or disguised targets. H2S had been standard equipment on the Lancaster since March 1944.

Bomber Command coupled these new devices with revised tactics. Navigation was now so accurate that decoy fires and spoof raids could be used within a few miles of the actual route. The navigators and bomb-aimers were now

Lancaster B.Mk.I (HK 541) fitted with 1,200 Imp (5,455 ltr) saddle-tank at the Aircraft & Armament Experimental Establishment, Boscombe Down, in the latter half of 1944.   (Imperial War Museum)

Lancaster B.Mk.I Specification

Power plant

Four Rolls-Royce Merlin XX or 22 12-cylinder 60° Vee-type
liquid cooled, two-speed supercharged engines.
: 1,460 hp each at 6,250 ft (1,905 m) in 'M' gear
: 1,435 hp each at 11,000 ft (3,350 m) in 'S' gear.
De Havilland type No.5140 or Nash Kelvinator type
No.A5/138 variable pitch, hydromatic constant speed
and feathering three-bladed propellers.
Diameter
: 12 ft 0 in (3.66 m)
Total fuel in six main tanks (three in each wing)
: 2,154 Imp gal (9,792 ltr)
Provision for one or two overload tanks in bomb-bay
: 400 Imp gal (1,818 ltr) each.

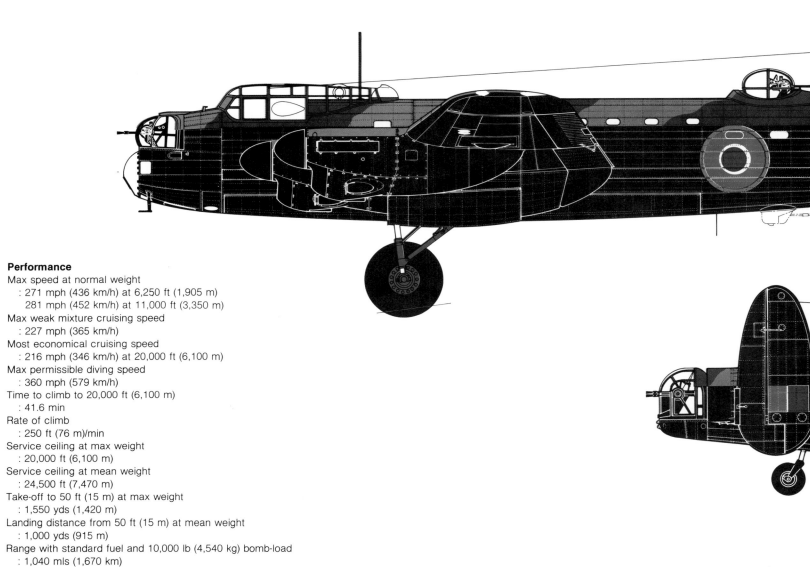

Performance

Max speed at normal weight
: 271 mph (436 km/h) at 6,250 ft (1,905 m)
281 mph (452 km/h) at 11,000 ft (3,350 m)
Max weak mixture cruising speed
: 227 mph (365 km/h)
Most economical cruising speed
: 216 mph (346 km/h) at 20,000 ft (6,100 m)
Max permissible diving speed
: 360 mph (579 km/h)
Time to climb to 20,000 ft (6,100 m)
: 41.6 min
Rate of climb
: 250 ft (76 m)/min
Service ceiling at max weight
: 20,000 ft (6,100 m)
Service ceiling at mean weight
: 24,500 ft (7,470 m)
Take-off to 50 ft (15 m) at max weight
: 1,550 yds (1,420 m)
Landing distance from 50 ft (15 m) at mean weight
: 1,000 yds (915 m)
Range with standard fuel and 10,000 lb (4,540 kg) bomb-load
: 1,040 mls (1,670 km)
Range with one auxiliary fuel tank and 7,000 lb (3,180 kg) bombs
: 2,680 mls (4,310 km)

Weights

Tare
: 36,900 lb (16,740 kg)
Empty equipped
: 41,000 lb (18,600 kg)
Mean weight
: 55,000 lb (24,950 kg)
Normal gross
: 68,000 lb (30,840 kg)
Max take-off
: 72,000 lb (32,660 kg)

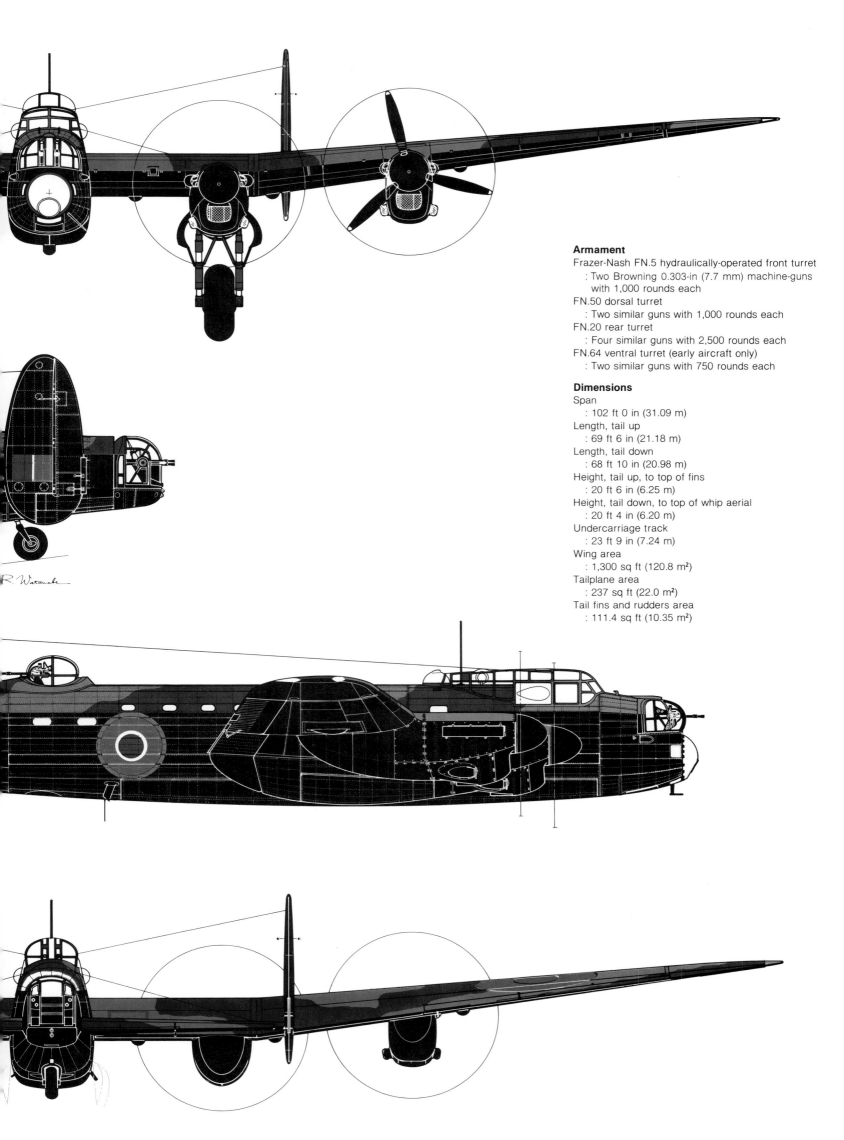

Armament
Frazer-Nash FN.5 hydraulically-operated front turret
 : Two Browning 0.303-in (7.7 mm) machine-guns
   with 1,000 rounds each
FN.50 dorsal turret
 : Two similar guns with 1,000 rounds each
FN.20 rear turret
 : Four similar guns with 2,500 rounds each
FN.64 ventral turret (early aircraft only)
 : Two similar guns with 750 rounds each

Dimensions
Span
 : 102 ft 0 in (31.09 m)
Length, tail up
 : 69 ft 6 in (21.18 m)
Length, tail down
 : 68 ft 10 in (20.98 m)
Height, tail up, to top of fins
 : 20 ft 6 in (6.25 m)
Height, tail down, to top of whip aerial
 : 20 ft 4 in (6.20 m)
Undercarriage track
 : 23 ft 9 in (7.24 m)
Wing area
 : 1,300 sq ft (120.8 m²)
Tailplane area
 : 237 sq ft (22.0 m²)
Tail fins and rudders area
 : 111.4 sq ft (10.35 m²)

Bombs

: Fourteen 1,000 lb (454 kg)—14,000 lb (6,350 kg) in all
: One 4,000 lb (1,814 kg) and six 1,500 lb (680 kg) mines— 13,000 lb (5,897 kg) in all
: six 2,000 lb (907 kg) and three 250 lb (113 kg)— 12,750 lb (5,783 kg) in all
: One 12,000 lb (5,443 kg)
: One 8,000 lb (3,623 kg) and six 500 lb (227 kg)— 11,000 lb (4,990 kg) in all
: One 4,000 lb (1,814 kg), six 1,000 lb (454 kg) and two 250 lb (113 kg)—10,500 lb (4,763 kg) in all

Accommodation
Standard crew of seven comprising pilot, flight engineer
or second pilot, navigator, bomb-aimer/front turret
gunner, wireless operator, dorsal turret gunner and rear
turret gunner.

sufficiently skilled to use an offset aiming point chosen for its visibility, and to aim their bombs at a given range and bearing from that point. The raid could also be controlled by a Master Bomber, circling the target and directing the hail of fire and explosive on areas which had escaped earlier waves of the attack. Dresden was just one of the cities levelled in an effort to hasten the end of the war. The technology of destruction by conventional weaponry had reached its peak.

The use of atomic weapons to end the war in Japan abruptly terminated RAF plans to take part in the anticipated conventional bombing and invasion. Under the code-name Tiger Force, a number of options had been considered to enable the RAF to match the range of US aircraft. The conversion of 600 Lancasters to tanker-receivers was planned for mid-1944, but following the successful 617 Squadron raid on the *Tirpitz* it was decided that a standard Lancaster could carry a useful bombload over the necessary range. Also tested, but abandoned, was a Lancaster version with a huge dorsal saddle-tank carrying 1,200 Imp gal (5,455 lit) of fuel, increasing capacity by 50 per cent. The handling of the version was unacceptable and only two saddle-tank conversions were made. Instead, the Lancaster B.I (F.E.) and B.VII (F.E.) were produced by conversions at maintenance units in the first half of 1945. With Merlin 24 engines, no mid-upper turrets and some other equipment removed, but retaining H2S Mk III bombing radars, the aircraft were expected to carry a 10,750 lb (4,877 kg) bombload to Japan from Okinawa. Also included in Tiger Force were the B.I (Special) aircraft of 617 Squadron, intended to use Grand Slam on the bridges connecting Kyushu, where the US forces intended to invade, to the main island of Honshu. Another special version of the Lancaster was the ASR.III, converted by Cunliffe-Owen to carry an airborne lifeboat under the fuselage. Intended to support the raids on Japan, these aircraft became the first Coastal Command Lancasters after Tiger Force was officially disbanded at the end of October 1945.

The Lancaster dropped its last bomb in anger on April 25, 1945, during an operation against submarine fuel stores. After the surrender of Germany, Bomber Command took part in operations to repatriate prisoners and bring the 8th Army back from the Middle East, and dropped supplies to refugees in the wreck they had done so much to create.

Lancaster production stopped in February 1946, and the much smaller post-war Bomber Command re-equipped rapidly with Lincolns. By the end of 1946 the mass scrapping of Lancasters had started in earnest, although the type remained in Bomber Command service, with two squadrons in Malta and a specialised survey unit, until 1954. Coastal Command used the Lancaster for a rather longer period. The ASR.IIIs surplus to requirements after the dismantling of Tiger Force, along with other converted Mk III Lancasters, went to replace Coastal Command's Liberators, which had been returned to the USA under Lend-Lease at the end of the war. In 1949 they were updated to GR.III standard by the installation of air-to-surface-vessel (ASV) radar equipment. These remained in service with Coastal Command, finally as trainers, until October 1956. The last Lancaster on RAF strength was a single aircraft leased to Handley

Page until the early 1960s to test laminar-flow wing sections. It reverted to the RAF in the mid-1960s and is now the pride of the service's Historic Aircraft Flight.

The Royal Canadian Air Force continued to operate Lancasters for maritime-reconnaissance long after the war, the last Lancaster 10-MR being retired from a special squadron in 1964. Some were then sold as water-bombers for fighting forest fires, and one survivor was ferried back to a private collection in Britain in the late 1970s. Another large post-war Lancaster operator was the French Aéronavale, which used a batch of 54 B.Is and B.VIIs for maritime-reconnaissance from 1952 until they were replaced by P2V-7 Neptunes in the late 1950s. Fifteen Lancasters were delivered from RAF surplus stocks to the Argentine, and in mid-1966 one bomber was reported as still operational.

Most mysterious of all Lancaster operations, however, involved the unmarked aircraft sighted by an RAF Mosquito pilot off the French coast during the Berlin crisis of 1948–49. It was believed at the time that the Soviet Air Force might have retained a few Lancasters which, for one reason or another, had force-landed in Soviet-held territory, and was using them to probe radar defences.

Although the Lancaster's post-war career was to be small beer compared to its wartime achievements, it was to be followed by a long line of descendants. In 1945, as the last Lancasters started their journey down the assembly line, their career was only just beginning.

Derivatives and developments

The first-born of the Lancaster's long progeny was actually developed in parallel with the bomber – the Avro 685 York. The prototype York was produced in less than six months from the start of design work and first flew in July 1942, but at that time production was not approved because it would have reduced the industrial capacity available for Lancasters.

The York was a straightforward transport adaptation of the Lancaster, with the same wing, powerplant, tail unit and undercarriage married to a square-section transport fuselage slung beneath the wing. A central tailfin was added to the tail unit after flight trials, offsetting the effects of the larger front fuselage. A few Yorks were produced during the war years, but large-scale production did not begin until 1945. Production eventually totalled 256 aircraft, the last being delivered in April 1948. In the absence of any competitive British airliners, Yorks were used for passenger services in the Middle East and Africa by the British Overseas Airways Corporation. Later, BOAC relegated the type to freighting duties, finally disposing of its last Yorks in 1957. The aircraft nevertheless remained in use with independent airlines, often on trooping contracts, until the early 1960s. Most of the Yorks were built for RAF Transport Command, and many of these were sold to civil operators in various parts of the world.

An even more basic adaptation of the Lancaster was the Lancastrian. This was developed from the modified Lancaster IIIs used by Trans-Canada Airlines to operate a

Avro York (MW 295) at an RAF airbase in the Far East in the early '50s.

high-priority transatlantic passenger/freight service from July 1943. With all defensive armament and armour removed, the eight modified aircraft had a range of 4,150 miles (6,680 km). With the easing of pressure on Lancaster production in 1945, new airframes could be delivered to the same standard, for use as Lancastrians. BOAC operated 20 of the type on North Atlantic services and on a high-speed Kangaroo service to Sydney.

The Lancastrian's career was prolonged by the failure of its cousin the Tudor, and by British economic policy which restricted the import of better airliners from the United States. With only nine passenger seats (13 in later versions) in the cramped, unpressurised rear fuselage, the Lancastrian was scarcely a practical airliner, and in the absence of political pressure on BOAC and British South American Airways (BSAA) to buy British it is unlikely that it would ever have been produced in quantity. Some Lancastrians were deli-

vered to Alitalia, Silver City Airways and Skyways, and some were used as tankers to carry fuel into Berlin during the Soviet blockade of 1948–49, but the last of them was retired in 1951.

The mainstream of Lancaster development had, however, taken a different course when production of the Lancastrian and York got under way. The decision to proceed with design and development of an improved, higher-flying Lancaster version using the then new two-stage-supercharged Rolls-Royce Merlin was taken in 1943, and prototypes of the Lancaster IV were ordered to Specification B.14/43.

To take advantage of the greater high-altitude output of the new engines, Roy Chadwick's team designed a new wing of greater span and area for the new Lancaster. To compensate for the greater weight and length of the new engines, and to restore stability and control with the larger

A civil transport Lancaster, operated by Trans-Canada Airlines, arrives at Prestwick after a transatlantic flight.

wing, the rear fuselage was slightly extended. The nose was redesigned to incorporate a more streamlined turret and an improved bomb-aiming position. The engines were installed in new-type "power eggs" with semi-annular radiators. The Lancaster IV was to have British-built Merlin 85 engines, and the Lancaster V was to be fitted with the equivalent Packard-built Merlin 66 or 68. In 1944 they were renamed Lincoln B.1 and B.2 respectively.

Development and production of the Lincoln took second place to increasing the output of Lancasters until late 1944, when it was planned to accelerate the production of the Lincoln so that the heavier, longer-range bomber would be available in time to form the backbone of the Tiger Force for bombing Japan. It was planned to wind down Lancaster production from November 1944, and to have more than 2,200 Lincolns completed by mid-1946.

The first Lincoln B.1 flew in June 1944, the second following in November. Development was not altogether smooth, the Merlin 85s giving trouble and the aircraft being plagued with vibration problems until four-blade propellers were fitted. Only about 50 aircraft had been flown by May 1945. With the end of the war, Lincoln production contracts were cut back sharply, the type being regarded as a stop-gap pending availability of the jet bombers ordered in 1945. Avro, Metropolitan-Vickers and Armstrong Whitworth participated in British production, but planned manufacture in Canada was terminated when the first Lincoln XV had been completed but not flown.

June 1945 saw the delivery of the first Lincoln B.2, and the Packard engines were found to be more reliable than the powerplants of the B.1. The later version was also better armed than the B.1, with twin 0.5-in (12.7 mm) machine-guns in the nose and tail and a dorsal Bristol B.17 turret, an electrically powered unit mounting a pair of 20 mm (0.79 in) Hispano cannon. It was decided in November that the B.1 would

be used only for training and conversion, and most of the 82 production B.1s were scrapped without seeing service.

The first unit to take delivery of operational Lincolns in February 1946 was 44 Squadron, which had been the first recipient of the Lancaster just over four years earlier. Replacement of the Lancaster got under way in 1947, and a total of 447 Lincoln B.2s were built before production ended in 1948. Later some Lincolns were modified, with Mk 4A H2S equipment replacing the older Mk 3G, and the defensive armament was progressively reduced, most aircraft ending their careers with neither nose nor dorsal armament. The latter, with its twin cannon, was regarded as operationally effective, but its 1,500 lb (680 kg) weight and the complexity of its electrical drive and ammunition feed were drawbacks. Some Lincolns were fitted with bulged bomb doors to accommodate a Tallboy penetration bomb, and the type was tested with Grand Slam.

From the RAF's point of view, the Lincoln's most serious drawback was that its speed and altitude were not high enough to escape safely from the blast of a nuclear weapon, and in mid-1950 one Lincoln squadron converted to Boeing Washington B.1s acquired second-hand from the US Air Force. Other Lincoln squadrons started to convert to Canberras in the following year, and the type was ultimately replaced by the Vickers Valiant in 1955.

Between 1950 and 1955 the Lincoln was used for anti-terrorist operatons in Malaya and Kenya, and during and after the type's employment with Bomber Command the Lincoln was extensively used for second-line roles. Two were employed for the development of electronic equipment such as Green Cheese, a pioneering side-looking airborne radar. Others were used for probing Soviet radar defences, one aircraft being shot down over Germany by Soviet MiG-15s in March 1953 after it strayed across the Eastern zone. Two Lincolns were stripped down, fitted with high-altitude-rated

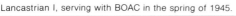 Lancastrian I, serving with BOAC in the spring of 1945. (Imperial War Museum)

Lincoln B.I fitted with H2S radome under the rear fuselage.

Merlin 113s and used by the Royal Aircraft Establishment for drop tests of nuclear stores. A quite bewildering number of engines were tested in Lincolns. Suffice it to say that the Lincoln and Lancaster between them tested nearly every large jet or turboprop engine built in Britain in the 1940s and 1950s.

A few Lincolns were used for RAF policing duties in Aden in 1956–57, but after that the type was confined to second-line roles, the last aircraft remaining in service for electronic-countermeasures training until 1963. The Argentine was the only export customer for the Lincoln, acquiring 30 of the type – 12 were B.1s which had escaped the acetylene torch, while the remainder were new B.2s built by Armstrong Whitworth, and all were stripped of H2S and other equipment. Some were still in service as transports in the Argentine's sector of the Antarctic in the mid-1960s. Two more British-built Lincolns were converted to freighter configuration in 1957, being intended for a meat transport company in Peru, but they were never delivered or even flown before being scrapped in 1959.

Unlike Canada, Australia persisted with production plans for the Lincoln. It had been decided early in 1944 to abandon plans for Australian production of the Lancaster III in favour of the newer aircraft. The first Lincoln B.30 flew from the Government Aircraft Factories facility at Fisherman's Bend in March 1946. Later aircraft were fitted with Merlin 102s built by the Commonwealth Aircraft Company, and the last few were completed as MR.31 maritime-reconnaissance aircraft. These had the nose-gun turret removed, and to compensate for the change in centre of gravity the nose was extended by 78 in (198 cm) forward of the cockpit. Fitted with ASV Mk 7 radar, developed from H2S, the MR.31 stayed in production until 1953, the rate of production having been kept low in order to keep Australia's aircraft industry in being. The Mk 30 bombers saw some action in Malaya in 1956–58, and many were converted to MR.31 standard. The last Australian Lincolns were the MR.31s, which were replaced by Lockheed Neptunes in mid-1961.

Developed in parallel with the Lincoln, as the York had been developed alongside the Lancaster, the Avro Tudor was far less successful. Planned as a British answer to the contemporary American four-engined airliners, the Tudor combined the wing, engines and landing gear of the Lincoln with a circular-section pressurised fuselage and a new tail unit. Basically smaller and less powerful than the contemporary Constellation and DC-6 – which had been developed while the British industry unavoidably concentrated on military aircraft – the Tudor flew in June 1945. The transatlantic Tudor 1 was finally rejected by BOAC in April 1947 after a long series of modifications, and the corporation ordered bigger American aircraft instead. The aircraft on the production line were modified into Tudor 4s, for British South American Airways, but airworthiness approval was withdrawn after two of the type vanished over the Caribbean.

The other main Tudor version was designed for operations over shorter stage lengths of the BOAC Eastern route system. This, the Tudor 2, had a greatly lengthened and wider fuselage with seats for 60 passengers. By 1945 no fewer than 79 Tudor 2s were on order for BOAC, Qantas and South African Airways, but the aircraft proved overweight and underpowered after it flew in March 1946. Production orders had been cancelled by the time the prototype crashed in August 1947. Tragically, chief designer Roy Chadwick was among the dead. A few of the Tudor 4s were re-certificated and used for freight services in the 1950s, but the long-fuselage Tudor was never used in scheduled service.

The ultimate descendant of the Lancaster was designed to meet a Coastal Command requirement for a successor to the Lancaster GR.III. Originally designated Lincoln ASR.III, the new aircraft underwent extensive redesign to suit the maritime-reconnaissance role. The Merlins gave way to the more powerful Griffons, driving six-blade contra-rotating airscrews, while the existing wing was married to a slightly shorter, fatter fuselage to provide more room for radar equipment and better working conditions, and the tail was redesigned.

Manchester I

Power units
2 × Rolls-Royce Vulture II engines
: 1,845 hp each at 5,000 ft (1,520 m)

Performance
Max speed at normal weight
: 264 mph (425 km/h at 17,000 ft (5,180 m)
Cruising speed at overload weight
: 205 mph (330 km/h) at 15,000 ft (4,570 m)
Service ceiling at mean weight
: 19,300 ft (5,880 m)

Weights
Tare
: 29,432 lb (13,350 kg)
Overload take-off
: 50,000 lb (22,680 kg)

Dimensions
Span
: 90 ft 1 in (27.46 m)
Length (tail up)
: 68 ft 10 in (20.98 m)
Height
: 19 ft 6 in (5.94 m)
Wing area
: 1,131 sq ft (105.1 m²)

Armament
8 × 0.303-in (7.7 mm) machine-guns
2 × 1,900 lb (862 kg), 2 × 1,000 lb
(454 kg) and 3 × 250 lb (113 kg)
bombs

Crew
7

Lancaster B.Mk.I

Power units
4 × Rolls-Royce Merlin XX or 22 engines
: 1,460 hp each at 6,250 ft (1,905 m)

Performance
Max speed at normal weight
: 271 mph (436 km/h) at 6,250 ft (1,905 m)
Most economical cruising speed
: 216 mph (348 km/h) at 20,000 ft (6,100 m)
Service ceiling at mean weight
: 24,500 ft (7,470 m)

Weights
Tare
: 36,900 lb (16,740 kg)
Max take-off
: 72,000 lb (32,660 kg)

Dimensions
Span
: 102 ft 0 in (31.09 m)
Length (tail up)
: 69 ft 6 in (21.18 m)
Height (tail up)
: 20 ft 6 in (6.25 m)
Wing area
: 1,300 sq ft (120.8 m²)

Armament
8 (early aircraft: 10) × 0.303-in (7.7
mm) machine-guns
14 × 1,000 lb (454 kg) bombs

Crew
7

Lincoln B.2

Power units
4 × Packard-built Marlin 68A engines
: 1,750 hp each at 5,500 ft (1,680 m)

Performance
Max speed at full load
: 305 mph (491 km/h) at 19,000 ft (5,790 m)
Cruising speed at mean weight
: 244 mph (393 km/h) at 22,500 ft (6,860 m)

Weights
Tare
: 44,188 lb (20,044 kg)
Max take-off
: 82,000 lb (37,200 kg)

Dimensions
Span
: 120 ft 0 in (36.58 m)
Length
: 78 ft 3 in (23.85 m)
Height (tail up)
: 20 ft 6 in (6.25 m)
Wing area
: 1,421 sq ft (132.0 m²)

Armament
2 × 20 mm cannon and 4 × 0.5-in
(12.7 mm) machine-guns
Bombs: Same as Lancaster

Crew
7

Shackleton MR.3

Power units
4 × Rolls-Royce Griffon 57A12 engines
: 2,450 hp each

Performance
Max speed at 85,000 lb (38,560 kg)
: 302 mph (486 km/h) at 12,000 ft (3,660 m)
Long range cruising speed
: 200 mph (322 km/h) at 1,500 ft (460 m)
Service ceiling
: 19,200 ft (5,850 m)

Weights
Tare
57,800 lb (26,220 kg)
Loaded
: 100,000 lb, approx. (45,360 kg)

Dimensions
Span
: 119 ft 10 in (36.53 m)
Length
: 92 ft 9 in (28.27 m)
Height
: 23 ft 4 in (7.11 m)
Wing area
:1,421 sq ft (132.0 m²)

Crew
11

Flown in March 1949, the new aircraft was renamed Shackleton MR.1. Seventy-seven MR.1s were followed, starting in 1952, by a batch of 69 MR.2s with improved operational equipment including a new radar with a retractable ventral scanner. The definitive development of the Shackleton was the MR.3 with a nosewheel undercarriage, further improved electronics and a modified wing. A proposed Shackleton MR.4 development with Napier Nomad compound diesel engines was not proceeded with, and production ended in 1960. From 1960 the Shackletons were brought up to MR.3 Phase 3 standards with auxiliary Viper jet engines in the outboard nacelles. These aircraft served until replaced by Nimrods in the early 1970s.

The line was not quite ended even with the Shackleton. The basic wing structure of the Lincoln was used in the Argosy freighter, with its twin tailbooms and four Dart turboprops. The commercial success expected for the Argosy failed to materialise, because its appearance in 1959 coincided with an influx of cheap DC-6s, DC-7s and Constellations on to the freight market as the big airlines bought jets. Fifty-six Argosy C.1s were acquired by the RAF, whose pilots christ-ened the aircraft "the whistling wheelbarrow". Production ended in 1964, and the Argosys were retired from transport duties following a mid-1970s review of defence costs.

At the time of writing, a few Shackleton MR.3s remain in service with the South African Air Force, but they are not the sole survivors outside the museums of the line which started with specification P.13/36 nearly half a century ago. In the late 1960s, faced with the emerging threat of low-level Soviet strike aircraft with the range to reach Britain from East Germany or the northern USSR, the RAF decided to improvise an airborne early warning system to replace carrier-borne aircraft which Britain's abandonment of carriers had left without a base. The American-built APS-20F radars from the carrier-based Gannet aircraft were transplanted into stored Shackleton MR.2 airframes. The converted aircraft, the Shackleton AEW.2, entered service in 1972, and the somewhat primitive radar equipment has been slightly updated since then. The Shackletons are due to be replaced by the incomparably more advanced Nimrod AEW.3 in mid-1982. Until then, the last of the Lancaster line is as vital as ever to the defence of Britain.

Lancasters returning from a bombing mission.

(Imperial War Museum)

MESSERSCHMITT
Bf 109

Text by
ROBERT GRINSELL

Acknowledgements

The information contained in this book has been researched from official records, photographs, correspondence and personal contacts, but due to the span of years since the Bf 109 first took flight and the fact that several company and personal files on the Bf 109 have been destroyed, a number of assumptions and conclusions had to be made, not only by this author, but by numerous others. My conclusions are, however, not without substance, being based on the information and recall of a number of individuals and organizations whose World War II relation to the Bf 109 was one of everyday dependence.

It is to these individuals and organizations who have provided the foundation for this book, that I wish to extend my gratitude for their cooperation, trust, and friendship which have made this effort possible.

Gerhard Barkhorn	Messerschmitt-Boelkow-Blohm, G.m.b.H.
Wilhelm Batz	Guenther Rall
Adolf Galland	Royal Air Force
Gemeinschaft der Jagdflieger	Johannes Steinhoff
Erich Hartmann	United States Air Force
Dietrich Hrabak	Office of Information
Hajo Herrmann	West German Air Force
Herbert Kaiser	West German Bundesarchiv/Koblenz
Hans-Joachim Kroschinski	Walter Wolfrum

(BUNDESARCHIV)

Introduction

The Bf 109 provides history with an interesting paradox. An unwanted fighter during its early development—due to unwarranted political influence and the high risk associated with its innovative and advanced design—it was to become the standard by which all other fighters of the World War II era would be judged.

Serving the Luftwaffe in almost every capacity including interceptor, fighter-bomber, night-fighter, photo-reconnaissance, escort fighter, and ground attack, the basic Bf 109 airframe survived the duration of the European conflict as the mainstay of the German air force, being produced in a greater number than any other plane (over 30,000 were delivered) past or present. The Bf 109 was also produced in more variants than any other aircraft of its era, with over eleven variants of the G version alone.

Although the Bf 109 had a number of inherent drawbacks that at times detracted from its adaptability to its multi-mission role, with a capable pilot at its controls it was normally more than a match for any of its counterparts. Its effectiveness is attested to by the fact that from its initial flight trials in 1935 until it was finally phased out of service with the Spanish Air Force in 1967, the basic Bf 109s career spanned over 30 years with various countries around the world.

Background

In 1940, some five years after its first introduction, the now famous Bf 109 remained superior to any fighter aircraft of the time. In 1945, with the ending of hostilities in Europe, the Bf 109 was still considered to be a more than formidable enemy in the hands of a competent pilot. The introduction of what was to become the standard dayfighter for the Luftwaffe, however, was anything but ordinary. It was, in fact, the result of a number of daring and unconventional business tactics and several fortunate twists of fate that eventually provided the Bf 109 with the opportunity it deserved to prove itself the capable and respected fighter it was to become.

One of the primary reasons for the success of the Bf 109 lay in the factors that influenced its advanced structural design and unique aerodynamic features. Although the concepts were radical for their time, the majority of them were not new, having been tried and tested on several earlier aircraft from various manufacturers around the world. It was, however, in the Bf 109 that all the concepts and aero-technological advances were married into a single aircraft. The risk of this approach was evident, but the relationship of the *Bayerische Flugzeugwerke* (Bavarian Aircraft Works) to the German government, left the company with no other alternative in the competition for a new Luftwaffe fighter.

The poor standing of the *Bayerische Flugzeugwerke* (BFW) and the *Luftwaffenfuehrungsstab* (Operations Staff) had its origin in 1929 and involved a disagreement between Dr. Willy Messerschmitt and Erhard Milch, the Director of *Lufthansa* Procurement. Messerschmitt had established his own aircraft manufacturing company, *Messerschmitt Flug-zeughbau G.m.b.H.*, in March, 1926 and, based on early successes, had been provided a subsidy from the Bavarian State Government. However, the government was also financially obligated to BFW, also formed in 1926 under the sponsorship of the Bavarian State Government, German Defense Ministry and a banking firm. It became apparent in 1927 that the Bavarian Government could not support both aircraft firms, and pressure was brought to bear on Messerschmitt to merge his company with BFW. On 8 September 1927, an agreement was signed which assigned total design and development responsibility for new aircraft to the Messerschmitt team and production responsibility to the BFW firm.

The initial aircraft to be designed and produced under this new arrangement was a 10-seat passenger plane designated M-20.

Numerous problems plagued the development schedule of the aircraft and after the first prototype crashed during flight trials in February, 1928, *Lufthansa,* represented by Erhard Milch, cancelled the order. A second prototype was quickly produced and after a successful flight test, the order was reinstated by *Lufthansa*. A year later, however, the order for 10 of the M-20s was again cancelled and *Lufthansa* requested its downpayment returned. The BFW, having utilized one portion of this funding to place long lead material and component orders, and still another portion to finance in-house development of more advanced aircraft, was unable to meet the repayment demands and filed bankruptcy on 1 June, 1931.

The heated exchanges between Messerschmitt and Milch during this period resulted in an irreversible hatred between the two men that was to last through future years and have a definite influence on the success of BFW and on the design of the Bf 109.

Under Messerschmitt's direction, the BFW was re-formed and reorganized; however, the bitterness that existed between Messerschmitt and Milch, who had risen to the position of Secretary of State of Aviation under Adolf Hitler, continued to restrict growth and progress of the firm. Milch was adamant in his objective of restricting the BFW's role in support of the new government's aircraft program to strictly a licensed, second-source producer of other German aircraft manufacturer's designs.

Due to the lack of German government support, either for commercial or military aircraft projects, Messerschmitt decided to chance the punishment of the Hitler regime and to solicit business outside of Germany in an effort to maintain his small design and manufacturing team. The company was successful in obtaining a pair of contracts from Rumania which placed orders for a commercial transport and a single-seat trainer under the designations M-36 and M-37.

It took Milch only a few days to publicly denounce Messerschmitt and the BFW for their support of a foreign government's (and possible future enemy's) aircraft industry. The Gestapo made a number of visits to Augsburg to discuss the matter with Messerschmitt and other officials of the *Bayerische Flugzeugwerke*. However, the young Messerschmitt held his ground and reiterated the fact that the only means of monetary support for his fledgling firm must come from foreign countries due to the prevailing attitudes of Milch and other members of the *Reichsluftministerium* (RLM).

No further actions were taken against Messerschmitt or the BFW, most likely due to the close relationship of Hermann Goering, Minister of Aviation, and Theo Croneiss, whom Goering had personally asked to join Messerschmitt in 1933 to assist in reorganizing and rebuilding the reformed BFW.

A fortunate turn of events for the BFW finally occurred in late 1933 when the Luftwaffe decided that the 4th *Challenge de Tourisme Internationale,* taking place in 1934, would provide the new German government with an opportunity to display its advanced aviation technology. The *Bayerische Flugzeugwerke* was, along with other German aircraft producers, requested to design and develop a competition sports plane for the races. BFW had, in fact, developed an aircraft for the 1932 *Challenge de Tourisme Internationale* under the designation M-29. However, the first of the four to be built crashed on 8 August. The following day, a second plane lost power in flight and although the pilot was able to bail out, the flight mechanic was killed in the ensuing crash, and the M-29 was grounded and prohibited from participating in the races.

Due to the limited time available and the advanced state of design progress made on the Rumanian-ordered M-37 trainer, Messerschmitt decided to base the new sports plane on the M-37 airframe. By October, 1933, the BFW was machining metal for the redesignated Bf 108. The aircraft was a two-seater with side-by-side controls, and incorporated a highly advanced monoplane construction with a flush-riveted stressed outer skin. Powered by a 250 hp Hirth HM-8U in-line V-8 or a 218 hp Argus AS-17, the Bf 108A attained airspeeds in excess of 320 km/h (200 mph) and was extremely maneuverable. The small wing of the Bf 108 was fitted with both leading and trailing edge slots for maximum lift and was constructed around a single-spar concept patented by Messerschmitt.

The initial Bf 108A was flown in February, 1934, at the BFW airfield near Augsburg, and the results of the trials exceeded even the most optimistic performance projections of the BFW staff. The next five aircraft rolled off the assembly lines at Augsburg between February and June and were accepted by the Luftwaffe for competition flying by a team of expert military pilots headed by Theo Osterkamp. Although minor problems with the aircraft appeared between May and June, no major setbacks were incurred and the flight testing proceeded without any substantial delays.

Then, on 27 July 1934, the bad luck which had been a constant nemesis to Messerschmitt, appeared again. The first prototype, coded D-LBUM, crashed and killed the pilot, a member of the Ministry of Aviation. In an effort to ensure that the Bf 108 would not be grounded as had the 1932 M-20, Messerschmitt and the design staff at the BFW worked feverishly to incorporate modifications into the remaining five aircraft to preclude reoccurrence of the mishap. The plane was finally certified before the end of July and cleared to race.

The Bf 108 performed admirably, but finished behind a pair of Polish RWD-9s (RWD-6s had won the rally in 1932) and a German Fieseler Fi 97. Proving itself the fastest of the aircraft entered, however, the Bf 108 had laid the groundwork for the entry of the BFW into the Luftwaffe's pending new fighter competition and had justified the firm's belief in the new construction techniques and advanced technological concepts employed in its design.

The initial specifications for a new Luftwaffe fighter were formulated and issued in early 1934 to Focke-Wulf, Arado and Heinkel. However, due to the influence of Erhard Milch, no request was forwarded to the BFW. The new fighter was the result of studies conducted by the *C-Amt* (Technical Office) of the German Air Ministry and required a low-wing monoplane configuration with a minimum armament of a pair of 7.9-mm MG 17 machine-guns and performance characteristics that emphasized structural integrity during a powered dive, spin recovery controls, and provisions for being fitted with a high performance liquid-cooled inverted V-12 cylinder powerplant. (Two companies, Junkers and Daimler-Benz, were actively engaged in the development of this powerplant at the time of the specification release by *C-Amt*).

A combination of events including the friendship of Goering and Croneiss, the respect of several Luftwaffe officers familiar with the Bf 108A and uninvolved in the Messerschmitt/Milch feud, and the workloads of the other aircraft firms, finally resulted in the issuance of a development contract to BFW in 1935 for a competitive fighter aircraft. Informed by Milch, that it was solely a development contract and that no production contract would be let to BFW, Messerschmitt was faced with a decision to accept the award and try to overcome Milch's bias with a superior aircraft, or to decline the contract, which at the time promised no long term security, and instead accept an offer for

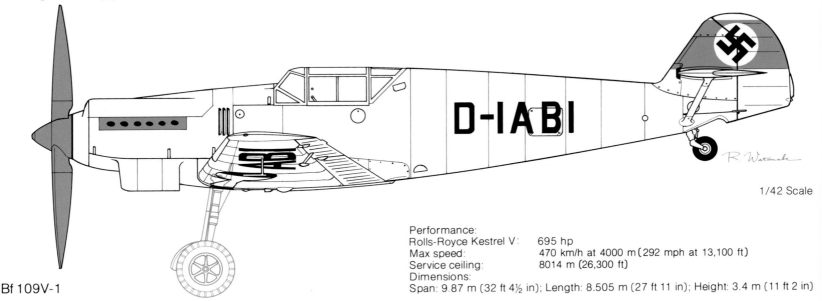

Bf 109V-1

1/42 Scale

Performance:
Rolls-Royce Kestrel V: 695 hp
Max speed: 470 km/h at 4000 m (292 mph at 13,100 ft)
Service ceiling: 8014 m (26,300 ft)
Dimensions:
Span: 9.87 m (32 ft 4½ in); Length: 8.505 m (27 ft 11 in); Height: 3.4 m (11 ft 2 in)

full professorship at Danzig Technical University. Fortunately for Germany, Messerschmitt opted for the former and pushed forward with his innovative and unique fighter design, the Bf 109.

Had Milch, even in his most far reaching fantasies, anticipated that the proposed Bf 109 would have even been an equal to the concepts submitted by the other firms, let alone far superior, he would surely never have approved the prototype development contract for the BFW.

The Bf 109 proposed by BFW had actually been on the drawing boards of Messerschmitt's staff since the initial flight of the Bf 108 in February, 1934, and was designed around the basic Bf 108A airframe. Like the Bf 108, the Bf 109A incorporated the cantilever low-wing monoplane configuration and retracting landing gear, and the single place cockpit was fitted with a fully hinged canopy.

The prototypes for the design were initiated in late 1934 and by August, 1935, the first of these was ready for ground trials at Augsburg. The aircraft was fitted with a Rolls-Royce Kestrel V-12 upright-vee liquid-cooled powerplant with a 695 hp rating at take-off. The Kestrel engine was used in the early prototype Heinkel He 112. Arado Ar 80 and the Bf 109 due to the lack of availability of the new Junkers Jumo 210 and Daimler-Benz DB 600 engines which were still undergoing development testing.

The trials at Augsburg, including extensive undercarriage testing on the struts and retraction, and extension mechanisms, were completed without problems. After undergoing minor modifications, the Bf 109A V1, (V designation for experimental) coded D-IABI, was flight-tested for the first time in September. Successful completion of these initial flight trials, which verified the handling characteristics and performances of the basic design, led to acceptance of the aircraft for flight testing at Rechlin (Luftwaffe Test Center). The Bf 109A V1 was flown to Rechlin and was immediately the object of suspicion by the assembled Luftwaffe test pilots. Used to the open cockpit, low wing loadings, and sturdy construction of the earlier biplanes, the test pilots could not accept the fully enclosed cockpit, innovative automatic wing slots, and the high ground angle of the new fighter which restricted the forward view during taxiing.

The exhibitions of the Bf 109As flight characteristics, including a 467 km/h (290 mph) airspeed which was 5% faster than the He 112 V1 (also at Rechlin for evaluation),

did little to overcome the test pilots' bias for the wide track, lower wing loading He 112. In the meantime, unconcerned that the He 112 was considered to be the forerunner in the fighter competition by knowledgeable Luftwaffe personnel, the BFW continued construction of the second and third prototypes. With the availability of the Junkers Jumo 210A powerplant, the second aircraft Bf 109A V2 was completed in October, 1935. The V2 differed from the V1 only in the powerplant installation, a few minor structural modifications to the undercarriage, and in the addition of an air intake for cooling of the proposed MG 17 machine-guns which would be installed in the aircraft's cowling. The fitting of the machine-guns occurred for the first time on the Bf 109A V3, and was the only change from the V2 aircraft. (The V3, however, did not roll off the Augsburg assembly line until May, 1936, due to delays in the delivery of the required Jumo 210A engine).

With the elimination of the Arado and Focke-Wulf prototypes from serious competition due to mechanical failures and low performance, the unwanted and unpopular design from the *Bayerische Flugzeugwerke* suddenly found itself in a position to become the next generation Luftwaffe fighter. Adding to the Bf 109s favor was the fact that German Intelligence had, in mid-1936, reported the production order of the new Royal Air Force Supermarine Spitfire, an aircraft much like the Messerschmitt in so far as it incorporated many similar technological advances.

In addition, continued superior performance demonstrated by the Bf 109 in comparison to the heavier and slower He 112 was beginning to influence even the most determined detractors of the BFW fighter at the RLM. As the flight evaluation trials continued through the fall of 1936 at Travemuende, the Bf 109 became an odds-on favorite. Demonstration of the Bf 109s ability to roll and recover at will, to maintain structural integrity under steep power dives from high altitudes, to turn inside and to outclimb the He 112, far outweighed the rumors and poor press that the new aircraft had been exposed to. Although not unanimous in its decision, the RLM recommended the selection of the Bf 109, and an order for 10 pre-production aircraft was placed with BFW.

Substantiation of this decision was to occur only weeks later when the Luftwaffe staged an aviation display at Rechlin for *Generalfeldmarschall* Goering and other high ranking officials of the RLM. The aerial display finished

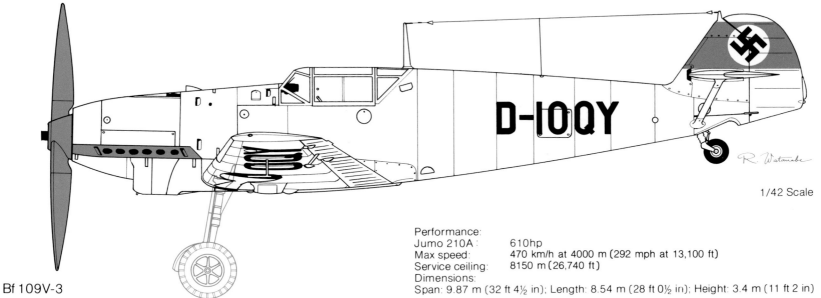

Bf 109V-3

1/42 Scale

Performance:
Jumo 210A : 610hp
Max speed: 470 km/h at 4000 m (292 mph at 13,100 ft)
Service ceiling: 8150 m (26,740 ft)
Dimensions:
Span: 9.87 m (32 ft 4½ in); Length: 8.54 m (28 ft 0½ in); Height: 3.4 m (11 ft 2 in)

with a mock air battle in which a force of bombers were to be intercepted by a flight of four He 51s. After this interception, *Oberst* Ernst Udet (famous fighter ace of World War I) was to take off in the Bf 109A V3 and intercept the four He 51s. Udet took off and destroyed the four He 51s in simulated combat, and then, on his own initiative, attacked the bombers and was credited with destroying the entire formation in his new single-place fighter.

Bf 109B *series (pre-production)*

The Bf 109B-0 designation was allocated to pre-production aircraft to be utilized in optimizing the basic Bf 109 airframe, powerplant and armament. They were therefore assigned the standardized series of experimental, or 'V' codes that identified developmental aircraft. The initial Bf 109B, coded V4, closely resembled its Bf 109A predecessors in that it was fitted with the Junkers Jumo 210A. However, it incorporated an additional MG 17 machine-gun located between the cylinders of the engine and firing through the propeller hub. This added armament was installed in response to the Luftwaffe Operations Staff's final evaluation review of the prototype tests which noted that the original requirement for only a pair of the 7.9-mm weapons provided insufficient firepower.

The Bf 109 V4, flown for the first time in November, 1936, was followed during the next two months by the V5 and V6. These aircraft were fitted with the improved performance Jumo 210B powerplant and included other minor refinements consisting of the replacement of the gun cooling intake with a trio of flush cooling slots, a modified and strengthened forward windscreen, and a change in the wing support structure to allow for removal of the wing panel stiffeners added to the second prototype aircraft during undercarriage load testing.

Not only did these three aircraft successfully complete their pre-flight trials, but they were actually evaluated under combat conditions, when in December, 1936, and January, 1937, the three planes were shipped to *Jagdgruppe* 88 in Spain to assist the Nationalist cause in the Spanish Civil War. Germany had, in mid-1936, committed itself to support of the Nationalists and assigned *Jagdgruppe*

88, equipped with He 51s, to Seville. However, during the initial engagements between the He 51s of *Jagdgruppe* 88 and the Soviet-built Polikarpov I-15 fighters used by the Republican Forces, the German fighter had continuously been out performed. It was decided by the Luftwaffe Command to send the new experimental fighters into the conflict to evaluate their strong points and shortcomings.

As would be expected, the new aircraft suffered from the vast array of minor mechanical problems which normally plague the early development of new fighters. However, it did prove its superior performance in service operations and verified the decision of the *Luftwaffenfuehrungsstab* in selecting the Bf 109 over the He 112. The three fighters were subsequently returned to Augsburg to be reinstated into the planned development program.

Bf 109 V7 started its flight testing in March, 1937, and was fitted with a Jumo 210G powerplant with fuel injection and a two-stage supercharger that provided over 700 hp for take-off compared to the 610 hp rating of the earlier Jumo 210A. This aircraft was to serve as the prototype for the Bf 109B-2.

The V8, V9 and V10 aircraft were identified as prototypes for the Bf 109C. The V8 and V9 models were powered by the Jumo 210Ga powerplant, while the V10 aircraft, initially flown with the same powerplant, was re-engined with a high-performance DB 600Aa which delivered over 900 hp for take-off. The V8 incorporated a pair of wing-mounted MG 17 machine-guns just outside of the undercarriage strut which required a few simple modifications to the wing's leading edge, and firing trials proved so successful that the new four machine-gun armament was adopted as standard for the later Bf 109C.

The V9 was similar to the V8 except that it was fitted with a pair of 20-mm MG FF cannon in the wings in place of the 7.9-mm machine-guns. However, minor problems with the higher caliber weapon restricted its incorporation into the production of aircraft until the evolution of the E-version.

The V10 model, with its DB 600 powerplant, crashlanded during an attempt by Ernst Udet (who had become one of the Bf 109's most ardent supporters) to set speed records at the Zurich-Duebendorf International Flying Meeting in July, 1937, and was replaced by the V11

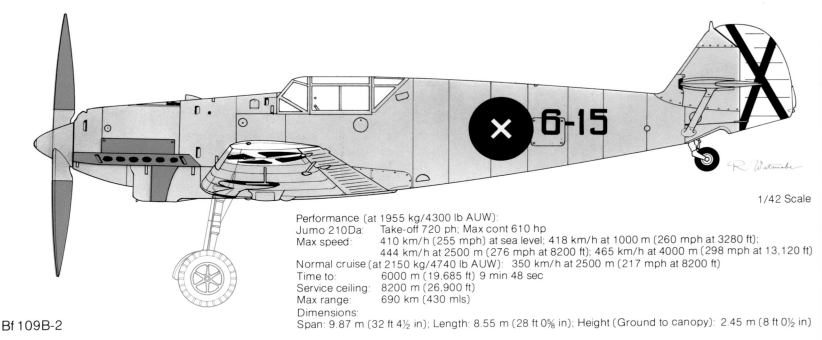

1/42 Scale

Bf 109B-2

Performance (at 1955 kg/4300 lb AUW):
Jumo 210Da: Take-off 720 ph; Max cont 610 hp
Max speed: 410 km/h (255 mph) at sea level; 418 km/h at 1000 m (260 mph at 3280 ft);
             444 km/h at 2500 m (276 mph at 8200 ft); 465 km/h at 4000 m (298 mph at 13,120 ft)
Normal cruise (at 2150 kg/4740 lb AUW): 350 km/h at 2500 m (217 mph at 8200 ft)
Time to: 6000 m (19,685 ft) 9 min 48 sec
Service ceiling: 8200 m (26,900 ft)
Max range: 690 km (430 mls)
Dimensions:
Span: 9.87 m (32 ft 4½ in); Length: 8.55 m (28 ft 0⅝ in); Height (Ground to canopy): 2.45 m (8 ft 0½ in)

for powerplant testing of the new Daimler-Benz engine. The Bf 109 V12 and V13 (the last of the original pre-production prototypes) were also originally fitted with the DB 600A. The V13 aircraft was later re-engined with the new and more powerful DB 601 and was the aircraft which set the world airspeed record for land-based aircraft in November, 1937. Covering a 3-km (1.86-mile) straight course twice in both directions, the Bf 109 V13 was clocked at an average airspeed of 610.5 km/h (379.38 mph).

Bf 109B *series (production)*

With the impressive success of the early prototype Bf 109Bs, production of the variant was ordered, and the initial Bf 109B-1 rolled off the assembly lines in February, 1937. The B-1 was essentially based on the V4, V5, and V6 models of the pre-production run and were powered by the super-charged Jumo 210Da engine driving a Schwarz twin-blade fixed-pitch wooden propeller which provided 680 hp at take-off. The armament was limited to a pair of cowling-mounted MG 17 machine-guns, with the through-propeller hub machine-gun being omitted due to cooling problems uncovered during the testing of the V4, V5, and V6 aircraft.

Originally scheduled to go into service with *Jagdgeschwader* 132 "*Richthofen,*" the initial B-1s were delivered to II *Gruppe* for combat training; however, the assignment of these aircraft to *Jagdgruppe* 88 in Spain was given top priority because of the proven advantages of the I-15 and I-16 over the Luftwaffe's He 51s. The pilots and aircraft of JG 132 therefore, were immediately transferred to *Jagdgruppe* 88 after training.

Only 30 of the B-1 models were produced before the *Luftwaffenfuehrungsstab* switched the Augsburg assembly line over to the Bf 109B-2, which differed from the B-1 only in the replacement of the wooden Schwarz airscrew with a variable-pitch VDM metal licence-built (Hamilton-Standard) propeller. By July, 1937, the Bf 109B-2s were being delivered to 1 *Staffel* of *Jagdgruppe* 88.

Because *Bayerische Flugzeugwerke* was producing the new fighter at maximum capacity, and still not meeting the Luftwaffe's need (although additional facilities were being constructed at Augsburg), a license agreement was signed with the Fieseler plant at Kassel for additional production. By December, aircraft from Fieseler began to supplement the deliveries from Augsburg.

Bf 109C *series*

The Bf 109C-1 was based on the V8, V9 and V10 prototype models and incorporated the improved Junkers Jumo 210Ga engine which developed 700 hp at take-off. (A few of the final batches of the Bf 109B-2 had been fitted with the Jumo 210Ga powerplant which was planned for initial incorporation into the Bf 109C.)

The C-1 also increased the basic Bf 109 armament through the addition of a pair of wing-mounted 7.9mm Rheinmetall MG 17 machine-guns and incorporated a revision of the powerplant exhaust exits and an increased radiator intake size which resulted in identifiable external differences from the B-1. In addition, the C-1 was fitted with an FuG 7 radio, providing direct communication between fighter-control ground forces and the plane, something that had not existed in the earlier models.

The Bf 109C-1s began leaving the assembly lines at Augsburg in March, 1938, and like its predecessors were immediately shipped to Spain to allow transition of the remaining He 51s and some of the initial Bf 109B-1s.

Three additional variants of the Bf 109C were produced at Augsburg, these being the C-2, C-3 and C-4 models. The Bf 109C-2 was an experimental development model and was identical to the C-1 except that it incorporated the engine-mounted MG 17 machine-gun that had been eliminated from earlier variants due to cooling problems. The cooling of the gun mechanism had been increased through a number of material changes and increases in insulation and ducting. The Bf 109C-3 was used as a test bed for the incorporation of using wing-mounted 20-mm MG FF cannons.

The Bf 109C-4, in turn, replaced the engine-mounted MG 17 with an MG FF cannon. The C-4s, however, were also utilized as developmental aircraft and were never delivered to operational units.

During the production of the C-version of the Bf 109, one other significant occurrence took place. That

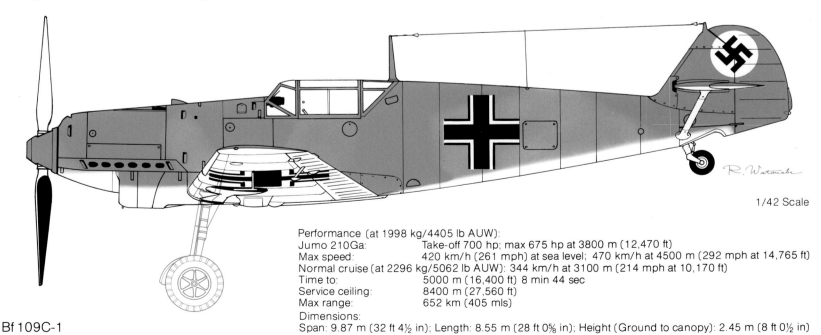

1/42 Scale

Bf 109C-1

Performance (at 1998 kg/4405 lb AUW):
Jumo 210Ga: Take-off 700 hp; max 675 hp at 3800 m (12,470 ft)
Max speed: 420 km/h (261 mph) at sea level; 470 km/h at 4500 m (292 mph at 14,765 ft)
Normal cruise (at 2296 kg/5062 lb AUW): 344 km/h at 3100 m (214 mph at 10,170 ft)
Time to: 5000 m (16,400 ft) 8 min 44 sec
Service ceiling: 8400 m (27,560 ft)
Max range: 652 km (405 mls)
Dimensions:
Span: 9.87 m (32 ft 4½ in); Length: 8.55 m (28 ft 0⅝ in); Height (Ground to canopy): 2.45 m (8 ft 0½ in)

was the change of name of the *Bayerische Flugzeugwerke* to *Messerschmitt A.G.* This change was essentially the result of not only the great success of the aircraft, but also because of the national hero status Messerschmitt had achieved during the previous two years with his innovative and successful new aircraft concepts. Wishing to capitalize on this growing fame, the German Air Ministry had suggested to the *Bayerische Flugzeugwerke* management (which included Messerschmitt) that it could provide the company with a more international image through the name change.

Bf 109D *series*

The Bf 109D version was produced only as an interim fighter (approximately 200 being built) filling the gap between the Jumo 210 powered Bf 109C and the planned DB 601 powered Bf 109E. The DB engines, both the basic 600 and the improved 601 models, provided increased performance to the Messerschmitt fighter. The availability of both, however, was limited during 1937-38. These limitations on availability were the influencing factors, not only on the decision to produce the D-variant, but also on the quantity built. Having been designed from the outset to accept the new Daimler-Benz 600 series powerplants, the incorporation of this engine into the Bf 109 was delayed until 1937 because the DB 600 was utilized in the He 111 bomber and the production of bombers had received the highest priorities during the mid-thirties. In addition, the service acceptance of the improved DB 601 engine was delayed due to difficulties with the new automatically-monitored supercharger system, which provided the engine with added power and eliminated cut-outs even under high G loadings.

    Realizing that the DB 600 would not be available in sufficient quantities for a large production run of the Bf 109D, and that the DB 601 would not be ready for some months, the German Air Ministry opted to produce the interim D-version with the limited supply of Jumo 210D and Jumo 210G powerplants, and to forestall the installation of the newer DB 601 until the Bf 109E series evolved.

    The Bf 109D program was initiated in mid-1937 with a pair of pre-production aircraft assigned the designation V14 and V15. However, these two planes were diverted to developmental efforts being started on the E-series aircraft, and the D-version was restricted to the utilization of the V11, V12 and V13 (Bf 109B-0 prototypes) for design and structural testing. The Bf 109D was to be the first model to feature the familiar lines that were to become the identification criteria for future variants. The aircraft would have been essentially identical to the earlier models from the cockpit aft, but the forward cowling would undergo a major change. The wide radiator intake would be replaced by a small, aerodynamically smooth, oil cooler intake and a pair of small glycol radiators would be added to the undersurface of each wing. A long supercharger air intake would also be added to the port side of the cowling just over the exhaust stubs. Structural strengthening was evident in the landing gear struts, undercarriage attach points and in the powerplant interface locations. However, all these modifications except for the structural changes, were delayed until the introduction of the E-version due to the reversion back to the Jumo powerplants.

    Armament for the Bf 109D consisted of the then-

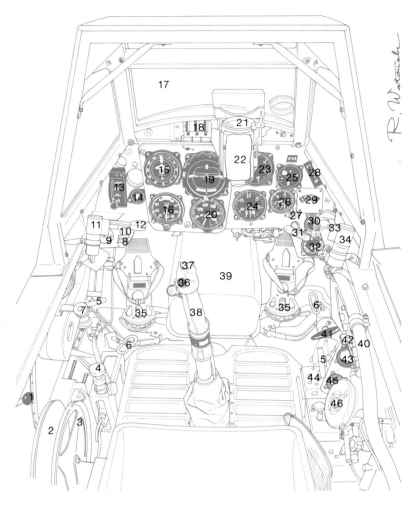

Bf 109G-6 Cockpit

1 Ventilation control lever
2 Undercarriage emergency lowering handwheel
3 Tailplane trim adjustment wheel
4 Fuel injection primer pump
5 Fuel cock lever
6 Radiator cut-off handle
7 Throttle
8 Undercarriage switch
9 Undercarriage position indicator
10 Undercarriage control switch
11 Instrument panel light
12 Canopy jettison lever
13 Ignition switch
14 Main light switch
15 Repeater compass
16 Altimeter
17 Laminated glass windscreen
18 Ammunition counters
19 Artificial horizon / turn and bank indicator
20 Airspeed indicator
21 Revi C/12D reflector gunsight. (Later series used Revi 16B)
22 Gunsight padding
23 Manifold pressure gauge
24 Tachometer
25 AFN2 homing indicator (for FuG16ZY only)
26 Propeller pitch position indicator
27 Fuel warning lamp
28 Tumbler switch
29 Combined coolant exit and oil intake temperature indicator
30 Fuel contents gauge
31 Undercarriage emergency release lever
32 Dual oil and fuel contents gauge
33 Auxiliary fuel contents indicator
34 Instrument panel light
35 Rudder pedal
36 Bomb release button
37 Firing trigger
38 Control column
39 20 mm MG151/20 cannon breech cover
40 Drop tank fuel pipe
41 Radiator shutter control lever
42 FuG16ZY radio control panel
43 Oxygen supply indicator
44 Radio control panel
45 Oxygen pressure gauge
46 Oxygen supply

(BUNDESARCHIV)　　　　(BUNDESARCHIV)

Bf 109G-5/R2 flown by *Major* Hermann Graf, *Kommandeur* of JGr 50(Jagdgruppe 50), 6 September, 1943.

The Bf 109G-5/R2 with the red tulip design on the nose and the Wfr.Gr.21 rocket mortars under both wings was flown by one of the best fighter pilots of the Luftwaffe, *Major* Hermann Graf, *Kommandeur* of *Jagdguppe* 50. He used it from summer 1943 until 22 March, 1944, when, as *Kommodore* of JG 11, he shot down two heavy US bombers but was himself badly wounded in a mid-air collision with a P-51 Mustang escort fighter.

Hermann Graf achieved his first victory on 3 August, 1941, flying as an *Oberfeldwebel* with JG 52. By 24 January, 1942, his score had risen to 42, and he was awarded the *Ritterkreuz* (Knights' Cross) and promoted to *Leutnant*. During the next four months Graf achieved another 62 victories on the Eastern Front increasing his score to 104, claiming his 100th on 14 May, 1942. Three days later he was awarded the Oak Leaves to the Knights' Cross as the 12th Luftwaffe pilot. By 4 September,

Graf's total had reached 150 victories, the second fighter pilot in the history to do so. Only twelve days later Graf's total had increased to 172 and he became the fifth Luftwaffe pilot to be awarded the Diamonds to the Oak Leaves and Swords of the Knights' Cross. However, on 2 October, 1942, after his 202nd victory, Graf was grounded by Propaganda Minister Goebbels who did not want to lose an exploitable national hero.

In early summer 1943 Graf was ordered to form and lead a special high-altitude unit, *Jagdgruppe* 50, remaining its *Kommandeur* until JGr 50 was disbanded in late autumn 1943. From November, 1943, to April, 1944, Graf was *Kommodore* of JG 11. After recuperation from his injuries Graf was appointed *Kommodore* of JG 52, and remained in this post until the capitulation with the rank of *Oberstleutnant*. By the end of the war Graf had flown 830 operational sorties and scored 212 confirmed victories.

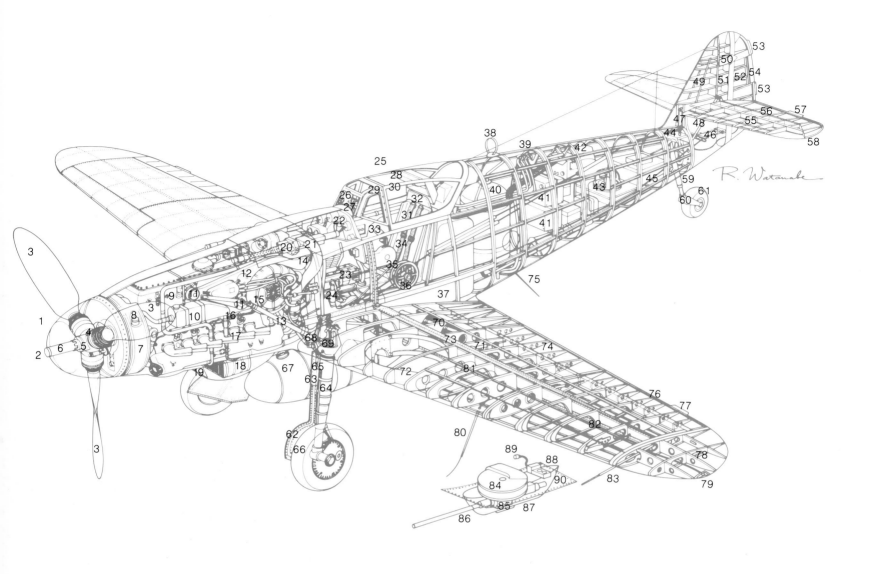

R. Watanabe

Bf 109G-10 Cutaway

1 Spinner
2 Engine-mounted cannon muzzle
3 VDM 9-12159 electrically-operated constant-
  speed propeller
4 Propeller pitch-change mechanism
5 Propeller hub
6 Blast tube
7 Oil tank (50 ltr/11 Imp. gal capacity)
8 Oil filler cap
9 Daimler Benz DB 605DCM twelve-cylinder
  inverted-vee liquid-cooled engine
10 Coolant header tank
11 Anti-vibration rubber engine-mounting pads
12 Electron forged engine bearer
13 Engine bearer support strut attachment
14 Engine bearer upper attachment
15 Supercharger assembly
16 Plug leads
17 Exhaust stubs
18 FO 987 oil cooler
19 Oil cooler intake
20 13-mm Rheinmetall Borsig MG 131 machine-
   gun breeches
21 13-mm machine-gun ammunition feed chute
22 Instrument panel
23 20-mm Mauser MG 151/20 cannon breech
24 Rudder pedals
25 'Galland'-type clear-vision hinged canopy
26 90-mm armourglass windscreen
27 Revi 16B reflector gunsight
28 Framed armourglass head/back panel

29 Armoured windshield frame
30 Canopy contoured frame
31 Pilot's seat
32 8-mm back armour
33 Throttle lever
34 Seat harness
35 Tail trim handwheel (in board)
36 Undercarriage emergency retraction
   handwheel (out board)
37 Underfloor contoured fuel tank
   (400 ltr/88 Imp. gal, 96 octane C3)
38 D/F loop antenna
39 Main fuel filler cap
40 MW 50 (methanol/water) tank
   (114 ltr/25 Imp. gal capacity)
41 Wireless equipment packs FuG16ZY
   (VHF 38.5 — 42.3MHz communications and
   FuG 25a IFF)
42 Methanol tank
43 Master compass
44 Tail trimming cables
45 Rudder cables
46 Rudder actuating linkage
47 Tail trim control
48 Elevator connecting rod
49 All-wooden tailfin construction
50 Rudder upper hinge bracket
51 Rudder post
52 Fabric-covered wooden rudder structure
53 Fixed rudder trim tub
54 Geared rudder tub
55 Tailplane structure
56 Port elevator
57 Fixed elevator trim tub

58 Elevator balance
59 Castoring non-retractable tailwheel leg
60 Wheel housing
61 Tailwheel tire: 350×135 mm (13.8×5.3 in)
62 Mainwheel fairing
63 Mainwheel leg fairing
64 Mainwheel oleo leg
65 Brake lines
66 Port mainwheel
67 Auxiliary fuel tank [Rüstsatz R3],
   300 ltr (66 Imp. gal)
68 Undercarriage retraction jak mechanism
69 Undercarriage pivot/bevel
70 Ducted coolant radiator
71 Flap actuating linkage
72 Port mainwheel well
73 Wing spar
74 Slotted flap structure
75 FuG 25a antenna
76 Metal-framed Frise-type aileron
77 Fixed trim tub
78 Wingtip construction
79 Port navigation light
80 FuG16ZY Morane antenna
81 Slot equalizer rod
82 Wing ribs
83 Pitot tube
84 Ammunition magazine drum
85 20-mm Mausar MG151/20 cannon
86 Cannon barrel
87 Gondola fairing
88 Electrical junction box
89 14-point plug connection
90 Underwing panel

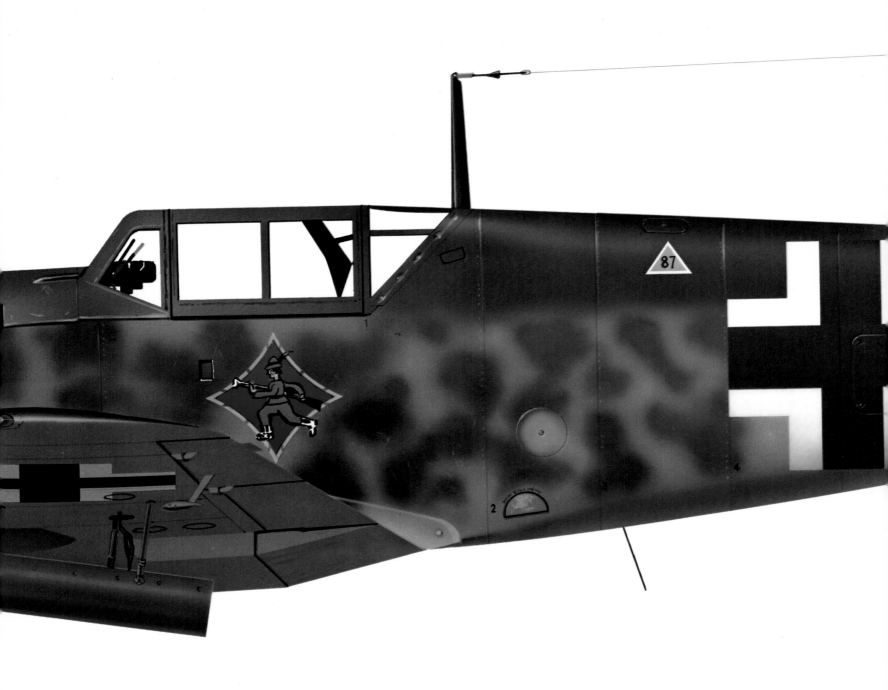

1m
3 ft

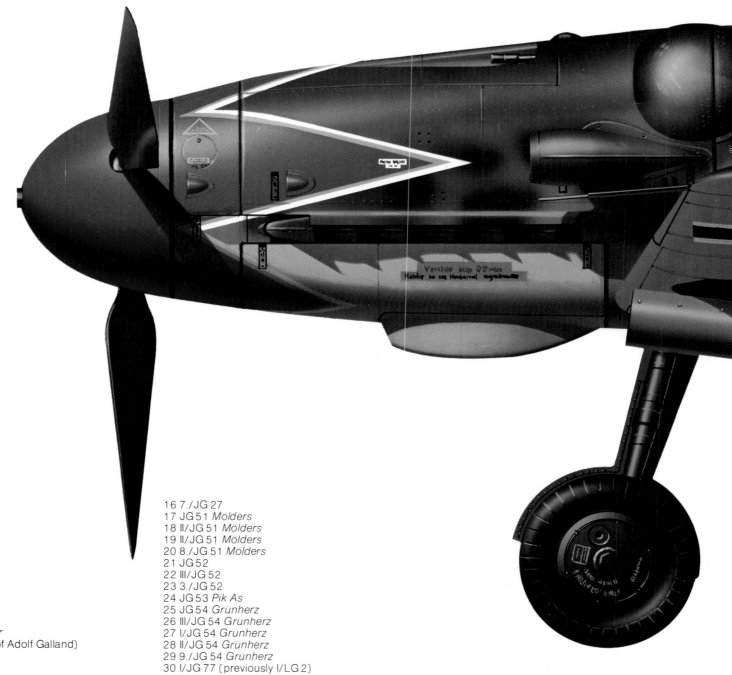

eft
)9F-4, flown by *Hauptmann* Reinhard Seiler,
mandeur, III/JG 54, on the Eastern Front at
nd of 1941. His final rank was *Major* and he
ed 109 victories in total including 16 night vic-
s over Russia.

◀ Right
Oberleutnant Hans-Ekkehard Bob, *Staffelkapitän,*
9./JG 54 and his Bf 109F-2 on the Eastern Front in
the winter of 1941 – 42. His final rank was *Major*
and he scored 59 victories in total including 21 victories on the Western Front.

1   2

Bf 109D, I/ZG 2, summer, 1939.   (BUNDESARCHIV)

standardized pair of cowl-mounted MG 17 machine-guns and a single 20-mm MG FF cannon between the cylinders of the inverted-Vee Jumo powerplant. The latter weapon was later removed from some of the aircraft, as operational use still resulted in numerous occurrences of jamming, and flight characteristics were adversely influenced when the cannon was fired.

In an effort to increase armament and overcome the still unresolved engine-mounted weapon problems, the Bf 109D-2 was ordered. The D-2 was identical to the D-1 except that the center-mounted weapon was omitted and the aircraft was fitted with a pair of wing-mounted MG 17 machine-guns. In addition, a small number of Bf 109D-3s were produced that differed from the D-2 only in that they incorporated a pair of 20-mm MG FF cannon in the wings in place of the MG 17 machine-guns.

Bf 109E series

The first large scale production version of the Bf 109 series was the Bf 109E. Powered by the DB 601A-1 engine, which had been fitted to the first pair of pre-production Bf 109D-0

aircraft (V14 and V15), ten pre-production Bf 109E-0s were ordered for service evaluation, basically for acceptance testing of the new powerplant. The testing of the DB 601 was necessitated by the RLM's decision to cancel further production of the DB 600 in early 1938 based on promises from Daimler-Benz that production quantities of the DB 601 would be available for the E-series by mid-1938. Problems with the early DB 601s, however, had delayed its service acceptance, and thus, production of the Bf 109E.

Assigning the first three pre-production codes (Bf 109E-01, -02, and -03) to the Bf 109 V13, V14, and V15, the remaining seven pre-production aircraft received designations of V16 through V22. These were utilized to test various armament and engine modifications.

Production deliveries of the Bf 109E-1 began early in 1939 with several of the initial aircraft being assigned to Spain with the Condor Legion, which began receiving the Bf 109E during February and March. Although these aircraft arrived too late to influence the outcome of the Spanish Civil War, a few scattered encounters between the new variant and the aircraft of the Republican Forces did take place, with the Bf 109E proving its vast superiority in almost every category.

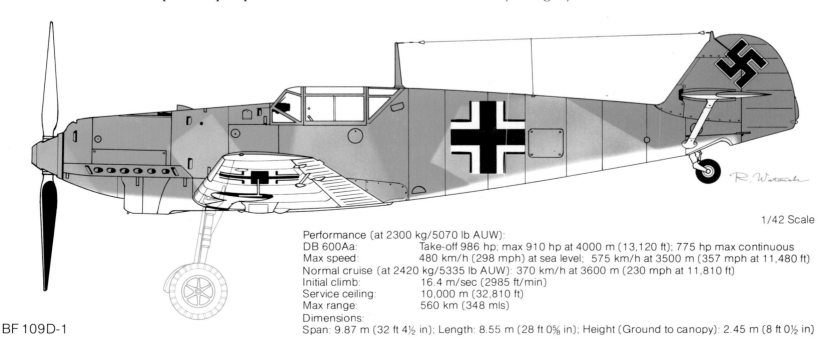

1/42 Scale

BF 109D-1

Performance (at 2300 kg/5070 lb AUW):
DB 600Aa: Take-off 986 hp; max 910 hp at 4000 m (13,120 ft); 775 hp max continuous
Max speed: 480 km/h (298 mph) at sea level; 575 km/h at 3500 m (357 mph at 11,480 ft)
Normal cruise (at 2420 kg/5335 lb AUW): 370 km/h at 3600 m (230 mph at 11,810 ft)
Initial climb: 16.4 m/sec (2985 ft/min)
Service ceiling: 10,000 m (32,810 ft)
Max range: 560 km (348 mls)
Dimensions:
Span: 9.87 m (32 ft 4½ in); Length: 8.55 m (28 ft 0⅝ in); Height (Ground to canopy): 2.45 m (8 ft 0½ in)

Bf 109E-4/Trop, I/JG 27, North Africa.   (BUNDESARCHIV)   Bf 109E-4/Trop, I/JG 27, North Africa.   (BUNDESARCHIV)

Armament of the early Bf 109E-1 included the standardized pair of cowl-mounted 7.9-mm MG 17 machine-guns and a pair of the same weapons installed in the wings. However, based on the successful results of both testing with the V14, and the favoring of heavier armament by the RLM, later batches of the E-1 were produced with a pair of 20-mm MG FF cannon in place of the wing-mounted machine-guns. Due to the increased size of the cannons, a specially designed cover with a bulged shape was fitted to the lower wing to provide space for the larger weapon and its ammunition drum. In addition, a selector switch for control of both, or one, of the wing weapons was installed in the cockpit allowing the pilot a choice of firepower.

By the end of the hostilities in Spain in late March, 1939, only twenty of the planned 40 Bf 109E-1s had been delivered to *Jagdgruppe* 88. Although the Luftwaffe units in Germany were also re-equipping with the Bf 109E at this time, the twenty aircraft were transferred to the Spanish National Forces, along with the remaining Bf 109Bs and Bf 109Cs.

The next variant of the Bf 109E to reach production was the E-3, incorporating the improved DB 601Aa which delivered nearly 1,200 hp at take-off and had provision for the installation of an MG FF cannon between the powerplant's cylinders. Problems of jamming, overheating and vibration, however, still plagued this modification, and most of the installations were either removed in the field, or seldom used. The Bf 109E-3 also incorporated other modifications, including a revised canopy design with heavier frame, and the addition of armor plate behind the pilot's head and under the seat.

The Bf 109E-3 supplanted the Bf 109E-1 on the assembly lines in late 1939 and by the end of the year they had started arriving for operational service with frontline Luftwaffe units.

Because of the apparent failure of the nose-mounted MG FF cannon, and its subsequent removal after installation, it was decided to produce the Bf 109E-3 without the center-firing weapon. The result was the designation change to Bf 109E-4, with production deliveries beginning during the summer of 1940.

It was also during this time that thoughts of employing the Bf 109 as a *Jagdbomber* (fighter-bomber) were being considered, based on the needs developed during fighting against the French. The concept was to attach a single bomb under the center fuselage and provide the pilot with an electrical release switch. To test the theory, an evaluation unit, *Erprobungsgruppe* 210, was formed and a number of Bf 109E-1s and Bf 110Cs were assigned as test aircraft.

With only very minimal training in dive-bombing techniques, the unit began their operational testing against British shipping in the English Channel. The results of the limited endeavor proved so successful that all Luftwaffe *Jagdgeschwader* were ordered to form one *Staffel* for *Jabo* operations. Normally consisting of nine *Staffeln*, this usually meant the addition of a tenth unit. To equip these new units, Bf 109E-1s, which were being replaced by the later model Bf 109E-3s and E-4s, were retrofitted with an ETC 50 rack for the carrying of a 50 kg (110-lb.) SC 50 bomb and assigned the designation Bf 109-E-1/B. In addition, several Bf 109E-4s still on the assembly lines were converted to Bf 109E-4/Bs through the incorporation of a central ETC 250 rack which was capable of handling a single 250 kg (550-lb.) bomb or four SC 50 bombs.

Continuing to strive for ever increasing performance, Daimler-Benz developed the DB 601N powerplant which not only delivered 1,200 hp at take-off, but also offered an emergency output of 1,250 hp for a duration of 1 minute at altitudes in the 4500 m (15,000 ft) range. The engine made use of flattened piston heads instead of the normal concave shape and increased the compression ratio by 15%. Due to this higher compression ratio the powerplant also required the use of higher octane fuel, necessitating a change from 87 to 96 octane. This powerplant was installed into the Bf 109E-4 series in mid-1940 and the aircraft were given the designation of Bf 109E-4/N.

The Bf 109E-5 was identical to the standard Bf 109E-4 except that it included the installation of a Rb 21/18 camera in the aft fuselage and deleted the wing-mounted MG FF cannon. Produced side-by-side with the E-4, the E-5 was assigned the task of fighter-reconnaissance. With the elimination of the wing armament and ammunition the aircraft's overall weight was reduced to give it increased airspeed for escape from Allied fighter-interceptors. A further refinement of the basic fighter-reconnaissance concept was reflected in the Bf 109E-6, which was identical to the E-5 model, except that it incorporated the higher performance DB 601N which had first been installed on the Bf 109E-4/N.

The next Bf 109E variant to appear was the E-7 which was identical to the Bf 109E-4/N except that it included a factory-installed ventrally-mounted ETC 250 rack capable of interfacing with an expendable auxiliary fuel tank (for extended range operation), or with an SC 250 bomb for use as a long-range fighter-bomber. This variant was further modified during 1941 to include the Bf 109E-7/U2, an early *Umruest-Bausatz* (factory conversion kit) which provided added armor plate protection for the underwing radiators, lower powerplant area and fuel tanks, and the Bf 109E-7/Z which incorporated a GM 1 injectant boost system to the engine. The injectant system tank, located behind the cockpit, contained nitrous oxide in liquid form which was fed to the powerplant by compressed air and injected into the supercharger where it provided added oxygen. This was, of course, advantageous at higher altitudes where the oxygen level is reduced, and the engine, dependent on oxygen for combustion, starts losing power. The injectant system, in effect, acted as an artificial altitude compensator.

The final two basic variants of the E-series were the Bf 109E-8 and the Bf 109E-9, which made their initial appearance in late 1940. The E-8 was almost identical to the basic E-1 variant, in that it was armed with a pair of fuselage-mounted MG 17 machine-guns and a similar pair of wing-mounted weapons. Designated as an extended-range fighter, the E-8 was fitted with the underfuselage rack to carry an auxiliary drop tank. The E-9 model was a combination of several of the earlier innovations and modifications made on the E-series and was assigned the role of long-range photo-reconnaissance. The aircraft, powered by the DB 601N engine, was fitted with the auxiliary fuel tank rack, and incorporated an Rb 50/30 camera aft of the cockpit. Armament consisted of the MG 17 fuselage machine-guns, and a pair of wing-mounted MG FF cannon.

Many other supplemental modifications were made to the basic Bf 109 E-series during its production career — late 1939 through early 1942. These included tropicalized versions of the Bf 109E-4, -5 and -7. The tropicalized modifications, resulting from the dusty environment of the North African area, included the installation of a filter over and in front of the supercharger air intake on the port side of the engine cowling and the packaging of a desert survival kit (including a lightweight carbine, food and water supply, signal equipment, etc.) inside the aircraft. The tropicalized versions of the Bf 109 were given the designation Trop. This term appeared after the basic model designation, as in Bf 109E-5/Trop.

Several one-of-a-kind experimental projects were also conducted with the Bf 109E series including the use of skis and the incorporation of overwing or underwing fuel tanks. The idea behind the use of skis was to provide for operations from snow covered landing areas and, even possibly, deep sand. A Bf 109E-8 was fitted with a pair of faired skis in place of wheels (in actuality, the skis appeared to be more like hollow pontoons) and was flight tested both with the skis alone and using a jettisonable wheeled dolly for assist in take-offs. By the time the tests had been completed, experience by the Luftwaffe in actual winter environments had resulted in minimal difficulties, and as the skied version of the Bf 109E suffered in performance due to the increased drag of the skis and fairings, the project was dropped.

The use of jettisonable over and under wing fuel tanks to improve the range of the fighter was tested on a modified Bf109E-4 in 1942. It was shown that the installation of these contoured tanks did not appreciably reduce overall airspeed, although they did, to a minor degree, decrease the aircraft's turning rate and overall handling characteristics. Because the need for this type of range was not critical (due in part to the installation of ventraly mounted drop tanks), the basic concept was cancelled. However, the possibility of utilizing the over-wing containers to carry personnel and equipment on behind-the-lines espionage missions added new life to the program. In the summer of 1943, a Bf 109E-4 had been modified with re-contoured over-wing containers capable of carrying a man, his parachute and necessary survival equipment, and was test-flown at Stuttgart-Ruit. Tests showed only a minimal loss in airspeed. By this time, however, interest in the project had subsided and no evidence exists that this concept was ever put to actual practice.

Bf 109F *series*

In early 1940, the Augsburg plant began a design improvement program with the intent of incorporating not only structural and aerodynamic modifications to the basic Bf 109 airframe, but also the installation of the higher per-

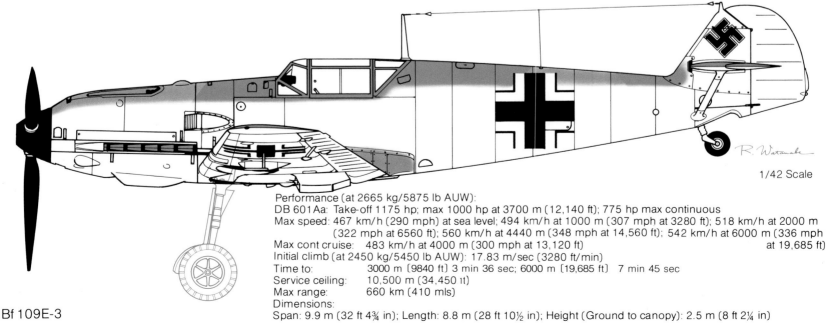

1/42 Scale

Bf 109E-3

Performance (at 2665 kg/5875 lb AUW):
DB 601Aa: Take-off 1175 hp; max 1000 hp at 3700 m (12,140 ft); 775 hp max continuous
Max speed: 467 km/h (290 mph) at sea level; 494 km/h at 1000 m (307 mph at 3280 ft); 518 km/h at 2000 m (322 mph at 6560 ft); 560 km/h at 4440 m (348 mph at 14,560 ft); 542 km/h at 6000 m (336 mph at 19,685 ft)
Max cont cruise: 483 km/h at 4000 m (300 mph at 13,120 ft)
Initial climb (at 2450 kg/5450 lb AUW): 17.83 m/sec (3280 ft/min)
Time to: 3000 m (9840 ft) 3 min 36 sec; 6000 m (19,685 ft) 7 min 45 sec
Service ceiling: 10,500 m (34,450 ft)
Max range: 660 km (410 mls)
Dimensions:
Span: 9.9 m (32 ft 4¾ in); Length: 8.8 m (28 ft 10½ in); Height (Ground to canopy): 2.5 m (8 ft 2¼ in)

Daimler Benz DB 601A engine

Year:	1937
Type:	12-cylinder inverted 60 degrees Vee supercharged liquid-cooled engine
Bore:	150 mm
Stroke:	160 mm
Total swept capacity:	33.9 lit (2069 in³)
Compression ratio:	6.9 : 1
Fuel:	92 octane
Maximum RPM:	2400 rpm
Reduction gearing:	1 : 1.55
Dry weight:	610 kg (1,344.7 lb)
Length:	1,352 mm (4 ft 5¼ in)
Width:	705 mm (2 ft 3¾ in)
Height:	1,027 mm (3 ft 4½ in)
Take-off power:	1,100 hp. max 1 min
Rated power at height:	1,020 hp at 4,500 m (14,800 ft), max 5 mins
Maximum continuous power:	960 hp at 5,000 m (16,400 ft), max 30 mins
Maximum cruise power:	890 hp at 5,700 m (18,700 ft)
Maximum economical cruise power:	800 hp at 5,500 m (18,000 ft)

1. Top cover of crankcase
2. Crankcase
3. Oil distributing joint
4. Reduction gear
5. Propeller shaft flange
6. Coolant injection pipe
7. Cylinder block
8. Spark plug
9. Air hose
10. Pilot pipe for coolant
11. Exhaust port
12. Bleeder
13. Balanced crankshaft

14. Connecting rod
15. Piston and rings
16. Valve
17. Valve spring
18. Overhead camshaft
19. Suction pipe (from oil feedback pump)
20. Ignition magnet
21. Hook-up bracket
22. Engine mount connecting joint
23. Air filter
24. Supercharger casing
25. Oil feedback pump
26. Valve gear cover

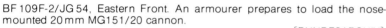

BF 109F-2/JG 54, Eastern Front. An armourer prepares to load the nose-mounted 20 mm MG151/20 cannon.

[BUNDESARCHIV]

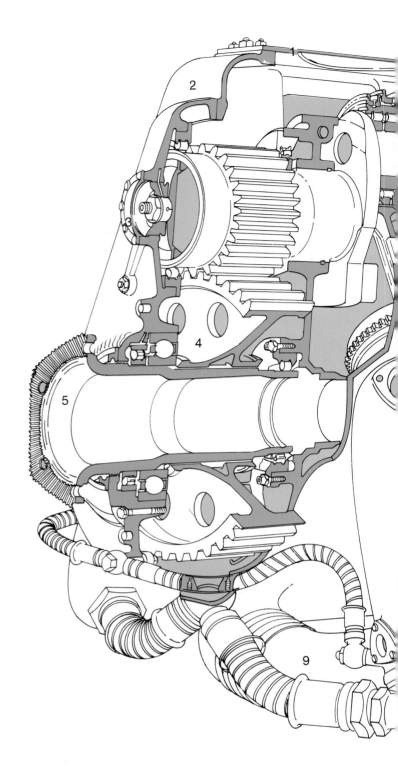

forming powerplants that were then under development at Daimler-Benz. The result of this program was the Bf 109F.

The airframe changes were numerous and resulted in an external configuration that was to remain essentially unchanged through the remainder of the Bf 109 variants. The wing, which had remained the same since the initial prototypes of the basic Bf 109, maintained the primary contours and spar structure, but incorporated a pair of significant modifications to reduce drag and improve lifting characteristics. First, the underwing radiators, which were a large contributor to the aircraft's drag, were decreased in height and recessed deeper into the wing through the use of a unique system of flaps and ducts which reduced the turbulence normally associated with the radiator protrusion into the airstream. The installation of this system also resulted in a change in the length and span of both the leading and trailing edge control flaps and the

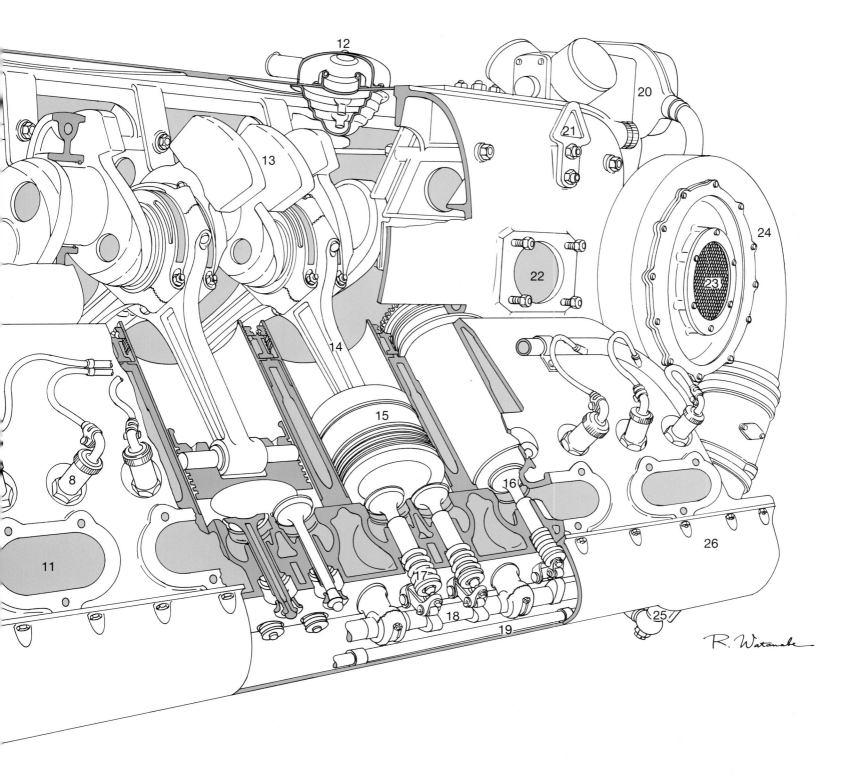

elimination of interconnecting linkage between the flaps and ailerons fitted previously.

A deeper, more streamlined cowling was also designed which tapered directly from the forward windscreen to the propeller hub and the air intake for the supercharger was moved farther into the airstream to increase the ram-effect of the scooped in air. The propeller hub, or spinner, was enlarged and lengthened to fit the new symmetrical cowling and contoured to reduce turbulent drag factors. In addition, the overall airscrew diameter was reduced by 10 cm (4 in) through the use of wider blades.

Major modifications also were incorporated into the tail assembly section where the rudder area was slightly reduced and the tail-plane bracing struts, which had become an identifying feature of earlier Bf 109s, were removed. With the removal of the struts, the new cantilevered tail-plane was moved slightly forward and below the

DB 601N engine

(BUNDESARCHIV)

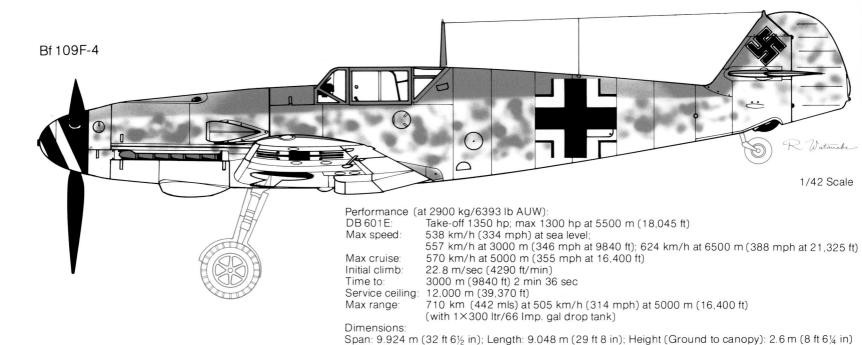

Bf 109F-4

1/42 Scale

Performance (at 2900 kg/6393 lb AUW):
DB 601E: Take-off 1350 hp; max 1300 hp at 5500 m (18,045 ft)
Max speed: 538 km/h (334 mph) at sea level;
                557 km/h at 3000 m (346 mph at 9840 ft); 624 km/h at 6500 m (388 mph at 21,325 ft)
Max cruise: 570 km/h at 5000 m (355 mph at 16,400 ft)
Initial climb: 22.8 m/sec (4290 ft/min)
Time to: 3000 m (9840 ft) 2 min 36 sec
Service ceiling: 12,000 m (39,370 ft)
Max range: 710 km (442 mls) at 505 km/h (314 mph) at 5000 m (16,400 ft)
                (with 1×300 ltr/66 Imp. gal drop tank)
Dimensions:
Span: 9.924 m (32 ft 6½ in); Length: 9.048 m (29 ft 8 in); Height (Ground to canopy): 2.6 m (8 ft 6¼ in)

original positioning and the chord thickness increased for structural rigidity.

Planned for installation of the DB 601E engine, which provided 1,350 hp for take-off, the four Bf 109F prototypes and ten pre-production aircraft were initiated in May, 1940. However, service testing and acceptance of the DB 601E had not yet been completed and, as a consequence, powerplant substitutions had to be made.

The first prototype, Bf 109 V21 utilized the DB 601Aa which had powered the later E-series while the last three prototypes all had early development DB 601E's installed. The Bf 109 V22 was to be utilized primarily for testing of the powerplant while the V23 and V24 aircraft were scheduled to be used for minor modifications to the new design in the area of structural and flight handling characteristics. The most significant change from the initial Bf 109F configuration was incorporated into V23, when el-

Oberleuntnant Viktor Bauer of JG 3 *Udet* achieved a total of 109 victories.

(BUNDESARCHIV)

liptically shaped detachable wingtips were added to increase the wing surface area (reducing wing loading) and to restore overall wingspan dimensions that had been reduced with the incorporation of the improved underwing radiator system. Armament for the Bf 109F was standardized with the retention of the cowling-mounted 7.9-mm MG 17 machine-guns and the addition of a 20-mm MG 151 cannon firing through the hollow propeller shaft. The reduction in armament from the Bf 109E, which had either a pair of MG 17 machine-guns or MG FF cannon mounted in the wings, was the result of several operational pilots' reports which maintained that the concentrated firepower of the center located weapons was more effective than the converging fire of the wing mounted weapons and that, in addition, the elimination of the wing armament added to the aircraft's handling characteristics.

Due to the continued delay in delivery of the planned DB 601E, the ten pre-production Bf 109F-0s, which began rolling off the assembly lines in October 1940, were powered by the DB 601N engine with its flattened piston heads. The F-0s also were fitted with the older MG FF cannon in the nose as deliveries of the proposed electronically armed MG 151 and MG 151/20 (15-mm and 20-mm) were delayed.

Deliveries of the initial Bf 109F-1 variant, very similar to its predecessor, the Bf 109F-0, began in November. The only real discernible difference in appearance was in the installation of the new extended supercharger air intake. This replaced the rectangular flush-mounted air intake from the E-series that had been used on the early pre-production aircraft until tests of the optimum contour and inlet size were completed on the improved design.

Within a few weeks of the initial deliveries of the Bf 109F-1s to Luftwaffe service evaluation units a number of them were lost, with the only clue as to the cause being a few pilot's messages reporting violent vibrations just prior to complete loss of control and crash. The Bf 109Fs were grounded and the cause of the vibration problem was investigated, with concentration in the powerplant attach interfaces and structural supports. Finding no irregularities, the investigation centered on the tail assembly, and it was discovered that the removal of the bracing struts had resulted in a high frequency vibration being set up in the fuselage at certain engine rpm levels. The aircraft were

Hauptmann Hans-Joachim Marseille, the 'Star of Africa,' and his *Gelbe-14* (Bf 109E-4N/Trop). His total score was 158, of which 151 were North African victories. His most sensational score record was that of 1 September, 1942. From 0926 to noon he downed eight planes, P-40s and one Spitfire, mostly Royal Air Force. From 1201 to 1853 he downed nine more, P-40s and Hurricanes, all SAAF and RAF. This gave him the total of 17 British aircraft in just nine hours.

(BUNDESARCHIV)

retrofitted with reinforcing plates in the tail-plane to fuselage attachment area and production was resumed.

In February and March, 1941, deliveries of the Bf 109F-1 gave way to the production of the Bf 109F-2 which varied from the F-1 only in that it replaced the nose-mounted MG FF cannon with the long awaited MG 151. The F-2 variant also was modified through the incorporation of a fuselage-mounted ETC 250 bomb rack or the addition of the GM 1 nitrous oxide power boost system on a number of aircraft. As the Luftwaffe had not standardized either the *Umruest-Bausatze* (factory installed modifications which were intended to increase performance or to utilize non-strategic materials) or the *Ruestsaetze* (bolt-on modifications that were added to the Bf 109 airframe for specific mission capabilities such as extended range and increased armament, and which could be incorporated either at the assembly line or in the field), the above noted modifications to the F-2 variant resulted in the designations of Bf 109F-2/Z (addition of GM 1 boost system) and the Bf 109F-2/B (addition of the ETC 250 ventral bomb rack) fighter-bomber. One further designation was allocated to the F-2 series, the Bf 109F-2/Trop, which was the tropicalized version. Like the previous Bf 109E-4/Trop, this sub-type was fitted with a dust filter over the supercharger air intake for use in the North African theater of operations.

The Bf 109F-3 and Bf 109F-4, which were produced simultaneously, replaced the F-2 variant on the assembly lines in early 1942 and differed from the F-2 in that they incorporated the long awaited DB 601E as the basic powerplant. The powerplant change was the only difference between the F-2 and F-3; however, the F-4 incorporated a number of additional modifications that were not externally discernible. These included an increase in the calibre of the MG 151 from 15-mm to 20-mm, the use of new self sealing fuel tanks, and an increase in the armor protection for the pilot. This protection included a thick steel plate behind the pilot's neck and upper back, and a similar plate mounted over his head under the bullet-resistant canopy glass. Both the F-3 and F-4 utilized the FuG 7a radio transmitter/receiver and Revi C/12D reflector gunsight that were standard on the earlier F-series.

A number of Bf 109F-4s were also modified like the F-2 variant with the incorporation of the GM 1 nitrous oxide boost system (Bf 109F-4/Z). In addition, two further

sub-type conversions were produced under the Bf 109F-4 designation. The first of these was the Bf 109F-4/R6 which was fitted with an extra pair of 20-mm MG 151 cannon in underwing gondolas. The increase in firepower was made at the request of General Adolf Galland and other top Luftwaffe fighter aces. The additional armament of the F-4/R6 was well received. The increased weight and added drag had a detrimental effect on the aircraft's handling qualities, however, reducing its capability as a "dogfighter," and the aircraft were used strictly as bomber-interceptors.

The second conversion was similar to that of the earlier fighter-bomber modifications to the Bf 109E-4/B and included the attachment of the ventrally-mounted ETC 250 bomb rack capable of carrying a 250 kg (550 lb) bomb, a 300 l (66 Imp gal) jettisonable fuel tank, or with an ER 4 adapter, four 50 kg (110 lb) SC 50 bombs.

The final two variants of the Bf 109F series were reconnaissance derivatives of the Bf 109F-4. The Bf 109F-5 eliminated the nose mounted cannon (for reduced weight and, thus, higher speed) and had a Rb 50/30 camera mounted in the aft fuselage. The Bf 109F-6 eliminated all armament and was fitted with a special camera bay in the underside of the fuselage just aft of the cockpit which was capable of utilizing the Rb 20/30, Rb 50/30 or RB 75/30 cameras. Both the F-5 and F-6 were fitted with a fuselage rack (R3 modification) for the 300 l (66 Imp gal) auxiliary fuel tank.

Bf 109G *series*

During late 1941 and early 1942, the RLM became increasingly concerned with higher aircraft speeds and was willing to accept higher wing and power loading risks. The necessity for a pressurized canopy was also among the requirements for higher altitude capability. The Bf 109G was to be their answer.

The G-version was planned to utilize the improved performance DB 605A powerplant with a take-off output of 1,450 hp and 1,250 hp at 20,000 feet. The only difference in the DB 605A and the then-popular DB 601E was that the new powerplant had a redesigned block which allowed oversized cylinders while maintaining the same centers. The increased volume raised the compression ratio

Hauptmann Gerhard Barkhorn, *Gruppenkommandeur,* II/JG 52 is congratulated on his 250th victory in his Bf109G-6/Trop *Christl.* 13 February, 1944. (BUNDESARCHIV)

while the basic dimensions of the overall engine remained the same. The installation of the DB 605A into the Bf 109G airframe, however, resulted in numerous structural changes as the new powerplant was not only more powerful (in torque), but was also heavier. As a consequence the weight spiral of the overall Bf 109 design continued upward, reducing handling and maneuvering characteristics.

To provide the necessary cockpit pressurization, Messerschmitt simply sealed the bulkheads, floorplate and sidewalls, incorporated a plate behind the pilot which seated with the fuselage wall on closure, and added seals to the hinged and open rails at the canopy to fuselage interfaces.

Construction of twelve pre-production Bf 109G-0s was started during the late summer of 1941, but the un-availability of the proposed DB 605A powerplant forced Messerschmitt to again substitute, this time with the DB 601E. The pre-production block was completed by October, 1941, and immediately, Messerschmitt set about initiation of the first production aircraft under the designation Bf 109G-1. The G-1, deliveries of which began in March, 1942, was fitted with a pressurized cockpit, incorporated the radio equipment of the Bf 109F-4 (FuG 7a) and was armed with an engine-mounted 20-mm Mauser MG 151 cannon with 200 rounds of ammunition and a pair of cowling mounted 7.9-mm MG 17 machine-guns with 500 rounds per gun. The G-1 was powered by the DB 605A-1 or DB 605B-1 and included provisions for mounting the GM 1 nitrous oxide power boost system, with the main tank and liquid oxygen bottles being located behind the cockpit.

One additional modification to the G-1 that was not present on the G-0 models included the fitting of a pair of small air scoops just aft of the propeller hub on both sides of the fuselage. These air scoops were to provide direct airstream cooling of the powerful DB 605A engine, which during prolonged ground operation (such as extended taxiing) had a tendency to overheat causing the nose-mounted oil tank to seep over the hot engine. Fires could

occur immediately, in which case shut-down solved the problem. In the air, where shut-down was not possible, the only solution was bailing out. In addition to the air scoops, the G-1 included an oil tank that was redesigned to allow for cooler operation and better sealing.

Sub-types of the G-1 variant during production included several *Ruestsaetze* and *Umruest-Bausatze* conversion kits.

G-1/U1 Evaluation aircraft incorporating a reversible-pitch Messerschmitt P-6 propeller. The propeller was to act like a thrust reverser on short field landings by redirecting airflow. Only a few of this model was delivered.

G-1/R3 Long range fighter with the addition of an under-fuselage rack for the fitting of a 300 l (66 Imp gal) auxiliary fuel drop tank.

G-1/R6 Fighter/interceptor with a pair of 20-mm MG 151 cannon in underwing gondolas assigned to the bomber attack role.

G-1/Trop. A specialized tropicalized version of the G-1 variant for use in North Africa. Because of continual over-heating problems with the engine-mounted cannon in the desert heat, this model also replaced the cowl-mounted 7.9-mm MG 17 machine-guns with a pair of 13-mm MG 131 machine-guns to provide greater firepower if malfunctioning of the nose cannon occurred. The aircraft also was fitted with the appropriate dust filters for the supercharger intake and radiator areas.

It should be noted here that the possibility of more than one conversion kit being added to an aircraft existed, and often became the rule as the war progressed. In most instances, however, the specified aircraft only carried a single designation. For example, a Bf 109G-1/R6 could have not only been fitted with the underwing MG 151 cannon, but could also have had an underfuselage bomb rack (fighter-bomber) or auxiliary fuel drop tank schackle (extended range fighter/interceptor) added.

Bf 109F-4/Trop

Oberleutnant Hans-Joachim Marseille as *Staffelkapitän* 3./JG 27 at Quotaifiya, North Africa, 15 September, 1942. Final rank/score: *Hauptmann*, 158 victories (all in the West).

Bf 109B

Spanish Nationalist air arm at Logroño, April, 1939. Transferred from 2./J 88 *Legion Condor*.

Bf 109E-4

Oberleutnat Helmut Wick as *Kommandeur* I/JG 2 at Mardyck, Belgium, 6 October, 1940. Final rank/score: *Major*, 56 victories.

Bf 109F-4/N Trop

Leutnant Werner Schroer, 2./JG 27, in North Africa, September, 1941. Final rank/score: *Major*, 114 victories.

R. Watanabe

◀ Me 309A-1

As a new fighter concept the Me 309 series bore little relationship to either the Bf 109 or the Me 209 series. It contained many innovative systems but by 1943 it was clear that the Me 309 had little chance of gaining official acceptance. The 309A-1 was a projected model, a fighter with two MG 131s and one MK 108.

▼ Bf 109Z Zwilling (Twin)

Offering an expedient solution to meet operational demands, the 'Twin 109' was initially projected as a *Zerstörer* (109Z-1) and high-speed bomber based on Bf 109G-6 airframes. The concept was also adapted for the intended Bf 109 replacements resulting in the Me 409 (twin Me 209) and Me 609 (twin Me 309) projects, which also had promising long-range reconnaissance potential.

The first and only Bf 109Z prototype assembled from two Bf 109F-4 airframes was completed in 1943 but damaged in an Allied air raid and never flown.

Due to changed operational requirements all further development work was abandoned in 1944.

Bf 109Z-1 (data based on project estimates)

Span:	13.270 m (43 ft 6¼ in)	Weight empty:	6,000 kg (13,224 lb)
Length:	9.048 m (29 ft 8 in)	Weight loaded:	7,280 kg (16,050 lb)
Height:	2.690 m (8 ft 10 in)	Max range:	1,995 km (1,240 mls)
Wing area:	23.2 m² (249.72 sq. ft)		
Max speed:	743 km/h at 8,000 m (462 mph at 26,250 ft)		
Cruising speed:	570 km/h at 3,000 m (354 mph at 9,840 ft)		
Service ceiling:	11,700 m (38,385 ft)		
Armamant:	2×30 mm MK 108 mounted in engines		
	2×30 mm MK 108 in underwing gondolas		
	1×30 mm MK 103 off centreline in wing center section		

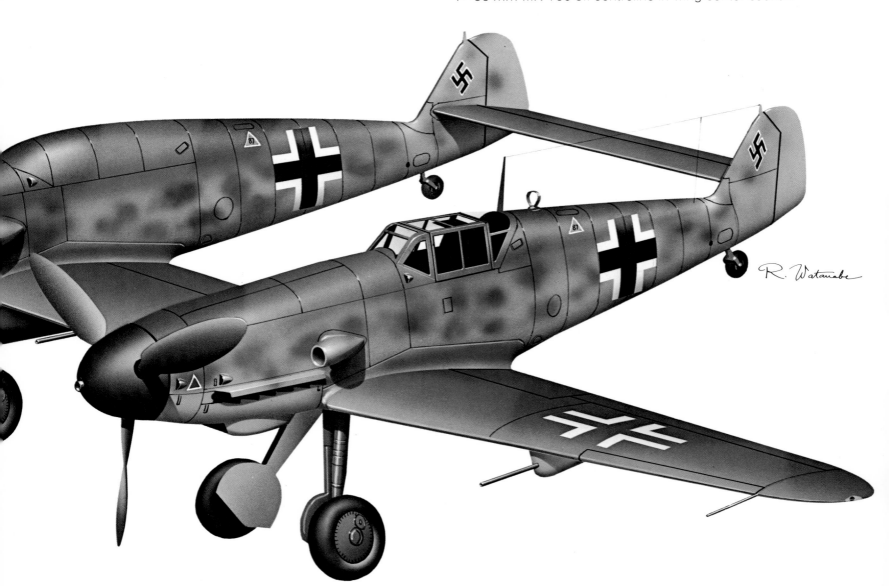

R. Watanabe

R. Watanabe

Bf 109F-2 'Special'
Oberst Adolf Galland as General of Fighters, December, 1941.
Final rank/score: *Generalleutnant*, 104 victories (all in the West).

Bf 109F-2
Oberstleutnant Werner Mölders as *Kommodore* JG 51, Eastern Front,
15 July, 1941. Final rank/score: *Oberst* (General of Fighters), 115 victories
(including 14 in Spain).

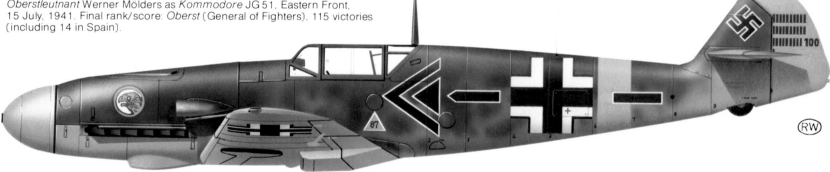

Bf 109F-2
Major Hannes Trautloft as *Kommodore* JG 54 at Siverskaya, Soviet Union,
winter 1941/42. Final rank/score: *Oberst*, 57 victories (including 4 in Spain).

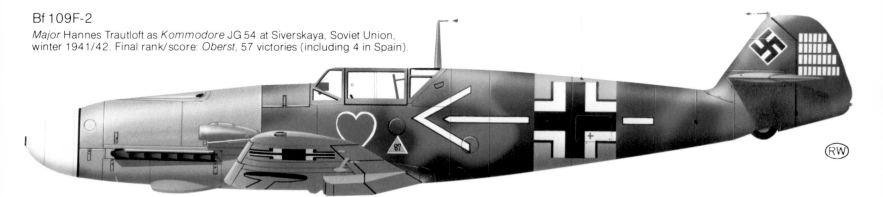

Bf 109F

Hauptmann Hans Philipp as *Kommandeur* I/JG 54 at Krasnogvardeisk,
Soviet Union, 31 March, 1942. Final rank/score: *Oberstleutnant*, 206 victories.

Bf 109F-4

Oberleutnant Siegfried Schnell as *Staffelkapitän* 9./JG 2 at Thêville, France,
late May, 1942. Final rank/score: *Major*, 93 victories.

Bf 109F-4

Oberleutnant Frank Liesendahl as *Staffelkapitän* 10. (Jabo)/JG 2 at
Beaumont, France, 31 March, 1942. Final rank: *Hauptmann;* his *Staffel*
reported sinking 20 ships (63,000 tons) by 26 June, 1942.

Bf 109G-2

Hauptmann Heinrich Ehrler as *Staffelkapitän* 6./JG 5 at Petsamo, Finland,
27 March, 1943. Final rank/score: *Major*, 209 victories.

◄ Bf 109H-1
High altitude interceptor. A limited number were completed from G-5 airframes in 1943. Early in 1944 a number of operational sorties were carried out including a few over England.

Span:	11.920 m (39 ft 1¼ in)	Height:	2.600 m (8 ft 6¼ in)
Length:	9.048 m (29 ft 8 in)	Service ceiling:	14,600 m (47,900 ft)

► Me 109TL

Proposed in January, 1943, to provide a quickly available jet-powered fighter utilizing many proven components in case the Me 262 series production should run into problems. The Me 109TL design was based on Me 155 fuselage with most equipment, combining it with wings of projected Me 409 and nose-wheel undercarriage of Me 309, with new nose section and tailplane. More detailed examination indicated the need for prolonged tests when those of the Me 262 had already been completed, and the project was dropped in March, 1943.

Two Jumo 004B-1 turbo-jet units
Take-off power 2×850 kgp (1874 lb/st. thr)

Span:	12.55 m (41 ft 2 in)	Weight empty:	3070 kg (6868 lb)
Length:	9.50 m (31 ft 2 in)	Weight loaded:	4750 kg (10,472 lb)
Height:	2.90 m (9 ft 6 in)		
Wing area:	19.50 m² (209.82 sq. ft)		

Performance estimates:
Max speed: 840 km/h (522 mph) at sea level,
                 980 km/h at 9000 m (609 mph at 29,530 ft)
Landing speed: 160 km/h (99 mph)
Service ceiling: 11,400 m (37,400 ft)

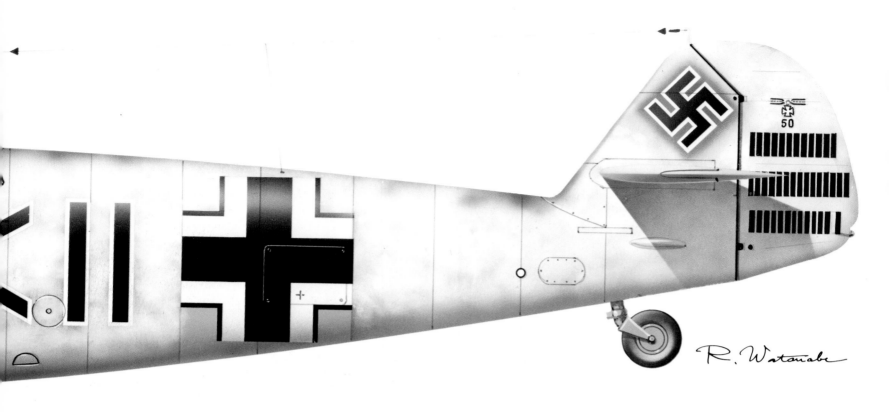

R. Watanabe

Bf 109G-2

Hauptmann Johannes Steinhoff as *Kommandeur* II/JG 52, Eastern Front, summer 1942. Final rank/score: *Oberst*, 176 victories.

Bf 109G-6

Leutnant Erich Hartmann of 9./JG 52 at Novo Zaporozhe, Soviet Union, summer 1942. Final rank/score: *Major*, 352 victories.

Bf 109K-4/R

Pilot unknown. I/JG 77, spring 1945.

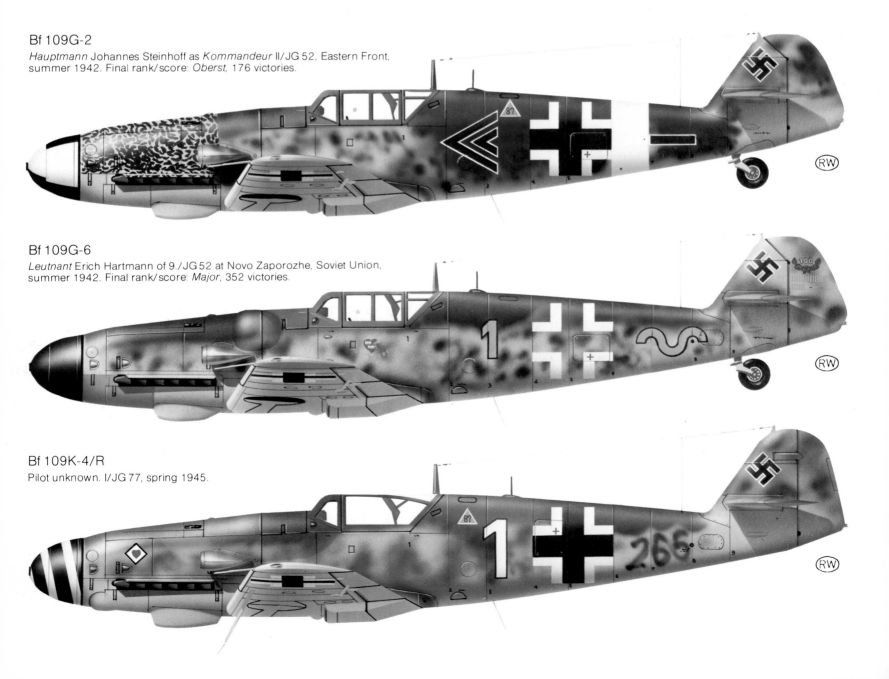

Produced in parallel with the Bf 109G-1, and in greater quantities, the Bf 109G-2 was identical except that it did not contain a pressurized cockpit or GM 1 power boost system. Sub-types of the basic Bf 109G-2 were also identical to those of the Bf 109G-1.

One unique experimental evaluation conducted on the Bf 109G-2 was a design for the development of an extended range fighter-bomber. A Bf 109G-0 (pre-production aircraft) was refitted with a DB 605A and redesignated Bf 109G-2/R1 for this test. The basic problem was in the size of the SC 500 bomb that was planned to be carried, in that it did not provide adequate clearance for takeoff when attached. To solve the problem, Fieseler designed an auxiliary single-wheel undercarriage component that could be attached to the underside of the fuselage just aft of the bomb, raising the aircraft off the ground. The undercarriage could be released after take-off through a series of explosive bolts and returned to the ground by parachute. To increase range, the plane was also fitted with two racks, or shackles for attachment of a pair of 300 l (66 Imp gal) drop tanks. After successful initial flight testing, however, the project was discontinued.

In April, 1942, the Bf 109G-4 was introduced into the assembly lines. The only major changes between it and the previous models were that it was not pressurized and had replaced the FuG 7a radio equipment with the newer and longer range FuG 16ZY equipment.

Although designated as a photo-reconnaissance fighter to be fitted with a camera installation in the aft fuselage, the Bf 109G-4 was delivered in several variants, and functioned in a number of additional roles for the Luftwaffe. In addition to the modified variants produced under the G-1 and G-2 designation, the G-4 also was ordered and/or delivered in the R1, R2, R4 and R7 models.

G-4/R1 Limited production fighter-bomber fitted with a ventral bomb rack for carrying a SC 250 bomb.

G-4/R2 Authorized fighter-bomber version incorporating the ETC 50/VIIId bomb rack capable of carrying four SC 50 bombs; however, this model was never delivered.

G-4/R4 Reconnaissance fighter incorporating an Rb 50/30 camera and a pair of wing mounted 300 l (66 Imp gal) drop tanks. This model, like the R2, never reached production.

G-4/R7 Standard fighter fitted with directional finding equipment installed inside the aft fuselage behind the cockpit, including a D/F loop antenna, to facilitate the locating of the aircraft in poor weather, poor visibility or after a crash landing.

With the introduction of the G-4 into service in August, 1943, the next version of the G-series to reach production status was the Bf 109G-3. This aircraft was nearly identical to the Bf 109G-4 in basic equipment, except that it incorporated the pressurized cockpit and GM 1 power boost system of the G-1 version and was designated for high altitude operation. Although relatively few Bf 109G-3s were delivered to Luftwaffe units, it was produced in a number of models including the R1, R2, R3, R6 and U2. The Bf 109G-3/U2 represented the first model of the Bf 109 series to use a non-strategic material in a major component. In this case, the tailplane was made of wood and a larger trim tab was included that was controllable from the cockpit. This aircraft was utilized for test and evaluation, with the wooden tailplane later being installed on several future G-series variants, except for the G-14 which utilized an entirely redesigned tailplane shape.

Bf 109G-6/R3, summer, 1944.

In addition, the Bf 109G-3 was the first G-series aircraft to exhibit wing surface bulges resulting from the use of larger tires necessitated by the increased weight of the G-series aircraft. The larger mainwheels, in addition to offering higher safety factors, required an increased area in the innerwing when retracted, and as the initial volume had been allocated to the smaller standard wheels of earlier variants, Messerschmitt either had to redesign the wing chord (which would mean complicated and extended testing), or add a slight drag-increasing bulge to the wing surface. The Bf 109G-5 entered production during the late June and early July of 1943, but did not appear with Luftwaffe units until January, 1944. The G-5 was powered by the DB 605A-1 engine, but in an effort to provide more efficient high altitude performance, was also delivered with an optional DB 605AS powerplant which was fitted with a larger supercharger. (Aircraft receiving the DB 605AS were designated with the letters AS after the variant, or *Ruestsaetze* (R), identification.) Armament of the Bf 109G-5 consisted of the engine mounted 20-mm MG 151 cannon and a pair of cowl-mounted 13-mm MG 131 machine-guns, which had been standardized for all future G-series variants. The increase in the size of the cowling weaponry resulted in still another set of external bulges, this time over the MG 131 breech blocks and ammunition feed chutes which were larger than those of the MG 17s.

The Bf 109G-5 was also fitted with a shorter radio mast and a directional finding loop antenna on later models, which incorporated the R7 directional transmitter inside the aft fuselage. One additional modification that was installed in the Bf 109G-5 was the improved vision "Galland" canopy which restructured the canopy braces and added bullet-resistant glass and thicker armor plate in key areas. This canopy was installed on a few late model G-5s, but did not become standard until the introduction of the G-14 variant.

Sub-type designations of the Bf 109G-5 to see service included the U2, R3, R6, R7, and the Trop., while authorization and plans for production of R1 and R2 models were received, but never started.

One unique modification incorporated into the G-5 was the addition of a pair of underwing Wfr. Gr. 210-mm mortar tubes for operations against Allied bomber streams. Designated as the Bf 109G-5/BR 21, the mortar tube concept was actually developed and flown initially on the Bf 109G-6 which preceded the G-5 variant in delivery to service units.

As noted above, the Bf 109G-6, although put into production at the same time as the Bf 109G-5, actually entered service first. It was identical to the G-5 variant except that it did not have provisions for cockpit pressurization. Produced in essentially the same models as previous G-series variants, the G-6 modifications also included the U2, U3, U4 and N designations. The Bf 109G-6/U3 identified the aircraft as being fitted with the MW 50 water-methanol supercharger boost system. Utilizing the tanks located behind the cockpit (used for the GM-1 system), the MW injectant, composed of 50% water and 50% methanol, was fed into the supercharger below the rated altitude of the powerplant to increase power through higher boost pressures. This system could increase take-off performance by over 300 hp, and provide similar power boosts up to altitudes of 6000 m (20,000 ft).

The Bf 109G-6/U4 was the result of continuing efforts by the RLM and Messerschmitt to increase the firepower of the Bf 109. The U4 modification incorporated an engine-mounted 30-mm MK 108 short barrel cannon in place of the 20-mm MG 151. Manufactured by Rheinmetall, the MK 108 had a rate of fire of 450 rounds per minute, was electrically actuated and automatically operated through a compressed air system separate from the weapon. Although a large number of G-6s were scheduled to receive the U4 modification, the limited supply of the MK 108s restricted its application and forced the retention of the MG 151 in most models.

The Bf 109G-6/N was a modification derived specifically for the night-fighting role. (As opposed to the use of the "N" designation in the E-series to identify use of the DB 601N.) The aircraft featured exhaust shields and flame dampers (to reduce the emission of light during night flying), the *Ruestsaetz* 6 (R6) conversion kit (which incorporated a pair of MG 151 cannon in underwing gondolas), and was fitted with the FuG 350 *Naxos* Z electronic receiver. This receiver was capable of homing on the H2S radar used by the Royal Air Force pathfinder aircraft, allowing the Bf 109G-6/N not only to locate the Allied bomber stream without ground guidance, but also to vector other airborne Luftwaffe interceptor units to the target. For the installation of the FuG 350, a transparent hemispherical dome was fitted just aft of the cockpit and the D/F loop was relocated to the underside of the fuselage.

The Bf 109G-8, entering production in late 1943, was a photo-reconnaissance variant of the Bf 109G-6. Incorporating the use of either an Rb 12.5/7 or Rb 32/7 camera, the only other changes were in the deletion of the cowl-mounted MG 131 machine-guns to reduce the overall aircraft weight, and the addition of a port wing-mounted gun-camera. The incorporation of the wing-mounted gun-camera, actuated by the gun-trigger button, was done on an experimental basis to gather data for its installation in future Bf 109 variants.

By April, 1944, production of the Bf 109G-6 and G-8 had given way to the Bf 109G-10, which was intended to standardize several of the *Umruest-Bausatze* modifications, including the wooden tailplane, MW 50 power boost system, and semi-retractable tailwheel assembly. Because of the numerous assembly plants engaged in producing the Bf 109G, however, and the limited availability of several of the components as a result of continuous Allied raids against the supplying plants, a formalized standard Bf 109G-10 was never achieved.

The Bf 109G-10 was powered by the DB 605D engine coupled with the MW 50 power boost system and delivered an impressive 1,850 hp at take-off. The new powerplant had been fitted with a larger diameter supercharger and the compression ratio was increased by 15% through redesign of the cylinders. The cowl-mounted MG 131 machine-guns were retained and either an engine-mounted MK 108 or MG 151 cannon was incorporated, depending on supply. The G-10 also was fitted with the FuG 16ZY radio and FuG 25a IFF equipment, and a Revi 16B reflector gunsight replaced the previous Revi 12D.

Like other variants of the Bf 109G series, the Bf 109G-10 was delivered in various sub-types which incorporated a number of *Umruest-Bausatz* and *Ruestsaetze* conversions.

G-10/U2 Adaptation of the non-strategic wooden tailplane.

G-10/U4 Adaptation of U2 wooden tailplane and the addition of a redesigned and enlarged rudder, also fabricated as a wooden structure.

G-10/R1 Fighter-bomber adaptation with a ventral rack for carrying a single 250 kg (550 lb) SC 250 bomb or four 50 kg (110 lb) SC 50 bombs.

G-10/R3 Extended range fighter with adaptation of fuselage rack for attachment of 300 l (66 Imp gal) drop tank.

G-10/R5 Interceptor with addition of a pair of underwing gondolas carrying 30-mm MK 108 short barrel cannon.

G-10/R7 Although not designated as R7 due to more than one *Ruestsaetze* modification being used, the installation of the R7 location signal device saw wide usage on the G-10 series.   One of the more unique of the G-series variant was the Bf 109G-12 which was a two-seat training conversion of the basic Bf 109G airframe. Studies for this sub-type had been started with the Bf 109E version in 1940 (under the designation Bf 109S), but the concept had not been authorized until late 1942 when pilot training in the Bf 109 had been accelerated. For the prototype of this variant, a Bf 109G-5 was modified through removal of the pressurization equipment, and the incorporation of an elongated canopy with a second set of controls and pilot instruments. The canopy housing was hinged in the student's location, with the aft portion being curved outward to give the instructor a better view. A large number of G-5 and G-6 aircraft were converted to the G-12 variant during 1943 and 1944, although production of a G-12 straight from the assembly line never became a reality due to the pressing need for increased fighter strength and the limited availability of components. One *Ruestsatz* that was added to the G-12 variant was the R3, which provided the training flights with increased range and endurance through the installation of the 300 l (66 Imp gal) auxiliary fuel drop tank.

By July, 1944, still a further variant of the Bf 109G series was being delivered to the Luftwaffe, this being the Bf 109G-14. Utilizing the DB 605AS or DB 605AM powerplants, and standardized in the incorporation of the "Galland" type canopy first used on the G-5, the G-14 was armed with the pair of cowl-mounted MG 131 machine-guns and an engine-mounted 20-mm MG 151 cannon. Although only a limited number of this variant were produced due to the impending introduction of the Bf 109K, several modifications were adapted including the U4, U6, R1, R3, and R6. The U6 conversion was the installation of the longer barrel 30-mm MK 103 cannon as an engine-mounted weapon in place of the 20-mm MG 151.

The final production variant of the Bf 109G series was the G-16, which was essentially identical to the G-14 except that it reverted back to use of the DB 605D powerplant and had standardized installation of the R1 (ventral bomb or drop tank rack) and R6 (underwing mounted 20-mm MG 151 cannon in gondolas) at the factory.

Bf 109H *series*

The Bf 109H was the result of a proposal by Messerschmitt A.G. to the RLM to provide a high-performance high-altitude interceptor. The request from the German Air Ministry in early 1943 was based on the increasing need of

Revi C/12D reflex gunsight

R. Watanabe

the Luftwaffe for a fighter plane that could intercept and combat the Allied bombers at high altitudes, or use the advantage of altitude for escape or to surprise the enemy.

The *Hochleistungsjaeger* (High performance fighter) was proposed to be produced in two separate phases. First, an interim or temporary aircraft would be delivered to the Luftwaffe to provide capabilities during the design and development of the advanced, or second phase, fighter. The Bf 109H was proposed to serve as the interim aircraft.

The original Bf 109H was almost identical to the Bf 109F, utilizing the basic airframe, but had an extended center section of the wing which increased surface area for high altitude operation. However, changing RLM requirements during 1943, especially increases in operating altitudes, resulted in the abandonment of the original Bf 109H concept. Instead, an alternate Messerschmitt proposal was made to proceed on the Me 209-II programme which was to incorporate either a DB 628A or DB 603E powerplant. These engines were specifically developed with turbo-supercharger for high altitude operations.

Realizing that Messerschmitt could not deliver the Me 209-II before 1944, and recognizing the importance of receiving a new interceptor as soon as possible, the RLM instructed Messerschmitt to proceed with the basic Bf 109H program, but to modify the configuration to utilize several of the Me 209-II components, including the DB 628A engine. Due to the fact that a Bf 109G airframe had already been modified to accept a mock-up of the DB 628A powerplant as a prototype (Bf 109 V49) and proved the concept's feasibility for the Me 209-II project, a second Bf 109G airframe was diverted from the assembly line (designated Bf 109 V50) and installed with a development engine for flight testing.

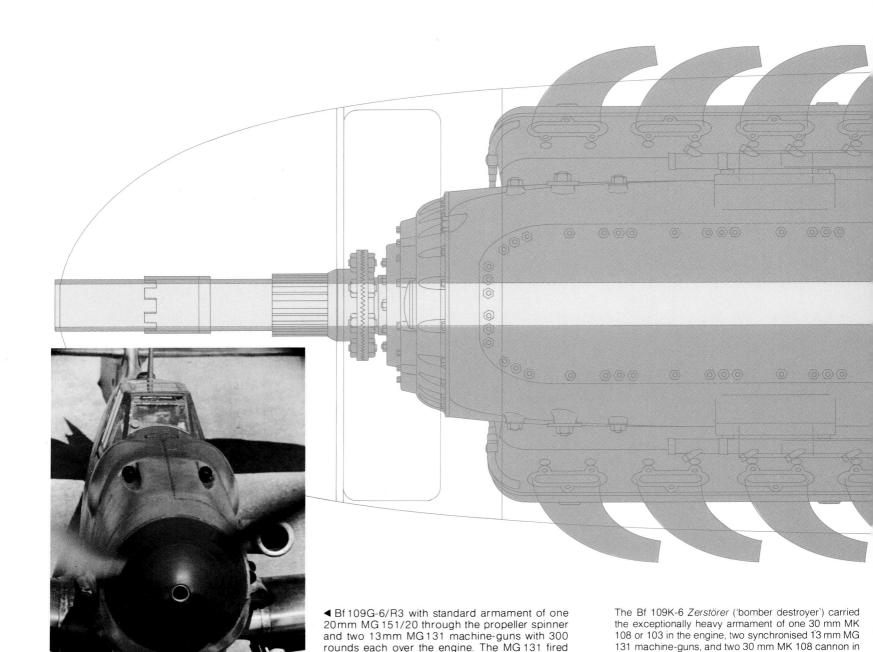

◄ Bf 109G-6/R3 with standard armament of one 20mm MG 151/20 through the propeller spinner and two 13mm MG 131 machine-guns with 300 rounds each over the engine. The MG 131 fired 930 rounds/min and had a muzzle velocity of 750 m/sec (2460 ft/sec).

(BUNDESARCHIV)

The Bf 109K-6 *Zerstörer* ('bomber destroyer') carried the exceptionally heavy armament of one 30 mm MK 108 or 103 in the engine, two synchronised 13 mm MG 131 machine-guns, and two 30 mm MK 108 cannon in the wings. Production began in January, 1945, but, only a limited number were ever used operationally. Heavy and unwieldy, the Bf 109K-6 was no match for Allied escort fighters.

Being nearly 180 kg (400 lbs) heavier and some 60 cm (2 ft) longer than the standard DB 605 powerplant used in the Bf 109G, the installation of the DB 628A into the Bf 109H prototype required the use of balance weights in the aft fuselage to insure maintaining of the aircraft center-of-gravity. This was to be compensated for in later models through the forward movement of the main wing attach points and an increase in the tail and rudder surfaces.

After initial flight trials at Augsburg, the V50 was transferred to Daimler-Benz for extended duration and altitude testing of the engine. While the testing of the V50 aircraft continued near Stuttgart, the Augsburg facility modified still another Bf 109G, under the designation Bf 109 V54, installing a DB 628 powerplant and incorporating the increased center wing section and tail surfaces.

In the meantime, while the testing of the new engine was being conducted at both Stuttgart and Augsburg, Messerschmitt initiated assembly of a number of modified Bf 109Fs under the designation Bf 109H-0 to conduct limit load tests of the widened undercarriage and increased surface areas. A number of Bf 109H-1s also were initiated and earmarked for delivery to the Luftwaffe for service evaluation. These aircraft utilized the DB 605A engine with the GM 1 injectant boost system.

The Bf 109H-1s were delivered to a Luftwaffe evaluation unit near Paris in early 1944, and while general handling characteristics were acceptable, the aircraft did exhibit a serious wing flutter in diving attitudes at high speed. To try and determine the cause and correction for the wing flutter, a number of Bf 109H-1s were returned to Augsburg for company testing and evaluation. During one of these tests, in April, 1944, the test pilot encountered the problem during a steep dive and pulled up sharply. In the pull-up the aircraft's wing was torn off. Limited testing continued on the aircraft; however, within the month, the Bf 109H program was cancelled and the RLM selected the Focke-Wulf Ta 152H for the high-altitude interceptor role.

Several additional proposals were offered by Messerschmitt based on the Bf 109H, including the H-2 (fitted with a Junkers Jumo 213E powerplant with GM 1 injection, engine-mounted 30-mm MK 103 cannon and a pair of wing-mounted 20-mm MG 151 cannon), the H-3 (fitted with the Jumo 213E engine and armed with a centre firing 30-mm MK 108 cannon and a pair of wing-mounted 13-mm

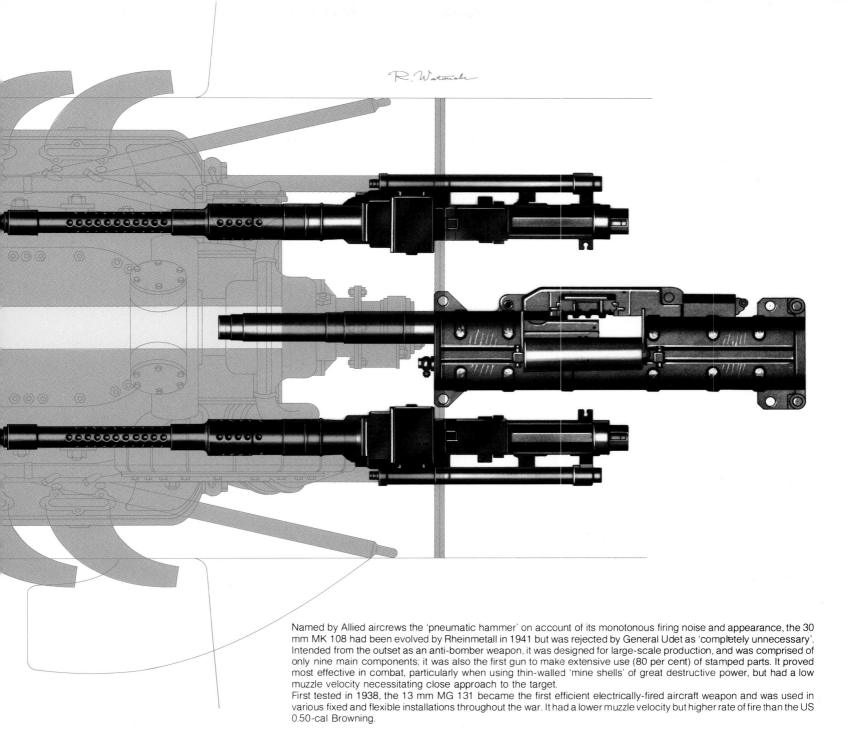

Named by Allied aircrews the 'pneumatic hammer' on account of its monotonous firing noise and appearance, the 30 mm MK 108 had been evolved by Rheinmetall in 1941 but was rejected by General Udet as 'completely unnecessary'. Intended from the outset as an anti-bomber weapon, it was designed for large-scale production, and was comprised of only nine main components; it was also the first gun to make extensive use (80 per cent) of stamped parts. It proved most effective in combat, particularly when using thin-walled 'mine shells' of great destructive power, but had a low muzzle velocity necessitating close approach to the target.

First tested in 1938, the 13 mm MG 131 became the first efficient electrically-fired aircraft weapon and was used in various fixed and flexible installations throughout the war. It had a lower muzzle velocity but higher rate of fire than the US 0.50-cal Browning.

MG 131 machine-guns), and the H-4 (reconnaissance aircraft with a camera installation in the aft fuselage). However, none of these proposals were ever accepted by the RLM for prototyping or development due to the success being enjoyed by both the FW 190D and Ta 152H.

Bf 109K *series*

The Bf 109K was the product of a standardization policy instituted by the RLM to reduce the number of variants and sub-types in the various basic airframes in use by the Luftwaffe. The plan was to select a basic variant, incorporating all the improvements that had evolved through the earlier sub-types, and establish a standard aircraft which would be manufactured by each of the aircraft plants involved in that particular design.

The Bf 109K was such an aircraft, and was based on the Bf 109G-10 variant, incorporating a number of the *Umruest-Bausatz* as well as several minor aerodynamic external features to improve streamlining. The pre-production aircraft, designated Bf 109K-0 for service evalu-

ation and acceptance, were similar to the late G-series production aircraft, but differed in that they had a raised cowling line just forward of the cockpit, a lengthened spinner, installation of the "Galland" type canopy, an enlarged tail assembly, and a fully retractable tailwheel which utilized a longer strut to raise the tail higher during take-offs and allow the pilot increased visibility in a forward attitude, and a modified rudder. In addition to the testing of the standardized G-10 armament of the nose-mounted 20-mm MG 151 cannon and cowling-mounted 13-mm MG 131 machine-guns, the K-0 prototypes also were evaluated with the incorporation of either a 30-mm MK 103 or an MK 108 nose-mounted cannon (the primary difference in the MK 103 and MK 108 was in the length of the barrel) and a pair of cowling-mounted 15-mm MG 151 machine-guns. The powerplant for the Bf 109K-0 was the DB 605B and included the installation of the GM 1 injectant boost system.

The initial production batch of K-series aircraft to be delivered consisted of both the Bf 109K-2 and the Bf 109K-4 models. Powered by either the DB 605 ASC or DB 605 DC engines rated at 2,000 hp for take-off and incorporating the GM 1 boost system, the K-2 and K-4 incorporated the

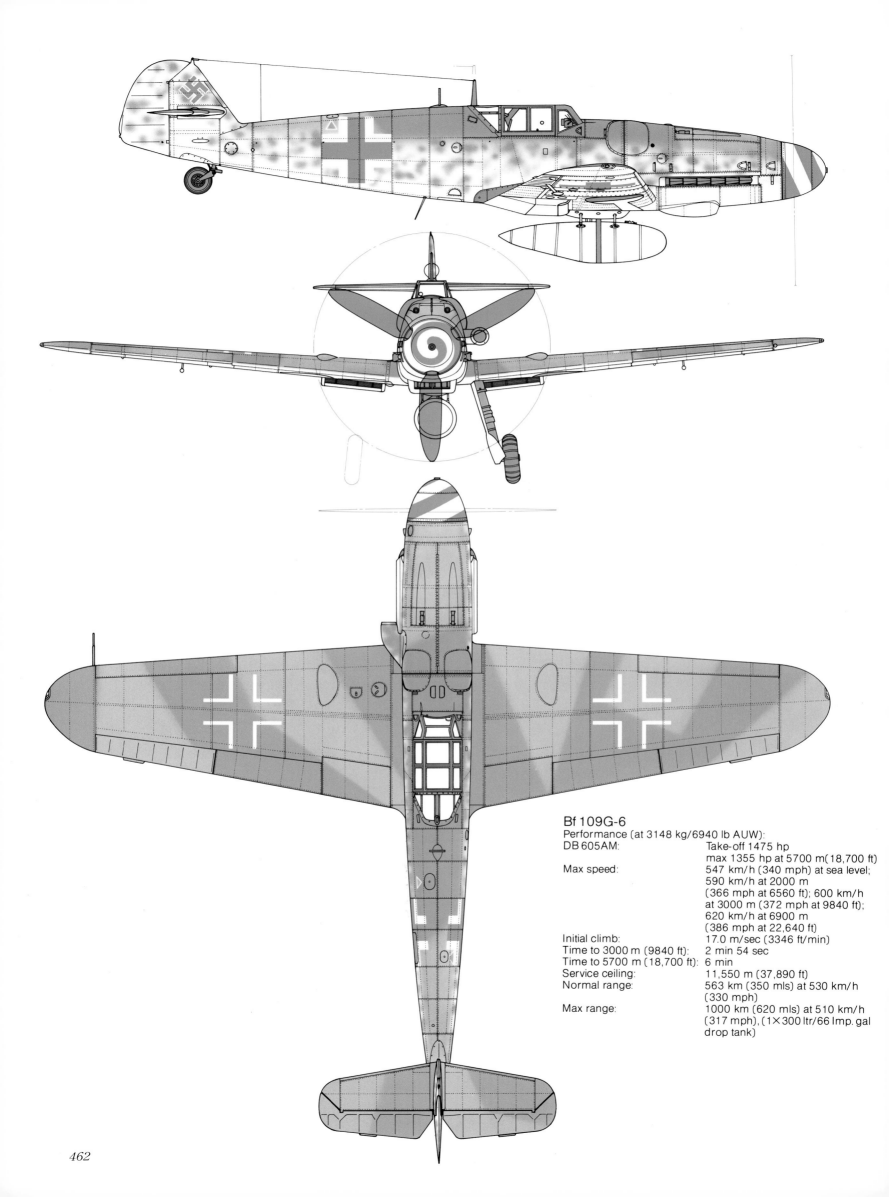

Bf 109G-6
Performance (at 3148 kg/6940 lb AUW):
DB 605AM: Take-off 1475 hp
                max 1355 hp at 5700 m(18,700 ft)
Max speed: 547 km/h (340 mph) at sea level;
                590 km/h at 2000 m
                (366 mph at 6560 ft); 600 km/h
                at 3000 m (372 mph at 9840 ft);
                620 km/h at 6900 m
                (386 mph at 22,640 ft)
Initial climb: 17.0 m/sec (3346 ft/min)
Time to 3000 m (9840 ft):   2 min 54 sec
Time to 5700 m (18,700 ft): 6 min
Service ceiling: 11,550 m (37,890 ft)
Normal range: 563 km (350 mls) at 530 km/h
                (330 mph)
Max range: 1000 km (620 mls) at 510 km/h
                (317 mph), (1×300 ltr/66 Imp. gal
                drop tank)

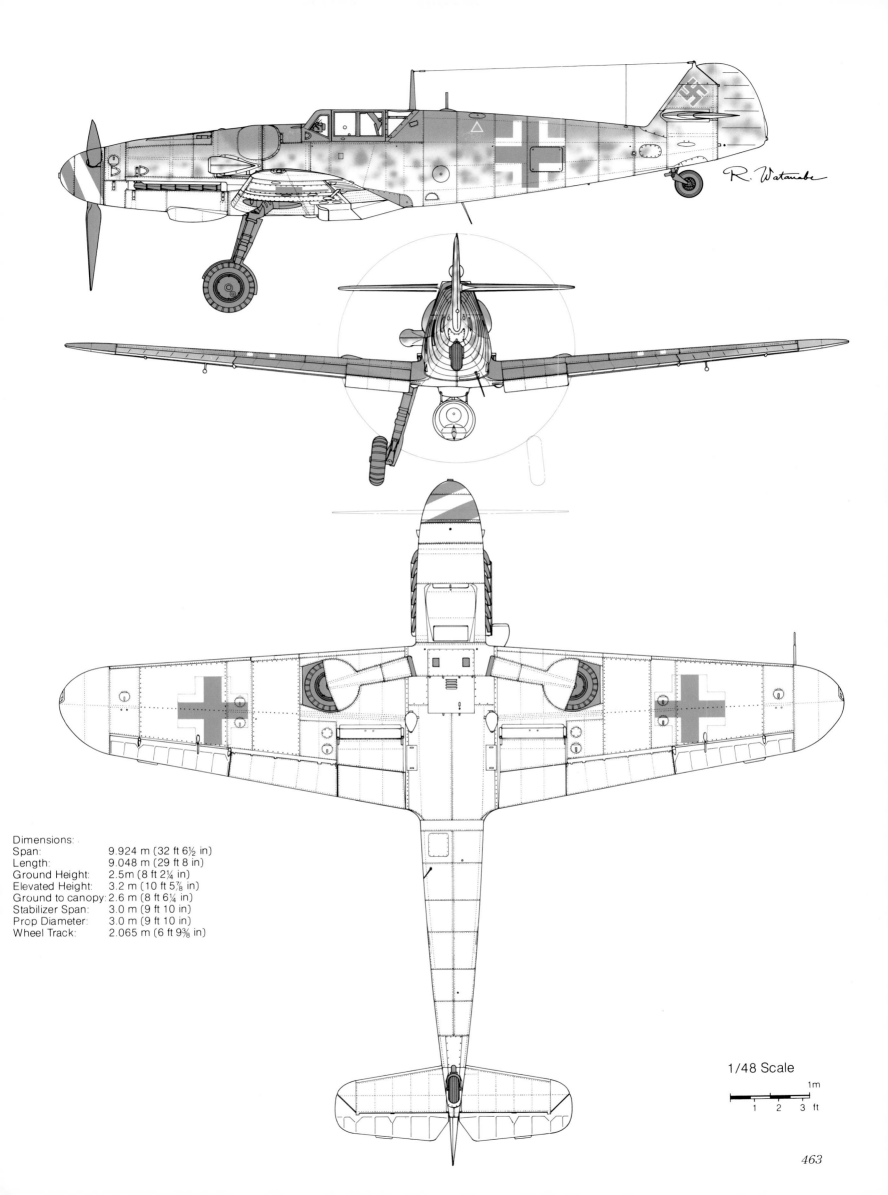

R. Watanabe

Dimensions:
Span: 9.924 m (32 ft 6½ in)
Length: 9.048 m (29 ft 8 in)
Ground Height: 2.5m (8 ft 2¼ in)
Elevated Height: 3.2 m (10 ft 5⅞ in)
Ground to canopy: 2.6 m (8 ft 6¼ in)
Stabilizer Span: 3.0 m (9 ft 10 in)
Prop Diameter: 3.0 m (9 ft 10 in)
Wheel Track: 2.065 m (6 ft 9⅜ in)

1/48 Scale

1m

1   2   3 ft

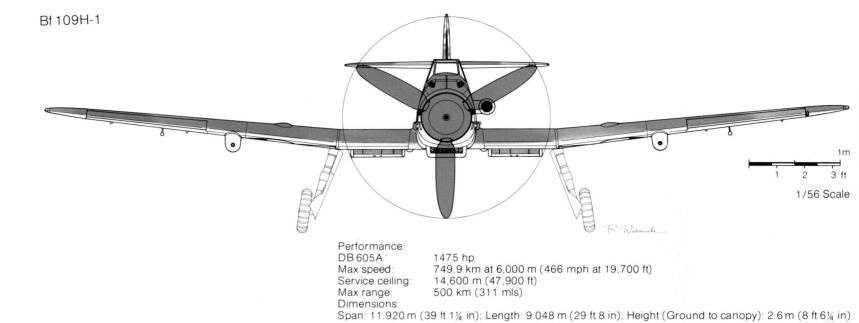

Performance:
DB 605A: 1475 hp
Max speed: 749.9 km at 6,000 m (466 mph at 19,700 ft)
Service ceiling: 14,600 m (47,900 ft)
Max range: 500 km (311 mls)
Dimensions:
Span: 11.920 m (39 ft 1¼ in); Length: 9.048 m (29 ft 8 in); Height (Ground to canopy): 2.6 m (8 ft 6¼ in)

1m
1   2   3 ft
1/56 Scale

modifications noted for the pre-production aircraft and standardized on the 30-mm nose cannon in combination with a pair of 15-mm MG 151 machine-guns. The only difference in the two models was in the installation of a pressurized cockpit into the K-4 model.

Ruestsaetze utilized on the Bf 109K-2 and K-4 models included the R1, R2, and R3 which provided the aircraft the capabilities of adapting to the fighter-bomber role with the use of the ETC racks (R1 and R2) or to the long range interceptor role with the R3 addition of the 300 l (66 Imp gal) ventraly-mounted drop tank.

With deliveries of the Bf 109K-2 and K-4 beginning in October, 1944, Messerschmitt undertook a further refinement of the basic K-series airframe to be used as a high-altitude bomber-interceptor. The designation assigned to this aircraft was Bf 109K-6. The aircraft was similar to the K-4, but reverted back to the 13-mm MG 131 fuselage mounted machine-guns and was fitted with a pair of 30-mm MK 108 cannons in the wings for added firepower, had a BSK 16 gun-camera installed inboard of the port wing cannon, and was equipped with a FuG 16ZY with underwing long range antenna on the port side.

A pair of *Ruestsaetze* were also available and utilized on the Bf 109K-6. These included the R3 (300 l [66 Imp gal] center mounted auxiliary fuel drop tank) and the R5 (30-mm MK 108 short barrel cannon in underwing gondolas). Both field conversions were rare and of an experimental nature due to the limited number of Bf 109K-6s delivered prior to the cessation of hostilities.

The Bf 109K-8 was produced as a photo-reconnaissance version of the K-6 variant, being fitted with a Rb 50/30 camera in the aft fuselage and fabricated without the fuselage mounted machine-guns, the cowling being faired over the gun troughs. These aircraft were scheduled to begin production during the early spring of 1945, however, with the end of the war, only a few of this variant ever left the assembly line.

The Bf 109K-10 variant represented a simple change in armament from the K-4 and the addition of one or more field conversions. Powered by the DB 601D engine, the K-10 was fitted with a pair of fuselage-mounted MG 131 machine-guns and a nose-mounted MK 103 cannon, and like the K-6 was fitted with a BSK gun camera and the FuG 16ZY

radio equipment. Conversion kits added to the few examples of this model to reach operational units included the auxiliary drop tank (R3), wing pylons for attachment of a pair of 300 l (66 Imp gal) jettisonable fuel tank (R4), and a pair of underwing 30-mm MK 108 short barrel cannon in gondolas (R5).

The final variant of the K-series to be produced was the Bf 109K-14 which reached operational Luftwaffe units during the last two weeks of the war. It was fitted with a DB 601L powerplant with a two-stage supercharger, offering over 1,700 hp at take-off with the use of 96 octane fuel. The obvious advantages of the new powerplant, which also made use of the MW 50 boost system, was that it could attain airspeeds of over 720km/h(450 mph) at altitudes in excess of 10,700 m (35,000 ft).

The only drawback to the Bf 109K-14 was in its armament which, like on the K-8, was limited to a pair of fuselage-mounted MG 131 machine-guns and a single nose-mounted MK 103 or MK 108 cannon. Like the earlier models of the K-series, the K-14 also incorporated the D/F loop and FuG 16ZY antenna to supplement the normal radio mast behind the cockpit, and was fitted with the Revi 16B reflector gunsight.

Bf 109L *series*

Never intended as a Bf 109 variant, the Bf 109L was the result of the cancellation of the Me 209 program at the Messerschmitt plant at Augsburg. The Me 209 program had been initiated in 1943 with the proposal for the mating of the new Jumo 213E-1 powerplant with a Bf 109F-1 airframe. By the spring of 1944 the prototype, designated Me 209 V6 was ready for flight testing. However, because of the success and progress of the Fw 190D and Ta 152H, the entire Me 209 program was halted.

Not willing to concede the production of the new high-performance high altitude fighter to Focke-Wulf, Messerschmitt decided to proceed with his project, changing the aircraft's designation to the Bf 109L. However, due to pressing production needs of the Bf 109G, and the work being conducted with the Bf 109H, no further efforts were expended on the Bf 109L.

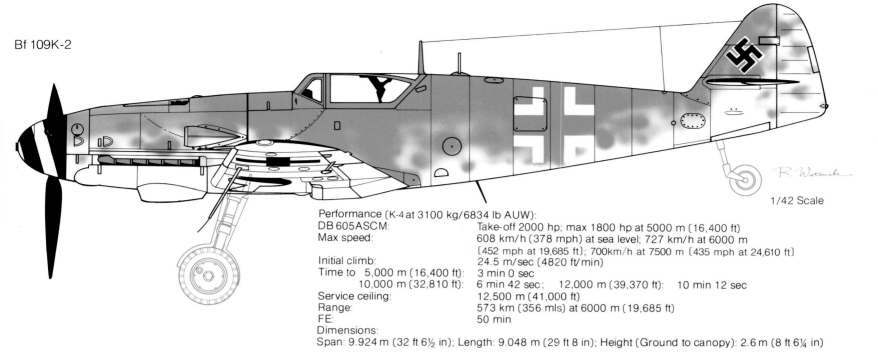

Bf 109K-2

Performance (K-4 at 3100 kg/6834 lb AUW):
DB 605ASCM: Take-off 2000 hp; max 1800 hp at 5000 m (16,400 ft)
Max speed: 608 km/h (378 mph) at sea level; 727 km/h at 6000 m
                           [452 mph at 19,685 ft]; 700km/h at 7500 m [435 mph at 24,610 ft]
Initial climb: 24.5 m/sec (4820 ft/min)
Time to 5,000 m (16,400 ft):   3 min 0 sec
        10,000 m (32,810 ft):   6 min 42 sec;   12,000 m (39,370 ft):   10 min 12 sec
Service ceiling: 12,500 m (41,000 ft)
Range: 573 km (356 mls) at 6000 m (19,685 ft)
FE: 50 min
Dimensions:
Span: 9.924 m (32 ft 6½ in); Length: 9.048 m (29 ft 8 in); Height (Ground to canopy): 2.6 m (8 ft 6¼ in)

1/42 Scale

Bf 109S *series*

The Bf 109S was the designation that resulted from a Messerschmitt project to transform the Bf 109E into a two place trainer. No immediate need was forecast for its use by the RLM and the proposal was rejected. However, in 1942 the program was resurrected utilizing the G-series and culminated in the delivery of several of this model to Luftwaffe *Jagdgeschwader* and fighter-training schools.

Bf 109T *series*

Not unlike other countries which would eventually be involved in World War II, Germany realized the importance that sea warfare would play in deciding the outcome of any future conflict. Therefore, in 1935 the *Kriegsmarine* initiated the procurement of a pair of aircraft carriers under the designations, *Graf Zeppelin* and *Peter Strasser*. To provide air units for the pair of carriers, to be part of the German Fleet by 1944, a special unit of Bf 109Bs and Ju 87s was assigned to Kiel-Holtenau, a large harbor on the Baltic Sea, for training as part of the first *Traegergruppe* (Carrier Group). The initial training was conducted with specially modified He 50s at Travemuende where landings and take-offs were conducted at low speeds on an outlined landing surface to simulate the deck of the *Graf Zeppelin*.

  Based on the initial success of the training operations, Messerschmitt was instructed to provide the *Kriegsmarine* with a carrier version of the Bf 109E. The design, designated Bf 109T *(Traeger),* was a simple modification of the basic Bf 109E-1 with an increased wing area, accomplished through the addition of approximately 60 cm (2 ft) to the outer panel length, the incorporation of an arrester hook just forward of the tailwheel, and the installation of catapult attach points and associated strengthening. The lengthened wings were also designed with a hinge to allow folding for storage which reduced the wing span of the plane to just over 4 m (13 ft), some 7 m (23 ft) less than the standard Bf 109E fighter.

  The design was accepted by the *Kriegmarine;* however, because of the demand on production being conducted at Augsburg, the program was transferred to Fieseler. Ten Bf 109E-1s were diverted from the assembly line as pre-production aircraft for the project and were given the designation Bf 109T-0.

  Sixty Bf 109T-1's were also ordered from Fieseler. However, in April, 1940, work on the carrier *Graf Zeppelin* was suspended and finally in early 1943, was cancelled entirely. Fieseler was ordered to complete the order of 60 Bf 109T-1s, but to ensure their usability, they were to omit the carrier equipment such as catapult hooks and arrester gear. Stripped of the carrier equipment, the variant was redesignated the Bf 109T-2 and fitted with a ventraly-mounted rack that would accept either an expendable auxiliary fuel tank or a variety of bomb loads, including four 50 kg (110 lb) SC 50s or a single 250 kg (550 lb) SC 250.

  The Bf 109T-2's deliveries started during March 1941 with the aircraft being assigned to units in Norway where operation from small airfields was a necessity. Being designed for carrier take-offs and incorporating the increased lift-producing wing surface made this variant especially suited to this mode of operation. This same short take-off and landing capability resulted in the few remaining Bf 109T-2s being transferred to the Heligoland fortress in 1943 as an island defense interceptor.

Bf 109Z *series*

Without question the most unique variant of the Bf 109 series was the Bf 109Z (*Zwilling,* or Siamese Twin). The concept for the aircraft had its origin in 1940 with the proposal for the joining together of a pair of He 111 bomber fuselages to provide enough power to tow the large Me 321 and Ju 322 attack gliders. The acceptance of this concept led Messerschmitt to initiate design drawings for the adaptation of a pair of Bf 109 fuselages joined in the center with a main wing and tailplane structure. The design was intended to offer the Luftwaffe a high performance fighter-bomber without the normal interference of already tooled production lines that would result with the introduction of a totally new aircraft design.

  The Messerschmitt proposal was received with interest by the RLM and approval to proceed with prototype assembly and testing was received in early 1942. To determine the feasibility of the concept and to verify flight characteristics, a pair of Bf 109F airframes were mated to the *Zwilling* configuration late in the year. The only modifications to the fuselages was the incorporation of the structural members necessary to interface with the center main wing and tailplane sections and the relocation of the undercarriage. Each outer wing was also fitted with a pylon capable of carrying an SC 250 bomb and a rack with a load capacity of over 500 kg (1,000 lb) was added to the center wing section. Because of the use of the two DB 601E powerplants, an extra pair of underwing glycol radiators were fitted to the center wing section.

During the assembly efforts related to the prototype, Messerschmitt also initiated design work on an improved *Zwilling* configuration that utilized a pair of Bf 109G airframes and incorporated either the DB 605A (standard powerplant of the Bf 109G) or the Jumo 213E engine. Planned armament included a pair of engine-mounted 30-mm MK 108 cannon, a 30-mm MK 103 cannon fitted in the center wing section and an additional pair of 30-mm MK 108s in weapon gondolas attached under the outer wings.

The improved Bf 109G configuration was also designated to fill the fighter-bomber role through installation of a pair of ETC 250 bomb racks under the outer wings and the inclusion of a center section rack for carrying auxiliary fuel or bombs. In addition, the aircraft would remain a single-place design, with the starboard cockpit area being closed in and utilized for storage of fuel.

The initial prototype Bf 109Z was completed in mid-1943; however, during pre-flight trials, the aircraft was damaged in an Allied bombing raid on the airfield. Repair efforts were immediately instituted, but before they could be completed, the entire *Zwilling* concept was abandoned in favor of the new jet powered aircraft and the fighter-bomber variants of the Focke-Wulf 190.

Foreign Production and Service

While the Bf 109 series saw active combat service with several of Germany's allies during World War II, it was also purchased by neutral countries such as Switzerland, which utilized it as a peacekeeping aircraft during the conflict. The countries which fought alongside Germany and took delivery of the Bf 109 in variants from the E-series through the G-series included Bulgaria, Finland, Hungary, Italy, Rumania and Croatia. Not all of these aircraft were of German manufacture, however, as assembly plants in Hungary and Rumania were put into operation late in the war to bolster the declining production resulting from Allied bombing.

With the end of hostilities in Germany, the attributes of the Bf 109 were not to be forgotten, however, and two countries, recognizing the need for an interim fighter to fill the gap between their obsolete, or non-existent, fighters and the jet age, initiated their own production or modification program to the later model variants of the Bf 109. The first of these countries was Czechoslovakia, which in 1944 had been selected as a dispersal site for a Bf 109G assembly plant. The plant was fortunate in that at war's end, a number of components and sub-assemblies had been left behind by the retreating German forces. Thus, in 1945, the

Avia factory started production of re-engined versions of the Bf 109G-12 and Bf 109G-14 under the designations CS 199 and S 199. The new powerplant was the Jumo 211F which was available due to stockpiles of this bomber engine being stored in Czechoslovakia. These aircraft were produced until 1949 and served with Czechoslovakian units until the mid-1950's.

The S 199 was also purchased by the newly forming Israeli Air Force in 1948 as the Czechoslovakian government, in need of hard foreign currency, ignored the United Nations arms embargo in the Middle East. The S 199 served as a stopgap fighter until 1949 when agreements with the major powers were worked out, allowing Israel to purchase newly developed aircraft for its Self Defense Forces.

Spain, the country which had received several of the initial BF 109s and had inherited several early models after the Spanish Civil War, also produced postwar Bf 109s. Actually, production of the Hispano Aviación Bf 109 had been initiated in 1942 with the signing of an agreement between Germany and Spain for the license building of the Bf 109G-2. Under the agreement, Germany was to supply Spain with the components and sub-assemblies to be assembled in Seville. However, as the war progressed, the delivery of these components was delayed and arrival of the DB 605 powerplants never occurred. Unable to secure the engines, Hispano Aviación, still under obligation to supply the Spanish Air Force with the Bf 109G-2, substituted the Hispano-Suiza 12Z 89 12-cylinder engine rated at 1,300 hp.

The first of these aircraft, designated HA-1109, flew in March, 1945, with disappointing results due in part to the opposite rotation of the Hispano powerplant in contrast to the Daimler-Benz. The opposite rotation resulted in forces that had to be accounted for through unconventional rudder and aileron control and drastically reduced handling characteristics of the aircraft.

During the next two years numerous design and component modifications were made to the HA-1109 with it finally being accepted for service in 1952. In 1953, cancellation of production of the Hispano-Suiza 12Z 17 powerplant resulted in a decision to re-engine with the British Rolls-Royce Merlin 500-45, with the initial Merlin powered Hispano-built Bf 109 lifting off from San Pablo Airfield in 1954. In just under 30 years, the Bf 109 had come full circle. It had started its career powered by a Rolls-Royce Kestrel and had received its operational baptism in Spain. It was now powered by the Rolls-Royce Merlin and would serve with the Spanish Air Force until 1967, when the last remaining unit was phased out of service.

Detailed Construction

Designed to be simple and inexpensive and yet provide a strong, but not heavy, overall construction, the basic Bf 109 design remained essentially unchanged throughout its career, even with the many modifications incorporated for performance, armament and structural improvements. The aircraft was comprised of several sub-assemblies which were designed to be fabricated by a number of factories, or dispersal plants, for assembly at a common point. In this manner no one plant was depended upon for the entire program, nor could delays of schedule by a single supplier impact other plants. The exception to this was the Daimler-Benz powerplant, but because of the number of engine variants, no serious problems were incurred.

Envisioned for assembly in a manner like the American automobile industry, Messerschmitt designed his aircraft to consist of sub-assemblies with near complete internal components already mated, including hydraulic, electrical and fuel lines. Simple interfacing couplings and fasteners locked the mating parts together. This also simplified maintenance and made repair and replacement of Bf 109 components a short and easy task.

The Bf 109 wings were built around a single mainspar construction concept with flanges and reinforcement braces at all key structural or support interfaces. The mainspar was located in the center of the wing chord to provide undercarriage and wheel retraction clearance without interference. The wing had a flush-riveted stressed-skin of aluminum alloy, while the control surfaces were covered with fabric for light weight and responsiveness. The pair of wing panels, fabricated as individual units, but complete with all necessary control and feed lines, were joined at the fuselage centerline and attached to the lifting body at three points. The forward interface was comprised of a large steel forging which also housed the undercarriage struts and the base for the aft engine mount. The wing's trailing edge consisted of slotted flaps (inboard) and ailerons (outboard) which were hinged at the pivot points and attached to the wing through aft extending flanges. The leading edge slots had a maximum extension of 5 cm (2 in) on the outboard side and 7.5 cm (3 in) on the inboard side.

The tail assembly, which was mated to the fuselage just under the tailplane assembly and included the rudder, was built around a stringer and reinforcement structure similar to the main wing, with all non-moving surfaces covered with an aluminum alloy skin while the rudder and elevators were covered in fabric.

The fuselage was an elliptically shaped configuration with an all-metal support structure which consisted of longerons and radial, or vertical, reinforcing frames. The fuselage was fabricated in two halves and joined at the top and bottom with a flanged longitudinal joint which formed a Z-frame.

On the upper forward fuselage section, just over the Daimler-Benz powerplant, a flat structure for the mounting of the cowl machine-guns was provided. The guns were synchronized to fire through the propeller's arc.

The upper and lower cowling were both hinged and locked in place by a pair of toggle switches which were easily accessible for the ground crew, but sturdy enough to sustain high flight loads without failure. The opening of these toggles allowed both cowlings to be removed in a matter of seconds and provided direct access to the armament and powerplant.

The Bf 109 cockpit was also simple and uncluttered, making use of only essential instruments, but locating them in easily readable locations, with the Revi reflector gunsight situated off-center to the right on top of the forward panel dash and the ignition switch located on the far left corner.

The right, or starboard, side of the cockpit wall contained the primary electrical panel and warning lights mounted in the forward upper quadrant, while the oxygen hose and mask were located just under the panel and se-cured in place with a pair of metal clips. The port side of the cockpit wall contained both the throttle and mixture control levers.

The flap and tailplane control was maintained through a pair of wheels just to the left of the pilot's seat with the vertical adjustment of the seat itself next to the wheels. The hinged canopy release was also located on the port side and was a simple mechanical lock which was pulled up and back to release the canopy seal.

Combat Operations

The Bf 109 was truly the backbone of the Luftwaffe during the war years. It performed in an operational status from 1936, when three developmental evaluation aircraft were sent to Spain to fight as part of *Jagdgruppe* 88, until the armistice of 8 May, 1945. It served in nearly every Luftwaffe *Jagdgeswader* as well as being the primary fighter for the air arms of Germany's axis allies. The only units it did not appear with were those specifically formed for a singular aircraft such as the famous JG 7 *Nowotny* which trained in, and entered combat with, the Me 262 twin-jet interceptor.

The Bf 109 achieved its first aerial victory of World War II on 4 September, 1939, only one day after war was declared between Germany and England. On this day, RAF Wellington bombers of No. 9 squadron attacked the German warships *Scharnhorst* and *Gneisenau* near Brunsbuettel on the North Sea. Unfortunately for the RAF, the Luftwaffe was expecting and prepared for the raid based on earlier attacks of 3 September. Bf 109Bs, Bf 109Cs and Bf 109Es of units based near Wilhelmshaven and Nordholz rose to meet the attack. In the encounter, two of the Wellingtons were destroyed by pilots of II *Gruppe* JG 77, the first losses of the war, and a further eight were destroyed by other fighter interceptor units and by fire from the German warships.

The initial recorded defeat for the Bf 109 occurred on 18 December when the RAF mounted still another heavy raid and reconnaissance mission over the German North Sea harbors in the Wilhelmshaven area. Again Luftwaffe units responded and destroyed a dozen of the intruding aircraft; however, a pair of Bf 109s were shot down. One of the Luftwaffe pilots who scored that day was *Leutnant* Johannes Steinhoff of 10 *Staffel* JG 26 who would go on to score 176 victories during the war and be given command of JG 7 in December, 1944.

For nearly a year, the Bf 109 ruled the skies over Europe, easily handling the RAF Hurricanes and early model Spitfires, the Curtiss Hawk 75s, Morane-Saulnier 406s and Dewoitine D.520s of the *Armée de l'Air* (French Air Force), and the various other obsolete fighters of the Belgium and Netherlands Air Forces. Its first real test came during the summer of 1940 when the Battle of Britain, one of the most important and decisive aerial confrontations of the conflict, at last vaulted the Bf 109 into worldwide attention and prominence.

For three months the Bf 109 found itself locked in a life and death struggle with its RAF counterparts for the right to air superiority over the English Channel and the British Isles themselves. The aircraft did everything asked of it and more. However, the distances from the bases in

France, and the continual utilization of the Bf 109 in an escort role, took its toll. Unprepared to perform in the long-range fighter escort function, its losses mounted. The Bf 109, in addition, suffered the disadvantage of fighting over enemy territory and when shot down, the pilots were unable to return to their bases to be assigned another aircraft as were their RAF counterparts. Finally, in September 1940, with heavy losses on both sides, the impending invasion of England was postponed and the beleaguered Bf 109 units in France took advantage of the time to reform and re-equip.

The experiences of these engagements over the British Isles resulted in the initial incorporation of the "U" and "R" conversions to the aircraft in an effort to compensate for its long-range deficiencies and to increase its multi-mission capabilities.

During the next few months, the Bf 109E continued to engage the enemy over the English Channel, in North Africa and in the Mediterranean, before it began to be phased out of service in early 1941 when the Bf 109F started transitioning into the Luftwaffe *Jagdgeschwader*. One of the first units to receive the new Bf 109s was JG 26 under *Oberst* Adolf Galland (later promoted to General and given command of the Luftwaffe Fighter Arm). It was Galland himself who scored one of the initial victories with the Bf 109F when on 1 April he was credited with a Supermarine Spitfire over the Southern English coast.

Two months later in June, 1941, Germany opened up a second front when it attacked the Soviet Union. The principal fighter during the early stages of "Operation Barbarossa" was the Bf 109F. The success of the first day alone can attest to the effectiveness, not only of the Bf 109, but of the Luftwaffe in general. Over 1,800 Soviet aircraft were destroyed on the ground and in the air for the loss of less than 50 German planes. Numerous Luftwaffe pilots were credited with five or more enemy planes shot down, among them Heinz Baer (final war-ending total of 220) and Werner Moelders (credited with 115 before his death in 1941 in a flying accident).

Another noteworthy Luftwaffe ace who piloted the Bf 109F was *Hauptmann* Hans-Joachim Marseille, who before his death on 30 September, 1942, accounted for 158 Allied aircraft destroyed. Flying his now-famous Bf 109F-4/Trop., "Yellow 14," Marseille had several multi-victory days including 6 June, 1942, when he claimed the destruction of six South African Air Force Curtiss P-40s.

In May, 1942, the Bf 109G began making its appearance with operational units in North Africa, France and the Russian-Crimea areas. By the end of the year it had virtually replaced the Bf 109F as the Luftwaffe's primary fighter aircraft. One of the first units to take delivery of the new variant was JG 52 based in Russia. The unit, which was credited with over 10,000 enemy aircraft during the war, had a pilot's roll that read like a "Wing of Aces." Among them were *Major* Gerhard Barkhorn (301 victories), *Major* Guenther Rall (275 victories), *Major* Wilhelm Batz (237 victories), *Oberst* Hermann Graf (212 victories), *Leutnant* Walter Wolfrum (137 victories), and *Oberst* Dietrich Hrabak (125 victories).

In August, 1942, a young replacement pilot was transferred to the unit. Assigned a Bf 109G as a member of the 7th *Staffel* of II *Gruppe,* this young pilot did not score until his 91st sortie. However, when he finally achieved his

30mm Ammunition: actual size

MK108 (A) Mine/tracer shell for air-to-air combat. Electric primer. Self-destructive. Fuze: ZZ1589A Muzzle velocity: 500m/sec (1640ft/sec)

(B) Incendiary shell for air-to-air combat. Electric primer. Self-destructive. Fuze: ZZ1589B. Muzzle velocity: 500m/sec (1640ft/sec)

MK103 (C) Tungsten-carbide core armour-piercing tracer, with additional incendiary effect, for use against heavy tanks. Not self-destructive. Muzzle velocity: 960m/sec (3150ft/sec), piercing 70mm armour plating at 60° up to 300m (984ft), 100mm armour plating at 90° up to 300m (984ft).

(D) Incendiary/tracer shell for air-to-air combat. Not self-destructive. Fuze: AZ1587 Muzzle velocity: 900m/sec (2950ft/sec)

(A)

Diameter of cartridge. 32.4mm (1.276in)

Length: Overall, 205mm (8.07in); Shell, 144mm (5.67in); Cartridge, 91mm (3.58in)

1. Fuze 2. Adaptor 3. Detonator 4. Booster 5. Paper disc 6. Explosive filler 7. Projectile body 8. Separator 9. Cover disc 10. Insert 11. Incendiary element 12. Closing plug

(B)

Diameter of cartridge, 32.5mm (1.28in)

Length: Overall, 205mm (8.07in); Shell, 146mm (5.75in); Cartridge, 91mm (3.58in)

RW

(D)

Length: Overall, 296.6mm (11.68in); Shell, 133.2mm (5.24in); Cartridge, 184mm (7.24in)   Diameter of cartridge, 39.5mm (1.56in)   Tungsten-carbide core, 85mm (7.24in) length, 16mm (90.63in) diameter

1. Fuze 2. Washer 3. Detonator 4. Projectile body 5. Incendiary element 6. Support ring 7. Rotating band 8. Equalizing body

Length: Overall, 298mm (11.73in); Shell, 144mm (5.67in); Cartridge, 184mm (7.24in)   Diameter of cartridge, 39.5mm (1.56in)

RW

initial victory in early 1943, it was only the beginning. By the end of the war, Erich Hartmann was to become the war's highest scoring ace with 352 aerial victories, all in the Bf 109G and K.

As previously noted throughout the description and discussions of the various Bf 109 variants, the plane was destined to fill many operational needs for the Luftwaffe. For the most part these were missions the basic aircraft was never designed for, and the required modifications usually detracted from its major advantages which included light weight and maneuverability. Among the more unique operational uses of the Bf 109 were the *Wilde Sau* (Wild Boar), the *Rammkommando* (Collision Commandos), and its attachment as a guiding aircraft to Ju 88s in the *Mistel* (flying bomb) configuration.

The *Wilde Sau* operations were the brainchild of *Major* Hajo Herrmann, who, during the summer of 1943 had proposed the use of single-place fighter aircraft in a night-fighter role over key German target areas where the enemy bomber stream would be illuminated by both searchlights and fires. The concept also had the advantage of visual contact, and was not dependent on the use of the *Himmelbett* line of FuG 220 *Lichtenstein* air-borne and *Wuerzburg* ground radar used by the Luftwaffe to guide its nightfighters to the incoming bombers.

With the advent of the use of chaff (small strips of aluminum foil dropped from the RAF pathfinder aircraft and bombers), the German radar systems became temporarily inoperative, providing only confusing readouts to the operators, not capable at that time of distinguishing contact with the metal strips from contact with the real aircraft. Until a number of modifications could be incorporated into the radar sets, *Wilde Sau* became the primary night-fighting weapon of the Luftwaffe.

In July, 1943, the decision was made to form an entire *Jagddivision*, with *Jagdgeschwader* 300 under Herrmann as the initial unit. Each of the new units, JG 300 near Bonn, JG 301 near Munich, and JG 302 near Berlin, were equipped with a single *Gruppe* of fighters modified with the incorporation of the underwing cannon or Wfr. Gr. 210-mm mortar tubes for increased firepower. Formed primarily around the heavily armored FW 190A, the limited availability of surplus aircraft forced each of the *Jagdgeschwader* to utilize the day fighters of other units operating from the same bases. This resulted in the use of several Bf 109G-6s in the new night-fighting role.

Even though victories by the *Wilde Sau* operations mounted, so did their losses. It became evident that although both the Fw 190 and Bf 109G were highly effective in this new role, the increased weight of the added armament reduced speed and handling characteristics and made the landing of the aircraft extremely hazardous in inclement weather, especially at night. With the arrival of the late fall and early winter of 1943, the weather conditions and overuse of the aircraft became the major enemy of the *Wilde Sau* units. Equipment malfunctions, structural failures due to fatigue, and pilots bailing out rather than landing under potentially fatal conditions, rapidly reduced the number of available planes and the operations were cancelled in early 1944.

During this same time period, a new method of daylight bomber interception was authorized under the leadership of *Major* von Kornatski. The new tactic was designated *Rammkommando* and was based on the use of heavily armored Fw 190A-8s which would attack the American bombers, getting as close as possible before opening fire. Although ramming of the bomber was not to be the primary objective, the suggestion was offered to the young pilots, who were instructed to bail out just prior to impact (a task more easily described than accomplished).

The success of the *Rammkommando* units lasted until late 1944 when the increase of Allied fighter escorts and the issuance of Allied Command orders to ignore the Bf 109G fighter cover and concentrate on the *Rammkommando* aircraft, spelled an end to this operation.

The use of the *Rammkommando* concept was revived, however, in April, 1945, when a special unit, *Rammkommando Elbe* was formed with Bf 109Gs. The special unit, composed of young volunteers inspired by patriotic conviction, flew only one mission. Over 80% of its aircraft never returned to base.

One of the strangest applications of the Bf 109 as an aerial weapon was in its use as the guidance plane for the *Mistel* or *Beethoven* flying bomb. The concept had been initiated in 1941, and revived in 1943 when Junkers proposed to the RLM that older Ju 88 airframes be loaded with high explosive and guided to a specified area by means of a fighter aircraft attached to the bomber by a center-mounted support structure which would be released near the target.

After a few successful tests with the Bf 109E, the prototypes were standardized utilizing a Ju 88A-4 and a Bf 109F-4, and production of the *Mistel* 1 began in May, 1944. The first unit to take delivery of the new *Mistel* system was *Kampfgeschwader* 101 which carried out its first *Mistel* operation in June. Although the success of the sorties flown by KG 101 was limited due to problems (among them, the aiming and releasing of the Ju 88), the potential of the concept was recognized, and further production was ordered which incorporated modifications in the support bracing and aiming instrumentation. The improved configuration was designated *Mistel* 2, and spelled the end of the Bf 109 participation in the *Mistel* project. The *Mistel* 2 and *Mistel* 3 were to utilize the Fw 190A as the guidance aircraft. Aside from the operation of *Rammkommando Elbe* in April, 1945 (as described above), the last major operation of the Bf 109 in World War II occurred on New Year's Day, 1945. Under the code name "Operation Herrmann" the Luftwaffe mounted a major offensive against Allied airfields in France, Holland and Belgium. The plan was to surprise the Allied command with an all-out attack and destroy the bulk of continent-based Allied aircraft on the ground. With Fw 190s and Bf 109s (including the use of the Bf 109K for the first time) the Luftwaffe force was composed of aircraft from nine separate *Jagdgeschwaders*. Claiming over 250 Allied aircraft destroyed, the Luftwaffe, however, suffered equally staggering losses and never fully recovered. The operational combat career of the Bf 109 was almost over.

Flying the Bf 109

Flying several variants of the Bf 109 for over seven years against almost every Allied aircraft, Herbert Kaiser, a Luftwaffe fighter pilot with 68 confirmed aerial victories, relates what it was like to pilot the Messerschmitt fighter and how it compared to its counterparts both on the Western and Eastern Fronts. As *Oberst* Kaiser describes it:

"The Bf 109B was not an easy aircraft to fly. It had to be directed with utmost attention from the split-second one gave it gas. The extremely narrow tracked undercarriage could not fully compensate for the normal tendency of the aircraft to pull to the right due to the prop torque. The maintaining of one's starting direction could be accomplished only by the smooth application of power, the balancing of the rudder, and the balancing of the elevators to lift the tail only after being airborne in order to keep constant aileron efficiency. Any casual disregard for those basic rules had a result of breaking the flight path and a possible crash.

"The cardinal rule during landing was that at the point of touchdown the gear and tail skid had to be oriented in the line of a projected roll without further attempt at directional control. Separation of aerodynamic lift due to insufficient approach speed, and excessive directional corrections performed during the landing procedure was the most common cause of crashes. The experienced pilot had these rules in his flesh and blood and this enabled him to make better use of his time by concentrating on other matters.

"Visibility from the cockpit was good, although during take-off it was quite restricted in the frontal area until the tail wheel left the ground. It was not at all reassuring to look forward and see only the large metal cowl, and this was why the aircraft had to be correctly oriented on take-off.

"Although the Bf 109B was useful as a frontline combat aircraft and far outclassed enemy aircraft of the time in speed and climbing ability, its initial Junkers-built engine was extremely sensitive and not sufficiently powerful.

"The Luftwaffe did not, in my estimation, have a truly superior and robust fighter aircraft until the appearance of the Bf 109E. The use of the DB 601 engine with 1200 hp, the increased speed, and the high climb rate made the Bf 109E, in relation to its counterparts, the best fighter of its time. Its armament of two machine guns and two cannon were more than enough to knock any enemy plane out of the air with a well placed burst of fire."

On 10 May, 1940, Kaiser, now flying as a part of III/JG 77, took part in the start of the Western Campaign against airfields in Holland and was credited with the destruction of two Dutch Fokker D.XXIs. He was then sent to France where he remained, flying patrol until the Dunkirk encirclement. Of these days Kaiser relates: "Although prior to the start of the Western Campaign in May, 1940, no German pilot could make a comprehensive comparison between British and French fighters and our Bf 109E, we firmly believed we had the best airplane based on comparative flying reports and an abundance of rumors. Personally, at the advent of hostilities, I had contact only with Dutch Fokker D.XXIs, and this fixed gear monoplane, approximately 80 km/h (50 mph) slower than a 109E, offered no particular challenge. Some of my comrades from neighboring units, however, had encountered the RAF Spitfires and Hurricanes, as well as the French Dewoitines and Morane Saulniers and thus affirmed what we all believed about our aircraft.

General Adolf Galland, commanded JG 26, one of the initial Luftwaffe units to take delivery of the Bf 109E. It was Galland himself, then an *Oberst*, who scored one of the first victories with the new fighter. He is now recognized by many aviation experts as one of the finest fighter pilots and tacticians of the war.

Oberst Erich Hartmann, known as the 'Ace of Aces' and the 'Blond Knight of Germany.' He ended the war as the world's highest scoring fighter ace, destroying 352 enemy aircraft. He did not join JG 53 until mid-1942 and remained with this unit throughout the war, flying various Bf 109 models, finishing in a Bf 109K. (ERICH HARTMANN COLLECTION)

Oberst Werner Moelders (left) and *Major* Hartmann Grasser (right) of JG 51. Moelders (115 victories) was later killed in a flying accident. Grasser (103 victories) survived the war. He served on Moelders' staff at JG 51 and was later assigned to JG 76. This photo was taken after both had safely returned from a mission over England.

"In personally facing the RAF in the air over the Dunkirk encirclement, I found that the Bf 109E was faster, possessed a higher rate of climb, but was somewhat less maneuverable than the RAF fighters. Nevertheless, during the campaign, no Spitfire or Hurricane ever turned inside of my plane, and after the war the RAF admitted the loss of 450 Hurricanes during the Battle of France."

On 19 June, 1941, III/JG 77 was posted to Bacau on the Russian border and on the 22nd engaged in their first missions against the Soviet Air Force. Taking off at 0400 hours Kaiser achieved his initial kill over the Eastern Front later in the day near Balti. *Oberst* Kaiser recalls the Russian campaign: "Against the early Russian aircraft the Bf 109E was untouchable. The Soviet planes were slower and could not climb with us. They were, however, highly maneuverable, especially the I-15 and I-16, and one could not allow an encounter to deteriorate into a contest of turns. This was easily avoided, because we always had the element of surprise, due to our high speed and advanced communication systems.

"In Russia I encountered many varied aircraft, particularly bombers, for the most part the twin-engined Ilyushin DB-3, and later the Pe-2, and Il-2 attack bombers. The greatest losses for the Soviets, at least in our sector, occurred with the DB-3. A military version of a Soviet long distance record-breaker, it had great range, but was incredibly slow, and possessed poor defensive firepower. All weapons were hand-held, rifle-caliber guns and the bomber was blind to a direct tail-on approach. A single burst between the left engine and the fuselage into the wing root and the unprotected fuel tanks guaranteed immediate burning and unavoidable crash. It was considerably more difficult to attack the Pe-2 because of her speed, twin-tail assembly and the unrestricted tail gunner's vision.

"The Ilyushin Il-2 (Shturmovik) was also tough. A single engine fighter bomber not exceptionally fast, but very well armored, this plane required a detailed knowledge of its construction and a well-executed approach to destroy. The unforgettable Moelders showed me personally how one downed this aircraft. The Il-2 possessed armor behind the pilot; but just behind this armor was a small tank which was utilized as a starter cartridge. Totally unprotected and vulnerable, this tank was exploded with a single incendiary burst. Of course, in this mode of attack, a precise and accurate burst was necessary. Later the Soviets installed a rear gunner's position and armored the starter cartridge.

"During my participation in the Russian campaign, I also encountered the LaGG-3 and the MiG-3. I did destroy some of these, but it would be extremely difficult to make any well founded comparison with the Bf 109 because of my limited confrontation."

It was in North Africa that Kaiser received his first Bf 109G; "Here I was introduced to the Bf 109G which had an even more powerful engine than the F-model and a larger compressor (supercharger). It also had extremely good high-altitude performance. The air density of the North African sky was considerably less than that over Russia, and our performance could be maintained only through the constant use of the compressor. From a pure flying standpoint, the Bf 109G offered little over the Bf 109F. She was considerably heavier and still had the difficult take-off and landing qualities inherent with all the Bf 109 variants.

"During the African campaign, we were short of aircraft and for the young pilots with little actual air or combat experience, it was very difficult to master the 109. In addition, landings and take-offs were aggravated by the general condition of the desert air strips, not to mention sand and blowing grit. Because of these conditions, the relatively few number of airworthy planes were usually flown by the older, more experienced pilots, and the appearance of the same familiar names dominated the victory totals."

Describing the tactics employed by the Luftwaffe in North Africa in late 1942 and his impressions of some of the aircraft he faced, *Oberst* Kaiser relates:

"The classic dogfight was still partly used in Africa, and the lone sortie was prevalent. We were forced to this lone sortie tactic of surprise due to the overwhelming supply of Allied aircraft and, in this way, were able to spread ourselves over more area. Any other tactics would be coupled with high losses on our side, a condition we could not allow. Additionally, the speed and durability of the Bf 109G lent itself very well to this type of tactic. If we were overmatched, we could always break off.

"The Curtiss P-40 was not as fast as the Bf 109G and in a confrontation with this plane we had nothing to worry about as long as the basic rules of combat tactics were followed. We did, however, have to avoid getting into the middle of a large formation, for the P-40 turned well and as an old German saying goes, 'Too many dogs are the death of the rabbit.'

"The P-38 Lightning was equal to our Bf 109G in performance, far superior in range, and was a much more difficult adversary in a dogfight. However, I never employed any special evasive maneuvers when I encountered one of them. Evasive tactics, as far as I am concerned, were dictated by the situation and were a reflex reaction. For the most part, independent of the aircraft on your tail, one would utilize a steep turn and pull out to get behind his enemy, or pull up on the stick in a succession of stuttering steps to reduce speed, hoping the abrupt velocity decrease would not be picked up in time by the aircraft behind you, forcing him to fly over, exposing his belly. I always considered a turn-out and dive a' high risk tactic and, to my knowledge, this particular move was not used to any great extent by Luftwaffe fighter pilots."

In January, 1943, Kaiser was detached from JG 77 and sent to a replacement depot in Southern France as an instructor. He stayed there for four months before rejoining III/JG 77 and was posted to Italy where he destroyed four more aircraft. Then in January, 1944, Kaiser was returned to Germany for a routine medical checkup after which he was assigned to I/JG 1 under the command of *Oberst* Walter Oesau. With this unit he flew until 6 June, 1944, in the Defense of the Reich. From 6 June until 9 August he was stationed on the Normandy Front flying in a defensive role against the Allied invasion forces and describes his experiences as follows:

"Near the end of June, 1944, while attached to I/JG 1, on an airfield just outside Paris, France, an excellent example of the almost complete Allied air superiority occurred. I was vectored out to intercept an incoming flight of Allied bombers which was attacking our troops in the Normandy area. Our take-off had to be only in the smallest of groups (usually 2 to 4 aircraft) due to the Allied fighters which almost always waited above the bases for our fighters to emerge from cloud cover. We would be forced to sneak from our base into our target area by hedge-hopping over the terrain to take advantage of all the camouflage possible. Flying only a few feet off the ground kept us off radar screens, but sometimes put us on the side of a hill. We would only climb to any height when we had reached the attack point under the enemy planes.

"My flight of four aircraft sighted a formation of escorting Spitfires, and we positioned ourselves to engage them. We were instead caught by a second group of Allied fighters and in the process I lost my three men. Escape from the onslaught seemed impossible. Only because of my experience and the lucky appearance of a nearby cloud was I able to save myself.

"At this time the Luftwaffe was being ground into the earth. One could not count on his hand the days he expected to live. It was surprising to me that the Luftwaffe pilot had any nerve left at all, let alone the ability to prepare himself for combat with the enemy under these conditions."

Glossary

Abbreviations

BFW	Bavarian Aircraft Works	FuG	Airborne Radio or Radar Set	R	Field Conversion Kit Designation
DB	Daimler-Benz	GM	Nitrous-Oxide Injectant	Rb	Automatic Camera
D/F	Directional Finder	JG	Luftwaffe Fighter Group	Revi	Reflector Sight
ETC	Electrically Operated Bomb Rack	KG	Luftwaffe Bomber Group	RLM	German Air Ministry
		MG	Machine-gun	SC	Fragmentation Bomb
		MK	Machine Cannon	U	Factory Conversion Kit Designati
		MW	Methanol-Water Injectant	Wfr. Gr.	Rocket Grenade

Terms

Erprobungsgruppe	Experimental Test Unit	Jagdgruppe	Interceptor or fighter squadron
Flugzeugbau	Aircraft Builder	Kampfgeswader	Bomber Group
Flugzeugwerke	Aircraft Factory	Kriegsmarine	German Navy
Generalfeldmarschall	General Fieldmarshall	Major	Major
Geschwader	Three *Gruppen* (Approx. 120 aircraft)	Leutnant	2nd Lieutenant
Gruppe	Squadron of three *Staffeln* (Approx. 36 aircraft)	Lufthansa	German Airline
Jagdbomber	Fighter-bomber	Oberst	Colonel
Jagddivision	Wing Composed of 3 or 4 Groups	Staffel	Flight (Approx. 12 aircraft)
Jagdgeschwader	Interceptor or Fighter Group	Traeger	Aircraft Carrier

Text by
ROBERT GRINSELL

R. Watanabe

Focke-Wulf
Fw190

Fw 190A-3   (BUNDESARCHIV)

Introduction

"When we designed the Focke-Wulf 190 in the summer of 1937, there were many in the *Reichluftfahrtsministerium* (RLM—German Air Ministry) who believed our fighter had little chance against the concepts then coming from Messerschmitt. But because we chose a radial engine that would not conflict with the short supply of the liquid-cooled powerplants earmarked for aircraft then in production, yet one that promised a great deal more horsepower than available at the time, several of our friends in procurement persuaded the technical bureau to give our proposals a chance. By the summer of 1939, they were glad they had done so.

"The Focke-Wulf 190 was designed to be built by a great number of small sub-assemblers. We designed it with ease of maintenance in mind, plus quick replacement of entire sections. It was a sturdy machine and extremely versatile. Although conceived as a fighter, it did double duty as an attack bomber and, in fact, throughout most of the war, was the only reliable, light attack bomber we possessed in numbers."

Kurt Tank

These words from Dipl. Ing. Kurt Tank, chief designer and technical director of the Focke-Wulf *Flugzeugbau,* provide a fitting epitaph for the Focke-Wulf 190, an aircraft considered by many aviation experts and enthusiasts to be the most beautifully proportioned and aerodynamically designed aircraft of World War II. It is, however, but a fraction of the Focke-Wulf 190 story.

Background

In the summer of 1937, although thoroughly committed to the Bf 109 as the standard day fighter for the Luftwaffe, a few knowledgeable military planners in the RLM began to give serious thought to a possible successor. While the majority of the technical staff maintained that the Messerschmitt Bf 109s technology was so advanced that any thought of a follow-on or sucessor was premature, the far-sighted planners persisted in their belief that the Luftwaffe's position as a world power was dependent upon continued development of new concepts. Thus, a specification was issued to the Focke-Wulf *Flugzeugbau* for supplementary design of a single seat fighter aircraft.

Over the next few months, numerous alternative designs were submitted to the RLM Technical Branch for approval. Most of the designs incorporated the newly developed liquid-cooled Daimler-Benz 12-cylinder 1,050 hp DB 601A in-line engine because of its low frontal area and reduced drag characteristics. These concepts all met with disapproval from most RLM technical and production staffs as they still could project no requirements for a back-up fighter, let alone one which would increase the demand on manufacturers for the already overstrained supply of the DB 601A.

However, the design that Tank favored, and the one for which he argued at length, was a radical configuration utilizing the powerful air-cooled 1,550 hp *Bayerische Motorenwerke* (Bavarian Motor Works) BMW 139. Arguments in favor of this approach included the powerplant's low susceptibility to combat damage and the fact that the radial engine put no demands on the liquid-cooled DB 601A delivery schedules for the Bf 109. Based on these points, and the fact that the Focke-Wulf was not at that time involved with any other major military project, the RLM issued a contract to Focke-Wulf for three prototype aircraft during the summer of 1938.

Detailed design effort was initiated immediately and the first prototype, designated Fw 190 V1, and carrying the code letters D-OPZE, was flown on 1 June, 1939, by Focke-Wulf chief test pilot Hans Sander. After five flights, the new aircraft, named *Wuerger* (Butcherbird) by Tank, was turned over to the Luftwaffe's Rechlin test facility for military evaluation. The new fighter was responsive and light on the controls, with a small turning radius (critical in close-in air combat), and offered quick acceleration both in climb and low level dash modes of operation. The tests, however, revealed the same major drawback which existed in many other famous and combat proven fighters. The large cowling, housing the big diameter air-cooled radial powerplant, reduced forward visibility on takeoff and landing and proved, in later years, to be a fatal flaw to many young and inexperienced pilots. One major advantage offered by the Fw 190V1, compared to its Messerschmitt counterpart, was the use of a wide-track-inward-retracting landing gear, structurally superior to the notoriously weak landing gear arrangement of the Bf 109.

During construction of the Fw 190V1, Focke-Wulf discovered that the selected BMW 139 powerplant was not meeting its performance expectations, and therefore opted for the use of the newer and more powerful 1,600 hp BMW 801C. Although the new powerplant was essentially the same diameter as the older BMW 139, and would fit easily into the cowling, it was somewhat longer and 160 kg (350 lbs) heavier. This required a redesign of the load carrying stress interfaces on the forward airframe, strengthening of the engine mounts, and an aft movement of the cockpit, due to critical center-of-gravity (c.g.) considerations. The redesign cycle also allowed the design team, headed by Chief Engineer R. Blaser, to solve and eliminate several minor type problems ("bugs") that are normal during early prototype development of any new aircraft. The only major problem to occur during the initial flight evaluation was the excessive

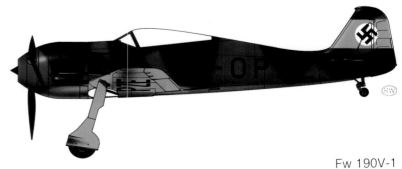

Fw 190V-1

temperatures reached in the cockpit (approximately 55°C) (130°F) as a result of the close proximity of the powerplant and exhaust manifolds to the cockpit firewall and the un-availability of the airscrew driven 10-bladed cooling fan planned for installation in front of the radial powerplant.

Shortly after its arrival at Rechlin, the Fw 190 V1 code identification was dropped and the call letters FO-LY assigned. Despite the almost constant overheating of the powerplant, the aircraft attained a maximum speed of 594 km/h (369 mph) in level flight and was praised almost unanimously by the many expert Luftwaffe test pilots who flew it.

The second prototype, Fw 190 V2, was flown for the first time in October, 1939, and after completion of some comparison and verification testing, was sent to Tarnewitz for gunnery tests of the wing mounted armament. After completing the firing trials, Fw 190 V2 was returned to Rechlin for more extensive handling and controls testing. However, after only a few hours of flight time, the crank shaft failed and the aircraft, coded FO-LZ, was destroyed.

The third test prototype to roll off the Focke-Wulf assembly line was designated Fw 190 V5 and incorporated the new BMW 801C powerplant, associated structural changes, and a return to a conventional spinner configuration rather than the unique ducted spinner used in the early Fw 190 V1 configuration. The latter change was based on the results of wind tunnel tests on the first prototype aircraft to determine the effects on engine cooling for both the conventional and unique ducted spinner. No appreciable cooling or aerodynamic advantages were found to exist with the ducted spinner.

With the increased powerplant weight and the added strengthening of the airframe, the overall weight of the new fighter had risen almost 25% to a gross of 3,400 kg (7,500 lbs). In addition, although the wing roots were extended to increase the area available for armament, the overall wing loading was also increased from nearly 186 kg/m² (38.1 lb/sq ft) to 227 kg/m² (46.6 lb/sq ft). The climb rate and responsiveness also suffered with the added weight burden. Nevertheless, Hermann Goering, after witnessing early flight tests, liked the new fighter and authorized a preliminary pre-production order of 40 Fw 190A-0 fighters.

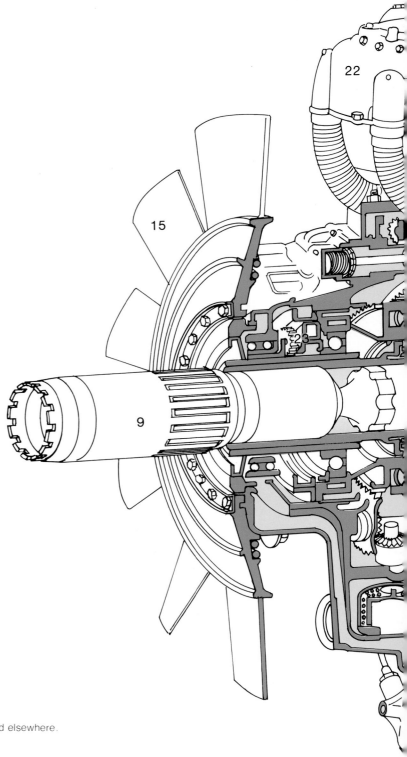

The BMW 801 engine

Manufacturer: Bayerische Motorenwerke Flugmotorenbau G.m.b.H., Munich, Eisenach, and elsewhere.
Type: 14-cylinder twin-row radial fitted with single-stage two-speed supercharger

Developed from the BMW 139 (which powered the Fw190V1 toV4) and produced in series first as BMW 801C-1 and C-2 (Fw 190V5 to Fw 190A-2) and then as BMW 801D-2 (Fw 190A-3 to Fw 190A-8: Fw 190F and G). The BMW 801 radials of course also powered many other Luftwaffe aircraft, from Arado Ar 232A to Junkers Ju 390.

Basic data

	BMW 801C-2	BMW 801D-2
Take-off and emergency power:	1600 hp at 2700 rpm	1700 hp at 2700 rpm
Climbing power:	1460 hp at 2400 rpm	1500 hp at 2400 rpm
Maximum power:	1380 hp at 15.100 ft (4600m)	1440 hp at 18.200 ft (5700 m)
Compression ratio:	6.5:1	7.22:1
High supercharger drive ratio:	7.46:1	8.31:1
Low supercharger drive ratio:	5.07:1	5.31:1
Dry weight:		2321 lb (1053 kg)
Overall diameter		1270 mm

1 Cooling fin
2 Valve
3 Rocker box cover
4 Piston
5 Connecting rod
6 Cylinder barrel
7 Push rod

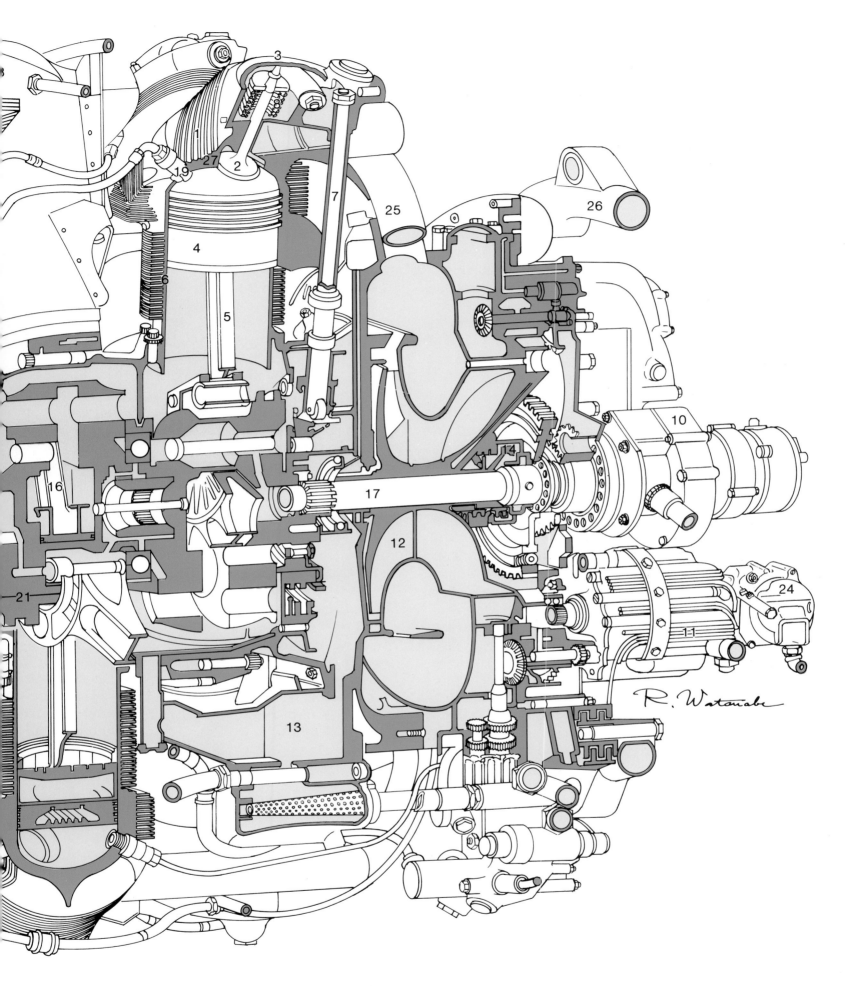

8 Valve spring	15 Cooling fan, 12-bladed	22 Twin magneto
9 Propeller shaft	16 Articulated connecting rod	23 Propeller pitch adjustment mechanism
10 Initial starter unit	17 Tail shaft	24 Fuel de-aerator
11 Generator	18 Valve push-rod casing	25 Cylinder drain
12 Supercharger impeller	19 Spark plug	26 Engine mounting ring
13 Oil sump	20 Crank shaft	27 Cylinder head
14 Supercharger clutch and gear drive	21 Crank throw	

Fw 190A *series (pre-production)*

Fw190A-0

Work on the pre-production aircraft proceeded in parallel with the construction of the Fw 190 V5, and when the third prototype was severely damaged in a ground collision with an airfield vehicle, the designers decided to rebuild the aircraft with an enlarged wing and increased tailplane surface, rather than wait and incorporate it on one of the early pre-production models as originally planned. The rebuilt development prototype was redesignated Fw 190 V5g. The changes resulted in only a 1% loss in maximum airspeed, but offered improved climb rate, and restoration of almost all of the handling and control benefits enjoyed by the lighter weight first prototype.

Aircraft Fw 190 V6 and Fw 190 V7 (the initial two pre-production models) were fabricated with the smaller wing and tailplane of the original Fw 190 V5 design. Fw 190 V7 was, however, the first BMW 801C powered model to incorporate armament, which included a pair of 7.9-mm MG 17 machine-guns in the forward fuselage upperbody over the powerplant, and a pair of similar weapons in the wing roots. The MG 17s were used in the wing roots in place of the planned Mauser 20-mm MG 151 cannon, as this new weapon had not yet been fully tested and was still in the development stages.

The remainder of the pre-production Fw 190A-0 aircraft began leaving the assembly line in November, 1940, with aircraft Fw 190 V8 and Fw 190 V9 still using the pre-production BMW 801C. From Fw 190 V10 on, the pre-production aircraft utilized the production BMW 801C-1 powerplant. In addition, it was not until Fw 190 V15 (tenth pre-production aircraft) that the assembly line could be completely retooled to add the larger wing and tailplane surface first tested on the third prototype.

A line of BMW 801 engine units in storage under a *No Smoking* sign.

(BUNDESARCHIV)

Of the total 40 pre-production aircraft ordered by the Luftwaffe, 14 received the ''V,'' or development, type classification. Six of these were delivered between February and April, 1941, to *Erprobungsstaffel* 190, a specially formed test unit under *Oberleutnant* Otto Behrens at Rechlin-Roggenthin for intensive combat simulation testing. The Luftwaffe personnel for this unit were selected from II *Gruppe* of the *Jagdgeschwader 26 Schlageter,* which had been designated by Luftwaffe Command as the first operational unit to receive the new fighter after acceptance testing was completed.

The test program at Rechlin (later transferred to Le Bourget, France) was anything but a success. Constant overheating problems with the BMW 801C-1 occurred during engine run up and during take off. Those aircraft that did manage to leave the ground usually returned in a short while trailing a long line of black smoke; cylinders seized due to the overheating; and numerous oil and coolant lines fractured under the high temperatures and working pressures.

Focke-Wulf naturally laid the blame for the problems on BMW, while BMW accused Focke-Wulf of insufficient design considerations in the powerplant cooling area. So serious were the problems being encountered that a visiting RLM Committee evaluating the new aircraft recommended cancellation of the entire Fw 190 project. However, the RLM was persuaded to postpone a final decision, giving Focke-Wulf and BMW an opportunity to coordinate their efforts in an attempt to solve the engine cooling deficiencies. After over 50 modifications in the design of the cooling fan, oil and cooling lines, and the oil cooling ring, the RLM accepted the Fw 190A for service production in mid-1941.

While the testing at Le Bourget was being conducted, and prior to official acceptance by the RLM, Focke-Wulf was completing the first production Fw 190A-1 fighters at the Marienburg facility. The first production Fw 190A-1s to reach 6 *Staffel* of JG 26 were delivered at Moorseele, Belgium, in July, 1941. By the first of September the entire II *Gruppe* of JG 26 had started their conversion from the Bf 109F-2 to the Fw 190A-1. The *Wuerger* had left its nest, and was ready to display its talons as a wartime bird of prey.

The Fw 190A-1 received its baptism of combat on 1 September 1941, when a *Schwarm* (four aircraft) of 6 *Staffel,* II *Gruppe,* JG 26 engaged several Supermarine Spitfire Vs over the Dunkirk beaches. Enjoying the advantage of altitude and surprise, the Fw 190s dove on the unsuspecting Spitfires and destroyed three while escaping without a loss. So superior in speed, climb and handling was the Fw 190, that the Luftwaffe pilots were able to engage and break off combat at will. These were the first kills of many to be recorded by the 'Butcherbird.' British reports of the first encounter with this new Luftwaffe fighter credited the victories to modified American manufactured Curtiss Hawks.

The first Fw 190 loss suffered by the Luftwaffe was unfortunately a costly one. *Gruppenkommandeur* Walter Adolf, commander of II *Gruppe,* and a bona fide air ace with 29 victories to his credit, was shot down on 18 September while engaging a Royal Air Force formation of Bristol Blenheims which were attacking a German convoy near Ostende.

Fw 190A *series (production)*

The Fw 190A-2, considered by the RLM to be the first "real production" model (most likely because of the many "band-aid" fixes on the Fw 190A-1) began leaving the Focke-Wulf assembly plant at Marienburg, the Arado *Flugzeugwerke* at Warnemuende and AGO at Oscherslebin in September and October of 1941. This variant incorporated the improved BMW 801C-2 powerplant and the wing root mounted 20-mm MG 151 cannon in place of the less effective MG 17 machine-guns. The incorporation of the pair of wing root cannon necessitated the addition of shallow bulges on the upper wing surfaces near the armament loading area. These bulges remained with all future variants and became one of the identifiable trademarks of the Fw 190 series.

Most Fw 190A-2s maintained the pair of Oerlikon 20-mm MG FF cannon that had been fitted to the Fw 190A-1s in the outer wings to increase firepower. With the 200 rounds per gun of the MG 151s stored and electro-pneumatically fed to the guns from directly behind the engine mounts, and the 55 rounds per gun fed from a rotary cylinder of the aft mounting plate of each MG FF, the heavy firepower of the Fw 190A-2 was devastating.

The Fw 190A-2 was truly a pilot's aircraft and the finest fighter the Luftwaffe had to offer in 1941 and early 1942. It was, more than likely, the finest fighter of its time. It, and the earlier Fw 190A-1, quickly proved its superiority over its main counterpart, the Spitfire Vb (which until the appearance of the Fw 190 had slowly, but unquestionably, gained the advantage over the Bf 109E and F).

The Fw 190 (A-1 and A-2 variants) received one of its strongest combat tests during the now famous "Channel Dash" of the German warships *Scharnhorst, Prinz Eugen* and *Gneisenau* from the French port at Brest to anchorages in Kiel and Wilhelmshaven, Germany, on 12 February, 1942. Fw 190s of II and III *Gruppen* and Bf 109Fs of I *Gruppe* of JG 26 provided continuous top cover for this operation from just after daylight until late in the day when the channel weather finally deteriorated sufficiently to restrict all air operations on both sides. The Fw 190s found themselves in a nearly constant running air battle with the Fairey Swordfish torpedo bombers of the Royal Navy and with the Spitfires and Hurricanes of the RAF.

For over six months the Fw 190A-2 was produced by the various assembly plants teamed with Focke-Wulf. Over 400 of this variants rolled off the assembly lines at Focke-Wulf, Arado and AGO before giving way to the Fw 190A-3 in the spring of 1942.

The Fw 190A-3 was identical to its predecessor, the Fw 190A-2, except for minor external changes in the powerplant cowling inspection panel location and geometry, a slight modification of the air cooling fairings and the addition of air outlet louvres just aft of the engine exhaust panel. The major internal change was the incorporation of the BMW 801D-2 engine which increased the compression ratio and provided added take-off and emergency power. The Fw 190A-3 was also the first of the Fw 190 variants to be modified with factory conversion kits that changed its role as an air superiority fighter into that of fighter-bomber *(Jabo)* and reconnaissance fighter. The conversion kits included the use of the ETC 250 and ETC 501 center-mounted bomb racks for carrying the 250 kg (551 lb) SC 250 and the 500 kg (1,102 lb) SC 500 bombs, ETC 50 wing mounted racks for carrying the 50 kg (110 lb) SC 50 bomb, and the incorporation of a pair of Rb 12.5 cameras mounted aft of the cockpit. The Fw 190A-3s incorporating these conversion kits were given additional suffix designations of U1, U3, and U4 with the "U" designation representing an abbreviation of *Umruest-Bausaetze* (factory conversion). The three variants and their respective conversions were:

A-3/U1   Fighter-bomber with ETC 501 rack and MG FF outboard cannons removed; ETC 501 rack could also be adapted to carry four SC 50 bombs.
A-3/U3   Fighter-bomber with ETC 250 rack; some aircraft also added ETC 50 racks to wings.
A-3/U4   Reconnaissance fighter with pair of Rb 12 cameras and outboard MG FF cannon removed.

The success of these modifications and combat roles was to lead to many other modifications made to the basic Fw 190 airframe, and would provide the Luftwaffe with a single aircraft that would eventually serve as fighter-bomber, ground attack, reconnaissance fighter, long range reconnaissance, allweather interceptor, night fighter, tank destroyer, torpedo plane and two seat trainer.

After production of over 500 Fw 190A-3s, the Fw 190A-4 variant began to make its appearance in late 1942. The Fw 190A-4 differed from the A-3 only in the addition of a methanol-water power boost system (MW 50) to the BMW 801D-2 to achieve added power under the rated altitude of 5000 m (16,000 ft), and a replacement of the FuG 7a radio with the newer and more powerful FuG 16z. Factory conversion kits were similar to those incorporated on the A-3 model. The U1 fighter-bomber was equipped with an ETC 501 under each wing and was stripped of all armament except the two wing-root-mounted MG 151 cannons. The U3 fighter-bomber was equipped with a single center mount ETC 250 rack that could carry either the SC 250 bomb or an auxiliary fuel drop tank. Standard armament was normally retained, although some instances of removal of the outboard MG FF wing cannons to reduce weight did occur. The U8 long-range fighter-bomber incorporated the center mount auxiliary fuel drop tank on an ETC 250 rack, a pair of wing-carried SC 50 bombs on each wing and full armament. With varying armament deletions (removal of the fuselage MG 17 machine-guns and/or the MG FF cannon) the U8 could increase its bomb load or external fuel-carrying capacity.

During the summer of 1942, the first examples of the Fw 190A-4/U1 were delivered to 10 *Staffel (Jabo)* of JG 26. By mid August, 10 *Staffel (Jabo)* of JG 2 had also transitioned into the new fighter-bomber. During the Allied raid on Dieppe, France, on 19 August, 1942, these units flew against positions captured by British and Canadian troops and the assorted landing craft and support ships in the harbor. The heavy toll of losses suffered by the Allied invasion force was a testament to the effectiveness of the Fw 190A in its new role.

Still another modification to the Fw 190A-4 was the R6 variant. The "R" designated a field conversion, rather than the "U" designation denoted factory conversions. The R6 model was an attempt by the Luftwaffe to stem the flow of the American bomber formations during the middle of 1943, through penetration and dispersal of their close formations from long ranges. The Fw 190A-4/R6 incorporated a pair of 210-mm rocket tubes under the wings just slightly outboard of the 20-mm MG FF cannon location. The basic plan was to attack the tight bomber box-defenses (flying in close proximity to each other to bring maximum firepower to bear and provide only a minimal target) with a wave of the rocket-firing Fw 190s and then follow up with standard equipped fighters, including the Bf 109 and Fw 190, which if all went according to plan, would be able to decimate the individual bombers which would scatter as the rockets took their toll of the USAAF formations.

Tests on this concept were carried out at Rechlin, where the feasibility was proven and the relative accuracy ranges, deviations and probabilities of success were determined. The Fw 190A-4/R6s first went into action on 14 October, 1943, against American B-17s that were targeted for Schweinfurt. The fighters launched their lethal load outside of the effective range of the more than 200 bombers and succeeded in breaking up the tight defensive boxes. Official reports of that raid indicated that the losses suffered by the American bombers was devastating. Over 50% of the bombers were destroyed during the attack of the R6 fighters and the standard interceptors, went down before reaching their home base, or were written off after landing due to the amounts of major damage inflicted. The Luftwaffe losses for the day were just under 40 fighters. The Fw 190 had been assigned still another combat role and once again had proven its versatility as an all-around fighter aircraft.

The Fw 190A-4 was also the initial operational variant to be sent to the Eastern Front in any quantity. *Hauptmann* Guenther Schack, a member of III/JG 51, was one of the first pilots to fly the newly arrived plane into combat in the Soviet Union. He relates this first mission:

"My first mission with the new plane occurred on 17 December, 1942, when I was assigned escort duty to a formation of Ju 88 bombers. As our flight approached the target area the unit was jumped by a flight of Soviet fighters;

however, upon seeing the new German fighters they quickly broke off the engagement. On the return flight at an altitude of approximately 2000 m (6500 ft), I came upon four Petlyakov Pe-2s intent on strafing the JG 51 base. My wingman and I immediately turned to the attack and in quick succession destroyed two of the Russian fighter-bombers. The remaining Pe-2s began to break away and turn to the east. I followed the aircraft, firing at them alternately. Suddenly, both aircraft burst into flames and crashed. My wingman and I had, however, crossed over the Russian lines and had to head for home as our fuel was running low. Once we crossed into German territory, we spotted three more Pe-2s and estimating that both fuel and ammunition were adequate for one last pass, we set upon the Soviet aircraft. I was able to add one more to my day's total before the remaining planes broke off. Over my own field there seemed to be no end to my 'waggling' (the German fighter pilots' sign of victory). In my first flight with the Fw 190, I had accounted for no less than five Russian Pe-2s."

Beginning in April, 1943, the Fw 190A-4 was being replaced on the production lines by the Fw 190A-5. The Fw 190A-5 differed from the A-4 only in that it included lengthened engine mounts to provide increased strength and reduced vibration. The overall aircraft length increase was only 15.5 cm (6.1 in), and the A-5 was distinguishable from earlier models only by comparing the hinged upper deck machine-gun cover panel.

The basis for the entire A-5 variant was to increase the amount and type of *Umruest-Bausaetze* (factory conversions) that would be made available for the Fw 190. The basic series served as prototype and pre-production test-beds for future variants. Twelve separate conversions of the A-5 were designed. These included the U2, U3, U4, U8, U9, U11, U12, U13, U14, U15, U16, and U17. These models and their respective modifications are described below:

A-5/U2 Extended range night-fighter-bomber with antiglare shields and exhaust flame dampers. Incorporated an ETC 501 rack beneath the fuselage and capacity for a pair of auxiliary fuel drop tanks. Armament was limited to the pair of wing root mounted 20-mm MG 151 cannon.

A-5/U3 Fighter-bomber variant with ETC wing and fuselage racks installed for carrying up to a ton of bombs, or for attaching four auxiliary fuel drop tanks. Aircraft was usually

Fw 190A-4 of I/JG 54 during engine warm up, winter, 1943.   (BUNDESARCHIV)

Emblems ▶

1 JG 1 until October, 1943
2 JG 1 from mid-1943 to the end of WW II; the *Oesau* emblem from May, 1944
3 I/JG 1 *Oesau*
4 III/JG 2 *Richthofen*
5 7./JG 2 *Richthofen*
6 10. (Jabo)/JG 2 *Richthofen*
7 JG 3 *Udet*
8 II/JG 1 from September, 1941; before that I/JG 3 (Bf 109)
9 II/SG 1; also used by II (Schlacht)/LG 2 and II/SG 2; identical to Adolf Galland's personal emblem
10 III/JG 54 *Grünherz*
11 I/JG 54 *Grünherz*
12 Personal emblem of *Oblt* Fritz Kause, 1./NJGr10, spring, 1944; his nickname 'Illo' superimposed on the *Wilde Sau* insignia
13 14. (Jabo)/JG5
14 9./JG 1 until April, 1943; afterwards 3./JG 1
15 IV (Sturm)/JG 3 *Udet* from spring, 1944
16 I/SG 4
17 II/JG 4
18 Personal emblem of *Oblt* Wolfgang Kosse, *Staffelkapitän* of 1./JG 5, 1942, the so-called *Eismeerjäger* (Polar Sea Fighters)

1   2   3   4   5   6

7   8   9   10   11   12

13   14   15   16   17   18

Fw190A-3 of II/JG1 on the Western Front in the summer of 194

(BUNDESARCHIV)

7334

60

Nicht verstellen

R. Watanabe

Photo:

Oberleutnant 'Sepp' Wurmheller at the tailplane of his Fw 190A-4 in summer, 1943. The rudder scoreboard shows 74 confirmed kills, with the last 14 marked according to nationality and type. In this photograph *Oblt* Wurmheller is wearing a standard Luftwaffe officers peaked cap, flying suit with attached shoulder tabs, and the Luftwaffe eagle insignia on his right breast. His decorations include the Oak Leaves to the Knights' Cross of the Iron Cross (neck), the German Cross in Gold (intermediate award between the Iron Cross, 1st Class and Knights' Cross), and the Iron Cross, 1st Class.

Drawing:

The Fw 190A-4 flown by Josef Wurmheller as *Staffelkapitän* of 9./JG 2 in summer, 1943. The rudder marking displays 78 kills.

1m

1   2   3   ft

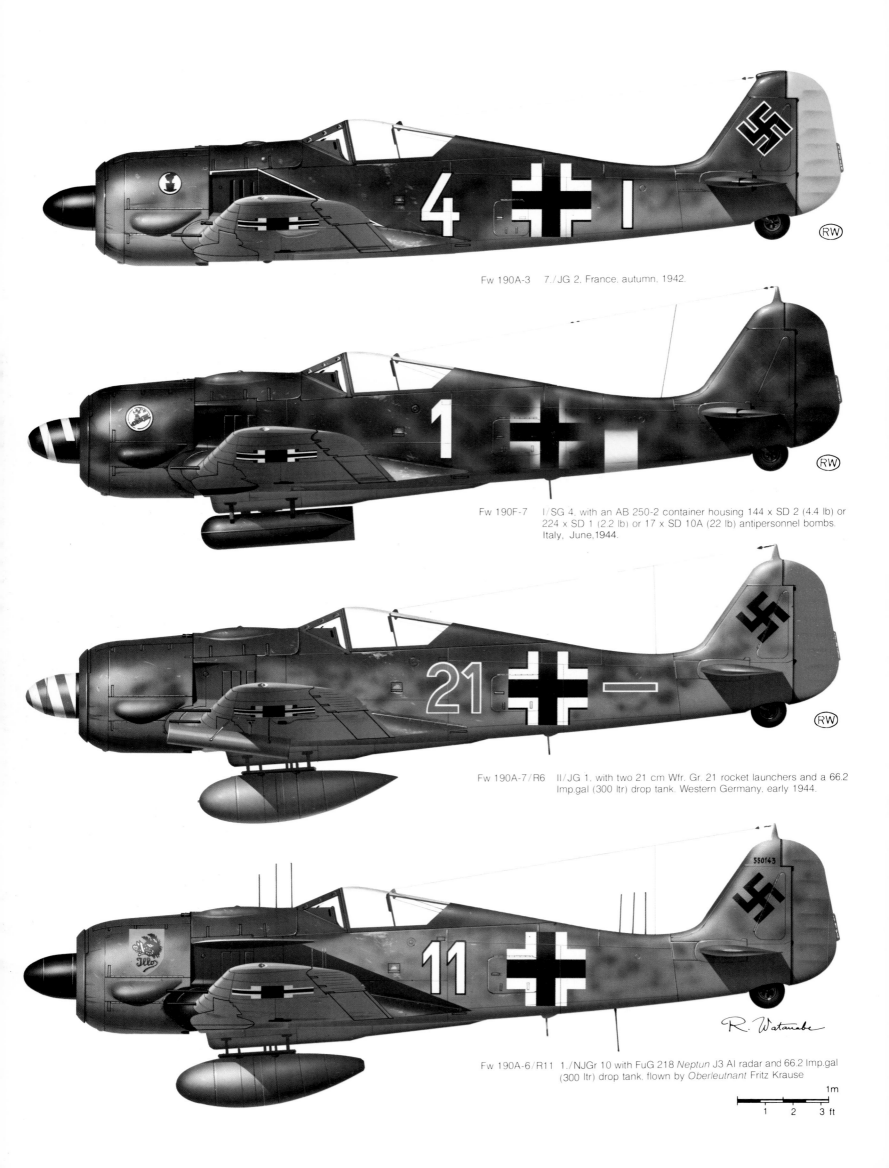

Fw 190A-3   7./JG 2, France, autumn, 1942.

Fw 190F-7   I/SG 4, with an AB 250-2 container housing 144 x SD 2 (4.4 lb) or 224 x SD 1 (2.2 lb) or 17 x SD 10A (22 lb) antipersonnel bombs. Italy, June,1944.

Fw 190A-7/R6   II/JG 1, with two 21 cm Wfr. Gr. 21 rocket launchers and a 66.2 Imp.gal (300 ltr) drop tank. Western Germany, early 1944

Fw 190A-6/R11   1./NJGr 10 with FuG 218 Neptun J3 AI radar and 66.2 Imp.gal (300 ltr) drop tank, flown by Oberleutnant Fritz Krause

1m
1   2   3 ft

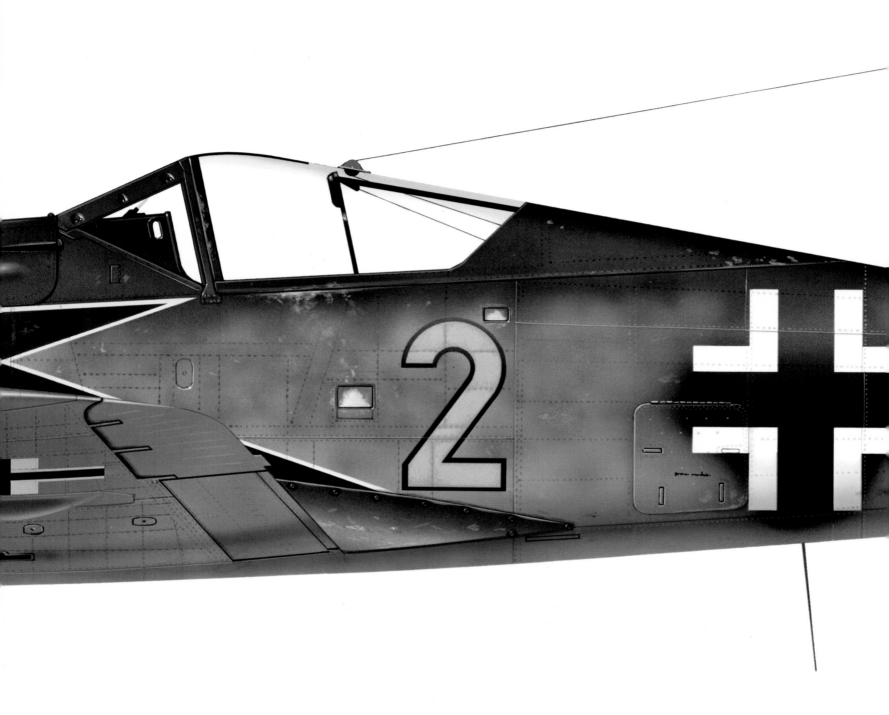

Joser Wurmheller, Fw 190 Ace

Josef 'Sepp' Wurmheller was born at Hausham/Upper Bavaria on 4 May, 1917, and worked as a miner before joining the Luftwaffe. He scored his first victory, a Faiery Battle, over Saarbrücken on 30 September, 1939, flying with I/JG 53; was then posted as instructor to a fighter school, rejoining his unit only in June 1940. Took part in the Battle of Britain (four victories, shot down twice himself) and the first three weeks of 'Operation Barbarossa' (nine victories). Transferred to III/JG 2 in July, 1941. Awarded *Ritterkreuz* (Knights' Cross) on 4

September, 1941, after 30 confirmed victories, then served another spell as fighter instructor, rejoining his unit in May, 1942.

Over Dieppe on 19 August, 1942, with one broken leg in plaster, shot down seven Spitfires and one Blenheim in three operational sorties. Awarded Oak Leaves to the Knights Cross on 13 November, 1942, after 60 confirmed victories. *Hauptmann* and *Kommandeur* of III/JG 2 on 10 June, 1944; killed in action (mid-air collision) on 22 June, 1944. Scored total of 102 kills (92 in the West, including 13 four-engined bombers; 9 in the East). Posthumously awarded Swords to the Oak Leaves of the Knights Cross; also promoted *Major*.

R. Watanabe

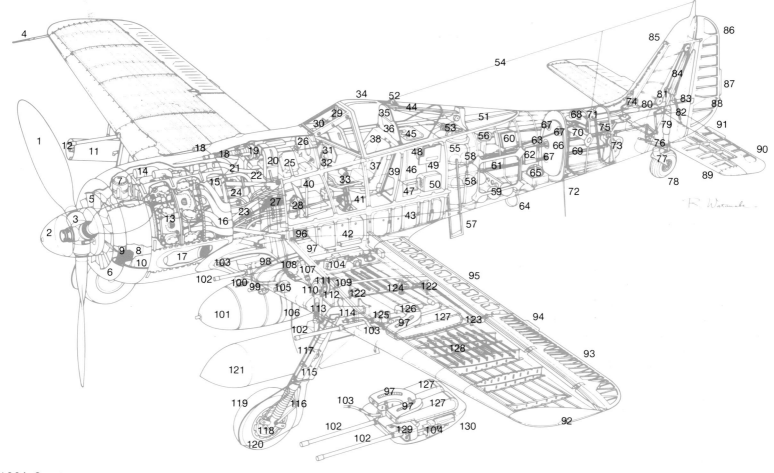

FW190A-8 cutaway

1 VDM three-blade adjustable-pitch constant-speed propeller
2 Spinner
3 Propeller hub
4 Pitot tube
5 Twelve-blade engine cooling fan
6 Cooler armoured ring (6.5 mm)
7 Magneto
8 Annular oil tank, 55 ltr. (12.1 Imp. gal)
9 Oil cooler, ring-shaped
10 Air cooler
11 Rocket-propelled shell launch tube
12 Rocket-propelled shell 21 cm Wfr. Gr. 21
13 BMW 801D-2 14 cylinder radial engine, take-off and emergency 1,700 hp
14 Supercharger air pressure pipe
15 Engine mounting ring
16 Exhaust pipe
17 Air intake duct
18 Rheinmetall MG 131 13 mm machine-gun
19 StL 131/5B weapon mount
20 Ammunition feed chute
21 Cold air pipe for ammunition cooling
22 MG 131 ammunition box (400 rounds each side)
23 Engine bearer assembly
24 Engine starter unit
25 Emergency power fuse and distributor box
26 Windscreen mounting frame
27 Fuel line
28 Rudder pedal
29 50 mm armoured glass windscreen
30 Reflector gunsight, Revi 16B
31 Instrument panel
32 Control column
33 Throttle lever
34 Canopy
35 Headrest
36 Head armour, 12 mm
37 Pilot's seat
38 Back armour, 5 mm
39 Side-section back armour, 5 mm
40 Rudder pedal arm
41 Adjustable rudder control push-rod
42 Forward fuselage fuel tank, 232 ltr. (51 Imp. gal)
43 Rear fuselage fuel tank, 293 ltr. (64.5 Imp. gal)

44 Head armour support strut
45 Baggage compartment hatch
46 Baggage compartment
47 Entry step cover panel
48 FuG 16ZY transmitter-receiver unit
49 FuG 16ZY power transformer
50 Transformer base plate
51 Canopy channel slide
52 Aerial attachment
53 Canopy emergency jettison unit
54 Aerial
55 Auxiliary fuel tank, 115 ltr. (25.3 Imp. gal)
56 Fuel filler point
57 Retractable entry step
58 Tri-spherical oxygen bottles, double, (broken lines) starboard side
59 Tri-spherical oxygen bottles, single, port side
60 FuG 25a IFF unit
61 Autopilot position integration unit
62 FuG 16ZY homer bearing converter
63 Rudder control DUZ-flexible rod
64 Fug 16ZY fixed loop homing antenna
65 Master compass sensing unit
66 Fabric panel
67 Rubber collar
68 Rudder differential unit
69 Elevator control cable
70 Read fuselage lift tube
71 Antenna matching unit
72 FuG 25a antenna
73 Elevator differential bellcrank
74 Horizontal stabilizer trim motor
75 Triangular stress frame
76 Drag yoke
77 Forked wheel housing
78 Tailwheel tyre, 350 x 135 mm
79 Tailwheel shock strut
80 Tailwheel retraction cable guide tube
81 Tailwheel retraction cable
82 Extension spring
83 Rudder control cable(s)
84 Shock strut guide
85 Vertical stabilizer
86 Rudder
87 Ground-adjustable rudder trim tab

88 Rear navigation light
89 Tailplane horizontal stabilizer
90 Elevator
91 Ground-adjustable elevator trim tab
92 Navigation light
93 Aileron
94 Ground-adjustable aileron trim tab
95 Flap
96 Wing root MG 151/20E ammunition box (250 rounds)
97 Ammunition feed chute
98 ETC 501 carrier unit
99 Spacer bar
100 Fuel filler cap
101 Auxiliary drop fuel tank, 300 ltr. (66 Imp. gal)
102 Mauser 20 mm MG 151/20E cannon
103 Hot air pipe for warming ammunition
104 Link belt segment/cartridge casing discard chute
105 BSK16 gun camera
106 FuG 16ZY Morane antenna
107 Sealed air-jack
108 Locking unit
109 Electric motor
110 Rotating drive outer cover
111 Main landing gear indicator rod
112 Rotating drive unit
113 Radius struts
114 Main struts mounting assembly
115 Main landing gear
116 Link arms
117 Brake line
118 Brake shoes
119 Mainwheel tyre, 700 x 175 mm
120 Main landing gear fairing
121 SC 500 bomb
122 Aileron control bellcrank
123 Aileron control linkage
124 Aileron control rod
125 Non-adjustable forward mount
126 Ammunition, 20 mm rounds
127 MG 151/20E ammunition box (125 rounds)
128 Stressed skin structure
129 Carrier frame
130 Underwing gun pack for A-8/R1

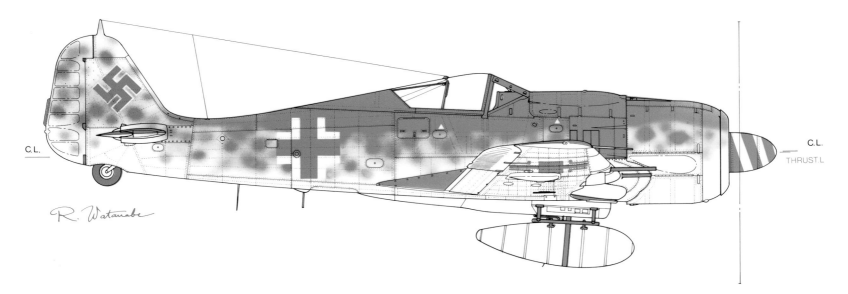

Fw 190A-8

flown with a combination of bomb and extra fuel capacity. Armament was limited to the fuselage mounted MG 17 machine-guns.

A-5/U4 Reconnaissance fighter with a pair of Rb 12.5/7 cameras or the installation of a single Rb 75/30 Rb 50/30 or Rb 20/30 camera installed in rear fuselage. Armament was limited to the MG 17 machine-guns as in the U2 version.

A-5/U8 Long range fighter-bomber with ETC rack under fuselage for SC 250 bomb and wing racks for a pair of auxiliary underwing fuel drop tanks. Armament was restricted to the wing root mounted 20-mm MG 151 cannon. This modification was very similar to the A-5/U2 and A-5/U3, but reflected a specific application of the bomb selection and auxiliary fuel capacity.

A-5/U9 Increased armament was the highlight of this factory conversion which incorporated a pair of 13-mm MG 131 machine-guns in the fuselage in place of the normal 7.9-mm MG 17s. It also had a pair of 20-mm MG 151 cannon installed in the wing just outboard of the undercarriage instead of the MG FF. Only two of this particular model were built and tested late in 1943.

A-5/U11 Another variant designed with the intent of increased firepower, this aircraft included a pair of 30-mm MK 103 cannon in place of the outboard 20-mm MG FF cannon. Only a single prototype of this model was ever produced. Problems with the larger, and higher power, cannon created numerous structural and design challenges that, at the time, were not considered worth the time of correction through major redesign.

A-5/U12 Another variant that included increased firepower, the U12 incorporated a pair of 20-mm MG 151 cannon in a pod mounted under each wing. The MG FF cannon were removed, but overall forward concentrated fire was increased from six guns to eight. Only two prototypes were built, but the concept of the dual cannon pod was to later be incorporated into several models of the basic A-7 and A-8 variants.

A-5/U13 Long range fighter-bomber with fuselage rack for SC 250 (500 lb) bomb and wing racks for attaching a pair of auxiliary fuel drop tanks. Only the wing mounted 20-mm MG 151 cannons were retained for armament. Again, only a

pair of these prototypes were produced, for testing and evaluation purposes.

A-5/U14 Torpedo bomber which incorporated a LT F5b torpedo onto a modified ETC 501 fuselage rack. To allow for the size and weight of the torpedo, this model also included an increased tail surface and an extended and strengthened tail-wheel strut to insure ground clearance. Armament was limited to the pair of wing root mounted MG 151 cannon. Only two prototypes were built.

A-5/U15 Torpedo bomber of essentially the same design as the U14, but which was intended to carry the Blohm and Voss LT 950 torpedo in place of the LT F5b. Only one prototype was produced.

A-5/U16 Experimental bomber version with a single 30-mm MK 108 cannon in a streamlined fairing under each wing; outboard MG151 cannon were deleted. Only once aircraft was built.

A-5/U17 Dive bomber and close support. Development aircraft for the Fw 190F series, incorporating a pair of ETC 50 wing racks. One prototype only.

The incorporation of the varied armament of the Fw 190 through its A-1 to A-5 variants increased its operating capabilities, however, even though each change and new mission environment assigned to the now much respected *Wuerger* met with more success than failure, these additions were not without disadvantages. The weight of the Fw 190 increased and resulted in the necessary redesign of the main wing structure to maintain the Fw 190s record of low maintenance and high combat survivability. This modified wing also incorporated a standardized armament of two 20-mm MG 151 electro-pneumatic operated cannon in each wing, the outboard MG FF cannon being replaced by the more effective MG 151. Additional armor was also added in critical areas such as the cockpit, cowling and cooling system to reduce damage susceptibility. Wing loading with the new wing was reduced to just over 226 kg/m² (46.3 lb/sq ft) and provided increased handling response over the previous models.

The first variant to include this new wing design and the increased armor protection was the Fw 190A-6, an aircraft specifically intended for operation on the Eastern

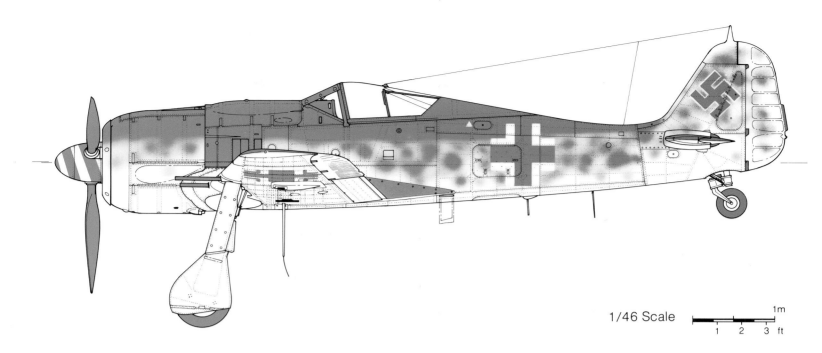

1/46 Scale

1m
1 2 3 ft

Front and one designed to accept a number of *Ruestsaetze* (field conversion kits) instead of the factory conversion kits. The reasoning behind this intention lay in the variety of missions required of an aircraft on that Front and the need for quick change. The Luftwaffe did not have, at the time, the numbers of aircraft needed, to assign individual units, or flights, to specific operational sorties, and therefore were in need of an all-purpose interceptor and fighter-bomber which could quickly and easily transition from one role to the other in the field.

The first Fw 190A-6s to be delivered were the A-6/R1 which incorporated the underwing pod with the pair of MG 151 cannon first evaluated on the A-5/U12. The Fw 190A-6/R2 never reached the front and was limited to one prototype. This modification included the deletion of the outboard MG 151 cannon and the incorporation of an underwing, 30-mm MK 108 cannon in its place.

Like the Fw 190A-6/R2, the R4 modification was also an experimental aircraft. The changes, however, were not in the area of increased armament, but instead were for the testing of a nitrous-oxide injection boost system (GM 1) for the BMW 801D powerplant and potential increased lift with extended wingtips.

The R6 configuration incorporated the 210-mm rocket tubes that had originally been installed on the Fw 190A-4/R6 and were intended for use, as was the A-4/R6 in the West, against massed USAAF bomber formations. Still another previous modification, the addition of ETC bomb racks to both the fuselage and wings, for the carrying of bomb loads, was installed on the Fw 190A-6 and given the identification of U3. The Fw 190A-6/U3 actually was identical in this respect, to the test evaluation Fw 190A-5/U3 model, as the Luftwaffe started using common ''U'' and ''R'' designations for different variants with the same factory or field conversions. A number of A-5s and A-6s were also equipped with the Nepture-J radar with wing antenna. These few aircraft became the world's first all-weather fighters.

The Fw 190A-7 reached production in December, 1943, and included only a few minor changes from the A-6. Among these were the standardized incorporation of a pair of

13-mm MG 131 machine-guns in place of the fuselage upper-deck 7.9-mm MG 17 machine-guns, and the addition of the new Revi 16b reflector gunsight. The installation of the newer and larger MG 131s also resulted in a change in the hinged upper deck fuselage panel which required a pair of protruding bulges to allow sufficient volume for housing the new guns. Approximately 80 of the A-7 variant were produced in late 1943 and early 1944, with over half of these incorporating the 30-mm MK 108 external cannon. Adhering to their standardized designation codes, these models were identified as Fw 190A-7/R2s. The only other major model of the A-7 to be delivered was the R6 model, which like its predecessors, incorporated a pair of underwing 210-mm Wfr.Gr. 21 rocket tubes. The last Fw 190A version to be produced was the Fw 190A-8 and was the variant produced in the largest numbers. The A-8 was similar to the A-7 variant in almost every respect, except that it included a few internal changes for increased performance capability. These changes consisted of the incorporation of the GM1 nitrous oxide tank, or additional fuel tank, located aft of the main cockpit area, and relocation of the radio and ETC bomb rack to compensate for the c.g. shifts resulting from the power boost tankage. No less than nine model designations were assigned to the Fw 190A-8 including:

A-8/R1 Heavy armed fighter incorporating the 20-mm MG 151 cannon pod under each wing.

A-8/R2 Heavy armed bomber destroyer aircraft incorporating a pair of 30-mm MK 108 cannon under the wings in place of the outboard WB 151 twin gun pods.

A-8/R3 Tank destroyer aircraft incorporating the long barrel 30-mm MK 103 cannon instead of the MK 108. The MK 103, although possessing a slower rate of fire, had demonstrated a much higher muzzle velocity (due to the longer barrel) and increased accuracy. This accuracy factor was critical when attacking fast moving Soviet tank columns on the extensive flat lands of the Eastern Front.

A-8/R7 This model became famous as the *Rammjaeger* and was designed for the ramming of USAAF bombers. The model carried standardized A-8 armament consisting of the pair of

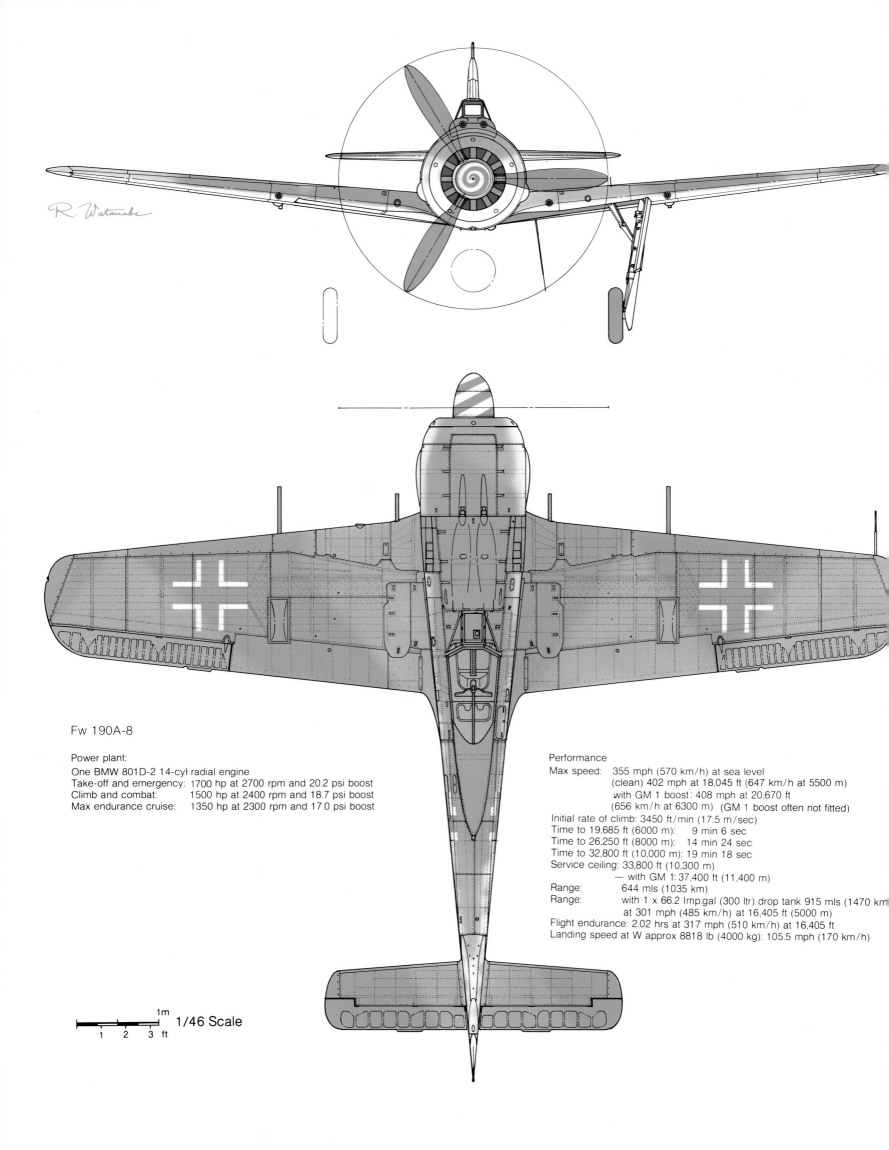

R. Watanabe

Fw 190A-8

Power plant:
One BMW 801D-2 14-cyl radial engine
Take-off and emergency: 1700 hp at 2700 rpm and 20.2 psi boost
Climb and combat: 1500 hp at 2400 rpm and 18.7 psi boost
Max endurance cruise: 1350 hp at 2300 rpm and 17.0 psi boost

Performance
Max speed: 355 mph (570 km/h) at sea level
             (clean) 402 mph at 18,045 ft (647 km/h at 5500 m)
             with GM 1 boost: 408 mph at 20,670 ft
             (656 km/h at 6300 m) (GM 1 boost often not fitted)
Initial rate of climb: 3450 ft/min (17.5 m/sec)
Time to 19,685 ft (6000 m):   9 min 6 sec
Time to 26,250 ft (8000 m):   14 min 24 sec
Time to 32,800 ft (10,000 m): 19 min 18 sec
Service ceiling: 33,800 ft (10,300 m)
              — with GM 1: 37,400 ft (11,400 m)
Range: 644 mls (1035 km)
Range: with 1 x 66.2 Imp.gal (300 ltr) drop tank 915 mls (1470 km
             at 301 mph (485 km/h) at 16,405 ft (5000 m)
Flight endurance: 2.02 hrs at 317 mph (510 km/h) at 16,405 ft
Landing speed at W approx 8818 lb (4000 kg): 105.5 mph (170 km/h)

1m
1/46 Scale
1 2 3 ft

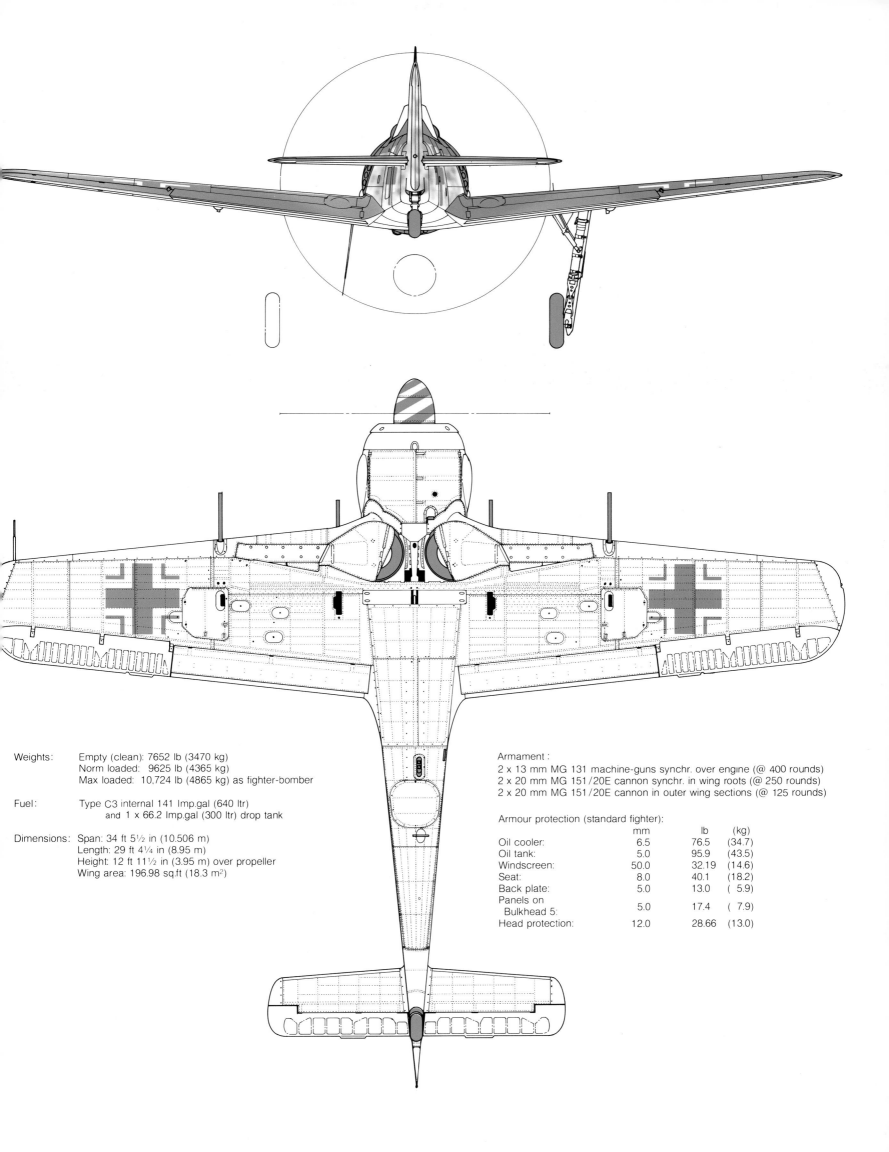

Weights: Empty (clean): 7652 lb (3470 kg)
              Norm loaded: 9625 lb (4365 kg)
              Max loaded: 10,724 lb (4865 kg) as fighter-bomber

Fuel: Type C3 internal 141 Imp.gal (640 ltr)
              and 1 x 66.2 Imp.gal (300 ltr) drop tank

Dimensions: Span: 34 ft 5½ in (10.506 m)
              Length: 29 ft 4¼ in (8.95 m)
              Height: 12 ft 11½ in (3.95 m) over propeller
              Wing area: 196.98 sq.ft (18.3 m²)

Armament :
2 x 13 mm MG 131 machine-guns synchr. over engine (@ 400 rounds)
2 x 20 mm MG 151/20E cannon synchr. in wing roots (@ 250 rounds)
2 x 20 mm MG 151/20E cannon in outer wing sections (@ 125 rounds)

Armour protection (standard fighter):

	mm	lb	(kg)
Oil cooler:	6.5	76.5	(34.7)
Oil tank:	5.0	95.9	(43.5)
Windscreen:	50.0	32.19	(14.6)
Seat:	8.0	40.1	(18.2)
Back plate:	5.0	13.0	(5.9)
Panels on			
Bulkhead 5:	5.0	17.4	(7.9)
Head protection:	12.0	28.66	(13.0)

Fw 190A-8: Loading the fuselage MG 131 machine-guns.

Fw 190A-3 undergoing gun adjusting tests.

fuselage mounted 13-mm MG 131 machine-guns and four wing mounted 20-mm MG 151 cannons, but had heavily increased frontal and cockpit armor.

A-8/R8   An experimental bomber formation interceptor for close engagements. The aircraft incorporated 30-mm MK 108 short barrel cannon in the outboard 20-mm MG 151 cannon receptacles.

A-8/R11   Designed as an all-weather fighter, this model was to incorporate the new BMW 801TS (TS for turbo-super-charged), FuG 125 D/F equipment, and the PKS 12 automatic pilot. Only a few of these were built due to more pressing needs of other models.

A-8/R12   Identical to the R11 except for the replacement of the outboard MG 151 cannon with the MK 108s of the A-8/R8 model. This model too was never built.

In addition to the various weapon and powerplant modifications to enhance the abilities of the Fw 190, another unique use was foreseen for the ever receptive *Wuerger*. The Luftwaffe had become disenchanted with its famous *Blitzkrieg* divebomber, the Junkers Ju 87, and had included in its varied mission plans for the Fw 190, the role of ground attacker, to replace the now vulnerable and obsolete Ju 87. To train pilots for this new role, the Air Ministry early in 1943 issued a set of requirements to Focke-Wulf to design and

develop a two-seat training aircraft design. The answer was not only obvious, but simple. Focke-Wulf engineers took the Fw 190 and made a two-seat training version from it to retrain the former Ju 87 crews.

Three prototypes were built under the designation Fw 190A-8/U1, the first of which was flown in January of 1944. The modifications included a second cockpit fitted just behind the original (with a new extended length canopy) with a set of simplified controls in the aft cockpit. This conversion was found to be applicable to any of the A-series variants and was given the official designation of Fw 190S (the "S" standing for *Schulflugzeug,* or flight training plane). Although only three of the Fw 190A-8/U1s were built, and only a few other S-5 and S-8 variants were manufactured, the Fw 190 had again demonstrated its ever amazing ability to adapt to any role assigned to it.

The Fw 190A-9, a proposed *Rammjaeger,* was built in six prototypes and incorporated the BMW801F-1 powerplant with heavily armored wing leading-edges. The Fw 190A-10 was a proposed long-range fighter-bomber which was to have used the BMW 80ITS or TH engine.

Several other different and highly unusual modifications were also tested on the basic Fw 190A airframe by the RLM. The first was the installation of a pair of auxiliary fuel tanks (*Doppelreiter*—Double Rider) that were attached to

Fw 190G-3 fighter-bombers had fuselage guns deleted.

Fw 190A-8 fighter-bomber, with an SC 500 bomb in the foreground. Eastern Front, summer 1944.

(BUNDESARCHIV)

(BUNDESARCHIV)

Fw 190A-3 of I/JG 51, summer, 1942.

Fw 190A-3 of I/JG 51. Eastern Front, summer, 1942.

the wing surface just inside of the outboard cannon and were jettisonable. The long, low profile tanks extended out over the trailing edge similar to many current day spoiler fairings. Another modification test was the incorporation of a series of upward firing single salvo cannon tubes on the side of the aft fuselage that were triggered by a photo-electric cell activated by a bomber's shadow. Many arrangements of these single salvo tubes were tested including three MK 103 tubes in line of the left side of the fuselage just aft of the cockpit with a 74-degree cant angle, and another which incorporated a cluster of seven MK 108 tubes.

Still another test evaluation aircraft was installed with a single aft-firing 21-cm rocket tube attached under the center of the fuselage. This concept was to be used by bomber interceptors as they pulled away from the bomber formations after a forward-firing pass through the stream.

Fw 190B *series*

The Fw 190 had proved its worth by late 1941 and early 1942; however, it had one serious drawback that was considered a major problem by both Focke-Wulf and the RLM. This was the aircraft's lack of adequate performance at altitudes above 4500 to 6000 m (15,000 to 20,000 ft). This was of concern

because in its interceptor role the Fw 190 was expected to vector to, and engage, high altitude Allied bomber formations. In early 1942, a temporary solution was conceived that included the addition of the GM 1 (nitrous-oxide) injection power boost system for the BMW 801 which would allow short duration performance increases for climb and high altitude acceleration. The nitrous-oxide was to be contained in a specialized tank that would be located behind the cockpit with a feeder line network to the BMW radial engine.

The concept was incorporated into a standard Fw 190A-0 and delivered to the RLM at the Focke-Wulf plant at Bremen for testing and evaluation. The results showed that the injectant indeed provided short term boosts in power up to altitudes of 7500 m (25,000 ft), but that the duration of the system was limited both by the size and weight of the tankage. To provide enough injectant for what was considered acceptable performance would increase the aircraft weight to unacceptable limits, and to work within the available weight and volume restrictions did not provide for sufficient injectant.

The failure of these tests, however, did not deter Focke-Wulf from their pursuit of a solution to the altitude performance deficiency. Although they felt that any modification to the BMW 801 powerplant was a matter of wasted effort (wanting to re-engine with a liquid-cooled in-line),

Fw 190F-3: SC 250 bomb being attached to the fuselage ETC 501 rack.

Fw 190A-5 '13' flown by *Major* Josef Priller, here with his BMW 328 roadster, France, 1943. BMW engineers powered both aircraft and motor car.

(BUNDESARCHIV)

(BUNDESARCHIV)

they abided by RLM wishes and under the designation Fw 190B embarked on an attempt to increase the high altitude performance of the Fw 190 and the BMW 801 through various design improvements. These included a turbo-supercharger for the powerplant, increased wing area and a pressurized cockpit.

The first of these prototypes, the Fw 190 V13 (a modified Fw 190A-0 pre-production model) was transferred to the B-series development program, however, BMW went on record as stating that there existed no possibility of their developing the supercharged BMW 801 engine within the scheduled dates. Based on these facts, Focke-Wulf re-engined the Fw 190 V13 with a DB 603A-0 inline liquid cooled 12-cylinder inverted-Vee powerplant which provided increased power and lighter weight. The second prototype, Fw 190 V16, was also fitted with the DB 603A-0 and was similar to the V13 in almost every respect, with neither aircraft including the pressurized canopy which Focke-Wulf felt could be separately tested and added at a later date.

In August 1942, the second prototype, V16, was sent to Daimler-Benz at Echterdingen for replacement of the DB 603A powerplant with the newer (initial development stages) and higher performing DB 603E and was then tested with both the GM 1 nitrous-oxide injectant boost system and the MW 50 methanol-water injection system to increase critical h.p. at altitude and during emergency combat situations.

The V16 was flown for altitude performance in October and attained maximum altitudes between 10,700 and 11,900 m (35,000 and 39,000 ft) as a matter of normality after the first two weeks, with duration at these altitudes for up to two hours.

Although the initial tests had proven successful with respect to the requirements for high altitude interception imposed on Focke-Wulf by the Luftwaffe, the technical staff at the RLM was becoming seriously concerned about the high altitude capabilities of the newer Allied bomber developments and modified the operational altitude requirements to 14,000 m (45,000 ft). After analytical evaluation of the required performance characteristics and the increased operational altitude, it was determined that the current airframe design and exhaust-driven supercharged DB 603 was not capable of compliance, and additional modifications in the powerplant/supercharger area would have to be made.

The remainder of the Fw 190B-series aircraft, using the BMW 801D with the GM 1 (less turbo/supercharger), incorporated pressurized high altitude canopies and were utilized basically as test vehicles for the pressurization system. Tests were scheduled, and then delayed, by continuous leaks around the rubber seal between the canopy hood frame and the fuselage guide rails. By November of 1942, both Focke-Wulf and the RLM had decided to discontinue efforts

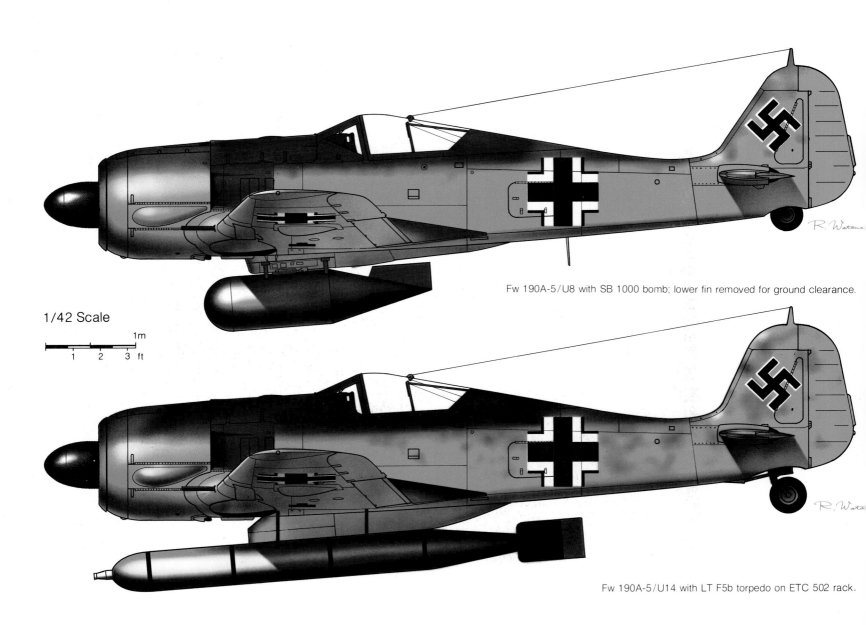

1/42 Scale

1m
1 2 3 ft

Fw 190A-5/U8 with SB 1000 bomb; lower fin removed for ground clearance.

Fw 190A-5/U14 with LT F5b torpedo on ETC 502 rack.

Fw 190A-5 Flown by *Leutnant* Otto Kittel, *Staffelkapitän* of 2./JG 54 'Grünherz'
in Courtand (Latvia), Eastern Front, spring, 1944.
Span 10.383 m (34 ft 0¾ in)
Length 8.950 m (29 ft 4 in)
Wing area 18.3 m² (196.98 sq.ft)

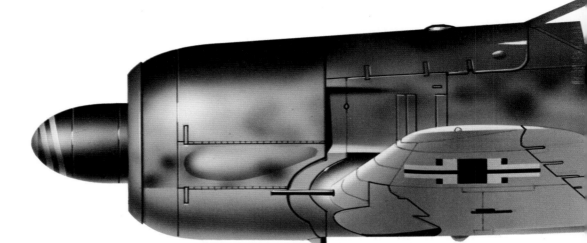

Fw 190D-9 Flown by *Oberleutnant* Oskar Romm, *Kommandeur* of IV/JG 3
'Udet', Berlin area, April, 1945.
Span 10.506 m (34 ft 5½ in)
Length 10.192 m (33 ft 5¼ in)
Wing area 18.3 m² (196.98 sq.ft)

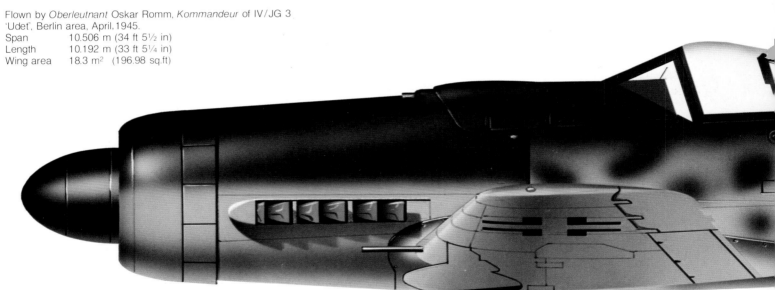

Ta 152H-1 *Stab*/JG 301, spring, 1945
Span 14.440 m (47 ft 4½ in)
Length 10.710 m (35 ft 1¾ in)
Wing area 23.3 m² (250.80 sq.ft)

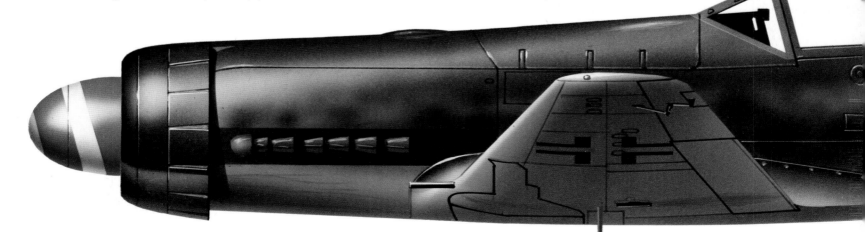

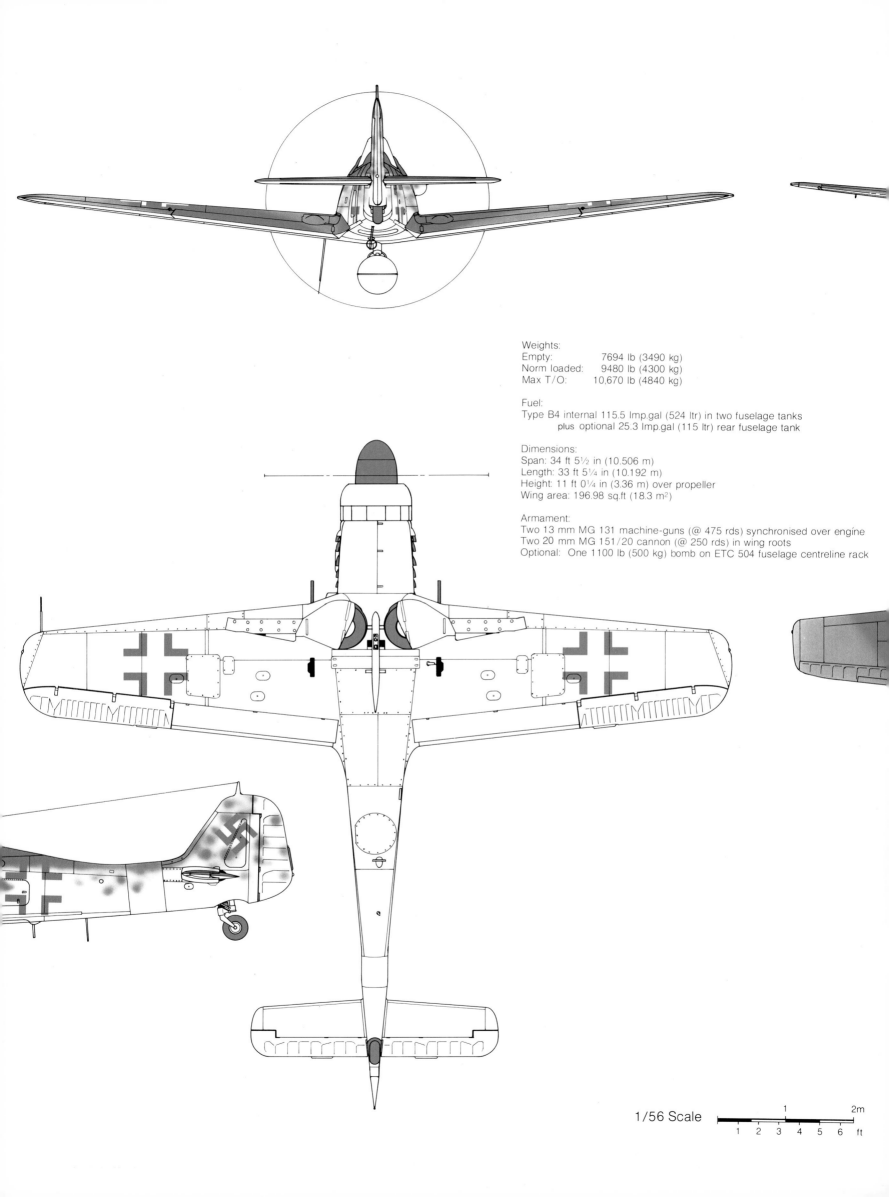

Weights:
Empty: 7694 lb (3490 kg)
Norm loaded: 9480 lb (4300 kg)
Max T/O: 10,670 lb (4840 kg)

Fuel:
Type B4 internal 115.5 Imp.gal (524 ltr) in two fuselage tanks
        plus optional 25.3 Imp.gal (115 ltr) rear fuselage tank

Dimensions:
Span: 34 ft 5½ in (10.506 m)
Length: 33 ft 5¼ in (10.192 m)
Height: 11 ft 0¼ in (3.36 m) over propeller
Wing area: 196.98 sq.ft (18.3 m²)

Armament:
Two 13 mm MG 131 machine-guns (@ 475 rds) synchronised over engine
Two 20 mm MG 151/20 cannon (@ 250 rds) in wing roots
Optional: One 1100 lb (500 kg) bomb on ETC 504 fuselage centreline rack

1/56 Scale

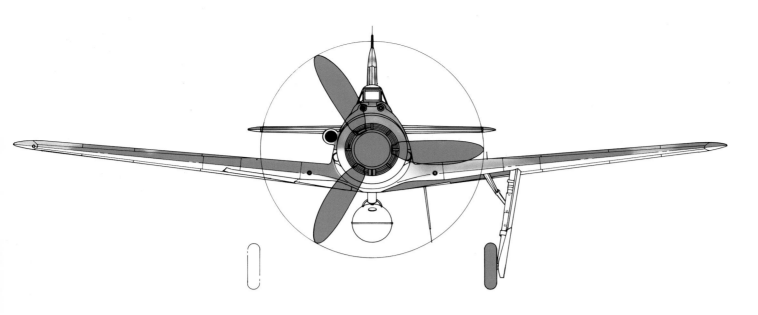

Fw 190D-9 data

Power plant: One Junkers Jumo 213A-1 12-cyl inverted-V inline engine
Take-off: 1776 hp
Maximum: 1600 hp at 18,045 ft (5500 m)

Performance at (9480 lb/4300 kg loaded weight) with MW 50 boost; clean
Max speed: 357 mph (575 km/h) at sea level
 397 mph at 10,830 ft (640 km/h at 3300 m)
 426 mph at 21,650 ft (686 km/h at 6600 m)
 397 mph at 32,810 ft (639 km/h at 10,000 m)
Time to 6560 ft (2000 m): 2 min 6 sec
Time to 13,120 ft (4000 m): 4 min 30 sec
Time to 19,685 ft (6000 m): 7 min 6 sec
Time to 32,810 ft (10,000 m): 16 min 48 sec
Range (clean): 520 mls (837 km) at 18,500 ft (5640 m)

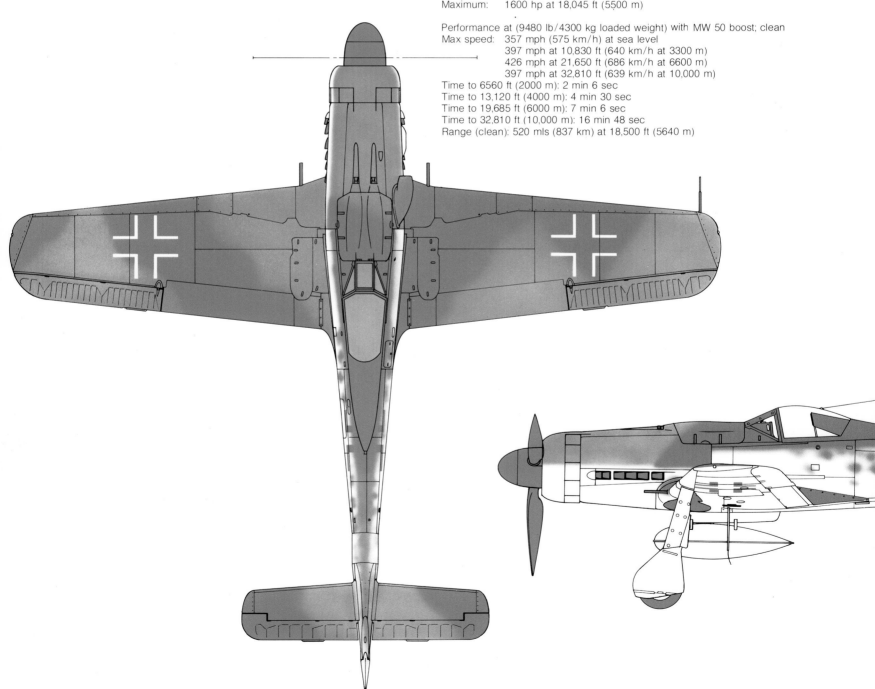

R. Watanabe

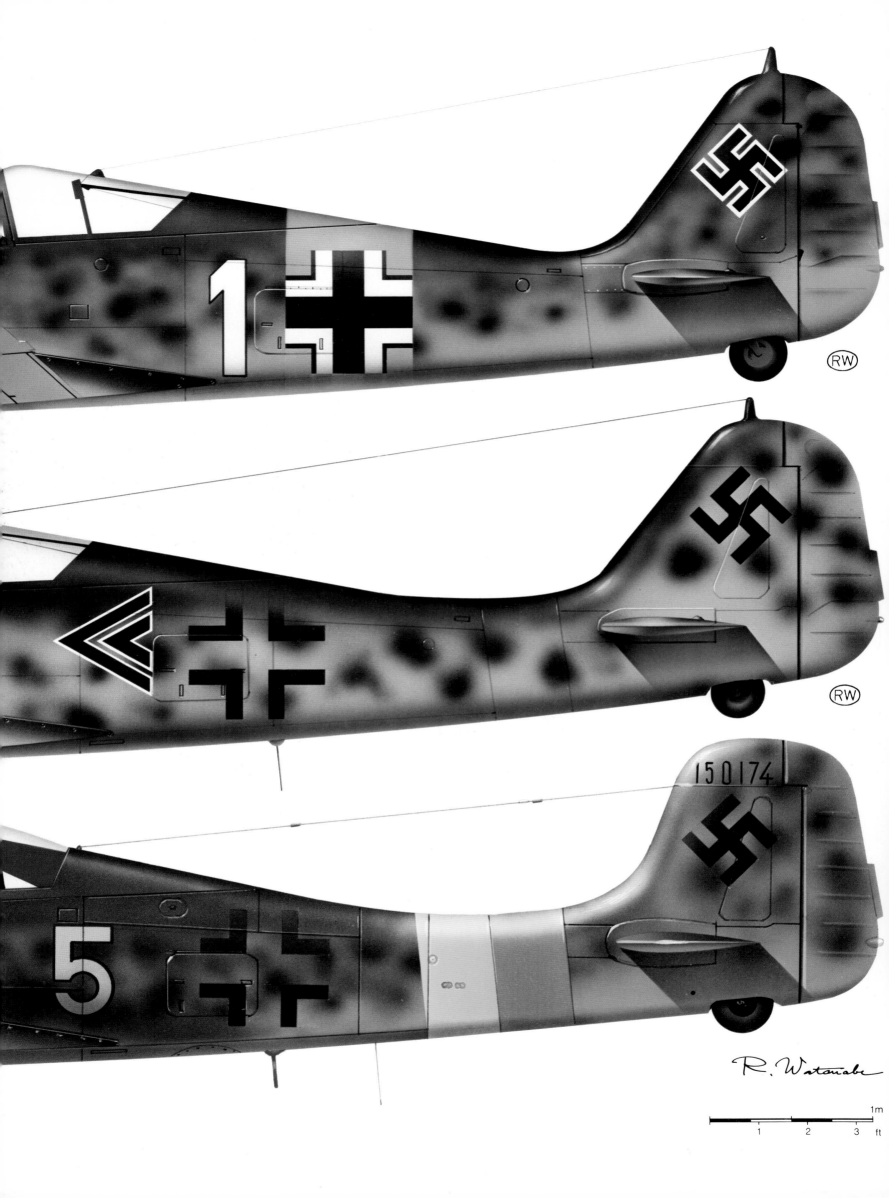

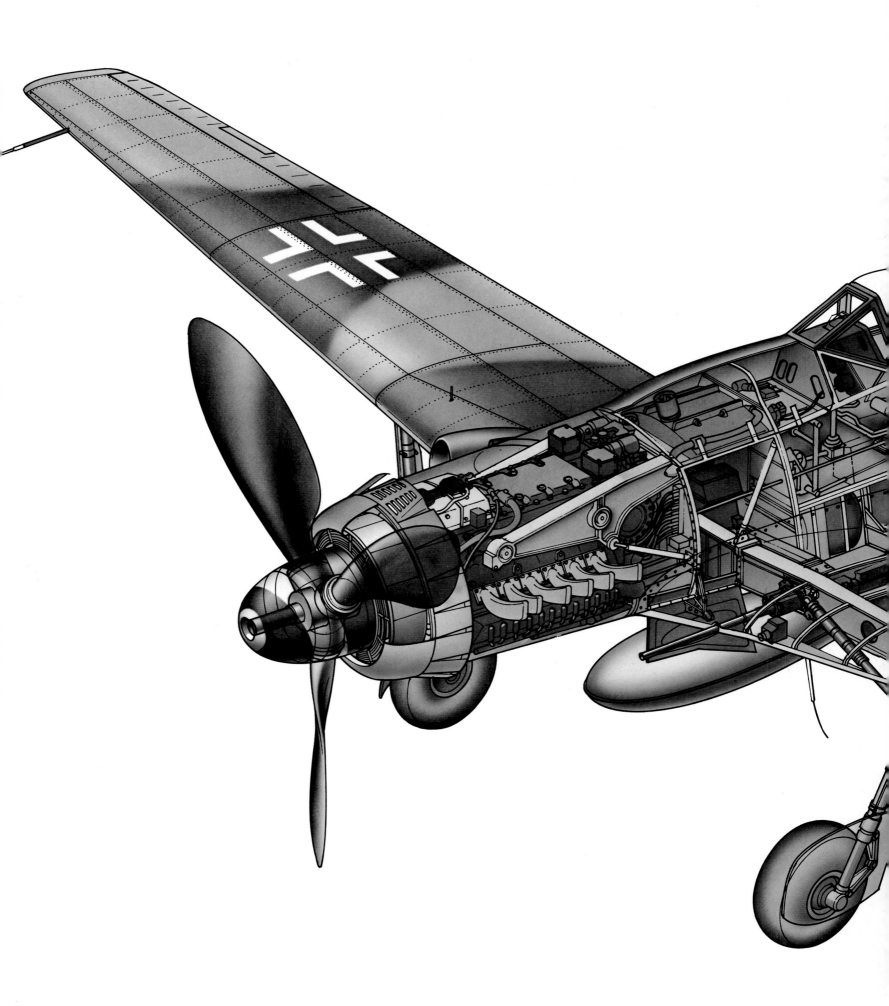

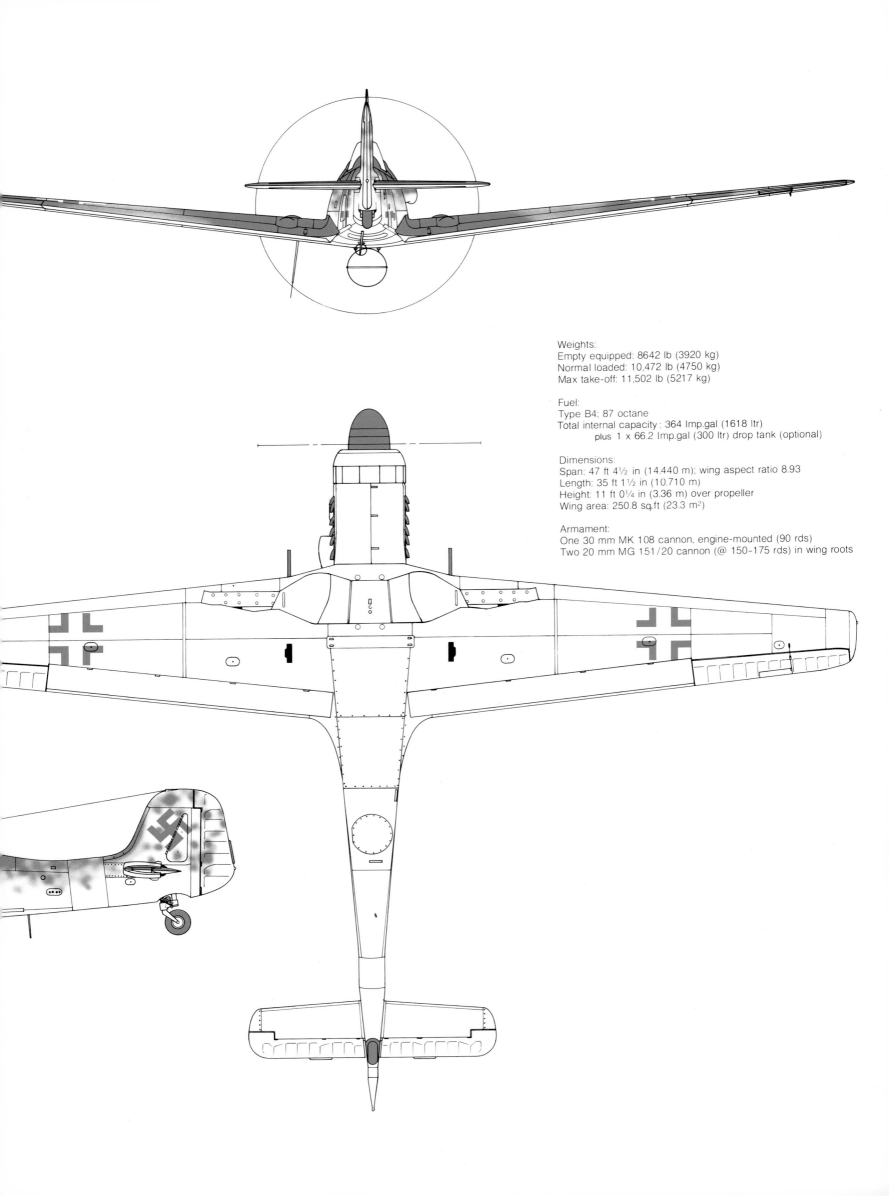

Weights:
Empty equipped: 8642 lb (3920 kg)
Normal loaded: 10,472 lb (4750 kg)
Max take-off: 11,502 lb (5217 kg)

Fuel:
Type B4; 87 octane
Total internal capacity : 364 Imp.gal (1618 ltr)
      plus 1 x 66.2 Imp.gal (300 ltr) drop tank (optional)

Dimensions:
Span: 47 ft 4½ in (14.440 m); wing aspect ratio 8.93
Length: 35 ft 1½ in (10.710 m)
Height: 11 ft 0¼ in (3.36 m) over propeller
Wing area: 250.8 sq.ft (23.3 m²)

Armament:
One 30 mm MK 108 cannon, engine-mounted (90 rds)
Two 20 mm MG 151/20 cannon (@ 150-175 rds) in wing roots

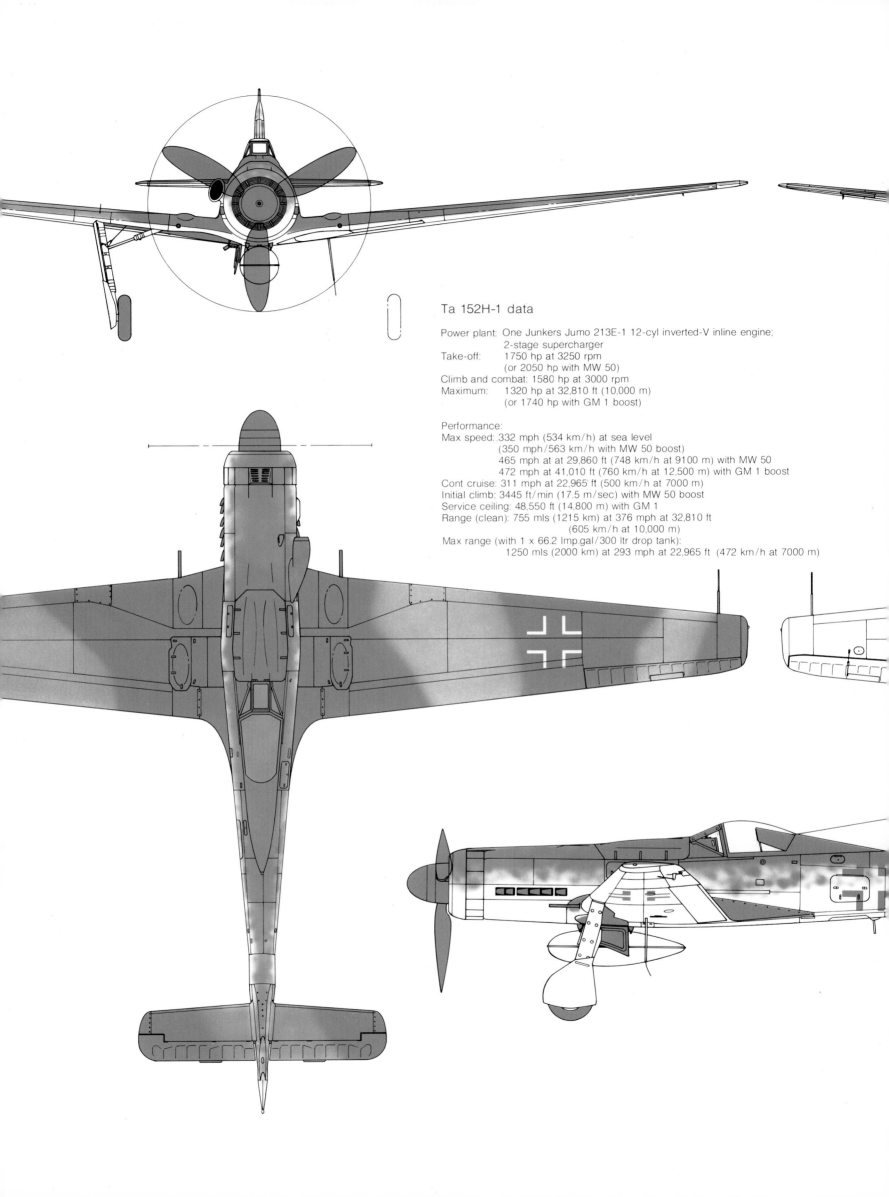

Ta 152H-1 data

Power plant: One Junkers Jumo 213E-1 12-cyl inverted-V inline engine;
2-stage supercharger
Take-off: 1750 hp at 3250 rpm
(or 2050 hp with MW 50)
Climb and combat: 1580 hp at 3000 rpm
Maximum: 1320 hp at 32,810 ft (10,000 m)
(or 1740 hp with GM 1 boost)

Performance:
Max speed: .332 mph (534 km/h) at sea level
(350 mph/563 km/h with MW 50 boost)
465 mph at at 29,860 ft (748 km/h at 9100 m) with MW 50
472 mph at 41,010 ft (760 km/h at 12,500 m) with GM 1 boost
Cont cruise: 311 mph at 22,965 ft (500 km/h at 7000 m)
Initial climb: 3445 ft/min (17.5 m/sec) with MW 50 boost
Service ceiling: 48,550 ft (14,800 m) with GM 1
Range (clean): 755 mls (1215 km) at 376 mph at 32,810 ft
(605 km/h at 10,000 m)
Max range (with 1 x 66.2 Imp.gal/300 ltr drop tank):
1250 mls (2000 km) at 293 mph at 22,965 ft (472 km/h at 7000 m)

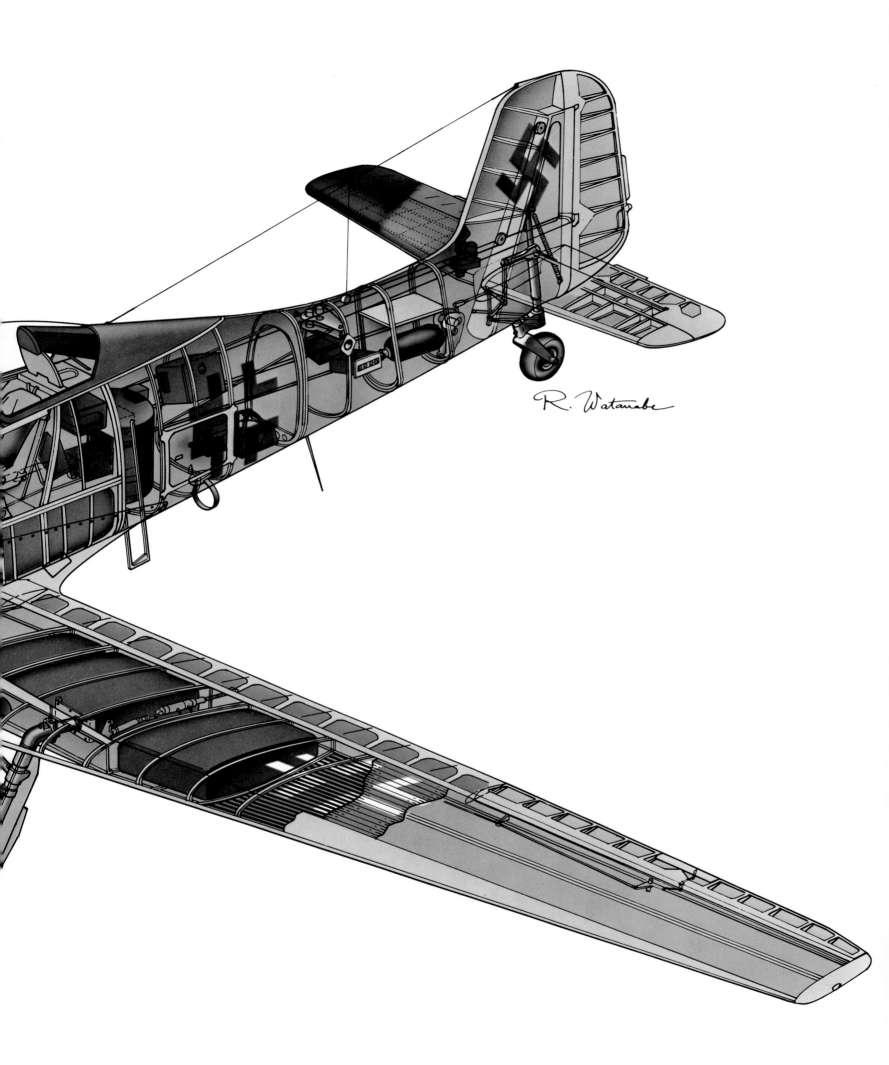

R. Watanabe

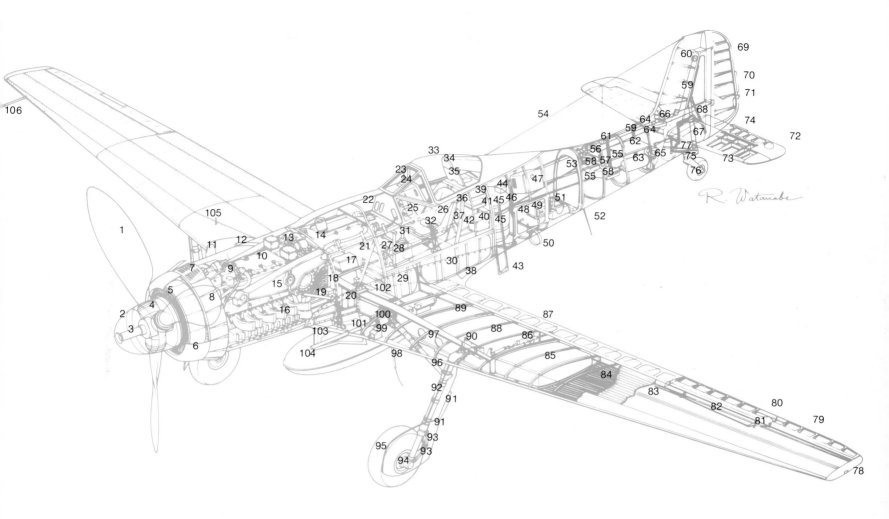

Ta152H-1 cutaway

1 Junkers three-blade constant-speed wooden
  propeller
2 Spinner
3 Blast tube for Reinmetall 30 mm MK108 cannon
4 Propeller hub
5 Annular radiator
6 Cooler armoured ring, 15 mm
7 Cooling louvres
8 Controllable cooling gill(s)
9 Engine accessories
10 Junkers Jumo 213E engine
11 Supercharger air intake
12 Auxiliary air intake
13 Generator
14 Oil tank 72 ltr. (15.8 Imp. gal)
15 Engine main bearer
16 Exhaust stub(s)
17 MK108 ammunition box (90 rounds)
18 Firewall
19 Engine bearer support member
20 Front spar carry-through
21 Cockpit forward pressure bulkhead
22 Space for two Mauser 20 mm MG151/20 cannon
   (Ta152C)
23 Laminated glass windscreen
24 Revi 16B gunsight
25 Instrument panel
26 Pilot's seat
27 Rudder pedal
28 Rudder pedal arm
29 Forward fuselage protected fuel tank, 233 ltr.
   (51.3 Imp. gal)
30 Rear fuselage protected fuel tank, 362 ltr. (80
   Imp. gal)
31 Control column
32 Throttle lever
33 Canopy
34 Headrest
35 Head armour, 20 mm

36 Two-piece shoulder armour, 5 mm
37 Two-piece back armour, 8 mm
38 Spring-loaded hand/foothold
39 Cut-out box
40 Dynamo
41 Cockpit rear pressure bulkhead
42 Lead storage battery
43 Retractable entry step
44 Distributor
45 FuG 125 navigation equipment (broken lines)
   (in Ta 152H-1/R11 bad-weather variant only)
46 Tank for GM 1 (N₂O: nitrous oxide) power
   boosting system, 85 ltr. (18.7 Imp. gal)
47 FuG 16ZY radio transceiver
48 Radio bay access hatch
49 LGW-Siemens K23 autopilot
50 FuG 16ZY fixed loop homing antenna
51 Master compass
52 FuG 125 aerial
53 Rudder control rod
54 Aerial
55 Elevator control cables
56 Rudder differential unit
57 Rear fuselage lift tube
58 AZA 10 signal cartridge(s)
59 Tailwheel retraction cable
60 Tail fin vertical stabilizer
61 Antenna matching unit
62 Oxygen cylinder storage shelf
63 Compressed air bottle for cannon operation,
   5 ltr. (1.1 Imp. gal)
64 Elevator control cable(s)
65 Elevator differential bellcrank
66 Master compass sensing unit
67 Tailwheel shock strut
68 Extension spring
69 Rudder
70 Ground-adjustable rudder trim tab
71 Rear position light

72 Elevator
73 Tailplane horizontal stabilizer
74 Ground adjustable elevator trim tab
75 Forked wheel housing
76 Tailwheel tyre, 380 x 150 mm
77 Drag yoke
78 Navigation light
79 Aileron
80 Controlable aileron trim tab
81 Aileron/trim tab control linkage
82 Aileron/trim tab control rod
83 Full span rear spar
84 Stressed skin structure
85 Outboard wing fuel tank
86 Flap actuating jack
87 Flap
88 Inboard wing fuel tank
89 Tank for MW 50 (50% methanol, 49.5% water and
   0.5% anti-corrosion fluid) injection system,
   70 ltr. (15.4 Imp. gal)
90 Main landing gear attachment plate
91 Main landing gear fairing
92 Main landing gear
93 Link arms
94 Brake shoes
95 Mainwheel tire, 740 x 210 mm
96 Retraction strut
97 Abbreviated steel front spar
98 FuG16 ZY Morane antenna
99 BSK 16 gun camera
100 MG 151/20 cannon forward mounting
101 Mauser MG 151/20 cannon
102 MG 151/20 ammunition box (175 rounds)
103 Undercarriage door
104 Auxiliary drop tank, 300 ltr. (66 Imp. gal)
105 Main landing gear indicator rod
106 Pitot tube

on the Fw 190B as a high altitude interceptor, and to concentrate on the powerplant modifications intended for the Fw 190C model.

Fw 190C *series*

The first Fw 190C prototype was, in fact, a modified Fw 190B (the V13 model) which had the BMW 801C-1 engine with GM 1 injectant system removed and replaced with a DB 603A-0 in-line. The aircraft was not fitted with either a turbo-supercharger or a pressurized cockpit, but was characterized by the use of a four-bladed propeller. Although designated as a B-series aircraft, because of the initial use of the BMW 801, the aircraft was, in truth, a pre-prototype C-model.

The first designated C-series prototype was the Fw 190 V18 which, from the beginning had been fitted with the DB 603A 12-cylinder in-line inverted-Vee powerplant. The original powerplant was then replaced by the DB 603G and a TK 11 exhaust-driven turbo-supercharger added. The turbo-supercharger, or compressor, was mounted under the center fuselage and was driven by the exhaust gas through over wing ducting to the turbine. The turbine, in turn, fed the compressed air back through a separate set of ducting into the supercharger. Additional modifications that were made to the V18 included the installation of an increased surface tailfin area and a pressurized cockpit.

In all, six Fw 190C prototype aircraft were produced (not including the V13), all with the DB 603G powerplant and all with under fuselage turbo-supercharger. Two incorporated the Hirth-Motoren 9-2281, while four of the aircraft, including the V18, were fitted with the DVL supplied TK 11. The test program with the C-series was discontinued in the fall of 1943 because of the lack of efficiency and reliability of the turbo-superchargers then in development. Still another major problem that was not solved was the overheating and failure of the exhaust gas transfer ducts which consistently cracked due to the exposure to the high temperature gases.

Fw 190D *series*

Simultaneously with the Fw 190B and Fw 190C projects, the RLM ordered full priority to the development of the Fw 190D with the Jumo 213A as its primary high altitude interceptor. This decision was also influenced by the same criteria which had almost cancelled the entire Fw 190 project in 1937, that of the availability of the DB 603 powerplant in quantity, due to its planned usage in numerous other Luftwaffe aircraft.

The Junkers Jumo 213A, a 12-cylinder in-line liquid cooled powerplant, was selected for installation into the basic Fw 190A-8 airframe because of the development status of the engine and because it was not at that time being

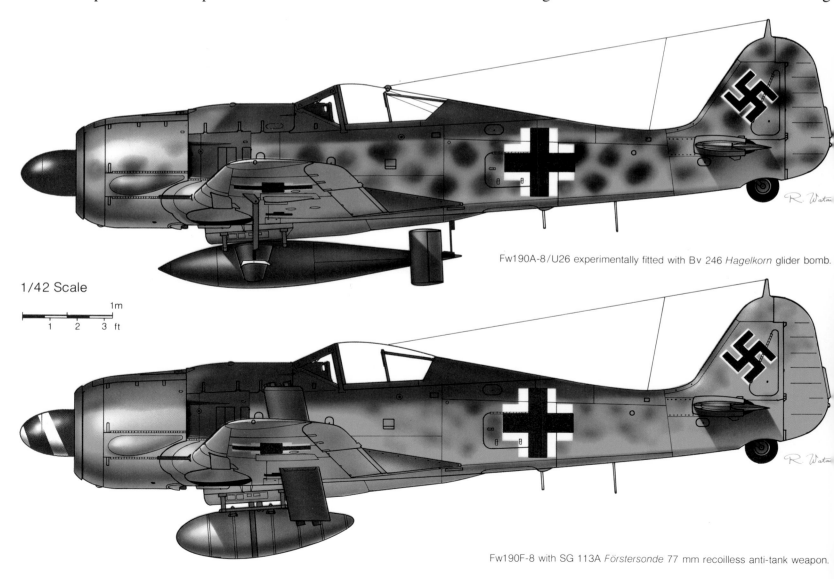

Fw190A-8/U26 experimentally fitted with Bv 246 *Hagelkorn* glider bomb.

1/42 Scale

1m
1 2 3 ft

Fw190F-8 with SG 113A *Förstersonde* 77 mm recoilless anti-tank weapon.

over utilized, or scheduled for extensive future use, in the long range plans of the RLM.

The initial Fw 190D prototype was produced with a standard Fw 190A-0 airframe (designated V17/U1) and made its initial flight in March of 1942. By the middle of 1942, five additional Jumo 213A powered Fw 190D prototypes were produced. All of these latter aircraft utilized the A-0 airframe with an increase in the nose cowling length and a commensurate increase just forward of the tail to insure maintaining of critical c.g. characteristics. The increase in length, of course, was required due to the installation of the Jumo 213A.

The prototypes were armed with the 7.9-mm MG 17 machine-guns in the upper fuselage deck and a pair of wing root mounted 20-mm MG 151 cannon. The aircraft performance trials met with immediate, if not total success, and in late 1943, Focke-Wulf received orders to proceed with pre-production of the D-series.

The Fw 190D-0 variant differed from the prototypes only in that it was based on the A-7 airframe in place of the A-0 airframe of the earlier models. The first Fw 190D-0 armament made use of the MG 17 fuselage mounted machine-guns and the pair of 20-mm MG 151 cannon in each wing, similar to the early A-7, but did not incorporate any of the D-series high altitude equipment or design modifications such as the increased tail and/or wing surface, and the pressurized cockpit. At the same time the Fw 190D-0 was rolling off the assembly line, the initial Fw 190D prototype, V17 was modified to resemble the Focke-Wulf proposed optimum configuration of airframe and powerplant, and designated as the Fw 190D-9.

The Fw 190D-9, which was to become the finest performing propeller-driven fighter to be supplied to the Luftwaffe, differed from the earlier variants of the D-series, in that it included the increased tail surface area to provide increased stability, replaced the 7.9-mm MG 17s with the added firepower of the 13-mm MG 131 machine-gun, included an ETC 504 center fuselage mounted rack for the installation of a single high explosive fragmentation bomb or an auxiliary fuel tank, quick mount bracketry for addition of wing racks and a MW 50 injection system. The Fw 190D-9 used the Jumo 213A-1 engine which, when combined with the MW 50 methanol-water injectant boost system, offered a horsepower rating of 2,240 at low level and 1,880 hp at 4,700 m (15,500 ft).

Initially seen as a stopgap solution by Dr. Tank (until he could fully develop his Ta 152, an improved version of the Fw 190D-9, which incorporated the new Jumo 213E with a three-speed supercharger with induction cooling, a 30-mm MK 108 cannon firing through the engine, and hydraulic flaps and undercarriage operation), the Fw 190D-9 more than proved to even its most serious skeptics that it was more than a match for the much vaunted North American P-51D of the Americans and the late model Supermarine Spitfires of the RAF.

With the assembly efforts beginning in June, de-

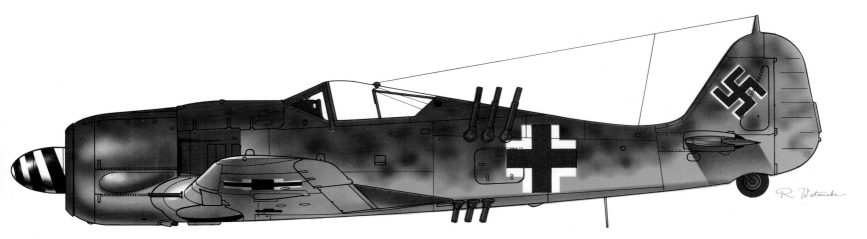

Fw190A-8 with SG 116 *Zellendusche* anti-bomber salvo weapon.

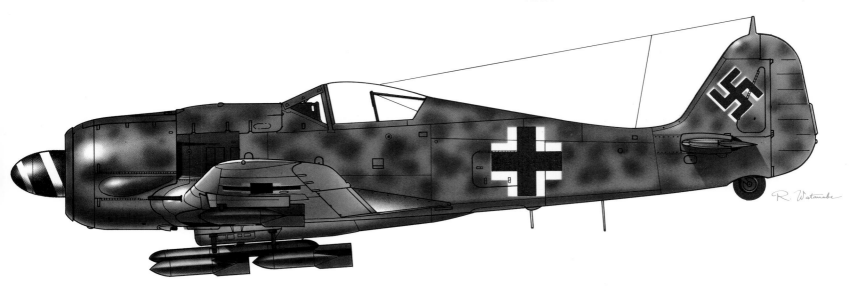

Fw190F-8 with eight SC 50 bombs (four on fuselage ER 4 and four on underwing ETC 50 racks).

(Vereinigte Flugtechnische Werke-Fokker GmbH)

liveries of the first units to the Luftwaffe took place in August, 1944, reaching combat service with III/JG 54 *"Gruenherz"* (Green Hearts) which transitioned into their new mounts in September. The first assignment for the new high altitude fighter fit its projected high altitude role perfectly. Based at airfields at Achmer, the III/JG 54 was assigned to fly top cover over the bases, and provide protection for the Me 262s of the newly formed Kommando Nowotny (Commanded by a famous ace pilot, *Major* Walter Nowotny. Reformed to III/JG7 in November, 1944). The new Me 262 jet fighter was an extremely potent aerial warfare weapon, but because it had to throttle back to land, it became vulnerable as it approached its home base, and Allied fighters, realizing this, would normally identify Me 262 bases, such as Achmer and Hesepe, and intercept the new jet during take-off or landing. The Fw 190D-9 was delivered to several other units in early 1945 in a belated attempt to stem the growing supremacy of Allied airpower. These units included JG 2, JG 3, JG 26 and JG 301. Most of the units, for the remainder of the war, were part of the "Home Defense" screen which was thrown into the air by Goering and Hitler in an ill-fated effort to turn the war again in their favor. The Fw 190D-9 and the Me 262 had the performance and armament to succeed; however, the overwhelming odds in favor of the Allies was too much for even these advanced aircraft to overcome.

Several other variants of the Fw 190D were fabricated, but very few reached front line units. All were modifications of the basic Fw 190D-9, but incorporated new technologies in the areas of powerplant performance increases, and various armament and external stores conversions. The D-series variants and conversions included:

D-9/R11   All-weather interceptor with PKS 12 automatic pilot and a FuG 125 directional-finder navigation and bad weather landing equipment.

D-10   Medium-level fighter with Jumo 213C powerplant which had provisions for the installation of a 30-mm MK 108 cannon firing through the propeller shaft. Only two prototypes were built.

D-11   Ground support/attack fighter powered by a supercharged Jumo 213F and incorporating increased armor protection for pilot and powerplant, a pair of 20-mm MG 151 cannon in the wing roots and a pair of outboard located 30-mm MK

108 cannon.

D-11/R5   Fighter-bomber with TSA 2D bombsight and ETC fuselage and wing racks for carrying eight SC 50 bombs, or a mix of SC 50 bombs and auxiliary fuel drop tanks. Only a few prototypes of this model were produced.

D-12   Ground support/attack aircraft powered by the Jumo 213F-1 with MW 50 power boost system, a pair of wing root mounted MG 151 cannon and an engine mounted 30-mm MK 108; production started in January, 1945.

D-12/R5   Long range fighter-bomber incorporating the Jumo 213EB engine with increased compression ratio and self-sealing internal wing fuel tanks in addition to the standard under cockpit tanks.

D-12/R11   All weather interceptor with PKS 12 auto-pilot and FuG 125 directional equipment. Powered by the Jumo 213EB with the MW 50 boost system, the D-12/R11 reached production status and several saw service with "Home Defense" units.

D-13   Similar to the D-12, differing only in the replacement of the 30-mm MK 108 cannon with a 20-mm MG 151 cannon firing through the engine.

D-13/R5   Fighter-bomber with the same conversions as the D-11 and D-12 variants. Only two prototypes were built. Other proposed D-13 variants included the D-13/R11, D-13/R21, and D13/R25.

D-14   High altitude interceptor utilizing the Fw 190D-9 design but powered by the DB 603LA engine. Concept had only reached the drawing board and tooling stage when hostilities ceased in Europe.

D-15   High altitude interceptor utilizing the Fw 109D-9 design with a DB 603G powerplant. Like the D-14, this concept was never built due to the end of the war. Fifteen of these aircraft were reportedly in various stages of assembly when U.S. forces overran the plant.

Fw 190E *series*

The Fw 190E was a proposed reconnaissance fighter development program using Fw 190A-4 airframes. This aircraft was never produced as its mission was accomplished through the use of various factory conversions to A-3 and A-5 fighters.

Fw 190F *series*

As has been stated earlier, the Fw 190 in its various configurations through the entire A-series had displayed a phenomenal ability to accept almost any mission requirement placed upon it, and through minor design modification, perform these roles in a highly successful manner. Several of these basic modifications were made to the Fw 190A-5/U17, which incorporated both an ETC 501 fuselage and a pair of ETC 50 wing mounted bomb racks. These models were intended for use as a replacement for the obsolete Ju 87 Stuka as a ground support/attack aircraft, and became the prototype and development aircraft for the Fw 190F series.

The basic Fw 190F was envisioned to incorporate a center fuselage mounted ETC 501 bomb rack to accept either a single 500 kg (1,100 lb) bomb or, with an adapter linkage, four 50 kg (110 lb) SC 50 bombs, and optional ETC 501 wing racks for single 250 kg (550 lb) bombs or, with adapters, a pair of 50 kg (110 lb) bombs. In addition, the undercarriage, including strut and shock assembly, was strengthened to accommodate the increased take-off weight.

The first of the F-series to be manufactured was the Fw 190F-1 of which only about two dozen were delivered. These aircraft were built around the A-4 airframe and were armed only with the fuselage mounted 7.9-mm machine-guns and the wing root located 20-mm cannon. The Fw 190F-2 appeared in early 1943 and although similar to the Fw 190F-1 in almost every respect, utilized the Fw 190A-5 airframe. The F-2 also incorporated a larger bulged canopy which was the result of pilot complaints on visibility during the ground support role both during training and initial early combat use.

The next variant to see production was the Fw 190F-3 which began rolling off Arado assembly lines at Warnemuende during the summer of 1943. Utilizing the A-6 airframe, the F-3 was produced in a pair of configurations, the F-3/R1 and F-3/R3. The basic Fw 190F-3/R1 configuration package consisted of the 7.9-mm MG 17 machine-guns in the fuselage upper deck and a pair of wing root mounted 20-mm MG 151 cannon as armament, a pair of ETC 50 racks under each wing, and an ETC 250 rack under the fuselage which could accept either a 250 kg (550 lb) bomb or an auxiliary fuel drop tank.

The Fw 190F-3/R3 configuration replaced the ETC 50 wing bomb racks with a 30-mm MK 103 cannon in gondolas under each wing. This aircraft provided an extremely versatile and potent ground attack weapon to the Luftwaffe.

The Fw 190F series continued with the F-8, F-9 and F-10 variants, all of which made use of the Fw 190A-8 airframe. The primary differences in the newer F variant were the incorporation of the A-8 variant's 13-mm MG 131 machine-guns in the fuselage in place of the earlier model 7.9-mm MG 17s, a pair of ETC 50 wing bomb racks under each wing as standard, and an improved bomb release system network for quicker and more accurate response to the pilot's command.

The F-8 was proposed for three different models of factory installed conversions. The first, the Fw 190F-8/U1, was similar in design to the basic Fw 190A-8/U1 in that it was a two seat training aircraft; however, it was never built. The Fw 190F-8/U2 and Fw 190F-8/U3 were designed to carry a center mounted torpedo bomb which could be used against both shipping and hardened ground targets. The U2 would carry the 700 kg (1,543 lb) BT 700 *(Bomben-Torpedo)* while the U3 would mount the 1400 kg (3,086 lb) BT 1,400.

Both aircraft were fitted with an elongated tail-wheel similar to those incorporated on the Fw 190A-5/U14. This added height at the aft end of the aircraft and, coupled with the foldable tail fins (used for flight stability) of the torpedo bombs, provided for more than adequate take-off clearance. Several of these torpedo aircraft were fabricated and assigned to KG 200 (the all purpose, and somewhat secretive, bomber and special unit of the Luftwaffe).

Various other configurations of the Fw 190F-8 were conceived, including a torpedo fighter along the lines of the Fw 190A-5/U14, and the Fw 190F-8/R13, which was a night ground-support aircraft with wing mounted racks for auxiliary fuel tanks, center mounted bomb rack, and flame dampening shrouds. While few ever reached more than prototype construction, still fewer of these modifications ever progressed farther than the drawing board.

The Fw 190F-8 also served as an experimental platform for a number of anti-tank weaponry. The first of these involved the incorporation of the single-salvo firing cannon barrels that had been installed as anti-bomber armament on the Fw 190A-8. In the F-8 configuration, the 30-mm MK 103 cannon barrels were reversed (firing downward). Testing of the concept, however, quickly illustrated its many drawbacks, including the major difficulty of target acquisition and accuracy, and the project was almost immediately cancelled.

The *Panzerschreck* (tank terror) project utilized an F-8 with a trio of 88-mm projectile launching tubes under each wing. Although an operational evaluation program was not completed, initial successes with the concept were enough to encourage the RLM to accept the system and several modified Fw 190Fs were used on the Eastern Front against Soviet armor.

In late 1944, the *Panzerschreck* was replaced by the *Panzerblitz I* (quick strike tank destroyer) which utilized modified launch tubes and projectiles with increased explosive charges. The increased charge allowed the attacking aircraft to unleash salvos from twice the distance of the original rockets.

Early in 1945, the basic concept was again improved, with the incorporation of 55-mm air-to-ground rockets with armor piercing warheads. These rockets were carried under the wing of the Fw 190F-8 on a pair of racks, each of which were capable of launching up to 6 rockets.

Still another tank destroyer configuration that was tested by the Luftwaffe was the 280-mm Wfr. Gr. 28/32 rocket. The basis for this concept had had its roots in the earlier use of the 210-mm Wfr. Gr. 21 rocket tubes on the Fw 190A-4/R6 and Fw 190A-7/R6 for use as an anti-bomber weapon. The newer and larger rocket tubes were evaluated in the field by Luftwaffe tank destroyer units, however, results proved disappointing due to the continued inaccuracy of the system and further testing was terminated.

The Fw 190F-8 gave way to the Fw 190F-9 in the summer of 1944. The Fw 190F-9 differed only in that it utilized the turbo-supercharged BMW 801TS, and in some cases, the MW 50 methanol-water boost system. Only a few of this type were produced before the end of hostilities.

Later models of the F-series included the Fw 190F-10 with a 2000 hp BMW 801F engine, the Fw 190F-15 with a BMW 801TH or TS engine and hydraulic rather than electrical undercarriage retraction, and the Fw 190F-16 with a BMW 801TS engine and a TSA 2D shallow-dive bombing sight. None of these reached production status.

Fw 190G *series*

Designed and produced in parallel with the F-series, the Fw 190G aircraft was conceived basically as an extended, or long range, fighter-bomber incorporating the standardized U13 armament and external stores conversion of fuselage and wing mounted guns, center mount bomb rack and wing racks for auxiliary fuel tanks. The only difference in these and earlier U13 models was the deletion of the fuselage mounted machine-guns to save weight and increase range.

Two models of the U13 modification were produced, with the Fw 190G-1 using the basic A-4 airframe while the Fw 190G-2 used the A-5 airframe which incorporated the slightly extended 15.5 cm (6.1 in) fuselage to allow for strengthened engine mounts.

Major internal and external changes were incorporated into the Fw 190G-3. These included the addition of the PKS autopilot and a fuel injection system that was pilot controlled to gain added power at take-off and during emergency situations. The addition of dust and particle filters to critical intake areas for use in the Mediterranean field of operations were also added to several of the G-3 models and the letters tp for Tropical were added to its designation code.

The Fw 190G-8 was basically a Fw 190A-8 which incorporated the modifications standardized for that particular model. These included the MW 50 fuel injection system (or auxiliary fuel tank) located aft of the cockpit, movement of the FuG 16Z radio forward, installation of the ETC 501 fuselage mounted bomb rack, and a pair of wing racks for bomb loads or auxiliary fuel drop tanks. The addition of the nitrous-oxide injection system was designated for the Fw 190G-8/R4, while the replacement of the 250 kg (550 lb) wing bomb rack with a pair of ETC 50 racks for the SC 50 bombs or 115 litre (25 Imp gallon) fuel tanks was assigned the designation of Fw 190G-8/R5.

Ta 152 *series*

As has been noted earlier, the concern of the *Reichsluftfahrtsministerium* with the marginal performance

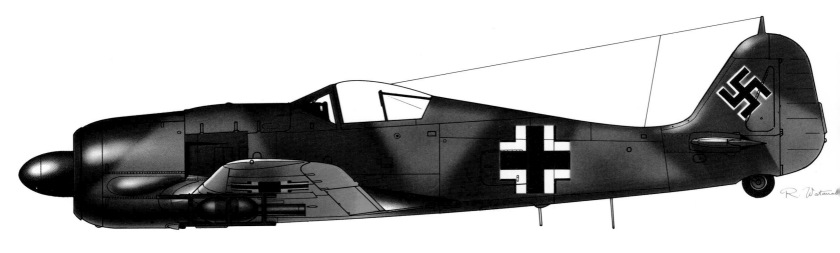

1/42 Scale

1m
1 2 3 ft

Fw190F-8 with Wfr.Gr. 28/32 rocket launchers.

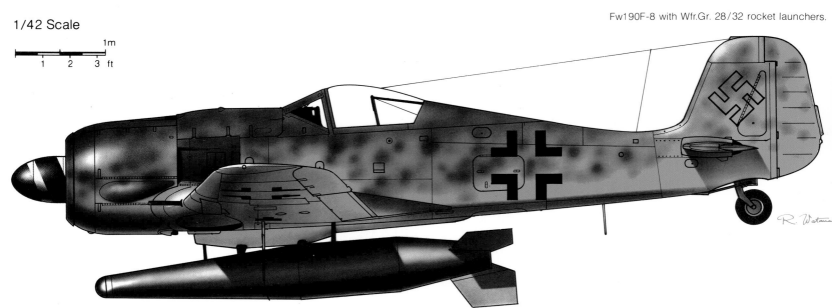

Fw190F-8/U3 with 3,086 lb BT 1400 bomb-torpedo. Its lower fin could be folded for increased ground clearance.

of its existing fighters against high-altitude Allied bombers resulted in the initiation of three developmental Focke-Wulf aircraft: the Fw 190B with pressurized cockpit and the basic BMW 801 air-cooled radial powerplant using the GM 1 nitrous oxide injection system (until an exhaust-driven superchanger could be incorporated); the Fw 190C with pressurized cockpit and a DB 603 powerplant coupled with a two-stage super-charger and GM 1 system, or a Hirth-Motoren turbo-supercharger; and the Fw 190D without cockpit pressurization and utilizing the Junkers Jumo 213 liquid-cooled engine. In addition, during the fall of 1942, Focke-Wulf submitted a proposal for a *Hochleistungsjaeger* (high-performance fighter) which offered the Luftwaffe an increased service ceiling and flexibility in the medium to high-altitude range of operation.

The proposed development consisted of two phases, the first of which would produce a fighter based on an existing airframe to make maximum use of commonality, and the second phase designed from the beginning, with new technology and major redesign where required, to fill the high-altitude intercept role. The Focke-Wulf design for the first phase resulted in the Fw 190 Ra-2 and Fw 190 Ra-3, based on the Fw 190D and Jumo 213 engine, while the second phase design was assigned the designation Fw 190 Ra-4D.

The only real significant difference between the Fw 190 Ra-2 and the Ra-3 was in the main wing size and armament. The Ra-2 incorporated the standard Fw 190D wing, engine-mounted 30-mm cannon, a pair of wing root 20-mm MG 151 cannon, and a pair of 20-mm MG 151 cannon in the cowling, while the Ra-3 had extended outer wing panels and deleted the cowling mounted machine-guns.

Because of the tremendous respect both Dr. Tank and Messerschmitt had gained at this time for their designs, new aircraft initiated by their respective companies were given the designer's initials. Thus, the Fw 190 Ra-2 and Fw 190 Ra-3 became the Ta 152B and Ta 152H. The Fw 190 Ra-4D was subsequently designated the Ta 153.

With the change in designation, two other variants of the Ta-series were proposed, the Ta 152C and the Ta 152E. The Ta 152C was similar in design to the Ta 152B, but incorporated the DB 603 powerplant in place of the Jumo 213, a request that Dr. Tank had pressed with the *Technische Amt* based on the superior performance at high altitudes of the DB engine. The Ta 152E was a camera-equipped reconnaissance derivative of the basic Ta 152B.

Various models of the Ta 152B, C, and H were proposed and/or planned by Focke-Wulf and the Luftwaffe; few, however, progressed further than the conceptual or prototype stage, with only several aircraft ever reaching combat units. The various sub-series of these variants included armament modifications that included incorporation of an 30-mm MK engine-mounted cannon, 30-mm wing-

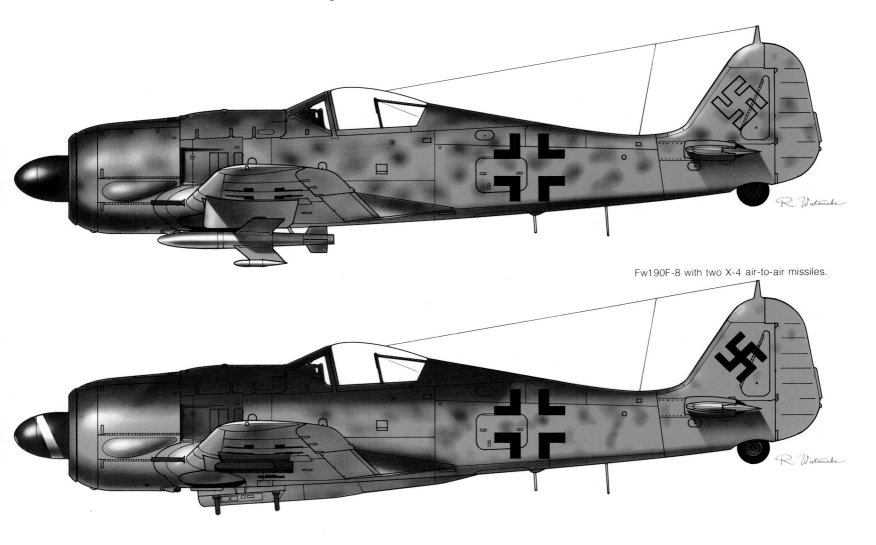

Fw190F-8 with two X-4 air-to-air missiles.

Fw190F-9 with 5 mm *Panzerblitz 2* (modified R4M) anti-tank rockets.

mounted cannon, and a number of 20-mm wing and 15-mm fuselage mounted machine-gun arrangements. Additionally, a number of camera installations and power boost systems were envisioned.

The most notable of the *Ruestsaetze* available for the Ta-series were the R11, R21 and R31 conversion sets. The R11 designation identified a Ta 152 that incorporated the FuG 125 D/F unit coupled with a LGW-Siemens K 23 autopilot. The R11 also was fitted with a specially constructed armour resistant windscreen and was proposed as an all-weather fighter.

ever, this aircraft was later rebuilt and re-engined with a Jumo 213 powerplant as a prototype for the Ta 152H program.

Design and Construction

The Focke-Wulf 190 offered the ultimate combination of simple, yet sturdy overall construction, housing highly complex sub-components. It was specifically designed from its inception for the pilot and the field maintenance man. What

Ta 152C-O/R11 pre-production all-weather fighter version.

(Imperial War Museum)

The R21 sub-series was fitted with an auxiliary fuel tank on a ETC 503 ventral rack and had the GM 1 system replaced with a methanol-water (MW 50) unit to increase lower altitude performance. The R31 sub-series was similar to the R11 all-weather fighter except that an additional fuel capacity aft of the cockpit was installed in place of the standard GM 1 injectant installation, which was relocated forward of the cockpit.

One additional Ta 152 variant was proposed, this being the Ta 152S-1. This aircraft was based on the Ta 152C-1 airframe with all armament and fuselage fuel tankage removed and a two seat tandem cockpit installed for training purposes. This variant, like most of its counterparts, was never built.

Ta 153 *series*

The Ta 153, as noted previously, was the designation assigned to the Fw 190 Ra-4D, an aircraft based on Fw 190D aerodynamic concepts, but incorporating a redesigned and structurally modified fuselage and a DB 603 powerplant with a DLV TK 15 turbo-supercharger. Other engines considered for use were the DB 622, DB 623 and DB 627, all with a turbo-supercharger and/or two-stage mechanical supercharger for high-altitude performance increases. One Fw 190C-series prototype aircraft was utilized as the testbed for this concept under the designation Ta 153 and incorporated a DB 603G engine, a short span wing, and four-bladed propeller; how-

at first inspection appeared to be unnecessarily complex, turned out to be well thought out, sturdy, self-contained, with quickly removable components designed and suited for a specific purpose, each one included with the idea of reducing field maintenance time to a minimum. The Fw 190 was created on the philosophy that it is easier to get components replaced as a unit than to repair them. Therefore, the aircraft was also designed to be fabricated and assembled through a widespread network of subcontracting and dispersal plants (these included not only Focke-Wulf, but AGO, Arado, Fieseler, Dornier and Junkers). The fuselage, for example, was comprised of only two major components, the fore section extending from the firewall, or what the Luftwaffe called the No. 1 bulkhead to bulkhead No. 8 aft of the pilot's seat, and the aft section which extended from bulkhead No. 8 to the aft empennage.

The forward fuselage section was the heart of the plane and was, in effect, a double-deck box type structure, with the top section making up the pilot's cockpit and the lower section serving as the fuel bays. The firewall or No. 1 bulkhead was constructed of light sheet steel backed by sheet aluminum alloy riveted to flanges extending from the top two engine mount fittings down to a second set of fittings, which served as attach points for the lower side engine mounts and front wing spar.

Longerons ran aft from these four points to the No. 8 bulkhead, where they were spliced to lighter supports in the aft section. The top longerons were 45 cm (1¾ in) wide U-sections made up of 4.8 mm (³/₁₆-in) aluminum alloy which also served as the tracks in which the cockpit canopy traveled. One stringer on each side, below the upper longerons, made up the only horizontal stiffeners in the upper portion of the fuselage. Aluminum alloy sheet, riveted to the lower longerons, formed the cockpit floor, separating the pilot from the fuel bays.

One skin panel, secured to longitudinal and transverse angle shaped stiffeners, was attached to the lower fuselage section by nine screws along each side and five on each end, thus offering quick access to the two self-sealing fuel tanks, which were suspended in the fuel bays with thick web fabric straps. On the upper fuselage section, immediately aft of the top engine mount fittings, the fuselage structure was flat, forming a shelf to which was bolted mounts for the 7.9-mm MG 17 machine-guns which were synchronized to fire through the propeller's arc. Directly behind the gun mount shelf, the fuselage extended to form the base for the windscreen, the front panel of which was 5.0 cm (2 in) bullet proof glass.

At the base of the front panel was the hinged fairing cover for the guns. This fairing, which hinged up and back for access to the guns and ammunition trays, was of waffle type construction, with a double skin being fastened together by a rivet in each inner skin dimple. Three heavy toggle locking switches were used on each side to hold the fairing in place. The heavy cowling, with easily removable hinges to keep it in place, added what appeared to be unnecessary weight. It was, however, in keeping with the apparent design theory. It was heavy enough to endure long, hard wear and, as an added feature, the side panels swung downward around the engine mounts to be used as work platforms by the maintenance crew. Also, in case the cowling was bent, the toggles were sturdy enough to pull it into shape for quick locking and take-off. The cowling on the Fw 190 averaged 8.54 kg/m² (1.75 lb/sq ft) in weight compared to the 6.1 kg/m² (1.25 lb/sq ft) for the typical British and American designs, and the Luftwaffe's persistent use of this cowling type through several model changes indicates their belief that the beating it could take and the speed with which it could be locked in place made it worth the added weight.

The cockpit cover and its fairing were built as an integral unit. The base of the structure was of tubular construction bent into an inverted U at the front to fit the windscreen. The plexiglass of the canopy was mounted between strips of synthetic rubber and a flat aluminum strip, and was held by screws driven into self-locking nuts in the tube. At the rear of the plexiglass was a stamped, flanged aluminum A-frame set between the tube-frame ends and riveted to an aluminum alloy fairing. The whole structure rode on three ball-bearing rollers, one on each side at the front of the plexiglass section in the top fuselage longerons, and one attached to the tube which ran in the channel section that was set in the fuselage turtle deck.

The canopy cover could be operated only from the inside by a crank attached to a sprocket which engaged a pin ratchet in the front end of the tubular frame. Emergency exit could be effected by pushing down on a small handle located near the crank. This disengaged the sprocket and then, through a series of rods and shafts, released a latch holding the firing pin. A cartridge was exploded and blew the rear end of the canopy backward far enough to let the slipstream get under it and pull it away. The explosive charge, about the size of a 12-gauge shotgun shell, was located aft of the armor plate in back of the pilot's head. The addition of the shotgun charge was necessary after early operational testing had resulted in uncovering the fact that the canopy would not leave the aircraft at airspeeds over 250 mph, being held in place by the air pressure distribution.

The radio antenna lead was fixed at the vertical fin and came over a pulley series in the plexiglass just behind the armor plate. It then was run through another pulley series to the radio, mounted just behind No. 8 bulkhead. Regardless of the canopy position, open or closed, the antenna maintained the same tension.

The cockpit itself did not give the appearance of being overcrowded. Nevertheless, there was no wasted space. Flight and engine controls and indicators were arranged in two panels beneath the windscreen and on horizon-

Fw190A-8

(Imperial War Museum)

tal panels along each side of the pilot's seat. The seat, the back of which was made of steel armor plate, was only adjustable in a vertical attitude over a range of 10 cm (4 in) and was designed for the use of seat-pack parachutes.

A departure from normal design construction showed up in the Fw 190 wing. It was built as a single unit from tip to tip. Thus, if damaged structurally, any place between the detachable tips, the entire unit would be replaced. The integral center section of the tapering front spar was a very heavy member, for it took the weight of the two lower side and bottom engine mounts, fuselage fitting attachments, 20-mm cannon and main landing gear assemblies. At the centerline of the wing was a built-up, triple-web I-beam reinforced by a heavy vertical channel shaped member containing at its lower end, a forged fitting for the lower engine mount structure. Between the centerline and the side engine mounts were two vertical shaped stiffeners. Engine mount members themselves were of similar shape, but were heavier and were riveted rather than bolted to the main spar.

The fabric covered metal Frise-type ailerons were as light in weight as they were on control. They were built around a channel monospar with beaded vertical stiffeners to which were riveted upper and lower two-layer metal leading edge skins, the inner ones having beaded stiffeners.

The main landing gear was a single-strut oleo shock unit with conventional torque scissors attached to a tapered roller bearing spindle assemble.

The front face of the mounting was flanged to bolt to the front spar. The fairing was in three sections, one attached to brackets extending up from the hub, another bolted to the oleo strut and the third hinged at the center of the fuselage. A scale painted on the two fairings attached to the landing gear told at a glance if proper pressure, about 1300 psia, was being maintained in the shock unit.

Retraction was electric, with a separate motor for each wheel. In the down position the oleo struts did not reach the perpendicular and there was no down lock on the gear. The two I-beams formed a straight line when the gear was down and this straight load, coupled with the high reduction from the motor, was enough to prevent the gear from shifting from the down position.

Small metal contacts on the faces of the I-beam joints automatically shut off the motor when the gear was in the full down position. On the rotating member of the landing gear mechanism was a small scaled rod which projected through a ball joint in the top of the wing as the gear went down so that the pilot could tell the exact position of the gear. The tail wheel assembly was attached by cables, which ran over pulleys, to the main gear. It was automatically lowered and retracted in parallel with the main gear through this mechanical link.

The Fw 190's fuel supply, less the external drop tank, was carried in two self-sealing tanks suspended by fabric web straps in the lower fuselage section. The forward tank, between spars, held 232 l (61.2 U.S. gl) while the aft tank had a capacity of 292 l (76.8 U.S. gl). Both tanks were filled from the right side of the fuselage, the filler pipe coverplates being quickly detachable flush units. Each tank contained a sealed electric pump. Gauges were all electric with the fuel warning light and pump indicator light being arranged vertically in the center of the lower instrument panel for easy recognition by the pilot.

Access to the Fw 190 was made via a retractable stirrup step provided on the left side of the plane. The stirrup was released by pressing a button near the top of the fuselage turtle deck. A handhold and a step, both covered by spring loaded panels, were also located in the left fuselage side.

Combat Operations

From its first combat encounter with RAF Spitfires on 1 September 1941 to its last on 8 May, 1945, with Soviet Pe-2s, the Fw 190 served the Luftwaffe during World War II in every major arena of combat and in almost every combat role. Nearly every *Jagdgeschwader* (fighter), *Schlachtgeschwader* (ground attack), *Jabo* (fighter-bomber) and *Aufkl. Gruppe* (photo reconnaissance) unit of the Luftwaffe, at one time or another, utilized this versatile airframe. Its performance and record speak for themselves.

As noted above, and throughout the descriptions and discussions of the various models of the Fw 190, it was destined to fill many operational needs of the Luftwaffe, both as a new innovation and as a replacement aircraft. Among the more unique operational needs filled by the *Wuerger* were the *Wilde Sau* (Wild Boar), *Sturmgruppe* (assauH or ramming) and the *Mistel* (Mistletoe) assignments.

The *Wilde Sau* operations had their origin during the summer of 1943 when the British initiated the use of chaff (small strips of tinfoil dropped from bombers) to confuse the *Lichtenstein* BC/C-1 AI radar and *Wuerzburg* ground radar used by the Luftwaffe to guide the twin-engined nightfighters to the bomber streams. Until a modification to the sets could be made, an alternate method of interception had to be found. *Major* Hajo Herrmann, a former Junkers Ju 88 bomber-pilot, had long been a proponent of utilizing fighter aircraft in a nighttime "seek and destroy through visual contact" mode on clear nights. He was given the go-ahead for his plan in July, 1943, and was placed in command of JG 300 to test his tactics. His unit, flying Bf 109Gs and Fw 109As quickly proved the logic of Herrmann's concept and two additional units were formed under the designation JG 301 and JG 302. Unfortunately, due to the scarcity of available aircraft, each unit had only one *Gruppe* (approximately 36 aircraft) of its own, while the other two *Gruppen* would share in the use of day fighters with nearby units. During the long summer of 1943 the victories of the *Wilde Sau* units continued to grow and they became the "darlings" of the German press, both because of their novelty and because of their actual achievements.

With the advent of late fall and early winter of 1943, the weather conditions and the overuse of the fighters became the most significant enemy of the *Wilde Sau* units. Losses began to mount due to equipment malfunctions, overstressed components and inclement flying conditions. The night-fighter sorties were discontinued and the pilots and aircraft of *Jagddivision* 30 were redesignated as a dayfighter unit.

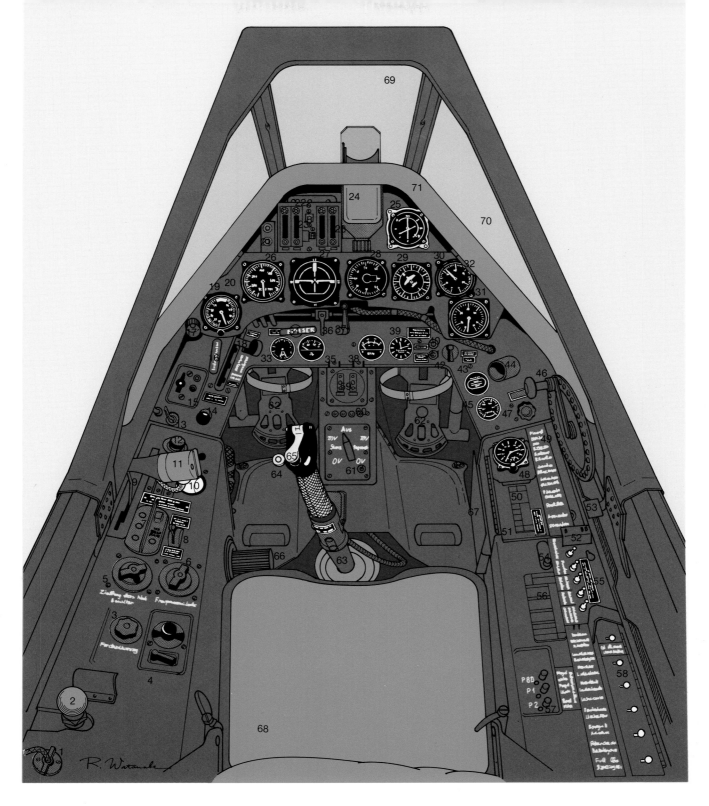

Fw 190 A-8 Cockpit

1 Headset R/T (Radio/Telephone) connection
2 Primer fuel pump handle
3 FuG 16ZY receiver fine tuning
4 FuG 16ZY volume control and FT (communications) — ZF (homing) switch
5 FuG 16ZY homing range switch
6 FuG 16ZY frequency selector
7 Undercarriage and landing flap actuation buttons
8 Horizontal stabilizer trim switch
9 Undercarriage position indicators (left and right), flap position (centre)
10 Horizontal stabilier trim indicator
11 Throttle lever with thumb-actuated propeller pitch control
12 Instrument panel lighting dimmer control
13 Stop cock control lever
14 Engine starter brushes withdrawal button
15 FuG 25a, *Erstling* IFF control unit
16 Undercarriage manual handle
17 Cockpit ventilation knob
18 Fuel tank selector lever
19 Altimeter
20 Pitot tube heater light
21 MG 131 armed indicator lights
22 SZKK 4 armament switch and control panel

23 Ammunition counters
24 Revi 16B reflector gunsight
25 AFN 2 homing indicator (FuG 16ZY)
26 Airspeed indicator
27 Artificial horizon
28 Rate of climb/descent indicator
29 Repeater compass
30 Supercharger pressure gauge
31 Tachometer
32 Ultra-violet cockpit light
33 Fuel and oil pressure gauge
34 Ventral stores manual release handle
35 Oil temperature gauge
36 Windscreen washer lever
37 Engine ventilation flap control lever
38 Fuel contents gauge
39 Propeller pitch indicator
40 Fuel low level warning light (red)
41 Rear tank switchover light (white)
42 Fuel gauge selector switch
43 Oxygen flow indicator
44 Flare pistol holder
45 Oxygen pressure gauge
46 Canopy acutator drive
47 Oxygen flow valve

48 Clock
49 Circuit breaker panel cover
50 Operations data card
51 Flare box cover
52 Starter switch
53 Canopy jettison lever
54 Flare box cover plate release button
55 Fuel pump circuit breakers
56 Compass deviation card
57 Armament circuit breakers
58 Circuit breaker panel cover
59 21cm Wfr.Gr. rocket control panel
60 External stores indicator lights
61 Bomb fusing selector panel
62 Rudder pedal with integral braking unit
63 Control column
64 Bomb release button
65 Wing cannon firing button
66 Throttle friction knob
67 Map/chart holder
68 Pilot's seat
69 Bullet resistant windscreen, 50mm armour glass (at 25°)
70 30mm armour glass
71 Padded coaming

With the termination of *Wilde Sau,* one of the Fw 190s more interesting escapades had terminated, but still another was just beginning. The autumn of 1943 saw increased Allied bombing raids inside Germany, which if allowed to continue, would eventually paralyze the armament industry and eliminate any potential of development on the newest ''secret'' weapons of the Third Reich. The answer was simple: provide more fighter interceptors. However, although production of fighters was up, the fighting along both the Western and the Eastern fronts was demanding these aircraft to support the operations in the field. To overcome the lack of fighters for ''Home Defense,'' the Luftwaffe in December, 1943, theorized a new method of attacking the bombers which led to the *Sturmstaffel* that flew the skies over Germany in 1944 and early 1945.

Calibre:	30 mm: 16 grooves
Weight of weapon:	145 kg
Weight fixed (nose):	198.9 kg
Length of weapon:	2335 mm

The concept of the *Sturm* tactics was the brainchild of *Major* von Kornatski, a close associate of Adolf Galland, and was based on the tactics used so successfully by *Hauptmann* Walter Krupinski (a high scoring Luftwaffe ace with 197 victories). The tactics involved were simply to get as close to the enemy bomber as possible before opening fire. It was dangerous and, to some extent, foolhardy, but the results of this type of infighting were enough to convince the Luftwaffe High Command that this approach was not only feasible, but necessary.

Major Kornatski was given orders to form a special *Sturmgruppe* (Storm Group) as part of the existing JG 3 ''Udet'' (World War I Luftwaffe hero). A number of the pilots were experienced combat aces with numerous victories and years of fighting under their belts, and they were not anxious to adopt this new tactic. The concept, of course, was to get as close as the pilot could without actual ramming of the enemy. Ramming was to occur only as a last resort and the pilot was to bail out just prior to, or at impact (this last statement, naturally, was not to the liking of most older pilots as the simultaneous ramming and evacuating was easier said than done). The experienced pilots therefore, began transferring to the newly formed Me 262 jet units or were reassigned, on request, to the training of new and younger pilots for the *Sturmgruppe* units being formed as part of each ''Home Defense'' *Jagdgeschwader.*

One of the most notable successes of the *Sturm* tactics occurred on 29 April, 1944, when the first operation *Sturmgruppe,* IV/JG 3, intercepted a formation of over 40 American B-17s on a mission to Berlin. In the first half hour of the engagement by the heavily armed, heavily armored Fw 109A-8s, the Luftwaffe interceptors destroyed nearly half of the bomber force. This success, however, was not to continue.

As additional *Sturmgruppe* interception sorties were completed, the need for escort cover for the heavy Fw 190s became painfully obvious as the unprotected and less maneuverable aircraft became susceptible to the long range fighter protection of the American bomber formation. The Luftwaffe assigned the Bf 109G to the fighter cover role for the *Sturmgruppe* and these tactics worked well until late 1944, when the Allied Command issued orders to the escort fighters to ignore the Bf 109 top cover and concentrate their attacks on the Fw 190 *Sturmgruppe* units.

At the same time, orders were issued to all Eighth U.S. Air Force fighter and ground attack units to destroy the *Sturmgruppen* on the ground whenever possible. This task was simplified for the Allies through reconnaissance overflights which identified *Sturmgruppe* bases, and the fact that once attacked, the heavy Fw 190s were cumbersome and slow to get off the ground because of the added armament and protective armor plating.

Rheinmetall 30 mm MK 103 cannon fitted in an early type underwing gondola. Later versions had a streamlined fairing over the barrel and vertically-ejecting muzzle brake.

Muzzle velocity:	HE/AP tracer	940 m/sec
	Mine shells	860 m/sec
Rate of fire (cyclic):	HE/AP tracer	380 rounds/min
	Mine shells	420 rounds/min
Weight of 100-round disintegrating link belt	HE/AP tracer: approx 94 kg
	Mine shells: approx 90.5 kg
Penetration	HE/AP tracer: 110 mm armour plate at 300 m

By October, most of the experienced aces had transferred out of the various *Sturmgruppen,* or had assumed command positions, and the younger pilots were actually carrying out the ''final resort'' of ramming the American bombers. However, the combined lack of available aircraft and available pilots spelled an end to large scale *Rammkommando* attacks by early spring of 1945. The concept had enjoyed unexpected success and had instilled fear in the minds of every Allied aircrew who was assigned a mission to Germany during 1944.

The *Rammkommando,* like the Japanese Kamikaze, had represented only a last ditch effort to turn back the inevitable: an effort which was, from the beginning, doomed.

One of the final wartime missions to be assigned to the Fw 190 series was in its use as the ''mother'' aircraft for the *Mistel* or *Beethoven* flying bomb. The concept consisted of the addition of a center mounted strut support structure to the Fw 190 fuselage which allowed it to guide an unmanned Junkers Ju 88 explosive-laden bomber. The fighter would carry the bomber to the target and ease into a slow glide, releasing the bomber and its lethal explosives just short of the target.

Initiated in 1943 with obsolete Ju 88s and Bf 109s, the project progressed through 1944 with numerous planned, but never executed missions, until late 1944 when Fw 190A-6 and Fw 190F-8 airframes were designated as the primary ''mother'' plane. The emphasis was placed on a planned all-out attack by the *Mistel* on Soviet armament plants in

March, 1945, in an effort to halt the Russian advances along the entire Eastern Front. The bases from which this operation was to have originated, however, were overrun by the advancing Red Army in February, 1945, and KG 200, which operated the Fw 190/Ju 88 combination, was ordered to concentrate the *Mistel* attacks against the bridges over the Oder and Neisse rivers in an effort to gain time for the retreating German forces. By April all available *Mistel* aircraft had been utilized and the units were disbanded with the pilots being reassigned to nearby fighter units or transferred to Berlin to join "Home Defense" *Jagdgeschwaders*.

Fw 190 had a very compact form, and undercarriage with a wide track, and a very impressive armament with two machine-guns and four cannons. It had a very noticeable and elegant streamlined cowl surface in which was housed a blower-cooled 14-cylinder double-row radial engine. This streamlined cowling defined to me the overall looks of this new fighter plane.

"The arrangement and execution of the canopy offered excellent visibility. Within the cockpit I found a vast

Trajectory:	Range	Elapsed time	Gravity drop	Shell velocity
	500 m	0.66 sec	1.9 m	676 m/sec
	1000 m	1.50 sec	9.4 m	519 m/sec
	1500 m	2.60 sec	26.3 m	400 m/sec
	2000 m	4.01 sec	58.2 m	323 m/sec

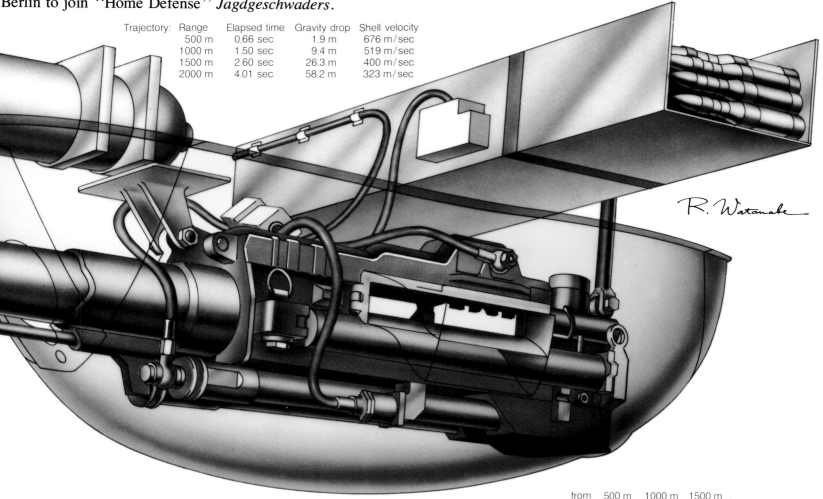

R. Watanabe

	from	500 m	1000 m	1500 m	
Theoretical performance: A 4-engined bomber could be shot down	with	40 rds	104 rds	308 rds	with 50% certainty
		76 rds	203 rds	650 rds	with 95% certainty

An insight into training and combat flying with the Fw 190 is described by *Oberleutnant* Oskar Romm (92 victories) who piloted the Fw 190A from its introduction on the Eastern Front in late 1942 through his final assignment as *Gruppenkommandeur* of IV Gruppe/JG 3 in February, 1945, where he flew the Fw 190D-9.

"My training as a fighter pilot was completed on a Bf 109 and progressed to completion without any problems. I became the master of this aircraft in every flying position and could hit gunnery targets with precise accuracy. When I completed my training in the summer of 1942 I had two big surprises: (1) I was posted to JG 51 on the Russian Front, and; (2) I was informed that my future combat flying would be done in our new fighter, the Focke-Wulf 190.

"I arrived at JG 51s base in Russia in September, 1942, and was immediately introduced to the Fw 190 through a series of technical lectures on its handling and flight characteristics. This was followed by actual flight training. The

array of installed electric indicators and instruments. I recognized some old ones which had appeared in front of me in other aircraft, but I also noticed some new ones. These included the controls and instruments for the powerplant, propeller, armament, landing gear, and trim which were all located in a logical and easily visible layout.

"My first flying assignments were to make normal rounds of the field where I would shoot landings and take-off again. I was to learn to start the Fw 190 from any position on the field whether I was standing still or rolling along the runway after engine shutdown. As far as taking-off was concerned, you just pulled back on the stick and she lifted her 'three legs' and away she went. With the simple punching of buttons she retracted her gear and flaps and provided trim. Her powerplant was unusually loud with a hard sound, but with growing airspeed one lost the sense of the noise.

"To set her down, one just choked the rpm's, with a punch of a button set the flaps to a lift position, and then let the gear down. To turn into the final landing pattern and to

Fw 190G-2 *Jabo-Rei* long-range fighter-bombers in camouflaged dispersal area.

Fw 190A-3 fighters of II/JG 26 in readiness. 1942.

trim the aircraft with the already extended flaps was a very simple matter. She would set herself down smartly and sure-footedly, almost landing herself. All flight maneuvers, including landing, presented no problems with this proud bird and as my training progressed my admiration for the Fw 190 grew.

"After completing the initial series of landings and take-offs, I began training in two plane formation flying while practicing combat maneuvers. This included strafing sorties and continuous gunnery practice. I became convinced that I could fly the Fw 190 as an armament platform with greater assurance and reliability under any and all conditions than I could the Bf 109.

"She reacted quickly for her size to any and all my control commands. She was fast, she could climb, she could maneuver with the best of her counterparts and she had an awesome gallery of firepower. My instructor, an already accomplished front line combat pilot, would engage in mock aerial combat with me and once I mastered my controls he was never able to turn inside one of my turns.

"My training continued with a specialized landing operation where we would land our Fw 190s from a very low formation with the goal of our efforts being that on our approach from any direction and while under possible enemy attack, we could set our aircraft down quickly and safely.

"As a fighter pilot in 1./I/JG 51 I started my combat in the fall of 1942 from a field near Ljuban in the vicinity of Leningrad as number four man in a *'Schwarm'* with the assignment or responsibility of 'free hunting' in a given sector. We would fly in two and four plane formations looking for enemy aircraft to attack. Climbing to my assigned altitude on my first sortie I noticed that my oil temperature had exceeded the maximum allowable limit (this was typical with the aircraft's powerplant during its early production). I realized I could not make it back to our base so I cinched up my harness and set her down in a large open marsh area. On impact, my head and body lunged forward and I injured myself on the Revi C/12D reflector gunsight. The next day my nose looked like a large potato. Our maintenance crews dragged my plane from the swamp and it was sent to the repair depot. After my own recovery, I was sent back to Germany where I picked up a new Fw 190 and flew it back to

our base in Russia. It was considered a matter of extra flight training time for me.

"A few days later I returned to combat status and began my second operational sortie with the Fw 190 from the unit's new base at Vyazma, south of Moscow. We encountered a formation of six Il-2s and immediately attacked. I destroyed one of the Il-2s, but as I pulled out of my dive to seek another target I saw for the first time a large fighter similar in design to my own Fw 190. It was a La-5 with a completely red cowl which identified it as being from the Stalin Squadron. The Russian had me at a speed disadvantage and with this edge he went into a series of sweeping, climbing curves to get above me. I was also trying to gain altitude, but in tight spiralling turns, while my wingman provided me with underside protection. I received a radio call from our commander to reform with the flight as we had exceeded our mission time and were being ordered back to our base. I stopped my chase, but before I pulled away I fired a burst at the Russian fighter as he flew through my six gun pattern. I saw no evidence of results as I banked over to reform with my wingman.

"I had now completed my first full combat sortie in the Fw 190 and although I had experienced an emergency landing in my initial effort, my faith in the Fw 190 increased. I had learned through my own experience that I must fly with greater precision and alertness and also I had learned the importance of height and a speed advantage in an aerial confrontation.

"In January, 1943, I flew my third sortie as part of an escort formation for Ju 88s and He 111s. After the bombers had deposited their lethal load, we turned homeward, but due to a low cloud bank we were forced to fly at near ground level. Suddenly my plane started to vibrate violently and the Russian landscape became nothing but a blur. I was too low to parachute so I prepared to again crash land. Keeping my wheels up because of the deep snow, my Fw 190 skidded over the surface for more than two miles before finally coming to a stop. I took the expensive clock from its panel and my signal pistol before climbing out. I jumped into the snow and inspected the aircraft to see if I could determine what had caused my problems. I discovered that two of the three propeller blades were on a negative setting and that the

Fw 190A-3 shortly after take-off.

A *Rotte* (pair) of Fw 190A-3 fighters of I/JG 51 'Mölders'. Eastern Front. 1942.

hydraulic limiters or stops had been rendered inoperable in the Russian cold.

"From this time on I flew my Fw 190s with greater care and with greater attention to detail. I still had the will to push this machine to its limits and oftentimes did. Shortly after this incident, I was called over by my crew chief to inspect a Fw 190 in which I had just completed a sortie. He showed me a series of 'ripples' on the upper wing surfaces. I had flown home on 'corrugated steel' as I had taken the wing skin beyond its design limits with some of my maneuvers. Only the strong main spar had held the wing together and saved the plane and possibly me.

"From this time on I concentrated harder than ever on my gunnery practice until I felt I was shooting true. I was able to gain my next six victories (Il-2s) in a matter of only seven minutes. My gunnery practice had paid off.

"I only attacked Russian fighters such as the Lavochkin, Yakovlev, and Mikoyan where I had to secure our airspace from interception, when our fighter-bomber or bomber formations needed protection, or when the Russian fighters were serving as escort to Russian bomber formations which we were attacking. We no longer went up like we did during the 'free hunts,' specifically looking for enemy fighters. 'A hot heart and a cool mind' became my motto for fighting.

"The time of massive and loose Russian formations was over, they were now flying in smaller, tighter, and more mobile units. We ran into numerous Pe-2 fighter-bombers in this new type of formation and against this aircraft I had great success. Short bursts into the powerplants of this machine almost certainly resulted in immediate and rapid burning or explosions.

"After gaining my 70th victory in the trusty Fw 190 I was relieved of combat duty and sent to Toulouse, France as an instructor, returning to JG 51 in February, 1944. Then in May, 1944, I was honored by being assigned to IV/JG 3 as part of the *Abschuss oder Rammen* unit. This unit was flying specially modified Fw 190s with increased armament and armor protection around the pilot and powerplant. They were to be used for interception and destruction, by ramming if necessary, of the American bomber streams then ranging far inside Germany.

"On 7 July I flew my first sortie with this unit and the heavier Fw 190 against a tight formation of Consolidated B-24Js. I searched out a bomber and from a very close range I gave it a short burst into the fuselage and into the starboard engines. The impact of our new improved shells was devastating. The attacked B-24J immediately lost altitude and sheet metal as it began to burn. The aircraft exploded as I completed my overflight. I watched as the wing split away from the fuselage and then the powerplants spun off the wing like Olympic torches. I had also received some hits from the bomber during the attack, both in my engine and fuselage, but the Fw 190 just kept flying.

"My next sortie was against a formation of Boeing B-17Gs and their P-51 Mustang escort fighters. To draw off the escort we would set up 'fighter traps' in the sky and these would develop into an aerial circus. (In the melee everyone would be shooting; sometimes even at the enemy.) I came so close to one of the Mustangs that I could observe the squadron marking of a 'sea-horse' on his nose.

"At about this time in the war the Luftwaffe fighters of the 'Home Defense' (of which JG 3 was a part) were being criticized by people at home who did not know the true field situation of overpowering odds, short supplies and almost constant alert. We were accused of cowardice in the face of the enemy and court martials were mounted by some officers in an effort to quiet the situation. I defended eight of my comrades in these proceedings and got them acquitted for they were truly innocent.

"In January, 1945, the badly depleted IV *Gruppe* of JG 3 was regrouping and I was given command of the 15th *Staffel*. We flew fighter-bomber sorties in our Fw 190s against the heavy armor and advancing convoys of the Soviet Army. My beloved Fw 190 performed beautifully in her new role. We flew in at low altitudes in a loose formation carrying bombs with delayed fuses. We would drop our load and then bank up and out to get out of range of the impending explosion.

"In February, 1945, we moved to Prenzlau near Berlin and I was given full command of IV *Gruppe*. My command flight received the new Focke-Wulf Fw 190D-9 which was, and is, the fastest prop-driven aircraft I have ever flown. It was supplied with a gyrostabilized EZ42 reflector gunsight and with this sight I found I could hit the cockpit of a Russian DB-7 from a very great distance. The Fw 190D-9 included all the good qualities of the regular Fw 190 with a higher speed and a higher climb rate. It also included a methanol-water (MW 50) injection system that not only boosted power output, but also reduced engine temperatures under high rpm situations.

"I accounted for my final aerial victories in the Fw 190D-9 before ending my fighting career on 24 April, 1945. On this day I was flying against the warnings of my *Geschwader Kommodore* who was insisting I reduce my flying time. I got into an engagement with a formation of Il-2s, and just as one of the enemy planes entered my sights I noticed my cooling manifold doors come open and my instruments registered overheating. I broke off my attack and luckily managed to elude the Russian fighter escorts. By the time I was free of the battle I had lost too much altitude to parachute. Suddenly, the engine quit and I tightened my harness and prepared for the inevitable. I set the Fw 190D-9 down in an open field and proceeded to smear its pieces all over the landscape. However, the same rugged construction that had saved my life in earlier emergency landings proved itself once again. The injuries I received from the crash, however, kept me from returning to active combat before the war came to an end."

Many achievements marked the scorecard of the *Wuerger* during its long and successful career as a fighter, fighter-bomber and ground attack aircraft, but perhaps one of the most memorable will never be proven. The incident not only poses an interesting question (was this the final air victory of World War II in Europe achieved by the Fw 190?), but provides a unique epitaph for not only the participation of Germany in World War II, but also for a truly fine fighting machine, the Fw 190. The story is related by *Oberleutnant* Gerhard Thyben of the JG 54 *Gruenherz*.

"The evacuation of fortress Courtland, Latvia, was started at 0730 on 8 May, 1945. It was to include multiple takeoffs of both small and large aircraft to save the time of forming up in the air, and to reduce the unnecessary usage of critical fuel. A strong air current was in evidence over Scandinavia and Central Europe and the sky was a cloudless light blue. Evidently even the God of Weather was happy about the end of the war.

"Quietly and evenly the engine of my Fw 190A-8 turned in front of my armor plate. My compass pointed west. At my left at the same altitude was 'Fritze' Hangebrauck, my usual 'sticky' wingman. We had not been airborne long when suddenly I sighted at a far distance to the left of us, and perhaps some 500 meters lower, a single twin-engine aircraft approaching. It was flying a typical stubborn straight-on Russian course and crossed directly under us. 'Fritze' noticed my mood (even without radio transmission). It was a Soviet Pe-2 on a recon sortie. My first thoughts were that a contact with the enemy was just what the doctor prescribed, but under our special circumstances I figured that this might be a Russian lead aircraft for the victorious forces. The Pe-2 was normally manned by three men (when the ladies were on vacation, stirring soup, or bearing children) of which two shot aft. This was deserving of special attention, especially when one was over cold water as we were.

"I happened to be busy at the time, closing the zipper of my flight outfit when 'Fritze' came within touching distance and indicated his wish to engage in offensive action. Completely against my better judgment I became courageous and the shooting started from a great distance. Instead of immediately diving, I tried my luck while maintaining altitude. This I should not have been done as it was really a fruitless effort. The range between us soon diminished and in spite of overheating weapons some of my shells hit his right motor and he began to smoke. The Russian soon realized his position and suddenly attempted to reach a lower altitude. Heading eastward he skimmed the surface on one engine at between one and two meters altitude, blinded by the morning sun and the glittering waves. A short burst of fire from my guns and the Soviet Pe-2 hit the water. The time was 0754, less than half an hour after we had taken off. I turned west and slowly gained altitude as 'Fritze' pulled up alongside and congratulated me with a hand victory sign.

"The chalk cliffs of the island of Ruegen began to appear and Fehmarn was now in sight. Over Grossenbrode my red fuel indicator light came on warning of only 15 to 20 minutes of flying time left. I knew we must hurry. We estimated that we had enough fuel to reach my home city of Kiel and we proceeded toward Kiel-Holtenau. An atmosphere of peaceful farming spread under us as the airfield was being made ready for our arrival. German farmers were working feverishly to fill in the bomb craters on our landing approach where, as a boy, I sailed in gliders. In the traditional manner of our forefathers, 'Fritze' and I wagged our wings as the crowds on the ground waved and cheered our arrival. We let down our wheels and softly lowered our machines onto the apron.

"Where former Luftwaffe aircraft with the Iron Cross once stood, RAF equipment now was apparent. British machines and personnel rushed toward us armed to the teeth. Their leader wore a beret on his head and stood in front of a rotating heavy machine-gun. Next to him sat his aide with a light machine-gun in his lap (I felt a bouquet of forget-me-nots would have been prettier). The war for Germany, myself and the Fw 190 was over."

Acknowledgement

I want to take this opportunity to express my personal appreciation to those individuals and institutions whose interest, assistance and trust have made this effort a reality.

Herbert Kaiser	Dipl. Ing. Kurt Tank	Gemeinschaft der Jagdflieger
Oskar Romm	Gerhard Thyben	Messerschmitt-Boelkow-Blohm
Guenther Schack	Bundesarchiv, West Germany	United States Air Force
Werner Schroer	Fokker G.m.b.H.	

STUKA

Text by ALEX VANAGS-BAGINSKIS

Ju87

1 Siren unit
2 Bottom plate
3 Attachment ring
4 Support cylinder
5 Set screw

Slipstream-driven dive bombing siren

Introduction

The Junkers Ju 87 was without doubt one of the most significant aircraft of World War II and has left its mark on history. There have been other dive bombers, but none have made such an impression on the popular mind, or captured so much imagination as the Ju 87 which eventually came to epitomize the term "Stuka". Although "Stuka" is a contraction of the German word *Sturkampfflugzeug* or dive bomber and could equally apply to the twin-engined Ju 88 when used in this role, it automatically conjures up visions of screaming Ju 87s diving onto a target like a flock of mechanized birds of prey. There is also no doubt that at least during the early stages of World War II the psychological effect of these screaming dives was almost as great as the actual damage, a fact appreciated and exploited by the German command.

And yet the dreaded Stuka was one of the most vulnerable of warplanes. It was an all-conquering weapon while the shock effect of its appearance held sway over the enemy, but once that had worn off the Ju 87 could only operate in areas dominated by the *Luftwaffe*. On their own, the Stukas were an easy prey to the fighters and a good target to the anti-aircraft guns once they were committed to a dive. Lacking armour protection and effective armament, they were not suited for close support tasks either until so modified, by which time the Ju 87 was already outdated.

Despite increasingly harder fighting and more frequent demands for support from the ground forces there was only a marginal increase in the establishment strength from nine to 13 *Stukagruppen* in summer 1943, but the actual combat strength was another matter. A detailed study by *Generalleutnant* (Rtd) Mahlke, one of the first Stuka *Gruppenkommandeure* shows that there were never more than about 360 Stukas and their crews in operational service at any one time. In fact, by late 1942 hardly 200 Stukas were available for operational use, and replacements could no longer keep up with losses. For instance, in 1942 St.G 2 alone lost 89 crews (including eight formation leaders with more than 600 operational sorties to their credit) in just eight months.

The official casualty reports compiled by the *Luftwaffe* General Staff list the loss of 1269 Stuka crews from 1 September 1939 to 30 September 1943 when the *Stukagruppen* lost their identity with hardly any change in their operational employment. However, the actual Stuka losses were much higher because thanks to the rugged construction of their mounts many shot-down Ju 87 crews survived to fight another day. In addition, many Ju 87s were also destroyed on the ground.

Nevertheless, the Ju 87 remained in the forefront of fighting for the better part of the war, particularly on the Eastern Front where their effect was out of all proportion to their numbers. And not only that: the Ju 87 even managed to make another name for itself as a flying tank destroyer during the late stages of fighting when the battlefields in the East were swarming with enemy fighters, and remained operational as a night ground attack bomber until the very end of hostilities. Indeed, few other warplanes have had such an

Ju 87B-2s of St.G 76 in V-formation, summer 1940.

intensive and effective combat life after being considered to be nearing obsolescence before World War II had even began.

It required special qualities and aptitude to be a Stuka pilot and those who survived the initial battles developed skills and an affection for their rugged mounts, eventually amassing an almost incredible number of operational sorties flying the Ju 87.

Apart from the unique Hans-Ulrich Rudel other Stuka pilots with many hundreds of combat flights to their credit included *Hptm* Alwin Boerst (1060), *Maj* Friedrich Lang (1007), *Maj* Dr Maximilian Otte (1179), *Hptm* Hendrik Stahl (1200), *Hptm* Herbert Bauer (1000+), *Maj* Karl Henze (1090) and literally dozens of others who had made over 600 operational flights.

In popular image the story of the Ju 87 is inextricably connected with Junkers and Ernst Udet ever since the name "Stuka" first appeared in print. Professor Hugo Junkers himself had in fact little to do with it. As pioneer of all-metal aircraft construction he unwittingly prepared the foundations, and the plant that built the Stuka bore his name, but that was all. Unlike other German aircraft firms the Junkers concern was State-controlled throughout the Third Reich period, while its founder died in banishment before the first Ju 87 was even flown. Likewise, it is not quite true that it was Ernst Udet, the most successful surviving German World War I fighter ace with 62 confirmed victories and aerobatic pilot extraordinary, who initiated Stuka development in Germany with his spectacular power-diving exhibitions flying the Curtiss Helldiver biplanes. By that time the basic Ju 87 design had already been finalized and in the mock-up stage. Ernst Udet did make a significant contribution to the development of the Stuka, but mainly because of his enthusiasm for the idea, great skill as an exhibition pilot and friendship and influence with some of the leading personalities of the Third Reich without which the Stuka would have had a much harder struggle.

Without the practical foundations laid by Junkers engineers the realisation of the Ju 87 Stuka would have taken much longer, a fact readily acknowledged by Erhard Milch, the Secretary of State for Air, who wrote on 22 February 1943: "The Junkers group was the first to take up the Stuka idea for Germany and carry it through technically. By his efforts, *GenOberst* Udet helped the Stuka idea to win through and make the work already available at Junkers effective and timely."

Birth of a weapon

After the end of the World War I and the total defeat of Germany and the Central Powers, the popular feeling in Western democracies was in favour of disarmament, combined with reliance on the new League of Nations. It is true that fighting in Eastern Europe and Russia went on for at least another three years, and the British, French and Italians had some colonial problems, but by and large the military were hard put to maintain their existence – except in the Soviet Union and Germany. The German air force commanded by General von Hoeppner officially ceased to exist on 8 May, 1920, four months after the Treaty of Versailles had become effective. Although the terms of the treaty forbade Germany to have an air force in the future an unexpected solution was provided by the Treaty of Rapallo between Germany and the Soviet Union, signed on 16 April 1922. This marked the beginning of years of close collaboration between the *Reichswehr* and the Red Army, one of the more tangible results being the establishment of a flying training centre at Lipetzk, north of Voronezh.

While these developments were taking place German military experts, just like their foreign counterparts, were debating the future role and significance of air power, but in more enclosed circles the first practical steps towards a new German air force were already being taken. World War I had shown the great importance of tactical and particularly ground-support aviation, and the term "flying artillery" was coined then, although as yet there were no means for such accurate delivery of bombs.

In the 1920s some attempts were made to build more or less "camouflaged" military aircraft in Germany, but it was obvious that to keep pace with technological development German aircraft designers and manufactures had to move abroad. Among these emigrants was Professor Hugo Junkers who, in the 1920s, established aircraft factories at Fili (near Moscow) and in Turkey, and a subsidiary firm, the AB Flygindustri, at Malmö-Limhamn in Sweden. A number of civil and military aircraft were either built under licence from Junkers or developed there, including the K 47 all-metal monoplane that was destined to play a major part in the Ju 87 story.

Designed by Dipl Ing Karl Plauth, a Junkers engineer, the K 47, which first flew in 1928 powered by a 480 hp Bristol Jupiter VII radial engine, represented a very advanced design for its time. Classed as a two-seat fighter, the K 47 was stressed for diving and featured specially braced wings to withstand the pull-out from high-speed power dives. (It was also the first Junkers aircraft with a smooth instead of a corrugated dural sheeting covered fuselage.)

In 1923, a newly graduated engineer and a former pilot of *Bombenversuchsabteilung* (Experimental Bomb Detachment), Hermann Pohlmann, had joined the Junkers works. Within a few years he proved to be a gifted and original designer and advanced to take charge of the development work on all-metal single-engined aircraft, his most notable successes being the Junkers W 33 and W 34.

Junkers K 47 two-seat fighter modified to A 48 standard in Germany.

Pohlmann had also collaborated on the design of the K 47, and after the death in an air crash of Karl Plauth he tok over its further development in Germany as the A 48. The foundations had been laid for the evolution of the Ju 87.

Meanwhile, dive bombing had appeared on the other side of the world. In the 1920s the US Marine Corps was called on to assist local governments threatened by various rebel factions in several Central American countries, particularly in Haiti and Nicaragua. Most of the fighting took place in dense jungle where the rebels often managed to avoid capture by withdrawing to their jungle encampments. As artillery was out of the question, and available air support limited to a few obsolete de Havilland D.H. 4B biplanes, the USMC pilots had to begin primitive dive-bombing attacks for better accuracy. These operations were so successful that the USMC included dive-bombing capability in their next request for general-purpose aircraft. Coincidentally, the Curtiss Aeroplane and Motor Company had just developed a new two-seat fighter, the F8C, which qualified for USMC service in 1928. Suitably modified and equipped, these machines were redesignated OC-1 and named Helldivers – a name subsequently carried by all Curtiss dive bombers.

It was, however, the earlier Curtiss developments that had attracted attention in both Japan and Germany. The Imperial Japanese Navy had been air-minded since the early days, having first carefully followed British experiments with aircraft and warships in 1911–12 and then various early air/sea operations during the final stages of World War I. By 1928 the Japanese Navy already possessed three aircraft carriers, including the 7,470-ton *Hosho*, completed in December 1922 as the world's first purpose-built aircraft carrier.

After the appearance of the first US Navy shipboard fighter/dive bombers the Japanese Navy was quick to realize the potential of this new method of attack and, late in 1930, commissioned the Ernst Heinkel Flugzeugbau at Warnemünde to design a suitable aircraft. Dr Heinkel had had business links with Japan since 1922 and his engineers began work on this new aircraft right away, with the dive-bombing requirement presenting an interesting challenge.

The He 50aW float biplane powered by a 390 hp Junkers L 5 inline engine was completed in the summer of 1931. It did not carry any military equipment, and was obviously underpowered. This fact was realized early on and the second prototype, the He 50aL landplane powered by a Siemens-built Bristol Jupiter VI radial of 450 hp was already a fully fledged dive bomber, the first such aircraft built in Germany. However, another event of far more significance took place in the autumn of 1931. While the second He 50 was still at the factory, Ernst Udet was invited to attend the National Air Races at Cleveland, Ohio. Among the aircraft demonstrated there was the latest Curtiss Helldiver performing near-vertical dives over the airfield dropping sand bags with amazing accuracy on marked targets. Udet was most impressed and, on returning home, submitted several enthusiastic reports about the military potential of such diving attacks. These reports soon gained the interested attention of the leading figures of the still "undercover" German military aviation, but that was all. However, as a result of the American demonstration dives the Junkers engineers at the Swedish branch works decided to modify their K 47 two-seat fighter and the first shallow dive bombing experiments began soon afterwards.

Dr Heinkel was well aware of the secret build-up of the clandestine German air force and its need for military aircraft. Being first and foremost an astute businessman, he tried everything possible to secure domestic orders in anticipation of the inevitable expansion that would come sooner rather than later. As far as the novel dive bomber was concerned he felt certain about his chances – he had already built one. Thus, while the details of the Japanese Navy contract were still being worked out, on Heinkel's instructions the He 50aL was redesignated He 50V1 and demonstrated to aviation experts from the RWM (Reichswehrministerium, the State Ministry of Defence) at Rechlin in the spring of 1932. With the second cockpit faired over, the He 50V1 carried out full performance trials, diving with 1,102 lb (500 kg) blocks of cement. This was the first such demonstration witnessed by the military in Germany, and they were most impressed. As a result, Heinkel was awarded a contract by the RVM (Reichsverkehrsministerium, the State Ministry of Transport, then also overtly and covertly looking after military aviation matters) for three evaluation aircraft. Knowing that there was no time to lose, Heinkel speeded up their completion and delivery by the late summer of 1932.

Generally similar to the He 50aL, these machines were powered by uncowled Siemens SAM 22B radials of 600 hp. Although completed as general-purpose two-seaters, the aircraft were delivered with interchangeable rear fuselage panels to convert them into single-seat dive bombers able to dive with a 1,102 lb (500 kg) bomb. Flight tests were passed successfully by July 1932 and Heinkel received a production order for 25 aircraft to be delivered as He 50A to various Verkehrsfliegerschulen (commercial pilot schools), all of which included military flying training groups. It was a promising start, but Heinkel's hopes were soon to be dashed.

Ernst Udet had never forgotten the small and sturdy American Helldiver, and during subsequent enquiries was told that he could have a similar export model for just 14,000 dollars. However, Udet did not have so much money and his attempts to persuade some business people in Germany were unsuccessful. He was still a civilian, and his interest in the Helldiver was based partly on his own desire to fly it at air shows as well as for its military potential.

On 30 January, 1933, Adolf Hitler took over the political leadership of Germany and from then on, there was no holding back on rearmament – money was no object. On 27 April, 1933, the Reichskommissariat für die Luftfahrt (State Inspectorate of Aviation) under Hermann Göring became the RLM (Reichsluftfahrtministerium); a month later, on 15 May, the whole hitherto secret and elaborate organisation of clandestine military aviation came under the control of the RLM – and the Air Minister, Hermann Göring. Ernst Udet now turned to Göring, his wartime squadron commander and comrade, if not a friend. Göring agreed to help provided Udet joined the new Reichsluftwaffe (the name suggested by Hitler, but soon changed to simply Luftwaffe). After some vacillation Udet agreed, on condition that he could test-fly any new aircraft he wanted to and delay the official date of joining (Udet rejoined as an Oberst only in June 1935).

The legend persists that it was Udet's spectacular demonstration dives with Curtiss Helldivers that convinced Göring and the leading officials of the RLM of the military potential of dive bombing, and resulted in the so-called Sofort-Programm (Immediate Programme) to build the first Luftwaffe dive bombers which led directly to the "real" Stuka, the Ju 87. This is only partly true. There is no doubt that Udet went out of his way to win support for "his" dive bomber idea – which eventually became almost an obsession with him – but that is by no means the fully story. To begin with, the Sofort-Programm was not a sudden decision, although it may have been influenced to some extent by Udet's enthusiasm and backing in higher quarters. In fact, dive bombing as a method of achieving greater accuracy of bomb delivery had been carefully considered already by the Fliegergeräte-Inspektion (Inspectorate of Aircraft Equipment) of the Luftschutzamt (Air Defence Office) already during the 1920s.

By 1932, these theoretical studies had progressed to the evaluation of foreign experiments and practical experience with the He 50 and the Junkers K 47 – where the tactical trials at Lipetzk played an important role. Early in 1933, the C-Amt of the Luftfahrtkommissariat in charge of the technical developments made a decision to initiate two consecutive stages of dive-bomber development, the immediate Sofort-Programm and the "second phase' to provide the Luftwaffe with the definitive dive bomber. The official request outlining initial requirements was issued – with Udet's encouragement – to the Fieseler Flugzeugbau at Kassel and the newly established Henschel Flugzeugwerke at Berlin-Johannisthal in the early spring of 1933. The specifications called for a single-seat all-metal biplane powered by a 650 hp BMW 132A radial engine (German licence-built version of the Pratt & Whitney Hornet); the aircraft were to be of conventional design; be suitable for series production, and have development potential. The stipulated date for the completion of prototypes (later allocated the RLM type designations Fi 98 and Hs 123) was February 1935.

However, by the summer of 1933 Göring too had become a supporter of the dive-bomber idea, but for different reasons, and readily agreed to Udet's suggestion that it would be prudent to purchase two American Helldivers, instead of just one. Göring also personally approved the transfer of dollars from government funds to the USA for the purchase of the Curtiss Hawk II biplanes (export designation of the F11C-2 Goshawk Helldiver). On 27 September, 1933, Udet was at the Curtiss factory at Buffalo, NY, to test-fly and collect his Hawk IIs, which were then loaded aboard the German liner *Europa*. On arrival at Bremerhaven on 19 October, the crates were assisted through the customs with the help of RLM Departmental Chief Fritz Müller, an early convert to the dive-bomber idea, who – on Göring's instructions – accompanied Udet and his acquisitions all the way to Berlin.

The Hawk II was powered by a 712 hp Wright SR-1820-F2 Cyclone radial engine and achieved a maximum speed of 202 mph (325 km/hr) at 3,300 ft (1,005 m) altitude. It weighed about the same as, and had similar range to, the Junkers K 47, but was smaller and much more manoeuvrable, and its diving characteristics were excellent. Compared to the Helldiver's lively performance the He 50 was clumsy and slow – one of the reasons some RLM officials were dubious about the military value of dive bombers. But the purchase of these Hawk IIs did not initiate dive-bomber development in Germany.

It was also in October 1933 that the RLM ordered the formation of the first dive-bomber *Gruppe* of the new *Luftwaffe*, which in fact did not take place until 17 months later. In December 1933 both Hawk IIs, sporting civilian registrations D-3165 and 3166 (later D-IRIS and D-ISIS) were transferred to Rechlin – the newly established test centre north of Berlin – where Udet personally demonstrated some spectacular mock diving attacks to RLM officials. Not all of them were convinced about the dive-bombing idea; in fact, the *Technisches Amt* (which had replaced the former *C-Amt*) was completely divided on this issue. The main opposition came from the chief of the Development section, *Major* Wolfram *Freiherr* von Richthofen (cousin of the famous Manfred) and the Secretary of State for Air, *Oberst* Erhard Milch, Richthofen – no doubt influenced by the poor showing of the He 50 – considered the whole Stuka concept as negative because of the apparent vulnerability of the dive bomber to ground fire, while Milch objected on the grounds that normal service aircrews would not stand up to the high gravitational forces. The only real support for Udet's ideas came from General Walther Wever, the first Chief of the *Luftwaffe* General Staff in everything but name. In the end it was agreed to give the idea a try and judge by results.

The first unit of the new *Luftwaffe* was activated at Döberitz, near Berlin, on 1 April, 1934 under *Major* Ritter von Greim, a well known World War I fighter pilot. Designated *Jagdgeschwader* 132 (JG 132) and largely based on the former so-called *Reklamestaffel Mitteldeutschland* this unit, in addition to its primary duties as a fighter formation, was also given the task of training dive-bomber pilots. To that end, the then standard Ar 65 and He 51 fighters were supplemented by a number of He 50A dive bombers, 60 of which had been ordered for that purpose for the still clandestine *Luftwaffe*.

By now though, a series of other events had taken place that had much more significance to the Ju 87 development. Soon after Adolf Hitler and his supporters had attained power in Germany, aircraft manufacturers were left in no doubt about the intended build-up of the armed forces, and were asked to collaborate. The Junkers works at Dessau was then the largest aircraft plant in Germany, essential for the planned expansion, but Professor Hugo Junkers was a convinced democrat and pacifist and refused to follow the Hitler line. Moreover, there was a long-standing enmity between the old professor and Erhard Milch. Junkers had never forgiven Milch, one of his former directors, for the incorporation of his small private airline into the State-subsidised Lufthansa and, even more so, for successfully insisting against Junkers' opposition that the Ju 52 should have three engines. There were also other, more political reasons. Pressure was nevertheless put on the stubborn professor, who was finally forced to give in to Milch's demands in May 1933. Control of his then near-bankrupt company was taken over by the State, and Hugo Junkers, the pioneer of all-metal aircraft construction, was banned from Dessau to Bavaria where he died on 3 February, 1935. The fact that Junkers was now State-controlled naturally had a certain influence on all future development and production contracts.

However, before these events took place the first determined steps leading to the Ju 87 had already been taken. A group of Junkers engineers had been quietly working on the problem of dive bombing since 1931 – in fact, since the K 47 was first flown in Sweden and revealed its remarkable diving characteristics. During 1931–34 the Junkers experimental group carried out methodical tests with the K 47 equipped with various measuring instruments flown by *Flugkapitän* Willy Neuenhofen, the Junkers chief test pilot. These tests took place in Sweden, initially at night due to the measuring method employed. The result of close German-Swedish collaboration, this involved the use of a strong searchlight attached underneath the K 47 and practice bombs fitted with light elements that could be accurately measured with a cine-theodolite.

After the evaluation of these results the tests were continued in daytime. Here, use was made of two cine cameras because it had been found that a pilot alone could not aim and read (and note) the instruments simultaneously. The development of the gyro-stabilized dive-bombing sight that automatically corrected the ballistic values according to the bank of the aircraft of course made it all so much easier. Another great help was the visual display of the correct bomb release altitude. Both of these still have to be developed, of course.

These tests were so successful and the target accuracy and bombing patterns so good that in 1934 the Junkers team in Sweden built and tested the first rocket-powered bombs. Once again, the trusty K 47 was used as a carrier and these tests showed clearly that the dive bomber could also attack moving shipping targets with a good chance of success. Two of the Swedish personnel deserving great credit for these developments were Capt Svensen and First Lt Bjuggrens; the Junkers team was led by Dipl Ing Ottfried Fuchs. He evolved the test instruments, determined the correct diving method, and was decisively involved in the development of the gyro-stabilized dive-bombing sight. His introduction to the final report dated 3 November, 1934 on these experimental dive-bombing tests concludes with the following prophetic words: "This final test has confirmed that the dive bomber (of German stamp) can be developed in time to be the sharpest weapon in the air force armoury."

In the meantime another group of Junkers engineers at Dessau led by Chief Designer Dipl Ing Hermann Pohlmann was converting the results of these tests into practical forms, and by 1933 the design of the Junkers dive bomber was taking shape. Over the years Hermann Pohlmann had gained invaluable experience in the construction of all-metal aircraft at Junkers, and from the outset he chose the typical Junkers monoplane configuration – despite the still prevalent official preference for biplanes. Although the design of Pohlmann's dive bomber was based on the K 47, it incorporated several novel features considered essential for a dive bomber. The most notable was the inverted gull wing which gave the pilot the best possible view forwards and downwards, combined with short but sturdy undercarriage legs. The fact that such a wing would take longer to produce was outweighed by its advantages.

The mock-up of this dive bomber, the Ju 87, was completed in 1934. That year was to be the most significant in the development history of German dive bombers, and of the Ju 87 itself. By then, the concept had gained more influential supporters, including Hitler himself (who had always liked Udet), and trials at Rechlin and elsewhere were pursued at an accelerated pace. There were now several He 50s and K 47s flying as test beds to evolve the most efficient bomb racks and dive brakes, as well as special dive-bombing sights. When the RLM issued its specifications for the "second phase" dive-bomber development in January 1935 it was in fact based on the Ju 87 proposal, although the competing firms were allowed a certain freedom of interpretation. The other contestants were the Arado Ar 81, the Heinkel He 118 and, as an outsider, the Ha 137. By then the RLM were thinking in terms of a single seat "light" Stuka and a two-seat "heavy" Stuka, but the Ju 87 was favoured for several reasons: the Junkers team were the only engineers to have a solid basis of experience in this sphere; their proposal promised the desired robustness combined with advanced features; and the design had already advanced to the mock-up stage.

As a result, the RLM had authorized the construction of three prototypes soon after an inspection of the Ju 87 mock-up in 1934, several months before issuing the official specifications to the other firms. Ostensibly the idea was to select the best design from all competitors, but the Ju 87 was clearly at a great advantage. While it was taking shape at Dessau another event took place that confirmed what most people already knew: by a decree effective from 1 March, 1935, Hitler made the *Luftwaffe* an independent branch of the armed forces, and officially revealed its existence to the world. Expansion began at once, and among the first new units activated was I *Gruppe* of *Stukageschwader* 162 (I/St.G 162) at Schwerin on 28 March, 1935 (named "Immelmann"

on 3 April, 1935), consisting of a collection of sedate He 50A dive bombers and Ar 65 fighters.

The two competing designs ordered under the *Sofort-Programm*, the Fi 98 and Hs 123, had flown early in 1935, and the faster and seemingly more robust Hs 123 was favoured right away. Detecting some wavering in support for the dive bomber, Udet gave another one of his masterly flying performances with the first Hs 123 over Johannisthal on 8 May, 1935. Everything seemed fine until the first three Hs 123 prototypes were tested at Rechlin the following month: two of them broke up in the air during power dives, killing the pilots. An immediate investigation discovered certain weaknesses in the upper wing which were rectified on the Hs 123V4. This aircraft passed its acceptance tests at Rechlin with top marks and the type was ordered in production at once. The first practical German dive bomber was on its way. In anticipation of production deliveries scheduled to commence in the summer of 1936 two new dive-bomber *Gruppen* were formed on 1 April, 1936: II/St.G 162 at Lübeck-Blankensee and I/St.G 165 at Kitzingen. (It is of interest to note that one Ha 137 single-seat prototype also competed against the Hs 123 at Rechlin. The construction of several Ha 137 prototypes had

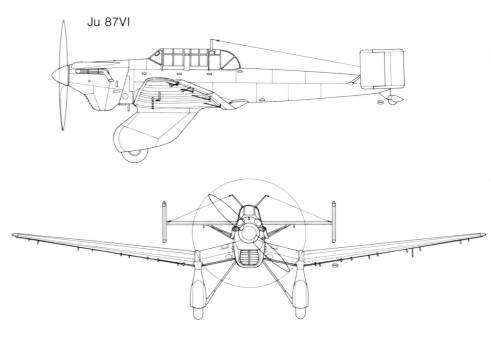

Ju 87VI

Modified first Ju 87 prototype with enlarged forward-set radiator.

been sanctioned by the RLM as a "back-up" design, but by that time the two-seat concept realized in the Ju 87 was already the accepted solution.)

The first Ju 87 was completed in the late summer of 1935 and made its maiden flight at Dessau on 17 September of that year. Like some other contemporary prototypes of German military aircraft, it was powered by a supercharged 525/640 hp Rolls-Royce Kestrel V engine; there were as yet no sufficiently powerful German aero engines available. The Ju 87 V1 featured a twin fin/rudder assembly as had the K 47. However, as the new wing dive brakes were still under development, the Ju 87 V1 had to fly without and during a test flight on 24 January, 1936, the aircraft went into an uncontrollable inverted spin and crashed. The pioneer dive bomber pilot, Willy Neuenhofen, and his observer died.

This unexpected tragic accident indicated a possible design fault and completion of the Ju 87 V2 was delayed pending the investigation. As a result, the tail assembly was completely redesigned to a large single fin/rudder configuration which made the Ju 87 almost spin-proof. Other changes were the installation of a German engine, the 610 hp Jumo 210Aa, and the special Junkers wing dive brakes. Registered D-UHUH, the Ju 87 V2 was completed in early March 1936, followed soon afterwards by the slightly modified Ju 87 V3 (D-UKYQ). Both aircraft were flown to Rechlin for the planned trials.

The official competition to chose the definitive dive bomber for the *Luftwaffe* was to take place in two stages: the preliminary evaluation in March 1936, and the final trials three months later. During the first, the Ju 87 and He 118 were selected as the main contenders and both firms awarded contracts for ten pre-production aircraft. The Ar 81 all-metal biplane was relegated to a "back-up" status, and the single-seat Ha 137, a late and unofficial entry – was to participate solely for comparison purposes; the two-seat dive bomber was now the accepted norm.

Although the He 118 was by far the more advanced and faster of the two finalists, it was also heavier and more complicated and not yet fully developed. It was also more an attack bomber than a Stuka, the second crew member acting as a bomb aimer. The He 118 design was based on the He 112 fighter being evolved in parallel, and Prof Heinkel was determined to overwhelm the opposition. However, the very advanced features of his contender were also its downfall. The first negative point came to light when the He 118 failed to participate in tests with the latest dive-bombing sight (*Stuvi* A3), planned to commence on 14 April, 1936. Also, its novel combined flaps/dive brakes were still under development when the time for the final tests arrived. These were flown at Rechlin during the first week of June 1936, and the participating He 118 V2 did not make a very good impression: while the Ju 87 performed a series of near-vertical dives with ease, the sleek He 118 dive bomber was restricted to an angle of 50°.

Then a curious thing happened. Although the Ju 87 had been awarded top marks and was about to be accepted, a confidential directive issued on 9 June, 1936 by *Oberst* von Richthofen – still one of the foremost opponents of the Stuka concept – called for the suspension of all further Ju 87

development! However, on the very next day Ernst Udet was appointed Chief of the RLM Technical Office and immediately cancelled von Richthofen's instructions. From this moment on, the dive bomber was firmly established as the main offensive weapon in the strategic sense as understood by the German military command. With Udet's now official support a considerable effort was soon placed behind the whole dive bomber programme and development.

One of his first tasks was to reach a quick final decision in the Ju 87/ He 118 matter. Despite the poor showing of the latter at Rechlin, Udet was loath to dismiss it completely. The best way to reach a decision was to test-fly the aircraft himself (Udet apparently never showed any interest in piloting the Ju 87). And this is when the advanced features of the He 118 ended Heinkel's hopes once and for all.

One of the innovations introduced on the He 118 was the combined flaps/dive brakes which were connected with the propeller pitch change, but this system was still not perfected when Udet arrived at the Heinkel works to try out the aircraft himself on 27 June 1936. Although the necessary procedure was explained to him, Udet did not seem to pay much attention and the inevitable happened. Soon after commencing his first dive from about 13,000 ft (3,962 m) the propeller suddenly feathered, shearing off the reduction gears, and the He 118 disintegrated around the pilot. Once again, Udet's parachute saved his life, but his interest in the Heinkel dive bomber had gone for good. Immediately afterwards the Ju 87 was officially declared winner of this contest and the State-controlled Junkers works awarded a production contract.

A few months earlier some *Luftwaffe* Stukas – still the biplane kind – had participated in the first adventure risked by Adolf Hitler, the "remilitarisation" of the Rhineland. In early March 1936, just four weeks after formation, I/St.G 162 was alerted and moved from its base at Kitzingen to Frankfurt/Main and Mannheim, and thence to the Rhineland.

In autumn of the same year, on Spanish request, the German government began assisting General Franco's Nationalist forces in Spain. By November 1936 the *Luftwaffe* contingent in Spain had grown to some 40 aircraft and 4,500 men and was organized as *Legion Condor*. Apart from the political considerations, the Spanish Civil war became an ideal testing ground for new weapons, tactics and equipment and was used as such particularly by the German and Soviet military.

The Ju 87 V4 (D-UBIP), the actual production prototype, was completed in the late autumn of 1936 and embodies various minor modifications and refinements. It was also the first Ju 87 to carry the proposed fixed armament of one 7.92 mm MG 17 in the starboard wing. Delivered to Rechlin in November 1936, this aircraft was used for intensive dive-bombing tests until the spring of 1937, with the main 551 lb (250 kg) and 1,102 lb (500 kg) as well as smaller anti-personnel bombs, and various fuses. There was no doubt now that the right choice had been made. The Ju 87 proved to be rugged, relatively easy to handle and, most important of all, could dive almost vertically and with great accuracy.

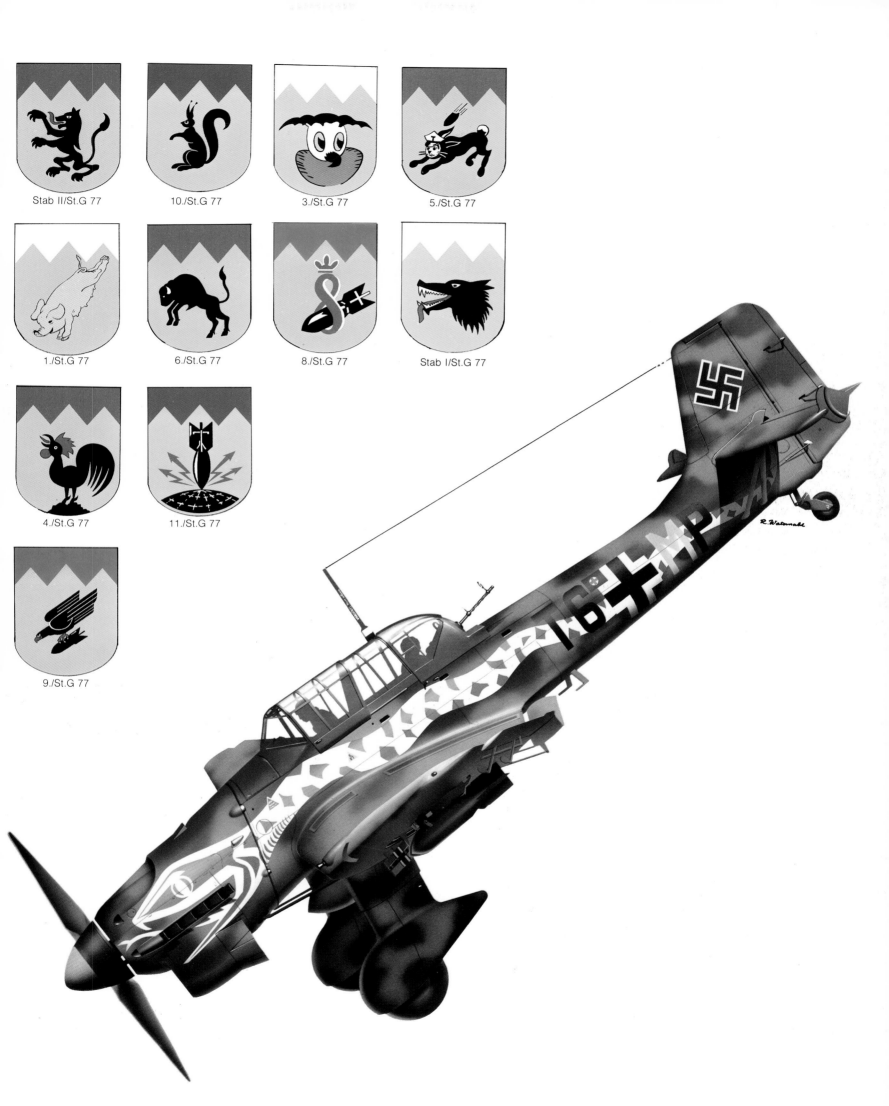

Stab II/St.G 77

10./St.G 77

3./St.G 77

5./St.G 77

1./St.G 77

6./St.G 77

8./St.G 77

Stab I/St.G 77

4./St.G 77

11./St.G 77

9./St.G 77

Ju 87B-2/trop of II/St.G 2 in North Africa, 1941.

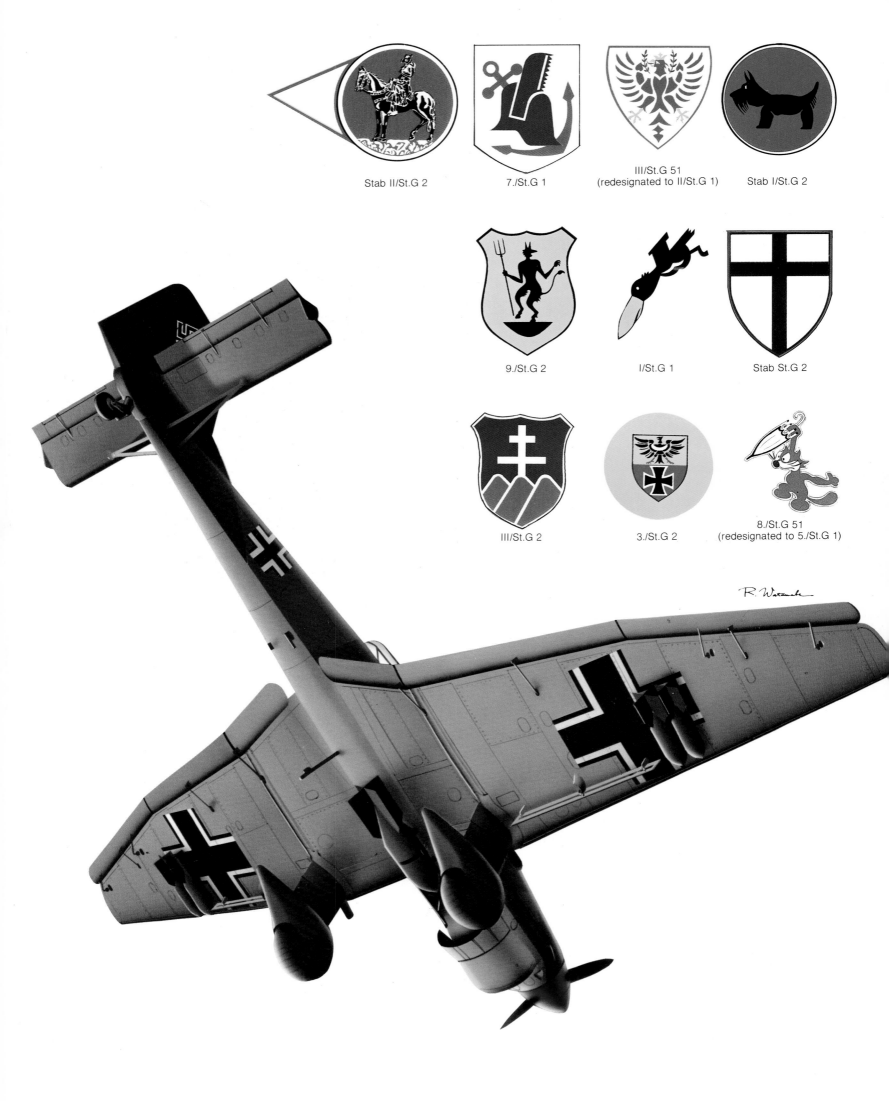

Stab II/St.G 2

7./St.G 1

III/St.G 51
(redesignated to II/St.G 1)

Stab I/St.G 2

9./St.G 2

I/St.G 1

Stab St.G 2

III/St.G 2

3./St.G 2

8./St.G 51
(redesignated to 5./St.G 1)

Ju 87B-2 with one SC 500 and four SC 50 bombs.

Ju 87B-2

Junkers Ju 87B-2 of 2./St.G 2 "Immelmann" in the Balkan region, spring 1941. It carries a 500 kg (1,102 lb) SC 500 bomb beneath the fuselage and four 50 kg (110 lb) SC 50 bombs under the wings.

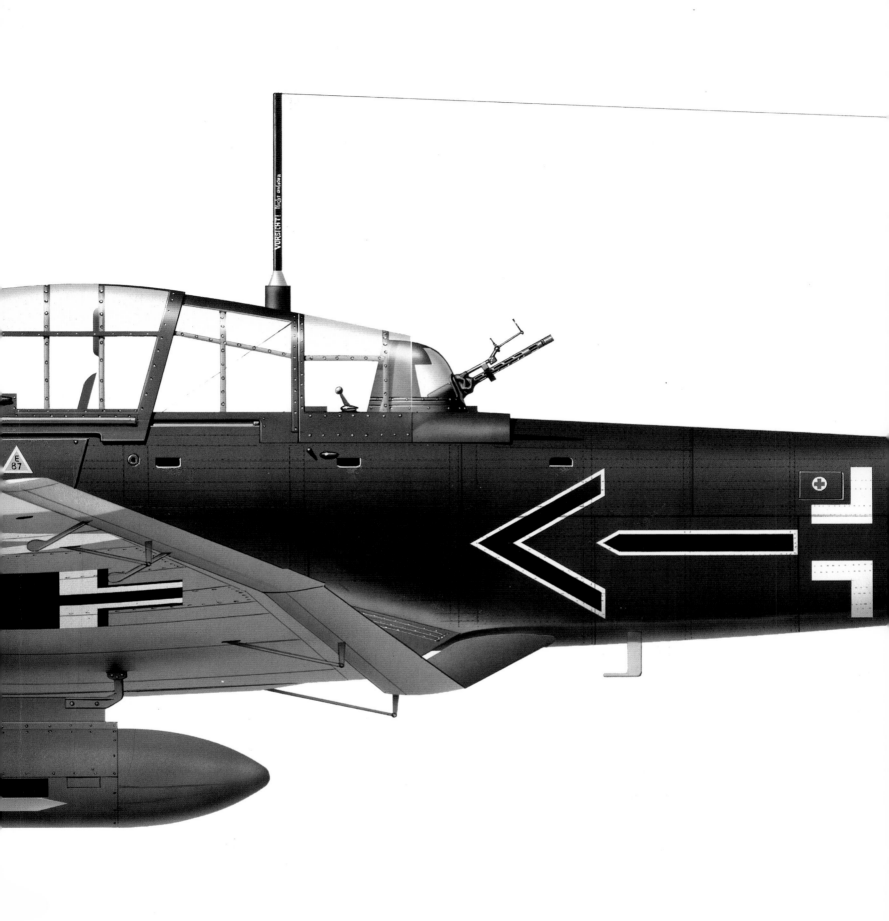

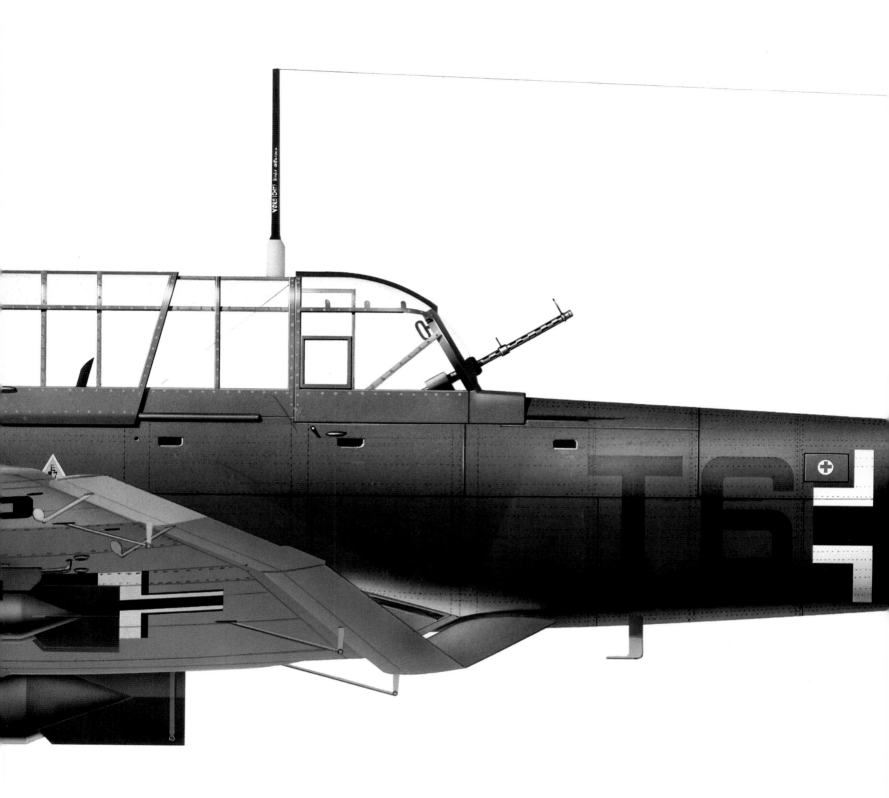

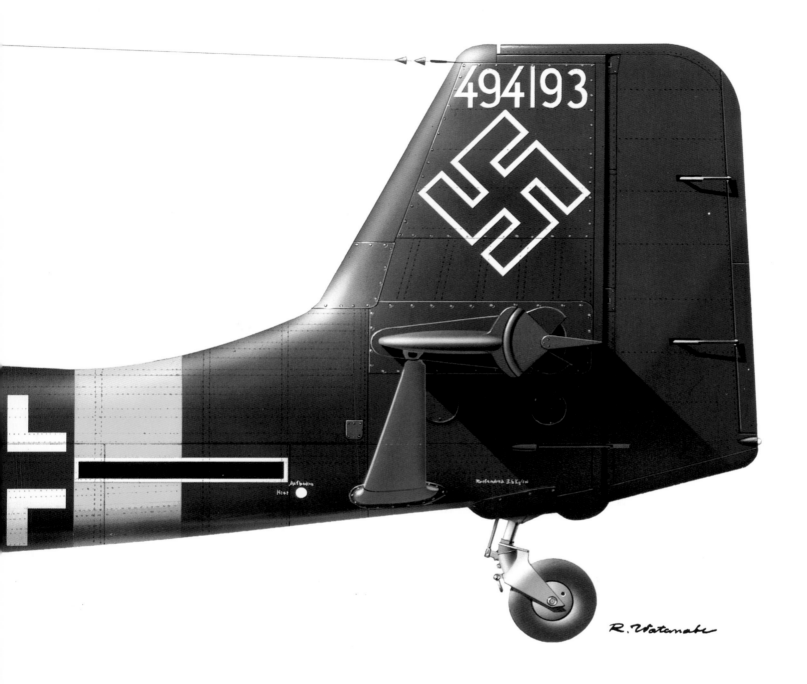

Ju 87G-1

Ju 87G-1 flown by *Oberstleutnant* Hans-Ulrich Rudel, *Kommodore* of SG 2 ''Immelmann'' (redesignated from St.G 2 on 18 October, 1943) on the Eastern Front in the autumn of 1944. The fighter style *Kommodore* markings are shown on both sides of the fuselage. As the only German soldier he was awarded the Golden Oak Leaves with Swords and Diamonds to the Knight's Cross of the Iron Cross, the highest German military decoration, on 29 December, 1944, and was promoted *Oberst* at the same time. During 2,530 combat sorties, Rudel destroyed at least 519 tanks, more than 800 vehicles, 150 artillery pieces, 70 landing craft and many bridges. His bombs also sank one battleship, one cruiser and one destroyer, and he shot down nine Soviet aircraft including seven fighters in air combat.

Ju 87A-2s of the *Stuka-Vorschule* (dive bomber training school) at Gratz, winter 1940/41.

(Imperial War Museum)

*The Ju 87 "Anton"** *

The first of the ten Ju 87A-0 pre-production aircraft were completed in late 1936. They differed from the four prototypes in having 600/640 hp Jumo 210Ca engines, constant taper wings of simplified structure, and an additional flexible 7.92 mm MG 15 in the rear cockpit. After factory tests these machines were immediately transferred to I/St.G 162 for service evaluation trials. Deliveries of the Ju 87A-1 began in the summer of 1937 but it took some time before production really got under way.

Although the German semi-voluntary *Legion Condor* had been in Spain since November 1936, it was not until September 1937 that the Ju 87A was considered fit for operational trials. Three aircraft were detached from I/St.G 163 (ex-I/St.G 162) and transferred to Spain, but their debut was delayed due to various technical problems. The first known operational use of the Ju 87A was in early March 1938. Dive-bomber crews from Germany were posted to this section – soon known as the *Jolanthe-Kette* – in rotation. In addition to providing a pool of operationally experienced personnel, this *Kette* also served to evolve combat tactics and point the way to further development much better than would have the most realistic exercises. At that time Wolfram von Richthofen was Chief of Staff of the *Legion Condor* and as

* It was the custom of Luftwaffe airmen to nickname many of their aircraft according to the version by using the contemporary service radio-telephone phonetic alphabet, 'Anton' for A, 'Bertha' for B, and so on.

the trio of Ju 87As began to show what they could do his long-standing scepticism of dive bombers gradually changed to admiration. Soon, he became one of the foremost protagonists of this weapon as part of ground-attack aviation, and was also instrumental in introducing the first ground-to-air controller system enabling the ground forces to vector aircraft visually to targets in the immediate combat zone. This method was later supplemented by *Luftwaffe* liaison officers attached to the ground troops who directed aircraft by radio. Both these developments revolutionized ground-to-air co-operation and are still valid today.

The Ju 87A-1 production run was relatively short, and the Ju 87A-2 had already replaced it on assembly lines at Dessau in late 1937. Generally similar to the first A-series model, the A-2 variant was powered by a 680 hp Jumo 210Da engine with two-speed supercharger and had modified radio equipment. Detailed reports about service and operational experience with the Ju 87A, combined with the availability of the more powerful Jumo 211 engine, then led to a major redesign.

The total Ju 87A-series production amounted to 262 aircraft, of which 192 were completed at Dessau (the last in May 1938) and the remainder at the new Weser plant at Berlin-Tempelhof.

"Bertha" joins the Luftwaffe

The complete range of trials with the Ju 87B-0 pre-production aircraft was completed almost without incident in less than 12 months.

From the operational point of view the main improvement on the Ju 87B series was the offensive power. This version could carry double the previous bombload – although this had to be balanced against reduced range caused by the higher fuel consumption of the new engine. Technically, the Ju 87B was an almost complete aerodynamic and structural redesign. Externally, these detail improvements included a reshaped cockpit canopy with sliding sections, enlarged vertical tail surfaces, and streamlined cantilever undercarriage fairings. Great attention was also paid to easier maintenance in the field – for instance, all parts of the undercarriages up to the upper attachment were interchangeable for both wheels. It was this version that gave the Ju 87 the characteristic shape that will forever be associated with the word Stuka.

The official *Luftwaffe* strength return of 1 August 1938 clearly shows the growth of the dive bomber force: Total
establishment: 3,714 aircraft (including 300 dive bombers)
Strength: 2,928 aircraft (including 207 dive bombers)
Available: 1,669 aircraft (including 159 dive bombers)

At the same time, only 80 dive-bomber crews were considered trained to full operational standards. This was to be remedied as a matter of urgency. In October 1938 five of the first Ju 87B-1s were sent to Spain where dive-bombing trials

Junkers Jumo 211Da (Ju 87B)

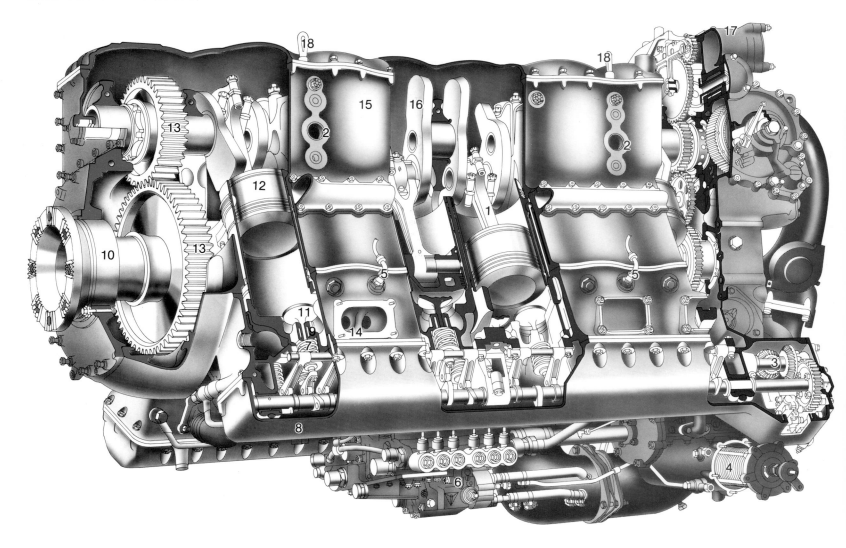

1 Connecting rod
2 Engine mount connecting joint
3 Camshaft bevel-drive gear
4 Oil filter
5 Spark plug
6 Fuel pump
7 Valve spring
8 Valve gear cover
9 Cylinder head
10 Propeller shaft
11 Valve
12 Piston and rings
13 Reduction gear
14 Exhaust port
15 Crank case
16 Balanced crank shaft
17 Engine accessories
18 Hook-up bracket

Type: Twelve-cylinder 60° inverted Vee liquid-cooled with direct fuel injection

Cylinders:
  Bore—150 mm (5.90 in)
  Stroke—165 mm (6.496 in)
  Capacity—35 litres
  Compression ratio—6.5 : 1

Dimensions:
  Length—2,173 mm (85.55 in)
  Width—804 mm (31.65 in)
  Height—1,053 mm (41.46 in)

Weight, dry: 660 kg (1,455 lb)

Supercharger: Two-speed centrifugal mounted on starboard side of engine
  Drive ratio—7.82 : 1 and 11.375 : 1

Propeller drive: Plain spur type
  Drive ratio—0.645 : 1

Performance
(at sea level):
  1,200 hp/2,400 rpm—Limit: 1 min (for take-off or emergency)
  1,020 hp/2,300 rpm—Limit: 5 min
  950 hp/2,300 rpm—Limit: 30 min (for climbing, etc.)
  800 hp/2,100 rpm—Continuous (for maximum cruising)
  660 hp/1,900 rpm—Continuous (for economical cruising)

were resumed with much better results. The "Bertha" was a great improvement and only one Ju 87B was lost in action, crash-landing behind Nationalist lines. One curious sidelight of this episode is that the Ju 87 was the only German aircraft the *Legion Condor* kept very much to themselves; no Spanish airmen were allowed either to examine or fly them.

In February 1939 Ernst Udet became *Generalluftzeugmeister (Luftwaffe* Director-General of Equipment) and the Stuka concept now had the highest official backing.

After the promising combat debut in Spain, the Ju 87B-1 quickly became the standard *Luftwaffe* dive bomber and output increased accordingly. The production orders were increased to 964 aircraft, of which the 187th had been delivered by 1 March, 1939. From the 697th aircraft (according to schedule, due for completion on 1 December, 1939) the airframes were to be fitted with the slightly more powerful Jumo 211D engines and incorporate other refinements (ejector exhausts, hydraulically operated radiator cooling gills, and an improved propeller with broader blades). Another improvement was that, when flown as a single-seater, this new variant could carry a 2,205 lb (1,000 kg) bomb. This aircraft was the Ju 87B-2.

By August 1939 all nine *Stukagruppen* were equipped with the "Bertha" and the Ju 87A was relegated to Stuka training schools. In the autumn of 1939 a new Weser plant at Bremen-Lemwerder was prepared for large-scale series production of the Ju 87B, and the total order was increased to 803 Ju 87Bs to be shared between both plants. This was to be followed by another order for no less than 827 Ju 87B-2s produced at Bremen, with the Junkers plant at Dessau being responsible for detail development. At that time the RLM stipulated that this would be the last production batch as it was planned to phase-out the Ju 87B from the first-line formations in the spring of 1941. In fact, because of its relatively low speed and vulnerability, the Ju 87B was considered already obsolescent by some *Luftwaffe* staff officers in 1939. This of course was known to both Udet and Erhard Milch, Göring's deputy and Secretary of State for Air, who were also looking forward to the planned re-equipment with the Me 210. In fact the Ju 87 was forced to soldier on when it was long past its prime.

Subsequently a number of field modifications were introduced in the light of operational experience and applied to both the Ju 87B-1 and B-2. These retrospective changes were as follows:

Ju 87B-1/U1 (B-2/U1) (1939/41)
Retrospective designation when variants introduced.
Ju 87B-1/U2 (B-2/U2) (1939/41)
Service version with revised radio equipment.
Ju 87B-1/U3 (B-2/U3) (1941/41)
Fitted with additional armour protection for the crew and engine.
Ju 87B-1/U4 (B-2/U4) (1941/41)
Provision for alternative ski undercarriage.
Ju 87B-1/trop (B-2/trop) (1941/41)
Tropicalized variant for use in hot and dry climates. Engine air intake dust filter; aircraft with desert survival equipment.

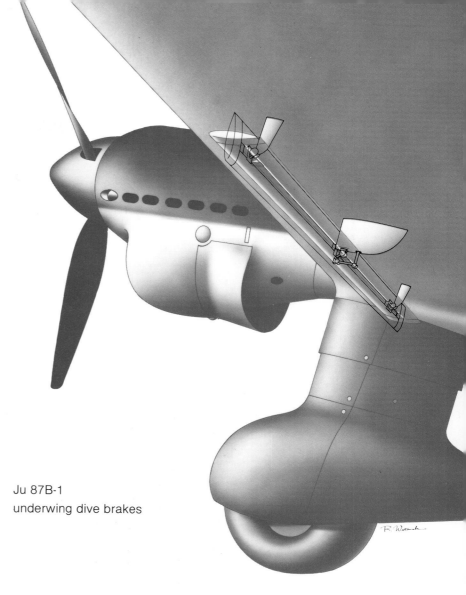

Ju 87B-1
underwing dive brakes

Beginning with the Ju 87B series all Stukas incorporated a special safety device to avoid too steep pull-out from a dive: the elevator movement was restricted by a "catch" that could be overcome in emergency. Another feature of the Bertha was a siren mounted in a fairing in the upper part of each undercarriage leg. Initially a simple whistle-type, operated by air passing through during a dive, later production series introduced a more elaborate type of siren in a streamlined fairing driven by a small propeller. An idea suggested by Ernst Udet, it became known as the "Jericho Trumpet" and was first used in France. The intended purpose was to add to the psychological effect of the dive bomber, and proved most successful. It also established the typical sound that is still immediately associated with the Ju 87 Stuka.

As Fate would have it, the Stuka suffered a tragic blow just before the war that affected its crews for some time to come. On 15 August, 1939, during the manoeuvres held in the Neuenhamm plain, I/St.G 1 led by *Hptm* Walter Sigel was to perform an early morning demonstration dive-bombing attack. Shortly before reaching the target area a freak spell of weather covered it in low cloud that was wrongly estimated to have a higher base than it actually had. The whole *Gruppe* dived as planned, but only some of the pilots pulled out in time when they realized the mistake. Others were fortunate to crashland, but 13 crews dived straight into the ground to their death. *Hptm* Sigel later went on to become one of the foremost Stuka experts but this terrible tragedy haunted him for ever.

Just two weeks later the Stukas were at war.

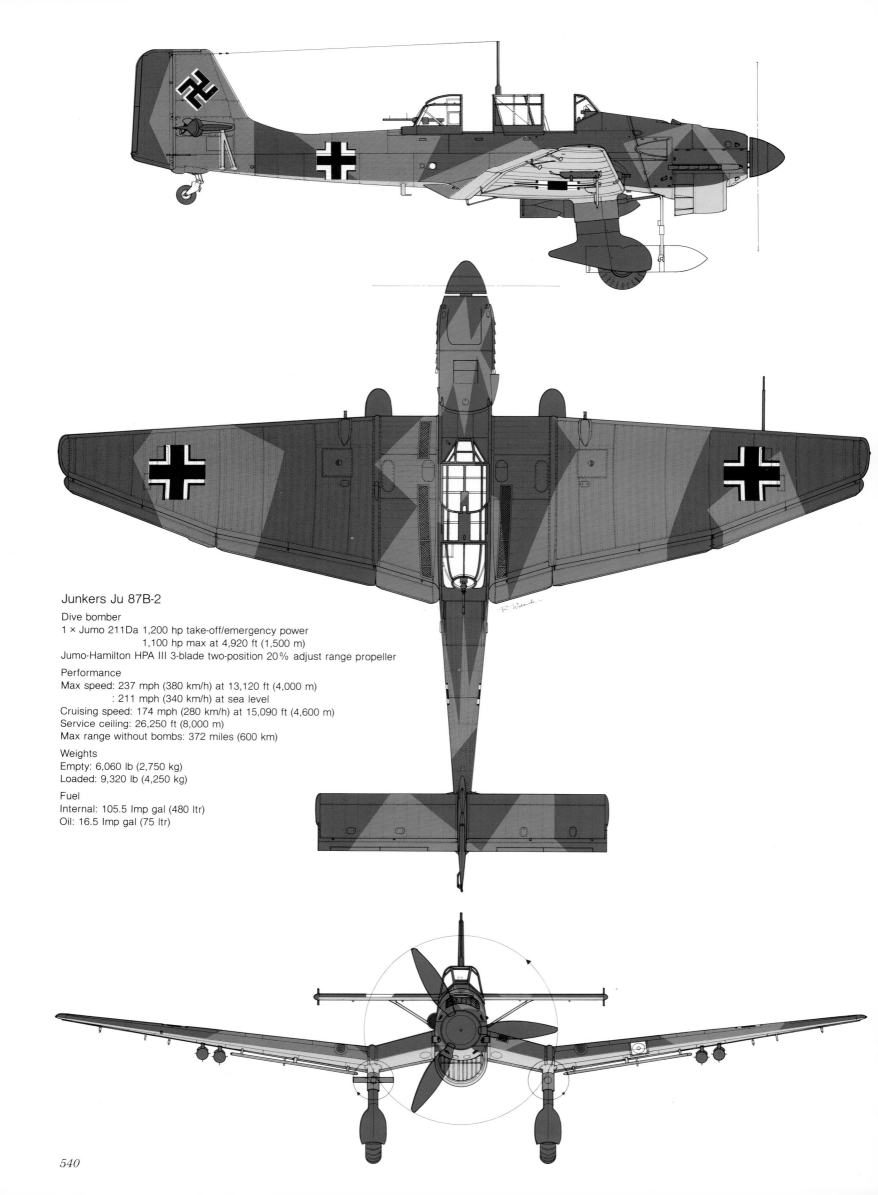

Junkers Ju 87B-2

Dive bomber
1 × Jumo 211Da 1,200 hp take-off/emergency power
        1,100 hp max at 4,920 ft (1,500 m)
Jumo-Hamilton HPA III 3-blade two-position 20% adjust range propeller

Performance
Max speed: 237 mph (380 km/h) at 13,120 ft (4,000 m)
       : 211 mph (340 km/h) at sea level
Cruising speed: 174 mph (280 km/h) at 15,090 ft (4,600 m)
Service ceiling: 26,250 ft (8,000 m)
Max range without bombs: 372 miles (600 km)

Weights
Empty: 6,060 lb (2,750 kg)
Loaded: 9,320 lb (4,250 kg)

Fuel
Internal: 105.5 Imp gal (480 ltr)
Oil: 16.5 Imp gal (75 ltr)

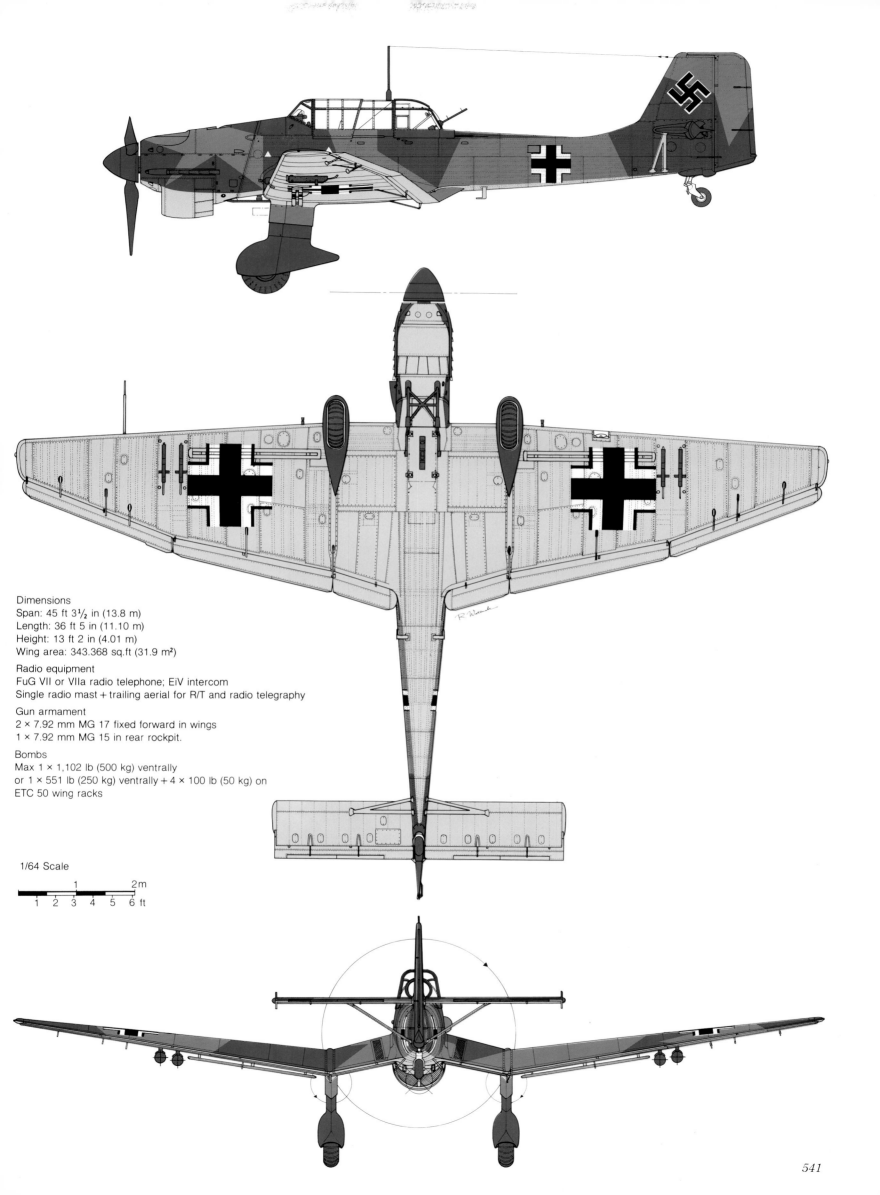

Dimensions
Span: 45 ft 3½ in (13.8 m)
Length: 36 ft 5 in (11.10 m)
Height: 13 ft 2 in (4.01 m)
Wing area: 343.368 sq.ft (31.9 m²)

Radio equipment
FuG VII or VIIa radio telephone; EiV intercom
Single radio mast + trailing aerial for R/T and radio telegraphy

Gun armament
2 × 7.92 mm MG 17 fixed forward in wings
1 × 7.92 mm MG 15 in rear rockpit.

Bombs
Max 1 × 1,102 lb (500 kg) ventrally
or 1 × 551 lb (250 kg) ventrally + 4 × 100 lb (50 kg) on
ETC 50 wing racks

1/64 Scale

1   2m
1   2   3   4   5   6 ft

The naval "Caesar"

In 1938, while construction work was still in progress on the first German aircraft carrier (to be launched on 8 December that year as *Graf Zeppelin*), and the second about to be laid down, it was decided that their air striking power should include a contingent of dive bombers. Work on this navalized and slightly smaller version of the Ju 87B began in the same year. However, contrary to the generally accepted view the development of the Ju 87C version was not abandoned in 1939 but completed in the summer of 1941, and the definitive Ju 87C-1 underwent its full trials at Rechlin in 1941–42.

During this development work great attention was paid to making the aircraft float for prolonged periods in case of forced landings on the water. These efforts were successful and subsequent tests determined that in calm seas the Ju 87C could remain afloat for as long as three days – long enough to be found by the carrier or rescue vessels. This was achieved by internal structural changes which incorporated four inflatable rubberised sacks (two in the wing leading-edges and two in the fuselage) with a total capacity volume of 550 Imp gal (2,500 l). The aircraft was fully stressed for catapult launches, and had other naval equipment: catapult spools, quick fuel release (1 min to empty all tanks), jettisonable undercarriage for ditching in water, landing hook and manually folding wings (time: 1 min; the wings could not be folded with attached drop tanks). The Ju 87C also carried a standard dinghy and was equipped with full heating installation.

Two modified Ju 87Bs were flown as Ju 87C prototypes during March and April 1939. The ten Ju 87C-0 pre-production aircraft were completed at the Weser plant, Tempelhof, in the summer of 1939 and delivered to 4. (Stuka)/*Trägergruppe* 186 which had been activated on Ju 87As at Kiel-Holtenau in December 1938. As such, it took part in the Polish campaign in September 1939, flying a mixture of Ju 87C-0s and B-1s.

When the construction work on the *Graf Zeppelin* was suspended in October 1939, the first batch of the 170 Ju 87C-1s ordered just two months before was already on the production line at the Weser works. However, only the first few machines were completed in the spring of 1940 and delivered to Rechlin, the remaining Ju 87C-1s being reconverted to normal Ju 87B-2 standards and delivered as such. Nevertheless, trials went on in case of need (work on the *Graf Zeppelin* was in fact later temporarily resumed), and the final Rechlin test report on the Ju 87C-1 was prepared in June 1942.

The far-reaching "Richard"

Work on this extended-range (R for *Reichweite*, range) anti-shipping version began in 1938, and the first variant, Ju 87R-1, went into production in 1939. Deliveries to the *Luftwaffe* began in early 1940, the first batch re-equipping I/St.G 1 before the invasion of Denmark and Norway. These were also the only Stukas participating in that campaign.

The Ju 87R was basically a B-series airframe incorporating some structural changes that allowed the installation of two additional fuel tanks in wing outer panels, and the fuel

Ju 87R-2s of St.G 2 over the Western Front. Each aircraft is carrying two 300 ltr (66 Imp gal) underwing drop tanks. (BUNDESARCHIV)

system was redesigned to use two 66 Imp gal (300 l) underwing drop tanks which were carried instead of wing bomb racks. This increased tankage almost doubled the effective range of the Stuka, although the offensive load was restricted to one 551 lb (250 kg) bomb. The Ju 87R first became operational off Norway in April 1940, and subsequently proved very successful in the anti-shipping role in the Mediterranean area in the spring and summer of 1941. The "Richard" was used in four variants differing only in minor equipment changes:

Ju 87R-1
Basic anti-shipping dive bomber
Ju 87R-2
As R-1 but with revised radio equipment. First operational off Sicily in April 1941; also in North Africa.
Ju 87R-2/trop
Field modification; engine air intake dust filter, revised lubrication system, emergency food and water packs.
Ju 87R-3
Limited series with different radio equipment
Ju 87R-4
As Ju 87R-2/trop but all tropical modifications incorporated on production line as standard.

The "Dora" arrives late

The Ju 87D was the outcome of the RLM's operational evaluation studies of the Polish campaign which indicated the need for the Stuka to carry heavier bombs, have an improved combat radius and incorporate better defensive armament. The key to this problem was a more powerful engine combined with an aerodynamically cleaner airframe. Work on this refined Ju 87 began in the spring of 1940, and the new version was officially designated Ju 87D in May. However, the intended powerplant, the new Jumo 211F, ran into serious development problems within a few months and the maiden flight of the first Ju 87D prototype (Ju 87 V21), planned for December 1940, had to be postponed. In the same year, Chief designer Dipl. Ing. Hermann Pohlmann, the creator of the Ju 87, left Junkers to join Blohm & Voss at Hamburg. It was also obvious that the Ju 87 had reached the end of its design potential, and the "Dora" was just an interim measure pending the availability of better aircraft.

Fortunately the Junkers engine works had another advanced powerplant under development, the Jumo 211J, and the first two Ju 87D prototypes were fitted with these engines

Ju 87D-5 of St.G 1 winging over before dive-bombing Soviet ground targets. This particular air-craft is carrying an SC 500 bomb ventrally and two SC 250 *Stabos* (from *Stachelbombe*, spike bomb) under the wings. (BUNDESARCHIV)

in the spring of 1941. Acceptance trials at Rechlin began in May 1941, when output of the Ju 87 was already being run down. Suddenly in the autumn of 1941 full production of the Ju 87D was ordered as an emergency measure. A total of 917 Ju 87Ds were to be delivered to the *Luftwaffe* in 1942.

The main reason for this was the failure of the expected replacement, the Me 210. Originally intended simply as a more powerful refinement of the Bf 110 and ordered as such in 1939, the Me 210 turned out to be anything but that. Without consulting Udet or other RLM officials, Professor Messerschmitt had designed a completely new aircraft, not less than 1,000 of which were ordered "off the drawing board" before the first prototype had even flown. Moreover, no change was made in the original delivery dates commenc-

ing in the spring of 1941. In practice, the basic design faults of the Me 210 could only be rectified by an almost complete redesign resulting in the Me 410 which did not appear until late 1942. This dismal failure was to cost Professor Messerschmitt the chairmanship of his concern. In the meantime, the *Luftwaffe* dive-bomber and ground-attack units had to operate with the Ju 87D.

The most obvious external changes characterizing the Ju 87D were the improved cowling shape, with the oil cooler transferred underneath the engine and the coolant radiator beneath the wing centre section, and the more streamlined cockpit canopy. The main undercarriage fairings were slimmer also, and the vertical tail surfaces slightly enlarged. Internally, the most important changes were the increased fuel tankage (same as on the Ju 87R) and added armour protection for the crew and equipment. The Jumo 211J-1 engine fitted on the Ju 87D-1 had many advanced features, such as a pressurized coolant system, induction air cooler, fully shrouded supercharger impeller, strengthened crankshaft and modified boost and injection pump controls.

The "Dora" was first operational on the Eastern Front in early February 1942, and subsequently served in North Africa, Italy and the Eastern Mediterranean. But by then the Stuka scare had passed, and the Ju 87D could sustain the fearsome reputation of the Bertha for just a few months before the increasingly more numerous Allied fighters practically precluded all daylight operations. The only exceptions were areas in which the *Luftwaffe* managed to hold a temporary local air superiority as on the Eastern Front, which was to be Dora's main battleground.

Gradual changes and improvements based on operational experience or requirements are reflected in the Ju 87D variants:

Ju 87D-1

The basic "Dora", and first of the most widely produced series. First operational on the Eastern Front in February 1942. Like all subsequent Ju 87D variants, often flown without mainwheel fairings due to the soft conditions of landing grounds in the East. Could be adapted for close-support tasks, with provisions for underwing gun packs. Retroactively fitted with explosive bolts to jettison the main undercarriage.

Ju 87D-1/trop

Tropicalized variant with engine air intake dust filters, protected lubrication system and desert survival equipment. First operational over Bir Hakeim in May 1942.

Ju 87D-2

Strengthened rear fuselage and combined tailwheel/hook for towing the Go 242 cargo glider. Intended for use in North Africa and the Mediterranean area.

Ju 87D-3

First specialized ground-attack variant. Basic "Dora" airframe with added armour protection for the crew, engine and radiators. Retained wing dive brakes, but deleted propeller-driven dive sirens in undercarriage fairings. Late production series had completely mass-balanced ailerons. In production from late 1942; operational principally on the Eastern Front. Frequently carried disintegrating plywood containers with 92 4.4 lb (2 kg) SD 2 anti-personnel bombs on underwing racks.

Total production amounted to 1,559 Ju 87D-3s completed at the Lemwerder (559) and Tempelhof (960) plants.

Ju 87D-4

Intended as a torpedo-bomber to carry one 1,687 lb (765 kg) LT F5b or similar torpedo. Evolved to a June 1941 requirement, only a small number of Ju 87D-1s and D-3s were so converted. None used operationally, and all aircraft reconverted to previous standards.

Ju 87D-5

Close-support aircraft. Basic Ju 87D-3 airframe but with tapered and extended wings. Deleted wing dive brakes (except on the first production series). Fixed armament changed to two 20 mm MG 151/20 cannon. Reinforced ground observation panel in the cockpit floor, mass-balanced ailerons, undercarriage jettison facility and revised bomb rack arrangement on late production aircraft. Production ceased at the Weser Bremen-Lemwerder plant in July 1944 after the completion of 771 Ju 87D-5s. Operational on the Eastern Front. Occasionally used 8.8 lb (4 kg) SD 4/HL hollow-charge bombs, fitted with rocket boosters, against Soviet tank concentrations.

Ju 87D-6

Proposed as a "rationalized" version in 1943, but not developed.

Ju 87D-7

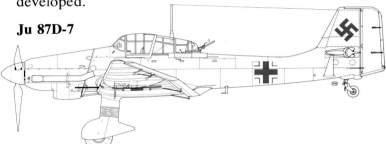

Night ground-attack bomber. Conversion of the Ju 87D-3 airframe and re-engined with the Jumo 211P of 1,500/1,410 hp with exhaust flame dampers and night flying equipment. No dive brakes; jettisonable main undercarriage; D-5 standard fixed and defensive gun armament. First Ju 87 night bomber, became operational on the Eastern Front in December 1943. Also used on the Western Front, in the Balkans and Italy until the end of hostilities.

Ju 87D-8

Night ground attack. Conversions of D-5 airframes to similar standards as the D-7 (Jumo 211P engine with exhaust flame dampers, night flying equipment). In early 1945 some Ju 87D-8s also flown in daytime with removed exhaust flame dambers.

Ju 87E-1

Proposed navalized version of the Ju 87D-1, intended to carry one LT F5W torpedo. Project work began in July 1941, and a modified early "Dora" designated Ju 87D-1to (for "Torpedo") was test-flown at the Travemünde test centre in spring and summer 1942. Development abandoned when construction work on the carrier *Graf Zeppelin* stopped for good in February 1943.

Ju 87F

Proposed development of the Ju 87D. Initial project submitted in late 1940 envisaged the use of the new Jumo 213 engine of over 1,700 hp then under development and featured reinforced undercarriage with larger tyres and a completely revised wing structure of increased span. After examination the proposal was rejected by the RLM in spring 1941 because the estimated performance was considered insufficient improvement to justify production. Project reworked as Ju 187.

Ju 87G-1 of 10.(Pz)/SG 3 taking off on a sortie against Soviet armour.

(BUNDESARCHIV)

Ju 87G-1

Specialized tank destroyer evolved in 1942–43. Basically a conversion of the Ju 87D-3 with attachment points to carry two 37 mm Flak 18 (BK 3,7) cannon in streamlined fairings outboard of the main undercarriage legs. (Cannon attachment points could be exchanged for bomb racks.) Standard defensive armament; often had improved ground vision panel in the cockpit floor.

The use of large-calibre cannon to combat the increasing number of Soviet tanks from the air was proposed by front-line aircrews in summer 1942, and first trials with various aircraft types (Ju 88P, Bf 110F and Ju 87D) were carried out in late 1942, when the Ju 87D was adjudged by far the best. Deliveries of converted D-3 airframes commenced immediately afterwards. On operations, some Ju 87G-1s were flown with, others without, the fixed wing armament. Operational principally on the Eastern Front, but small numbers also used in North Africa in spring 1943 and on the Western Front late in 1944 and early in 1945.

Ju 87G-2

Tank destroyer. As Ju 87G-1, but conversion of the Ju 87D-5 airframes. Deleted fixed wing armament. Some machines fitted with exhaust flame dampers and used at night. Operational areas as Ju 87G-1.

Ju 87H series

Dual-control trainers for conversion training of ex-bomber and other pilots. The Ju 87H-1, -3, -5, -7 and -8 were conver-

sions of Ju 87D-1, -3, -5, -7 and -8 dive bombers respectively incorporating the following major changes: gunner's seat replaced by a forward-facing seat from the Ar 96 trainer; dual controls and instrumentation; new rear cockpit canopy with side blisters; deleted armament and wing bomb racks. Some impressed into operational service in spring 1945.

Ju 187

Proposed second Ju 87 replacement after rejection of the Ju 87F. Project envisaged a heavily armoured two-seat low-wing aircraft loosely based on the Ju 87 (and with some influence of the Soviet Il-2 *Shturmovik*) powered by a 1,776/1,480 hp Jumo 213A engine. Main undercarriage designed to turn through 90° to retract backwards into wing wells. The proposed gun armament consisted of two 20 mm MG 151/20 cannon fixed forward in the wings and a remotely controlled dorsal barbette with one 15 mm MG 151 and one 13 mm MG 131; the offensive load included one 2,205 lb (1,000 kg) bomb ventrally and attachment points for four 551 lb (250 kg) bombs or gun or rocket packs outboard of the main undercarriage legs.

Allocated the RLM designation 8-187, design work on this new aircraft was completed in summer 1943 but the performance estimates were only slightly better than those of the Ju 87D (estimated maximum speed: 248 mph [400 km/hr]) and the development of the Ju 187 was cancelled in autumn 1943.

Ju 187 project

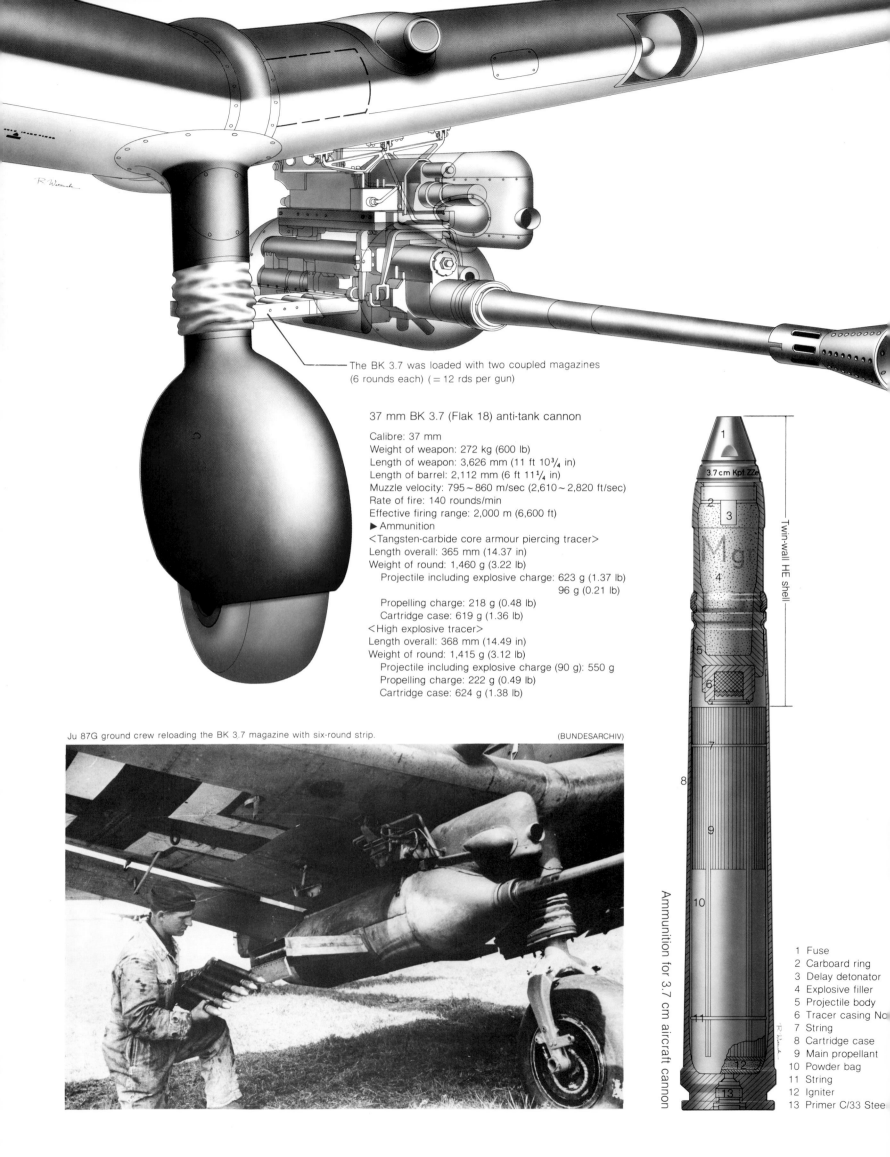

The BK 3.7 was loaded with two coupled magazines
(6 rounds each) (= 12 rds per gun)

37 mm BK 3.7 (Flak 18) anti-tank cannon

Calibre: 37 mm
Weight of weapon: 272 kg (600 lb)
Length of weapon: 3,626 mm (11 ft 10¾ in)
Length of barrel: 2,112 mm (6 ft 11¼ in)
Muzzle velocity: 795~860 m/sec (2,610~2,820 ft/sec)
Rate of fire: 140 rounds/min
Effective firing range: 2,000 m (6,600 ft)
▶ Ammunition
<Tangsten-carbide core armour piercing tracer>
Length overall: 365 mm (14.37 in)
Weight of round: 1,460 g (3.22 lb)
   Projectile including explosive charge: 623 g (1.37 lb)
                                     96 g (0.21 lb)

   Propelling charge: 218 g (0.48 lb)
   Cartridge case: 619 g (1.36 lb)
<High explosive tracer>
Length overall: 368 mm (14.49 in)
Weight of round: 1,415 g (3.12 lb)
   Projectile including explosive charge (90 g): 550 g
   Propelling charge: 222 g (0.49 lb)
   Cartridge case: 624 g (1.38 lb)

Ju 87G ground crew reloading the BK 3.7 magazine with six-round strip.

(BUNDESARCHIV)

3.7 cm Kpf. ZZe

Mg

Twin-wall HE shell

Ammunition for 3.7 cm aircraft cannon

1 Fuse
2 Carboard ring
3 Delay detonator
4 Explosive filler
5 Projectile body
6 Tracer casing No
7 String
8 Cartridge case
9 Main propellant
10 Powder bag
11 String
12 Igniter
13 Primer C/33 Stee

World War II

On 1 June, 1939, three months before the start of hostilities, the existing Stuka formations were redesignated once again according to their re-organized regional origin:

I/St.G 160 became I/St.G 1 (Insterburg)
I/St. G. 162 became II/St.G 2 (Stolp-Reitz)
I/St.G 163 became I/St. G 2 (Cottbus)
II/St.G 163 became III/St.G 2 (Langensalza)
I/St.G 165 (Kitzingen) became I/St.G 77 (Brieg)
II/St.G 165 (Schweinfurt) became II/St.G 77 (Breslau)
III/St.G 165 (Wertheim) became III/St.G 51
I/St.G 168 (Graz since 1 March,1938) became I/St.G 76

The odd unit out was 4.(Stuka)/Tr.Gr. 186 formed on 1 October, 1938, the carrier dive bomber *Staffel* intended for the *Graf Zeppelin* then under construction. It remained operational as an independent *Staffel* until 8 November, 1939, later being reinforced to full *Gruppe* strength as I/Tr.G 186 (sometimes referred to as I/St.G 186).

Poland (1 September – 27 September, 1939)

A total of 1,939 combat aircraft were deployed by the *Luftwaffe* against Poland, including 366 Stukas, of which 348 were serviceable on 1 September.

This concentration of airpower was opposed by some 800 Polish aircraft of which only 463 could be regarded as first-line. This total included 277 fighters which, although highly manoeuvrable, were of obsolescent design.

In this first *Blitzkrieg* campaign the Stukas proved a decisive weapon and an outstanding success, and their achievements more than justified all expectations. In some cases the target accuracy was an amazing ± 30 m when bombing from near-vertical dives, and evidence of Ju 87 precision attacks was abundant. Apart from various important pin-point targets on land, such as bridges, road or rail junctions, armoured trains, individual factory buildings and radio stations, on 3 September the Stukas also hit the 1,540-ton Polish destroyer *Wicher* and the 2,227-ton minelayer *Gryf* at Hela, the first warships sunk by dive bombers in World War II.

An important contributing factor to the quick German victory was the demoralizing effect of repeated diving attacks on troops (and particularly cavalry), in some cases causing panic. From then on the screaming, diving Stuka became the symbol of this new kind of war, and remained so in imagination and reality for some time to come. Whilst this was a most gratifying boon for the Stuka supporters, it blinded them to the fact that successes were only made possible because the Stukas could operate almost without enemy interference in the air. The attrition was lower than expected from such intensive use of airpower. Although the *Luftwaffe* lost 285 aircraft of various types (plus another 229, more than 50 per cent damaged), only 31 Stukas were lost in action, most of them ground fire.

Ju 87B-1 of 1./St.G 1 over Poland in September, 1939.   (BUNDESARCHIV)

It was during the Polish campaign that names of such Stuka pioneers and leaders as *Oberst* Günther Schwarzkopff (I/St.G 77), *Major* Oskar Dinort (I/St.G 2), *Hptm* Walter Sigel (I/St.G 76) and *Hptm* Paul-Werner Hozzel (I/St.G 1) first gained prominence. Apart from *Oberst* Schwarzkopff who was to be killed in action over France eight months later, the others went on to leave their mark in military history: Oskar Dinort for inventing the highly successful stand-off impact fuse (later known as *Dinortstab*), Walter Sigel for his pinpoint precision attacks, and Paul-Werner Hozzel for his skilful and successful anti-shipping attacks in the Mediterranean.

Among the more notable Ju 87 exploits during this brief campaign was the daring low-level attack on 1 September by three aircraft led by *Hptm* Dinort on a Polish blockhouse controlling the demolition charges attached to the vital railway bridge over the Vistula at Tczew (Dirschau) – due to an error almost a quarter of an hour before the official declaration of war. (It was accurate but only partly successful – part of the bridge was blown up by the Polish pioneers shortly afterwards.) Apart from actually "opening World War II," the Stukas can also claim another unusual credit: a Ju 87B of I/St.G 2 piloted by *Uffz* Frank Neubert shot down the first enemy aircraft of the war, a Polish P.11 fighter, on the same morning. By the end of the Polish campaign the Stuka was firmly established as a decisive weapon and played an increasingly important role in the plans then being finalized for the Western campaign.

Norway (9 April – 9 June, 1940)

Unternehmen Weserübung (Weser Exercise) was the first true combined operation carried out by the armed forces of any nation. It was also the first time paratroops were used to capture airfields, and the first large-scale air transport operation, including air supply of large troop units. Although fighting in Norway will always be associated with the town of Narvik, the main outlet for Swedish iron ore – and the main reason for the campaign – this operation also had a much wider significance. Apart from the important support role of air power, it also convincingly demonstrated the effect dive-bombing attacks had on naval vessels sailing without air cover.

A total of 878 *Luftwaffe* aircraft were assigned to *Weserübung* consisting of 240 bombers and Stukas, 95 fighters and *Zerstörer* and 534 transports, reconnaissance and other types (including seaplanes). During the main phase of fighting in May this force was increased by an additional 70 bombers, 20 fighters, 60 seaplanes and ten Stukas, in part as replacement for losses. The expected opposition was negligible comprising some 20 biplane fighters in Norway, and every effort was made to capture the airfields to deny their possible use by British aircraft. This time, the Stuka contingent was small – only I/St.G 1 (*Hptm* Hozzel) with 40 Ju 87Bs (replaced in mid-May by longer-ranging Ju 87R-1s). Nevertheless, this small force of dive bombers (initially only about 20 aircraft on Norwegian soil) made an important contribution to the German operations on land, and particularly against Allied warships and transports off Norway.

In fact, the danger posed by this incomplete *Gruppe* of Stukas was considered so great that on 14 April the RAF mounted a long-range (over 450 miles) bombing raid from Scotland to Stavanger-Sola, the temporary base of I/St.G 1. (It was unsuccessful; only one Ju 87 was damaged.) On 17 April the cruiser HMS *Suffolk* was ordered to shell the Stuka base at Stavanger and, caught in the open seas by He 111s and Ju 87s on withdrawal, had to suffer 33 air attacks (12 by Stukas) lasting for seven hours. No damaging hits were scored, but the message was clear: ships without air cover were running a great risk when sailing within the range of enemy bombers.

As if to emphasize this point, during the evacuation of the so-called "Maurice Force" from Namsos between 30 April and 3 May, Stukas sank the destroyer HMS *Afridi* and bombed the French destroyer *Bison* to standstill. On 14–15 May I/St.G 1 hit and so badly damaged the 11,440-ton troop transport *Chrobry* near Bodø that she had to be abandoned; and finally on 28 May the same Stukas damaged the AA cruiser HMS *Cairo*, flagship of the British admiral in charge of the Narvik operation. But this was also the first time the Ju 87s had run into determined opposition by Hurricane I and Gloster Gladiator fighters flown off British aircraft carriers, and they were forced to abandon regular diving attacks to defend themselves. The Norwegian campaign introduced a number of new factors in warfare and the lessons were there for all to learn.

From the *Luftwaffe* point of view it had been another victory, achieved under far more difficult conditions than in Poland. The Ju 87R long-range anti-shipping dive bomber had been blooded in combat, and a lot of new and valuable experience gained in dive bombing of shipping targets. And not only that, the balance was most favourable – only 16 Stukas (including four shot down in air combat) were lost in action.

Such details (and even some of the lessons) were almost immediately forgotten because of the name the Stuka was making for itself in another campaign which in the meantime had already reached its climax.

Western Campaign
(10 May – 22 June 1940)

The *Luftwaffe* formations deployed for this campaign totalled 3,834 aircraft consisting of 1,482 bombers and Stukas, 42 close-support aircraft, 1,016 fighters, 248 *Zerstörer* and 1,046 reconnaissance, transport and other types. This concentration of offensive and support airpower was opposed by 2,372 first-line Allied aircraft – which, however, did not have or operate under a unified command. These Allied air forces were composed as follows (operational strength on 10 May, 1940):

France – 764 fighters, 260 bombers, 180 reconnaissance and 400 army co-operation aircraft
British AASF (Advanced Air Striking Force) – 261 fighters, 135 bombers and 60 reconnaissance aircraft
Belgium – 81 fighters and 99 other types
Holland – 58 fighters (35 single-, 23 twin-engined) and 74 other types.

(It has to be added that in the case of the French *Armée de l'Air* only the modern aircraft have been included; there were also several hundred more dated types, quite a few of which participated in the war in some capacity. Also, several hundred new aircraft were produced during hostilities and a number delivered to operational units.)

The main effort of the German assault was indicated by the concentration of all *Stukagruppen* in *Luftflotte* 2 against France. This force totalled 380 Ju 87s of which 358 were available for operations on 10 May 1940.

The German Western campaign, having been postponed several times, was finally launched at 0535 hrs on 10 May 1940 and unleashed the full fury of another *Blitzkrieg* upon Holland, Belgium and France. It was to be surprisingly quick and decisive and a textbook example of modern mobile warfare: surprise air attacks to destroy as much as possible of the enemy air force on the ground; selective use of paratroops to take key objectives; concentrated use of air power to breach the enemy defences; and intense and close air support of advancing troops. In all this, the Stuka formations again played a major and often decisive role, repeating the success of the Polish campaign on a larger and more convincing scale. As before, it was a matter of achieving aerial superiority within the shortest possible time, and then proceeding according to the proven recipe: Stukas to shatter the resistance; breakthrough by armoured forces; and "pincer" drives deep into the enemy rear. The fighting took place in almost ideal conditions for this kind of warfare, with a well developed network of roads to speed the advance of motorized troops, and the whole campaign had a limited objective – the only way it could succeed. What is more important, the Stukas were once again able to operate without much enemy interference in the air; half of the *Luftwaffe* force committed to battle consisted of fighters to ensure that.

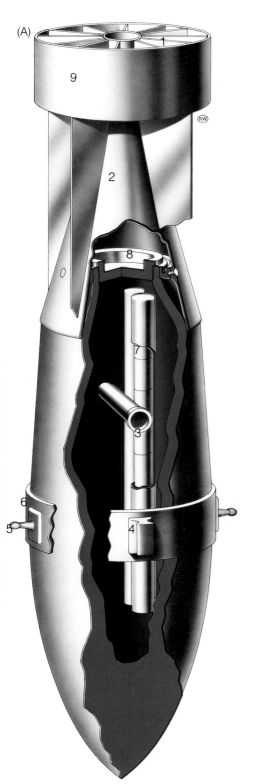

▲
1 Tail fins
2 Tail cone
3 Base plate
4 End plate
5 Bomb body
6 Explosive cavity
7 Suspension lug
8 Fuse pocket

◄ 1 Tail fins
2 Tail cone
3 Fuse pocket
4 Suspension lug
5 Trunnion bolt
6 Suspension band
7 Central exploder tube
8 Base plate
9 Ring strut

(A) PC 1000

1,000 kg (2,205 lb) cylindrical armour piercing bomb. The bomb body is made of one-piece forged steel. The tail unit is constructed of magnesium alloy.

Length overall: 217 cm (85.5 in)
Body length: 149 cm (58.5 in)
Body diameter: 50 cm (19.8 in)
Weight of filling: 160 kg (353 lb)

(B) SC 50 Bi

50 kg (110 lb) high explosive cylindrical general purpose bomb. The bomb body is made of one-piece cast steel. The tail cone is sheet steel constructed in four pieces, and welded together.

Length overall: 117 cm (46.1 in)
Body length: 76 cm (30.0 in)
Body diameter: 20 cm (7.9 in)
Weight of filling: 24.4 kg (54 lb)

Ju 87B ground crew use the standard bomb trolly to load the ventral 551 lb SC 250 (above) and manhandle the 110 lb SC 50 underwing bombs (below). (BUNDESARCHIV)

As expected, most resistance was met at the beginning and the *Luftwaffe* losses reflect the intensity of fighting, totalling 304 aircraft (plus 51 damaged) on the first day of this campaign. Under conditions of almost complete aerial superiority and with fighters sweeping the sky clear ahead of them, the Stukas did well – only 14 were lost during the first four days of fighting, increasing to 55 by 17 May (not counting damaged aircraft crash-landing at their own bases). Another week later the pace was beginning to tell. From the outset, the *Luftwaffe* had been intended and prepared only for short champaigns of limited range and objective, a fact too readily overlooked.

Beginning 25 May the first Stuka formations were switched to attacks on shipping off Boulogne, Calais and then Dunkirk, and, for the first time faced some determined fighter opposition. "Operation Dynamo", the evacuation of British (and some French) troops from France, ran for seven days beginning 28 May and, although a success, the cost was high – nine Allied destroyers and 20 larger and smaller transports were sunk, and 27 destroyers and smaller warships and numerous transports damaged. Due to fog or low cloud the Stukas could only operate over Dunkirk for four days when, according to official German records, 11 Ju 87s were lost to British fighters. For that, the Stukas claimed the largest share of Allied shipping losses due to *Luftwaffe* operations.

Even before the end of "Dynamo" the Stukas were moved south to force a decision during the second phase of the French campaign. For the last week of the campaign the Stukas had almost everything their way, with only an occasional attack by French fighters. The last two Stukas lost before the Armistice collided in mid-air on a transfer flight on 18 June, 1940.

After the victorious conclusion of the French campaign the word "Stuka" was on everybody's lips – the all-conquering "wonder weapon", the very image of *Blitzkrieg*, and the German propaganda machine did not waste any time in exploiting this reputation to the full for domestic and export purposes. Soon after the French campaign, a special Stuka song was composed. Not many months later there was also a film entitled *Stukas!* which was immensely popular in Germany and was also shown in quite a few foreign countries. The Stuka had indeed arrived in great style.

Stukas against Britain
(4 July – 14 November, 1940)

After the conclusion of fighting in France the Stuka units were first regrouped and then re-organized. It was also time for rest and replacement of aircraft and crews in preparation for the next target that was obvious to all – Britain.

This campaign consisted of two distinct kinds of operations: Stuka attacks on British shipping in the Channel and selected ports; and then starting from "*Adlertag*" (13 August), dive-bombing attacks mainly on land targets within reach. The first stage, which began with an attack on the Royal Navy base at Portland on 4 July 1940, was quite successful from the *Luftwaffe* point of view. On 18 separate raids on shipping targets and British ports over the next 38 days the Stukas lost only 18 of their number in exchange for two smaller warships and ten transports sunk and many damaged – not counting the damage caused to port installations. Most of these raids had taken place with heavy fighter escort that enabled the Stukas to operate almost as before, but the Channel was soon to prove more than "just another, wider river" as it had been described.

By the end of that period the RAF fighter pilots had the measure of their opponents and knew the weak spots. In particular when the Stuka had just commenced its dive, or just after the automatic pull-out at the end of one when, for a few seconds, the Ju 87 was almost helpless. The straight dive itself was a good opportunity to close with a Stuka, and the best time for the AA gunners to score. Most of the Ju 87s dived with their air brakes out, accurately limiting their diving speed.

The ten *Stukagruppen* deployed against Britain in August, 1940 had an establishment strength of 316 Ju 87s but were 36 aircraft short on 13 August, and of the 280 on strength only 220 were serviceable that day.

The second phase of *England-Einsatz* (operations against Britain) was to prove very costly indeed, and destroy the Stuka myth in no uncertain fashion – not that this was admitted officially. But the *Luftwaffe* command now knew what had been obvious to many for some time – the Ju 87 could only operate successfully in conditions of near-complete aerial mastery.

The facts spoke for themselves. Not less than 41

Fully loaded Ju 87B-2 of 3./St.G 2 immediately before take-off during the Battle of Britain.

A section of Ju 87B-2s returning from a raid during the Balkan campaign. (BUNDESARCHIV)

Stukas were lost in just six days beginning 13 August, 1940, not counting more than 20 damaged machines that force-landed or crashed in France on their way back. The Stukas had also had some successes, such as a most effective raid on the RAF airfield at Detling on the first day when they destroyed 22 aircraft on the ground without loss to themselves (the only Stuka raid out of four to find its target that day), and the classic dive-bombing attack on Tangmere on 16 August that devastated the airfield before the four RAF fighter squadrons patrolling in the air could interfere. There were also the precision attacks on several radar stations which, at some cost, succeeded in temporarily putting them out of action – but overall the loss rate was too high.

As a result, the Stuka units were withdrawn on Göring's orders to the Pas de Calais, officially "for the big blow after the RAF resistance had been broken". For a while four *Stukagruppen* were retained within reach of Britain for "special tasks", such as anti-shipping strikes and night operations, but that could not camouflage the true reason. These units did in fact carry out four raids on shipping in the Thames Estuary, the Stukas making their last appearance over British territory on 14 November, 1940, but the Spitfires were waiting as usual.

Another chapter in the career of the Junkers dive bomber had come to an end, but this by no means ended its useful operational life.

The Balkans
(6 April – 27 April 1941)

By early spring 1941 the ill-conceived Italian invasion of Greece had bogged down, and the whole Balkan situation became a problem. The Romanian oil supplies were vital to Germany, and now in addition to the potential Soviet threat there was also the danger of a possible British intervention in that area. British troops were already in Crete, and advancing rapidly into Italian North Africa; Romanian oilfields were within reach of RAF bombers from both. Apart from this, plans for "Operation Barbarossa", the invasion of the Soviet Union, were already at an advanced stage and the southern flank was insecure.

In December 1940, without much enthusiasm, Hitler had ordered preparations for another quick campaign to conquer all Greece if necessary to help his Italian ally, and pressure was put on Yugoslavia to join the Tripartite Pact already signed by Bulgaria and Romania. The Yugoslav government finally resigned on 25 March. By that time there were 490 *Luftwaffe* combat aircraft in Bulgaria and Romania for the planned attack on Greece. This forced comprised 40 bombers, 120 Stukas, 120 single- and 40 twin-engined fighters, and 50 long-range and 120 short-range reconnaissance aircraft. Suddenly, the whole situation changed literally overnight: a military *coup d'etat* in Belgrade on 26 March immediately annulled the Tripartite Pact and adopted an open pro-British attitude. The German reaction was swift – within 12 hours another 480 combat aircraft were ordered into the Balkans, to be followed by a second wave of 120. The Stuka force was doubled before the attack. On 6 April 1941 *Luftwaffe* bombers including Stukas raided Belgrade and targets in northern Greece, and German and Italian troops crossed the frontiers in force.

Once again, the pre-combat balance was most favourable: The Yugoslav Air Force of 420 aircraft could muster just 110 modern fighters of which the 40 or so operational Bf 109Es (of the 100 supplied by Germany) might cause some problems, at least by creating confusion; the Greek Air Force had only 80 aircraft, most of them dated.

Despite the mountainous character of the countries it was to be another typical *Blitzkrieg* campaign. Organized

Ju 87D-1 Cutaway

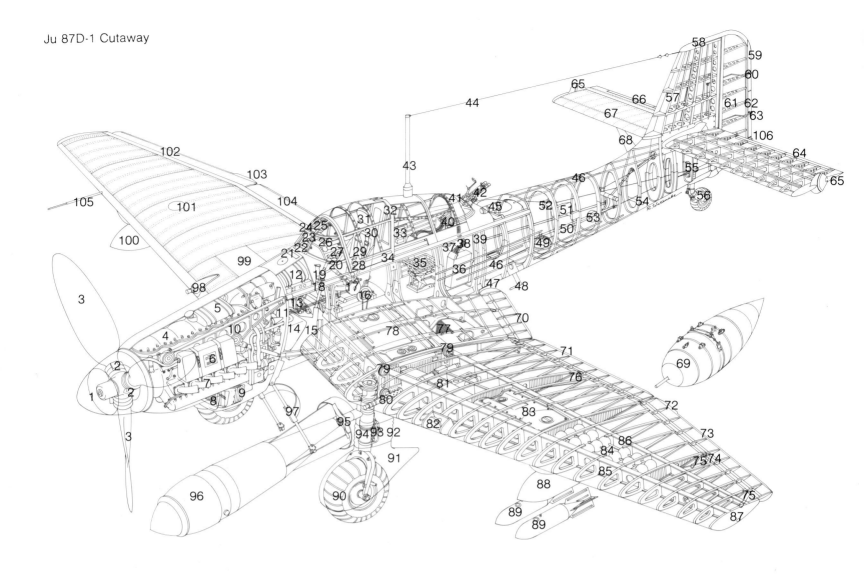

1 Spinner
2 Pitch-change counterweight
3 Junkers VS 11 constant speed propeller
4 Junkers Jumo 211J-1 12-cylinder inverted-vee liquid cooled engine
5 Auxiliary oil tank (5.9 Imp gal/ 26, 8 ltr capacity)
6 Coolant (Glysantin-water) header tank
7 Ejector exhaust stubs
8 Armoured coolant radiator (centre)
9 Oil cooler
10 Magnesium alloy forged engine mount
11 Firewall bulkhead
12 Oil tank (6.8 Imp gal/31 ltr capacity)
13 Rudder pedals
14 Main oil tank (9.9 Imp gal/45 ltr capacity)
15 Ventral vision panel
16 Tail trim control handle
17 Throttle lever
18 Ventral vision panel control
19 Control column
20 Signal flare tube
21 Fresh air intake flap
22 De-icing air intake flap
23 Revi C/12C or D reflector sight
24 Reinforced armoured windscreen
25 Handhold
26 Padded crash bar
27 Switchbox
28 Sliding canopy handgrip
29 Pilot's seat
30 Pilot's back armour (8 mm)
31 Headrest
32 Radio equipment
33 Radio switch control box
34 Upper main stringer

35 Radio-operator/gunner's seat (folding)
36 Ammunition box
37 Spent metal belt link and cartridge container
38 Ammunition belts
39 Armoured bulkhead (8 mm)
40 Sliding canopy handgrip and lever
41 Upper armoured shield
42 Twin 7.92 mm Mauser MG 81Z machine gun on GSL-K 81 mount
43 Radio mast
44 Radio aerial
45 Peil G IV D/F equipment
46 Ω type stringers
47 Lower main stringer
48 Crew entry step (port and starboard)
49 Master compass
50 Elevator control rod
51 First-aid stowage
52 Stiffener
53 Internal elevator mass balance
54 Jacking tube
55 Tailwheel leg
56 Tailwheel
57 Tailfin
58 Rudder horn balance
59 Rudder trim tab
60 Rudder trim tab controls
61 Rudder
62 Rudder balance tab
63 Rudder balance tab rod
64 Elevator tab
65 Faired elevator mass balance
66 Starboard elevator
67 Tailplane
68 Tailplane brace
69 Drop fuel tank (2 x 33 Imp gal/150 ltr)
70 Inboard flap
71 Port outboard flap
72 Aileron trimming tab

73 Port aileron
74 Aileron hinge
75 Aileron mass balance
76 Flap hinge
77 Armoured coolant radiator (port and starboard)
78 Self-sealing port inner wing fuel tank (52.8 Imp gal/240 ltr capacity)
79 Ball-and-socket wing attachment points
80 7.92 mm MG 17 machine gun
81 Ammunition box (1,000 rounds capacity)
82 Landing lamp
83 Self-sealing port outer fuel tank (33 Imp gal/150 ltr capacity)
84 Spherical oxygen bottles
85 Front spar
86 Rear spar
87 Port navigation light
88 SC 250 (551 lb) bomb on multi-purpose carrier
89 SC 50 (110 lb) bombs
90 Mainwheel
91 Wheel spat
92 Leather shroud
93 Torque link arm
94 Oleo-pneumatic shock absorber
95 Siren fairing
96 SC 1000 (2,205 lb) bomb (max 1,800 kg/3,968 lb)
97 Bomb release trapeze
98 Starboard machine gun
99 Ammunition panel
100 SC 250 (551 lb) bomb
101 Fuel filler cap
102 Starboard aileron
103 Aileron trimming tab
104 Starboard flap
105 Pitot head
106 Rear navigation light

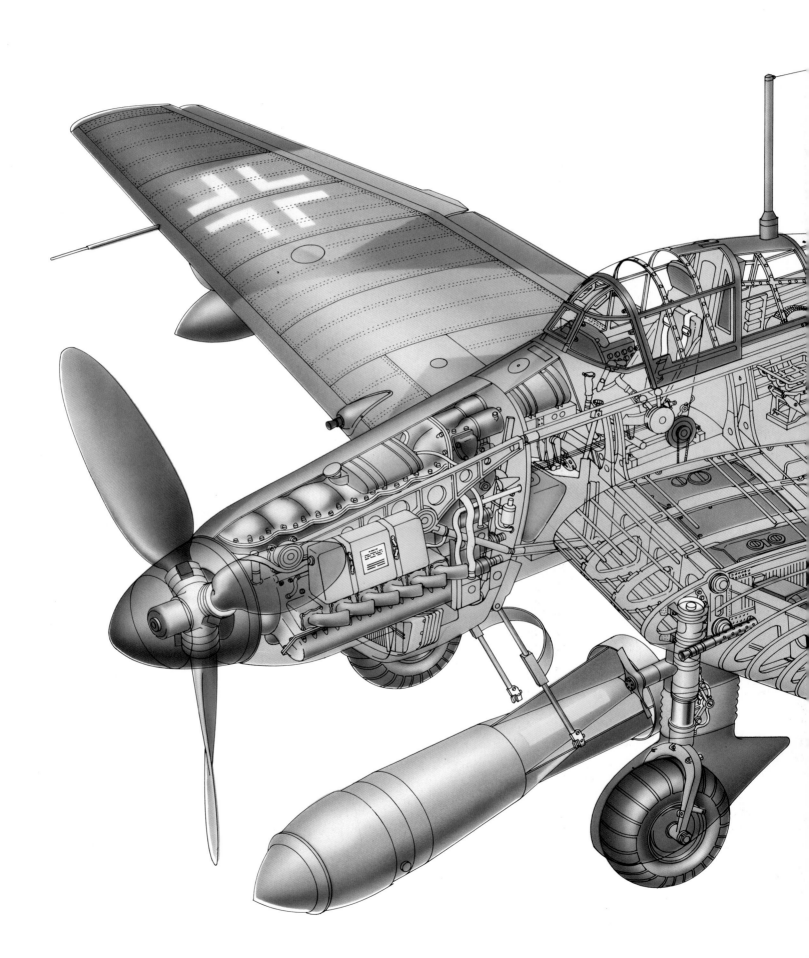

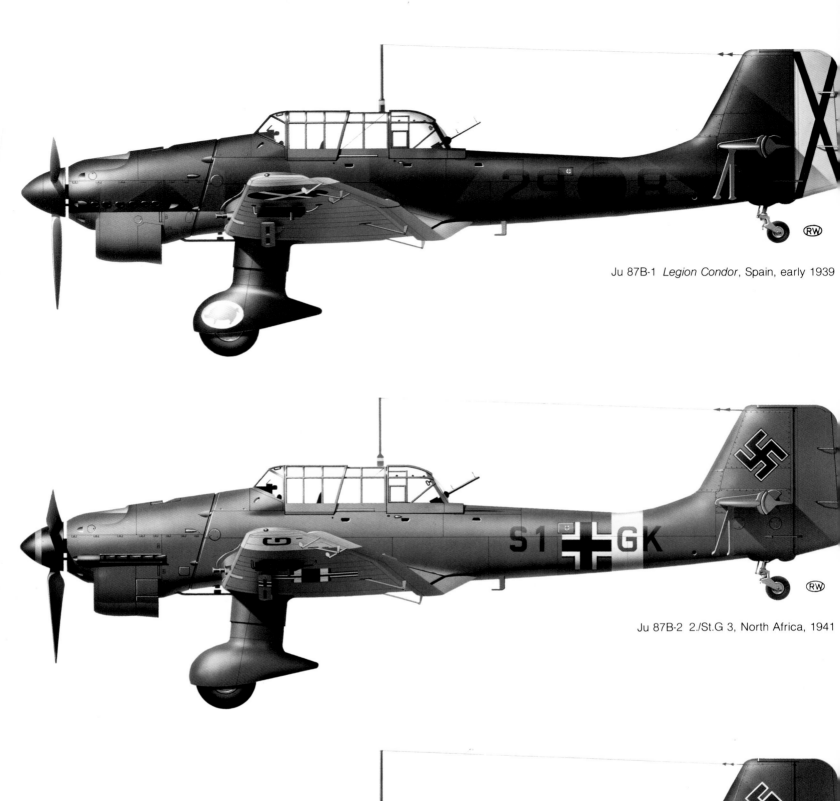

Ju 87B-1 *Legion Condor*, Spain, early 1939

Ju 87B-2 2./St.G 3, North Africa, 1941

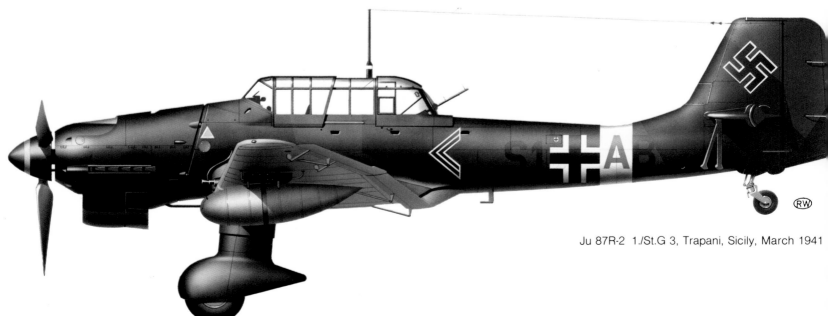

Ju 87R-2 1./St.G 3, Trapani, Sicily, March 1941

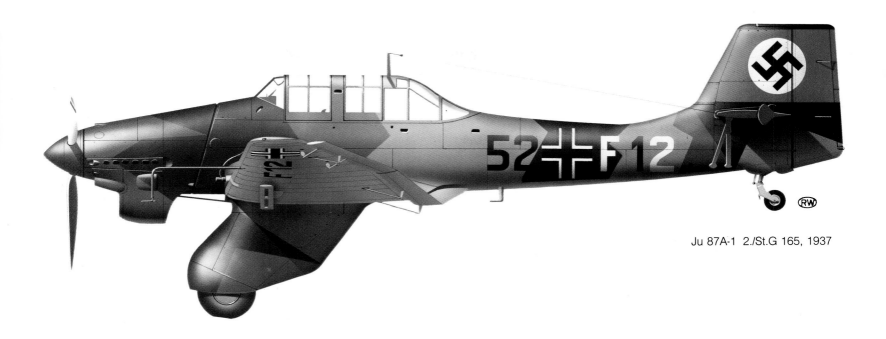

Ju 87A-1 2./St.G 165, 1937

Ju 87A-1 *Jolanthe Kette* of St.G 163, Spain, 1938

Ju 87B-1, 1938

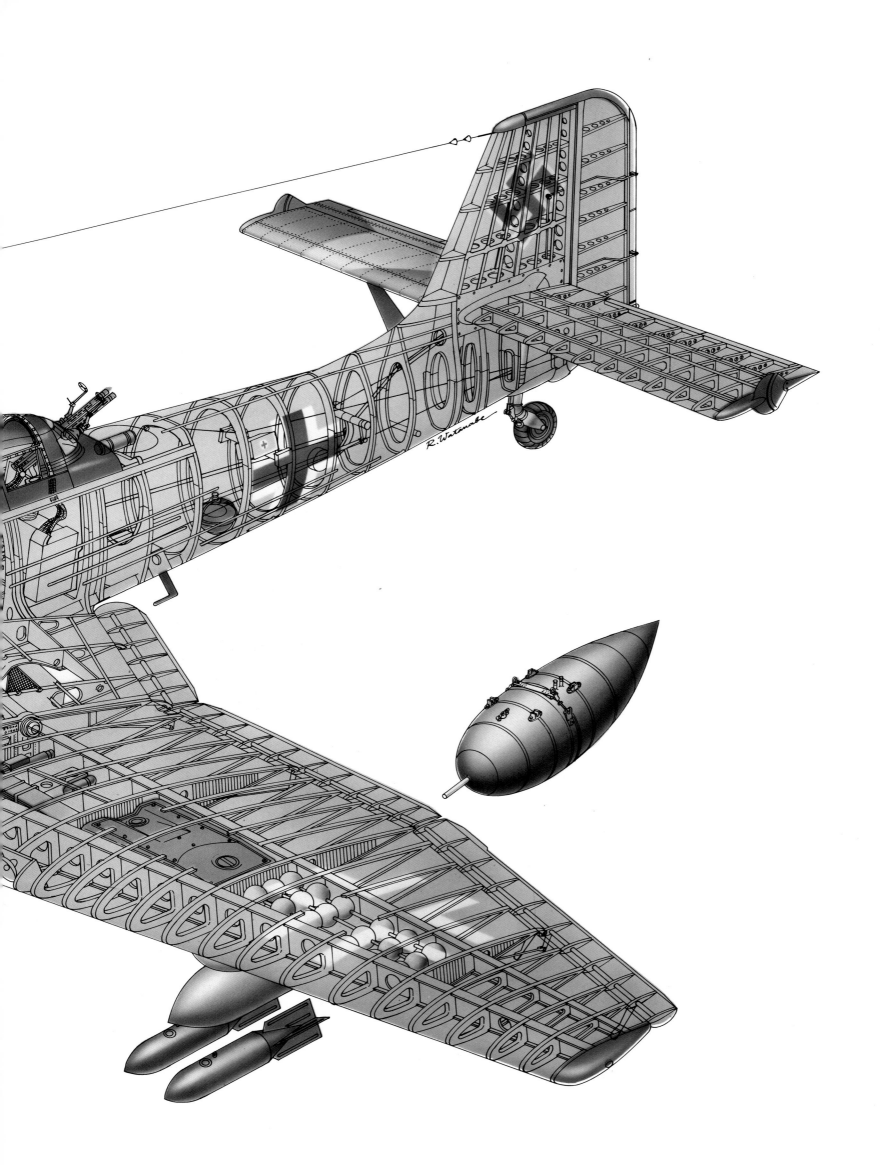

R. Watanabe

Ju 87D-1/trop Stab/St.G 3, North Africa, 1942

Ju 87D-3 9./St.G 77, Eastern Front, 1943

Ju 87G-2 10.(Pz)/SG 3, Eastern Front, late 1943

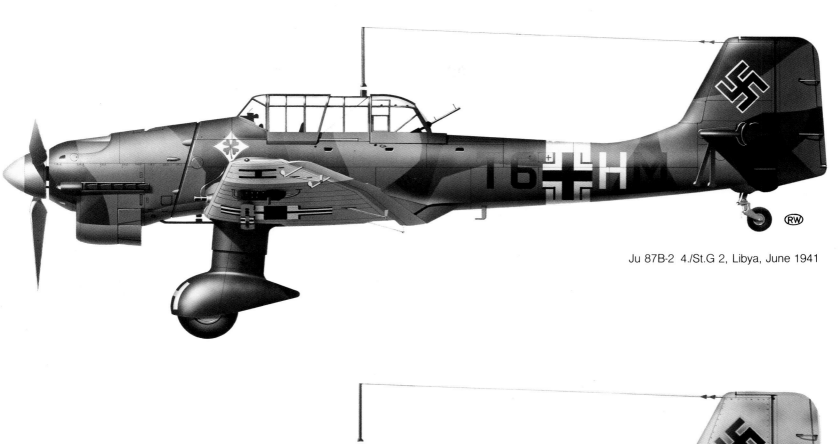

Ju 87B-2 4./St.G 2, Libya, June 1941

Ju 87B-2 3./St.G 5, Leningrad, early 1943

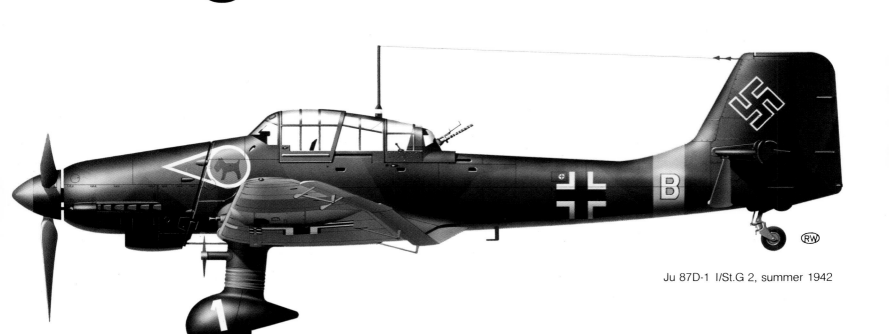

Ju 87D-1 I/St.G 2, summer 1942

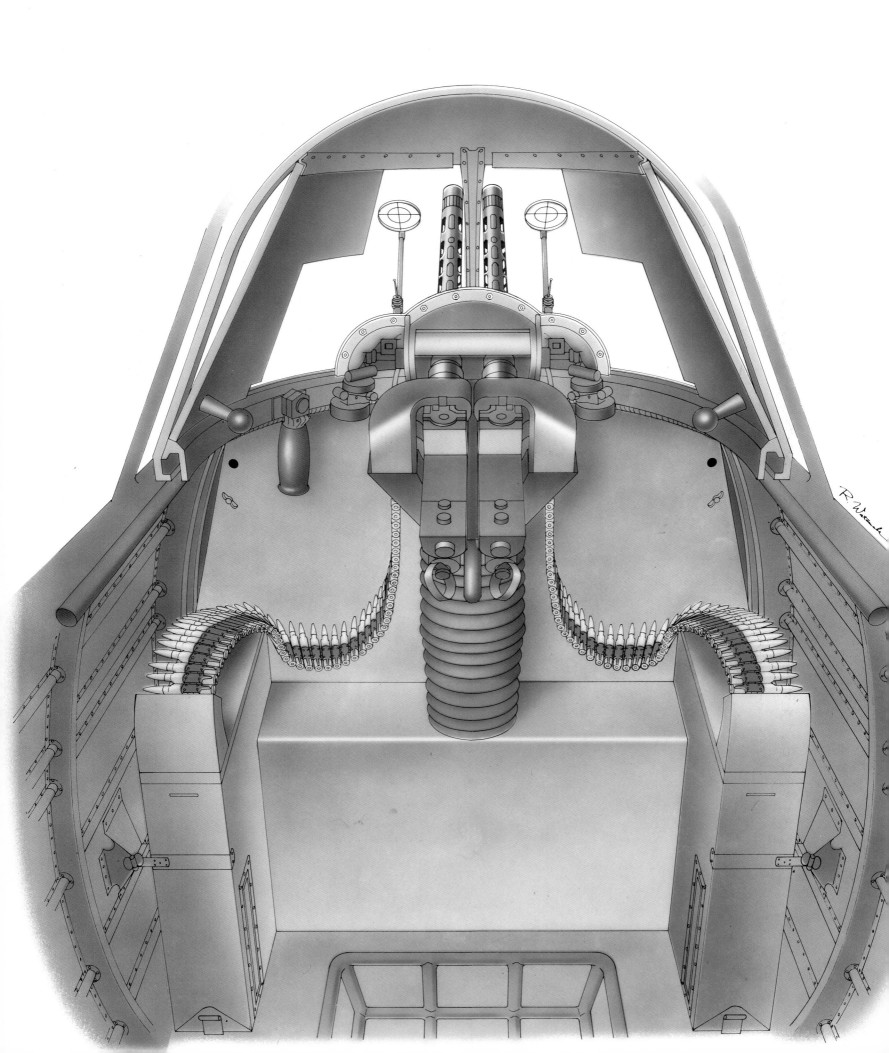

Ju 87D Pilot's Cockpit Instrumentation Key

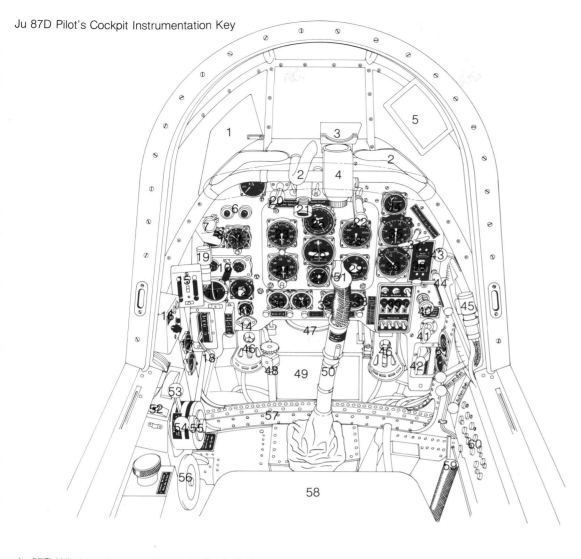

Ju 87D Wireless Operator/Gunner's Cockpit Key

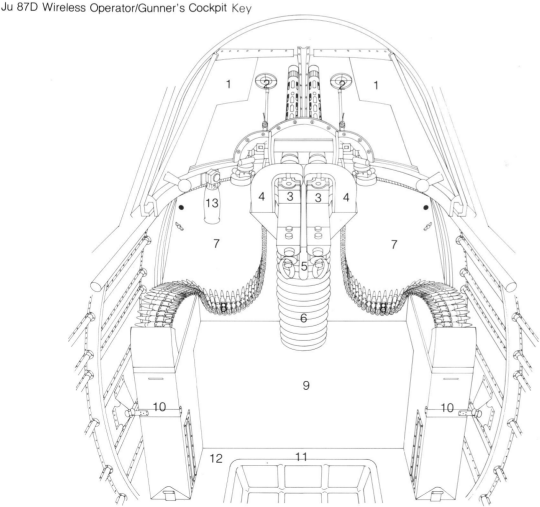

Ju 87D
Pilot's Cockpit Instrumentation Key

1 Visual dive indicator
2 Windscreen washer ducts
3 Reflector sight
4 Crash pad
5 Rear view mirror
6 Wind machine gun armed lights
7 Signal flare pistol tube
8 Dive pre-set indicator
9 Clock
10 Direction finder control unit
11 Compass
12 Instrument panel lighting dimmer
   control
13 Mains switch
14 Starter
15 Ammunition round counter
16 Armament selector switch box
17 Dive brake oil pressure gauge
18 Fuel priming pump lever
19 Cockpit light
20 Boost control
21 Windscreen washer actuator
22 Fresh air control
23 Rate of climb indicator
24 Radio altimeter
25 Repeater compass
26 Artificial horizon
27 Propeller pitch indicator
28 Airspeed indicator
29 Altimeter
30 Fuel contents gauge
31 Coolant temperature indicator
32 Oil temperature indicator
33 Oil contents gauge
34 Rate of climb/descent indicator
35 Revcounter (rpm)
36 Boost pressure indicator
37 Emergency bomb release lever
38 Bombing control panel
39 Radio switch panel
40 Manual fuel pump
41 Engine priming pump
42 Oil cooler flap control
43 Flare case release lever
44 Flap deflection indicator
45 Cockpit light
46 Rudder bar pedal
47 Oil tank
48 Target view panel flap control
49 Target view panel
50 Control column
51 Gun firing-button
52 Dive-bombing siren (Jericho siren)
53 Propeller pitch control lever
54 Throttle lever
55 Camera release button
56 Elevator trim hand wheel
57 No. 1 bulkhead
58 Pilot's seat
59 Seat up/down lever
60 Main switch panel
61 Oxygen indicator

Ju 87D
Wireless Operator/Gunner's
Cockpit Key

1 Upper armour olating
2 Gun sight
3 Twin 7.92-mm Mauser MG 81Z
   machine guns
4 Ammunition belt guide chute
5 Hand grip
6 Spent metal belt link and
   cartridge case chute
7 Rear armoured bulkhead (8 mm)
8 Disintegrating metal link
   ammunition belts
9 Spent metal belt link and
   cartridge case box
10 7.92 mm ammunition boxes
11 Gunner's seat
12 Floor armour (5 mm)
13 GSL-K 81 mount's grip

Ju 87R-2s of St.G 2 accompany Ju 52/3m transports of KGzbV 1 to North Africa.

(BUNDESARCHIV)

resistance in Yugoslavia was broken after 12 days (and five bombing raids on Belgrade in one day), and Greece once more provided the ideal operational conditions for Stukas – the *Luftwaffe* had almost complete mastery of the air. VIII *Fliegerkorps* under the skilful command of von Richthofen functioned like a well-oiled machine, and the campaign in Greece was short and decisive. The small Greek Air Force was neutralized, while the British air contingent hurriedly sent over from North Africa lacked any early warning systems and was largely destroyed on the ground.

Once again, the Stuka ruled supreme and the German victory was complete. In addition to demonstrating their accuracy on land, the Stukas also made short work of the Greek Navy by sinking the old 16,500-ton battleship *Kilkis*, a destroyer and nine other warships between 21 and 24 April, 1941. A ship, even in port, was always a more rewarding target for dive bombing. Throughout the campaign, the Stuka losses had been negligible.

Mediterranean and North Africa (January 1941 – May 1943)

Although the Ju 87s were used in the Mediterranean area from early 1941 to the summer of 1943 (and until the end of hostilities as night ground-attack aircraft) their operations show several distinct phases of concentrated effort.

The first was in January 1941 when the initial attempt was made to neutralize Malta, the important British naval and air base controlling the central Mediterranean.

In late December 1940 the X *Fliegerkorps* commanded by *General der Flieger* Geisler began transferring to Sicily, completing the move in less than a week. This force included three *Stukagruppen*, I and III/St.G 1 and II/St.G 2.

Just then, two strongly protected British convoys were on their way to Malta, approaching from the east and west. The east-bound convoy was spotted by Italian reconnaissance aircraft on 9 January and attacked by a combined force of level bombers and Stukas within hours. This was the first time the Ju 87 "Richards" had an aircraft carrier in their sights, and the HMS *Illustrious* was hit six times. Saved by her metal deck and strong internal construction, HMS *Illustrious* managed to reach Malta but was unable to sail for some time. This was an auspicious start: despite very heavy AA fire only one Stuka was lost in this action by I/St.G 1 (*Hptm* Hozzel) and II/St.G 2(*Maj* Enneccerus). Two days later Stukas of II/St.G 2 intercepted the cruisers HMS *Gloucester* and *Southampton* leaving Malta. In concentrated dive-bombing attacks both cruisers were hit several times, the 11,350 ton (full load) HMS *Southampton* had to be abandoned and was sunk by British naval forces the following day. The lessons of dive-bombing attacks on warships off Norway eight months before had been assimilated by the Stukas, if not by the navy.

Attention then turned to Malta itself. This island fortress had been raided by the *Regia Aeronautica* on and off for some five months, but without much effect. This time both Axis air forces were going to deal concentrated blows, including precision attacks by Stukas. (The Italian-manned Ju 87Bs had been operational over Malta in small numbers since the previous September)

Between 16 and 26 February, 1941 Malta was the target for a series of heavy air raids, with Stukas participating in most. More hits were achieved on HMS *Illustrious*, the heavy cruiser HMS *Perth* was seriously damaged, and many port and airfield installations destroyed, but the results were still inconclusive. The AA defences of Malta did not slacken, and the naval and air bases could not be completely neutralized. There was no time to press it home – the Stukas were needed elsewhere. The only real consolation was that the carrier HMS *Illustrious* was out of action for several months, being repaired by special arrangement in the USA, then still a neutral country.

The Stukas arrived in North Africa in January 1941 and the first Ju 87 (a "Richard") was lost at El Agheila on 14 February. The strength of Stuka formations based in North Africa was to fluctuate between two and four *Gruppen*, limited by the fuel and general supply situation. Their operations were also dogged by maintenance problems on open desert landing grounds and the serviceability was never as high as in Europe. There was also none of that close co-operation between ground forces and Stukas that characterized the other campaigns. In fact, there were no *Luftwaffe* liaison officers attached to ground force staffs which on occasion resulted in Stuka attacks on their troops. In any case, instead of ground support the North Africa-based Ju 87s were often given anti-shipping tasks more in line with X *Flieger-korps* usual operations

Then there was Tobruk. For five months beginning April 1941 the *Luftwaffe* and *Regia Aeronautica* tried their hardest to subdue this British-held port in Cyrenaica, with Stukas participating in many of these attacks. According to the records kept by the Tobruk AA command not less than 1,185 Stukas were engaged in 62 separate dive-bombing attacks between 10 April and 9 October, 1941. But Tobruk held, this time. The highlights of the Stuka operations in North Africa in 1942 were Bir Hakeim and once more Tobruk. The fortified but isolated oasis of Bir Hakeim, held by Free French forces under General Koenig, was on the extreme southern flank of the British lines and its capture was essential for Rommel's *Afrika Korps* to advance eastwards. Between 26 May and 10 June this relatively small and open target was subjected to repeated attacks by St.G 3 before the

French garrison was forced to withdraw – an amazing record of fortitude under Stuka bombardment.

The Stukas also played a major role in the second Axis assault on Tobruk. This time the tactics were different and the battle was decided in just two days. The aerial bombardment began on 20 June, 1942: relays of Stukas from St.G 3 blasted a wide gap in the extensive minefields enabling the German and Italian infantry to advance. Just 90 minutes later the Stukas were back again, precision-bombing the strongpoints and fortifications holding up the advance without respite. The Tobruk garrison of 32,000 men surrendered next day, together with enormous stocks of military supplies of which by far the most important were nearly 1.5 million Imp gallons of fuel. The cost to St.G 3 had been minimal.

In the meantime another determined effort had been made to subdue Malta which nearly succeeded. Together with other *Luftwaffe* units and *Regia Aeronautica* bombers the Stukas of III/St.G 3 were out in force, and by mid-April 1942 Malta had hardly any fighter defences left. This was the critical phase, but no more Stukas could be spared. On 15 April Malta was awarded the George Cross by the grateful British government. In more practical terms, 47 replacement Spitfires were flown off the US carrier *Wasp* 660 miles west of Malta, a flight made possible by two oversize drop tanks. Within three days only six of these Spitfires were still operational – but by then the worst was over. By the end of April *Luftwaffe* units were moving away to other tasks, and the last Stuka raid on Malta (by III/St.G 3) took place on 10 May. 1942. Malta had proved too hard a nut to crack with the forces available.

Between 14 and 16 June, 1942 the Stukas carried out their most successful operation in the Mediterranea area when St.G 3 and Italian-manned Ju 87s of 102° *Gruppo*

Ju 87D-1/trop of St.G 3 armed with four 77 kg (170 lb) SD 70 *Stabo* bombs underwing shortly before take-off in North Africa, summer 1942. (BUNDESARCHIV)

together with *Luftwaffe* and *Regia Aeronautica* level bombers attacked and practically annihilated one of two British convoys bound for Malta. Only two ships from the eastbound convoy got through to their destination, while the other convoy was forced to turn back.

By the end of June 1942 the Stuka units in North Africa were practically grounded for lack of fuel, spare parts and other supplies, even food. Thus during the most critical phase of his advance at El Alamein, when everything hung in the balance, Rommel and his *Afrika Korps* were left without Stuka support. The number of Stukas in the Mediterranean area never increased to more than 60 in 1941–42, of which about half were based in North Africa, but their effect on operations after July 1942 was insignificant.

On 8 November, 1942, the first day of "Operation Torch", the US/British landing in North-West Africa, the *Luftwaffe* strength in the whole Mediterranean area was 400 operational aircraft including just 30 Stukas. This was temporarily increased to nearly 640 combat aircraft and 60 Stukas by 31 December, 1942 (including the Tunisian sector), but the Allied aerial superiority could no longer be challenged.

It was then that the first Fw 190 fighter-bombers used in the close-support role appeared in Tunisia – a clear indication that the days of the Stuka were over at least as far as their use against the Western Allies was concerned.

Crete
(20 May – 1 June, 1941)

The battle of Crete occupies a place of its own in the annals of military history. Crete is the only island to have been conquered by an airborne assault with close air support in the face of a numerically superior defensive force fully informed about it in advance. What the defenders lacked was air support, without which even detailed knowledge of enemy plans could not help. The event also provided another most con-

Newly arrived Ju 87D-1s and older Ju 87B-2s rest their wings at an operational base.

(BUNDESARCHIV)

vincing demonstration of the superiority of aircraft over warships sailing without air cover, and the Stukas were there in force to underline it.

Crete had been occupied by British toops since 29 October, 1940, a day after the Italian attack on Greece and, after the very successful conclusion of "Operation Marita", was one of the two obvious strategic objects for the Axis command. Although tentative plants were drawn up for an airborne invasion of Malta – considered by many the more important – the final choice fell on Crete. The order for this assault ("Operation Merkur") was given on 25 April, 1941 and the complete VIII *Fliegerkorps* with a force of 650 aircraft (including 150 Stukas) was concentrated on recently completed airfields in southern Greece and on the island of Scarpathos. The opposition was negligible, just 24 British fighters, including some Gloster Gladiator biplanes.

The assault began after a heavy preliminary bombardment on 20 May at Maleme, one of the three vital airfields on the island. By then the British and Greek troops evacuated from the Greek mainland had been in Crete for three weeks and had had sufficient time to prepare. The defenders of Crete were in a unique position because their commander, General Freyberg VC, had received from London detailed advance information about the coming assault ("Operation Ultra", the highly secret computerized decoding of German radio traffic) on special orders from Winston Churchill – probably the only time in military history when a general had such details about the enemy's intentions. The force under his command numbered not less than 42,640 (32,112 British and 10,258 Greek troops).

But it proved impossible to provide air cover from Egypt, or even fly in regular supplies or reinforcement aircraft: the German air blockade of the island was too tight, and eventually the Stukas of I and III/St.G 2 and I/St.G 3, together with relentless attacks by strafing fighters and other bombers hammered the Allied defences into submission. With this close air support and despite appalling losses the German paratroops, together with mountain troops airlifted straight into battle, were finally able to consolidate and take Maleme and, later, the other two airfields. By the next day the *Luftwaffe* had complete air mastery over Crete and, although the battle for Crete went on until 1 June, its outcome had been decided on the night of 22 May.

The Stukas played an important part in the conquest of Crete, but their greatest hour was yet to come in the classic aircraft versus warship contest. On 22 May British warships had intercepted and largely destroyed a German seaborne support force on its way to Crete, and the complete St.G 2 was immediately ordered to leave targets in Crete and concentrate on the Royal Navy. On the same day the Stukas found and sank the destroyer HMS *Greyhound* and damaged two cruisers (HMS *Gloucester* and HMS *Fiji*). The day after, on 23 May, Ju 87s of I/St.G 2 sank the destroyers HMS *Kelly* and HMS *Kashmir* after a memorable fight.

The Royal Navy struck back on the night of 25–26 May when a strong force comprising the carrier HMS *Formidable* accompanied by two battleships (HMS *Barham* and HMS *Queen Elizabeth*) and a screen of destroyers tried to neutralize the Stuka base on Scarpathos by an air strike using carrier-borne aircraft. Like a similar attempt at a Stuka base in Norway a year before, this sortie by the Royal Navy also achieved little – the Stukas could only be deterred by fighters.

On 26 May, Ju 87 "Richards" of II/St.G 2 were directed to another force of British warships sailing to assist operations around Crete and so badly damaged the carrier HMS *Illustrious* that she was out of action again for several months. Two days later, during the evacuation of Crete, the Stukas hit and severely damaged the cruisers HMS *Dido* and HMS *Orion*, incapacitated the destroyer HMS *Hereward*, and damaged HMS *Imperial*. The only air cover the Royal Navy had were some twin-engined Blenheim fighters sent from Egypt which proved quite useless against the Stukas.

On 1 June, 1941 the battle for Crete was over. 18,600 of the 42,640 Allied troops had been evacuated – but at a cost of three cruisers and six destroyers lost and two battleships, one aircraft carrier, six cruisers and seven destroyers damaged to some extent, much of it done by Stukas commanded and piloted by *Maj* Enneccerus, *Hptm* Hozzel and *Hptm* Hitschhold who had specialized in this task.

Eastern Front
(22 June, 1941 – 8 May, 1945)

"Operation Barbarossa", the German invasion of the Soviet Union, was optimistically intended to be over by Christmas 1941. It turned out to be the longest and bloodiest campaign in which the German armed forces were to be involved in World War II, largely contributing to the downfall of the Third Reich. At the end of it at least 8 million Red Army troops and more than 3.5 million German and satellite soldiers had been killed in battle, and perhaps 22 million Soviet, German and other civilians slaughtered in the fighting or its aftermath. Only approximate estimates can be made about the material losses.

Compared to the previous campaigns, the length and extent of the new battlefield was enormous, and the main front was 995 miles (1,600 km) long (expanding to 1,490 miles [2,500 km] during the campaign). There were another 620 miles (1,000 km) along the Finnish frontier.

And yet the number of *Luftwaffe* aircraft deployed for Operation Barbarossa totalled only 2,875, of which only 1,945 were combat aircraft, less than had been made available for the Western campaign.

On the morning of 22 June, 1941, only 1,407 of the 1,945 aircraft on strength were available for operations: 510 bombers, 197 Stukas, 440 fighters, 40 close-support and 120 reconnaissance aircraft under *Luftwaffe* control. The opposing Red Air Force was estimated to possess at least 18,000 aircraft of all types, of which some 9,000 were stationed in the Western districts – but only about 20 per cent of the aircraft were really modern, and the re-equipment and retraining on new types was still going on. Apart from that, many of the combat units seemed to be concentrated close to the western borders of the Soviet Union where most of the bases had been carefully photographed by the high-flying clandestine He 111

and Ju 86P reconnaissance aircraft from *Gruppe Rowehl*. It was an ideal situation to use the proven *Luftwaffe* maxim of surprise attack to destroy most of the enemy air force on the ground with one massive blow before turning attention to tactical-support tasks.

Although the Red Air Force was largely an unknown quantity, judged by its performance in Finland (with some reference to earlier experiences in Spain) it did not seem to present a serious threat. By June 1941 the *Luftwaffe* had gained combat experience in four victorious campaigns, and the technique of co-operation between aircraft and the ground forces had been perfected to a fine pitch. The morale was high, and so was self-confidence – Operation Barbarossa was to be the biggest, and last campaign.

A total of 66 selected Soviet airfields were raided the first day and 1,811 aircraft destroyed on the ground and in the air for the loss of only 35 *Luftwaffe* machines. The surprise had been complete, but was never to be repeated on the same scale. Despite a series of remarkable successes on the ground and in the air the campaign bogged down within four months, and the Soviet resistance was far from broken. The official *Luftwaffe* records of losses on the Eastern Front tell their own story: from 22 June to 31 December, 1941 they list 2,093 aircraft as total loss (including 758 bombers, 568 fighters and 767 others), while another 1,361 aircraft (473 bombers, 413 fighters and 475 other types) were damaged to some extent. In other words, in just six months the *Luftwaffe* had lost more aircraft than it had started with at the beginning of the campaign. While aircraft could always be replaced, the loss of experienced crews would gradually begin to have an effect.

Ju 87B-2s in winter camouflage on the Eastern Front early in 1942.   (BUNDESARCHIV)

Ju 87D-3s taking off in *Kette* formation from a snow covered advanced base on the Eastern Front. Each "Dora" is carrying one 500 kg and four 70 kg bombs.   (BUNDESARCHIV)

The Stukas were in the thick of fighting from the very beginning and regained much of their earlier reputation as hard-hitting precision bombers with nerve-shattering screaming dives that panicked men and animals. One of the most notable Stuka exploits in 1941 was the sinking of the 26,170-ton Soviet battleship *Marat* at Kronshtadt on 21 September by a young *Oberleutnant* named Hans-Ulrich Rudel of III/St.G 2. He had scored a direct hit on *Marat* with an ordinary 1,102 lb (500 kg) bomb already on 16 September, but the 2,205 lb (1,000 kg) armour-piercing bomb dropped with great precision five days later split the ship in half. These were probably the most dangerous and difficult attacks ever flown by a dive-bomber pilot – Kronshtadt was defended by more than 1,000 AA guns of all calibres on land and afloat, and the fire concentration was much more intense than over London or Malta. Hans-Ulrich Rudel was destined to become the most famous dive-bomber pilot of all time, preferring to fly the Ju 87, with almost unbelievable success, until the end of the war.

In 1942, with few notable exceptions, the use of Stukas became much more tactical and close support in character. It was this type of aircraft that the *Luftwaffe* needed most of all on the Eastern Front to counter the increasing number of Soviet Il-2 *Shturmoviks*. Because of the great length and depth of the battlefield the well-tried recipe of concentrated air strikes in support of armoured troops did not work in the East and it was becoming clear that no decisive victory could be achieved. On the other hand, the Stuka was still a powerful weapon as long as the *Luftwaffe* fighter pilots had the edge over their Soviet counterparts. Thus, the great "pincer battles" of 1941 and 1942 resulting in

enormous numbers of prisoners and captured war material would have hardly been possible without the participation of the Ju 87 formations, but the object was always limited – there was no way the enemy's nerve centre could be hit decisively as during the previous campaigns.

One of the most remarkable battles of that year was the German assault on Sevastopol, probably the strongest fortified naval base in the world at the time and in this the Stukas of VIII *Fliegerkorps* played a decisive role. The concentrated Stuka attacks began on 7 June and went on between raids by other bombers and artillery fire of all calibres until 1 July when the half-dazed survivors of the garrison finally surrendered. Once again, this dive bombing was only possible because of the superior performance of *Luftwaffe* fighter pilots.

It was also at about this time that on the other side of the world the Ju 87 was allocated the SW Pacific reporting name of "Irene" in the mistaken belief it would be used by the Japanese. The year 1942 also saw the battle for Stalingrad, which had since become a symbol of Soviet fortitude and German defeat. The Stukas, as always, were in the forefront of this offensive and Ju 87s of St.G 1, 2 and 77 took part in the first concentrated attacks on the town itself on 3 September. The battle for Stalingrad gradually degenerated into vicious street fighting with no hope of capturing it before the onset of winter. When the Soviet counter-attack began on 19 November many Stuka units based on advanced airfields between the Chir and Don rivers were right in the path of Soviet armour and, unable to escape in time, suffered great losses in personnel and equipment. That, and the intense cold and primitive maintenance conditions combined with lack of

spares held up in the hinterland, reduced the serviceability as never before, and the Stukas became a shadow of their former power.

According to the official *Luftwaffe* documents, on 31 December, 1942 there was a total of 1,355 bombers (including 270 Stukas) in front-line units spread across Europe and in North Africa – 65 Ju 87s less than in September 1939. In mid-January 1943 the total number of combat aircraft on the Eastern Front (bombers, fighters, *Zerstörer* and reconnaissance aircraft) was barely 1,700, of which just 40 per cent were operational. At this stage, the Soviet numerical superiority in the air was 5 : 1.

With one temporary exception, 1943 was the year of defensive battles all along the front. In January strong *Luftwaffe* forces, including five undermanned *Stukagruppen* (II/St.G 1, St.G 2 and I and II/St.G 77) were assembled to hold the Donetz line, but could not stop the Red Army crossing the river on 15 January. From then on, the *Luftwaffe* command was hard pressed to achieve even local air mastery.

The outcome of another Soviet thrust was the "Kursk bulge" that practically invited a pincer operation. Despite objections from many of his generals Hitler decided to attack with the strongest armoured force the German army had ever assembled for one battle. Known as "Operation Zitadelle", this final German offensive in the East began on 5 July. The *Luftwaffe* had deployed 1,830 combat aircraft for this operation, including nine *Stukagruppen* but it was not enough. After some initial successes the Soviet resistance became even more tenacious and it was soon obvious that the depth of their defensive positions and combat strength were much greater than assumed. (The fact that all the details of

this offensive had been known to Soviet intelligence thanks to their spy "Werther" in the German High Command, had a lot to do with it of course.) The offensive was called off after ten days, but the losses suffered by the German tank forces and the *Luftwaffe* close-support formations were severe. In July, the *Luftwaffe* lost 911 aircraft on the Eastern Front, most of them in the central and southern sectors.

By the summer of 1943 it was clear that the Ju 87 was fast becoming outdated as a first line combat aircraft and, on the Eastern Front, needed replacing as a matter of urgency. During the previous six months the Red Air Force had exchanged most of its obsolescent aircraft by modern types quite up to *Luftwaffe* standard and far better suited to the local conditions – and their fighter pilots had become much more aggressive. The Ju 87 had long since ceased to be the dreaded weapon it once was, although it could still deal out some hefty blows.

Another change, long since overdue, was the re-organisation of the *Luftwaffe* ground attack and close-support aviation. However, this did not take place until after the suicide, on 18 August 1943, of the *Luftwaffe* Chief of the General staff, Hans Jeschonnek, and the appointment of General Korten in his place. He immediately ordered the formation of a separate *Schlachtflieger* command to unify all the units hitherto partly subordinated to the General of Fighters and General of Bombers, causing obvious delays and clashes in command competences. The first *General der Schlachtflieger* was *Oberst* Dr Ernst Kupfer, former commander of St.G 2, appointed on 1 September 1943. He immediately initiated the formation of *Schlachtgeschwader* by renaming all existing *Stukageschwader* and ordered their re-equipment

Ju 87D-5s escorted by Bf 109G-5s of JG 51 returning from a raid on the Eastern Front.

(BUNDESARCHIV)

with the Fw 190F and G close-support aircraft. This re-equipment and conversion began in October and was to take place at the rate of about two *Gruppen* every six weeks.

After *Oberst* Kupfer's death in a flying accident on 6 November, 1943, *Oberst* Hubertus Hitschhold, another very experienced Stuka pilot and commander, was appointed to take his place and continued to speed up the re-equipment of former Stuka formations with the Fw 190.

However, the Ju 87 still had two operational roles left to play until the very end of the war.

Ju 87D-3 carrying an AB 500-1 plywood container loaded with thirty-seven SD 10A fragmentation bombs ventrally and four SD 70 *Stabo* bombs underwing over the Eastern Front.

(BUNDESARCHIV)

The "Flying anti-tank gun"

The Ju 87G "flying tank destroyer" is always associated with the name of *Oberst* Hans-Ulrich Rudel whose personal score amounted to 519 Soviet tanks. He was also actively involved in the development of this novel weapon and participated in trials at Rechlin and Tarnewitz in early 1943 before taking the first Ju 87Gs to the Crimea for operational trials.

The idea of using aircraft armed with large-calibre cannon to combat tanks was first mooted in 1942 and by the end of that year a special *Versuchskommando für Panzerbekämpfung* commanded by *Oberst* Otto Weiss, an experienced ground attack pilot, had been set up. After a series of tests with several aircraft types the Ju 87D armed with two 37 mm Flak 18 cannon was found the most suitable solution and a special *Panzerjagdkommando Weiss* was formed in February 1943. Among the pilots of this detachment was *Hptm* Rudel, who had already flown the Ju 87G at Rechlin. The first operational trials took place on 16 March, but it was *Hptm* Rudel's skilful use of the "Gustav" on detachment in the Crimea that attracted attention. By 5 July 1943, the start of Operation "Zitadelle", the first two Ju 87G-equipped *Staffeln* were operational: Pz.J.Sta./St.G 1 and Pz.J.Sta./St.G 2. On the same day *Hptm* Rudel, who by then had evolved his own tactics later adopted by all "flying tank destroyers" (low approach and attack from the rear or side, aiming for the tank engine) destroyed a complete company of 12 attacking Soviet T-34s.

On 17 July *Hptm* Rudel took over command of III/St.G 2, the formation where he had started his amazing career as a dive bomber pilot in June 1941, and went on to develop it into an elite tank destroyer unit. Within a few

Ju 87G-1 just before touch-down. The white tank emblem on the engine indicates the anti-tank trial unit led by *Hptm* Rudel in 1943. (BUNDESARCHIV)

months III/St.G 2 became literally a "flying anti-tank brigade" called upon for support wherever the situation was critical or the Soviet tanks had broken through, which, from late 1943 onwards, was becoming more and more frequent. Although the Ju 87G could only manage about 217 mph (350 km/h) at ground level, *Hptm* Rudel's skill as a pilot and gunner, and stamina, were truly unique, and his score mounted: by 28 March, 1944 it had reached 202 tanks, increased to 300 by 6 August, and to 463 by 23 December. After being wounded on 17 November, 1944 Rudel continued flying with one leg in plaster, was awarded the Golden Oakleaves for exceptional bravery on 1 January 1945, and promoted *Oberst* at the age of

Oberleutnant Hans-Ulrich Rudel as *Staffelkapitän* of 9./St.G 2 in his Ju 87D, summer 1942. (BUNDESARCHIV)

28. By the end of the war his record as a combat pilot was unique: in 2,530 operational flights as a dive bomber pilot and tank destroyer, he had accounted for 519 Soviet tanks, sunk the battleship *Marat*, one Soviet cruiser, one destroyer, destroyed 70 landing craft, four armoured trains, and much other war material – in addition to shooting down nine enemy aircraft with his Ju 87. In that time Rudel himself had been shot down 30 times (by ground fire only, never by a fighter) and wounded five times, ending the war with an artificial leg, and still flying.

What is more surprising about this exceptional man and pilot is that he failed twice to make the grade as a Stuka pilot in 1939 and 1940, and did not fly his first operational sortie until 23 June 1941 – and then almost by accident. However, his performance on that day and afterwards singled Rudel out as an above-average Stuka pilot, and soon his achievements became a legend on the Eastern Front. By summer 1944 his blue-nosed Ju 87G was high on the Soviet 'wanted' list: in August 1944 when Rudel was shot down near Érgli in Latvia and once again managed to evade capture, he had a price of 100,000 roubles on his head, dead or alive!

But there were other Ju 87G pilots who also ran up quite respectable scores of tank kills, such as *Lt* Anton Korol (99), *Lt* Wilhelm Joswig (88+) and *Ofw* Jakob Jenster (58), as well as many who never survived the first few low-level sorties in the slow Ju 87 against the murderous fire from automatic AA weapons which now protected the Soviet tanks – as a rule fired without any tracer and spotted too late.

Diminishing numbers of Ju 87Gs, the "flying anti-tank gun", remained in action on the Eastern Front until the end of the war.

The Ju 87 had honourably fulfilled another role for which it had never been intended.

Nocturnal Finale

The last operational role of the Stuka no longer involved screaming dive-bombing attacks in daytime but stealthy nocturnal flights using quite different tactics.

The idea of night harassment aircraft originated with the Red Air Force which began using obsolete U-2 and R-5 biplanes for this task already in late 1941. Despite the small bomb load carried and the limited range of these "night nuisance raiders" they were so effective just by their presence in the air near the combat zone that in October 1942 the idea was also officially adopted by the *Luftwaffe* on the Eastern Front.

Initially known as *Behelfskampfstaffeln* (Auxiliary bomber flights), these units were equipped with a mixture of older aircraft such as the Junkers W 34, He 45, Go 145 and Ar 66. A month later these flights were re-designated *Störkampfstaffeln* (harassing bomber flights), but with the general re-organization of ground support aviation on 18 October, 1943 formed into *Nachtschlachtgruppen* (NSGr).

The idea of using reconditioned and/or modified Ju 87s as night ground attack aircraft was first proposed in summer 1943 and in August work put in hand at a factory in Hamburg-Harburg to convert 300 Ju 87Ds for night operations. The first 78 Ju 87D-7s and D-8s were completed as a matter of urgency and immediately delivered to various NS-*Gruppen* for re-training and operational use. By June 1944 the number of NS-*Gruppen* had grown to 12, but re-equipment and re-training on the Ju 87 was very gradual. In late autumn of that year several night harrassment formations were disbanded (NSGr 11, NSGr 12 and the *Ostfliegerstaffel*). Of the remaining formations only six were equipped with the Ju 87 and were operational as follows:

NSGr 1: Ju 87 from August 1943; 3 *Staffeln*. Operational on the Eastern Front until August 1944, then in the West until May 1945.

NSGr 2: Ju 87 from February 1944; 4 *Staffeln*. Operational on the Eastern Front until September 1944, then in the West (except one *Staffel* remaining in the East) until April 1945.

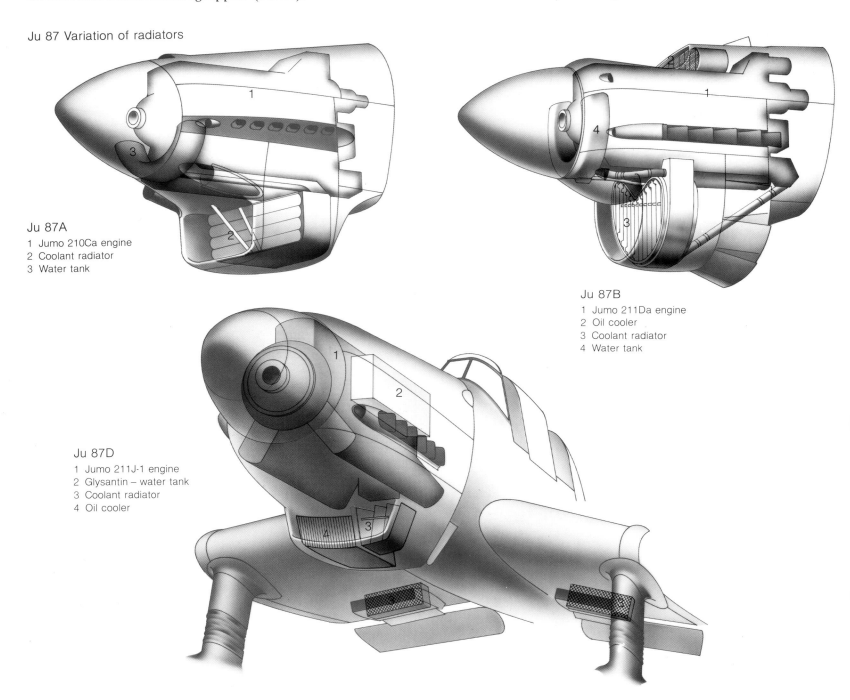

Ju 87 Variation of radiators

Ju 87A
1 Jumo 210Ca engine
2 Coolant radiator
3 Water tank

Ju 87B
1 Jumo 211Da engine
2 Oil cooler
3 Coolant radiator
4 Water tank

Ju 87D
1 Jumo 211J-1 engine
2 Glysantin – water tank
3 Coolant radiator
4 Oil cooler

Ju 87D-8 night harassment bomber of NSGr 9 on an Italian airfield. Note the absence of underwing dive brakes. (BUNDESARCHIV)

NSGr 4: Ju 87 from August 1944; 3 *Staffeln*. Operational over South-eastern Europe. Two newly-formed *Staffeln* transferred to West late 1944.

NSGr 8: Ju 87 from May 1944; 2 *Staffeln* only. Operational in Finland until September 1944, then Norway. In January 1945 transferred to the Oder front, Berlin area.

NSGr 9: Ju 87 from May 1944; 3 *Staffeln*. Operational in Northern Italy until capitulation.

NSGr 10: Ju 87 from October 1944; 2 *Staffeln* only. Operational in the Balkan area.

From this brief summary it is evident that from autumn 1944 onwards most of these Ju 87-equipped night ground attack/harassment units were deployed against the Western allies. The main reason for this was the lack of conventional bombers and shortage of fuel: the Ju 87 was able to carry an effective bomb load over the enemy hinterland on one engine, was more manoeuvrable, and could fly lower if necessary. And so another wheel had turned a full circle: the *Luftwaffe* had relied on the Ju 87 on the Western Front in 1940, and had to do so again in late 1944, only this time for different reasons and at night.

In action, the nocturnal Ju 87 proved effective and comparatively invulnerable to Allied defences. What is more, its low cruising speed was used to advantage by Ju 87 crews in avoiding attacks by Allied night fighters (usually Mosquitoes), and losses at night to anti-aircraft fire were minimal.

As a rule, these aircraft operated only during periods of moonlight, as it was considered too dangerous to fly at low level to and from the target in complete darkness. The usual targets were tank and troop concentrations near the front line, trains and railway stations and junctions, bridges and road transport, as well as individual buildings suspected as staff quarters. Weather conditions permitting, a whole *Staffel* would normally be used against one specific target, the aircraft attacking in pairs: the leader would drop flares to illuminate the target, and his partner would bomb. Both aircraft were in radio contact via their FuG 16 R/T sets – an essential pre-requisite for successful co-operation. When the first pair had used up their combat loads they would be replaced by the next two Ju 87s summoned by radio. This tactic enabled the attack to continue non-stop for several hours. The usual attack altitude was between 3,000 and 800 ft, but in good visibility individual Ju 87s sometimes approached their target with throttled-back engines lower than that. Quite frequently, some Ju 87s would also drop *Düppel* (metallic strips) to jam the Allied radar, dispensed in bundles by the rear gunner, and the FuG 25a IFF sets were required equipment when operating in the West.

The importance attached by the *Luftwaffe* command to night ground attack aircraft in the West is shown by the increase in their numbers: from 70 Ju 87s in late October 1944 to 130 on 16 December, the first day of the German Ardennes offensive.

In an emergency, these nocturnal Ju 87s were also used in daytime, both in the East and West, the most notable occasion being the series of desperate and costly raids on the Remagen bridge in March 1945.

The last known Ju 87 night ground attack operations in the West were flown by NSGr 1 on 4 May 1945 – over German territory. The war was all but over, but the descendants of the dreaded Stukas that filled the skies on the first day of World War II fought on till the last. Early in the morning on 8 May 1945 the indomitable *Oberst* Rudel made his last tank hunting flight but had to turn back empty handed. A few hours later, as a final act of defiance, the crews of NSGr 2 destroyed their remaining aircraft at Holzkirchen.

The Stuka was no more, but it had left an indelible mark on history.

Epilogue

Among the thousands of *Luftwaffe* aircraft dealt with by the Allied forces after the German surrender in May 1945 were only a small number of Ju 87s – probably no more than 200. After the usual search for ammunition they were all destroyed, mostly by blowing off the engines, and then scrapped.

Quite by chance, one partly converted Ju 87D was saved and is now exhibited at the RAF Battle of Britain Museum, Hendon in London. Another Stuka, a Ju 87B-2/trop found abandoned by British forces in North Africa, was taken to the USA during the war and restored in 1974 by the Experimental Aircraft Association of Wisconsin.

These are the only two representatives still extant of the 5,709 Stukas built, the aircraft that to many symbolized the power of the *Luftwaffe* during World War II.

Ju 87R-2s of Italian 97° *Gruppo Tuffatori* at their base in Sicily, summer 1941.

(BUNDESARCHIV)

Satellite Stukas

Italy

The first of Germany's allies to receive Stukas was Italy.

The initial 50 ex-*Luftwaffe* Stukas consisted of Ju 87 B-2/trop and ordinary B-2 dive bombers. These were followed by a second batch of 50 Ju 87R-2 anti-shipping dive bombers, all being delivered during 1940. Subsequently the *Regia Aeronautica* received a delivery of 46 Ju 87D-2 and D-3 dive bombers and some Ju 87R-2s. The following *Regia Aeronautica* units were equipped at various times with the Ju 87:

96° *Gruppo Tuffatori* (also known as *Gruppo Bombardamenti a Tuffi*) (236a and 237a *Squadriglia*).
Formed at Comiso 22 August, 1940 with 15 Ju 87s. Commanded by *Maggiore* E. Ercolani. First operational over Malta 2 September, 1940.

97° *Gruppo Tuffatori* (238a and 239a *Squadriglia*).
Formed at Comiso November 1940 with 13 Ju 87s. Commanded by *Tenente Col* A. Moscatelli, then *Magg* Larcher

101°*Gruppo Tuffatori* (208a and 209a *Squadriglia*).
Formed March 1941 with 16 Ju 87s. Commanded by *Magg* G. Donadio. First operational March 1941.

102°*Gruppo Tuffatori* (209a and 239a *Squadriglia*).
Formed 1 May, 1942 of reconstituted squadrons. Commanded by Capt G. Cenni

103° *Gruppo Tuffatori* (207a and 237a *Squadriglia*).
Formed 1 February 1943 with 12 Ju 87D-3s Commanded by *Tenente Col* A. Savarino

121° *Gruppo Tuffatori* (206a and 216a *Squadriglia*).
Formed 9 July, 1943 with eight Ju 87B-2s, later replaced by Ju 87Ds. Commanded by *Magg* L. Orlandini

Romania

A batch of Ju 87B-2 dive bombers was supplied to Romania in the autumn of 1940 and, after the necessary retraining of aircrew, equipped the newly formed *Grupul 6 Pikaj* (consisting of *Escadrile* 81, 82 and 83) dive-bombing wing of 30 aircraft. This unit became operational on the Eastern Front under I *Fliegerkorps* in July 1941 in support of the Romanian 3rd and 4th Armies.

In 1942–43 the *Luftwaffe* supplied 115 Ju 87D-1, -3 and -5 dive bombers to the Royal Romanian Air Force of which the Ju 87D-3s were used to re-equip *Grupul 6 Pikaj* for close-support tasks and the Ju 87D-1s and D-5s to equip the newly formed *Grupul 3 Pikaj* (*Escadrile* 84, 85 and 86). All these units were operational in concert with German forces until the *coup d'etat* in Romania and her capitulation to the Soviet forces on 23 August, 1944. While some Romanian aircrews remained loyal to the *Luftwaffe*, most others changed sides and the surviving Ju 87Ds (repainted in pre-war Romanian markings) were formed into *Escadrile* 74, and briefly used against the German troops near Cluj (Klausenburg) in September 1944.

Hungary

The Royal Hungarian Air Force came under the German direction soon after the annexation of Austria in the spring of 1938. With German assistance the formation of an independent dive-bomber squadron was initiated in 1941. Designated 1.*Önálló Zuhanöbombázö Osztály*, this unit was equipped with ten Ju 87B-2s, but these aircraft were used for training purposes only. In 1942–43 Hungarian aircrews were retrained on the Ju 87D-5 and, following the re-organization of the air force, a new dive-bomber squadron was formed with 12 Ju 87D-3/D-5s in May 1943. Designated 102/I *Zuhanöbomázö Osztály* this unit became operational from Gomel in Byelorussia in August 1943. After intensive combat operations and heavy losses the survivors were withdrawn to Hungary in October 1943. The squadron became operational again in June 1944, flying mostly from Polish bases, until late August 1944 when it began retraining on the FW 190. Apart from *Oberst* Rudel's III/SG.2 tank-destroyers, this Hungarian unit was the last to fly the Ju 87 on the Eastern Front.

Bulgaria

Among the various other German aircraft types delivered to the Royal Bulgarian Air Force were 12 Ju 87R-2/R-4 dive bombers in 1942, followed by 32 Ju 87D-5s in 1943. Some of the latter were used against anti-Royalist partisans in the Bulgarian mountains in the summer of 1944. After Bulgaria capitulated to the Soviets in September 1944 a few Bulgarian Ju 87Ds were reportedly flown against the retreating German troops.

Croatia

The Croatian Air Force was established under German authority in 1941. The Croat squadrons served as part of various *Luftwaffe* fighter and bomber formations, and the aircrew wore *Luftwaffe* uniforms with the Croat "Ustashi" insignia on the right sleeve (and on their aircraft). Fifteen Ju 87D dive bombers and a few Ju 87R-2 extended range dive bombers are known to have been supplied to the Croat Air Force, and six of these were flown operationally against the Soviet troops in the late summer of 1944. By that time many of the Croat personnel were deserting to the partisan forces led by Tito and within a few more months the Croat Air Force had ceased to exist.

Slovakia

Founded as a semi-independent "State" after the German occupation of Czechoslovakia in 1939, Slovakia established a small air force under *Luftwaffe* patronage in the same year. A number of Slovak personnel served with *Luftwaffe* units, but there were also two fighter squadrons equipped with progressively more modern aircraft operational on the Eastern Front. A small number of Ju 87D-5 dive bombers were delivered to the Slovak Air Force in 1943 and equipped part of the 3rd Air Regiment in 1944, but there is no confirmation of their operational use. In fact, the Slovak Air Force never exceeded more than 70 first-line aircraft.

Ju 87 production

Unlike some other German warplanes, the Ju 87 production figures are known with some degree of accuracy: 1935–36: 4; 1937–38: 395; 1939: 557; 1940: 613; 1941: 476; 1942: 960; 1943: 1,692; 1944: 1,012; 1945: –. Total: 5,709. (Total German aircraft production 1939–45: 113,514 of all types, incl. gliders.)

Remarks: The official *Luftwaffe* records show the receipt of 4,811 Ju 87s of all versions, leaving a discrepancy of 828 aircraft. No documents seem to have survived to account for these Ju 87s but this figure is probably made up of some 480-500 Ju 87s supplied to various German allied and satellite air forces ex-factory, completed aircraft lost in air raids or in transit, and some 40 prototypes and test aircraft retained by the factory and various test centres.

Ju 87D-5 fuselages on the assembly line. (BUNDESARCHIV)

Junkers Ju 87A-1

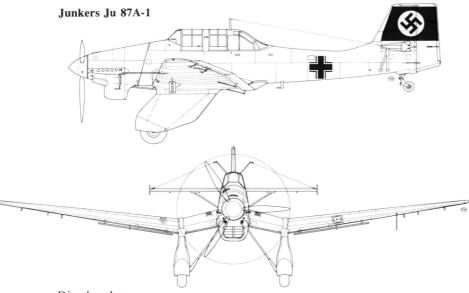

Dive bomber

1 × Jumo 210Ca 600 hp take-off
640 hp at 8,860 ft (2,700 m)

Jumo-Hamilton HPA 3-blade two-position 10% adjustable range (initial series) or HPA III 20% adj range propeller

Performance
Max speed: 183 mph (295 km/hr) at 9,840 ft (3,000 m) with
1 × 551 lb (250 kg) bomb
199 mph (320 km/hr) at 13,120 ft (4,000 m) clean
Max cruise: 171 mph (275 km/hr) at 8,860 ft (2,700 m)
Max diving speed: 279 mph (450 km/hr)
Landing speed: 62 mph (100 km/hr)
Service ceiling: 22,965 ft (7,000 m)
Max range: 620 miles (1,000 km) at 162 mph (260 km/hr)
Max flight endurance appr. 2.5 hrs

Weights
Empty: 5,004–5,104 lb (2,270–2,315 kg)
Max loaded: 7,495 lb (3,400 kg)

Dimensions
Span: 45 ft 3½ in (13.80 m)
Length: 35 ft 5¼ in (10.78 m)
Height: 12 ft 9½ in (3.89 m)
Wing area 343.368 sq.ft (31.9 m²)

Radio equipment
FuG VII with twin mast aerials for R/T

Bombs
Normally 1 × 551 lb (250 kg) ventrally – increased to max 1 × 1,102 lb (500 kg) when flown solo (with ballast in rear cockpit for CG reasons).

Gun armament
1 × 7.92 mm MG 17 fixed in port wing
1 × 7.92 mm MG 15 in rear cockpit

Junkers Ju 87B-1

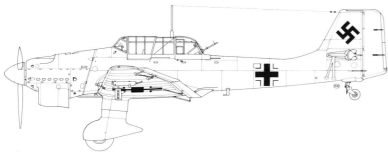

Dive bomber

1 × Jumo 211Da 1,200 hp take-off/emergency power
1,100 hp max at 4,920 ft (1,500 m)
Jumo-Hamilton HPA III 3-blade two-position 20% adjust range propeller.

Performance
Max speed: 211 mph (340 km/hr) at sea level
238 mph (383 km/hr) at 13,410 ft (4,090 m)
Max cruise: 209 mph (336 km/hr) at 12,140 ft (3,700 m)
Econ cruise: 174 mph (280 km/h) at 15,090 ft (4,600 m)
Max diving speed: 404 mph (650 km/h)
Landing speed: 67 mph (108 km/h)
Time to altitude: 3,280 ft (1,000 m) 2 min
6,560 ft (2,000 m) 4 min 18 sec
13,120 ft (4,000 m) 12 min
Max ceiling: 26,250 ft (8,000 m)
Max range: (with 1 × 1,102 lb (500 kg) bomb) 370 miles (595 km) at 202 mph (325 km/hr); without external load 490 miles (790 km)

Weights
Empty: 5,980 lb (2,710 kg)
Empty equipped: 6,090 lb (2,760 kg)
Max loaded: 9,480 lb (4,250 kg)

Dimensions
Span: 45 ft 3½ in (13.8 m)
Length: 36 ft 5 in (11.10 m)
Height: 13 ft 2 in (4.01 m)
Wing area: 343.368 sq. ft (31.9 m²)

Radio equipment
FuG VII or VIIa radio telephone; EiV intercom
Single radio mast + trailing aerial for R/T and radio telegraphy

Gun armament
2 × 7.92 mm MG 17 fixed forward in wings
1 × 7.92 mm MG 15 in rear rockpit.

Bombs
Max 1 × 1,102 lb (500 kg) ventrally
or 1 × 551 lb (250 kg) ventrally + 4 × 110 lb (50 kg) on
ETC 50 wing racks

Junkers Ju 87C-1
Carrier-borne dive bomber

1 × Jumo 211Da 1,200 hp take-off/emergency power
1,100 hp max at 4,920 ft (1,500 m)

Performance
Max speed (at 11,684 lb/5,300 kg) (i.e. with 1 × 1,102 lb/500 kg bomb and both drop tanks):
178 mph (286 km/hr) at sea level
193 mph (310 km/hr) at 9,840 ft (3,000 m)
199 mph (320 km/hr) at 16,405 ft (5,000 m)
Max cruise (same weight):
190 mph (306 km/hr) at 16,405 ft (5,000 m)
Max speed (at 10,586 lb/4,802 kg) (i.e. with 1 × 1,102 lb/500 kg bomb but no drop tanks):
184 mph (296 km/hr) at sea level
214 mph (344 km/hr) at 16,405 ft (5,000 m)
Time to altitude (at 11,684 lb/5,300 kg):
3,810 ft (1,000 m) 4 min 6 sec
9,840 ft (3,000 m) 13 min 36 sec
16,405 ft (5,000 m) 27 min 48 sec
Norm range (with 1,102 lb/500 kg bomb, no drop tanks):
332 miles (534 km)
Max range (with 1,102 lb /500 kg bomb and drop tanks):
721 miles (1,160 km)

Weights
Empty equipped 8,058–8,157 lb (3,655–3,700 kg):
depending on bomb load and fuel
Loaded 8,818–11,773 lb (4,000–5,340 kg):
(as above)

Dimensions
Span: 43 ft 3½ in (13.20 m) (folded: 16 ft 5 in/5.00 m)
Length: 36 ft 0¾ in (11.00 m)
Height: 12 ft 4½ in (3.77 m)
Wing area: 336.91 sq.ft (31.3 m²)

Radio equipment
FuG VII radio telephone; EiV intercom

Gun armament
2 × 7.92 mm MG 17 (@ 500 rds) fixed forward in wings
1 × 7.92 mm MG 15 (900 rds) in rear cockpit

Bombs
1 × 1,102 lb/500 kg + 2 × 66 Imp. gal (300 l) drop tanks *or*
4 × 110 lb/50 kg bombs

Junkers Ju 87R-2
Extended range anti-shipping dive bomber
1 × Junkers Jumo 211Da 1,200 hp take-off/emergency power
1,100 hp max at 4,920 ft (1,500 m)

Performance
Max speed: 211 mph (340 km/hr) at 13,120 ft (4,000 m)
Max diving speed: 404 mph (650 km/hr)
Max range: 779 miles (1,254 km) with 1,102 lb (500 kg) bomb at
180 mph (290 km/h) outwards and 205 mph (330 km/h) return at
13,120 ft (4,000 m)
Service ceiling: with 1,102 lb (500 kg) bomb and external fuel tanks
19,030 ft (5,800 m); clean 26,250 ft (8,000 m)

Weights
Max loaded: 12,456 lb (5,650 kg)

Dimensions, **armament**, **radio equipment**: as Ju 87B-2
(FuG 25a IFF set as retroactive fitting)

Junkers Ju 87D-1

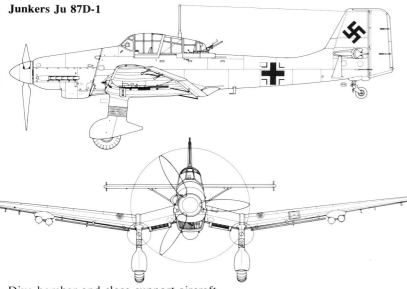

Dive bomber and close-support aircraft
1 × Jumo 211J-1 1,420 hp take-off/emergency power
1,190 hp max continuous
960 hp cruise
Junkers VS 11 constant speed propeller

Performance
Max speed (at 12,600 lb/5,715 kg):
255 mph (410 km/hr) at 13,450 ft (4,100 m)
Max cont cruise with extra bombs: 193 mph (310 km/hr) at 16,730 ft
(5,100 m)
Econ cruise (with 3,968 lb/800 kg bomb load):
115 mph (185 km/hr) at 16,730 ft (5,100 m)
Landing speed: 68 mph (110 km/hr)
Time: to 16,405 ft (5,000 m) 19 min 48 sec
Service ceiling: (at 12,600 lb/5,715 kg) 23,905 ft (7,285 m)
(at max loaded weight) 15,520 ft (4,730 m)
Norm range: 510 miles (820 km)
Max range: 954 miles (1,535 km) on econ cruise

Weights
Empty, equipped: 8,598 lb (3,900 kg)
Loaded (normal): 12,880 lb (5,842 kg)
Max overload: 14,550 lb (6,600 kg)

Dimensions
Span: 45 ft 3⅓ in (13.80 m)
Length: 37 ft 8¾ in (11.50 m)
Height: 13 ft 9¼ in (3.88 m)
Wing area: 343.37 sq.ft (31.9 m²)

Armour protection
Pilot: 8 mm black plate, 10 mm headshield, 8 mm ventral,
8 mm rear plate, 4 mm side
Gunner: 8 mm bulkhead, 5 mm floor

Radio equipment
FuG 16 radio-telephone; EiV intercom
Peil G IV D/F set
2 × 7.92 mm MG 17 fixed forward in wings
1 × 7.92 mm twin-barrel MG 81Z on GSL-K 18 mount in rear cockpit
For ground strafing: 2 × WB 81 (each 3 × MG 81), or 2 × 20 mm MG FF
cannon, or 2 plywood bomb containers (@ 94 × 4.4 lb/2 kg SD 2 bombs)

Gun armament
2 × 7.92 mm MG 17 fixed forward in wings
1 × 7.92 mm twin-barrel MG 81Z on GSL-K 18 mount in rear cockpit
For ground strafing: 2 × WB81(each 6 × MG 81), or 2 × 20 mm MG FF
cannon, or 2
plywood bomb containers (@ 94 × 4.4 lb/2 kg SD 2 bombs)

Bombs
1 × 3,968 lb (1,800 kg) for short-range overload operations
max 1 × 2,205 lb (1,000 kg)
norm 1 × 1,102 lb (500 kg) or 1 × 551 lb (250 kg) under fuselage
+ 4 × 110 lb (50 kg) or 2 × 551 lb (250 kg) under wings

Junkers Ju 87D-8
Night ground attack/harassment bomber
1 × Jumo 211P(dev of Jumo 211J with increased rpm and boost pressure)
1,500 hp take-off/emergency power
1,410 hp at 14,440 ft (4,400 m)
1,010 hp max cruise at 17,060 ft (5,200 m)

Performance
Max speed: 249 mph (400 km/hr) at 14,400 ft (4,400 m)
Landing speed: 68 mph (110 km/h)
Max range: 985 miles (1,585 km)
Service ceiling: 24,610 ft (7,500 m)

Weights
Empty equipped: 8,682 lb (3,938)
Max loaded: 14,566 lb (6,607 kg)

Dimensions
Span: 49 ft 2½ in (15.00 m)
Length: 36 ft 6 in (11.13 m)
Height: 13 ft 9¼ in (3.88 m)
Wing area: 362.528 sq.ft (33.68 m²)

Armour protection
Basically as on D-1, with some field additions

Radio equipment
FuG 16 radio-telephone; EiV intercom
Peil G IV D/F set; often FuG 25a IFF

Gun armament
2 ×20 mm MG 151/20 cannon fixed in wings
1 × 7.92 mm twin-barrel MG 81Z in rear cockpit

Bombs
often two plywood containers with 92 × 4.4 lb/2 kg SD 2 anti-personnel
bombs.

Ju 87D-1 of 7/St.G 1 on final approach in summer of 1942. (BUNDESARCHIV)

零戦
ZERO FIGHTER

Text by ROBERT C. MIKESH

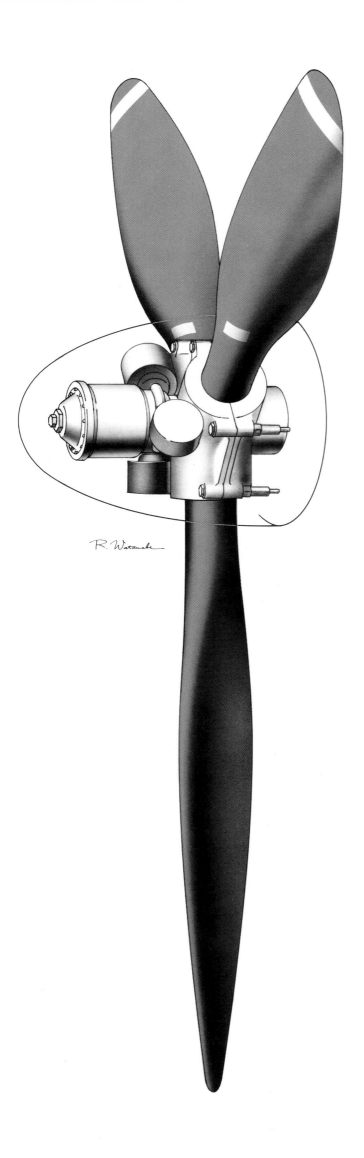

R. Watanabe

Acknowledgements

My sincerest thanks go to all who have helped in developing this story of the Zero fighter. Particular appreciation goes to Shorzoe Abe, David A. Anderton, Walter J. Boyne and René J. Francillon. The letters, books and personal contact with Jiro Horikoshi and Saburo Sakai have provided the foundation on which this history has been developed. To all, I give my deepest thanks.

First Blood

Twelve Mitsubishi Zero fighters of the 12th *Kokutai* turned away from the Chinese city of Chungking and headed back toward Hankow. Below, billowing columns of smoke mushroomed from the stricken city, the result of well-placed bombs dropped by an Imperial Japanese Navy force of 54 Mitsubishi G3M2 Type 96 Bombers (later to be code-named "Nell" by the Allies). The Zeros, flying on their first combat mission, had been detailed to escort the bombers to the target and back.

Lieutenant Tamotsu Yokoyama, a recent arrival from Omura Naval Air Base, led the fighter formation. Earlier in the flight he had given the signal to his pilots to arm their weapons, but much to their disappointment, not a single enemy fighter was sighted. This first mission of the new A6M2 fighter, on 19 August, 1940, was a bloodless one.

Previous escort missions had been flown by another Mitsubishi fighter, the A5M4 model (known later by the Allies as "Claude"), with open cockpits, fixed landing gear, and limited range. They had gone with the bombers as far as they could. More aggressive Chinese interceptions during the past six months had begun to hurt the Japanese; their losses were rising. The new Zero fighter arrived on the scene none too soon, for the vulnerable bombers needed protection all the way to the target and back, and the Zero had been designed to do just that.

Type 96 "Nell" bombers over China in the late 1940's.

Type 96 Carrier-borne Fighter (Mitsubishi A5M4) "Claude"

But where was the Chinese opposition that had been so plentiful on previous missions? The Zero pilots could hardly wait to engage the enemy, for they knew they had the superior machine. But the Chinese, noted for their intelligence-gathering ability, apparently could foresee the Zero's deadly capability, and knew when this first mission was taking place. There was no contest in the air that day.

The next day it was the same. Formation leader Lieutenant Saburo Shindo hoped he would have the chance to engage the enemy for the first time with the Zero. He and his wingmates returned to Hankow without firing a shot.

These Zeros, introduced to operations in the late summer of 1940, were part of a pre-production batch of 15 used to test the design in actual squadron service. Mitsubishi

engineers had been reluctant to clear these fighters for combat before they had been fully tested. Navy engineers differed; the Zero was so promising that they believed any changes could be handled in the combat zone, and technicians and engineers were sent along with the Zeros to make what ever modifications were found necessary after battle experience.

On 12 September, the Zeros were airborne again to escort 27 bombers over Chungking and back. The Japanese pilots were determined to fire their guns at the enemy even if they had to leave the bombers to do it. As the bomber force left the target area, the Zero pilots spotted what appeared as five enemy aircraft on the ground, and dived to attack. They proved to be decoys, but the Zeros shot up at will the Shihmachow Air Field and other ground installations. Their actions goaded the Chinese to come up and fight, but none rose to the challenge. Despite the lack of aerial opposition to the Zero, post-strike aerial photography taken by a Mitsubishi C5M ("Babs") reconnaissance aircraft confirmed the presence of 32 Chinese planes at dispersed locations around the city.

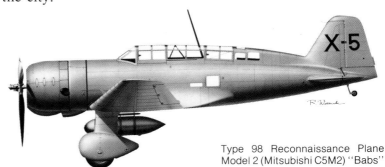

Type 98 Reconnaissance Plane Model 2 (Mitsubishi C5M2) "Babs"

The situation changed, however, when the Zero's fourth mission was flown on 13 September. This became their day of "first blood," creating a legend that would build and remain throughout World War II and beyond. Once again, the Zeros were escorting the bomber force deep into mainland China for an attack on Chungking. As before, not one Chinese fighter rose to the attack and the Japanese bombs rained on the city.

As the attacking force left the target area, a lone Japanese reconnaissance plane high above the burning city spotted Chinese fighters converging over the area. Wasting no time, the observer reported this sighting to the departing formation of Zeros. Wheeling back toward the city and climbing for an advantage in altitude, Lieutenant Shindo led his squadron of Zeros in a classic situation of surprise and pounced on the unsuspecting Chinese pilots.

Polikarpov I-16/10

For the Chinese, a painful one-sided air duel took place. The Zeros swarmed over the startled enemy pilots, cutting their aircraft out of the sky with their machine-guns and cannon fire. The Russian-made Polikarpov I-15 biplanes and chunky I-16 monoplane fighters were totally outclassed by the swift and agile Zeros and within minutes plumes of smoke from falling Chinese planes filled the sky. When the slaughter ended, all 27 Chinese fighters were destroyed. If there was any disappointment to the Japanese pilots, it was that a few enemy planes were not destroyed until they were landing, and one, in his effort to escape, crashed when flying too low to the ground, depriving the Japanese pilots of aerial targets. Not one Zero was lost in this opening air battle, which was the birthplace of an image of invincibility for the new fighter and the skill of its pilots.

With the threat of Zeros engaging any Chinese aircraft that might appear, twin-engined as well as single-engined Japanese bombers could attack at will with little threat of opposition. On 16 September, a single large Chinese aircraft of an unrecorded type was spotted over the city of Chungking and was immediately shot down by the six Zeros that were committed to strikes that day. This was the last mission flown in the month of September for these service test aircraft. For the remaining two weeks of that month, mechanics prepared the Zeros for the forthcoming flights that would take them even deeper into enemy territory where the Chinese had retreated.

When this small experimental force of Zero fighters was ready for more combat flying, they were sent on a very long-range mission against Chengtsu in Szechwan Province on 4 October, 1940. Twenty-seven bombers escorted by eight Zeros were to flush out the Chinese at this remote retreat.

The Model 11 Zero fighter, the first production version. This flight of two was

Again the attack was unchallenged. As the bombers departed the target area, the formation of Zeros broke off and circled back, undetected, in a wide arc above broken clouds. Bursting in among unsuspecting Chinese pilots flying at Taipingssu Air Field, they downed five Chinese I-16 fighters and one Russian-made Tupolev medium bomber before resorting to ground strafing attacks. Reconnaissance photos later confirmed as many as 19 aircraft of various types were destroyed on the ground. Only two Zeros received light damage.

From these encounters, the Chinese considered the Zero fighter to be invincible, and their pilots treated it with such caution that interceptions virtually came to an end. Thus, the Japanese gained air superiority over almost the entire Chinese theatre of war. This complete control of the air meant that bombers of all descriptions would be sent on operations deep into Chinese territory at will, protected by the awe-inspiring Zero. During the four months from 19 August, 1940, until the end of that year, a total of 153 Zero sorties were flown in 22 missions during which 59 Chinese aircraft were shot down and 101 destroyed on the ground without any loss in the Zero force.

From October, 1940, to April, 1941, the Mitsubishi G3M2 ("Nell") bomber squadrons were withdrawn from the mainland for reorganization. During this six-month period, the Zero was the only aircraft that could attack the Chinese on all fronts since they had retreated beyond the effective range of the single-engined Japanese Navy bombers and A5M4 ("Claude") fighters, and meanwhile the Zero pilots continued to taunt Chinese pilots into combat and maintaining their one-sided superiority.

part of a group of 15 first committed to combat over China.

The air war over China in the early part of 1941 followed consistently the events of 1940. By September that year, the Zeros had flown 354 sorties, shot down 44 enemy aircraft, damaged 62 more, and by now had lost two Zeros as a result of anti-aircraft fire. From this point, a number of air units were systematically withdrawn from the China front in preparation for an even greater conflict. For the Zero this air war over China had been decidedly a one-sided affair. As the opening of the Pacific war against the United States drew near, Japanese planners had unshaking faith in the ability of the Zero against the then existing American and British aircraft. A few recognized however that should such a war be prolonged, the Japanese and their Zero would face an array of weapons whose qualities and quantities could only be guessed at. The days of crushing superiority would be short lived.

Early Generations

When the Zero was in the design stage, its concept was far more advanced than any other carrier-borne fighter then in existence anywhere in the world, or in any stage of development at that time. To trace the historic development of the Zero, it is well to examine briefly the lineage of the five previous generations of operational carrier-borne fighters used by the Imperial Japanese Navy and their counterparts of other nations.

This line of fighters and other tactical aircraft began when aircraft carriers came into fleet use by the world's major naval powers in the early 1920s. The Japanese were first to complete and launch a true aircraft carrier, the *Hosho*. Completed in December, 1922, she was designed and built as a carrier from the keel up; in contrast, the later USS *Langley*, recommissioned in 1925, was a conversion from the USS *Jupiter*, a 1913 collier. During World War I the British had converted a battle-cruiser into HMS *Furious*, a hybrid carrier recommissioned as an aircraft carrier in 1925. In her 1917 configuration she had a limited flight deck area forward of the superstructure; aft, she kept her battle-cruiser armament.

In February, 1923, initial take offs and landings were made on the *Hosho* by Mitsubishi's British pilot Lieutenant William Jordan late of the Royal Flying Corps, flying one of the company's Type 10 Carrier-borne fighters.

Two years previously in January, 1921, a British Air Mission led by Captain Sir William Francis Sempill, RN, (Also known as Capt. The Master of Sempill) had been invited to Japan to advise the Imperial Japanese Navy on equipping and training its air arm. British Gloster Sparrowhawk fighters were selected as Japan's first carrier-borne fighters. Their design, of 1919–1920 vintage, was basically that of the Nieuport Nighthawk, modified and re-engined by the Gloucestershire Aircraft Co. Ltd. Fifty were purchased, and parts of 40 more were acquired. Most of the latter were assembled into complete aircraft by the Navy Arsenal at Yokosuka. Many of these lively Sparrowhawks powered by 230-hp Bentley B.R. 2 nine-cylinder rotary engines remained in service up to 1928.

As Japan embarked on its own aircraft industry, it was heavily influenced by foreign designs and designers. The Mitsubishi Internal Combustion Engine Manufacturing Co., located then in Kobe and beginning a new venture in manufacturing aircraft, employed the services of Herbert Smith, formerly with Sopwith as their chief designer. From this company came the first in a series of carrier-borne aircraft for various missions. Because of this engineering team leadership, the new fighter carried the influence seen in earlier Sopwith designs. Completed in October, 1921, these were identified as Type 10 Carrier-borne Fighters (signifying the 10th year of Emperor Taisho). These aircraft have the distinction of being the first fighters designed for carrier operation, while aircraft of other nations at that time were adaptations of existing land-based fighters. A total of 128 machines was produced, and they remained in service for nine

Type 10 Carrier-borne Fighter

years — until 1929, serving simultaneously with the Sparrowhawks. At the onset, the performance of the Type 10 Fighter, powered by the Mitsubishi-built Hispano-Suiza 300-hp engine, was comparable to, if not better than, that of other fighters operated from aircraft carriers of other nations of the world. Their greatest drawback was that they remained in service far too long.

The second generation of Japanese shipboard fighters which entered service in 1929 was also influenced by foreign design. This time the Nakajima Aircraft Company had won the competition with their license-built Gloster Gambet. This British design, stemming from the Gloster Grebe of 1923 vintage, became the Type 3 Carrier-borne Fighter (Type 3 identified the 3rd year of the Showa period – 1928). Unfortunately, this fighter design was already sadly outdated upon delivery. At the same time the US Navy was outfitting its three carriers with new Boeing F4B-1s, supplementing late model Curtiss F6C-3 fighters.

The type 3 Carrier-borne Fighters saw action during the Shanghai Incident and the initial stage of the Sino–Japanese Incident, but under the circumstances their obsolescence was not critical. These 420-hp, Jupiter-powered fighters served until 1935, their latter years in second line roles. Approximately 150 fighters of this type were manufactured by Nakajima.

For this time period, nearly all carrier based fighters were equipped with engines of the 400–500-hp range including the Nakajima Type 3 fighter. Although the Type 3 was an outdated design for worldwide front-line carrier fighters, it was the lightest and considered the most manoeuvrable. In combat, however, it would have lacked speed and firepower.

When Japan adopted a new designation system for its Navy aircraft in 1927, the Type 3 fighter was assigned the earliest designation in this system as A1N1. The "A" series signifies carrier-based fighter, first in the new designation series, while "N" shows this as having been designed by Nakajima. This closely resembles the U.S. Navy method of designations used from 1922 to 1963, an organizational system that Japan greatly admired.

As the Japanese aviation industry grew, they became less dependent on foreign designs, yet were not hesitant to use the best forms of technology found in foreign equipment and improve upon it. The third set of Japanese carrier-borne fighters to be selected in 1930 for its growing fleet, now containing three carriers, was the Nakajima Type 90, identified by the Japanese year 2590 (AD 1930). When these came off the production line in 1931, they were modern fighters by world standards. Japan had caught up. Production of 100 of these fighters rapidly replaced the two-year-old A1N1s which by now were actually outdated by eight years in comparable design technology. The design, although Japanese, was influenced by the Boeing Model 69B the export version of the F2B of which Japan had purchased one example in 1928. This very manoeuvrable Japanese fighter, designated A2N1 after it was accepted by the Navy, was powered by a Nakajima-built Bristol Jupiter engine, called the Kotobuki 2 generating 460 hp.

When the A2N1 entered service in 1932, its counterparts in the U.S. Navy were the all metal fuselage Boeing F4B-3s and -4s which remained front-line equipment for the next three years. On Great Britain's two carriers were the one-year-old sleek-lined Hawker Nimrod biplanes. This navalized and strengthened version of the RAF's Fury was highly regarded by pilots and had a long life with the Fleet Air Arm. Nimrods were powered by a 525-hp Rolls-Royce Kestrel inline engine which gave a very pleasing appearance to this fighter. In order to remain abreast of modern design trends, Japan succeeded in purchasing one Nimrod for study in 1934.

France was the fourth country to have an aircraft carrier prior to the birth of the Zero: the *Béarn*, launched in 1926. She carried French-built fighters throughout her career, parasol-wing designs that were adaptations of land-based aircraft. The threat of World War II prompted the order of American-made Grumman G-36A fighters (equivalent to F4F-3 model with Wright GR-1820 "Cyclone" engines) to replace the French-built designs, but France capitulated in 1940 before any of the American aircraft were delivered.

Japan held the biplane design for its fourth generation of carrier-borne fighters which began in the mid-1930s. This was a refinement of the A2N, Type 90, which became the Nakajima A4N, Type 95 fighter. These cleaner biplanes entered production in 1935 and 221 machines were delivered. A little faster than the A2N, the A4N was heavier, and not fully compensated for by the increase in power of the 670-hp *Hikari* engine, thus, pilots preferred the agility of the earlier model. This pilot preference would emerge again in a heated discussion over the design of the Zero when a choice in performance between speed and range became an issue. Due to the shorter range of the A4N, its activities were limited during the initial stage of the Sino–Japanese Incident. These were the last biplane fighters for the Imperial Japanese Navy.

Era of the Monoplanes

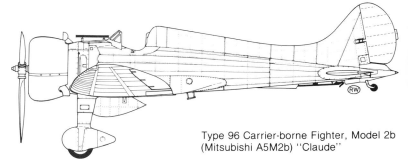

Type 96 Carrier-borne Fighter, Model 2b
(Mitsubishi A5M2b) "Claude"

It was at this point – the generation of Navy fighters preceding the Zero – that the Japanese not only equalled, but in some standards surpassed other nations in aircraft of this type. The new Mitsubishi Type 96 Carrier Fighter, having been designated A5M as a service aircraft, was the first of the low wing monoplanes for carrier duty, a configuration that all future designs would follow. A compromise had been made here, often with verbal objections by Navy pilots, for improving speed and range at some sacrifice to manoeuvrability by departing from the biplane arrangement. These monoplanes went into service on 18 September, 1937, and were soon

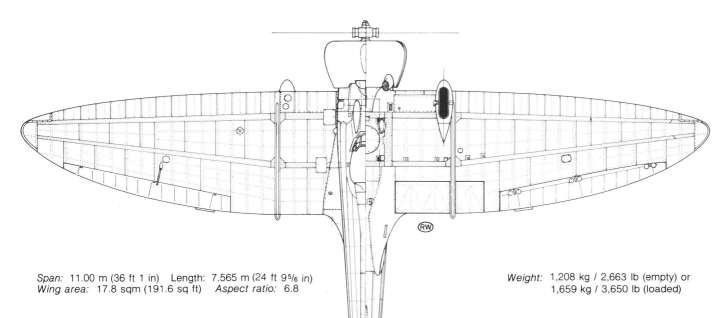

Span: 11.00 m (36 ft 1 in)   *Length:* 7.565 m (24 ft 9⁵/₆ in)
Wing area: 17.8 sqm (191.6 sq ft)   *Aspect ratio:* 6.8

Weight: 1,208 kg / 2,663 lb (empty) or
1,659 kg / 3,650 lb (loaded)

operating from the aircraft carrier *Kaga*. The A5M, later given the code name "Claude" by the Allies, arrived none too soon for the Japanese in the stiffening air war over China as the second Sino-Japanese conflict flared up again. Replacing obsolete A2N and A4N biplanes that were now being heavily mauled by Chinese fighters, they escorted bombing attacks over Nanking and other parts of the mainland of China, quickly gaining mastery of the air. They were a superior opponent to all aircraft types the Chinese could muster. The overall performance of these new all-metal monoplanes seemed ignored by other nations – perhaps not only because of Japan's apparent isolation from the rest of the world, but also because pilots at that time still clung to the biplane concept with emphasis on manoeuvrability. Continuing with this philosophy, the U.S. Navy carriers had, as standard equipment, Grumman's stubby F2F and F3F biplanes featuring a retractable landing gear. The British Fleet Air Arm was newly equipped in 1937 with Gloster Sea Gladiator fixed-gear biplanes. Their service life extended into the early war years until they were replaced by Grumman G-36A aircraft that were originally ordered by the French for the *Béarn*, and later by G-36 Martlets supplied under head-lease by the British.

The success of Mitsubishi's new fighter did not come without its failures in this attempt to use a monoplane configuration. In an effort to meet an earlier requirement of the Navy for a 7-*Shi* (1932) experimental fighter, little time was granted to Mitsubishi to perfect its design for a new low-wing carrier based monoplane before being pushed into

premature production. Specifications issued by the Navy for the 7-*Shi* fighter left little latitude for designers based on current capabilities. Due to the engineering level of Japan's aviation industry, the undertaking was too advanced and the new test series of only two aircraft was an almost total failure.

When the specifications were issued that eventually became the A5M ("Claude") fighter, no mention was made of carrier-based equipment. Only five basic requirements for what was then known as the 9-*Shi* fighter were specified; speed, climb, fuel capacity, armament, and maximum wing span and length were given. This gave the Mitsubishi design team led by a young engineer named Jiro Horikoshi, more latitude in which to design a suitable aircraft. Given a freedom that he did not have on his first design attempt with the 7-*Shi*, Horikoshi was able to innovate. He was quoted later as saying: "Since each man, and the group as a whole, had benefited from the knowledge and experience of working on the 7-*Shi* fighter, I was able to incorporate into my new design several novel ideas which represented a marked change over former practices. I could determine without hesitation the general policy, the aircraft's basic configuration, and details of the design, and expect full support from every member of the team."

In the design concept of the new fighter, the thickness of both the wing and the fuselage were kept to a minimum. The landing gear remained fixed, but was streamlined to the greatest extent possible. Its length was shortened through the use of an inverted gull wing. Retractable landing gear was an essential feature on modern aircraft, yet

Engine: Kotobuki 3-Kai, rated at 600 hp for take-off,
dry weight 410 kg (902 lb)
Wing loading: 93.2 kg/sqm (19.1 lb/sq ft)
Power loading: 2.77 kg/hp (6.1 lb/hp)

Max speed: 217 kt (252 mph) at 4,000 m (13,120 ft)
Time to climb 5,000 m (16,400 ft): 7 min 18 sec
Armament: 2 × 7.7 mm machine-guns,
2 × 30 kg (66 lb) bomb

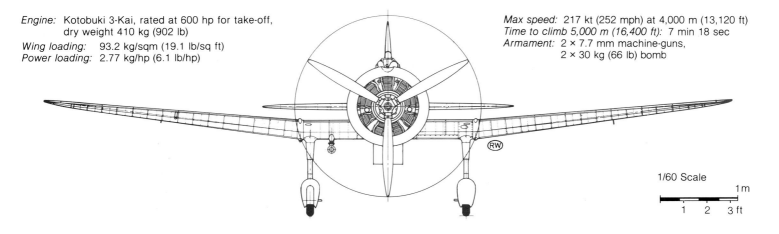

1/60 Scale

1m

1   2   3 ft

Horikoshi estimated that disadvantages in increased weight and mechanical linkage problems would not justify the speed increase. The fixed gear accounted for ten per cent of the minimum resistance of the entire aircraft; if retracted, it would only have given about three per cent increase in overall airspeed.

Great effort was given to perfecting flush riveting for the exterior skin of the airframe. This was an innovation just being introduced in German and American designs. Every consideration in streamlining was given careful study. When the structure was completed, skin crevices and irregularities were filled and painted to a smooth finish. Although a 218 mph maximum speed in level flight was called for in the design specification, the 9-*Shi* fighter reached 280 mph during initial tests. Powered by a 600-hp Nakajima *Kotobuki* 5 engine, its high speed was attributed to its very clean design, rather than an abundance of power.

Every weight-saving measure was also taken. Engineers concluded that even 90 to 110 pounds saved could affect the ultimate success in an air engagement. Horikoshi said, "The margin of 100 pounds between two opposing fighters was considered comparable with the difference between a veteran pilot and an unskilled novice. The fighter pilots compared themselves with the old *kendo* [Japanese fencing] champions, and asked for fighters with the quality of the master craftsman's Japanese swords. As a result of our pilot's figurative demand for the blades and arts of the old masters, the Japanese fighter planes were the lightest in weight and amongst the most manoeuvrable in the world. Our pilots sought tenaciously to master every trick of the superior fighter pilot, and they became well known for their prowess."

The delay between the final approval of the 9-*Shi* airframe and its acceptance as the Type 96 Carrier-borne Fighter A5M1 ("Claude") stemmed from the lack of a suitable engine. A number of radial engines and one inline engine, varying from 600 to 800 hp, were considered by the Navy. Finally, the 600-hp Nakajima *Kotobuki* 2-*Kai-1*, having the most reliability, was adopted for the initial production models. The gull wing was dropped in favour of a more conventional form to simplify production.

The performance of the early models was lower than that which was demonstrated by the prototypes, but they went into service anyway in the Sino-Japanese war which began in July, 1937. They became the backbone of the Imperial Japanese Navy's fighter force, and over 1,000 were built in several models. The model produced in greatest quantities was the A5M4 which remained in production at Mitsubishi's Nagoya plant until 1940. As power plants improved, these late models were equipped with the Nakajima *Kotobuki* 41 and 41 Kai engine, rated at 710 hp for take-off.

"Claude's" involvement in the Pacific War was very limited. With the exception of a token number used for the early attack against Davao in the Philippines, and again in the Aleutians, most of these open-cockpit, fixed-landing-gear fighters were retained in Japan by second-line and training units, giving way to its successor, the Zero Fighter.

The Zero is Born

At an earlier time, even while the A5M "Claude" was enjoying initial success as a combat aircraft in the conflict with China, the Imperial Japanese Navy recognized that the aircraft lacked range to escort the bombers to targets deep in the mainland. The aircraft would soon be obsolete compared to foreign equipment that was then being shown by potential enemy nations. From these elements developed new requirements by the Japanese Navy in 1937 for the 12-*Shi* fighter, the results of which became the Zero.

The study determined the requirements for a new-generation aircraft based on a number of situations, some hypothetical, others real. What was needed in a fighter operating over China in the existing situation was clear, but the requirements needed to combat an enemy which might materialize during the operational career of the aircraft took much planning. Not only was the theatre of operation to be taken into consideration in determining distances to be flown, but also the type and quality of opposition the enemy might have to offer. Considering all factors often called for aircraft with a performance reflecting technology that exceeded the actual capabilities of the aviation industry. Planners believed that the performance demands for the Zero were far in excess of the industry's capabilities to deliver; in spite of that, the Navy further increased the required performance of the proposed fighter.

Specifications submitted to Japan's aviation industry for the 12-*Shi* Carrier-borne Fighter were as follows:

Mission: A fighter capable of intercepting and destroying enemy attack bombers, and of serving as an escort fighter with combat performance greater than that of enemy interceptors.
Dimensions: Wing span less than 12 metres (39 ft 4 in).
Speed: Maximum speed exceeding 500 km/h (270 kt, 310.5 mph) at 4000 m (13,123 ft) in level flight. (*315.5 mph).
Climb: Climb to 3000 m (9,843 ft) within 3 min. 30 sec.
   (*3 min. 54 sec. achieved from takeoff start.)
Endurance: Normal flight duration of 1.2 to 1.5 hours with normal rated power (maximum continuous) at 3000 m (9,843 ft) fully loaded with auxiliary fuel tank; 1.5 to 2 hours at 3000 m (9,843 ft) using normal rated power, or 6 to 8 hours at maximum range cruising speed. (†10 hours, 18 gph, 115 kt at 12,000 ft, 1,700 to 1,850 rpm.)
Takeoff: Less than 70 m (229.7 ft) with head wind of 12 m/sec (43.2 km/h, 30 mph).
   Approximately 175 m (574 ft) in calm wind.
Landing speed: Less than 107 km/h (58 kt, 66.7 mph).
   (*55 mph)
Gliding descent/min: 210 m (690 ft) to 240 m (787).
Manoeuvrability: Equal or better than Type 96 Fighter A5M
Armament: Two Type 99, 20-mm cannon Mk.1, Model 3, and two Type 97, 7.7-mm machine guns.
Bombs: Two 30-kg (66-lb) bombs or two 60-kg (132-lb) bombs.
Radio: Type 96-ku-1 airborne radio and Type Ku-3 radio homer.

Nakajima Type 3 Model 2 carrier-borne fighter (A1N2)
of the Kaga Fighter Unit. Flown by Lt. Nogiji Ikuta in Feb., 1932.

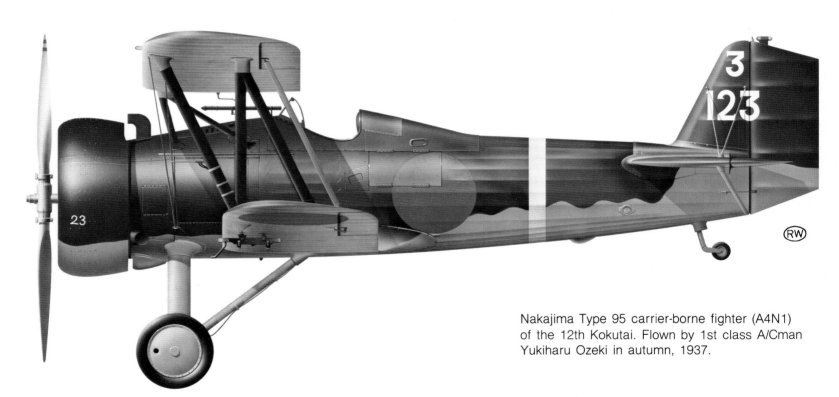

Nakajima Type 95 carrier-borne fighter (A4N1)
of the 12th Kokutai. Flown by 1st class A/Cman
Yukiharu Ozeki in autumn, 1937.

Nakajima Type 3, and Type 95

The license manufacture of the British Gloster Gambet by Nakajima as the Navy Type 3 Carrier-borne Fighter was characteristic of Japanese dependency on foreign designs in their early years of aviation. Light weight and maneuverable, the Type 3 was the best Japanese Navy fighter during the early 1930s. Equipped with two 7.7-mm machine-guns, these airplanes were used extensively during the Shanghai Incident in 1932 and performed well though limited opposition was encountered. They remained in first line service until 1935 despite their outdated design based on 1923 technology which stemmed from the early Gloster Grebe. Retroactively, when a new designation system was initiated by the Japanese Navy, Type 3

Fighters with 520 hp Jupiter VI engines became A1N1s, and 520 hp Kotobuki 2 powered models were the A1N2s.

As a successor to the Type 3, Nakajima produced the Type 90 Carrier-borne Fighter, A2N series. This 1930 design was developed in Japan but was influenced heavily by foreign technologies found on imported aircraft. They entered service in 1932. Nakajima refined the Type 90 design in 1935, which became the A4N, Type 95 Carrier-Borne Fighter (bottom). This model was a little faster with its 670 hp Hikari engine, than its predecessor, but its increased weight made it less maneuverable and it had shorter range. They too were armed with two 7.7-mm machine-guns. The A4Ns saw limited activity during the initial stage of the Sino-Japanese Incident and were the last biplane fighters for the Imperial Japanese Navy. About 221 were built by Nakajima.

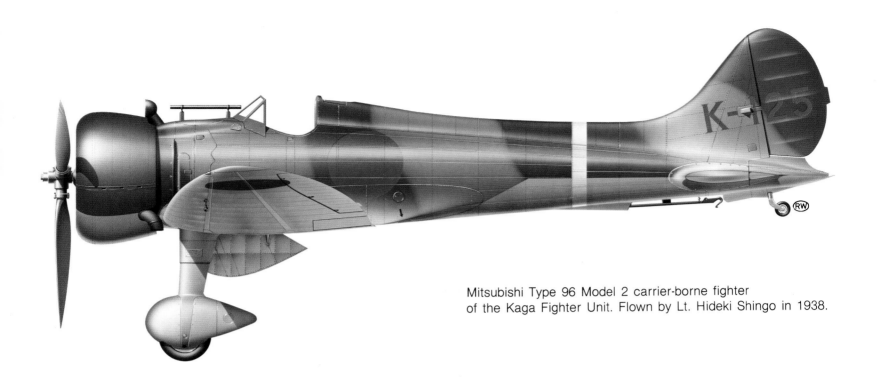

Mitsubishi Type 96 Model 2 carrier-borne fighter
of the Kaga Fighter Unit. Flown by Lt. Hideki Shingo in 1938.

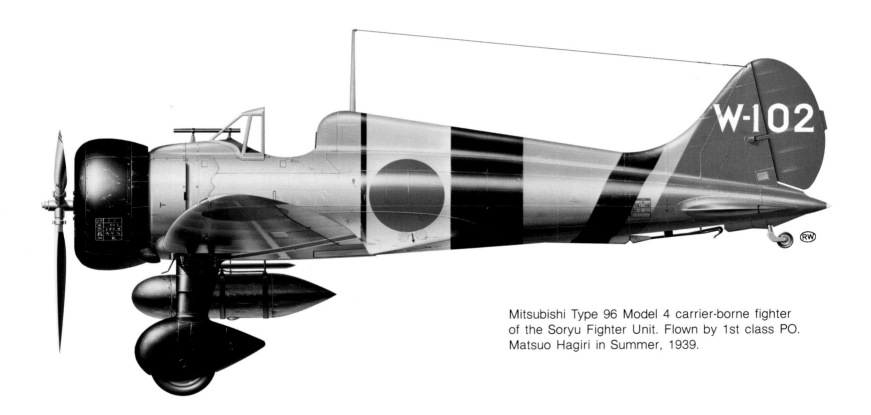

Mitsubishi Type 96 Model 4 carrier-borne fighter
of the Soryu Fighter Unit. Flown by 1st class PO.
Matsuo Hagiri in Summer, 1939.

Mitsubishi Type 96

The Type 96 Fighter was the world's first operational low-wing carrier-borne fighter. Developed from the experimental Mitsubishi 9-*Shi* fighter with an inverted gull wing and remarkable performance, the design was simplified for production and military use. Drag was minimized by adopting an airframe of small cross-section with flush-riveted aluminum stressed-skin covering. Based upon combat experi-

ence gained over China, several models evolved over the three years of production that began in late 1936. Most noticable changes were the deeper looking fuselage and larger wheels and pants on later models. The Model 24 or A5M4 was built in larger numbers than any other variant of this fighter. When superseded by the Zero as a first-line air-craft, A5M4s, code named 'Claude' by the Allies, served as single-place fighter-trainers. A two-seat model was also built and used as an advanced trainer.

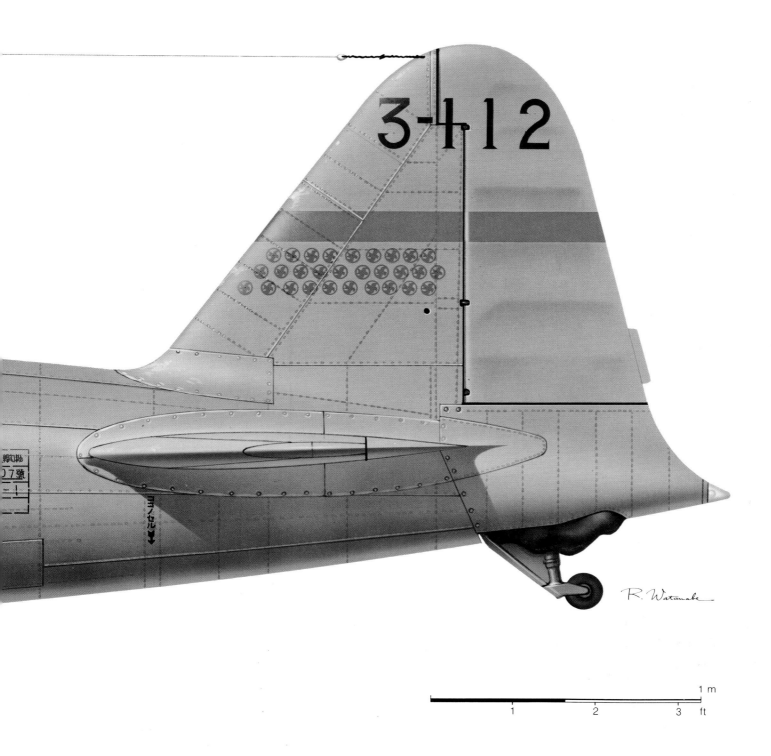

1 m

| 1 | 2 | 3 | ft |

Kokutai in Aug., 1941.

pilots, but was also due to the limitations in horsepower that was available at that time. Performance was remarkable for only having a 950 hp Sakae engine, while opponents were above 1,000 hp and would soon reach 2,000 hp.

When the heavier armed and faster American fighters reached the combat zone, the frailties of the Zero became apparent. Armor plating for the pilot and protection for the fuel tanks had been sacrificed for lightness in the airframe. The only defense for the Zero was to outmaneuver the enemy during its many encounters with Allied fighters. Despite its weaknesses the Model 21 remained a lethal weapon in the hands of capable pilots in the early part of the Pacific War.

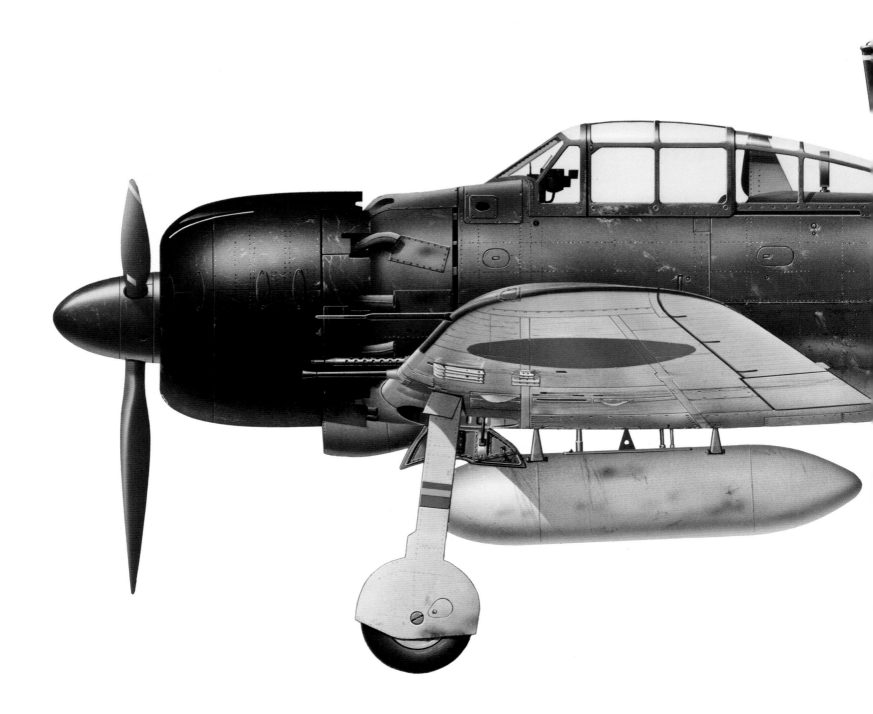

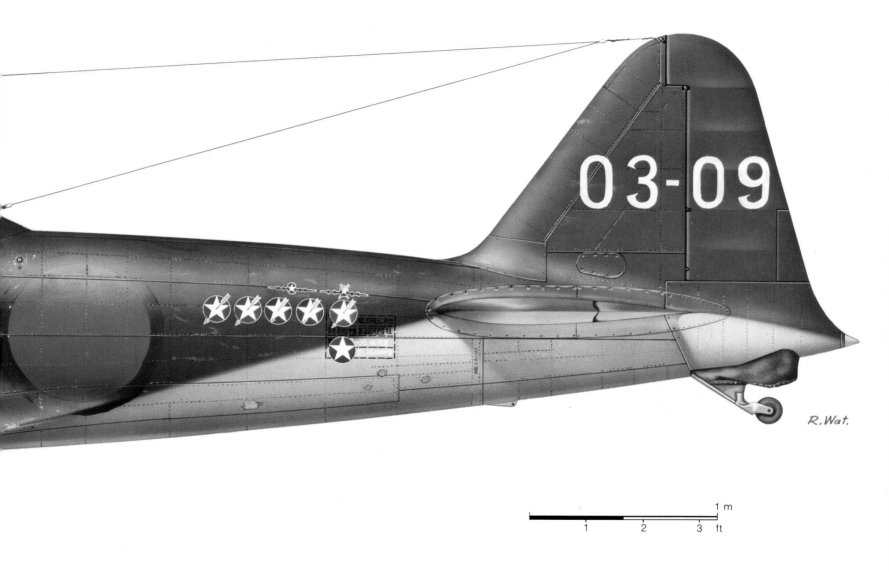

1 m

1   2   3   ft

Mitsubishi Type 0, Model 52c (A6M5c) carrier-borne fighter of the 303 Fighter Hikotai, 203 Kokutai. Flown by Chief PO. Takeo Tanimizu in June, 1945.

In an attempt to keep abreast of newer Allied fighters, since a replacement for the Zero was not close at hand, the Model 52, A6M5, was developed. This version with a 1,100 hp Sakae engine incorporated jet-effect exhaust stacks and a new rounded wing tip with reduced wing span compared to the Model 21. When it entered combat in August, 1943, its improved performance was negated by the Grumman F6F Hellcat that entered service at the same time.

Continuing modifications were made in an effort to keep pace with the changing war situation. The Model 52a carried 25 more rounds for each of its two cannon and had thicker wing skin for improved diving speed. The Model 52b increaséd the size of one nose gun, added a bullet resistant windshield, and included a fire ex-

tinguisher system around the fuselage fuel tank. These additions were improved again in the Model 52c which also included two additional wing guns. With each succeeding model, engine horsepower was to increase, but this was very slight. With these changes to the Zero, dictated by the combat situation when there was little hope for more advanced fighter aircraft, the weight of late model Zeros had increased 1,050 lbs, or 28-percent, with engine power only increasing by 16-percent over that of the Model 21.

Despite these disadvantages, the Zero remained a deadly weapon in the hands of experienced pilots. However, by mid-1943, the loss of these seasoned veterans was severely felt by the Japanese Navy and the Zero was unable to be used to its fullest ability.

Mitsubishi Type 0, Model 21 (A6M2) carrier-borne fighter o

The Mitsubishi Zero became world famous from the opening day of the Pacific War and carried respect for its fighting capability to the very end of that conflict. It surprised the Allies with its very long range, strong fire power, maneuverability, and high rate of climb. It seemed to appear everwhere in large numbers on every fighting front —diving from the sun and firing its lethal 20-mm cannon in high speed attacks. Zeros first engaged in combat over China, and when the Pacific War began, the airplane was a proven weapon in the hands of veteran naval pilots.

Designed as a carrier-borne fighter it was exceptionally light weight compared to its combat opponents. This was not only necessary in order to provide the maneuverability that was demanded by its

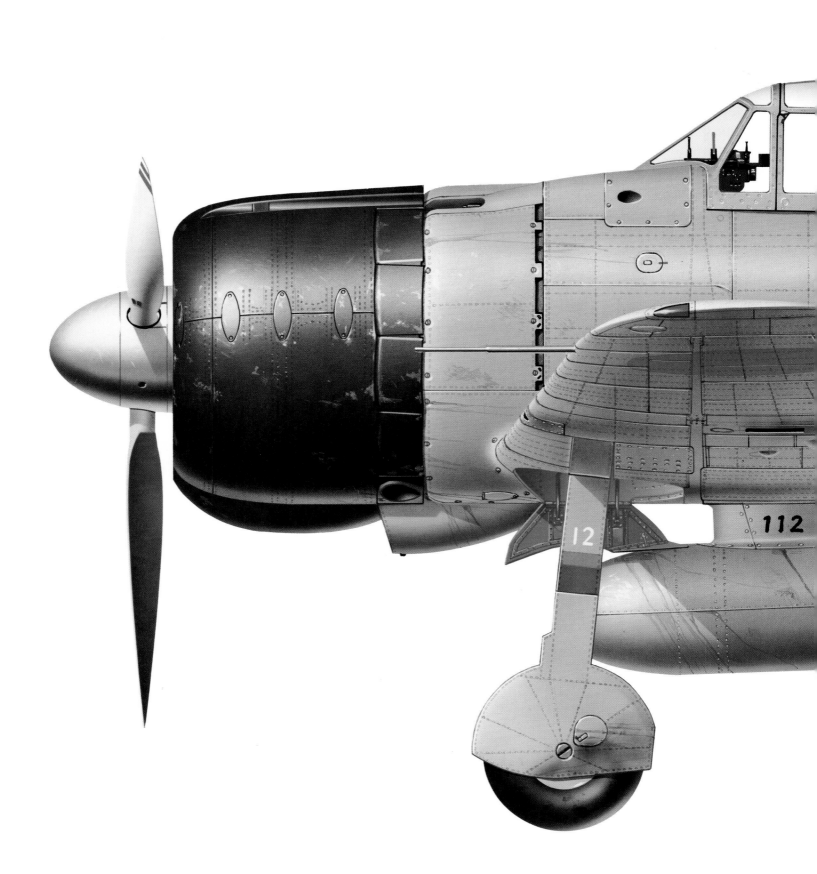

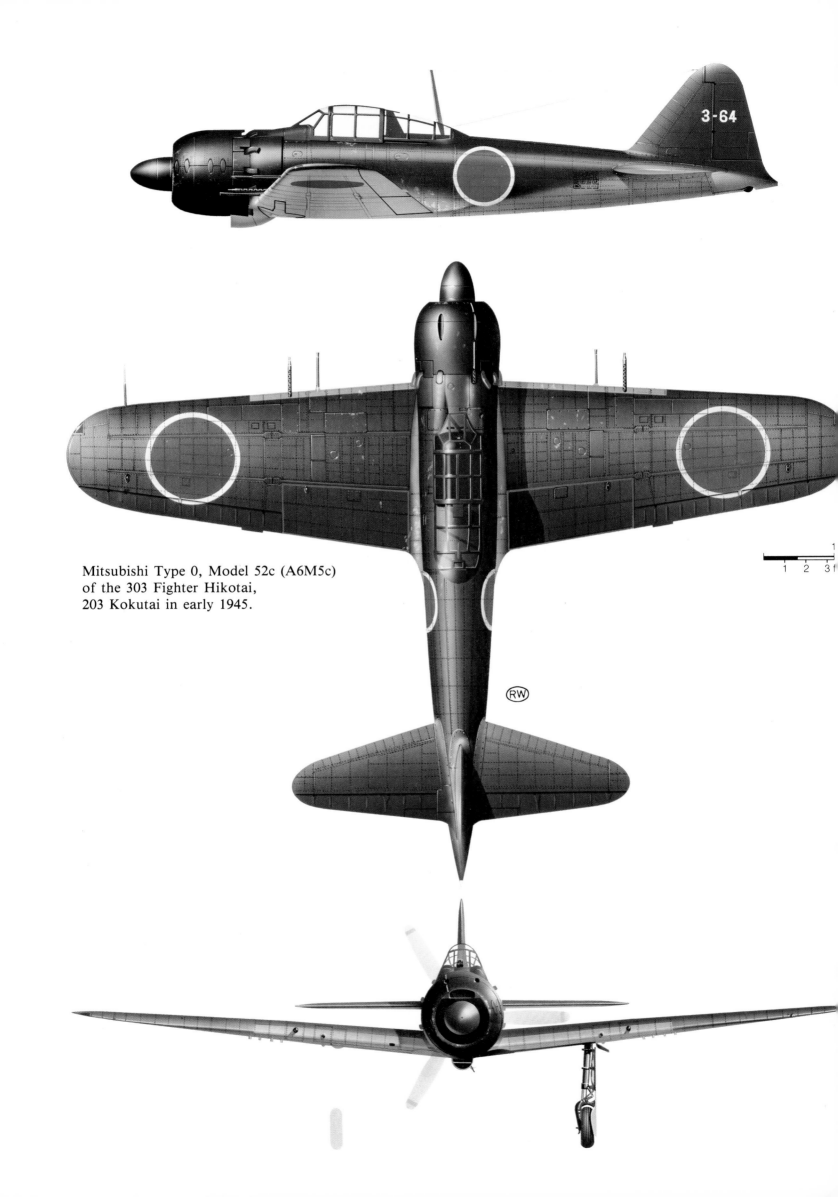

Mitsubishi Type 0, Model 52c (A6M5c)
of the 303 Fighter Hikotai,
203 Kokutai in early 1945.

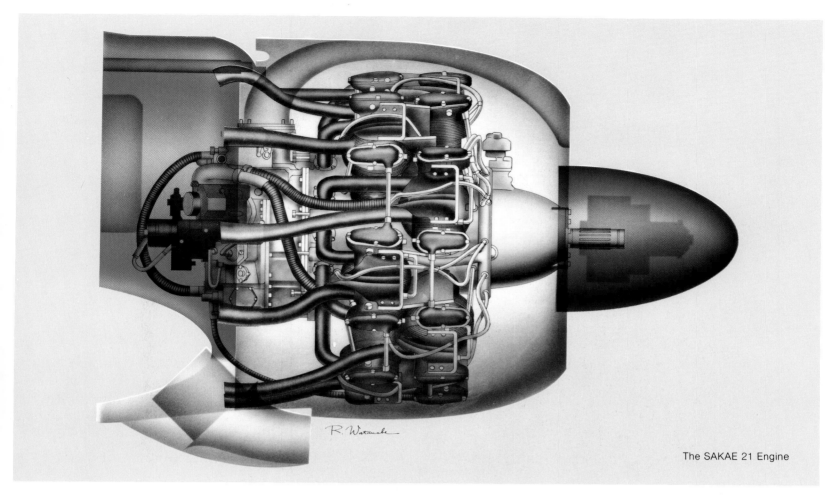

The SAKAE 21 Engine

Auxiliary equipment: Oxygen system, engine fire extenguisher, lighting equipment and standard aircraft and engine instruments. (It is interesting to note that specifications for the 12-*Shi* Carrier-borne Fighter had the same omissions of maximum weight restrictions, and carrier-borne operating equipment as the 9-*Shi* "Claude" fighter plus no mention of size restriction. Without these design limitations or requirements, the Zero was still to emerge as the best carrier-based fighter in the world.)

The requirements for this new fighter were revealed to representatives of Nakajima and Mitsubishi at a meeting held at the Naval Air Arsenal at Yokosuka on 17 January, 1938. Nakajima withdrew from the competition that seemingly posed impossible requirements. Mitsubishi was absorbed in the development of the Navy 11-*Shi* bomber and was hesitant to attempt an undertaking that showed little hope of success. The company was persuaded to accept the project however, in favour of not continuing with the 11-*Shi* bomber in spite of the risk of failure. With reluctance put aside, Jiro Horikoshi organized his design team to prepare for the new project as he did for the successful A5M "Claude." To assist him was a select staff of engineers, including Yoshitoshi Sone and Teruo Tojo for mathematical calculations; Sone and Yoshio Yoshikawa for structural work; Denichiro Inoue and Shotaro Tanaka for powerplant installation; Yoshimi Hatakenaka for armament and auxiliary equipment; and Sadahiko Kato and Takeyoshi Mori for landing gear and related equipment.

Note: *Based on US evaluation of captured A6M2, December, 1942.
†Performances recorded in flight by Saburo Sakai.

The immediate problem facing Horikoshi was the selection of the correct engine around which to design the airframe. A number of advanced engines were in the design and experimental stages, but to avoid the risk of failure caused by an unproven engine, the selection would be made from only existing and reliable engines. There were three possible choices: the 875-hp Mitsubishi *Zuisei* 13, the 950-hp Nakajima *Sakae* 12 and the 1,070-hp Mitsubishi *Kinsei* 46. The Mitsubishi design team did not favour the *Sakae*, at first, since it was produced by a competitor. Horikoshi favoured the larger and heavier, yet more powerful *Kinsei*, but with the Navy's insistence of a power loading not to exceed 5.5 lb/hp, the *Zuisei* 13 was selected and installed in the first two prototype aircrafts. This must have been an issue of frustration to this chief of design, for he was developing an aircraft expected to compete with a generation of potential enemy fighters that were already being fitted with engines over 1,000 hp, some of which were about to reach 2,000 hp. Beginning with the third prototype, the 950-hp *Sakae* 12 engine was installed which produced better performance than that with the Mitsubishi engine, and production of the new fighter began with this combination.

In order to achieve the performance demanded by the Navy, weight conservation was the prime order in the 12-*Shi* design. The wing, for instance, was built in one piece, thus eliminating heavy centre-section fittings for joining two halves. None of the structure in joining the wing had to be built into the fuselage, therefore these attachment fittings were kept very light.

A unique light weight material called Extra-Super Duralumin, E.S.D., was used extensively for the first time in

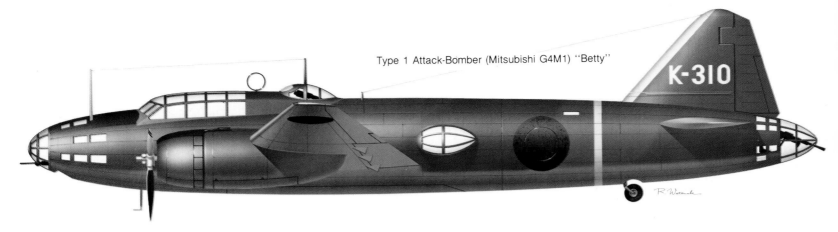

Type 1 Attack-Bomber (Mitsubishi G4M1) "Betty"

this aircraft as a main part of the wing spar. This was very similar to 75S aluminium adapted several years later by the United States. This new alloy, manufactured by the Sumitomo Metal Industry, had a tensile strength 30 to 40 per cent higher than that of previously used Super Duralumin, comparable to 24S aluminium. Acquired from the manufacturer in the form of angle bar stock, it was then cut and milled to taper with the wing form and used for the main wing spar caps, creating a very light yet strong wing structure.

(After nearly 40 years, when examining aircraft of this type that survived, most of which are in the hands of museums, this E.S.D. material has crystallized in many places to the point that it can be scooped away with the blade of a screwdriver. This is the main deterrent in restoring Zeros and other Japanese aircraft that used this metal, for exhibit or flying today, but longevity to this extent was not a factor at the time of their manufacture.)

The design of the fuselage followed a non-standard method in another effort to save additional weight. The centre section was built integrally with the wing and, in fact, was not structurally complete until riveted to the top wing skin which forms the cockpit floor. Since the fuselage did not come free from the wing, it separated in two sections just aft of the wing trailing edge by removing a series of bolts joining the forward and aft fuselage sections at two fuselage ring formers. This avoided the awkwardness and impracticality of moving essentially a one-piece aircraft in restricted areas, and facilitated depot storage, as well as granting unobstructed access into the cockpit for major repairs. As can be seen, then, the entire design philosophy of the 12-*Shi* design team emphasized lightness, simplicity, and utility. This weight-saving design could indicate that the craft was flimsily built, but such was not the case. Its strength compared favourably with many American-built aircraft that were known for their durable structures.

Aerodynamically, the aircraft was designed for minimal drag, and good stability and control. A desire to reduce the wing loading below 105 kg/m² (21.5 lb/sq ft) for reasons of enhancing take-off, climb, and manoeuvrability characteristics resulted in the craft having a wing area of 22.44 m² (241.54 sq ft). The designers selected the wing airfoil section after carefully considering the desired mission requirement. This new airfoil became the Mitsubishi 118, with a similar mean camber line to that of a NACA 23012 series which offered minimal centre of pressure travel. Mitsubishi used this same refined airfoil with a great success on the G4M Navy Type 1 Attack-Bomber which became well known to the Allies as "Betty".

To prevent tip stall, the wing was given a 2½ degree washout angle which had also been used on the A5M "Claude". The tail surfaces of the Zero were designed to give exceptional longitudinal and directional stability characteristics.

Selecting the Armament

The purpose of any fighter aircraft is to provide a stable platform for a weapon system that can be placed in the best position to destroy the enemy. As the design of the Zero was evolved, these requirements were satisfied with a lightweight airframe to give it the manoeuvrability, and the optimum engine for pursuit. Selecting the best armament was the next consideration.

Throughout the world, there were several combinations of armament being considered during the time that the Zero was in the planning stage. For this period, around 1938, here is a sampling of these trends.

The Browning .30 calibre machine-gun had been the standard in the United States for a number of years, but the new generation of fighters was being armed with the large Browning .50 calibre machine-gun. Aircraft cannon were gaining popularity also at this time, but not to the extent of replacing machine-guns. When the Lockheed XP-38 prototype first appeared during this period, its nose contained a cluster of one 23 mm Madsen cannon and four .50 calibre machine-guns. Bell's new XP-39 Airacobra used its propeller drive shaft to house the cannon barrel for firing 37-mm projectiles, a feature which carried through to the P-63 Kingcobra. Augmenting the one cannon of the Airacobra were two .50 calibre and two .30 calibre Browning machine-guns. The sole experimental XF4F-2 Wildcat was flying with four .50 calibre machine-guns; models so equipped would initially

slug it out with the Zero. Already well into production at this time was the Curtiss P-36 with the somewhat archaic firepower of one .30 calibre and one .50 calibre Browning machine-gun installed in the fuselage to fire through the propeller arc. The P-36 Hawk fighter was developed into the P-40 a few years later and armed then with four .50 calibre machine-guns to pit it against the Zero fighters.

The British had adopted the .303-in Browning machine-gun for most of its fighters at that time. The Hawker Hurricanes and Supermarine Spitfires which figured so prominently in the Battle of Britain in 1940 carried eight of these smaller calibre weapons so that more in number could be concentrated on the target.

The Germans on the other hand were relying on heavier weapons rather than quantity. Early production Messerschmitt Bf 109Es mounted four 7.9-mm MG 17 machine-guns, but later machines standardized on two MG 17s over the engine and two wing mounted 20-mm cannon.

Changes in weapon systems and combinations took place as these aircraft were advanced in different stages during the war. The trends were fairly well established however, and the designers of the Zero had to select and fit the best combination to their airframe. Their preceding design, the A5M "Claude," like all other Japanese service fighters of this period, was equipped with two 7.7-mm fixed weapons which were versions of the Vickers machine-gun. This weapon proved adequate for air combat over China for the opposition that was presented, but would be inadequate for the new 12-*Shi* Fighter.

A search had already started by the Technical Division of Japan's Naval Bureau of Aeronautics to find the most suitable armament for its next generation of fighters. One that brought the greatest interest was the Swiss 20-mm Oerlikon cannon, which was in use in several European air forces. One aircraft fitted with this gun was the French Dewoitine D.510, of which two were purchased by Japan in 1935 for close study and evaluation by the Japanese military and aviation industry. The major fault with this cannon, however, was its low muzzle velocity as compared to weapons of similar size. The advantages of the weapon, however, were its very low profile for installing in a wing, its light weight, and its ability to fire explosive shells. These features made it particularly attractive for fighter aircraft. When a determination was made that licence agreement could be acquired for the manufacture of

this cannon in Japan, it was adopted as the standard Japanese naval aircraft cannon, Type 99.

Manufacturers of the new licence built weapon became the Dai-Nihon Heiki Company, Ltd. (The Japan Munitions Company Ltd.) which also mass produced the ammunition. In time, six additional factories were set up, and by the end of the war, thirty-five thousand of these cannon had been produced.

Adapting this weapon into the 12-*Shi* Fighter design was not an arbitrary decision. The fighter specifications called for two Type 99 20-mm cannon. It was not an easy task to design a sturdy gun platform for this relatively heavy firing weapon to be installed into such a lightweight airframe. Horikoshi and his design team devoted considerable attention to this detail. When the initial design was completed, the Zero emerged with one of these 20-mm cannon in each wing just outboard of the landing gear, able to carry 60 rounds each. Augmenting the cannon were the tried and proven Type 97 7.7-mm machine guns; two were snugly fitted between the top of the engine and the cockpit.

Historians rightfully comment on the advanced performance qualities of the Zero when discussing its combat capabilities. Often overlooked however is credit for this selection of armament. The Type 99 cannon was a very large calibre weapon to be used by the Zero at this time when compared to the world standards already described. True, it did have shortcomings in low muzzle velocity and slow rate of fire, but reports of these cannon rounds hitting their targets and exploding brought a much higher total in kill records than if the lighter armament had been used as some proposed. The success of the new fighter was so profound when first introduced in combat over China, that Vice-Admiral Teijiro Toyoda, Chief of Naval Bureau of Aeronautics, forwarded a letter of appreciation to not only the manufacturer of the airframe, Mitsubishi, and to Nakajima for the sound performance of the engine, but also to Dai-Nihon Heiki for the effectiveness of the 20-mm cannon.

A6M5

R. Watanabe

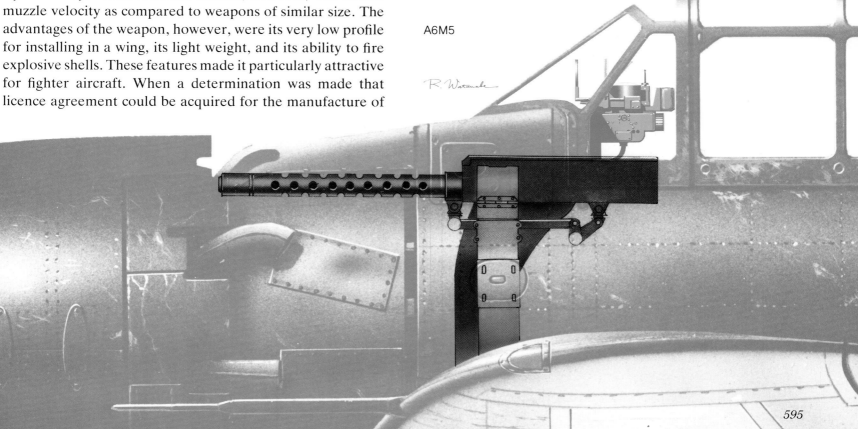

Design Uncertainties

There were times that uncertainties were raised concerning design philosophies being incorporated into the 12-*Shi* Fighter. The greatest controversy arose at a time when the prototype was nearly completed. Based on experience gained in combat over China, some navy planners felt that the new aircraft would fail to meet some of the requirements they thought to be necessary. To discuss these problems, a conference was held on 13 April, 1938, with all parties concerned.

Opening a major aspect of what turned into a debate was Lieutenant-Commander Minoru Genda, a highly respected combat leader, test pilot, and tactician. He held different opinions as to the course the future development of the fighter should take.

He argued that in a fighter, particularly a carrier-based fighter, the single most important characteristic is the ability of the aircraft to engage successfully in close-in fighting. Having this quality, the need for heavyweight cannon can be replaced by lighter guns and thus improve the aircraft's manoeuvrability. To further achieve this quality, a sacrifice of speed and range could also be made.

Opposing these views was Lieutenant-Commander Takeo Shibata, a man with equal qualifications, whose words carried the same authority as those of Genda. Shibata pointed out that Japanese Navy fighters were already superior in dogfighting performance to those of other nations of the world. Unfortunately, the air battles over China where fighter protection was needed to defend the bombers was taking place far beyond the range of Japan's fighters then in existence. Therefore, the next fighter must have not only long range but high speed as well. Even the slightest edge in speed would provide the margin needed to destroy the enemy. Shibata was convinced that the Japanese fighter pilots could be trained to maintain a clear superiority over enemy fighters, even with aircraft of inferior turning radius. To defend his theory he clearly pointed out that the maximum speed of an aircraft is strictly limited by its power and the design of the aircraft, a factor over which the pilot has no control. On the other hand, in dogfighting, pilot skill can compensate for any lack in manoeuvrability.

These arguments created much soul searching on the part of those responsible for the success of the new fighter. The conference was spilt without a decision since there were no grounds on which to challenge the wisdom of either man. To evade the stalemate, the Mitsubishi design team was asked to review the requirements set forth by the 12th *Kokutai* (Air Corps) that had a need for the new fighter in China, along with discussions just heard, and evaluate the embryonic 12-*Shi* Fighter with these demands in mind.

At this point, the new fighter was just a few weeks away from its maiden flight, yet at this moment it appeared on the brink of extinction. Horikoshi checked his earlier computations against the 12-*Shi* written specifications as well as the desires needed in the new fighter that were just debated. His findings were more convincing than before and once again he

The SAKAE 21 Engine (Nakajima NK1F)

14-cylinder twin-row radial, fitted with two-speed supercharger. Rated at 1,130 hp for take-off 1,100 hp at 2,850 m (9,350 ft) and 980 hp at 6,000 m (19,685 ft) *Maximum RPM:* 2,700 rpm *Reduction gearing:* 05833 : 1 (7/12) *Overall diameter:* 1.115 m (3 ft 9 in)

submitted them to the Navy. With these facts he was quick to point out that the aircraft as requested by the 12th Air Corps would fail to match the overall efficiency of the aircraft already under construction. After fully supporting his case that the 12-*Shi* Fighter would possess not one or even two, but all three qualities asked for – superior speed, manoeuvrability, and range – the Navy relented and once again gave full support to the project.

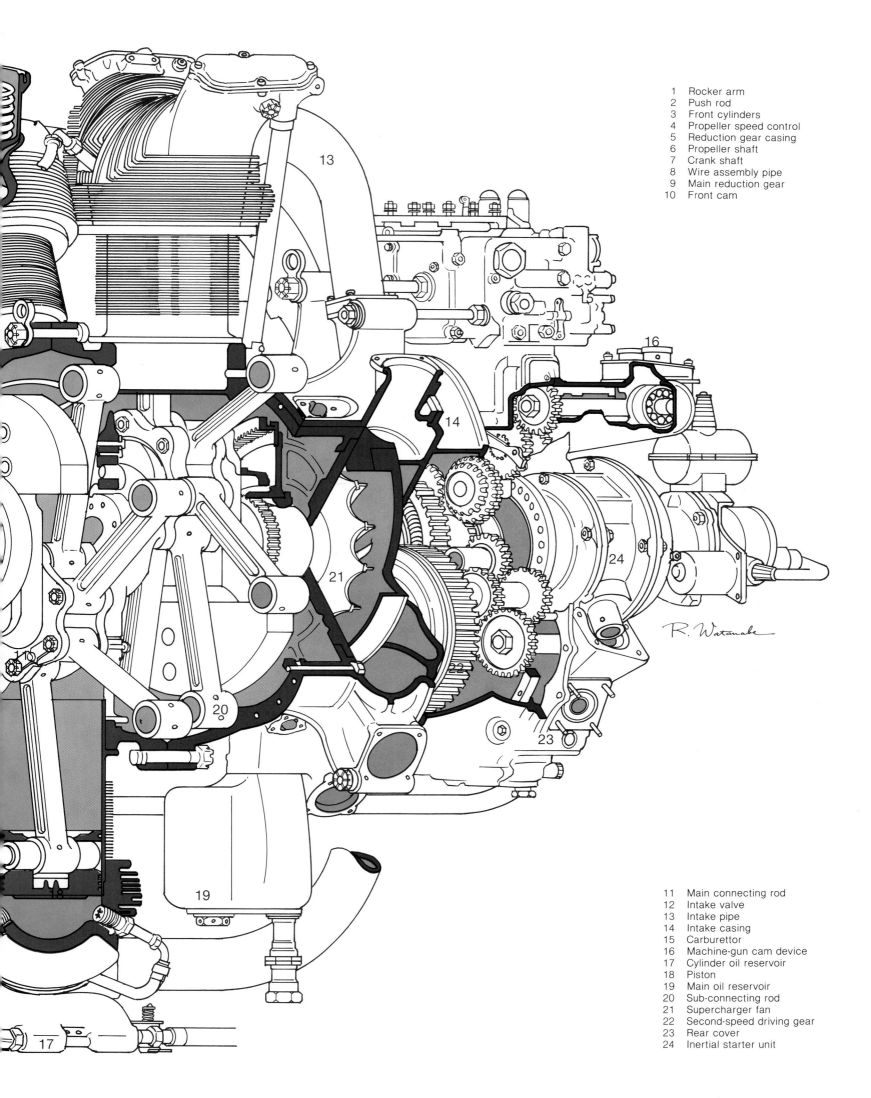

1 Rocker arm
2 Push rod
3 Front cylinders
4 Propeller speed control
5 Reduction gear casing
6 Propeller shaft
7 Crank shaft
8 Wire assembly pipe
9 Main reduction gear
10 Front cam

11 Main connecting rod
12 Intake valve
13 Intake pipe
14 Intake casing
15 Carburettor
16 Machine-gun cam device
17 Cylinder oil reservoir
18 Piston
19 Main oil reservoir
20 Sub-connecting rod
21 Supercharger fan
22 Second-speed driving gear
23 Rear cover
24 Inertial starter unit

The Prototype Zero

Model 21 (A6M2)

On 16 March, 1939, eleven months after the 12-*Shi* Carrier-Borne Fighter requirements were announced by the Navy, the first in this series was completed. Three days later, after weight and balance calculations were completed, and functional tests were run on the engine and other systems, the aircraft was ready to be moved to the flying field.

Partially due to poor planning, coupled with an aircraft industry that was a spin-off from factories established for the manufacture of other goods, few had adjacent runways. In the case of the Mitsubishi factory in southern Nagoya, the nearest suitable flying field was Kagamigahara Airfield, twenty-five miles to the north. The glistening new fighter, a product of the most advanced technology of its day, had to be disassembled and trundled to the airfield on two cumbersome, ox-drawn wagons.

The maiden flight of any new aircraft is a never-to-be-forgotten occasion, particularly for the men that created it. Zero designer Jiro Horikoshi reflected upon that day in April, 1939, as all concerned in building it waited for their machine to come to life.

"The long months of painstaking labour invested in the airframe, the wings, the engine, and the thousands of small parts all appeared in final form as a complete, but as yet inert machine. This silent machine was more than merely an assemblage of mechanical devices; the aircraft's sweeping, graceful curves expressed our attempt to master the air space which would be its medium. We hoped that our efforts would not have been in vain."

On that first afternoon in April, this "silent machine" did come to life as Mitsubishi's test pilot, Katsuzo Shima, signaled for engine start. When he was satisfied it was running properly, there was the routine of taxi tests to ensure that the brakes, controls and systems were working properly. Then with all eyes upon the shining fighter, Shima advanced the throttle, allowed the aircraft to roll forward, gaining speed until it was airborne. Assessment of control responses was quick and deliberate, and the power was reduced which allowed the aircraft to settle back on to the runway after a brief jump-flight. The Zero had taken wing for the first time.

In the days that followed, the tests became more extensive and more demanding. Aside from slight teething problems with the landing gear, a disturbing vibration persisted with each flight, for no apparent reason. Horikoshi felt that the two-bladed propeller was the cause of the vibration and substituted a three blade unit. Used for the first time on the 17 April flight, it almost entirely eliminated the vibration. This was also the first time that a constant speed propeller was used on a Japanese-made aircraft.

▲ A6M2 with light anti-personnel bombs (US Navy)

◄ Identification Plate Affixed inside Fuselage

(1) *Place of Manufacture:* Mitsubishi Heavy Industry Co., Nagoya Aircraft Factory.
(2) *Name:* Reishiki Type No. 1 Carrier-borne Fighter Plane, design 2.
(3) *Model:* A6M2   (4) *Motor:* Nakajima NK1 (   ) horsepower.
(5) *Manufacture Serial Number:* No.4593.   (6) *Net Weight:* 1715.0 kgs.
(7) *Load:* 650.3 kgs.   (8) *Weight, fully equipped:* 2365.3 kgs.
(9) *Date completed:* February 19, 1942.   (10) *Inspection mark:* 'Na-Ko.'

When all were satisfied that the 12-*Shi* Fighter had filled the Imperial Japanese Navy requirements, the first prototype was officially accepted on 14 September, 1939. Its military designation became A6M1 Type 0 Carrier-borne Fighter. The "0" was derived from the last number of the Japanese calendar year in which the aircraft would be placed into full service; 2600, equivalent to 1940. The alpha numeric designator A6M1 was seldom the identifier used by the Japanese, who preferred instead the term Type 0 Carrier-Borne Fighter. In the Japanese language, the words became *Rei Shiki Sento Ki* (Type Zero Fighter), often shortened to the abbreviation of Rei-sen or Reisen. Without question, this word identified the Mitsubishi fighter to every Japanese, but in this case, even for the Japanese after World War II, the most used name became "Zero-sen".

The entire and often changing designation system of Japanese Army and Navy aircraft was never fully understood by Allied intelligence during the war years. The inability to properly identify types made the task of defence difficult. To help solve the problem, a simple, easy to remember code-name system was developed. Male names were given to fighters, female names assigned to bombers. In the case of the Zero-sen, the name "Zeke" was applied, but by this time the term "Zero" was already popular and was more often used than "Zeke". In fact, the Zero became so well publicized at the opening phase of the war that even today people often identify nearly any low-wing radial-engined fighter having a Japanese insignia as a "Zero" – regardless of its type.

After the Navy took delivery of this first A6M1 the second prototype, which included among other things a correction in elevator control force, passed company testing and went into Navy hands on 25 October, 1939. The Navy was anxious to begin test firing the cannon system on this new fighter. Beginning in late October, the first firing mission scored nine hits out of twenty rounds fired in the first pass at a ground target 19 m (62.3 ft) square. Expectations of the Zero fighter were aroused even more by these rewarding results.

It is rare that all goes well continually with any new aircraft, and the Zero was no exception. On 11 March, 1940, test pilot Okuyama took off from Oppama Airfield in the A6M1 prototype No. 2 to investigate engine overspeeding during steep dives. On his second dive at about a 50-degree angle from 1500 m (4,920 ft) a loud engine roar at about 900 m (2,950 ft) was followed by an immediate explosion.

The Zero disintegrated instantly, and the pilot separated from the aircraft. His parachute opened, but at approximately 300 m (985 ft) the pilot's body slipped out of the harness and plunged into the sea. It was believed that Okuyama died in the explosion and that the parachute opened of its own accord.

The cause of the accident was never fully determined as there were a number of circumstantial possibilities. The most plausible cause was felt to be that the elevator mass-balance failed just prior to the accident, and during the dive and acceleration it is possible that elevator flutter started, causing severe vibration throughout the aircraft which led to complete disintegration.

The Tiger Unleashed

Despite this setback, production continued with only slight modifications becoming necessary as flight tests revealed them. On the last day of July, 1940, the Zero became a regular Navy service Type aircraft. Navy air force personnel at the China combat front heard about the outstanding performance of the Zero and asked for shipments of the new fighter at the earliest possible moment. As already described, 15 pre-production A6M2s were dispatched to Hankow in spite of cooling problems with the *Sakae* 12 engine. Technicians at Hankow corrected this problem and their solution appeared later on production aircraft. One that would not be solved until later was the frequent hang-up of the drop tank when pilots would attempt to jettison these expendable fuel tanks, especially at speeds of 207 mph or above. Pilots felt that their skill and their advantage in aircraft performance would outweigh the disadvantages in combat with the tanks still attached.

Historians have often said that the confidence gained by Japan with the outstanding success of the Zero fighter had much to do with initiating a war with the United States. Japanese intelligence and statisticians stated unequivocally that the superiority of the Zero fighter meant that, in battle, one Zero would be the equal of from two to five enemy fighter planes, depending on their type. Taking into consideration that the potential enemy had endless resources, Japanese victories had to be achieved quickly. The Zero would play an important part in achieving that goal by maintaining control of the air over any battle area. Because of this extreme confidence in the Zero, most Japanese Navy commanders were unshakable in their faith in victory for their planned military operations.

From the Zero's first day in combat over China, it was another sixteen months before the Zero fighter, along with Aichi D3A ("Val") dive-bombers and Nakajima B5N ("Kate") torpedo-bombers, slashed into their attack on Pearl

Type 99 Carrier-borne Bomber, Model 11 (Aichi D3A1) "Val"

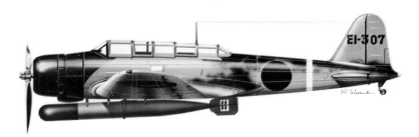

Type 97 Carrier-borne Attack Bomber, Model 3 (Nakajima B5N2) "Kate"

Zero 21 taking off from carrier *Zuikaku* for the battle of Santa Cruz, 26 October, 1942.

Harbor. The allies were completely astonished at the sight of the new fighter and were totally unaware of the Zero's performance. Observers in China had submitted reports about the new aircraft but whether performance figures were exaggerated or not, these reports were thought to describe an aerodynamic impossibility and were filed away without further study or interest. The Japanese were equally surprised at Allied ignorance after having exposed their Zero for more than the year in the air battles over China.

The Zero left no doubt of its existence after its appearance at Pearl Harbor. Lack of knowledge and uncertainty of the potential of an unknown adversary creates a camp for fear, and from this the superiorities about the "won-

der fighter" became wildly exaggerated. In an attempt to put down its true or mythical qualities, stories mushroomed that the sole genius of the Japanese was imitative. Early in the Pacific war, when the agile fighter was consistently victorious over obsolete US made equipment, the embarrassed U.S. authorities were quick to claim that it was merely a poor copy of this or that American design. Depending on the depth of the critic's aeronautical ignorance, the parent design was often claimed to have been based on Howard Hughes' racer or, the Vought V-143, which was bought by the Japanese in 1937. Once the Zero was accepted as a copy of American technology, it then became possible to speak highly of it.

Lieutenant Hideki Shingo, in command of carrier *Shokaku* fighter squadron, taking off in a *Zero 21* to attack *USS Enterprise*. 26 October, 1942.

Made In Japan

The Zero was, as we now know, a completely original design. No one will more vigorously defend this than the designer himself, Jiro Horikoshi. In his words, this is the response to this very old controversy:

"The Zero fighter was no more a copy than any other fighter used in the world today. All single-engined all-metal low-wing monoplanes are to some extent progressive 'copies' of the original Junkers 'Blechesel', the father of all these machines. There is a certain pool of common information from which all engineers draw. There is a certain reciprocal borrowing of detail ideas without permission during wartime, and by cross-licensing in times of peace.

"As virtually all competent aircraft designers will hold with me, the business of creating any new aircraft is a process of adapting the existing art and science to the problem at hand. For example, I will state that the undercarriage retraction on the Zero was inspired by the Vought 143, and that the system of fastening the engine cowl and the method of mounting the engine came from other foreign planes. And nothing else, so far as the airframe is concerned. It is no exaggeration to say that we did not look upon the general design or basic configuration of foreign aircraft with great respect. Any designer who fails, out of vanity, to adapt the best techniques available to him, fails his job. All engineers are influenced by their teachers, by their experience and by the constant stream of scientific information that is placed at their disposal.

"As foreigners inspected our aircraft in the combat zone, they were quick to identify accessories that looked familiar to them as copies of their own products. What they did overlook was that these were built under licence from abroad; wheels were manufactured by Okamoto Engineering Company under licence from Bendix and Palmer, instruments were built by the Tokyo Instrument Company under licence, or later in the war, by direct copy from Sperry, Pioneer and Kollsman. Sumitomo built hydromatic propellers under a licence from Hamilton Standard, as well as the German VDM propeller. The Nihon Musical Instrument. Co. built the Junkers and Schwarz propellers, while the Kokusai Aircraft Company built the French Ratier prop. We built 20-mm cannon licensed by Oerlikon of Switzerland and copies of the 13-mm (.50 cal.) Browning.

"I can claim, however, in the study of the Zero, its ancestors and descendants, that it was original to the same degree as other planes are, and that while it contains certain special features that were all its own, it serves as a prime example of a special design created to suit an unusual set of circumstances."

The Aleutian Zero Unmasked

Many months had passed in the war and little intelligence information about the Zero was in the hands of the Allies. Most of what was available was obtained from pilots that engaged the Zero in combat. Even line drawings showing the shape of the aircraft were misleading and highly inaccurate. It was essential that the Allies should obtain an intact Zero at the earliest moment for close examination and flight evaluation.

Damaged A6M2 flown by 1st class PO Koga on Akutan Island.   (National Archives)

That opportunity occurred during the diversionary attacks on Dutch Harbour in the Aleutian Islands during the Battle of Midway. On 3 June, 1942, Petty Officer Tadayoshi Koga's A6M2 engaged in an attack, developed engine trouble and was forced to make a landing on a remote clear area of Akutan Island. Landing with the gear down, the plane settled in the unexpected marsh surface and flipped on its back, killing the pilot. Little thought was given to retrieving this aircraft because of its inaccessibility until a U.S. Navy scouting party went to the crash site five weeks later and found the craft not too badly damaged.

Transfer work for the A6M2 at seaside.   (National Archives)

A captured Zero (A6M2) made ready for flight testing. (National Archives)

This Zero Model 21 was carefully removed and sent on a cargo vessel to the Assembly and Repair Department at NAS North Island, San Diego, arriving there in August, 1942. There, in a secure area of the blimp hangar, it was carefully inspected and repaired so that it could be flown for flight evaluation.

Major repairs were required for the tail, canopy and nose. The broken Sumitomo propeller was probably replaced with an American-made Hamilton Standard, for both were reported to be identical. This task of repair without technical data to work from was difficult, yet it was completed in early October the same year.

The mere gathering of flight data figures to be compared with similar data of another aircraft is often inconclusive since flight conditions are not always the same. A true test was to have both aircraft pitted together under the same set of circumstances. In order to do this, one of each American-type fighter was sent to San Diego for flight evaluation with the Zero. Army Air Forces pilots from the AAF Proving Ground Group at Eglin Field, Florida, brought an example of the Lockheed P-38F Lightning, Bell P-39D-1 Airacobra, Curtiss P-40F Warhawk, and the still very new North American P-51 Mustang. Navy pilots flew the Grumman F4F-4 Wildcat and an early model Vought F4U-1 Corsair for the tests. An intelligence summary of these findings, recorded in December, 1942, provides an excellent account of these comparisons. The often sought after results of this report are reproduced here in part for what is believed to be the first time in print:

To begin this test, both ships took off in formation on a pre-arranged signal. The Zero left the ground first and was about 300 feet in the air before the P-38F was airborne. The Zero reached 5,000 feet about five seconds ahead of the Lightning. From an indicated speed of 200 mph (174 kts) the Lightning accelerated away from the Zero in straight and level flight quite rapidly. The Zero was superior to the P-38 in manoeuvrability at speeds below 300 mph (260 kts).

The planes returned to formation and both ships reduced to their best respective climbing speed. Upon signal the climb was started to 10,000 feet. Again the Zero was slightly superior in straight climbs reaching 10,000 feet about four seconds ahead of the P-38. Comparable accelerations and turns were tried with the same results.

In the climb from 15,000 feet to 20,000 feet, the P-38 started gaining at about 18,200 feet. At 20,000 feet the P-38 was superior to the Zero in all manoeuvres except slow speed turns. This advantage was maintained by the P-38 at all altitudes above 20,000 feet.

One manoeuvre in which the P-38 was superior to the Zero was a high speed reversal. It was impossible for the Zero to follow the P-38 in this manoeuvre at speeds above 300 mph (260 kts).

The test was continued to 25,000 and 30,000 feet. Due to the superior speed and climb of the P-38F at these altitudes, it could out manoeuvre the Zero by using these two advantages. The Zero was still superior in slow speed turns.

P-38F Lightning vs Zero 21:

P-39D-1 Airacobra vs Zero 21:

Takeoff was accomplished in formation on signal to initiate a climb from sea level to 5,000 feet indicated. The P-39D-1 was drawing 3000 rpm and 70 inches manifold pressure on takeoff when the engine started to detonate, so manifold pressure was reduced to 52 inches. The Airacobra left the ground first and arrived at 5,000 feet indicated just as the Zero was passing 4,000 feet indicated. This manifold pressure of 52 inches could be maintained to 4,500 feet indicated. At 5,000 feet from a cruising speed of 230 mph (200 kts) indicated, the P-39 had a marked acceleration away from the Zero. Climb from 5,000 feet to 10,000 feet at the respective best climbing speeds, (thus eliminating zoom effect) the P-39 reached 10,000 feet approximately six seconds before the Zero. At 10,000 feet indicated, from a cruising speed of 220 mph (191 kts) indicated, the Airacobra still accelerated away from the Zero rapidly. Climbing from 10,000 feet to 15,000 feet, both aircrafts maintained equal rates of climb to 12,500 feet. Above this altitude the Zero walked away from the P-39.

Climb from 15,000 to 20,000 feet indicated, the Zero took immediate advantage and left the Airacobra. The climb from 20,000 feet to 25,000 feet was not completed as the P-39 was running low on fuel.

On a straight climb to altitude from takeoff under the same conditions as before, the Airacobra maintained the advantage of the climb until reaching 14,800 feet indicated. Above this altitude the P-39 was left behind reaching 25,000 feet indicated approximately 5 minutes behind the Zero. At 25,000 feet from a cruising speed of 180 mph (156 kts) indicated, the Zero accelerated away from the P-39 for three ship lengths. This lead was maintained by the Zero for one and a half minutes and it took the P-39D-1 another thirty seconds to gain a lead of one ship length.

P-51 Mustang vs Zero 21:

The P-51 was drawing 3,000 rpm and 43 inches manifold pressure for its takeoff and climb to 5,000 feet. The low manifold pressure was due to the setting on the automatic manifold pressure regulator. (This was the early Allison-powered Mustang.) The Zero left the ground and reached its best climb speed approximately six seconds before the P-51. It also reached 5,000 feet approximately six seconds before the Mustang. At 5,000 feet from a cruising speed of 250 mph (217 kts) indicated, the P-51 accelerated sharply away from the Zero.

Climb from 5,000 to 10,000, and from 10,000 to 15,000 feet produced the same results having the Zero accelerate away from the P-51 in rate of climb. At 10,000 feet from a cruising speed of 250 mph (217 kts) indicated, the Mustang moved sharply away from the Zero, and at 15,000 feet from a cruising speed of 240 mph (208 kts) indicated the P-51 had the advantage over the Zero, but slightly slower than at 5,000 and 10,000 feet.

The P-51 could dive away from the Zero at any time. During this test, the P-51's power plant failed to operate properly above 15,000 feet so the comparison was not continued above this altitude.

P-40F Warhawk vs Zero 21:

These tests were not completed with the P-40F because it was found impossible to obtain maximum engine operation.

[Author's note: An interesting observation on the foregoing accounts are the mechanical problems mentioned in this report which included one aborted flight, yet no problems were indicated with the Zero. Also of interest are the acceleration comparisons at altitude that were started at optimum airspeeds for the respective American fighters. The Zero being the older designed fighter, performed admirably.]

F4F-4 Wildcat vs Zero 21:

The Zero was superior to the F4F-4 in speed and climb at all altitudes above 1,000 feet, and was superior in service ceiling and range. Close to sea level, with the F4F-4 in neutral blower, the two planes were equal in level speed. In a dive, the two planes were equal with the exception that the Zero's engine cut out in pushovers. There was no comparison between the turning circles of the two aircraft due to the relative wing loadings and resultant low stalling speed of the Zero. In view of the foregoing, the F4F-4 type in combat with the Zero was basically dependent on mutual support, internal protection, and pull-outs or turns at high speeds where minimum radius is limited by structural or physiological effects of acceleration (assuming that the allowable acceleration on the F4F is greater than that of the Zero.) However, advantage should be taken where possible, of the superiority of the F4F in pushovers and rolls at high speed, or any combination of the two.

F4U-1 Corsair vs Zero 21:

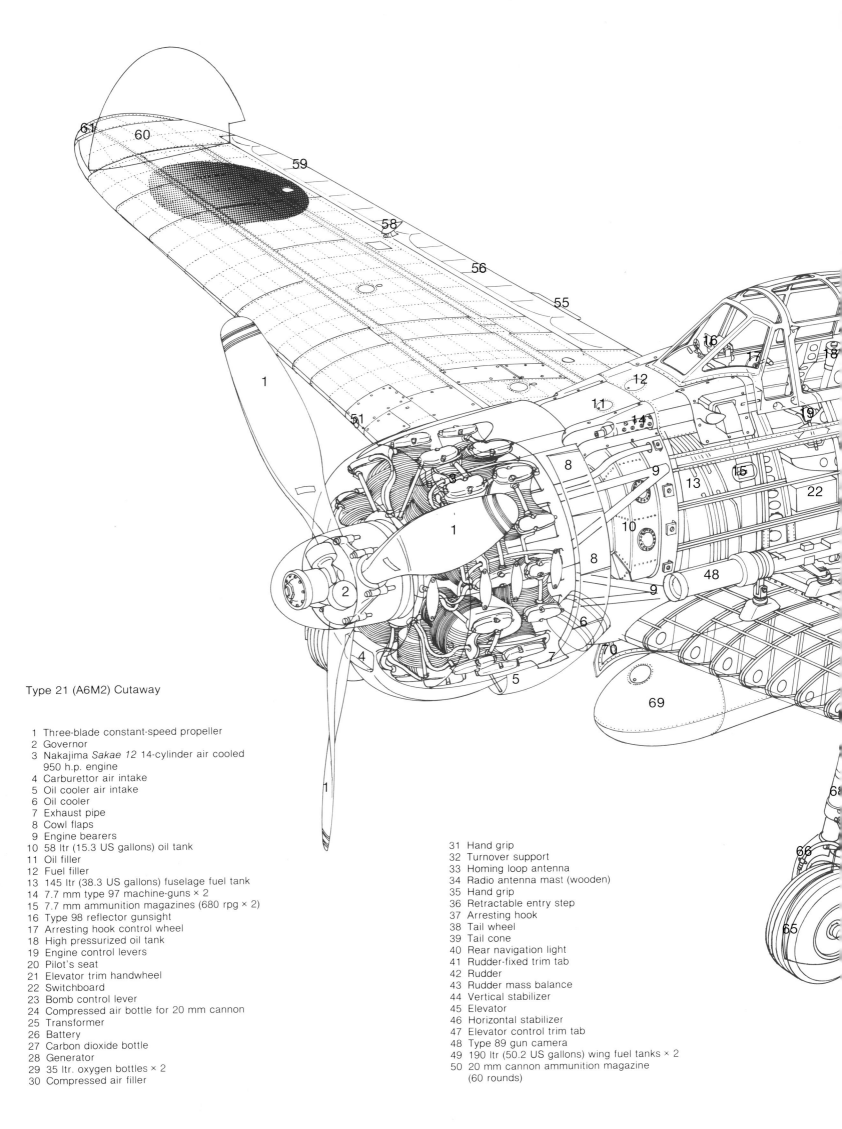

Type 21 (A6M2) Cutaway

 1 Three-blade constant-speed propeller
 2 Governor
 3 Nakajima *Sakae 12* 14-cylinder air cooled
   950 h.p. engine
 4 Carburettor air intake
 5 Oil cooler air intake
 6 Oil cooler
 7 Exhaust pipe
 8 Cowl flaps
 9 Engine bearers
10 58 ltr (15.3 US gallons) oil tank
11 Oil filler
12 Fuel filler
13 145 ltr (38.3 US gallons) fuselage fuel tank
14 7.7 mm type 97 machine-guns × 2
15 7.7 mm ammunition magazines (680 rpg × 2)
16 Type 98 reflector gunsight
17 Arresting hook control wheel
18 High pressurized oil tank
19 Engine control levers
20 Pilot's seat
21 Elevator trim handwheel
22 Switchboard
23 Bomb control lever
24 Compressed air bottle for 20 mm cannon
25 Transformer
26 Battery
27 Carbon dioxide bottle
28 Generator
29 35 ltr. oxygen bottles × 2
30 Compressed air filler

31 Hand grip
32 Turnover support
33 Homing loop antenna
34 Radio antenna mast (wooden)
35 Hand grip
36 Retractable entry step
37 Arresting hook
38 Tail wheel
39 Tail cone
40 Rear navigation light
41 Rudder-fixed trim tab
42 Rudder
43 Rudder mass balance
44 Vertical stabilizer
45 Elevator
46 Horizontal stabilizer
47 Elevator control trim tab
48 Type 89 gun camera
49 190 ltr (50.2 US gallons) wing fuel tanks × 2
50 20 mm cannon ammunition magazine
   (60 rounds)

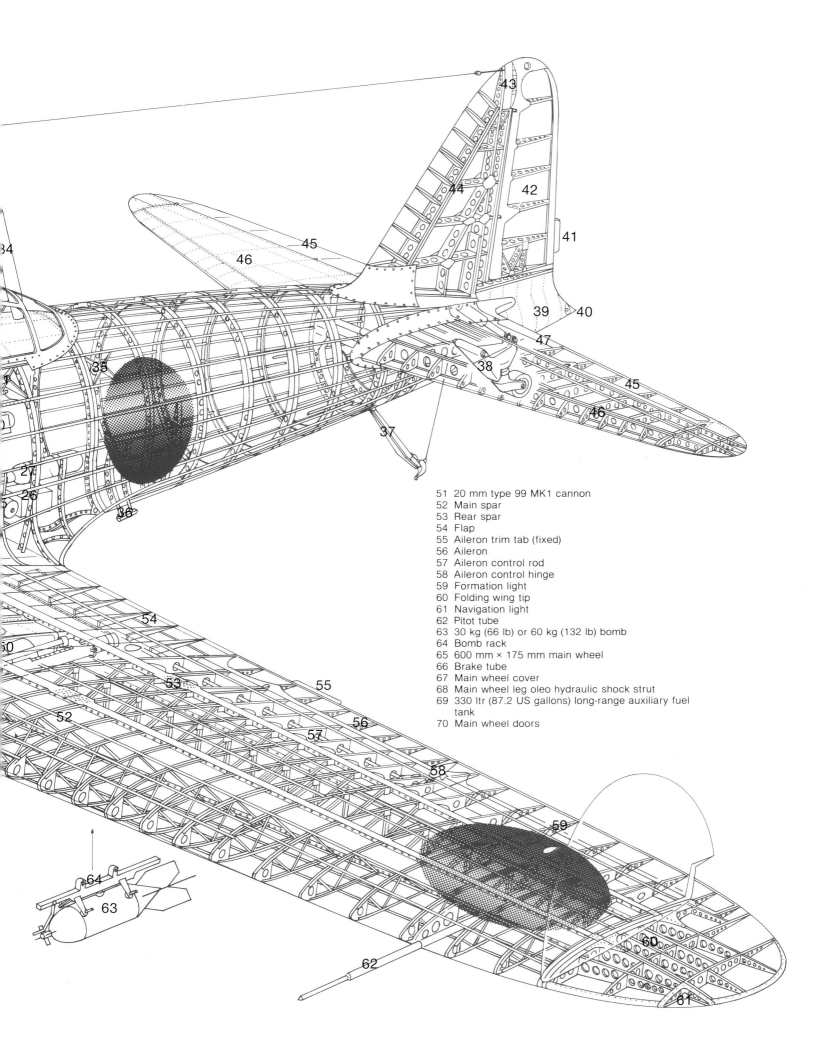

51 20 mm type 99 MK1 cannon
52 Main spar
53 Rear spar
54 Flap
55 Aileron trim tab (fixed)
56 Aileron
57 Aileron control rod
58 Aileron control hinge
59 Formation light
60 Folding wing tip
61 Navigation light
62 Pitot tube
63 30 kg (66 lb) or 60 kg (132 lb) bomb
64 Bomb rack
65 600 mm × 175 mm main wheel
66 Brake tube
67 Main wheel cover
68 Main wheel leg oleo hydraulic shock strut
69 330 ltr (87.2 US gallons) long-range auxiliary fuel
   tank
70 Main wheel doors

R. Watanabe

A captured Zero (A6M2) flying over San Diego area for testing, in early 1943.

The Zero was far inferior to the F4U-1 in level and diving speeds at all altitudes. It fell short in climbs starting at sea level, and also above 20,000 feet. Between 5,000 and 19,000 feet the situation varied. With slightly more than the normal fighter load, which may be distributed to give equal range and gun power, the Zero was slightly superior in average maximum rate of climb. This superiority became negligible at altitudes where carburettor air temperatures in the F4U were down to normal; close to the blower shift points it was more noticeable. However, the Zero could not stay with the Corsair in high speed climbs. The superiority of the F4U at 30,000 feet was very evident, and would persist when carrying heavier loads.

In combat with the Zero, the Corsair could take full advantage of its speed along with its ability to pushover and roll at high speed if surprised. Due to its much higher wing loading, the F4U had to avoid any attempt to turn with the Zero unless at high speed, and could expect the latter to outclimb the Corsair at moderate altitudes and low airspeeds. In this case, the F4U should be climbed at high airspeed and on a heading which would open the distance and prevent the Zero from reaching a favourable position for diving attacks. After reaching 19,000 to 20,000 feet, the Corsair had superior performance in climb and could choose its own position for attack.

During and after these tests, the first of subsequent Zeros to be captured and flown became an object of great curiosity. Charles A. Lindbergh is said to have been one of many noted airmen that were given a turn at flying this Zero. Several museums have since indicated that they possess this aircraft, but the truth is that prior to a routine flight at NAS North Island, in the summer of 1944, the pilot of a Curtiss SB2C Helldiver inadvertently taxied into it and chopped it to pieces from the tail to the cockpit. The Zero was a total loss.

The Zero Matures

As a war situation changes, so must combat aircraft be changed to adapt to the new environment and take advantage of advances in technology until fully replaced by new aircraft designs. In the case of the Zero, the Japanese Navy failed to substantially introduce an improved replacement for the Zero, to match the speed, armament and protection of the modern Allied fighters which began arriving in the Pacific in late 1942. Consequently, the Zero faced an even more potent enemy having both quantity and quality in its aircraft, while the Japanese pilots were left to rely on an array of improvements made to the Zeros basic 1939 vintage design. Its obsolescence could no longer be shielded through these modifications after 1943 yet, by necessity, it was kept in production until the surrender of Japan. As a consequence of being the first-line fighter of the Japanese Navy throughout the entire Pacific war, more Zeros were built than any other type of Japanese aircraft.

The life span of the Zero ranged from the superiority it enjoyed over China and the first year of the Pacific war, to the final desperate attempts to ward off swarms of Allied carrier based aircraft and the B-29s over the home islands of Japan. By examining each modification made to the Zero over this time period, it becomes clearly evident that the trend changed from being the aggressor to the defender. These changes in themselves encapsulate the history of the Zero, and in a way, the Pacific war itself.

As each of the Zero models is described, it may appear that a duel system of identification had been used; one being an alpha-numeric system closely resembling a method used by the U.S. Navy up until 1963, the other having the name of an aircraft followed by two digits. In fact, two distinct systems did exist. Officially, both were used by the Japanese Navy, but of the two, the use of its name designator was more commonly used.

With the letter system, the first letter identifies the aircraft mission. For the A6M5 Zero, a carrier-borne fighter, "A" signifies the naval mission. The 6 shows it to be the sixth basic design in the carrier-borne fighter series. "M" is for Mitsubishi, the design company, and the last number represents the modification number after initial acceptance of the design. This system was seldom used publicly since it revealed too much information about the aircraft in relation to other models in the Japanese Navy.

The two digit system that followed the aircraft name such as Zero 21 or Reisen 21, identifies the aircraft model. This designation is actually two numbers, not one double digit number as it appears, and is expressed as Zero Two-One. The first of the two numbers relate to the basic airframe and subsequent changes which are numbered consecutively. The second number identified the engine type changes made after the basic design acceptance by the Navy.

Mitsubishi 12-Shi, A6M1:

When the Imperial Japanese Navy accepted the *12*-Shi fighter in September, 1939, it was assigned the designation A6M1. It is believed that this designation applied only to the first two prototypes since both were powered by the 875 hp Mitsubishi *Zuisei* 13 engine, and it was from the evaluation of this configured model that the aircraft was accepted by the Navy and given this Navy designator.

Zero 11, A6M2:

The third prototype was powered by the more powerful 950 hp Nakajima *Sakae* 12 engine which gave it improved performance and production status. It was the model that first saw combat in China; 64 were built, commencing in December, 1939.

Zero 21, A6M2:

Service test model 11's proved the effectiveness of the design. The Zero performed well aboard Japan's aircraft carriers, but their snug fit while riding on the elevators between the flight and hangar decks put them in danger of damaging their wing tips. To solve the problems, the wing tip sections were made to be folded manually, reducing the span by 500 mm (20 in) on each side for added elevator clearance. This structural change warranted a new designation, making this Zero, Model 21. Had the entire wing been made to fold to save space like that of the Wildcat, Hellcat and others of the U.S. Navy, it would have increased the weight in the structure, a penalty that the Japanese did not want to pay.

With this model, Nakajima Aircraft Company also began manufacturing the Zero in November, 1941, and together with Mitsubishi produced 740 of this type. Beginning with the 127th aircraft, a new balance tab arrangement was installed on the ailerons. The amount of tab action was linked to the landing gear retraction system. This reduced the required stick force that was needed for lateral manoeuvrability during high speed flight, yet provided responsive ailerons while at traffic pattern speeds.

By now, the Allies had learned the meaning of the model designation system used by the Japanese Navy, so the Allies referred to this Zero with its code name as "Zeke 21."

Zero 32, A6M3:

To compete with the expected increase performance in allied fighter aircraft, it was necessary to improve the Zero's altitude and climb performance. This brought about the most apparent design change in the basic appearance of the Zero.

Additional power was given to the Zero in the form of the new *Sakae* 21 engine with its increased output of 1,100 hp. This engine had a change in reduction gearing, allowed for a larger propeller, and incorporated a two speed supercharger for improved high altitude performance. The most visible feature in this engine change was the placement of the air-scoop for its down draft carburettor at the top front of the cowling and the nose guns firing out closer to the front of the cowling rather than along gun troughs at the top of the cowling. This engine change alone accounted for most of the 280 pound weight increase over the earlier Model 21. Fuel quantity was reduced by approximately 21 U.S. gallons due to the increase in dimensional size of the engine as a measure to retain the original overall fuselage length. Although the difference in fuel consumption of the *Sakae* 21 compared to the *Sakae* 12 was negligible in normal cruise performance, the tactical combat radius of the Model 32 was reduced considerably because of the difference in fuel capacity and fuel consumption at full power.

Despite this increase in power for the Zero, the performance anticipated to be gained by the designers did not materialize. Pilots flying the test models recommended removing the folding wing tips entirely, which was done, and a fairing was added to cover the exposed end. This brought some loss in overall performance but did provide the increase in maximum speed. With a shorter aileron that was necessitated by removing the wing tip, the two-speed ratio aileron tab arrangement was eliminated which simplified production.

When this squared off wing model was first encountered by the Allies in October, 1942, over the Solomon Islands, it was thought to be a new Japanese fighter. It was given the Allied code name "Hap" in honour of General "Hap" Arnold of the Air Force, but when Arnold found out about the name he was less than flattered and it was recoded to "Hamp". When the first close inspection of this type was conducted by the Americans on New Guinea in December, 1942, they discovered it to be a modification of the basic Zero form, and the code name was changed to "Zeke" 32.

The reduction in wing area by just over nine square feet gave slightly improved manoeuvrability at high speeds. This had been a shortcoming in the earlier configurations. Ammunition for the 20-mm cannon was increased from 60 to 100 rounds per gun. From production which started in July, 1941, 343 machines were delivered to the Japanese Navy.

Type 98 Reflector Gunsight

increase was due to a small fuel tank outboard of the main fuel cell in each wing which provided for an additional total of 24 U.S. gallons. This gave the Model 22 the longest range of all models, about 100 miles more than that which the astonishing Model 21 had tactically demonstrated. By August, 1942, this increase in the Zero's range was necessitated when required to fly as far as 560 nautical miles (644 statute miles) from Rabaul to the combat area over Guadalcanal. There they engaged the numerically superior and more modern allied aircraft such as the Vought F4U-1 Corsair, Lockheed P-38 Lightning and Supermarine Spitfire, and suffered heavy losses in this campaign.

When the earlier Type 99 Mark 1 Oerlikon wing cannons were changed in favour of the higher muzzle velocity, longer barrel Type 99, Mark 2, Model 3 cannons, this Zero became the Model 22a. A small number of Model 22s were operationally tested at Rabaul with wing-mounted experimental 30-mm cannon.

Zero Model 32, A6M4:

The assignment of this designation to a model of the Zero had been questionable for a long period of time since there was no record of its use. The Japanese use the number "4" with the same reservations that Westerners treat the number "13", and therefore it was presumed not to have been used for this reason although not avoided in numbering systems for other aircraft. (The number "4" which is *shi* in Japanese also has the meaning of the word "death.") It was not until 1968 that Horikoshi revealed that a Model 32 was equipped with an experimental turbo-supercharged engine, and this designation A6M4 was reserved for this configured model had it gone into production.

Zero Model 52, A6M5:

Despite promises in 1943 of a new interceptor that later was known to the Allies as "Jack," production as well as development lagged far behind. Again it became necessary to modify the existing Zero fighter in an attempt to counter the new American fighters which in many respects now clearly out-performed the earlier Zero models.

This new Zero Model 52 was an effort to simplify and speed production, as well as to increase the diving speed. Once again, effort was directed at redesigning the wing tip. The wing span remained the same as with the squared off tip, Model 32, but modifications included the elimination of the unused wing tip folding mechanism which was merely faired over, and rounding off the otherwise square wing tip. This not only simplified production, but saved weight although an overall increase of 150 to 170 pounds (68–78 kg) over the Zero 32 was experienced. For gaining the needed increase in diving speed, heavier gauge wing skin allowed this airspeed to be moved up to 355 knots (410 mph).

Another measure taken to improve speed performance was to replace the exhaust collector ring with straight individual stacks. This change directed the high velocity exhaust gas backward for additional thrust. These changes produced a Zero having a maximum speed which reached 305 knots (351 mph) in level flight at 6,000 m (19,700 ft), and

Zero Model 22, A6M3:

This reversal in a portion of the model number was a result of adding once again the round wing tip which matched the airframe of the earlier Model 21, yet retaining the larger *Sakae* 21 engine. The reason for this reversal was to gain back the loss in range which was partly a result of the decreased wing area. This aircraft actually preceded the square wing Model 32 in design concept but was presumably set aside to meet the request to eliminate the folding portion of the wing tip. By the time the Model 22 reached the production stage, the next generation, Zero 52, was rapidly approaching operational status. Therefore Zero 22, which appeared in combat after Model 32s, had a relatively short operational life despite the fact that 560 of this type were manufactured. They first appeared in combat in late 1942 when they were rushed to Buna, on New Guinea, and Buka, in the Solomon Islands where they frequently provided escort cover for vessels operating between the fighting on Guadalcanal and the northern supply bases.

This return of the "round-wing" model made a net weight increase of 123 pounds over the Zero 32. Some of this

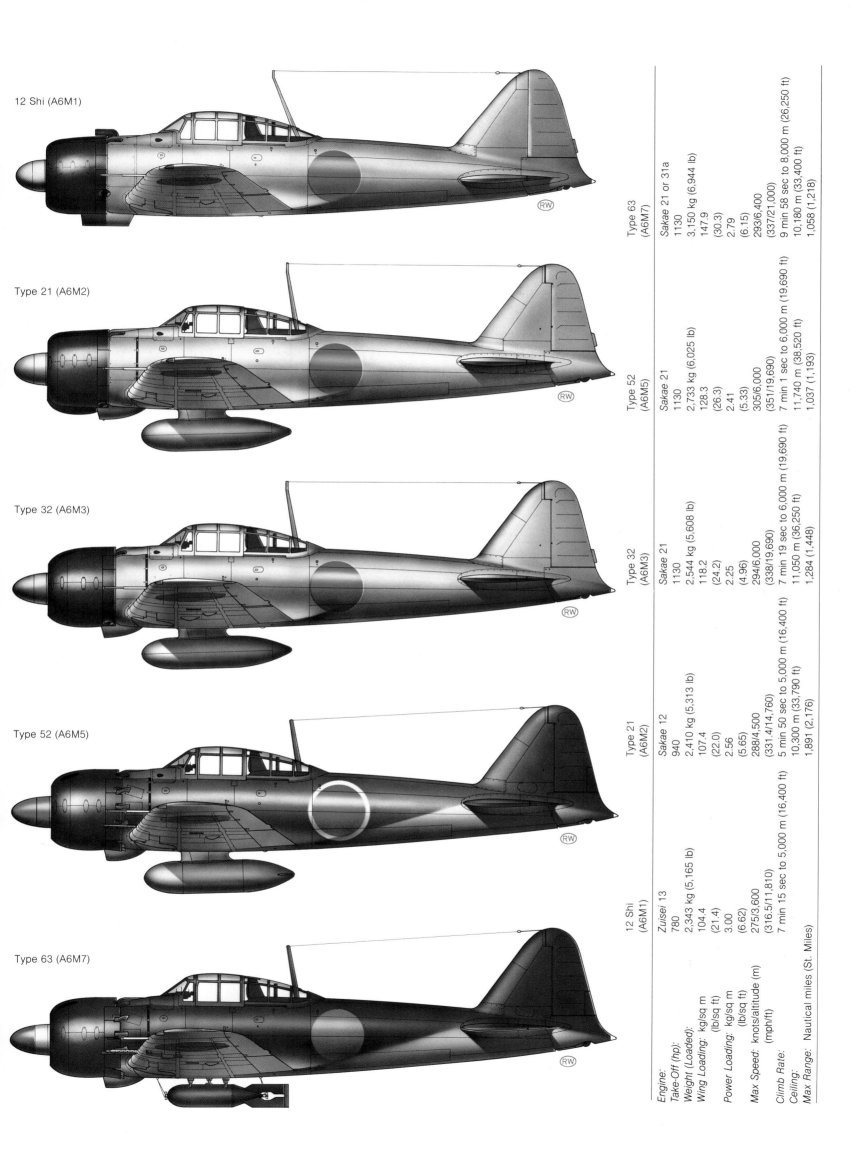

12 Shi (A6M1)

Type 21 (A6M2)

Type 32 (A6M3)

Type 52 (A6M5)

Type 63 (A6M7)

	12 Shi (A6M1)	Type 21 (A6M2)	Type 32 (A6M3)	Type 52 (A6M5)	Type 63 (A6M7)
Engine:	Zuisei 13	Sakae 12	Sakae 21	Sakae 21	Sakae 21 or 31a
Take-Off (hp):	780	940	1130	1130	1130
Weight (Loaded):	2,343 kg (5,165 lb)	2,410 kg (5,313 lb)	2,544 kg (5,608 lb)	2,733 kg (6,025 lb)	3,150 kg (6,944 lb)
Wing Loading: kg/sq m	104.4	107.4	118.2	128.3	147.9
(lb/sq ft)	(21.4)	(22.0)	(24.2)	(26.3)	(30.3)
Power Loading: kg/sq m	3.00	2.56	2.25	2.41	2.79
(lb/sq ft)	(6.62)	(5.65)	(4.96)	(5.33)	(6.15)
Max Speed: knots/altitude (m)	275/3,600	288/4,500	294/6,000	305/6,000	293/6,400
(mph/ft)	(316.5/11,810)	(331.4/14,760)	(338/19,690)	(351/19,690)	(337/21,000)
Climb Rate:	7 min 15 sec to 5,000 m (16,400 ft)	5 min 50 sec to 5,000 m (16,400 ft)	7 min 19 sec to 6,000 m (19,690 ft)	7 min 1 sec to 6,000 m (19,690 ft)	9 min 58 sec to 8,000 m (26,250 ft)
Ceiling:	10,300 m (33,790 ft)	10,300 m (33,790 ft)	11,050 m (36,250 ft)	11,740 m (38,520 ft)	10,180 m (33,400 ft)
Max Range: Nautical miles (St. Miles)	1,891 (2,176)		1,284 (1,448)	1,037 (1,193)	1,058 (1,218)

Zero fighters (Type 21/22) of the First Naval Air Corps prepare to take off from Rabaul in support of 'Operation *Ro-Go*.' November, 1943.

clearly improved rate of climb. This became the most widely used model of the Zero series with 1,701 manufactured, beginning in the summer of 1943.

This new model was pressed into service in the fall of 1943 in time to meet the initial appearance of the new Grumman F6F Hellcat. The Zero 52 could hold its own in performance against the slightly less manoeuvrable Hellcat, but the Zero was too often the victim of the heavier armament of the F6F due to its lighter construction and inadequate protection.

Zero 52a, A6M5a:

Within the Zero Model 52 series, three sub series followed. By the fall of 1943, the Zero Model 52a emerged with additional firepower that was now needed to encounter the Hellcat. This was effected by using a belt feed rather than a drum whereby the ammunition supply could be increased for each wing cannon from 100 to 125 rounds each.

To again improve the diving speed a partial increase in wing skin was made at high stress locations. This raised the maximum speed limitation from 355 kts (410 mph) to 400 kts (460 mph). Engineers were hesitant to push the limit beyond this point, but this did close the speed margin between 17 to 26 kts (20 to 30 mph) short of the diving limitations of the heavier F4U Corsair.

Zero Model 52b, A6M5b:

Some of the harsh lessons learned in combat with the lack of pilot and aircraft protection were applied to this model of the Zero. To fill the gap while waiting for the next generation of fighters to replace the Zero design, a study was begun in early 1944 to add protection features to the Zero. These began emerging in the Zero 52b. Most significant was the use of an automatic CO_2 fire extinguisher system built into the fuel tank areas of the fuselage and around the engine fire wall. For the pilot, a 50 mm (2 in) bullet resistant windshield was provided which consisted of two plates of glass with clear

plastic sandwiched between. For increasing firepower, one of the two fuselage mounted Type 97, 7.7-mm machine-guns was replaced by a larger Type 3, 13-mm machine-gun, the first change in armament size since the first prototype of the Zero.

This added fire power and improved survivability was in preparation for the pending battle of the Philippines which took place beginning 19 June, 1944. Mitsubishi turned out 470 of this model and Nakajima an unknown quantity.

Zero Model 52c, A6M5c

Every attempt was being made to maintain the survivability of the Zero which was destined to carry the fight without a replacement. Another attempt at improvement was in the Model 52C which concentrated on increased firepower, more fuel tank protection and an over-all performance increase. Operational pilots felt that this would return the Zero's qualitative superiority it had lost to the Grumman F6F Hellcat. Designers knew, however, that they would severely overload their 1938-designed airframe in trying to assume 1944 standards. There were no options but to try.

The Navy issued a top priority order on 23 July, 1944, which called for a number of equipment changes and additions. Armament was again increased by adding two Type 3 13-mm wing mounted machine-guns outboard of the two 20-mm cannon. To adjust for some of this weight increase, the newly installed 13-mm nose machine-gun was eliminated altogether. Armament now consisted of five guns.

Adding to this firepower were the addition for the first time of underwing racks to accommodate small air-to-air rocket bombs.

Recognizing that the Zero was now far too often in front of the foe, armour plate was installed for the first time behind the pilot's seat and several panels of bullet resistant glass were added within the rear canopy.

To compensate for the loss in operational range that had occurred over previous modifications with the addition of weight, a 37-gallon self-sealing fuel tank was installed behind the pilot seat. All these modifications added up to more than 300 kg (660 lbs) over that of the previous model.

By now, the Zero's designer, Jiro Horikoshi, had moved on to the urgent project of designing the A7M *Reppu*, Allied code name "Sam," as Mitsubishi's replacement for the Zero. The task of these late modifications to the Zero were left to designer engineer Eitaro Sano. He could readily see that, with this vast increase in weight, the performance of the A6M5c would be greatly impaired if the *Sakae* 21 engine was to be retained. His team's proposal to the Naval Bureau of Aeronautics was to incorporate Mitsubishi's own engine of greater horsepower into the Zero. This new engine was the 1,350 hp *Kinsei* 62, which would provide an increase of 250 hp. With this engine, the design staff felt that the Zero might well be restored to a performance equal to that of the American F6F Hellcat.

To the grave disappointment of the designers, the Navy refused to release any of the larger engines, for most were already committed as an emergency replacement engine for the troublesome Aichi-built *Atsuta* in-line water-cooled engine used on the carrier dive bomber D4Y ("Judy") which was urgently needed in combat. Besides, the Navy claimed that the engineering time required for adapting this engine to the Zero airframe was prohibitive. As an alternate measure, the Navy recommended water-methanol injection be used with the *Sakae* engine for emergency power when needed. Mitsubishi's engineers were left with no choice, but this engine modification, now called the *Sakae* 31a, was slow in coming and the project had to continue with the existing series of the *Sakae* 21.

Nevertheless, the airframe modifications that were planned for, did continue. When the first A6M5c was completed in September 1944, the flight tests were disappointing, but were expected under the circumstances. The added weight without increase in power reduced performance considerably. Production was interrupted with this model when the new A6M6c showed promise, but with its failing, A6M5c production was resumed until 93 of this series was completed by the end of 1944.

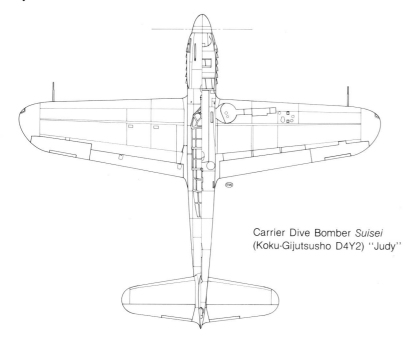

Carrier Dive Bomber *Suisei*
(Koku-Gijutsusho D4Y2) "Judy"

Zero Model 53c, A6M6c

By November of that year, the water-methanol *Sakae* Model 31a was installed in a Zero airframe. Engineers also felt that self-sealing tanks were developed sufficiently for operational use and incorporated them for the first time in a Japanese aircraft. What was hoped to be a smooth transition on the existing A6M5c Model 52c assembly line to this new model, produced one more of many disappointments. The new engine failed to perform as expected. Not only was this engine reduced in power due to the modification, but the value on the new water-methanol metering system failed repeatedly during engine functional tests. A solution to the problem did not seem forthcoming. This uncertainty slowed production until the plan for using the modified engine and the equally troublesome self-sealing tanks was abandoned and production was resumed with the preceding Model 52c. Mitsubishi produced only one Zero 53c. Although its designation followed the prescribed pattern for airframe and engine model changes, the reason for the use of the suffix "c" in this case remains unclear.

Zero Model 63, A6M7:

The requirements for war continued to move ahead at a rate faster than Japan's aircraft industry could match. Deprived of its larger aircraft carriers by the fall of 1944, the Japanese Navy had difficulties in equipping its smaller carrier-borne units with suitable dive bombers. The Aichi D3A "Val" was far too slow and virtually defenseless against new Allied fighters. Its replacement, the Aichi D4Y3 "Judy" landed too fast to be safely operated from these carriers. A substitute had to be found in time to defend the Philippines against the coming Allied invasion.

Zeros were modified for the fighter-bomber mission which resulted in the Model 63. The armament remained the same as on the previous Model 52c, but a replacement of the normal 330 ltr (87 U.S. Gal) centre-line expendable auxiliary fuel tank, was a Mitsubishi-developed bomb rack capable of carrying a 250 kg (550 lb) bomb. Replacing the centre-line fuel tank were two wing-mounted 150 ltr (40 U.S. Gal) drop tanks, fitted outboard of the landing gear.

To compensate for added stresses encountered in the dive-bomber role, increased skin thickness was added to the tail of these models.

When this new model – many of which were modified from earlier types – was committed to combat in the Philippines, difficulty was often encountered with the bomb release mechanism. This frustration coupled with the desperate war situation for Japan led to some of the first recognized *kamikaze* attacks of the war by Zeros that carried their bomb loads directly into their targets.

Although existing records do not show a change back to the *Sakae* 21 engine for this model, some measure of success must have been achieved in the water-methanol modified engines. In addition to the "3" being retained instead of changing the designation to Zero Model 62, the one known example of a Model 63, which is in the collection of the U.S. National Air and Space Museum in Washington, is fitted with a *Sakae* 31b engine. Mitsubishi produced an undetermined

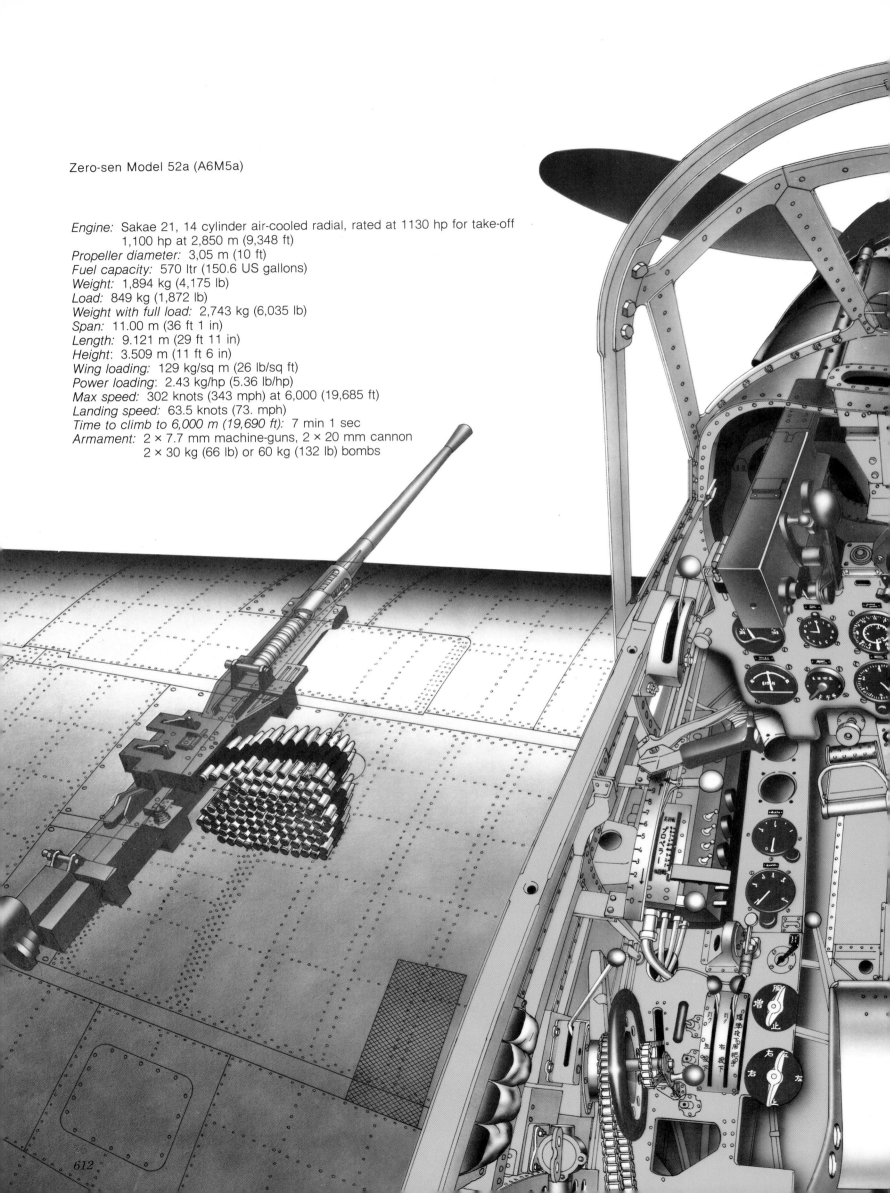

Zero-sen Model 52a (A6M5a)

Engine: Sakae 21, 14 cylinder air-cooled radial, rated at 1130 hp for take-off
      1,100 hp at 2,850 m (9,348 ft)
Propeller diameter: 3,05 m (10 ft)
Fuel capacity: 570 ltr (150.6 US gallons)
Weight: 1,894 kg (4,175 lb)
Load: 849 kg (1,872 lb)
Weight with full load: 2,743 kg (6,035 lb)
Span: 11.00 m (36 ft 1 in)
Length: 9.121 m (29 ft 11 in)
Height: 3.509 m (11 ft 6 in)
Wing loading: 129 kg/sq m (26 lb/sq ft)
Power loading: 2.43 kg/hp (5.36 lb/hp)
Max speed: 302 knots (343 mph) at 6,000 (19,685 ft)
Landing speed: 63.5 knots (73. mph)
Time to climb to 6,000 m (19,690 ft): 7 min 1 sec
Armament: 2 × 7.7 mm machine-guns, 2 × 20 mm cannon
      2 × 30 kg (66 lb) or 60 kg (132 lb) bombs

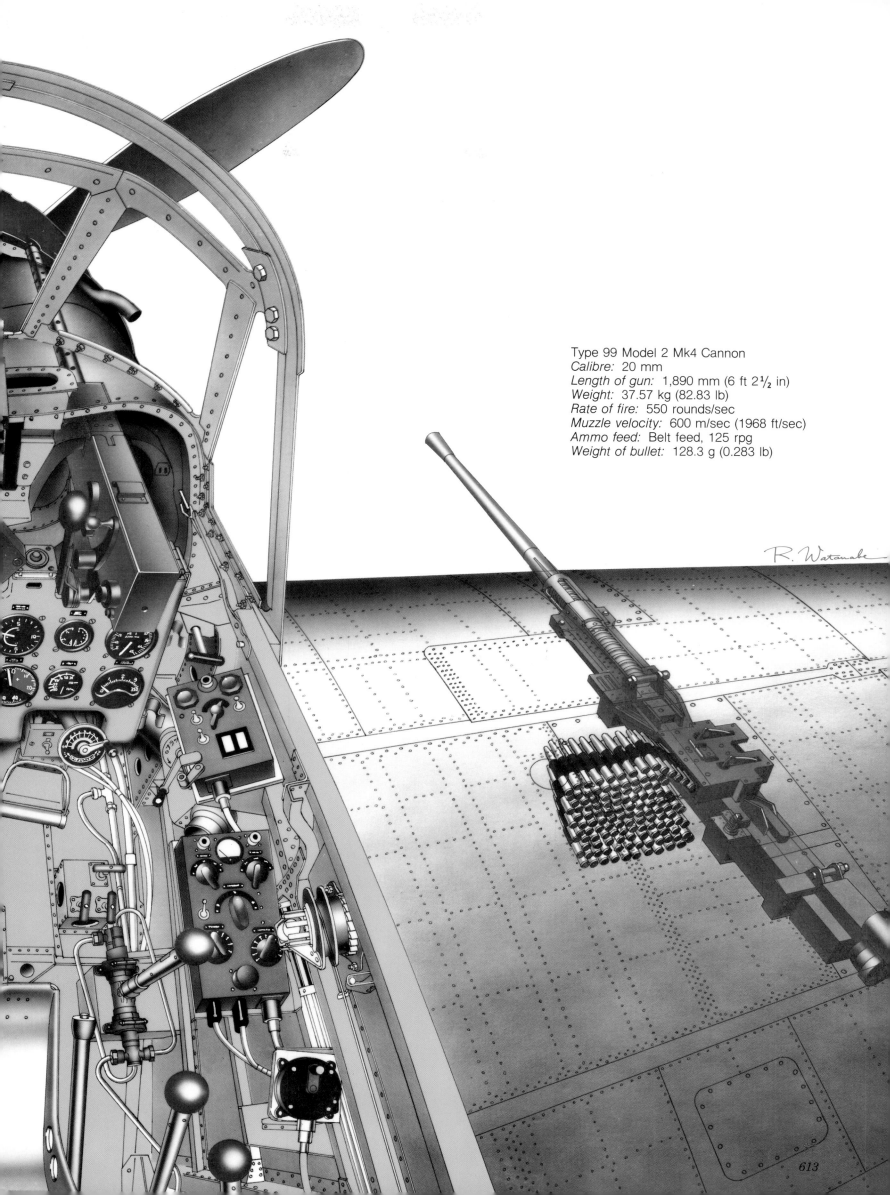

Type 99 Model 2 Mk4 Cannon
Calibre: 20 mm
Length of gun: 1,890 mm (6 ft 2½ in)
Weight: 37.57 kg (82.83 lb)
Rate of fire: 550 rounds/sec
Muzzle velocity: 600 m/sec (1968 ft/sec)
Ammo feed: Belt feed, 125 rpg
Weight of bullet: 128.3 g (0.283 lb)

R. Watanabe

613

number of these models, starting their manufacture in May, 1945. Zeros within this group included Model 62, with the *Sakae* 21 engine, for some Allied Intelligence reports mention such a model designation along with Model 63.

Zero Model 54c, A6M8c:

Despite the resistance of the Japanese Navy to place a more powerful engine in the Zero airframe, a number of events finally reversed this decision. Not only had the aircraft continued to gain structural weight with each modification, but little or no added power was ever introduced to compensate. In addition, the clean lines of the fighter were being interrupted with bomb racks, drop tanks, more guns, and some external strengthening of the skin, all of which detracted from performance. Quality in production of both airframe and engines lessened as the war persisted with unskilled and drafted labour, and the relentless B-29 bombing raids. The Zero fighter may have retained the appearance of the earlier "hunter" when it first ruled the Pacific in the

opening months of the war, but now it was the "hunted," manned with under-trained pilots and having to cope with superior Allied fighters and better trained crews.

To follow the plan of replacing the Zero with Mitsubishi's new fighter the A7M1 *Reppu*, "Sam," production of the *Sakae* engine began tapering off to increase production of the new and more powerful *Homare* engine. Problems with the new aircraft necessitated continual production of the Zero but the supply of *Sakae* engines became critical. As a result, in November, 1944, the Navy agreed to install the Mitsubishi *Kinsei* 62 engine in newly produced Zero fighters. This had been Horikoshi's preference from a very early stage of development but its reality came too late, for now it was only a matter of time as the air war was all but lost.

Among other changes included in the new model were the elimination of the troublesome self-sealing fuel tanks, replacing their protection with a fire extinguishing system. Also included was an increase in fuel capacity for the thirstier engine in order to retain a flight time of 30 minutes at

1	Type 99 Model 2 Mk4 20mm cannon
2	20mm ammunition belt (125 rpg)
3	Gadget pocket
4	Emergency float blower lever
5	Machine-gun lock lever
6	Elevator trimming tab control
7	Rudder trimming tab control
8	Bomb release lever
9	Auxiliary fuel tank jettison lever
10	Wing tanks selector lever
11	Fuselage/wing-tanks switching cock
12	Wing tanks fuel gauge switching cock
13	Emergency fuel jettison lever
14	Wing tanks fuel gauge
15	Fuselage tank fuel gauge
16	Circuit breakers
17	Supercharger control
18	Propeller pitch control lever
19	Mixture control lever
20	Throttle lever
21	20mm cannon firing lever
22	High altitude automatic mixture control
23	Emergency power boost
24	Radio direction indicator
25	Magneto switch
26	Altimeter
27	Magnetic compass
28	Manifold pressure gauge
29	Oil temperature gauge
30	Cylinder head temperature gauge
31	Tachometer
32	Fuel & oil pressure gauge
33	Rate of climb indicator
34	Airspeed indicator
35	Clock
36	Exhaust temperature gauge
37	Artificial horizon
38	Turn & bank indicator
39	7.7mm type 97 machine-gun
40	Type 98 reflector gunsight
41	Inertia starter lever
42	Cowl flap control
43	Direction finder control unit
44	Fresh air duct
45	Radio control unit
46	Arresting hook winding wheel
47	Loop antenna handle
48	Flap control
49	Landing gear lever
50	Emergency fuel pump lever
51	Emergency gear-down lever
52	Wing tanks cooling air intake control
53	Oil cooler shutter control
54	Ignition booster switch
55	20mm cannon master switch
56	Oxygen supply gauge
57	Hydraulic pressure gauge
58	Primer
59	Foot pedal
60	Foot pedal position adjuster
61	Control column
62	Seat
63	Seat up/down lever

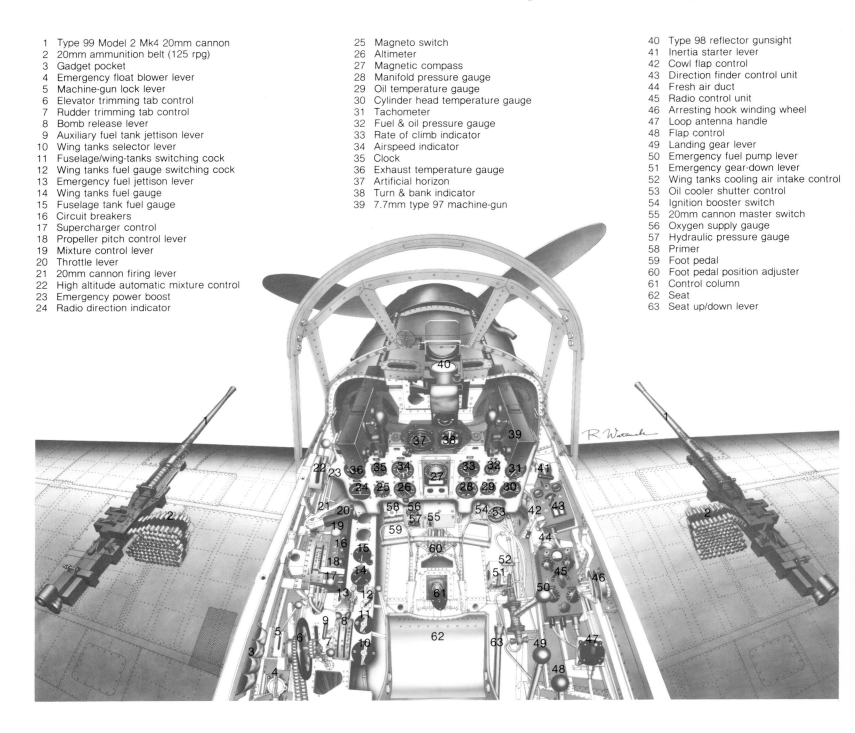

combat power, plus 2½ hours at normal cruise. The new engine increased the size of the nose appreciably, and with this added weight, the single nose-mounted Type 3, 13-mm machine-gun was eliminated.

By the end of March, 1945, the first prototype of the new series was expected to be completed, but extensive air-raid damage to the Mitsubishi dispersal plants had drastically delayed production. The effort for delivering the new machine was pressed home by Engineers Eitaro Sano, Kazuaki Izumi and Shiro Kushibe, and the first machine was flown in late April. The continuing war effort was taking its toll on everything being produced, and the new engine suffered from such things as low oil pressure, high oil temperature, and fluctuations in fuel pressure at various altitudes. Changes were made to correct these faults until finally the new aircraft achieved the expectations of Mitsubishi and the demands of the Navy.

The Navy accepted the first prototype of the A6M8c on 25 May, 1945, and one month later took delivery of the second. Maximum level-flight speed was recorded at 308 kts (355 mph) at 6,000 m (19,700 ft) along with the ability to climb to that altitude in 6 min 50 secs. Although this maximum level speed was 48 kts (55 mph) slower than the F4U-1D at that altitude, it showed a halt in the trend toward deteriorating performance which had prevailed since the spring or summer of 1944 in all Japanese aircraft. Test pilots who flew the Model 54c overwhelmingly agreed that this was the best model of the Zero yet produced.

Type 2 Seaplane Fighter, A6M2-N:

Before departing from these accounts in the development of the Zero, there was another model of this fighter that deserves mention in addition to two-seat trainer versions. This is the seaplane version of the Zero that the Allies code named "Rufe." In late 1940, Nakajima was already in production of the A6M2 when the Japanese Navy issued the 15-*Shi* specification calling for a single-seat seaplane fighter pending the development and production of the Kawanishi N1K1 *Kyofu*, known as "Rex." Its purpose was to provide air cover during the early phases of amphibious landing operations or over military bases of the small islands where the construction of airfields was not practical. As an interim aircraft, the Navy instructed Nakajima to develop a float fighter version of the Zero using the aircraft of the Model 11 without folding wing tips. The design modification that followed had the main float supported by a unique triangular type strut, and the wing tip float at both sides was attached by one slender strut. This float system ensured the least amount of drag, yet was sturdy enough for practical seaplane use.

A total of 327 "Rufe" fighters was manufactured early in the war, making them the first seaplane fighters to actually engage in combat. "Rufes" were active in the Aleutian Operation and in the Solomons. Despite the weight and drag of the floats, these fighters were fast and manoeuvrable. They served their mission very well initially, but in a short time they were unable to effectively counter Allied land-based fighters.

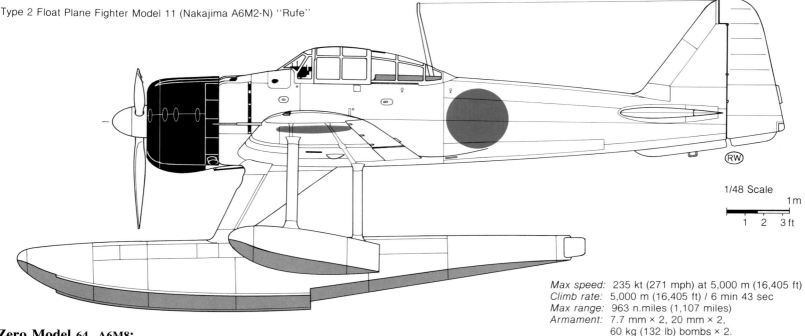

Type 2 Float Plane Fighter Model 11 (Nakajima A6M2-N) "Rufe"

1/48 Scale

1 m

1   2   3 ft

Max speed: 235 kt (271 mph) at 5,000 m (16,405 ft)
Climb rate: 5,000 m (16,405 ft) / 6 min 43 sec
Max range: 963 n.miles (1,107 miles)
Armament: 7.7 mm × 2, 20 mm × 2,
                  60 kg (132 lb) bombs × 2.

Zero Model 64, A6M8:

With this model, the final development of the Zero went into production with an overly optimistic order of 6,300 machines. Satisfied with the promising results demonstrated with the 1,350 hp *Kinsei* 62 powered Model 54, this Model 64 would have the fighter-bomber airframe of the earlier Model 63. Six major aircraft plants of both Mitsubishi and Nakajima were pressed into continued production of the Zero. But Japan failed to see another of the improved models come from their production lines, for time had run out and the surrender of Japan ended production.

Combat Rages On

First Allied experience with the Zero fighter was during missions for which it was designed. For the attack on Pearl Harbor, aircraft carriers of the Japanese fleet delivered the Zeros and bombers used in this attack within 200 nautical miles of the target. From that moment on the name "Zero Fighter" would never be forgotten.

The Zeros next appeared over Wake Island, destroying all opposing aircraft and gaining their superiority so that the invasion of that island was successful. From there, the Japanese military strength pushed further south in a string of victories, eventually attacking Port Darwin, Australia, by mid-February, 1942. Zero fighters provided air cover for each of these operations during which air superiority was maintained throughout. For this campaign, instead of operating from aircraft carriers as the Allies were again certain was

The day following this attack, Clark Air Base in the Philippines was left in burning rubble by Japanese bombers escorted by Zeros of the Tainan *Kokutai* (Air Corps). The Americans were convinced that the fighters had been launched from nearby aircraft carriers, which is the way the plan was first intended. Instead, after confirming the long range capabilities of the Zero, these strikes at targets in the Philippines originated and terminated from bases on Formosa, a round trip distance of 900 nautical miles (nearly 1,125 statute miles) leaving sufficient time for combat engagements in the target area. The long range designed into the Zero was put to the ultimate test, which freed the otherwise needed aircraft carriers for other strikes. By 13 December, after five days of attack, the U.S. air forces had been virtually annihilated throughout the Philippines.

the case, they did in reality fly from newly captured land bases on Timor Island, 400 nautical miles (460 statute miles) to the northwest. The Allies could not fully grasp the true capabilities of the Zero to cover such distances and then function so well as a fighter.

The tide of the Japanese military power went unchecked over the vast area of the Pacific and its many islands until the great naval engagement in the Coral Sea on 7 and 8 May, 1942. This was the first battle engagement ever to be fought entirely by aircraft with the surface ships out of sight of each other. During the two-day battle, the A6M2s fought ruthlessly in this first real challenge to Japanese air superiority. This situation was not a matter of superiority of one fighter against another, but one fighter force against another fighter force. The Zero was challenged by the chunky

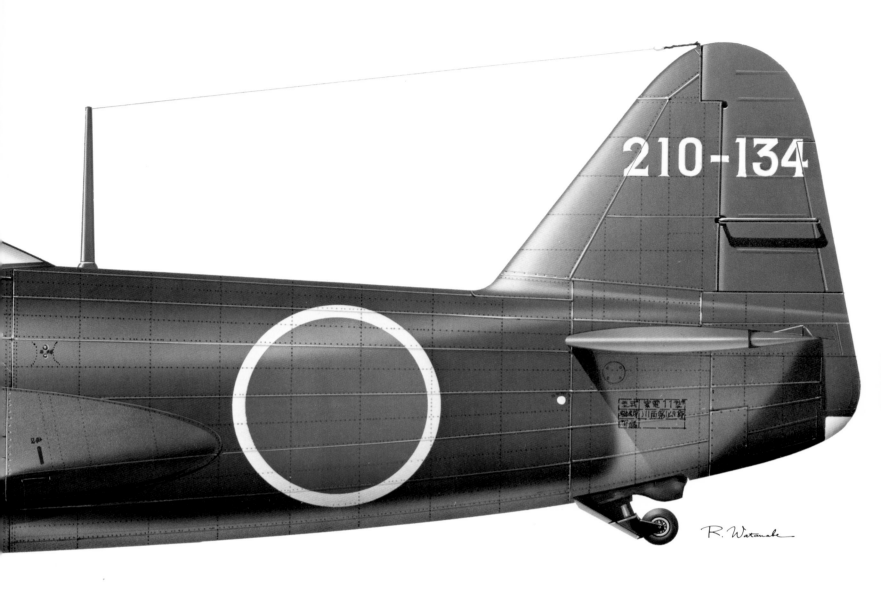

Kawanishi N1K1-J *Shiden* Model 11a
of the 210 Kokutai in early 1945.

Delays with the *Raiden* fighter ('Jack') prompted the Japanese Navy to look into other possibilities for an air superiority fighter. In March, 1944, the decision was made to redirect priorities from that of the ailing *Raiden* to the Kawanishi N1K1-J *Shiden*, better known as 'George,' while continuing with the production of the Zero fighter. At first, the Navy was reluctant to fully recognize the potential of the *Shiden* since Kawanishi made it a private venture to convert their *Kyofu* N1K1 seaplane fighter design 'Rex' into a land-based fighter.

This conversion had its own share of technical problems. Utilizing the 1,990 hp Homare engine which was over 500 hp more than the seaplane version, its resultant large propeller required a long landing gear from its mid-wing configuration for sufficient ground clearance. From the start of flight testing in December, 1942, its progress was marred by problems. Like so many of the unproven engines, the Homare failed to develop its rated power. The long landing gear legs which contracted as they retracted into the wheel wells often failed.

Many of the airframe design problems were resolved by a new version of 'George,' designated N1K2-J. With a redesigned fuselage to simplify manufacture, the wing was relocated to the bottom of the fuselage, thus allowing for a shorter and more reliable landing gear retracting arrangement.

In combat, 'George' was regarded as an inefffictive interceptor due to its relatively poor climbing capability. However, the *Shiden Kai*, as it was named, was considered an outstanding fighter in air engagements on equal terms with the best Allied fighter aircraft.

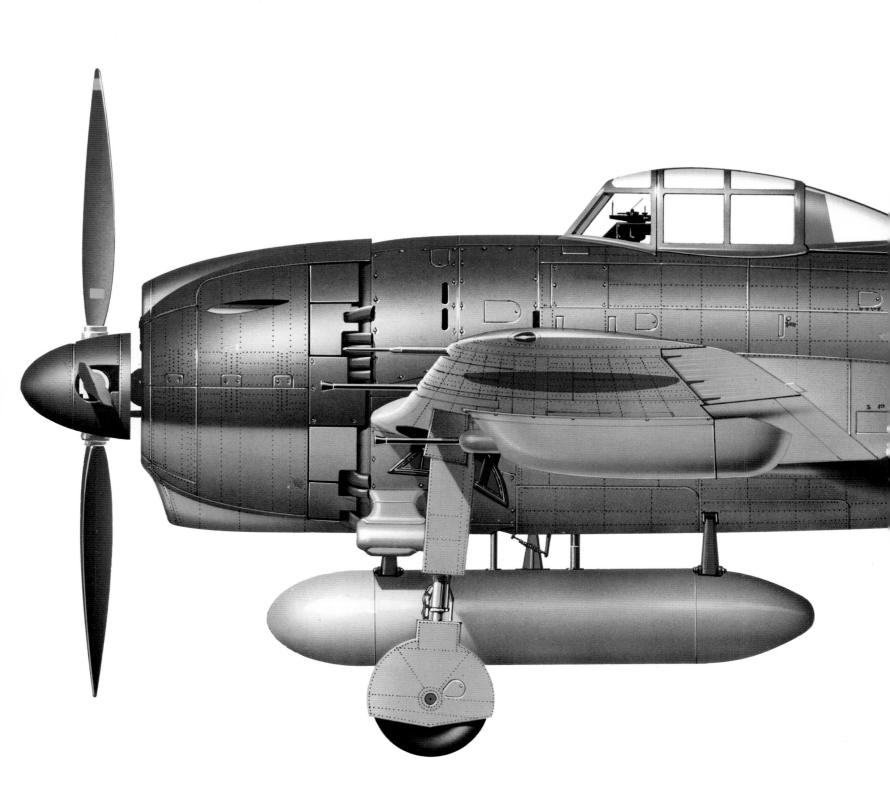

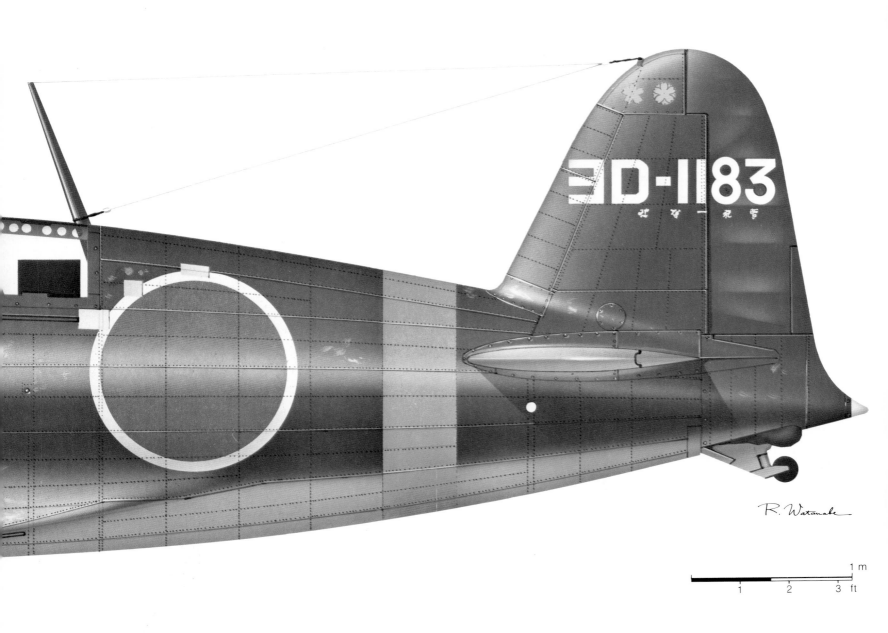

1 m

1 2 3 ft

Mitsubishi J2M3 *Raiden* Model 21
of the 2nd Hikotai, 302 Kokutai in May, 1945.

'Jack,' as the Allies code named the Mitsubishi J2M *Raiden*, was
the Japanese Navy's first purely air defense interceptor. Conceived as
the 14-*Shi* Interceptor Fighter in 1939, after proposal for the Zero had
been established, the *Raiden* was intended to augment, not replace the
Zero. As the war progressed, however, and the air war for Japan became that of defense, there was a greater need for this type aircraft
than first envisioned.

The design concept of the *Raiden* centered around a snuggly cowled 1,800 hp Kasei radial engine, aircooled by a fan at the front. An extended drive shaft placed the propeller well forward of the engine
which allowed the shape of the nose to be slender and give a more

aerodynamic teardrop shape to the fuselage. The wings incorporated
the newly developed laminar airflow section.

Problems with the engine and related vibration delayed its acceptance by the Navy as a service airplane until October, 1942. The first
production airplane was not delivered until December, 1943. Preoc-
cupation by Mitsubishi in the manufacture of the Zero contributed to
some of this delay in solving technical problems and accelerating production. Finally, in despair, the Navy transferred the production of
Raiden to a satellite plant of Mitsubishi, while the main Nagoya plant
concentrated on the Zero. In all of several models, about 470 *Raidens*
were built. Although it still retained the undesirable features of poor
visibility, engine vibration, and short flight duration, its outstanding
speed and climb made 'Jack' the most successful fighter used against
the B-29 Superfortress.

Kyushu J7W1 *Shinden*

A prime example of Japanese aircraft design ingenuity after the development of the Zero was the *canard*-type Kyushu J7W1 *Shinden* fighter. Having the appearance of a futuristic fighter for the World War II time-period, it was the only tail-first design of several through-out the world that was regarded as a production aircraft. Plans were laid for mass production even before the first prototype was completed.

Unaware of experiments conducted in other countries with fighters of the *canard* type, a design team at the Naval Aero-Technical Arsenal conceived a short-range intercepter early in 1943 which embodied this configuration. None of the existing interceptor programs in Japan were attaining success and the state of the art was surpassing their design before any of these fighters could be produced. The

Shinden was to be of advanced technology in hopes of closing this gap.

Much of the design work for the J7W1 was carried out at the Air Arsenal which included a series of tests with gliders and powered craft of the *canard* configuration. Results were so successful that the Navy ordered the *Shinden* into immediate production. The project for this unorthodox fighter was passed to the Kyushu Airplane Company since they were the only major airframe manufacturer not already committed to a priority fighter production. Navy engineers were so confident of the potentialities of this fighter that their chief designer, Captain M. Tsuruno was sent to Kyushu to supervise development until production status was attained. The *Shinden* was an all metal air-plane with a 2,000 hp Mitsubishi Ha 43-42 eighteen cylinder air-cooled radial engine mounted in the rear, driving a 6-blade propeller. The front-mounted horizontal surface acted as an elevator for flight

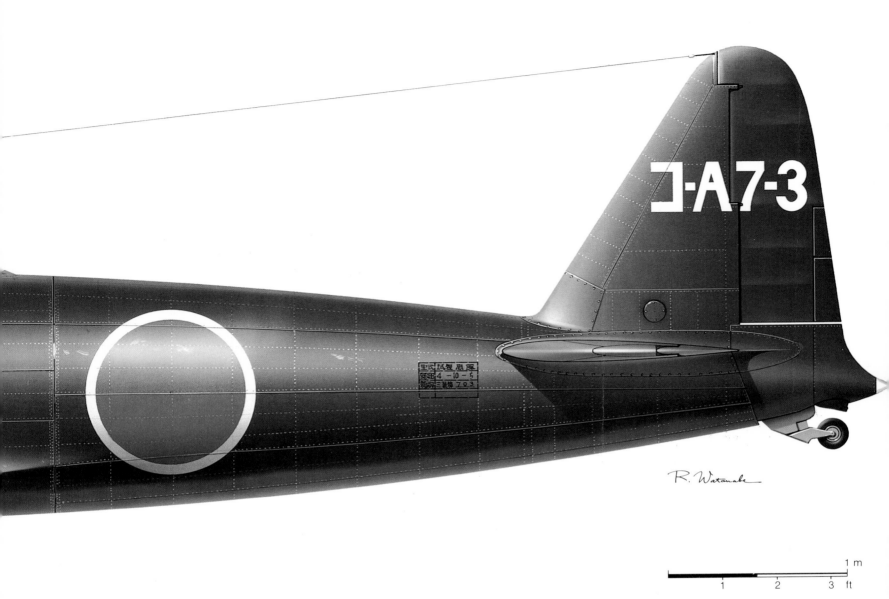

R. Watanabe

1 m

1 2 3 ft

Mitsubishi A7M2 *Reppu* of Koku-Gijutsusho in 1945.

Had the Japanese Navy's plan succeeded for producing the Mitsubishi A7M *Reppu*, code-named 'Sam,' it could well have restored the air superiority Japan enjoyed in the first year of the war. Initially designed to be powered by a Mitsubishi 2,200 hp Ha 43 engine, the plane's size was comparable to the Republic P-47N Thunderbolt, yet the P-47s empty weight was 1.6 times greater than 'Sam.' With combat flaps, 'Sam's' maneuverability was said to have equaled that of the Zero fighter.

Conceived as early as April, 1942, when Mitsubishi was instructed to begin the design of the *Reppu* carrier-borne fighter to the 17-*Shi* specifications, it met with nothing but indecisions on the part of the Japanese Navy. After months of delays, the Navy finally insisted on a lesser-powered engine than the design had intended for meeting per-

formance requirements. Redesigning the airframe to carry the smaller engine further delayed completing the test airplane. This lack of sufficient power proved itself during the initial flight tests in May, 1944. Despite this handicap, 'Sam' demonstrated the handling qualities of being a formidable opponent against Allied fighters.

The Navy now reversed its decision and approved the originally intended engine. With reengineering needed once again, the new A7M2, was finally flight tested in October, 1944. Having achieved the expected performance, the Navy ordered *Reppu* into production. By now serious material shortages, Allied bombing attacks, and the destructive earthquake of December, 1944, prevented more than the eight prototype aircraft from being completed. After more than three years in the development program, not one combat capable *Reppu* was produced—an airplane intended to replace the ageing and outclassed Zero fighter which had to see the war through to the last day.

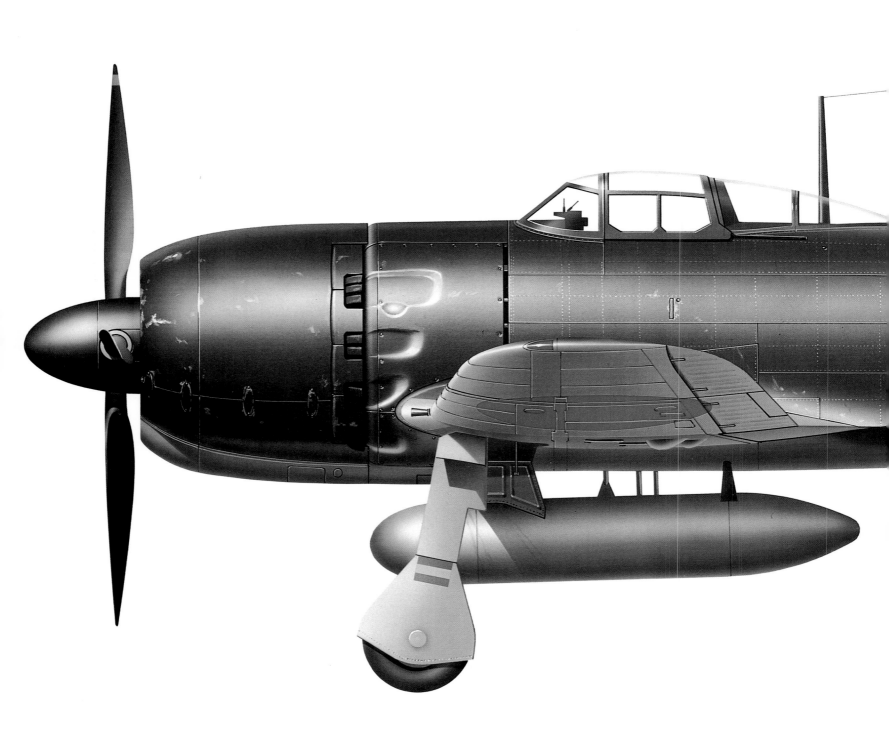

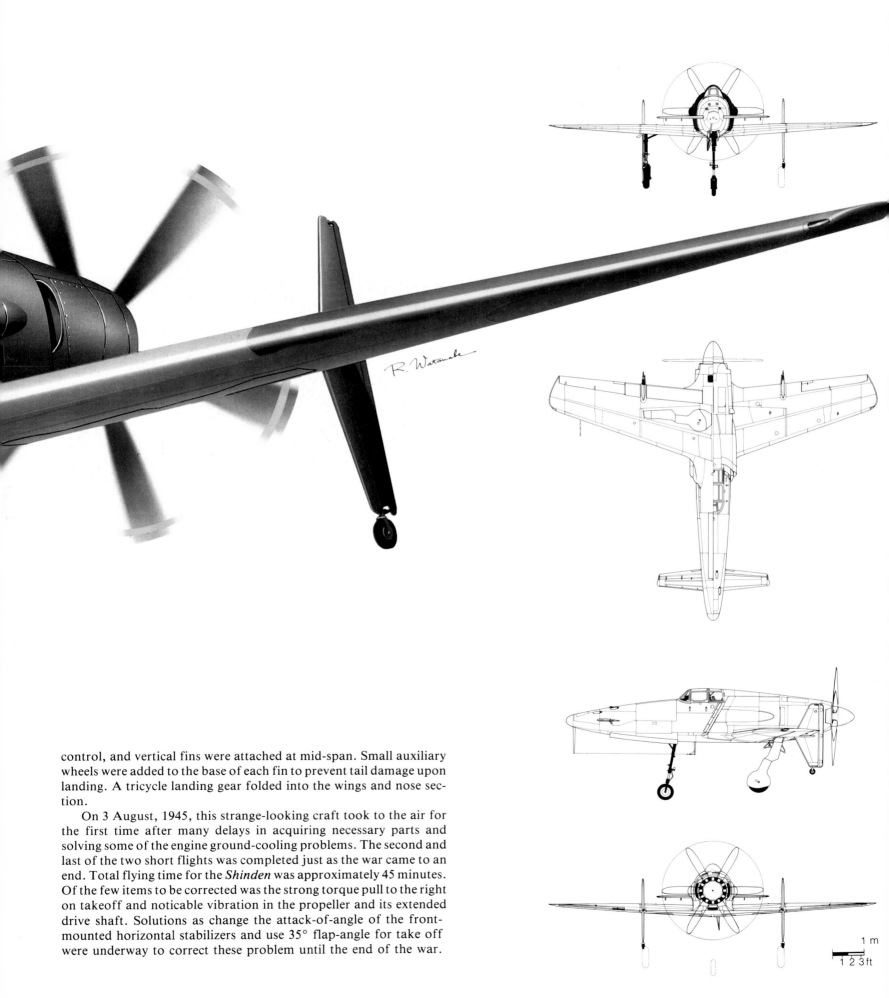

control, and vertical fins were attached at mid-span. Small auxiliary wheels were added to the base of each fin to prevent tail damage upon landing. A tricycle landing gear folded into the wings and nose section.

On 3 August, 1945, this strange-looking craft took to the air for the first time after many delays in acquiring necessary parts and solving some of the engine ground-cooling problems. The second and last of the two short flights was completed just as the war came to an end. Total flying time for the *Shinden* was approximately 45 minutes. Of the few items to be corrected was the strong torque pull to the right on takeoff and noticable vibration in the propeller and its extended drive shaft. Solutions as change the attack-of-angle of the front-mounted horizontal stabilizers and use 35° flap-angle for take off were underway to correct these problem until the end of the war.

1 m

1 2 3 ft

Grumman F4F of near equal power, but the Japanese fighter with its lighter weight gave it the advantage of manoeuvrability, speed, rate of climb and acceleration – everything that was planned in its design. The ability of the Wildcat to absorb punishment was without a doubt its redeeming feature, but this did not give the American pilots any great advantage where flight performance was generally the deciding factor. Fighter team tactics by the U.S. Navy pilots had much to do with shifting the advantage to the Wildcat.

longer dominated the ocean. Thus ended the Zero's operations from the heavy carriers of the Japanese fleet, and the only thing Japan had accomplished during this battle was the seizing of the tiny, uninhabited islands of Attu and Kiska in the Aleutians as a diversionary effort of the major battle at Midway. This gain was perhaps countered, for it was from this northern operation that the Americans were able to gain a downed Zero and discover, for the first time, its innermost secrets.

◄ Admiral Yamamoto, Commander-in-Chief of the Japanese Combined Fleet, watching a *Zero 21* taking off from Rabaul. He died on 18 April, 1943, while on his way to Buin Airbase, about ten days after this picture was taken.

▼ *Zero 22s* of the First Naval Air Corps in Rabaul engaging in Operation *Ro-Go*. The operation (November 2-12, 1943), involving 80 pilots and 82 Zeros, ended with a loss of 24 pilots and 43 planes.

By June, 1942, the Japanese fleet, supported by carrier-based Zeros, attempted to invade Midway Island. The element of surprise was thought by the Japanese to be on their side, but the Americans were prepared for the attack. The battle started favourably for the Japanese when they successfully defended their carriers against attack and the American forces took heavy aerial losses. As the battle progressed and the attention of the Japanese was switched to the low flying U.S. torpedo bombers attacking their ships, U.S. dive bombers came in steeply overhead and unloaded their 1,000 pound bombs, many of them squarely on the Japanese carriers. Three were sunk and a fourth set on fire. With them went 234 Japanese aircraft. This became the turning point of the Pacific War. With these losses of principal ships and the fighter cover provided by the Zero, Japanese warships no

With Japan's shortage of aircraft carriers, the heavy arresting gear hooks were removed from a number of Zeros as air units were assigned to land base operations only. During the late spring and early summer of 1942, the only major Japanese Navy air action against the Allies came from the 25th Air Flotilla, headquartered at Rabaul. Aircraft from this air unit engaged in constant air attacks, concentrated against Allied installations at Port Moresby in New Guinea. Lesser attacks were directed at such places as Port Darwin and Timor, to prevent the Allies from concentrating all their defences on centralized points. Japanese medium bombers were escorted by a comparative number of Zero fighters on these sorties.

To support the ultimate plan for taking Port Moresby, the Japanese attacked Buna in mid-July, 1942, on the north-east coast of New Guinea. This erupted in fierce fighting as each side tried to counter their enemy's next move. When the Allies launched their invasion of Guadalcanal in the southern group of the Solomon Islands, this was the first attempt by the Americans to strike back at the Japanese. This combined air, land and sea assault by the Allies started the long road to recovering lost ground.

In this early phase of fighting, the Zero fighters operating from Salumaua and Lae, put up what was unquestionably the toughest fighter opposition Allied pilots experienced throughout the Pacific war. At these advanced bases were Japan's greatest aces of the Imperial Navy. The Zero was still superior to the P-39s and P-40s as well as the Wildcats they were encountering, but the American pilots were gaining in skill and tactics which were able to defeat the Zero. The long period of repeated victories for the Japanese was nearing the end as the year 1942 came to a close.

An assortment of superior American fighters was beginning to be introduced to the Pacific conflict in late 1942 at the same time the Japanese had programmed for their replacement of the Zero. Japan's new Navy fighters were slow to be developed and the Zero was left to hold the line as best it could. Starting in 1943, the most frequent opponent of the Zero was the Grumman Hellcat, a carrier-based fighter that could take on the Japanese opposition under any conditions. One reason was that its original pre-Pearl Harbor design had been specifically altered to combat the Zero, based on the lessons learned by U.S. Navy pilots in the early days of fighting. When the Lockheed P-38 Lightning and Vought F4U Corsair appeared on the scene, they were superior to the Zero in nearly every respect except manoeuvrability. Allied aircrews developed tactics of a type that countered the Japanese attempt to engage in dogfights which would give the Zero the advantage. Other fighters followed such as the Republic P-47 Thunderbolt, and much later, the North American P-51 Mustang. There were many air battles during the months that followed in which the Zero was often present. The most often recorded and discussed is the battle of the Philippine Sea. This battle erupted when the Japanese fleet attempted to counter the Allied invasion of the Marianas Islands.

The Japanese task force west of the islands, consisting of nine aircraft carriers and other major ships, had prepared for shuttle attacks against the American invading Task Force that was positioned between the Japanese fleet and the Japanese-held islands. Shortly after dawn on 19 June, 1944, the Japanese carriers began sending their planes on their strike mission against the American ships and landing assault forces. Having guessed the plan of the Japanese, the F6F Hellcats were already waiting high above the fleet. As the Japanese planes appeared, the American fighters dived down upon them in a devastating coordinated attack.

Over a period of eight hours, four successive waves of Japanese planes flew in from the southwest, in groups averaging about one hundred each. The same fate was experienced by each wave. Only about forty of the Japanese aircraft got through the defending fighters, and half of these were shot down by the ships' curtain of intense anti-aircraft fire.

About 370 Japanese planes were shot down during this spectacular aerial battle which history refers to as the "Marianas Turkey Shoot." Counting the land-based Japanese planes that took off for these islands earlier that morning and were shot down, total Japanese losses for the day were more than 400 aircraft. Of the original 450 Japanese planes used during the battle, only one in 10 had survived. On the remaining carriers not sunk that day, only six torpedo-bombers, two dive bombers, 12 attack-bombers, and a mere 25 of the original compliment of 225 Zero fighters remained. Twenty-six American planes were lost, and about half of their pilots were saved.

These results, of course, are very one-sided. The Zero fighter had not lessened in its performance or capability, in fact it had improved. Either because of Japanese tactical error, or because of the poor state of training of the Japanese pilots for an operation of this size, the attack came in widely separated and ill-coordinated waves. This allowed the American aircraft time to reservice and rearm. The Japanese pilots were also in a semi-exhausted state after flying nearly 350 nautical miles from their carriers, supposedly out of reach of U.S. planes, and were therefore at a disadvantage to evade the fierce and overwhelming attacks by the F6F Hellcats.

There was more to be blamed for these heavy losses than undertrained crews and outdated equipment. A trait found in most Japanese aircraft that were encountered early in the war was their inability to withstand enemy gunfire, and the Zero was no exception. Their lack of pilot protection devices, such as armour plate and fire-resisting self-sealing fuel tanks were items omitted from nearly all these early war period aircrafts, a concept based on recommendations made by seasoned combat pilots. They were more concerned in obtaining the best performance resulting from minimum weight for concentrating on *attack*, than the lack of safety features which to them represented encumbering luxury. It was not uncommon that pilots left their parachutes on the

(National Archives)

ground in order to reduce weight for an added advantage in any air duel.

The point must be stressed, however, that these design shortcomings from adequate protection were not an oversight by the designers. What was missing from the very beginning was a good 1,200 hp engine to carry the necessary safeguards for aircraft and pilot without sacrificing performance. As was the case with Allied planes, more power should have been added over the years as the Zero was improved with its inherent weight penalties. Horikoshi did extremly well with the limited horsepower that was available to him for the Zero.

As the Pacific war went on, and the Allies introduced new fighters possessing greater firepower and speed, the attitudes of Japanese pilots began to change as their losses continued to increase. Beginning with the Zero 52, modifications including pilot protective features and fire suppression devices originally scorned were being added at a sacrifice in performance. But the tide of battle had already turned against Japan and the previous lack of protective measures through much of the war had already cut deeply into their equipment and highly skilled pilots.

Model 52 and the Americans

The battle of the Marianas and the capture of Saipan in June, 1944, placed the improved Model 52 Zero into American hands for the first time. Allied airmen had been encountering the newer model as early as the previous fall, recognizing it primarily by a surprising increase in performance. Now they had their first chance for a closer look and flight evaluation of the improved Zero.

Twelve of these newly captured Zeros were sent from Saipan to the United States for study by the Technical Air Intelligence Centre. Several were rebuilt to be flown and

by the end of 1944, comparison flight tests had been made with various American fighters. The narrative report made of these findings has evaded publication over the years, though often sought by many historians. The intelligence summary gives comparative details recorded when the Zero was flown against the Vought F4U-1D Corsair, Grumman F6F-5 Hellcat and Eastern (Grumman) FM-2 Wildcat.

F4U-1D vs Zero 52:

Both aircrafts were flown side by side, making all things equal at the beginning of this flight comparison test. In a race for altitude, the best climb of the F4U-1D was equal to the Zero up to 10,000 ft, above 750 ft/min better at 18,000 feet and above 500 ft/min better at 22,000 feet and above. Best climb speeds of the F4U and Zero were 156 mph (135 kts) and 122 mph (105 kts) indicated air speed, respectively.

The F4U-1D was faster than the Zero 52 at all altitudes, having the least margin of 42 mph (37.5 kts) at 5,000 feet and the widest difference of 80 mph (70 kts) at 25,000 feet. Top speeds attained were 413 mph (360 kts) TAS at 20,400 feet for the Corsair and 335 mph (290 kts) TAS at 18,000 feet for the Zero.

Rate of roll for the Zero was equal to that of the Corsair at speeds under 230 mph (200 kts) and inferior above that speed due to the high control forces. Manoeuvrability of the Zero was remarkable at speeds below 202 mph (175 kts). being far superior to that of the Corsair. In slow speed turns the Zero could gain one turn in three and a half at 10,000 feet. At speeds around 202 mph (175 kts) however, the F4U could, by using flaps, stay with the Zero for about one-half turn, or until its speed fell off to 173 mph (150 kts).

Initial dive accelerations of the Zero and the Corsair were about the same after which the Corsair was far superior, and slightly superior in zooms after dives.

F6F vs Zero 52:

The Zero climbed about 600 ft/min better than the F6F up to 9,000 feet, after which the advantage fell off gradually until the two aircraft were about equal at 14,000 feet.

(National Archives)

Above this altitude the Hellcat had the advantage, varying from 500 ft/min better at 22,000 ft, to about 250 ft/min better at 30,000 feet. Best climb speeds of the F6F-5 and Zero 52 were 150 mph (130 kts) and 122 mph (105 kts) indicated, respectively.

The F6F-5 was faster than the Zero 52 at all altitudes, having the least margin of 25 mph (21.5 kts) at 5,000 feet and the widest difference of 75 mph (65 kts) at 25,000 feet. Top speeds attained were 409 mph (355 kts) at 21,600 feet for the Hellcat, and 335 mph (290 kts) at 18,000 feet for the Zero.

(Comments on rate of roll, dive, maneouvrability and turns for the Hellcat were identical to those made on the F4U except that attempts at turning with flaps was not mentioned.)

FM-2 vs Zero 52:

The FM-2 was a General Motors built Wildcat having a 1,350 hp engine replacing the 1,200 hp engine on the earlier F4F-4 previously described. In climbs, the Zero was about 400 ft/min less than that of the Wildcat starting at sea level, becoming equal at 4,000 feet and 400 ft/min better at 8,000 feet. Climbs became equal again passing 13,000 feet, and the Zero was only slightly inferior above 13,000 feet. Best climb speeds of the FM-2 and Zero were 138 mph (120 kts) and 122 mph (105 kts) indicated, respectively.

The FM-2 was 6 mph (5 kts) faster than the Zero at sea level becoming 4 mph (3.5 kts) slower at 5,000 feet and dropped to 26 mph (22.5 kts) slower at 30,000 feet. Top speeds attained were 321 mph (288 kts) TAS at 13,000 feet for the FM-2 and 335 mph (290 kts) at 18,000 feet for the Zero.   Rate of roll of the two fighters was equal at 184 mph (160 kts) and under. The Zero became inferior at higher speeds due to heavy stick forces. Turns of the FM-2 and Zero were very similar, with a slight advantage in favour of the Zero 52. The Zero could gain one turn in eight at 10,000 feet.

The Zero was slightly superior to the FM-2 in initial dive acceleration, after which the dives were about the same. Zooms after dives were about equal for the two aircraft.

Suggested Tactics: For engaging in combat with the Zero, all three American aircraft were not to dogfight with the Japanese fighter and not to follow it in a loop or half-roll with pull-through. When attacking, the superior power and speed performance of the F6F-5 and F4U-1D was to be used for engaging the Zero at the most favourable moment. For the FM-2, any altitude advantage possible was to be maintained. In all three cases, to evade a Zero, the best method was to roll and dive away in a high speed turn.

From this American report describing the performance of the later model Zero and how to cope with it, the point was obvious that the aircraft was still a serious threat in any air battle. The weakest aspect of the Zero fighter at this stage of its operational life was the lack of skilled pilots to fly them. It can be safely assumed that the American pilots flying the Zero for these tests were far more qualified through experience and training than the Japanese pilots normally encountered in combat.

Offspring of the Zero

The Imperial Japanese Navy had not expected the war to be prolonged as it was, nor for the service life of the Zero to be so extended. In addition to an array of Japanese Army fighters that opposed Allied air power, there were other Navy fighters, proposed or in being, to augment the Zero fighter. Technical production problems prevented these aircraft to do much to overshadow the dependency that the Navy placed upon the Zero.

Among these aircraft was Mitsubishi's J2M1 *Raiden*, code named "Jack" by the Allies. This was a radical change in Japanese single-seat fighter concepts in that for the first time, manoeuvrability became a secondary consideration to speed and climb. "Jack" was purely an interceptor intended to destroy enemy bombers as well as to out-perform enemy escort fighters. This concept from which evolved the 14-*Shi* fighter *Raiden*, began only two years after that of the Zero and before it had made its first flight.

By the time of the first test flight of the new aircraft on 20 March, 1942, Mitsubishi's production and technical skills were heavily committed to the Zero and other military aircraft that were in great demand. The project languished in development due primarily to problems with engine vibration and poor visibility for the pilot. These were not resolved until 1943, at which time limited production did get underway. Because of poor production management for an aircraft that was slowly to replace the Zero in the production lines, emphasis remained with the Zero and production of "Jack" was transferred to a subsidiary plant of Mitsubishi. In all, only 470 of the J2M1 interceptors were manufactured.

Meanwhile, as "Jack" was suffering with ever mounting technical problems, the Navy looked to Kawanishi with possibilities of converting their 15-*Shi Kyofu* seaplane fighter design into a land based interceptor. This design change became the N1K1-J *Shiden*, that the Allies code named "George". Due to its mid-wing that was suited for the seaplane design, and its huge propeller turned by a 1,990 hp Nakajima *Homare* 21 engine, the landing gear for the land based version had to be unusually long. This brought about numerous problems with strength and linkage that prompted the design to evolve into a low wing configuration in order to shorten the landing gear length.

In March, 1944, the Japanese Navy decided to replace the languishing production of "Jack" with the "George," while still continuing production with the proven Zero until it could adequately be replaced. In all 1,400 "George" interceptor fighters were produced in the mid-wing and low-wing versions.

All this while, the Japanese Navy was counting on Mitsubishi's A7M1 *Reppu* carrier-borne fighter, code named "Sam" as a replacement for the Zero. The A7M design was initiated in 1942 by Horikoshi to restore to Japan the air superiority it enjoyed in the brief first year of the war. With intentions of powering the new fighter with a 2,200 hp engine, there was every reason to believe that this new fighter would be superior to the American fighters it would one day oppose.

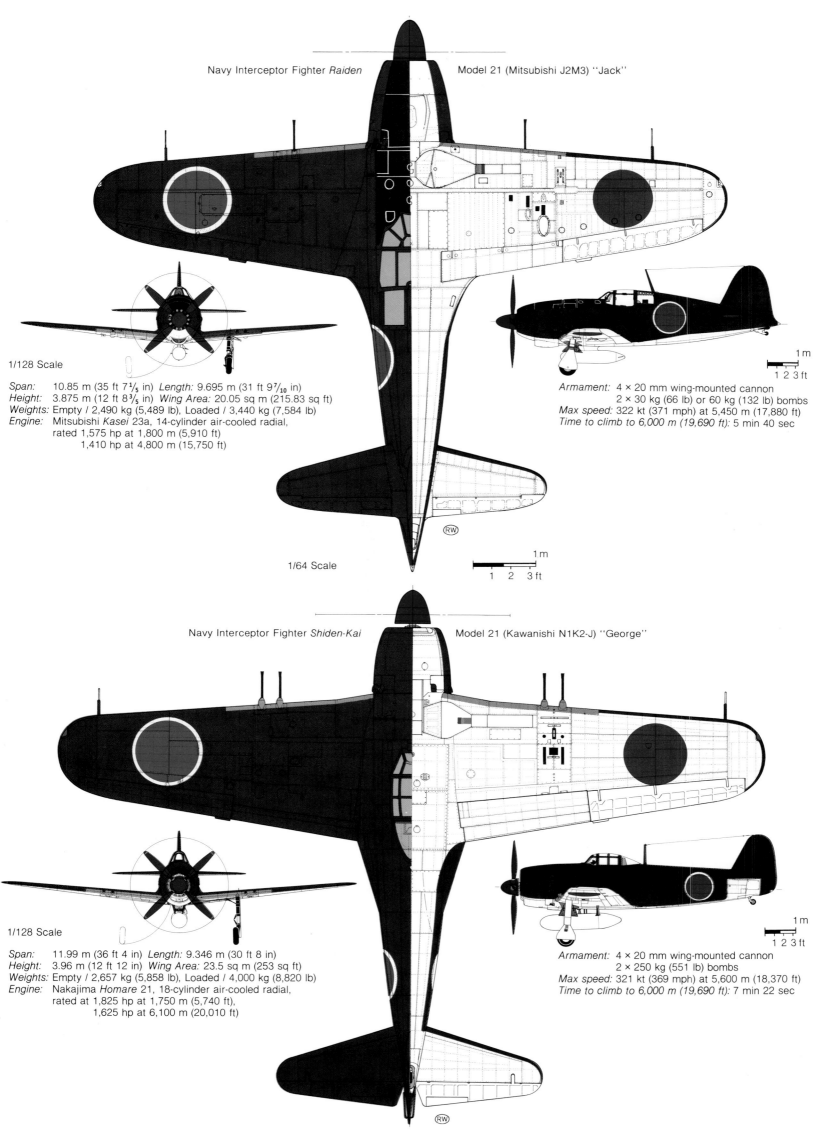

Navy Interceptor Fighter *Raiden* Model 21 (Mitsubishi J2M3) "Jack"

1/128 Scale

Span: 10.85 m (35 ft 7¹/₅ in) *Length:* 9.695 m (31 ft 9⁷/₁₀ in)
Height: 3.875 m (12 ft 8³/₅ in) *Wing Area:* 20.05 sq m (215.83 sq ft)
Weights: Empty / 2,490 kg (5,489 lb), Loaded / 3,440 kg (7,584 lb)
Engine: Mitsubishi *Kasei* 23a, 14-cylinder air-cooled radial,
        rated 1,575 hp at 1,800 m (5,910 ft)
        1,410 hp at 4,800 m (15,750 ft)

Armament: 4 × 20 mm wing-mounted cannon
          2 × 30 kg (66 lb) or 60 kg (132 lb) bombs
Max speed: 322 kt (371 mph) at 5,450 m (17,880 ft)
Time to climb to 6,000 m (19,690 ft): 5 min 40 sec

1/64 Scale

Navy Interceptor Fighter *Shiden-Kai* Model 21 (Kawanishi N1K2-J) "George"

1/128 Scale

Span: 11.99 m (36 ft 4 in) *Length:* 9.346 m (30 ft 8 in)
Height: 3.96 m (12 ft 12 in) *Wing Area:* 23.5 sq m (253 sq ft)
Weights: Empty / 2,657 kg (5,858 lb), Loaded / 4,000 kg (8,820 lb)
Engine: Nakajima *Homare* 21, 18-cylinder air-cooled radial,
        rated at 1,825 hp at 1,750 m (5,740 ft),
        1,625 hp at 6,100 m (20,010 ft)

Armament: 4 × 20 mm wing-mounted cannon
          2 × 250 kg (551 lb) bombs
Max speed: 321 kt (369 mph) at 5,600 m (18,370 ft)
Time to climb to 6,000 m (19,690 ft): 7 min 22 sec

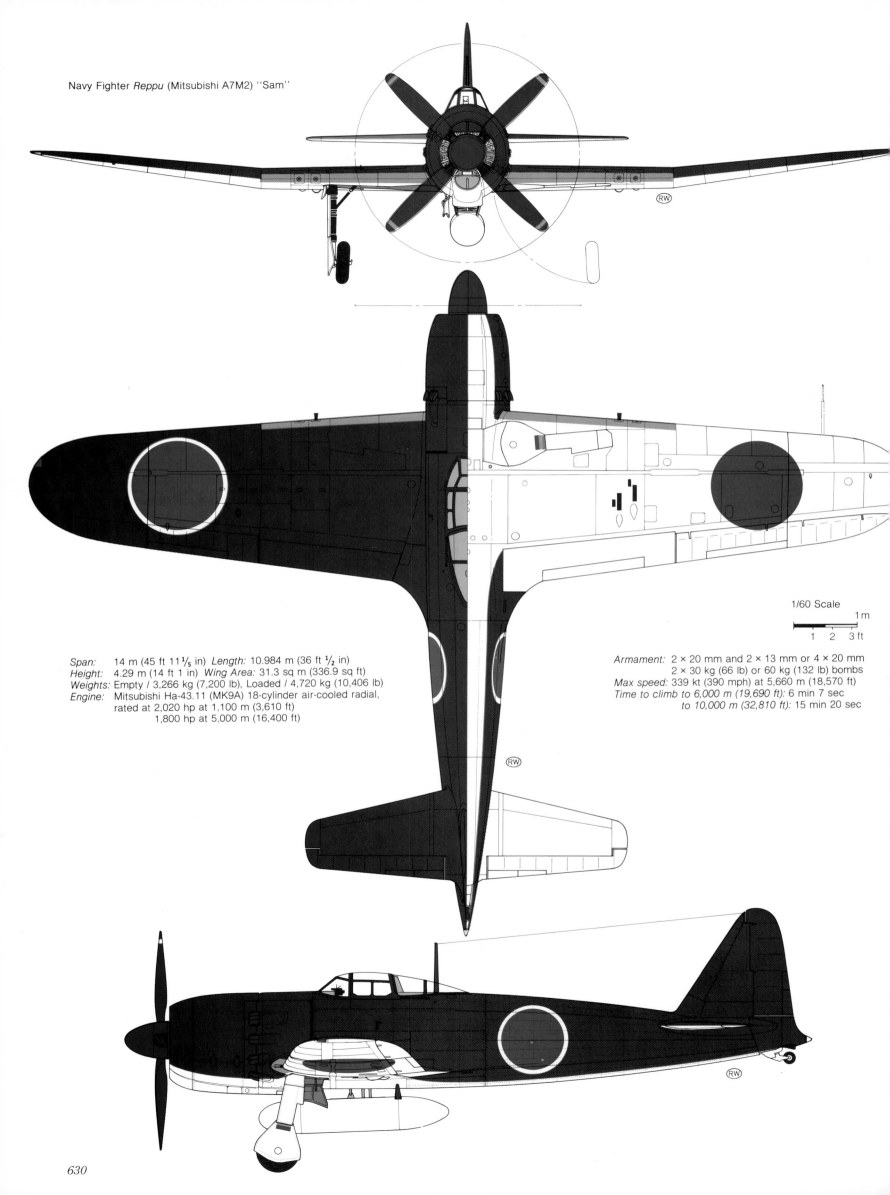

Navy Fighter *Reppu* (Mitsubishi A7M2) "Sam"

Span: 14 m (45 ft 11⅕ in) *Length:* 10.984 m (36 ft ½ in)
Height: 4.29 m (14 ft 1 in) *Wing Area:* 31.3 sq m (336.9 sq ft)
Weights: Empty / 3,266 kg (7,200 lb), Loaded / 4,720 kg (10,406 lb)
Engine: Mitsubishi Ha-43.11 (MK9A) 18-cylinder air-cooled radial,
　　　　rated at 2,020 hp at 1,100 m (3,610 ft)
　　　　1,800 hp at 5,000 m (16,400 ft)

1/60 Scale
1 m
1　2　3 ft

Armament: 2 × 20 mm and 2 × 13 mm or 4 × 20 mm
　　　　2 × 30 kg (66 lb) or 60 kg (132 lb) bombs
Max speed: 339 kt (390 mph) at 5,660 m (18,570 ft)
Time to climb to 6,000 m (19,690 ft): 6 min 7 sec
　　　　to 10,000 m (32,810 ft): 15 min 20 sec

A single Zero in a *kamikaze* attack the instant before it crashed into the battleship *USS Missouri* off Okinawa.

Due to many underlying factors, the ultimate production goal of the "Sam" was never achieved. The indecisiveness between Mitsubishi and the Navy over the selection of the engine to be used was the first of many delays. Once the decision was made, which was contrary to designer Horikoshi's choice, the necessary redesign caused additional delays, later to be compounded by material shortages, Allied bombing and the devastating earthquake in December, 1944.

When the prototype first flew 6 May, 1944, it possessed excellent stability and controllability, but was decidedly underpowered. At the Navy insistence, a less-powerful engine was used than Mitsubishi had planned. The *Homare* 22 engine, rated at 1,999 hp at take-off fell off with altitude until at 6000 m (19,700 ft) the engine was yielding only 1,300 hp. Intending to eliminate this shortcoming, a later prototype flew with the 2,200 hp Mitsubishi Ha 43 engine, and it was immediately obvious that manoevrability, rate of climb, and maximum speed were noticably improved, while it retained its excellent stability and control features.

When the war ended, only eight prototype A7M "Sam" fighters, with a few additional production models in the assembly stage, had been achieved. Thus, the true intended replacement fighter for the Zero had not flown one operational strike against the enemy, which by then was destroying the very factories from which these fighters were to come.

Kamikaze

From the early days over China and the first year of the Pacific war, the Zero was a living legend. Countless hordes of these nimble fighters would appear, seemingly from out of nowhere, attacking and sending their enemies to the ground in flames, then flamboyantly departing the battle area with barrel rolls pronouncing victory. The success of the Zero fighter in the early stages of the war can scarcely be overemphasized. It was justifiably respected as the aggressor and victor.

As the final stages of the war turned to successive defeats for the Japanese, the Zero remained essentially the same aircraft that had fought four years earlier. With increased demands placed upon it, improvements were frequently made in attempts to at least match its opponents. Its engine was more reliable and somewhat more powerful. Design changes had improved its performance in some areas, and downgraded it in others due to added weight. An increase in weaponry gave it a bigger punch in striking power.

None the less, as the newer generation of Allied aircraft came on the scene, it became a losing battle whichever way the Zero turned to disengage from its enemy. The Japanese pilots were still just as courageous as in the early years of the Zero. For the young Japanese pilots who first flew the Zero, it was the modern weapon of the *samurai*, a nimble fighter not unlike the slashing sword with which Japan would defeat all its enemies. Now the situation in combat was reversed and the Zero had become the *hara-kiri* blade, an instrument of sacrificial suicide, a one-way expendable weapon that carried its pilot to death and glory. Consequently, the Zero itself, once victorious in combat was being expended in a cause that would elude its certain defeat.

The story of *kamikaze* attacks is not new. Few may realize, however, that more Zeros were expended in those attacks than any other aircraft, including special craft designed for these suicide missions. Normally the older Zeros, such as A6M2s, were fitted with a 250 kg (550 lb) bomb for these one-way missions. Initially volunteer crews were limited to those having less flying experience and who stood little chance of survival in air-to-air combat or accurate dive-bombing, but who would be able to guide their aircraft in a final death dive upon an Allied ship. The few experienced pilots that remained often flew escort in the later model Zeros that had a better chance of survival while acting as decoys to draw the fire of the aggressive F6F Hellcat fighter screens, and the walls of anti-aircraft which the U.S. fleet was able to set up.

The Battle of the Philippines, in October, 1944, was the first major operation to employ these tactics. Several American aircraft carriers were either sunk or severely damaged, along with other surface craft. Although these attacks were effective, they failed to prevent the U.S. forces from landing on Luzon, completing their invasion operations when and where they chose. Of the 331 Zeros launched in the Philippine Operation in *kamikaze* attacks, 158 were able to reach their targets, destroying themselves in this desperate manner of attack.

These tactics were used again during the invasion of Okinawa and other lesser locations throughout the ever tightening ring of combat around Japan. Had it not been for the surrender that took place before the pending invasion of Japan became necessary, the plan called for every Zero and comparable aircraft to be expended against the invading force in *kamikaze* attacks.

The philosophy of the *kamikaze* pilots had never been properly understood by Western minds, although many Western pilots died in missions which were virtually suicidal. Anyone having flown numerous combat missions has at one time or other felt that "his number" was up on a particular mission, yet continued on after there was still time to turn back to safety. A vivid example is the story of U.S. Navy Torpedo Squadron Eight at Midway as each plane attacked and was successively shot down. Not only have airmen demonstrated this bravery, but other combatants as well. One of many examples was the case of 20-mm gun crews remaining at their stations aboard the USS *Essex* until enveloped in flames, in an effort to beat off a *kamikaze* attack.

There was a fundamental difference however in the heroism of these opposing military men. The Japanese accepted the situation that there was no avenue of hope and escape – the American never did. To the Western mind there must be that last slim chance of survival, the feeling that

(National Archives)

although a lot of other men around him may die, it was he that somehow was going to make it back.

The Japanese pilots who accepted the principle of suicide tactics most wholeheartedly were, as a general rule, those whose religious or patriotic conviction were highly developed. These self-sacrificing attacks offered them a chance to attain several goals. Uppermost was to inflict losses on the enemy that might make them lose their overwhelming material advantage, while another motivation was to die bravely in the purest style of ancient Japanese tradition. Those who succeeded in returning from the typical type of combat encounters in which most of their comrades had been shot down were convinced that their survival was only temporary. A *kamikaze* mission afforded the opportunity to control this destiny in the form of a devastating blow against the enemy for love of family and country.

These examples of human self-sacrifice on a group scale have not been witnessed since the Pacific conflict. Perhaps a combat situation since then has not fostered such extreme measures. However, it seems doubtful, based on the attitudes so often expressed today, that a trend of such emotional human involvement would not be given a fleeting chance for consideration.

And yet the attraction of the hero remains in all the world; people still like to read about bravery and self sacrifice, even if it seems that there are fewer around who would appreciate it. Perhaps it is a cyclical thing; heroism may once again come into fashion, and the bravery of the men who flew the Zeros will become not only admirable, but understandable.

AIRCRAFT INDEX

Makers

---

*Numbers in bold face refer to the original volume.

---

*Numbers in bold face refer to the original volume.

Designations

*Numbers in bold face refer to the original volume.

Official Names and Nicknames

---

*Numbers in bold face refer to the original volume.

Categories

FIGHTERS/ FIGHTER BOMBERS

Czechoslovakia
Avia S199

France
Dewoitine D.510
Dewoitine D.520
Morane-Saulnier MS.406
Nieuport Nighthawk

Germany
Arado Ar65
Arado Ar80
Dornier Do335
Focke-Wulf Fw190
Focke-Wulf Ta152
Focke-Wulf Ta153
Focke-Wulf Ta154
Heinkel He51
Heinkel He100/He113
Heinkel He112
Heinkel He219
Messerschmitt Bf109
Messerschmitt Bf109Z
Messerschmitt Bf110
Messerschmitt Me109TL
Messerschmitt Me209II
Messerschmitt Me210
 /Me410
Messerschmitt Me262
Messerschmitt Me309

Italy
Macchi C.202
Reggiane Re2000

Japan
Kawanishi N1K1
Kawanishi N1K1-J
Kawanishi N1K2-J
Kawasaki Ki45-Kai
Kawasaki Ki61
Kawasaki Ki64
Kyushu J7W
Mitsubishi 7-Shi carrier-based fighter
Mitsubishi 9-Shi carrier-based fighter
Mitsubishi A5M
Mitsubishi A6M
Mitsubishi A7M
Mitsubishi J2M
Mitsubishi Type 10 carrier-based fighter

Nakajima A1N
Nakajima A2N
Nakajima A4N
Nakajima A6M2-N
Nakajima Ki43
Nakajima Ki84

Netherlands
Fokker D.XXI

Poland
P.Z.L. P.11

Spain
Hispano HA-1109

Sweden
SAAB J32

United Kingdom
Boulton Paul Defiant
Bristol Beaufighter
Bristol Bulldog
de Havilland Hornet
 /Sea Hornet
de Havilland Mosquito
de Havilland Vampire
Fairey Firefly
Gloster Gambet
Gloster Gauntlet
Gloster Gladiator
 /Sea Gladiator
Gloster Meteor
Gloster Sparrowhawk
Hawker Demon
Hawker Fury
Hawker Hurricane
Hawker Nimrod
Hawker Sea Fury
Hawker Tempest
Hawker Typhoon
Saunders-Roe SR.A1
Supermarine Scimitar
Supermarine Spiteful
 /Seafang
Supermarine Spitfire
 /Seafire
Supermarine Swift
Vickers Jockey
Westland Welkin
Westland Whirlwind

U.S.A.
Bell P-39
 /P-400

Bell P-63
Boeing F2B
Boeing F4B
Boeing P-26
Curtiss F6C
Curtiss F11C
Curtiss P-36
Curtiss P-40
Douglas F3D
Douglas P-70
Goodyear F2G
Grumman F2F
Grumman F3F
Grumman F4F
 /G-36
 /Eastern (GM) FM
Grumman F6F
Grumman F8F
Grumman F9F
Grumman XF5F
Lockheed F-94
Lockheed P-38
Lockheed P-80
Lockheed XP-49
Lockheed XP-58
Lockheed-Vega XB-40/YB-40
McDonnell F-4
North American P-51/F-51
North American P-82/F-82
Northrop P-61
Republic P-47
Vought F4U
 /Goodyear FG
 /Brewster F3A
Vought V-143

U.S.S.R.
Lavochkin La-5
Lavochkin La-9
Lavochkin LaGG-3
Mikoyan-Gurevich MiG-3
Mikoyan-Gurevich MiG-15
Polikarpov I-15
Yakovlev Yak-1 ~ Yak-9

BOMBERS/ DIVE BOMBERS/ ATTACKERS

Germany
Arado Ar81
Arado Ar234
Blohm und Voss Ha137

Dornier Do17
Dornier Do19
Dornier Do217
Fieseler Fi98
Focke-Wulf Fw200
Heinkel He50
Heinkel He111
Heinkel He118
Heinkel He119
Heinkel He177
Henschel Hs123
Junkers A48
Junkers J1
Junkers Ju87
Junkers Ju88
Junkers Ju88 Mistel
Junkers Ju89
Junkers Ju187
Junkers Ju188
Junkers K47

Japan
Aichi D3A
Koku-Gijutsusho D4Y
Mitsubishi G3M
Mitsubishi G4M
Mitsubishi Ki51
Nakajima B5N
Nakajima B6N

United Kingdom
Armstrong Whitworth Whitley
Avro Lancaster
Avro Lincoln
Avro Manchester
Avro Valcan
Blackburn Buccaneer
Blackburn Roc
Boulton Paul Overstrand
Boulton Paul Sidestrand
Bristol Blenheim
Bristol Brigand
de Havilland D.H.4
de Havilland D.H.9
de Havilland Mosquito
 /Sea Mosquito
English Electric Canberra
Fairey Battle
Fairey Fox
Fairey Swordfish
Handley Page Halifax
Handley Page Hampden
Handley Page Harrow
Hawker Hart
Short Stirling
Vickers Valiant
Vickers Warwick
Vickers Wellington

U.S.A.
Boeing B-17
Boeing B-29
Boeing B-50
Boeing XB-15
Boeing YB-9
Consolidated B-24
 /PB4Y-1
Convair B-36
Curtiss F8C
 /OC-1
Curtiss SB2C
Douglas A-26

Douglas AD/A-1
Douglas B-18
Douglas DB-7/A-20
Douglas SBD
Douglas TBD
Grumman TBF
 /Eastern (GM) TBM
Lockheed XB-38
Martin 146
Martin B-10
North American B-25
 /PBJ

U.S.S.R.
Ilyushin DB-3
Ilyushin Il-2
Petlyakov Pe-2
Polikarpov R-5

RECON. AIRCRAFT/
PATROL AIRCRAFT

Germany
Junkers Ju86

Japan
Mitsubishi C5M

United Kingdom
Avro Anson
Avro Shackleton
de Havilland Mosquito
Fairey Gannet
Hawker Siddeley Nimrod
Short Sunderland
Vickers Warwick

U.S.A.
Boeing F-9
Boeing PB-1
Consolidated PB4Y-2
Consolidated PBY
Lockheed P2V/P-2
Lockheed F-4
 /F-5
North American F-6

TRANSPORTS

Germany
Arado Ar232
Fieseler Fi97
Fieseler Fi156
Heinkel He70
Junkers Ju52
Junkers Ju390
Junkers W33
Junkers W34
Messerschmitt M20
Messerschmitt M37/Bf108

Netherlands
Fokker F.VIIB/3m

United Kingdom
Armstrong Whitworth Albemarle
Avro 642
Avro Five
Avro Lancastrian
Avro Ten
Avro Tudor
Avro York
de Havilland Albatross
de Havilland D.H.34

de Havilland Hercules
Hawker Siddeley Argosy

U.S.A.
Boeing C-97
Boeing C-108
Boeing Model 247
Boeing Monomail
Boeing Stratoliner
Douglas C-54
Douglas DC-1
 /DC-2
Douglas DC-3
 /C-47
Douglas DC-6
Douglas DC-7
Lockheed Constellation
Lockheed Lodestar

U.S.S.R.
Polikarpov U-2
 /Po-2
(for night harassment)

TRAINERS

Czechoslovakia
Avia CS199
Avia C210

Germany
Arado Ar66
Arado Ar96
Gotha Go145
Heinkel He45

United Kingdom
Avro 504
Avro Tutor
de Havilland Hammingbird
de Havilland Moth
 /Gipsy Moth
 /Tiger Moth
Short Sturgeon
(for target tug)

U.S.A.
North American T-6

RACERS

Germany
Messerschmitt M29
Messerschmitt Me209

Poland
P.W.S. RWD-6
P.W.S. RWD-9

United Kingdom
de Havilland Comet
Supermarine S.4
Supermarine S.5
Supermarine S.6B

U.S.A.
Curtiss CR-3

FLYINGBOATS/
SEAPLANES

Japan
Kawanishi N1K1
Nakajima A6M2-N

United Kingdom
Saunders-Roe SR.A1
Short Sunderland
Supermarine Walrus

U.S.A.
Consolidated PBY
Curtiss CR-3
Grumman J2F

HELICOPTER

U.S.A.
Sikorsky HO3S

GLIDERS

Germany
Gotha Go242
Junkers Ju322
Messerschmitt Me321

MISSILES

Germany
Blohm und Voss Bv246
Fiseler Fi103/V-1
HVP A-4/V-2
Ruhrstahl/Kramer X-4